A Catalogue
of the Tract Collection
of Saint David's University College,
Lampeter

Mansell 1975

© 1975 Saint David's University College, Lampeter

Mansell Information/Publishing Limited, 3 Bloomsbury Place, London WC1A 2QA

ISBN: 0 7201 0538 2

Text reproduced from catalogue cards,
printed by photolithography and bound at
The Scolar Press Limited, Ilkley, Yorkshire

To

John Roland Lloyd Thomas

Principal of Saint David's University College, Lampeter

1953–1975

Contents

Foreword   vii

Acknowledgements   xi

Introduction   xiii

The Catalogue   I

Index   287

Foreword

I count as one of the outstanding moments of a career till then largely devoted to the pursuit and cataloguing of old books, the occasion in February 1972 when I was first confronted with the tract collection in Lampeter Old Library. The revision of the Bibliographical Society's *Short-Title Catalogue, 1475–1640*, had offered a few hints to those in bibliographical circles that the books at Lampeter were of more than usual interest. Most old libraries have STC books, however, and very many have more and better than those at Lampeter. But the quantity of the later tracts was of a different order, and the realization that there existed 'on a pastoral forehead of Wales' a largely unknown archive of what was surely the great age of pamphlet-writing in English remains a vivid memory. The writing of a preface to a chronological catalogue of the tracts is thus a pleasant duty.

As Mr James proves in his introduction, the Lampeter collection in this catalogue is that of the Bowdler family with minor additions. Almost all libraries of any age—and many of newer foundation—in Britain have on their shelves a row of quarto pamphlets, usually bound to a uniform size and with lists of contents on their fly-leaves. The rise of the quarto pamphlet and its multiplication at a rate which faithfully indicates the religious and political temperature of the period is itself a phenomenon that deserves more study than it has had. However, the collection—some twenty-seven volumes—which can be attributed to Thomas Bowdler I is not particularly large by the standards of the day; though any collection of this kind is particularly valuable in Wales, in view of the political importance of the principality during the civil wars when Bowdler was collecting. The first Bowdler lacked the omnivorousness of his nephew, who would not have overlooked one of the most voluminous pamphleteers of the day, John Milton, though he would certainly have detested his opinions.

Whether Thomas Bowdler II began, as Mr James suspects, himself to collect at the time of the Popish plot, or whether the strength of his collection from 1678 onwards derives from retrospective purchases made by him, we have arrived at a point where the volume and quality of collecting change perceptibly.

> About this time the presse abounds with all sorts of pamphlets and libells; one side running down the papists and upholding the dissenters; the other side cryeing down both, asperseing the two last houses of commons and ridiculing their proceedings, and sounding nothing but 41; publick intelligencers or pamphlets of news abounding, every day spawning two, sometimes three, filling the town and country with notorious falsehoods.[1]

The words, curiously disparaging in view of his own obsessive acquisition of these pamphlets and libels, are those of Narcissus Luttrell, a collector with whom Thomas Bowdler II may, at least in mid-career, be compared.

---

1   N. Luttrell. *A brief historical relation of state affairs* Vol. 1 (1857), p. 76.

No doubt the fact that the licensing of the press lapsed from 1679 to 1685 encouraged the proliferation of pamphlets. But the mere absence of prohibition does not amount to the stimulus that drove the greatest writers of the day, Marvell and Dryden, to name but two, to channel their energies into the ephemeral mode of satire. Marvell died before it was possible to print *The Last Instructions to a Painter*, but the *Account of the Growth of Popery* printed in 1677 provoked official anger. Part of the satirical flood was *Absalom and Achitophel*. Luttrell bought it and noted 'Agt Mr Thomas Shadwell. A good poem'. Bowdler, no doubt in political sympathy with Dryden, agreed; he had six copies of various editions of the first part.

The literary vigour and quality of controversial literature, emphasized by such collections as *Poems on Affairs of State*, deserves more attention. It is possible, I think, to detect a change from the destructive (even remembering the part played by the press in broadcasting Oates's lies) to the persuasive. The tone of reasoned conversation finds its way into Defoe's titles, for example, 'An answer to the question that no body thinks of, viz. But what if the Queen should die?' And Defoe is the author most copiously represented in Bowdler's collections.

There is surely bibliographical confirmation, independent of the lapse in the licensing laws and their final abolition in 1695, that pamphlet controversy was not felt likely, in the end, to destroy the social fabric. In 1680 there was published 'A compleat catalogue of all the stitch'd books and single sheets printed since the first discovery of the Popish Plot.' This is itself a rare piece, and Lampeter's possession of a copy is cause for rejoicing. The *Continuation* and *Second continuation* are even rarer, and are not at Lampeter, but Luttrell's copies have survived in the British Library as evidence of his truly amazing zeal as a collector of ephemera.[2]

The three catalogues were reissued as 'A General Catalogue of all the stich'd books and single sheets' in 1680, and with the addition of the following highly significant words, 'Very useful for Gent. that make collections.' The implication is surely that however monstrous the libels, however terrible their consequences, those on all sides might be comprehended in the library of a gentleman, aloof from the fray, who might 'make collections.' The *General Catalogue* itself is rare, and we do not know how many gentlemen accepted its invitation, and followed in George Thomason's footsteps. Thomas Bowdler II, as Mr James makes clear in his introduction, had interests of a circumscribed kind, and his collections are those of a man of affairs, of a certain political and religious complexion. The flourishing drama of the period is not particularly evident. We shall look in vain for such tracts as those once owned by Luttrell and now in the Newberry Library, which describe the lowest of low London life at the end of the seventeenth century. But if Bowdler does not, as it were, move into the same league as Luttrell until the reign of Queen Anne, the balance is somewhat redressed by the fact that we have Bowdler's tracts in one place, catalogued in chronological order, while Luttrell's are scattered all over the world. In the week that I write this, I have seen one sheet in the museum of the Oxford University Press; the Bodleian has bought another from an American bookseller.

As Mr James points out, 'the most interesting phase of Bowdler's activity as a collector lies in the years 1709–18, when he appears to have been buying pamphlets at, or close upon, their publication.' Many of the pamphlets bought in these years bear manuscript dates. We may thus have invaluable information on exact dates of publication. Many, though alas not all, the poetical pamphlets collected by Luttrell during these years survive, particularly in the King's Library, and it will be instructive to compare the dates given by the two collectors. Thomas Bowdler II's period of intensive collecting seems to have ended about 1720. We do not know why. The entries under each year in the catalogue become fewer, though no collection which contained so much pamphlet verse by Pope (including three copies of *The New Dunciad*) could be considered insignificant. Swift is present, as are early works by Fielding and even Johnson's *Marmor Norfolciense*.

Among the most obvious features of English literature of this period are that it is largely topical in content and that it is bibliographically ephemeral. Thus the importance of the Lampeter tract collection is that it has preserved this literature, often in flawless condition. Every scholar knows the suggestive value of the contemporary binding together of pamphlets—particularly of this period—and of their later association in a specialized catalogue. Serendipity may thrive on the alphabetical route from Defoe to Ward.

Dr Thomas Bowdler by an act of folly gave a new word to the English language, and posterity has till now

2 *Narcissus Luttrell's Popish Plot Catalogues.* Introduction by F. C. Francis (Oxford, 1956).

found him absurd. But he also gave a collection of books to a small Welsh college. This catalogue for the first time gives scholars an opportunity of judging the full value of his gift. It is one that would have been welcome to older and greater universities. The value to students of literature and history of such a comprehensive collection of tracts so near to the academic heart of Wales would be enormously enhanced if Lampeter could add either originals or photocopies in the period 1680–1720, where it is so strong. This is not an auspicious time to look for benefactors, but there must be such, Welsh, English or American, who would help to augment the more memorable work of the Bowdlers.

Julian Roberts. Oxford, May 1975.

Acknowledgements

It is a pleasure to acknowledge formally the help and advice so readily given by Mr R. C. Rider, the Rev. D. G. Selwyn and Professor P. H. Davison of Saint David's University College, Lampeter; by Mr L. J. Harris of the College of Librarianship Wales, Llanbadarn Fawr; by Miss Eiluned Rees and Mr Gwyn Walters of the National Library of Wales, Aberystwyth; by Mr John Horden and Mr Peter Grant (who permitted reference to their materials for a new edition of Halkett and Laing); by Mr Robert Latham of Magdalene College, Cambridge; by Dr R. A. Sayce of Worcester College, Oxford; by Mr J. E. C. Palmer, editor of the British Union Catalogue of Books Printed before 1801, British Library Reference Division; and by the staffs of the British Library Reference Division, the Bodleian Library, Bath Public Library, and the libraries of Trinity College, Dublin, the University of Glasgow, the National Maritime Museum, the University of London and Trinity College, Cambridge.

The trustees of the Catherine and Lady (Grace) James Foundation, Aberystwyth, generously contributed an annual grant towards the cost of typing this catalogue.

Finally, I wish to express my personal thanks to my typists, and especially to Mrs Clar Parri whose skill greatly eased my editorial burden.

Brian Ll. James, *Editor, Dydd Gŵyl Dewi, 1975.*

Introduction

The Tract Collection in the Old Library of Saint David's University College, Lampeter, consists of 828 volumes, containing 11,395 separate pieces. (The total includes 1,572 duplicates and 1,184 parts of serials; the whole is catalogued in 8,692 entries.) The range of dates of the pamphlets and serials included in the Collection is from *circa* 1520 to 1843, but the table on page xviii shows that the bulk of them (rather more than three out of four) are dated between 1641 and 1720. Even within these eighty years there is a shorter period extending from 1679 to 1719 which is the real core of the Collection. There is a remarkably rich concentration in the years 1709–13, with as many as 2,015 pieces (1,295 catalogue entries), probably representing a substantial proportion of the output of pamphlets in England during those years.

Within the Collection there are copies of 176 pamphlets published in the British Isles (or in the English language abroad) before 1641; of these, six are not recorded in Pollard and Redgrave's *Short-title catalogue* (1926). There are 3,352 items similarly published from 1641 to 1700, and 162 of these do not appear in the first edition of Wing's *Short-title catalogue*. The number of pamphlets in the Collection printed in the eighteenth century is 4,477 but there is, alas, no short-title catalogue against which to measure them. There are 101 pamphlets carrying foreign imprints (excluding those falling within the scope of Pollard & Redgrave and Wing) of the sixteenth and seventeenth centuries. In fact the pamphlets hereafter catalogued are mostly the products of the London book-trade; other places of printing and publication appear in the catalogue in small numbers: Oxford and Cambridge, the major English provincial cities, Edinburgh and Dublin. An analysis of the 344 entries for the year 1710 reveals that 90 per cent have a London imprint, 6 per cent have no imprint (though most of these almost certainly would have been printed in London), the remaining 4 per cent originating from Oxford, Exeter, Dublin, Norwich, Worcester and Amsterdam. It is a London-centred collection, therefore.

The tracts reflect in a particularly vivid way the events and concerns of their age. Religious controversies and political crises were the weighty matters which most engaged the attention of the pamphleteers and preachers of the eventful eighty years which began with the outbreak of the Civil War in 1642. But there is a leaven of pamphlets treating of all manner of subjects—literary, philosophical, economic, scientific, medical —while others, lighter still, give accounts of contemporary scandals, supernatural occurrences and whatever was of that moment occupying the public attention. The writings of some of the most eminent intellectuals of their day—Milton, Jeremy Taylor, Dryden, George Hickes, Locke, Defoe, Swift, Pope—are to be found in the Tract Collection side by side with the effusions of now barely-remembered controversialists such as Roger L'Estrange, Charles Leslie, Henry Sacheverell and Benjamin Hoadly, or of minor versifiers and hack writers such as Ned Ward and Tom Brown[1].

---

1 A very general description of the subject content of the Collection has appeared in an article by L. J. Harris and B. Ll. James, 'The tract collection at Saint David's University College, Lampeter', *Trivium*, 9 (1974), pp. 100–9.

In addition to the mass of printed material there is in the Collection, interspersed among the pamphlets, a considerable number of manuscript items in various seventeenth- and eighteenth-century hands. Many of these seem to be copies of printed pamphlets, among which sermons predominate, though there is not a little verse. The manuscript material is not included in this catalogue.

The volumes which now compose the Lampeter Tract Collection were given to the College by a number of benefactors in the first half of the nineteenth century.

By far the most significant constituent of the Collection was a single donation of some 550 volumes containing perhaps between nine and ten thousand separate pieces. The College has no record of the donor's name, but the history of the volumes, reconstructed from association marks and from other documentary evidence, leads to the almost certain conclusion that the donor was Dr Thomas Bowdler, editor of the *Family Shakespeare*, and that the pamphlets had been collected by his family over a century and a half. Since these volumes contain as much as four-fifths of the Tract Collection it is clear that the Collection here catalogued is really the Bowdler Collection with minor additions.

At least five members of the Bowdler family[2] had a part in the building up of their collection, the earliest being Thomas Bowdler I (*fl.* 1638–1700), a merchant of the city of London; he had his pamphlets bound in a uniform set of numbered volumes, of which 27 are extant;[3] each volume has a table of contents or an index in his hand, and in most he has signed his name and added 'Consider the end of all things'. The earliest of his dated signatures is 1638. In this small group of volumes occur the most important of the Civil War tracts at Lampeter. On the title-pages of two pamphlets appears the signature of John Bowdler, Thomas' brother and the father of Thomas Bowdler II (1661–1738) the major collector of the family.

The second Thomas was born in Dublin where his father was in the government's service; his mother was the daughter of Henry Jones, Bishop of Meath. After his father's early death and his mother's remarriage he was sent as a boy to London to be brought up by his uncle, the City merchant. By the age of fifteen he had entered the Navy Office as a clerk, and so began a long association with the great Samuel Pepys, an association which ripened into a life-long friendship. The real turning point of his life came in 1689 when, following the example of his admired superior, Bowdler resigned his place rather than take the oath to William and Mary. He was still a very young man with a long life in front of him, but he remained a resolute Jacobite and a devout member of the Non-juring communion to the end; a particularly close friend was George Hickes (1642–1715), the eminent scholar and Non-juring bishop. Bowdler seems to have become a man of considerable means, probably as the heir to his uncle, and perhaps also through his marriage in 1692 to the daughter of Sir Joseph Martin, a Turkey merchant; it seems likely that Bowdler himself had an interest in Martin's business. He also had shares in the East India Company.

It is not easy to determine exactly when Thomas Bowdler II began to collect pamphlets. His son wrote in a letter to Richard Rawlinson that his father was 'very curious and made Collections from his Youth'.[4] He may therefore have begun collecting at the time of the Popish Plot when a spate of ephemeral literature issued from the London presses. His vital dates (1661–1738) are so close to those of Narcissus Luttrell (1657–1732) that a comparison with that well-known pamphlet collector suggests itself; Luttrell himself became a serious collector during the Popish Plot crisis.[5]

It is clear however that it was many years later that Bowdler became a considerable—indeed an obsessive —collector of ephemera. He did not inherit his uncle's collection until after 1700; in 1701 he bought at least eighteen volumes[6] (containing 239 pamphlets) at the auction of the goods of Francis Turner, the deposed Bishop of Ely; he paid £3 2s. 6d. for these. Some years later Bowdler acquired a substantial ready-made collection of unbound pamphlets some of which bore annotations by John Gauden (1605–1662),[7] Bishop of

---

2 The most useful printed sources on the Bowdlers are: *D.N.B.*; Thomas Bowdler, *Memoir of the life of John Bowdler, Esq.* (London, 1824); Noel Perrin, *Dr. Bowdler's legacy* (London, 1970).
3 These now have the following numbers: T.61, 86, 116, 118, 122–4, 126–30, 174, 176–8, 182, 183, 287, 309, 313, 317, 504, 508.
4 Bodleian Library MS. Rawl. D.923, fol. 290.
5 J. M. Osborn, 'Reflections on Narcissus Luttrell (1657–1732)', *The Book Collector*, 6 (1957), pp. 15–27.
6 These now have the numbers: T.32, 63, 65, 114, 173, 175, 181, 185, 236, 320, 380, 393, 494, 496–8, 503.
7 A manuscript work by Gauden, contained in T.145, is the subject of an article by A. J. Sambrook, 'Milton's creation heresy paralleled', *English Studies*, 46 (1965), pp. 330–1.

Worcester, the supposed author of Εἰκὼν Βασιλικη, and other members of the Gauden family; it is conceivable that Bowdler obtained these from the estate of William Hewer of Clapham (1642–1715) of which he was one of the executors.[8] His position as executor may also have enabled him to get hold of pamphlets that had belonged to George Hickes, for there are many which either bear his name or have annotations in his distinctive handwriting.[9]

The most interesting phase of Bowdler's activity as a collector lies however in the years 1709–18 when he appears to have been buying pamphlets at, or close upon, their publication. A large number of pieces occur, scattered through eighty-five volumes of the Lampeter Collection, having a note written as near as possible to the bottom edge of the title-page or half-title. The note consists of initials and a date. Two alternative groups of initials occur (though the hand is the same, presumably that of a clerk employed by Bowdler) seeming to be either G.Str^n or N.W^n. It would seem fairly safe to claim that they represent the names of agents through whom Bowdler obtained his supply of pamphlets, and it would not be unreasonable to interpret the former as the name of George Strahan, a London bookseller. The date must be that of acquisition by Bowdler.

Having come to possess a vast accumulation of pamphlets, most of them unbound but tied up in bundles, Bowdler embarked in 1717 upon the labour of cataloguing. In his own hand he listed the contents of each bound volume on its fly-leaf (following his uncle's practice), but the contents of the bundles of loose papers he methodically and with exemplary neatness and accuracy entered in a book which still forms a part of the Lampeter Collection. Another habit which places us even further in his debt is that where he could he wrote —either on the title-page or in the manuscript catalogue—the name of the author of anonymous works. His deep involvement with the Non-jurors makes him a particularly valuable authority upon the authorship of their numerous publications.

The subject range of Thomas Bowdler II's collecting during his most active years was wide; his pamphlets are representative of English publishing of the time, comprising everything from serious religious work to scurrilous and indeed bawdy satirical verse. The uncut condition of so many pamphlets of the 1709–18 period suggests that the collector was not necessarily interested in reading his multifarious acquisitions. Outside these years, however, one can detect the range of Bowdler's particular interests; there is ample evidence that he was a close and critical reader of the numerous pamphlets relating to Ireland, the Navy and foreign trade. But, above all, he was interested in those crucial areas of controversy which hinged upon the vital theme of the relationship between Church and State, religion and politics, from the years of the Popish Plot and the Exclusion Crisis, through the reign of James II and the Revolution, and into the era of the Non-jurors. It would seem not too much to claim this as one of the best extant collections of Non-juring literature. As an instance of the richness of the Collection in this literature one may cite the Usages Controversy—a disagreement among the Non-jurors over a proposed change in the communion office; Thomas Wagstaffe listed forty contributions to this controversy, of which thirty-five are present in the Lampeter Collection[10]. Other aspects of Church and State gave rise to many pamphlets, for example the Convocation Controversy, Occasional Conformity, the impeachment of Sacheverell and the Bangorian Controversy. Bowdler's sympathies lay, of course, with the High-Church Tories in these disputes, but he collected the opposing publications of Catholics, Low Churchmen and Dissenters. In fact the Dissenter Daniel Defoe is the writer most voluminously represented in the Lampeter Tract Collection!

Thomas Bowdler II's interest in collecting pamphlets waned rapidly after 1720, and thus the Collection at Lampeter contains remarkably few publications of the 1720s and 1730s. Bowdler had retired to live at Boulogne by 1735 and had already divided much of his property among his children before making his will in that year; he died in 1738. The pamphlet collection passed to his elder son, Thomas Bowdler III (1706–85)

8   Hewer, the protégé and close friend of Pepys, had bought the house at Clapham from Sir Denis Gauden, victualler to the Navy, after he (Gauden) had been ruined; Sir Denis had built the house originally for his brother, the Bishop. R. Ollard, *Pepys* (London, 1974), p. 148.
9   Hickes's will was published as a pamphlet (no. 6050 in this catalogue). Hilkiah Bedford was appointed literary executor and received Hickes's papers and his controversial pamphlets—though some at least of these evidently found their way into Bowdler's hands. The major part of Hickes's library was sold by auction in 1716.
10   Wagstaffe's list is printed in H. Broxap, *The later Non-jurors* (Cambridge, 1924), pp. 63–5.

and his collection of naval documents to his other son, Captain John Bowdler, R.N.[11] The third Thomas Bowdler lived at Ashley near Bath from 1749 and later in Bath itself, where he died in 1785; he was apparently a gentleman of private means. His marriage in 1742 to Elizabeth Stuart Cotton,[12] the daughter of Sir John Cotton and a descendent of the founder of the Cottonian Library, confirmed him in the family's Non-juring and Jacobite tradition. It would seem that Thomas Bowdler III was not a collector of books in the strict sense of the term, but he was a cultivated and well-read man and the owner of an excellent library; he had, however, a not inconsiderable quantity of pamphlets since he added to the family's collection some 350 pieces in thirty-seven volumes and noted their contents at the end of his father's catalogue. There are also in the Lampeter Collection three sets of uniformly bound and numbered volumes[13] which may be the result of another phase of his acquisitions; they contain only one pamphlet dated after his death, but another pamphlet carries a note of presentation to Dr Thomas Bowdler IV.[14] This particular group of volumes could thus either have been Thomas Bowdler III's (but inherited by and bound to the order of Dr Bowdler, his son), or it could have been assembled by Dr Bowdler himself; a view of the contents, which are mainly of the middle decades of the eighteenth century, suggests that the former is the more likely explanation. The Bowdlers ceased to add to their collection after this time (1785–87).

What happened between the death of Thomas Bowdler III in 1785 and the gift of the collection to St David's College some time between about 1810 and 1827 is not certain, but it is certain that it came to Lampeter as part of what might be called the 'Foundation Collection' of the Library. There are two assumptions: first, that Dr Thomas Bowdler (1754–1825) inherited the entire collection from his father and, second, that he presented it to the College. The circumstantial evidence bearing upon the second point is fairly strong, depending as it does upon the long-standing friendship which existed between Bishop Burgess, the College's founder, and the Bowdler family,[15] and upon the fact that Dr Bowdler lived for the last fourteen years of his life near Swansea, at that time within Burgess' diocese of Saint David's, and some forty-five miles from Lampeter. Both he and his sister, the bluestocking, Henrietta Maria Bowdler, were sufficiently interested in the College to contribute to its funds. There is no reference to the tract collection in his will, neither is there any specific reference to it in the brief advertisement of the sale of his library which took place at Swansea in June 1825.[16]

In the time of Thomas Bowdler II the greater part of his collection of pamphlets had been in loose bundles. By the time of their arrival at Lampeter the bundles had been rather cheaply bound, and the volumes were numbered to correspond to the manuscript catalogue. Entries relating to the tracts appeared in the printed catalogue of the College Library published in 1836, but only in the form of 'Tracts and Pamphlets, principally of the reigns of James II, William III and Queen Anne, *bound together* in 491 vols. . . . all numbered; with a manuscript catalogue of their contents.' The sets of volumes associated with the third and fourth Bowdlers were given similar collective treatment—though these had no tables of contents, neither were they included in the manuscript catalogue.

At the time of the first printed catalogue of its contents the Library at Lampeter was small and undistinguished; the bulk of its 5,000 miscellaneous volumes had been contributed by well-wishers—many of whose names are unrecorded—in response to an appeal that Bishop Burgess had first issued in 1807. We surmise that Dr Bowdler had been one of these early and uncommemorated benefactors. Some other donor gave a set of seventeen numbered volumes of 'miscellanies',[17] containing some eighty-five pamphlets of the later seventeenth and early eighteenth centuries; these had evidently once been the property of Alexander and Thomas Scott,

11 These had once been official papers belonging to the Navy Office; they now form an important group in the Rawlinson MSS in the Bodleian Library, and are a major source of the history of Pepys's administration of the Navy. Several letters from Thomas Bowdler III to Richard Rawlinson, of various dates in 1749, tell the story of how 'my Father's naval papers' were acquired by Rawlinson from Captain Bowdler (surely a black sheep in the family), but the writer did not know how Thomas Bowdler II had obtained them. MS. Rawl. D 912 and 923.
12 Mrs Bowdler was the author of a paraphrase of the Song of Solomon (no. 7661 in this catalogue). Noel Perrin, *op. cit.*, pp. 65–67.
13 These are now numbered T.539–543 (the folios), T.554–559 (the large quartos) and T.626–678 (the small quartos and octavos).
14 No. 7809 in this catalogue.
15 See, for example, the dedication to Burgess in Dr Thomas Bowdler's *Select chapters from the Old Testament* (Swansea, 1823); also Noel Perrin, *op. cit.*, pp. 78–79.
16 *The Cambrian*, 28 May 1825. No copy of the sale catalogue is known to exist.
17 These are now numbered: T.56, 286, 339–41, 345–6, 349, 354, 356, 386, 477–81, 690.

Lincolnshire parsons of that period. But it was some years before further volumes of tracts were acquired, and then only as a minor part of two benefactions of a size and richness that immediately made the Lampeter Library the largest and most important in Wales: the gifts of Thomas Phillips, and the bequest of his personal library by Bishop Burgess.

Thomas Burgess (1756–1837) was Bishop of Saint David's from 1803 to 1825 and of Salisbury from 1825 to 1837; it was he who was principally responsible for the founding of Saint David's College to provide for the education of young men of the diocese who intended to take holy orders but who could not afford to go to Oxford or Cambridge. First adumbrated in 1804, the scheme for a college was eventually realized, after a long period of planning and collecting, in 1822–27. Burgess had been one of the leading classical scholars in the country in the latter part of the eighteenth century, and his library was well stocked in this field, as well as in biblical and patristic scholarship. Among his books were fifty-one volumes (containing 440 pamphlets) which have subsequently been added to the Tract Collection. These are eighteenth- and nineteenth-century pamphlets mainly, though there are two volumes from the Popish Plot era and others of the reign of James II. Most of the pamphlets are sermons and religious polemics, but learned controversies (such as that between Richard Bentley and Conyers Middleton) are also represented.

Thomas Phillips (1760–1851), the Library's principal benefactor, had no connection with the famous bibliophile Sir Thomas Phillipps of Middle Hill. He was a Radnorshire man who became a surgeon employed by the East India Company and in the course of many years' service in India he accumulated a substantial fortune. Returning to this country in 1817 he began to seek out ways of using his money to promote educational projects, mainly in South Wales; his chief monument is the public school which he founded at Llandovery, but his generosity towards the young and struggling college at Lampeter is also notable. Between 1834 and 1852 the College received at intervals sixty consignments of books, numbering altogether more than 22,500 volumes and comprising a most remarkable (but quite random) sample of the literature of Western Europe published since about 1470. Among these riches were found 169 volumes of pamphlets which are now part of the Tract Collection. The most interesting items that came from Phillips were sets of 'miscellanies'[18] and 'political tracts'[19] of the 1790s.

It is not very certain when the volumes of tracts given by Burgess, Phillips and several others were added to the Bowdler collection; it was probably some time in the second half of the last century. It would not appear, however, that the importance and value of the Collection was really recognized until the 1880s, when T. F. Tout came to the College as professor and librarian. Together with his friend C. H. Firth,[20] an external examiner at the College for several years, Tout rescued the Tract Collection from neglect. Several volumes were found to be decayed and were disposed of; the binding of many others was in urgent need of renewal. Tout and Firth proceeded to study the Collection, to re-arrange the contents of part and to have seventy-two volumes rebound, each volume being given a useful binder's title instead of a number. For example, they brought together, arranged in chronological order and bound in four volumes all the Civil War and Commonwealth newspapers which they found scattered through the Collection. Firth was allowed to buy some of the duplicates from the Collection and these seem to have been included among the books bequeathed by him to Worcester College, Oxford.[21] Many other volumes were rebound early in the present century but no more attempts were made to arrange the contents in a logical way; just a few of the Bowdler volumes (that is, the bundles of the 1717 catalogue) now remain in their original bindings.

By the turn of the century the Bowdler numbering system had been lost and the other tract volumes had become mixed up with the Bowdler volumes. The Collection was re-numbered in a single sequence as far as T.579 probably at the same time as a partial attempt was made, in 1902–5, to create a card-index for the tracts (and for the Library as a whole). The remaining volumes were not numbered until the whole Collection was catalogued in 1972–74, when further additions of comparable material hitherto in other parts of the Library were made.

18 T.607–615.
19 T.586–589.
20 Firth described his work in the Library in a letter to the College's Principal, 3 Nov. 1898.
21 Information from Dr R. A. Sayce, Librarian of Worcester College.

The following is a summary of the provenance of the volumes composing the Lampeter Tract Collection:

Bowdler: 1–53, 55, 57–92, 94–116, 118–71, 173–8, 180–5, 189–209, 211–13, 215–34, 236–75, 278–83, 285, 287, 289–310, 312–14, 316–38, 342–4, 347–8, 350–1, 355, 358–75, 377–83, 385, 387–418, 421–44, 446–9, 452, 455–9, 461–3, 465–76, 482–7, 489–98, 500–28, 539–43, 546–51, 554–9, 565, 626–78, 774, 801.

Phillips: 93, 172, 179, 186, 188, 235, 277, 311, 315, 357, 376, 419, 420, 445, 451, 488, 529–34, 536–7, 545, 552, 560–4, 566–75, 577, 581–2, 586–99, 601, 604–16, 618, 620–1, 624–5, 680–1, 683–8, 692–703, 705–10, 715–18, 722–8, 730, 732–7, 739, 741, 744–6, 748–51, 755–7, 764–6, 769, 771, 773, 775–6, 778–81, 783–4, 790, 792, 794, 797, 799, 803, 807–13, 815, 817, 819–20, 822–3, 825–8.

Burgess: 54, 117, 210, 214, 288, 353, 384, 460, 499, 538, 553, 576, 578, 603, 619, 623, 679, 691, 704, 712–14, 719–21, 731, 738, 743, 758–61, 767–8, 777, 782, 785–6, 788, 791, 793, 796, 800, 802, 804, 806, 814, 816, 818, 821, 824.

Others: 56, 187, 249, 276, 284, 286, 339–41, 345–6, 349, 352, 354, 356, 386, 450, 453–4, 464, 477–81, 535, 544, 579–80, 583–5, 600, 602, 617, 622, 682, 689–90, 711, 729, 740, 742, 747, 752–4, 762–3, 770, 772, 787, 789, 795, 798, 805.

The following table gives a total for each decade of the number of catalogue entries (which is nearly equivalent to the number of different pamphlets in the Collection), the number of duplicate pamphlets and the number of parts of serials. The right-hand column gives for each decade the total number of separate pieces in the Collection.

	Catalogue Entries	Duplicates	Serial Parts	Total		Catalogue Entries	Duplicates	Serial Parts	Total
1511–20	1	.	.	1	1701–10	1,356	426	348	2,130
1521–30	1	.	.	1	1711–20	1,498	343	160	2,001
1531–40	.	.	.	.	1721–30	281	26	6	313
1541–50	2	.	.	2	1731–40	194	11	1	206
1551–60	2	.	.	2	1741–50	341	27	13	381
1561–70	3	1	.	4	1751–60	138	6	1	145
1571–80	3	.	.	3	1761–70	155	2	4	161
1581–90	9	.	.	9	1771–80	144	8	3	155
1591–1600	5	.	.	5	1781–90	170	13	.	183
1601–10	23	.	.	23	1791–1800	200	2	.	202
1611–20	43	2	.	45	1801–10	114	1	.	115
1621–30	44	1	.	45	1811–20	101	1	4	106
1631–40	72	5	.	77	1821–30	176	.	.	176
1641–50	681	43	60	784	1831–40	90	3	1	94
1651–60	297	13	87	397	1841–50	9	.	.	9
1661–70	177	18	54	249					
1671–80	510	131	6	647		8,598	1,572	1,184	11,354
1681–90	1,210	343	28	1,581	Undated				8
1691–1700	548	146	408	1,102	Uncatalogued fragments, etc.				33
									11,395

Editor's Note

The catalogue has been reproduced from a card-index of the Tract Collection compiled in 1972–74; the object in cataloguing was to provide a finding-list of the contents of the Collection, giving for each item the bibliographical information normally found in a library catalogue; more elaborate description was not attempted. In publishing the card-index it was decided to arrange the entries chronologically since so much of the material included in the Collection is significant only in relation to contemporary events and to other pamphlets published in the same year. The added entries prepared for the alphabetical card-index have been relegated to the index.

Chronological arrangement is so dependent upon accurate dating that some statement upon this awkward problem is called for. The date adopted is that actually printed on the pamphlet, e.g. 1710, even though it is realized that this may indicate printing (or publication) at any time from October 1709 to March 1711 (New Style), a period of eighteen months.[22] (It would have been a difficult and laborious task to discover, in a large proportion of cases, the actual year of issue expressed in New Style.) Where the printer has chosen to indicate the year in both Old and New Style (either as $171\frac{9}{1}$ or $17\frac{10}{11}$) then the item is filed under the year 1711. Where a pamphlet is undated a date is supplied in the catalogue entry within square brackets; where there is some doubt about its accuracy a question mark is added [1710?], and where the date is only approximate c. is prefixed [c. 1710]. Eight pamphlets which could not be dated within a decade are listed at the end of the main section of the catalogue (see page 282). Serials are listed in an appendix (see also page 282).

Many pamphlets of the seventeenth and eighteenth centuries were published either anonymously or pseudonymously. Where authorship can be established to a reasonable degree of certainty the entry is made under that author's name; where attribution is uncertain or disputed entry is made under the title, but a statement of attribution is inserted in brackets after the title or, in a few cases, is included as a footnote. Following the practice of the short-title catalogues, entry is made under initials where these are the only indication of authorship, but pseudonyms are avoided except in the cases of Isaac Bickerstaff and Caleb D'Anvers. In general the authority of the British Museum catalogue on questions of authorship is accepted in preference to that of Halkett and Laing, but evidence has also been taken from other major catalogues and bibliographies such as the *New Cambridge bibliography of English literature*, the *National Union Catalog* and John Robert Moore, *A checklist of the writings of Daniel Defoe*. Wing is not a good authority on questions of authorship. Manuscript attributions on title-pages or in the 1717 catalogue are not accepted for entry if they are unsupported by other evidence, but they are recorded in footnotes.

Reference is made where appropriate to numbers assigned by Pollard and Redgrave's *Short-title catalogue* (1926), the first edition of Wing's *Short-title catalogue* (including the *Gallery of ghosts* and the Christ Church supplement), and H. M. Adams, *Catalogue of books printed on the continent of Europe, 1501–1600, in Cambridge libraries*. Because the Tract Collection includes so many of Daniel Defoe's publications reference is made to the numbers assigned in J. R. Moore's *Checklist*.

Each catalogue entry is given a serial number from 1 to 8,690; since this bears no relation to the location of the pamphlet on the Library's shelves, the tract volume number is cited on each card, beneath the entry, in the form, for example, of T.402.

The index consists principally of the names of authors and the titles of anonymous works; the names of persons and the titles of anonymous pamphlets referred to or written against are also included. In the index titles have been ruthlessly abbreviated, but only omissions within the part of the title actually quoted have been indicated by three dots; initial articles have been omitted. Where known, the names of authors of anonymous works are given in square brackets.

22   cf. L. W. Hanson, *Contemporary printed sources for British and Irish economic history* (Cambridge, 1963), pp. xiii–xiv.

The Catalogue

1520—1529

1

ANGLIARA (Juan de)

Die Schiffung mitt dem Lanndt der Gulden Insel
gefundē durch Hern Johan vō Angliara... gar hübsch
ding zū hōre mit allen yren leben und sitten.
[No imprint, 1520?]   4°

Three leaves only.

T.248

1530—1539

2

ELIAS, *Levita*.

[Hebrew] Capitula cantici, specierum, proprietatum,
& officiorum, in quibus scilicet agitur de literis,
punctis, & quibusdam accentibus Hebraicis... Per
Sebastianum Munsterum iam pridem Latine iuxta
Hebraismum uersum. Basilae [Col: apud Io. Frobenium]
anno 1527.   8°

Adams E 113.

T.452

1540—1549

3

AUGSBURG CONFESSION.

Abtrucke der verwarungs schrifft, der Chur vnd
Fürsten, auch Graffen, Herrn, Stette vnd Stende der
Augspurgischen Confession Eynungs verwandten, Irer
yetzigen hochgenottrangten, vnd verursachten
Kriegssrüstung halben, an Keyserliche Mayestat
aussgangen, vnd beschehen. [Nuremberg, Johann vom
Berg und Ulrich Neuber], 1546.   4°

T.248

4

JOHN FREDERICK, *Elector of Saxony and* PHILIP,
Landgrave of Hesse.

Meiner genedigsten und genedigen Herrn Hertzog Johans
Friderichen Churfürsten zu Sachssen etc. und Herren
Philipsen Landgrauen zu Hessen etc. warhafftige
ausfürung/ das Marggraue Hansen von Brandenburgk nicht
gebürt sich in der Keiser. Maiestat dienst wider ir
Chur/ und fürstliche gnad/ und ander derselben
Religions verwandte einzulassen/... [Wittenberg?],
1546.   4°

T.248

1550—1559

5

STANDISH (John) *Archdeacon of Colchester.*

A discourse wherein is debated whether it is expedient
that the scripture should be in English... Londini,
in aedibus R. Caly, 1554.   8°

STC 23207.
The title-page and many other leaves wanting.

T.457

6

CHARLES V, *Holy Roman Emperor.*

Oratio Caroli. V. Romanorum imperatoris habita in
conuentu Bruxellensi ad ordines, as Belgicae regionis
proceres, in declarando Philippum filium eiusdē
regionis principem. Florentiae, 1556.   4°

P 1849.
Incomplete.

T.248

1560—1569

7

PIGNA (Giovanni Battista)

Il principe di Gio. Battista Pigna ... Nel qual
si discriue come debba essere il principe heroico,
sotto il cui gouerno vn felice popolo, possa
tranquilla & beatamente viuere. In Venetia, [col:
appresso Francesco Sansovino, 1561.   4°

Adams P 1207.
The first gathering is in T.689, the rest of the book
in T.249.

T.249 T.689

8

SANCTOTISIUS (Christophorus)

Concio R.P. Mag. Christophori Sanctotisii, Hispani,
Burgensis ... habita ad sacrosanctam oecumenicam
Synodum Tridentinam. De signis uerae Ecclesiae
agnoscendae ... Venetiis, ex officina Iordani
Ziletti, 1563.   4°

Not in Adams.

T.138

9

GREGORY, *of Nazianzus.*

Sententiae et regulae vitae ex Gregorii Nazanzeni
scriptis collectae. Eiusdem Iambi aliquot, nunc
primum in lucem editi: per Ioannem Sambucum
Pannonium. Antuerpiae, ex officina Christophori
Plantini, 1568.   8°

Adams G 1164.
The first two gatherings only.

T.585

1570—1579

10

BĒZE (Théodore de)

Theodori Bezae Modesta et Christiana defensio ad D.
Nicolai Selnecceri maledicam & virulentam
responsionem. Genevae apud Ioan. Crispinum, 1572.
8°

T.451

11

MERCERUS (Johannes)

Ioannis Merceri Regii quondam in Academia Parisiensi
literarum professoris commentarij in
librum Iob. Adiecta est Theodori Bezae epistola, in
qua de huius viri doctrina, & istorum commentariorum
utilitate disseritur. Genevae, excudebat Eustathius
Vignon, 1573. Fol.

Adams M 1314.

T.687

WHITGIFT (John) *Archbishop of Canterbury.*

A godlie sermon. 1574.

See no. 5924.

12

FOXE (John)

A sermon preached at the christening of a certaine
Iew, at London. Conteining an exposition of the
xi. chapter of S. Paul to the Romanes. Translated
out of Latine into English by Iames Bell. Imprinted
at London by Christopher Barker, anno. 1578.   8°

STC 11248.
Signature of Hugh Cowper.

T.457

1580—1589

13

CHURCH OF ENGLAND. *Articles of Religion.*

Articles whereupon it was agreed by the archbishops
and byshops of both prouinces and the whole cleargie,
in the Conuocation holden at London in the yeere of
our Lorde God 1562... Imprinted at London by
Christopher Barker, 1581.   4°

STC 10042.

T.55

14

DUDLEY (Robert) *Earl of Leicester.*

Lawes and ordinances, set downe by Robert Earle
of Leycester, the Queenes Maiesties lieutenant
and captaine general of her armie... in the Lowe
Countries... Imprinted at London by Christopher
Barker, [1586].   4°

STC 7288.

T.306

15

BEZE (Théodore de)

Ad acta colloquii Montisbelgardensis Tubingae edita,
Theodori Bezae responsio. Geneuae, excudebat Joannes
le Preux, 1587.   4°

Adams B 882.

T.138

16

JAMES I, *King of England.*

Ane fruitfull meditatioun contening ane plane and
facill expositioun of ye 7.8.9. and 10 versis of
the 20 chap. of the Reuelatioun in forme of ane
sermone... Imprentit at Edinburgh be Henrie
Charteris, 1588.   8°

STC 14376.

T.475

17

COOPER (Thomas) *Bishop of Winchester.*

An admonition to the people of England: wherein
are answered not onely the slaunderous untruethes,
reprochfully uttered by Martin [Marprelate] the
libeller, but also many other crimes objected
generally against all bishops... [The address
signed T.C.] London, the deputies of Christopher
Barker, 1589.   4°

STC 5682.
Wanting the title-page, and other pages.

T.247

18

SOME (Robert)

A godly treatise, wherein are examined and confuted
many execrable fancies, giuen out and holden, partly
by Henry Barrow and Iohn Greenewood: partly, by other
of the anabaptistical order... Imprinted at London
by G.B. deputie to Christopher Barker, 1589.   4°

STC 22912.

T.55

19

WRIGHT (Leonard)

A summons for sleepers. Wherein most grieuous and
notorious offenders are set foorth true
frutes of repentance... Hereunto is annexed, A
patterne for pastors... Newly reprinted, corrected
and amended... [No imprint, 1589.]   4°

STC 26034.

T.754

1590—1599

20

BĒZE (Théodore de)

Tractatus pius et moderatus de vera excommunicatione,
& christiano presbyterio, iampridem pacis
conciliandę causa, Cl.V. Th. Erasti D. Medici centum
manuscriptis thesibus oppositus, & nunc primum,
cogente necessitate, editus. Geneuae, apud
Ioannem le Preux, 1590.   4°

Adams B 961 (?)

T.138

21

CHURCH OF SCOTLAND.

The confession of faith, subscribed by the Kingis
Maiestie and his houshould: togither with the copie
of the bande, maid touching the maintenance of the
true religion, the Kingis Majesties person and
estate... At Edinburgh, Robert Walde-grave, 1590. 4°

STC 22023.

T.55

22

BIBLE. *New Testament. Revelation.*

Apocalypsis S. Iohannis Apostoli et Euangelistae,
methodica analysi argumentorum, notisque breuibus
ad rerum intelligentiam & Catholicae ac Christianae
Ecclesiae historiam pertinentibus illustrata per
Franciscum Iunium Biturigem. Heidelbergae,
[Hieronymus Commelinus], 1591.   8°

Adams B 1950
The first six leaves only. Signature of Iacobus
Usher.

T.585

23

BARLAAMUS, *Bishop of Gerace.*

Του σοφωτατου Βαρλααμ λογος περι της του κατα
αρχης. Barlaami de papae principatu libellus.
Nunc primum Graece & Latine editus opera Ioannis
Luidi... Oxoniae, excudebat Iosephus Barnesius,
1592.   4°

STC 1430.

T.254

24

PISCATOR (Johannes)

Analysis logica quinque postremarum epistolarum
Pauli... Una cum scholiis & observationibus
locorum doctrinae... Editio tertia, ab autore
recognita... Sigenae Nassoviorum ex officina
Christophori Corvini, 1598.   8°

Not in Adams.
The first gathering only.

T.585

1590−1599 (Cont'd.)

25

FREHER (Marquard)

De numismate census, a pharisaeis in quaestionem vocato. Dissertatio theologistorica. Editio auctior Heidelbergae, apud Andream Cambierum, 1599.   4°

Adams F 1000.

T.620

1600

26

DU PERRON (Jacques Davy) *Archbishop of Sens.*

A discourse of the conference holden before the French King at Fontain-bleau, betweene the L. Bishop of Eureaux, and Munsieur du Plessis L. of Mornay, the 4. of May 1600. Concerning certaine pretended corruptions of authors, cyted by the sayd Munsieur du Plessis in his booke against the Masse. Faithfully translated out of the French. London, E.A. for Mathew Selman and William Ferbrand, 1600.   4°

STC 6381

T.55

1601

27

ABBOT (Robert) *Bishop of Salisbury.*

The exaltation of the kingdome and priesthood of Christ. In certaine sermons upon the 110. psalme: preached in the cathedrall church and city of Worcester... 1596. Londini. impensis G. Bishop, 1601.   4°

STC 51.

T.475

28

BACON (Francis) *Viscount St. Albans.*

A declaration of the practises & treasons attempted and committed by Robert late Earle of Essex and his complices, against her Maiestie and her kingdoms, and of the proceedings... Together with the very confessions and other parts of the euidences themselues... [Anon.] Imprinted at London by Robert Barker, anno 1601.   4°

STC 1133.

T.127

1603

29

M. (T.)

The copie of a letter written from Master C.S. [but signed T.M.] neere Salisbury, to Master H.A. at London, concerning the proceedings at Winchester; where the late L. Cobham, L. Gray, and Sir Griffin Marckham, all attainted of hie treason, were ready to be executed on Friday the 9. of December 1603... Imprinted at London by R.B., 1603.

STC 17151a.

T.129

1604

30

BACON (Francis) *Viscount St. Albans.*

Certaine considerations touching the better pacification, and edification of the Church of England: dedicated to his most excellent Maiestie. [Anon.] Printed for Henry Tomes, [1604?]   4°

STC 1120.

T.306

31

CHURCH OF ENGLAND. *Constitutions and Canons.*

Constitutions and canons ecclesiasticall, treated upon by the Bishop of London... and the rest of the bishops and clergie of the... Prouince: and agreed upon... 1603. Imprinted at London by Robert Barker, 1604.   4°

STC 10070.
Wanting the title-page.

T.251

32

JACOB (Henry)

Reasons taken out of Gods word and the best humane testimonies proving a necessitie of reforming our churches in England... [No imprint], 1604.   4°

STC 14338.

T.251

33

PONT (Robert)

De unione Britanniae, seu de regnorum Angliae et Scotie omniumque adjacentium insularum Britanicarum in unam monarchiam consolidatione... dialogus, per R.P. Edinburgi, R. Charteris, 1604.   8°

STC 20103.
Wanting the title-page.

T.481

34

The SUPPLICATION of certaine masse-priests falsely called Catholikes. Directed to the Kings most excellent Maiestie, now this time of Parliament, but scattered in corners, to mooue mal-contents to mutinie... (An answere unto the principall points, and reasons of the Supplication praecedent.) London imprinted for William Aspley, 1604.   2 parts. 4°

STC 14431.

T.251

1605

35

BROUGHTON (Hugh)

... The familie of David, for the sonnes of the kingdome, with a chronicle unto the redemtion. Printed at Amstelredam, by Zacharias Heyns, 1605.   8°

Part of STC 3881.

T.390

36

SYMONDS (William)

Pisgah evangelica, or a commentary upon the book of Revelation. Imprinted at London by Felix Kyngston, for Edmund Weauer, 1605 [or 1606].   4°

STC 23592 or 23593.
Wanting the title-page.

T.213

1606

37

BARLOW (William) *Bishop of Lincoln.*

One of the foure sermons preached before the Kings Maiestie, at Hampton Court in September last. This concerning the antiquitie and superioritie of bishops... By... William Lord Bishop of Rochester. London, I.W. for Matthew Law, 1606.   4°

STC 1451.

T.475

38

EPICEDIA, quae clarissimi aliquot viri, et D. Theodoro Bezae charissimi: sicut & illis ipse Beza viuus charissimus, & mortuus est honoratissimus: scripserunt in ipsius obitum. Geneuae, apud Iacobum Chouet, 1606.   4°

T.138

39

WHETENHALL (Thomas)

A discourse of the abuses now in question in the churches of Christ... Imprinted. 1606.   4°

STC 25332.

T.251

1607

40

BLACKWELL (George)

Mr. George Blackwel, (made by Pope Clement 8. Archpriest of England) his answeres upon sundry his examinations... Imprinted at London by Robert Barker, 1607.   4°

STC 3105.

T.306

WILKINSON (Robert) *Pastor of St. Olave's Southwark.*

The merchant royall. 1607.

See no. 4487.

1608

41

DOWNAME (George) *Bishop of Derry.*

Two sermons, the one commending the ministerie in generall: the other defending the office of bishops in particular... At London imprinted by Felix Kyngston, and are to be sold by Matthew Lownes, 1608. 2 parts. 4°

STC 7125.

T.475

1609

42

BROUGHTON (Hugh)

Principal position for groundes of the holy Bible. Short oration of the Bibles translation. Positions historique: and of the Apocrypha... Printed in the yeare of our Lord, 1609.   4°

STC 3880.
Signature of Francis Russell.

T.251

43

OXLEY (Thomas)

The shepheard, or A sermon, preached at a synode in Durisme minster, vpon Tuesday, being the fifth of April. 1608... London for Eleazar Edgar, 1609.   4°

STC 19053.

T.754

44

WYBARNE (Joseph)

The new age of old names. By Ios. Wib... London, for William Barret, and Henry Featherstone, 1609.   4°

STC 26055.

T.251

1610

45

ANTHONIE (Francis)

Medicinae chymicae, et veri potabilis auri assertio, ex lucubrationibus Fra. Anthonii... Cantabrigiae, ex officina Cantrelli Legge, 1610.   4°

STC 668.

T.138

46

CARPENTER (John) *and* JOHNSON (Francis)

Quaestio de precibus et leiturgijs, ab hominibus praescriptis ... Duabus epistolis tractata: quarum altera scripta erat, per Iohannem Carpenterum ... Altera, per Franciscum Iohnsonum ... Francofurti, prostat apud viduam Levini Hulsij, anno 1610.   4°

T.138

47

CRASHAW (William)

A sermon preached in London before the right honorable the Lord Lawarre, Lord Gouernour and Captaine Generall of Virginea... At the said Lord Generall his leaue taking... and departure for Virginea, Febr. 21. 1609... London, for William Welby, 1610.   4°

STC 6029.
"Reverendo patri Dno D Doct Jamesio Episcopo Dunelmensi officii et amoris ergo."

T.475

48

ENGLAND.

The rates of marchandizes, as they are set downe in the booke of rates, for the custome and subsidie of poundage, and for the custome and subsidie of clothes... [No imprint, 1610.]   8°

STC 7693.

T.448

49

VINSEMIUS (Dominicus)

Contra tragicos Ecclesiastes libellus defensandae veritatis apologiam. Atque ad Ecclesiasticam concordiam exhortationem complectens. [Leiden?], excusus anno Domini ... 1610.   4°

Incomplete.

T.138

1611

50

CASAUBON (Isaac)

Isaaci Casauboni ad Frontonem Ducaeum S.J. theologum epistola; in qua de apologia disseritur communi Iesuitarum nomine ante aliquot menses Lutetiae Parisiorum edita. Londini excudebat Ioannes Norton, 1611. 4°

STC 4742.

T.138

51

HARRIS (Robert)

Absaloms funerall: preached at Banburie by a neighbour minister: or The lamentation of a loving father for a rebellious child... London, William Hall, for Thomas Man, 1611. 4°

STC 12818.

T.475

52

HIGGONS (Theophilus)

A sermon preached at Pauls crosse the third of March, 1610... At London imprinted by William Hall, for William Aspley, 1611. 4°

STC 13456.

T.475

53

L.N., *Sieur de.*

La veritable response a l'Anticoton sans falcification de son texte. Mis en forme de dialogue. Par le Sieur de L.N. Iouxte la copie imprimée à Nantes, M.CD.XI [i.e. 1611]. 8°

T.388

54

SANFORD (John)

Προπυλαιον, or an entrance to the Spanish tongue... London, Th. Haueland, for Nath. Butter, 1611. 4°

STC 21738.

T.306

1612

55

AD Roberti Cardinalis Bellarmini librum de temporali potestate papae, commentatio ... Heidelbergae, typis Johannis Lancelloti. Prostat Francofurti in bibliopolio Jonae Rosae, 1612. 8°

T.304

56

ADAMS (Thomas) *D.D.*

The gallants burden. A sermon preached at Paules Crosse, the twentie nine of March... 1612. London, W.W. for Clement Knight, 1612. 4°

STC 117.

T.475

57

BECANUS (Martinus)

The English iarre. Or disagreement amongst the ministers of great Brittaine, concerning the Kinges supremacy. Written in Latin by the Reuerend Father, F. Martinus Becanus... And translated into English by I.W.P. [St. Omer], imprinted anno 1612. 4°

STC 1702.

T.96

58

BROUGHTON (Hugh)

Obseruations upon the first ten Fathers. Imprinted at London by W. White, 1612. 4°

STC 3874.

T.251

59

HOOKER (Richard)

A learned and comfortable sermon of the certaintie and perpetuitie of faith in the elect... At Oxford, Ioseph Barnes, and are to be sold by John Barnes, 1612. 4°

STC 13707.

T.475

60

JAMES I, *King of England.*

His Maiesties declaration concerning his proceedings with the States generall of the Vnited Prouinces of the Low Countreys, in the cause of D. Conradus Vorstius... Imprinted at London by Robert Baker, 1612. 4°

STC 9233.

T.129

61

SCLATER (William)

The Christians strength. At Oxford, Ioseph Barnes, 1612. 4°

STC 21833.

T.246

62

SCLATER (William)

The ministers portion. At Oxford, Ioseph Barnes, 1612. 4°

STC 21841.

T.246

63

SCLATER (William)

The sick souls salve. At Oxford, Ioseph Barnes, 1612. 4°

STC 21845.

T.246

64

WARMINGTON (William)

A moderate defence of the oath of allegiance; wherein the author proveth the said oath to be most lawfull, notwithstanding the Pope's breves prohibiting the same... [No imprint], 1612. 4°

STC 25076.
Pp.26-138 only.

T.321

65

WILLET (Andrew)

A treatise of Salomons mariage, or, A congratulation for the happie and hopefull mariage between... Frederike the V. count palatine of Rhine... and... the Ladie Elizabeth, sole daughter unto the high and mighty Prince Iames... At London imprinted by F.K. for Thomas Man the elder, and William Welby, 1612. 4°

STC 25705.

T.475

1613

66

ROBARTES (Foulke)

The revenue of the Gospel is tythes, due to the ministerie of the word, by that word... Printed by Cantrel Legge printer to the Vniuersitie of Cambridge, 1613. 4°

STC 21069.

T.246

67

ROMAN CATHOLIC CHURCH.

Consilium quorundam episcoporum Bononiae congregatorum quod de ratione stabilendae Romanae Ecclesiae Iulio 3. Pont. Max. datum est... Ex bibliotheca W. Crashauij... Londini excudebat Gulih. White, 1613. 4°

STC 3218.

T.138

68

SPEGHT (James)

A briefe demonstration, who haue, and of the certainty of their saluation, that haue the spirit of Christ... London, William Hall, for Thomas Man, 1613. 8°

STC 23055.

T.457

1614

69

ADAMS (Thomas) *D.D.*

The white devil, or The hypocrite uncased: in a sermon preached at Pauls Crosse, March 7. 1612... The third edition reuiued and corrected by the author. London, Thomas Purfoot for William Erondell, 1614. 4°

STC 132.

T.215

70

ANDREWES (Lancelot) *Bishop of Winchester.*

A sermon preached before his Maiestie, at Whitehall, on Easter day last, 1614. By the Bishop of Elie. Imprinted at London by Robert Barker, 1614. 4°

STC 622.

T.340

71

MOSSE (Miles)

Iustifying and saving faith distinguished from the faith of the deuils. In a sermon preached at Pauls crosse in London, May 9. 1613... Cantrell Legge, printer to the Vniuersitie of Cambridge, 1614. And are to be sold by Matthew Law. 4°

STC 18209.

T.215

72

PALATINATE.

A faithfull admonition of the Paltsgraves churches, to all other protestant churches in Dutchland. That they would consider the great danger that hangeth ouer their heads as well as our by the popedome... Englished by Iohn Rolte. Imprinted at London by Edward Griffin for George Gibbes, 1614. 4°

STC 19129.

T.246

73

S. (T.)

A iewell for gentrie. Being an exact dictionary, or true method, to make any man understand all the art, secrets, and worthy knowledges belonging to hawking, hunting, fowling and fishing... [Based on the Book of hawking, hunting and fishing, attributed to Dame Juliana Berners.] Printed at London for Iohn Helme, 1614. 3 parts. 4°

STC 21520.

T.321

1615

74

HIERON (Samuel)

The dignitie of preaching: in a sermon upon I. Thessal. 5. 20... At London printed by Felix Kyngston for William Welby, 1615. 4°

STC 13396.

T.215

1616

75

BESCHREIBUNG dess new entsprungnen heylbruñens, bey Delbing zwischen Bopffingen und dem Kloster Nerreshaimb ligendt, welcher entsprungen ist den 12. Mayen, dises 1616. Jahrs. Gsangweiss gestelt... Zu Augspurg, bey Jeremias Gath, [1616]. brs.

T.817

76

HAKEWILL (George)

An answere to a treatise written by Dr. Carier, by way of letter to his Maiestie: wherein he layeth downe sundry politike considerations... Imprinted at London by Iohn Bill, 1616. 2 parts. 4°

STC 12610.

T.341

1617

77

CORNWALLIS (*Sir* William)

Essayes of certaine paradoxes. The second impression, inlarged. (Essays or rather, Encomions, prayses of sadnesse: and of the Emperour Iulian the Apostata.) London, (George Purslowe), for Richard Hawkins, 1617, 16. 2 parts. 4°

STC 5780, 5778.
Wanting the title-page of Part I.

T.287

78

DOMINIS (Marco Antonio de) *Archbishop of Spalatro.*

A sermon preached in Italian... the first Sunday in Aduent, anno 1617. In the Mercers chappel in London... First published in Italian by the author, and thereout translated into English. London, Iohn Bill, 1617. 4°

STC 7004.
2 copies.

T.112 T.215

1617 (Cont'd.)

79

FISCUS papalis. Sive, Catalogus indulgentiarum & reliquiarum septem principalium ecclesiarum urbis Romae... A part of the popes exchequer, that is a catalogue of the indulgences and reliques belonging to the seauen principall churches in Rome... Taken out of an antient manuscript, and translated [by William Crashaw]... London, Nicholas Okes, for George Norton, 1617.   4°

STC 19174.

T.306

1618

80

A DECLARATION of the demeanor and cariage of Sir Walter Raleigh, Knight, as well in his voyage, as in, and sithence his returne; and of the true motiues and inducements which occasioned his Maiestie to proceed in doing iustice upon him... London, Bonham Norton and Iohn Bill, 1618.   4°

STC 20654.

T.129

1619

81

BOHEMIA.

The reasons which compelled the States of Bohemia to reiect the Archiduke Ferdinand &c. & inforced them to elect a new king. Togeather with the proposition which was made vpon the first motion of the chocie [sic] of th' Elector Palatine to be King of Bohemia... Translated out of the french copies [by John Harrison?]. at Dort, printet by George Waters, [1619].   4°

STC 3212.

T.253

82

DORT, *Synod of.*

Iudicium synodi nationalis, reformatarum Ecclesiarum Belgicarum, habitae Dordrechti, anno 1618. & 1619 ... Dordrechti, apud Ioannem Berewout, & Franciscum Bosselaer, socios Caninij, 1619.   4°

T.304

83

SEMPILL (*Sir* James)

Sacrilege sacredly handled. That is, according to Scripture onely... An appendix also added; answering some obiections mooued, namely, against this treatise: and some others, I finde in Ios. Scaligers Diatribe, and Ioh. Seldens Historie of tithes... London, William Iones, for Edmund Weaver, 1619.   4°

STC 22186.

T.253

84

A TRUE discovery of those treasons of which Geilis van Ledenberch was a practiser against the Generall States of the united Netherlands Prouinces; through the aduise, and assistance of Iohn van Olden Barneuelt... London, E. Griffin for N. Butter, 1619. 4°

STC 15352.

T.127

85

WHATELY (William)

Gods husbandry: the first part. Tending to shew the difference betwixt the hypocrite and the true-hearted Christian. As it was delivered in certaine sermons, and is now published... London, Felix Kyngston for Thomas Man, 1619.   4°

STC 25305.

T.215

86

WHATELY (William)

The new birth: or, A treatise of regeneration, delivered in certaine sermons... London, Felix Kyngston for Thomas Man, 1619.   4°

STC 25309.

T.215

1620

87

FREDERICK, *Elector Palatine and King of Bohemia.*

A declaration of the causes, for which, wee Frederick, by the grace of God King of Bohemia... haue accepted of the crowne of Bohemia... Middleburg, Abraham Schilders, 1620.   4°

STC 11351.

T.253

88

GATAKER (Thomas)

Marriage duties briefely couched togither; out of Colossians, 3. 18, 19. London, William Iones, for William Bladen, 1620.   4°

STC 11667.
2 copies.

T.112 T.243

89

GOODWIN (George)

Melissa religionis pontificiae. Eiusdemque apotrope. Elegiis decem conclusa... Londini, impensis Nathanaelis Butter, 1620.   4°

STC 12029.

T.75

90

THOMAS (Thomas) *Lexicographer.*

Dictionarium linguae Latinae et Anglicanae. Duodecima editio. Londini, ex officina J. Legati, 1620.   4°

STC 24017.
Gatherings Yy and Zz only.

T.168

91

VIRGINIA.

A declaration of the state of the colonie and affaires in Virginia: with the names of the aduenturors, and summes aduentured in that action. By his Maiesties Counsell for Virginia. 22. Iunij. 1620. London: T.S., 1620. 5 parts.   4°

STC 24835.

T.94

92

WHITBOURNE (Richard)

A discourse and discovery of New-found-land, with many reasons to prooue how worthy and beneficiall a plantation may there be made... Imprinted at London by Felix Kyngston, for William Barret, 1620.   4°

STC 25372.

T.253

1621

93

GODWIN (Francis) *Bishop of Hereford.*

Ad commentarium de praesulibus Angliae, per Franciscum Godwinum... editum anno 1616. Appendix. [No imprint, 1621?]   4°

STC 11942.

T.138

94

LANGLOIS DE FANCAN (François)

The favourites chronicle. London, 1621.   4°

STC 15203.
2 copies, both imperfect.

T.287 T.306

1622

95

BREREWOOD (Edward)

Enquiries touching the diuersity of languages, and religions, through the chiefe parts of the world. London, Iohn Bill, 1622.   4°

STC 3619.

T.246

96

COOKE (Alexander)

Yet more worke for a masse-priest... London, William Iones, and are to be sold by William Sheffard, 1622.   4°

STC 5664.

T.253

97

GROTIUS (Hugo)

Hugonis Grotii Silva, ad Franciscum Augustum Thuanum, Iac. Augusti F. Excudebatur Lutetiae Parisiorum, 1622.   12°

T.453

98

OXFORD. *University.*

Vltima linea Savilii sive in obitum... Henrici Savilii... iusta academica. Oxonii, excudebant Iohannes Lichfield, & Iacobus Short, 1622.   4°

STC 19025.

T.75

99

SHELDON (Richard)

Christ, on his throne; not in popish secrets. A prophecie of Christ, against his pretended presence in popish secrets; laid open in a sermon preached before his Maiestie at Wansted... London, Humfrey Lownes, 1622.   4°

STC 22394.

T.243

100

WHITBOURNE (Richard)

A discourse containing a loving invitation both honourable, and profitable to all such as shall be aduenturers... for the aduancement of his Maiesties most hopefull plantation in New-found-land... (A letter from Captaine Edward Wynne, gouernour of the colony of Ferryland... in Newfound-land...) Imprinted at London by Felix Kyngston, 1622. 2 parts.   4°

STC 25375a.

T.253

1623

101

CHASTEIGNER DE LA ROCHE-POZAI (Henri Louis)

Celebriorum distinctionum tum philosophicarum, tum theologicarum synopsis. Coloniae, sumptibus Conradi Butgenii, 1623.   4°

T.75

102

CRACKANTHORP (Richard)

De providentia Dei tractatus. Cantabrigiae, impensis Leonardi Greene unius ex typographis Academiae, 1623. 4°

STC 5973.

T.75

103

GATAKER (Thomas)

The ioy of the iust; with the signes of such. A discourse tending to the comfort of the deiected and afflicted... London, Iohn Haviland for Fulke Clifton, 1623.   4°

STC 11665.

T.243

104

HIERON (Samuel)

Aarons bell a-sounding. In a sermon, tending cheiftly to admonish the ministerie, of their charge, & duty... Printed, 1623.   4°

STC 13385.

T.669

105

TAYLOR (John) *the Water-Poet.*

A new discovery by sea. With a wherry from London to Salisbury. London, E. Allde, 1623.   8°

STC 23778.
Wanting the title-page.

T.448

1624

106

ABBOT (George) *Archbishop of Canterbury.*

A treatise of the perpetuall visibilitie, and succession of the true Church in all ages. [Anon.] At London, Humfrey Lownes, for Robert Milbourne, 1624.   4°

STC 39.

T.321

107

GATAKER (Thomas)

A iust defence of certaine passages in a former treatise concerning the nature and use of lots, against such exceptions and oppositions as haue beene made thereunto by Mr. I.B... London, Iohn Haviland for Robert Bird, 1624.   4°

STC 11666.

T.253

108

GEE (John)

Hold fast, a sermon preached at Pauls crosse upon Sunday being the XXXI. of October, anno Domini 1624. London, A.M. and I.N. for Robert Mylbourne, 1624.   4°

STC 11705.

T.381

109

MORE (*Sir* Thomas)

Sir Thomas Moore's Vtopia... translated... by Raphe Robinson... Now after many impressions newly corrected... London: Bernard Alsop, 1624. 4°

STC 18097.
Wanting the title-page.

T.306

110

WADSWORTH (James)

The copies of certaine letters which have passed betweene Spaine and England in matter of religion ... Betweene Master Iames Wadesworth... and W. Bedell... London, William Stansby for William Barret and Robert Milbourne, 1624.   4°

STC 24925.

T.106

1625

111

ABBOT (Robert) *Minister of St. Austin's, Watling Street.*

The danger of popery; or a sermon preached at... Ashford... London, J.L. for P. Stephens and C. Meredith, 1625.   4°

STC 57.
Wanting the title-page.

T.754

112

CAMBRIDGE. *University.*

Cantabrigiensium dolor & solamen: seu decessio beatissimi regis Iacobi pacifici: et successio augustissimi regis Caroli: Magnae Britanniae, Galliae, & Hiberniae monarchae. Excudebat Cantrellus Legge, Almae Matris Cantabrigiae typographus, 1625.   4°

STC 4478.

T.552

113

CHURCH OF ENGLAND.

A forme of common prayer, together with an order of fasting: for the auerting of Gods heavy visitation upon many places of this Kingdome... Imprinted at London by Bonham Norton and Iohn Bill, 1625.   4°

STC 16540.

T.246

114

CRASHAW (William)

Londons lamentation for her sinnes: and complaint to the Lord her God. Out of which may bee pickt a prayer for priuate families, for the time of this fearefull infection... By W.C. London, for G. Fayerbeard, 1625.   12°

STC 4324.
Signature of Eliz. Andrews.

T.448

115

WILLIAMS (John) *Archbishop of York.*

Great Britains Salomon. A sermon preached at the magnificent funerall, of the most high and mighty king, Iames... the seuenth of May 1625. London, Iohn Bill, 1625.   4°

STC 25723.

T.112

1626

116

CHARLES I, *King of England.*

A declaration of the true causes which moued his Maiestie to assemble, and after inforced him to dissolue the two last meetings in Parliament. London Bonham Norton, and Iohn Bill, 1626.   4°

STC 9246.

T.129

117

GUMBLEDEN (John)

Three sermons preached in severall places... London, Augustine Mathewes for Henry Crips of Oxford, 1626.   4°

STC 12515.

T.381

118

HARRIS (Robert)

Peters enlargement upon the prayers of the Church. 4th ed... London, Robert Young for John Bartlet, 1626.   4°

STC 12841.

T.112

119

WOTTON (Anthony)

A dangerous plot discovered. By a discourse, wherein is proved, that, Mr. Richard Mountague, in his two bookes; the one called A new gagg; the other, A iust appeale: laboureth to bring in the faith of Rome... [Anon.] London, for Nicholas Bourne, 1626. 2 parts. 4°

STC 26003.

T.246

1627

120

MUSAEUS.

Musaei vetustissimi venustissimique poetae Graeci Erotopaegnion Herus et Leandri. Cum versione Latinâ ... collegit, & commentario libro illustrauit Daniel Pareus. Francofurti, impensis Gulielmi Fitzeri, 1627.   4°

T.75

121

VICARS (Thomas)

Ρομφαιοφορος. The sword-bearer. Or, The byshops of Chichester's armes emblazoned in a sermon preached at a synod. By T.V. London, B.A. and T. Fawcet, for R. Milbourne, 1627.   4°

STC 24705.

T.754

1628

122

BURTON (Henry)

Israels fast. Or a meditation upon the seuenth chapter of Ioshuah... By H.B. Printed at London, 1628.   4°

STC 4146.
Title-page broken.

T.669

123

CHARLES I, *King of England.*

His Maiesties declaration to all his louing subjects, of the causes which moued him to dissolue the last Parliament. Imprinted at London by Bonham Norton and Iohn Bill, 1628.   4°

STC 9249.

T.129

124

CHURCH OF ENGLAND.

A forme of prayer, necessary to bee vsed in these dangerous times of warre: wherein we are appointed to fast... for the preseruation of his Maiestie, and his realmes, and all reformed churches. London Bonham Norton, and Iohn Bill, 1628.   4°

STC 16547.

T.246

125

DRAKE (*Sir* Francis) *the Younger.*

Sir Francis Drake reuiued: calling vpon this dull or effeminate age, to follow his noble steps for gold and siluer... Faithfully taken out of the report of M. Christopher Ceely, Ellis Hixom, and others... By Philip Nichols... Set forth by Sir Francis Drake Baronet (his nephew) now liuing. London, for Nicholas Bourne, 1628.   4°

STC 18545.
Wanting gathering B, which is supplied in manuscript.

T.508

126

RALEIGH (*Sir* Walter)

The prerogative of parliaments in England: proued in a dialogue (pro & contra) betweene a councellour of state and a iustice of peace... Preserued to be now happily (in these distracted times) published, and printed at Midelburge, 1628.   4°

STC 20648a.

T.389

127

WILLIAMS (John) *Archbishop of York.*

Perseuerantia sanctorum. A sermon of persevering in patience, repentance, and humiliation, in time of afflictions, preached before the Lords of the Parliament... the 18. day of February 1628... London, Iohn Bill, 1628.   4°

STC 25727.

T.381

1629

128

BURRELL (Percival)

Sutton's synagogue or, The English centurion: shewing the unparralleled bounty of protestant piety... Printed at London, by T.C. for Ralph Mabb, 1629.   4°

STC 4126.

T.380

129

MARTINI (Matthias)

Graecae linguae fundamenta: quae sunt tanquam epitome lexici & etymologici Graeci; limatiora & pleniora ex quarta editione... Londini, excusum typis Ioannis Hauiland, impensis Io. Partridge, 1629.   8°

STC 17522.

T.460

1630

130

CLEMENS (Venceslaus)

Gedanum sive Dantiscum urbs illustris et regia urbs venustiss. ampliss. florentiss... Gedani, typis Rhetianis sumptibus autoris, [1630].   4°

T.820

131

CROMPTON (Richard)

Star-chamber cases. Shewing what causes properly belong to the cognizance of that court. Collected for the most part out of Mr. Crompton, his booke, entituled, The iurisdiction of divers courts. London, for Iohn Grove, 1630.   4°

STC 6056

T.473

132

GOLIUS (Jacobus)

Libri MSS. Arabici, quos ex Oriente advexit I. Golius, cum genuinis Arabicis eorundem titulis. [Leiden, c.1630.]   4°

"Quem mihi dono dedit doctissimus autor Lugduni Bat. Aug. 10. 1638" (Possibly in hand of John Gauden.)

T.168

1630 (Cont'd.)

133

HOLYDAY (Barten)

Τεχνογαμια: or the marriages of the arts. A
comedie... London, Iohn Haviland for Richard
Meighen, 1630. 4°

STC 13618.
Wanting title-page and other pages.

T.508

134

JONSON (Benjamin)

Loves triumph through Callipolis. Performed in a
masque at court 1630. by his Maiestie with the
lords and gentlemen assisting. The inuentors.
Ben. Ionson. Inigo Iones... London, I.N. for
Thomas Walkley, 1630. 4°

STC 14776.

T.677

135

The ORIGINALL of popish idolatrie, or The birth of
heresies [sic], and called-in the same yeare, upon
misinformation. But now upon better consideration
reprinted with alowance... [Translated by Abraham
Darcie.] Published by S.O. Printed in the yeare
of our Saviour, 1630. 4°

STC 4748.

T.314

136

PRYNNE (William)

God; no impostor, nor deluder. (A coppie of a
recantation... made by Maister Barret... The nine
assertions, or articles of Lambheth.) [London,
1630?] 4°

cf. STC 20460-1. Probably published with *Anti-
Arminianisme*, though this is not present here;
there is no title-page; the signatures run a-b⁸, c⁴.

T.306

1631

137

BENEDETTO, *da Mantova.*

The benefit of Christs death, or the glorious riches
of Gods free grace... First compiled and printed in
the Italian tongue: and afterwards translated and
printed in the French tongue. And out of French into
English. By A.G... London, I.L. for Andrew Hebb,
1631. 8°

Not in STC. Other editions there attributed to
Antonio dalla Paglia.

T.481

138

CHAPMAN (George)

Caesar and Pompey: a Roman tragedy, declaring
their warres... London: Thomas Harper, and are
to be sold by Godfrey Emondson, and Thomas
Alchorne, 1631. 4°

STC 4993.
Wanting the final gathering.

T.667

139

DENISON (Stephen)

The monument or tombe-stone: or, A sermon preached
at Laurence Pountnies church in London, Nouemb. 21.
1619. at the funerall of Mrs. Elizabeth Iuxon...
The fifth impression. (The new creature. A sermon
preached at Pauls crosse, January 17. 1619.)
London, George Miller, 1631. 4°

STC 6606.

T.215

140

PRESTON (John)

The saints daily exercise. A treatise, unfolding
the whole dutie of prayer. Delivered in five
sermons, upon I Thes. 5.17. The sixth edition,
corrected... London, W.I. for Nicolas Bourne,
1631. 4°

STC 20256.

T.381

141

PRESTON (John)

Sermons preached before his Maiestie; and vpon other
speciall occasions... London, for Michael Sparke,
1631. 2 parts. 4°

STC 20272.

T.381

1632

142

AURELIUS (Abraham)

Iobus, sive de patientia liber poetica metaphrasi
explicatus. Londini, impress. in aedibus Roberti
Junii, 1632. 4°

STC 961.

T.75

143

FEATLEY (John)

The honor of chastity. A sermon... London: G.P.
for Nicholas Bourne, 1632. 4°

STC 10741.

T.381

144

HUGHES (George)

The saints losse and lamentation. A sermon preached
at the funerall of the worshipfull Captaine Henry
Waller... Octob. 31. 1631... London, I.B. for
Ralph Mab, 1632. 4°

STC 13913.

T.674

145

ROGERS (Nehemiah)

A sermon preached at the second trienniall visitation
of... William Lord Bishop of London, holden at
Keluedon in Essex: September.3. 1631... London,
George Miller for Edward Brewster, 1632. 4°

STC 21198.

T.754

1633

146

CHURCH OF ENGLAND. *Constitutions and Canons.*

Constitutions and canons ecclesiasticall, treated
upon by the Bishop of London, president of the
Conuocation for the prouince of Canterbury, and
the rest of the bishops and clergy... And agreed
upon with the Kings Maiesties licence in their synod
begun at London, anno Dom. 1603... London, Iohn
Norton, for Ioyce Norton, Richard Whitaker, 1633. 4°

STC 10076.

T.473

147

The CONTINUATION of the German history. The fifth
part [of the Swedish intelligencer]. Collected
out of the truest intelligences... briefly brought
downe, to the late treaty in Silesia... London,
for Nath. Butter, and Nicholas Bourne, 1633. 4°

STC 11783.
Signature of Elis. Lewkenor.

T.473

148

DONNE (John)

Iuuenilia or certaine paradoxes and problemes,
written by I. Donne. The second edition,
corrected. London, E.P. for Henry Seyle, 1633. 4°

STC 7044.

T.129

149

FISHER (Jasper)

Fuimus Troes Aeneid. 2. The true Troianes, being a
story of the Britaines valour at the Romanes first
invasion: publikely represented by the gentlemen
students of Magdalen Colledge in Oxford... [Anon.]
London, I.L. for Robert Allot, 1633. 4°

STC 10886.

T.672

150

HOARD (Samuel)

Gods love to mankind. Manifested, by dis-prooving
his absolute decree for their damnation... [Anon.]
Imprinted, anno, 1633. 4°

STC 13534.

T.473

1634

151

BLAXTON (John)

The English usurer. Or, Usury condemned, by the
most learned, and famous divines of the Church
of England... The second impression, corrected
by the authour... London, Iohn Norton, and are
to be sold by Francis Bowman, in Oxford, 1634. 4°

STC 3129a.

T.316

152

FITZ-GEFFREY (Charles)

The blessed birth-day celebrated in some pious
meditations, on the angels anthem... Oxford,
Iohn Lichfield, and are to be sold by Ed. Forrest,
1634. 4°

STC 10935.

T.407

153

ROSS (Alexander)

Virgilius evangelisans. Sive historia Domini &
Salvatoris nostri Iesu Christi, Virgilianis verbis
& versibus descripta... Londini, per Iohannem
Legatum pro Richardo Thralo, 1634. 8°

STC 24826.

T.585

1635

154

AEDO Y GALLART (Diego de)

Le voyage du prince Don Fernande Infant d'Espagne,
cardinal, depuis le douziéme d'Avril de l'an 1632 ...
jusques au jour de son entrée en la ville de Bruxelles
le quatriéme du mois de Novembre de l'an 1634.
Traduict de l'Espagnol ... par le Sr. Iule Chifflet.
En Anvers, chez Iean Cnobbaert, 1635. 4°

Signature of Joanes Vershuylen.

T.552

155

BURTON (Henry)

A briefe answer to a late treatise of the Sabbath
day [by Francis White]... [Anon. Also attributed
to William Prynne and to Richard Byfield.]
Amsterdam, J.F. Stam, [1635?] 4°

Not in STC.
Wanting the title-page.

T.316

156

DRAKE (*Sir* Francis) *the Younger.*

The world encompassed by Sir Francis Drake. Being
his next voyage to that to Nombre de Dios, formerly
imprinted; carefully collected out of the notes of
Master Francis Fletcher... and divers others...
London, E.P. for Nicholas Bourne, 1635. 4°

STC 7162
"Thomas Bowdler his booke 1638."

T.508

157

GROTIUS (Hugo)

Hugonis Grotii tragoedia Sophompaneas. Accesserunt,
tragoedia ejusdem Christus patiens, et sacri
argumenti alia. Edito nova... Amsterdami, apud
Guilielmum Blaeu, 1635. 12°

T.453

158

RAINBOW (Edward) *Bishop of Carlisle.*

Labour forbidden, and commanded. A sermon preached
at St. Pauls church, September 28. 1634... London:
for Nicholas Vavasour, 1635. 4°

STC 20603.

T.670

159

SENECA (Lucius Annaeus)

L.A. Seneca the philosopher, his booke of consolation
to Marcia. Translated into an English poem [by Sir
Ralph Freeman]. London, E.P. for Henry Seile, 1635.
4°

STC 22215a.

T.407

160

SPANHEIM (Frédéric)

Geneva restituta. [Anon.] [No imprint], 1635. 4°

"Pour Monsr Battier/v.s.L.D."

T.75

161

WALL (George)

A sermon at the Archbishop of Canterbury his visitation... Iun.3. 1635. Preached by G.W... London, Tho. Cotes, for Robert Allot, 1635. 4°
STC 24984.

T.754

1636

162

BLOUNT (*Sir* Henry)

A voyage into the Levant. A breife relation of a journey, lately performed by Master H.B. Gentleman, from England... unto Gran Cairo... 2nd ed. London, I.L. for Andrew Crooke, 1636. 4°
STC 3137.

T.123

163

DALECHAMP (Caleb)

Haereseologia tripartita: vel, de pernicie, necessitate, et utilitate haeresium in Ecclesia. Concio ad clerum habita Cantabrigiae 21 Junii 1633 pro gradu baccalaureatus in theologia... Cantabrigiae, ex Academiae celeberrimae typographeo, anno 1636. 4°
STC 6194.

T.733

164

ERPENIUS (Thomas)

Thomae Erpenii Grammatica Arabica. Ab autore emendata & aucta. Cui accedunt Locmanni Fabulae, et Adagia quaedam Arabum ... Lugduni Batavorum, apud Ioannem Maire, 1636. 2 parts. 4°

T.168

165

FEATLEY (John)

Obedience and submission. A sermon preached at St. Saviours-church in South-warke... the eigth day of December: anno Dom. 1635... London, R.B., 1636. 4°
STC 10742.

T.753

166

GORE (John)

The way to prosper. A sermon preached at St. Pauls crosse on Sunday the 27. day of May, being Trinity Sunday. 3rd ed. London, Thomas Cotes for Thomas Alchorn, 1636. 4°
STC 12085.

T.243

167

PHILIPOT (John)

The catalogue of the chancellors of England, the lord keepers of the great seale: and the lord treasurers of England... By J.P. Printed at London by Tho. Cotes, and are to be sold by Andrew Crooke, 1636. 2 parts. 4°
STC 19846.

T.316

168

POCKLINGTON (John)

Sunday no Sabbath. A sermon preached before the Lord Bishop of Lincolne, at his Lordships visitation at Ampthill in the county of Bedford, Aug. 17. 1635... London, Robert Young, 1636. 4°
STC 20077.
2 copies.

T.580 T.753

169

REYNOLDS (Edward) *Bishop of Norwich.*

The shieldes of the earth. A sermon preached before the reverend judges... at the assizes holden at North-hampton: February 25. 1634. London, Felix Kyngston, for Robert Bostock, 1636. 4°
STC 20932.

T.243

170

SIBBS (Richard)

Two sermons upon the first words of Christs last sermon Iohn XIIII. I... London, Thomas Harper, for Lawrence Chapman, 1636. 4°
STC 22515.

T.243

171

STANBRIDGE (John)

Stanbrigii embryon relimatum, seu vocabularium metricum olim a Iohanne Stanbrigio digestum, dein a Thoma Newtono aliquantulum repurgatum... Nunc vero locupletatum... industria Ioh: Brinslaei. Londini excusum typis T. Cotes, & venales prostant a Tho. Alchorne, 1636. 4°

Not in STC.

T.316

1637

172

COMENIUS (Johannes Amos)

Conatuum Comenianorum praeludia ex bibliotheca S.H. Oxoniae, excudebat Guilielmus Turnerus Academiae typographus, 1637. 4°
STC 15077.
A second title-page has the title Porta sapientiae reserata.

T.304

173

CROWNE (William)

A true relation of all the remarkable places and passages observed in the travels of... Thomas Lord Howard, Earle of Arundell and Surrey... Ambassadour extraordinary to his sacred Majesty Ferdinando the second, Emperour of Germanie, anno Domini 1636. London, for Henry Seile, 1637. 4°
STC 6097.

T.316

174

FREDERICK, *Elector Palatine and King of Bohemia.*

A declaration of the Pfaltzgraves: concerning the faith and ceremonies professed in his churches. According to the originall printed in the High Dutch, translated by I.R. London, for Thomas Iones, 1637. 4°
STC 19131.

T.316

175

HEYLYN (Peter)

A briefe and moderate answer, to the seditious and scandalous challenges of Henry Burton, late of Friday-Streete; in the two sermons, by him preached on the fifth of November. 1636... London: Ric. Hodgkinsonne; and are to be sold by Daniel Frere, 1637. 4°
STC 13269.

T.247

176

LAUD (William) *Archbishop of Canterbury.*

A speech delivered in the Star-chamber, on Wednesday, the XIVth of Iune, MDCXXXVII. at the censure, of Iohn Bastwick, Henry Burton, & William Prinn; concerning pretended innovations in the Church. London, Richard Badger, 1637. 4°
STC 16306.
Another copy, of a different setting of type, STC 15307.

T.123 T.247

177

MEDE (Joseph)

The name altar, or θυσιαστηριον, anciently given to the holy table... London, M.F. for John Clark, 1637. 4°
STC 17768.

T.318

178

MORTON (Thomas) *Bishop of Durham.*

Antidotum adversus Ecclesiae Romanae de merito proprie dicto ex condigno venenum... Cantabrigiae, ex Academiae celeberrimae typographeo, 1637. 4°
STC 18172.

T.304

179

SENNERTUS (Daniel)

The weapon-salves maladie: or, A declaration of its insufficiencie to performe what is attributed to it ... Translated out of his 5th booke, Part 4. chap. 10. Practicae medicinae. London, for Iohn Clark, 1637. 4°
STC 22232.
Incomplete.

T.316

180

SPARROW (Anthony) *Bishop of Norwich.*

A sermon concerning confession of sinnes, and the power of absolution. Preached by Mr. Sp. London, R. Bishop for Iohn Clark, 1637. 4°
STC 23029.
2 copies, having variations in the wording of the imprint.

T.243 T.669

181

TEDDER (Richard)

A sermon preached at Wimondham, in Norfolke, at the primary visitation of... Matthew, Lord Bishop of Norwich, on the third of Iune, ann. 1636. London, Thomas Harper, for Godfrey Emerson, 1637. 4°
STC 23858.

T.754

182

WHITE (Francis) *Bishop of Ely.*

An examination and confutation of a lawlesse pamphlet [by Henry Burton], intituled, A briefe answer to a late treatise of the Sabbath-day... London, R.B. for Andrew Crooke, 1637. 4°
STC 25379a.
2 copies.

T.96 T.316

183

WILLIAMS (John) *Archbishop of York.*

The holy table, name & thing, more anciently, properly, and literally used under the New Testament, then that of an altar: written long ago by a minister in Lincolnshire, in answer to D. Coal, a judicious divine of Q. Maries dayes. [Actually a reply by Bishop Williams to Peter Heylyn, A coale from the altar.]... Printed for the diocese of Lincoln, 1637. 4°
STC 25725.

T.247

184

WILLIAMS (John) *Archbishop of York.*

The holy table name and thing more antiently, properly, and literally used under the New Testament, then that of an altar: written long agoe by a minister in Lincolnshire, in answer to D. Coal, a judicious divine of Queene Maries daies. [Actually a reply by Bishop Williams to Peter Heylyn, A coale from the altar.]... Printed for the diocesse of Lincoln, 1637. 4°
STC 25725.

T.96

185

YATES (John)

A treatise of the honor of God's house... London, T.C. for W. Cooke, 1637. 4°
STC 26089.
Wanting the title-page.

T.251

1638

186

The ANSWERS of some brethren of the ministerie [i.e. Alexander Henderson and David Dickson] to the replies of the ministers and professors of divinitie in Aberdene, concerning the late Covenant. Also, Duplies of the ministers and professors of Aberdene, to the second answers of some reverend brethren, concerning the late Covenant... Printed by R.Y. his Majesties printer for Scotland, 1638. 2 parts. 4°
STC 70.

T.378

187

CHURCH OF SCOTLAND.

The confession of faith of the Kirk of Scotland, subscribed by the Kings Majestie and his housholde, in the year of God, 1580... And subscribed by the nobles, barrons, gentlemen, burgesses, ministers, and commons, in the yeare of God, 1638... [Edinburgh, George Anderson, 1638.] 4°
Not in STC. cf. 22025.

T.121

1638 (Cont'd.)

188

CHURCH OF SCOTLAND.

The confession of the faith, and doctrine believed and professed by the protestants of Scotland, exhibited to the Estates of the first Parliament of King James the sixt... Edinburgh, George Anderson, 1638. 4°

STC 22027.

T.121

189

GENERALL demands concerning the late Covenant: propounded by the ministers and professors of divinity in Aberdene, to some reverend brethren, who come thither to recommend the late Covenant to them... Together with the answers of those reverend brethren... As also the replyes of the foresaid ministers and professors to their answers ... Printed by his Majesties printer for Scotland, anno 1638. 4°

STC 65.

T.378

190

HAMILTON (James) *1st Duke of Hamilton.*

Begin. It will, no doubt, seeme strange to see my name in print... [Hamilton's vindication of himself against the charge of having accepted the Covenant.] Imprinted by his Majesties printer for Scotland, anno 1638. 4°

Part of STC 65.

T.378

191

HARDWICK (William)

Conformity with piety, requisite in Gods service. Delivered in a visitation sermon at Kingston upon Thames September 8. 1638... London: I. Okes for Richard Cartwright, 1638. 4°

STC 12766.

T.754

192

MEDE (Joseph)

Churches, that is, appropriate places for Christian worship; both in, and ever since the Apostles times... London, M.F. for John Clark, 1638. 4°

STC 17765.

T.247

193

MEDE (Joseph)

The reverence of Gods house. A sermon preached at St. Maries in Cambridge before the Universitie on St. Matthies day, anno 1635/6... London, M.F. for Iohn Clark, 1638. 4°

STC 17769.

T.243

194

REYNOLDS (Edward) *Bishop of Norwich.*

A sermon touching the peace & edification of the Church. Preached at the second trienniall visitation of... Francis Lord Bishop of Peterborough, at Daventrie... London, Felix Kyngston for Robert Bostock, 1638. 4°

STC 20931.

T.243

195

SICTOR (Joannes)

Panegyricon inaugurale honoratissimi... praetoris regii, sive majoris... reipublicae Londinensis, Richardi Fenn, sub finem anni Christi 1637... Ex chalcographia Thomae Harperi, [1638.] 4°

STC 22533.

T.304

196

SICTOR (Joannes)

Panegyricon inaugurale honoratissimi... praetoris regii, sive majoris... urbis Londinensis, a forma reipublicae breviter conscriptum... Cantabrigiae, ex officina Rogeri Danielis, [1638?] 4°

STC 22533a.

T.304

197

USSHER (James) *Archbishop of Armagh.*

Immanuel or the mystery of the incarnation of the Son of God... London, I.H. for John Parker, &c., 1638. 4°

STC 24553.

T.247

1639

198

HUNGERFORD (*Sir* Anthony)

The advise of a sonne professing the religion established in the present Church of England to his deare mother a Roman Catholike... Oxford, L. Lichfield, for Henry Cripps, 1639. 4°

STC 13972.

T.246

199

ROBARTES (Foulke)

Gods holy house and service, according to the primitive and most Christian forme thereof... London, Tho. Cotes, 1639. 4°

STC 21068.

T.247

200

SARPI (Paolo)

The history of the Inquisition... Translated out of the Italian... by Robert Gentilis. London, J. Okes, for Humphrey Mosley, 1639. 4°

STC 21765.

T.320

201

VERTUES reward wherein the living are incouraged unto good workes, from the blessed memory which they [sic] dead for so doing, doe leave behinde them... (Sions suite, or a treatise conteyning many waighty reasons...) [Amsterdam], printed in the yeare 1639. 2 parts. 4°

Not in STC.

T.318

1640

202

BAYLY (Richard)

The shepheards starre, or the ministers guide... London, E.G. for Iohn Rothwell, 1640. 8°

STC 1625.

T.452

203

CARTER (John) *Deacon.*

Vindiciae decimarum. Of tithes, a plea for the ius divinum... Printed at London by T. Cotes, 1640. 4°

STC 4694.

T.146

204

CHARLES I, *King of England.*

His Majesties declaration: to all his loving subjects, of the causes which moved him to dissolve the last Parliament. London: Robert Barker: and by the assignes of John Bill, 1640. 4°

STC 9262.
Signature of Thomas Bowdler.

T.129

205

CHURCH OF ENGLAND. *Constitutions and Canons.*

Constitutions and canons ecclesiasticall; treated upon by the archbishops of Canterbury and York... and the rest of the bishops and clergie of those provinces; and agreed upon with the Kings Majesties licence in their severall synods begun at London and York. 1640... London: Robert Barker: and by the assignes of John Bill, 1640. 4°

STC 10080.
2 copies.

T.128 T.465

206

CORBET (John)

The epistle congratulatorie of Lysimachus Nicanor of the Societie of Jesu, to the Covenanters in Scotland... Anno Domini 1640. 4°

STC 5751.

T.378

207

FLETCHER (John)

The tragoedy of Rollo Duke of Normandy. Acted by his Majesties servants. Oxford, Leonard Lichfield, 1640. 4°

STC 11065.

T.287

208

SADLER (John)

Masquarade du ciel: presented to the great Queene of the little world... By J.S. London, R.B. for S.C., 1640. 4°

STC 21542.

T.146

1641

209

An ANSWER to the new motions: or, A serious and briefe discussion of certaine motions now in question. London, for Robert Bostock, 1641. 4°

Wing A 3427.

T.278

210

BACON (*Sir* Nicholas)

Arguments exhibited in Parliament by Sir Nicholas Bacon ... Whereby it is proved, that the persons of noble men are attachable by law, for contempts by them committed in the ..., Court of Chancery, for disobeying the decrees of that court. Printed in the yeare, 1641. 4°

Wing B 367.

T.136

211

BURGESS (Cornelius)

A sermon preached to the honourable House of Commons assembled in Parliament, at their publique fast, Novem. 17. 1640 ... London, T. Badger, for P. Stephens, and C. Meredith, 1641. 4°

Wing B 5682.

T.252

212

BURGESS (Cornelius)

Two sermons preached to the honorable House of Commons assembled in Parliament, at their publique fast, Novem. 17. 1640. By Cornelius Burges and Stephen Marshall ... London, T. B. and I. O. for S. Man, P. Stephens, and C. Meredith, 1641. 4°

Wing B 5687.
Marshall's sermon is entered separately.

T.252

213

BY the Kings Maiestie, were accused with seven articles of high treason these worthy members in the house of Commons in Parliament, Munday Ian. 3. 1641 ... London, for Iohn Thomas, 1641. 4°

Wing B 6364.

T.130

214

CARY (Lucius) *Viscount Falkland.*

A speech made to the House of Commons concerning episcopacy. London, for Thomas Walkely, 1641. 4°

Wing F 324.

T.278

215

CASE (Thomas)

Two sermons lately preached at Westminster, before sundry of the honourable House of Commons. London, I. Raworth for Luke Fawne, 1641. 2 parts. 4°

Wing C 845.

T.670

216

A CERTIFICATE from Northampton-shire. 1. Of the pluralities. 2. Defect of maintenance. 3. Of not preaching. 4. Of scandalous ministers ... London, for William Sheares, 1641. 4°

Wing C 1766.

T.278

217

CHARLES I, *King of England.*

Articles of the large treaty, concerning the
establishing of the peace betwixt the Kings
Majesty, and his people of Scotland, and betwixt
the two kingdomes. Agreed upon by the Scottish, and
English commissioners in the city of Westminster
the 7th day of August, 1641 ... Printed by Henry Seile,
1641. 4°

Wing C 2148.

T.387

218

CHARLES I, *King of England.*

His Majesties declaration, to all his loving
subjects ... London: Robert Barker: and the assignes
of John Bill, 1641. 4°

Wing C 2251.

T.129

219

CHARLES I, *King of England.*

His Majesties declaration to both Houses of
Parliament; ... in answer to that presented to him
at New-market the 9th of March 1641. London:
Robert Barker, and the assignes of John Bill, 1641.
4°

Wing C 2268.

T.130

220

CHARLES I, *King of England.*

The Kings Majesties demand of the House of Commons,
concerning those members who were accused of high
treason, Jan. 4. 1641 ... With his Maiesties speech
in Guild-Hall ... London, for Iohn Thomas, 1641. 4°

Wing C 2292.

T. 66

221

CHARLES I, *King of England.*

His Maiesties letter January the 24. 1641. In
answer to the petition of both Houses of Parliament
... Likewise the copie of a letter sent from
Scotland by the Lord Rothes, to the lords
commissioners here in England for that kingdome ...
London, for Iohn Thomas, 1641. 4°

Wing C 2391 A.

T.248

222

CHURCH OF SCOTLAND.

The doctrine and discipline of the Kirke of
Scotland, as it was formerly set forth by publicke
authority... The first and second booke...
Printed by Rob. Young, and are to be sold by
John Sweeting, 1641. 4°

Wing C 4224.
2 copies.

T.121   T.146

223

COTTON (*Sir* Robert Bruce)

Serious considerations for repressing of the
increase of Iesuites, priests, and papists,
without shedding of blood. Written by Sir R. C.
... [London], printed anno Dom. 1641. 4°

Wing C 6497.

T.249

224

DERING (*Sir* Edward)

A consideration and a resolution. First, concerning
the right of the laity in nationall councells.
Secondly, concerning the power of bishops in affaires
secular. Prepared for the honorable House of
Parliament. By S. E. D. London, Tho. Paine, for
John Stafford, 1641. 4°

Wing D 1107.

T.146

225

DIGBY (George) *Earl of Bristol.*

The speeches of the Lord Digby in the high court of
Parliament, concerning grievances, and the
trienniall parliament. Printed for Thomas Walkely,
1641. 4°

Wing B 4774.

T.130

226

DURY (John)

Consultatio theologica super negotio pacis
ecclesiasticae promovendo, exhibita submissaq;
judicio reverendae Facultatis Theologicae in
Academia Regia Vpsaliensi ... Londini, excudebat
G. M. pro Andrea Crooke, 1641. 4°

Wing D 2847.

T.304

227

DURY (John)

A memoriall concerning peace ecclesiasticall amongst
protestants. London, for W. Hope, anno 1641. 4°

Wing D 2872.

T.146

228

EAST INDIA COMPANY.

The petition and remonstrance of the governour and
company of merchants of London trading to the
East Indies, exhibited to the ... Lords and
Commons in the high court of Parliament assembled.
London, printed in the year, 1641. 4°

Wing E 100 F.

T.324

229

EGERTON (Thomas) *Viscount Brackley.*

The priviledges and prerogatives of the High Court
of Chancery. Written by the Right Honourable
Thomas Lord Elsmere ... London, for Henry
Sheapheard, 1641. 4°

Wing E 540.

T.389

230

ENGLAND, *Parliament.*

The articles or charge exhibited in Parliament
against Sir Francis Windebanck, Secretary of State
to his Majesty ... Printed anno Dom. 1641. 4°

Wing E 1235.

T.130

231

ENGLAND, *Parliament.*

A declaration of the Lords and Commons in Parliament:
with the additional reasons, last presented to his
Maiestie ... London, for Iohn Wright and I, Franke,
1641. 4°

Wing E 1484.

T.130

232

ENGLAND, *Parliament.*

A remonstrance of the state of the Kingdom ...
London, printed 1641. 4°

Wing E 2221 B.

T. 95

233

ENGLAND, *Parliament. House of Commons.*

The petition of the House of Commons, which
accompanied the declaration of the state of the
Kingdome, when it was presented to his Majestie
at Hampton Court. London, printed in the yeare
1641. 4°

Wing E 2680.

T. 66

234

ENGLAND, *Parliament. House of Commons.*

The true coppie of an act, or, declaration of the
honourable House of Commons, touching the care
they have in chusing of a lieutenant of the
Tower ... London, for T. B., 1641. 4°

Wing E 2747.

T.208

235

FANNANT (Thomas)

An historicall narration of the manner and forme of
that memorable parliament, which wrought wonders.
Begun at Westminster 1386 ... Related and
published by Thomas Fannant, clerke. Printed in
the yeare 1641. 4°

Wing F 415.

T.389

236

FIENNES (Nathaniel)

A speech... in answere to the third speech of
the Lord George Digby, concerning bishops and
the city of London's petition... 9th of Feb.
1640... [London], 1641. 4°

Wing F 880.
Incomplete, wanting the title-page and other
leaves.

T.278

237

GAUDEN (John) *Bishop of Worcester.*

Love of truth and peace. A sermon preached before
the honourable House of Commons ... Novemb. 29.
1640 ... London, T. C. for Andrew Crooke, 1641. 4°

Wing G 362.
2 copies.

T.252

238

HALL (Joseph) *Bishop of Norwich.*

A defence of the humble remonstrance, against the
frivolous and false exceptions of Smectymnuus.
Wherein the right of leiturgie and episcopacie is
clearly vindicated from the vaine cavils, and
challenges of the answerers. By the author of the
said humble remonstrance ... London, for Nathaniel
Butter, 1641. 2 parts. 4°

Wing H 378.

T.146

239

HENDERSON (Alexander)

The government and order of the Church of Scotland
... [Anon.] [Edinburgh], printed, anno 1641. 4°

Wing H 1432.

T.121

240

HOWARD (Thomas) *Earl of Arundel and Surrey.*

The true coppy of a letter sent from Thomas Earle
of Arundell, Lord Marshall, from Middleborough in
Zealand, to Mr. Pym... Whereunto is added the
coppy of another letter sent to Mr. Pym also
from the Committee in Scotland... London, for
Iohn Thomas, 1641. 4°

Wing N 1236.

T.249

241

The HUMBLE petition of the ministers of the Church of
England desiring reformation of certain ceremonies
and abuses of the Church: with the answer of the
Vice chancelor, the doctors, both the proctours, and
other the heads of houses in the University of
Oxford. Printed anno, 1641. 4°

Wing H 3562.

T.146

242

KILVERT (Richard)

A reply to a most untrue relation made and set forth
in print, by certaine vintners, in excuse of
their wine project. [Anon.] Printed in the yeare,
1641. 4°

Wing K 478.

T.81

243

L'ESTRANGE (Hamon)

Gods Sabbath before/ under the law and under the
gospel. Briefly vindicated from novell and heterodox
assertions ... Cambridge, Roger Daniel, 1641. 4°

Wing L 1188.

T.316

244

MARSHALL (Stephen)

Meroz cursed. Or, A sermon,preached to the
honourable House of Commons, at their late solemn
fast, Feb. 23. 1641 ... London, R. Badger, for
Samuel Gellibrand, 1641. 4°

Wing M 762.

T.252

245

MARSHALL (Stephen)

A sermon preached before the honourable House of Commons, now assembled in Parliament, at their publike fast, November 17. 1640 ... London: J. Okes, for Samuel Man, 1641. 4°

Wing M 776.
2 copies, with different type-settings.

T.252

246

MEDE (Joseph)

The apostasy of the latter times ... or, The gentiles theology of daemons, i.e. inferiour divine powers ... London, Richard Bishop for Samuel Man, 1641. 4°

Wing M 1590.

T.318

247

NAUNTON (Sir Robert)

Fragmenta regalia, or observations on the late Queen Elizabeth, her times and favorits. Printed, anno Dom. 1641. 4°

Wing N 249.

T.129

248

PAREUS (Joannes Philippus)

Oratio panegyrica pro musis Hanovicis instaurandis... In praesentia illustrium ac generosum comitum in Hanau & Isenburg... Publice habita a Philippo Pareo... Londini, in typographio I.O., 1641. 4°

Wing P 355.

T.304

249

PARTINGTON (Thomas)

Worse and worse newes from Ireland being the coppy of a letter read in the House of Parliament, the 14. of this instant moneth of December, 1641 ... [Anon.] London, for Nath: Butter, 1641. 4°

Wing P 611.

T.208

250

PIERREPONT (Henry) Marquess of Dorchester.

Two speeches spoken in the house of the Lords, by the Lord Viscount Newarke. The first concerning the right of bishops to sit in Parliament ... The second about the lawfulnes and conveniency of their intermedling in temporall affaires ... London, printed 1641. 4°

Wing D 1921.

T.278

251

The PRIVILEDGES and practice of parliaments in England. Collected out of the common lawes of this land... Printed in the yeare, 1641. 4°

Wing P 3534.

T.270

252

PURY (Thomas)

Mr. Thomas Pury alderman of Glocester his speech, upon that clause of the bill against episcopacy, the which concernes deanes, and deanes and chapters, at a committee of the whole House. Printed in the yeare 1641. 4°

Wing P 4247.

T.278

253

PYM (John)

Master Pimmes speech to the lords in Parliament, sitting in Westminster Hall the twelfth of Aprill, 1641. London, printed, 1641. 4°

Wing P 4297.
Signature of Thomas Bowdler.

T.130

254

SEVEN arguments plainly proving that papists are trayterous subjects to all true Christian princes. With a touch of Iesuites treacheries. Printed in the yeare 1641. 4°

Wing S 2735.

T.140

255

SHERMAN (John)

A Greek in the temple; some common-places delivered in Trinity Colledge chapell in Cambridge... Printed by Roger Daniel printer to the Universitie of Cambridge, 1641. 4°

Wing S 3385.

T.472

256

A SHORT treatise of archbishops and bishops, Lords spirituall: (viz.) whether they be in lesse fulnesse lords then the temporall; and whether to be tryed by peeres as the lords temporall... Printed in the yeare, 1641. 4°

Wing S 3635.

T.379

257

SICTOR (Joannes)

Continuatio epicediorum super octo senatores Londinenses, duos equites ex-praetores & sex armigeros, hoc triennio mortuos... Cantabrigiae, ex officina Rogeri Danielis, 1641. 4°

Wing S 3753.

T.304

258

STAPLETON (Sir Phillip)

Sir Phillip Stapleton his worthy speech in the House of Commons in Parliament, Ian, 15. 1641. Concerning the accusation of the Lord Digby and Colonell Lynsford of high treason, London, for John Thomas, 1641. 4°

Wing S 5258.

T.130

259

SUCKLING (Sir John)

A letter sent by Sir Iohn Suckling from France, deploring his sad estate and flight: with a discoverie of the plot and conspiracie, intended by him and his adherents against England. Imprinted at London, 1641. 4°

Wing S 6131.

T.407

260

SYMONDS (Joseph)

A sermon lately preached at Westminster, before sundry of the honourable House of Commons... London, for Luke Fawne, 1641. 4°

Wing S 6358.

T.670

261

TO the Kings most excellent Majestie, The humble petition of the inhabitants of the county of Glocester. With their protestation to his Majestie ... London, for John Thomas, 1641. 4°

Wing T 1540.

T.66

262

TO the Kings most excellent Majestie. The petition of the inhabitants of the county of Buckingham, concerning Mr. Hampden, Mr. Hollis, Mr. Pym, Sir Arthur Haslerigge, and Mr. Strowde. With his Maiestie's answer ... London, for John Thomas, 1641. 4°

Wing T 1554.

T.66

263

UDALL (Ephraim)

Τὸ πρεπον εὐχαριστιχον i,e, Communion comlinesse. Wherein is discovered the conveniency of the peoples drawing neere to the table in the sight thereof when they receive the Lords supper ... London, T. Bates, 1641. 4°

Wing U 13.

T.146

264

UNITIE, truth and reason. Presented in all humility petition-wise to the honourable, the knights, citizens and burgesses, for the Commons House of Parliament. By some moderate, and peace-desiring ministers, for the more happy and certaine reconciling of the Church-differences. Printed anno Dom. 1641. 4°

Wing P 38 (entered under H.P.)
Wanting title-page.

T.142

265

WENTWORTH (Sir Peter)

A pack of puritans, maintayning the unlawfulnesse, or unexpedience or both of pluralities and non-residency. Unpreaching prelates and ministers... As also a defence of the authority of princes and parliaments to intermeddle with matters of religion .... [Anon.] London, for William Sheeres, 1641. 4°

Wing W 1357.

T.142

266

WENTWORTH (Thomas) Earl of Strafford.

The conclusion of the Earle of Strafford's defence, the twelfth of Aprill, 1641. Printed in the yeere, 1641. 4°

Wing S 5784.

T.130

267

WENTWORTH (Thomas) Earl of Strafford.

The two last speeches of Thomas Wentworth, late Earle of Strafford ... The one in the Tower, the other on the scaffold on Tower-hill, May the 12th. 1641. [London, 1641.] 4°

Wing S 5800 A.

T.130

268

WHITE (John) Counsellor at Law.

Mr. Whites speech in Parliament on Munday, the 17th. of January. Concerning the triall of the XII. bishops, an. Dom. 1641. London, for F. Coules & T. Bancks, [1641]. 4°

Wing W 1772.

T.278

269

WILKINSON (Henry) Canon of Christ Church.

A sermon against lukwarmenesse in religion. Preached at Saint Maries in Oxford, the sixt of September, 1640 ... London, John Beale, for Humphrey Robinson, 1641. 4°

Wing W 2226.

T.252

270

WRAY (Sir John)

A speech, delivered in parliament; Novemb.13. 1641... Concerning the unlawfulnesse of bishops, and episcopall authoritie. London: for Tho. Banks, 1641. 4°

Wing W 3669.

T.278

1642

271

ANIMADVERSIONS upon those notes which the late Observator hath published upon the seven doctrines and positions which the King by way of recapitulation (he saith) layes open so offensive. London, for William Sheares, 1642. 4°

Wing A 3209.

T.270

272

BOECLER (Johann Heinrich)

Dissertatio Ioannis Henrici Boecleri de politicis Iusti Lipsii. Accessit oratio, De historia C. Cornelii Taciti. Argentorati, anno Christiano 1642. 12°

T.453

273

BOOTH (William)

The humble petition of Captain William Booth of Killingholme, in the county of Lincoln: with his Majesties answer thereunto. York, 30 June, 1642. London: Robert Barker, and the assignes of John Bill, 1642. 4°

Wing B 3741.

T.130

274

BRIDGE (William)

A sermon preached unto the volunters of the city of Norwich and also to the volunters of Great Yarmouth... London, J.F. for Ben. Allen, 1642. 4°

Wing B 4466.

T.516

275

BRIDGE (William)

The wounded conscience cured, the weak one strength-
ened, and the doubting satisfied.   By way of answer
to Doctor Fearne... London, for Benjamin Allen,
1642.   4°

Wing B 4476.

T.516

276

CALAMY (Edmund) *the Elder*.

Gods free mercy to England: presented as a
precious, and powerfull motive to humiliation: in
a sermon preached before the honorable House of
Commons at their late solemne fast, Feb. 23. 1641
... London, for Christopher Meredith, 1642.   4°

Wing C 253.

T.252

277

CALVERT (George) *1st Baron Baltimore*.

The answer to Tom-Tell-Troth.   The practise of
princes and the lamentations of the Kirke.   London,
printed 1642.   4°

Wing B 611.

T.508

278

CARTER (William)

Israels peace with God Beniamines overthrow.
A sermon preached before the honourable House
of Commons, at their late solemne fast, August
31. 1642 ... London, for Giles Calvert, and to
be sold by Christopher Meredith, 1642.   4°

Wing C 679A.

T.472

279

A CATALOGUE of the names of the dukes, marquesses,
earles and lords, that have absented themselves
from the Parliament, and are now with his Majesty
... Printed 1642.   4°

Wing C 1393.

T.372

280

CERTAINE observations touching the two great
offices of the seneschalsey or high-stewardship,
and high-constableship of England.   London, for
L. Chapman, Octob. 17. 1642.   4°

Wing C 1713.

T.287

281

CHARLES I, *King of England*.

His Majesties answer, by way of declaration to a
printed paper, entitled, A declaration of both
houses of Parliament, in answer to his Majesties
last message concerning the militia ... London:
Robert Barker, and the assigns of John Bill, 1642.
4°

Wing C 2090.

T.130

282

CHARLES I, *King of England*.

His Majesties answer to a book, entitled, The
declaration, or remonstrance of the Lords and
Commons, of the 19th of May, 1642.   London: Robert
Barker, and the assignes of John Bill, 1642.   4°

Wing C 2092.

T.130

283

CHARLES I, *King of England*.

His Majesties answer to a printed book, entitled,
A remonstrance, or, The declaration of the Lords
and Commons now assembled in Parliament, May 26.
1642 ... London: Robert Barker, and the assignes of
John Bill, 1642.   4°

Wing C 2103.

T.130

284

CHARLES I, *King of England*.

His Maiesties answer to the declaration of both
Houses of Parliament.   Concerning the commission of
array.   Of the first of July, 1642... Yorke, printed
by Robert Barker, and now reprinted at London, 1642.
4°

Wing C 2114.

T.508

285

CHARLES I, *King of England*.

His Majesties answer to the petition of both Houses
of Parliament.   Presented at York the 23, of May
1642.   Concerning the disbanding of his guard ...
London, for S. E, in the yeere 1642.   4°

Wing C 2131 B.

T.130

286

CHARLES I, *King of England*.

His Majesties answer to the petition of the Lords
and Commons in Parliament assembled: presented to his
Majestie at York, June 17, 1642.   London: Robert
Barker, and the assignes of John Bill, 1642.   4°

Wing C 2137.

T.130

287

CHARLES I, *King of England*.

His Majesties answer to the XIX. propositions of
both Houses of Parliament.   London: Robert Barker,
and the assignes of John Bill, 1642.   4°

Wing C 2122.

T.130

288

CHARLES I, *King of England*.

His Majesties declaration concerning leavies ...
London: Robert Barker, and the assignes of John
Bill, 1642.   4°

Wing C 2190.

T.130

289

CHARLES I, *King of England*.

His Majesties declaration, made the 13, of June,
1642, to the Lords, attending his Majestie at York
... Also, the copie of a letter, sent from divers
knights and gentlemen of Notinghamshire, to the
knights serving for that country in Parliament.
1 July, 1642.   Printed at York, and re-printed at
London, by Robert Young, [1642].   4°

Wing C 2211,

T.130

290

CHARLES I, *King of England*.

His Majesties declaration to all his loving subjects,
after his late victory against the rebels, on Sunday
the 23. of October.   Together with a relation of the
battell lately fought betweene Keynton and Edge-hill...
Oxford, Leonard Lichfield, 1642.   And now re-printed
at London.   4°

Wing C 2223.

T.508

291

CHARLES I, *King of England*.

His Majesties declaration to all his loving subjects,
occasioned by a false and scandalous imputation
laid upon his Majesty of an intention of raising
or leavying war against his Parliament ... London:
Robert Barker, and the assignes of John Bill, 1642,
4°

Wing C 2237.

T.130

292

CHARLES I, *King of England*.

His Majesties declaration to all his loving
subjects, Of August 12 1642.   Cambridge, Roger
Daniel, 1642.   4°

Wing C 2241.

T.130

293

CHARLES I, *King of England*.

His Majesties declaration to all his loving subjects,
of his true intentions in advancing lately to
Brainceford.   Oxford, Leonard Lichfield, 1642.   4°

Wing C 2246.

T.508

294

CHARLES I, *King of England*.

His Majesties declaration to all his loving subjects
shewing his true intentions in advancing lately
to Brainford ... London: Robert Barker: and the
assignes of John Bill, 1642,   4°

Wing C 2254.

T.129

295

CHARLES I, *King of England*.

His Maiesties declaration to all his loving
subjects, upon occasion of a late printed paper
entituled, A declaration and protestation of the
Lords and Commons in Parliament of this Kingdome,
and the whole world... Oxford. Leonard Lichfield,
1642.   4°

Wing C 2255.

T.508

296

CHARLES I, *King of England*.

His Maiesties declaration to all his loving
subjects, upon occasion of his late messages to
both Houses of Parliament, and their refusall, to
treat with him for the peace of the Kingdom ...
Oxford, Leonard Lichfield, 1642.   4°

Wing C 2257.

T.130

297

CHARLES I, *King of England*.

His Maiesties declaration to all his loving subjects,
upon occasion of the ordinance and declaration of the
Lords and Commons, for the assessing of all such who
have not contributed sufficiently for raising of mony,
plate, &c... Oxford, Leonard Lichfield, December 8.
1642.   4°

Wing C 2262.

T.508

298

CHARLES I, *King of England*.

His Majesties gracious message to both Houses of
Parliament, sent from Nottingham, August 25.   With
the answer of the Lords and Commons to the said
message ... London: Robert Barker, and the assigns
of John Bill, 1642.   4°

Wing C 2334.

T.130

299

CHARLES I, *King of England*.

His Majesties letter and declaration to the
sheriffes and citty of London.   Ianuary 17.1642.
Oxford, Leonard Lichfield, Ianuary 18.1642.   4°

Wing C 2385.

T.209

300

CHARLES I, *King of England*.

His Majesties message sent to the Parliament, April
8. 1642, concerning his resolution to go into
Ireland for suppressing the rebells there.   London:
Robert Barker, and the assignes of John Bill, 1642.
4°

Wing C 2447.
Signature of Tho. Bowdler.

T.130

301

CHARLES I, *King of England*.

His Majesties message to both Houses of Parliament,
April 28, 1642, concerning his refusall to passe
the bill for the militia.   London: Robert Barker,
and the assignes of John Bill, 1642.   4°

Wing C 2453.

T.130

302

CHARLES I, *King of England*.

His Majesties message to both Houses of Parliament,
of the eleventh of Iuly, 1642,... London: Robert
Barker, and the assignes of John Bill, 1642.   4°

Wing C 2456.

T.130

303

CHARLES I, *King of England*.

His Majesties speech and protestation, made in the
head of his armie, between Stafford and Wellington,
the 19th of September, 1642 ... London: Robert
Barker, and the assignes of John Bill, 1642.   4°

Wing C 2776.

T.130

304

CHARLES I, *King of England.*

His Majesties two speeches: one to the knights, gentlemen, and freeholders of the county of Nottingham at Newark, The other to the knights, gentlemen, and freeholders of the county of Lincoln at Lincoln. London: Robert Barker, and the assignes of John Bill, 1642. 4°

Wing C 2866.

T.130

305

CHURCH OF SCOTLAND.

To the King's most excellent Maiesty. The humble petition of the commissioners of the generall assembly of the Kirk of Scotland, met at Edenborough Ianuary, 4. 1642 ... With his Maiesties gratious answer thereunto March 16. 1642. Oxford, Leonard Lichfield, March 20. 1642. 4°

Wing C 4271.

T.387

306

The CITIES propositions, and the Parliaments answer. London, Richard Cotes, 1642. 4°

Wing C 4332.

T.209

307

A COMPLAINT to the House of Commons, and resolution taken up by the free protestant subjects of the cities of London and Westminster, and the counties adjacent. Oxford, Leonard Lichfield, 1642. 4°

Wing C 5622 (?)
"Ex libris Thomae Bowdler, 1642."

T.508

308

CORBETT (Edward)

Gods providence, a sermon preached before the honourable House of Commons, at their late solemne fast, Decemb. 28. anno 1642 ... London, Tho: Badger, for Robert Bostock, 1642. 4°

Wing C 6241.

T.514

309

COTTON (*Sir* Robert Bruce)

The forme of government of the kingdome of England: collected out of the fundamental lawes and statutes of this kingdome ... [Anon.] London, for Tho. Bankes, 1642. 4°

Wing C 6492.

T.270

310

A COUNTER-PLOT against popery. Suggested by way of short considerations, touching the necessity and usefulnesse of some agents, to correspond betwixt the protestant churches, in matters of publike edification. London: printed, anno Domini, 1642. 4°

Wing C 6521.

T.278

311

CUDWORTH (Ralph)

A discourse concerning the true notion of the Lords supper. By R. C. London, for Richard Cotes, 1642. 4°

Wing C 7466.

T.146

312

CUDWORTH (Ralph)

The union of Christ and the Church; in a shadow. By R. C. London, for Richard Bishop, 1642. 4°

Wing C 7472.

T.146

313

DERING (*Sir* Edward)

A collection of speeches made by Sir Edward Dering, knight and baronet, in matter of religion ... London, printed, 1642. 4°

Wing D 1103.

T.508

314

DEVEREUX (Robert) *3rd Earl of Essex.*

Two proclamations by his Excellency Robert Earl of Essex; captain generall of all the forces raised, or to be raised for the defence of the king and parliament, and kingdom ... London, for Iohn Frank, March 8. 1642. 4°

Wing E 3339.

T.372

315

DIGBY (George) *Earl of Bristol.*

The Lord George Digbies apologie for himselfe, published the fourth of Ianuary, anno Dom. 1642.

Wing B 4761.

T.504

316

DIGBY (John) *Earl of Bristol.*

A speech, made by the right honourable, Iohn Earle of Bristoll, in the high court of Parliament, May 20, 1642. concerning an accomodation. London, for Richard Marriot, 1642. 4°

Wing B 4794.

T.130

317

DIGGES (Dudley)

An answer to a printed book [by Henry Parker], intituled, Observations upon some of his Maiesties late answers and expresses. [Anon.] Printed by his Maiesties command at Oxford, by Leonard Lichfield, 1642. 4°

Wing D 1454.
2 copies.

T.270   T.124

318

DU CHESNE (André)

Behold! Two letters, the one written by the Pope to the (then) Prince of Wales, now King of England: the other, an answere to the said letter, by the said Prince ... Being an extract out of the history of England, Scotland and Ireland; written in French by Andrew du Chesne ... and now translated into English. Printed in the yeare of discoveries, 1642. 4°

Wing D 2424.

T. 81

319

DURY (John)

A petition to the honourable House of Commons in England now assembled in Parliament. Whereunto are added certaine considerations, shewing the necessity of a correspondencie in spirituall matters betwixt all protestant churches. London, for William Hope, 1642. 4°

Wing D 2879.

T.216

320

The ECCLESIASTICALL discipline of the reformed churches in France or, the order whereby they are governed. Faithfully transcribed into English out of a French copy. London: E. P. for Nicholas Bourne, 1642. 4°

Wing E 137.

T.121

321

ECKHOLT (Jacob)

Aigenschafft, Krafft und Würckung dess Brandtbronnens: das Krumbad genannt: in dess 16bl. Gottshaus Ursperg, gebiett ein Feldwegs von dem Marckht Krumbach... Gedruckt zu Augspurg, durch Andream Aperger, 1642. brs.

T.817

322

EIGHT speeches spoken in Guild-hall, upon Thursday night, Octob. 27, 1642 ... By the Lo: Wharton [and others] ... London: for Peter Cole, 1642. 4°

Wing E 262.

T.130

323

ENGLAND. *Parliament.*

Another declaration of the Lords and Commons assembled in Parliament, concerning subscriptions for bringing in money, plate, and horses ... London, Luke Norton and Iohn Field, for Edward Husbands and Iohn Franck, July 6. 1642. 4°

Wing E 1215.

T.130

324

ENGLAND. *Parliament.*

The answer of both houses of Parliament, presented to his Majestie at York the ninth of May, 1642. To two messages sent to them from his Majestie, concerning Sir Iohn Hothams refusall to give his Majestie entrance into his town of Hull. With his Majesties reply thereunto ... London: Robert Barker, and the assignes of John Bill, 1642. 4°

Wing E 1219.

T.130

325

ENGLAND. *Parliament.*

Certaine propositions of both Houses of Parliament, concerning the raising of horse, horsemen, and arms, for the defence of the King ... London, for Ioseph Hunscott, 1642. 4°

Wing E 1274.

T.129

326

ENGLAND. *Parliament.*

A declaration and ordinance of the Lords and Commons assembled in Parliament, for new loans, and contributions, as well as from the united Provinces of Holland, as from England and Wales, for the speedy relief of the miserable and distressed estate of the protestants in the kingdom of Ireland ... London, J. R. for Edw. Husbands, Feb. 2. 1642. 4°

Wing E 1297.

T.217

327

ENGLAND. *Parliament.*

A declaration and protestation of the Lords and Commons in Parliament, to this Kingdome, and to the whole world. Wherein ... is discovered, how severall commissions under the Kings authority have bin granted to many profest papists ... London, for John Wright, Octob. 23. 1642. 4°

Wing E 1309.

T.508

328

ENGLAND. *Parliament.*

A declaration and resolution of the Lords and Commons assembled in Parliament, concerning his Majesties late proclamation for the suppressing of the present rebellion... London, for Edward Husbands and Iohn Franck, August 15. 1642. 4°

Wing E 1313.

T.130

329

ENGLAND. *Parliament.*

A declaration and resolution of the Lords and Commons assembled in Parliament, in answer to the Scots declaration ... London, for Edward Husbands and John Franck, September 23. 1642. 4°

Wing E 1319.

T.129

330

ENGLAND. *Parliament.*

A declaration and resolution of the Lords and Commons assembled in Parliament. In answer to the Scots declaration ... London, for John Wright, Septemb. 23. [1642]. 4°

Wing E 1321.

T.387

331

ENGLAND. *Parliament.*

A declaration and votes of the Lords and Commons assembled in Parliament: concerning some scruple in their late ordinance, for the assessing of persons according to their abilities ... Printed for Iohn Wright, Decem. 8. 1642. 4°

Wing E 1328.

T.129

332

ENGLAND. *Parliament.*

The declaration and votes of the Lords and Commons assembled in Parliament: concerning the late treaty of peace in York-shire ... London, for Iohn Wright, October 5. 1642. 4°

Wing E 1327.

T.130

333

ENGLAND. *Parliament*.

A declaration of both houses of Parliament, in
answer to his Majesties last message, concerning
the militia ... Printed for Joseph Hunscott, May
5, 1642. 4°

Wing E 1342.

T.130

334

ENGLAND. *Parliament*.

The declaration of the Lords and Commons assembled
in Parliament, concerning his Maiesties letter,
and the petition of diverse noblemen, gentleman,
burgesses and ministers, to the Privy Councell
of Scotland ... London, for Joseph Hunscott and
John Wright, 1642. 4°

Wing E 1370.

T.387

335

ENGLAND. *Parliament*.

A declaration of the Lords and Commons assembled
in Parliament, concerning the pressing necessities
of this kingdome ... London, for Iohn Wright,
January, 10. 1642. 4°

Wing E 1397.

T.217

336

ENGLAND. *Parliament*.

A declaration of the Lords and Commons assembled in
Parliament, for the appeasing and quieting of all
unlawfull tumults and insurrections ... London,
for J. Wright, Septemb. 3, 1642. 4°

Wing E 1411.

T.130

337

ENGLAND. *Parliament*.

A declaration of the Lords and Commons assembled
in Parliament, for the association of all well-
affected persons in Lincoln-shire ... [London],
for I. Wright, Ian. 10. 1642. 4°

Wing E 1412.

T.217

338

ENGLAND. *Parliament*.

A declaration of the Lords and Commons assembled
in Parliament, for the incouragement of all such
apprentices as have or shall voluntarily list
themselves to go in this present expedition ...
[London], for John Wright, Novemb. 8, 1642. 4°

Wing E 1416.

T.130

339

ENGLAND. *Parliament*.

A declaration of the Lords and Commons assembled
in Parliament, for the preservation and safety of
the Kingdom, and the town of Hull ... London,
Luke Norton and Iohn Field, for Edward Husbands
and Iohn Franck, July 13, 1642. 4°

Wing E 1419 A.

T.130

340

ENGLAND. *Parliament*.

A declaration of the Lords and Commons assembled in
Parliament. For the raising of all power, and
force, as well trained bands as others, in severall
counties of this Kingdome ... London, for E.
Husbands and I. Franck, August. 9, 1642. 4°

Wing E 1423.

T.130

341

ENGLAND. *Parliament*.

A declaration of the Lords and Commons assembled in
Parliament, for the speedy putting this city into
a posture of defence ... London,for I. Wright,
Octob. 27. 1642. 4°

Wing E 1430.

T.130

342

ENGLAND. *Parliament*.

A declaration of the Lords and Commons assembled i:
Parliament, in answer to a proclamation, set forth
in his Majesties name, concerning the receipt and
payment of customs ... (An ordinance of Parliament,
concerning the subsidie of tonnage and poundage.)
London, for Lawrence Blaiklock, 1642. 2 parts. 4°

Wing E 1441.

T.130

343

ENGLAND. *Parliament*.

A declaration of the Lords and Commons assembled in
Parliament, setting forth the grounds and reasons,
that necessitate them at this time to take up
defensive arms for the preservation of his Majesties
person, the maintenance of the true religion, the
laws and liberties of this Kingdom, and the power
and privilege of Parliament... London, for Edward
Husbands, and Iohn Franck, August 3. 1642. 4°

Wing E 1450.

T.130

344

ENGLAND. *Parliament*.

A declaration of the Lords and Commons assembled in
Parliament that all such persons who shall advance
present moneyes ... shall be repaid ... Printed for
Iohn Wright, Decemb. 3, 1642. 4°

Wing E 1462.

T.129

345

ENGLAND. *Parliament*.

A declaration of the Lords and Commons assembled in
Parliament, upon information received, that divers
of his Majesties souldiers under colour of his
command ... have violently attempted to seize on
the magazine in sundry places ... London, for
Iohn Wright, Iuly 30, 1642. 4°

Wing E 1474.

T.130

346

ENGLAND. *Parliament*.

A declaration of the Lords and Commons assembled
in Parliament upon the statute of 5 H, 4 whereby
the commission of array is supposed to be
warranted ... London, for Edw. Husbands and John
Frank, 1642. 4°

Wing E 1475.

T.130

347

ENGLAND. *Parliament*.

The declaration of the Lords and Commons in
Parliament assembled. Willing, that no messenger
or officer, by colour of his Majesties command or
warrant under his hand, shall arrest, take, or carry
away any of his Majesties subjects against their
wils ... London, for John Wright, July 28. 1642. 4°

Wing E 1478.

T.130

348

ENGLAND. *Parliament*.

A declaration of the Lords and Commons in Parliament,
concerning an illegall writt sent to the high
sheriff of Essex ... London, A, Norton for Edw.
Husbands and Iohn Franke, June 20, 1642. 4°

Wing E 1360.

T.130

349

ENGLAND. *Parliament*.

A declaration of the Lords and Commons in Parliament:
concerning his Majesties proclamation, and the
declaration of the county of Essex ... London:
for Tho: Banks, Novemb. 4, 1642. 4°

Wing E 1373.

T.129

350

ENGLAND. *Parliament*.

The declaration or remonstrance of the Lords and
Commons, in Parliament assembled. With divers
depositions and letters therunto annexed ... London,
for Joseph Hunscott and John Wright, 1642. 4°

Wing E 1517.
Signature of Thomas Bowdler.

T.130

351

ENGLAND. *Parliament*.

The declaration, votes, and order of assistance, of
both houses of Parliament, concerning the magazine
at Hull ... And his Majesties answer thereunto ...
London: Robert Barker, and the assignes of John
Bill, 1642. 4°

Wing E 1520.

T.130

352

ENGLAND. *Parliament*.

The humble petition and advice of both Houses of
Parliament, with, XIX propositions, and the
conclusion sent unto his Majestie the second of
June, 1642 ... Printed for J, Hunscott, and I,
Wright, [1642]. 4°

Wing E 1565.
Signature of Thomas Bowdler.

T.130

353

ENGLAND. *Parliament*.

The humble petition of both Houses of Parliament:
presented to his Majesty on the 24th of November,
With his Majesty's gracious answer thereunto ...
Oxford, Leonard Lichfield, 1642. 4°

Wing E 1570.

T.130

354

ENGLAND. *Parliament*.

The humble petition of the Lords and Commons
assembled in Parliament; sent, to ... Robert Earl
of Essex, to be presented to his Majestie ...
London, for Edward Husbands and John Franck,
September 27. 1642. 4°

Wing E 1580 (?)

T.130

355

ENGLAND. *Parliament*.

The humble petition of the Lords and Commons to
the King, for leave to remove the magazine at Hull
to the Tower of London ... London: Robert Barker,
and the assignes of John Bill, 1642. 4°

Wing E 1583.
Signature of Thomas Bowdler.
Another copy, P 1838.

T.311   T.130

356

ENGLAND. *Parliament*.

June 21, 1642. A new declaration of the Lords and
Commons in Parliament, in answer to his Maiesties
letter, dated the 14 of June ... London, E, G, for
Edward Husbands, and Iohn Franke, 1642. 4°

Wing E 1667.

T.130

357

ENGLAND. *Parliament*.

An ordinance and declaration of the Lords and
Commons assembled in Parliament, allowing and
authorising any of his Majesties ...subjects in the
Kingdom of England, to furnish with all manner of
warlike provision, and send to sea what ships and
pinaces they shall thinke fit, to make stay of all
such supplies, as they shall seize upon by sea or
land, going to assist the rebels in Ireland ...
London, for I. Wright,   Octob.21. 1642. 4°

Wing E 1765,

T.130

358

ENGLAND. *Parliament*.

An ordinance and declaration of the Lords and
Commons assembled in Parliament. For the assessing
of all such as have not contributed upon the
propositions of both Houses of Parliament, for
raising of money ... London, for I. Wright,
Decemb. 1. 1642. 4°

Wing E 1770.
2 copies.

T.508   T.130

359

ENGLAND. *Parliament*.

An ordinance and declaration of the Lords and
Commons assembled in Parliament, that the Lord
Major and citizens of the city of London ... shall
have full power and authority .. to trench, stop,
and fortifie all high-waies leading into the said
city ... London, for I. Wright, March 8. 1642. 4°

Wing E 1775.

T.217

360

ENGLAND. *Parliament.*

An ordinance of the Lords and Commons assembled in Parliament, exhorting all his Majesties good subjects ... to the duty of repentance, (as the onely remedy for their present calamities) ... London, for John Wright, Feb. 16. 1642. 4°

Wing E 1849.

T.217

361

ENGLAND. *Parliament.*

An ordinance of the Lords and Commons assembled in Parliament: for the relieving of all persons over rated by the ordinance for weekly assessments ... London, for Edw. Husbands, March 10. 1642. 4°

Wing E 2030.

T.217

362.

ENGLAND. *Parliament,*

An ordinance of the Lords and Commons in Parliament assembled; for the better observation of the monthly fast ... London, for Laurence Blaiklock, 1642. 4°

Wing E 1943.

T.130

363

ENGLAND. *Parliament.*

The Parliaments answer to the two petitions of the county of Buckingham, as they were presented to both Houses ,.. Printed, the 13 of January, 1642. 4°

Wing E 2130.

T. 66

364

ENGLAND. *Parliament,*

The petition of both Houses of Parliament, presented to his Majestie at York, March 26. 1642. With his Majesties answer thereunto ... London: Robert Barker, and the assignes of John Bill, 1642. 4°

Wing E 2164.

T.130

365

ENGLAND. *Parliament.*

The petition of the Lords and Commons in Parliament, delivered to his Majestie the 16, day of July: together with his Majesties answer thereunto ... London: Robert Barker, and the assignes of John Bill, 1642. 4°

Not in Wing.

T.130

366

ENGLAND. *Parliament.*

The petition of the Lords and Commons, presented to his Majestie by the Earle of Stamford ... April 18, 1642. Together with his Majesties answer thereunto. London: Robert Barker, and the assignes of John Bill, 1642. 4°

Wing E 2179.

T.130

367

ENGLAND. *Parliament.*

Propositions and orders by the Lords and Commons now assembled in Parliament, for bringing in of money or plate, to maintaine horse, horse-men, and armes ,.. London, for Edward Husbands, and I. F., 1642. 4°

Wing E 2202 (?)

T.130

368

ENGLAND. *Parliament.*

A second remonstrance or, declaration of the Lords and Commons assembled in Parliament, concerning the commission of array, occasioned by a booke lately published, intituled His Majesties answer to the declaration ... concerning the said commission ... London, for Iohn Wright, and Richard Best, Ianuary 18. 1642. 4°

Wing E 2287.

T.217

369

ENGLAND. *Parliament.*

To the Kings most excellent Majesty, the humble answer of the Lords and Commons assembled in Parliament, to his Majesties last message the 11, September, 1642... London, for J. Wright, 17, Septemb, 1642. 4°

Wing E 2371.

T.130

370

ENGLAND. *Parliament.*

Two declarations of the Lords and Commons assembled in Parliament, The one, concerning the releasing of diverse worthy ministers ... The other, for the repaying of all such sums of money, as are, or shall be brought towards this publicke charge ... London, for Iohn Wright, September 9, 1642. 4°

Wing E 2391.

T.130

371

ENGLAND. *Parliament.*

Two orders of the Lords and Commons assembled in Parliament: concerning a committee of citizens, chosen and appointed by the Parliament to see that no gun-powder be conveyed out of London, without speciall warrant ... [London], for Iohn Wright, Decem. 5. 1642. 4°

Wing E 2397.

T.130

372

ENGLAND. *Parliament.*

The votes agreed on by the Lords and Commons concerning a treatise ... With his Majesties gracious answer thereunto ... London: Robert Barker: and the assignes of John Bill, 1642. 4°

Wing E 2437.

T.217

373

ENGLAND. *Parliament.*

Votes and declarations of both Houses of Parliament, concerning the taking away and disanulling the power of the clergie in making constitutions ... Printed for Francis Leach and William Gay, 1642, Iuly 14. 4°

Wing E 2439 (?)

T.130

374

ENGLAND. *Parliament. House of Commons.*

A declaration of the House of Commons in vindication of divers members of their House, from a false, and scandalous pamphlet, intituled, The humble petition of Captain William Booth ... London, Luke Norton and John Field, for Edward Husbands and Iohn Franck, July 22, 1642. 4°

Wing E 2567.

T.130

375

FAIRFAX (Ferdinando) *2nd Baron Fairfax.*

The answer of Ferdinando Lord Fairfax to a declaration of William Earle of Newcastle, touching a late warrant issued by the Lo: Fairfax, dated 2. February. 1642 ... London, for Iohn Franke, March 3. 1642. 4°

Wing F 111.

T.372

376

FAIRFAX (Ferdinando) *2nd Baron Fairfax.*

A second letter from the Right Honorable the Lord Fairfax, of his late prosperous proceedings against the Earle of New-castle, and his popish army in Yorke-shire ... London, for Iohn Wright, January 5. 1642. 4°

Wing F 123.
Title-page broken.

T.372

377

FERNE (Henry)

The resolving of conscience, upon this question, Whether ... subjects may take arms and resist ? and whether that case be now? ... Printed at Cambridge, and re-printed at London, 1642. 4°

Wing F 803.
3 copies.

T.516   T.146   T.124

378

FIENNES (Nathaniel)

An extraordinary deliverance, from a cruell plot, and bloudy massacre contrived by the malignants in Bristoll, for the delivering up the said city to Prince Rupert ... London, for I. Wright, March 15. 1642. 4°

Wing F 873.

T.372

379

A FRIVOLOUS paper, in forme of a petition: framed and composed by a disaffected party in this citie of London ... With certaine considerations propounded by way of advertisement and caution unto those who through unadvisednesse, are apt to subscribe the same. By a wel-wisher to peace and truth. Enlarged with new additions ... London, for Stephen Bowtell, 1642. 4°

Wing F 2232.

T.209

380

FULLER (Thomas) *Prebendary of Salisbury.*

A fast sermon preached on Innocents day ... London, L.N. and R.C. for John Williams, 1642. 4°

Wing F 2423.

T.470

381

GOODWIN (John)

Anti-cavalierisme, or, Truth pleading as well the necessity, as the lawfulness of this present war ... London, G. B. and R. W. for Henry Overton, [1642]. 4°

Wing G 1146.

T.122

382

GRIFFITH (Matthew)

A patheticall perswasion to pray for publick peace: propounded in a sermon preached in the cathedrall church of Saint Paul, Octob. 2. 1642 ... London, for Richard Royston, 1642. 4°

Wing G 2016.
2 copies.

T.668   T.146

383

HALES (John)

A tract concerning schisme and schismatiques. Wherein is briefly discovered the originall causes of all schisme. Written by a learned and judicious divine. London, printed for R. B., 1642. 4°

Wing H 277.

T.369

384

HARRIS (Robert)

A sermon preached to the honourable House of Commons assembled in Parliament, at a publike fast, May, 25. 1642 ... London, M.F. for Iohn Bartlet, 1642.   4°

Wing H 875.
2 copies.

T.472   T.674

385

HASLERIGG (*Sir* Arthur)

Sir Arthur Haslerigg his speech in Parliament, Whereby, hee cleareth himselfe of the articles of high treason, exhibited against himselfe ... London, for F. C. and T. B., 1642. 4°

Wing H 1129.

T.130

386

HERBERT (Philip) *4th Earl of Pembroke.*

Two speeches made in the House of Peers, on Munday the 19. of December, for, and against accomodation. The one by the Earl of Pembroke, the other by the Lord Brooke ... London, for Joh. Thompson, 1642. 4°

Wing P 1125.

T.187

387

HERLE (Charles)

A fuller answer to a treatise written by Doctor
Ferne, entituled The resolving of conscience upon
this question ... Done by another authour. And by
him revised and enlarged by occasion of some late
pamphlets ... London, for Iohn Bartlet, 1642. 4°

Wing H 1558.

T.124

388

HILL (Thomas) *Master of Trinity College, Cambridge.*

The trade of truth advanced. In a sermon preached
to the honourable House of Commons, at their solemne
fast, July 27, 1642... London, I.L. for Iohn
Bellamie, Philemon Stephens, and Ralph Smith, 1642.
4°

Wing H 2031.
2 copies.

T.472 T.674

389

HOLBORNE (Robert)

The reading in Lincolnes-Inne, Feb. 28. 1641. upon
the stat. of 25.E.3. cap.2. being the Statute of
treasons ... Oxford; Leonard Lichfield, 1642. 4°

Wing H 2374.

T.504

390

The HONEST informer or Tom-Tell-Troth's observations
upon abuses of government. Directed to his
Maiesty by way of an humble advertisement ...
Printed in the yeare 1642.   4°

Wing H 2586.

T.508

391

The HUMBLE petition and representation of the gentry,
ministers, and others of the counties of Cumberland
and Westmerland, to his sacred Maiestie: with his
Majesties answer thereunto ... London: Robert
Barker, and the assignes of John Bill, 1642. 4°

Wing H 3442.

T.130

392

The HUMBLE petition of the gentry and commons of
the county of York, presented to his Majesty,
April 22. 1642 ... London, for S. E., 1642. 4°

Wing H 3504.

T.130

393

The HUMBLE petition of the inhabitants of the
county of Essex to his Majesty. With his Maiesties
gratious answer thereunto ... Printed, by his
Majesties command, at Oxford, Ianuary II. By
Leonard Lichfield, 1642. 4°

Wing H 3518.

T. 81

394

The HUMBLE petition of the peacefull, obedient,
religious, and honest Protestants, of this
Kingdome, presented unto the Honourable House of
Commons, in their behalfe, by Doctor Hynton ...
Printed in the yeare 1642. 4°

Wing H 3569.

T. 66

395

A IUST complaint, or loud crie, of all the well-
affected subiects in England. Against that false
and scandalous pamphlet, intituled, A complaint to
the House of Commons, and resolution taken up by
the free protestant subjects of the cities of
London and Westminster, and the counties adjacent
... London, printed in the yeare of our Lord, 1642.
4°

Wing J 1232.

T.209

396

JOHNSON (William)

The resolution of the gentry and commonalty in the
county of Nottingham, presented to his Excellence
the Earle of Essex, the 12. of September ...
London, for Henry Fowler, Septem. 15. 1642.   4°

Wing J 863.

T.372

397

L.

A letter intercepted at a court-guard of the city of
London: wherein is discovered a most desperate and
bloody act to be performed on divers good ministers
and their congregations ... [Signed L.] London,
for Edw: Husbands, February 28. 1642.   4°

Wing L 1.

T.209

398

LOFTUS (Edward)

Ioyfull newes from Ireland, or, A true relation of
the great overthrow which the English gave the
rebels before Droheda, sent in a letter ... to Sir
Robert King ... [Anon.] London, for Iohn Franke,
1642. 4°

Wing L 2831.

T.208

399

LONDON.

The humble petition of the Major, aldermen, and
commons of the citie of London: and his Majesties
gracious answer the fourth of January 1642 ...
London: Robert Barker: and the assignes of John
Bill, 1642. 4°

Wing H 3554.

T.217

400

LONDON.

Propositions agreed upon at a court of common
councell, in Guild Hall. London. Feb. 21. 1642.
London, Richard Cotes, 1642. 4°

Wing P 3776.

T.217

401

The MANNER of the impeachment of the XII. bishops
accused of high treason, for preferring a petition,
and making a protestation, to the subverting the
fundamentall laws and being of Parliament ...
London, for Joseph Hunscott, 1642. 4°

Wing M 474.

T.278

402

MARSHALL (Stephen)

Reformation and desolation: or, A sermon tending to
the discovery of the symptomes of a people to
whom God will by no meanes be reconciled. Preached
to the honourable House of Commons at their late
solemne fast, Decemb. 22. 1641 ... London, for
Samuel Gellibrand, 1642. 4°

Wing M 770.

T.252

403

MEDE (Joseph)

Diatribae. Discourses on divers texts of
scripture: delivered upon severall occasions ...
London, M. F. for John Clark, 1642. 4°

Wing M 1596.

T.318

404

MORTON (Thomas) *Bishop of Durham.*

The presentment of a schismaticke. In his sermon
preached at the cathedrall church of Saint Pauls the
19. of Iune 1642. London, T. Badger, for R. Whitaker,
and S. Broun, 1642. 4°

Wing M 2846.

T.472

405

MORTON (Thomas) *Bishop of Durham*

The presentment of a schismaticke. In his sermon
preached at the cathedrall church of Saint Pauls the
19. of Iune. 1642. The second impression carefully
corrected and amended. London: I. Okes, for R.
Whitaker, and S. Broun, 1642. 4°

Wing M 2845.
Incomplete.

T.754

406

A MOST exact and true relation of the proceedings
of his Maiesties armie at Shelborne. Written by a
lover of the truth. London, for R. M. and G. B.,
1642. 4°

Wing M 2876.

T.130

407

A MOST true relation of the present state of his
Majesties army; wherein also the truth of that
declaration published by the Parliament, of their happy
victory in the battaile at Keynton, is both justly
asserted and abundantly proved, humbly presented by the
author who was personally present, to the honourable the
Lords and Commons in Parliament assembled... London,
for I.E., 1642. 4°

Wing M 2931.

T.508

408

OBSERVATIONS upon his Majesties answer, to the
city of Londns [sic] petition. Sent from his
Majestie by Captaine Hearne. And read at a
common-hall on fryday the 13. of Ianuary 1642.
Printed in the yeare 1642. 4°

Wing O 111.

T.209

409

OBSERVATIONS upon the Prince of Orange and the
States of Holland. [London, 1642.] 4°

Wing O 105.

T.287

410

The OBSERVATOR defended in a modest reply to the
late animadversions upon those notes the Observator
published upon the seven doctrines and positions
which the King by way of recapitulation layes open
so offensive. [London, 1642.] 4°

Wing O 108.

T.270

411

The ORDERS for ecclesiastical discipline. According
to that which hath been practised since the
Reformation of the Church ... by the auncient ministers,
elders, and deacons of the Isles of Garnsey, Gersey,
Spark, and Alderny ... London: printed in the yeare,
1642. 4°

Wing O 399.

T.121

412

PARKER (Henry)

Observations upon some of his Majesties late
answers and expresses. [Anon.] [No imprint,
1642.] 4°

Wing P 412.

T.270

413

PARKER (Henry)

Observations upon some of his Majesties late
answer and expresses. The second edition corrected
from some grosse errors in the presse. [Anon.]
[London, 1642.] 4°

Wing P 413.
2 copies.

T.122 T. 129

414

The PETITION of the nobilitie, gentrie, burrows,
ministers, and commons of the kingdom of Scotland,
to the lords of his Majesties most honourable Privie
Councell. London: printed by Robert Barker: and
by the assignes of John Bill, 1642. 4°

Wing P 1824.

T.387

415

QUESTIONS resolved, and propositions tending to
accomodation and agreement betweene the King being
the royall head, and both Houses of Parliament being
the representative body of the Kingdome of England...
[London, 1642] 4°

Wing Q 186.

T.270

416

R.(T.)

An honest letter to a doubtfull friend, about the
rifling of the twentieth part of his estate. Printed
in the yeare 1642. 4°

Wing R 84.

T.270

417

RAYNSFORD (John)

The yong souldier. London, J.R. for Joseph Hunscott, 1642. 4°

Wing Y 132.

T.372

418

REASONS why this Kingdome ought to adhere to the Parliament. [London, 1642.] 4°

Wing R 592.

T.270

419

The REMONSTRANCE and protestation, of the gentry, and commonalty of the counties of Buckingham, Hartford, Bedford, and Cambridge ... London, L. N. and R. C, for F. Eaglesfield, December 9, 1642. 4°

Wing R 971.

T. 81

420

REYNOLDS (Edward) *Bishop of Norwich.*

Israels petition in time of trouble. A sermon preached in St. Margarets Church... before the honourable House of Commons... at the late publique and solemn fast, July 27. 1642. London, George Bishop, and Robert White, for Robert Bostock, 1642. 4°

Wing R 1256.

T.668

421

RICH (Henry) *1st Earl of Holland.*

Two speeches delivered by the Earl of Holland, and Mr. Io: Pym, Esquire. Concerning a petition to his Majestie for peace. Spoken in Guild-hall ... London: J. F. for Peter Cole, 1642. 4°

Wing H 2422.

T.209

422

SACKVILLE (Edward) *4th Earl of Dorset.*

The Earle of Dorset his speech for propositions of peace, delivered to his Majesty at Oxford, on January 18. London, printed in the yeare 1642. 4°

Wing D 1951.

T.187

423

SAINT LEGER (*Sir* William)

True and happy news from Ireland, being the coppy of a letter written from Sir W. Saintliger Lord Presidant of Munster, to the Lord Lieutenant of Ireland ... London, for Iohn Wright, 1642. 4°

Wing S 338.

T.208

424

The SECOND part of Vox populi. Being the peoples report unto the King, upon the severall appeales declared in his Majesties name ... [No imprint, 1642?] 4°

cf. Wing S 2323.

T.270

425

SEDGWICK (Obadiah)

England's preservation or, A sermon discovering the onely way to prevent destroying judgements: preached to the honourable House of Commons... May, 25. 1642... London, R.B. for Samuel Gellibrand, 1642. 4°

Wing S 2372.
2 copies.

T.472 T.670

426

SEDGWICK (William)

Zions deliverance and her friends duty: or the grounds of expecting, and meanes of procuring Jerusalems restauration. In a sermon preached... before the honourable House of Commons. London, for John Bellamy, & Ralph Smith, 1642. 4°

Wing S 2392.

T.670

427

SOME speciall passages from Hull, Anlaby, and Yorke: truly informed Munday the first of August 1642. (Number 10.) London, R.O. and G.D., 1642. 4°

Not in Wing.

T.372

428

SPELMAN (*Sir* John)

A view of a printed book [by Henry Parker] intituled Observations upon his Majesties late answers and expresses. [Anon.] Oxford, Leonard Lichfield, 1642. 4°

Wing S 4941.
2 copies.

T.508   T.270

429

STOUGHTON (William) *Professor of Civil Law.*

An assertion for true and Christian church-policie. Wherein certain politike objections made against the planting of pastours and elders in every congregation, are sufficiently answered ... London, for Iohn Bartlett, 1642. 4°

Wing S 5761.

T.146

430

A SUDDAINE answer to a suddaine moderatour; who, directed by reason and no more, expects suddaine peace, or certaine ruine ... London, printed in the yeare of restauration, when the times always have been, are, and will be troublous, 1642. 4°

Wing S 6141.

T.124

431

SYMMONS (Edward)

Foure sermons wherein is made a foure-fold discovery... London, R.C. for Andrew Crooke, 1642. 4°

Wing S 6343.

T.252

432

TAYLOR (Jeremy) *Bishop of Down and Connor.*

Of the sacred order, and offices of episcopacy, by divine institution, apostolicall tradition, & catholike practice... Oxford, Leonard Lichfield, 1642. 4°

Wing T 353.

T.747

433

A TREATIE of peace, concluded the 29. of September, 1642 ..., that all forces assembled together in any part of Yorkshire ... shall be disbanded ... London, for I. Benson, 1642. 4°

Wing T 2100.
Signature of T. Bowdler.

T.130

434

TWO petitions, of the knights, gentlemen, freeholders, and others of the inhabitants of the county of Hertford ... London, printed by a perfect copie, by R. O. & G. Dexter, and are to be sold by John Sweeting, 1642. 4°

Wing T 3511.
3 copies.

T.81 T.66

435

A VINDICATION of the King, with some observations upon the two houses: By a true son of the Church of England, and a lover of his countries liberty. London, printed anno Domini, 1642. 4°

Wing V 509.
Signature of Thomas Bowdler.

T.270

436

The VINDICATION of the Parliament and their proceedings. Or, Their military designe proved loyall and legall ... London, printed in the yeare 1642. 4°

Wing V 521.

T.270

437

WARD (Richard)

The anatomy of warre, or, Warre with the wofull fruits, and effects thereof, laid out to the life: wherein from scripture, and experience, these things are clearely handled... By R.W... London, for Iohn Dalham, and Rich. Lownds, [1642]. 4°

Wing W 800
Incomplete.

T.270

438

WARMSTRY (Thomas)

Ramus Olivae; or, An humble motion for peace: presented to his sacred Maiestie, and the honourable Houses of Parliament... Oxford, Henry Hall, 1642. 4°

Wing W 888 (?)

T.270

439

WHARTON (Philip) *4th Baron Wharton.*

The two speeches of the Lord Wharton, spoken in Guild-hall Octob.27.1642. In which are contained a full and true relation of the battell between the two armies at Kinton... London, for Sa. Gellibrand, 1642. 4°

Wing W 1574.

T.372

440

WILCOCK (James)

The true English protestants apology, against the blacke-mouth'd obloquie of ignorance and innovation... London, printed by I.R., 1642. 4°

Wing W 2119.

T.472

441

WILDE (John)

A letter sent from Mr. Sergeant Wilde, and Humphrey Salwey, Esq; both members of the House of Commons, to the Honorable, William Lentall ... concerning divers passages at the quarter sessions in Worcester, about the execution of the Commission of Array ... London, Luke Norton and John Field, for Edward Husbands and Iohn Franck, July 18. 1642. 4°

Wing W 2163.

T.81

442

WYNELL (Thomas)

The covenants plea for infants: or, The covenant of free grace, pleading the divine right of Christian infants unto the seale of holy baptisme... Oxford, Henry Hall for the author, 1642. 4°

Wing W 3778.

T.472

1643

443

An ANSWER to a pamphlet intituled the Lord George Digby his apologie for himselfe: plainly discovering the cunning untruths, and implicit malice in the said pamphlet ... London, for Thomas Iohnson, anno Dom. 1643. 4°

Wing A 3326.

T. 81

444

An ANSWER to a seditious pamphlet [by Edward Bowles], intituled, Plain English... Printed in the yeare, 1643. 4°

Wing A 3351.

T.124

445

ARTICLES of impeachment and accusation, exhibited in Parliament, against Colonell Nathaniel Fiennes, touching his dishonorable surrender of the city and castle of Bristoll; by Clement Walker and William Prynne, esquires. Together with a letter from Mr. Prynne to Colonell Fiennes. London: printed in the yeer, 1643. 4°

Wing A 3856.

T.372

446

BAILLIE (Robert)

Satan the leader in chief to all who resist the reparation of Sion. As it was cleared in a sermon to the honourable House of Commons at their late solemn fast, Febr.28.1643...   London, for Samuel Gellibrand, 1643.   4⁰

Wing B 468.
2 copies.

T.470 T.669

447

BARTON (Thomas)

Λογος αγωνιος; or, A sermon of the Christian race, preached before his Maiesty at Christ-Church in Oxford, May 9. 1643... [Oxford], printed by L.L., 1643.   4⁰

Wing B 999.

T.468

448

BIRKENHEAD (*Sir* John)

A letter from Mercurius Civicus to Mercurius Rusticus: or, Londons confession but not repentance. Shewing, that the beginning and the obstinate pursuance of this accursed horrid rebellion is principally to be ascribed to that rebellious city... [Anon.] [Oxford], printed, 1643.   4⁰

Wing B 6323 (attributed to Samuel Butler).

T.217

449

BOWLES (Edward)

Plaine English: or, A discourse concerning the accomodation, the armie, the association ... [Anon.] Printed (unlesse men be the more carefull, and God the more mercifull) the last of liberty, 1643. 4⁰

Wing B 3878.
2 copies.

T.122 T.124

450

BURROUGHES (Jeremiah)

The glorious name of God, the lord of hosts. Opened in two sermons, at Michaels Cornhill, London... With a postscript, briefly answering a late treatise by Henry Ferne... London, for R. Dawlman, 1643. 4⁰

Wing B 6074/5.

T.468

451

CALAMY (Edmund) *the Elder*.

The noble-mans patterne of true and reall thankfulnesse. Presented in a sermon preached before the ... House of Lords, at their late solemne day of thanksgiving, Iune 15. 1643... London, G.M. for Christopher Meredith, 1643.   4⁰

Wing C 261.
2 copies.

T.252 T.468

452

CARDENAS (Alonso de)

A speech, or complaint, lately made by the Spanish embassadour to his Maiestie at Oxford, upon occasion of the taking of a ship called Sancta Clara in the port of Sancto Domingo ... by one Captaine Bennet Strafford, and by him brought to Southampton ... Translated out of the Spanish, in Oxford, by Sr Torriano ... London, for Nathaniel Butter, Jan. 17. 1643. 4⁰

Wing C 496.

T.369

453

CARTER (Thomas)

Prayers prevalencie for Israels safety. Declared in a sermon preached in Saint Margarets Westminster, before the honourable House of Commons ... June 28. 1643. London, Richard Cotes, and are to be sold by John Bellamie and Ralph Smith, 1643.   4⁰

Wing C 668.
2 copies.

T.474 T.670

454

CAWDREY (Daniel)

The good man a publick good, 1. passively, 2. actively. As it was manifested in a sermon preached to the honourable House of Commons, at the late solemne fast: January 31. 1643... London, Tho. Harper, for Charles Greene, and P.W., 1643. 4⁰

Wing C 1628.

T.468

455

CHALONER (Richard)

Mr. Challenor his confession and speech made upon the ladder before his execution on Wednesday the fifth of July 1643 ... London, Peter Cole, 1643. 4⁰

Wing C 1800.

T.209

456

CHAMBERS (Humfry)

A divine ballance to weigh religious fasts in. Applyed to present use, in a sermon preached before the honourable House of Commons... Sept.27.1643... London, M.F. for Samuel Man, 1643. 4⁰

Wing C 1915.
2 copies.

T.474 T.670

457

CHARLES I, *King of England*.

His Majesties declaration to all his loving subjects, in answer to a declaration of the Lords and Commons upon the prceedings of the late treaty of peace and severall intercepted letters ... Oxford, 3. June 1643. Oxford, Leonard Lichfield, 1643. 4⁰

Wing C 2233.

T.217

458

CHARLES I, *King of England*.

His Majesties declaration to all his subjects of his kingdom of Scotland, upon occasion of a printed paper, entiled [sic], The declaration of the kingdom of Scotland, concerning the present expedition into England, &c ... Oxford, Leonard Lichfield, January 9. 1643. 4⁰

Wing C 2263.

T.387

459

CHARLES I, *King of England*.

His Majesties gracious message of the fifth of this instant May, to both Houses of Parliament; occasioned by a bill delivered to his Majesty ... intituled, An act for the speedy payment of moneys subscribed towards the reducing of the rebels in Ireland, which yet remains unpaid. Oxford, Leonard Lichfield, 1643. 4⁰

Wing C 2326.

T.217

460

CHARLES I, *King of England*.

The grounds and motives inducing his Maiesty to agree to a cessation of armes for one whole yeare, with the Roman Catholiques of Ireland ... Oxford, Leonard Lichfield, 1643. 4⁰

Wing G 2134.

T.208

461

CHARLES I, *King of England*.

His Maiesties message to both Houses Aprill 12. 1643. concerning disbanding of both armies; and his Maiesties returne to both Houses of Parliament ... Oxford, 19. May 1643. Oxford, Leonard Lichfield, 1643. 4⁰

Wing C 2458.

T.217

462

CHARLES I, *King of England*.

Military orders, and articles, established by his Maiestie, for the better ordering and government of his Maiesties armie... Re-printed at Oxford, by Leonard Lichfield, [1643]. 4⁰

Wing C 2496.

T.504

463

CHEYNELL (Francis)

The rise, growth, and danger of Socinianisme... London, for Samuel Gellibrand, 1643.   4⁰

Wing C 3815.

T.471

464

CHEYNELL (Francis)

Sions memento, and Gods alarum. In a sermon at Westminster, before the honourable House of Commons, on the 31. of May 1643... London, for Samuel Gellibrand, 1643.   4⁰

Wing C 3816.

T.474

465

CHURCH OF SCOTLAND.

The reformation of the discipline and service of the Church ... With the forme of the common prayers and administration of the sacraments ... London, for Mathew Walbanck, and Lawrence Chapman, 1643. 4⁰

Wing R 743.

T.121

466

COLE (Robert)

The true coppies of two letters sent from Ireland [by Robert Cole]: shewing the severall battailes and victories obtained on the rebels there. London, for J. B. and R. Smith, 1643. 4⁰

Wing C 5027.

T.208

467

The COLLECTION of all the particular papers that passed between his Maiestie, both Houses, and the Committee, concerning the late treaty. Oxford, Leonard Lichfield, 1643. 4⁰

Wing C 5112.

T.217

468

A CUNNING plot to divide and destroy, the Parliament and the city of London. Made knowne (at a common hall) by the Earle of Northumberland, Master Solliciter, and Sir Henry Vane ... London, Peter Cole, January 16, 1643. 4⁰

Wing C 7586.

T. 86

469

The DECLARATION of the kingdomes of England and Scotland, ioyned in armes for the vindication and defence of their religion, liberties, and lawes, against the popish, prelaticall, and malignant party ... London, for Iohn Wright, Februar. 1. 1643. 4⁰

Wing D 691.

T.387

470

DEVEREUX (Robert) *3rd Earl of Essex*.

Laws and ordinances of warre, established for the better conduct of the army, by his Excellency the Earl of Essex, lord generall of the forces raised by the authority of the Parliament ... London, for Luke Fawne, 1643. 4⁰

Wing E 3316.

T.217

471

DIGBY (George) *Earl of Bristol*.

A true and impartiall relation of the battaile betwixt, his Maiesties army, and that of the rebels neare Newbery in Berkshire, Sept. 20. 1643 ... [Anon.] Oxford, L. Lichfield, 1643. 4⁰

Wing B 4778.

T.217

472

DU MOULIN (Louis)

Αὐτομαχια: or, The selfe-contradiction of some
that contend about church-government ... By
Irenaeus Philalethes ... London, printed anno
Dom. 1643.   4°

Wing D 2531.

T.369

473

E. (R,)

An answer to a letter written out of the country,
to Master John Pym ,.. London, printed anno Dom.
1643.   4°

Wing E 26,

T.81

474

An ELEGIACALL commemoration of the pious life,
and most lamented death, and funerals, of Mr.
Josiah Shute... London, printed in the yeare
of our Lord, 1643.   4°

Wing E 337.

T.369

475

ENGLAND. Laws, Statutes.

A collection of certaine statutes in force, with
full and ready notes in the margent containing
their effect in briefe... London, printed in the
yeare, 1643.   4°

Wing E 886.

T.369

476

ENGLAND. Parliament.

The articles of cessation of the Lords and Commons
in Parliament. Presented to his Majesty upon
consideration of the former articles ... And his
Maiesties gracious answer thereunto. March 22.
1642. Oxford, Leonard Lichfield, March 25. 1643.
4°

Wing E 1231.

T.217

477

ENGLAND. Parliament.

The copies of such bills as were presented unto
his Majestie at Oxon ... Unto the which bills
his Majestie hath not as yet given his royall
assent ... London: for Edward Husbands, July 19.
1643. 4°

Wing C 6081.

T.217

478

ENGLAND, Parliament.

A declaration and ordinance of the Lords and
Commons assembled in Parliament; touching the
great seale of England ... [London], for Edward
Husbands, November 11, 1643. 4°

Wing E 1305.

T.217

479

ENGLAND, Parliament.

The declaration of the Lords and Commons of
Parliament assembled at Oxford according to his
Majesties proclamation, concerning their endeavours
since they came thither for the peace of the
kingdom ... Oxford, Leonard Lichfield, 1643. 4°

Wing E 1402.

T, 86

480

ENGLAND, Parliament.

A declaration of the Lords and Commons of Parliament
assembled at Oxford, of their proceedings touching
a treatie for peace, and the refusall thereof; with
the severall letters and answers that passed
therein ... Oxford, Leonard Lichfield, 1643. 4°

Wing E 1445

T, 86

481

ENGLAND. Parliament.

A declaration and ordinance of the Lords and
Commons in Parliament; for the speedy raising of
a body of horse, for the preservation, safety, and
peace of the Kingdom ... [London], for Edward
Husbands, July 27. 1643. 4°

Wing E 1304.

T.217

482

ENGLAND. Parliament.

A declaration or ordinance of the Lords and
Commons assembled in Parliament, Concerning the
taking of horses for the service of the
Parliament in the severall counties of England ...
[London], for John Wright, May 11. 1643.   4°

Wing E 1515.

T.217

483

ENGLAND. Parliament.

An ordinance by the Lords and Commons assembled in
Parliament, enabling all persons approved of by
Parliament, to set forth ships in war-like manner
... London, for Laurence Blaiklocke, 1643. 4°

Wing E 1840.

T.217

484

ENGLAND. Parliament.

An ordinance of the Lords and Commons assembled in
Parliament; concerning the proceedings of divers
ill-affected persons and papists within the
counties of Denbigh, Mountgomery, Flint, Merioneth,
Carnarvon and Anglesey ... [London], for Edw,
Husbands, July 11. 1643. 4°

Wing E 1828

T.217

485

ENGLAND, Parliament.

An ordinance of the Lords and Commons assembled in
Parliament, explaining the former ordinance for
the raising of a body of horse for the preservation,
peace, and safety of the Kingdome ... London, for
Iohn Wright, Aug. 26. 1643. 4°

Wing E 1850.

T.217

486

ENGLAND, Parliament.

An ordinance of the Lords and Commons assembled in
Parliament. For the calling of an assembly of
learned, and godly divines ... for the settling
of the government and lyturgy of the Church of
England ... London, for Iohn Wright, June 13.
1643. 4°

Wing E 1952

T.217

487

ENGLAND, Parliament.

An ordinance of the Lords and Commons assembled
in Parliament: for the leaving of moneys, by
way of excise, or, new impost ... London: for
Edward Husbands, Septemb. II. 1643. 4°

Wing E 1988.

T.217

488

ENGLAND, Parliament.

An ordinance of the Lords and Commons assembled in
Parliament; for the raising of a new loan and
assessment in the county of Middlesex ... [London],
for Edw. Husbands, Febr. 19, 1643. 4°

Wing E 2013.

T, 86

489

ENGLAND. Parliament.

An ordinance of the Lords and Commons assembled in
Parliament, for the securing those apprentices
from indempnity, that will list themselves under
the command of Sir William Waller ... [London],
for Edward Husbands, September 26. 1643. 4°

Wing E 2037.

T.217

490

ENGLAND. Parliament.

An ordinance of the Lords and Commons assembled in
Parliament, for the speedy raising and impresting
of men, for the defence of the Kingdom ...
[London], for Edward Husbands, August II. 1643. 4°

Wing E 2048.

T.217

491

ENGLAND. Parliament.

An ordinance of the Lords and Commons assembled in
Parliament, for the speedy raising and levying of
money for the maintenance of the army ... London,
for Edw, Husbands, 1643. 4°

Wing E 2050.

T.217

492

ENGLAND. Parliament.

An ordinance of the Lords and Commons assembled in
Parliament, for the speedy raising and leavying of
money thorowout the whole kingdom ... London, for
Edward Husbands, May 11. 1643. 4°

Wing E 2051.
Incomplete.

T.217

493

ENGLAND. Parliament.

An ordinance of the Lords and Commons assembled in
Parliament. For the speedy raising and levying
of moneyes, by way of excise, or new impost, upon
severall commodities ... London, for John Wright,
Iuly 27. 1643. 4°

Wing E 2052.

T.217

494

ENGLAND. Parliament.

An ordinance of the Lords and Commons assembled in
Parliament; for the upholding the government and
fellowship of merchants of England trading in the
Levant seas ... London, for Edward Husbands, 1643.
4°

Wing E 2068.

T. 86

495

ENGLAND. Parliament.

An ordinance of the Lords and Commons assembled in
Parliament. Shewing that all his Majesties, the
Queenes, and princes honours, mannors, lands ...
and profits whatsoever ... shall be seized upon
... London, for Iohn Wright, Septemb. 23. 1643. 4°

Wing E 2082.

T.217

496

ENGLAND. Parliament.

An ordinance of the Lords and Commons assembled in
Parliament; to prevent the coming over of the
Irish rebells ... London, for Edward Husbands,
Septemb. 12. 1643. 4°

Wing E 2097.

T.217

497

ENGLAND. Parliament.

Die Martis, 9. Ianuarii, 1643. An ordinance of the
Lords and Commons assembled in Parliament, touching
the excise of flesh-victualls, and salt. London,
Rich. Cotes and Joh. Raworth, 1643. 4°

Wing E 2100.

T. 86

498

ENGLAND. Parliament.

An ordinance of the Lords and Commons assembled in
Parliament; with instructions for the taking of the
league and covenant ... [London], for E. Husbands,
[1643]. 4°

Wing E 2110.

T, 86

499

ENGLAND. *Parliament.*

The reasons of the Lords and Commons in Parliament
why they cannot agree to the alteration and
addition in the articles of cessation offered by
his Maiesty. With his Maiesties gratious answer
thereunto ... Oxford, Leonard Lichfield, 1643. 4°

Wing E 2215.

T.504

500

ENGLAND. *Parliament.*

A sacred vow and covenant taken by the Lords and
Commons assembled in Parliament: upon the
discovery of the late horrid and treacherous
designe, for the destruction of this Parliament,
and the Kingdom ... London: for Edward Husbands,
June 12. 1643. 4°

Wing E 2284.

T.217

501

ENGLAND. *Parliament.*

Three ordinances of the Lords and Commons
assembled in Parliament. Containing the names
and divers knights and gentlemen, to be added to
the committees in the counties of Kent and Sussex,
for the weekly assessements ... London, for
Iohn Wright, May 19. 1643. 4°

Wing E 2360.

T.217

502

ENGLAND. *Parliament.*

Two ordinances of the Lords and Commons assembled
in Parliament. Concerning the trained bands of
the cities of London and Westminster, and the
county of Middlesex ... [London], for John Wright,
May 4. 1643. 4°

Wing E 2399.

T.217

503

ENGLAND. *Parliament.*

Two ordinances of the Lords and Commons assembled
in Parliament. One, that all sellers of wine who
shall pay the excise ... The other, concerning
Northampton ... London, for Iohn Wright, Octob.
10. 1643. 4°

Wing E 2415.

T.217

504

ENGLAND. *Parliament.*

Two ordinances of the Lords and Commons assembled
in Parliament; viz. The first, enabling the
committee of the Admiralty to grant commissions
... The second, for the sequestring of the estates
of spyes and intelligencers ... [London], for
Edw. Husbands, November 10. 1643. 4°

Wing E 2428.

T.217

505

ENGLAND. *Parliament.*

The vow and covenant appointed by the Lords and
Commons assembled in Parliament. To be taken by
every man ... throughout the whole Kingdome ...
Printed for Iohn Wright, Iune 22. 1643. 4°

Wing E 2461.

T.128

506

ENGLAND. *Parliament. House of Commons.*

Articles of the Commons assembled in Parliament,
in maintenance of their accusation, against
William Laud Archbishop of Canterbury, whereby he
stands charged with high treason ... Printed for
John Wright, Jan. 19. 1643. 4°

Wing E 2527.

T.278

507

ENGLAND. *Parliament. House of Commons.*

A declaration of the Commons assembled in
Parliament; concerning the rise and progresse of
the grand rebellion in Ireland ... London, for
Edw. Husbands, July 25. 1643. 4°

Wing E 2557.

T.217

508

ENGLAND. *Parliament. House of Commons.*

Two orders of the Commons in Parliament of
great consequence ... London, for Edw. Husbands,
March 30. 1643. 4°

Wing E 2751.

T.217

509

FERNE (Henry)

Conscience satisfied. That there is no warrant for
the armes now taken up by subjects. By way of reply
unto several answers ... Especially unto that which
is entituled A fuller answer ... Oxford, Leonard
Lichfield, 1643. 4°

Wing F 791.

T.124

510

FERNE (Henry)

A reply unto severall treatises pleading for the
armes now taken up by subjects in the pretended
defence of religion and liberty ... Oxford,
Leonard Lichfield, 1643. 4°

Wing F 799.
2 copies.

T.146   T.124

511

FISHER (Edward)

An appeale to thy conscience: as thou wilt answere
it at the great and dreadfull day of Christ Iesus
... [Anon.] Printed in the nineteenth yeare of
our gracious lord King Charles, [1643]. 4°

Wing F 987.

T. 88

512

FOSTER (Henry)

A true and exact relation of the marchings of the
two regiments of the trained bands of the city of
London ... As also of the three regiments of the
auxiliary forces ... who marched forth for the
reliefe of the city of Gloucester ... London, for
Ben. Allen, Octo. 2. 1643.   4°

Wing F 1625.

T.508

513

FREEMAN (John)

A sermon preached without a text, at the Inner-
Temple, March the 12. anno Dom. 1643... London
printed in the yeere 1643.   4°

Wing F 2134.
Wanting the title-page. Signature of Thomas Bowdler.

T.128

514

FULLER (Thomas) *Prebendary of Salisbury.*

Truth maintained, or positions delivered in a
sermon at the Savoy: since traduced for dangerous:
now asserted for sound and safe ... Printed at
Oxford, anno Dom. 1643. 3 parts.   4°

Wing F 2474.

T.470

515

GARROWAY (*Sir* Henry)

A speech made by Alderman Garroway, at a common-
hall, on Tuesday the 17. January. Upon occasion
of a speech delivered there the Friday before, by
M. Pym, at the reading of his Majesties answer to
the late petition ... Printed in the year 1643.
4°

Wing G 281.

T.508

516

GENEVA.

The lawes and statutes of Geneva, as well concerning
ecclesiasticall discipline, as civill government ...
Faithfully translated out of the French tongue ...
London, Tho. Fawcet, for Mathew Wallbanck and
Lawrence Chapman, 1643. 4°

Wing L 697.

T.121

517

GOODWIN (Thomas) *and others.*

An apologeticall narration, humbly submitted to
the honourable Houses of Parliament. By Tho:
Goodwin, Philip Nye, William Bridge, Jer:
Burroughes, Sidrach Simpson. London, for Robert
Dawlman, 1643. 4°

Wing G 1225.

T.278

518

GREY (Henry) *1st Earl of Stamford.*

A true relation of the late victory obtained by the
Right Honourable the Earle of Stanford, at Plimmouth,
and Modbury, the 21th of February, 1643. Being
extracted out of a letter sent by his Lordship to
his Excellency at Windsor.. . Printed for S.G.,
1643.   4°

Wing T 2992.

T.372

519

The HARMONY of our oathes. Shewing, an agreement
betwixt the oathes of supremacie, allegeance, the
freemans oath, protestation and covenant ... London,
T. Pain, and M. Simonds for Thomas Underhill, 1643.
4°

Wing H 801.

T.217

520

HERLE (Charles)

An answer to Doctor Fernes reply, entitled Conscience
satisfied: especially to as much of it as
concerned that answer to his treatise which went
under the name of the Fuller answer ... By the same
author ... London: Tho, Brudenell for N, A,, 1643.
4°

Wing H 1552.

T.124

521

HERLE (Charles)

The independency on scriptures of the independency
of churches ... London: Tho. Brudenell for N. A.,
1643. 4°

Wing H 1559.

T.369

522

HEYLYN (Peter)

The rebells catechism. Composed in an easy and
familiar way; to let them see, the heinousness of
their offence ... [Anon.] Printed, 1643. 4°

Wing H 1731 A.

T.60

523

HILL (Thomas) *Master of Trinity College, Cambridge.*

The militant church, triumphant over the dragon and
his angels. Presented in a sermon, preached to both
Houses of Parliament assembled on Friday the 21. of
July, 1643 ... London, for John Bellamie and Ralph
Smith, 1643.   4°

Wing H 2024.
2 copies.

T.466   T.669

524

HUNTON (Philip)

A treatise of monarchie, containing two parts:
1. Concerning monarchy in generall, 2. Concerning
this particular monarchy ... [Anon.] London, for
John Bellamy, and Ralph Smith, 1643. 4°

Wing H 3781.
2 copies.

T.369   T.124

525

KNOWNE lawes. A short examination of the counsells
and actions of those that have withdrawne the King
from the governement and protection of his people.
London, printed in the yeare, 1643. 4°

Wing K 736.

T.270

526

A LETTER to a noble lord at London from a friend at
Oxford: upon occasion of the late covenant taken
by both Houses. [London], printed, 1643. 4°

Wing L 1690.

527

A LETTER without any superscription, intercepted in the way to London. Published, that the poore people of England may see the intentions of those whom they have followed. Printed in the yeare, 1643. 4°

Wing L 1757.

T.86

528

LEY (John)

The fury of warre, and folly of sinne, (as an incentive to it) declared and applyed, for caution and remedy against the mischiefe and misery of both. In a sermon preached at St. Margarets Westminster, before the honourable House of Commons... April 26. 1643... London, G.M. for Christopher Meredith, 1643. 4°

Wing L 1879

T.468

529

LIGHTFOOTE (John)

Elias redivivus: a sermon preached before the honourable House of Commons, in the parish of Saint Margarets Westminster, at the publike fast, March 29, 1643. London, R. Cotes, for Andrew Crooke, 1643. 4°

Wing L 2053.

T.468

530

MARSHALL (Stephen)

A copy of a letter written by Mr Stephen Marshall to a friend of his in the city, for the necessary vindication of himself and his ministry... London, for John Rothwell, 1643. 4°

Wing M 750.

T.278

531

MARSHALL (Stephen)

The song of Moses the servant of God, and the song of the lambe: opened in a sermon preached to the honorable House of Commons, at their late solemne day of thanksgiving, June 15. 1643... London, for Sam: Man and Sam: Gellibrand, 1643. 4°

Wing M 789.

T.474

532

MAURICE, *Prince.*

Articles of agreement betweene his Excellency Prince Maurice, and the Earle of Stamford, upon the delivery of the city of Excester, the fifth of September, 1643 ... London, for Tho. Walkley, 1643. 4°

Wing M 1357.

T.217

533

MEDE (Joseph)

Daniels weekes. An interpretation of part of the prophecy of Daniel. London, M. F. for John Clark, 1643. 4°

Wing M 1595.

T.318

534

MERCURIUS Davidicus, or A patterne of loyall devotion, Wherein King David sends his pietie to King Charles, his subjects ... Oxford, Leonard Leichfield, 1634 [i.e. 1643]. 8°

Wing M 1761 (= STC 17829 a).

T.285

535

MILTON (John)

The doctrine and discipline of divorce: restor'd to the good of both sexes, from the bondage of canon law... [Anon.] London, T.P. and M.S., 1643. 4°

Wing M 2108.
Incomplete.

T.314

536

MONTAGU (Edward) *2nd Earl of Manchester.*

Two speeches spoken by the Earl of Manchester, and Jo: Pym Esq; as a reply to his Maiesties answer to the city of Londons petition ... read at a common-hall, on Friday the 13th of January, 1642 ... London, for Peter Cole, 1643. 4°

Wing M 402.
2 copies.

T.209 T.217

537

MORTON (Thomas) *Bishop of Durham.*

Christus Dei, the Lords annoynted. Or, A theologicall discourse, wherein is proved, that the regall or monarchicall power of our soveraigne lord King Charles is not of humane, but of divine right... [Anon.] Printed at Oxford, 1643. 4°

Wing J 961 A (attributed to John Jones).
2 copies.

T.129 T.369

538

A NARRATIVE of the disease and death of that noble gentleman John Pym Esquire, late a member of the honourable House of Commons. Attested under the hands of his physitians, chyrurgions and apothecary ... London, for John Bartlet, 1643. 4°

Wing N 183.

T.217

539

A NEW diurnall of passages more exactly drawne up then heretofore. [Satirical verse.] Printed at Oxford for H. H., 1643. 4°

Wing N 631.

T.217

540

NEWCOMEN (Matthew)

The craft and cruelty of the churches adversaries: discovered in a sermon preached at St. Margarets in Westminster, before the honorable House of Commons... Novemb. 5. 1642... London: for Peter Cole, 1643. 4°

Wing N 908 B.

T.472

541

OWEN (David)

Puritano-Iesuitismus, the Puritan turn'd Jesuite; or rather out-vying him in those diabolicall and dangerous positions, of the deposition of kings ... Printed for William Sheares, 1643. 4°

Wing O 704 B.
Signature of Thomas Bowdler.

T.122

542

PARKER (Henry)

A political catechism, or, Certain questions concerning the government of this land, answered in his Majesties own words, taken out of his answer to the 19 propositions ... [Anon.] London, for Samuel Gellibrand, 1643. 4°

Wing P 416.

T.270

543

POVEY (Thomas)

The moderator expecting sudden peace, or, certain ruine ... [Anon.] London, printed anno Domini, 1643. 4°

Wing P 3043.
Signature of Thomas Bowdler.

T.124

544

The PROCEEDINGS in the late treaty of peace. Together with severall letters of his Majesty to the Queen, and of Prince Rupert to the Earle of Northampton, which were intercepted and brought to Parliament ... London, for Edward Husbands, 1643. 4°

Wing P 3571.

T.217

545

PRYNNE (William)

The Popish royall favourite: or, A full discovery of his Majesties extraordinary favours to, and protections of notorious Papists, priests, Jesuits, against all prosecutions and penalties ... Imprinted at London for Michael Spark Senior, 1643, 4°

Wing P 4039.

T.19

546

PRYNNE (William)

Romes master-peece. Or, The grand conspiracy of the Pope and his Iesuited instruments, to extirpate the Protestant religion ... [Anon.] Printed at London for Michael Sparke, senior, 1643, 4°

Wing P 4055.
2 copies.

T.504 T.19

547

QUERES and coniectures, concerning the present state of this Kingdome. London, for Richard Royston, 1643. 4°

Wing Q 165.

T.270

548

A REMONSTRANCE to vindicate his excellence Robert Earle of Essex from some false aspersions cast upon his proceedings. To the 17. of August. 1643. Printed for T. W., 1643. 4°

Wing R 1o32.

T.217

549

RICH (Henry) *1st Earl of Holland.*

A declaration made to the Kingdome, by Henry Earle of Holland. London, for Mathew Walbancke, 1643. 4°

Wing H 2419.

T.217

550

RUTHVEN (Patrick) *Earl of Forth.*

A letter from the Earle of Forth, to his Excellency Robert Earle of Essex, Lord Generall, &c ... and his Excellencies answer thereunto ... Also a petition of the well-affected nobility and gentry of the realm of Ireland ...London, for J, C, and T. G., 1643. 4°

Wing F 1615.

T. 86

551

SATISFACTION concerning mixt communions: in answer to the doubts of some, who abstain from the sacrament of the Lords supper; because wicked persons are present... London, John Raworth for Samuel Gellibrand, July 8. 1643. 4°

Wing S 726.

T.369

552

SCOTLAND. *Privy Council.*

A declaration of the lords of his Majesties Privie-Councell in Scotland; and commissioners for conserving the articles of the treaty: for the information of his Majesties good subjects of this Kingdom... Edinburgh, Evan Tyler; and now re-printed at London for Edward Husbands, 27 Junii, 1643. 4°

Wing S 1491.

T.387

553

SEDGWICK (Obadiah)

Haman's vanity, or, A sermon displaying the birthlesse issues of church-destroying adversaries. Preached to the honourable House of Commons... June 15. 1643... London, R. Bishop, for Samuel Gellibrand, 1643. 4°

Wing S 2374.

T.474

554

SEDGWICK (William)

Scripture a perfect rule for church-government delivered in a sermon at Margarets Westminster, before sundry of the House of Commons. London, for Ralph Smith, [1643]. 4°

Wing S 2388.

T.670

555

SIMPSON (Sidrach)

A sermon preached at Westminster before sundry of the House of Commons. London, for Peter Cole, 1643. 4°

Wing S 3826.

T.674

556

SMART (Peter)

Septuagenarii senis itinerantis cantus epithalamicus. [No imprint, 1643.] 4°

Not in Wing.

T.407

557

SMITH (George)

Great Britains misery; with the causes and cure ... By G. S. Gent. London, for Laurence Chapman, 1643. 4°

Wing S 4037.

T.270

558

SMITH (William) *Captain.*

Severall letters of great importance, and good successe. Lately obtained against the Fellowship of Bristow, by Captain William Smith... London, for Lawrence Blaiklock, 1643. 4°

Wing S 4265.

T.372

559

SPELMAN (*Sir* John)

The case of our affaires, in law, religion, and other circumstances briefly examined, and presented to the conscience. Oxford, H. H. for W. W., 1643. 4°

Wing S 4936.

T.124

560

SPURSTOWE (William)

Englands patterne and duty in it's monthly fasts presented in a sermon, preached to both Houses of Parliament assembled, on Friday the 21. of July, an. Dom. 1643... London, for Peter Cole, 1643. 4°

Wing S 5094.

T.674

561

STAMPE (William)

A sermon preached before his Maiestie at Christ-Church in Oxford, on the 18. of April 1643. Oxford, Printed in the yeare 1643. 4°

Wing S 5194.

T.468

562

The SUBJECTS liberty: set forth in the royall and politique power of England... London: for Ben: Allen, 1643. 4°

Wing S 6105.
P 1842.

T.248

563

SYMMONS (Edward)

A loyall subjects beliefe, expressed in a letter to Master Stephen Marshall, minister of Finchingfield in Essex, from Edward Symmons... occasioned by a conference betwixt them... Oxford, for W. Webb, 1643. 4°

Wing S 6345.

T.252

564

THREE speeches delivered at a common-hall, on Saturday the 28 of July, 1643. At the reading of a proclamation from the King: viz. I. By Edward Earl of Manchester... II. By John Pym... III. By Henry Martin... London, for Peter Cole, August 1. [1643]. 4°

cf. Wing T 1119.

T.217

565

TOMPKINS (Nathaniel)

The whole confession and speech of Mr. Nathaniel Tompkins, made upon the ladder at the time of his execution, on Wednesday the fifth of July; 1643 ... London, for Peter Cole, [1643]. 4°

Wing T 1865.

T.217

566

TRAY (Richard)

The right way to protestantisme. Delivered in a sermon at Serjeants Inne in Chancery Lane... London, L.N. and R.C. for John Williams, 1643. 4°

Wing T 2068.

T.470

567

TUCKNEY (Anthony)

The balme of Gilead, for the wounds of England: applyed in a sermon preached at Westminster, before the honourable House of Commons... August 30. 1643 ... London, Richard Bishop for Samuel Gellibrand, 1643. 4°

Wing T 3210.

T.474

568

URBAN VIII, *Pope.*

The Popes brief: or Romes inquiry after the death of their catholiques here in England, during these times of warre... London, for Edw: Husbands, Decem.7.1643. 4°

Wing U 128.

T.278

569

V.(G.L.)

Brittish lightning or suddaine tumults, in England, Scotland and Ireland; to warne the united Provinces to understand the dangers, and the causes thereof... Written first in lowe-dutch by G.L.V. and translated for the benefit of Brittaine. Printed in the yeare 1643. 4°

Wing V5.

T.369

570

VICARS (John)

The opinion of the Roman judges touching imprisonment, and the liberty of the subject, or, A sermon preached at the Abby at Westminster, at a late publique fast, Jan.25.1643... By J.V. prisoner. Printed in the year of our Lord, 1643. 4°

Wing V 320.

T.468

571

WALKER (Clement)

An answer to Col: Nathaniel Fiennes relation concerning his surrender of the city and castle of Bristol... [London], printed in the yeere, 1643. 4°

Wing W 320.

T.217

572

WALLIS (John)

Truth tried: or, Animadversions on a treatise published by the right honorable Robert Lord Brook, entituled, The nature of truth, its union and unity with the soule... By I.W. London, Richard Bishop for Samuel Gellibrand, 1643. 4°

Wing W 615.

T.314

573

WILKINSON (Henry) *Canon of Christ Church.*

Babylons ruine, Jerusalems rising. Set forth in a sermon preached before the honourable House of Commons on the 25 Octob... London, for Chr. Meredith, and Sa. Gellibrand, 1643. 4°

Wing W 2220.

T.474

574

WILLIAMS (Griffith) *Bishop of Ossory.*

Vindiciae regum; or, The grand rebellion that is, a looking-glasse for rebels... Oxford, Henry Hall, 1643. 4°

Wing W 2675.

T.369

1644

575

AINSWORTH (Henry)

A seasonable discourse, or, A censure upon a dialogue of the Anabaptists, intituled, A Description of what God hath predestinated concerning man... London, for Benjamin Allen, 1644. 4°

Wing A 812.

T.471

576

The ARTICLES of peace, concluded lately in Italy: the first, betweene the Pope and the Duke of Parma. The second, betweene the Pope and the Republicke of Venice, the gran Duke of Florence, and other princes of the late league. [Translated by I. H., James Howell?] London, Richard Heron, 1644. 4°

Not in Wing.

T. 86

577

BACKHOUSE (Robert)

A true relation of a wicked plot intended and still on foot against the city of Glocester, to betray the same into the hands of the Cavaliers. Discovered by Captaine Backhouse ... London, for Ed. Husbands, May 7. 1644. 4°

Wing B 265.

T.372

578

BEWICK (John)

Confiding England under conflicts, triumphing in the middest of her terrors... First preached in Bengeo, and Hitchin in Hartfordshire, and now published for the common comfort of the nation. London, I.D. for Andrew Crooke, 1644. 4°

Wing B 2193.

T.472

579

BOND (John)

Salvation in a mystery: or A prospective glasse for Englands case. As it was laid forth in a sermon preached at Margarets in Westminster... March 27.1644... London, L.N. for Francis Eglesfeild, 1644. 4°

Wing B 3574.

T.674

580

BOOKER (John)

Mercurius coelicus; or, A caveat to all the people of the Kingdome, that now have, or shall hereafter happen to reade the counterfeit and most pernicious pamphlet written under the name of Naworth: or, A new almanack, and prognostication for... 1644... London, J. Raworth, for John Partridge, [1644]. 4°

Not in Wing. Ch. Ch. B 3728+.

T.86

581

BOREEL (Willem) *Baron.*

The propositions of their excellencies the ambassadours of the high and mighty States Generall of the United Provinces, in the Netherlands ... London, T. Badger, 1644. 4°

Wing B 3752.

T. 81

582

CARYLL (Joseph)

The saints thankfull acclamation at Christs
resumption of his great power and the initials
of his kingdome. Delivered in a sermon at
Westminster ... April 23rd, 1644 ... London,
G.M. for Giles Calvert, 1644.   4°

Wing C 787.

T.670

583

CATO.

Catonis Disticha de moribus. Cum scholiis Des.
Erasmi Roterodami... Londini, typis E.P.
impensis Societatis Stationar., 1644.   8°

Not in Wing.

T.452

584

CHARLES I, *King of England.*

His Majesties speech to the Lords and Commons of
Parliament assembled at Oxford, delivered at their
recesse ... Oxford, Leonard Lichfield, 1644. 4°

Wing C 2812.

T. 86

585

CHEYNELL (Francis)

Chillingworthi novissima. Or, The sicknesse,
heresy, death, and buriall of William
Chillingworth... London, for Samuel Gellibrand,
1644.   4°

Wing C 3810.

T.471

586

A COPY of the articles for the surrender of the
city of Yorke. July the 16. 1644. London, G. B.
for Robert Bostock, and Samuell Gellibrand, 1644.
4°

Wing C 6204.

T.387

587

DERING (*Sir* Edward)

A declaration by Sir Edward Dering knight and
baronet. With his petition to the honourable
House of Commons assembled in Parliament ...
London, J. Raworth, for Philemon Stephens, April 1.
1644. 4°

Wing D 1108.

T. 86

588

A DIRECTORY for the publique worship of God...
Together with an ordinance of Parliament for the
taking away of the Book of Common-Prayer...
London: for Evan Tyler, Alexander Fifield, Ralph
Smith, and John Field, 1644.   4°

Wing D 1545.
2 copies.

T.128   T.672

589

DOUGLAS (*Lady* Eleanor)

Prophetia de die novissimo novissimis hisce
temporibus manifestando; item de excisione
ecclesiae & redemtione ex inferis. Verbum Dei a
Domina Eleonora, Legato Lusitaniae in Anglia
residenti... Londini, excudebat Tho: Paine, 1644.
4°

Wing D 2005.
Wanting leaf D2 (pp.25-6).

T.304

590

DURY (John)

An epistolary discourse wherein (amongst other
particulars) these following questions are
briefly resolved. I. Whether or no the state
should tolerate the independent government ...
London, for Charles Greene, 1644. 4°

Wing D 2859.

T.278

591

ENGLAND. *Parliament.*

All the severall ordinances and orders of the Lords
and Commons assembled in Parliament: for the speedy
establishing of a court martiall ... London, for
Iohn Wright, August 19 1644, 4°

Wing E 1204.

T. 86

592

ENGLAND, *Parliament.*

A declaration of the Lords and Commons assembled
in Parliament, concerning his Majesties late
proclamation threatning fire and sword to all
inhabitants in the county of Oxford and Berks ...
London, for Iohn Wright, April, 23. 1644. 4°

Wing E 1369.

T. 86

593

ENGLAND. *Parliament.*

A declaration of the Lords and Commons assembled in
Parliament, with the advice and concurrence of the
Commissioners of Scotland, to publish their
proceedings upon his Majesties letter, touching a
treaty of peace ... London, for Edward Husbands,
March 29, 1644. 4°

Wing E 1486 (?)

T. 86

594

ENGLAND. *Parliament.*

An ordinance of the Lords and Commons assembled
in Parliament, for providing of draught-horses for
carriages of the traine of artillery to the army ...
London, for Edward Husbands. March 15, 1644. 4°

Wing E 1900.

T. 86

595

ENGLAND. *Parliament.*

An ordinance of the Lords and Commons assembled in
Parliament, for raising and maintaining of forces
for the defence of the Kingdom ... London, for Edw,
Husbands Febr. 17, 1644. 4°

Wing E 1906.

T. 86

596

ENGLAND. *Parliament.*

An ordinance of the Lords and Commons assembled in
Parliament, for raising of fourscore thousand pounds
by a weekly assessment ... for the present relief
of the British army in Ireland ... London: for
Edw, Husbands. October 23. 1644. 4°

Wing E 1913.

T. 86

597

ENGLAND. *Parliament.*

An ordinance of the Lords and Commons assembled in
Parliament, for re-imbursing of Captaine William
Edwards the moneys to him due for the service of
the state ... London, for J. Wright, 1644. 4°

Wing E 1916.

T. 86

598

ENGLAND. *Parliament.*

An ordinance of the Lords and Commons assembled in
Parliament, for the raising and levying of the
monethly sum of one and twenty thousand pounds,
towards the mainteinance of the Scotish army ...
London, for Edw. Husbands Febr. 24, 1644. 4°

Wing E 2010,

T. 86

599

ENGLAND. *Parliament.*

An ordinance of the Lords and Commons assembled in
Parliament, for the speedy raising and leavying of
monyes, for the advance and mainteinance of the
forces now sent forth for this present expedition
... London, for Iohn Wright, October 14. 1644. 4°

Wing E 2053,

T,86

600

ENGLAND. *Parliament,*

Three ordinances of the Lords and Commons assembled
in Parliament. For the better observation of the
monethly fast ... London, for I, Wright, Decemb. 21.
1644. 4°

Wing E 2365,

T.86

601

ENGLAND. *Parliament.*

Two ordinances of the Lords and Commons assembled
in Parliament: one commanding that no officer or
souldier either by sea or land, shall give any
quarter to any Irishman ... The other for the
better observation of the monethly fast ... London,
for Iohn Wright, 26. Octob. 1644. 4°

Wing E 2409,

T. 86

602

ESTWICK (Nicolas)

Christ's submission to his fathers will. Set
forth in a sermon preached at Thrapston in
Northampton-shire. London, George Miller, 1644.
4°

Wing E 3358.

T.470

603

GEREE (John)

Vindiciae ecclesiae Anglicanae: or Ten cases
resolved, which discover, that though there bee
need of reformation in, yet not of separation from
the churches of Christ in England ... London,
Richard Cotes, for Ralph Smith, 1644. 4°

Wing G 602.

T.369

604

GOODWIN (John)

θεομαχια; or the grand imprudence of men running the
hazard of fighting against God, in suppressing any
way, doctrine, or practice, concerning which they know
not certainly whether it be from God or no ... London;
for Henry Overton, 1644.   4°

Wing G 1206.

T.470

605

GREENE (John)

Nehemiah's teares and prayers for Judah's affliction,
and the ruines and repaire of Jerusalem. Delivered
in a sermon in the church of Magarets [sic]
Westminster, before the honourable House of Commons
... April 24. 1644... London, G.M. for Philemon
Stephens, 1644. 4°

Wing G 1822.

T.668

606

HAMMOND (Henry)

Of conscience ... [Anon.] Oxford, Henry Hall,
1644.   4°

Wing H 548.
Wanting title-page.

T.471

607

HAMMOND (Henry)

Of resisting the lawfull magistrate under colour
of religion, and appendant to it, Of the word
χριμα, rendred damnation, Rom. 13 ... [Anon.]
Oxford, for H. H. and W. W., 1644. 4°

Wing H 557.

T.369

608

HAMMOND (Henry)

Of scandall ... [Anon.] Oxford, Henry Hall, 1644.
4°

Wing H 560.

T.471

609

HAMMOND (Henry)

Of will-worship ... [Anon.] Oxford, Henry Hall, 1644.   4°

Wing H 571.

T.471

610

HAUSTED (Peter)

Ad populum: or, A lecture to the people. [Anon.] Printed in the yeare 1644.   4°

Wing H 1154.

T. 81

611

HENDERSON (Alexander)

Reformation of church-government in Scotland, cleared from some mistakes and prejudices, by the Commissioners of the Generall Assembly of the Church of Scotland, now at London. [Anon.] Printed for Robert Bostock, 1644.   4°

Wing H 1436.

T.121

612

HILL (Thomas) *Master of Trinity College, Cambridge.*

The good old way, Gods way, to soule-refreshing rest: discovered in a sermon preached ... Apr. 24. 1644 ... London, Ric. Cotes, for John Bellamie and Philemon Stephens, 1644.   4°

Wing H 2023.

T.669

613

HILL (Thomas) *Master of Trinity College, Cambridge.*

The season for Englands selfe-reflection, and advancing temple-work: discovered in a sermon preached to the two Houses of Parliament; at Margarets Westminster, Aug. 13. 1644 ... London, Richard Cotes, for John Bellamy, and Philemon Stephens, 1644.   4°

Wing H 2027.

T.474

614

The LATE proceedings of the Scotish army, certifying their passing over Tyne; with the particulars... Sent by an expresse, from his Excellency the Lord Generall Lesley his quarters, and dated at Sunderland, March 12. (Numb. 4.) London, for Robert Bostock and Samuel Gellibrand, March 21. 1644.   4°

Not in Wing. cf. L 557.

T.387

615

LAUD (William) *Archbishop of Canterbury.*

The Archbishop of Canterbury's speech or his funerall sermon, preacht by himself on the scaffold on Tower-Hill, on Friday the 10. of January, 1644 ... All faithfully written by John Hinde ... London, Peter Cole, 1644.   4°

Wing L 599.

T.86

616

LILLY (William)

Merlinus Anglicus junior: the English Merlin revived; or, His prediction upon the affaires of the English Common-wealth ... By W. L. London, R. W. for T. U, and are to be sold by I. S., 1644.   4°

Wing A 1919.

T.81

617

MARSHALL (Stephen)

A sacred panegyrick, or a sermon of thanks-giving, preached to the two Houses of Parliament... London, for Stephen Bowtell, 1644.   4°

Wing M 772.

T.474

618

MARSHALL (Stephen)

A sermon of the baptizing of infants. Preached in the abbey-church at Westminster ... London, Richard Cotes for Stephen Bowtell, 1644.   4°

Wing M 774.
2 other copies, one with a different type-setting.

T.474   T.354

619

MARSHALL (Stephen)

θρηνωδια.   The churches lamentation for the good man his losse: delivered in a sermon... at the funerall of that excellent man John Pym... London, for Stephen Bowtell, 1644.   4°

Wing M 793.

T.474

620

MAXWELL (John) *Archbishop of Tuam.*

Sacro-sancta regum majestas: or; The sacred and royall prerogative of Christian kings ... Printed at Oxford, ann. Dom. 1644.   4°

Wing M 1384.

T.124

621

A PARAENETICK or humble addresse to the Parliament and Assembly for (not loose, but) Christian libertie. The second impression. London: Matthew Simmons for Henry Overton, 1644.   4°

Wing W 2769 (attributed to Roger Williams).
Incomplete.

T.270

622

PINDAR (Martin) *and others.*

A letter sent to the Honourable William Lenthall... wherein is truely related the great victory obtained by Gods blessing, by the Parliaments army, against the Kings forces, neer Newbery... London: for Edw. Husbands, October 29. 1644.   4°

Wing P 2248.

T.372

623

PRYNNE (William)

A full reply to certaine briefe observations and anti-queries on Master Prynnes twelve questions about church-government ... London, F. L. for Michael Sparke Senior, 1644.   4°

Wing P 3966.

T.19

624

PRYNNE (William)

Independency examined, unmasked, refuted, by twelve new particular interrogatories ... London, F. L. for Michael Sparke Senior, 1644.   4°

Wing P 3985.

T.19

625

QUARLES (Francis)

The loyall convert, (according to the Oxford copy.) A convert will be loyall: or, Some short annotations on this book; by W. Bridges. [Anon.] London, for Edward Husbands, 1644.   4°

Wing Q 106.

T.369

626

QUARLES (Francis)

The whipper whipt. Being a reply upon a scandalous pamphlet, called The Whip: abusing that excellent work of Cornelius Burges... entituled, The fire of the sanctuary newly discovered... [Anon.] Imprinted, 1644.   4°

Wing Q 121.

T.471

627

REYNER (William)

Babylons ruining-earthquake and the restauration of Zion. Delivered in a sermon before the honourable house of Commons at Margarets Westminster... August 28. 1644... London: T.B. for Samuel Enderby, 1644. 4°

Wing R 1324.

T.472

628

RICH (Robert) *2nd Earl of Warwick.*

A letter from the Right Honourable Robert Earle of Warwicke, lord high-admiral of England: to the speaker of the House of Peeres... London, for Iohn Wright, June 11. 1644.   4°

Wing W 1000.

T.372

629

RUTHERFORD (Samuel)

A sermon preached to the honorable House of Commons: at their late solemne fast, Wednesday, Janu. 31. 1643... London, Richard Cotes, for Richard Whittakers & Andrew Crooke, 1644.   4°

Wing R 2391.

T.468

630

SCOTLAND. *Parliament.*

Articles and ordinances of warre; for the present expedition of the army of the Kingdome of Scotland. By the committee of Estates, and his Excellence, the Lord Generall of the army. Printed at Edinburg by Evan Tyler. And reprinted at London for Robert Bostocke, 1644.   4°

Wing S 1187.
2 copies.

T.387   T.218

631

The SCOTS army advanced into England certified in a letter, dated from Addarston, the 24 of January: from his excellencies the Lord Generall Lesley's quarters... London, for Robert Bostock, 1644.   4°

Wing S 2022.

T.387

632

SELDEN (John)

Ioannis Seldeni de anno civili & calendario veteris ecclesiae seu reipublicae Judaicae, dissertatio... Londini, excudebat Richardus Bishopius, 1644.   4°

Wing S 2423.

T.304

633

SHUTE (Josiah)

Divine cordials: delivered in ten sermons, upon part of the ninth and tenth chapters of Ezra, in a time of visitation... London, for Robert Bostock, 1644.   4°

Wing S 3714.

T.470

634

STAUNTON (Edmund)

Rupes Israelis: the rock of Israel. A little part of its glory laid forth in a sermon preached at Margarets in Westminster before the honorable House of Commons... Apr. 24. 1644. London, for Christopher Meredith, 1644.   4°

Wing S 5342.

T.674

635

STRICKLAND (John)

A discovery of peace: or, The thoughts of the Almighty for the ending of his peoples calamities. Intimated in a sermon at Christ-Church London... upon the 24th of April, 1644... London, M. Simmons for Henry Overton, 1644.   4°

Wing S 5969.

T.674

636

TORSHELL (Samuel)

A helpe to Christian fellowship: or, A discourse tending to the advancement and spirituall improvement of holy societie... London, G.M. for John Bellamy, 1644.   4°

Wing T 1937.

T.471

637

TORSHELL (Samuell)

The hypocrite discovered and cured... London, G.M. for John Bellamy, 1644.   4°

Wing T 1938.
Incomplete.

T.471

1644 (Cont'd.)

638

WERE (John)

The apologie of Colonell John Were, in vindication
of his proceedings since the beginning of this
present Parliament. London, printed in the yeare,
1644. 4°

Wing W 1364.

T.86

639

WILKINSON (Henry) *Canon of Christ Church.*

Babylons ruine, Jerusalems rising. Set forth in a
sermon preached before the honourable House of
Commons... London, for Chr. Meredith, and Sa.
Gellibrand, 1644. 4°

Wing W 2221.

T.553

640

YOUNG (Thomas)

Hopes incouragement pointed at in a sermon, preached
in St. Margarets Westminster, before the honorable
House of Commons... at the last solemn fast, February
28. 1643... London, for Ralph Smith, 1644. 4°

Wing Y 92.

T.470

1645

641

AINSWORTH (Samuel)

A sermon preached at the funerall of that
religious gentle-woman Mis Dorothy Hanbury, wife
to Edward Hanbury Esq. living at Kelmarsh in
Northampton-shire... London, Richard Cotes, for
Stephen Bowtell, 1645. 4°

Wing A 816.

T.468

642

BASTWICK (John)

The Church of England a true church: proved in a
disputation held by John Bastwick, against Mr. Walter
Montague in the Tower ... London, for A. Crooke and
I. Rothwell, 1645. 4°

Wing B 1058.

T.88

643

BELLAMIE (John)

Lysimachus enervatus, Bellamius reparatus: or, A
reply to a book, intituled, A full answer to a plea
for the commonaltie of London... London, G. Miller,
1645. 8°

Wing B 1815.

T.448

644

BELLAMIE (John)

A plea for the Commonalty of London, or, a vindication
of their rights... in the choice of sundry city
officers... 2nd ed. London, George Miller, 1645.
8°

Wing B 1817.
Wanting the first two gatherings.

T.448

645

BLACKWELL (Elidad)

A caveat for magistrates. In a sermon, preached at
Pauls, before the right honorable Thomas Atkin,
esquire, Lord Mayor of the city of London, November
the third; 1644... London, Robert Leyburn for
Richard Wodenothe, 1645. 4°

Wing B 3090.

T.674

646

BOUGHEN (Edward)

Observations upon the ordinance of the Lords and
Commons at Westminster. After advice had with
their Assembly of Divines, for the ordination of
ministers pro tempore ... [Anon.] Oxford, Leonard
Lichfield, 1645. 4°

Wing B 3815.

T.278

647

BRINSLEY (John) *the Younger.*

The sacred and soveraigne church-remedie: or, The
primitive and apostolicall way of composing
ecclesiasticall differences, and establishing the
churches of Christ... London, Moses Bell for
Edward Brewster, 1645. 4°

Wing B 4725.

T.472

648

C. (A.)

A letter to a friend. Shewing, the illegall
proceedings of the two houses of Parliament: and
observing God's aversenesse to their actions ...
Oxford printed in the year 1645. 4°

Wing C 7.
title-page and other pages broken.

T.270

649

CALAMY (Edmund) *the Elder.*

An indictment against England because of her selfe-
murdering divisions... Presented in a sermon
preached before the right honourable House of Lords
... December 25. 1644... London, I.L. for
Christopher Meredith, 1645. 4°

Wing C 256.

T.468

650

CHARLES I, *King of England.*

A declaration of the Kings Majesties most gracious
messages for peace... Printed at Oxford by Leonard
Lichfield, 1645 ..., and reprinted at London for
Mathew Walbank, February 2. 1645. 4°

Wing C 2214.

T. 86

651

CHARLES I, *King of England.*

The Kings cabinet opened: or, Certain packets of
secret letters & papers, written with the Kings
own hand, and taken in his cabinet at Nasby-Field
... London, for Robert Bostock, 1645. 4°

Wing K 591.

T.86

652

COLEMAN (Thomas)

Hopes deferred and dashed, observed in a sermon
to the honourable House of Commons, in
Margarets Westminster, July 30. 1645 ...
London, for Christopher Meredith, 1645. 4°

Wing C 5053.

T.466

653

CORPUS disciplinae: or the discipline together with
the form of all ecclesiasticall administrations
used in the Dutch-churches within this Kingdom ...
Published by the ministers and elders of the Dutch
congregation in London. London, John Field for
Ralph Smith, 1645. 4°

Wing C 6344.

T.121

654

D. (N.)

Vindiciae Caroli Regis: or, A loyall vindication
of the King. In answer to The popish royall
favourite [by William Prynne] ... Imprinted,
1645. 4°

Wing D 71.

T.326

655

DELL (William)

Power from on high: or, the power of the holy ghost
dispersed through the whole body of Christ ...
delivered in two sermons ... London, for Henry
Overton, 1645. 4°

Wing D 925.
Wanting title-page.

T.473

656

ENGLAND, *Parliament.*

Directions of the Lords and Commons assembled in
Parliament, after advise had with the Assembly of
Divines, for the electing and choosing of ruling-
elders ... London, for John Wright, August 20. 1645.
4°

Wing E 1523.

T.128

657

ENGLAND, *Parliament.*

Four ordinances of the Lords and Commons assembled
in Parliament, for raising moneys for Sir Thomas
Fairfax army ... London, for Edw. Husbands, January
23. 1645. 4°

Wing E 1544.

T. 86

658

ENGLAND, *Parliament.*

An ordinance of the Lords and Commons assembled in
Parliament, for constituting commissioners and
councell of warre, for triall of all persons in the
late rising in the county of Kent ... Printed by
T. W. for Ed. Husband, Iune the 10. 1645. 4°

Wing E 1873.

T.129

659

ENGLAND, *Parliament.*

An ordinance of the Lords and Commons assembled in
Parliament, for securing of the eighty thousand
pounds advanced by, and under the eight treasurers
hereafter named ... London, for Edward Husbands,
April 2. 1645. 4°

Wing E 1923.

T. 86

660

ENGLAND, *Parliament.*

An ordinance of the Lords and Commons assembled in
Parliament, for the more effectuall puting in
execution the directory for publique worship ...
T. W. for Ed. Husband, 1645. 4°

Wing E 1995.

T.128

561

ENGLAND, *Parliament.*

An ordinance of the Lords & Commons assembled in
Parliament, for the raising of twenty thousand pounds,
to be imployed towards the reducing of Oxford ...
London, T. W. for Ed. Husband, 1645. 4°

Wing E 2023.
Endorsed: "Mr. Penoire at Mr Carters."

T. 86

662

ENGLAND, *Parliament.*

An ordinance of the Lords and Commons assembled in
Parliament, for Thursday next to be a day of
thanksgiving within the lines of communication ...
for the great victory obtained against the Kings
forces, nere Knasby ... London, for Ed. Husband,
Iune the 17. 1645. 4°

Wing E 2072.

T.86

663

ENGLAND, *Parliament.*

An ordinance of the Lords and Commons assembled in
Parliament: inabling the Lord Maior and Court of
Alderman to seize and sequester ... all the houses,
rents and revenues belonging to ... the Cathedrall
Church of Pauls London ... London, for John Wright.
12. May. 1645. 4°

Wing E 1847.

T. 86

664

ENGLAND. *Parliament.*

An ordinance of the Lords and Commons assembled in Parliament. Together with rules and directions concerning suspention from the sacrament of the Lords Supper ... London, for John Wright, 21 Octob. 1645. 4°

Wing E 2098.

T.128

665

ENGLAND. *Parliament.*

A second declaration of the Lords and Commons assembled in Parliament; of the whole proceedings with the late extraordinary ambassadors from the ... States Generall of the United Provinces; concerning restitution of ships, and the course of trade. London: for Edward Husband. Sept. 18.1645. 4°

Wing E 2286.

T. 86

666

ENGLAND and Scotlands covenant with their God ... Printed for Edw. Husband, 1645. 12°

Wing E 2931.

T.457

667

FAIRFAX (Thomas) *3rd Baron Fairfax.*

Sir Thomas Fairfax's letter to the Honoble William Lenthal ... Concerning the agreement between Sir Tho: Fairfax's commissioners and Sir Ralph Hoptons at Truro in Cornwal ... London: for Edw. Husband, March 23. 1645. 4°

Wing F 196.

T.372

668

FAIRFAX (Thomas) *3rd Baron Fairfax.*

Sir Thomas Fairfax's letter to the Honorable William Lenthall ... of all the particulars concerning the taking of Bridgewater ... London, for Edw. Husband, July 28. 1645. 4°

Wing F 193.

T.372

669

FARY (John)

Gods severity on mans sterility. Taken from the parable of the fruitlesse fig-tree, and delivered in a sermon ... London, J. D. for Andrew Crook, 1645. 4°

Wing F 538.

T.466

670

A FULLER relation of the taking of Bath by Sir Thomas Fairfax his forces: with the conditions of the surrender ... London, for Thomas Bates, 1645. 4°

Wing F 2492.

T.372

671

GOODWIN (John)

Calumny arraign'd and cast. Or a briefe answer to some extravagant and rank passages, lately fallen from the pen of William Prynne, in a late discourse, entituled, Truth triumphing over falshood ... London; M. Simmons for Henry Overton, 1645. 4°

Wing G 1153.

T.128

672

HAMMOND (Henry)

Of a late, or, a death-bed repentance ... [Anon.] Oxford, Henry Hall, 1645. 4°

Wing H 547.

T.471

673

HAMMOND (Henry)

Of sinnes of weaknesse, wilfulnesse, and appendant to it, A paraphrasticall explication of two difficult texts, Heb. 6 and Heb. 10 ... [Anon.] Oxford, Henry Hall, 1645. 4°

Wing H 564.

T.471

674

HAMMOND (Henry)

Of superstition ... [Anon.] Oxford, Henry Hall, 1645. 4°

Wing H 566.

T.471

675

HARRIS (Robert)

True religion in the old way of piety and charity, delivered in a sermon to the Lord Major and court of aldermen of this city of London... at the Spittle, 1645... London, for John Bartlet, 1645. 4°

Wing H 878.
2 copies.

T.466   T.674

676

HOYLE (Joshua)

Jehojadahs iustice against Mattan, Baals priest: or the covenanters iustice against idolaters. A sermon preacht upon occasion of a speech utter'd [by Archbishop Laud] upon Tower-Hill ... By J.H. minister of the gospel ... London; M. Simmons for Henry Overton, 1645. 4°

Wing H 3203.

T.472

677

HUDSON (Samuel)

The essence and unitie of the Church Catholike visible, and the prioritie thereof in regard of particular churches discussed. London, George Miller for Christopher Meredith, 1645. 4°

Wing H 3265.

T. 88

678

The KENTISH conspiracy: or, An order and narration declaring the late plot for the surprizing of Dover Castle ... Taken and extracted out of the examination of the severall conspirators ... London, R. Cotes, for Michael Spark, junior, 1645. 4°

Wing K 322.

T.129

679

A LETTER sent to the Right Honourable William Lenthall ... concerning the raising of the siege of Taunton by the Parliaments forces. By a worthy gentleman in Sir Thomas Fairfax his army ... London, Edward Husbands, July 10. 1645. 4°

Wing L 1625.

T.372

680

LONDON.

The humble petition of the Lord Mayor, aldermen, and commons of the city of London ... concerning church-government: presented to the House of Peers upon Fryday the 16, of Ianuary 1645 ... London, for John Wright, 17, Ian. 1645. 4°

Wing H 3532.

T.128

681

The PARLIAMENTS severall late victories in the West, obtained by Sir Thomas Fairfax army ... London, for Edw. Husbands, January 21. 1645. 4°

Wing P 524.

T.372

682

The PERSWASION of certaine grave divines ... to such as suffer for the King, that they persevere in their sufferings ... Oxford, Leonard Lichfield, 1645. 4°

Wing P 1669.

T.88

683

The PREROGATIVE of man: or, The immortality of humane soules asserted against the vain cavils of a late worthlesse pamphlet, entituled, Mans mortality, &c. [By Richard Overton,] Whereunto is added the said pamphlet it selfe ... Oxford, printed in the yeare, 1645. 2 parts. 4°

Wing P 3220.

T.88

684

ROBINSON (Henry)

The falsehood of Mr. William Pryn's Truth triumphing, in the antiquity of Popish princes and Parliaments ... [Anon.] Printed in London, 1645. 4°

Wing R 1672.

T.19

685

ROBINSON (Henry)

A moderate answer to Mr. Prins full reply to certaine observations on his first twelve questions... By the same author. London, for Benjamin Allen, 1645. 4°

Wing R 1676.

T.278

686

ROSS (Alexander)

Medicus medicatus: or the physicians religion cured, by a lenitive or gentle potion: with some animadversions upon Sir Kenelme Digbie's Observations on Religio medici. London, James Young, and are to be sold by Charles Green, 1645. 8°

Wing R 1961.
Incomplete.

T.452

687

RUTHERFORD (Samuel)

A sermon preached before the right honourable House of Lords, in the Abbey Church at Westminster, Wednesday the 25. day of Iune, 1645... London, R.C. for Andrew Crook, 1645. 4°

Wing R 2393.

T.466

688

SHUTE (Josiah)

Judgement and mercy: or, The plague of frogges inflicted, removed. Delivered in nine sermons. Whereunto is added a sermon preached at his funerall, by Mr. Ephraim Vdall... London, for Charles Greene, 1645. 2 parts. 4°

Wing S 3715.

T.466

689

The STATE of the Irish affairs, for the honourable members of the Houses of Parliament: as they lye represented before them, from the Committee of adventurers in London for lands in Ireland ... London, G. Miller, 1645. 4°

Wing S 5318.

T.208

690

WHINCOP (John)

Israels tears for distressed Zion. Shown in a sermon before the right honourable House of LOrds assembled in Parliament, at their late solemn fast, in the Abby-Church of Westminster, Sept.24.1645... London, R.C. for Andrew Crooke, 1645. 4°

Wing W 1664.
Incomplete.

T.466

1646

691

The ANSWER of the Commissioners of the Navie, to a scandalous pamphlet, published by Mr. Andrewes Burrell. Printed by Will. Bentley, anno Dom. 1646. 4°

Wing A 3289.

T. 18

692

ANTI-TOLERATION, or a modest defence of the letter of the London ministers to the reverend Assembly of Divines. By a wel-wisher of peace and truth ... London, John Field for Ralph Smith, 1646. 4°

Wing A 3515.

T.128

693

ARTICLES concerning the surrender of Newark to the Commissioners of both Kingdoms: and sent from Colonel General Poyntz to the Honorable William Lenthal ... London, for Edw. Husband, May 11. 1646. 4°

Wing A 3814.

T. 86

694

ARTICLES for the delivering up of Lichfield-Close on Thursday the 16, of this instant July... London, for Edward Husband, July 18.1646. 4°

Wing A 3825.

T.86

695

BALL (William)

Constitutio liberi populi. Or, The rule of a free-born people ... Printed, anno Dom. 1646. 4°

Wing B 588.

T.389

696

BASIRE (Isaac)

Deo et ecclesiae sacrum. Sacriledge arraigned by Saint Paul, and prosecuted in a treatise, by Isaac Basire ... Oxford, Leonard Lichfield, 1646. 4°

Wing B 1032.

T.216

697

BELLAMIE (John)

A vindication of the humble remonstrance and petition of the Lord Major, aldermen, and commons, of the city of London ... presented to both Houses of Parliament, the 26 of May, 1646. Or, An answer to two late libels published by two annonymusses, against the said remonstrance ... London, for Richard Cotes, 1646. 4°

Wing B 1818.
Wanting pp. 3-6.

T.209

698

BIRKENHEAD (Sir John)

An answer to a speech without doores: or animadversions upon an unsafe and dangerous answer to the Scotch-papers, printed under the name of M. Challener his speech ... [Anon.] [London, 1646.] 4°

Wing B 2960.

T.387

699

BIRKENHEAD (Sir John)

The speech without doores defended without reason. Or, A vindication of the Parliaments honour: in a rejoynder to three pamphlets published in defence of M. Chaloners speech. [Anon.] Printed in the yeare 1646. 4°

Wing B 2972.

T.387

700

BOLTON (Samuel)

The arraignment of errour: or, A discourse serving as a curb to restrain the wantonnesse of mens spirits ... London, G. Miller for Andrew Kembe, 1646. 4°

Wing B 3517.

T.216

701

BRIDGES (Walter)

Division divided: or, Ruines fore-runner discovered and decyphered, in a sermon before the... Lord Major and aldermen of the city of London, preached on the Lords-day, September 20.1646... London, for Andrew Crooke, 1646. 4°

Wing B 4484.

T.466

702

CAMPBELL (Archibald) Marquess of Argyle.

A speech by the Marquesse of Argile to the honourable lords and Commons in Parliament. 25. June 1646. With a paper concerning their full consent to the propositions to be presently sent to his Majesty for a safe and well grounded peace ... London: for Iohn Wright, 27 June 1646. 4°

Wing A 3666.

T.218

703

CAMPBELL (John) 1st Earl of Loudoun.

Several speeches, spoken by the Right Honourable the Earle of Loudoun, Lord High Chancellor of the Kingdome of Scotland: at a conference with a committee of the honourable Houses ... Edinburgh: Evan Tyler, 1646. 4°

Wing L 3087.

T.387

704

CASAUBON (Meric)

A discourse concerning Christ his incarnation, and exinanition. As also, concerning the principles of Christianity: by way of introduction. London, M. F. for R. Mynne, 1646. 4°

Wing C 803.

T.216

705

CHALONER (Thomas)

An answer to the Scotch papers. Delivered in the House of Commons in reply to the votes of both Houses ... concerning the disposall of the Kings person ... London, Francis Leach, 1646. 4°

Wing C 1801.

T.387

706

CHARLES I, King of England.

His Majesties last most gracious message of Decemb. 20. 1646. to the Lords & Commons of the Parliament of England ... and to the commissioners of the Parliament of Scotland at London, for a personall treaty. Printed in the yeere, 1646. 4°

Wing C 2373.

T.387

707

DELL (William)

Right reformation: or, The reformation of the church of the New Testament, represented in Gospel-light. In a sermon preached to the honourable House of Commons, on Wednesday, November 25. 1646 ... London, R. White, for Giles Calvert, 1646. 4°

Wing D 927.

T.466

708

DIGBY (George) Earl of Bristol.

The Lord George Digby's cabinet a Dr Goff's negotiations; together with his Majesties, the Queens, and the Lord Jermin's, and other letters: taken at the battel at Sherborn ... London: for Edward Husband, March 26. 1646. 4°

Wing B 4763.

T.86

709

DURY (John)

Israels call to march out of Babylon unto Jerusalem: opened in a sermon before the honourable House of Commons assembled in Parliament, Novemb. 26. 1645 ... London, G.M. for Tho. Underhill, 1646. 4°

Wing D 2867.
Incomplete.

T.466

710

ENGLAND. Parliament.

The answer of the Lords and Commons assembled in the Parliament of England at Westminster, to several papers of the Commissioners of Scotland ... London: for Edward Husband, April 16. 1646. 4°

Wing E 1224.
2 copies.

T.218 T.387

711

ENGLAND. Parliament.

An ordinance of the Lords and Commons assembled in Parliament: for the ordination of minister by the classicall presbyters ... London, for Iohn Wright, 31 Aug. 1646. 4°

Wing E 2000.

T.128

712

ENGLAND. Parliament.

An ordinance of the Lords and Commons assembled in Parliament for the present setling (without further delay) of the Presbyteriall government in the Church of England ... London, for Iohn Wright, 1646. 4°

Wing E 2002.

T.128

713

ENGLAND. Parliament.

An ordinance of the Lords and Commons assembled in Parliament. For the selling of the lands of all the bishops ... for the service of the Common-wealth ... London, for John Wright, Novemb 18. 1646. 4°

Wing E 2038.

T. 86

714

ENGLAND, Parliament.

The Parliaments answer to his Majesties two letters, concerning his Majesties personall treaty with them. The one dated the 26. and the other the 29. of December last. London: for Edward Husband, Jan. 17. 1646. 4°

Wing E 2127.

T.387

715

ENGLAND. Parliament.

The propositions of the Lords and Commons assembled in Parliament. For a safe and well grounded peace. Sent to his Majestie at Newcastle ... London, for Iohn Wright, 17 July 1646. 4°

Wing E 2209.
2 copies.

T.387 T. 86

716

ENGLAND. Parliament. House of Commons.

The answer of the Commons assembled in Parliament, to the Scots Commissioners papers of the 20th, and their letter of the 24th of October last ... London, for Edward Husband, December 4. 1646. 4°

Wing E 2520.
2 copies.

T.218 T.387

717

ENGLAND. Parliament. House of Commons.

A declaration of the Commons assembled in Parliament, against all such persons as shall take upon them to preach or expound the scriptures ... London, for Edward Husband, January 2. 1646. 4°

Wing E 2553.

T.128

718

ENGLAND. Parliament. House of Commons.

A declaration of the Commons of England assembled in Parliament, of their true intentions concerning the ancient and fundamental government of the kingdom ... Printed for Edward Husband, April 18. 1646. 4°

Wing E 2562.

T.387

719

FAIRFAX (Thomas) 3rd Baron Fairfax.

Orders established the 14th of this present January, by his Excellency Sir Thomas Fairfax, for regulating the Army... London, for Edward Husband, January 26. 1646. 4°

Wing E 740.
Wanting title-page.

T.129

720

FORTIN (Pierre) *Sieur de la Hoguette.*

Catechisme royal. [Anon.] A Paris, 1646.   8°

"Ex libris St. Geo. Ashe".

T.585

721

The GENERALL and particular acts and articles of
the late national synod of the reformed churches of
France ... London, T. W. for G. Emerson, 1646. 4°

Wing G 488.

T.121

722

GREGORY (John)

Notes and observations upon some passages of
scripture. By I. G. ... Oxford, H. Hall, for
Ed. Forrest iunior, 1646. 4°

Wing G 1920.

T.312

723

HAMMOND (Henry)

A new view of the new directory and a vindication
of the ancient liturgy of the Church of England;
in answer to the reasons pretended in the ordinance
and preface, for the abolishing the one, and
establishing the other. [Anon.] 2nd ed. Oxford,
Henry Hall, 1646. 4°

Wing H 613.

T.312

724

The HUMBLE petition of many thousands of young men
and apprentices of the city of London, to the ...
knights, citizens and burgesses, in the supreme
court of Parliament assembled ... London, for
George Whittington, 1646. 4°

Wing H 3477.

T.129

725

JUS divinum regiminis ecclesiastici: or, The divine
right of church-government, asserted and
evidenced by the holy scriptures ... By sundry
ministers of Christ within the city of London ...
London, J. Y. for Joseph Hunscot and George
Calvert, 1646. 4°

Wing J 1217.

T.312

726

The JUSTIFICATION of a safe and wel grounded answer
to the Scottish papers, printed under the name of
Master Chaloner his speech ... London, A. Griffin,
1646.   4°

Wing J 1256.

T.387

727

The LAST articles of peace made, concluded,
accorded and agreed upon the 30. day of Iuly, 1646.
by and between his Excellency, James Lord Marques
of Ormond ... and Donogh Lord Viscount Muskery ...
Imprinted first at Dublin by William Bladen; and now
reprinted at London for Edw. Husband, Sept. 7,
1646. 4°

Wing L 475.
2 copies.

T.208   T.86

728

LESLIE (Alexander) *lst Earl of Leven.*

The declaration of his Excellency the Earl of Leven,
the general officers, and all the inferior officers
and soldiers of the Scotish army. Together with
their petition to his Majesty ... and his Majesties
answer to the said petition. London: for Laurence
Chapman, July 6. 1646.   4°

Wing L 1812.

T.387

729

A LETTER to the Honoble William Lenthal ... from
the commissioners imployed by the Parliament for
the reducing of Newark ... London: for Edw. Husband,
April 6. 1646. 4°

Wing L 1737.

T.372

730

LILBURNE (John)

An unhappy game at Scotch and English. Or, A full
answer from England to the papers of Scotland ...
Edinburgh, Evan Tyler, 1646. 4°

Wing L 2195.

T.129

731

MARSHALL (Stephen)

A defence of infant-baptism: in answer to two
treatises, and an appendix to them concerning it;
lately published by Mr. Jo. Tombes ... London, Ric.
Cotes, for Steven Bowtell, 1646. 4°

Wing M 751.

T.216

732

MARTEN (Henry)

A corrector of the answerer [Sir John Birkenhead]
to the speech out of doores. Iustifying the
worthy speech of Master Thomas Cheloner a faithful
member of the Parlement of England. [Anon.]
Edinburgh, as truly printed by Evan Tyler... as
were the Scotish papers, anno. 1646. 4°

Wing M 818.

T.387

733   T.378

MAXWELL (John) *Archbishop of Tuam.*

The burthen of Issachar: or, the tyrannicall power
and practises of the presbyteriall government in
Scotland. [Anon.] Printed, 1646. 4°

Wing M 1379.
Title page broken.

T.378

734

MAYNE (Jasper)

A sermon against false prophets. Preached in
St. Marjes church in Oxford, shortly after the
surrender of the garrison... Printed in the
yeere, 1646. 4°

Wing M 1473.

T.754

735

MORNAY (Philippe de) *Seigneur du Plessis Marly.*

The soules own evidence, for its own immortality. In a
very pleasant and learned discourse, selected out of
that excellent treatise entituled, The trunesse of
Christian religion, against atteists, epicures, &c.
First compiled in French by famous Phillip Mornay, lord
of Plessie Marlie, afterward turned into English by elo-
quent Sir Phillip Sydney... and now re-published. By
John Bachiler... London, M.S. for Henry Overton, 1646.
4°
Wing M 2802.

T.216

736

NEWCOMEN (Matthew)

The duty of such as would walke worthy of the gospel:
to endeavour union, not division nor toleration.
Opened, in a sermon at Pauls, ... Feb. 8. 1646 ...
London, G. M. for Christopher Meredith, 1646. 4°

Wing N 909.

T.128

737

PARKER (Thomas) *of Newbury, New England.*

The visions and prophecies of Daniel expounded:
wherein the mistakes of former interpreters are
modestly discovered, and the true meaning of the
text made plain... London, for Edmund Paxton, and
are to be sold by Nathanael Webb and William Grantham,
1646. 4°

Wing P 481

T.466

738

PRICE (John) *Citizen of London.*

A moderate reply to the Citie-remonstrance; presented
to the high court of Parliament the 26 of May, 1646.
Containing severall reasons why many well affected
citizens cannot assent thereunto... [Anon.] London,
for Matthew Simmons, and Henry Overton, 1646. 4°

Wing M 2331.

T.209

739

PRYNNE (William)

Diotrephes catechised: or sixteen important questions
touching the ecclesiastical jurisdiction and
censures (contradistinct to civill) now eagerly
pretended to and challenged by a divine right, by
some over-rigid Presbyterians, and Independents
... London, for Michael Sparkes, 1646. 4°

Wing P 3945 (?)

T.83

740

R. (S.)

The Kings march with the Scots, and a list of the
names of 3. lords, 12. knights ... with other
gentlemen that submit to the Parliament upon the
surrender of Newarke ... London: Elizabeth
Purslow, May 11, 1646. 4°

Wing R 74.

T.86

741

SALTMARSH (John)

An end of one controversie: being an answer or
letter to master Ley's large last book, called
Light for smoke ... London, Ruth Raworth, for
G. Calvert, 1646. 4°

Wing S 479.

T.128

742

SALTMARSH (John)

Perfume against the sulpherous stinke of the snuffe
of the Light for smoak, called, Novello-mastix ...
London, Elizabeth Purslow, April 19, 1646. 4°

Wing S 495.

T.128

743

SCOTLAND. *Parliament.*

Letters from the committee of Estates at Newcastle,
and the commissioners of the Kingdom of Scotland
residing at London to both Houses of Parliament.
Together with two papers delivered in to his Maiesty
by the committee of Estates... London: for
Laurence Chapman, June 17. 1646.   4°

Wing S 1291.

T.387

744

SCOTLAND. *Parliament.*

Papers delivered in by the Commissioners of the
Kingdom of Scotland at London, to the honourable
Houses of Parliament of England ... Printed at
Edinburgh, by Evan Tyler, 1646. 4°

Wing S 1300.

T.86

745

SCOTLAND. *Parliament.*

Papers lately delivered in to the honorable Houses of
Parliament by the Commissioners of the Kingdom of
Scotland, concerning the proceedings of the Scotish
army, and their intentions ... London: for Laurence
Chapman, June 9. 1646. 4°

Wing S 1301.
2 copies.

T.387 T.218

746

SCOTLAND. *Parliament.*

Several letters from the Parliament and General
Assembly of the Kirk of Scotland, to the Houses
of Parliament of England, the Lord Mayor...   and
the Assembly of Divines at Westminster.   London:
for Laurence Chapman, July 13. 1646. 4°

Wing S 1337.

T.387

747

SCOTLAND. *Parliament.*

Some papers given in by the commissioners of the
Parliament of Scotland, to the honourable Houses
of the Parliament of England...   Concerning the
disposing of his Majesties person. Edinburgh:
Evan Tyler, 1646. 4°

Wing S 1343.

T.387

1646 (Cont'd.)

748

SCOTLAND. *Parliament.*

Some papers of the commissioners of Scotland, given in lately to the Houses of Parliament, concerning the propositions of peace. London, for Robert Bostock, April 11. 1646. 4°

Wing S 1346.

T.387

749

TAYLOR (Jeremy) *Bishop of Down and Connor.*

A discourse concerning prayer ex tempore, or, by pretence of the spirit. In justification of authorized and set-formes of lyturgie ... [Anon.] Printed in the yeere, 1646. 4°

Wing T 312.

T.312

750

TOLLERATION iustified, and persecution condemnd. In an answer or examination, of the London-ministers letter ... London, printed in the year, 1646. 4°

Wing T 1773.

T.128

751

A VINDICATION of a printed paper, entituled, An ordinance presented to the honorable House of Commons, for the preventing of the growth and spreading of heresies, against the irreligious and presumptuous exceptions call'd Some humble and modest queries ... London, T. R. and E. M. for Ralph Smith, 1646. 4°

Wing V 465.

T.128

752

VINES (Richard)

The hearse of the renowned, the Right Honourable Robert Earle of Essex... As it was represented in a sermon, preached in the Abbey Church at Westminster, at the magnificent solemnity of his funerall, Octob. 22. 1646... London, T.R. and E.M. for Abel Roper, 1646. 4°

Wing V 553.

T.466

753

WHITE (John) *of Dorchester.*

The troubles of Jerusalems restauration, or the churches reformation. Represented in a sermon preached before the right honorable House of Lords, in the Abby Church Westminster, Novemb.26.1645... London, M. Simmons for John Rothwel, and Luke Fawne, 1646. 4°

Wing W 1784.

T.466

1647

754

ANDREWES (Lancelot) *Bishop of Winchester.*

Of episcopacy. Three epistles of Peter Moulin ... Answered by ... Lancelot Andrews, late Lord Bishop of Winchester. Translated for the benefit of the publike ... Printed in the yeer, 1647. 4°

Wing A 3143.

T.158

755

CASE (Thomas)

Spirituall whordome discovered in a sermon preach'd before the honourable House of Commons... May 26.1647. London, J. Macock, for Luke Fawne, 1647. 4°

Wing C 843.

T.670

756

CHARLES I, *King of England.*

His Majesties message to both houses of Parliament, from the Isle of Wight, Novemb. 17, 1647 ... London: Robert Austin, 1647. 4°

Wing C 2465.

T.129

757

CHARLES I, *King of England.*

His Majesties most gracious message, May the 12th. from Holdenby, to the Lords and Commons in the Parliament of England, assembled ... London, for Rich. Royston, 1647. 4°

Wing C 2511.

T.129

758

A CLEERE and full vindication of the late proceedings of the armie under the conduct of his Excellencie, Sir Thomas Fairfax, by certain positions, built upon principles and grounds both of religion and sound reason... London, for William Larnar, 1647. 4°

Wing C 4618.

T.292

759

CULME (Arthur)

A diary and relation of passages in, and about Dublin: from the first of August, 1647. to the tenth of the same. Brought this day ... by Lieutenant Colonell Arthur Culme ... By him presented to the Parliament. London, for Godfrey Emerson, 1647. 4°

Ch. Ch. C 7477+.

T.208

760

DIGGES (Dudley)

The unlawfulnesse of subjects taking up armes against their soveraigne, in what case soever... Printed in the Yeare of our Lord, 1647. Since the 25. day of March. 4°

Wing D 1465.
2 copies.

T.122   T.291

761

DIVERS papers from the army: viz. 1. Marshall Generall Skippons speech to the army, May the 15th. 2. The answer of the army: wherein they set downe their grievances ... London; for Hanna Allen, 1647. 4°

Wing D 1709.

T.292

762

EDWARDS (Thomas) *Puritan Divine.*

The casting down of the last and strongest hold of Satan. Or, A treatise against toleration and pretended liberty of conscience ... The first part ... London, T.R. and E.M. for George Calvert, 1647. 4°

Wing E 225.
"Edward Willmore his booke."

T.264

763

ENGLAND. *Parliament.*

A declaration of the Lords and Commons assembled in Parliament, concerning the papers of the Scots Commissioners ..., London, for Edward Husband, March 13. 1647. 4°

Wing E 1392.

T.129

764

ENGLAND. *Parliament.*

The four bills sent to the King to the Isle of Wight to be passed. Together with the propositions ... And also the articles of the Church of England ... Unto all which doth refer, the late declaration ... concerning the papers of the Scots Commissioners ... London: for Edward Husband, March 20. 1647. 4°

Wing E 1541.

T.129

765

ENGLAND. *Parliament.*

An ordinance of the Lords and Commons assembled in Parliament: for the putting out of the cities of London and Westminster ... all delinquents, papists, and others that have been in arms against the Parliament ... London, for John Wright, 1647. 4°

Wing E 2009.

T.129

766

ENGLAND. *Parliament.*

An ordinance of the Lords and Commons assembled in Parliament. For the raising and securing of 42000. li. for the payment of the guards of the city of London ... London, for John Wright, 1647. 4°

Wing E 2011.

T.129

767

ENGLAND. *Parliament.*

Three ordinances of the Lords and Commons assembled in Parliament ... London, for John Wright, 1647. 4°

Wing E 2368.

T.129

768

ENGLAND. *Parliament. House of Commons.*

A declaration of the Commons of England in Parliament assembled; expressing their reasons and grounds of passing the late resolutions touching No farther address or application to be made to the King ... London, for Edward Husband, Feb. 15, 1647. 4°

Wing E 2559.

T.129

769

FAIRFAX (Thomas) *3rd Baron Fairfax.*

Another letter from his Excellency Sir Thomas Fairfax to the Speaker of the House of Commons, of his Majesties removall from Childersley to New-market, and the grounds thereof ... London, for Lawrence Chapman, 1647. 4°

Wing F 134.

T.292

770

FAIRFAX (Thomas) *3rd Baron Fairfax.*

A declaration: or, Representation from his Excellencie, Sir Tho. Fairfax, and the army under his command ..., concerning the just and fundamental rights and liberties of themselves and the Kingdom ... London, for George Whittington, 1647. 4°

Wing F 156.
2 copies.

T.86   T.129

771

FAIRFAX (Thomas) *3rd Baron Fairfax.*

An humble representation from his Excellencie Sir Thomas Fairfax, and the councel of the armie; concerning their past endeavours, and now finall desires for the putting of the souldiery into constant pay ... London, John Clowes, for George Whittington, 1647. 4°

Wing F 169.

T.292

772

FAIRFAX (Thomas) *3rd Baron Fairfax.*

A letter from his Excellency Sir Thomas Fairfax, sent to both Houses of Parliament June the 6. concerning the Kings being brought from Holmby towards the army ... London, for George Whittington, [1647]. 4°

Wing F 172.

T.292

773

FAIRFAX (Thomas) *3rd Baron Fairfax.*

A particular charge or impeachment in the name of his Excellency Sir Thomas Fairfax ... against Denzill Holles [and others], members of the honorable House of Commons. London; for George Whittington, 1647. 4°

Ch. Ch. F 210+.

T.292

774

FAIRFAX (Thomas) *3rd Baron Fairfax.*

A remonstrance from his Excellency Sir Thomas Fairfax, and his councell of warre, concerning the late discontent and distraction in the army ... London, for George Whittington, 1647. 4°

Wing F 226.

T.292

775

FAIRFAX (Thomas) *3rd Baron Fairfax.*

Three letters from his Excellency Sir Thomas Fairfax, and the officers and soldiers under his command ... London, for Laurence Chapman, Iune 28. 1647. 4°

Wing F 241.

T.292

776

FAIRFAX (Thomas) *3rd Baron Fairfax.*

Two letters from his Excellencie Sir Thomas Fairfax
... giving an accompt of what transactions and
proceedings have been betwixt the Kings Majesty and
the Army ... London, for Laurence Chapman, Iuly 10,
1647. 4°
2 copies.

Wing F 245.

T.292   T.129

777

FAIRFAX (Thomas) *3rd Baron Fairfax.*

Two letters from his Excellencie Sir Thomas Fairfax,
sent to both Houses of Parliament; with the
humble advice of the councel of warre ... upon
the votes of both Houses, sent to the army for
their disbanding ... London: for George Whittington,
1647. 4°

Wing F 248.

T.292

778

GRENE (Giles)

A declaration in vindication of the honour of the
Parliament, and of the Committee of the Navy and
Customes; against all traducers ... London, for
Laurence Blaiklock, 1647. 4°

Wing G 1817.

T. 18

779

HAMMOND (Henry)

A copy of some papers past at Oxford, betwixt the
author of the Practicall catechisme [i.e.
Henry Hammond] and Mr. Ch. [i.e. Francis
Cheynell] ... London, R. Cotes for Richard Royston,
1647. 4°
2 copies.

Wing H 530.

T.312

780

HAMMOND (Henry)

Of the power of the keyes: or, Of binding and
loosing ... [Anon.] London, for Richard Royston,
1647. 4°

Wing H 567.

T.158

781

HUGHES (George)

Vae-euge-tuba. Or, The wo-ioy-trumpet, sounding
the third and greatest woe to the Antichristian
world ... Unfolded in a sermon before the
honourable House of Commons ... May 26. 1647 ...
London, E.G. for Iohn Rothwell, 1647. 4°

Wing H 3310.

T.674

782

JAMES (Francis)

A proclamation to the King; in a sermon preached the
15. of June, 1647. before his Majesty, and the head
of Sir Thomas Fairfax his army ... London, John
Hammond, 1647. 4°

Wing J 424.

T.466

783

LILBURNE (John)

Regall tyrannie discovered: or, A discourse,
shewing that all lawfull (approbational) instituted
power by God amongst men, is by common agreement,
and mutual consent ... [Anon.] London, printed
anno Dom. 1647. 4°

Wing L 2172.

T.88

784

LONDON.

A declaration of the Lord Maior, aldermen, and
commons of the city of London, in common-councell
assembled. [London], Richard Cotes, 1647. 4°

Wing D 704.

T.129

785

LUBIN (Eilhard)

Clavis Graecae linguae, duabus partibus distincta ...
Editio novissima ... opera & cura I.H. Londini, in
officina Roberti White, sumptibus Johannis Partridge,
1647. 8°

Wing L 3386.

T.460

786

MONTAGU (Edward) *2nd Earl of Manchester.*

A letter from the Right Honourable Ed. Lord Montagu,
one of the commissioners attending his Majesty. With
a perfect narration of all the passages betwixt his
Majesty and those forces that brought him from
Holdenby ... London, for John Wright, 1647. 4°

Wing M 392.

T.292

787

NEWCOMEN (Matthew)

The all-seeing unseen eye of God. Discovered, in
a sermon preached before the honourable House of
Commons; at Margarets Westminster, December 30. 1646...
London, A.M. for Christopher Meredith, 1647. 4°

Wing N 904.

T.466

788

The PETITION and vindication of the officers of the
Armie under ... Sir Thomas Fairfax ... London, for
George Whittington, 1647. 4°

Wing P 1745.

T.129

789

The PETITION of the officers and souldiers in the
Army, under the command of ... Sr. Thomas Fairfax,
with the severall votes of the councell of war at
Saffron Walden ... London, for Robert White, April.
2. 1647. 4°

Wing P 1825.

T.129

790

PRYNNE (William)

A full vindication and answer of the XI. accused
members, viz. Denzill Holles [and others] to a late
printed pamphlet intituled, A particular charge or
impeachment, in the name of Sir Thomas Fairfax...
[Anon.] London, printed in the year, 1647. 4°

Wing P 3968.

T.292

791

PRYNNE (William)

The sword of Christian magistracy supported: or A
full vindication of Christian kings and magistrates
authority under the Gospell, to punish idolatry,
apostacy, heresie, blasphemy, and obstinate schism
... London, John Macock for John Bellamie, 1647.
4°

Wing P 4098.

T.19

792

SANDERSON (Robert) *Bishop of Lincoln.*

Reasons of the present judgement of the University
of Oxford, concerning the Solemne League and
Covenant, the Negative Oath, the Ordinances
concerning discipline and worship ... Printed in
the yeare, 1647. 4°

Wing S 623.

T.88

793

The SCOTCH souldiers speech concerning the Kings
coronation-oath. Printed in the yeare, 1647. 4°

Wing S 963.

T.187

794

SCOTLAND. *Parliament.*

The answer of the Commissioners of the Kingdome of
Scotland, to both Houses of Parliament, upon the
new propositions of peace, and the foure bills to be
sent to his Majestie. London, for Robert Bostock,
1647. 4°
2 copies.

Wing S 1180.

T.218   T.129

795

SEDGWICK (Obadiah)

The nature and danger of heresies. Opened in a
sermon before the honourable House of Commons,
Ianuary 27. 1646. at Margarets Westminster, being
the day of their solemn monthly fast... London,
M.F. for Samuel Gellibrand, 1647. 4°

Wing S 2377.

T.466

796

SHEPARD (Thomas)

The day-breaking, if not the sun-rising of the
Gospell with the Indians in New-England ... [Anon.]
London, Rich. Cotes, for Fulk Clifton, 1647. 4°

Wing S 3110.

T.158

797

WARD (Nathaniel)

The simple cobler of Aggawam in America. Willing
to help 'mend his native country ... By Theodore
de la Guard, London, J. D. & R, I, for Stephen
Bowtell, 1647. 4°

Wing W 787.

T.94

798

WENTWORTH (Thomas) *Earl of Strafford.*

A briefe and perfect relation, of the answeres and
replies of Thomas Earle of Strafford; to the articles
exhibited against him, by the House of Commons on
the thirteenth of Aprill, an. Dom. 1641. London,
printed, 1647. 4°

Wing R 68.

T.127

799

WESTMINSTER ASSEMBLY OF DIVINES.

The humble advice of the Assembly of Divines, now
by the authority of Parliament sitting at Westminster;
concerning a larger catechism... Printed at London;
and re-printed at Edinburgh by Evan Tyler, 1647. 4°

Wing W 1437 A.

T.312

800

WILBEE (Amon)

Secunda pars, De comparatis comparandis: seu
justificationis regis Caroli, comparate, contra
Parliamentum. Or the second part of Things compared,
&c ... Printed at Oxford, 1647. 4°

Wing W 2114.

T.270

1648

801

An ANSWER to the chief, or materiall heads &
passages in the late declaration, called, The
declaration of the kingdome of Scotland: and
answer of the Commissioners to both Houses of
Parliament, upon the new propositions of peace, and
the foure bills. London, for Robert White, Ian.
4. 1648. 4°

Wing A 3398.

T.292

802

ASHHURST (William)

Reasons against agreement with a late printed paper
[by John Lilburne], intituled, Foundations of
freedome: or, The agreement of the people ...
London: for Tho: Underhill, 1648. 4°

Wing A 3977.

T.292

803

ASHHURST (William)

The state of the Kingdome represented to the people
concerning the King, parliament, army, and the whole
land. In a rejoynder, by way of animadversions upon
the Answer to the agreement of the people. London,
Robert Ibbitson, 1648. 4°

Wing S 5319.

T.292

804

BADILEY (Richard)

The sea-men undeceived: or, Certaine queries to a
printed paper, intituled, The humble tender and
declaration of many wel-affected sea-men, commanders
of ships, and members of Trinity-House, to the
Commissioners of the Navy... By R.B. ... London,
Matthew Simmons, 1648. 4°

Wing B 389.

T.18

805

BOXHORN (Marcus Zuerius)

Marci Zuerii Boxhornii Oratio panegyrica de pace, inter potentiss. Philippum IV. Hispaniarum regem, et foederatorum Belgarum ordines ... Lugduni Batavorum, ex officina Davidis Lopez de Haro, 1648. Fol.

T.810

806

CHARLES I, *King of England.*

The Kings Majesties answer to the paper delivered in by the reverend divines attending the honourable Commissioners concerning church-government. London, E. Griffin, for T. Hewer, 12 October, 1648. 4°

Wing C 2125.

T.292

807

CHARLES I, *King of England.*

His Majesties finall answer concerning episcopacie. Delivered in to the Commissioners of Parliament the first of Novemb. 1648. London, for Richard Best, 1648. 4°

Wing C 2306.

T.292

808

CHARLES I, *King of England.*

The Kings most gracious messages for peace, and a personal treaty ... Printed in the yeare, 1648. 4°

Wing C 2520.

T.292

809

CHARLES I, *King of England.*

His Maiesties reason why he cannot in conscience consent to abolish the episcopall government. Delivered by him in writing to the divines that attend the honorable Commissioners of Parliament at the treaty at Newport ... With the answer of the said divines delivered to his Majestie ... London, William Wilson, 1648. 4°

Wing C 2738.

T.292

810

COBBET (Thomas)

A just vindication of the covenant and church-estate of children of church-members: as also of their right unto baptisme... London, R. Cotes for Andrew Crooke, 1648. 4°

Wing C 4778.
Wanting title-page and prelims.

T.318

811

COLLECTIONS of notes taken at the Kings tryall, at Westminster Hall, on Saturday last, Janua. 20. 1648 ... Which notes were taken by H. Walker, who was present at the tryall that day. London, Robert Ibbitson, 1648. 4°

Wing C 5217.

T.292

812

The COMMENCEMENT of the treaty between the King's Majesty, and the commissioners of Parliament at Newport. A prayer drawne by his Majesties speciall direction and dictates, for a blessing on the treaty at Newport. [No imprint, 1648.] brs.

Wing C 5546 (?)

T.292

813

An ENDEVOUR after the reconcilement of that long debated and much lamented difference between the godly Presbyterians, and Independents; about church-government. In a discourse touching the Iews synagogues ... London, M. S. for John Bellamy, 1648. 4°

Wing E 727.

T.158

814

ENGLAND. *Parliament.*

The form of church-government to be used in the Church of England and Ireland: agreed upon by the Lords and Commons assembled in Parliament, after advice had with the Assembly of Divines ... London, for John Wright, 1648. 4°

Wing E 1539.

T.321

815

ENGLAND. *Parliament.*

An ordinance of the Lords and Commons assembled in Parliament: for the speedy getting in the arreares of such money as is assessed on the citie of London ... London, Richard Cotes, 1648. 4°

Wing E 2046.

T.129

816

FAIRFAX (Thomas) *3rd Baron Fairfax.*

The declaration of his Excellency the Lord General Fairfax, and his general councel of officers, shewing the grounds of the armies advance towards the city of London ... London, John Field for John Partridge, Novemb. 1, 1648. 4°

Wing F 145.

T.129

817

FAIRFAX (Thomas) *3rd Baron Fairfax.*

The humble proposals and desires of his Excellency the Lord Fairfax, and of the general councel of officers, in order to a speedy prosecution of justice ... London, John Field for John Partridge, Decemb. 7, 1648. 4°

Wing H 3597.

T.129

818

FAIRFAX (Thomas) *3rd Baron Fairfax.*

A remonstrance of his Excellency Thomas Lord Fairfax ... and of the generall councell of officers held at St. Albans the 16, of November, 1648 ... London, for John Partridge and George Whittington, 1648. 4°

Wing F 229.
2 copies.

T.126 T.129

819

GATFORD (Lionel)

Englands complaint: or, A sharp reproof for the inhabitants thereof; against that now raigning sin of rebellion. But more especially to the inhabitants of the county of Suffolk. With a vindication of those worthyes now in Colchester ... London, printed in the yeere 1648. 4°

Wing G 332.

T.291

820

GAUDEN (John) *Bishop of Worcester.*

The religious & loyal protestation, of John Gauden ... against the present declared purposes and proceedings of the army and others; about the trying and destroying our soveraign lord the King ... London, for Richard Royston, 1648. 4°

Wing G 367.

T.292

821

HARTLIB (Samuel)

A further discoverie of the office of publick addresse for accomodations. [Anon.] London, printed in the yeer, 1648. 4°

Wing H 987.
Wanting the title-page and the next leaf.

T.373

822

HERBERT (Philip) *4th Earl of Pembroke.*

The Earl of Pembroke's speech in the House of Peers, when the seven lords were accused of high-treason. [A satire.] Printed in the year 1648. 4°

Ch. Ch. P 1118+

T.123

823

HORTON (Thomas) *Colonel.*

Die Mercurii, 17 Maii, 1648. A true confirmation of the great victory in Wales: sent in a letter to the speaker ... London, for Edward Husband, May 18. 1648. 4°

Wing H 2887.

T.372

824

HOWELL (James)

The instruments of a king: or, A short discourse of the sword, the scepter, the crowne ... London, printed in the yeare, 1648. 4°

Wing H 3083.

T.504

825

HOWELL (James)

A Venice looking-glasse: or, A letter [signed J.B.C.] written very lately from London to Rome, by a Venetian clarissimo to Cardinal Barberino, protector of the English nation, touching these present distempers ... Faithfully rendred out of the Italian ... Printed in the yeare 1648. 4°

Wing H 3126.

T.504

826

The HUMBLE petition of the knights, gentlemen, citizens, free-holders, and inhabitants of the county of Surrey ... to ... both Houses of Parliament ... Likewise the petition of the county of Essex, and the answer of both Houses to the same ... May 16. 1648. London, printed 1648. 4°

Wing H 3527.

T.209

827

HYDE (Edward) *Earl of Clarendon.*

A full answer to an infamous and trayterous pamphlet, entituled, A declaration of the Commons of England in Parliament assembled, expressing their reasons and grounds of passing the late resolutions touching no further addresse or application to be made to the King ... [Anon.] Printed for R. Royston, 1648. 4°

Wing C 4423.

T.126

828

I. (T.)

A perfect narrative of the proceedings of the army under the command of Col. Michael Iones... in their last advance from Dublin; with the taking of the strong castles and forts of Ballysonan, Allan, Black-hall, Raville, and Granye... London, for John Wright, Octob.17.1648. 4°

Wing I 14.

T.208

829

KNELL (Paul)

A looking-glasse for Levellers: held out in a sermon, preached ... Sept. 24. 1648 ... London, printed in the year, 1648. 4°

Wing K 683.

T.126

830

LILLY (William)

An astrologicall prediction of the occurrances in England, part of the yeers 1648. 1649. 1650 ... London: T. B. for John Partridge and Humfrey Blunden, 1648. 4°

Wing L 2211.

T.126

831

LONDON.

The humble petition of the Lord Major, aldermen, and commons of the city of London, in Common-Councell assembled, presented to the ... Lords and Commons ... With the answer of the Lords to the said petition. [London], Richard Cotes, August 8. 1648. 4°

Wing H 3544.

T.292

832

MARESIUS (Samuel)

Quaestionum aliquot theologicarum, regimen, ordinem, praxim & eutaxiam Ecclesiae spectantium, decisio academica. Groningae, typis Johannis Nicolai, 1648. 4°

T.168

833

A NARRATIVE and declaration of the dangerous design against the Parliament & Kingdom, carried on in the county of Kent and elswhere ... London, for Edward Husband, June 8. 1648. 4°

Wing N 166.

T.129

834

P. (A.)

An appendix to the Agreement for the people. Published for the satisfaction of tender consciences. London, for G. Calvert, 1648. 4°

Wing P 2.

T.292

835

A PAIRE of spectacles for the Citie. Printed in the yeare, 1648. 4°

Wing P 196.

T.209

836

PAPERS presented to the Parliament, against the Lord Inchequin Lord President of Munster in Ireland, sent from Captain Crowther ... And the Lord Inchequins declaration ... London, Robert Ibbitson, 1648. 4°

Wing P 300.

T.129

The PARLIAMENT arraigned, convicted... 1648.

See no. 4855.

837

PARSONS (Robert)

Severall speeches delivered at a conference concerning the power of Parliament, to proceed against their King for misgovernment ... [Anon.] London, Robert Ibbitson, 1648. 4°

Wing P 573.

T.270

838

PRYNNE (William)

A briefe memento to the present un-parliamentary iunto, touching their present intentions and proceedings, to depose & execute Charles Steward, their lawfull king ... London, printed anno Dom. 1648. 4°

Wing P 3909 (?)
Incomplete.

T.20

839

RAVIUS (Christian)

Christiani Ravii Berlinatis Sesqi-decuria epistolarum adoptivarum ex varijs orbis partibus commissarum circa orientalium studiorum promovendorum curam. London: W. Wilson, for T. Iachson, 1648. 12°

Wing R 315.

T.458

840

S. (G.)

A letter from an ejected member of the House of Commons, to Sir Jo: Evelyn: shewing the constitution of that councell... Printed in the yeare, 1648. 4°

Wing S 26.

T.126

841

The SAD, and bloody fight at Westminster between the souldiers of the Parliaments guard and the club-men of Surrey. With a copy of their petition to the Parliament ... London, for H. Becke, 1648. 4°

Wing S 227.

T.209

842

SALUS populi solus rex. The peoples safety is the sole soveraignty, or The royalist out-reasoned: calculated for the hopefull recovery of the considerate royalist, from the dangerous infecton of the slie sophistry of Iudge Ienkings ... [London], printed, 1648. 4°

Wing S515.
Imprint cropped.

T.88

843

SCOTLAND. *Commissioners.*

... The humble representation of the Commissioners of the Generall Assembly, to the honorable Estates of Parliament; upon their declaration lately communicated to us ... London, for John Dallom, 1648. 4°

Wing S 983 A.
Incomplete.

T.218

844

WALKER (Clement)

Relations and observations, historicall and politick, upon the Parliament, begun anno Dom. 1640... [Anon.] Printed in the yeare, 1648. 4°

Wing W 334.

T.250

845

WARNER (John) *Bishop of Rochester.*

Church-lands not to be sold. Or, A necessary and plaine answer to the question of a conscientious protestant; whether the lands of the bishôps, and churches in England and Wales may be sold? ... [Anon.] Printed in the yeare, 1648. 4°

Wing W 900.
2 copies.

T.291   T.379

846

WARNER (John) *Bishop of Rochester.*

The devilish conspiracy, hellish treason, heathenish condemnation, and damnable murder, committed, and executed by the Iewes, against the anointed of the Lord ... As it was delivered in a sermon on the 4. Feb. 1648... [Anon.] London, printed in the yeare, 1648. 4°

Wing W 902.

T.466

847

WELDON (Robert)

The doctrine of the scriptures, concerning the originall of dominion. Wherein Gods perpetuall propriety in the soveraignty of the whole earth, and the Kings great charter for the administration thereof, are justified... Printed for Richard Royston, 1648. 4°

Wing W 1280.

T.158

848

WENDELIN (Marcus Frederik)

Admiranda Nili. Commentatione philologica geographica, historica, physica, & hieroglypica, ex CCCXVIII. autoribus, Graecis & Latinis, vetustis & recentibus illustrata... Ex officine Rogeri Danielis, 1648. 4°

Wing W 1348.

T.168

1649

849

CHARLES I, *King of England.*

The princely pellican. Royall resolves presented in sundry choice observations, extracted from his Majesties Divine meditations... Printed in the yeare, 1649. 4°

Wing P 3491. Almack 74.

T.291

850

CHARLES I, *King of England.*

The royall legacies of Charles the first of that name ... king and martyr; to his persecutors and murderers. Being a short paraphrase upon his Majesties most Christian, and most charitable speech, delivered immediately before his translation ... Printed in the year 1649. 4°

Wing C 2764

T.291

CLEVELAND (John)

The character of a country committee-man. 1649.

See no. 3722.

851

DU MOULIN (Pierre) *the Younger.*

Ecclesiae gemitus sub anabaptistica tyrannide ... [Anon.] Anno Dom. 1649. Aerae Martyrii Caroli I. Britanniarum Regis, anno primo. 8°

Wing E 136.

T.585

852

The ESSEX watchmen's watchword to the inhabitants of the said county respectively, dwelling under their several charges, by way of apologetical account, of the true grounds of their first engagement with them in the cause of God, King and parliament, for their vindication from unjust aspersions ... London, for Ralph Smith, 1649. 4°

Wing E 3342 A.
Signature of John Bowdler.

T.292

853

FAIRFAX (Thomas) *3rd Baron Fairfax.*

A petition from his Excellency Thomas Lord Fairfax and the general councel of officers of the army, to the honorable the Commons of England ... concerning the draught of an agreement of the people for a secure and present peace ... London, for John Partridge, R. Harford, G. Calvert, and G. Whittington, 1649. 4°

Wing F 213.

T.292

854

GEREE (John)

Καταδυναστης: might overcoming right. Or a cleer answer to M. John Goodwin's Might and right well met ... London, for Robert Bostock, 1649. 4°

Wing G 598.

T.292

855

HAMMOND (Henry)

To the Right Honourable, the Lord Fairfax, and his councell of warre: the humble addresse of Henry Hammond. London, for Richard Royston, 1649. 4°

Wing H 606/7.

T.158

856

HARMAR (John) *the Younger.*

Ad spectatissimum virum Lambertum Osbalstonum epistola: cui intexitur apologia pro Joanne Williams, Angliae Primate. Londini, venundantur apud Octavianum Pullenum, 1649. 8°

Wing H 781.
Wanting title-page.

T.458

857

HOWELL (James)

A winter dreame ... [Anon.] Printed anno Domini QuanDo ReX AngLoruM *VectI* vIctItabat CaptIvus, 1649. 4°

Wing H 3129.

T.504

858

JENKINS (David)

God and the king: or, The divine constitution of the supreme magistrate; especially in the kingdome of England: against all popular pretenders whomsoever ... [Anon.] Printed in the yeare, 1649. 4°

Wing J 591.

T.321

1649 (Cont'd.)

LESLIE (Henry) *Bishop of Meath.*

The martyrdome of King Charles. 1649.

See no. 3741.

859

LILBURNE (John)

Englands new chains discovered; or, The serious apprehensions of a part of the people, in behalf of the Commonwealth; (being presenters, promoters, and approvers of the large petition of September II. 1648.) Presented to ... the representers of the people in Parliament assembled. By Lieut. Col. John Lilburn ... whereunto his speech delivered at the bar is annexed. [London, 1649.]   4°

Wing L 2106.

T.292

860

LILBURNE (John)

The hunting of the foxes from New-market and Triploe-heaths to White-hall, by five small beagles (Late of the armie) ... By Robert Ward, Thomas Watson, Simon Graunt, George Jellis, and William Sawyer. [By John Lilburne.] Printed in a corner of freedome, right opposite to the councel of warre, 1649.   4°

Wing L 2115.

T.287

861

MARTEN (Henry)

A word to Mr. Wil. Prynn Esq; and two for the Parliament and army.   Reproving the one, and justifying the other in their late proceedings... [Anon.]   London, for T. Brewster, 1649.   4°

Wing M 825.
Incomplete.

T.289

862

PRYNNE (William)

A legall vindication of the liberties of England, against illegall taxes and pretended acts of Parliament lately enforced on the people ... London, for Robert Hodges, 1649.   4°

Wing P 3996.
2 copies.

T.289   T.30

863

PRYNNE (William)

The substance of a speech made in the House of Commons ... on Munday the fourth of December, 1648. Touching the Kings answer to the propositions of both houses upon the whole treaty ... London, for Michael Spark, 1649.   4°

Wing P 4092.
2 copies.

T.289   T.126

864

PRYNNE (William)

A vindication of the imprisoned and secluded members of the House of Commons, from the aspersions cast upon them, and the majority of the House, in a paper lately printed and published: intituled, An humble answer of the general conncel of the officers of the army under his Excellency Thomas Lord Fairfax... [Anon.]   London, for Michael Spark, 1649.   4°

Wing P 4128.

T.292

865

ROUS (Francis) *The Elder.*

The grand case of conscience stated, about submission to the new and present power, Or, An impassionate answer to a modest book concerning the lawfullnesse of submitting to the present government ... [Anon.] [London, 1649.] 4°

Wing R 2015.

T.84

866

RR.

The armies remembrancer.   Wherein they are presented with a sight of their sinnes and dangers.   And also with a scripture expedient for their preservation... By a cordiall friend to the Kingdomes welfare. Rr. London, for Stephen Bowtell, 1649.   4°

Wing R 2166.

T.292

867

A SERIOUS and faithfull representation of the judgements of ministers of the Gospell within the province of London. Contained in a letter from them to the Generall and his councell of warre ... Imprinted at London by M. B. for Samuel Gellibrand, and Ralph Smith, 1649. 4°

Wing S 2604.
2 copies.

T.552 T.145

868

The SEVERAL speeches of Duke Hamilton Earl of Cambridg, Henry Earl of Holland, and Arthur Lord Capel, upon the scaffold ... London, for Peter Cole, Francis Tyton, and John Playford, 1649. 4°

Wing H 482.
Signature of John Bowdler.

T.126

869

TAYLOR (Jeremy) *Bishop of Down and Connor.*

An apology for authorized and set forms of liturgie: against the pretence of the spirit. 1. For ex tempore prayer, and 2. Formes of private composition ... London, for R. Royston, 1649. 4°

Wing T 289.

T.214

870

WARD (Nathaniel)

A religious demurrer, concerning submission to the present power: contained in a letter... [Signed A.B.C.D.] [London, 1649.] 4°

Wing R 2o26 (attributed to Francis Rous).

T.84

1650

871

AUCHER (John)

Arguments and reasons to prove the inconvenience & unlawfulness of taking the New Engagement ... [Anon.] [No imprint, 1650.] 4°

Wing A 4190 A.

T. 23

872

CONSCIENCE puzzel'd, about subscribing the new engagement ... Printed in the year, 1650. 4°

Wing C 5899.

T. 84

873

COOK (John)

A true relation of Mr. Iohn Cook's passage by sea from Wexford to Kinsale in that great storm Ianuary 5. Wherein is related the strangeness of the storm, and the frame of his spirit in it ... Printed at Cork, and re-printed at London, and are to be sold by T. Brewster and G. Moule, 1650. 4°

Wing C 6022.

T.249

874

DURY (John)

Just re-proposals to humble proposals. Or an impartiall consideration of, and answer unto, the humble proposals ... concerning the Engagement which the Parliament hath ordered to be taken ... London, J.C. for Richard Wodenothe, 1650.   4°

Wing D 2868 A.

T.493

875

ENGLAND. *Parliament.*

The answer of the Parliament of England, to a paper, entituled, A declaration by the Kings Majesty, to his subjects of the kingdoms of Scotland, England and Ireland ... Whereunto is annexed, copies of four letters to the King of Scotland, which were found in the Lord Loudouns cabinet ... London, Edward Husband and John Field, 1650. 4°

Wing E 1227.

T.287

876

The EXERCITATION [i.e. the pamphlet by Edward Gee] answered, in the assertions following made good against it... London, for John Wright, 1650.   4°

Wing E 3865.

T.23

877

GEE (Edward) *the Elder.*

An exercitation concerning usurped powers wherein the difference betwixt civil authority and usurpation is stated ... [Anon.] Printed in the yeare, 1650. 4°

Wing G 449.

T.23

878

GEE (Edward) *the Elder.*

A plea for non-subscribers. Or, The grounds and reasons of many ministers in Cheshire, Lancashire, and the parts adjoyning for their refusall of the late engagement modestly propounded ... [Anon.] Printed in the yeere 1650. 2 parts. 4°

Wing G 450.

T.84

879

GEE (Edward) *the Elder.*

A vindication of the oath of allegiance in answer to a paper disperst by Mr. Sam: Eaton ... By the author of The Exercitation concerning usurped powers ... Printed in the year, 1650. 4°

Wing G 452.
2 copies.

T.308   T. 23

880

HEARNE (Thomas)

A seasonable word, or a plain and tender-hearted epistle to all sincere hearts in Parliament, army and countrey ... Printed at London, in the year 1650.   4°

Wing H 1309 A.

T.469

881

HUDSON (Samuel)

A vindication of The essence and unity of the Church Catholike visible. And the priority thereof in regard of particular churches. In answer to the objections made against it, both by Mr John Ellis junior, and by ... Mr Hooker, in his Survey of church discipline. London, A.M. for Christopher Meredith, 1650. 4°

Wing H 3266.

T.493

882

HYDE (*Sir* Henry)

A true copy of Sir Henry Hide's speech on the scaffold, immediately before his execution before the Exchange, on the 4th of March, 1650. Taken in short-hand from his mouth, by John Hinde. London: Peter Cole, 1650. 4°

Wing H 3871.

T.287

883

The LAST will and testament of the E[ar]l of P[e]mbr[o]ke. [Attributed to Samuel Butler.] [No imprint, 1650?] 4°

Not in Wing.

T.283

884

LEPORINUS (Johannes)

Kurtze Beschreibung dess Dainacher Saurbrunnens, seiner fürnämbsten Krüfften und Eygenschafften... Getruckt zu Stuttgart bey Matthia Kautten, 1650. brs.

T.817

885

NEVILLE (Henry)

Newes from the new exchange, or the commonwealth of ladies, drawn to the life, in their severall characters and concernments ... [Anon.] London, printed in the year, of women without grace, 1650. 4°

Wing N 510.

T.81

886

A PACK of old puritans maintaining the unlawfulness & inexpediency of subscribing the new engagement ... London, printed by the Company of Covenant-Keepers, dwelling in Great Brittain, 1650. 4°

Wing P 155.

T.84

887

A PERTINENT & profitable meditation, upon the history of Pekah, his invasion and great victory over Judah... Upon occasion of the thanksgiving appointed Octob. 8. for the late successe in Scotland... London, printed in the year, 1650. 4°

Wing P 1673.

T.493

888

REYNOLDS (Edward) *Bishop of Norwich.*

The humble proposals of sundry learned and pious divines within this Kingdome. Concerning the Engagement, intended to be imposed on them for their subscriptions... [Anon.] London, printed in the year, 1650. 4°

Wing R 1254.

T.493

889

A VINDICATION of the presbyteriall-government, and ministry... Published, by the ministers, and elders, met together in a provinciall assembly, Novemb.2d.1649... London, for C. Meredith, 1650. 4°

Wing V 523.

T.493

1651

890

GOODWIN (John)

The pagans debt, and dowry. Or a brief discussion of these questions ... London, J, Macock, for H. Cripps, and L, Lloyd, 1651. 4°

Wing G 1186.
Signature of Thomas Bowdler.

T.128

891

HALL (Thomas)

The pulpit guarded with XX arguments proving the unlawfulness, sinfulness and danger of suffering private persons to take upon them publike preaching, and expounding the scriptures without a call ... Occasioned by a dispute at Henly in Arden in Warwick-shire, Aug. 20. 1650 ... The third edition, with additions ... London, J. Cottrel, for E. Blackmore,1651. 4°

Wing H 438.

T.493

892

The HUMBLE petition of many cordial friends, to this present Parliament, inhabiting within the city of London, and places adjacent, in behalf of Mr. Christopher Love, prisoner in the Tower ... London, J. C., 1651. 4°

Wing H 3469.

T. 84

893

LILLY (William)

Monarchy or no monarchy in England. Grebner his prophecy concerning Charles son of Charles, his greatnesse, victories, conquests ... London, for Humfrey Blunden, 1651. 4°

Wing L 2228.
Signature of Thomas Bowdler.

T.122

894

MILTON (John)

Joannis Miltoni Angli Pro populo Anglicano defensio contra Claudii Anonymi, alias Salmasii, Defensionem regiam. Londini, typis Du Gardianis, anno Domini, 1651. 12°

Wing M 2167-8 (?)

T.499

895

OVERBURY (*Sir* Thomas)

Observations upon the Provinces United. And on the state of France. London, T. Maxey for Richard Marriot, 1651. 8°

Wing O 609.

T.479

896

A SHORT plea for the common-wealth, in this monstrous and shaking juncture, wherein treason is scarcely accounted an offence, and traitors have so manie advocates ... London, W. D. July 11, anno Domini, 1651. 4°

Wing S 3610.

T.84

897

VERITAS pacifica: seu Articulorum fidei Christianae delineatio, haustam de verbo Dei veritatem salutiferam, solidae pacis coagulum, complexa ... Amstelodami, apud Ludovicum Elzevirium, 1651. 12°

T.481

1652

898

The ADVOCATE. London, William Du-Gard; and are to bee sold by Nicolas Bourn, 1652. Fol.

Wing A 670.

T.543

899

DOMINIUM maris: or, The dominion of the sea. Expressing the title, which the Venetians pretend unto the sole dominion, and absolute sovereigntie of the Adriatick Sea ... Translated out of Italian. [London, William Du Gard, 1652.] 4°

Wing D 1843.

T. 23

900

DURHAM (William)

Maran-atha: the second Advent, or, Christ's coming to judgment. A sermon preached before the honourable judges of assize, at Warwick: July 25. 1651 ... London, T. Maxey, for M.M.G. Bedell, and T. Collins, 1652. 4°

Wing D 2832.

T.469

901

FULLWOOD (Francis)

The churches and ministery of England, true churches and true ministery. Cleared, and proved, in a sermon preach'd the 4th of May at Wiviliscombe ... London, A.M. for George Treagle at Taunton, and are to be sold at London by William Roybould, 1652. 4°

Wing F 2498.

T.469

902

HALL (Thomas)

The font guarded with XX arguments. Containing a compendium of that great controversie of infant-baptism, proving the lawfulness thereof ... London, R. W. for Thomas Simmons book-seller in Birmingham, and are to be sold in London by George Calvert, 1652. 4°

Wing H 432.

T.354

903

JUDGMENT of the reformed churches, that a man may lawfully not only put away his wife for her adultery, but also marry another. London, for Andrew Crook, 1652. 4°

Wing J 1184.
The title-page is bound between pages 128-9 of HALL (T.) The font guarded with XX arguments.

T.354

904

PHILLIPS (John)

Joannis Philippi Angli Responsio ad apologiam Anonymi cujusdam tenebrionis pro Rege & populo Anglicano infantissimam. Londini, typis Du-Gardianis, an. Dom. 1652. 12°

Wing P 2098.

T.499

905

ROBINSON (Henry)

Certain proposalls in order to the peoples freedome and accommodation in some particulars. With the advancement of trade and navigation of this Common-Wealth in generall ... London, M. Simmons, 1652. 4°

Wing R 1670.

T.145

906

USSHER (James) *Archbishop of Armagh*

Jacobi Usserii Armachani De textus Hebraici Veteris Testamenti variantibus lectionibus ad Ludovicum Cappellum epistola ... Londini, typis J. Flesher, impensis J. Crook, & J. Baker, 1652. 4°

Wing U 169.

T.168

WELDON (Sir Anthony)

A cat may look upon a king. 1652.

See no. 5920.

907

ZIEGLER (Caspar)

Casparis Ziegleri Lipsiensis circa regicidium Anglorum exercitationes. Lipsiae, apud haered. Grossi, literis Lanckisianis exscribebat Christoph. Cellarius, 1652. 12°

T.499

1653

908

BADILEY (Richard)

Capt. Badiley's reply to certaine declarations from Capt. Seamen, Cap. Ell, & Cap. Fisher. As he found them divulged abroad in a fallacious pamphlet [by Henry Appleton] called The remonstrance of the fight neer legorn, between the English and the Dutch ... London, Matthew Simmons, 1653. 4°

Wing B 388.

T.287

909

BAR-ISAJAH (Eliazar)

A vindication of the Christians Messiah, (viz.) that Jesus Christ the sonne of God is the true Messiah prophesied of ... Written by Eliazar Bar-isajah P. a Jew born, but now a converted and baptized Christian. London, Gartrude Dawson, 1653. 4°

Wing B 765.

T.375

910

BOREMAN (Robert)

Παισεια θριαυβος. The triumph of learning over ignorance, and of truth over falsehood. Being an answer to foure quaeries... which were lately proposed by a zelot, in the parish church at Swacie neere Cambridge, after the second sermon, October 3.1652. Since then enlarged by the answerer, R.B... London, For R. Royston, 1653.

Wing B 3760.

T.754

911

C. (E.)

The Wiltshire-petition for tythes explained, for the better understanding of the people of this Commonwealth ... By E. C. and R. E. London, for William Larnar, 1653. 4°

Wing C 29.

T.375

912

COOTE (Edmund)

The English school-master, teaching all his scholers, of what age soever, the most easie, short, and perfect order of distinct reading, and true writing our English tongue, that hath ever yet beene known or published by any ... By Edward Cook [sic] ... Now the 24 time imprinted ... London, T. Maxey, for the Company of Stationers, 1653. 4°

Not in Wing.

T.375

1653 (Cont'd.)

913

DAILLÉ (Jean)

An apologie for the reformed churches; wherein is shew'd the necessitie of their separation from the Church of Rome ... Translated out of French. And a preface added; containing the judgement of an university-man, concerning Mr. Knot's last book against Mr. Chillingworth. [By Thomas Smith.] Printed by Th. Buck, printer to the Universitie of Cambridge, 1653. 8°

Wing D 113.

T.447

914

DESCARTES (René)

Renatus Des-cartes excellent compendium of musick: with necessary and judicious animadversions thereupon. By a person of honour. London, Thomas Harper, for Humphrey Moseley, and are to be sold at his shop ... and by Thomas Heath, 1653. 4°

Wing D 1132.

T.672

915

GAUDEN (John) *Bishop of Worcester.*

The case of ministers maintenance by tithes, (as in England,) plainly discussed in conscience and prudence ... London, Thomas Maxey, for Andrew Crook, 1653. 4°

Wing G 344.
Annotated by the author.

T.493

916

HARTLIB (Samuel)

A discoverie for division or settling out of land, as to the best form. Published... for direction and more advantage and profit of the adventurers and planters in the Fens and other waste and undisposed places in England and Ireland... London, for Richard Wodenothe, 1653. 4°

Wing H 985.

T.23

917

MASTER John Goodwins quere's questioned, concerning the power of the civil magistrate in matters of religion: by one quere opposed to the thirty... London, for Tho. Underhill, 1653. 4°

Wing M 1062.

T.493

918

LYFORD (William)

An apologie for our publick ministerie, and infant-baptism ... London, William Du-Gard, and are to bee sold by Joseph Cranford, 1653. 4°

Wing L 3545.

T.375

919

ROBINSON (Henry)

Certaine proposals in order to a new modelling of the lawes, and law-proceedings, for a more speedy, cheap, and equall distribution of justice throughout the Common-wealth ... London: M. Simmons, 1653. 4°

Wing R 1669.

T.23

920

SA (Pantaleao)

A narration of the late accident in the New-Exchange, on the 21. and 22.of November, 1653 ... Written by the most noble and illustrious lord, Don Pantaleon Sa ... to his much esteemed nobilitie of England, and to all of the beloved and famous city of London, from Newgates prison. London, printed in the yeare, 1653. 4°

Wing S 210.

T.287

921

SANDERSON (Robert) *Bishop of Lincoln.*

A sermon preached at Newport in the Isle of Wight, October 1648. In the time of the treaty. London, T.M. for Andrew Crook, 1653. 4°

Wing S 628.

T.341

922

SEDGWICK (Joseph)

A sermon, preached at St. Marie's in the University of Cambridge May 1st, 1653. Or, An essay to the discovery of the spirit of enthusiasme and pretended inspiration, that disturbs and strikes at the universities... London: R.D. for Edward Story, bookseller in Cambridge, 1653. 4°

Wing S 2362.

T.469

923

SOCIETY OF JESUS. *Collegium S.J. Dusseldorpii.*

Monumentū, quod aere perennius ... D. Wolfgangus Wilhelmus, comes palatinus Rheni ... non intermorituris virtutum suarum exemplis in vita erexit, et omnia posteritati, post mortem spectandum reliquit. Ab humanoribus Societatis Jesu musis Dusseldorpii ... Typis viduae Hartgeri Woringen, 1653. Fol.

T.810

924

SPITTLEHOUSE (John)

The army vindicated, in their late dissolution of the Parliament: with several cautions and directions in point of a new representative ... London, for Richard Moone, 1653. 4°

Wing S 5004.

T.84

925

WATERHOUSE (Thomas)

Disputationum physicarum de monstris & prodigiis, disputatio tertia; quam ... sub praesidio ... Adami Steuarti, publicè ventilandam proponit Thomas Waterhousius, ad diem 10. Decembris ... Lugd. Batavor., ex officina Johannis & Danielis Elsevier, 1653. 4°

T.168

1654

926

CAMBRIDGE, *University.*

Oliva pacis. Ad illustrissimum celsissimuq; Oliverum, Reipub. Angliae, Scotiae, and Hiberniae Dominum Protectorem; de pace cum foederatis Belgis feliciter sancita, carmen Cantabrigiense. Cantabrigiae: ex celeberrimae Academiae Typographeo, anno Dom. 1654. 4°

Wing C 348.

T.407

927

CARREUS (Johannes)

Dissertatio theologica de descensu Christi ad inferos ... Hagae-Comitum, ex typographia Adriani Vlacq, 1654. 12°

T.481

928

A COPY of a letter concerning the election of a Lord Protector. Written to a member of Parliament. London, Tho. Newcomb, 1654. 4°

Wing C 6113.

T.287

929

CROMWELL (Oliver)

His Highnesse the Lord Protector's speech to the Parliament in the painted chamber, on Tuesday the 12th of September. 1654 ... London, T. R. and E. M. for G. Sawbridge, 1654. 4°

Wing C 7170.

T.287

930

CROMWELL (Oliver)

His Highnes speech to the Parliament, in the painted chamber, at their dissolution, upon Monday January 22. 1654. London, Henry Hills, 1654. 4°

Wing C 7171.
Wanting title-page.

T.287

931

CROMWELL (Oliver)

His Highnesse the Lord Protector's speeches to the Parliament in the painted chamber, the one on Munday the 4th of September; the other on Tuesday the 12. of September. 1654 ... London, T. R. and E. M. for G. Sawbridge, 1654. 4°

Wing C 7175.

T.287

932

GACHES (Raymond)

Le consolateur promis aux apostres. Ou sermon sur le chapitre XVI. de l'Euangile selon Saint Jean verser 7. Prononcé à Charenton ... 25. May 1654. Se vend a Charenton, par Louis Vendosme, 1654. 8°

T.444

933

GAUDEN (John) *Bishop of Worcester.*

Ἱεροτελεστια γαμικη. Christ at the wedding: the pristine sanctity and solemnity of Christian marriages, as they were celebrated by the Church of England ... London, E. Cotes, for Andrew Crook, 1654. 4°

Wing G 360.
2 copies.

T.469 T.341

934

GERRARD (John)

The true and perfect speeches of Colonel John Gerhard upon the scaffold at Tower Hill ... and Mr. Peter Vowel at Charing-Cross ... Likewise, the speech of the Portugal ambassadors brother [Pantaleao Sá] upon the scaffold ... Taken by an ear witness, and impartially communicated for general satisfaction. Imprinted at London for C. Horton, 1654. 4°

Wing G 615.

T.287

935

HALL (Thomas)

Comarum ἀκοσμεια: the loathsomenesse of long haire ... with the concurrent judgement of divines both old and new against it. With an appendix against painting, spots, naked breasts ... London, J.G. for Nathanael Webb and William Grantham, 1654. 8°

Wing H 429.
Wanting title-page and all before p.7.
Signature of Richard Munkland, 1685.

T.457

936

HAMMOND (Henry)

A vindication of the dissertations concerning episcopacie: from the answers, or exceptions offered against them by the London ministers, in their Jus divinum ministerii evangelici. London, J. G. for Richard Royston, 1654. 4°

Wing H 618.
2 copies.

T.747 T.319

937

JUS divinum ministerii evangelici. Or the divine right of the gospel-ministry ... Published by the provincial assembly of London. London, for G. Latham, J. Rothwell, S. Gellibrand, T. Underhill, and J. Cranford, 1654. 2 parts. 4°

Wing J 1216 (?)
Signature of Thomas Bowdler.

T.319

938

PRYNNE (William)

A seasonable, legall, and historicall vindication and chronologicall collection of the good, old, fundamentall, liberties, franchises, rights, laws of all English freemen... London, for the authour, and are to be sold by Edward Thomas, 1654. 4°

Wing P 4062.
2 copies (one incomplete).

T.30 T.289

939

SADLER (Anthony)

Inquisitio Anglicana: or, The disguise discovered. Shewing the proceedings of the commissioners at Whitehall, for the approbation of ministers. In the examinations of Anthony Sadler cler... London, J. Grismond, for Richard Royston, 1654. 4°

Wing S 265.

T.375

940

TRAPNEL (Anna)

The cry of a stone: or a relation of something spoken in Whitehall, by Anna Trapnel, being in the visions of God. Relating to the governors, army, churches, ministry, universities: and the whole nation... London printed. 1654. 4°

Wing T 2031.

T.375

941

A TRUE account of the late bloody and inhumane conspiracy against his Highness the Lord Protector, and this Commonwealth... London, Thomas Newcomb, 1654. 4°

Wing T 2381.

T.287

942

A TRUE state of the case of the Commonwealth of England, Scotland, and Ireland...; in reference to the late established government by a lord protector and a parlament... London, Tho. Newcomb, 1654. 4°

Wing T 3114.

T.84

943

VOSSIUS (Gerardus Joannes)

Gerardi Joannis Vossii de cognitione sui libellus. Accedunt & alia opuscula. Amstelodami, apud Cornelium Joannis, 1654. 2 parts. 12°

T.453

944

VOSSIUS (Gerardus Joannes)

Gerardi Joannis Vossi in epistolam Plinii de Christianis, et edicta caesarum Romanorum adversus Christianos, commentarius. Amstelodami, apud Cornelium Joannis, 1654. 12°

T.453

945

WARREN (Albertus)

A new plea for the old law, extracted from reason, and experience ... London, T. R. for Henry Twyford, 1654. 4°

Wing W 953.

T.84

1655

946

BAXTER (Richard)

The Quakers catechism, or, The Quakers questioned, their questions answered, and both published ... London; A. M. for Thomas Underhill, and Francis Tyton, 1655. 4°

Wing B 1362.
Signature of Thomas Bowdler, 1655.

T.128

947

CROMWELL (Oliver)

A declaration of his Highnes, by the advice of his council, shewing the reasons of their proceedings for securing the peace of the Commonwealth, upon occasion of the late insurrection and rebellion ... London, Henry Hills and John Field, 1655. 4°

Wing C 7082.

T.287

948

FISHER (Edward)

A Christian caveat to the old and new sabbatarians. Or, A vindication of our gospel-festivals ... Together with questions preparatory to the better, free, and more Christian administration of the Lords Supper. London, for Edw. Blackmore, and R. Lowndes, 1655. 2 parts. 4°

Wing F 992.

T.467

949

GILPIN (John)

The Quakers shaken, or, A warning against quaking ... London, S.G. for Simon Waterson, 1655. 4°

Wing G 771.

T.469

950

HAMMOND (Henry)

An account of Mr. Cawdry's triplex diatribe concerning superstition, wil-worship, and Christmas festivall. London, J. Flesher, for Richard Royston, and for Richard Davis bookseller in Oxford, 1655. 4°

Wing H 511.

T.747

951

HODGES (Thomas) *of Kensington.*

Inaccessible glory. Or the impossibility of seeing Gods face, whilst we are in the body. Delivered in a sermon preached at the funeral of ... Sir Theodore de-Mayerne ... London, for William Leak, 1655. 4°

Wing H 2316.

T.469

952

MARVELL (Andrew)

The first anniversary of the government under his Highness the Lord Protector. [An anonymous poem.] London, Thomas Newcomb, and are to be sold by Samuel Gellibrand, 1655. 4°

Wing M 871.

T.117

953

PHILLIPS (John)

A satyr against hypocrites... [Anon.] London, for N.B., an. Dom. 1655. 4°

Wing P 2101.

T.317

954

PIERCE (Thomas)

A correct copy of some notes concerning Gods decrees, especially of reprobation. Written for the private use of a friend in Northamptonshire. And now published to prevent calumny... [Anon.] London, E. Cotes for R. Royston, 1655. 4°

Wing P 2170.

T.467

955

RATIO constitutae nuper reipublicae Angliae, Scotiae, & Hiberniae... penes D. Protectorem & Parliamentum... Ex Anglico in Latinum versa. Hagae-Comitum, typis Adriani Vlacq, 1655. 12°

A translation of A true state of the case of the Commonwealth of England...

T.499

956

TERTULLIANUS (Quintus Septimius Florens)

Tertullians apology, or defence of the Christians, against the accusations of the gentiles. Now made English by H. B. London, Tho. Harper, and are to be sold by Thomas Butler, 1655. 4°

Wing T 785.

T.96

957

W. (J.)

Romae ruina finalis, anno Dom. 1666, mundiq; finis sub quadragesimum quintum post annum... Londini, excudebat T.C. veneuntq; apud Johannem Sherlaeum, & Sam. Thomson, 1655. 4°

Wing W 67.

T.168

1656

958

BELLERS (Fulk)

Abrahams interment: or The good old mans buriall in a good old age. Opened in a sermon, at Bartholomews Exchange, July 24. 1655. at the funerall of the worshipfull John Lamotte... London: R.I. for Tho. Newberry, 1656. 4°

Wing B 1826.

T.469

959

CLARKE (William) *of North Crawley, Bucks.*

Ἀγαπαι ἀσπιλοι, or The innocent love-feast. Being a sermon preached at S. Lawrence Jury in London, the sixth day of September, anno Domini 1655. On the publick festival of the county of Hertford ... London, for William Lee, 1656. 4°

Wing C 4566.

T.514

960

DILLINGHAM (William)

Prove all things, hold fast that which is good ... Handled in two sermons at S. Maries in Cambridge ... Cambridge: John Field. And are to be sold by William Morden, 1656. 4°

Wing D 1486.

T.754

961

ENGLANDS remembrancers. Or, A word in season to all English men about their elections of the members for the approaching parliament. [London, 1656.] 4°

Wing E 3037.

T. 84

962

GILPIN (Richard)

The agreement of the associated ministers & churches of the counties of Cumberland, and Westmorland: with something for explication and exhortation annexed ... [Anon.] London, T. L. for Simon Waterson, & are sold ... by Richard Scott bookseller in Carlisle, 1656. 4°

Wing G 774.

T. 84

963

GURNALL (William)

The magistrates pourtraiture drawn from the world, and preached in a sermon at Stowe-Market in Suffolk, upon August, the 20. 1656 before the election of parliament-men for the same county ... London, for Ralph Smith, 1656. 4°

Wing G 2259.

T.469

964

HAMMOND (Henry)

Δευτεραι φροντιδες, or, A review of the Paraphrase & annotations on all the books of the New Testament. With some additions & alterations ... London, J. Flesher for R. Royston, 1656. 8°

Wing H 534.

T.386

965

HOARD (Samuel)

Gods love to man-kinde. Manifested, by disproving his absolute decree for their damnation ... [Anon.] London, for John Clark, 1656. 4°

Wing H 2201 (?)
Signature of Thomas Bowdler.

T.309

966

HUMBLE proposals to the Parliament now assembled. Whereby the profession of the civil law may be used in certain cases, to the great ease and benefit of the people ... London, E. C. for R. Royston, 1656. 4°

Wing H 3600.

T. 84

967

OWEN (John)

God's work in founding Zion, and his peoples duty thereupon. A sermon preached in the Abby Church at Westminster, at the opening of the Parliament Septemb. 17th 1656... Oxford, Leon: Lichfield, for Tho: Robinson, 1656. 4°

Wing O 758

T.469

968

PRYNNE (William)

The second part of a short demurrer to the Iewes long discontinued remitter into England ... London, Edward Thomas, 1656. 4°

Wing P 4073.

T.30

969

PRYNNE (William)

A short demurrer to the Jewes long discontinued remitter into England ... London, for Edward Thomas, 1656. 4°

Wing P 4078.

T.289

1656 (Cont'd.)

970

PRYNNE (William)

A summary collection of the principal fundamental rights, liberties, proprieties of all English freemen ... London, printed for the author, 1656. 4°

Wing P 4094.

T.122

971

RAIE (C)

Gemitus plebis: or a mournful complaint and supplication in behalf of the more weak and ignorant of the people of this nation ... London, R. Ibbitson, for Tho. Newberry, 1656. 4°

Wing R 137.

T.84

972

TAYLOR (Jeremy) *Bishop of Down and Connor.*

A further explication of the doctrine of originall sin. London, James Flesher for R. Royston, 1656. 8°

Not in Wing. Primarily intended to be inserted as chapter 7 in *Unum necessarium* (Wing T 415, q.v.); some copies were sold as separate pamphlets.

T.375

973

USSHER (James) *Archbishop of Armagh.*

The reduction of episcopacie unto the form of synodical government received in the ancient church... A true copy set forth by Nicolas Bernard... London, E.C. for R. Royston, 1656. 4°

Wing U 217.
2 copies.

T.375

1657

974

C. (R.)

A copie of a letter written by a friend, to one who would be owned for minister of that parish from whom he with-holds all ordinances but preaching ... London, for William Ley, 1657. 4°

Not in Wing.

T.84

975

CALAMY (Edmund) *the Elder.*

The city remembrancer. Or, A sermon preached to the native-citizens, of London, at their solemn assembly in Pauls on Tuesday, the 23 of June, A.D. MDCLVII... London, S.G. for John Rothwell, 1657. 8°

Wing C 228.

T.447

976

DRAYTON (Thomas)

The proviso or condition of the promises, the strait, but the straight-way that leadeth unto happiness. Being the substance of two sermons preached at Wilton, March the first. 1656 ... London; Tho. Newcomb, 1657. 4°

Wing D 2148.

T.514

977

FIENNES (Nathaniel)

The speech of the right honourable the Lord Fiennes, Commissioner of the great seal; made before his Highness and both houses of Parliament ... London, Henry Hills, and John Field, 1657. 4°

Wing F 881.

T. 84

978

HAMMOND (Henry)

Some profitable directions both for priest & people, in two sermons preached before these evil times ... London, J. F. for R. Royston, 1657. 8°

Wing H 605.

T.386

979

PHILIP IV, *King of Spain.*

A proclamation of his Majesty the King of Spaine, For the conservation of the contrabando, revocation of the permissions, prohibition of the use of the merchandises ... and reformation of vestures ... Translated out of Spanish. London, G, Dawson, for Iohn Sweeting, anno 1657. 4°

Wing P 1986 A.

T.16

980

The WHOLE business of Sindercome, from first to last. It being a perfect narrative of his carriage, during the time of his imprisonment in the Tower of London... London, Tho. Newcomb, 1657. 4°

Wing W 2054.

T.287

1658

981

GILPIN (Richard)

The temple re-built. A discourse on Zachary 6,13. Preached at a generall meeting of the associated ministers of the county of Cumberland ... London, E. T. for Luke Fawne, and are to be sold by Richard Scott, bookseller in Carlisle, 1658. 4°

Wing G 778.

T.112

982

HARDY (Nathaniel)

The olive-branch presented to the native citizens of London, in a sermon preached at S. Paul's Church, May 27 ... London, J.G. for John Clark, 1658. 4°

Wing H 737.

T.469

983

HEYDON (John)

[Hebrew] A new method of Rosie Crucian physick: wherein is shewed the cause; and therewith their experienced medicines for the cure of all diseases ... London, for Thomas Lock, 1658. 4°

Wing H 1672.

T.321

984

HEYLYN (Peter)

Respondet Petrus: or, the answer of Peter Heylyn to so much of Dr. Bernard's book entituled, The judgement of the late Primate of Ireland, &c, as he is made a party to by the said Lord Primate in the point of the Sabbath ... London, for R, Royston, 1658. 4°

Wing H 1732.
2 copies.

T.375 T.127

985

PIERCE (Thomas)

Ἀυτοκαταχρισις, or, Self-condemnation, exemplified in Mr. Whitfield, Mr. Barlee, and Mr. Hickman. With occasional reflexions on Mr Calvin, Mr Beza, Mr Zuinglius, Mr Piscator, Mr Rivet, and Mr Rollock... London, J.G. for R. Royston, 1658. 2 parts. 4°

Wing P 2164.

T.467

986

PIERCE (Thomas)

Ἐαυτουτιμωρουμενος, or the self-revenger, exemplified in Mr. William Barlee: by way of rejoynder to the first part of his reply... London, R. Daniel, for Richard Royston, 1658. 4°

Wing P 2181.
Wanting title-page and final leaf.

T.23

987

PIERCE (Thomas)

Φιλαλληλια. Or, The grand characteristick whereby a man may be known to be Christ's disciple. Delivered in a sermon at St. Paul's, before the gentlemen of Wilts. Nov. 10. 1658... London, J.G. for R. Royston, 1658. 4°

Wing P 2189.

T.469

988

POOLE (Matthew)

A model for the maintaining of students of choice abilities at the university, and principally in order to the ministry... Printed anno Domini, 1658. 4°

Wing P 2842.

T.375

989

PRYNNE (William)

A plea for the Lords, and House of Peers: or, A full, necessary, seasonable, enlarged vindication, of the just, antient hereditary right of the lords, peers, and barons of this realm to sit, vote, judge in all the Parliaments of England... London: printed for the author, 1658. 4°

Wing P4034.
Wanting the title-page and other pages.

T.30

990

PRYNNE (William)

A probable expedient for present and future publique settlement... By a well-wishing philopater... London, printed in the year 1658. 4°

Wing P 4041.

T.287

991

PRYNNE (William)

The subjection of all traytors, rebels, as well peers, as commons in Ireland, to the laws, statutes, and trials by juries of good and lawfull men of England ... London, J. Leach for the author, 1658. 4°

Wing P 4090.

T.30

992

SANDERSON (*Sir* William)

Peter pursued, or Dr, Heylin overtaken, arrested, and arraigned upon his three appendixes ... Patch'd together in his Examen historicum, for which the doctor is brought to censure ... London, Tho. Leach, 1658. 4°

Wing S 649.
First two leaves only.

T.96

993

SANDERSON (*Sir* William)

Post-haste: a reply to Peter (Doctor Heylin's) appendix; to his treatise intituled Respondet Petrus &c. London, printed for the use of the author, 1658. 4°

Wing S 650.

T.96

994

SHAW (Samuel)

Holy things for holy men: or, The lawyers plea non-suited... in some Christian reproofe and pitie expressed towards Mr Prynn's book; intituled, The Lord's supper briefly vindicated... By S.S. London, for Tho. Parkhurst, 1658. 4°

Wing S 3037.
T.289

1659

995

ANNESLEY (Arthur) *1st Earl of Anglesey.*

England's confusion: or A true and impartial relation of the late traverses of state in England; with the counsels leading thereunto ... Written by one of the few English men that are left in England ... London, printed in the year of our Lord, 1659. 4°

Wing A 3167.

T.287

996

An APOLOGIE and vindication of the major part of the members of Parliament excluded from sitting and speaking for themselves and the Common-wealth ... London, Tho. Ratcliffe, 1659. 4°

Wing A 3542.
T. 15

997

The ARMY'S plea for their present practice: tendered to the consideration of all ingenuous and impartial men ... London, Henry Hills, 1659. 4°

Wing A 3716.

T.287

998

B. (I.)

A new map of England. Or, Forty six quaeries ... London, printed in the year, 1659. 4°

Wing B 86.

T.271

999

BAGSHAW (Edward) *the Younger.*

A practicall discourse concerning Gods decrees... Oxford, Hen. Hall, for Tho. Robinson, 1659. 2 parts. 4°

Wing B 420.

T.467

1000

BAGSHAW (Edward) *the Younger.*

A true and perfect narrative of the differences between Mr Busby and Mr Bagshawe... Written long since, and now published, in answer to the calumnies of Mr. Pierce. London, A.M. in the year 1659. 4°

Wing B 426.

T.23

1001

BILS (Louis de)

The coppy of a certain large act [obligatory] of Yonker Lovis de Bils, Lord of Koppens-damme, Bonen, &c. Touching the skill of a better way of anatomy of mans body... London, 1659. 8°

Wing B 2914.

T.447

1002

BRADSHAW'S ghost: being a dialogue between the said ghost, and an apparition of the late King Charles... [London], printed, 1659. 4°

Wing B 4164.
Wanting title-page.

T.509

1003

A BRIEF account of the meeting, proceedings, and exit of the committee of safety. Taken in short-hand by a clerk to the said committee. London: printed for Thomas Williamson, 1659. 4°

Wing B 4510

T. 15

1004

BURGESS (Cornelius)

A case concerning the buying of bishops lands with, the lawfulness thereof. And the difference between the contractors for sale of those lands, and the Corporation of Wells ... London, printed in the year of our Lord, 1659. 4°

Wing B 5670.

T. 23

1005

BUTLER (Samuel) *Poet.*

Mola asinaria, or, The unreasonable and insupportable burthen now press'd upon the shoulders of this groaning nation... By William Prynne [actually by Samuel Butler]... Printed at London, in the year MDCLVIX [i.e. 1659]. 4°

Wing P 4012.

T.289

1006

C. (C.) *of Gray's Inn.*

A word to purpose: or, a Parthian dart, shot back to 1642. and from thence shot back again to 1659. swiftly glancing upon some remarkable occurrences of the times... [Anon.] [No imprint, 1659?] 7pp. 4°

Not in Wing (cf. W3566/7).

T.508

1007

The CHARACTER or ear-mark of Mr. William Prynne bencher of Lincolnes Inne, and author of a great many late scandalous pasquils ... 2nd ed. corrected and inlarged. London: printed in the year 1659. 4°

Wing C 2033.

T.290

1008

COLE (William)

Severall proposals humbly tendered to the consideration of those that are in authority, for the ease, security, & prosperity of this Common-wealth ... London: printed 1659. 4°

Wing C 5040.

T. 15

1009

A COPIE of quaeries, or, A comment upon the life, and actions of the grand tyrant and his complices; Oliver the first and last of that name ... Printed in Utopia, that shall be 1659. To be sold by the haukers at St. Magnus, and Pye-Corner. 4°

Wing C 6197.

T.271

1010

CROMWELL (Richard)

The speech of his Highness the Lord Protector, made to both houses of Parliament... the 27th of January 1658. As also the speech of the Right Honourable Nathaniel Lord Fiennes... London, Henry Hills and John Field, [1659]. 4°

Wing C 7191.
Fiennes' speech is catalogued separately.

T.84

1011

D. (E.)

Complaints and queries upon Englands misery: acted Octob. 13, 1659. By some officers of the Army, against the Parliament of the Common-wealth of England. By a true lover of the lawes and liberties of England. E. D. London, printed by J. C., 1659. 4°

Wing D 14.

T. 15

1012

The DECLARATION of the Army in Ireland. Declaring their resolutions for a free Parliament, and the re-admitting of all the members secluded in 1648. and for the establishing of a learned and orthodox ministry ... Printed at Dublin, and now re-printed at London, by S. Griffin, for John Playford, 1659. 4°

Wing D 634.

T. 15

1013

A DECLARATION of the general council of the officers of the army: agreed upon at Wallingford-house, 27th Octob. 1659 ... London, Henry Hills, 1659. 4°

Wing D 673.

T.287

1014

A DECLARATION of the officers of the army, inviting the members of the Long Parliament, who continued sitting till the 20th of April, 1653. to return to the exercise and discharge of their trust ... London, Henry Hills, for him and William Mountfourt, 1659. 4°

Wing D 730.

T.287

1015

DENHAM (*Sir* John)

A panegyrick on his Excellency the Lord General George Monck: commander in chief of all the forces in England, Scotland, and Ireland. [Anon.] London, for Richard Marriot, 1659. 4°

Wing D 1004.

T.407

1016

DU MOULIN (Louis)

Proposals, and reasons whereon some of them are grounded: humbly presented to the Parliament towards the settling of a religious and godly government in the Commonwealth ... London, Iohn Redmayne, 1659. 4°

Wing D 2552.

T. 15

1017

EIGHT and thirty queries propounded by one that is setting forth sail, and desires to steer his course aright ... Touching things past, present, and to come ... London, for Richard Andrews, 1659. 4°

Wing E 257.

T.271

1018

EIGHTEEN new court-quaeries humbly offered to the serious consideration, and mature deliberation of all the good honest hearted people of the three nations... By several well-wishers to our settlement. London, printed in the year 1659. 4°

Wing E 263.

T.271

1019

ENGLAND. *Parliament.*

A declaration of the Parliament assembled at Westminster ... London, John Streater and John Macock, 1659. 4°

Wing E 1491

T.287

1020

ENGLANDS repentance Englands only remedy: religiously propounded in a serious resolve of this enquiry, Q. What is to be desired by all such as wish well to England? In a letter written by a minister in London, in answer to one sent from a worthy member of the late Long Parliament. London, D. Maxwell, 1659. 4°

Wing E 3041.

T.271

1021

ENGLANDS safety in the laws supremacy. London: printed in the year 1659. 4°

Wing E 3044.
2 copies.

T.388   T. 15

1022

FEAKE (Christopher)

A beam of light, shining in the midst of much darkness and confusion: being (with the benefit of retrospection) an essay toward the stating (and fixing upon its true and proper basis) the best cause under heaven ... London, J. C. for Livewell Chapman, 1659. 4°

Wing F 567.

T.375

1023

FELL (John) *Bishop of Oxford.*

The interest of England stated: or A faithful and just account of the aims of all parties now pretending ... [Anon.] Printed in the year, 1659. 4°

Wing F 613.

T. 15

1024

FIENNES (Nathaniel)

The speech of the right honourable Nathaniel Lord Fiennes, one of the lord keepers of the great seale of England, made before his Highnesse, and both houses of Parliament: on Thursday the 27th. of January, 1658 ... London, for Henry Twyford, 1659. 4°

Wing F 882.

T. 84

1025

FLEETWOOD (Charles)

The Lord General Fleetwoods answer to the humble representation of Collonel Morley, and some other late officers of the Army ... [No imprint], 1659. 4°

Wing F 1239.

T. 15

1026

FOURTY four queries to the life of Queen Dick [i.e. Richard Cromwell]. By one who will at any time work a job of journey-work, to serve his countrey. Printed in the year, 1659. 4°

Wing F 1622.

T.271

1027

FRESE (James)

The out-cry¦ and just appeale of the inslaved people of England, made to the Right Honourable the Parliament ... London, T. Fawcet, 1659. 4°

Wing F 2197 D.

T. 15

1028

The GAME is up: or, XXXI new quaeries and orders; fitted for the present state of affairs, and recommended to the councell of officers...
Printed in the year 1659. 4°

Wing G 189.

T.271

1029

GAUDEN (John) *Bishop of Worcester.*

A petitionary remonstrance, presented to O. P. Feb. 4. 1655. By J. G. ... in behalf of many thousands his distressed brethren (minister of the gospel, and other good schollars) who were deprived of all publique imployment ... by his declaration, Jan. 1. 1655 ... London, Thomas Milbourn for Andrew Crook, 1659. 4°

Wing G 365.

T. 84

1030

A GENERAL, or, no general over the present army of the Common-wealth: in twenty two queries briefly handled. Printed in the year, 1659. 4°

Wing G 505.

T.271

1031

GERY (William)

Proposals for reformation of abuses and subtilties in practise against the law and in acandall of it. London, for William Shears, 1659. 4°

Wing G 622.

T. 15

1032

HARRINGTON (James) *the Elder.*

Aphorisms political. London: J. C. for Henry Fletcher,[1659.] 4°

Wing H 804.

T.287

1033

HARRINGTON (James) *the Elder.*

Valerius and Publicola: or, The true form of a popular commonwealth extracted e puris naturalibus ... London: J. C. for Henry Fletcher, 1659. 4°

Wing H 824.

T.277

1034

HOWELL (James)

A brief admonition of some of the inconveniences of all the most famous governments known to the world: with their comparisons together. [The preface signed J. H.] London printed, 1659. 4°

Wing H 3058.
2 copies.

T.277 T. 15

1035

The HUMBLE petition and addresse of the officers of the Army, to the Parliament of the Common-wealth of England ... London, Henry Hills, for him and Francis Tyton, 1659. 4°

Wing H 3428.

T. 84

1036

The HUMBLE petition of divers well-affected persons, delivered the 6th day of July, 1659. to the supreme authority, the Parliament of the Common-wealth of England ... London, for Thomas Brewster, 1659. 4°

Wing H 3463.

T. 84

1037

The HUMBLE petition of many inhabitants, in and about the city of London, Presented to the Parliament by Mr. Sam. Moyer and others, May 12. 1659. Together with the answer of the Parliament thereunto. London,for Tho. Brewster & Livewell Chapman, 1659. 4°

Wing H 3471.

T. 84

1038

The HUMBLE representation and petition of the officers of the Army, to the Parliament of the Commonwealth of England ... London, Henry Hills, 1659. 4°

Wing H 3634.

T. 84

1039

The HUMBLE representation of some officers of the Army, to the Right Honourable Lieutenant General Fleetwood. [No imprint], 1659. 4°

Wing H 3639.

T. 15

1040

INVISIBLE John made visible: or, A grand pimp of tyranny portrayed, in Barkstead's arraignment at the barre, where he stands impeached of high treason ... Printed at London, in the year 1659. 4°

cf. Wing B 812.

T.287

1041

LAMBERT (John)

The Lord Lambert's letter to the Right Honorable the Speaker of the Parliament, concerning the victory which it hath pleased God to give the forces of this Commonwealth over the rebels under Sir George Booth in Cheshire ... London, Tho. Newcomb, 1659. 4°

Wing L 237.

T.15

1042

LAMBERT (John)

Colonell Iohn Lambert's speech at the council of state, or the Lord President's report unto the Parliament, of the discourse of Colonell Iohn Lambert before the Council. London, Iohn Redmayne, 1659. 4°

Wing L 243.

T.15

1043

LET me speake too? Or, Eleven queries, humbly proposed to the officers of the army concerning, the late alteration of government ... London, printed 1659. 4°

Wing L 1329.

T.271

1044

A LETTER from the commanders and officers of the Fleet of this Common-wealth, unto General Monck in Scotland ... London, Sarah Griffin for Thomas Hewer, 1659. 4°

Wing L 1516.

T.15

1045

A LETTER of comfort to Richard Cromwell Esq; alias Lord Richard, alias Richard Protector. Sent him since the alteration of his titles and our government: from a servant of his late Highness ... London, printed 1659. 4°

Wing L 1572.

T.15

1046

A LETTER of November the 16th: from an eminent officer in the Army at Edenburgh to a friend at London, declaring the true number of the horse and foot now under General Monck ... Printed in the year 1659. 4°

Wing L 1573 C.

T.15

1047

A LETTER sent to the Right Honourable, William Lenthal Esq; Speaker of the Parliament ... concerning the securing of Windsor Castle for the Parliament ... London, John Streater, 1659. 4°

Wing L 1624 (=B 6274).

T.15

1048

LONDON.

The humble petition of the Lord Major, aldermen, and Common-Council of the city of London, presented to the Parliament on Thursday June 2. 1659. Together with the answer of the House thereunto. London, D. Maxwell, 1659. 4°

Wing H 3549.

T.84

1049

LONDON.

Two letters; the one sent by the Lord Mayor, aldermen, and Common Council of London, to his Excellency, the Lord Gen. Monck... The other, his Excellencies answer thereunto. London, John Macock, 1659. 4°

Wing T 3481.

T.287

1050

LOYAL queries, humbly tendred to the serious consideration of the Parliament, and army. By a peaceable-minded man, and a true lover of his country. London, printed in the year 1659. 4°

Wing L 3361.

T.271

1051

MONCK (George) *Duke of Albemarle.*

General Monck's last letter to his Excellency the Lord Fleetwood. Declaring his resolution to send Col. Wilkes ... by way of treaty, in order to a happy union between the two armies of England and Scotland ... London, for Francis Smith, 1659. 4°

Wing A 846.

T.15

1052

MONCK (George) *Duke of Albemarle.*

A letter of November 12. from General Monck, directed (& delivered) to the Lord Mayor, Aldermen, and Common Council of the City of London; inciting them ... to give their assistance, for redemption of the almost lost liberties of England. Printed in the year, 1659. 4°

Wing A 860.

T.15

1053

MONCK (George) *Duke of Albemarle.*

The speech and declaration of his Excellency the Lord Generall Monck delivered at White-hall upon Tuesday the 21. of February 1659 ... London, S. Griffin, for John Playford, 1659. 4°

Wing A 867.

T.287

1054

A NEGATIVE voyce: or, A check for your check: being a message (by a black-rod) of non-concurrence, for the ballancing-house, or co-ordinate snnate: fairly discussing the security it can give to the good old cause ... Printed in the year, 1659. 4°

Wing N 414.

T.15

1055

NINETEEN cases of conscience. Submissively tendred to Mr. Hugh Petrs, and the rest of his fellow commissioners, the Triars. By sundry weak brethren. London, printed in the year 1659. 4°

Wing N 1163.

T.271

1056

The NORTHERN queries from the Lord Gen: Monck his quarters; sounding an allarum, to all loyal hearts, and free-born English-men ... Printed in the year of Englands confusions [1659?], and are to be sold at the sign of Wallingford-House, right against a free Parliament .4°

Wing N 1297.

T.271

1057

ONE and thirty new orders of Parliament, and the Parliaments declaration: published for the satisfaction of the people off the three nations ... Together with the Parliaments ghost ... Printed in the year, 1659. 4°

Wing O 331.

T.287

1058

ONE and twenty Chester queries, or, Occasional scruples, reflecting upon the late memorable affairs at the places adjacent to, and in Cheshire. By several of the officers and souldiers then under the conduct of the Lord Lambert ... London, printed in the year, 1659. 4°

Wing O 332.

T.271

1059

OWEN (John)

Unto the questions sent me last night, I pray accept of the ensuing answer, under the title of two questions concerning the power of the supream magistrate about religion, and the worship of God ... London, for Francis Tyton, 1659. 4°

Wing O 820.
2 copies.

T.493   T.271

1060

The PARLIAMENTS plea: or XX. reasons for the union of the Parliament & Army presented to publick consideration ... Printed in the year, 1659. 4°

Wing P 521.

T.23

1061

PIERCE (Thomas)

Ἔμψυχον νεκρον. Or the lifelesness of life on the hether side of immortality. With (A timely caveat against procrastination.) Briefly expressed and applyed in a sermon preached at the funerall of Edward Peyto of Chesterton in Warwick-shire... London, for R. Royston, 1659. 4°

Wing P 2182.

T.469

1062

PRIDE (Thomas)

The last words of Thomas Lord Pride, taken in short hand by T. S. late clerk to his lordship's brew-house. [London, 1659?] 4°

Wing P 3411.

T.81

1063

PRYNNE (William)

An answer to a proposition in order to the proposing of a commonwealth or democracy. Proposed by friends to the commonwealth by Mr. Harringtons consent... [Anon.] Londoon, printed in the year 1659. 4°

Wing P 3889.

T.277

1064

PRYNNE (William)

A brief necessary vindication of the old and new secluded members, from the false malicious calumnies ... 1. Of John Rogers, in his un-christian concertation with Mr. Pryne, and others. 2. Of M: Nedham in his Interest will not lie... London, Edward Thomas, 1659. 4°

Wing P 3913.

T.290

1065

PRYNNE (William)

Concordia discors, or the dissonant harmony of sacred publique oathes, protestations, leagues, covenants, ingagement, lately taken by many time-serving saints... London, for Edward Thomas, 1659. 4°

Wing P 3928.

T.290

1066

PRYNNE (William)

The privileges of Parliament which the members, army, and this Kingdom have taken the protestation and covenant to maintain. Reprinted for consideration and confirmation on the 5th. of January, 1659... [Anon.] [London, 1659.] 4°

Wing P 4040.

T.270

1067

PRYNNE (William)

The re-publicans and other superious good old cause. Briefly and truly anatomized... Printed in the year of our Lord, 1659. 4°

Wing P 4052.
The word "superious" has been altered to "spurious".

T.289

1068

PRYNNE (William)

Ten considerable quaeries concerning tithes ... London, for Edward Thomas, 1659. 4°

Wing P 4100.

T.289

1069

PRYNNE (William)

Ten quaeres, upon the ten new commandements of the general council of the officers of the armies Decemb. 22. 1659. [Anon.] [London, 1659.] 4°

Wing P 4101.

T.287

1070

PRYNNE (William)

A true and perfect narrative of what was done, spoken by and between Mr. Prynne, the old and newly forcibly late secluded members, the army officers, and those now sitting, both in the Commons lobby, house, and elswhere; on Saturday and Monday last... Printed in the year 1659. 4°

Wing P 4113.

T.317

1071

PRYNNE (William)

The true good old cause rightly stated, and the false un-cased. [Anon.] [London, 1659.] 4°

Wing P 4114.

T.287

1072

QUAEREES on the proposalls of the officers of the armie, to the Parliament... & tending towards the clearing and settlement of the constitution, for securing the peace of the three nations. Printed in the year of our Lord, 1659. 4°

Wing Q 170.
2 copies.

T.271   T.287

1073

RETZ (Jean François Paul) *Cardinal*.

France no friend to England. Or, The resentments of the French upon the success of the English. As it is expressed in a most humble and important remonstrance to the King of France, upon the surrendring of the maritime ports of Flanders into the hands of the English... [Anon.] Translated out of French. London, printed in the year, 1659. 4°

Wing R 1186.
Incomplete

T.321

1074

RIX (John)

Innocencie vindicated. Or, A brief answer to part of a scandalous paper, entituled A true narrative of the occasion and causes of the late Lord General Cromwel's anger against Lieutenant Colonel Joyce ... Printed at London, by J. C., 1659. 4°

Wing R 1569.

T.15

1075

ROGERS (John) *Fifth Monarchy Man*.

Mr. Pryn's good old cause stated and stunted 10. years ago. Or, A most dangerous designe, in mistating the good, by mistaking the bad old cause... [Anon.] London, J.C. for L. Chapman, 1659. 4°

Wing R 1812.

T.290

1076

A SEASONABLE question soberly proposed, argued and resolved. London, printed 1659. 4°

Wing S 2240.

T.271

1077

A SEASONABLE speech, made by a worthy member of Parliament in the House of Commons, concerning the Other House. March 1659. [Attributed to Silas Titus and to the Earl of Shaftesbury.] [London, 1659.] 4°

Wing S 2898.

T.129

1078

SEEK and you shall find; or, Certaine queryes of highest import. Most humbly tendered to be considered on as no little conducing to the laying a foundation of a more rigrteous [sic] government ... Printed in the year, of care and fear, [1659]. 4°

Wing S 2409.

T.271

1079

SEVERAL resolves prepared by the commanding junto to pass the House. Printed in the year, 1659. 4°

Wing S 2810.
Incomplete.

T.15

1080

SMITH (Thomas) *Librarian of Cambridge University*.

The Quaker disarm'd, or a true relation of a late publick dispute held at Cambridge. By three eminent Quakers, against one scholar of Cambridge [i.e. Thomas Smith]... London, J.C., 1659. 4°

Wing S 4227.
2 copies.

T.23   T.794

1081

STREATER (John)

The continuation of this session of Parliament, justified; and the action of the Army touching that affair defended ... By J. S. London, printed, 1659. 4°

Wing S 5945.

T.15

1082

STUBBE (Henry)

A light shining out of darknes: or Occasional queries submitted to the judgment of such as would enquire into the true state of things in our times ... [Anon.] London, printed in the year 1659. 4°

Wing S 6056.

T.271

1083

STUBBE (Henry)

A vindication of that prudent and honourable knight, Sir Henry Vane, from the lyes and calumnies of Mr. Richard Baxter ... By a true friend and servant of the Commonwealth of England ... London: for Livewel Chapman, 1659. 4°

Wing S 6068.

T.15

1084

THREE speeches made to the right honorable the Lord Maior, aldermen, and Common-Council of London, by the Lord Whitlock, Lord Fleetwood, [and] Lord Disbrowe ... London, printed in the year, 1659. 4°

Wing T 1120 A.

T.84

1659 (Cont'd.)

1085

TITUS (Silas)

Killing, no murder. With some additions briefly
discourst in three questions, fit for publick
view; to deter and prevent single persons, and
councils, from usurping supream power. By William
Allen [i.e. Silas Titus] ... London, printed 1659.
4°

Wing T 1311.
2 copies.

T.15 T.83

1086

TREVANIAN (John)

The fair dealer: or, A modest answer to the sober
letter of his Excellency, the Lord General Monck
... By the private hand of a Gent. of Devon.
London: for James Hanzen, 1659. 4°

Wing T 2128.

T.15

1087

The TRUE and exact particulars of the articles of
peace & mariage agreed confirmed and published at
the heads of both the armies of the two great
monarchs of Europe ... Sent in a letter from an
eminent person in France to an honourable lord in
England ... London, printed in the year 1659. 4°

Wing T 2437.

T.81

1088

A TRUE narrative of the proceedings in parliament,
councell of state, general councell of the army,
and committee of safetie; from the 22. of Septemb.
untill this present ... London, John Redmayne,
1659. 4°

Wing E 2382.

T.287

1089

TWELVE queries humbly proposed to the consideration
of the Parliament & army, for the better security
of, and advantage to the present government...
By divers well-affected persons. London: printed
1659. 4°

Wing T 3402.

T.271

1090

TWELVE seasonable quaeries proposed to all true
zealous protestants and English free-men: occasioned by our late and present revolutions... Printed
in the year, 1659. 4°

Wing T 3403.

T.271

1091

TWENTY five modest, and sober queries, propounded
at the coffee club; concerning parliament, army,
common-council of London, and universities, &c.
London, printed in the year, 1659. 4°

Not in Wing.

T.271

1092

XXV queries: modestly and humbly, and yet sadly
and seriously propounded, to the Commons of England,
and their representatives: and likewise to the
army in this juncture of affairs... London: for
L. Chapman, 1659. 4°

Wing T 3409.

T.271

1093

TWENTY four queries touching the Parliament & army,
and the interest of the royal-party, and others of
this nation... By several friends to publick good.
Printed in the year, 1659. 4°

Wing T 3410.

T.271

1094

TWENTY quaking queries, having been clowded, and
now brought forth to light. By Mad-Tom. London,
for Robert Page, 1659. 4°

Wing T 3415.

T.271

1095

TWENTY seven queries relating to the general good
of the three nations. Which will neither please
mad-men nor displease rational men. London, printed
in the year, 1659. 4°

Wing T 3416.

T.271

1096

XXIII. punctilio's or caprichio's of state among
the present grandees... By Count Gundomar.
Printed at Madrid in the year, 1659. 4°

Not in Wing.

T.271

1097

The UNHAPPY marks-man: or, Twenty three queries
offered to the consideration of the people of these
nations. Printed in the year, 1659. 4°

Wing U 69.

T.15

1098

UNIVERSITY queries, in a gentle touch by the by.
Cambridge; printed in the year 1659. 4°

Wing U 80.

T.271

1099

A VINDICATION of the London apprentices petition.
And the legality of their subscriptions asserted.
London, printed in the year 1659. 4°

Wing V 513.

T.15

1100

WITHER (George)

Epistolium-vagum-prosa-metricum: or, An epistle at
randome ... Printed at London, in the year 1659.
4°

Wing W 3156.

T.15

1101

YOUR servant gentlemen, or What think you of a
query or two more? London, printed in the year
1659. 4°

Wing Y 202.

T.271

1660

1102

The ANATOMY of Dr. Gauden's Idolized non-sence
and blasphemy, in his pretended analysis, or
setting forth the true sense of the Covenant...
London: printed in the year 1660. 4°

Wing A 3055.

T.465

1103

An APOLOGY for purchases of lands late of
bishops deans and chapters. [London, 1660.] fol.

Wing A 3547.

T.379

1104

ARDERNE (James)

The kingdom of England the best Commonwealth. A
discourse concerning obedience to kingly
government ... London, J. H. for Matthew Keinton,
1660. 4°

Wing A 3627.

T.277

1105

ASTON (Sir Thomas)

A collection of sundry petitions presented to the
Kings most excellent Majesty, As also, to the two
most honourable houses, now assembled in
Parliament ... Collected by a faithfull lover of
the Church ... [Anon.] London, T. Mabb for
William Shears, 1660. 4°

Wing Q A 4075 A.

T. 23

1106

BAGSHAW (Edward) the Elder.

A just vindication of the questioned part of the
reading of Edward Bagshaw, Esq; an apprentice of
the common law. Had in the Middle Temple Hall
the 24th day of February ... 1639 ... With a true
narrative of the cause of silencing the reader by
the then Archbishop of Canterbury ... London,
[printed], [1660]. 4°

Wing B 396.
Title-page broken.

T.247

1107

BAGSHAW (Edward) The Younger.

The great question concerning things indifferent
in religious worship, briefly stated; and tendred
to the consideration of all sober and impartiall men.
[Anon.] 3rd ed ... London, printed in the year,
1660. 4°

Wing B 414.

T.142

1108

BAXTER (Richard)

The life of faith, as it is the evidence of things
unseen. A sermon preached (contractedly) before
the King at White-hall, upon July the 22th 1660...
London, R.W. and A.M. for Francis Tyton and Jane
Underhill; and are to be sold... by Nevil Simmons
at Kederminster, 1660. 4°

Wing B 1299

T.669

1109

BERNARD (Nicholas)

A letter of Dr. Bernards to a friend of his at
court... [No imprint, 1660?] 4°

Wing B 2010.

T.23

1110

CALFINE (Gyles)

The Book of Common Prayer confirmed by sundry acts
of Parliament, and briefly vindicated against the
contumelious slanders of the fanatique party,
tearming it porrage... London, T.M. for William
Potter, 1660. 4°

Wing C 293.

T.23

1111

CAMBRIDGE. University.

Academiae Cantabrigiensis Σωστρα. Sive, ad Carolum
II reducem, de regnis ipsi, musis per ipsum feliciter
restitutis gratulatio. Cantabrigiae, excudebat
Joannes Field, 1660. 4°

Wing C 333.

T.407

1112

CAMPANELLA (Tommaso)

Thomas Campanella ... his advice to the King of
Spain for attaining the universal monarchy of the
world ... Translated into English by Ed. Chilmead
... With an admonitorie preface by William Prynne.
London, for Philemon Stephens, [1660]. 4°

Wing C 400 (including C 401).
The title page of A discourse of the Spanish monarchy
is dated 1654.

T.122

1113

The CASE of the purchasers of publick lands, fee-
farms, &c. stated: or a plea for such purchasers
enjoying their purchased estates, and for the
payment of publick faith debts. London, for L.H.,
1660. 4°

Wing C 1150.

T.465

1114

CHARLES II, King of England.

His Maiesties letter to his Excellency the Lord
General Monck, to be communicated to the officers
of the Army ... London, John Macock, 1660. 4°

Wing C 3101.

T. 23

1115

A COFFIN for the good old cause; or, A sober word by way of caution to the Parliament and Army, or such in both as have prayed, fought, and bled for its preservation ... London, printed for the author, 1660. 4°

Wing C 4889.

T.23

1116

COMPLAINTS concerning corruptions and grievances in church-government. Dedicated and directed to the Kings most excellent Majesty ... By certain peaceably affected presbyters, of the Church of England ... Printed in the year 1660. 4°

Not in Wing.

T.24

1117

CONYERS (Tobias)

A pattern of mercy. Opened in a sermon at St. Pauls, before the ... Lord Mayor, and the Lord General Monck. February 12. 1659. London, M. I., 1660. 4°

Wing C 5994.

T.234

1118

The COPPY of a letter to Generall Monck. London, printed, 1660. 4°

Wing C 6163.

T.23

1119

CRADOCKE (Francis)

An expedient for taking away all impositions, and for raising a revenue without taxes ... London, for Henry Seile, 1660. 4°

Wing C 6742.

T.373

1120

CROFTON (Zachary)

Ἀναληψις, or Saint Peters bonds abide: for rhetorick worketh no release, is evidenced in a serious and sober consideration of Dr. John Gauden's sence and solution of the Solemn League and Covenant ... London, for Ralph Smith, 1660. 4°

Wing C 6984.

T.465

1121

DUNCON (Eleazar)

Eleazaris Dunconi ss. theol. apud Britannos professoris celeberrimi Carolo I° Τρισμακαριστω a sacris de adoratione Dei versus altare. Determinatio Cantabrigiae habita Martij 15 1633. Pro gradu doctoratus. Editio postuma. [No imprint], 1660. 16°

Wing D 2601.

T.458

1122

ENGLAND. *Laws, Statutes.*

Acts of Parliament now in force, establishing the religion of the Church of England. London, for Robert Pawley, 1660. 4°

Wing E 1166.

T.465

1123

ENGLAND. *Parliament.*

The standard of common liberty: or, The petition of right: exhibited to his late Majestie K. Charles the I .., by the Lords spiritual and temporal, and Commons in Parliament assembled ... London; printed, and are to be sold at several book-sellers shops in London and Westminster-Hall, 1660. 4°

Wing S 5202.

T.23

1124

ENGLAND. *Parliament. House of Lords.*

The humble answer of the House of Peers to his Majesties gracious letter and declaration ... London, John Macock, and Francis Tyton, 1660. 4°

Wing E 2806.

T. 23

1125

FANATIQUE queries, propos'd to the present assertors of the good old cause. London, printed for Praise-God-Barebones, the Rumps leather-seller, [1660]. 4°

Wing F 399.

T.271

1126

FEATLEY (Daniel)

The league illegal. Wherein the late Solemn league and Covenant is seriously examined ... Written long since in prison, by Daniel Featley ... Published by John Faireclough, vulgo Featley ... London: for R. Royston, 1660. 4°

Wing F 591.

T.23

1127

FINCH (Heneage) *Earl of Nottingham.*

An exact and most impartial accompt of the indictment, arraignment, trial, and judgment of ... nine and twenty regicides, the murderers of his late Majesty ... [Anon.] London, for Andrew Crooke, and Edward Powel, 1660. 4°

Wing N 1403.
Wanting title-page.

T.120

1128

FOX (George)

Margarita in Anglia reperta pro pauperibus, afflictis, & dispersis, in gentibus exteris ... [By] G. F. Pro Roberto Wilson, apud officinam ejus, 1660. 4°

Wing F 1861.

T.321

1129

FOX (George)

The pearle found in England this is for the poor distressed, scattered ones in forraigne nations. From the royall seed of God, and heires of salvation, called Quakers ... [By] G. F. London, for Robert Wilson, 1660. 4°

Wing F 1880.

T.321

1130

GAUDEN (John) *Bishop of Worcester.*

Ἀναλυσις. The loosing of Saint Peter's bands; setting forth the true sense and solution of the covenant in point of conscience, so far as it relates to the government of the Church by episcopacy... London, J. Macock, for Andrew Crook, 1660. 4°

Wing G 341.

T.378

1131

GAUDEN (John) *Bishop of Worcester.*

Antisacrilegus. Or, a defensative against the plausible pest, or guilded poyson, of that nameless paper... which tempts the Kings Majestie by the offer of five hundred thousand pounds, to make good by an Act of Parliament to the purchasers of bishops, deans and chapters lands, their illegal bargain, for ninety nine years. London, J.B. for Andrew Crook, 1660. 4°

Wing G 343.
2 copies.

T.465 T.145

1132

GAUDEN (John) *Bishop of Worcester.*

Certain scruples and doubts of conscience about taking the solemne league and covenant; first printed in the yeare 1643 ... Being now reprinted and in all love tendered to the consideration of Sir Lawrence Bromfield and Mr. Zach. Grofton ... [Anon.] London, printed in the year, 1660. 4°

Wing G 346.

T.201

1133

GAUDEN (John) *Bishop of Worcester.*

Κακουργοι sive medicastri: slight healings of publique hurts. Set forth in a sermon preached in St. Pauls Church, London, before the ... Lord Mayor, Lord General, aldermen, common council, and companies of the honourable city of London, February 28. 1659 ... London, for Andrew Crook, 1660. 4°

Wing G 361   Annotated by the author.

T.467

1134

GAUDEN (John) *Bishop of Worcester.*

The religious and loyal protestation of John Gauden ... against the declared purposes and proceedings of the Army and others, about the trying and destroying ... the King ... London, for Richard Royston, 1660. 4°

Wing G 369.

T.145

1135

GEREE (John)

Σινιορραγια, the sifters sieve broken: or a treatise clearly proving, that bishops are not jure divino ... Printed at London, 1660. 4°

Not in Wing.

T.465

1136

HALL (Joseph) *Bishop of Norwich.*

A modest offer of some meet considerations tendered to the learned prolocutor, and to the rest of the Assembly of Divines, met at Westminster, 1644. Concerning a form of church-government. London, re-printed and are to be sold by Tho. Basset, 1660. 4°

Wing H 395.

T.248

1137

HEYLYN (Peter)

Historia quinqu-articularis: or, A declaration of the judgement of the western churches, and more particularly of the Church of England, in the five controverted points, reproched in these last times by the name of Arminianism ... London, E. C. for Thomas Johnson, 1660. 4°

Wing H 1721.

T.309

1138

L. (W.)

King Charles vindicated, or the grand cheats of the nation discovered ... By W. L. a lover of his country. Printed, for Theodorus Microcosmus, 1660. 4°

Wing L 89.
Incomplete.

T.23

1139

LA TOUR D'AUVERGNE (Anne de) *Vicomtesse de Turenne.*

Certain letters evidencing the Kings stedfastness in the protestant religion: sent from the Princess of Turenne, and the ministers of Charenton, to some persons of quality in London. London, Thomas Newcomb for Gabriel Bedell, and Thomas Collins, 1660. 4°

Wing C 1702 (=L 577).
Wanting the first three leaves.

T.326

1140

L'ESTRANGE (*Sir* Roger)

L'Estrange his apology; with a short view of some late and remarkable transactions leading to the settlement of these nations under the government of our lawfull and gracious soveraign Charles the II ... By R.L.S. London, for Henry Brome, 1660. 4°

Wing L 1200.
Wanting gatherings A and B.

T.287

1141

L'ESTRANGE (*Sir* Roger)

No blinde guides, in answer to a seditious pamphlet of J. Milton's, intituled Brief notes upon a late sermon titl'd, The fear of God and the King; preach'd, and since publishd, by Matthew Griffith ... Addressed to the author ... [Anon.] London, for Henry Broome, April 20. 1660. 4°

Wing L 1279.

T.287

1142

L'ESTRANGE (*Sir* Roger)

Physician cure thy self: or, An answer to a seditious pamphlet, entitled Eye-salve for the English army, &c... [Anon.] London, for H.B., 1660. 4°

Wing P 2146.
A note (in Bowdler I's hand) in the contents list of T.287: Roger Lestrange's answer to Milton's Eyesalve.

T.287

1143

L'ESTRANGE (*Sir* Roger)

A plea for limited monarchy, as it was established
in this nation, before the late war. In an humble
addresse to ... General Monck. By a zealot for
the good old laws of his country ... [Anon.]
London, T. Mabb, for William Shears, 1660. 4°

Wing L 1285.

T.23

1144

L'ESTRANGE (*Sir* Roger)

Sir Politique uncased, or, a sober answer to a
juggling pamphlet [by N.D.], entituled, A letter
intercepted. Printed for the use and benefit of
the ingenuous reader: in which the two different
forms of monarchy, and popular government are
briefly controverted... By D.N. Gent. London,
printed in the year 1660. 4°

Wing N 10.

T.23

1145

LONDON.

A common-councell holden the first day of May 1660.
Ordered by this court that the Kings Majesties
letter and declaration directed to this court, &
now read, be forthwith printed and published.
Printed by James Flesher, 1660. 4°

Wing L 2887.

T.23

1146

LONDON.

A declaration and vindication of the Lord Mayor,
aldermen and commons of the city of London in
common-councell assembled ... Printed by James
Flesher, 1660. 4°

Wing D 559.

T.287

1147

The LONG Parliament twice defunct: or, An answer
to a seditious pamphlet [by Sir William Drake],
intituled, The Long Parliament revived... By a
zealous yet moderate oppugner of the enemies of
his prince and country... London, for Henry Brome,
1660. 4°

Wing P 4003 (attributed to William Prynne).

T.287

1148

LOVE (Richard)

Oratio habita in Academia Cantabrigiensi, in solenni
magnorum comitiorum die, anno domini MDCLX ...
Cantabrigiae, excudebat Joannes Field, 1660. 4°

Wing L 3192.

T.465

1149

MONCK (George) *Duke of Albemarle.*

A letter from his Excellencie the Lord General Monck,
and the officers under his command, to the Parliament
... London: John Macock, 1660. 4°

Wing A 854.

T.23

1150

MONCK (George) *Duke of Albemarle.*

The Lord General Monck his speech delivered by him
in the Parliament on Munday, Feb.6.1659.
London: John Macock, 1660. 4°

Wing A 869.

T.15

1151

MOORE (John) *of Weohicombe.*

A leaf pull'd from the tree of life: medicinall
for the healing of Englands divisions. Or, A
glimpse of the excellency of a kingly government
... London, for E. Brewster, 1660. 4°

Wing M 2560.

T.23

1152

MORE (Henry)

Free-parliament quaeres: proposed to tender
consciences; and published for the use of the members
now elected. By Alazonomastix Philalethes...
Printed in the year of our redemption, 1660. 4°

Wing M 2661A.

T.271

1153

MOSSOM (Robert) *Bishop of Derry.*

An apology in the behalf of the sequestered
clergy; presented to the high court of Parliament...
London, for William Grantham, 1660. 4°

Wing M 2860.

T.754

1154

N. (N.)

Mutiny maintained: or, Sedition made good from its
unity, knowledge, wit, government, Being a
discourse, directed to the armies information.
[London, 1660.] 4°

Wing N 46.
2 copies.

T.88 T.95

1155

NO new parliament: or some queries or considerations
humbly offered to the present parlament-members.
By a friend to them and their cause. London, printed
in the year, 1660. 4°

Wing N 1183.

T.271

1156

OGILVY (Michael)

Fratres in malo, or the matchles couple;
represented in the writings of Mr. Edward Bagshaw,
and Mr. Henry Hickman ... All in vindication of
Dr. Heylin and Mr. Pierce. By one of the meanest
of their admirers M. O. ... Printed by R. Wilks,
and are to be sold by the booksellers of London
and Oxford, 1660. 4°

Wing O 186.

T.178

1157

OXFORD. *University.*

Britannia rediviva. Oxoniae, excudebat A. &
L. Lichfield, 1660. 4°

Wing O 863.
Signature of Nathanael Bowne.

T.552

1158

P. (H.)

The coffin opened: or, Self-interest discovered, to
be laid up in the coffin, under the name of the
good old cause. In answer to a late pamphlet ...
entituled, A coffin for the good old cause . By
H. P. a known friend to the cause and Commonwealth.
London, for James Johnson, 1660. 4°

Wing P 26.

T.23

1159

PEIRCE (*Sir* Edmond)

Anglorum singultus: or, The sobbs of England, poured
out. To be presented to ... George Monke. [Anon.]
London, for D. L., 1660. 4°

Wing P 1059.

T.23

1160

PEIRCE (*Sir* Edmond)

Englands monarchy asserted, and proved to be the
freest state, and the best common-wealth throughout
the world. With a word to the present authority,
and ... General Monck. [Anon.] London, W. G. for
Richard Lowndes, 1660. 4°

Wing P 1061.

T.23

1161

A PERTINENT speech made by an honourable member of
the House of Commons, tending to the establishment
of kingly government, as the only way to the setling
of these three distracted nations in their due
rights ... London, printed in the year, 1660. 4°

Wing P 1674.

T.23

1162

PIERCE (Thomas)

Englands season for reformation of life. A sermon
delivered in St. Paul's church, London. On the Sunday
next following his sacred Majesties restauration.
London, for Timothy Garthwait, 1660. 4°

Wing P 2183.

T.321

1163

PRYNNE (William)

A brief narrative of the manner how divers members of
the House of Commons, that were illegally and unjustly
imprisoned or secluded by the armies force, in
December, 1648. and May 7. 1659... [Anon.] London,
for Edward Thomas, 1660. 4°

Wing P 3912.

T.287

1164

PRYNNE (William)

The case of the old secured, secluded, and now
excluded members, briefly and truly stated...
London, Edward Thomas, 1660. 4°

Wing P 3921.

T.355

1165

PRYNNE (William)

Conscientious, serious theological and legal quaeres,
propounded to the twice-dissipated, self-created
anti-parliamentary Westminster juncto, and its
members... London, Edward Thomas, 1660. 4°

Wing P 3930.

T.355

1166

PRYNNE (William)

A full declaration of the true state of the
secluded members case ... [Anon.] London, printed,
and are to be sold by Edward Thomas, 1660. 4°

Wing P 3965.

T.23

1167

PRYNNE (William)

A seasonable vindication of the supream authority
and jurisdiction of Christian kings, lords,
parliaments, as well over the possessions, as
persons of delinquent prelates and churchmen ...
Transcribed out of the printed works of Iohn
Hus, and Mr. Iohn Fox ... London, T. Childe, and
L. Parry, and are to be sold by Edward Thomas,
1660. 4°

Wing H 3802.

T.379

1168

PRYNNE (William)

Seven additional quaeres in behalf of the secluded
members, propounded to the twice-broken Rump now
sitting ... [Anon.] [London, 1659/60.] 4°

Wing P 4077.

T.271

PRYNNE (William)

The title of kings proved to be jure divino.
1660.
See no. 4868.

1169

QUAESUMUS te, &c. Or, The supplement to the new
letany for these times: being a further expedient
in order to the perfecting of a reformation in the
three nations; but chiefly of the city of London.
London, for Cauda Draconis: in English, the Rump,
1660. 4°

Wing Q 8.

T.271

1170

The REMONSTRANCE & address of the armies of England, Scotland, and Ireland, to the Lord General Monck ... London, John Macock, 1660. 4°

Wing R 959.

T.15

1171

REYNOLDS (Edward) *Bishop of Norwich.*

A seasonable exhortation of sundry ministers in London to the people of their respective congregations. [Anon.] London, E.M. for Samuel Gellibrand; and Robert Gibbs, 1660. 4°

Wing R 1276.

T.465

1172

RUSSELL (John) *of Chingford.*

The solemn league and covenant discharg'd. Or St. Peter's bonds not only loosed but annihilated ... [Anon.] Attested by John Gauden ... London, for Henry Brome, 1660. 4°

Wing R 2343.

T.201

1173

SANCROFT (William) *Archbishop of Canterbury.*

A sermon preached in S. Peter's Westminster, on the first Sunday in Advent, at the consecration of ... John Lord Bishop of Durham, William Lord Bishop of S. David's ... By W. S. ... London, T. Roycroft, for Robert Beaumont, 1660. 4°

Wing S 566.
2 copies.

T.310 T.175

1174

SANDERSON (Robert) *Bishop of Lincoln.*

Reasons of the present judgement of the Universitie of Oxford, concerning the Solemn League and Covenant, the Negative Oath, the Ordinances concerning discipline and worship ... London, re-printed for R. Pawley, 1660. 4°

Wing S 626.

T.129

1175

SANDERSON (Robert) *Bishop of Lincoln.*

Reasons of the present judgement of the University of Oxford, concerning the Solemne League and Covenant, the negative oath, the ordinances concerning discipline and worship... London, for R. Royston, 1660. 4°

Wing S 627.

T.378

1176

SCOTLAND. *Commissioners.*

A letter sent from the Commissioners of Scotland, to his Excellency the Lord General Monck, in the behalf of themselves and the whole nation ... London, for Daniel White, 1660, 4°

Wing L 1606.

T.23

1177

SELECT city quaeries: discovering several cheats, abuses and subtilties of the city bawds, whores, and trapanners. By Mercurius Philalethes ... Part. I. London: printed in the year 1660. 4°

Wing S 2447.

T.271

1178

A SHORT discourse upon the desires of a friend: wherein, upon observation of the late governments and revolutions, it is made evident, what alone can be the perfect settlement of this nation, and the composure of all differences. London, for H.H., anno 1660. 4°

Wing S 3590.

T.508

1179

The SPEECHES and prayers of some of the late King's judges ... Printed anno Dom. 1660. 4°

Wing S 4875.

T.120

1180

STRODE (William)

A sermon preached at a visitation held at Lin in Norfolk, June the 24th anno 1633... London, W. Wilson for Samuel Brown, 1660. 4°

Wing S 5986.

T.753

1181

TATHAM (John)

London's glory represented by time, truth and fame, at the magnificent triumphs and entertainment of his most sacred Majesty Charles II... at Guildhall on Thursday being the 5th day of July 1660... [Anon.] London, William Godbid, 1660. 4°

Wing T 222.
Wanting the first gathering.

T.321

1182

W.(T.)

The oaths of supremacy & allegiance, which have lain dead for many years, now taken by both Houses of Parliament, and all officers and souldiers, and are to be taken by all that fear God and honour the King ... London, for William Sheares, 1660. 4°

Wing W 124.

T.378

1183

WALLER (*Sir* Edmund)

To the King, upon his Majesties happy return. [London], for Richard Marriot, [1660]. Fol.

Wing W 529.

T.699

1184

WILD (Robert)

Iter boreale. Attempting somthing upon the successful and matchless march of the Lord General George Monck, from Scotland to London, the last winter, &c... By a rural pen. London, printed on St. George's day, being the 23d of April, 1660. 4°

Wing W 2133.
Signature of Thomas Bowdler.

T.508

1185

WILD (Robert)

The tragedy of Christopher Loue at Tower-Hill. By the ingenious author of Iter boreale. London, for R. Crofts, 1660. 4°

Wing W 2150.

T.508

1186

A WORD in due season to the ranting royallists, and rigid presbyterians, &c. By a person wholly disinterested in any of the late, or present factions. Printed, in the year, 1660. 4°

Wing W 3542.

T.465

1661

1187

An ANSWER to this quodlibetical question. Whether the bishops make a fundamental, and essential part of the English parliament: collected out of some memorials in a larger treatise... London, for A. Seile, 1661. 4°

Wing A 3454.

T.465

1188

BACON (Francis) *Viscount St. Albans.*

A letter of advice written by Sr. Francis Bacon to the Duke of Buckingham, when he became favourite to King James, never before printed. London, for R.H. and H.B., 1661. 4°

Wing B 302.

T.287

1189

BAXTER (Richard)

A petition for peace: with the reformation of the liturgy. As it was presented to the right reverend bishops, by the divines appointed by his Majesties commission to treat with them about the alteration of it. [Anon.] London, printed, anno Dom. 1661. 4°

Wing B 1343.
Wanting the first gathering.
T.23

1190

BERNARD (Nicholas)

Clavi trabales; or, Nailes fastned by some great masters of assemblyes. Confirming the kings supremacy. The subjects duty. Church government by bishops... London: R. Hodgkinson, to be sold by R. Marriot, 1661. 4°

Wing B 2007.
Pp.1-64 only, containing two speeches by James Ussher, a sermon by Bernard and his account of "The late Primate Usher's judgment and practice."

T.253

1191

CAMBRIDGE. *University.*

Threni Cantabrigienses in funere duorum principum, Henrici Glocestrensis, & Mariae Arausionensis, serenissimi Regis Caroli II, fratris & sororis. Cantabrigiae: excudebat Joannes Field, ann. Dom. 1661. 4°

Wing C 354.

T.407

1192

CAMPBELL (Archibald) *Marquess of Argyle.*

The speech and plea of Archibald Marquesse of Argyle to the Parliament of Scotland ... In answer to the charge of high treason against him. London, H. Lloyd, and R. Vaughan, for Thomas Johnson, 1661. 4°

Wing A 3665 A.

T.287

1193

The CHARGE of high treason, murders, oppressions, and other crimes, exhibited to the Parliament of Scotland against the Marquess of Argyle and his complices, January 23. 1661. London, for Richard Lowndes, 1661. 4°

Wing C 2056.

T.287

1194

CHARLES II, *King of England.*

Articles of peace & alliance between the most serene and mighty princes, Charles II ... and Frederick III. hereditary king of Denmark and Norway, &c. Concluded the thirteenth day of February, in the year of our Lord, 1660. Translated out of Latine into English. London, John Bill and Christopher Barker, 1661. 4°

Not in Wing.

T.287

1195

CHARLES II, *King of England.*

Articuli pacis & confaederationis inter serenissimos & potentissimos principes, Carolum II... et Fridericum III... Daniae & Norwegiae regum haereditarium, &c. Conclusi decimo tertio die mensis Februarii, anno Domini M.DC.LX. Londini, excusum per Johannem Bill & Christophorum Barker, 1661. 4°

Not in Wing.

T.287

1196

CHURCH OF ENGLAND.

A form of common prayer, to be used upon the thirtieth of January ... London: John Bill and Christopher Barker, 1661. 4°

Wing C 4114.

T.126

1661 (Cont'd.)

1197

CHURCH OF ENGLAND.

A form of prayer, to be used upon the twelfth of June, in all churches and chappels within the cities of London and Westminster ... for the averting those sicknesses and diseases, that dearth and scarcity, which justly may be feared from the late immoderate rain and waters ... London: John Bill and Christopher Barker, 1661. 4°

Wing C 4143.

T.313

1198

CLARKE (Samuel) *Minister of Grendon Underwood.*

Ministers dues and peoples duty; or a bill of accounts between ministers and people: shewing what people owe unto their ministers... London, A.M. for William Miller, 1661. 4°

Wing C 4494.

T.754

1199

COLET (John)

A sermon of conforming and reforming: made to the convocation at S. Pauls Church in London ... To which is now added an appendix of Bp. Andrews, and Dr. Hammonds solemn petition and advice to the convocation; with his directions to the laity, how to prolong their happiness ... [Edited by Thomas Smith.] Printed by J. Field, (printer to the Universitie of Cambridge) for William Morden, 1661. 8°

Wing C 5096   (Ch.Ch. C 5096 +).
2 copies.

T.441 T.478

1200

COPLESTON (John)

Moses next to God, and Aaron next to Moses subordinate and subservient: opened, in a sermon preached at St. Peters in Exon on Wednesday the 29th of May 1661 ... London, W. Godbid for Richard Thrale, 1661. 4°

Wing C 6083.

T.234

1201

CROFTON (Zachary)

A serious review of presbyters re-ordination by bishops: in a letter written unto a minister in Warwickshire ... London, for Ralph Smith, [1661]. 4°

Wing C 7003.

T.465

1202

EUSTACE (*Sir* Maurice)

The speech of the Right Honourable the Lord Chancellor of Ireland made as he was one of the lords justices in their name and behalf of the opening of the parliament there, the 8th. of may 1661. London, for Abel Roper, 1661. 4°

Wing E 3428.

T.287

1203

GATAKER (Thomas)

The Covenanters plea against absolvers. Or, a modest discourse, shewing why those who in England & Scotland took the Solemn League and Covenant, cannot judge their consciences discharged from the obligation of it ... Written out by Theophilus Timorcus ... London, for T. B. and are to be sold in Westminster Hall and Pauls Church-yeard, 1661. 4°

Wing G 314.

T.378

1204

GAUDEN (John) *Bishop of Worcester.*

Considerations touching the liturgy of the Church of England. In reference to his Majesties late gracious declaration, and in order to an happy union in church and state ... London: J.G. for John Playford, 1661. 4°

Wing G 348.

T.465

KING (Henry) *Bishop of Chichester.*

A sermon preached at White-hall. 1661.

See no. 5681.

1205

LANGBAINE (Gerard) *the Elder.*

A review of the covenant: wherein the original, grounds, means, matter and ends of it are examined ... London, for Humphrey Robinson, 1661. 4°

Wing L 372.
2 copies.

T.378 T.552

1206

L'ESTRANGE (*Sir* Roger)

A caveat to the Cavaliers. The third impression ... London, for Henry Brome, August the 21. 1661. 8°

Wing L 1213.

T.359

1207

L'ESTRANGE (*Sir* Roger)

Interest mistaken, or, The holy cheat; proving, from the undeniable practises and positions of the presbyterians, that the design of that party is to enslave both king and people ... By way of observation upon a treatise, entituled, The interest of England in the matter of religion, &c. [by John Corbet] ... London, for Henry Brome, 1661. 4°

Wing L 1261.

T.317

1208

L'ESTRANGE (*Sir* Roger)

A modest plea both for the Caveat, and the author of it. With some notes upon Mr. James Howell, and his Sober inspections ... London, printed Aug. 28. 1661. for Henry Brome. 8°

Wing L 1272.
2 copies.

T.359 T.447

1209

L'ESTRANGE (*Sir* Roger)

The relaps'd apostate: or, Notes upon a presbyterian pamphlet [by Richard Baxter], entituled, A petition for peace, &c. wherein the faction and design are laid as open as heart can wish ... London, for Henry Brome, 1641 [i.e. 1661]. 4°

Wing L 1293.

T.146

1210

L'ESTRANGE (*Sir* Roger)

State-divinity; or a supplement to the Relaps'd apostate. Wherein is prosecuted the discovery of the present designe against the King, the Parliament, and the publick peace: in notes upon some late presbyterian pamphlets ... London, for Henry Brome, 1661. 4°

Wing L 1311.

T.330

1211

L'ESTRANGE (*Sir* Roger)

To the right honorable, Edward Earl of Clarenden ... the humble apology of Roger L'Estrange ... London, for Henry Brome, 1661. 4°

Not in Wing. Ch, Ch, L 1314 +.

T,85

1212

MORLEY (George) *Bishop of Worcester.*

A sermon preached at the magnificent coronation of ... King Charles the IId ... London: R, Norton for T. Garthwait, 1661. 4°

Wing M 2794.

T,65

1213

PARTRIDGE (Seth)

The description and use of an instrument, called the double scale of proportion ... London, William Leybourn for William Wright, 1661. 4°

Not in Wing.

T.391

1214

PIERCE (Thomas)

Concio synodica ad clerum Anglicanum, ex provincia praesertim Cantuariensi ... Londini, typis R, Nortoni, impensis Timoth.Garthwait, 1661. 4°

Wing P 2169.

T.65

1215

PRYNNE (William)

A short sober pacific examination of some exuberances in, and ceremonial appurtenances to the Common Prayer ... London, T.C. and L.P. and are to be sold by Edward Thomas, 1661. 4°

Wing P 4081.

T.355

1216

RELAÇAO da vitoria que o Conde de Villa Flor D, Sancho Manoel, e Ioão de Mello governador das armas da provincia da Beira, ganharão aos Castelhanos, Sabbado 29. de Outubre de 1661. Lisboa, 1661. 4°

Part of the imprint has been cut away.

T.287

1217

A RENUNTIATION and declaration of the ministers or congregational churches and publick preachers of the same judgment, lying in, and about the city of London: against the late horrid insurrection and rebellion acted in the said city. London: Peter Cole and Edward Cole, 1661. 4°

Wing R 1042.

T.287

1218

RUST (George) *Bishop of Dromore.*

A letter of resolution concerning Origen and the chief of his opinions. Written to the learned and most ingenious C.L. Esquire; and by him published. [Anon.] London, printed in the year 1661. 4°

Wing R 2365.

T.465

1219

SCOTLAND. *Parliament.*

The last proceedings of the Parliament in Scotland, against the Marquesse of Argyle. Together with the speech and defence of the said Marquesse, in vindication of himself ... London, T. M. for T. J. 1661. 4°

Wing S 1251.

T.287

1220

STEPHENS (Jeremiah)

An apology for the ancient right and power of the bishops to sit and vote in parliaments... [Anon.] London, W. Godbid, for Richard Thrale, 1661. 4°

Wing S 5447.

T.379

1221

TAYLOR (Jeremy) *Bishop of Down and Connor.*

A sermon preached at the opening of the Parliament of Ireland, May 8.1661... London, J.F. for R. Royston, 1661. 4°

Wing T 393.
On the final leaf: A catalogue of some books written by Jeremy [Taylor], and printed for R. Royston.

T.380

1222

VIOLET (Thomas)

Two petitions of Thomas Violet of London goldsmith, to the Kings Majestie... London, printed anno Dom. 1661. 4°

Wing V 594 A.

T.504

1223

WAAD (John)

Charitable admonition, or, A few lines of good advice, to the people called Quakers... The substance of which was written in a letter from Morlaix... to N.C. of Plymouth, to be communicated to George Fox... London, printed for the author, in the year 1661. 4°

Not in Wing.

T.465

1224

WALSH (Peter)

Some few questions concerning the oath of allegiance, propos'd by a Catholick gentleman in a letter to a person of learning and honour... [Anon.] Printed in the year, 1661.   4°

Wing W 641.

T.248

1662

1225

BAGSHAW (Edward) *the Younger.*

A letter unto a person of honour and quality, containing some animadversions upon the Bishop of Worcester's letter. [Anon.] London, printed in the year, 1662. 4°

Wing B 417.

T.313

1226

BOREMAN (Robert)

Αὐτοκατακριτος: or hypocrisie unvail'd, and Jesuitisme unmaskt. In a letter to Mr. R. Baxter, by one that is a lover of unity, peace, and concord, and his well-wisher... [Anon.] London: for R. Royston, 1662. 4°

Wing B 3756.

T.465

1227

CAMBRIDGE, *University.*

Epithalamia Cantabrigiensia in nuptias auspicatissimas serenissimi Regis Caroli II, Britanniarum monarchae, et illustrissimae principis Catharinae... Cantabrigiae: ex officina Joannis Field, ann. Dom. 1662. 4°

Wing C 335.

T.407

1228

CARYLL (Joseph)

The white robe: or, The undefiled Christian clothed in a white garment; held forth in a farewel sermon preached... at Magnus, August the 17. 1662. Printed anno Domini, 1662. 4°

Wing C 789.

T.234

1229

CHILLINGWORTH (William)

Mr. Chillingworths letter touching infallibility. London, D. Maxwell for Timothy Garthwait, 1662. 4°

Wing C 3888.

T.320

1230

COSIN (John) *Bishop of Durham.*

Articles of inquiry, concerning matters ecclesiastical, exhibited to the ministers, church-wardens, and side-men of every parish within the diocess of Durham... London, T. Garthwait, 1662.   4°

Wing C 4033.

T.465

1231

DARLEY (John)

The glory of Chelsey Colledge revived ... London, for J. Bourn, 1662.   4°

Wing D 259.

T.465

1232

DUREL (Jean)

The liturgy of the Church of England asserted in a sermon preached at the chappel of the Savoy, before the French congregation ... Translated into English by G. B. London, for R. Royston, 1662. 4°

Wing D 2692.

T.341

1233

The EXAMINATIONS of Henry Barrow, John Greenwood, and John Penry, before the high commissioners and lords of the council ... London: for William Marshall, [1662]. 4°

Wing E 3731.
(Formerly assigned to [1594?] STC 1520.)

T. 55

1234

GAUDEN (John) *Bishop of Worcester.*

Articles of visitation and enquiry concerning matters ecclesiasticall, according to the laws and canons of the Church of England, exhibited to the ministers, church-wardens, and side-men of every parish within the diocese of Worcester. London, J.G. for Richard Royston,1662.   4°

Wing C 4090.

T.465

1235

GAUDEN (John) *Bishop of Worcester.*

Χαρις και Εἰρηνη: or some considerations upon the Act of Uniformity; with an expedient for the satisfaction of the clergy within the province of Canterbury. By a servant of the God of peace. London, for Edward Thomas, and Henry Marsh, 1662. 4°

Wing G 347.

T.314

1236

GAUDEN (John) *Bishop of Worcester.*

Στρατοστη λιτευτικον. A iust invective against those of the army, and their abettors, who murthered King Charles I ... London, T.L. for James Davies, and are to be sold by Phil. Stephens, 1662.   4°

Wing G 372.

T.465

1237

L'ESTRANGE (*Sir* Roger)

A memento: directed to all those that truly reverence the memory of King Charles the martyr ... The first part ... London: for Henry Brome, Aprill the 11. 1662.   4°

Wing L 1270.

T.317

1238

L'ESTRANGE (*Sir* Roger)

A whipp a whipp, for the schismaticall animadverter [i.e. Edward Bagshaw] upon the Bishop of Worcester's [i.e. George Morley's] letter... London: for Henry Brome, February the 7th. 1662.   4°

Wing L 1325.

T.465

1239

L'ESTRANGE (*Sir* Roger)

A whipp for the schismaticall animadverter [i.e. Edward Bagshaw] upon the Bishop of Worcester's letter. With an answer to a second, and impudent libell from the same hand, entituled some further animadversions, &c ... The second impression. London: for Henry Brome, February the 12th. 1662.   4°

Wing L 1326.

T.287

1240

LILY (William)

Lilies rules construed. Whereunto are added Tho. Robinsons [i.e. Robertson's] Heteroclites, the Latine syntaxis, and qui mihi ... [Edited by William Haine.] London, Roger Norton, 1662.   8°

Not in Wing.

T.447

1241

MEINERTZHAGEN (Geruinus à)

Monumentum honoris immortalis a sacra themide et beneficentia erectum ... D. Francisco ab Eick ... Coloniae Agrippinae, typis Petri Hilden, anno 1662. Fol.

T.810

1242

MORLEY (George) *Bishop of Winchester.*

The Bishop of Worcester's letter to a friend for vindication of himself from Mr. Baxter's calumny... London, R. Norton for Timothy Garthwait, 1662.   4°

Wing M 2790.
2 copies.

T.313 T.465

1243

PATRICK (Symon) *Bishop of Ely.*

A brief account of the new sect of latitude-men together with some reflections upon the new philosophy. By S.P. of Cambridge. In answer to a letter from his friend at Oxford... London, printed and are to be sold in St.Pauls Church-yard, and in Westminster-Hall and Oxford and Cambridge, 1662. 4°

Wing P 754.

T.354

1244

PHILIPPS (Fabian)

Restauranda: or the necessity of publick repairs, by setling of a certain and royal yearly revenue for the King... [Anon.] London, Richard Hodgkinson, for the author, and are to be sold by Abel Roper, 1662. 4°

Wing P 2017.

T.689

1245

SANDERSON (Robert) *Bishop of Lincoln.*

Articles of visitation and enquiry concerning matters ecclesiastical: exhibited to the ministers, church-wardens, and side-men of every parish within the diocess of Lincoln... London: for A. Seile, 1662.   4°

Wing C 4054.

T.465

1246

The SPEECHES, discourses, and prayers, of Col. John Barkstead, Col. John Okey, and Mr. Miles Corbet; upon the 19th of April, being the day of their suffering at Tyburn ... Printed in the year, 1662. 4°

Wing B 817.

T.120

1247

TAYLOR (Jeremy) *Bishop of Down and Connor.*

Via intelligentiae. A sermon preached to the University of Dublin: shewing by what means the scholars shall become most learned and most usefull ... London: for R. Royston, 1662. 4°

Wing T 416.

T.340

1248

The TRYAL of Sir Henry Vane, Kt. at the Kings Bench, Westminster, June the 2d. and 6th. 1662... [London], printed in the year, 1662.   4°

Wing T 2216.
"A certaine venimous Booke wrot in defence of Sir Harry Vane the grand traitor."

T.120

1249

WATERHOUSE (William)

One tale is good, until another is told. Or, some sober reflections upon the Act for chimney-money... London, R. Norton, 1662.   4°

Wing W 1052.

T.465

1250

WHITE (Thomas) *Roman Catholic Priest.*

A copy of a letter sent by Mr. Thomas White, to be delivered to his Holiness in the congregation of the Holy Office: in obedience to his Holinesse's command requiring him to clear himself. [English and Latin.] [No imprint; the letter dated Amsterdam, 1662.] 4°

Not in Wing.

T.321

1662 (Cont'd.)

1251

WOMOCK (Laurence) *Bishop of St. David's.*

Pulpit-conceptions, popular-deceptions: or, The grand debate resumed, in the point of prayer... Being an answer to the presbyterian papers presented to the most reverend the ls. bishops at the Savoy upon that subject... [Anon.] London, for Richard Royston, 1662. 4°

Wing W 3347.
2 copies.

T.313 T.326

1252

WREN (Matthew) *Bishop of Ely.*

An abandoning of the Scotish covenant. London, D. Maxwell for Timothy Garthwait, 1662. 4°

Wing W 3674.

T.465

1663

1253

B. (I.) *Philomathes.*

Ancilla grammaticae: or, An epitome of grammar. Containing all the necessary rudiments of the Latine tongue... By I.B. Φιλομαθης. With short rules of spelling orthographie, pointing, construing, parsing, making Latine, variation, imitation, &c. By Ra. Johnson. London, for Tho. Pierrepont, 1663. 2 parts. 8°

Wing B 89.

T.447

1254

BIRD (John) *Rector of Cheddington.*

The divine and spiritual ambassadour described in a sermon preached at the visitation at Alisbury, com. Bucks. Octob.14.1662... London, Sarah Griffin, for Robert Pawlet, 1663. 4°

Wing B 2952.

T.753

1255

BIRKENHEAD (*Sir* John)

The assembly-man; written in the year 1647... [The preface signed J.B.] London: for Richard Marriot, 1662/3. 4°

Wing B 2961.

T.119

1256

BIRKENHEAD (*Sir* John)

Cabala, or an impartial account of the non-conformists private designs, actings and wayes, from August 24. 1662. to December 25. in the same year. [Anon.] London, printed in the year, 1663. 4°

Wing B 2965 (?)

T.201

1257

CERTAIN queries upon Dr. Pierces sermon at Whitehall Feb. 1. London, printed in the year 1663.

Wing C 1745.

T.271

1258

DOBSON (John)

Queries upon queries: or Enquiries into certain queries upon Dr. Pierce's sermon at Whitehall, Feb. 1. [Anon.] [London], for R. Royston, [1663]. 4°

Wing D 1755.

T.514

1259

The HORRID conspiracie of such impenitent traytors as intended a new rebellion in the Kingdom of Ireland... Verbatim out of the expresses sent to his Majesty from the Duke of Ormond... London: for Samuel Speed, 1663. 4°

Wing H 2863.

T.17

1260

KEN (Thomas) *Bishop of Bath and Wells.*

Ichabod: or, The five groans of the Church ... [Anon.] Cambridge: for J. Greaves, 1663. 4°

Wing K 348.
Wanting title-page.

T.142

1261

MAXWELL (John) *Archbishop of Tuam.*

Presbytery display'd for the justification of such as do not like the government; and for the benefit of those, that do not understand it ... [Anon.] London, for Henry Brome, 1663. 4°

Wing M 1381.
pp. 41-8 supplied in Thomas Bowdler's hand.

T.309

1262

PIERCE (Thomas)

The primitive rule of reformation: delivered in a sermon before his Majesty at Whitehall, Febr. 1. 1662. in vindication of our church against the novelties of Rome. London, for Timothy Garthwait, 1663. 4°

Wing P 2191.
2 copies.

T.340 T.553

1263

PIERCE (Thomas)

The primitive rule of reformation: delivered in a sermon before his Majesty at Whitehall, Feb. 1. 1662. in vindication of our church against the novelties of Rome. 8th ed. Oxford, H.H. for Ric. Royston, and Ric. Davis in Oxon, 1663. 4°

Wing P 2194.

T.742

1264

PRICE (John) *D.D.*

Moderation not sedition: held forth in a sermon partly preached at St. Matthews Friday-street, the 5. of July 1663... London, printed for the author, 1663. 4°

Wing P 3334.

T.309

1265

SANCHES (Manuel) *Conde de Villa Flor.*

A relation of the great success the King of Portugal's army had upon the Spaniards, the 29th of May (Engl. stile) 1663. London, Alice Warren, for William Garret, 1663. 4°

Wing V 389.

T.4

1266

SCIALITTI (Moses)

A letter written to the Jewes. By Rabbi Moses Scialitti, a Jew of Florence, baptized June 14. 1663. Declaring the reasons of his conversion, and exhorting them to embrace the Christian faith. London, printed 1663. 4°

Wing S 908.

T.17

1267

SOUTH (Robert)

A sermon preached at the cathedral church of St. Paul, Novemb. 9. 1662. London: J.G. for Tho. Robinson, bookseller in Oxon, 1663. 4°

Wing S 4738.
2 copies.

T.380 T.764

1268

TAYLOR (Jeremy) *Bishop of Down and Connor.*

A sermon preached in Christ-Church, Dublin: at the funeral of ... John [Bramhall], late Lord Archbishop of Armagh ... London, for John Cooke, 1663. 4°

Wing T 395.

T.127

1269

A TRUE account of the tryal of Mrs. Mary Carlton, at the sessions in the Old-Bayly, Thursday the 4th of June, 1663. She being indicted by the name of Mary Mauders alias Stedman... London, for Charls Moulton, 1663. 4°

Not in Wing.

T.17

1664

1270

A BRIEF relation of the present state of Tangier, and of the advantages which his Excellence the Earle of Tiveot has obteyned against Gayland. London, T. Mabb, 1664. 4°

Not in Wing.

T.248

1271

A CATALOGUE of the damages for which the English demand reparation from the United-Netherlands ... London, for Henry Brome, 1664. 4°

Wing C 1371.

T.315

1272

CHARLES II, *King of England.*

Articles of peace between his sacred Majesty, Charles the II ... and the city and kingdome of Algiers, concluded by Thomas Allen Esq... London, Thomas Mabb, 1664. 4°

Wing C 2907.

T.261

1273

CORNEILLE (Pierre)

Pompey the great. A tragedy. [Anon.] As it was acted by the servants of his Royal Highness the Duke of York. Translated out of French by certain persons of honour ... London, for Henry Herringman, 1664. 4°

Wing C 6319.

T.504

1274

An EXACT narrative of the tryal and condemnation of John Twyn, for printing and dispersing of a treasonable book ... London, Thomas Mabb for Henry Brome, 1664. 4°

Wing E 3668.

T.120

1275

HOWE (Obadiah)

Βασιλιδι δωρον: or, The royal present. As it was delivered in a sermon, in the parish-church of Boston, Octob. 9. 1663 ... London, E. Cotes, for A. Seile, 1664. 4°

Wing H 3049.

T.753

1276

PELL (John)

Easter not mis-timed. A letter written out of the countrey to a friend in London concerning Easter-day. [Anon.] London, for Timothy Garthwait, 1664. 4°

Wing P 1070.

T.17

1277

A TRUE relation of the late great and bloudy fight, betwixt the English and the Dutch upon the coast of Spain... Imprinted for Charles Robinson, 1664. 4°

Not in Wing.

T.248

1278

BELL (John)

Londons remembrancer: or, A true account of every
particular weeks chrisnings and mortality in all the
year of pestilence within the cognizance of the bills
of mortality being XVIII years... London: E. Cotes,
1665.   4°

Wing B 1800.

T.504

1279

BEUTTEL (Johann Caspar)

Krafft und Würckung dess Gesund-Bronnens, sonst das
Dalfinger Badt genandt, welches in dess Heil. Röm.
Reichs freyen Stadt Ulm gebiet... Gedruckt zu Ulm,
durch Balthasar Kühnen, 1665.   brs.

T.817

1280

BUXTORF (Johann) *the Elder.*

Masora. A collection out of the learned Master
Joannes Buxtorfius's Commentarius Masorethicus.
By Clement Barksdale... London, for Matthias
Thurston, 1665.   8°

Not in Wing.

T.481

1281

CASAUBON (Meric)

To J. S. (the author of Sure-footing) his letter,
lately published: the answer of Mer. Casaubon,
D.D. concerning the new way of infallibility,
lately devised to uphold the Roman cause ...
London, for Timothy Garthwait, 1665.   4°

Wing C 811.

T.320

1282

DOLBEN (John) *Archbishop of York.*

A sermon preached before his Majesty on Good-Friday
at Whitehall, March 24. 1664/5. London, for
Timothy Garthwait, 1665.   4°

Wing D 1831.
Signature of J.M. Newbolt e don: R. Shipman S.T.P.

T.708

1283

DOWNING (*Sir* George) *1st Baronet.*

A reply of Sir George Downing, knight and baronet,
envoy extraordinary from his Majesty of Great
Britain, &c. To the remarks of the deputies of
the Estates General, upon his memorial of the 20th
of December, 1664. London, 1665. 4°

Wing D 2109.
Wanting title-page.

T.315

1284

FORD (Simon)

θαυμασια κυριου ἐν βυθῳ. Or the Lords wonders in
the deep. Being a sermon preached at the time of
the publique assises at Allhallows in Northampton
July 4. 1665 ... Oxford, W. Hall for Samuel
Pocock, 1665.   4°

Wing F 1504.

T.380

1285

GUIS (Joseph)

Description des arenes, ou de l'amphitheatre d'Arles.
A Arles, par François Mesnier, 1665.   4°

T.12

1286

LUSUS Neo-Gamelii gentilitiis Neo-Gamorum deprompti,
quando ... D. Joannes Petrus ab Althoven ... nec
non ... Clara Sophia à Cronenberg ... feliciori
omine dextras porrigebant ... Coloniae Agrippinae,
imprimebat Petrus Hilden, 1665. Fol.

T.810

1287

REMONSTRANCE du clergé de France, faite au Roy, par
Monseigneur ... Iacques Adhemar de Monteil de
Grignan, Euesque & comte d'Vzes ... A Paris, chez
Antoine Vitré, 1665.   4°

T.326

1288

SOUTH (Robert)

A sermon preached before the court at Christchurch
chappel in Oxford. Oxford, W.H. for William Nott,
and are to be sold by Richard Davis, 1665.   4°

Wing S 4741.

T.764

1289

WAIGHTY and demonstrative reasons why Monsr. Peter
du Moulin, ought not to be made gouvernour of the
colonie of Syrinam. London, A.B. for C.P.,
[*c*.1665].

Not in Wing.
2 copies.

T.118   T.504

1666

1290

FORDE (*Sir* Edward)

Experimented proposals how the King may have money
to pay and maintain his fleets with ease to his
people. London may be rebuilt, and all propietors
satisfied ... London, William Godbid, 1666. 4°

Wing F 1520.

T. 16

1291

HOBBES (Thomas)

Ad nobilissimum dominum Gulielmum Comitem Devoniae,
&c. De Mirabilibus Pecci, carmen Thomae Hobbes.
[London.]   4°

Wing H 2222.
Wanting the first leaf.

T.668

1292

HOLLAND (Richard) *Mathematician.*

Globe notes per R.H. [Oxford?] 1666.   8°

Not in Wing.

T.455

1293

KILLIGREW (Henry)

A sermon preach'd before the King the first Sunday
of Advent. 1666 ... London, Tho. Roycroft, for
Thomas Hacker, 1666. 4°

Wing K 446.

T.234

1294

LANEY (Benjamin) *Bishop of Ely.*

A sermon preached before the King at White-hall,
March 18. 1665/6. By ... B. Lord Bishop of Lincoln.
London, for Timothy Garthwait, 1666.   4°

Wing L 349.

T.313

1295

OWEN (Richard)

Paulus multiformis. Concio ad clerum Londinensem
habita Maii 8. 1666. in ecclesia Sancti Alphagii...
Londini, typis S. Griffin, vaeneuntque apud Joh.
Williams, 1666.   4°

Not in wing.

T.668

1296

RELATION succinte de l'estat ou sont maintenant les
eglises reformées de France. 1666. [No imprint.]
4°

T.326

1297

SOUTH (Robert)

A sermon preached at Lambeth-chappel on the 25th
of November, upon the consecration of ... John
Dolben Lord Bishop of Rochester. Savoy, Tho.
Newcomb for William Nott, 1666. 4°

Wing S 4739.

T.234

1298

STUBBE (Henry)

The miraculous conformist: or An account of severall
marvailous cures performed by the stroaking of the
hands of Mr Valentine Greatarick... Oxford, H. Hall,
for Ric: Davis, 1666.   4°

Wing S 6062.
Signature of George Hickes.

T.326

1299

VOSSIUS (Gerardus Joannes)

Ger. Jo. Vossii Elementa rhetorica, oratiis
ejusdem partitionibus accomodata... Amstelodami,
apud Joannem Ravesteinium, 1666.   8°

Signature of Dar. Osborn.

T.454

1300

WALLER (*Sir* Edmund)

Instructions to a painter, for the drawing of the
posture & progress of his Maties forces at sea,
under the command of his Highness Royal... London,
for Henry Herringman, 1666.   Fol.

Wing W 500.

T.699

1667

1301

ALLESTREE (Richard)

A sermon preached before the King at Whitehall on
Sunday Nov. 17. 1667. London, J. Flesher, for
James Allestree, 1667. 4°

Wing A 1167.

T.65

1302

BAXTER (Richard)

The judgment of Mr. Baxter concerning ceremonies
and conformity. With a short reflection upon a
scandalous pamphlet [by David Jenkins], intituled,
A proposition for the safety and happiness of the
king and kingdom. In a letter to a gentleman of
the House of Commons. London, for R. Jenaway,
1667. 4°

Wing B 1290.

T.313

1303

The CHARACTER of a London scrivener. Printed in
the year 1667. 4°

Wing C 1979.

T.262

1304

CHARLES II, *King of England.*

Articles of peace, commerce, & alliance, between
the crowns of Great Britain and Spain. Concluded in
a treaty at Madrid ... in the year of our Lord God,
1667. Translated out of Latin ... (The copy of a
patent, containing several gracious priviledges
lately granted ...) In the Savoy, the assigns of
John Bill and Christopher Barker, 1667. 4°

Wing C 2910.

T. 16

1305

ETHEREGE (*Sir* George)

The comical revenge; or, Love in a tub. Acted at
his Higness the Duke of York's theatre in
Lincolns-Inn-Fields. London, for Henry Herringman,
1667.   4°

Wing E 3369.
Signature of Thomas Bowdler.

T.504

1306

GLANVILL (Joseph)

A loyal tear dropt on the vault of our late martyred
sovereign, In an anniversary sermon on the day
of his murther, [Anon.] London, E. Cotes, and are
to be sold by James Collins, 1667, 4°

Wing G 813.
2 copies.

T.764   T.73

1667 (Cont'd.)

1307

GLANVILL (Joseph)

Some philosophical considerations touching the being of witches and witchcraft. Written in a letter to ... Robert Hunt Esq; by J. G. ... London, E. C. for James Collins, 1667. 4°

Wing G 832.

T.96

1308

LLOYD (William) *Bishop of Worcester.*

The late Apology in behalf of the papists [by Roger Palmer, Lord Castlemaine] re-printed and answered, in behalf of the royallists. [Anon.] London, for M.N., 1667. 4°

Wing L 2683.

T.313

1309

M. (P.)

A letter to the answerer [i.e. William Lloyd] of the Apology for the Catholicks [by Roger Palmer, Lord Castlemaine]. [London, 1667.] 4°

Wing M 65 A.

T.313

1310

MULERIUS (Carolus)

Linguae Italicae, compendiosa institutio... Oxonii, impensis Joh. Crosley, 1667. 8°

Wing M 3053.

T.458

1311

OWEN (John)

Indulgence and toleration considered: in a letter unto a person of honour, [Anon.] London, printed in the year 1667. 4°

Wing O 763.

T.17

1312

ROYAL AFRICAN COMPANY.

The several declarations of the Company of Royal Adventurers of England trading into Africa, inviting all his Majesties native subjects in general to subscribe, and become sharers in their joynt-stock... Anno Dom. 1667. 4°

Wing S 2759.

T.324

1313

SOUTH (Robert)

Musica incantans, sive poema exprimens musicae vires, juvenem in insaniam adigentis, et musici inde periculum. Oxonii, typis W.H. impensis G. West, anno Dom. 1667. 4°

Wing S 4736.

T.668

1314

TOMKINS (Thomas)

The inconveniencies of toleration, or an answer to a late book [by David Jenkins], intituled, A proposition made to the King and Parliament, for the safety and happiness of the King and Kingdom... [Anon.] London, for W. Garret, 1667. 4°

Wing T 1835.

T.201

1315

A TRUE relation of the terrible earthquake which happened at Ragusa, and several other cities in Dalmatia and Albania. The sixth of April 1667 ... In the Savoy, Tho: Newcomb, 1667. 4°

Wing T 3059.

T.127

1668

1316

BETHEL (Slingsby)

The world's mistake in Oliver Cromwell; or, A short political discourse, shewing that Cromwell's mal-administration ... layed the foundation of our present condition, in the decay of trade. [Anon.] London, printed in the year 1668. 4°

Wing B 2079.

T.317

1317

CHILD (Sir Josiah)

A short addition to the observations concerning trade, and interest of money. By the same hand. London, for Henry Mortlock, 1668. 4°

Wing C 3864.

T. 16

1318

CULPEPER (Sir Thomas)

A discourse, shewing the many advantages which will accrue to this kingdom by the abatement of usury ... Humbly presented to the High Court of Parliament now sitting. London, Tho. Leach, for Christopher Wilkinson, 1668. 4°

Wing C 7555.

T. 16

1319

FRANCO (Solomon)

Truth springing out of the earth: that is, The truth of Christ proved out of the earthly promises of the law ... London, J. Flesher, for the authour, 1668. 4°

Wing F 2066 A.

T.320

1320

LAUNOY (Jean de)

Conspectus epistolarum Ioannis Launoii Constantiensis, theologi Parisiensis, quae in sex partes distributae prostant. Parisiis, apud Edmundum Martinum, 1668. 8°

T.458

1321

LINGARD (Richard)

A sermon preached before the King at White-hall, July 26. 1668. in defence of the liturgy of our Church. London, J.M. for John Crook, 1668. 4°

Wing L 2353.

T.764

1322

LIONNE (Hugues de)

Memoires de Monsieur de Lyonne au Roy, interceptez par ceux de la garnison de Lille ... [No imprint], 1668. 12°

T.458

1323

LLOYD (William) *Bishop of Worcester.*

A sermon preached before the King at White-hall, on Decémb.1. M.DC.LXVII... London: E. Cotes, for Henry Brome, 1668. 4°

Wing L 2702.
2 copies.

T.764   T.234

1324

LONDON.

An act for preventing and suppressing of fires within the city of London, and liberties thereof. London, for Nath: Brook, 1668. 4°

Wing L 2854.

T.17

1325

PERRINCHIEF (Richard)

A discourse of toleration: in answer to a late book, intituled, A discourse of the religion of England [by John Corbet] ... [Anon.] London, E. C. for James Collins, 1668. 4°

Wing P 1593 B.

T.201

1326

The TRYALS of such persons as under the notion of London-apprentices were tumultuously assembled in Moore-Fields ... under colour of pulling down bawdy-houses ... London, for Robert Pawlet, 1668. 4°

Wing T 2262.

T.120

1327

UNIVERSUM totale, sive compendium rerum visibilium. [Probably an advertisement for the series of atlases and cosmographies published by Blaeu and Waesberghe in the 1660s.] [No imprint, c. 1668.] Fol.

T.810

1328

WETENHALL (Edward) *Bishop of Kilmore and Ardagh.*

Miserere cleri. A sermon presenting the miseries of the clergy, and assigning their true causes in order to redress: preached... in the cathedral of Saint Peter, Exon, at the assizes, on Sunday, July 26. 1668... In the Savoy, T.N. for James Collins, and are to be sold by Abisha Brocas bookseller in Exon, 1668. 4°

Wing W 1505.

T.504

1669

1329

BOREMAN (Robert)

A mirrour of Christianity, and a miracle of charity: or, A true and exact narrative of the life and death of ... Alice Dutchess Duddeley ... London, E. C, for R. Royston, and for J. Collins, 1669 . 4°

Wing B 3758.

T.127

1330

BRETT (Arthur)

A demonstration how the Latine tongue may be learn't with far greater ease and speed then commonly it is. [Signed A.B. Z.W.] London, for J.S., 1669. 4°

Wing B 4395.

T.262

1331

CONNANT (Malachi)

Urim and thummim; or, The clergies dignity and duty recommended in a visitation sermon preached at Lewes. April, 27. 1669 ... London: for James Collins, 1669. 4°

Wing C 5691.

T.753

1332

FINCH (Heneage) *2nd Earl of Winchilsea.*

A true and exact relation of the late prodigious earthquake & eruption of Mount Etna... as it came in a letter written to his Majesty from Naples by... the Earle of Winchilsea... Printed by T. Newcomb in the Savoy, 1669. 4°

Wing W 2967.
2 copies.

T.127   T.262

1333

GLANVILL (Joseph)

Catholick charity recommended in a sermon, before the ... Lord Mayor, and aldermen their sermon: in order to the abating the animosities among Christians, that have been occasion'd by differences in religion. London: for H. Eversden, and J. Collins, 1669. 4°

Wing G 801.
2 copies.

T.742   T.764

1334

LITTLETON (Adam)

The Churches peace asserted upon a civil account. As it was ... deliver'd in a sermon before the Right Honourable the Lord Mayor, in Guild-hall-chappel, July 4 ... London, for Philip Chetwind, 1669. 4°

Wing L 2560.
2 copies.

T.764   T.380

1335

SHERLOCK (Richard)

A sermon preached at a visitation, held at Warrington in Lancashire May 11, 1669. London, for Rich. Royston, 1669. 4°

Wing S 3256.
3 copies.

T.625   T.754   T.764

1336

STILLINGFLEET (Edward) *Bishop of Worcester.*

A sermon preached before the King, January 30. 1668/9 being the day of the execrable murther of King Charles I. London, Robert White, for Henry Mortlock, 1669. 4°

Wing S 5642.
2 copies.

T.504   T.764

1337

ASSHETON (William)

Toleration disapprov'd and condemn'd by the authority and convincing reasons of... Faithfully collected by a very moderate hand, and humbly presented to the serious consideration of all dissenting parties. [Anon.] London, for Francis Oxlad sen. to be sold by John Williams, 1670. 4°

Wing A 4047 (?)
Wanting title-page and leaf A4.

T.142

1338

ASSHETON (William)

Toleration disapprov'd and condemn'd by the authority and convincing reasons of ... Faithfully collected by a very moderate hand, and humbly presented to the serious consideration of all dissenting parties. [Anon.] Oxford, William Hall, for Francis Oxlad sen: anno Dom. 1670. 4°

Wing A 4048.

T.313

1339

BAGSHAW (Edward) *the Younger.*

An antidote against Mr. Baxters palliated cure of church divisions. Or, An account of several weighty and just exceptions against that book ... [Anon.] Printed in the year, 1670. 4°

Wing B 403.

T.201

1340

BREVAL (François Durant de)

Faith in the just victorious over the world. A sermon preached at the Savoy in the French church, on Sunday Octob.10.1669. Translated into English by Dr. Du-Moulin. London, for Will. Nott, 1670. 4°

Wing B 4402.

T.742

1341

CAMBRIDGE. *University.*

Musarum Cantabrigiensium threnodia in obitum incomparabilis herois ac ducis illustrissimi Georgii Ducis Albaemarlae... Cantabrigiae, ex officina Joann. Hayes, 1670. 4°

Wing C 347.

T.407

1342

DRAKE (Samuel)

θεου διακονος. Or the civil deacon's sacred power. In a sermon... preached in the cathedral church of St. Peter, York, at the summer assize, 1669... London, for William Grantham, 1670. 4°

Wing D 2133.

T.764

1343

DRAKE (Samuel)

Totum hominis; or, The decalogue in three words, viz. justice, mercy, and humility. Being a sermon ... preached in the cathedral of St. Peters, York, upon Monday the 15th day of March, 1668/9 ... London, for William Grantham, 1670.   4°

Wing D 2134.

T.764

1344

The ENGLISHMAN, or A letter from a universal friend, perswading all sober protestant to hearty and sincere love of one another ... Printed in the year 1670.   4°

Wing E 3097.

T.314

1345

FORD (*Sir* Richard)

The speech of Sr Richard Ford knight, and alderman of London: made at Guild-hall to the liveries of the several companies of that city, on Michaelmas day, 1670 ... London, for N. B., 1670. 4°

Wing F 1472.

T.262

1346

GADBURY (John)

A brief relation of the life and death of the late famous mathematician and astrologer, Mr. Vincent Wing ... By J. G. Φιλομαθηματικος ... London, T. Milbourn for John Stephens, 1670. 4°

cf. Wing G 76.

T.262

1347

GLANVILL (Joseph)

Λογου θρησκεια: or a seasonable recommendation, and defence of reason, in the affairs of religion; against infidelity, scepticism, and fanaticism of all sorts. [Anon.] London, E.C. and A.C. for James Collins, 1670. 4°

Wing G 812.

T.764

1348

INQUEST after blood. Being a relation of the several inquisitions of all that have died by any violent death in the city of London, and borough of Southwark ... London, printed, 1670. 4°

Wing I 209 B.

T.262

1349

LOCKYER (Nicholas)

Some seasonable and serious queries upon the late Act against conventicles ... By a friend to truth and peace ... Printed in the year 1670. 4°

Wing L 2801.

T.17

1350

LUCAS (Charles) *2nd Baron Lucas.*

My Lord Lucas his speech ... upon the reading of the Subsidy Bill the second time, in the presence of his Majesty ... London, printed in the year 1670. 4°

Wing L 3392.

T.17

1351

MEGGOTT (Richard)

A sermon preached at St. Martins in the Fields, at the funeral of the Reverand Doctor Hardy, Dean of Rochester, June 9th. 1670. London, E. Tyler and R. Holt, for Joseph Clark, 1670. 4°

Wing M 1620.

T.618

1352

OVERING (John)

Hadadrimmon: or, Josiah's lamentation. Being a sermon preached upon the anniversary for Charles I ... London: Thomas Johnson, 1670.   4°

Wing O 616.

T.380

1353

P. (J.)

A caveat to conventiclers: being a letter from an English gentleman in Stockholme... relating the manner of the devils appearance in the Dutchy of Finland. [Signed J. P.] London, printed in the year 1670. 4°

Wing P 45.

T.17

1354

PATRICK (Symon) *Bishop of Ely*

A sermon preached at the funeral of Mr. Thomas Grigg, B.D. and rector of St. Andrew-Undershaft, September. 4. 1670... London, Robert White, for Francis Tyton, 1670. 4°

Wing P 838

T.764

1355

POPE (Walter)

The memoires of Monsieur Du Vall: containing the history of his life and death. Whereunto are annexed his last speech and epitaph ... [Anon.] London, for Henry Brome, 1670. 4°

Wing P 2912.

T.118

1356

PRAETORIUS (Johann)

Q.D.B.V. de ritu veterum Christianorum precandi versus orientem... Literis Christiani Michaelis, [1670]. 4°

T.819

1357

SANDERSON (Robert) *Bishop of Lincoln.*

Ad clerum. A sermon preached at a visitation holden at Grantham... 8° Octob. 1641. By a late learned prelate... Oxford, H.Hall for Ric. Davis, 1670. 4°

Wing S 580.
2 copies.

T.753   T.764

1358

STUBBE (Henry)

A censure upon certaine passages contained in the history of the Royal Society [by Thomas Sprat], as being destructive to the established religion and Church of England... Oxford, for Ric. Davis, A.D. 1670. 4°

Wing S 6033.

T.262

1359

STUBBE (Henry)

Lex talionis; sive vindiciae pharmacoporum: or a short reply to Dr Merrett's book; and others, written against the apothecaries ... [Anon.] London, Moses Pitt, 1670. 4°

Wing S 6055.

T.262

1360

A TRUE relation of the victory and happy success of a squadron of his Majesties fleet in the Mediterranean, against the pyrates of Algiers: taken as well out of letters from Sir Thomas Allen... and from Sir Wil. Godolphin...   as also from a relation made by the Heer Van Ghent... Printed by T. Newcomb in the Savoy, 1670.   4°

Wing T 3069.

T.325

1361

VERNON (George)

A letter to a friend concerning some of Dr. Owens principles and practices: with a postscript to the author [Samuel Parker] of the late Ecclesiastical polity, and an Independent catechism ... [Anon.] London, J. Redmayne for Spencer Hickman, 1670. 4°

Wing V 247.

T.118

1362

WARD (Seth) *Bishop of Salisbury.*

The Christians victory over death. A sermon at the funeral of the most honourable George Duke of Albemarle, &c... London, for James Collins, 1670. 4°

Wing W 818.

T.742

1363

WILKINS (John) *Bishop of Chester.*

A sermon preached before the King, upon the twenty seventh of February, 1669/70. London: A. Maxwell, for Sa: Gellibrand, 1670. 4°

Wing W 2210.

T.764

1364

AUSTIN (Samuel)

The character of a Quaker in his true and proper colours; or, The clownish hypocrite anatomized ... [Anon.] London, for T. Egglesfield, 1671. 4°

Wing A 4256.

T. 79

1365

BARROW (Isaac)

The duty and reward of bounty to the poor: in a sermon preached at the Spittal... London, Andrew Clark, for Brabazon Aylmer, 1671. 8°

Wing B 933.

T.478

1671 (Cont'd.)

1366

DUNCUMB (Thomas)

The great efficacy and necessity of good example especially in the clergy: recommended in a visitation sermon preached at Guilford...
London, John Winter, for William Cadman, 1671. 4°

Wing D 2610.

T.752

1367

HOLLES (Denzil) *Baron Holles*.

A true relation of the unjust accusation of certain French gentlemen, (charged with a robbery, of which they were most innocent) ... Published by Denzell Lord Holles ... London, J. Darby, for Richard Chiswel, 1671. 4°

Wing H 2480.

T.136

1368

LITTLETON (Adam)

A sermon preached in Lent-assizes, holden for the county of Bucks, at Alesbury. March 8th 1670/1 ... London, J. Macock, for R. Davis of Oxon, 1671. 4°

Wing L 2570.

T.764

1369

LLOYD (William) *Bishop of Worcester*.

A sermon preached at the funeral of Mr. Francis Mitchel, who dyed the 19th. and was buried the 24th. of July, 1671 ... [Anon.] London, Thomas Milbourn, for Thomas Johnson, 1671.   4°

Wing L 2702 A.

T.380

1370

MAYNWARING (Everard)

Praxis medicorum antiqua & nova: the ancient and modern practice of physick examined, stated, and compared ... London, J. M. and are to be sold by T, Archer, 1671, 4°

Wing M 1512.

T.17

1371

NORTH (John)

A sermon preached before the King at Newmarket October 8. 1671 ... Cambridge, John Hayes, and are to be sold by Edw. Story, 1671. 4°

Wing N 1289.
2 copies.

T.314   T.380

1372

S.(W.)

An answer to a letter of enquiry into the grounds and occasions of the contempt of the clergy.
London, for Nath. Ranew, and J. Robinson, 1671.   8°

Wing S 188.

T.457

1373

SANDERSON (Robert) *Bishop of Lincoln*.

Judicium Universitatis Oxoniensis, de 1. Solenni ligā & foedere. 2. Juramento negativo. 3. Ordinationibus Parlamenti circa disciplinam, & cultum. In plenā convocatione 1. Junii 1647 ... Londini, typis R. N. impensis R. Royston, 1671. 8°

Wing S 609.

T.157

1374

SCANDRETT (Stephen)

An antidote against Quakerisme: wherein these Following questions are opened, the truth concerning them proved, the contrary arguments examined and confuted...   London, for Tho. Parkhurst, 1671. 4°

Wing S 817.

T.354

1375

TUKE (*Sir* Samuel)

The adventures of five houres: a tragi-comedy. As it is acted at his Royal Highness the Duke of York's theatre.   The third impression, revis'd and corrected by the author... London, T,N, for Henry Harringman, 1671.   4°

Wing T 3231.

T.504

1376

WEST (Richard) *Rector of Shillingston*.

The profitableness of piety, opened in an assize sermon preach'd at Dorchester, March 24. 1670/1...
London, for R. Royston, 1671.   4°

Wing W 1380.

T.742

1377

WETENHALL (Edward) *Bishop of Kilmore and Ardagh*.

Two discourses for the furtherance of Christian piety and devotion...   By the author of the Method of private devotion.   [Anon.] London, J.M. for John Martyn, 1671.   8°

Wing W 1522.
Signature of A. Scot.

T.480

1378

WHITEHEAD (George) *and* PENN (William)

A serious apology for the principles & practices of the people call'd Quakers. Against the malicious aspertions, erronious doctrines and horrid blasphamies of Thomas Jenner and Timothy Tayler ... Printed in the year, 1671. 4°

Wing W 1957.
Title-page broken.

T.249

1379

WILKINS (John) *Bishop of Chester*.

A sermon preached before the King, upon the nineteenth of March, 1670/1.   London: A. Maxwell, for Sa: Gellibrand, 1671. 4°

Wing W 2211.

T.340

1672

1380

CHARLES II, *King of England*.

Articles of alliance and commerce, between ... Charles II ... and ... Christian V ... King of Denmark, Norway, &c. Concluded at Copenhagen, the 11th day of July, 1670 ... In the Savoy, the assigns of John Bill, and Christopher Barker, 1671/2. 4°

Wing C 2892.

T.17

1381

DU MOULIN (Pierre) *the Younger*.

A sermon preached in the metropolitical church of Canterbury, October 17. MDCLXXII. at the funeral of the very Reverend Thomas Turner ... London: for Henry Brome, 1672. 4°

Wing D 2567.

T.380

1382

EACHARD (John)

Moon-shine: or the restauration of Jews-trumps and bagpipes. Being an answer to Dr. R.Wild's letter &c. and his Poetica licentia, &c... London, for R.C., 1672. 4°

Wing A 439.

T.314

1383

FULLWOOD (Francis)

The necessity of keeping our parish-churches, argued from the sin and danger of the schisms in the church of Corinth, and of the present separations. In a sermon before the honourable judges, at the last assizes, held at Exeter ... London, E. T. and R. H. for James Collins, 1672. 4°

Wing F 2510.

T.380

1384

FULLWOOD (Francis)

Toleration not to be abused. Or, A serious question soberly debated, and resolved upon presbyterian principles ... By one that loves truth and peace ... London, S. and B. Griffin, for James Collins, 1672. 4°

Wing F 2519.
2 copies.

T.308   T.176

1385

GOOGE (Barnaby)

A prophecie lately transcribed from an old manuscript of Doctor Barnaby Googe ... predicting the rising, meridian, and falling condition of the states of the United Provinces ... London: J. C. for R, Robinson, 1672. 4°

Wing G 1271.

T.17

1386

GOULD (William)

Domus mea, domus orationis, a sermon preached in the cathedral of St. Peter in Exon. On Palm-Sunday. An. Dom. 1672. London, for R. Royston, and are to be sold by Abisha Brocas, 1672.   4°

Wing G 1439.

T.764

1387

JEMSON (Nathaniel)

A true and perfect account of a strange and dreadful apparition which lately infested and sunk a ship bound for New-Castle ... And of the strange deliverance of John Pye master ... London, for Robert Clavel, 1672. 4°

Wing J 555 (=P 4253).

T.127

1388

A LETTER to Mr. S. a Romish priest concerning the impossibility of the publick establishment of popery here in England, May 19. 1672. [London, 1672.]
Fol.

Wing L 1718.

T.688

1389

LORENZ (Justus)

[Hebrew] sive Exercitatio academica de ritu benedictionis sacerdotalis... Jenae, typis Johannis Jacobi Bauhoferi, [1672]. 4°

T.819

1390

RAPIN (René)

Reflections upon the use of the eloquence of these times. [Anon.]   Translated out of French. Oxford, printed and sold by the booksellers there, anno 1672. 8°

Wing R 275.

T.458

1391

STUBBE (Henry)

A justification of the present war against the United Netherlands...   In answer to a Dutch treatise entituled, Considerations upon the present state of the United Netherlands. By an English man...   London, for Henry Hills and John Starkey, 1672. 4°

Wing S 6050.

T.325

1392

STUBBE (Henry)

Rosemary & bayes: or, Animadversions upon a treatise called, The rehearsall trans-prosed [by Andrew Marvell]. In a letter to a friend in the countrey ... [Anon.] London, for Jonathan Edwin, 1672. 4°

Wing S 6064.
2 copies.

T.201   T.248

1393

A TRUE and impartial narrative of the eminent hand of God that befell a Quaker and his family, at the town of Panton in Lincolnshire ... London, for Francis Smith, 1672. 4°

Wing T 2498.

T.79

1394

VILLIERS (George) *2nd Duke of Buckingham*.

A letter to Sir Thomas Osborn, one of his Majesties Privy Council, upon the reading of a book, called, The present interest of England stated. [Anon.] London:for Henry Brome, 1672. 4°

Wing B 5312 (?)
Incomplete. A different setting of type from copy in T.118

T.17

1395

VILLIERS (George) *2nd Duke of Buckingham.*

A letter to Sir Thomas Osborn, one of his Majesties Privy Council, upon the reading of a book, called, The present interest of England stated. [Anon.] London: for Henry Brome, 1672. 4°

Wing B 5313.
A different setting of type from copy in T.17

T.118

1396

WILD (Robert)

A letter from Dr. Robert Wild to his friend Mr. J.J. upon occasion of his Majesty's declaration for liberty of conscience: Together with his Poetica licentia... London, for T. Parkhurst, J. Starkey, F. Smith, and D. Newman, 1672. 4°

Wing W 2140.

T.407

1673

1397

ASSHETON (William)

The danger of hypocrisie. A sermon preached at Guild-hall chappel, August 3d. 1673. London, for R. Royston, 1673. 4°

Wing A 4027.

T.380

1398

BUSHELL (Seth)

A warning-piece for the unruly; in two sermons at the metropolitical visitation of... Richard Lord Archbishop of York, held at Preston... London, for Will. Cademan: and Tho. Passinger, 1673. 4°

Wing B 6238.

T.753

1399

EGAN (Anthony)

The book of rates, now used in the sin custom-house of the Church of Rome ... London, for Benjamin Southwood, 1673. 4°

Wing E 245.

T.106

1400

EGAN (Anthony)

The Franciscan convert: or a recantation-sermon of Anthony Egan, late confessor general of the kingdom of Ireland ... London, for Robert Clavel, 1673. 4°

Wing E 248.
2 copies.
T.733 T.380

1401

ENGLAND, *Laws, Statutes,*

Summary account of all the statute-laws of this Kingdom now in force, made against Jesuites, seminary priests, and Popish recusants: drawn up for the benefit of all Protestants ... London, for John Starkey, 1673. 4°

Wing E 924.

T.106

1402

FORTREY (Samuel)

Englands interest and improvement. Consisting in the increase of the store, and trade of this kingdom. London, for Nathanael Brook, 1673. 8°

Wing F 1617.

T.391

1403

The FRIENDLY vindication of Mr. Dryden from the censure of the Rota by his cabal of wits ... Cambridge, printed in the year 1673. 4°

Wing F 2229.

T. 69

404

GREGORY (Francis)

Concio ad clerum, or a visitation sermon, preached at Great Wycomb within the diocess of Lincoln, May 13. 1673 ... London, R.N. for Richard Royston, 1673. 4°

Wing G 1887.

T.764

1405

HALES (John)

Sermons preach'd at Eton. 2nd ed. London, T. Newcomb, for Richard Marriot, 1673. 4°

Wing H 275.

T.504

1406

HILL (Joseph)

The interest of these United Provinces. Being a defence of the Zeelanders choice ... By a well wisher to the reformed religion, and the wellfare of these countries. Middelburg, Thomas Berry, according to the Dutch copie. Printed at Amsterdam, anno 1673. 4°

Wing H 2000.

T.83

1407

LEIGH (Richard)

The censure of the Rota. On Mr Driden's Conquest of Granada. [Anon.] Oxford, H. H. for Fran, Oxlad, 1673. 4°

Wing L 1018.

T.69

1408

LLOYD (William) *Bishop of Worcester.*

A conference between two protestants and a papist; occasion'd by the late Seasonable discourse [by William Lloyd]. [Anon.] Anno Dom, 1673. 4°

Wing L 2675.

T.320

1409

LLOYD (William) *Bishop of Worcester.*

A seasonable discourse shewing the necessity of maintaining the established religion, in opposition to popery. [Anon.] London: for Henry Brome, 1673. 4°

Wing L 2693.

T.140

1410

LLOYD (William) *Bishop of Worcester.*

A seasonable discourse shewing the necessity of maintaining the established religion, in opposition to popery. [Anon.] 2nd ed. corrected. London: for Henry Brome, 1673. 4°

Wing L 2694.
"Dr. Floyd's booke."
T.763

1411

LLOYD (William) *Bishop of Worcester.*

A seasonable discourse shewing the necessity of maintaining the established religion, in opposition to popery. [Anon.] The fourth edition corrected according to the mind of the author. London: for Henry Brome, 1673. 4°

Wing L 2696.
2 copies.
T.313 T.553

1412

LLOYD (William) *Bishop of Worcester.*

A seasonable discourse shewing the necessity of maintaining the established religion, in opposition to popery. The fifth edition corrected according to the mind of the author. London: for Henry Brome, 1673. 4°

Wing L 2697.

T.320

1413

A NARRATIVE of the siege and surrender of Maestricht, to the Most Christian King. On the 30 of June. In the Savoy, Tho. Newcomb, 1673. Fol.

Wing N 225.

T.4

1414

PEARSON (John) *Bishop of Chester.*

A sermon preached November V.MDCLXXIII. at the Abbey-church in Westminster. London: Andrew Clark, for John Williams, junior, 1673. 4°

Wing P 1009.

T.380

1415

SANDYS (*Sir* Edwin)

Europae speculum; or a view or survey of the state of religion in the western parts of the world... London, for Thomas Basset, 1673. 8°

Wing S 666.
Signature of Thomas Bowdler.

T.359

1416

A SERIOUS expostulation with B. E. an eminent Quaker, about his late breaking, for near forty thousand pounds. A great part whereof was moneys of the Quakers publique-stock. Printed for J. C. in the year, 1673. 4°

Wing S 2615.

T.79

1417

TILLOTSON (John) *Archbishop of Canterbury.*

A sermon lately preached, on 1 Corinth.3.15. By a reverend divine of the Church of England. Printed in the year, 1673. 8°

Wing T 1223.
Another copy, of a different impression.

T.359 T.659

1418

W. (E.)

The continuaticn of the case between Sir William Courten, his heyres and assignes, and the East India Company of the Netherlands, concerning the shipps Bona Esperanza and Henry Bonadventure, to the 23. of December 1673 ... Recollected by E. W. ... Printed in the year 1673. 4°

Part of Wing W 21 (?)

T. 194

1419

WARD (Seth) *Bishop of Salisbury.*

An apology for the mysteries of the Gospel. Being a sermon preached at White-hall, Feb.16.1672/3. London, Andrew Clark, for James Collins, 1673. 4°

Wing W 814.
Another copy, of a different impression.

T.733 T.764

1674

1420

BAXTER (Richard)

An appeal to the light, or, Richard Baxter's account of four accused passages of a sermon on Eph.1.3... London, for Nevil Simmons, 1674. 4°

Wing B 1190.

T.504

1421

CHARLES II, *King of England.*

Articles of peace, between ... Charles II ... and the high and mighty lords, the States General of the United Netherlands ... London, the assigns of John Bill and Christopher Barker, 1673/4. 4°

Wing C 2905.

T. 16

1422

DAVIES (*Sir* John)

England's independency upon the papal power historically and judicially stated, by Sr. John Davis ... and by Sr. Edward Coke ... With a preface written by Sir John Pettus. London, E. Flesher, J. Streater, and H. Twyford, assigns of Richard Atkins and Edward Atkins, 1674. 4°

Wing E 2984 (=D 397)

T.187

1423

DIGBY (George) *Earl of Bristol.*

Two speeches of George Earl of Bristol, with some observations upon them ... London, printed in the year, 1674. 4°

Wing B 4786.
2 copies.

T.313 T.95

1424

GOULD (William)

Conformity according to canon justified; and the new way of moderation reproved: a sermon preached at Exon ... London, A. Maxwell, for R. Royston, and are to be sold by Abisha Brocas, bookseller in Exon, 1674. 4°

Wing G 1438.
2 copies.

T.733 T.380

1425

GRAVEROL (François)

Francisci Graverolii Nemausensis I.V.D. Miles missicius. [No imprint], 1674. 8°

2 copies.

T.391 T.458

1426

HOOKE (Robert)

An attempt to prove the motion of the earth from observations ... London, T. R. for John Martyn, 1674. 4°

Wing H 2613.

T. 12

1427

JAMES (Henry)

A sermon preached before the King at Newmarket, October 11. 1674. London, W. Godbid, and are to be sold by M. Pitt, 1674. 4°

Wing J 426.

T.176

1428

A JUST vindication of the principal officers of his Majesties ordnance from the false and scandalous aspersions laid upon them in a printed libel, entituled An exact relation of the several engagements and actions of his Majesties fleet ... London, for Nathanael Brooke, 1674. 4°

Wing J 1244.
2 copies.

T.17 T.18

1429

A LETTER from a gentleman of the Romish religion, to his brother a person of quality of the same religion; perswading him to go to church, and take those oaths the law directs ... London, for John Starkey, 1674. 4°

Wing L 1399.

T.321

1430

LLOYD (William) Bishop of Worcester.

The difference between the church and court of Rome, considered: in some reflections on a dialogue entituled, A conference between two protestants and a papist. By the author of the late Seasonable discourse. London: Andrew Clark for Henry Brome, 1674. 4°

Wing L 2677.

T.320

1431

LLOYD (William) Bishop of Worcester.

A reasonable defence of The seasonable discourse: shewing the necessity of maintaining the established religion in opposition to popery. Or, A reply to a treatise, called, A full answer and confutation of a scandalous pamphlet, &c. [by Roger Palmer, Lord Castlemaine]. [Anon.] London, for H. Brome, 1674. 4°

Wing L 2692.
2 copies.

T.313 T.320

1432

LODINGTON (Thomas)

The honour of the clergy vindicated from contempt of the laity, in a sermon preached at the arch-deacon of Lincoln his visitation, holden at Grantham, Oct. 15. 1672 ... London, John Macock, for Joseph Clarke, 1674. 4°

Wing L 2812.

T.752

1433

PENN (William)

A just rebuke to one & twenty learned and reverend divines (so called). Being an answer to an abusive epistle against the people call'd Quakers ... Printed in the year 1674. 4°

Wing P 1311.

T.176

1434

PRINCE (John)

A sermon preached at Exon, in the cathedral of St. Peter: at the visitation of... Anthony... Lord Bishop of Exeter. London, A. Maxwell, for R. Royston; and are to be sold by Abisha Brocas, bookseller in Exon, 1674. 4°

Wing P 3478.

T.753

1435

ROLEGRAVIUS (Johannes)

Iohannis Rolegravii Tractatus de religionum conciliatoribus ... Lauzannae, typis Martini Vigel, 1674. 12°

T.458

1436

SHARP (John) Archbishop of York.

The things that make for peace. Delivered in a sermon preached before the Right Honourable the Lord Mayor, and the court of aldermen, at Guild-hall chappel, upon the 23. of August, 1674. London, Andrew Clark for Walter Kettilby, 1674. 4°

Wing S 3003
2 copies.

T.504 T.764

1437

SHERLOCK (Richard)

The irregularitie of a private prayer in a publick congregation. In a letter to a friend. [Anon.] [Oxford, Leonard Lichfield], 1674. 4°

Wing S 3241.

T.461

1438

STILLINGFLEET (Edward) Bishop of Worcester.

A sermon preached November V. 1673, at St. Margarets Westminst. 3rd ed, London, Robert White, for Henry Mortlock, 1674. 4°

Wing S 5643.
2 copies.

T.728 T.65

1439

TURNOR (Thomas)

The case of the bankers and their creditors. Stated and examined... By a true lover of his King and country, and a sufferer for loyalty... [The preface signed Sma. Ro.] Printed in the year, 1674. 4°

Wing T 3335.
3 copies.

T.17 T.95 T.118

1440

WARD (Hamnet)

A sermon preacht at Shaftsbury, at the primary visitation of... Guydo... Lord Bishop of Bristol. London, A. Maxwell for R. Clavel, 1674. 4°

Wing W 768.

T.753

1441

WARD (Seth) Bishop of Salisbury.

The case of Joram. A sermon preached before the House of Peers in the abby-church at Westminster, January 30. 1673/4. London: Andrew Clark, for James Collins, 1674. 4°

Wing W 817.

T.764

1442

WHALLEY (Peniston)

The religion established by law, asserted to conduce most to the true interest of prince and subject... London, for John Place; and Thomas Bassett, 1674. 4°

Wing W 1535.

T.313

1443

The WOMEN'S petition against coffee. Representing to publick consideration the grand inconveniences accruing to their sex from the excessive use of that drying, enfeebling liquor... London, printed 1674. 4°

Wing W 3331.

T.262

1675

1444

BONHOME (Joshua)

A new constellation: discovered in a sermon preached at the visitation held at Leicester the 29th of April, 1675. London, W.G. and are to be sold by Moses Pitt, 1675. 4°

Wing B 3594.

T.733

1445

BOYCE (Thomas)

The Quakers cruelty, deceit & wickedness, presented to the King and Parliament by Thomas Boyce. With a copy of the paper the Quakers put forth against me ... London, printed in the year, 1675. 4°

Wing B 3902.

T.79

1446

A BRIEF and true narration of the late wars risen in New-England: occasioned by the quarrelsom disposition, and perfidious carriage of the barbarous, savage and heathenish natives there. London, for J. S., 1675. 4°

Wing B 4534.

T. 94

1447

BURNET (Gilbert) Bishop of Salisbury.

Subjection for conscience-sake asserted: in a sermon preached at Covent-Garden-Church, December the sixth, 1674. London, for R. Royston, 1675. 4°

Wing B 5928.
2 copies (one wanting title-page).

T.65 T.742

1448

A COLLECTION of several treatises concerning the reasons and occasions of the penal laws. Viz. I. The execution of justice in England, not for religion, but for treason: 17 Dec. 1583. [By William Cecil.] II. Important considerations, by the secular priests: printed A.D. 1601. [By William Watson.] III. The Jesuits reasons unreasonable: 1662. London. for Richard Royston, 1675. 4°

Wing C 5192A.

T.320

1449

COOPER (Anthony Ashley) 1st Earl of Shaftesbury.

A letter from a Parliament man to his friend, concerning the proceedings of the House of Commons this last session ... [Anon.] Printed in the year, 1675. 4°

Wing S 2896.

T.95

1450

COOPER (Anthony Ashley) 1st Earl of Shaftesbury.

A letter from a person of quality, to his friend in the country. [Anon.] Printed in year, 1675. 4°

Wing S 2897.

T.17

1451

CREAMER (Charles)

A journey into the country; being a dialogue between an English Protestant physitian and an English Papist ... In some answer to Peter Walsh, and pursuant to the directions of a person of honor ... [Anon.] London, for Henry Brome, 1675. 4°

Wing C 6867.

T.95

1452

CROFT (Herbert) *Bishop of Hereford.*

The naked truth. Or, The true state of the
primitive Church. By an humble moderator...
[Anon.] Printed in the year, 1675. 4°

Wing C 6970.
2 copies.

T.83 T.142

1453

DESMARETS (Jean)

La defense de la poësie, et de la langue françoise.
Addressée a Monsieur Perrault, A Paris, chez Nicolas
le Gras, et Claude Audinet, 1675, 8°

T.204

1454

DU MOULIN (Pierre) *the Younger.*

A replie to a person of honour [Roger Earl of
Castlemaine] his pretended answer to the vindication
of the protestant religion in the point of
obedience to soveraigns, and to the book of papal
tyranny. London, for Henry Brome, 1675. 4°

Wing D 2564.
2 copies.

T.106 T.176

1455

GLANVILL (Joseph) *and* SHERLOCK (William)

An account of Mr. Ferguson his common-place-book,
in two letters. London: Andrew Clark, for
Walter Kettilby, 1675. 4°

Wing G 798 (= F 729).

T.176

1456

The GRAND-jurors of the city of Bristoll, their
address to the general sessions of the peace, there
assembled: wherein are shewed their reasons for the
putting the laws in due execution against the
phanaticks and papists ... Printed with allowance,
1675. 4°

Wing G 1501.

T.504

1457

H. (C.)

The golden rule made plain and easie: by a short
method, different from that which is commonly
found in books of arithmetick. The second edition,
with additions. London: first printed 1660,
and now reprinted by J. C. for William Crook,
1675. 8°

Wing H 13.

T.391

1458

JACKSON (William) *D.D.*

Of the rule of faith. A sermon at the visitation
of... William Lord Bishop of Lincolne... Cambridge,
John Hayes for Henry Dickinson in Cambridge, and
are to be sold by R. Chiswel in London, 1675. 4°
Wing J 95.
3 copies.

T.65 T.605 T.733

1459

JANE (William)

A sermon preached at the consecration of the
Honourable Dr. Henry Compton, Lord Bishop of Oxford,
in Lambeth-chappel, on Sunday, December 6. 1674.
London, W. Godbid, and are to be sold by R. Littlebury,
1675. 4°

Wing J 455.
2 copies.

T.380 T.733

1460

JORDAN (Thomas)

The triumphs of London, performed on Friday, Octob.
29. 1675. for the entertainment of the Right
Honourable ... Sir Joseph Sheldon Kt, Lord Mayor
of the city of London ... London, J. Macock, for
John Playford, 1675. 4°

Wing J 1068.

T.262

1461

LA MOTTE (François de)

The abominations of the Church of Rome: delivered
in a recantation-sermon, lately preached in
the French church in the Savoy ... English'd.
London: W. G. and are to be sold by Moses Pitt,
1675. 4°

Wing L 393.

T.320

1462

LEWIS (Mark)

Plain, and short rules for pointing periods, and
reading sentences grammatically, with the great
use of them. [London, 1675?] 8°

Wing L 1845.

T.391

1463

LILY (William)

A synopsis of Lillies grammar. The second edition
corrected and enlarged by the author ... Oxford,
H. Hall: for Thomas Hancox, bookseller in Hereford;
1675. 8°

Not in Wing.

T.458

1464

LLOYD (William) *Bishop of Worcester.*

The late Apology in behalf of the papists [by Roger
Palmer, Lord Castlemaine], reprinted and answered
in behalf of the royalists. [Anon.] The fourth
edition corrected. London, for Henry Brome, 1675.
4°

Wing L 2685.
2 copies.

T.106 T.320

1465

MEGGOTT (Richard)

A sermon preached before the King, at Windsor-
Castle, August 15. 1675. London, for Nathanael
Brooke, 1675. 4°

Wing M 1622.

T.503

1466

NAILOUR (William)

A commemoration sermon, preached at Darby, Feb. 18.
1674, for the Honourable Colonel Charles Cavendish,
slain in the service of King Charles the first ...
London, Andrew Clark, for Henry Brome, 1675. 4°

Wing N 85.

T.127

1467

OBRECHT (Ulrich)

Vlrici Obrechti de nummo Domitiani Isiaco ad ...
Eliam Brackenhofferum ... epistola. Argentorati,
apud Joh. Eberhardum Zetznerum, 1675. 4°

T.620

1468

A PASSIONATE satyr upon a devillish great he-whore
that lives yonder at Rome. [London, 1675.] brs.

Wing P 662

T. 532

1469

PROSOPOPOEIA protreptica. By which is represented
the non-conformist counsel for conformity to the
Church of England. In a letter to ... John Owen ...
Printed in the year, 1675. 4°

Not in Wing.

T.118

1470

SARDI (Alessandro)

Johannis Seldeni Angli Liber de nummis. In quo
antiqua pecunia Romana & Graeca metitur precio ejus,
quae nunc est in usu. Hiuc accedit Bibliotheca
nummaria... [by Philippe Labbe]. Londini, prostant
venales apus Mosem Pitt, 1675. 2 parts. 4°

Wing S 688.

T.618

1471

SMITH (Thomas) *of Magdalen College, Oxford.*

Ενωτικον, sive De causis remediisque dissidiorum,
quae orbem Christianum hodiè affligunt, exercitatio
theologia. Authore T.S. Oxonii, excudebat H. Hall,
impensis Ric. Davis, 1675. 4°

Wing S 4239.

T.733

1472

SMITH (Thomas) *of Magdalen College, Oxford.*

A sermon of the credibility of the mysteries of the
Christian religion, preached before a learned audience. London, Tho. Roycroft, for Ric. Davis
bookseller in Oxford, 1675. 4°

Wing S 4250.

T.733

1473

STILLINGFLEET (Edward) *Bishop of Worcester.*

A sermon preach'd before the King Feb. 24. 1674/5.
London, Rob. White, for Hen. Mortlock, 1675. 4°

Wing S 5647.

T.742

1474

STRADLING (George)

A sermon preach'd before the King at White-hall,
Jan. 30. 1674/5... London, for Henry Mortlock,
1675. 4°

Wing S 5782.

T.742

1475

T.(R.)

The art of good husbandry, or, the improvement of
time; being a sure way to get and keep money...
In a letter... by R.T. London, for J.G., 1675.
4°

Wing T43.
Wanting title-page.

T.262

1476

TILLOTSON (John) *Archbishop of Canterbury.*

A sermon preached before the King, Febr. 26th 1674/5.
London: A. Maxwell, for Samuel Gellibrand, 1675. 4°

Wing T 1227.

T.709

1477

TILLOTSON (John) *Archbishop of Canterbury.*

A sermon preached before the King, April 18th 1675.
London: A. Maxwell, for Samuel Gellibrand, 1675. 4°

Wing T 1228.
2 copies.

T.380 T.709

1478

TWO seasonable discourses concerning this present
Parliament. [The second discourse, entitled A
letter from a parliamentman to his friend, is signed
T.E. Attributed to the Earl of Shaftesbury.]
Oxford, printed in the year, 1675. 2 parts. 4°

Wing S 2906.

T.95

1479

WOOLLEY (John)

A sermon preached at the Oxfordshire-feast, Novemb.
25. 1674. In the church of St. Michael's Cornhill,
London. London, A. Maxwell, for R. Royston, 1675.
4°

Wing W 3525.
Signature of Jo. Hopkinson.

T.602

1676

1480

An ANSWER to Two letters, concerning the East-
India Company. Printed in the year 1676. 4°

Wing A 3457.

T.324

1481

B, (A,)

A letter of advice concerning marriage, By A, B,
London, for William Miller, 1676. 4°

Wing B 15.

T. 17

1482

BAGSHAW (Henry)

A sermon preached before the King at White-hall,
January xxx. 1675/6. London, William Godbid,
and are to be sold by Moses Pitt, 1676. 4°

Wing B 432.
3 copies.

T.61 T.65 T.602

1483

BURNET (Gilbert) *Bishop of Salisbury.*

A modest survey of the most considerable things in a discourse lately published [by Herbert Croft], entitled Naked truth. Written in a letter to a friend. [Anon.] London, for Moses Pitt, 1676. 4°

Wing B 5835.

T.176

1484

CARTWRIGHT (Thomas) *Bishop of Chester.*

A sermon preached before the King at White-hall, January the 9th 1675/6. In the Savoy: Tho. Newcomb, and are to be sold by Jonathan Edwyn, 1675/6. 4°

Wing C 702.

T.234

1485

CARTWRIGHT (Thomas) *Bishop of Chester.*

A sermon preached before the King at White-hall, January the 9th 1675/6. In the Savoy: T. Newcomb, and are to be sold by Jonathan Edwyn, 1676. 4°

Not in Wing (cf. C 702)

T.733

1486

CARTWRIGHT (Thomas) *Bishop of Chester.*

A sermon preached July 17. 1676. in the cathedral church of St. Peter in York, before ... his Majesties judges of assize for the northern circuit. In the Savoy: Thomas Newcomb; and are to be sold by Richard Lambert, bookseller in York, 1676. 4°

cf. Wing C 703.

T.340

1487

CHARPENTIER (François)

A treatise touching the East-Indian trade: or, A discourse (turned out of French into English) concerning the establishment of a French company for the commerce of the East-Indies ... [Anon.] London, for H. B. and are to be sold by Robert Boulter, 1676. 4°

Wing C 3715.

T.324

1488

DUPORT (James) *Dean of Peterborough.*

Three sermons preached in St. Maries Church in Cambridge, upon the three anniversaries ... London: for Henry Brome, 1676. 4°

Wing D 2655.
Signature of Jo. Hopkinson.

T.602

1489

E. (R.)

A scriptural catechism; or, The duty of man laid down in express words of scripture, chiefly intended for the benefit of the younger sort ... London; H.C. for Moses Pitt, 1676. 8°

Wing E 32.

T.520

1490

An EARNEST request to Mr. John Standish, &c. Upon occasion of a sermon of his preached at White-hall, before his Majesty. September 26. 1675. From Patropolis, directly over against Irenopolis. Printed in the year 1676. 4°

Wing E 98 A.

T.118

1491

FELL (Philip)

Lex talionis: or, The author of Naked truth [i.e. Herbert Croft] stript naked. [Anon.] London, for Henry Brome, 1676. 4°

Wing F 644.
Also ascribed to William Lloyd, Bishop of Worcester.

T.176

1492

GOULD (William)

The generosity of Christian love: with some reflexions upon that sordid self-love that now governs the world ... Delivered in a sermon ... London: J. Grover for R. Royston, 1676. 4°

Wing G 1440.

T.765

1493

GROVE (Robert) *Bishop of Chichester.*

A vindication of the conforming clergy from the unjust aspersions of heresie, &c. in answer to some part of M. Jenkyn's funeral sermon upon Dr. Seaman ... [Anon.] London, for Walter Kettilby, 1676. 4°

Wing G 2161.

T.118

1494

HAYWARD (Roger)

A sermon preached before the King at White-hall, January xvj. 1675/6. London, for Thomas Basset, 1676. 4°

Wing H 1236.

T.605

1495

HOLDEN (Samuel) *M.A.*

Two sermons preach'd at the funerals of the Right Honourable Robert Lord Lexington, and the Lady Mary his wife. London, for J. Edwyn, 1676. 4°

Wing H 2382.

T.65

1496

HOLLES (Denzil) *Baron Holles.*

The Long Parliament dissolved ... [Anon.] Printed in the year, 1676. 4°

Wing H 2463.

T. 17

1497

HORDEN (John)

A sermon preached at St. Martin in the Fields, to the natives of that parish: upon the 29th. of May, 1676 ... London: for Henry Brome, 1676. 4°

Wing H 2788.

T.602

1498

IS not the hand of Joab in all this? Or An enquiry into the grounds of a late pamphlet [by J.R.] intituled, The mystery of the new-fashioned-goldsmiths. or bankers, &c. And answering the exceptions in it to the bankers trade. Printed in the year, 1676. 4°

Wing I 1056.

T.118

1499

LATHOM (Paul)

Victory over death. A sermon preached at Steeple-Ashton ... at the funeral of Mr. Peter Adams ... London, H.C. for Edward Gellibrand, 1676. 4°

Wing L 575.

T.602

1500

MARVELL (Andrew)

Mr. Smirke. Or, the divine in mode. Being certain annotations, upon the Animadversions of the naked truth. Together with a short historical essay, concerning general councils, creeds, and impositions, in matters of religion ... By Andreas Rivetus, Junior ... [i.e. Andrew Marvell]. [London], printed anno Domini 1676. 4°

Wing M 873.

T.83

1501

MEGGOTT (Richard)

A sermon preached to those who had been scholars of St. Paul's school, in St. Michael's Cornhil, London, at their anniversary-meeting on St. Paul's day. 1675/6. London, for John Baker, 1676. 4°

Wing M 1624.

T.733

1502

The MIRACULOUS recovery of a dumb man at Lambeth ... London: for D. M., 1676. 4°

Wing M 2217.

T.127

1503

MURRAY (Robert)

A proposal for the advancement of trade, upon such principles as must necessarily enforce it. [Anon.] London, A.M. and R.R. for Dorman Newman, and Jonathan Edwin, 1676. Fol.

Wing M 3118.

T.543

1504

NEDHAM (Marchamont)

A pacquet of advices and animadversions, sent from London to the men of Shaftsbury ... Occasioned by a seditious phamphlet, intituled, A letter from a person of quality to his friend in the country. [Anon.] London: printed in the year 1676. 4°

Wing N 400.
2 copies.

T.17   T.118

1505

PARKER (Timothy)

A sermon preached before the Lord Bishop of Chichester at Lewes, at his first visitation there. London, for John Baker, 1676. 4°

Wing P 484

T.752

1506

PATRICK (Symon) *Bishop of Ely.*

A sermon preached before the King, on St. Stephen's-day, London, A. Maxwell, for R. Royston, 1676. 4°

Wing P 839.
2 copies.

T.602   T.65

1507

R. (J.)

The mystery of the new fashioned goldsmiths or bankers. Their rise, growth, state, and decay, discovered in a merchant's letter to a country gent. who desired to bind his son apprentice to a goldsmith. Printed in the year 1676. 4°

Wing R 28.

T.118

1508

SCATTERGOOD (Samuel)

A sermon preached before the King at New-market April 2. 1676. Cambridge, John Hayes, 1676. 4°

Wing S 843.

T.602

1509

SHARP (John) *Archbishop of York.*

A sermon preached before the ... Lord Mayor, and aldermen of London, atBow-Church. London: Andrew Clark, for Walter Kettilby, 1676. 4°

Wing S 3001.
2 copies.

T.602   T.176

1510

SOCIETY OF JESUS.

Nuptiae Pelei et Thetidos renovatae. Hoc est auspicatissimum Leopoldi I. Romanor. Imperat ... et serenissimae Eleonorae Magdalenae Theresiae ... connubium ... A tribus Societ. Iesu collegijs, Dusseldorpiensi, Marcodurano, et Monasteriensi Eifflae ... Coloniae Agrippinae, typis Petri Alstorff, 1676. Fol.

T.810

1511

STAINFORTH (William)

A sermon preached March 6. 1675. in the cathedral church of S. Peter in York; before... Sir Timothy Littleton, Kt. and Vere Bertie, esquire... London, for R. Royston, and R. Lambert bookseller in York, 1676. 4°

Wing S 5172.

T.602

1512

STANDFAST (Richard)

A sermon preached at Christ-Church in Bristol,
before... Sr Francis North... at the assizes held
there, August 7th, anno Dom. 1675. London, A.M.
for Charles Allen, bookseller in Bristol, 1676. 4°

Wing S 5213.

T.602

1513

STANDISH (John) *Rector of Conington.*

A sermon preached before the King at White-hal,
Septem. the 26th 1675. London: for Henry Brome,
1676. 4°

Wing S 5215.

T.380

1514

STANDISH (John) *Rector of Conington.*

A sermon preached before the King at White-hall,
Septemb. the 26th. 1675. 2nd ed. London: for
Henry Brome, 1676. 4°

Wing S 5216.
2 copies.

T.602   T.625

1515

TEMPLER (John)

The reason of episcopall inspection asserted in a
sermon at a visitation in Cambridge. Cambridge, John
Hayes, for William Morden, 1676. 4°

Wing T 665.
2 copies.

T.605   T.753

1516

TILLOTSON (John) *Archbishop of Canterbury.*

A sermon preached before the King, Febr. 25th 1675/6.
London: A. Maxwell, for Edward Gellibrand, 1676. 4°

Wing T 1229.

T.602

1517

A TRUE relation of the confession and execution of
Drinkwater the deer-stealer... London: D.M.,
1676. 4°

Not in Wing.

T.262

1518

A TRUE relation of the unexpected proceedings of
the King of Denmark, against the Duke of Holstein,
and Gottorp ... Communicated by a letter from a
gentleman out of Holstein, to an intimate friend
of his in London ... London, printed in the year
1676. 4°

Not in Wing.

T.61

1519

TURNER (Francis) *Bishop of Ely.*

Animadversions upon a late pamphlet [by Herbert
Croft] entituled The naked truth; or, The true
state of the primitive Church. [Anon.] London,
T. R. and are to be sold by Benj. Tooke, 1676. 4°

Wing T 3274.

T.176

1520

TWO letters concerning the East-India Company.
Printed in the year 1676. 4°

Wing T 3455.

T.324

1521

VERITABLE relation en forme de lettre, escritte à
un amy à Paris du camp de l'Armée de sa Majesté
tres-Chrestienne de St. Jean des Choux pres de
Sauerne, qui contient tout ce qui s'est passé entre
les deux armées. [No imprint, 1676?] 4°

T.820

1522

WAHRHAFFTIGE Erzehlungen Kayserlicher und
Frantzösischer Kriegs-Geschichten/ von der
Campagnia dises 1676-sten Jahrs/...
Strassburg/ zu finden bey Friderich Wilhelm
Schmuck, [1676]. 6 parts. 4°

T.820

1523

WYLLYS (J.)

Suum cuiq; or, Every one his own. In a short
discourse on the 21th. ver. of the 22th. chapt. of
St. Matthew... London, for Henry Brome, 1676. 4°

Wing W 3771.

T.602

1677

1524

ARDERNE (James)

A sermon preached at the visitation of... John
Lord Bishop of Chester, at Chester. London:
for H. Brome, 1677. 4°

Wing A 3625.

T.497

1525

BARROW (Isaac)

A sermon upon the passion of our blessed Saviour:
preached at Guild-hall Chappel on Good Friday, the
13th day of April, 1677 ... London, for Brabazon
Aylmer, 1677. 4°

Wing B 954.

T.176

1526

BIBLE. *New Testament.* [Malay]

Jang ampat evangelia ... That is, The four gospels
of our Lord Jesus Christ, and the Acts of the holy
Apostles, translated into the Malayan tongue.
[Edited by Thomas Hyde.] Oxford, H. Hall, 1677. 4°

Wing B 2796.
Prelims. only.

T.314

1527

The CASE of Sir Robert Viner, Edward Backwel...
goldsmiths, humbly offered to the consideration
of Parliament. [No imprint, 1677?] brs.

Not in Wing.

T.17

1528

A CATHOLICK pill to purge popery. With a preparatory
preface, obviating the growing malignity of popery
against Catholick Christianity. By a true son of the
Catholick Apostolick Church... London: for J.
Coles, and Will. Miller, 1677. 8°

Wing C 1495.

T.447

1529

CHARLES II, *King of England.*

His Majesties gracious patent to the goldsmiths,
for payment and satisfaction of their debt. London,
John Bill, Christopher Barker, Thomas Newcomb and
Henry Hills, 1677. Fol.

Wing C 3039.

T.543

1530

CHARLES II, *King of England.*

A treaty marine between ... Charles II ... and ...
Lewis XIV ... Concluded at St. Germains in Laye,
the twenty fourth day of February 1676/7 ... London,
the assigns of John Bill and Christopher Barker,
1677. 4°

Wing C 3617.

T.16

1531

A DIALOGUE between Lod. Muggleton and the Quakers:
shewing forth the damnable blasphemies of that
impudent impostor, collected out of their own
printed letters ... London, printed for J. C.,
1677. 4°

Wing D 1315.

T.79

1532

FERGUSON (Robert)

The East-India-trade a most profitable trade to the
Kingdom. And best secured and improved in a company,
and a joint-stock. Represented in a letter written
upon the occasion of two letters lately published,
insinuating the contrary. [Anon.] London, printed
in the year, 1677. 4°

Wing P 305 (attributed to Thomas Papillon).

T.324

1533

FRANÇOIS (Claude)

A sermon at the funeral of ... Henry de la Tour
d'Auvergne, Viscount of Turenne, Mareschal General
of France ... Englished out of French. London,
W. G. and are to be sold by Moses Pitt, 1677. 4°

Wing F 2073.

T. 65

1534

FRANTZÖSISCHE Plünderung und Verbrennung der Statt
Cron-Weissenburg, so geschehen im Januario dieses
1677.sten Jahrs. [No imprint, 1677.] 4°

T.820

1535

FRANTZÖSISCHE Verstörung der alten statt Hagenaw,
welche im Januario dieses 1677. Jahrs vollzogen
worden... [No imprint, 1677.] 4°

T.820

1536

GOODMAN (John)

A sermon preached at Bishops-Stortford, August 29.
1677. before ... Henry, Lord Bishop of London, &c.
at his lordship's primary visitation. London, for
R. Royston, 1677. 4°

Wing G 1123.

T.753

1537

The HOLY fast of Lent defended against all its
prophaners: or, A discourse, shewing that Lent-fast
was first taught the world by the apostles, as Dr.
Gunning... proved in a sermon printed by him in
the year, 1662... London, printed in the year,
1677. 4°

Wing H 2525.

T.17

1538

INGELO (Nathaniel)

A discourse concerning repentance ... London, T.R.
for Richard Marriott, and sold by William Bromwich,
1677. 8°

Wing I 182.

T.451

1539

JAMES II, *King of England.*

James Duke of York and Albany... Lord High
Admiral... Instructions for the better ordering
his Majesties fleet in sayling. (Instructions to
be observed by all masters... attending the fleet.)
(Instructions for the better ordering his Majesties
fleet in fighting.) [No imprint, 1677?] 3 parts.
Fol.

Not in Wing.

T.539

1540

JÄMMERLICHE Zerstörung der uhralten bischofflichen
Straßburgischen Residentz-Statt Zabern, welche
im Mayo dieses lauffenden 1677sten Jahrs von
denen im Elsaß liegenden Frantzosen, werckstellung
gemacht worden. [No imprint, 1677.] 4°

T.820

1541

JORDAN (Thomas)

Londons triumphs: illustrated with many magnificent
structures & pageants ... Performed October 29, 1677.
for the celebration, solemnity, and inauguration of the
Right Honourable Sir Francis Chaplin knight, Lord
Mayor of the city of London ... London, for John
Playford, 1677. 4°

Wing J 1043.

T.262

1542

A LETTER from a gentleman in Ireland to his brother
in England, relating to the concerns of Ireland in
matter of trade. London, Langley Curtiss, 1677. 4°

Wing L 1385.

T.118

1543

LEWIS (Mark)

Proposals to the King and Parliament, how this tax
of one hundred sixty thousand pounds per moneth, may
be raised ... London, printed in the year, 1677.
8°

Wing L 1847.

T.136

1677 (Cont'd.)

1544

A LIST of several ships belonging to English
merchants, taken by French privateers, since
December, one thousand six hundred seventy and three
... Amsterdam, printed in the year, 1677. 4°

Wing L 2405.
Incomplete.
Signature of John Forster.

T.90

1545

MARSCH der Kayserl. Armée in Lothringen, wie auch
Relation Dessen was bey Belägerund Eroberung der
Statt Saarbrücken sich begeben. [No imprint, 1677.]
4°

T.820

1546

MERITON (John)

A sermon preached before the King, at White-hall
July 30, 1676. London, for Simon Miller, 1677.
4°

Wing M 1821.

T.605

MULLINER (John)

A testimony against periwigs. 1677.

See no.4441.

1547

NEDHAM (Marchamont)

Honesty's best policy; or, Penitence the sum of
prudence: being a brief discourse, in honour of the
right honourable Anthony Earl of Shaftesbury's
humble acknowledgment and submission for his
offences ... at the bar of the House of Lords ...
[Anon.] [London, 1677.] 4°

Wing N 390.

T.123

1548

NEDHAM (Marchamont)

A second pacquet of advices and animadversions
sent to the men of Shaftesbury. Occasioned by
several seditious pamphlets ... [Anon.] Printed at
London, and are to be sold by Jonathan Edwin, 1677.
4°

Wing N 403.

T.118

1549

PHILLIPS (John)

A satyr against hypocrites ... [Anon.] London, for
O. B. and R. H., 1677. 4°

Wing P 2107.

T.269

1550

POOR Robins answer to Mr. Thomas Danson, author of
the late Friendly debate between Satan and Sherlocke
... By the author of Poor Robin's Weekly intelligence.
London, printed in the year, 1677. 4°

Wing P 2875.

T.176

1551

The PRESENT state of Christendome and the interest
of England, with a regard to France. In a letter
to a friend. London, J. B. for H. Brome, 1677. 4°

Wing P 3257.

T.90

1552

SHERLOCK (William)

An answer to a late scandalous pamphlet, entituled,
A friendly debate between Satan and Sherlock,
written by Thomas Danson, London: A. C. for
Walter Kettilby, 1677, 4°

Wing S 3262.

T.176

1553

SUNDRY considerations touching naturalization of
aliens: whereby the alledged advantages thereby
are confuted, and the contrary mischiefs thereof
are detected and discovered. [London, 1677?] 4°

Wing S 6178.

T.80

1554

THORPE (George)

A sermon preached before ... the Lord Mayor, and
aldermen of London, at Guild-hall chappel. London:
Andrew Clark, for Walter Kettilby, 1677. 4°

Wing T 1072.

T.175

1555

TURNOR (Thomas)

The joyful news of opening the Exchequer to the
gold-smiths of Lombard-street, and their creditors.
As it was celebrated in a letter [signed Tho. Turnor]
to the same friend in the countrey, to whom the
bankers case was formerly sent. By the author of the
same case... London, T.N. for William Place; and
Thomas Basset, 1677. Fol.

Wing T 3339.

T.543

1556

A VINDICATION OF Mr. Sherlock and his principles from
the malicious calumnies and cavils of Mr. Danson,
in a late scurrilous pamphlet, rudely entituled, A
friendly debate between Satan and Sherlock. London,
for Benj. Shirley, 1677. 4°

Wing V 483.

T.201

1557

WAHRHAFFTIGE Erzehlung von Hinrichtung dess
berühmbten Mordbrenners de La Brosse. [No
imprint], im Jahr 1677. 4°

T.820

1558

The WONDER of this age: or, God's miraculous
revenge against murder. Being a relation of an
undoubted truth out of the West... London, for
B.H., 1677. 4°

Wing W 3358 A.

T.262

1678

1559

BATTIE (William)

A sermon preached before the ... Lord Mayor of
London, at Guild-hall Chapell, November the 18th.
1677. London, F. Flesher for R. Royston, 1678.
4°

Wing B 1160.
2 copies.

T.175   T. 61

1560

BROWN (John) *of Wamphray.*

The history of the Indulgence shewing its rise,
conveyance, progress and acceptance: together with
a demonstration of the unlawfulness thereof ...
By a presbyterian. Printed in the year 1678. 4°

Wing B 5029.

T.142

1561

BUTLER (John) *Canon of Windsor.*

Christian liberty asserted in oposition to the
Roman yoke, delivered in a sermon preached in his
Majesties royal chappel of Windsor. The 8th. of
Decemb. 1678. London: M.C. for Walter Kettilby,
1678. 4°

Wing B 6277.
2 copies.

T.617 T.771

1562

CADE (William)

The foundation of popery shaken: or, The Bishop of
Rome's supremacy opposed. In a sermon, upon Matth.
XVI. 18, 19. London, T.M. for Robert Clavel, 1678.
4°

Wing C 194.

T.729

1563

CAMFIELD (Benjamin)

A sermon preached on the fast-day, November the xiiith.
1678... London, J. Macock, for Henry Brome, 1678.
4°

Wing C 385.
2 copies.

T.503 T.617

1564

CHARLES II, *King of England.*

His Majesties gracious speech, together with the
Lord Chancellors, to both Houses of Parliament,
on Thursday the 23d of May, 1678. London, John
Bill, Christopher Barker, Thomas Newcomb and Henry
Hills, 1678. Fol.

Wing C 3085.

T.543

1565

CHURCH OF ENGLAND.

A form of prayer, to be used on Wednesday November
the thirteenth; being the fast-day appointed by
the King... London, John Bill, Christopher Barker,
Thomas Newcomb, and Henry Hills, 1678. 4°

Wing C 4145.
2 copies.

T.321 T.411

1566

CRADOCK (Zachary)

A sermon preached before the King, February 10th
1677/8. London, for Richard Royston, 1678. 4°

Wing C 6766.

T.178

1567

CRADOCK (Zachary)

A sermon preached before the King, February 10th
1677/8. 2nd ed. London, for Richard Royston, 1678.
4°

Wing C 6767.
3 copies.

T.771 T.314 T.175

1568

CROFT (Herbert) *Bishop of Hereford.*

A second call to a farther humiliation. Being
a sermon preached the 24th of Novemb. last past.
London, for Charles Harper, 1678. 4°

Wing C 6973.

T.729

1569

DRYDEN (John)

All for love: or, The world well lost. A tragedy,
as it was acted at the Theatre-Royal ... In the
Savoy: Tho. Newcomb, for Henry Herringman, 1678.
4°

Wing D 2229.

T.501

1570

ENGLAND. *Parliament.*

Anno regni Caroli II. Regis ... decimo tertio ...
An Act for the establishing articles and orders for
the regulating and better government of his
Majesties navies, ships of war, and forces by sea.
London, S. and B. Griffin, 1678. 4°

Not in Wing.

T. 18

1571

An EXACT account of the trials of the several
persons arraigned at the sessions-house in the
Old-Bailey for London & Middlesex ... London,
G. Hills, and are to be sold by L. Curtiss, 1678.
4°

Wing E 3590.

T.310

1572

HICKES (George)

Ravillac redivivus, being a narrative of the late
tryal of Mr. James Mitchel, a conventicle-preacher,
who was executed the 18th of January last, for an
attempt which he made on the sacred person of the
Archbishop of St. Andrews ... In a letter from a
Scottish to an English gentleman. [Anon.] London,
Henry Hills, 1678. 4°

Wing H 1860.

T.177

1573

HOSPINIANUS (Rodolphus)

The Jesuit's manner of consecrating both the
persons and weapons imploy'd by them for the murdering
kings and princes by them accounted hereticks ...
Translated out of Hospinian's History of the
Jesuits ... London, T. S., 1678. 4°

Wing H 2888.

T.106

1574

HUMFREY (John)

The healing paper: or, A Catholick receipt for
union between the moderate bishop & sober nonconformist ... By a follower of peace, and lover
of sincerity ... London, for B. T. and T. M., 1678.
4°

Wing H 3680.

T. 17

1575

An IMPARTIAL and exact accompt of the divers
Popish books, beads, crucifixes and images, taken
at the Savoy, by Sr. William Waller ... Written in
a letter to a friend in the countrey. London:
for R. G., 1678. 4°

Wing I 79.

T,17

1576

JAMES (John)

Ad clerum. A visitation sermon preached at
Beckonsfield in the county of Bucks, April the 9th.
1678. London, T.H. for R. Chiswel, 1678.   4°

Wing J. 427.

T.733

1577

JANE (William)

The present separation self-condemned, and proved to
be schism: as it is exemplified in a sermon preached
upon that subject, by Mr. W. Jenkyn: and is further
attested by divers others of his own persuasion. All
produced in answer to a letter from a friend ...
[Anon.] London, for Edward Croft, 1678.   4°

Wing J 454.
2 copies.

T.310 T.517

1578

LAMPLUGH (Thomas) *Archbishop of York.*

A sermon preached before the House of Lords on the
fifth of November, in the abby-church at Westminster.
By the Right Reverend ... Thomas, Lord Bishop of
Exeter.   In the Savoy: Tho. Newcomb; and are to be
sold by Henry Brome, 1678. 48p.   4°

Wing L 305.

T.492

1579

LAMPLUGH (Thomas) *Archbishop of York.*

A sermon preached before the House of Lords on the
fifth of November, in the abby-church at Westminster.
By Thomas, Lord Bishop of Exeter.   In the Savoy,
Tho.Newcomb, and are to be sold by Henry Brome,
1678. 4° 43pp.

Wing L 305.
2 copies.

T.729   T.183

1580

L'ESTRANGE (*Sir* Roger)

An account of the growth of knavery, under the
pretended fears of arbitrary government, and Popery.
With a parallel betwixt the reformers of 1677,
and those of 1641, in their methods, and designs.
In a letter to a friend. [Anon,] London, H. H.
for Henry Brome, 1678. 4°

Wing L 1193.

T.61

1581

L'ESTRANGE (*Sir* Roger)

Tyranny and Popery lording it over the consciences,
lives, liberties, and estates both of King and
people. [Anon.] London, for Henry Brome, 1678,
4°

Wing L 1321.

T.61

1582

A LETTER from Amsterdam, to a friend in England.
London: for G. H., 1678. 4°

Wing L 1439.

T.177

1583

LLOYD (William) *Bishop of Worcester.*

A sermon at the funeral of Sir Edmund-Bury Godfrey...
Preached on Thursday the last day of October 1678.
in the parish church of St. Martin in the Fields.
London, Tho. Newcomb, for Henry Brome, 1678. 4°

Wing L 2700.
2 copies (one wanting title-page).

T.183 T.771

1584

MARVELL (Andrew)

An account of the growth of popery, and arbitrary
government in England... Printed at Amsterdam, and
recommended to the reading of all English protestants.
[London, 1678.] Fol.

Wing M 861
2 copies.

T.538   T.694

1585

NEDHAM (Marchamont)

Christianissimus Christianandus. Or, Reason for
the reduction of France to a more Christian state
in Europ ... [Anon.] London, Henry Hills, for
Jonathan Edwin, 1678. 4°

Wing N 383.

T,123

1586

PATRICK (Symon) *Bishop of Ely.*

Angliae speculum: A glass that flatters not;
presented to a country congregation at the late
solemn fast, April 24. 1678... By a dutiful son
of this Church.   London, for Richard Royston, 1678.
4°

Wing P 744
2 copies.

T.728 T.742

1587

PATRICK (Symon) *Bishop of Ely.*

A sermon preached at S. Paul Covent-Garden.   On
the late day of fasting & prayer.   Novemb. 13.
London: R. E. For J. Magnes and R. Bentley, 1678.
4°

Wing P 840.

T.728

1588

PATRICK (Symon) *Bishop of Ely.*

A sermon preached before the King, on the second
Sunday in Advent, Decemb. viii. 1678.   London,
J. Macock for R. Royston, 1678. 4°

Wing P 841.
2 copies.

T.729   T.175

1589

The PEACEABLE Christian.   A sermon.   London,
Tho. Snowden, for Tho. More, 1678.   4°

Wing P 923.

T.729

1590

REYNOLDS (John)

Vituli labiorum.   Or, A thanksgiving sermon, in
commemoration of our great deliverance from the
horrid powder-plot, 1605... Preached at St. Peter's,
Exon, Nov. 5. 1678... London, for Tho. Cockeril:
and Walter Dight bookseller in Exceter, 1678.   4°

Wing R 1318.

T.605

1591

SANCROFT (William) *Archbishop of Canterbury.*

A sermon preach'd to the House of Peers, Novemb.
13th 1678.   Being the fast-day appointed by the
King... In the Savoy: Tho. Newcomb, for Robert
Beaumont, 1678.   4°

Wing S 568.
5 copies.

T.78   T.234   T.503   T.728   T.729

1592

SCOTLAND. *Privy Council.*

A true narrative of the proceedings of his Majesties
Privy-Council in Scotland, for securing the peace
of that kingdom, in the year 1678 ... Reprinted at
London for A. F., 1678. 4°

Wing S 2003.
2 copies.

T.495   T,83

1593

SIXTUS V, *Pope.*

The Catholick cause; or, The horrid practice of
murdering kings, justified, and commended by the
Pope, in a speech to his cardinals, upon the
barbarous assassination of Henry the Third of
France ... London, for Walter Kettilby, 1678.   4°

Wing S 3931.

T.106

1594

SPRAT (Thomas) *Bishop of Rochester.*

A sermon preached at the anniversary meeting of the
sons of clergy-men.   In the church of St. Mary-le-Bow,
Nov. vii. 1678.   London, J. Macock, for Henry Broome,
1678. 4°

Wing S 5055.
2 copies.

T.503   T.729

1595

SPRAT (Thomas) *Bishop of Rochester.*

A sermon preached before the... House of Commons...
January 30, 1677/8.   London, T.N. for Henry Brome,
1678. 4°

Wing S 5053.
Wanting title-page.

T.310

1596

SPRAT (Thomas) *Bishop of Rochester.*

A sermon preached before the King at White-hall
December the 22. 1678.   London, S.R. for Henry
Brome, 1678. 4°

Wing S 5056.

T.497

1597

STANLEY (Charles) *8th Earl of Derby.*

The Jesuites policy to suppress monarchy, proving
out of their own writings that the Protestant
religion is a sure foundation and principle of a
true Christian.   Written by a person of honor.
London, for William Cademan, 1678. 4°

Wing D 1088.

T. 83

1598

STILLINGFLEET (Edward) *Bishop of Worcester.*

A sermon preached on the fast-day, November 13. 1678.
at St Margarets Westminster, before the honourable
House of Commons.   London, Margaret White, for Henry
Mortlock, 1678. 4°

Wing S 5649.

T.503

1599

STILLINGFLEET (Edward) *Bishop of Worcester.*

A sermon preached on the fast-day, November 13. 1678.
at St Margarets Westminster, before the honourable
House of Commons.   2nd ed.   London, Margaret White,
for Henry Mortlock, 1678.   4°

Wing S 5650.
2 copies.

T.310   T.729

1600

STRANGE and terrible news from sea.   Or: A true
relation of a most wonderful violent tempest of
lightning and thunder ... Printed by A. P. and T. H.
for John Clarke, 1678. 4°

Wing S 5831.

T.262

1601

THOMAS (William) *Bishop of Worcester.*

A sermon preached before the right honourable, the
lords assembled in Parliament, in the Abbey Church
of St. Peters, Westminster, upon the fast-day
appointed April 10. 1678. By William, Lord Bishop
of St. Davids. London, Tho. Newcomb for Tho.
Collins; and William Leach, 1678. 4°

Wing T 982.

T.175

1602

TILLOTSON (John) *Archbishop of Canterbury.*

A sermon preached November 5. 1678. at St. Margarets
Westminster, before the honourable House of Commons.
London, J. D. for B. Aylmer, and William Rogers,
1678. 4°

Wing T 1230.
2 copies.

T.729   T.183

1603

TILLOTSON (John) *Archbishop of Canterbury.*

A sermon preached November 5. 1678. at St. Margarets
Westminster, before the honourable House of Commons.
6th ed. London, J.D. for Brabazon Aylmer. And
William Rogers, 1678. 4°

Wing T 1231.
3 copies.

T.234 T.709 T.728

1604

The TRYAL of Edward Coleman, gent., for conspiring the death of the King, and the subversion of the government of England... London, for Robert Pawlet, 1678. Fol.

Wing T 2185.

T.686

1605

The TRYAL of William Stayley, goldsmith; for speaking treasonable words against his most sacred Majesty... London, for Robert Pawlet, 1678. Fol.

Wing T 2237.

T.687

1606

The TRYALS of William Ireland, Thomas Pickering, and John Grove; for conspiring to murder the King: who upon full evidence were found guilty of high treason... London, for Robert Pawlet, 1678. Fol.

Wing T 2268.

T.690

1607

TURNER (Bryan)

A sermon preached before the ... Lord Mayor, and aldermen of London, at the Guild-hall chappel, Octob. the 28th, 1677. London, for Henry Brome, 1678. 4°

Wing T 3270.

T.175

1608

TURNOR (Thomas)

Three seasonable considerations upon his Majesty's gracious letters patents lately granted to the goldsmiths, their heirs and assigns, for security and satisfaction of their debt. By a friend to debtor and creditor, who hath taken the same advice he now gives. London, for W.B., 1678. 4°

Wing T 3341.

T.495

1609

WILLIAMS (John) *Bishop of Chichester.*

A sermon preached upon the fifth of November, 1678. By a protestant divine. London: for Dorman Newman, 1678. 4°

Wing W 2723.

T.729

1679

1610

An ABSTRACT of the contents of several letters relating to the management of affairs with Rome, by the D. of Y. and others... Published for satisfaction of the people, with a preface, Shewing our present dangers, and the authors thereof. By a protestant. [London, 1679?] Fol.

Wing A 131.

T.688

1611

An ACCOUNT of the proceedings at the Guild-hall of the city of London, on Saturday, September 12.1679. With the substance of Sir Thomas Player's speech, and the Lord Mayor's answer thereunto. [London, 1679.] Fol.

Wing A 357.

T.688

1612

ADVICE to a painter, &c. [By John Ayloffe or Henry Savile.] [London, 1679.] Fol.

Not in Wing. 2 copies.
Attributions in *Poems on affairs of state*, I,213-9.

T.532 T.688

1613

ALSOP (George)

A sermon preached at sea, before the Honourable Sir Robert Robinson, Knight, principal commander of his Majestie's squadron of ships, now riding at Spitt-Head, November the 24th, 1678 ... London, for Langley Curtis, 1679. 4°

Wing A 2903.

T.234

1614

ANANIAS and Saphira discover'd. Or, The true intent of a pamphlet called Omnia comesta belo: in a letter by way of answer... London: M.Clark, for Henry Brome, 1679. 4°

Wing A 3048.
2 copies.

T.90 T.580

1615

B. (A.)

The reasons for non-conformity examined and refuted, in answer to a late letter from a minister to a person of quality, shewing some reasons for his non-conformity. London, for Walter Kettilby, 1679. 4°

Wing B 26.

T.123

1616

B.(J.)

A compleat and true narrative of the manner of the discovery of the popish plot to his Majesty, by Mr. Christopher Kirkby. With a full answer to a late pamphlet entituled [Reflections upon the Earl of Danby.] Relating to the murther of Sir Edmundbury Godfrey... London, Henry Million, 1679. Fol.

Wing B 98.

T.688

1617

B.(J.)

Some reflections upon the Earl of Danby, in relation to the murther of Sir Edmondbury Godfrey. In a letter to a friend. [London, 1679.] Fol.

Wing B 127.

T.688

1618

B. (R.)

A word in season: or, A letter from a reverend divine to a justice of the peace in London ... [Signed R. B.] London, for R. G. in the year, 1679. 4°

Wing B 173 A.

T. 17

1619

BARLOW (Thomas) *Bishop of Lincoln.*

A discourse of the peerage & jurisdiction of the lords spiritual in Parliament. Proving... that they have no right in claiming any jurisdiction in capital matters. [Anon.] London, printed in the year 1679. Fol.

Wing B 829.

T.688

1620

BARLOW (Thomas) *Bishop of Lincoln.*

Popery: or, The principles & positions approved by the Church of Rome (when really believ'd and practis'd) are very dangerous to all... In the Savoy: T. Newcomb, and sold by James Collins, 1679. 4°

Wing B 839.
2 copies.

T.83 T.495

621

BARROW (Isaac)

A sermon preached on the fifth of November, MDCLXXIII. London, J.D. for Brabazon Aylmer, 1679. 4°

Wing B 953.

T.580

1622

BEDLOE (William)

The excommunicated prince: or, The false relique. A tragedy. As it was acted by his Holiness's servants. Being the popish plot in a play. London: for Tho. Parkhurst, D. Newman, Tho. Cockerill, and Tho. Simmons, 1679. Fol.

Wing B 1676.

T.538

1623

BEDLOE (William)

A narrative and impartial discovery of the horrid popish plot: carried on for the burning and destroying the cities of London and Westminster... London, for Robert Boulter, John Hancock, Ralph Smith, and Benjamin Harris, 1679. Fol.

Wing B 1677.
2 copies.

T.533 T.538

1624

BETHEL (Slingsby)

An account of the French usurpation upon the trade of England, and what great damage the English do yearly sustain by their commerce ... [Anon.] London: printed in the year, 1679. 4°

Wing B 2062.

T. 90

1625

BLOUNT (Charles)

An appeal from the country to the city, for the preservation of his Majesties person, liberty, property and the protestant religion... [Anon.] London, printed in the year 1679. Fol.

Wing B 3300.
Incomplete.

T.538

1626

BOROVIUS (Georgius)

Vox rugientis leonis; sive epistola exhortatoria ad papismum patris Georgii Borovii ... una cum responsoria ad eandem cura G. J. Londini, excudebat anno, 1679. 4°

Wing B 3776 (=V 739).

T.341

1627

BRADSHAW (John) *Political Writer.*

The Jesuite countermin'd, or, An account of a new plot carrying on by the Jesuites... [The preface signed J.Br.] London, printed in the year 1679. 4°

Wing B 4087.

T.106

1628

BROME (James)

The famine of the word threatned to Israel, and Gods call to weeping and to mourning. Being two sermons... London, M. Clark, for Richard Chiswel. 1679.

Wing B 4856.

T.580

1629

BRYDALL (John)

The clergy vindicated, or the rights and privileges that belong to them, asserted; according to the laws of England. More particularly, touching the sitting of bishops in Parliament... [Anon.] London, E.T. and R.H., 1679. Fol.

Wing B 5255.

T.688

1630

BURY (John)

A true narrative of the late design of the papists to charge their horrid plot upon the protestants... As appears by the depositions taken before... Sir Joseph Williamson... and the several examinations before Sir William Waller... [Anon.] London: for Dorman Newman, 1679. Fol.

Wing B 6215.

T.538

1631

C.

The deposition, and farther discovery of the late horrid plot, by one Mr. C---, late servant to Sir Tho. G--- in York-shire ... London, for F. F., [1679]. 4°

Wing C 1.

T. 90

1632

CARKESSE (James)

Lucida intervalla: containing divers miscellaneous poems, written at Finsbury and Bethlem by the doctors patient extraordinary... [Anon.] London, printed anno Dom. 1679. 4°

Wing C 577.

T.407

1633

CARYLL (John)

Naboth's vinyard: or, The innocent traytor: copied from the original of holy Scripture, in heroick verse ... [Anon.] London, for C.R., 1679. Fol.

Wing C 745A.
2 copies.

T.532 T.543

1634

CHARLES II, *King of England.*

His Majesties declaration for the dissolution of his late Privy-Council, and for constituting a new one, made... April the twentieth, 1679. London, John Bill, Thomas Newcomb, and Henry Hills, 1679. Fol.

Wing C 2967.

T.688

1635

CHARLES II, *King of England.*

His Majesties most gracious speech, together with the Lord Chancellors, to both houses of Parliament, on Thursday the 6th of March 1678/9. London, John Bill, Christopher Barker, Thomas Newcomb, and Henry Hills, 1678/9. Fol.

Wing C 3184A.

T.688

1636

CHARLES II, *King of England.*

His Majesties most gracious speech together with the Lord Chancellors, to both Houses of Parliament, on Wednesday the 30th of April, 1679. London, John Bill, Thomas Newcomb, and Henry Hills, 1679. Fol.

Wing C 3186.

T.688

CHRISTIAN (Edward)

Reflections upon a paper intituled, Some reflections upon the Earl of Danby. 1679.

See no. 5267.

1637

CHURCH OF ENGLAND.

A form of prayer, to be used on Friday the eleventh of April; being the fast-day appointed by the Kings proclamation ... London, John Bill, Thomas Newcomb, and Henry Hills, 1679. 4°

Wing C 4146.

T.123

1638

CLOAK in its colours; or the Presbyterian unmasked, and proved as dangerous as Papists to the Church of England ... London, printed anno Dom. 1679. 4°

Wing C 4719.

T. 17

1639

CROFT (Herbert) *Bishop of Hereford.*

The legacy of the right reverend ... Herbert Lord Bishop of Hereford: to his diocess. Or, A short determination of all controversies we have with the papists, by Gods holy word. The second impression corrected ... London, for Charles Harper, 1679. 4°

Wing C 6967.

T.106

1640

D. (J.)

A word without-doors concerning the bill for succession. [London, 1679.] 4°

Wing D 48.

T.90

1641

DANGERFIELD (Thomas)

Mr. Tho. Dangerfields particular narrative, of the late popish design to charge those of the presbyterian party with a pretended conspiracy against his Majesties person, and government. London, for Henry Hills, John Starkey, Thomas Basset, John Wright, Richard Chiswell, and Samuel Heyrick, 1679. Fol.

Wing D 192.

T.533

1642

DAVIES (James)

A sermon on Psal. CXIX. v.57. Shewing wherein the good man's portion and dependence consists. London: for Henry Brome, 1679. 4°

Wing D 386.
2 copies.

T.617 T.742

1643

The DECLARATION of the rebels in Scotland. [Edinburgh, 1679.] Fol.

Wing D 760.

T.538

1644

A DIALOGUE between Duke Lauderdale and the Lord Danby. [London, 1679.] brs.

Wing D 1309.

T.688

1645

The DISCOVERY of the Popish Plot, being the several examinations of Titus Oates D.D. before the high court of Parliament, the Lord Chief Justice, Sir Edmund-Bury Godfry, and several other of his Majesties justices of the peace. London, printed, 1679. 4°

Wing D 1658 (= O 34).
Numerous MS amendments to the text.

T.139

1646

ELIZABETH I, *Queen of England.*

The last speech and thanks of Queen Elizabeth of ever blessed memory, to her last Parliament, after her delivery from the popish plots, & c. London, printed, 1679. Fol.

Wing E 530 (?)

T.538

1647

ENGLAND. *Laws, Statutes.*

An abstract of all the penal-laws now in force against Jesuites, priests, and Popish recusants. Collected for the ease of justices of the peace, and others who are obliged to put the laws in execution. London, for John Starkey, 1679. 4°

Wing E 862.

T. 95

1648

ENGLAND. *Parliament.*

An exact collection of all orders, votes, debates, and conferences in the House of Peers, and House of Commons ... concerning Thomas Earl of Danby, and the other five lords in the Tower ... London, for Francis Smith, 1679. Fol.

Wing E 1531.
3 copies

T.538 T.688 T.694

1649

ENGLAND. *Parliament.*

An impartial account of divers remarkable proceedings the last sessions of Parliament relating to the horrid popish plot, & c ... London, printed anno 1679. Fol.

Wing E 1588 (=I 62)

T.690

1650

ENGLAND. *Parliament, House of Commons.*

The reasons and narrative of proceedings betwixt the two houses: which were delivered by the House of Commons to the Lords, at the conference touching the tryal of the lords in the Tower. On Monday, the 26th. of May, 1679. [London, 1679.] Fol.

Wing E 2693.
2 copies

T.538 T.688

1651

EPISCOPAL government and the honour of the present bishops proved necessary to be maintained: in a modest and seasonable address to the citizens of London. By a zealous lover of the Protestant religion, and a hearty friend to the City of London. London, for Henry Brome, 1679. 4°

Wing E 3160.
3 copies. (The T. 17 copy is incomplete.)

T.580 T. 17 T. 61

1652

The ESTABLISHED test, in order to the security of his Majesties sacred person, and government, and the Protestant religion. Against the malitious attempts and treasonable machinations of Rome ... London, T. N. for Jonathan Edwin, 1679. 4°

Wing E 3344.
"By Dr. Nalson as Mr. Proudfoot assured me."

T. 61

1653

EVERARD (Edmund)

Discourses on the present state of the protestant princes of Europe ... Wherein the general scope of this horrid popish plot is laid down, and presented to publick view ... London, for Dorman Newman, 1679. Fol.

Wing E 3528.

T.538

1654

The EXECUTION of Mr. Rob. Foulks, late minister of Stanton-Lacy in Shropshire. With some account of his most penitent behaviour, confession, last speech, &c ... London: for R. G., 1679. 4°

Wing E 3853 (?)

T.310

1655

F. (E.)

A letter from a gentleman of quality in the country, to his friend, upon his being chosen a member to serve in the approaching Parliament ... Being an argument relating to the point of succession to the Crown ... Printed in the year 1679. Fol.

Wing F 14.

T.688

1656

FIAT justitia, & ruat coelum. Or, Somewhat offer'd in defence of the imperial crown of England, and its successor. In answer to a speech, pretended to be spoken in the honourable House of Commons, upon reading the bill against the D[uke]. By a true Englishman. [London, 1679?]. Fol.

Wing F 845.

T.688

1657

FOULKES (Robert)

An alarme for sinners: containing the confession, prayers, letters, and last words of Robert Foulkes, late minister of Stanton-Lacy ... With an account of his life ... London, for Langley Curtis, 1679. 4°

Wing F 1644.
2 copies.

T.310 T. 17

1658

G. (W.)

The case of succession to the Crown of England stated, in a letter to a member of the Honorable House of Commons. Being an answer to that pamphlet that pretends to prove the Parliament hath no power to alter succession. By W.G. Gent. Printed, 1679. 4°

Wing G 67.
2 copies.

T.17 T.688

1659

GOD'S wonderful judgment in Lincoln-shire: or, A dreadful warning to children that are undutiful to their parents ... London, for L.C., 1679. 4°

Not in Wing.

T.411

1660

GREAT and weighty considerations relating to the D. or successor of the Crown. Humbly offer'd to the Kings most excellent Majesty, and both Houses of Parliament. By a true patriot. [London, 1679.] Fol.

Wing G 1660.

T.688

1661

HARRIS (Walter)

A farewel to Popery: in a letter to Dr. Nicholas, Vice-Chancellor of Oxford ... from W. H. ... London, for Walter Kettilby, 1679. 4°

Wing H 884.
2 copies.

T.617 T. 61

1662

HASCARD (Gregory)

A sermon preached upon the fifth of November, 1678. at St. Clements Danes. London, S. and B.G. for William Crook, 1679. 4°

Wing H 1113.

T.617

1663

HESS (Joannes Armondus de)

A letter from a Jesuite: or, The mysterie of equivocation ... [Anon.] London, for W. W., 1679. 4°

Wing H 1624.

T.17

1679 (Cont'd.)

1664

An HUMBLE proposal to cause bancrupts make better and more speedie payment of their debts to their creditors ... By a well-wisher to trade, and the publick good. London, printed in the year, 1679. 4°

Wing H 3594.

T. 95

1665

An IMPARTIAL account of the trial of the Lord Cornwallis. London, printed in the year. 1679. Fol.

Wing I 78.

T.688

1666

An IMPARTIAL state of the case of the Earl of Danby, in a letter to a member of the House of Commons. London, printed in the year, 1679. Fol.

Wing I 88.

T.688

1667

JACOB (John)

... The Jew turned Christian; or, The corner-stone: wherein is an assertion of Christ being the true Messiah. London: A.M. and R.R. for Tho. Cockerill, 1678/9. 4°

Wing J 98.

T.729

1668

JANE (William)

A sermon preached on the day of the publick fast, April the 11th, 1679. at St. Margarets Westminster; before the honourable House of Commons. London: M.C. for Henry Brome, and Richard Chiswel, 1679. 4°

Wing J 456.
4 copies.

T.123   T.497   T.617   T.728

1669

JENISON (Robert)

The narrative of Robert Jenison, of Grays-Inn, Esquire. Containing. I. A further discovery and confirmation of the late horrid and treasonable popish plot ... London, for F. Smith, T. Basset, J. Wright, R. Chiswel and S. Heyrick, 1679. Fol.

Wing J 561.
2 copies.

T.533   T.538

1670

The JESUITES new discoveries. Printed in the year, 1679. 4°

Not in Wing.

T.106

1671

The JESUITS letter of thanks to the covenanters in Scotland: for their compliance in divers material points of Roman Catholick doctrine and practice. 2nd ed. London, printed in the year, 1679. 4°

Wing J 721.

T.142

1672

The JESUITS unmasked: or Politick observations upon the ambitious pretensions and subtle intreagues of that cunning society... London, for Henry Brome, 1679. 4°

Wing J 728.

T.106

1673

JONES (Henry) *Bishop of Meath*.

A sermon at the funeral of James Margetson, D.D. late Arch-Bishop of Armagh ... preached at Christ Church, Dublin, Aug. 30. 1678 ... London, for Nathanael Ranew, 1679. 4°

Wing J 947.
2 copies.

T.580   T.144

1674

JONES (Henry) *Bishop of Meath*.

A sermon of antichrist, preached at Christ- Church, Dublin, Novemb. 12, 1676. 2nd ed. revised and corrected. Reprinted at London for Nathaniel Ponder, 1679. 4°

Wing J 950.
2 copies.

T.144   T.61

1675

JORDAN (Thomas)

London in luster: projecting many bright beams of triumph ... Performed with great splendor on Wednesday, October XXIX. 1679. at the initiation and instalment of the Right Honourable Sir Robert Clayton, knight, Lord Mayor of the city of London ... London, for John Playford, 1679. 4°

Wing J 1035.

T.407

1676

L'ESTRANGE (*Sir* Roger)

The case put, concerning the succession of his Royal Highness the Duke of York, [Anon,] London: M. Clark, for Henry Brome, 1679. 4°

Wing L 1206.
2 copies.

T.61   T.95

1677

L'ESTRANGE (*Sir* Roger)

The case put, concerning the succession of his Royal Highness the Duke of York. With some observations upon The political catechism [by Henry Parker], The appeal, &c. and three or four other seditious libels. [Anon.] The second edition enlarged. London: M.C. for Henry Brome, 1679. 4°

Wing L 1207.

T.330

1678

L'ESTRANGE (*Sir* Roger)

The free-born subject: or, The Englishmans birth-right: asserted against all tyrannical usurpations either in church or state. [Anon.] London, for Henry Brome, 1679. 4°

Wing L 1248.

T.61

1679

L'ESTRANGE (*Sir* Roger)

The reformed Catholique: or, The true Protestant ... [Anon.] London, for Henry Brome, 1679. 4°

Wing L 1289.

T.61

1680

A LETTER from no body in the city, to no body in the countrey. Published at the importunity of no body. London, printed for some-body, 1679. 4°

Wing L 1491.

T.17

1681

A LETTER from some-body in the country: in answer to no-bodies letter: directed from London: in vindication of some-body. London, printed for D. M., 1679. 4°

Wing L 1510.

T.17

1682

A LETTER to an honourable member of the House of Commons; in the vindication of the Protestant Reformed Church (as established by law) in opposition to the superstitious and idolatrous Church of Rome. London, printed, and are to be sold by the booksellers, 1679. 4°

Wing L 1699.

T.17

1683

A LETTER to the Right Honorable A. Earl of Essex, from Dublin. Declaring the strange obstinacy of papists (as hope, so) in Ireland ... London, for Langley Curtis, 1679. 4°

Wing L 1747.

T.106

1684

LLOYD (William) *Bishop of Worcester*.

Papists no Catholicks: and Popery no Christianity. 2nd ed. much enlarged. [Anon.] London: for Henry Brome, 1679. 4°

Wing L 2689.

T.106

1685

LLOYD (William) *Bishop of Worcester*.

A sermon preached at St. Martins in the Fields, on November the fifth, 1678. London: T.N. for Henry Brome, 1679. 4°

Wing L 2709.
2 copies.

T.617   T.728

1686

LLOYD (William) *Bishop of Worcester*.

A sermon preached before the King at White-hall. The 24th. of Novemb. 1678. London: M. C. for Henry Brome, 1679. 4°

Wing L 2711.
2 copies.

T.497   T.132

1687

LONDON'S flames: being an exact and impartial account of divers informations given in to the committee of Parliament ... concerning the dreadful fire of London in the year 1666, and the many other strange fires which have happened since ... London, printed in the year 1679. 4°

Wing L 2927.

T.95

1688

LYNFORD (Thomas)

A sermon preached before ... the Lord Mayor and aldermen of the city of London at the Guild-hall chappel, Novem. xvi. 1679. London, for Walter Kettilby, 1679. 4°

Wing L 3568.

T.175

1689

MONTAGU (Ralph) *Duke of Montagu*.

Two letters from Mr. Montagu to the Ld Treasurer ... which were read in the House of Commons. Together with the Lord Treasurer's speech in the House of Peers, upon an impeachment of high treason ... London, Jonathan Edwin, 1679. 4°

Wing M 2468.

3 copies.

T.17   T.95   T.123

1690

MORTON (Thomas) *Bishop of Durham*.

An exact account of Romish doctrine in the case of conspiracy and rebellion, by pregnant observations collected out of the express dogmatical principles of popish priests and Jesuites. [Anon.] ... Reprinted and published. By Ezerel Tonge. London, for John Starkey, 1679. 4°

Wing M 2839.
2 copies (one copy incomplete).

T.83   T.515

1691

NALSON (John)

A letter from a Jesuit at Paris, to his correspondent in London; shewing the most effectual way to ruine the government and Protestant religion. [Anon.] London, Jonathan Edwin, 1679. 4°

Wing N 110.
2 copies.

T.95   T.123

1692

NEEDHAM (Robert)

Six sermons, preached (most of them) at S. Maries in Cambridge. London, M. Clark for Walter Kettilby, 1679. 8°

Wing N 410.

T.451

1693

NEVILLE (Robert)

The necessity of receiving the holy sacrament ... Declared in a sermon, at a conference of the several ministers of the deanery of Braughin in the county of Hertford ... London, J.D. for Benj. Billingsly, 1679. 4°

Wing N 523

T.580

1694

NEVILLE (Robert)

A sermon preached before the Right Honourable, the Lord Mayor, and court of aldermen, of the city of London, at Guildhall-chappel, August 18. 1678.   London, for Benj. Billingsley, 1679.   4°

Wing N 525.
2 copies.

T.605   T.729

1695

OATES (Titus)

A sermon preached at St. Michaels Wood-street, at the request of some friends; and now published to prevent mistakes ... London, H. Hills and T. Newcomb, for Gabriel Kunholt, 1679.   4°

Wing O 53.
2 copies.

T.617   T.234

1696

OATES (Titus)

A true narrative of the horrid plot and conspiracy of the popish party against the life of his sacred Majesty, the government and the protestant religion.. London: for Thomas Parkhurst, and Thomas Cockerill, 1679.   Fol.

Wing O 59.
2 copies.

T.533   T.687

1697

OBSERVATIONS on the last Dutch wars, in the years 1672, and 1673. With some reflections upon the city and country ... London, printed in the year, 1679.   4°

Wing O 104.

T.17

1698

OMNIA comesta a bello: or, An answer out of the west, to a question out of the north ... Printed in the year, 1679.   4°

Wing O 291.

T.187

1699

OWEN (John)

The Church of Rome no safe guide ... London, for Nathaniel Ponder, 1679.   4°

Wing O 727.

T.106

1700

PALMER (Roger) *Earl of Castlemaine.*

The compendium: or, A short view of the late tryals, in relation to the present plot against his Majesty and government: with the speeches of those that have been executed... [Anon.] London, printed in the year 1679.   4°

Wing C 1241.

T.495

1701

The PAPISTS plot of firing dicovered, in a perfect account of the late fire in Fetter-Lane, London ... London, for A. B., 1679.   4°

Wing P 318,

T.106

1702

A PARADOX against liberty.   Written by the lords, during their imprisonment in the Tower.   A poem... London, printed in the year, 1679.   Fol.

Wing P 330
Title-page only.

T.538

1703

A PATERN for true Protestants. Setting forth divers examples by way of encouragement to all the Kings subjects, to be liberal in their contributions towards the rebuilding of S. Pauls Cathedral ... London, for T, Burrel, 1679, 4°

Wing P 870.

T.17

1704

PELLING (Edward)

A sermon preached on the thirtieth of January, 1678/9.   Being the anniversary of the martyrdom of King Charles...   London, for Jonathan Edwin, 1679.   4°

Wing P 1091.
2 copies.

T.310   T.497

1705

PELLING (Edward)

A sermon preach'd to the Artillery Company at S. Mary le Bow, October 21. 1679...   London, for Jonathan Edwin, 1679.   4°

Wing P 1092.

T.669

1706

A PERFECT catalogue of all the lords treasurers that have been in England to this present year, 1679. With particular observations on Thomas Earl of Danby. [London, 1679.]   Fol.

Wing P 1474.

T.688

1707

PINDAR (William)

A sermon of divine providence, in the special preservation of governments and kingdoms... London: M. Clark, for H. Brome, 1679.   4°

Wing P 2250
2 copies.

T.503   T.729

1708

POPE (Walter)

The Catholick ballad: or, An invitation to popery, upon considerable grounds and reasons.   [Anon.] London: for Henry Brome, 1679.   Fol.

Wing P 2908 A.

T.532

1709

The POPISH plot more fully discovered: being a full account of a damnable and bloody design of murdering his sacred Majesty...   London, for H.B., 1679.   Fol.

Wing P 2955.

T.538

1710

PRANCE (Miles)

The additional narrative of Mr. Miles Prance of Covent-Garden, goldsmith, who was the discoverer of the murder of Sr. Edmondbury Godfrey...   London, for Francis Smith, Thomas Basset, John Wright, Richard Chiswel and Samuel Heyrick, 1679.   Fol.

Wing P 3170.

T.538

1711

PRANCE (Miles)

A true narrative and discovery of several very remarkable passages relating to the horrid popish plot: as they fell within the knowledge of Mr Miles Prance...   London, for Dorman Newman, 1679. Fol.

Wing P 3177.
3 copies.

T.533   T.538   T.686

1712

The PROCEEDINGS against Mr. J, Reading, who being found guilty of high misdemeanours, was fined to the King in one thousand pounds ... London, for B, W., 1679.   4°

Not in Wing.

T.90

1713

RAMSAY (William)

Mirmah, or, The deceitful witness.   A prophecy of Solomon now first and seasonably discovered... Being a sermon preached Novemb.5. on Prov. 14, 25... London, for Benj. Billingsley, 1679.   4°

Wing R 219.

T.605

1714

A REJOYNDER to the reply concerning the peerage and jurisdiction of the lords spiritual in Parliament, &c ...   London, A.G. and J.P. for Jonathan Edwin, 1679. Fol.

Wing R.770.

T.688

1715

S. (T.)

Several weighty considerations humbly recommended to the serious perusal of all, but more especially to the Roman Catholicks of England. To which is prefix'd an epistle from one who was lately of that communion, to Dr. Stillingfleet... London, for, and to be sold by John Holford; and John Harding, 1679. 4°

Wing S 183.
2 copies.

T.106   T.495

1716

SCROGGS (*Sir* William)

The Lord Chief Justice Scroggs his speech in the Kings-bench the first day of this present Michaelmas Term 1679, .Occasion'd by the many libellous pamph-lets which are publisht against law...   London, for Robert Fawlet, 1679.   Fol.

Wing S 2122.

T.538

1717

SHARP (John) *Archbishop of York.*

A sermon preached on the day of the public fast, April the 11th. 1679. at St. Margarets Westminster; before the House of Commons.   London: M.C. for Walter Kettilby, 1679.   4°

Wing S 2984.

T.617

1718

SMITH (John) *of Walworth.*

The narrative of Mr. John Smith of Walworth... Containing a further discovery of the late horrid and popish-plot...   London, Robert Boulter, 1679. Fol.

Wing S 4127.
3 copies.

T.533   T.538   T.687

1719

STILLINGFLEET (Edward) *Bishop of Worcester.*

A sermon preached before the King at White-hall, March 7. 1678/9.   London, for Henry Mortlock, 1679. 4°

Wing S 5654.
2 copies.

T.605   T.617   T.234

1720

STILLINGFLEET (Edward) *Bishop of Worcester.*

A sermon preached on the fast-day, November 13. 1678. at St. Margarets Westminster, before the honourable House of Commons. 5th ed. London, Margaret White, for Henry Mortlock, 1679.   4°

Wing S 5653.
2 copies.

T.728   T.234

1721

TILLOTSON (John) *Archbishop of Canterbury.*

A sermon preached at the first general meeting of the gentlemen, and others in and near London, who were born within the county of York.   In the church of S. Mary-le-Bow, Decemb.3.1678.   London, for Brabazon Aylmer: and William Rogers, 1679.   4°

Wing T 1232.
2 copies.

T.709   T.742

1722

TILLOTSON (John) *Archbishop of Canterbury.*

A sermon preached at White-hall, April the 4th, 1679, London, for Brabazon Aylmer: and William Rogers, 1679.   4°

Wing T 1233.
3 copies.

T.733   T.234   T.123

1723

TOSIER (John)

A letter from Captain John Tosier, commander of his Majesties ship the Hunter at Jamaica. With a narrative of his embassy and command in that frigat to the captain general and governour of Havannah ... Printed in the year 1679.   4°

Wing T 1950,

T.17

1724

The TRUE narrative of the proceedings at the sessions for London and Middlesex, begun on Thursday the 5th of June 1679...   London: for L.C., 1679.   4°

Wing T 2815.

T.310

1725

A TRUE relation of what is discovered concerning the murther of the Archbp of St. Andrews, and of what appears to have been the occasion thereof. [London, 1679.] Fol.

Wing T 3080.

T.538

1726

TRUTH and honesty in plain English, or, A brief survey of some of those libels & pamphlets printed and published since the dissolution of the last Parliament ... By a true lover of monarchy and the Anglicane-Church. London, printed in the year, 1679. 4°

Wing T 3149.

T.61

1727

The TRYAL of Philip Earl of Pembroke and Montgomery, before the Peers in Westminster-Hall, on Thursday the 4th. of April 1678. Printed in the year 1679. Fol.

Wing T 2209.

T.688

1728

The TRYALS of Sir George Wakeman Barronet. William Marshall, William Rumley, and James Corker, Benedictine monks, for high treason, for conspiring the death of the King... London, for H. Hills, T. Parkhurst, J. Starkey, D. Newman, T. Cockeril, and T. Simmons, 1679. Fol.

Wing T 2259.

T.686

1729

TURNER (John) *Hospitaller.*

Animadversions upon the doctrine of transub-stantiation. A sermon preached before the Right Honourable the Lord Mayor and the court of aldermen, Octob.XIX. 1679... London, for Walter Kettilby, 1679. 4°

Wing T 3299.

T.580

1730

WALLER (*Sir* William)

The tragical history of Jetzer: or, A faithful narrative of the feigned visions, counterfeit revela-tions, and false miracles of the Dominican Fathers of the covent of Berne... Collected from the records of the said city by the care of Sir William Waller... London, for Nathanael Ponder, 1679. Fol.

Wing W 548.

T.533

1731

WILLES (Samuel)

A sermon preach'd at the funeral of the Right Honble the Lady Mary, daughter to Ferdinando late Earl of Huntingdon, and wife to William Jolife... London, J.D. for John Baker, 1679. 4°

Wing W 2305.

T.580

1732

WILLIAMS (John) *Bishop of Chichester.*

A sermon preached before the Right Honourable the Lord Mayor, and aldermen of the city of London, at the Guild-hall chappel, October 12. 1679. London: M. Clark, for R. Chiswel, and W. Kettilby, 1679. 4°

Wing W 2724.

T.580

1733

WILSON (Thomas) *Rector of Arrow.*

A sermon on the gunpowder treason, with reflections upon the late plot. London: for Henry Brome, 1679. 4°

Wing W 2936.

T.617

1734

A WORD within-doors: or, A reply to a Word without-doors [by J.D.]: in which the divers opinions of succession to the Crown of England, are compared. In a letter to a person of worth. [London, 1679?] Fol.

Wing W 3576.

T.688

1735

WYATT (William)

A sermon preached to those, who had been scholars of St. Paul's School, in Guild-hall chapel, London, at their anniversary-meeting on St. Pauls Day, 1678/9. London, for Benj. Tooke, 1679. 4°

Wing W 3735.

T.175

1736

YARRANTON (Andrew)

A coffee-house dialogue: or A discourse between Captain Y—— and a young barrester of the Middle Temple; with some reflections upon the bill against the D. of Y. [Anon.] [London, 1679?] Fol.

Wing Y 10.

T.688

1680

1737

A. (M.)

Speculum Baxterianum: or, Baxter against Baxter. Being sober and usefull reflections upon a treatise of Mr. Richard Baxter's, stiled, Sacriliegious desertion of the holy ministry rebuked, and tolerated preaching of the gospel vindicated... London; for Richard Chiswell, 1680. 4°

T.330

1738

An ACCOUNT of the new sheriffs, holding their office. Made publick, upon reason of conscience, respecting themselves and others, in regard to the Act for corporations...London, Thomas Snowden, 1680. Fol.

Wing A 333.
2 copies.

T.532 T.537

1739

ALSOP (Vincent)

The mischief of impositions: or, An antidote against a late discourse, partly preached at Guild-Hall chappel, May 2. 1680. called The mischief of separation [by Edward Stillingfleet] ... [Anon.] London: for Benj. Alsop, 1680. 4°

Wing A 2917.

T.308

1740

ARTICLES stipulated and required from Old Nick, by the Duke of L-- , a person of great quality in France, when he resigned and made himself over to the devil. Translated from the French. London: printed in the year 1680. 4°

Wing A 3886.

T. 90

1741

B, (H.)

A true copy of a letter (intercepted) going for Holland, directed thus for his (and his wives) never failing friend Roger Le Strange at the Oranges Court with care and speed ... London, for H. B., Feb. 10th. 1680. Fol.

Wing B 80.

T. 85

1742

B.(S.)

A letter wherein is shewed, first, what worship is due to images according to the second Council of Nice. Secondly, that the papists are very unjust in charging schism on the Church of England... London, for William Churchill bookseller in Dorchester, 1680. 4°

Wing B 176.

T.763

1743

BAXTER (Richard)

Richard Baxters answer to Dr Edward Stillingfleet's charge of separation ... London, for Nevil Simmons, and Thomas Simmons, 1680. 4°

Wing B 1183.

T.330

1744

A BRIEF method of the law. Being an exact alpha-betical disposition of all the heads necessary for a perfect common-place... London, the Assignees of Richard and Edward Atkins, for John Kidgell, 1680. Fol.

Wing B 4605.

T.531

1745

BRYDALL (John)

The white rose: or a word for the House of York, vindicating the right of succession, in a letter from Scotland to a peer of this realm... [Anon.] London, printed anno Dom. 1680. Fol.

Wing B 5268.

T.688

1746

BUCHANAN (George)

De jure regni apud Scotos... Translated out of the original Latine into English by Philalethes. Printed, 1680. 12°

Wing B 5275.
Wanting title-page.

T.459

1747

CAMFIELD (Benjamin)

The commination prescribed in the liturgy of the Church of England, vindicated... in a sermon, preached to a countrey audience on the first Sunday in Lent, 1679/80... London, for H. Brome, and R. Chiswell, 1680. 4°

Wing C 377.

T.580

1748

CELLIER (Elizabeth)

Malice defeated: or a brief relation of the accusation and deliverance of Elizabeth Cellier... London, for Elizabeth Cellier, 1680. Fol.

Wing C 1661.

T.684

1749

CLARK (Margaret)

The true confession of Margret Clark, who consented to the burning of her masters Mr. Peter Delanoy's house in Southwark... London: Joseph Collier, 1680. 4°

Wing C 4482.

T.411

1750

A COMPLEAT catalogue of all the stitch'd books and single sheets printed since the first discovery of the Popish Plot, (September 1678.) to January 1679/80 ... Printed in the year 1680. 4°

Wing C 5630.

T. 90

1751

CONSTABLE (Robert)

God and the king: or, Monarchy proved from holy writ, to be the onely legitimate species of politick government, and the onely polity con-stituted and appointed by God ... London, for W. L., 1680. 4°

Wing C 5935.

T. 90

1752

CORKER (James)

A rational account given by a young gentleman to his uncle, of the motives and reasons why he is become a Roman Catholick ... [Anon.] [No imprint, c. 1680.] 4°

Not in Wing.

T.181

1753

The COUNTER-PLOT, or the close conspiracy of atheism and schism opened, and, so defeated ... By a real member of this most envy'd as, most admired, because, best reformed protestant Church of England ... London, for Henry Brome, 1680. 4°

Wing C 6522.

T.178

1754

CROFT (Herbert) *Bishop of Hereford.*

Naked truth: the first part, or, The true state of the primitive Church. By an humble moderator ... Printed in the year 1680. Fol.

Wing C 6971.

T.532

1755

CROMWELL (Oliver)

A most learned, conscientious, and devout excercise, or sermon, held forth the last Lords-day of April, in the year 1649 ... As it was faithfully taken in characters by Aaron Guerdon. London: printed in the year 1680. 4°

Wing C 7118.

T. 90

1756

DAILLÉ (Jean)

A lively picture of Lewis du Moulin, drawn by the incomparable hand of Monsieur Daille, late minister of Charenton. London, for Rich. Royston, 1680. 4°

Wing D 116.

T.310

1757

DANGERFIELD (Thomas)

The information of Thomas Dangerfield, gent. delivered at the bar of the House of Commons ... London, the assigns of John Bill, Thomas Newcomb, and Henry Hills, 1680. Fol.

Wing D 187.

T.533

1758

A DIALOGUE between the Pope and a phanatick, concerning affairs in England. By a hearty lover of his prince and country. London: printed in the year 1680. 4°

Wing D 1333.
2 copies.

T.178   T. 90

1759

DISCOURSES upon the modern affairs of Europe, tending to prove, that the illustrious French monarchy may be reduced to terms of greater moderation ... Printed in the year, 1680. 4°

Wing D 1630.
2 copies.

T.90   T.117

1760

DOVE (Henry)

A sermon preached before the honourable House of Commons, at St. Margarets Westminster, November 5. 1680. London, M.C. for H. Brome, and Benj. Tooke, 1680.   4°

Wing D 2048.

T.492

1761

DUGDALE (Stephen)

The further information of Stephen Dugdale, gent. Delivered at the bar of the House of Commons ... London: for Thomas Parkhurst: and Thomas Simmons, 1680. Fol.

Wing D 2474.
3 copies.

T.533   T.686   T.694

1762

DUGDALE (Stephen)

The information of Stephen Dugdale, gent. Delivered at the bar of the House of Commons ... London, the assigns of John Bill, Thomas Newcomb, and Henry Hills, 1680. Fol.

Wing D 2475.
2 copies.

T.533   T.694

1763

DU MOULIN (Louis)

The last words of Lewis du Moulin: being his retraction of all the personal reflections he had made on the divines of the Church of England... London, for Rich. Royston, an Dom. 1680. 4°

Wing D 2542.

T.182

1764

DU MOULIN (Louis)

A short and true account of the several advances the Church of England hath made towards Rome: or, A model of the grounds upon which the Papists for these hundred years have built their hopes and expectations ... London: printed in the year, 1680. 4°

Wing D 2553.

T.117

1765

ELYS (Edmund)

Edmundi Elisii ... ad Samuelem Parkerum, S. T. P., epistola tertia. Cui accesserunt Epistola ad authorem [i.e. John Williams] libelli cujusdam cui titulus, Dr. Stillingfleet against Dr. Stillingfleet: Ac breviuscula paraenesis ad authorem [i.e. William Jenkyn] Celeusmatis, seu clamoris ad theologos ... Londini, typis A. G. & J. P. pro Roberto Clavel, 1680. 3 parts. 8°

Wing O E 656 A.

T.388

1766

ENGLAND. *Parliament. House of Commons.*

The report of the Committee for receiving informations concerning the Popish Plot; upon the complaint of Mr. Peter Norris. Presented to the House of Commons, upon Thursday the 9th. day of Decemb. 1680. London, for John Wright, and Richard Chiswell, 1680.   Fol.
Part of a collection of reports, no.47, pp.123-9. cf. Wing R 1084A.

T.694

1767

ENGLAND. *Parliament. House of Commons.*

The resolutions of the House of Commons, for the impeachment of Sir William Scroggs... Sir Thomas Jones... Sir Richard Weston... Upon the report of the Committee of the Commons appointed to examine the proceedings of the judges in Westminster-Hall... London, for John Wright, and Richard Chiswell, 1680. Fol.
Part of a collection of reports, no.50, pp.148-159. cf. Wing R 1084A.

T.531

1768

ENGLAND. *Parliament. House of Commons.*

A true and perfect collection of all messages, addresses, &c. from the House of Commons, to the Kings most excellent Majestie, with his Majesties gracious answers thereunto. From 1660 ... untill the dissolution of the Parliament, 14. August, 1679. London, printed in the year, 1680. Fol.

Wing E 2746.

T.538

1769

The EXAMINATION of Captain William Bedlow deceased, relating to the popish plot, taken in his last sickness, by Sir Francis North ... London, the assigns of John Bill, Thomas Newcomb, and Henry Hills, 1680. Fol.

Wing E 3714.
2 copies.

T.533   T.694

1770

An EXAMINATION of the Impartial state of the case of the Earl of Danby. In a letter to a member of the House of Commons. London: Walter Davis, 1680. Fol.

Wing E 3727.

T.688

1771

FARIA (Francisco de)

The information of Francisco de Fario, delivered at the bar of the House of Commons ... London, the assigns of John Bill, Thomas Newcomb, and Henry Hills, 1680. Fol.

Wing F 425.
3 copies.

T.533   T.686   T.694

1772

FELL (John) *Bishop of Oxford.*

A sermon preached before the House of Peers on December 22, 1680. Being the day of solemn humiliation. Printed at the Theater in Oxford, anno Dom. 1680. 4°

Wing F 621.
2 copies.

T.495   T.175

1773

FITZGERALD (David)

A narrative of the Irish popish plot for the betraying that kingdom into the hands of the French ... London: for Tho. Cockerill, 1680. Fol.

Wing F 1072.

T.533

1774

The FRENCH politician found out, or considerations on the late pretensions that France claims to England and Ireland; and her designs and plots in order thereunto. By a well-wisher of his countrey. London, for Robert Harford, 1680. 2 parts. 4°

Wing F 2194.

T. 90

1775

A FULL and true account of the penitence of John Marketman, during his imprisonment in Chelmsford gaol for murthering his wife ... To which is prefixed, A sermon preached ... immediately before his execution. By Richard Hollingworth. London, for Samuel Walsall, 1680. 2 parts, 4°

Wing F 2308 A.

T.90

1776

A FULL relation of the contents of the black box. With some other remarkable occurrences. Printed in the year, 1680. 4°

Wing F 2361.

T. 90

1777

GOODMAN (John)

A sermon preached before the Right Honourable Sir Robert Clayton ... at Guild-hall chappel, January XXV. 1679. London, for R. Royston, 1680. 4°

Wing G 1125.

T.310

1778

GREBNER (Paul)

Paul Grebners prophecy concerning these times. Written in the reign of Queen Elizabeth, anno 1582. Taken out of the original copy ... with a paraphrase thereupon, by a person of honour. London, for Thomas Burrel, 1680. brs.

Wing G 1809.

T.537

1779

GROVE (Robert) *Bishop of Chichester.*

Roberti Grovii S.T.B. Responsio ad nuperum libellum qui inscribitur Celeusma seu clamor ad theologos hierarchiae Anglicanae, &c. [by William Jenkyn]. Londini, typis J. M. pro Gualt. Kettilby, 1680. 4°

Wing G 2157.
2 copies.

T.495   T. 1

1780

HANCOCKE (Robert)

A sermon preached before the Right Honourable the Lord Mayor, and the court of aldermen, at Guildhall-chappel, Septemb. 19. 1680. London, S. Roycroft for Tho. Flesher, and W. Leech, 1680.   4°

Wing H 645.
2 copies.

T.625   T.670

1781

HAWLES (*Sir* John)

The English-mans right. A dialogue between a barrister at law, and a jury-man ... [Anon.] London: for Richard Janeway, 1680. 4°

Wing H 1185.

T. 90

1782

HAWLES (*Sir* John)

The grand-jury-man's oath and office explained: and the rights of English-men asserted. A dialogue between a barrister at law, and a grand-jury-man. [Anon,] London, for Langley Curtis, 1680. 4°

Wing H 1187.

T. 90

1783

HICKERINGILL (Edmund)

Curse ye meroz, or the fatal doom. In a sermon preached in Guild-hall-chappel London... London, J. R. for J. Williams, 1680. 4°

Wing H 1803.
2 copies.

T.178   T.765

1784

HINDMARSH (Thomas)

A sermon preach'd in the cathedral of Lincoln, August 1. 1680. (Being the assize Sunday.) London, for Joseph Hindmarsh, 1680. 4°

Not in Wing.

T.175

1785

HOBBES (Thomas)

An historical narration concerning heresie, and the punishment thereof. London: printed in the year 1680. Fol.

Wing H 2238.

T.538

1786

HOLLINGWORTH (Richard)

An account of the spirits working upon the minds of men, in the several ages of the Christian Church. In a visitation sermon, before... Henry Lord Bishop of London; at Burntwood in Essex, Septemb. 14. 1680. London, for Hen. Brome, 1680. 4°

Wing H 2485.

T.753

1787

HONEST Hodge & Ralph holding a sober discourse, in answer to a late scandalous and pernicious pamphlet, called, A dialogue between the Pope and a phanatick concerning affairs in England, Written by a person of quality. London, for John Kidgell, 1680. 4°

Wing H 2584.

T.90

1788

HORATIUS FLACCUS (Quintus)

Horace's Art of poetry. Made English by ... the Earl of Roscommon. London, for Henry Herringman, 1680. 4°

Wing H 2768,
2 copies.

T.314   T.117

1789

HOWARD (William) *Viscount Stafford.*

The speech of William late Lord Viscount Stafford, on the scaffold on Tower-Hill, immediately before his execution, Wednesday, Decemb. 29. 1680. London: for W. Bailey, 1680. Fol.

Wing S 5156.

T.684

1790

HUMFREY (John)

An answer to Dr. Stillingfleet's sermon, by some nonconformists, being the peaceable design renewed. Wherein the imputation of schism wherewith the Doctor hath charged the nonconformists meetings, is removed ... [Anon.] London, for J. Janeway, 1680. 4°

Wing H 3668.

T.492

1791

HUNT (Thomas) *Lawyer.*

The great and weighty considerations, relating to the Duke of York, or, successor of the Crown. Offered to the King, and both houses of Parliament: considered. With an answer to a letter, from a gentleman of quality in the country [E.F.] to his friend, relating to the point of succession to the Crown... [Anon.] London, printed in the year, 1680. Fol.

Wing H 3751.
2 copies.

T.531   T.688

1792

HYDE (Edward) *Earl of Clarendon.*

Two letters written by the Right Honourable Edward Earl of Clarendon... one to his Royal Highness the Duke of York: the other to the Dutchess, occasioned by her embracing the Roman Catholick religion. [London, 1680?] Fol.

Wing C 4429.
2 copies.

T.538   T.688

1793

The INTEREST of the three kingdom's, with respect to the business of the black box, and all the other pretensions of his grace the Duke of Monmouth, discuss'd and asserted. In a letter to a friend. London, printed in the year, 1680. 4°

Wing I 270 A.
2 copies.

T. 90   T. 95

1794

The INTEREST of the three kingdom's, with respect to the business of the black box, and all the other pretensions of his grace the Duke of Monmouth, discuss'd and asserted; in a letter to a friend. The second impression; with large additions, upon the subject of the black box. London, for James Vade, 1680. 4°

Wing I 270 (?)

T.178

1795

An INTIMATION of the deputies of the States General, in a late discourse with Mr. Sidney, extraordinary envoy from his Majesty of Great Britain. [London, 1680.] Fol.

Wing I 275.

T.537

1796

JENISON (Robert)

The information of Robert Jennison of Grays-Inn, Gent. Delivered at the bar of the House of Commons ... London, the assigns of John Bill, Thomas Newcomb, and Henry Hills, 1680. Fol.

Wing J 559.
2 copies.

T.533   T.694

1797

JORDAN (Thomas)

London's glory, or, the lord mayor's show: containing an illustrious description of the several triumphant pageants ... Performed on Friday, October XXIX. 1680. for the entertainment of the Right Honourable Sir Patience Warde, knight, Lord Mayor of the city of London ... London, for John and Henry Playford, 1680. 4°

Wing J 1037.

T.407

1798

A JUST and modest vindication of his Royal Highness the Duke of York: in observation upon a late revived pamphlet, intituled, A word without doors ... London, for Thomas Benskin, 1680. 4°

Wing J 1222.
2 copies.

T.182   T.90

1799

The KNAVERY of astrology discover'd, in observations upon every month, for the year 1680... By Tim. Tell-Troth... London, for T.B. and R.E., 1680. 4°

Wing K 676.

T.123

1800

LAMBE (John)

A sermon preached before the King, at his Majesties free-chappel of Windsor, June 13. 1680. London, for Walter Kettilby, 1680. 4°

Wing L 220.

T.492

1801

The LATE keepers of the English liberties drawn to the life: in the qualifications of persons by them declar'd capable to serve in Parliament. London, printed in the year 1680. 4°

Wing L 549.

T.90

1802

L'ESTRANGE (*Sir* Roger)

Citt and Bumpkin. In a dialogue over a pot of ale, concerning matters of religion and government. [Anon.] London, for Henry Brome, 1680. 4°

Wing L 1216.

T.310

1803

L'ESTRANGE (*Sir* Roger)

Citt and Bumpkin. Or, A learned discourse upon swearing and lying, and other laudable qualities tending to a thorow reformation. The second part. [Anon.] London, for Henry Brome, 1680. 4°

Wing L 1221.

T.178

1804

L'ESTRANGE (*Sir* Roger)

Discovery upon discovery, in defence of Doctor Oates against B. W.'s libellous vindication of him, in his Additional discovery; and in justification of L'Estrange against the same libell. In a letter to Doctor Titus Oates ... London, for Henry Brome, 1680. 4°

Wing L 1238.

T.178

1805

L'ESTRANGE (*Sir* Roger)

A further discovery of the plot: dedicated to Dr. Titus Oates. London, for Henry Brome, 1680. 4°

Wing L 1252.
2 copies.

T.310   T.330

1806

L'ESTRANGE (*Sir* Roger)

L'Estrange's case in a civil dialogue betwixt 'Zekiel and Ephraim. London, for H. Brome, 1680. 4°

Wing L 1204.
2 copies.

T.183   T.330

1807

L'ESTRANGE (*Sir* Roger)

Lestrange's narrative of the Plot. Set forth for the edification of his Majesties liege-people. London, J. B. for Hen. Brome, 1680. 4°

Wing L 1275.

T.178

1808

L'ESTRANGE (*Sir* Roger)

The Presbyterian sham, or, A commentary upon the new old answer of the assembly of divines to Dr. Stillingfleet's sermon ... [Anon.] London, printed in the year, 1680. 4°

Wing L 1286.

T.90

1809

L'ESTRANGE (*Sir* Roger)

A seasonable memorial in some historical notes upon the liberties of the presse and pulpit ... [Anon.] London, for Henry Brome, 1680. 4°

Wing L 1301.

T.61

1810

L'ESTRANGE (*Sir* Roger)

A short answer to a whole litter of libellers. London, J. B. for Hen. Brome, 1680. 4°

Wing L 1307.

T.85

1811

L'ESTRANGE (*Sir* Roger)

A short answer to a whole litter of libels. London, J.B. for Hen. Brome, 1680. 4°

Wing L 1307 A.

T.178

1812

L'ESTRANGE (*Sir* Roger)

The state and interest of the nation, with respect to his Royal Highness the Duke of York, discours'd at large; in a letter to a member of the Honourable House of Commons. [Anon.] London, printed in the year, 1680. 4°

Wing L 1309.

T.90

1813

A LETTER from a gentleman in the city, to one in the country; concerning the bill for disabling the Duke of York to inherit the imperial crown of this realm. London, printed in the year, 1680. 4⁰

Wing L 1390.

T.95

1814

A LETTER to Dr du Moulin, containing a charitable reproof for his schismatical book entituled, A short and true account of the several advances the Church of England hath made towards Rome ... London, printed in the year 1680. Fol.

Wing L 1700.

T.532

1815

A LETTER to the Earl of Shaftsbury this 9th of July, 1680. From Tom Tell-Troth a downright Englishman. [London, 1680.] Fol.

Wing L 1734.

T.537

1816

LEWIS (William)

The information of William Lewis, gent. Delivered at the bar of the House of Commons ... Together with his further narrative relating thereto ... London, for Randal Taylor, 1680. Fol.

Wing L 1851.
2 copies.

T.533 T.694

1817

LLOYD (William) *Bishop of Worcester.*

A sermon preached before the House of Lords, on November 5, 1680. By ... William Lord Bishop of St. Asaph. London, M. C. for Henry Brome, 1680. 4⁰

Wing L 2712.

T.175

1818

LONDON.

The humble petition of the Right Honourable the Lord Mayor, aldermen, and commons of the city of London, in common-council assembled, on the thirteenth of January, 1680. To the King's most excellent Majesty, for the sitting of this present Parliament prorogu'd to the twentieth instant ... London, Samuel Roycroft, 1680. Fol.

Wing H 3577.

T.537

1819

LONDON,

The proceedings at the Guild-hall in London, on Thursday July the 29th, 1680. [London, 1680.] Fol.

Wing P 3559.

T.537

1820

LONDON.

To the Kings most excellent Majesty. The humble petition and address of the Lord Mayor, aldermen, and commons of the city of London. London, for Francis Smith, 1680. brs.

Wing T 1520.

T.537

1821

MALLET (*Sir John*)

Concerning penal laws: a discourse or charge at sessions in the burrough of Bridgewater, 12 July, 1680 ... London, for Thomas Cockeril, 1680. Fol.

Wing M 338.

T.537

1822

MANNINGHAM (Thomas) *Bishop of Chichester.*

A sermon preach'd before the Right Honourable Sir Robert Clayton Lord Mayor of London, at Guild-hall-chappel, December 7. 1679. London: for William Crooke, 1680. 4⁰

Wing M 502.

T.234

1823

MANSELL (Roderick)

An exact and true narrative of the late popish intrigue, to form a plot, and then to cast the guilt and odium thereof upon the protestants ... London: for Tho. Cockerill and Benj. Alsop, 1680. Fol.

Wing M 514.

T.687

1824

A MOST serious expostulation with several of my fellow citizens in reference to their standing so high for the D.Y 's interest at this juncture of time. [London, 1680?] Fol.

Wing Y 1.

T.688

1825

N. (N.)

The arts and pernicious designs of Rome. Wherein is shewn what are the aims of the Jesuits & friers ... By a person of their own communion ... [Signed N.N.] London: for Henry Brome, 1680. 4⁰

Wing A 3895.

T.106

1826

NALSON (John)

Foxes and fire-brands: or a specimen of the danger and harmony of Popery and separation... [Anon. The preface signed Philirenes.] London, for Benjamin Tooke, 1680. 4⁰

Wing N 102.
2 copies.

T.90 T.178

1827

OATES (Titus)

An exact and faithful narrative of the horrid conspiracy of Thomas Knox, William Osborne and John Lane, to invalidate the testimonies of Dr. Titus Oates, and Mr. William Bedlow... London: for Tho. Parkhurst, Tho. Cockerill and Benj. Alsop, 1680. Fol.

Wing O 41.

T.533

1828

OLDHAM (John)

The clarret drinkers song: or, the good fellows design. By a person of quality. London, printed 1680. Brs.

Wing O 233

T.532

1829

ONSLOW (Richard)

A sober discourse of the honest cavalier: wherein, the author of the Dialogue between the Pope and a fanatick vindicates himself ... By a person of quality ... London, for Henry Brome, 1680. 4⁰

Wing O 350.

T.178

1830

OSBORNE (Thomas) *1st Duke of Leeds.*

The answer of the Right Honourable the Earl of Danby to a late pamphlet, entituled, An examination of the Impartial state of the case of the Earl of Danby. London, E.R. to be sold by Randal Taylor, 1680. Fol.

Wing L 920.

T.688

1831

OSBORNE (Thomas) *1st Duke of Leeds.*

The Earl of Danby's answer to Sr. Robert Howard's book, entituled An account of the state of his Majesties revenue; as it was left by the Earl of Danby at Lady-day, 1679. London, for Randall Tayler, 1680. Fol.

Wing L 921.

T.537

1832

OTWAY (Thomas)

The orphan: or, the unhappy-marriage: a tragedy, as it is acted at... The Duke's theatre... London, for R. Bentley, and M. Magnes, 1680. 4⁰

Wing O 552.

T.502

1833

OWEN (John)

A brief vindication of the non-conformists from the charge of schisme. As it was managed against them in a sermon preached before the Lord Mayor; by Dr. Stillingfleet... [Anon.] London, for Nathaniel Ponder, 1680. 4⁰

Wing O 723

T.492

1834

P.
A letter to a friend, reflecting upon the present condition of this nation, and demonstrating, an exclusion of his Royal Highness from the succession, to be unlawful and unjust. [London, 1680?] Fol.

Wing P 1.

T.688

1835

PARSONS (Robert)

A sermon preached at the funeral of the Rt Honorable John Earl of Rochester, who died at Woodstock-Park, July 26. 1680, and was buried at Spilsbury in Oxford-shire, Aug. 9. Oxford, printed at the Theater for Richard Davis and Tho: Bowman, in the year, 1680. 4⁰

Wing P 570.
3 copies.

T.182 T.605 T.742

1836

A PLEA to the Duke's answers. Fiat justitia, ruat coelum. Anglice, the bill in the honourable the late House of Commons against the D. was their duty. [London, 1680.] Fol.

Wing P 2526.

T.688

1837

The POPES letter, to Maddam Cellier in relation to her great sufferings for the Catholick cause, and likewise Maddam Celliers lamentation standing on the pillory... London, D. Mallet, 1680. Fol.

Wing P 2935.

T.684

1838

The POPISH plot, taken out of several depositions made and sworn before the Parliament. [London, 1680?] Fol.

Wing P 2956.

T.538

1839

The PRESBYTERIANS loyalty, and zeal for religion, briefly demonstrated in a letter, by way of reply to a late fanatical pamphlet, intituled, The knave uncloak'd; or, The Jesuit in its colours ... Printed in the year 1680. 4⁰

Wing P 3228.

T.90

1840

The PRIVILEGES and practice of Parliaments in England: collected out of the common laws of this land ... London, for Robert Harford, 1680. 4⁰

Wing P 3535.
2 copies.

T.321 T.117

1841

R, (M.)

Three great questions concerning the succession and the dangers of popery, fully examin'd. In a letter to a member of this present Parliament. London, for M. R., 1680. 4⁰

Wing R 49.

T.182

1842

RAMSAY (William)

Maroum: the destruction of the Lord of Rome, and of all Romish kings and powers, and of the whole Roman Church... Being a sermon preacht in Istleworth church, Decemb. 7. 1679... London, J.A. for Benj. Billingsley, 1680. 4⁰

Wing R 218.

T.580

1843

REYNER (Samuel)

A sermon preached at the funeral of the Right
Honourable Denzell Lord Holles... London, for
William Churchill bookseller in Dorchester, 1680.
4°

Wing R 1233.

T.234

1844

The RISE and fall or degeneracy of the Roman Church
... London, for Benjamin Billingsley, 1680. 4°

Wing R 1535.

T.106

1845

The ROMAN wonder. Being truth confest by papists
wherein the clergy of the Church of England in their
charge of heretical and damnable doctrines upon the
Jesuits are fully and fairly justified... Written
originally in Latine and French, and now translated
into English... London, for Walter Kettilby, 1680.
Fol.

Wing R 1893.

T.687

1846

ROME'S overthrow, in a fatal blow at her greatest
idol ... By a son of the Church. London, for John
Kidgell, 1680. 4°

Wing R 1903

T.106

1847

SCOTLAND. *Parliament.*

A summary of the acts of the parliaments of Scotland
againt popery and papists. [London, 1680?] Fol.

Wing S 1347A.

T.688

1848

SCOTT (John)

A sermon preached before the Artillery Company of
London, September 15, 1680, at St. Mary Le Bow ...
London, for John Baker, and to be sold by him, and
by Walter Kettilby, 1680. 4°

Wing S 2066.
2 copies.

T.732   T.175

1849

A SEASONABLE address to the Right Honourable, the
Lord Mayor, court of aldermen, and commoners of the
city of London, upon their present electing of
sherifs. By Philo-patris, citizen, &c. [London,
1680.] Fol.

Wing S 2205.

T.537

1850

A SEASONABLE memento both to king and people upon
this critical juncture of affaires ... London,
printed in the year 1680. 4°

Wing S 2232.

T.90

1851

The SENTIMENTS. A poem to the Earl of Danby in
the Tower. By a person of quality. London: for
James Vade, 1679 [overprinted 1680]. Fol.

Wing S 2558.

T.53.

1852

The SEVERAL informations of John Mac-Namarra,
Maurice Fitzgerald, and James Nash: relating to
the horrid popish plot in Ireland... London, for
John Wright, and Richard Chiswell, 1680. Fol.

Wing S 2766.

T.533

1853

SHARP (John) *Archbishop of York.*

A sermon preached before the right honourable the
Lord Mayor and aldermen, in Bow-Church; on the
feast of St. Michael, 1680... London, M.F. for
Walter Kettilby, 1680. 4°

Wing S 2987.

T.492

1854

SHEERES (*Sir* Henry)

A discourse touching Tanger: in a letter to a
person of quality. To which is added, The interest
of Tanger: by another hand. [Anon.] London,
printed in the year 1680. 4°

Wing D 1621.

T.248

1855

A SHORT reply to M.L'Estrange's short answer to a
litter of libels in a letter to a friend ...
London, printed in the year 1680. 4°

Wing S 3623 A.
Incomplete.

T.85

1856

SMITH (William) *Prebendary of Norwich.*

A sermon preached on the fourth Sunday in Lent,
in the cathedral church of Norwich. Wherein is
represented the great sin and danger of neglecting
the holy communion. London, for Walter Kettilby,
1680. 4°

Wing S 4282.

T.605

1857

The SOVEREIGN: or a political discourse upon the
office and obligations of the supreme magistrate
... London, printed in the year, 1680. 4°

Wing S 4777.

T.90

1858

SPEED (John) *1628-1711.*

Batt upon Batt. A poem upon the parts, patience,
and pains, of Barth. Kempster, clerk, poet, cutler,
of Holy-Rood-Parish in Southampton. By a person
of quality... London: for Samuel Crouch, 1680. 4°

Wing S 4887.

T.310

1859

STILLINGFLEET (Edward) *Bishop of Worcester.*

The mischief of separation. A sermon preached at
Guild-hall chappel ... London, for Henry Mortlock,
1680. 4°

Ch. Ch. S 5604 +.
3 copies.

T.728   T.605   T.178

1860

STUDY to be quiet: or serious and seasonable advice
to the citizens of London. Written by a citizen of
London. London: for Henry Brome, 1680. 4°

Wing S 6092.

T.90

1861

TILLOTSON (John) *Archbishop of Canterbury.*

The protestant religion vindicated, from the charge
of singularity & novelty: in a sermon preached
before the King at White-hall, April the 2d. 1680.
London: for Brabazon Aylmer: and William Rogers,
1680. 4°

Wing T 1214.
6 copies.

T.709   T.728   T.178   T.497   T.580   T.605

1862

TREASON, Popery, &c. Brought to a publique test:
with regard to the grounds of his Majesties late
declaration concerning the succession of the
Crown ... London, printed in the year 1680. 4°

Wing T 2079.

T.90

1863

A TRUE narrative of the popish-plot against King
Charles I. and the protestant religion: as it
was discovered by Andreas ab Habernfeld to Sir
William Boswel... Also a compleat history of the
papists late Presbyterian plot discovered by Mr.
Dangerfield... London, for Robert Harford, 1680.
Fol.

Wing T 2805 (=H164).

T.687

1864

The TRYAL and sentence of Elizabeth Cellier; for
writing, printing, and publishing, a scandalous
libel, called Malice defeated &c... London, for
Thomas Collins, 1680. Fol.

Wing T 2171.

T.684

1865

The TRYAL of Sr. Tho. Gascoyne Bar. for high-
treason in conspiring the death of the King, the
subversion of the government, and alteration of
religion, on Wednesday the 11th of February 1679...
London: for Tho. Basset, and Sam. Heyrick, 1680.
Fol.

Wing T 2219.

T.684

1866

TURBERVILL (Edward)

The information of Edward Turbervill of Skerr in
the county of Glamorgan, gent. Delivered at the
bar of the House of Commons... London, the assigns
of John Bill, Thomas Newcomb, and Henry Hills, 1680.
Fol.

Wing T 3252.
3 copies.

T.533   T.686   T.694

1867

UNDERWOOD (John)

The Church-papist (so called;) his religion and
tenets fully discovered ... By one of the children of
the late captivity. London, for Robert Hartford,
1680. 4°

Wing U 46.

T.106

1868

WARD (*Sir* Patience)

The speech of the Right Honourable Sir Patience
Warde, Lord Mayor elect, at Guild-hall, London,
September 29, 1680... London, for Thomas Collins,
and Brabazon Aylmer, 1680. Fol.

Wing W 794.

T.537

1869

WARNING for servants: and a caution to protestants.
Or, the case of Margret Clark, lately executed
for firing her masters house in Southwark...
London: for Tho. Parkhurst; and are to be sold
by Joseph Collier, 1680. 4°

Wing C 4483.

T.411

1870

The WAY of peace: or, A discourse of the dangerous
principles and practices of some pretended
protestants... Being certain brief collections out
of the late writings of several learned protestant
authors... By the author, a protestant of the
Church of England [i.e. Philemon Angell?]...
London: for Henry Brome, 1680. 4°

Wing W 1162.

T.90

1871

WILKINSON (Richard)

A true and perfect relation of Elizabeth Freeman
of Bishops-Hatfield in the county of Hertford,
of a strange and wonderful apparition which appeared
to her several times, and commanded her to declare
a message to his most sacred Majesty. [Anon.]
London, for J.B. anno Domini 1680. brs.

Wing W 2248.

T.537

1872

WOMOCK (Laurence) *Bishop of St. David's.*

Two treatise the first, proving both by history & record that the bishops are a fundamental & essential part of our English Parliament: the second, that they may be judges in capital cases. [Anon.] London, Tho. Braddyll for Robert Clavell, 1680. 2 parts. Fol.

Wing W 3355.

T.688

1873

YARRANTON (Andrew)

A continuation of the Coffee-house dialogue, between Captain Y. and a young baronet [sic] of the Middle-Temple; wherein the first dialogue is vindicated... [Anon.]   [London, 1680?] Fol.

Wing Y 12.

T.688

1681

1874

ADDISON (Lancelot)

The Moores baffled: being a discourse concerning Tanger, especially when it was under the Earl of Teviot; by which you may find what methods and government is fittest to secure that place against the Moors. In a letter from a learned person (Lon. resident in that place)... London: for William Crooke, 1681.   4°

Wing A 525.

T.689

1875

An ANSWER of a letter from a friend in the country to a friend in the city: or some remarks on the late comet. Being a relation of many universal accidents that will come to pass in the year, 1682... London, George Croom, 1681.   4°

Wing A 3282.

T.411

1876

An ANSWER to a paper, entituled, A brief account of the designs of the papists against the Earl of Shaftsbury, occasioned by his commitment, July 2. 1681. London; for T. Davies, 1681.   Fol.

Wing A 3328.

T.531

1877

An ANSWER to Pereat papa: or, A reply by way of letter from a gentlewoman to a person of quality; commending to her consideration a paper entituled Pereat papa; or, Reasons why popery should not inherit the Crown. [London, 1681?] Fol.

Wing A 3372.

T.688

1878

An APOLOGY for the protestants: being a full justification of their departure from the Church of Rome, with fair and practicable proposals for a re-union. Done out of French into English by Roger L'Estrange. London: T. B. for Henry Brome, 1681. 4°

Wing A 3554

T.182

1879

The ARRAIGNMENT and plea of Edw. Fitz-Harris, Esq; with all the arguments in law, and proceedings of the court of Kings-Bench thereupon, in Easter term 1681.   London, for Fr. Tyton, and Tho. Basset, 1681. Fol.

Wing A 3746.

T.684

1880

The ARRAIGNMENT, tryal and condemnation of Stephen Colledge for high treason, in conspiring the death of the King, the levying of war, and the subversion of the government... London, for Thomas Basset, and John Fish, 1681. Fol.

Wing A 3761.

T.684

1881

The ASSENTERS sayings, published in their own words, for the information of the people: being in requital of Roger L'Estrange's Dissenters sayings. By an indifferent hand. London, for Henry Jones, 1681. 4°

Wing A 4019.

T. 85

1882

B. (J.) *Philalelos,*

Good and joyful news for England: or, The prophecy of the renowned Michael Nostradamus, that Charles the II ... shall have a son of his own body lawfully begotten ... With observations concerning the present blazing-comet. By J.B. Philalelos. [London, for A. Banks, 1681.] 4°

Wing B 105.

T.17

1883

B. (T.)

The loyalty of the last Long Parliament: or, a letter to an English gentleman at Florence ... London, for Francis Smith, senior, 1681. 4°

Wing B 187.
2 copies.

T.90   T.117

1884

BAKER (Thomas)

The head of Nile: or the turnings and windings of the factious since Sixty, in a dialogue between Whigg and Barnaby ... [Anon.] London, Walter Davis, 1681. 4°

Wing B 518.

T.90

1885

BEANE (Richard)

A discourse concerning Popish perjurers in an addresse to the honorable the Commons of England, in Parliament assembled at Oxford. London, for H. Brome, 1681. 4°

Wing B 1561.

T. 90

1886

A BRIEF account of the designs which the papists have had against the Earl of Shaftsbury, occasioned by his commitment, July 2. 1681. Printed for R. Baldwin, 1681.   Fol.

Wing B 4504.

T.532

1887

BROWNE (John) *Quaker.*

Kedarminster-stuff. A new piece of print: or, A remnant of Mr. Baxter's piae fraudes unravelled. Being an appendix to Nonconformists plea for peace impleaded. By J. B. Worcestershire ... London: for Randal Taylor, 1681. 4°

Wing B 5121.

T.330

1888

BURNET (Gilbert) *Bishop of Salisbury.*

An exhortation to peace and union. A sermon preached at St. Lawrence-Jury, at the election of the Lord-Mayor of London, on the 29th of September, 1681. London; for Richard Chiswell, 1681. 4°

Wing B 5787.

T.175

1889

BURNET (Gilbert) *Bishop of Salisbury.*

A sermon preached before the aldermen of the city of London, at St. Lawrence-Church, Jan 30. 1680/1 ... London, for Richard Chiswel, 1681. 4°

Wing B 5875.

T.175

1890

BURNET (Gilbert) *Bishop of Salisbury.*

A sermon preached on the fast-day, Decemb.22.1680. At St. Margarets Westminster, before the honourable House of Commons.   London, J.D. for Richard Chiswell, 1681.   4°

Wing B 5874.

T.492

1891

BUTLER (Samuel) *Poet.*

The priviledge of our saints in the business of perjury. Useful for grand-juries. By the author of Hudibras. London, for Benj. Tooke, 1681. brs.

Wing B 6328.

T.532

1892

BYROM (John) *Rector of Stanton St. Quintin.*

The necessity of subjection, asserted in an assise-sermon preached in the cathedral church at Sarum. July 17. 1681. London, for Benj. Took, 1681.   4°
Wing B 6408.

T.492

1893

CAUSAE veteris epitaphium, in antecessum, ab anonymo autore scriptum. [London, William Abington, 1681?] 4°

Wing C 1532.
Incomplete.

T.69

1894

CHARLES II, *King of England.*

The answers commanded by his Majesty to be given by... the Earl of Nottingham... upon several addresses presented to his Majesty in Council at Hampton-Court, the 19th of May, 1681. London, the assigns of John Bill, Thomas Newcomb, and Henry Hills, 1681. brs.

Wing C 2890.

T.537

1895

CHARLES II, *King of England.*

Aurea dicta. The King's gracious words for the Protestant religion of the Church of England ... To which is added Salus populi suprema lex. London, Grantham, for Walter Davis, and are to be sold by John Barksdale, bookseller in Cirencester, 1681. 4°

Wing C 2929.

T. 90

1896

CHARLES II, *King of England.*

His Majesties letters to the Bishop of London and the Lord Mayor. London, S. Roycroft, 1681.   brs.

Wing C 3120.

T.537

1897

CHILD (*Sir* Josiah)

A treatise wherein is demonstrated, I. That the East-India trade is the most national of all foreign trades ... By Φιλοπατρις [i.e. Sir Josiah Child]. London, T. J. for Robert Boulter, 1681. 4°

Wing C 3866.

T.324

1898

A CHOICE collection of wonderful miracles, ghosts and visions.   London, for B.R. and D.W. [1681]. Fol.

cf. Wing C 3915.

T.537

1899

CLAGETT (William)

A reply to a pamphlet [by Vincent Alsop] called The mischief of impositions; which pretends to answer the Dean of St. Paul's [Edward Stillingfleet] sermon concerning the mischief of separation. [Anon.] London, for Walter Kettilby, 1681. 4°

Wing C 4393.

T.182

1900

CLARKSON (David)

The case of Protestants in England under a Popish prince, if any shall happen to wear the imperial crown. [Anon.] London: for Richard Janeway, 1681. 4°

Wing C 4569.

T. 95

1901

COLLEGE (Stephen)

The speech and carriage of Stephen Colledge at Oxford, before the castle, on Wednesday August 31. 1681. Taken exactly from his own mouth at the place of execution. London, for Thomas Basset, and John Fish, 1681. Fol.

Wing C 5229.

T.684

1902

COLLEGE (Stephen)

A true copy of the dying words of Mr. Stephen Colledge, left in writing under his own hand, and confirmed by him at the time of execution, August 31. 1681. at Oxford. London, for Edith Colledge, 1681.   brs.

Wing C 5231.

T.684

1903

COLLINGES (John)

The history of conformity: or a proof of the mischief of impositions, from the experience of more than one hundred years. [Anon.] London: A. Maxwell, and R. Roberts, 1681. 4°

Wing C 5319.

T.411

1904

DANGERFIELD (Thomas)

More shams still: or a further discovery of the designs of the papists, to impose upon the nation the belief of their feigned protestant or presbyterian plot. London, for Richard Baldwin, 1681.   4°

Wing D 191.

T.411

1905

The DELIQUIUM: or, The grievances of the nation discovered in a dream. [No imprint, 1681.] brs.

Wing D 908.

T.532

1906

A DIALOGUE at Oxford between a tutor and a gentleman, formerly his pupil, concerning government. London, for Rich. Janaway, 1681. 4°

Wing D 1290.
2 copies.

T.95 T.277

1907

The DIALOGUE between the Pope and a fanatick concerning affairs in England, revived. London, for John Kidgell, 1681.   4°

Wing D 1333 B.

T.411

1908

A DIALOGUE betwixt Sam. the ferriman of Dochet, Will. a waterman of London, and Tom. a bargeman of Oxford. Upon the Kings calling a Parliament to meet at Oxford. London, printed in the year, 1681. 4°

Wing D 1353.
2 copies.

T.201 T. 95

1909

DRYDEN (John)

Absalom and Achitophel. A poem ... [Anon.] London, for J.T. and are to be sold by W. Davis, 1681. Fol.

Wing D 2212.
2 copies.

T.532 T.698

1910

DRYDEN (John)

Absalom and Achitophel. A poem ... [Anon.] The second edition; augmented and revised. London, for J.T. and are to be sold by W. Davis, 1681. 4°

Wing D 2216.

T.495

1911

DRYDEN (John)

An elegy on the usurper O.C. By the author of Absalom and Achitophel ... London, for J. Smith, 1681. brs.

Wing D 2268.

T.117

1912

An ELOGY, against occasion requires upon the Earl of Shaftsbury. Calculated for the meridion of eight one. London, for Ab. Green, 1681. brs.

Wing E 341.

T.698

1913

ELYS (Edmund)

Summum bonum: seu vera, atq; unica beatitudo hominibus per Christum communicanda, sex dissertationibus aliquatenus explicata... Londini, postant apud Henricum Faithorne, & Johannem Kersey, 1681.   8°

Not in Wing.

T.441

1914

ENGLISH loyalty vindicated by the French divines; or, A declaration and subscription of threescore doctors of Sorbonne, for the oath of allegiance, as it was originally deliver'd by them in Latin. Faithfully done in English, by W. H. ... London, for Nath. Thompson, 1681. 4°

Wing E 3096.

T. 90

1915

The EXAMINATION of Edw. Fitzharris, relating to the popish plot, taken the tenth day of March, 1680/1 ... London: for Thomas Fox, 1681. Fol.

Wing E 3717.
2 copies.

T.533 T.684

1916

FERGUSON (Robert)

No Protestant-plot: or The present pretended conspiracy of Protestants against the King and government, discovered to be a conspiracy of the Papists against the King and his Protestant-subjects. [Anon.] London: for R. Lett, 1681. 4°

Wing F 756.
4 copies.

T.90 T.95 T.117 T.125

1917

FERGUSON (Robert)

A second dialogue between the Pope and a phanatick, concerning affairs in England. By the author of the first ... London: for H. Jones, 1681. 4°

Wing F 758.

T.125

1918

The FIRST steps, and following degrees whereby popish pomp, superstition & idolatry succeeded, and is now, vainly, endeavouring to extirpate Gospel innocency... London, T. Dawks: who formerly publish'd (from this author) A chronology of the rise and growth of popery... [1681?] 4°

Not in Wing.

T.106

1919

FITZ-HARRIS (Edward)

The confession of Edward Fitz-harys, esquire, written with his own hand, and delivered to Doctor Hawkins minister of the Tower, the first of July, 1681. Being the day of his execution. Together with his last speech. London, for S. Carr, 1681. Fol.

Wing F 1092.

T.684

1920

FITZ-HARRIS (Edward)

The last speech of Edward Fitz-harris, at the time of his execution at Tyburn the first of July, 1681. London, for R. Harbottle, and sold by R. Janeway, 1681. brs.

Wing F 1094.

T.684

1921

FIVE important queries humbly propounded to all true lovers of the peace and safety of the church and state. By a sincere well-wisher to the old Protestant religion ... London: Nathaniel Thompson, 1681. 4°

Wing F 1107.
2 copies.

T.509 T. 90

1922

FLATMAN (Thomas)

A pindarique ode on the death of the Right Honourable Thomas Earl of Ossory ... London, J.G. for Benjamin Tooke, 1681. Fol.

Wing F 1150.

T.699

1923

GLANVILL (Joseph)

The zealous, and impartial protestant, shewing some great, but less heeded dangers of popery. In order to thorough and effectual security against it. In a letter to a member of Parliament. [Anon.] London: M. C. for Henry Brome, 1681. 4°

Wing G 837.
3 copies.

T.763 T.330 T.182

1924

GODWYN (Morgan)

A supplement to The negro's α Indian's advocate: or, Some further considerations and proposals for the effectual and speedy carrying on of the negro's Christianity in our plantations ... By M.G. ... London, printed by J.D., 1681.   4°

Wing G 973.

T.517

1925

The GRAND question resolved: viz. A king having protested to defend ... the true protestant religion, with the rights and liberties of all his subjects: but if they, fearing that he will violate this his protestation, take up arms to prevent it, what may be judged hereof? London, for R. Baldwin, 1681.   Fol.

Wing G 1509.

T.532

1926

The GREAT case put home in some modest queries humbly proposed and tendred to consideration, by a true loverof the Protestant religion and English loyalty ... Oxford, for R. Davis, and are to be sold by T. Taylor, 1681. 4°

Wing G 1674.
2 copies.

T. 24 T. 90

1927

GROVE (Robert) *Bishop of Chichester.*

A short defence of the Church and clergy of England. Wherein some of the common objections against both are answered: and the means of union briefly considered. [Anon.] London, J. Macock for Walter Kettilby, 1681. 4°

Wing G 2160.

T.177

1928

GUNNING (Peter) *Bishop of Ely.*

Reasons why all good Christians should observe the holy fast of Lent. Extracted out of my Lord of Ely's Paschal fast. London, for Joseph Hindmarsh, 1681. 4°

Wing G 2236 A.

T. 17

1929

HARANGUE au roy: fait par un ministre de l'eglise Francoise de la Savoye, le 19, d'Octobre, 1681 ... A Londres, 1681. 4°

Not in Wing.

T.117

1930

HAWKINS (Francis)

A narrative, being a true relation of what discourse passed between Dr. Hawkins and Edward Fitz-Harys, Esq; late prisoner in the Tower; with the manner of taking his confession. London, for Samuel Carr, 1681. Fol.

Wing H 1173

T.532

1931

HICKERINGILL (Edmund)

The horrid sin of man-catching: explain'd in a sermon... preach'd at Colchester, July 10, 1681... London, for Francis Smith, 1681. 4°

Wing H 1811.

T.117

1932

HICKERINGILL (Edmund)

The horrid sin of man-catching: explain'd in a sermon... preach'd at Colchester, July 10. 1681... 2nd ed. London, for Francis Smith, 1681. 4°

Wing H 1812.

T.765

1933

HICKERINGILL (Edmund)

The naked truth. The second part. In several inquiries concerning the canons and ecclesiastical jurisdiction, canonical obedience ... and visitations. Also of the Church of England, and church-wardens ... [Anon.] London, for Francis Smith, 1681. Fol.

Wing H 1821.
2 copies.

T.532 T.537

1934

HICKES (George)

Peculium Dei. A discourse about the Jews, as the peculiar people of God. In a sermon preached before the honourable the aldermen and citizens of London, on the sixth of February, 1680/81 ... London, for Walter Kettilby, 1681. 4°

Wing H 1858.
2 copies.

1935

HICKES (George)

The spirit of enthusiasm exorcised. In a sermon preached before the University of Oxford, On Act-Sunday, July 11. 1680 ... 2nd ed. London, for Walter Kettilby, 1681. 4°

Wing H 1872.

T.177

1936

HICKES (George)

The true notion of persecution stated. In a sermon preached at the time of the late contribution for the French Protestants ... London, for Walter Kettilby, 1681. 4°

Wing H 1875.
2 copies.

1937

HICKMAN (Charles)

A sermon preached before the Right Honourable George Earl of Berkeley, governour, and the Company of Merchants of England trading into the Levant Seas ... London: for Henry Brome, 1681. 4°

Wing H 1896.
2 copies.

T.732   T.132

1938

HOLLINGWORTH (Richard)

Christian principles no abettors of popish practices, discovered in a sermon before the Lord Mayor, at Guild-hall chappel, January 23. 1680. London, for Robert Boulter, 1681. 4°

Wing H 2489.

T.492

1939

HOWARD (William) *Baron Howard of Escrick.*

A letter from my Lord Howard of Escrick, to his friend. Together with his protestation, at his receiving the blessed communion in the Tower, on July the third, 1681. London: Robert Roberts, 1681. Fol.

Wing H 3012.
2 copies.

T.531 T.684

1940

The HUMBLE petition of the protestants of France lately presented to his most Christian Majesty, by the Mareschal Schomberg, and the Marquis of Ruvigny. London: for L. Curtis, [1681]. Fol.

Wing H 3575.

T.532

1941

IGNORAMUS: an excellent new song. London: printed in the year 1681. brs.

Wing I 42.

T.698

1942

An IMPARTIAL account of the nature and tendency of the late addresses, in a letter to a gentleman in the country. [Attributed to the Earl of Shaftesbury] London: for R. Baldwyn, 1681. 4°

Wing I 73.
2 copies.

T.95 T.117

1943

JAMES I, *King of England.*

Vox regis: or, The difference betwixt a king ruling by law, and a tyrant by his own will ... In two speeches of King James to the Parliaments in 1603, and March 21. 1609. And in his Basilicon doron. Which may be an appendix to Vox populi . London, for Francis Smith, 1681. 4°

Wing J 148.
2 copies.

T.90 T.117

1944

JEKYLL (Thomas)

Righteousness and peace the best means to prevent ruin: recommended in a sermon preached at Guild-hall Chappel, (Sept. 25. 1681.) before the Lord-Mayor, &c. 2nd ed. London; for Jonathan Robinson, 1681. 4°

Wing J 537.

T.175

1945

The JESUITE in masquerade: or the sheriffs case uncas'd. In some brief observations upon the danger of taking oaths otherwise than according to the plain and literal meaning of the imposers ... London: for C. Mearne, 1681. Fol.

Wing J 704.

T.531

1946

JONES (Thomas) *Almanack Maker.*

An astrological speculation of the late prodigy. Or a clear discovery of the approaching miseries signified by that comet, or blazing star, which hath so long been visible... London, printed for the author, and are sold by him, 1681. 4°

Not in Wing.

T.411

1947

JORDAN (Thomas)

London's joy, or, the lord mayors show: triumphantly exhibited in various representations ... Performed on Saturday, October XXIX. 1681. at the inauguration of the Right Honourable Sir John Moore, knight, Lord Mayor the city of London ... London, for John and Henry Playford, 1681. 4°

Wing J 1038.

T.407

1948

K. (H.)

An arrest on the East India privatier, as per advice and copy sent to its commander Sr. J. C. [i.e. Sir Josiah Child] from H. K. near Hamburgh. (Reasons for constituting a new East-India Company in London.) [No imprint, 1681.] 4°

Wing K 10.

T.324

1949

L. (L.)

Scotland against popery, or Christs day against AntiChrist; or An account of the manner of the burning of the Popes effigies upon Christmas Day last 1680. in the city of Edenborough. Sent in two letters from two several friends to a citizen of London. London, for Richard Janeway, 1681. Fol.

Wing L 43.

T.537

1950

L. (T.)

The true notion of government ... In vindication of kingly-prerogative. London: for Edward Gellibrand, 1681. 4°

Wing L 82.

T.90

1951

The LAWYERS demurrer, to the addresses in fashion. Or, the several declarations and orders of the honourable societies of the Middle Temple, and Grays-Inn, lately made in relation to that affair. London, for Richard Janeway, 1681. brs.

Wing L 740.

T.537

1952

LEE (*Sir* Charles)

Notes of the evidence given against the Lord Howard of Escrick to the grand inquest of the hundred of Edmonton and Gore ... taken by Sir Charles Lee their foreman ... London, for S. Carr, 1681. brs.

Wing L 838.

T.684

1953

L'ESTRANGE (*Sir* Roger)

The casuist uncas'd, in a dialogue betwixt Richard and Baxter, with a moderator between them, for quietnesse sake. London, for Henry Brome, 1681. 4°

Wing L 1210.

T.183

1954

L'ESTRANGE (*Sir* Roger)

The character of a papist in masquerade; supported by authority and experience. In answer to the Character of a popish successor [by Elkanah Settle]. London, for H. Brome, 1681. 4°

Wing L 1215.

T.183

1955

L'ESTRANGE (*Sir* Roger)

The dissenter's sayings, in requital for L'Estrange's sayings. Published in their own words, for the information of the people. London, for Henry Brome, 1681. 4°

Wing L 1240.

T.174

1956

L'ESTRANGE (*Sir* Roger)

The dissenters sayings, in requital for L'Estrange's sayings, published in their own words, for the information of the people. 3rd ed. London, for Joanna Brome, 1681. 4°

Wing L 1242.

T.83

1957

L'ESTRANGE (*Sir* Roger)

Dissenters sayings. The second part ... London, for Joanna Brome, 1681. 4°

Wing L 1245.

T.174

1958

L'ESTRANGE (*Sir* Roger)

The dissenters sayings. The second part ... 2nd ed. London, for Joanna Brome, 1681. 4°

Wing L 1246.

T.83

1959

L'ESTRANGE (*Sir* Roger)

L'Estrange his appeal humbly submitted to the Kings most excellent Majesty and the three estates assembled in Parliament. London, for Henry Brome, 1681. 4°

Wing L 1202.

T.183

1960

L'ESTRANGE (*Sir* Roger)

L'Estrange no Papist: in answer to a libel entituled L'Estrange a Papist, &c. [by Miles Prance]. In a letter to a friend. With notes and animadversions upon Miles Prance ... London, T. B. for H. Brome, 1681. 4°

Wing L 1267.
2 copies.

T.183   T.85

1961

L'ESTRANGE (*Sir* Roger)

L'Estrange no papist nor Jesuite. Discussed in a
short discourse between Philo-L'Estrange and
Pragmaticus ... London: for Henry Brome, 1681. 4°

Wing L 1267 A.
Not another edition of L 1267.

T.330

1962

L'ESTRANGE (*Sir* Roger)

Notes upon Stephen College. Grounded principally
upon his own declarations and confessions, and
freely submitted to publique censure. London, for
Joanna Brome, 1681. 4°

Wing L 1281.
2 copies.

T.174   T.117

1963

L'ESTRANGE (*Sir* Roger)

The relaps'd apostate: or, Notes upon a presbyterian
pamphlet [by Richard Baxter], entituled, A petition
for peace, &c. 3rd ed ... London, for Henry Brome,
1681. 4°

Wing L 1295.

T.183

1964

L'ESTRANGE (*Sir* Roger)

A reply to the second part of The character of a
popish successor [by John Phillips]. London, for
Joanna Brome, 1681.   4°

Wing L 1298.
2 copies.

T.174   T.177

1965

L'ESTRANGE (*Sir* Roger)

The shammer shamm'd: in a plain discovery, under
young Tong's own hand, of a designe to trepann
L'Estrange into a pretended subornation against the
Popish Plot. London, for Joanna Brome, 1681. 4°

Wing L 1306.
2 copies.

T.177   T.411

1966

L'ESTRANGE (*Sir* Roger)

A word concerning libels and libellers, humbly presented
to the Right Honourable Sir John Moor, Lord-Mayor of
London ... London, for Joanna Brome, 1681.   4°

Wing L 1327.

T.411

1967

A LETTER written to the French King, by the lords
spiritual the arch-bishops and the bishops ...
about the last breve of the Pope, upon the subject
of the regale. [London, 1681.] Fol.

Wing L 1772.

T.537

1968

LEVANT COMPANY.

The allegations of the Turky Company and others
against the East-India-Company, relating to the
management of that trade ... Together with the
answer of the said East-India-Company thereunto
... [No imprint, 1681.] Fol.

Wing A 954.

T.324

1969

LONDON.

At the general sessions of the peace, and gaol delivery,
held for the city of London, on Wednesday the 31st of
August, at justice-hall in the Old-Bayly, in the three
and thirtieth year of our sovereign lord, Charles, &c.
[Prosecution of Nathanael Thompson, Ben. Tooke and
Johanna Broom, printers.] London, for Rich. Janeway,
1681. brs.

Not in Wing.

T.698

1970

LONDON.

The humble petition and address of the Right
Honourable the Lord Mayor, aldermen and commons
of the city of London, in common-councel assembled.
London, Samuel Roycroft, 1681. brs.

Wing H 3429.

T.537

1971

LONDON.

The proceedings of the Common-hall of London the 24th
of June, 1681. At the choice of sheriffs, and other
officers: as also the proceedings there the 27th
instant, at the declaring of the sheriffs, &c. London,
for Richard Janeway, 1681. brs.

Wing P 3578.

T.532

1972

LONDON.

A true narrative of the proceedings at Guild-hall,
London, the fourth of this instant February, in
their unanimous election of their four members to
serve in Parliament... London, for Francis Smith,
1681. brs.

Wing T 2809.

T.532

1973

MARVELL (Andrew)

Miscellaneous poems. London, for Robert Boulter,
1681. Fol.

Wing M 872.

T.532

1974

A MODEST vindication of the Earl of S[haftesbur]y:
in a letter to a friend concerning his being elected
King of Poland. London,for   Smith, 1681. Fol.

Wing M 2375.

T.537

1975

The MORNING-star out of the north, or the ruine and
destruction of the Pope and Church of Rome ...
discovered to be at hand ... [No imprint, 1681.] 4°

Wing M 2805.

T.106

1976

MULTUM in parvo, aut vox veritatis: wherein the
principles, practices, and transactions of the
English nation... are most faithfully and impartially
examined, collected, and compared together for the
present seasonable use, benefit and information of
the publick... By Theophilus Rationalis... London:
for Rich. Janeway, 1681. Fol.

Wing M 3061.

T.531

1977

NALSON (John)

Vox populi, fax populi. Or, A discovery of an
impudent cheat and forgery put upon the people of
England by Elephant Smith, and his author of Vox
populi ... [Anon.] London, S. R. for Benj. Tooke,
1681 . 4°

Wing N 121.
2 copies.

T.182   T.90

1978

A NEW ignoramus: being the second new song.
London, for Charles Leigh, 1681. brs.

Wing N 648.

T.698

1979

The NEW popish sham-plot discovered: or, the
cursed contrivance of the Earl of Danby, Mrs. Celier,
with the popish lords, and priests, in the Tower and
Newgate, fully detected in villanously suborning
witness to swear that Sr Edmundbury Godfrey wilfully
murdered himself. London, for T. Davies, [1681].
brs.

Wing N 718A.

T.698

1980

NICOLS (Daniel)

A sermon preach'd in the cathedral of Lincoln,
July XVIII. 1681. Being the assize-Monday.
London, A.G. and J.P. for Joseph Lawson, bookseller
at the Bail of Lincoln; and sold by Richard
Chiswell; and Thomas Sawbridge, 1681. 4°

Wing N 1142.

T.492

1981

NONE but the sheriffs ought to name and return jurors
to serve in inquests before commissioners of oyer
and terminer. London: for R. Baldwyn, [1681].
brs.

Wing N 1226.

T.537

1982

The OATHS of Irish papists no evidence against
protestants: or, A warning piece to jurors. In a
letter to a friend. [Signed Philanglus.] London:
for William Inghall the Eld. book-binder, 1681.
4°

Wing P 1333 (attributed to William Penn).
2 copies, one incomplete.

T.106   T.117

1983

P.(J.)

A letter to a friend in the country: being a
vindication of the Parliaments whole proceedings
this last session. With the state of the plot,
and manner of its discovery. [London, 1681.]
Fol.

Wing P 55.
2 copies.

T.538   T.688

1984

PARIS. *Parlement.*

The decrees of the Parlement of Paris, upon a
copy of the Pope's brief of the first of
January, 1681 ... London, for Benj. Tooke,
1681. 4°

Wing D 807.

T.411

1985

A PARTICULAR account of the proceedings at the Old-
Bayly... with relation to the Earl of Shaftsbury,
and others, prisoners in the Tower... In the
Savoy, Thomas Newcomb, 1681. brs.

Wing P 586.

T.698

1986

PASQUIER (Etienne)

The Jesuits catechism, according to St. Ignatius
Loyola ... Wherein the impiety of their principles,
perniciousness of their doctrines, and iniquity of
their practices are declared ... [Anon.] 2nd ed.
London, for Robert Harford, 1681. 4°

Wing P 653.

T.117

1987

PATRICK (Symon) *Bishop of Ely.*

Christs counsel to his Church. In two sermons
preached at the two last fasts ... London, J. Macock,
for R. Royston, 1681. 4°

Wing P 770.

T.132

1988

PENN (William)

The Protestants remonstrance against Pope and
presbyter: in an impartial essay upon the times, or
plea for moderation. By Philanglus ... London:
N.T. for Walter Davis, 1681. 4°

Wing P 1345.
2 copies.

T.90   T.125

1989

The PETITION of divers eminent citizens of London
presented to the Lord Mayor and court of aldermen
the 28th of April, 1681. London, for B.A. and
published by Richard Janaway, 1681. brs.

Wing P 1762.

T.537

1990

The PLOTTING cards reviv'd, or, the new game at forty one. [London, 1681.] brs.

Wing P 2605 B.

T.532

1991

PLUNKET (Oliver)

The last speech of Mr. Oliver Plunket, titular primate of Ireland, who was executed at Tyburn on Friday the 1st. of this instant July, 1681. London, N. Thompson, 1681. Fol.

Wing P 2626.

T.684.

1992

The POWER and privilege of juries asserted: in opposition to the willfully blind, and malitious humour of some ill and uncharitable men. Published for the information of Heraclytus Ridens, and the doting Observator. London, for Richard Janeway, 1681. 4°

Wing P 3103.
Incomplete.

T.90

1993

The PROCEEDINGS at the sessions house in the Old-Baily, London... upon the bill of indictment for high-treason against Anthony Earl of Shaftsbury. London, for Samuel Mearne and John Baker, 1681. Fol.

Wing P 3564.

T.698

1994

The PROTESTANT admirer or, An answer to the vindication of a popish successor. [London, 1681.] Fol.

Wing P 3819.

T.688

1995

PROTESTANT loyalty fairly drawn, in an answer to a pair of scandalous and popish pamphlets. The first intituled, A dialogue at Oxford ... The other intituled, An impartial account of the nature and tendency of the late addresses ... London, for Walter Kettilby, 1681. 4°

Wing P 3837.

T.125

1996

The PROTESTANT petition and addresse. London, April 30. 1681. Upon Thursday last there was presented to the Lord-Mayor and court of aldermen... this following address. Printed for the subscribers, April 30. 1681. brs.

Wing P 3839.

T.537

1997

PRYNNE (William)

The subjection of all traytors, rebels, as well peers, as commons in Ireland, to the laws, statutes, and tryals by juries of good and lawful men of England... London, for Edward Thomas, 1681. 4°

Wing P 4091.

T.562.

1998

RADCLIFFE (Alexander)

The lawyers demurrer argued. By the loyall addressers (the gentlemen) of Grays-Inne, against an order made by the bench of the said society. [Anon.] London, for A.B., 1681. brs.

Wing L 740 A.

T.537

1999

RESBURY (Nathanael)

A sermon preach'd at the anniversary-meeting of the Charter-house scholars ... On Monday, December 13th. 1680. London, for Walter Kettilby, 1681. 4°

Wing R 1130.

T.132

2000

RONQUILLO (Pedro)

The last memorial of the Spanish ambassador, faithfully translated into English. London, for Francis Smith, 1681. brs.

Wing R 1916.

T.537

2001

ROSS (John)

Tangers rescue; or a relation of the late memorable passages at Tanger ... London, for Hen. Hills, 1681. 4°

Wing R 1988.

T.248

2002

S.(J.)

A new letter from Leghorn, from aboard the Van-Herring to a merchant in London, fully discovering the present state of that ship. London, for Joseph Hindmarsh, 1681. Fol.

Wing S 76.

T.537

2003

SALGADO (James)

A confession of faith of James Salgado, a Spaniard, and sometimes a priest in the Church of Rome ... London: for William Marshall, 1681. 2 parts. 4°

Wing S 375.

T.106

2004

SALUS populi, &c. or the case of King and people. Modestly handled, and impartially stated, very useful for these distracted times... London, for John Place, 1681. 4°

Wing S 514.

T.326

2005

SAVILE (George) *Marquess of Halifax.*

A seasonable address to both houses of Parliament concerning the succession, the fears of popery, and arbitrary government. By a true protestant, and a hearty lover of his countrey. London, printed in the year, 1681. 4°

Wing H 320.

T.182

2006

SAYWELL (William)

A serious inquiry into the means of an happy union: or, What reformation is necessary to prevent popery, and to avert God's judgments from the nation... London: A.G. and J.P. and are to be sold by Rand. Taylor, 1681. 4°

Wing S 805.

T.517

2007

SCLATER (Edward)

A sermon preached in the church of Putney in the county of Surrey, upon the 24th of April, 1681. His Majesty's declaration being read that day... London, for R. Horne, 1681. 4°

Wing S 912.

T.514

2008

The SHERIFFS case. Whether, and how they may lawfully qualifie themselves for their holding the office, according to the Act for corporations? London, Thomas Snowden, 1681. Fol.

Wing S 3234.

T.537

2009

SMITH (John) *of Walworth*

No faith or credit to be given to papists. Being a discourse occasioned by the late conspirators dying in denial of their guilt. With particular reflections on the perjury of Will. Viscount Stafford... in relation to Mr. Stephen Dugdale, and Mr. Edward Turbervill. London, for Tho. Cockerill, 1681. 4°

Wing S 4128
2 copies.

T.531 T.684

2010

SMITH (*Sir* William)

Midd. ss. Ad general. sessionem pacis Domini Regis... quinto die Decembris, anno regni Caroli Regis Secundi... tricesimo tertio. The justices then assembled, directed Sir William Smith to speak to the grand-jury to some points, which he did as followeth. [London, 1681?] Fol.

Not in Wing.

T.698

2011

A SOBER and seasonable discourse, by way of dialogue, between a states-man, and a country-gentleman... Written by a true lover of his King and country, for the quieting the spirits of all sorts of people. London: N. Thompson, and are to be sold by Randal Taylor, 1681. 4°

Wing S 4401.

T.411

2012

SOME modest reflections upon the commitment of the Earl of Shaftsbury, arising from the late indictment against Mr. Stephen Colledge. London, for R. Baldwin, July 12, 1681. Fol.

Wing S 4524.

T.531

2013

SOME seasonable remarks upon the deplorable fall of the Emperour Julian, with an epistle of his to the citizens of Bostra. Now made English. By Philaretus Anthropopolita... London: for J. Gellibrand, 1681. 4°

Wing S 4610.

T.326

2014

SOME short but necessary animadversions on the paper delivered to Dr. Hawkins, together with a copy of the paper it self entituled, The confession of Edward Fitz-Harris, Esq... London, for Richard Janeway, 1681. brs.

Wing S 4612.

T.684

2015

STRANGE news from Hicks's Hall. Or, An order of some of the justices of the peace for the county of Middlesex for the bailiffs of liberties to return juries... London, for R. Harbottle, 1681. Fol.

Wing S 5891.

T.537

2016

T. (L.)

A short account, or state of Mr. Sheridan's case before the late House of Commons. In a letter to J.T. London, for J. Hindmarsh, 1681. 4°

Wing T 25.
3 copies.

T.90 T.145 T.183

2017

TENISON (Thomas) *Archbishop of Canterbury.*

A sermon concerning discretion in giving alms preached at St Sepulchres Church in London ... April vi. MDCLXXXI. London, J. Macock, for Francis Tyton, 1681. 4°

Wing T 709.
3 copies.

T.492 T.132 T.175

2018

THOMSON (William)

A sermon preached at the assizes held at Stafford August. 4. MDCLXXX ... London, for the author, 1681. 4°

Wing T 1020.

T.145

2019

TILLOTSON (John) *Archbishop of Canterbury.*

The lawfulness, and obligation of oaths. A sermon preach'd at the assises held at Kingston upon Thames, July 21. 1681. London, for Brabazon Aylmer: and William Rogers, 1681. 4°

Wing T 1200.
4 copies.

2020

The TRADE of England revived: and the abuses thereof rectified... Humbly offered to this present Parliament. London: for Dorman Newman, 1681. 4°

Wing T 2004.

T.373

2021

TREBY (*Sir* George)

A collection of letters and other writings, relating to the horrid popish plot: printed from the originals in the hands of George Treby Esq; chairman of the committee of secrecy of the honourable House of Commons. London, for Samuel Heyrick, Thomas Dring, and John Wickins, 1681.

Wing T 2102.
2 copies.

T.533 T.694

2022

TREBY (*Sir* George)

The second part of the collection of letters and other writings, relating to the horrid popish plot: printed from the originals in the hands of Sir George Treby ... chairman of the committee of secrecy of the honourable House of Commons. London, for Samuel Heyrick, Thomas Dring, and John Wickins, 1681. Fol.

Wing T 2104.

T.533

2023

TREBY (*Sir* George)

Truth vindicated: or A detection of the aspersions and scandals cast upon Sir Robert Clayton [and others], in a paper published in the name of Dr. Francis Hawkins, intituled, The confession of Edward Fitz-Harris ... [Anon.] London: for Rich. Baldwin, 1681. 4°

Wing T 2107.
2 copies.

T.117 T.311

2024

The TRIUMPHS of justice over unjust judges... Humbly dedicated to the Lord Chief Justice Scroggs... London, for Benjamin Harris, 1681. Fol.

Wing T 2297.

T.537

2025

The TRUE and wonderful relation of the dreadful fighting and groans that were heard and seen in the ayr, on the fifteenth of this instant January, in Carmarthen, in South-Wales, by Mr. Henry Lewys, and his whole family... Printed for W.T. and J.C., 1681. 4°

Wing T 2588.

T.411

2026

A TRUE copy of the indictment which is preferred against Archibald Earl of Argile, for high-treason, who is to be tryed on Monday the 12th. day of this instant December 1681... Edenbrough: for James Alexander, 1681. brs.

Wing T 2643.

T.698

2027

The TRYAL and condemnation of Edw.Fitz-Harris, Esq; for high-treason... As also the tryal and condemnation of Dr Oliver Plunket, titular primate of Ireland, for high-treason... London, for Francis Tyton, and Thomas Basset, 1681. Fol.

Wing T 2140.

T.684

2028

The TRYAL and condemnation of George Busby, for high-treason, as a Romish priest and Jesuite, upon the statute of 27. Eliz. cap.2... As it was faithfully taken, by a person of quality. London, for Randolph Taylor, 1681. Fol.

Wing T 2142.

T.684

2029

The TRYAL of Roger Earl of Castlemaine for high treason in conspiring the death of the King, the subversion of the government, and introducing of popery and arbitrary power... London, for S.G. and N.E. and are to be sold by Randal Taylor, 1681. Fol.

Wing T 2214.

T.684

2030

The TRYAL of Sr. Miles Stapleton Bar. for high treason, in conspiring the death of the King, &c. at York assizes on the 18th. day of July, 1681... To which is added the Tryal and condemnation of Mr. Thomas Thwing for high treason, at the summer assizes before. London, for Richard Baldwin, 1681. 2 parts. Fol.

Wing T2217.

T.684

2031

The TRYAL of William Viscount Stafford for high treason in conspiring the death of the King, the extirpation of the protestant religion... upon an impeachment... begun in Westminster-Hall the 30th day of November 1680, and continued until the 7th of December following... London: the assigns of John Bill, Thomas Newcomb, and Henry Hills, 1680/1. Fol.

Wing T 2238.
2 copies (copy T.686 incomplete)

T.684 T.686

A TRYAL of witches. 1682.

See no. 8554.

2032

TURNER (Bryan)

Testimonium Jesu; or, The demonstration of the spirit, for the confirmation of Christian faith, and conviction of all infidelity. A sermon preached before the ... Lord Mayor and aldermen of the city of London, at the Guildhall-chappel. London, S. Roycroft for Walter Kettleby, 1681. 4°

Wing T 3271.

T.175

2033

TURNER (Francis) *Bishop of Ely.*

A sermon preached before the King on the 30/1 of January 1680/1. Being the fast for the martyrdom of King Charles I ... London, J. Macock, for R. Royston, 1681. 4°

Wing T 3280.

T.73

2034

The TWO associations. One subscribed by CLVI members of the House of Commons in the year 1643. The other seized in the closet of the Earl of Shaftesbury... London: for Samuel Mearne and John Baker, 1681. Fol.

Wing T 3428.

T.698

2035

A VINDICATION of the honourable the sheriffs & recorder of London, from those impudent reflections cast upon them in Fitzharris's libel, entituled His confession, &c. London: for Richard Baldwyn, [1681]. brs.

Wing V 506.

T.684

2036

VOX patriae: or the resentments & indignation of the free-born subjects of England, against popery, arbitrary government, the Duke of York, or any popish successor; being a true collection of the petitions and addresses lately made... London, for Francis Peters, 1681. Fol.

Wing V 725.

T.531

2037

VOX populi: or the peoples claim to their Parliaments sitting, to redress grievances, and provide for the common safety ... London, for Francis Smith, 1681. 4°

Wing V 729.
2 copies.

T.90 T.117

2038

WEYER (Florence)

The honesty and true zeal of the kings witnesses justified and vindicated against those un-christian-like equivocal protestations of Dr. Oliver Plunkett ... London, for T. Baldwin, 1681. Fol.

Wing W 1525.

T.531

2039

WHITAKER (Edward)

The bishops courts dissolved: or, The law of England touching ecclesiastical jurisdiction stated... By E.W. London, for T. Reyner, to be sold by Rich. Janeway, 1681. Fol.

Wing W 1701.
2 copies.

T.531 T.537

2040

WHITAKER (Edward)

The ignoramus justices: being an answer to the order of sessions at Hicks's Hall... Also a short account of all the acts that relate to protestant dissenters... By Drawde Kekatihw. London, for Ab. Green, 1681. 4°

Wing W 1702.

T.117

2041

WILKINSON (Henry) *Captain.*

The information of Capt. Hen. Wilkinson, of what hath passed betwixt him and some other persons, who have attempted to prevail with him to swear high treason against the Earl of Shaftsbury. London: for Henry Wilkinson, 1681. Fol.

Wing W 2218.
2 copies.

T.694 T.698

2042

WILLIAMS (*Sir* William)

A specimen, of the rhetorick, candour, gravity, and ingenuity of Wi. Williams, Speaker to the late House of Commons at Westminster, in his speech to Sir Robert Peyton, when he expell'd him that house. [London, 1681.] brs.

Wing W 2779.

T.698

2043

YARRANTON (Andrew)

A full discovery of the first Presbyterian sham-plot, or a letter form one in London, to a person of quality in the country. London: for Francis Smith, 1681. 4°

Wing Y 15.

T.90

1682

2044

An ANSWER to Mr. Read's case. Wherein is a full discovery of his dissimulation with God and man ... London: printed for the author [by R. Janeway], 1682. 4°

Wing A 3370.

T.307

2045

AQUILA Furstenbergica in petra moriens, sive reverendissimus ... dominus, D. Franciscus Egon, Episcopus Argentoratensis ... Coloniae, excudebat Petrus Alstorff, 1682. Fol.

T.810

2046

AZARIA and Hushai, a poem ... [Attributed to Elkanah Settle and to Samuel Pordage.] London, for Charles Lee, an. Dom. 1682. 4°

Wing S 2662.

T.117

2047

BALL (Richard)

The true Christian-man's duty both to God and the King: deliver'd in a sermon preached in the Temple-Church on Sunday, November VI. 1670. London, A. G. and J. P. for John Playford, 1682. 4°

Wing B 583.

T.234

2048

BARNE (Miles)

A discourse concerning the nature of Christ's kingdom, with relation to the Kingdoms of this world; in two sermons preach'd at St. Maries before the University of Cambridge. Cambridge, J. Haynes; for R. Green, 1682. 2 parts. 4°

Wing B 857.

T.733

2049
BAYLY (Thomas)

The royal charter granted unto kings by God himself:
and collected out of his holy word in both
Testaments ... London: for W. Leach, 1682.   4°

Wing B 1515.

T.307

2050
BEVERIDGE (William) *Bishop of St, Asaph,*

A sermon concerning the excellency and usefulness of
the common prayer. Preached ... 27th of November,
1681. London, T. James for Richard Northcott, 1682.
4°

Wing B 2100.

T.177

2051
BEVERIDGE (William) *Bishop of St.Asaph.*

A sermon concerning the excellency and usefulness
of the Common prayer. Preached... 27th of
November. 1681. 3rd ed. London, T.James for
Richard Northcott, 1682.   4°

Wing B 2102.

T.771

2052
BOHUN (Edmund)

An address to the free-men and free-holders of the
nation. [Anon.] London: for George Wells, 1682.
4°

Wing B 3445.
2 copies.

T.307   T.177

2053
BOHUN (Edmund)

The second part of the Address to the free-men and
free-holders of the nation. By the same author.
London, A. Godbid and J. Playford for George Wells,
1682.   4°

Wing B 3460.
2 copies.

T.307   T.174

2054
A BRIEF account of the proceedings of the French
clergy, in taking away the Pope's usurp'd supremacy
... London, for Tho. Simmons, 1682.   2 parts.
4°

Wing B 4516.

T.411

2055
BROWNE (Philip) *of Halstead.*

The sovereign's authority, and the subject's duty,
plainly represented in a sermon preached at the
visitation, April the 12th. 1681... London,
M. Flesher, for Walter Kettilby, 1682.   4°

Wing B 5139.

T.733

2056
BRYDALL (John)

A new-years-gift for the anti-prerogative-men: or,
A lawyers opinion, in defence of his Majesties
power-royal, of granting pardons, as he pleases.
Wherein is more particularly discussed the
validity of the E. of D's pardon ... [Anon.]
London, H. H. for John Fish, 1682. 4°

Wing B 5264.

T.307

2057
BURNET (Gilbert) *Bishop of Salisbury.*

An answer to the Animadversions on the History of
the rights of princes, &c. [by Thomas Comber].
London, for Richard Chiswell, 1682. 4°

Wing B 5761.

T.307

2058
BURNET (Gilbert) *Bishop of Salisbury.*

News from France: in a letter giving a relation of
the present state of the difference between the
French King and the court of Rome... [Anon.]
London, for Richard Chiswel, 1682.   4°

Wing B 5839.

T.411

2059
BURNET (Gilbert) *Bishop of Salisbury.*

A sermon preached at the funeral of Mr. James
Houblon, who was buried at St. Mary Wolnoth Church
in Lombard-street, June 28. 1682. London, for
Richard Chiswel, 1682.   4°

Wing B 5878.

T.333

2060
BUTLER (James) *1st Duke of Ormonde.*

A letter from his Grace James Duke of Ormond, lord
lieutenant of Ireland, in answer to the Right
Honourable Arthur Earl of Anglesey lord privy-seal,
his Observations & reflections upon the Earl of
Castlehaven's Memoires concerning the rebellion
of Ireland... London, printed in the year 1682.
And are to be sold by R. Baldwin. Fol.

Wing O 448

T.532

2061
CARE (Henry)

A perfect guide for protestant dissenters, in case
of prosecution upon any of the penal statutes made
against them... [Anon.] London, for R. Baldwin,
1682. 2 parts. Fol.

Wing C 531.
2 copies

T.531   T.698

2062
CARTWRIGHT (Thomas) *Bishop of Chester.*

A sermon preached at Holy-roodhouse, January 30.
1681/2. Before her Highness the Lady Anne.
Edinburgh, printed by David Lindsay, and
reprinted at London, and sold by Walter Davis,
1682. 4°

Wing C 704A.

T.333

2063
The CHARGE of a Tory plot maintain'd in a dialogue
between the Observator, Heraclitus and an inferior
clergy- man at the Towzer-tavern ... By the same
author. London, for N. L. to be sold by Richard
Janeway, 1682. 4°

Wing C 2052.

T.95

2064
CLIFFORD (William)

The power of kings, particularly the British
monarchy asserted and vindicated, in a sermon
preached at Wakefield ... October the 30th,
1681. London, Samuel Roycroft, for Robert
Clavell, 1682.   4°

Wing C 4715.

T.492

2065
COMBER (Thomas)

Animadversions on Dr. Burnet's History of the
rights of princes in the disposing of ecclesiastical
benefices and church-lands. In a letter to a
friend. [Anon.] London: printed in the year
1682. 4°

Wing C 5440.

T.307

2066
COMBER (Thomas)

The nature and usefulness of solemn judicial
swearing, with the impiety and mischief of vain
and false-swearing: in a sermon preached July
14th, 1681. in the cathedral church of S.Peter
in York ... London, Samuel Roycroft, for
Robert Clavell, 1682.   4°

cf. Wing C 5479.

T.492

2067
A CONGRATULATORY poem on his R. H's
entertainment in the City. London: for Joanna
Brome, 1682. brs.

Wing C 5822.

T.407

2068
D. (M.)

An account of the arraignment, tryal, escape,
and condemnation, of the dog of Heriot's
Hospital in Scotland, that was supposed to have
been hang'd, but did at last slip the halter.
London, printed for the author, M.D., 1682. brs.

Wing D 55.

T.698

2069
DRYDEN (John)

Absalom and Achitophel. A poem ... 4th ed.;
augmented and revised. [Anon.] London, for J. T.
and are to be sold by W. Davis, 1682. 4°

Wing D 2219.
2 copies

T.117 T.119

2070
DRYDEN (John)

Absalom and Achitophel. A poem. [No imprint,
1682?] 4°

Not in Wing.
No. 12L in H. Macdonald, *John Dryden: a
bibliography.* 8pp. printed in double columns.

T.204

2071
DRYDEN (John)

The medall. A satyre against sedition. By the
authour of Absalom and Achitophel ... London,
for Jacob Tonson, 1682.   4°

Wing D 2311.

T.495

2072
DRYDEN (John)

Prologue to his Royal Highness, upon his first
appearance at the Duke's theatre since his return
from Scotland. Written by Mr. Dryden. Spoken by
Mr. Smith. London, for J. Tonson, [1682.] brs.

Wing D 2336.

T.532

2073
DRYDEN (John)

The second part of Absalom and Achitophel. A
poem ... [Anon.] London: for Jacob Tonson,
1682. Fol.

Wing D 2350.

T.532

2074
ELLIOT (Adam)

A modest vindication of Titus Oates the
Salamanca-doctor from perjury: or an essay to
demonstrate him only forsworn in several
instances ... London, for the author, and are to
be sold by Joseph Hindmarsh, 1682. Fol.

Wing E 543.

T.687

2075
ENGLAND'S most dreadful calamity by the late floods:
being a most lamentable account of the great
damages sustained by the fearful inundations;
caused by the unparalell'd rain which fell on the
24th of April, 1682 ... Printed for P. Brooksby,
1682.   4°

Wing E 2999.

T.307

2076
EVANS (John) *Rector of St. Ethelburga, London.*

Moderation stated: in a sermon preached before the
Right Honourable the Lord Mayor .. at Guild-hall
chappel. Octob. 22. 1682. London, for Walter
Kettilby, 1682.   4°

Wing E 3450.

T.514

2077
EVERETT (George)

A second letter to Mr. Miles Prance, in reply to
the ghost of Sir Edmond-bury Godfrey. [Signed
Trueman.] London, for N. Thompson, 1682. Fol.

Wing P 192 (attributed to William Paine).

T.694

2078
FERGUSON (Robert)

A just and modest vindication of the proceedings of the two last parliaments. [Anon,] [London, 1682.] 4°

Wing F 741.
2 copies.

T.95 T.117

2079
FERGUSON (Robert)

The second part of No Protestant plot. By the same hand. London: for R. Smith, 1682. 4°

Wing F 759.
3 copies.

T.90 T.117 T.125

2080
FERGUSON (Robert)

The third part of No Protestant plot: with observations on the proceedings upon the bill of indictment against the E. of Shaftesbury ... [Anon.] London: for Richard Baldwin, 1682. 4°

Wing F 762.
3 copies.

T.95 T.117 T.125

2081
FORE-WARN'D, fore-arm'd: or, England's timely warning in general, and London's in particular. By a collection of five prophetical predictions published by Mr. William Lilly forty years ago: two of Mr. John Gadbury's, anno 1678 ... London, for John Powel, 1682.   4°

Wing F 1556A. (=L 2222).

T.411

2082
The FORFEITURES of Londons charter, or an impartial account of the several seisures of the city charter ... since the reign of King Henry the third ... Printed for the author, and are to be sold by Daniel Brown, and Thomas Benskin, 1682. 4°

Wing F 1557.

T. 95

2083
FREEMAN (Samuel)

The Israelite indeed. A sermon preached at the funeral of Mark Cottle Esq; late register of the Prerogative-office, on Thursday, Jan. 5, 1681. London, for Edward Gellibrand, 1682. 4°

Wing F 2141.

T.314

2084
FYLER (Samuel)

A sermon preach'd in the cathedral church at the triennial visitation of ... Seth, Lord Bishop of Sarum. London, E.T. and R.H. for Thomas Flesher, 1682.   4°

Wing F 2568.
3 copies.

T.605 T.733 T.752

2085
GARBRAND (John)

The royal favourite clear'd: with an admonition to the Roman Catholicks, and an address to his Royal Highness, James, Duke of York, &c. By a barrister of the Inner-Temple. London, for James Vade, 1682. 4°

Wing G 206.

T. 90

2086
GROVE (Robert) *Bishop of Chichester*.

Roberti Grovii S.T.D. Defensio suae responsionis ad nuperum libellum, qui inscribitur Celeusma, &c. adversus refutationem ab authore Celeusmatis editam [i.e. William Jenkyn] ... Londini, typis J. M. impensis G. Kettilby, 1682. 4°

Wing G 2150.
2 copies.

T.495   T.1

2087
HAMMOND (Henry)

Considerations of present use, concerning the danger resulting from the change of our church-government. [Anon.] London, T. M. for Fin. Gardiner, 1682. 4°

Wing H 528.

T.307

2088
HICKERINGILL (Edmund)

Scandalum magnatum: or the great trial at Chelmsford assizes, held March 6, for the county of Essex, betwixt Henry Bishop of London, plaintiff, and Edm. Hickeringill ... defendant, faithfully related ... London, for E. Smith, 1682. Fol.

Wing H 1825.

T.531

2089
HICKES (George)

A discourse of the soveraign power, in a sermon preached at St. Mary Le Bow, Nov.28. 1682. Before the Artillery Company of London... London: for John Baker, 1682. 4°

Wing H 1845.
3 copies.

T.132 T.173 T.514

2090
HICKES (George)

The moral schechinah: or a discourse of Gods glory. In a sermon preached at the last Yorkshire-feast in Bow-church, London. June 11. 1682. London: J. Wallis, for Walter Kettilby, 1682.   4°

Wing H 1857.

T.514

2091
HICKES (George)

A sermon preached before the Lord Mayor, aldermen, and citizens of London, at Bow Church, on the 30th. of January, 1681/2 ... London, for Walter Kettilby, 1682. 4°

Wing H 1864.
2 copies.

T.175 T.177

2092
The HISTORY of the association, containing all the debates in the last House of Commons ... concerning an association, for the preservation of the Kings person, and the security of the protestant religion... London, for R. Janeway, 1682. Fol.

Wing H 2144.

T.698

2093
HOOPER (George) *Bishop of Bath and Wells*.

A sermon preached before the King at White-hall, on the fifth of November, 1681. London, for Mark Pardoe, 1682.   4°

Wing H 2706.

T.492

2094
HUNT (Thomas) *lawyer*.

Mr. Emmertons marriage with Mrs. Bridget Hyde considered ... In a letter from a gentleman in the country to one of the commissioners delegates in that cause ... [Anon.] London, printed for the author, and published by Richard Baldwin, 1682. 4°

Wing H 3757.

T.314

2095
JEKYLL (Thomas)

True religion makes the best loyalty. Discovered and recommended in a sermon, prepar'd for that assembly which intended to meet at St. Michael's Cornhil, April 21. 1682 ... London; for Jonathan Robinson, 1682. 4°

Wing J 539.

T.333

2096
JORDAN (Thomas)

The lord mayor's show: being a description of the solemnity at the inauguration of the truly loyal and Right Honourable Sir William Prichard, Kt. Lord Mayor of the city of London ... [Anon.] London, for T. Burnel, 1682.   4°

Wing J 1044 A.

T.407

2097
KEN (Thomas) *Bishop of Bath and Wells*.

A sermon preached at the funeral of the Right Honourable Lady Margaret Mainard, at Little Easton in Essex. On the 30th. of June, 1682. London, M. Flesher, for Joanna Brome; and William Clarke bookseller in Winchester, 1682. 4°

Wing K 279.

T.333

2098
The KINGDOM of Sweden restored to its true interest. A political discourse. London, M. Flesher, for Joanna Brome, 1682. 4°

Wing K 581 (?)

T.411

2099
LAXTON (Thomas)

Grief allayed, death sweetned, hope raised. A sermon preached at the funeral of the Honourable Christopher Sherard ... February the 28th, 1681. London, S. Roycroft, for Robert Clavell, 1682.   4°

Wing L 744.

T.333

2100
L'ESTRANGE (*Sir* Roger)

The accompt clear'd: in answer to a libel, intituled, A true account from Chichester, concerning the death of Habin the informer, &c. London, for Joanna Brome, 1682. 4°

Wing L 1192.
2 copies.

T.201 T.307

2101
L'ESTRANGE (*Sir* Roger)

A memento. Treating, of the rise, progress, and remedies of seditions: with some historical reflections upon the series of our late troubles. 2nd ed. Printed in the year 1642, and now reprinted for Joanna Brome, 1682.   4°

Wing L 1271.

T.307

2102
L'ESTRANGE (*Sir* Roger)

Remarks on the growth and progress of non-conformity ... [Anon.] London, for Walter Kettilby, 1682.   4°

Wing L 1296.
3 copies.

T.177 T.307 T.326

2103
L'ESTRANGE (*Sir* Roger)

A sermon prepared to be preach'd at the interment of the renowned Observator. With some remarques on his life, by the reverend Toryrorydammeeplotshammee Younkercrape. To which is annexed an elegy and epitaph, by the rose-ally-poet, and other prime wits of the age. London, Langley Curtiss, 1682.   4°

Wing L 1305.

T.307

2104
A LETTER from a person of quality to his friend, about abhorrers and addressors, &c. London, for John Frith, 1682. brs.

Wing L 1427.

T.698

2105
LONDON.

A brief collection out of the records of the City, touching elections of the sheriffs of London and the county of Middlesex. [London], S. Roycroft, 1682. Fol.

Wing B 4556.

T.532

2106

LONDON.

The city of London's plea to the quo warranto, (an information) brought against their charter in Michaelmas Term 1681 ... London, printed in the year 1682. And published by Randal Taylor. Fol.

Wing C 4360.

T.532

2107

LONDON.

The city of Londons rejoinder, to Mr. Attorney General's replication in the quo warranto brought by him against their charter ... London, L. Curtiss, 1682. Fol.

Wing C 4361.

T.532

2108

LOUIS XIV, *King of France.*

The French King's edict upon the declaration made by the clergy of France, of their opinion, concerning the ecclesiastical power ... London, printed in the year 1682. Fol.

Wing L 3122.

T.532

2109

LOUIS XIV, *King of France.*

An edict of the French Kings upon the declaration made by the clergy of France, of their opinions touching ecclesiastical power ... London, for Robert Clavell, 1682. Fol.

Wing L 3122 A.

T.698

2110

MANNINGHAM (Thomas) *Bishop of Chichester.*

Praise and adoration. Or, a sermon on Trinity-Sunday before the University of Oxford. 1681. London: for William Crooke, and William Cadman. Also sold by R. Davis in Oxford, 1682.   4°

Wing M 497.

T.492

2111

MAURICE (Henry)

A sermon preached before the King at White-hall, on January the 30th, 1681. London, Samuel Roycroft, for Robert Clavell, 1682. 4°

Wing M 1370.

T.333

2112

MEGGOTT (Richard)

A sermon preached at the assises for the county of Surrey, held in the burrough of Southwark, March 23. 1681/2. London, A. Grover, for Thomas Rowe Jun., 1682. 4°

Wing M 1626.
2 copies.

T.618   T.333

2113

MEREDITH (Edward)

Some remarques upon a late popular piece of nonsence called Julian the apostate, &c. [by Samuel Johnson]. Together, with a particular vindication of his Royal Highness the Duke of York... By a lover of truth, vertue, and justice... London, for T. Davies, 1682. 2 parts. Fol.

Wing M 1784.

T.687

2114

MIRACLES reviv'd, in the discovery of the Popish Plot, by the late reverend Dr. of Salamanca. London, for A. Banks, 1682. brs.

Wing M 2208.

T.177

2115

MR. Emerton's cause now depending before the delegates, briefly stated and unfolded.   London: for R. Dew, 1682. Fol.

Wing M 2264.

T.698

2116

A MODEST enquiry concerning the election of the sheriffs of London. And the right of chusing demonstrated to belong unto, and to have been always adjudged to reside in the lord mayor, the court of aldermen, and the common-hall. London: for Henry Mead, 1682. 4°

Wing M 2365.

T.411

2117

MOORE (John) *Bishop of Ely.*

A sermon preach'd before the Lord Mayor, and the court of aldermen, at Guild-hall chappel, on the 28th of May, 1682. London, for Walter Kettilby, 1682. 4°

Wing M 2552.
2 copies.

T.314   T.670

2118

N.(N.)

The heu and cry: or, A relation of the travels of the devil and Towzer... in search after the lost Heraclitus. Written by N.N. M.A. and chaplain errant to his excellency the guide to the inferiour clergy... London, printed for Roger Catflogger, [1682]. 4°

Wing N 36.

T.411

2119

OBSERVATIONS touching appeals from Chancery. Collected out of the authorities of law. London: printed anno Domini, 1682. brs.

Not in Wing.

T.698

2120

The OPINIONS of the barons of the Exchequer. And directions to all justices of the peace, and constables, &c. For the legally convicting of all persons, that are taken in conventicles... Given at the court of Exchequer, upon Justice Balch's case. London, for R.H. and are to be sold by Walter Davies, 1682. brs.

Wing O 358.

T.698

2121

OSBORNE (Thomas) *1st Duke of Leeds.*

An account at large of the Right Honourable the Earl of Danby's arguments at the court of King's-Bench at Westminster, upon his lordship's motion for bail ... 2nd ed. London, for Charles Mearne, 1682. Fol.

Wing L 919.
2 copies.

T.531   T.698

2122

OSBORNE (Thomas) *1st Duke of Leeds.*

The arguments of the Right Honourable the Earl of Danby the second time, at the court of King's-Bench at Westminster, upon his lordship's motion for bail ... London, for Richard Tonson, 1682. Fol.

Wing L 922.
2 copies.

T.531   T.698

2123

A PANEGYRICK on their Royal Highnesses, and congratulating his return from Scotland. London, A. Godbid and J. Playford for Jos. Hindmarsh, 1682. Fol.

Wing P 264

T.699

2124

PELLING (Edward)

A sermon preached on the anniversary of that most execrable murder of K. Charles the first royal martyr... London, for J. Williams, and Joanna Brome, 1682. 4°

Wing P 1090.

T.333

2125

PELLING (Edward)

The true mark of the beast: or the present degeneracy of the Church of Rome from the faith once delivered to the saints. A sermon on November 5. 1681 ... London, for Joseph Hindmarsh, and Walter Davis, 1682. 4°

Wing P 1106.

T.177

2126

PENN (William)

William Penn's last farewel to England: being an epistle containing a salutation to all faithful friends, a reproof to the unfaithful, and a visitation to the enquiring... London, for Thomas Cooke, 1682. 4°

Wing P 1317.

T.307

2127

PENNSYLVANIA. *Free Society of Traders.*

The articles, settlement and offices of the Free Society of Traders in Pennsilvania: agreed upon by divers merchants and others for the better improvement and government of trade in that province. London, for Benjamin Clark, 1682. Fol.

Wing A 3885.

T.543

2128

PERSE (William)

A sermon preached at the anniversary meeting of the Eton-scholars, at St. Mary le Bow, on Decemb. the 6. 1681. London, for Samuel Carr, 1682. 4°

Wing P 1653.

T.492

2129

PHILLIPS (John)

Speculum crape-gownorum, the second part. Or a continuation of observations and reflections upon the late sermons of some that would be thought Goliah's for the Church of England.   By the same author. London: for R. Baldwin, 1682. 4°

Wing P 2111.

T.411

2130

PIERCE (Thomas)

Two letters containing a further justification of the Church of England, against the dissenters. The first, by one of the reverend commissioners for the review of the liturgy, at the Savoy, 1661. The second, by Dr. Laurence Womock ... London: for Robert Clavell, 1682. 8°

Wing P 2207.

T.211

2131

A PINDARIQUE ode, on their Royal Highnesses happy return from Scotland after his escape at sea. London, A. Godbid and J. Playford for Jos. Hindmarsh, 1682. Fol.

Wing P 2254 B.

T.532

2132

PITTIS (Thomas)

An old way of ending new controversies; in a sermon preached to the comptroller, and the rest of the gentlemen of the... Inner Temple: on Sunday the 8th January 1681/2... London, J.R. for Joanna Brome, 1682. 4°

Wing P 2315.

T.625

2133

A PLEASANT conference upon the Observator, and Heraclitus: together with a brief relation of the present posture of the French Affairs. London: for H. Jones, 1682. 4°

Wing P 2540.

T.307

2134

PLEYDELL (Josias)

Loyalty and conformity asserted; in two sermons... London, for Joanna Brome, 1682. 4°

Wing P 2568.
2 copies.

T.492   T.765

2135

The PRESENT alteration in religion in France.
Discours'd of in two letters, the one from a person
of quality to an abbot. The other the abbot's
answer thereunto. Which may serve as an appendix
to the Mistery of Jesuitisme. London, for Rich.
Janeway, 1682. 4°

Wing P 3233.

T.411

2136

The PRIVILEDGES of the citizens of London:
contained in the charters, granted to them by the
several kings of this realm ... London, printed for
the translator of it, and published by Langley Curtiss
1682. 4°

Wing P 3537.

T.117

2137

The PROCEEDINGS at the sessions of the peace held at
Hicks-Hall, for the county of Middlesex, Decemb.5.
1681. With his Majesties two orders and Sir William
Smith's speech to the grand jury, concerning putting
the laws in execution against popish recusants...
London: for Walter Davies, 1682. Fol.

Wing P 3567.

T.531

2138

REFLECTIONS upon the conduct of the King of Great
Britain in the late wars. Contained in a letter from
a subject of one of the confederated princes, to a
friend in Holland. London, for H.R., 1682. Fol.

Wing R 727.

T.698

2139

REFLECTIONS upon two scurrilous libels [by John
Phillips], called Speculum crape-gownorum. By a
lay-man. London, for Benjamin Tooke, 1682. 4°

Wing R 734 A.

T.411

2140

The RIGHTS of the City farther unfolded: and the
manifold miscarriages of my Lord Mayor, as well as
the punishments he hath rendred himself obnoxious
unto, for his misbehaviour in relation to the present
election of sheriffs, display'd and laid open.
London, for J. Johnson, 1682. Fol.

Wing R 1516.

T.532

2141

S.(T.)

Δετμα βασιλκη: a sermon preached at the Kings prison
the Fleet, on the 30th. of January, 1681... London:
for Walter Davies, 1682. 4°

Wing S 156.

T.333

2142

SANDERSON (Robert) *Bishop of Lincoln.*

Judicium Universitatis Oxoniensis de 1. Solenni liga
& foedere. 2. Juramento negativo. 3. Ordinationibus Parlamenti circa disciplinam, & cultum. In plena
convocatione 1. Junii 1647... Editio tertia.
Londini typis M.C. impensis R. Royston, 1682. 8°

Wing S 610.
Title-page broken.

T.478

2143

A SEASONABLE warneing to the poor persecuted Church
of Scotland, or a dissuasive to all true non-conformists, from sinful complying with, owneing of, and
active submitting to abjured prelates... By
Philalethes... Printed in the year 1682. 8°

Not in Wing.

T.441

2144

The SECOND character of an informer: wherein his
mischievous nature and leud practises are detected.
London, for S.M., 1682. 4°

Wing S 2262.

T.411

2145

SETTLE (Elkanah)

Absalom senior: or, Achitophel transpros'd.
A poem... [Anon.] London: for S.E. and sold
by Langley Curtis, 1682. Fol.

Wing S 2652.
2 copies.

T.532 T.698

2146

SEYMOUR (Thomas)

Advice to the readers of the Common-prayer, and to
the people attending the same... By a well-meaning
(though unlearned) layick of the Church of England.
London: for Randal Taylor, 1682. 4°

Wing S 2827.

T.411

2147

SMITH (Benjamin)

A sermon preached July 17. 1681. at the assizes at
Huntingdon... London, for Tho. Parkhurst, 1682.
4°

Wing S 4021B.

T.492

2148

SMITH (Thomas) *of Magdalen College, Oxford.*

A sermon concerning the doctrine, unity, and
profession of the Christian faith. Preached
before the University of Oxford... London, for
Walter Kettilby, 1682. 4°

Wing S 4249.

T.670

2149

SMITH (*Sir* William)

The charge given by Sr William Smith, Brt. at the
quarter-sessions of the peace held for the county
of Middlesex, at Westminster, on Monday the 24th of
April, 1682. London, Tho. Hodgkin, 1682. Fol.

Wing S 4255A.

T.698

2150

SPRAT (Thomas) *Bishop of Rochester.*

A sermon preached before the Artillery Company of
London at St. Mary Le Bow, April 20. 1682. 2nd ed.
London, for John Baker, 1682. 4°

Wing S 5059.

T.333

2151

SPRAT (Thomas) *Bishop of Rochester.*

A sermon preach'd before the Lord Mayor, and the court
of aldermen, at Guild-hall chappel, on the 29th of
January, 1681/2. London: M.C. for Joanna Brome, 1682.
4°

Wing S 5057.

T.333

2152

STILLINGFLEET (Edward) *Bishop of Worcester.*

Of the nature of superstition. A sermon preached
at St Dunstans West, March 31. 1682. London, for
H. Mortlock, 1682. 4°

Wing S 5614.

T.132

2153

A TORY plot: or the discovery of a design carried
on by our late addressers and abhorrers, to alter
the constitution of the government, and to betray the
Protestant religion. By Philanax Misopappas.
London, for N. L., to be sold by Richard Janeway,
1682. 4°

Wing T 1946.

T.95

2154

A TRUE account of the whole proceedings betwixt his
Grace James Duke of Ormond, and the Right Honor.
Arthur Earl of Anglesey late lord privy-seal, before
the King and Council... London, for Thomas Fox,
1682. Fol.

Wing T 2408.

T.532

2155

The TRYAL and condemnation of George Borosky alias
Boratzi, Christopher Vratz, and John Stern; for the
barbarous murder of Thomas Thynn... London, for
Thomas Basset, 1682. Fol.

Wing T 2141.

T.698

2156

TURNER (Francis) *Bishop of Ely.*

A sermon preached before the Lord Mayor and the
court of aldermen at Guild-hall chappel on the 7th
of May 1682. London, J. Macock, for R. Royston,
1682. 4°

Wing T 3281.

T.503

2157

ULMORUM Acherons; or the history of William Pen's
conversion from a gentleman to a quaker. Or a
stop to the Call of the unconverted... London, for
Tho. Lee, 1682. 4°

Wing U 21.

T.307

2158

UNDERHILL (Cave)

Vox lachrymae. A sermon newly held forth at
Weavers-hall upon the funeral of the famous T.O.
Doctor of Salamancha. By Elephant Smith [i.e. Cave
Underhill]. Printed at Francfort... 1681.
Reprinted at London for R. Davies, 1682. 4°

Wing U 42.

T.411

2159

VERNEY (Robert)

Englands interest or the great benefit to trade by
banks or offices of credit in London, &c. As it hath
been considered and agreed upon by a committee of
aldermen and commons, thereunto appointed, by the...
Lord Major, aldermen and commons, in Common-Council
assembled... [Anon.] London, John Gain, 1682. 4°

Wing V 243.

T.373

2160

WALL (Thomas)

A brief answer to an indictment presented by the jury
upon oath, at Surry-sessions... against several of
the inhabitants in Southwark... London: for
T. Wall, G. Hampton, and the rest of the persons
indicted, and sold by W. Marshall, 1682. 4°

Wing W 475.

T.411

2161

WHITAKER (Edward)

The second part of the ignoramus justices: or an
answer to the scandalous speech of Sir W.S.
Barronet, spoken to the grand-jury at the sessions
of peace held for the county of Middlesex...
Together with several remarks upon the order of
sessions, for the printing and publishing the same.
By the same authour. London, for E. Smith, 1682.
4°

Wing W 1705.

T.411

2162

WHITFIELD (John)

The dreadfulness of the sin of despising dominion,
and speaking evil of dignities: represented in a
sermon preached before the... Lord Mayor, and court
of aldermen, at the Guild-hall chappel, July 30. 1682.
London, for Samuel Carr, 1682. 4°

Wing W 2004.

T.495

2163

WOMOCK (Laurence) *Bishop of St. Davids.*

Billa vera: or, The arraignment of Ignoramus. Put
forth out of charity, for the use of grand inquests
and other jury's ... [Anon.] London, for Robert
Clavel, 1682. 4°

Wing W 3340.

T.90

1683

2164

An ACCOUNT of Monsieur de Quesne's late expedition
at Chio; together with the negotiation of Monsieur
Guilleragues the French ambassadour at the Port
... Translated into English. London, for Richard
Tonson: and Jacob Tonson, 1683. 4°

Wing A 211.

T.194

2165

ANNESLEY (Arthur) *1st Earl of Anglesey.*

A letter of remarkes upon Jovian [by George Hickes].
By a person of quality. London, for H. Jones,
1683. 4°

Wing A 3174.

T.137

2166

An APOLOGY for the protestants of France, in
reference to the persecutions they are under at
this day; in six letters... London, for John
Holford, 1683. 2 parts. 4°

Wing A 3555A

T.411

2167

ATWOOD (William)

A seasonable vindication of the truly Catholick
doctrine of the Church of England: in reply to
Dr. Sherlock's answer to Anonymus his three letters
concerning Church-communion... [Anon.] London:
for Jonathan Robinson, 1683. 4°

Wing A 4182.

T.745

2168

ATWOOD (William)

Three letters to Dr. Sherlock concerning Church-
communion. Wherein 'tis enquired whether the
Doctor's notion of Church-communion be not too
narrow and uncharitable, both to dissenters, and
men of larger principles. By a lay-man... London,
for Jonathan Robinson, 1683. 4°

Wing A 4183.

T.745

2169

B. (W.)

A funeral sermon preached on the occasion of the
Right Honourable the Earl of Sh---y's late
interment in Dorset-shire. By W. B. ... London,
George Croom, 1683. 4°

Wing B 211.

T.144

2170

BARNE (Miles)

A sermon preach'd before the University of Cambridge
on the ninth of September, being the day of publick
thanksgiving for the deliverance of his Majesties
sacred person... London, for R. Royston, 1683. 4°

Wing B 862.

T.514

2171

BARROW (John)

A sermon preached at the triennial visitation of
... Seth, Lord Bishop of Sarum, held at Reading,
Sept.6. 1683. London, Ralph Holt, for John Gelli-
brand, 1683. 4°

Wing B 966.

T.503

2172

BLOUNT (Charles)

Miracles no violations of the laws of nature ...
[Anon.] London: for Robert Sollers, 1683. 4°

Wing B 3310.
Attributed by Wing (following Halkett & Laing) to
Blount; a manuscript attribution on the title-
page to Walter Charleton.

T.144

2173

BOHUN (Edmund)

Reflections on a pamphlet [by Robert Ferguson],
stiled A just and modest vindication of the
proceedings of the two last parliaments: or, A
defence of his Majesties late declaration. By the
author of the Address to the freemen and freeholders of the nation... London, M. Clark, for
George Wells, 1683. 4°

Wing B 3459.

T.174

2174

BOHUN (Edmund)

The third and last part of the Address to the free-
men and free-holders of the nation. By the same
author. London, for George Wells, 1683. 4°

Wing B 3461.
2 copies.

T.307 T.174

2175

BUTLER (John) *B.D.*

God's judgments upon regicides: a sermon preached
in the Fleet-Prison, on the 30th day of January.
1681/2 ... London, T. Moore, and J. Ashburne, for
Awnsham Churchill, 1683. 4°

Wing B 6273.

T. 73

2176

C.(C.)

Sylla's ghost: a satyr against ambition, and the
last horrid plot... [By C.C., Caleb Calle?]
London, John Harefinch, 1683. Fol.

cf. Wing C 18.

T.532

2177

C. (J.)

The nonconformists plea for the conformists: or,
The Church of England and the dissenters
reconciled ... London, for James Chick and sold
by Benj. Harris, 1683. 4°

Wing C 68

T.326

2178

CALAMY (Benjamin)

A discourse about a scrupulous conscience, preached
at the parish-church of St. Mary Aldermanbury,
London ... London, for Rowland Reynolds, 1683. 4°

Wing C 211.
2 copies.

T.495   T.333

2179

CALAMY (Benjamin)

A discourse about a scrupulous conscience, preached
at the parish-church of St. Mary Aldermanbury,
London ... 2nd ed. London, for Rowland Reynolds,
1683. 4°

Wing C 212.

T.273

2180

CALAMY (Benjamin)

A sermon preached before the ... Lord Mayor, and
the court of aldermen, at Guild-hall chappel, upon
the 30th of September, 1683. London, for W.
Kettilby, 1683. 4°

Wing C 218.

T.132

2181

The CASE of the charter of London stated.
Shewing, 1. What a corporation is. 11. Whether
a corporation may be forfeited. 111. Whether
the mayor, commonalty, and citizens have done
any act in their common council, whereby to
forfeit their corporation and franchises.
London, for John Kidgell, 1683. Fol.

Wing C 1026.

T.532

2182

CHARLES II, *King of England.*

His Majesties declaration to all his loving
subjects, concerning the treasonable conspiracy
against his sacred person and government ...
London, printed by the assigns of John Bill
deceas'd: and by Henry Hills, and Thomas Newcomb,
1683. 4°

Wing C 2998.
2 copies.

T.116 T.315

2183

CHARLETON (Walter)

Three anatomic lectures, concerning 1. The motion
of the bloud through the veins and arteries; 2. The
organic structure of the heart; 3. The efficient
causes of the hearts pulsation ... London, for
Walter Kettilby, 1683. 4°

Wing C 3693.

T. 12

2184

CHURCH OF ENGLAND.

A form of prayer with thanksgiving, to be used on
Sunday September the 9th; being the day of
thanksgiving, appointed by the Kings declaration...
London, printed by the assigns of John Bill
deceas'd: and by Henry Hills, and Thomas Newcomb,
1683. 4°

Wing C 4172.
3 copies.

T.315 T.411 T.514

2185

CHURCH OF ENGLAND. *Articles of Religion.*

Articles agreed upon by the archbishops and bishops
of both provinces, and the whole clergy, in the
convocation holden at London in the year 1562...
London, the assigns of John Bill deceas'd: and by
Henry Hills, and Thomas Newcomb, 1683. 4°

Not in Wing.

T.327

2186

The CIVIL wars of Bantam: or, An impartial relation
of all the battels, sieges, and other remarkable
transactions, revolutions and accidents that happened
in the late civil war between that king, and his
eldest son... London, H.C. for Tho. Malthus, 1683.
Fol.

Wing G 409 (attributed to Edmund Gayton).

T.531

2187

CLAGETT (William)

The difference of the case, between the separation
of protestants from the Church of Rome, and the
separation of dissenters from the Church of England.
[Anon.] London, for Thomas Basset, and Fincham
Gardiner, 1683. 4°

Wing C 4377.
2 copies.

T.606 T.691

2188

COMBER (Thomas)

Religion and loyalty supporting each other. Or, A
rational account how the loyal addressers
maintaining the lineal descent of the crown is very
consistent with their affection to the established
protestant religion. By a true son of the Church
of England ... 2nd ed., corrected and enlarged by
the author. London, for Robert Clavel, 1683. 4°

Wing C 5487.

T.308

2189

CROWNE (John)

City politiques. A comedy. As it is acted by
his Majesties servants. London, for R. Bently,
and Joseph Hindmarsh, 1683. 4°

Wing C 7378.

T.502

2190

EVANS (John) *Rector of St. Ethelburga, London.*

The case of kneeling at the holy sacrament stated
and resolved. Part II ... [Anon.] London: for
T. Basset; B. Took; and F. Gardiner, 1683. 4°

Wing E 3448.

T.746

2191
FERGUSON (Robert)

Mr. Ferguson's lamentation, for the destruction of
the association and the good old cause. London,
for J. Smith, 1683. 4°

Wing F 745.

T.134

2192
FITZGERALD (Robert)

Salt-water sweetned: or, a true account of the
great advantages of this new invention both by sea
and by land ... A letter of the Honourable Robert
Boyle to a friend upon the same subject. 3rd ed.,
with additions. London, for William Cadman, 1683.
4°

Wing F 1088 A.

T. 16

2193
FITZ-WILLIAM (John)

A sermon preach'd at Cotenham, near Cambridge, on
the 9th. of September, 1683. Being the day set
a-part for publick thanksgiving for the deliverance
of his sacred Majesty and the government from the
late treasonable conspiracy. London: for Will.
Nott, 1683. 4°

Wing F 1106.
2 copies.

T.514   T. 83

2194
FOWLER (Edward) *Bishop of Gloucester.*

A discourse of offences. Delivered in two sermons
Aug. 19. and Sept. 2. 1683. in the cathedral
church of Gloucester ... London, J. Heptinstall,
for Brabazon Aylmer, 1683. 4°

Wing F 1702.

T.497

2195
FOWLER (Edward) *Bishop of Gloucester.*

The resolution of this case of conscience, whether
the Church of England's symbolizing as far as it
doth with the Church of Rome, makes it unlawful to
hold communion with the Church of England? [Anon.]
London: Henry Hills, jun. for Fincham Gardiner,
1683. 4°

Wing F 1713.

T.106

2196
A FUNERAL sermon on the occasion of the death of
Algernon Sidney, Esq. Who was beheaded on Tower-
Hill ... for high-treason. London, for J. Smith,
1683. 4°

Not in Wing.

T.107

2197
HASCARD (Gregory)

A discourse about edification: in answer to a
question, Whether it is lawful for any man to
forsake the communion of the Church of England, and
go to the separate meetings, because he can better
edifie there? [Anon.] London: Henry Hills, Jun.
for Fincham Gardiner, 1683. 4°

Wing H 1108.

T.745

2198
HASCARD (Gregory)

A discourse about the charge of novelty upon the
reformed Church of England, made by the papists
asking of us the question, Where was our religion
before Luther? [Anon.] London, for Robert Horn,
and Fincham Gardiner, 1683. 4°

Wing H 1110.

T.691

2199
HICKES (George)

The case of infant-baptism. In five questions.
[Anon.] London, for Tho. Basset; Benj. Tooke;
and F. Gardiner, 1683. 4°

Wing H. 1842.
Signature of John Jenkins, 1690.

T.746

2200
HICKES (George)

Jovian. Or, an answer to Julian the Apostate.
By a minister of London. London, Sam. Roycroft,
for Walter Kettilby, 1683. 8°

T.56

2201
HICKES (George)

A sermon preached before the Lord Mayor, aldermen,
and citizens of London, at Bow-Church, on the 30th.
of January, 1681/2 ... London, for Walter
Kettilby, 1683. 4°

Wing H 1865.

T.132

2202
HICKES (George)

The spirit of enthusiasm exorcised. In a sermon
preached before the University of Oxford, on Act-
Sunday, July 11. 1680 ... 3rd ed. London, for
Walter Kettilby, 1683. 4°

Wing H 1873.
Signature of John Midgley.

T.742

2203
HILDEYARD (John)

A sermon preached at the funeral of the Right
Honourable Robert Earl and Viscount Yarmouth ...
London, for Robert Clavel, 1683. 4°

cf. Wing H. 1982.
2 copies.

T.514   T.765

2204
HOUSCHONE (William)

Scotland pulling down the gates of Rome: or,
Christ against Antichrist ... [Anon.] London: for
Joseph Roberts, 1683. 4°

Wing H 2944.

T.106

2205
HUGHES (John) *Fellow of Balliol College.*

A sermon preach'd before the Right Honourable
George Earl of Berkley, governour, and the
Company of Merchants of England trading in the
Levant seas. At St. Peter's church in Broadstreet,
Nov. 18. 1683. London, for Fincham Gardner,
1683. 4°

Wing H 3312 A.

T.333

2206
JENKES (Henry)

The Christian tutor, or, A free and rational discourse
of the sovereign good and happiness of man ...
London, for Henry Faithorne, and John Kersey, 1683.
8°

Wing J 628.

T.480

2207
JOHN III SOBIESKI, *King of Poland.*

A letter from the King of Poland to his Queen. In
which is incerted many particulars relateing to
the victories obtained against the Turks...
Translated from the Cologne Gazette, Octob.19.
1683. London, for R. Baldwin, 1683. brs.

Wing J 448.

T.532

2208
The JUDGEMENT upon the arguments, for and against the
charter of London. Delivered at Westminster, the 12th
day of June, 1683. London, George Croom, 1683. brs.

Wing J 1184 A.

T.532

2209
KIMBERLEY (Jonathan)

Of obedience for conscience-sake. A sermon
preach'd at the assizes held at Warwick. August
the 7th. 1683. London, J.H. for Benj. Tooke, and
John Smith, 1683. 4°

Wing K 479.

T.132

2210
KINGSTON (Richard)

Vivat rex. A sermon preached before the right
worshipful the mayor, aldermen, council and citizens
of Bristol: upon the discovery of the late
treasonable phanatick plot ... London: for Joseph
Hindmarsh, 1683. 4°

Wing K 617.

T.514

2211
The LAST speech & behaviour of William late Lord
Russel, upon the scaffold ... Also the last speeches,
behaviour, and prayers of Capt. Thomas Walcot, John
Rouse Gent. & Willam [sic] Hone joyner ... London:
J.C. and F.C. for Thomas Fox, 1683. Fol.

Wing L 504 (= R 2351).

T.694

2212
L'ESTRANGE (*Sir* Roger)

Considerations upon a printed sheet entituled the
speech of the late Lord Russel to the sheriffs:
together with the paper delivered by him to them,
at the place of execution, on July 21. 1683. The
fourth impression. London, T. B. for Joanna Brome,
1683. 4°

Wing L 1233.

T.201

2213
L'ESTRANGE (*Sir* Roger)

The lawyer outlaw'd; or a brief answer to Mr. Hunt's
defence of the charter. With some useful remarks
on the Commons proceedings ... In a letter to a
friend. [Anon.] Printed by N. T. for the author,
1683. 4°

Wing L 1266.
2 copies.

T.119   T.201

2214
LOUIS XIV, *King of France.*

Conditions upon which the most Christian King
consents, that the difference between him and
the Catholick King be ended. London: J.C. and
F. Collins, 1683. brs.

Wing C 5724.

T.532

2215
The LOYAL Observator: or, Historical memoirs of the
life and actions of Roger the fidler; alias, the
Observator. London: for W. Hammond, 1683. 4°

Wing L 3356.

T.307

2216
LUCAS (Richard)

Unity and peace: or, The duty of the people in
respect of communion with our church. Delivered
in two sermons at St. Steven's Coleman-street.
London, H. Hills, for Robert Pawlet, 1683. 4°

Wing L 3422.
2 copies.

T.489   T.333

2217
MARSHALL (Thomas)

The catechism set forth in the Book of Common-Prayer,
briefly explained by short notes, grounded upon holy
scripture... [Anon.] 5th ed. Printed at the
Theater in Oxford, anno Domini 1683. 8°

Wing M 802.

T.459

2218
MEGGOTT (Richard)

A sermon preached at White-hall in Lent, March the
16. 1682/3. London, for Walter Kettilby, 1683. 4°

Wing M 1627.

T.333

2219
MILBOURNE (Luke)

Samaritanism reviv'd. A sermon preached at the
parish church of Great Yarmouth, upon the ninth
of September; being the day appointed for a
solemn thansgiving for the discovery of the late
horrid plot ... London, Samuel Roycroft, for
Walter Kettilby, 1683. 4°

Wing M 2037.

T.333

2220

MODERATION a vertue: or, A vindication of the principles and practices of the moderate divines and laity of the Church of England, represented in some late immoderate discourses, under the nick-names of Grindalizers and trimmers. By a lover of moderation... London: for Jonathan Robinson, 1683. 4°

Wing O 772 (attrib. to John Owen).

T.517

2221

A MODEST examination of The resolution [by Edward Fowler] of this case of conscience, whether the Church of England's symbolizing in some things so far as it doth with the... Church of Rome, makes it unlawful to hold communion with the Church of England... In a letter to a friend. London, for Thomas Parkhurst, 1683. 4°

Wing M 2364.

T.745

2222

NALSON (John)

The present interest of England; or A confutation of the Whiggish conspiratours anti-monyan principle, shewing from reason and experience the ways to make the government safe... [Anon.] London, for Thomas Dring, 1683. 4°

Wing N 111.
2 copies.

T.201 T.326

2223

NORRIS (John)

An idea of happiness, in a letter to a friend: enquiring wherein the greatest happiness attainable by man in this life does consist ... London, for James Norris, 1683. 4°

Wing N 1252.

T.119

2224

NYE (Philip) *and* ROBINSON (John)

The lawfulnes of hearing the publick ministers of the Church of England proved, by Mr. Philip Nye, and Mr. John Robinson, two eminent Congregational divines ... London: for Jonathan Robinson, 1683. 4°

Wing N 1496.

T.201

2225

OXFORD. *University.*

The judgment and decree of the University of Oxford past in their convocation July 21. 1683, against certain pernicious books and damnable doctrines destructive to the sacred persons of princes... and of all humane society... Printed at the Theater, 1683. Fol.

Wing O 891.

T.531

2226

PARTRIDGE (John)

Mr. John Partrige's, new prophesie of this present year 1684. Wherein are foretold the most consider-able events and mutations... According to the opinion of the best astrologers. London, George Croom, 1683. 4°

Wing P 623

T.307

2227

PATRICK (Symon) *Bishop of Ely.*

A discourse about tradition; shewing what is meant by it, and what tradition is to be received, and what tradition is to be rejected. [Anon.] London, Miles Flesher, for Robert Horne, and Fincham Gardiner, 1683. 4°

Wing P 787
2 copies.

T.691 T.746

2228

PELLING (Edward)

A sermon preached before the Lord Mayor and court of aldermen, at St. Mary le Bow, on Nov.5.1683. Being the commemoration-day of our deliverance from a popish conspiracy. London, for Will. Abington, 1683. 4°

Wing P 1095.

T.333 T.669 T.732

2229

PELLING (Edward)

A sermon preached upon September the 9th, 1683. Being a thanksgiving-day for a late deliverance from a fanatick-conspiracy... London, for Will. Abington, 1683. 4°

Wing P 1094.

T.333

2230

PETTY (*Sir* William)

Another essay in political arithmetick, concerning the growth of the city of London: with the measures, periods, causes, and consequences thereof. 1682. London: H.H. for Mark Pardoe, 1683. 8°

Wing P 1915.

T.443

2231

PRYNNE (William)

Concordia discors, or the dissonant harmony of sacred publique oaths, protestations, leagues covenants, ingagements, lately taken by many time-serving saints ... London, for Edw. Thomas, in 1659. And now reprinted by Samuel Lowndes, in 1683. And are to be sold by R. Davis. 4°

Wing P 3929.

T.355

2232

RODERICK (Richard)

A sermon preached at Blandford-forum in Dorset-shire, December the 19th, 1682. At the Lord Bishop of Bristol's visitation. London, M. Flesher, for Henry Clements book-seller in Oxford, 1683. 4°

Wing R 1770.

T.733

2233

SCOTT (John)

Certain cases of conscience resolved, concerning the lawfulness of joyning with forms of prayer in publick worship. Part II... [Anon.] London: H. Hills Jun. for T. Basset; B. Tooke; and F. Gardiner, 1683. 4°

Wing S 2041.

T.746

2234

SHERLOCK (William)

A letter to Anonymus [i.e. William Atwood], in answer to his Three letters to Dr. Sherlock about Church-communion. London, for Fincham Gardiner, 1683. 4°

Wing S 3300.
Signature of Edward Jenkins 1699.

T.745

2235

SHERLOCK (William)

The protestant resolution of faith, being an answer to three questions... [Anon.] London, for F. Gardiner, 1683. 4°

Wing S 3332.
2 copies.

T.515 T.691

2236

SHERLOCK (William)

A resolution of some cases of conscience which respect church-communion... [Anon.] London, Henry Hills, Jun. for Fincham Gardiner, 1682/3. 4°

Wing S 3336.
2 copies.

T.411 T.746

2237

SHERLOCK (William)

Some seasonable reflections on the discovery of the late plot. Being a sermon preacht on that occasion. London: for Thomas Basset, and Fincham Gardiner, 1683. 4°

Wing S 3366.
3 copies.

T.497 T.514 T.765

2238

SHORT dull remarks, upon the long dull Essay upon poetry [by John Sheffield, Duke of Buckingham]. London: J. Grantham, for J. Walthoe, 1683. 4°

Wing S 3592.

T.407

2239

SIDNEY (Algernon)

The very copy of a paper delivered to the sheriffs, upon the scaffold on Tower-Hill, on Friday Decemb. 7. 1683. By Algernoon Sidney, Esq; before his execut-ion there. London, for R.H. J.B. and J.R. and are to be sold by Walter Davis, 1683. Fol.

Wing S 3766.

T.694

2240

SMITH (William) *Prebendary of Norwich.*

A sermon preached in the cathedral church of Norwich, on the ninth of September, 1683... London, Samuel Roycroft, for Walter Kettily, 1683. 4°

Wing S 4281.

T.514

2241

SOCIETY OF JESUS. *Collegium S.J. Coloniae.*

Virgo in mitra gloriosior; id est, Argentinensis urbs et ecclesia in ... D. Guilielmo Egone, episcopo Argentoratensi ... Extemporanea musa prosequitur Collegium Societatis Jesu Coloniae ... Coloniae Agrippinae, imprimebat Petrus Alstorff, 1683. Fol.

T.810

2242

TENISON (Thomas) *Archbishop of Canterbury.*

An argument for union, taken from the true interest of those dissenters in England, who profess, and call themselves protestants. [Anon.] London, for Tho. Basset; Benj. Tooke; and F. Gardiner, 1683. 4°

Wing T 688.

T.308

2243

TENISON (Thomas) *Archbishop of Canterbury.*

A discourse concerning a guide in matters of faith; with respect, especially, to the Romish pretence of the necessity of such a one as is infallible. [Anon.] London, for Ben. Tooke, and F. Gardiner, 1683. 4°

Wing T 695.
2 copies.

T.606 T.691

2244

THOMSON (William)

The treasures of the sea. A sermon to the mariners upon Deut. XXXIII. xviii, xix ... London, for Robert Kettlewell, 1683. 4°

Not in Wing.
2 copies.

T.514 T.145

2245

TILLOTSON (John) *Archbishop of Canterbury.*

A letter written to my Lord Russel in Newgate, the twentieth of July, 1683. London, for R. Baldwin, 1683. brs.

Wing T 1201.

T.694

2246

TILLOTSON (John) *Archbishop of Canterbury.*

A persuasive to frequent communion in the holy sacrament of the Lord's supper. In a sermon upon I Corinth.XI. 26,27,28. [Anon.] London, M. Flesher, for Brabazon Aylmer, and William Rogers, 1683. 4°

Wing T 1206.

T.461

2247

TILLOTSON (John) *Archbishop of Canterbury.*

A sermon preached at the funeral of the Reverend Benjamin Whichcot, D.D... May 24th, 1683. London, M. Flesher, for Brabazon Aylmer, and William Rogers, 1683. 4°

Wing T 1235.

T.709

2248

The TOLERATION intolerable. In a full and clear answer to a nameless printed letter to a member of parliament for liberty of conscience... London, J.C. for Blanch Pawlet, 1683. 4°

Wing T 1772.

T.308

1683 (Cont'd)

2249

The TRYALS of Thomas Walcot, William Hone, William Lord Russell, John Rous & William Blagg. for high-treason for conspiring the death of the King, and raising a rebellion in this Kingdom... London, for Richard Royston, Benjamin Took and Charles Mearn, 1683. Fol.

Wing T 2265.

T.687

2250

TURNER (Francis) *Bishop of Ely.*

A sermon preach'd before the King in the cathedral church of Winchester, upon Sunday, Septemb. 9. 1683. Being the day of publick thanksgiving for the deliverance of his sacred Majesties person and government from the late treasonable conspiracy. London: for Benj. Tooke, 1683. 4°

Wing T 3282.
2 copies.

T.497 T.333

2251

TURNER (John) *Hospitaller.*

A sermon preached at Epsom upon the 9th of September, being the day of thanksgiving appointed by his Majesty for the discovery and disappointment of the republican plot... London, for W. Kettilby, 1683. 4°

Wing T 3317.
2 copies.

T.497 T.514

2252

VESEY (John) *Archbishop of Tuam.*

A sermon preached at Clonmell, on Sunday the sixteenth of September, 1683. at the assizes held for the county palatine of Tipperary... Dublin, Joseph Ray, for Sam. Helsham, 1683. 4°

Wing V 281.

T.333

2253

VILLIERS (Pierre de)

L'art de prêcher à un abbé. Par le Sieur D.***. à Amsterdam, ches Henri Desbordes, 1683. 8°

T.444

2254

A VINDICATION of the Lord Russell's speech and innocence, in a dialogue betwixt Whig & Tory: being the same that was promis'd to the Observator in a peny-post-letter. London: printed for the author, anno Domini, 1683. 4°

Wing V 516.

T.201

2255

WAGSTAFFE (Thomas)

A sermon preached at Stow, in the county of Bucks, on the ninth of September, 1683. Being the day of thanksgiving... for acknowledging God's great mercy in discovering and defeating the late treasonable conspiracy... London, Samuel Roycroft, for Walter Kettilby, 1683. 4°

Wing W 212.

T.333

2256

WILKENS (Johann)

Q.D.B.V. [Hebrew] Sive Functio pontif. m. in adyto anniversaria... Ienae, ex officina Nisiana, [1683]. 4°

T.818

2257

WILLIAMS (John) *Bishop of Chichester.*

The case of indifferent things used in the worship of God, proposed and stated ... [Anon.] London, T. Moore, & J. Ashburne, for Fincham Gardiner, 1683. 4°

Wing W 2690.

T.308

2258

WILLIAMS (John) *Bishop of Chichester.*

The case of lay-communion with the Church of England considered; and the lawfulness of it shew'd from the testimony of above an hundred eminent non-conformists of several perswasions... [Anon.] London, for Dorman Newman, 1683. 4°

Wing W 2691.

T.745

2259

YOUNG (Edward) *Dean of Salisbury.*

A sermon preached before the Right Honourable the Lord Mayor and aldermen at Guild-hall chappel, February 4. 1682. London: J. Wallis, for Walter Kettilby, 1683. 4°

Wing Y 67.
2 copies (one wanting title page).

T.497 T.709

1684

2260

The ARRAIGNMENT, tryal & condemnation of Algernon Sidney, Esq; for high-treason. For conspiring the death of the King... London, for Benj. Tooke, 1684. Fol.

Wing A 3754.

T.694

2261

ASSHETON (William)

The royal apology: or, An answer to the rebels plea: wherein, the most noted anti-monarchical tenents ... are distinctly consider'd ... [Anon.] London, T. B. for Robert Clavel, and are to be sold by Randolph Taylor, 1684. 4°

Wing A 4038.
2 copies.

T.119 T.134

AUCHER (John)

The arraignment of rebellion. 1684.

See no. 6257.

2262

BARNE (Miles)

A sermon preach'd at the assizes at Hertford, July 10th. 1684 ... Cambridge, J. Hayes; for R. Green, 1684. 4°

Wing B 864.
2 copies.

T.496   T.107

2263

BEVERIDGE (William) *Bishop of St. Asaph.*

A sermon concerning the excellency and usefulness of the Common prayer. Preached... 27th of November, 1681. 7th ed. London, T. James for Richard Northcott, 1684. 4°

Wing B 2105.

T.742

2264

BISBIE (Nathaniel)

Two sermons. The first shewing the mischiefs of anarchy. The second, the mischiefs of sedition. And both of them, the mischiefs and treasons of conventicles... London, for Walter Kettilby, 1684. 4°

Wing B 2984.

T.625

2265

BOSSUET (Jacques Benigne) *Bishop of Meaux.*

A relation of the famous conference held about religion at Paris, between M. Bossuet... and Monsieur Claude, minister of the reformed church at Charenton... Translated from the French copy, as it was lately published by Monsieur Claude. London, H.C. for Thomas Malthus, 1684. Fol.

Wing B 3790.

T.687

2266

BOYLE (Robert)

Experiments and considerations about the porosity of bodies, in two essays. London, for Sam. Smith, 1684. 8°

Wing B 3966.

T.454

2267

BROWNE (Philip) *of Halstead.*

The observation of holy days justified, and recommended in a sermon preached before ... Henry Lord Bishop of London ... London, for Walter Kettilby, 1684. 4°

Wing B 5138.

T.107

2268

BURNET (Gilbert) *Bishop of Salisbury.*

A sermon preached at the chappel of the Rolls, on the fifth of November, 1684 ... London: for the author, and are to be sold by R. Baldwin, 1684. 4°

Wing B 5879.

T.107

2269

BUTLER (John) *B.D.*

A sermon preached on the 30th. of January, 1683/4 ... By John Buttler. London, for Randall Tayler, 1684. 4°

Not in Wing.

T.333

2270

BYFIELD (Timothy)

The artificial spaw, or mineral-waters to drink: imitating the German spaw-water in its delightful and medicinal operations on humane bodies, &c. London, James Rawlins for the author, and are to be sold by Matthew Keinton, 1684. 8°

Wing B 6396.

T.447

2271

CAMFIELD (Benjamin)

Of God almighty's providence both in the sending and dissolving great snows & frosts ... A sermon occasioned by the late extreme cold weather ... London, for R. Chiswell, 1684. 4°

Wing C 382.

T.314

2272

CARTWRIGHT (Thomas) *Bishop of Chester.*

A sermon preached to the gentlemen of Yorkshire, at Bow- Church in London, the 24th of June, 1684... London, for Tho. Flesher, 1684. 4°

Wing C 705.

T.503

2273

CAVE (William)

A discourse concerning the unity of the Catholick Church maintained in the Church of England. [Anon.] London, for B. Toke, and F. Gardner, 1684. 4°

Wing C 1594.

T.691

2274

CAWDREY (Zachary)

The certainty of salvation to them who dye in the Lord. A sermon preached at the funeral of ... George Lord Delamer; at Boden ... London, for Peter Gillworth, book-seller in New-Castle, in Staffordshire; and James Thurston, book-seller in Nantwich, 1684. 4°

Wing C 1645.

T.107

2275

CHURCH OF ENGLAND.

Prayers for the King; to be used in all churches, and chapels immediately before the prayer of S. Chrysostom... London, the assigns of John Bill: and by Henry Hills, and Thomas Newcomb, Febr. 4. 1684. 4°

Not in Wing.

T.514

2276

CHURCH OF ENGLAND. *Articles of Religion.*

Articles agreed upon by the archbishops and bishops of both provinces, and the whole clergy, in the convocation holden at London in the year 1562... London, the assigns of John Bill deceas'd: and by Henry Hills, and Thomas Newcomb, 1684. 4°

Wing C 4005.

2277

CRUSIUS (Thomas Theodorus)

The origine of atheism in the popish and protestant churches, shew'n by Dorotheus Sicurus, 1684. Made English, and a preface added by E.B. Esquire. London, for Walter Kettilby, 1684. 4°

Wing S 3756.

T.463

2278

DE LAUNE (Thomas)

Εἰκων του θηριου or the image of the beast, shewing, by a paralell scheme, what a conformist the Church of Rome is to the pagan, and what a nonconformist to the Christian Church ... By T. D. ... Printed in the year, 1684. 4°

Wing D 891.

T.326

2279

DE LAUNE (Thomas)

A narrative of the sufferings of Thomas Delaune, for writing, printing and publishing a late book, called, A plea for the nonconformists ... Printed for the author, 1684. 4°

Wing D 892.

T.326

2280

DE LAUNE (Thomas)

A plea for the non-conformists, giving the true state of the dissenters case ... In a letter to Dr. Benjamin Calamy, upon his sermon, called, Scrupulous conscience, inviting hereto ... London, printed for the author, 1684. 4°

Wing D 893,

T.326

2281

The DEPUTIES of the republick of Amsterdam to the States of Holland convicted of high-treason, written and proved by the minister of state ... London, for Randal Taylor, 1684. 4°

Wing D 1085,

T.134

2282

DILLON (Wentworth) *Earl of Roscommon.*

An essay on translated verse... London, for Jacob Tonson, 1684. 4°

Wing R 1930.

T.407

2283

DU BOURDIEU (Isaac)

A discourse of obedience unto kings & magistrates ... Done from the French by J, W, ... London: for Samuel Lowndes, 1684. 4°

Wing D 2408.

T.107

2284

FORSTER (Richard)

Prerogative and privilege represented in a sermon in the cathedral church of Rochester in Kent, March 18. 1683/4. at the assizes ... London, for B. Tooke and W. Kettilby, 1684. 4°

Wing F 1606.
2 copies.

T.496 T.497

2285

FOWLER (Edward) *Bishop of Gloucester.*

A defence of The resolution of this case, viz. Whether the Church of England's symbolizing so far as it doth with the Church of Rome, makes it unlawful to hold communion with the Church of England. In answer to a book intituled A modest examination of that resolution. [Anon.] London, J.H. for B. Aylmer, 1684. 4°

Wing F 1697.

T.745

2286

FREEMAN (Samuel)

A discourse concerning invocation of saints ... [Anon.] London, for Ben. Tooke, and F. Gardiner, 1684. 4°

Wing F 2140.

T.691

2287

GOODMAN (John)

A discourse concerning auricular confession, as it is prescribed by the Council of Trent, and practised in the Church of Rome. With a post-script on occasion of a book [by Jacques Boileau] lately printed in France, called Historia confessionis auricularis. [Anon.] London, H. Hills Jun. for Benj. Tooke; and Fincham Gardiner, 1648, [i.e. 1684.] 4°

Wing G 1104.

T.691

2288

GRENVILLE (Denis)

The compleat conformist, or seasonable advice concerning strict conformity, and frequent celebration of the holy communion, in a sermon ... London, for Robert Clavell, 1684. 4°

Wing G 1938.
Signature of Tho. Martyn.
2 copies.

T.497   T.73

2289

GUIDOTT (Thomas)

Gideon's fleece: or, The Sieurde Frisk, An heroick poem. Written on the cursory perusal of a late book, call'd The conclave of physicians [by Gideon Harvey]. By a friend to the muses ... London, for Sam, Smith, 1684. 4°

Wing G 2194.

T.119

2290

HALE (*Sir* Matthew)

The judgment of the late Lord Chief Justice Sir Matthew Hale, of the nature of true religion, the causes of its corruption, and the churches calamity, by mens additions and violences: with the desired cure... [Published by] Richard Baxter... London, for B. Simmons, 1684. 4°

Wing H 247.

T.83

2291

HESKETH (Henry)

A sermon preach'd before the King in his royal chappel of Windsor, July the 27th 1684. London, for Henry Bonwicke, 1684. 4°

Wing H 1618.

T.107

2292

HICKES (George)

The harmony of divinity and law, in a discourse about not resisting of soveraign princes. [Anon.] London, R. E. and are to be sold by Randal Taylor, 1684. 4°

Wing H 1850.
2 copies.

T.24   T.137

2293

HICKES (George)

A sermon preached at the cathedral church of Worcester, on the 29th of May, 1684 ... London, R. E. for Walter Kettilby, and John Jones bookseller in Worcester, 1684. 4°

Wing H 1867.
2 copies.

T.503   T.132

2294

HICKES (George)

A sermon preached at the church of St. Bridget, on Easter-Tuesday, being the first of April, 1684. Before ... Sir Henry Tulse, Lord Mayor of London ... together with the governors of the hospitals, upon the subject of alms-giving. London, for W. Kettilby, and R. Kettilwell, 1684. 4°

Wing H 1866.
2 copies.

T.503   T.132

2295

HOLLOWAY (James)

The free and voluntary confession and narrative of James Holloway (addressed to his Majesty) written with his own hand, and delivered by himself to Mr. Secretary Jenkins ... London, for Robert Horn, John Baker, and John Redmayne, 1684. Fol.

Wing H 2509.
Another copy, with a variant imprint.

T.687 T.694

2296

HOOKE (Richard)

The royal guard: or The King and Kingdoms sure defensative ... [Anon.] London, H, H, Jun, for Francis Bently in Hallifax, & sold by Rand. Taylor, 1684. 4°

Wing H 2610.

T.134

2297

JOHNSON (Samuel) *Rector of Corringham.*

A sermon preach'd before the Lord Mayor and aldermen at Guildhall-chappel, on Palm-Sunday, 1679 ... London; printed for the author, and are to be sold by Richard Baldwin, 1684. 4°

Wing J 845.

T.314

2298

JORDAN (Thomas)

London's royal triumph for the city's loyal magistrate ... Performed on Wednesday, October XXIX. 1684. at the instalment and inauguration of the Right Honourable Sir James Smith, knight, Lord Mayor of the city of London ... London, for John and Henry Playford, 1684. 4°

Wing J 1041.

T.407

2299

KETTLEWELL (John)

A discourse explaining the nature of edification ... In a visitation sermon at Coventry, May 7, 1684. London, for Robert Kettlewell, 1684. 4°

Wing K 365.
3 copies.

T.754   T.496   T.107

2300

KETTLEWELL (John)

A funeral sermon for the Right Honourable the Lady Frances Digby, who deceased at Coles-hill in Warwickshire, on the 29th of September, 1684. London, for Robert Kettlewell, 1684. 4°

Wing K 368.

T.496

2301

KREHER (Matthias)

[Hebrew] usus phylacterior: Judaicor: quem benivolo superiorum indultu in illustri salana publicae ventilationi exponent. Jenae, literis Bauhoferianis, 1684. 4°

T.819

2302

LAKE (Edward)

A sermon preached at the church of S. Mary le Bow, before the Right Honourable the Lord Mayor, and court of aldermen, on the thirtieth of January, MDCLXXXIII ... London: M. C. for C. Wilkinson, 1684. 4°

Wing L 193.
3 copies.

T.732   T.514   T.333

2303

MESMES (Jean Antoine de) *comte d'Avaux.*

An exact copy of a letter from the Count d'Avaux his most Christian Majesties ambassador at the Hague... which was intercepted by the Marquess de Grana governour of the Spanish Netherlands. As also the copies of other three letters relating to the same affair. Printed at the Hague by Jacobus Sekeltus, and re'printed at London for Randall Taylor, 1684. brs.

Wing A 4267.

T.532

2304

MR. Sidney his self-conviction: or, his dying-paper condemn'd to live, for a conviction to the present faction, and a caution to posterity. London, H. Hills jun. for Robert Clavell, 1684. 4°

Wing M 2274 C.

T.95

2305

The OBSERVATOR reproved, more especially in
relation to the controversie between that
eminently pious, charitable and worthy divine
Mr. Smithye... and himself.
London, printed for the author, and published by
Langley Curtis, 1684.   4°

Wing O 114.

T.307

2306

An ODE to the King on his return from New-Market.
Set by Mr. Baptist, master of the Queen's musick.
London, for R. Bentley, 1684.   4°

Not in Wing.

T.407

2307

OXFORD. *University.*

Verses by the University of Oxford. On the death
of the most noble, and right valiant Sir Bevill
Grenvill, alias Granvill, Kt ... Printed at
Oxford in the year of our Lord, 1643, and now
reprinted at London, 1684. 4°

Wing O 989.

T.262

2308

PEARSON (Richard)

The study of quietness explained, recommended, and
directed, in a sermon preached... at the Guild-
Hall chappel, March 16. 1683/4... London, R. H.
for Henry Bonwicke, 1684. 4°

Wing P 1017.

T.514

2309

PECK (Samuel)

A sermon preached at the funeral of Sir Henry
Johnson, Kt. who was interr'd in the chappel at
Popler, November the 19th. 1683. London: for
Tho. Parkhurst, 1684. 4°

Wing P 1037.

T.333

2310

PELLING (Edward)

A sermon preacht on January 30th. 1683. in
Westminster-Abby, before the reverend and
honourable, the Kings judges... London, H. Hills
Jun. for William Abington, 1684. 4°

Wing P 1096.
2 copies.

T.514   T.669

2311

PETER (John)

A relation or diary of the siege of Vienna ...
London, for William Nott, and George Wells, 1684.
4°

Wing P 1690.

T.4

2312

PETRE (William) *4th Baron Petre.*

The declaration of the Lord Petre upon his death
touching the plot, in a letter to his most sacred
Majestie. London, T.B. for R. Mead, 1684. brs.

Wing P 1877.

T.532

2313

The PROCEEDINGS against Sir Thomas Armstrong, in
his Majesties court of Kings-Bench, at Westminster,
upon an outlawry for high-treason, &c... London,
for Robert Horn, John Baker, and John Redmayne, 1684.
Fol.

Wing P 3546.

T.694

2314

RAM (Robert)

The souldiers catechism, composed for the
Parliaments army...   Written for the encouragement
and instruction of all that have taken up arms in
the cause of God and his people... And now
republisht to satisfie tender consciences in the
grounds upon which the late thorough reformation
proceeded... [Anon.] London, re-printed by T.B. and
are to be sold by R. Taylor, 1684.   4°

Wing R 198.

T.509

2315

RESBURY (Nathanael)

The case of the cross in baptism considered.
Wherein is shewed, that there is nothing in it,
as it is used in the Church of England, that can
be any just reason of separation from it...
[Anon.] London, for Fincham Gardiner, 1684. 4°

Wing R 1126.

T.746

2316

The REVISION revised: or, A vindication of the
right reverend... George, Lord Bishop of Winton,
against a late pamphlet, published by L.W. [i.e.
John Warner]..., and entituled, A revision of Dr.
Morley's judgment in matters of religion...
London, for Randal Taylor, 1684. 4°

Wing R 1204.

T.106

2317

SCOTT (John)

A sermon preached before the Right Honourable the
Lord Mayor, and court of aldermen, at the Guild-hall
chappel, the 16th of December, 1683. London,
Ralph Holt, for Robert Horn, and Walter Kettilby,
1684. 4°

Wing S 2067.
6 copies.

T.132   T.340   T.503   T.618   T.732

2318

A SECOND letter to Dr. Burnet, London, for R.
Taylor, 1684. 4°

Wing S 2287.
2 copies.

T.463   T.76

2319

SMYTHIES (William)

A letter to the Observator, from William Smythies...
in his own vindication. London, for John Southby,
1684. 4°

Wing S 4368.

T.307

2320

SMYTHIES (William)

A reply to the Observator; together with a sermon
preached on the 24th of August ... (most unjustly
reflected upon by him.) The third impression, with
a further reply. London, for John Southby, 1684.
4°

Wing S 4372.
3 copies.

T.85   T.95   T.107

2321

SPRAT (Thomas) *Bishop of Rochester.*

A sermon preach'd before the Right Honourable Sir
Henry Tulse, Lord Mayor... On May the 29th. 1684
... London, for Jacob Tonson, 1684.   4°

Wing S 5060.

T.732

2322

STILLINGFLEET (Edward) *Bishop of Worcester.*

A sermon preached before the King, February the 15.
1683/4. London, J.M. for Henry Mortlock, 1684.
4°

Wing S 5655.
2 copies.

T.333   T.503

2323

TAAFFE (Francis) *3rd Earl of Carlingford.*

Count Taaffe's letters from the Imperial camp, to
his brother the Earl of Carlingford here in London
... London, for T, B, and are to be sold by William
Abbington, 1684. 4°

Wing C 592.

T.4

2324

A THIRD dialogue between the Pope and a phanatick,
concerning affairs in England. By the author of
the first and second, who is a hearty lover of his
prince and country. London: J. P. and are to be
sold by Randolph Tayler, 1 684. 4°

Wing T 907.

T.201

2325

TILLOTSON (John) *Archbishop of Canterbury.*

A discourse against transubstantiation. [Anon.]
London, M. Flesher, for Brabazon Aylmer: and
William Rogers, 1684.   4°

Wing T 1190.

T.691

2326

TILLOTSON (John) *Archbishop of Canterbury.*

A discourse against transubstantiation. [Anon.]
2nd ed. London, for Brabazon Aylmer: and William
Rogers, 1684.   4°

Wing T 1191.

T.743

2327

TO his Royal Highness the Duke of York, upon his
return to the care and management of the Navy of
England. [A poem.] London, for Benj. Tooke, 1684.
4°

Wing T 1376.

T.407

2328

TO the Prince of Orange, upon the opening of the
campagne, 1684. [A poem.] London, for R. Bentley,
1684.   4°

Wing T 1597 A.

T.407

2329

The TRYAL and conviction of John Hambden, Esq.,
upon an indictment of high-misdemeanour, for
contriving and practising to disturb the peace of
...   the King, and stirring up sedition in this
Kingdom...   London, for Benjamin Tooke, 1684. Fol.

Wing T 2160.

T.694

2330

The TRYAL and conviction of Sr. Sam Bernardiston,
Bart. for high-misdemeanor at the session of nisi
prius... London: for Benjamin Tooke, 1684. Fol.

Wing T 2164.

T.694

2331

The TRYAL of Laurence Braddon and Hugh Speke, Gent.
upon an information of high-misdemeanor, subornation
and spreading false reports... London: for
Benjamin Tooke, 1684. Fol.

Wing T 2196.

T.694

2332

TURNER (Francis) *Bishop of Ely.*

A sermon preached before the King on Easter-day,
1684. By Francis Lord Bishop of Rochester...
London, J. Macock for R. Royston, 1684. 4°

Wing T 3283.

T.503

333

TURNER (Francis) *Bishop of Ely.*

A sermon preach'd before the Right Honourable Sir
Henry Tulse, Lord Mayor... together with the
governors of the hospitals.   At the parish-church
of St. Bridget...   March 31.1684. By...   Francis
Lord Bishop of Rochester. London: for Benj. Tooke,
1684.   4°

Wing T 3284.
2 copies.

T.503 T.732

334

WILLIAMS (John) *Bishop of Chichester.*

A sermon preached at the Northampton-shire feast,
November 8. 1683... London: J.G. for Benjamin
Alsop, 1684.   4°

Wing W 2725.

T.333

1685

2335

A. (P.)

Sober and serious considerations: occasioned by the
death of ... King Charles II. (of ever blessed
memory,)and the serious time of Lent, following it
... By a gentleman in communion with the Church of
England ... London, John Leake, for Luke Meredith,
1685. 4°

Wing A 26.

T.17

2336

ACTS of the general assembly of the French clergy
in the year MDCLXXXV. concerning religion.
Together with the complaint of the said general
assembly against the calumnies, injuries and
falsities, which the pretended reform'd have, and
do, every day publish ... London, printed 1685.
4°

Wing A 458.

T.331

2337

ADEE (Nicholas)

A plot for a crown, in a visitation-sermon, at
Cricklade, May the fifteenth, 1682 ... London,
R. W. and are to be sold by Walter Davis, 1685.   4°

Wing A 573.

T.333

2338

ALLESTREE (Charles)

A sermon preach'd at Oxford, before Sir Will. Walker
... upon the 26th. of July 1685: being the day of
thanksgiving, for the defeat of the rebels in
Monmouth's rebellion. Oxford, for Henry Clements,
and sold by Joseph Hindmarsh, 1685.   4°

Wing A 1081.

T.33

2339

ARWAKER (Edmund) *the Younger.*

The second part of the vision, a pindarick ode:
occasioned by their Majesties happy coronation...
London, J. Playford for Henry Playford, 1685.
Fol.

Wing A 3912.

T.699

2340

ARWAKER (Edmund) *the Younger.*

The vision: a pindarick ode: occasion'd by the
death of our late gracious sovereign King Charles
II... London, J. Playford, for Henry Playford,
1685. Fol.

Wing A 3913.

T.699

2341

ASSHETON (William)

An admonition to a deist. Occasioned, by some
passages in discourse with the same person...
[Anon.] London, T.B. for Robert Clavel, 1685.
4°

Wing A 4022.

T.463

2342

ASSHETON (William)

The royal apology: or, An answer to the rebels plea:
wherein, the most noted anti-monarchical tenents
... are distinctly consider'd. 2nd ed. London,
T. B. for Robert Clavel and are to be sold by
Randolph Taylor, 1685. 4°

Wing A 4039.

T.134

2343

The ATHEIST unmasked, or a confutation of such as
deny the being of a supream deity, that governs
heaven and earth.   By unanswerable arguments
deduc'd... By a person of honour...   London,
for Langley Curtiss, 1685.   4°

Wing A 4108.

T.463

2344

BARBON (Nicholas)

An apology for the builder: or a discourse
shewing the cause and effects of the increase of
building. [Anon.] London, for Cave Pullen,
1685. 4°

Wing B 704.

T.373

2345

BARNE (Miles)

The authority of church-guides asserted in a sermon
preach'd before our late gracious sovereign ...
2nd ed. London, for Richard Green bookseller in
Cambridge, 1685. 4°

Wing B 856.

T.234

2346

BARZIA Y ZAMBRANA (Joseph de)

A discourse of the excellency of the soul, and the
care every Christian ought to have of it. In a
sermon preach'd in Spanish ... London, for
Matthew Turner, 1685. 4°

Wing B 1011.
2 copies.

T.515   T.108

2347

BEHN (Aphra)

A pindarick on the death of our late sovereign:
with an ancient prophecy on his present Majesty.
London, J. Playford, for Henry Playford, 1685.   Fol.

Wing B 1750.

T.532

2348

BEHN (Aphra)

A pindarick poem on the happy coronation of his
most sacred Majesty James II. and his illustrious
consort Queen Mary. London, J. Playford for Henry
Playford, 1685. Fol.

Wing B 1753.

T.532

2349

BERNARD, *Saint.*

A looking-glass for all new-converts to whatsoever
perswasion. London: printed, 1685. 4°

Wing B 1980 A.

T.331

2350

BEVERLEY (Thomas)

A disquisition upon our Saviour's sanction of
tithes ... Wherein the whole case is most impartially
stated and resolved ... [Anon.] London, Th.
Dawks, 1685. 4°

Wing B 2139.

T.108

2351

BLECHYNDEN (Richard)

Two useful cases resolved.   I. Whether a certainty
of being in a state of salvation be attainable?
II. What is the rule by which this certainty is to
be attained? [Anon.] London: for Henry Bonwicke,
1685. 4°

Wing B 3183.

T.463

2352

BOHUN (Edmund)

An apologie for the Church of England, against the
clamours of the men of no-conscience: or the Duke
of Buckingham's seconds. By E. B. ... London, for
W. Kettilby, 1685. 4°

Wing B 3447.

T.201

2353

BOSSUET (Jacques Benigne) *Bishop of Meaux.*

An exposition of the doctrine of the Catholic Church
in matters of controversie. Done into English
from the fifth edition in French. London, printed
in the year, 1685. 2 parts. 4° 22 + 48p.

Wing B 3783.

T.105

2354

BOSSUET (Jacques Benigne) *Bishop of Meaux.*

An exposition of the doctrine of the Catholic Church
in matters of controversie. Done into English
from the fifth edition in French. London, printed
in the year 1685. 3 parts. 4° 24,51 + 16p.

Wing B 3783.

T.331

2355

BRIDGE (Francis)

A sermon preached before ... the Lord Mayor, aldermen,
and citizens of London, at the Church of S, Mary
le Bow, the fifth of November 1684. London, for
Walter Kettilby, 1685. 4°

Wing B 4444.
2 copies.

T.73 T.107

2356

BRIEF reflections upon the inconveniencies attending
wilful and malitious forgery and perjury, with some
reasons why such crimes ought to be made felony.
By a truly loyal subject, and a sincere lover of
his king, country, and the laws of this realm.
London: for Mark Pardoe, 1685.   Fol.

Wing B 4620.

T.531

2357

BRYAN (Matthew)

The certainty of the future judgment asserted and
proved, in a sermon preached at St. Michael's
Crooked Lane, London, Octob. XXVI. 1684. London,
for Walter Kettilby, 1685. 4°

Wing B 5246.

T.107

2358

BULKELEY (Richard) *Prebendary of Hereford.*

A sermon preached at the cathedral-church of
Hereford, on May the 29th 1684... London, for
William Crook, 1685. 4°

Wing B 5406.
Nine pages of Books printed for, and sold by
William Crooke.

T.107

2359

BURNET (Gilbert) *Bishop of Salisbury.*

An answer to a letter to Dr. Burnet, occasioned by
his Letter to Mr. Lowth. [Anon.] London: for
Richard Baldwin, 1685. 4°

Wing B 5758.
3 copies.

T.463 T.330

2360

BURNET (Gilbert) *Bishop of Salisbury.*

A letter from Gilbert Burnet, D. D. to Mr. Simon
Lowth ... occasioned, by his late book of the
subject of Church-power. London: for Richard
Baldwin, 1685. 4°

Wing B 5818.
3 copies.

T.463 T.330 T. 76

1685 (Cont'd)

2361

BURNET (Gilbert) *Bishop of Salisbury.*

A letter occasioned by the second Letter to Dr. Burnet, written to a friend. London, for Richard Baldwyn, 1685. 4°

Wing B 5819.
2 copies.

T.463   T.330

2362

BURY (Jacob)

Advice to the Commons within all his Majesties realms and dominions ... London, Henry Hills, Jun. for Richard Northcott, 1685. 4°

Wing B 6212.

T.134

2363

CALAMY (Benjamin)

A sermon preached before the Artillery-Company of London, at St. Mary-le-Bow, December 2, 1684. London, for John Baker, 1685. 4°

Wing C 220.
2 copies.

T.496   T.107

2364

CAMFIELD (Benjamin)

A sermon preach'd upon the first Sunday after the proclamation of ... James the II ... which was made at Leicester, February the 10th. 1684/5 ... London, for Charles Brome, 1685. 4°

Wing C 386.

T.112

2365

CARE (George)

A reply to the answer of the man of no name, to his Grace the Duke of Buckingham's paper of religion, and liberty of conscience. By G.C. London, John Leake, for Luke Meredith, 1685. 4°

Wing C 504.

T.463

2366

CAUSAE veteris epitaphii editio altera. Accedit Causa vetus conclamata... Neapoli sive Augustae Trinobantum: prostant in officina B. Tooke, 1685. 4°

Wing C 1531.

T.501

2367

CAVE (William)

A sermon preached before the King at White-hall, on Sunday, January 18th. 1684/5. London, for Richard Chiswel, 1685. 4°

Wing C 1607.

T.496

2368

CHAMBERLAYNE (Edward)

Englands wants: or, Several proposals probably beneficial for England, humbly offered to the consideration of all good patriots in both Houses of Parliament. By the authour of The present state of England. London, Randal Taylor, 1685. 4°

Wing C 1841.

T.373

2369

The CHURCH catechism with scripture proofs. London: for the Company of Stationers, 1685. 8°

Ch.Ch. C 3994+.

T.544

2370

CHURCH OF ENGLAND.

A form of prayer with fasting, to be us'd yearly upon the 30th of January, being the day of the martyrdom of the blessed King Charles the first... London, by the assigns of John Bill deceas'd: and by Henry Hills, and Thomas Newcomb, 1685. 4°

Wing C 4167.

T.463

2371

CHURCH OF ENGLAND.

A form of prayer, with thanksgiving to almighty God for having put an end to the Great Rebellion by the restitution of the King and royal family ... London, by the assigns of John Bill deceas'd: and by Henry Hills, and Thomas Newcomb, 1685. 4°

Wing C 4173.

T.463

2372

CLAGETT (Nicholas)

A perswasive to an ingenuous tryal of opinions in religion. [Anon.] London: for Tho. Basset, 1685. 4°

Wing C 4370.

T.691

2373

CONSIDERATIONS moving to a toleration, and liberty of conscience. With arguments inducing to a cessation of the penal statutes against all dissenters... Occasioned by an excellent discourse upon that subject, publish'd by his Grace the Duke of Buckingham... [Attributed to William Penn.] London, for R. Hayhurst, 1685. 4°

Wing P 1269.

T.463

2374

COOKE (Shadrach)

A sermon preached at Islington, upon the 26th day of July, 1685 ... being the day of solemn thanksgiving ... for his Majestie's late victories over the rebels ... London, R. N. for Walter Kettilby, 1685. 4°

Wing C 6038.

T. 33

2375

COVENTRY (*Sir* William)

A letter written to Dr. Burnet, giving an account of Cardinal Pool's secret powers ... To which are added, Two breves that Card. Pool brought over, and some other of his letters, that were never before printed. [Anon.] London, for Richard Baldwin, 1685. 4°

Wing C 6631.

T.463

2376

The DANGER and unreasonableness of a toleration: in reference to some late papers which have passed concerning liberty of conscience ... London, for Walter Davis, 1685. 4°

Wing D 177.

T.463

2377

DANGERFIELD (Thomas)

Dangerfield's memoires, digested into adventures, receits, and expences. By his own hand. London, J. Bennet, for Charles Brome, 1685. 4°

Wing D 190.
2 copies.

T.134   T.139

2378

DAVENANT (*Sir* William)

The seventh and last canto of the third book of Gondibert, never yet printed. London, for William Miller and Joseph Watts, 1685. 8°

Wing D 338.

T.447

2379

A DEFENCE of the Duke of Buckingham, against the answer to his book, and the reply to his letter. By the author of the late considerations. London, for W.C. 1685. 4°

Wing D 816 A.

T.463

2380

DOVE (Henry)

A sermon preached before the King at Whitehall, Sunday January 25, 1684/5 ... London: for Benjamin Tooke, 1685. 4°

Wing D 2050.
2 copies.

T.496   T.108

2381

DUBOURDIEU (Jean Armand) *and others.*

A true copy of a project for the reunion of both religions in France. London, for Randal Taylor, 1685. Fol.

Wing D 2410.

T.532

2382

ELLESBY (James)

The doctrine of passive obedience: asserted in a sermon preach'd on January 30, 1684 ... London, for William Crooke, 1685. 4°

Wing E 537.

T.107

2383

'EYXAPIΣTIA, Or, A grateful acknowledgment unto heaven for the happy discovery of the late horrid plot... By a country presbyter, in the diocess of Chichester. The second impression, more correct, and enlarged... London, H.C. and are to be sold by Walter Davis, 1685. 4°

Not in Wing.

T.108

2384

FOWLER (Edward) *Bishop of Gloucester.*

The great wickedness, and mischievous effects of slandering, represented in a sermon ... London, for Brabazon Aylmer, 1685. 4°

Wing F 1707.
2 copies.

T.496   T. 33

2385

FOWLER (Edward) *Bishop of Gloucester.*

A sermon preached at the general meeting of Gloucestershire-men for the most part inhabitants of the city of London ... London, T. B, for Braybazon Aylmer, 1685. 4°

Wing F 1718.
2 copies.

T.496   T.107

2386

FREZER (Augustine)

The divine original and the supreme dignity of kings, no defensative against death . A sermon, preached ... before the right worshipful the Fellowship of Merchants Adventurers of England, resideing at Dort ... Oxford, L. Lichfield, and are to sold by Nicholas Cox, 1685. 4°

Wing F 2203.

T.108

2387

FYSH (Thomas)

A sermon preached upon the 29th of May, in the parish-church of St. Margaret, in Lyn-Regis, in Norfolk ... London, T. Snowden, for Sam. Smith, 1685. 4°

Wing F 2569.

T.108

2388

GADBURY (John)

Cardines coeli: or, An appeal to the learned and experienced observers of sublunars and their vicissitudes, whether the cardinal signs of heaven are not most influential upon men and things ... London: for M. G. and sold by Daniel Brown, Sam. Sprint, John Guillim, 1685. 4°

Wing O G 78 A.

T.134

2389

ASKARTH (John)

... sermon preached before ... John, Lord Bishop of Bristol, at his primary visitation in Bristol, October 30 ... London, for Walter Kettilby, 1685. ...

Wing G 288.

.752

2390

GODWYN (Morgan)

Trade preferr'd before religion, and Christ made to give place to Mammon: represented in a sermon relating to the Plantations ... London, for B. Took, and for Isaac Cleave, 1685. 4°

Wing G 974.
2 copies.

T.184   T.108

2391

GOODRICK (John)

A sermon preached before the Honble Society of Lincolns-Inne, upon the 26th of July, 1685, being the thanksgiving-day for his Majesty's victory over the rebels. London, J. D. and to be sold by Israel Harrison, 1685. 4°

Wing G 1144.

T.33

2392

GOSTWYKE (William)

A sermon preached at St. Michaels Church in Cambridge, on the 26th of July 1685. Being appointed the day of publick thanksgiving for his Majesties late victory over the rebels. Cambridge, John Hayes. And are to be sold by H. Dickinson, and by Walter Davis, 1685. 4°

Wing G 1323.

T.33

2393

GOTHER (John)

A papist mis-represented and represented: or, A twofold character of popery ... By J.L. [i.e. John Gother]. Printed anno Domini 1665 [i.e. 1685]. 4°

Wing G 1333.

T.406

2394

GOTHER (John)

A papist mis-represented and represented: or, A two-fold character of Popery ... By J.L. [i.e. John Gother]. Printed anno Dom. 1685. 2 parts. 4°

Wing G 1335 A.

T.515

2395

GOTHER (John)

A papist mis-represented and represented: or, A two-fold character of Popery ... By J, L, [i.e. John Gother]. To which is annexed, Roman-Catholick principles, in reference to God and the King. Printed anno Domini, 1685. 2 parts. 4°

Wing G 1335.
2 copies.

T.760   T.105

2396

GOWER (Humfrey)

A sermon preached before the King at White-hall on Christmas-Day, 1684. London, S. Roycroft, for Robert Clavell, 1685. 4°

Wing G 1459.

T.107

2397

GREY (Thomas) *M.A.*

Loyalty essential to Christianity: being a sermon preached the thirtieth of June, 1685. Upon the occasion of the news of the damnable rebellion in the West ... London, Henry Clark, and sold by Walter Davis, 1685. 4°

Wing G 1971.

T.108

2398

GROVE (Robert) *Bishop of Chichester.*

Roberti Grovii Carmen de sanguinis circuitu, a Gulielmo Harvaeo Anglo, primum invento ... Londini, typis R. E. impensis Gualteri Kettilby, 1685. 4°

Wing G 2148.

T.1

2399

GROVE (Robert) *Bishop of Chichester.*

Seasonable advice to the citizens, burgesses, and free-holders of England, concerning Parliaments, and the present elections. By a divine of the Church of England. London, for Walter Kettilby, 1685. 4°

Wing G 2158.

T.134

2400

HASCARD (Gregory)

A sermon preached before ... the Lord Mayor, Sir James Smith ... London, for William Crook, 1685. 4°

Wing H 1115.

T.108

2401

HAYNE (Samuel)

An abstract of all the statutes made concerning aliens trading in England from the first year of K. Henry the VII ... Printed by N. T. for the author, and are to be sold by Walter Davis, 1685. 4°

Wing H 1216.

T.373

2402

HESKETH (Henry)

A sermon preached in his Majesty's Chapel-Royal at White-hall, upon the 26th day of July, 1685. Being the day of publick thanksgiving ... for his Majesty's late victory over the rebels ... London, for Jo. Hindmarsh, 1685. 4°

Wing H 1620.
2 copies.

T.732   T. 33

2403

HEYRICK (Thomas)

The character of a rebel. A sermon preached at Market Harborow, on the 26th of July, 1685. Being the day of thanksgiving appointed for his Majesties victory over the rebels. London, for Samuel Heyricke, 1685. 4°

Wing H 1752.

T.33

2404

HEYRICK (Thomas)

A sermon preached at Market Harborow in the county of Leicester, on the 17th day of February, 1684/5 ... London: for Samuel Heyrick, 1685. 4°

Wing H 1755.

T.108

2405

HICKES (George)

A letter from a person of quality to an eminent dissenter, to rectifie his mistakes concerning the succession, the nature of persecution and a comprehension. [Anon.] London, T, B, for Randolph Taylor, 1685. 4°

Wing H 1854 A.

T.134

2406

HINTON (John)

A sermon preached in the parish church of Newbury, Berks, on the 26th of July, 1685. Being the day of thanksgiving for his Majesty's late victory over the rebels ... London, for Walter Kettilby, 1685. 4°

Wing H 2068.

T. 33

2407

HORNE (Thomas) *Fellow of Eton College.*

A sermon preached in his Majesties chappel at Whitehall on the eighth of February 1684/5 ... London: for Robert Horne, 1685. 4°

Wing H 2814.
2 copies.

T.489   T.108

2408

HOWELL (John) *Rector of New Radnor.*

A discourse on persecution, or, Suffering for Christ's sake ... London, for Robert Kettlewell, 1685. 4°

Wing H 3130.

T.463

2409

IRONSIDE (Gilbert) *Bishop of Hereford.*

A sermon preached before the King at White-hall November 23, 1684. Oxford, Leonard Lichfield, for James Good, 1685. 4°

Wing I 1049.
2 copies.

T.496   T.107

2410

JAMES II, *King of England.*

To the most reverend fathers in God, William Lord Archbishop of Canterbury ... and John Lord Archbishop of York ... (Directions concerning preachers.) London, Charles Bill, Henry Hills, and Thomas Newcomb, 1685. 4°

Wing J 389.
3 copies.

T.308   T.144   T.116

2411

JEWEL (John) *Bishop of Salisbury.*

An apology for the Church of England. Written originally in Latine ... and newly made English from the most correct edition ... London, R. R. and are to be sold by Randall Taylor, 1685. 4°

Wing J 735.

T.463

2412

KEN (Thomas) *Bishop of Bath and Wells.*

An exposition on the Church-catechism, or the practice of divine love. Composed for the Diocese of Bath & Wells. London, for Charles Brome; and William Clarke in Winchester, 1685. 8°

Wing K 262.

T.144

2413

L. (N.)

The way to good success. Propounded in a sermon, preached upon November the 24th, 1684. at Trinity-house-Chappel ... York, John White, and are to be sold by Thomas Clark bookseller in Hull, 1685. 4°

Wing L 49.

T.107

2414

The LAUREL, a poem on the poet-laureat [i.e. John Dryden]... London, for Benj. Tooke, 1685. 4°

Wing L 622.
Wrongly attributed to Robert Gould.

T.407

2415

LEE (Nathaniel)

Sophonisba: or, Hannibal's overthrow. A tragedy. Acted at the Theatre-Royal, by their majesties servants... London, for R. Bently and S. Magnes, 1685. 4°

Wing L 872.

T.501

2416

L'ESTRANGE (*Sir* Roger)

L'Estrange no papist ... London, F. Leach, for Charles Brome, 1685. 4°

Wing L 1268.

T.307

1685 (Cont'd)

2417

L'ESTRANGE (*Sir* Roger)

The Observator defended, by the author of the observators. In a full answer to several scandalls cast upon him, in matters of religion, government, and good manners. [Anon.] London, for Charles Brome, 1685. 4°

Wing L 1283.
3 copies.

T.184   T.201   T.307

2418

A LETTER to a lawyer: containing an essay to prove the compassing and imagination of the death of the King's brother and heir to be high-treason within 25. Ed. 3. Written by a gentleman in the country ... London, for John Eglesfeild, 1685.   4°

Wing L 1664.

T.509

2419

LONG (Thomas)

The unreasonableness of rebellion. In a sermon preached at St. Peters, Exon. on the 26th of July, 1685. Being the day appointed for thanksgiving for his Majesties victory over the rebels... London: J.C. and Freeman Collins, and are to be sold by Randal Taylor, 1685.   4°

Wing L 2983.

T.33

2420

LOUIS XIV, *King of France*.

Articles of agreement concluded between his most Christian Majesty, and the Republik of Geneva. London, George Croom, 1685. Fol.

Wing L 3102.

T.532

2421

LOWTH (Simon)

A letter to Dr. Burnet, occasioned by his late Letter to Mr. Lowth. [Anon.] London: for Randal Taylor, 1685.   4°

Wing L 3327.
2 copies.

T.330   T.463

2422

MANNINGHAM (Thomas) *Bishop of Chichester*.

A short view of the most gracious providence of God in the restoration and succession ... [Anon.] London, for William Crook, 1685.   4°

Wing M 507.
2 copies.

T.496   T.108

2423

MASTERS (Samuel)

A discourse of friendship, preached at the Wiltshire-feast, in St. Mary Le-Bow-Church December the 1st. 1684... London, T.B. for Marm. Foster and Awnsham Churchill, 1685. 4°

Wing M 1069.
3 copies.

T.314   T.107   T.618

2424

MAURICE (Henry)

The antithelemite, or an answer to certain quaeres by the D. of B. and to the considerations of an unknown author concerning toleration.   [Anon.] London, for Sam. Smith, 1685.   4°

Wing M 1359.
2 copies.

T.330   T.463

2425

The MISCHIEF of cabals: or, The faction expos'd. With some considerations for a lasting settlement. In a letter to a member of Parliament ... London, Randal Taylor, 1685.   4°

Wing M 2233,
3 copies.

T.509   T.83   T.134

2426

NALSON (John)

Toleration and liberty of conscience considered, and proved impracticable, impossible, and, even in the opinion of dissenters, sinful and unlawful.   [Anon.] London, for Thomas Dring, 1685,   4°

Wing N 115.
Signature of Thomas Bowdler, May 1685.

T.201

2427

NICOLSON (William) *Bishop of Carlisle*.

A sermon preach'd in the cathedral church of Carlisle, on Sunday Feb. 15. 1684/5 ... London, for John Gellibrand, 1685.   4°

Wing N 1149.

T.108

2428

The OBSERVATOR prov'd a trimmer: or, Truth and justice vindicated, in the history of the murther of Sir Edmundbury Godfrey, and the several popish shams... Being a full answer to certain late pamphlets, intituled, Observators...   The third impression corrected, with additions...   London: for J. Allen, 1685.   Fol.

WingO 113.

T.531

2429

The OBSERVATOR vindicated, or an answer to Mr. Smythies's reply to the Observator: together with a brief, but just, censure on his sermon annex'd to it ... London, for Walter Davis, 1685.   4°

Not in Wing.
2 copies.

T.307   T.201

2430

OWEN (Vincent)

A plain sermon preached to a country congregation in the beginning of the late rebellion in the West ... London, Randal Taylor, 1685.   4°

cf. Wing O 832 A.

T.108

2431

P.(W.)

Tears wip'd off, or the second essay of the Quakers by way of poetry: occasioned by the coronation of James and Mary.   Written in the sincerity of the spirit, by W.P. a servant to the light.   London, J.P. for Henry Playford, 1685. Fol.

Wing P 138.

T.532

2432

PAYNE (William) *D.D.*

A discourse concerning the adoration of the Host, as it is taught and practised in the Church of Rome. Wherein an answer is given to T.G. on that subject, and to Monsieur Boileau's late book De adoratione Eucharistiae.   Paris 1685.   [Anon.] London: for Brabazon Aylmer, 1685.   4°

Wing P 898.

T.331

2433

PELLING (Edward)

The apostate protestant.   A letter to a friend, occasioned by the late reprinting of a Jesuites book, about succession to the crown of England, pretended to have been written by R. Doleman [ie. Robert Parsons].   2nd ed.   London, for W. Davis and J. Hindmarsh, 1685.   4°

Wing P 1076.
Wanting title page.

T.330

2434

PELLING (Edward)

A sermon preached at Westminster-Abbey on the 26th. of July, 1685. Being the thanksgiving-day for his Majesties victory over the rebels ... London, for Samuel Keble, and Walter Davis, 1685,   4°

Wing P 1098.
4 copies.

T.618   T.496   T.489   T.33

2435

PELLING (Edward)

A sermon preached on the 30th of January, 1684, The day of the martyrdom of King Charles I ... London, for T. M. and are to be sold by Randal Taylor, 1685. 4°

Wing P 1097.

T.107

2436

PELLING (Edward)

A sermon preacht at St. George's Church at Windsor, Septemb. 27. 1685.   London, for Sam Keble, and Walter Davis, 1685.   4°

Wing P 1099 (?)

T.489

2437

PELLING (Edward)

The true mark of the beast: or the present degeneracy of the Church of Rome from the faith once delivered to the saints. A sermon on November 5 ... London, for Joseph Hindmarsh, 1685. 4°

Wing P 1107.

T.33

2438

PENN (William)

A defence of the Duke of Buckingham's book of religion & worship, from the exceptions of a nameless author.   By the Pensilvanian... London, for A. Banks, 1685.   4°

Wing P 1275.

T.463

2439

PETTER (John)

A sermon preached July, 5th, on the occasion of the late rebellion. London, for Samuel Walsal, 1685. 4°

Wing P 1889.

T.33

2440

PHELPS (Thomas)

A true account of the captivity of Thomas Phelps, at Machaness in Barbary ... London, H. Hills, Jun. for Joseph Hindmarsh, 1685. 4°

Wing P 1982.

T.134

2441

RICH (S.)

A sermon preached at Chard, June 21. 1685. Before the right honourable John Lord Churchill, and his Majesties' forces ... London, R. N. for Charles Brome, 1685. 4°

Wing R 1365,
2 copies.

T.496   T.108

2442

ROBERTS (Richard)

A sermon preached at St. Thomas Church in Bristol. September 3, 1685. Before the Right Honourable the Lord Arthur Somerset, and the Society of the Loyal Young Men and Apprentices of Bristol, at the time of their anniversary feast. London: for Joseph Hindmarsh, 1685. 4°

Wing R 1604.

T.33

2443

RULES and articles for the better government of his Majesties land-forces in pay during this present rebellion. London, the assigns of John Bill deceas'd: and by Henry Hills and Thomas Newcomb, 1685. 8°

Wing R 2239.

T.443

2444

S. (S.)

A sermon preach'd at the funeral of the reverend George Pain, late rector of Maltby, in the county of Lincoln ... London, for Joseph Lawson bookseller, in the Bayl of Lincoln, 1685. 4°

Not in Wing.

T.108

2445

SAINT EVREMOND (Charles Marguetel de Saint-Denis)
Seigneur de.

Mixt essays upon tragedies, comedies, Italian
comedies, English comedies, and opera's.
London: for Timothy Goodwin, 1685. 4°

Wing S 307.

T.134

2446

SALUS Britannica: or, The safety of the protestant
religion, against all the present apprehensions of
popery fully discust and proved... London, for Tho.
Graves, 1685. Fol.

Wing S 511.

T.531

2447

SAUNDERS (Sir Edmund)

Observations upon the statute of 22 Car.11. cap.1.
entituled, An act to prevent and suppress seditious
conventicles. London, for Tho. Dring, 1685. 8°

Wing S 742.

T.479

2448

SCOTT (John)

A sermon preached before the Right Honourable the
Lord Mayor ... at St. Mary le Bow, July 26. 1685.
being the day of publick thanksgiving for his
Majesties late victory over the rebels. London,
R. N. for Rob. Horne, and Walter Kettilby, 1685.
4°

Wing S 2069.
2 copies.

T.732   T.33

2449

SHARP (John) *Archbishop of York.*

A discourse of conscience. The second part.
Concerning a doubting conscience. [Anon.] London,
for Walter Kettilby, 1685. 4°

Wing S 2973.

T.273

2450

SHARP (John) *Archbishop of York.*

A sermon preached at White-hall, in Lent, on Friday,
March 20. 1684/5. London, for Walter Kettilby,
1685. 4°

Wing S 2988.
3 copies.

T.771   T.496   T.108

2451

SHERIDAN (William) *Bishop of Kilmore and Ardagh.*

St. Pauls confession of faith: or, A brief account
of his religion. In a sermon preach'd ... in
Dublin, March 22. 1684/5. Printed at Dublin for
William Norman: and re-printed at London by
W. Downing, for W. Whitwood; and published by
Randal Taylor, 1685. 4°

Wing S 3232.

T.108

2452

SHERLOCK (William)

A discourse concerning the object of religious
worship. Or, a scripture proof of the unlawfulness
of giving any religious worship to any other being
besides the one supreme God. Part I. [Anon.]
London: for Abel Swalle, 1685. 4°

Wing S 3292.

T.331

2453

SHERLOCK (William)

A sermon preached at St. Margarets Westminster,
May 29. 1685. Before the honourable House of
Commons. London: for J. Amery, and A. Swalle, 1685.
4°

Wing S 3345.
4 copies, one copy wanting t.p.

T.765   T.108   T.112

2454

SHERLOCK (William)

A vindication of a passage in Dr. Sherlock's
sermon preached before the honourable House of
Commons, May 29. 1685. from the remarks of a late
pretended remonstrance... London: for John
Amery; and Abel Swalle, 1685. 4°

Wing S 3369.
2 copies.

T.108   T.273

2455

A SHORT answer to his Grace the D. of Buckingham's
paper, concerning religion, toleration, and liberty
of conscience. London: for S.G. and are to be sold
by Randal Taylor, 1685. 4°

Wing S 3561.

T.463

2456

SMITH (Thomas) *of Magdalen College, Oxford.*

A sermon about frequent communion, preached before
the University of Oxford, August the 17th. 1679.
London, for Samuel Smith, 1685. 4°

Wing S 4248.

T.234

2457

SOME cursory reflexions impartially made upon Mr.
Richard Baxter his way of writing notes on the
Apocalypse, and upon his advertisement and postscript.
By Phililicrines Parrhesiastes... London, for Walter
Kettilby, 1685. 4°

Wing S 4499.
2 copies.

T.330   T.463

2458

STANLEY (William)

A discourse concerning the devotions of the Church of
Rome, especially, as compared with those of the Church
of England... [Anon.] London, for Benj. Tooke,
1685. 4°

Wing S 5244.

T.691

2459

STILLINGFLEET (Edward) *Bishop of Worcester.*

A sermon preached at a publick ordination at St.
Peter's Cornhill, March 15th. 1684/5. London,
M. Flesher, for Henry Mortlock, 1685. 4°

Wing S 5657.
2 copies.

T.108   T.112

2460

STRATFORD (Nicholas) *Bishop of Chester.*

A discourse concerning the necessity of reformation,
with respect to the errors and corruptions of the
Church of Rome. The first part. [Anon.] London,
for Richard Chiswell, 1685. 4°

Wing S 5930.

T.691

2461

TAUBMAN (Matthew)

London's annual triumph: performed on Thursday,
Octob. 29. 1685. for the entertainment of the Right
Honourable Sir Robert Jeffreys, Kt. Lord Mayor of the
city of London... London, for Hen. Playford, 1685.
4°

Wing T 241.

T.407

2462

The THIRD commandment; an essay tending to prove that
perjury deserves not only the pillory, but a much
severer punishment ... London, for Joseph Hindmarsh,
1685. 4°

Wing T 904.

T.134

2463

THOMPSON (Richard)

A sermon preached in the cathedral church of Bristol,
June xxi. MDCLXXXV. before his grace Henry Duke of
Beaufort ... London, for Luke Meredith, 1685. 4°

Wing T 1007.

T.108

2464

The TRYALS of Henry Cornish, Esq; for conspiring
the death of the King, and raising a rebellion...
and John Fernley, William Ring, and Elizabeth Gaunt,
for harbouring and maintaining rebels... London:
George Croom, 1685. Fol.

Wing T 2250.

T.686

2465

TURNER (Francis) *Bishop of Ely.*

A sermon preached at the anniversary meeting of the
sons of clergy-men, in the church of St Mary-le-Bow,
December 4, 1684. London, John Playford, for
Henry Bonwick, 1685. 4°

Wing T 3286.

T.107

2466

TURNER (Francis) *Bishop of Ely.*

A sermon preached before the King at White-Hall,
November 5. 1684. London, for Benj. Tooke, 1685. 4°

Wing T 3285.

T.107

2467

TURNER (Francis) *Bishop of Ely.*

A sermon preached before the King on the 30th of
January, 1684/5 ... London, for Robert Clavell,
1685. 4°

Wing T 3287.

T.108

2468

TURNER (Francis) *Bishop of Ely.*

A sermon preached before their Majesties K. James
II. and Q. Mary, at their coronation in Westminster-
Abby, April 23, 1685. London: for Robert Clavell,
1685. 4°

Wing T 3288.
3 copies.

T.756   T.93   T.112

2469

TURNER (Thomas) *D.D.*

A sermon preached in the King's chappel at White-
hall, upon the 29th of May, 1685. London, for
Walter Kettilby, 1685. 4°

Wing T 3340.
2 copies.

T.314   T.496

2470

VERBUM diei: or, A word in season. London: for
Robert Clavel, 1685. 4°

Wing V 237.

T.134

2471

VILLIERS (George) *2nd Duke of Buckingham.*

The Duke of Buckingham his grace's letter to the
unknown author of a paper, entituled, A short
answer to his Grace the Duke of Buckingham's paper,
concerning religion, toleration, and liberty of
conscience. London, J.L. for Luke Meredith, 1685.
Fol.

Wing B 5314.

T.463

2472

VILLIERS (George) *2nd Duke of Buckingham.*

A short discourse upon the reasonableness of men's
having a religion, or worship of God. London, John
Leake, for Luke Meredith, 1685. 4°

Wing B 5329.

T.463

2473

VINCENT (Nathaniel)

The right notion of honour: as it was delivered in
a sermon before the King at Newmarket, Octob. 4.
1674... London, for Richard Chiswell, 1685.
2 parts. 4°

Wing V 419.

T.496

1685 (Cont'd)

2474
WAGSTAFFE (Thomas)

A sermon preached before ... the Lord Mayor, and the court of aldermen, at the Guild-hall chappel on November the 23d. 1684. London, for Walter Kettilby, 1685. 4°

Wing W 213.
2 copies.

T.489   T.107

2475
WAGSTAFFE (Thomas)

A sermon preached on the 26th day of July, 1685. Being the day of thanks-giving appointed for his Majesty's victory over the rebels .,. London, for Walter Kettilby, 1685. 4°

Wing W 214.

T.33

2476
WARREN (Erasmus)

Religious loyalty, or old allegiance to the new King. A sermon preached on the eighth of February 1684... in the parish church of Worlington in Suffolk. London, for Robert Clavell, 1685. 4°

Wing W 968.

T.108

2477
WERGE (Richard)

The trouble and cure of a wounded conscience. Set out in a sermon preached in St. Mary's Church at Gates-head... London: for Joseph Hall, New-Castle upon Tine, 1685. 4°

Wing W 1367.

T.108

2478
WHITBY (Daniel)

Three sermons preach'd at Salisbury ... London, for T. Basset, 1685. 3 parts. 4°

Wing W 1737.

T.333

2479
WILLIAMS (John) *Bishop of Chichester*.

A discourse concerning the celebration of divine service in an unknown tongue. [Anon.] London, for Richard Chiswell, 1685. 4°

Wing W 2702.

T.691

2480
WILLIAMS (John) *Bishop of Chichester*.

A sermon preached July 26, 1685. Being the day of publick thanksgiving appointed by his Majesty for the late victory over the rebels ... London: R. R, and are to be sold by Walter Davis, 1685. 4°

Wing W 2726.

T.33

2481
WILLIAMS (William) *Minister*.

Religion exprest by loyalty: in a sermon preach'd before... Samuel Swift Esq; mayor... of Worcester ... the 19th day of October, 1684. London, for the author, by T. Braddyll, and are to be sold by Walter Davies, 1685. 4°

cf. Wing W 2790.

T.107

2482
WOODROFFE (Benjamin)

A sermon preach'd January XXX. 1684/5. Being the fast for the martyrdom of King Charles I ... London: J.P. for John Blyth, and are to be sold at John Playford's shop, 1685. 4°

Wing W 3469.
3 copies.

T.496   T.73   T.108

2483
YOUNG (Edward) *Dean of Salisbury*.

A sermon preached at Lambeth January the 25th. at the consecration of... Thomas [Ken] Lord Bishop of Bath and Wells. London, for William Grantham, 1685. 4°

Wing Y 68.
3 copies.

T.108   T.496   T.709

1686

2484
ARWAKER (Edmund) *the Younger*.

Fons perennis. A poem on the excellent and useful invention of making sea-water fresh... London, for Henry Bonwicke, 1686. 4°

Wing A 3908.

T.407

2485
ATTERBURY (Lewis)

The grand charter of Christian feasts, with the right way of keeping them. In a sermon preach'd at a meeting of several of the natives and inhabitants of the county of Buckingham... London, for Christopher Wilkinson, 1686. 4°

Wing A 4156.

T.637

2486
BISBIE (Nathaniel)

The bishop visiting: or a sermon on I Cor. XI. xxxiv. Preached at Bury St. Edmunds, before... William Lord-Bishop of Norwich... May the 3d 1686. London, for Walter Kettilby, 1686. 4°

Wing B 2981.

T.753

2487
CANARIES (James)

Rome's additions to Christianity shewn to be inconsistent with the true design of so spiritual a religion ... Edinburgh, printed in the year 1686. 4°

Wing C 421.

T.236

2488
CARTWRIGHT (Thomas) *Bishop of Chester*.

A sermon preached upon the anniversary solemnity of the happy inauguration of our dread soveraign lord King James II. In the collegiate church of Ripon, February the 6th, 1685/6. London, J. Leake, and are to be sold by Walter Davis, 1686. 4°

Wing C 706.
2 copies.

T. 33

2489
CARTWRIGHT (Thomas) *Bishop of Chester*.

A sermon preached upon the anniversary solemnity of the happy inauguration of our dread soveraign lord King James II. in the collegiate church of Ripon, February the 6th. 1685/6. 2nd ed. London, J. Leake, and are to be sold by Walter Davis, 1686. 4°

Wing C 707.

T.489

2490
CAUSTON (Peter)

Tunbrigialia. P.C. Merc. Lond. Ad G.F. Londini, typis J. Richardson, 1686. 8°

Wing C 1553.

T.204

2491
The CHARACTER and qualifications of an honest loyal merchant. London: Robert Roberts, 1686. 4°

Wing C 1961.

T.332

2492
CHURCH OF ENGLAND,

A form of prayer and thanksgiving to Almighty God, for the prosperity of the Christian arms against the Turks, and expecially for taking the city of Buda ... London, Charles Bill, Henry Hills, and Thomas Newcomb, 1686. 4°

Wing C 4124.

T.116

2493
The CHURCH of England truly represented, according to Dr. Heylins History of the Reformation, in justification of her Royal Highness the late Dutchess of Yorks paper ... London, for the author, and sold by Matthew Turner, 1686. 4°

Wing C 4192.

T.144

2494
COLOMIES (Paul)

Ad Guilielmi Cave canonici Windesoriensis Chartophylacem ecclesiasticum paralipomena. Londini, impensis Richardi Chiswell, 1686. 8°

Wing C 5404.

T.451

2495
CRISP (Samuel)

A sermon preach'd at the primary visitation of... William Lord Bishop of Norwich. Held at Beccles the 23rd of April, 1686. London, for Robert Clavell, and are to be sold by George Rose bookseller in Norwich, 1686. 4°

cf. Wing C 6920.

T.752

2496
The DESIGNS of France against England and Holland discovered: or, the intrigues of that crown, for the utter ruine of both those nations, laid open. [No imprint, 1686.] 4°

Wing D 1177.

T.332

2497
A DIALOGUE between a new Catholic convert and a protestant, shewing the doctrin of transubstantiation to be as reasonable to be believ'd as the great mystery of the Trinity by all good Catholicks. London, Henry Hills, 1686. 4°

Wing D 1297.

T.406

2498
DRYDEN (John)

A defence of the papers written by the late King of blessed memory, and Duchess of York, against the answer made to them. [Anon.] London, H. Hills, 1686. 4°

Wing D 2261.
3 copies.

T.331   T.105   T.116

2499
ELLIS (Philip)

A sermon preach'd before the King, on November the 13. 1686. Being the feast of all the saints of the H. Order of St. Benedict ... London, Henry Hills, 1686. 4°

Wing E 598.
2 copies.

T.515   T.116

2500
An ESSAY to ecclesiastical reconciliation, humbly offered to the consideration of all peaceable and good Christians. By a lover of peace. London, printed anno Domini, 1686. 4°

Wing E 3293.

T.331

2501
FRANCIS (William)

A discourse concerning the holy fast of Lent: together with the sentiment of Dr. John Cosens, late Bishop of Durrham, concerning the same holy fast. Printed for the author, William Francis, 1686. 4°

Wing F 2060.

T. 17

2502

GOTHER (John)

An amicable accomodation of the difference between the representer and the answerer. In return to the last reply against The papist protesting against protestant popery. [Anon.] London, H. Hills, 1686. 4°

Wing G 1325.
3 copies.

T.406 T.515 T.760

2503

GOTHER (John)

The papist misrepresented and represented. [Anon.] Second part. London, Henry Hills, 1686. 4°

Wing G 1337-8, cf. Wing G1327.
Each gathering has a colophon and a caption title. From gathering F the title changes to The Catholic representer. Another copy of the first three gatherings in T.406.

T.515

2504

GOTHER (John)

Papists protesting against Protestant-Popery. In answer to a discourse entituled, A papist not mis-represented by Protestants, Being a vindication of the Papist mis-represented and represented, and the Reflections upon the answer, [Anon.] London, Hen. Hills, 1686. 4° 39pp.

Wing G 1340.
2 copies.

T.760 T.105

2505

GOTHER (John)

Papists protesting against Protestant-Popery. In answer to a discourse [by William Sherlock] entituled, A papist not mis-represented by Protestants. Being a vindication of the Papist mis-represented and represented, and the Reflections upon the answer. [Anon.] London, Hen. Hills, 1686. 38pp.   4°

Wing G 1341.   2 copies

T.125 T.406

2506

GOTHER (John)

Reflections upon the answer to the Papist mis-represented, &c. Directed to the answerer [i.e. Edward Stillingfleet]. [Anon.] [London, 1686.] 4°

Wing G 1348.
5 copies.

T.105 T.125 T.406 T.515 T.760

2507

GOTHER (John)

A reply to the Answer [by William Sherlock] of the Amicable accomodation. Being a fourth vindication of the Papist mis-represented and represented ... [Anon.] London, Henry Hills, 1686. 4°

Wing G 1349.
2 copies.

T.406 T.515

2508

GRENVILLE (Denis)

A sermon preached in the cathedral church of Durham, upon the revival of the ancient laudable practice of ... having sermons on Wednesdays and Fridays, during Advent and Lent. By D.G. London: for Robert Clavel, 1686.   4°

Wing G 1941.

T.496

2509

HICKES (George)

Speculum Beatae Virginis. A discourse of the due praise and honour of the Virgin Mary. By a true Catholick of the Church of England. London, Randal Taylpr, 1686. 4°

Wing H 1869.

T.371

2510

JAMES II, *King of England.*

Treaty of peace, good correspondence & neutrality in America, between ... James II ... and ... Lewis XIV ... concluded the 6/16th day of Novemb. 1686. Printed by Thomas Newcombe in the Savoy, 1686.   4°

Wing J 393.

T.332

2511

JOANNES, *Parisiensis.*

Determinatio Fr. Joannis Parisiensis praedicatoris, de modo existendi corpus Christi in sacramento altaris, alio quam sit ille quem tenet Ecclesia: nunc primum edita ex MS. codice S. Victoris Paris ... Londini, excudebat B.G. impensis J. Cailloue, 1686. 8°

Wing J 746.

T.388

2512

JURIEU (Pierre)

Lettres pastorales addressées aux fideles de France, qui gemissent sous la captivité de Babylon... [Anon.] Seconde edition. A Rotterdam, chez Abraham Acher, 1686.   8°

T.388

2513

KETTLEWELL (John)

The religious loyalist: or, A good Christian taught how to be a faithful servant both to God and the King. In a visitation-sermon preached at Coles-hill in Warwickshire, Aug. 28, 1685 ... London, for Robert Kettlewell, 1686. 4°

Wing K 381.
2 copies.

T.754   T.33

2514

LEYBURN (John)

A reply to the answer made upon the three royall papers. [Anon.] London, for Matthew Turner, 1686.   4°

Wing L 1941.

T.331

2515

LUCILLA and Elizabeth, or, Donatist and Protestant schism parallel'd. London, Henry Hills, 1686.   4°

Wing L 3441.

T.406

2516

MAIMBOURG (Louis)

A peaceable method for the re-uniting protestants and Catholicks in matters of faith: principally in the subject of the holy Eucharist... Written in French by Lewis Maimbourg. Printed for G. W. 1686. 4°

Wing M 294.

T.331

2517

MANNINGHAM (Thomas) *Bishop of Chichester.*

A sermon preached at the Hampshire-feast, on Shrove-Tuesday, Feb. 16, 1685/6. London: F. Collins, for W. Crooke, 1686. 4°

Wing M 503.

T.112

2518

MANNINGHAM (Thomas) *Bishop of Chichester.*

A solemn humiliation for the murder of K. Charles I. With some remarks on those popular mistakes, concerning popery, zeal, and the extent of subjection, which had a fatal influence in our Civil Wars. [Anon.] London: F. Collins for W. Crooke, 1686. 4°

Wing M 509.
2 copies.

T.496 T.112

2519

MILTON (John)

Paradisus amissa, poema heroicum, quod à Joanne Miltono Anglicè scriptum in decem libros digestum est: nunc autem à viris quibusdam natione eadem oriundis in linguam Romanam transfertur. Liber primus. Londini: impensis Thomae Dring, 1686.   4°

Wing M 2155.

T.407

2520

A NEW plot newly discovered, by the help of the London belman; if wicked and hellish conspiracies against the peace of this kingdom ... The first part. Printed for J. Conyers, 1686. 4°

Wing N 708 (?)

T.332

2521

PENN (William)

A perswasive to moderation to church dissenters, in prudence and conscience: humbly submitted to the king and his great councel. By one of the humblest and most dutiful of his dissenting subjects ... [London, 1686.] 4°

Wing P 1338 A.
2 copies.

T.201 T.119

2522

PETTY (*Sir* William)

An essay concerning the multiplication of mankind: together with another essay in political arithmetick; concerning the growth of the city of London... 2nd ed. revised and enlarged. London: for Mark Pardoe, 1686.   8°

Wing P 1923.

T.447

2523

RANDOLPH (Bernard)

The present state of the Morea, called anciently Peloponnesus... Printed at Oxford, 1686.   4°

Wing R 236.

T.332

2524

A REQUEST to protestants, to produce plain scriptures directly authorizing their tenets. London, Henry Hills, 1686. 4°

Wing R 1119.
3 copies.

T.105 T.406 T.515

2525

SCARISBRIKE (Edward)

A sermon preached before her Majesty the Queen Dowager, the 13th. Sunday after Pentecost, 1686... London, for Matthew Turner, 1686.   4°

Wing S 825.

T.637

2526

SCLATER (Edward)

Consensus veterum: or, The reasons of Edward Sclater, minister of Putney, for his conversion to the Catholic faith and communion ... London, Henry Hills; and for him and Matt. Turner, 1686. 4°

Wing S 910.
3 copies.

T.786 T.406 T.105

2527

SCOTT (John)

A sermon preached at the assizes at Chelmsford, in the county of Essex, August 31, 1685 ... London, M. Flesher, for Rob, Horn, and Walter Kettilby, 1686. 4°

Wing S 2070.
2 copies.

T.618 T.33

2528

SCOTT (John)

A sermon preached before the Right Honourable the Lord Mayor, aldermen, and citizens of London; at the church of St. Mary le Bow, September the second, 1686... London, for Walter Kettilby, and Thomas Horn, 1686.   4°

Wing S 2071.

T.618

2529

A SEASONABLE memento both to King and people upon this critical juncture of affaires... London, printed in the year 1686.   4°

Not in Wing.
The date is probably a printer's error for 1680.

T.371

2530
SHERLOCK (William)

An answer to a discourse intituled, Papists protesting against Protestant-Popery [by John Gother] being a vindication of Papists not misrepresented by Protestants ... [Anon.] London: for John Amery, and William Rogers, 1686. 4°

Wing S 3259.

T.125

2531
SHERLOCK (William)

An answer to the Amicable accomodation of the difference between the representer and the answerer [by John Gother]. [Anon.] London: for John Amery, and William Rogers, 1686. 4°

Wing S 3263.

T.406

2532
SHERLOCK (William)

A discourse concerning a judge of controversies in matters of religion. Being an answer to some papers asserting the necessity of such a judge... [Anon.] London, for Robert Clavell, 1686. 98p. 4°

Wing S 3285.

T.406

2533
SHERLOCK (William)

A discourse concerning a judge of controversies in matters of religion. Being an answer to some papers asserting the necessity of such a judge. With an address to wavering protestants... [Anon.] London, for Robert Clavell, 1686. 82p. 4°

Wing S 3285.
2 copies.

T.265 T.606

2534
SHERLOCK (William)

A discourse concerning the object of religious worship. Or, a scripture-proof of the unlawfulness of giving any religious worship to any other being besides the one supream God. Part I. [Anon.] London: for Abel Swalle, 1686. 4°

Wing S 3293.

T.746

2535
SHERLOCK (William)

A papist not misrepresented by protestants. Being a reply to the Reflections upon the answer to A papist mis-represented and represented [by John Gother]. [Anon.] London : for Ric. Chiswel, 1686. 4°

Wing S 3306.
3 copies.

T.760 T.406 T.105

2536
SHERLOCK (William)

A protestant of the Church of England, no Donatist. Or, some short notes on Lucilla and Elizabeth. [Anon.] London, for T. Basset, 1686. 4°

Wing S 3331.

T.406

2537
SHERLOCK (William)

The protestant resolution of faith, being an answer to three questions ... [Anon.] London: for T. Basset, and Abel Swalle, 1686. 4°

Wing S 3334.
Another copy, of a different impression.

T.406 T.265

2538
SHERLOCK (William)

A sermon preached at the funeral of the reverend Benj. Calamy ... Jan. 7th 1685/6. London: for John Amery, and William Rogers, 1686. 4°

Wing S 3347.
2 copies.

T.286 T.78

2539
STILLINGFLEET (Edward) *Bishop of Worcester.*

An answer to some papers lately printed, concerning the authority of the Catholick Church in matters of faith, and reformation of the Church of England. [Anon.] London, for Ric. Chiswel, 1686. 4°

Wing S 5562.

T.116

2540
STILLINGFLEET (Edward) *Bishop of Worcester.*

The doctrines and practices of the Church of Rome truly represented; in answer to a book [by John Gother] intituled A papist misrepresented, and represented, &c. 3rd ed. corrected. [Anon.] London: for W. Rogers, 1686. 4°

Wing S 5592.
2 copies.

T.760 T.105

2541
STILLINGFLEET (Edward) *Bishop of Worcester.*

A sermon preached at White-hall, February the 19th, 1685/6... London, for Henry Mortlock, 1686. 4°

Wing S 5658.

T.637

2542
The SUCCESSION of the Church and sacraments, from Christ and his apostles, to the end of the world. Cleared, and stated according to the antient doctrine of the Greek and Latine fathers... London: for N.T., 1686. 4°

Wing S 6114.

T.371

2543
TAUBMAN (Matthew)

London's yearly jubilee: perform'd on Friday, October XXIX. 1686. for the entertainment of the Right Honourable Sir John Peake, knight, Lord Mayor of the city of London... London, for H. Playford, 1686. 4°

Wing T 244.

T.407

2544
THURLIN (Thomas)

The necessity of obedience to spiritual governours, asserted in a sermon at an episcopal visitation in Kings-Lyn, Norfolk, on the tenth day of May. 1686. Cambridge, John Hayes. And are to be sold by H. Dickinson, 1686. 4°

Wing T 1138.

T.752

2545
TILLOTSON (John) *Archbishop of Canterbury.*

A sermon preached at White-hall, before his late Majesty. London: for Brabazon Aylmer, 1686. 8°

Not in Wing.

T.33

2546
TURNER (Francis) *Bishop of Ely.*

Articles of visitation and enquiry concerning matters ecclesiastical exhibited to the minister, church-wardens and side-men of every parish within the diocess of Ely ... Cambridge, J. Hayes, 1686. 4°

Not in Wing.

T.181

2547
W.(R.)

Two letters to a friend, concerning the distempers of the present times. London, for Charles Brome, 1686. 4°

Wing W 104.

T.332

2548
WAKE (William) *Archbishop of Canterbury.*

A defence of the Exposition of the doctrine of the Church of England, against the exceptions of Monsieur de Meaux [Bossuet], and his vindicator... [Anon.] London, for Richard Chiswell, 1686. 4°

Wing W 236.

T.371

2549
WAKE (William) *Archbishop of Canterbury.*

An exposition of the doctrine of the Church of England, in the several articles proposed by Monsieur de Meaux [Bossuet] ... in his Exposition of the doctrine of the Catholick Church ... [Anon.] London, for Richard Chiswell, 1686. 4°

Wing W 243.
2 copies.

T.371 T.105

2550
WENSLEY (Robert)

Ferguson's text explain'd and apply'd, in a sermon before the Right Honourable, Sir Robert Geffery ... at Guild-Hall chappel, December the 6th, anno Dom. 1685. London, Tho. Milbourn, for Benjamin Tooke, 1686. 4°

Wing W 1352.
2 copies.

T.732 T.33

2551
WOODHEAD (Abraham)

The protestants plea for a Socinian: justifying his doctrine from being opposite to scripture or church-authority; and him from being guilty of heresie, or schism. In five conferences. [Anon.] London, Henry Hills, 1686. 4°

Wing W 3451.

T.331

1687

2552
ADVICE to freeholders and other electors of members to serve in Parliament. In relation to the penal laws and the tests. In a letter to a friend in the country. London, Andrew Sowle, 1687. 4°

Wing P 1250 (attributed to William Penn).

T.66

2553
ADVICE to the confuter of Bellarmin, with some consideration upon the antiquity of the Church of England. London, Henry Hills, 1687. 4°

Wing A 653.

T.114

2554
ALDRICH (Henry)

A reply to two discourses [by Abraham Woodhead]. Lately printed at Oxford concerning the adoration of our blessed Savior, in the Holy Eucharist ... [Anon.] Oxford, printed at the Theater, anno 1687. 4°

Wing A 899.
2 copies.

T.784 T.7

2555
ALTHAM (Michael)

The creed of Pope Pius the IV. or a prospect of popery taken from that authentick record. With short notes. [Anon.] London, for L. Meredith, 1687. 4°

Wing A 2932.

T.744

2556
ALTHAM (Michael)

A vindication of the Church of England from the foul aspersions of schism and heresie unjustly cast upon her by the Church of Rome. [Anon.] Part. I ... London, J.H. for Luke Meredith, 1687. 4°

Wing A 2936.

T.406

2557
An ANSWER to a late pamphlet, intituled, The judgment and doctrine of the clergy of the Church of England, concerning one special branch of the King's prerogative; viz. in dispensing with the penal-laws... In a letter to a friend. London, for Ric. Chiswell, 1687. 4°

Wing A 3309.
2 copies.

T.517 T.744

2558

An ANSWER to a letter to a dissenter, upon occasion of his Majesties late gracious declaration of indulgence [by Lord Halifax]. London, printed anno 1687.   4°

Wing A 3319.
A different pamphlet from the one with the same title by Sir Roger L'Estrange.

T.509

2559

An ANSWER to Monsieur de Meaux's book, intituled, A conference with Mr. Claude. Also the author's letter to a friend of his.   Wherein he answers a discourse of M. de Condom, now Bishop of Meaux, concerning the Church.   London: for T. Dring, 1687.   2 parts.   4°

Wing A 3364.

T.616

2560

ATTERBURY (Francis) *Bishop of Rochester.*

An answer to some considerations on the spirit of Martin Luther and the original of the Reformation [by Abraham Woodhead]; lately printed at Oxford... [Anon.] Oxford, printed at the Theater, anno 1687.
4°

Wing A 4146.
2 copies.

T.7   T.784

2561

BAINBRIDGE (Thomas)

An answer to a book [by Joshua Basset], entituled, Reason and authority: or, The motives of a late protestant's reconciliation to the Catholick Church. Together with a brief account of Augustine the monk, and conversion of the English.   In a letter to a friend. [Anon.] London, J.H. for Brabazon Aylmer, 1687.   4°

Wing B 473.

T.616

2562

BEAULIEU (Luke de)

A discourse shewing that protestants are on the safer side, notwithstanding the uncharitable judgment of their adversaries; and that their religion is the surest way to heaven. [Anon.] London: for Richard Chiswell, 1687.   4°

Wing B 1572.
3 copies.

T.616   T.498   T.144

2563

BEAUMANOIR (Henri Charles de) *Marquis de Lavardin.*

Protestation de Monsieur le Marquis de Lavardin, ambassadeur extraordinaire de France à Rome. [Paris, 1687?]   4°

T.236

2564

BOYLE (Robert)

Reasons why a protestant should not turn papist: or, Protestant prejudices against the Roman Catholic religion; propos'd, in a letter to a Romish priest. By a person of quality. London: H. Clark, for John Taylor, 1687.   4°

Wing B 4018.

T.140

2565

BRIDOUL (Toussain)

The school of the Eucharist established upon the miraculous respects and acknowledgments, which beasts, birds, and insects upon several occasions, have rendred to the holy sacrament of the altar... Printed in French at Lille, 1672.   And now made English... London: for Randall Taylor, 1687. 4°

Wing B 4495.
2 copies.

T.616   T.743

2566

BURNET (Gilbert) *Bishop of Salisbury.*

The citation of Gilbert Burnet D.D. to answer in Scotland on the 27. Iune... for high treason: together with his answer; and three letters, writ by him, upon that subject, to the Right Honourable the Earl of Midletoune...   [The Hague? 1687.]   4°

Wing B 5767.

T.565

2567

BURNET (Gilbert) *Bishop of Salisbury.*

Six papers ... Printed in the year, 1687.   4°

Wing B 5912.
2 copies.

T.236   T. 66

2568

BYFIELD (Timothy)

A short and plain account of the late-found balsamick wells at Hoxdon.   And of their excellent virtues above other mineral waters...   London, printed and are to be sold by Christopher Wilkinson, Thomas Fox, and John Harris, 1687.   8°

Wing B 6398.

T.455

2569

C, (J.)

An answer to the query of a deist, concerning the necessity of faith. [No imprint, 1687?] 4°

Wing C 51.

T, 72

2570

CARE (Henry)

Draconia: or, An abstract of all the penal-laws touching matters of religion; and the several oaths and tests thereby enjoyned... Published for more general information and satisfaction, by H.C... London: George Larkin, 1687.   Fol.

Wing C 510.

T.531

2571

CARE (Henry)

A modest enquiry, whether St. Peter were ever at Rome, and bishop of that church ... [Anon.] London: for Randall Taylor, 1687. 4°

Wing C 529.

T.114

2572

CHURCH OF ENGLAND.

A form or order of thanksgiving, and prayer, to be used in London ... and throughout England ... in behalf of the King, the Queen, and the Royal Family, upon occasion of the Queen's being with child, London, Charles Bill, Henry Hills, and Thomas Newcomb, 1687. 4°

Wing C 4182.

T,116

2573

CLAGETT (William)

The present state of the controversie between the Church of England and the Church of Rome, or, An account of the books written on both sides. In a letter to a friend. [Anon.] London: for Tho. Basset, James Adamson, and Tho. Newborough, 1687. 4°

Wing C 4390.

T.140

2574

CLAGETT (William)

A view of the whole controversy between the representer [i.e. John Gother] and the answerer, with an answer to the representer's last reply: in which are laid open some of the methods by which protestants are misrepresented by papists. [Anon.] London: for William Rogers, 1687. 4°

Wing C 4402.

T.760

2575

CLIFFORD (Martin)

Notes upon Mr. Dryden's poems in four letters ... London, printed in the year 1687. 4°

Wing C 4706.
Incomplete.

T, 12

2576

COMBER (Thomas)

The plausible arguments of a Romish priest from antiquity, answered by the author of the Answer to the plausible arguments from scripture. London, for Robert Clavell, 1687.   8°

Ch.Ch. C 5482 +.

T.405

2577

CROSS, *alias* MORE (John)

An apology for the Contemplations on the life and glory of holy Mary, mother of Jesus ... By J. C. London, Nath. Thompson, 1687.   8°

Wing C 7249.

T.322

2578

DARRELL (William)

The lay-mans opinion, sent in a private letter to a considerable divine of the Church of England. [Signed W. D.] Printed in the year 1687. 4°

Wing D 266.
2 copies.

T.315   T.144

2579

A DIALOGUE between two Church of England-men concerning maters of religion, as set forth in the pulpit. [London, 1687.]   8°

Not in Wing.

T.801

2580

DOVE (Henry)

A sermon preached at the anniversary meeting of the sons of clergy-men, in the Church of S. Mary Ie Bow, on Thursday, Decemb. 2. 1686 ... London: for Benj. Tooke, 1687. 4°

Wing D 2051.

T. 33

2581

DRUMMOND (John) *Earl of Melfort.*

The Earle of Melfort's letter to the presbyterian-ministers in Scotland, writ in his Majesty's name upon their address; together with some remarks upon it. [Edinburgh, 1687.] 4°

Wing M 1641.

T.236

2582

DRYDEN (John)

The hind and the panther. A poem, in three parts ... [Anon.] London, for Jacob Tonson, 1687.   4°

Wing D 2281.
The final leaf wanting; the missing text supplied in Thomas Bowdler II's hand.

T.502

2583

DRYDEN (John)

A poem upon the death of the late usurper, Oliver Cromwel. By the Author of the H[in]d and the P[anthe]r. London, for S.H. and to be sold by the booksellers of London and Westminster, 1687.   4°

Wing D 2331.

T.502

2584

DRYDEN (John) *and* LEE (Nathaniel)

Oedipus: a tragedy. As it is acted at his Royal Highness the Duke's Theatre. 3rd ed ... London, for Richard Bentley, 1687. 4°

Wing D 2324.

T.501

2585

DU FOUR DE LONGUERUE (Louis)

A treatise written by an author of the communion of the Church of Rome. Touching transubstantiation ... [Anon.] London, for Richard Chiswell, 1687. 4°

cf. Wing D 2456.

T.265

2586

FREEMAN (Samuel)

A plain and familiar discourse by way of dialogue betwixt a minister and his parishioner, concerning the Catholick Church ... By a divine of the Church of England. London: for R. Clavel, and B. Tooke, 1687.   4°

Wing F 2142.

T.406

1687 (Cont'd)

2587

GEE (Edward) *the Younger.*

Veteres vindicati, in an expostulatory letter to Mr. Sclater of Putney upon his Consensus veterum ... [Anon.] 2nd ed. corrected. London, for Henry Mortlock, 1687.   4°

Wing G 463.

T.786

2588

The GOOD old test reviv'd and recommended to all sincere Christians. London, Randal Taylor, 1687. 4°

Wing G 1080.

T. 66

2589

GOODEN (Peter)

The sum of a conference had between two divines of the Church of England, and two Catholic lay-gentlemen, at the request, and for the satisfaction of three persons of quality, August 8. 1671. [Anon.] London, Henry Hills, for him and Matthew Turner, 1687.   4°

Wing G 1099.

T.745

2590

GORDON (James)

A request to Roman Catholicks to answer the queries upon these their following tenets ... By a moderate son of the Church of England. London, for Brab. Aylmer, 1687. 4°

Wing G 1282.

T.356

2591

GOTHER (John)

The Catholic representer, or the papist misrepresented and represented. Second part. [Anon.] London, Henry Hills, 1687. 4°

Wing G 1327.

T.184

2592

GOTHER (John)

Good advice to the pulpits, deliver'd in a few cautions for the keeping up the reputation of those chairs, and preserving the nation in peace. [Anon.] London, Henry Hills, 1687. 4°

Wing G 1329.
2 copies.

T.184   T.515

2593

GOTHER (John)

A letter from a dissenter to the divines of the Church of England, in order to a union. [Anon.] London: Randal Taylor, 1687.   4°

Wing G 1330.

T.744

2594

GOTHER (John)

The Papist misrepresented and represented: with a preface, containing reflections upon two treatises, the one the State, the other the View of the controversie between the representer and the answerer. [Anon.] Third part. London, Henry Hills, 1687. 4°

Wing G 1339.

T. 63

2595

GOTHER (John)

The primitive fathers no Protestants: or, A vindication of Nubes testium from the cavils of the answerer [Edward Gee]. [Anon.] London, Henry Hills, 1687. 4°

Wing G 1345.

T. 63

2596

GOTHER (John)

Transubstantiation defended, and prov'd from scripture: in answer to the first part of a treatise [by John Tillotson], intitled, A discourse against transubstantiation. [Anon.] The first part ... London, Henry Hills, 1687.   4°

Wing G 1350.

T.515

2597

GRIFFITH (Evan)

Pax vobis: or, Gospel and liberty: against ancient and modern papists. By E.G. The fourth edition, corrected and amended ... Printed, anno Dom. 1687. 12°

Wing G 1993.

T.459

2598

H. (W.)

A letter concerning the test, and persecution for conscience, To an honourable member of the House of Lords. London, for Matthew Turner, 1687. 4°

Wing H 156.

T. 66

2599

HAYLEY (William)

A sermon preached before the Right Honourable George Earl of Berkeley governour, and the Company of Merchants of England trading into the Levant Seas. At St. Peter's Church in Broadstreet Jan. 30 being Sunday, 1686/7. London, for Samuel Smith, 1687. 4°

Wing H 1210.

T.732

2600

HENRY VIII, *King of England.*

Assertio septem sacramentorum: or, An assertion of the seven sacraments, against Martin Luther ... Faithfully translated into English by T. W. London, Nath. Thompson, 1687. 4°

Wing H 1468.
2 copies.

T.743   T.184

2601

HEYRICK (Thomas)

The new Atlantis. A poem, in three books. With some reflections upon the Hind and the panther [by John Dryden] ... [Anon.] Printed for the author, 1687.   4°

Wing H 1754.

T.502

2602

HICKES (George)

An apologetical vindication of the Church of England: in answer to those who reproach her with the English heresies and schisms, or suspect her not to be a Catholick Church, upon their account. [Anon.] London: for Walter Kettilby, 1687.   4°

Wing H 1840.
2 copies.

T.498   T.639

2603

HILL (Samuel)

The Catholic balance: or a discourse determining the controversies concerning I. the tradition of Catholic doctrines. II. the primacy of S. Peter and the bishop of Rome. III. the subjection and authority of the Church in a Christian state ... [Anon.] London, for Robert Clavell, 1687.   4°

Wing H 2006.

T.498

2604

HOW the members of the Church of England ought to behave themselves under a Roman Catholic king, with reference to the test and penal laws. In a letter to a friend by a member of the same Church. London, Randal Taylor, 1687. 8°

Wing H 2961.

T.388

2605

HUTCHINSON (C.)

Of the authority of councils, and the rule of faith. By a person of quality. With an answer [by William Clagett] to the eight theses laid down for the trial of the English reformation, in the book [by Abraham Woodhead] that came last week from Oxford. London; for R. Clavel, W. Rogers, and S. Smith, 1687.   4°

Wing H 3828B.

T.616

2606

An INSTANCE of the Church of England's loyalty. London: Henry Hills, 1687.   4°

W ing I 231.

T.509

2607

JAMES (Elinor)

Mrs. James's Defence of the Church of England, in a short answer to the Canting address, &c. With a word or two concerning a Quakers good advice to the Church of England, Roman Catholick, and protestant dissenter ... Printed for me Elinor James, 1687. 4°

Wing J 417.
2 copies.

T.565   T.328

2608

JAMES (Elinor)

Mrs. James's Vindication of the Church of England, in an answer to a pamphlet entituled, A new test of the Church of England's loyalty ... London, printed for me Elinor James, 1687. 4°

Wing J 423.
2 copies.

T.565   T.328

2609

JOHNSON (Samuel) *Rector of Corringham.*

The tryal and examination of a late libel, intituled, A new test of the Church of Englands loyalty. With some reflections upon the additional libel, intituled, An instance of the Church of Englands loyalty. [Anon.] [London, 1687?]   4°

Wing J 846.

T.565

2610

JOHNSTON (Joseph)

A full answer to the second defence of the exposition of the doctrin of the Church of England; in a letter to the defender. [Anon.] London, Henry Hills, 1687. 4°

Wing J 868.

T.63

2611

KIDDER (Richard) *Bishop of Bath and Wells.*

A second dialogue between a new Catholick convert and a protestant. Shewing why he cannot believe the doctrine of transubstantiation, though he do firmly believe the doctrine of the trinity. [Anon.] London, for B. Aylmer, 1687.   4°

Wing K 411.

T.331

2612

LA PLACETTE (Jean de)

Six conferences concerning the Eucharist. Wherein is shewed, that the doctrine of transubstantiation overthrows the proofs of Christian religion. [Anon.] London: for Richard Chiswell, 1687.   4°

Wing L 430.
2 copies.

T.356   T.498

2613

LE CAMUS (Etienne) *Bishop of Grenoble.*

A pastoral letter of the Lord Cardinal Le Camus, bishop and prince of Grenoble to the curats of his diocess; touching the methods they ought to take, and in what manner they should behave themselves towards their new converts. Faithfully translated from the original in French. London, Nath. Thompson, 1687. 4°

Wing L 806.

T.236

2614

L'ESTRANGE (*Sir* Roger)

An answer to a letter to a dissenter, upon occasion of his Majesties late gracious declaration of indulgence, [by Lord Halifax], London, for R. Sare, 1687. 4°

Wing L 1195.
2 copies.

T.509   T.66

2615

L'ESTRANGE (*Sir* Roger)

A reply to the reasons of the Oxford-clergy against addressing. [Anon.] London, Henry Hills, 1687. 4°

Wing L 1297.

T.509

2616

LOWTH (Simon)

A letter to Edw. Stillingfleet... In answer to the epistle dedicatory before his sermon, preached at a publick ordination... March 15. 1684/5. Together with some reflections upon certain letters, which Dr. Burnet wrote on the same occasion... London, J.L. and are to be sold by Randal Taylor, 1687. 4°

Wing L 3328.
2 copies.

T.76   T.326

2617

MANBY (Peter)

A reformed catechism, in two dialogues concerning the English reformation ... Printed by Nathaniel Thompson, 1687. 4°

Wing M 388.

T.63

2618

MEREDITH (Edward)

A letter desiring information of the conference at the D. of P. mentioned in the Letter to Mr. G. [by Edward Stillingfleet]. [Anon.] London, Henry Hills, 1687. 4°

Wing M 1781.

T.515

2619

A NEW test of the Church of Englands loyalty. London, for N.T. in the year, 1687. 4°

Wing N 783

T.509

2620

PATRICK (John)

Transubstantiation no doctrine of the primitive fathers: being a defence of the Dublin letter herein, against the Papist misrepresented and represented, part 2. cap. 3. [by John Gother]. [Anon.] London: for Benjamin Tooke, 1687. 4°

Wing P 735.

T.140

2621

PATRICK (Symon) *Bishop of Ely.*

The pillar and ground of truth. A treatise shewing that the Roman Church falsly claims to be that church, and the pillar of that truth, mentioned by S. Paul ... [Anon.] London, for Richard Chiswell, 1687. 4°

Wing P 833.
2 copies.

T.744   T.114

2622

PATRICK (Symon) *Bishop of Ely.*

A private prayer to be used in difficult times. [Anon.] London, for Ric. Chiswell, 1687. 8°

Wing P 834.
2 copies.

T.441 T.32

2623

PAYNE (Henry)

An answer to a scandalous pamphlet [by Lord Halifax], entitled A letter to a dissenter concerning his Majesties late declaration of indulgence, &c. London, for N.T. anno Domini 1687. 4°

Wing P 887.

T.509

2624

PELLING (Edward)

The antiquity of the protestant religion: with an answer to Mr. Sclater's reasons, and the collections made by the author [i.e. John Gother] of the pamphlet entitled Nubes testium. In a letter to a person of quality. [Anon.] London, for Ben Griffin, and are to be sold by Randal Taylor, 1687. 2 parts. 4°

Wing P 1072, 1073.

T.406

2625

PELLING (Edward)

A third letter to a person of quality, being a vindication of the former, in answer to a late pamphlet [by John Gother] intituled a Discourse of the use of images, &c. [Anon.] London, for Ben. Griffin, and are to be sold by Randal Taylor, 1687. 4°

Wing P 1105.

T.140

2626

PENDLEBURY (Henry)

A plain representation of transubstantiation, as it is received in the Church of Rome ... By a countrey divine ... London, for J. Johnson, 1687. 4°

Wing P 1141.

T.140

2627

PENN (William)

Good advice to the Church of England, Roman Catholick, and protestant dissenter. In which it is endeavoured to be made appear that it is their duty, principles & interest to abolish the penal laws and tests... [Anon.] London, Andrew Sowle, 1687. 4°

Wing P 1296.

T.509

2628

PENN (William)

A letter from a gentleman in the country, to his friends in London, upon the subject of the penal laws and tests ... [Anon.] Printed in the year 1687. 4°

Wing P 1318.
2 copies.

T.509   T.66

2629

PENN (William)

A third letter from a gentleman in the country, to his friends in London, upon the subject of the penal laws and tests. [Anon.] London, for J. H. and T. S., 1687. 4°

Wing P 1381.

T.66

2630

PETTY (*Sir* William)

Five essays in political arithmetick... London, for Henry Mortlock, 1687. 8°

Wing P 1924.

T.391

2631

PETTY (*Sir* William)

Observations upon the cities of London and Rome. London, for Henry Mortlocke, and J. Lloyd, 1687. 8°

Wing P 1930.

T.391

2632

PETTY (*Sir* William)

Two essays in political arithmetick, concerning the people, housing, hospitals, &c. of London and Paris... London, for J. Lloyd, 1687. 8°

Wing P 1942.
2 copies.

T.391   T.443

2633

The POPISH doctrine of transubstantiation not agreeable to the opinion of the primitive fathers. Shewed in a letter to a friend. Dublin, printedy b Jo. Ray at Colledg green, and are to be sold by most booksellers, [1687?]. 4°

Wing P 2949.

T.331

2634

PRIOR (Matthew) *and* MONTAGU (Charles) *Earl of Halifax.*

The hind and the panther transvers'd to the story of the country mouse and the city-mouse... [Anon.] London: for W. Davis, 1687. 4°

Wing P 3511.

T.502

2635

The PROPHECIE of a Turk concerning the downfall of Mahometism, and of the setting up the kingdom and glory of Christ ... London, Andrew Sowle, 1687. 4°

Wing P 3678.

T.66

2636

RANDOLPH (Bernard)

The present state of the island in the archipelago (or arches) sea of Constantinople, and gulph of Smyrna; with the islands of Candia, and Rhodes ... Printed at the Theater in Oxford, 1687. 4°

Wing R 234.
2 copies.

T.12 T.235

2637

RAVENSCROFT (Edward)

Titus Andronicus, or the rape of Lavinia. Acted at the Theatre Royall, a tragedy, alter'd from Mr Shakespears works, by Mr. Edw. Ravenscroft. London, J.B. for J. Hindmarsh, 1687. 4°

Wing S 2949.

T.502

2638

REASONS for the repeal of the tests.. In a letter to a friend in the country. London, Andrew Sowle, 1687. 4°

Wing R 519.

T.509

2639

REED (John)

Animadversions by way of answer to a sermon preached by Dr. Thomas Kenne... on Ascension-day last, being the fifth day of May, 1687. [Anon.] London, for Nathaniel Thompson, 1687. 4°

Wing R 665.

T.308

2640

REFLECTIONS upon the new test, and the reply thereto with a letter of Sir Francis Walsingham's concerning the penal laws made in the reign of Queen Elizabeth. London: printed in the year 1687. 4°

Wing R 732.

T.66

2641

A REPLY to the new test of the Church of England's loyalty. London, for J. D. assignee of N. T., 1687. 4°

Wing R 1077.

T.66

2642

The REVOLTER. A trage-comedy acted between the Hind and panther, and Religio laici, &c. London, printed in the year 1687. 4°

Wing R 1206.

T.502

2643

RICHARDS (Jacob)

A journal of the siege and taking of Buda, by the Imperial army ... [London], for M. Gilliflower, and J. Partridge, 1687. 4°

Wing R 1371.
2 copies.

T.4 T.144

2644

SABRAN (Lewis)

Dr. Sherlock sifted from his bran and chaff: or, A certain way of finding the true sense of the Scriptures ... in a dialogue between the Master of the Temple, and a student there. [Anon.] London: Henry Hills, 1687. 4°

Wing S 216.

T.63

2645

SAVILE (George) *Marquess of Halifax.*

A letter [signed T.W.] to a dissenter, upon occasion of his Majesties late gracious declaration of indulgence. [London, 1687.] 7p. 4°

Wing H 311 (?)

T.565

2646

SAVILE (George) *Marquess of Halifax.*

A letter [signed T.W.] to a dissenter, upon occasion of his Majesties late gracious declaration of indulgence. London: for G.H., 1687. 10p. 4°

Wing H 312 (?)
2 copies.

T.93 T.509

2647

SAVILE (George) *Marquess of Halifax.*

A letter [signed T.W.] to a dissenter, upon occasion of his Majesties late gracious declaration of indulgence. London: for G.H., 1687. 17p. 4°

Wing H 313(?)
2 copies.

T.66 T.332

2648

SAVILE (George) *Marquess of Halifax.*

Remarkes upon a pamphlet stiled, A letter to a dissenter, &c. In another letter to the same dissenter. [Anon.] [London, 1687.] 4°

Wing H 318.

T.66

2649

SCHUYL (Frans)

A catalogue of all the cheifest rarities in the publick theater and anatomie-hall of the University of Leyden ... [Anon.] In Leyden, Jacobus Voorn, 1687. 4°

Wing S 904.

T.262

2650

A SEEKERS request to Catholick priests, and Protestant ministers, for satisfying his conscience in the truth of what he ought to believe of the Lords Supper ... London, for J. F., 1687. 4°

Wing S 2411.

T.63

2651

SHERLOCK (William)

An answer to a late dialogue between a new Catholick convert and a Protestant, to prove the mystery of the Trinity to be as absurd a doctrine as transubstantiation. By way of short notes on the said dialogue. [Anon.] London, for Thomas Bassett, 1687. 4°

Wing S 3261.
Incomplete.

T.406

2652

SHERLOCK (William)

An answer to the Request to protestants, to produce plain scriptures directly authorizing these tenets. [Anon.] London: for Tho, Basset, 1687. 4°

Wing S 3264.

T.406

2653

SHERLOCK (William)

An answer to three late pamphlets. Viz. I. A request to Protestants, to produce plain scripture ... II. A dialogue between a new Catholick convert and a Protestant. III. Lucilla and Elizabeth. London, for Tho. Basset, 1687. 3 parts. 4°

Wing A 3455 (including S 3261, 3264, 3331).

T.1o5

2654

SHERLOCK (William)

A short summary of the principal controversies between the Church of England, and the Church of Rome. Being a vindication of several protestant doctrines, in answer to a late pamphlet intituled, Protestancy destitute of scripture-proofs. [Anon.] London, for Richard Chiswell, 1687. 4°

Wing S 3365.

T.498

2655

SMALRIDGE (George) *Bishop of Bristol.*

Animadversions on the eight theses laid down, and the inferences, deduced from them, in a discourse entitl'd Church-government. Part, V. [by Abraham Woodhead] .., Oxford, printed at the Theater, anno 1687. 4°

Wing S 4001.
2 copies.

T.784 T.7

2656

SMALRIDGE (George) *Bishop of Bristol,*

Reflections on the historical part of Church-government, part, V. [by Abraham Woodhead] ... Oxford, printed at the Theater, anno 1687. 4°

Wing S 4003.

T.7

2657

STILLINGFLEET (Edward) *Bishop of Worcester.*

The doctrine of the Trinity and transubstantiation compared, as to scripture, reason, and tradition. In a new dialogue between a protestant and a papist. The first part ... [Anon.] London, J. D. for W. Rogers, 1687. 4°

Wing S 5587.

T.144

2658

STILLINGFLEET (Edward) *Bishop of Worcester.*

A second letter to Mr. G. in answer to two letters lately published concerning the conference at the D. of P. [Anon.] London, for H. Mortlocke, 1687. 4°

Wing S 5635.

T.140

2659

STILLINGFLEET (Edward) *Bishop of Worcester and* BURNET (Gilbert) *Bishop of Salisbury.*

A relation of a conference held about religion, at London, by Edw. Stillingfleet, D,D, &c. With some gentlemen of the Church of Rome. London: Randal Taylor, 1687. 4°

Wing B 5863.

T.180

2660

TAYLOR (Jeremy) *Bishop of Down and Connor.*

A copy of a letter written to a gentlewoman newly seduced to the Church of Rome. London, for L. Meredith, 1687. 8°

Wing T 306.

T.441

2661

TENISON (Thomas) *Archbishop of Canterbury.*

The difference betwixt the protestant and Socinian methods: in answer to a book written by a Romanist [i.e. Abraham Woodhead], and intituled, The protestants plea for a Socinian. [Anon.] [London], for Benjamin Tooke, 1687. 4°

Wing T 694.

T.180

2662

TENISON (Thomas) *Archbishop of Canterbury.*

A discourse concerning a guide in matters of faith. With respect, especially, to the Romish pretence of the necessity of such a one as is infallible. [Anon.] The second edition, corrected. London, for T. Basset, and Ben. Tooke, 1687. 4°

Wing T 696.

T.406

2663

TENISON (Thomas) *Archbishop of Canterbury.*

Mr. Pulton consider'd in his sincerity, reasonings, authorities. Or a just answer to what he hath hitherto published in his True account; his True and full account of a conference, &c. his Remarks; and in them his pretended confutation of what he calls D. Ts rule of faith. London, for Richard Chiswell, 1687. 4°

Wing T 703.
2 copies.

T.140 T.180

2664

TENISON (Thomas) *Archbishop of Canterbury.*

A true account of a conference held about religion at London, Septemb. 29, 1687. Between A, Pulton, Jesuit, and Tho. Tenison ... London: for Ric. Chiswell, 1687. 4°

Wing T 723.

T.180

2665

The USE and great moment of The notes of the Church, as deliver'd by C. Bellarmine De notis Eccl. justified. In answer to a late discourse [by William Sherlock] concerning The notes of the Church... London, Nathaniel Thompson, 1687. 4°

Wing U 144.

T.114

2666

WAKE (William) *Archbishop of Canterbury.*

A discourse of the holy Eucharist, in the two great points of the real presence and the adoration of the host. In answer to the two discourses lately printed at Oxford... [Anon.] London, for Richard Chiswell, 1687. 4°

Wing W 240.

T.743

2667

WAKE (William) *Archbishop of Canterbury.*

Two discourses: of purgatory, and prayers for the dead. [Anon.] London, for Ric. Chiswell, 1687. 4°

Wing W 272.

T.498

2668

WARD (Thomas)

Monomachia: or a duel between Dr. Tho, Tenison ... and a Roman Catholick souldier; wherein the Speculum ecclesiasticum is defended against the frivolous cavils ... of Doctor Tenison ... London, printed for the author [by N.T.], 1687. 4°

Wing W 834.

T.63

2669

WARD (Thomas)

Some queries to the protestants concerning the English reformation. By T.W. Gent. London, Nathaniel Thompson, 1687. 4°

Wing W 836.

T.515

2670

WILLIAMS (John) *Bishop of Chichester.*

The papist represented, and not misrepresented; being in answer to the first sheet of the second part of the Papist misrepresented and represented [by John Gother]. And for a further vindication of the Catechism truly representing the doctrine and practices of the Church of Rome. [Anon.] London: for Ric. Chiswell, 1687. 4°

Wing W 2713.

T.406

2671

WOODHEAD (Abraham)

Church-government part V. A relation of the English Reformation, and the lawfulness thereof examined ... [Anon.] Printed at Oxford, 1687. 4°

Wing W 3440.
2 copies.

T.7

2672

WOODHEAD (Abraham)

Two discourses concerning the adoration of our B. Saviour in the H. Eucharist... [Anon.] At Oxford printed, anno 1687. 2 parts. 4°

Wing W 3459.

T.265 T.784

2673

WOODHEAD (Abraham)

Two discourses. The first, concerning the spirit of Martin Luther, and the original of the Reformation. The second, concerning the celibacy of the clergy. [Anon.] Printed at Oxford. An. 1687. 2 parts. 4°

Wing W 3460.

T.784

1688

2674

An ABRIDGMENT of the prerogatives of St. Ann, mother of the mother of God. With the approbation of the doctors at Paris: and thence done into English to accompany The contemplations on the life and glory of holy Mary ... London: for Ric. Chiswell, 1688. 4°

Wing A 108.

T.178

2675

An ACCOUNT of the late persecution of the protestants in the Vallys of Piemont; by the Duke of Savoy and the French King, in the year 1686 ... Oxford, printed at the Theatre for John Crosley, 1688. 4°

Wing A 315.
Signature of Ann Wentworth & Lovelace.

T.249

2676

ADVICE from a dissenter to those of the Church of England; who are against taking off the penal laws and tests: shewing their calumnies cast upon his Majesty, to be false and unchristian... London: printed in the year, 1688. 4°

Wing A 633.

T.565

2677

ADVICE to the English youth: relating to the present juncture of affairs. London: George Larkin, 1688. 4°

Wing A 655.

T.509

2678

ALLIX (Peter)

A discourse concerning penance. Shewing how the doctrine of it, in the Church of Rome, makes void true repentance ... London: for Ric. Chiswell, 1688. 4°

Wing A 1220.

T.393

2679

ANNESLEY (Arthur) *1st Earl of Anglesey.*

The king's right of indulgence in spiritual matters, with the equity thereof, asserted. By a person of honour, and eminent minister of state lately deceased. [Edited by Henry Care.] London: Randall Taylor, 1688. 4°

Wing A 3169.

T.332

2680

An ANSWER to a paper, intitled, Reflections on the Prince of Orange's declaration. [London, 1688.] 4°

Wing A 3331.

T.565

2681

The BALLANCE adjusted: or, the interest of church and state weighed and considered upon this revolution. [London, 1688?] 4°

Wing B 540.
3 copies.

T.511 T.328 T.64

2682

BARLOW (Thomas) *Bishop of Lincoln.*

A few plain reasons why a protestant of the Church of England should not turn Roman Catholick. By a real Catholick of the Church of England ... London, for R. Clavel, 1688. 4°

Wing B 831.

T.236

2683

BROWN (Thomas) *of Shifnal.*

The reasons of Mr. Bays [i.e. John Dryden] changing his religion. Considered in a dialogue between Crites, Eugenius, and Mr. Bays... [Anon] London, for S.T. and are to be sold by the booksellers of London and Westminster, 1688. 4°

Wing B 5069.

T.502

2684

BROWNE (Thomas) *Fellow of St. John's College, Cambridge.*

Concio ad clerum habita coram Academia Cantabrigiensi ... ubi vindicatur vera & valida cleri Anglicani, ineunte Reformatione, ordinatio... Cui accessit concio habita Julii 3.1687. de canonica cleri Anglicani ordinatione... Cantabrigiae, ex officina Joan. Hayes, impensis H. Dickinson & Sam. Smith, 1688. 2 parts. 4°

Wing B 5184.

T.112

2685

BURNET (Gilbert) *Bishop of Salisbury.*

An apology for the Church of England, with relation to the spirit of persecution: for which she is accused. [Anon.] [Amsterdam, 1688.] 4°

Wing B 5762.

T.66

2686

BURNET (Gilbert) *Bishop of Salisbury.*

The case of compulsion in matters of religion stated. By G.B. Addressed to the serious consideration of the members of the Church of England, in this present juncture. London, printed by T.S. in the year 1688. 8°

Wing B 5765.

T.144

2687

BURNET (Gilbert) *Bishop of Salisbury.*

A discourse concerning transubstantiation and idolatry. Being an answer to the Bishop of Oxford's Plea relating to those two points. [Anon.] London, printed in the year, 1688. 4°

Wing B 5775.

T.763

2688

BURNET (Gilbert) *Bishop of Salisbury.*

An enquiry into the measures of submission to the supream authority... [Anon.] [London, 1688.] 4°

Wing B 5808.
3 copies.

T.66 T135 T.199

2689

BURNET (Gilbert) *Bishop of Salisbury.*

An enquiry into the reasons for abrogating the test imposed on all members of Parliament. Offered by Sa. Oxon. [Anon.] [London, 1688]. 4°

Wing B 5813.
2 copies.

T.66

2690

BURNET (Gilbert) *Bishop of Salisbury.*

Reflections on the relation of the English Reformation, lately printed at Oxford ... By G.B. Amsterdam: for J. S., 1688. 4°

Wing B 5856.

T.144

2691

BURNET (Gilbert) *Bishop of Salisbury.*

A vindication of the ordinations of the Church of England... In answer to a paper written by one of the Church of Rome to prove the nullity of our orders... [Anon.] 2nd ed. London: for Ric. Chiswell, 1688. 4°

Wing B 5940.
2 copies.

T.236 T.744

2692

CANNING (William)

Gesta Grayorum: or, The history of the high and mighty prince, Henry Prince of Purpoole... who reigned and died, A.D. 1594... [Anon.] London, for W. Canning, 1688. 4°

Wing C 444.

T.502

2693

CARE (Henry)

Draconia: or, An abstract of all the penal laws touching matters of religion; and the several oaths and tests thereby enjoyned... The second edition, with considerable additions... London: George Larkin, 1688. 4°

Wing C 511.

T.565

2694

CARE (Henry)

The legality of the court held by his Majesties Ecclesiastical Commissioners, defended. Their proceedings no argument against the taking off penal laws & tests. [Anon.] London, Richard Janeway, 1688. 4°

Wing C 527.
4 copies.

T.308 T.66 T.116 T.236

2695

CARE (Henry)

A vindication of the proceedings of his Majesties Ecclesiastical Commissioners, against the Bishop of London, and the fellows of Magdalen-College. [Anon.] London, Tho. Milbourn, and published by Richard Janeway, 1688. 4°

Wing C 536.
3 copies.

T.327 T.236 T.116

2696

CHAP. I. Of magistracy. [London, 1688.] Fol.

Not in Wing.

T.531

2697

CHURCH OF ENGLAND.

A form of prayer and thanksgiving to almighty God, for having made his Highness the Prince of Orange the glorious instrument of the great deliverance of this Kingdom from popery and arbitrary power... In the Savoy: Edw. Jones, 1688. 4°

Wing C 4125.
4 copies.

T.461 T.463 T.489

2698

CHURCH OF ENGLAND.

A form of prayer with thanksgiving for the safe delivery of the Queen, and happy birth of the young prince... London, Charles Bill, Henry Hills, and Thomas Newcomb, 1688. 4°

Wing C 4168.

T.411

2699

CHURCH OF ENGLAND.

A prayer for his Highness the Prince of Orange, to be used immediately after the prayer for the royal family. In the Savoy: Edward Jones; and for James Partridge, Matthew Gyllyflower, and Samuel Heyrick, 1688. 4°

Wing C 4188 I.
2 copies.

T.461   T.463

2700

CHURCH OF ENGLAND.

Prayers to be used in all cathedral, collegiate, and parochial churches, and chapels, within this kingdom, during this time of publick apprehensions from the danger of invasion ... [London, 1688.] 4°

Wing P 3196 A.

T.144

2701

CLAGETT (William)

An answer to the representers [i.e. John Gother's] reflections upon the state and view of the controversy. With a reply to the vindicator's [i.e. Joseph Johnston's] full answer; shewing, that the vindicator has utterly ruined the new design of expounding and representing popery. [Anon.] London: for Ric. Chiswell, 1688.

Wing C 4376.

T.760

2702

CLAGETT (William)

The queries offered by T. W. [i.e. Thomas Ward] to the protestants concerning the English reformation reprinted and answered ... [Anon.] London: H. Clark, for James Adamson, 1688. 4°

Wing C 4391.

T.236

2703

A CLEAR proof of the certainty and usefulness of the Protestant rule of faith, Scripture, after the help of ministerial guides, finally interpreted by each man's private sense ... London, Henry Hills, 1688. 4°

Wing C 4620.

T. 63

2704

A COLLECTION of papers relating to the present juncture of affairs in England ... Printed in the year, 1688. 4°

Wing C 5169A.

T.137

2705

COMBER (Thomas)

A discourse concerning the second Council of Nice, which first introduced and established image-worship in the Christian Church, anno Dom. 787. [Anon.] London, for Walter Kettilby, 1688. 4°

Wing C 5461.

T.180

2706

COMBER (Thomas)

Three considerations proposed to Mr. William Pen, concerning the validity and security of his new Magna Charta for liberty of conscience, by a Baptist ... [Anon.] [London, 1688.] 4°

Wing C 5496.

T.509

2707

COURTILZ DE SANDRAS (Gatien de)

Nouveaux interets des princes de l'Europe. Revûs, corrigés & augmentés par l'auteur... Troisième edition. [Anon.] A Cologne, chez Pierre Marteau, 1688. 8°

T.323

2708

DARRELL (William)

The vanity of human respects, in a sermon ... London, for John Tottenham, 1688. 4°

Wing O D269 A.

T.173

2709

DELLON (Gabriel)

The history of the inquisition, as it is exercised at Goa. Written in French, by the ingenious Monsieur Dellon, who laboured five years under those severities ... Translated into English. London, for James Knapton, 1688. 4°

Wing D 942.

T.265

2710

DEPOSITIONS made upon the birth of his Royal Highness the Prince of Wales: Printed in the year 1688. 8°

Not in Wing.
2 copies.

T.446   T.368

2711

DODWELL (Henry)

An account of the fundamental principle of popery, as it is a distinct communion ... London: for Benj. Tooke, 1688. 4°

Wing D 1802.

T.185

2712

DODWELL (Henry)

An answer to six queries, proposed to a gentlewoman of the Church of England, by an emissary of the Church of Rome; fitted to a gentlewomans capacity. London: for Benj. Tooke, 1688. 4°

Wing D 1803.

T.185

2713

The DREAM. [No imprint, 1688.]   4°

Wing D 2157.
A poem, beginning: Weary'd with Business, and with Cares oprest ...

T.502

2714

The DUTCH design anatomized, or, A discovery of the wickedness and unjustice of the intended invasion, and a clear proof, that it is the interest of all the King's subjects to defend his Majesty and their country against it. Written by a true member of the Church of England ... London, Randal Taylor, 1688.   4°

Wing D 2897.

T.511

2715

DU VIGNAN, *Sieur*.

The Turkish secretary, containing the art of expressing ones thoughts, without seeing, speaking, or writing to one another; with the circumstances of a Turkish adventure ... [Anon.] Translated by the author of the Monthly account. London, J. B. and sold by Jo. Hindmarsh, and Randal Taylor, 1688. 4°

Wing D 2922.

T.315

2716

ELLIS (Clement)

The reflector's defence of his letter to a friend, against the furious assaults of Mr. I. S. in his second Catholick letter. In four dialogues. [Anon.] London: for William Rogers, 1688.   4°

Wing E 570.

T.786

2717

ENGLAND. *Parliament.*

The history of the Parliament of England, from MDCLXI. Printed in the year, 1688. Fol.

Not in Wing.

T.531

2718

An EXACT account of the whole proceedings against the Right Reverend father in God, Henry Lord Bishop of London, before the Lord Chancellor, and the other ecclesiastical commissioners. London, printed in the year 1688. 4°

Wing E 3591.

T.332

2719

FAGEL (Gaspar)

A letter, writ by Mijn Heer Fagel, pensioner of Holland, to Mr. James Stewart, advocate; giving an account of the Prince and Princess of Orange's thoughts concerning the repeal of the test, and the penal laws. London, printed in the year 1688. 4°

Wing F 89.

T. 66

2720

FAIRFAX (Henry)

An impartial relation of the whole proceedings against St. Mary Magdalen Colledge in Oxon, in the year of our Lord 1687. Containing only matters of fact as they occurred. Printed in the year, 1688. 4°

Wing F 125.
2 copies.

T.236   T.327

2721

A FORM of prayer, &c. [for the Prince of Orange, 1688.] Translated from the Dutch. [London, 1688.] brs.

Wing F 1569.

T.461

2722

FOWLER (Edward) *Bishop of Gloucester*.

A sermon preached before the Right Honourable, the Lord Maior of London, and the court of aldermen, &c. on Wednesday in Easter week ... London, T.M. for Brabazon Aylmer, 1688.   4°

Wing F 1719.

T.494

2723

FREE thoughts of the penal laws, tests, and some late printed papers touching both. In a letter from a person of quality. Printed in the year 1688.   4°

Wing F 2123.

T.565

2724

GEE (Edward) *the Younger*,

An answer to the compiler of the Nubes testium [John Gother] ... Together with a vindication of the Veteres vindicati from the weak and disingenuous attempts of the author of Transubstantiation defended [i.e. John Gother]. By the author of the answer to Mr. Sclater of Putney. London, for Henry Mortlock, 1688. 4°

Wing G 453.

T.140

2725

GEE (Edward) *the Younger*.

A vindication of the principles of the author of the Answer to the compiler of the Nubes testium [i.e. John Gother] from the charge of popery. In answer to a late pretended Letter from a dissenter to the divines of the Church of England ... London, for Henry Mortlock, 1688.   4°

Wing G 464.

T.744

2726

GILES (William)

A defence of Dr. Sherlock's Preservative against popery, in relpy to a Jesuit's answer: wherein the R. Father's reasonings are fully confuted. By W. G. a protestant foot-man. London: for Brab. Aylmer, 1688. 4°

Wing G 739.

T.315

2727

GILES (William)

A defence of Dr. Sherlock's Preservative against
popery, in reply to a Jesuit's answer: wherein the
R. Father's reasonings are fully confuted. 2nd ed.
London, for B. Aylmer, 1688.   4°

Wing G 740.

T.606

2728

GOTHER (John)

The Pope's supremacy asserted, from the considerations
of some Protestants, and the practice of the
primitive Church, in a dialogue between a church-
divine and a seeker: in a vindication of Nubes
testium. [Anon.] London, Henry Hills, 1688. 4°

Wing G 1344.

T. 63

2729

GOTHER (John)

Pulpit-sayings, or, The characters of the pulpit-
Papist examined in answer to the Apology for the
pulpits, and in vindication of the representer
against the stater of the controversie. [Anon.]
London, Henry Hills, 1688. 4°

Wing G 1347.

T. 63

2730

GRASCOMBE (Samuel)

A letter to a friend, in answer to a letter written
against Mr. Lowth, in defence of Dr. Stillingfleet.
[Anon.] London, Randal Taylor, 1688. 4°

Wing G 1573.
3 copies.

T.330 T. 76

2731

HARLAY (Achille de) *Comte de Beaumont*.

Acte d'appel interjetté par Monsieur le Procureur
General au Concile, au sujet de la bulle du Pape,
concernant les franchises dans la ville de Rome ...
A Paris, chez Francois Muguet, 1688.   4°

T.236

2732

HARRINGTON (James) *Barrister*.

Some reflexions upon a treatise call'd Pietas
Romana & Parisiensis [by Thomas Carre, i.e. Miles
Pinkney]... To which are added I. A vindication
of Protestant charity, in answer to some passages
in Mr. E.M.'s Remarks on a late conference. II.
A defence of the Oxford reply to two discourses...
[Anon.] Oxford, printed at the Theater, anno
Domini 1688. 4°

Wing H 834.

T.7

2733

HELLIER (Henry)

A sermon preached before the University of Oxford
December 4. 1687 concerning the obligation of
oaths. Oxford, printed at the Theater for John
Crosley, 1688.   4°

Wing H 1380 A.

T.494

2734

HERBERT (*Sir* Edward)

A short account of the authorities in law, upon
which judgement was given in Sir Edw. Hales his
case ... London: for M. Clark, 1688. 4°

Wing H 1496.
3 copies.

T.487 T.332 T.131

2735

HUDLESTON (Richard)

A short and plain way to the faith and Church.
Composed many years since by ... Richard Hudleston
... And now published for the common good by his
nephew Mr. Jo. Hudleston ... London, Henry Hills,
1688. 4°

Wing H 3257.
2 copies.

T.63 T.116

2736

I. (P.)

A letter written by a minister, for the
satisfaction of a person doubting in religion.
Shewn to be unsatisfactory. London, Henry Hills,
1688. 4°

Wing I 10.
2 copies.

T.515   T.331

2737

JENKIN (Robert)

An historical examination of the authority of
general councils, shewing the false dealing that
hath been used in the publishing of them ...
[Anon.] London, for Henry Mortlock, 1688. 4°

Wing J 568.

T.761

2738

JOHNSTON (Nathaniel)

The dear bargain. Or, A true representation of
the state of the English nation under the Dutch.
In a letter to a friend. [Anon.] [London, 1688].
4°

Wing J 874.

T.64

2739

JURIEU (Pierre)

Monsieur Jurieu's pastoral letters, directed to
the protestants in France, who groan under the
Babylonish captivity. Translated out of the French.
London, for Jo. Hindmarsh, 1688. 4°

Wing J 1207.

T.332

2740

KEN (Thomas) *Bishop of Bath and Wells*.

A pastoral letter from the Bishop of Bath and Wells
to his clergy, concerning their behaviour during
Lent. London, for Charles Brome, and W. Clark in
Winchester, 1688. 4°

Wing K 276.

T.332

2741

LANGBAINE (Gerard) *the Younger*.

Momus triumphans: or, The plagiaries of the English
stage; expos'd in a catalogue... London: for N.C.
and are to be sold by Sam. Holford, [1688]. 4°

Wing L 377.
Title-page cropped.

T.502

2742

LA PLACETTE (Jean)

Of the incurable scepticism of the Church of Rome.
[Anon.] London: for Ric. Chiswel, 1588 [i.e. 1688].
4°

Wing L 429.
2 copies.

T.761 T.180

2743

L'ESTRANGE (*Sir* Roger)

The free-born subject: or, The Englishmans birthright:
asserted against all tyrannical usurpations either
in church or state. By a person of quality. London,
for B.C. and are to be sold by the booksellers of
London and Westminster, 1688.   4°

Not in Wing.

T.199

2744

A LETTER from a gentleman in the city, to a clergy-
man in the country. London, for D.C. and are to be
sold by the booksellers of London and Westminster,
1688.   4°

Wing L 1387.

T.509

2745

A LETTER to the author [i.e. Henry Care] of the
Vindication of the proceedings of the Ecclesiastical
Commissioners, concerning the legality of that court.
By Philonomus Anglicus. Printed Eleutheropolis.
[Oxford, 1688] 4°

Wing L 1728.
2 copies.

T.66 T.236

2746

LLOYD (William) *Bishop of Worcester*.

An answer to the Bishop of Oxford's reasons for
abrogating the test, impos'd on all members of
Parliament ... By a person of quality. London,
printed in the year 1688. 4°

Wing L 2673.

T.66

2747

LOUIS XIV, *King of France*.

The French king's memorial to the Pope. [French and
English.] London, for Joseph Hindmarsh, 1688.   4°

Wing L 3130.
2 copies.

T.332

2748

MARSDEN (Thomas)

Roman Catholicks uncertain whether there be any true
priest or sacraments in the Church of Rome: evinced
by an argument urg'd and maintain'd ... against Mr
Edward Goodall ... London, for Walter Kettilby,
1688.   4°

Wing M 725.

T.743

2749

MAURICE (Henry)

Doubts concerning the Roman infallibility ... [Anon.]
London, for James Adamson, 1688. 4°

Wing M 1362.
2 copies.

T.140 T.185

2750

MEREDITH (Edward)

Some farther remarks on the late account given by
Dr. Tenison of his conference with Mr. Pulton ...
London: Henry Hills, 1688. 4°

Wing M 1783.

T.63

2751

MILBOURNE (Luke)

A short defence of the orders of the Church of
England, as by law established: against some
scatter'd objections of Mr. Webster of Linne. By
a presbyter of the diocess of Norwich.   London,
Randal Taylor, 1688.   4°

Wing M 2038.

T.236

2752

MILNER (John)

A collection of the church-history of Palestine;
from the birth of Christ, to the beginning of the
empire of Diocletian. By J. M. London, for Thomas
Dring, 1688. 4°

Wing M 2077.
2 copies.

T.140 T.144

2753

MONRO (Andrew)

Compendium rhetoricae.   Ad scholas, & provectiorum
discipulorum captum quam diligentissime accomodatum...
Londini, typis G. Wilde, impensis autoris prostat
vaenale apud S. Crouch; & apud B. Crayle, 1688. 8°

Wing O M 2446A.

T.448

2754

N.(N.)

Old popery as good as new. Or the unreasonableness
of the Church of England in some of her doctrines
and practices, and the reasonableness of liberty
of conscience. In a letter from a private
gentleman in the country to his friend a clergy-man
in the city.   Printed in the year 1688. 4°

Wing N 47.

T.236

2755

NELSON (Robert)

Transubstantiation contrary to scripture: or, The
protestant's answer to the seeker's request ...
[Anon.] London: for Dorman Newman, 1688. 4°

Wing N 417.

T.236

2756

The NOTES of the Church, as laid down by Cardinal Bellarmin; examined and confuted... [By William Sherlock and others.] (A vindication [By William Sherlock] of the brief discourse concerning The notes of the Church... A defence [by George Tully] of the confuter of Bellarmin's second note of the Church, Antiquity, against the cavils of the adviser.) London, for Richard Chiswell, 1688. 3 parts. 4°

Wing N 1392 (Including S 3374 and T 3236).
2 copies.

T.761 T.114

2757

PARIS. *Parlement.*

Arrest rendu en la cour de Parlement, les Grande Chambre & Tournelle assemblées, sur la bulle du Pape, concernant les franchises dans la ville de Rome, & l'ordonnance renduë en consequence le 26. du mois de decembre dernier. A Paris, chez François Muguet, 1688. 4°

T.236

2758

PARIS. *Parlement.*

The proceedings of the parliament of Paris, upon the pope's bull, concerning the franchises in the city of Rome, and the following ordonnance of the 26th of December. Translated into English ... London, for R. Bentley, and are to be sold by Randal Taylor, 1688. 4°

Wing F 2053.

T.236

2759

PARKER (Henry)

The true portraiture of the kings of England; drawn from their titles, successions, raigns and ends... To which is added the political catechism. [Anon.] London, printed in the year 1688. 4°

Wing P 430.

T.516

2760

PARKER (Samuel) *Bishop of Oxford.*

Reasons for abrogating the test, imposed upon all members of Parliament anno 1678 ... London, for Henry Bonwick, 1688. 4°

Wing P 467.
3 copies.

T.565 T.7 T.131

2761

PARTRIDGE (John)

Mene tekel ou jugement astrologique pour l'annee MDCLXXXVIII. Dans lequel on montre par les principes de cette science la catastrophe prochaine du papisme en Angleterre. [Anon.] Traduite de l'Anglois sur la copie de Londres. [No imprint, 1688.] 8°

A translation of Wing G 88 (attributed to John Gadbury).

T.32

2762

PASTON (James)

A discourse of penal laws in matter of religion: endeavouring to prove that there is no necessity of inflicting or continuing them. First delivered in a sermon ... occasioned by his Majesties late gracious declaration for liberty of conscience... London, printed for the author, 1688. 4°

Wing P 665.
2copies.

T.236 T.273

2763

A PASTORAL letter from the four Catholic bishops to the lay-Catholics of England. London: Henry Hills, 1688. 4°

Wing P 675.

T.515

2764

PATRICK (John)

A full view of the doctrines and practices of the ancient church relating to the Eucharist... Being a sufficient confutation of Consensus veterum, Nubes testium, and other late collections of the fathers, pretending the contrary... [Anon.] London, for Richard Chiswell, 1688. 4°

Wing P 729.

T.498

2765

PAYNE (William) *D.D.*

A discourse of the sacrifice of the mass. [Anon.] London, for Brabazon Aylmer, 1688. 4°

Wing P 901.
2 copies.

T.498 T.144

2766

PENN (William)

The great and popular objection against the repeal of the penal laws & tests briefly stated and consider'd and which may serve for answer to several late pamphlets upon that subject. By a friend to liberty for liberties sake. London, Andrew Sowle, 1688. 4°

Wing P 1298.

T.236

2767

PHILLIPS (John)

Sam. Ld. Bp. of Oxon, his celebrated reasons for abrogating the test, and notions of idolatry, answered by Samuel, Arch-deacon of Canterbury... London, printed in the year, 1688. 4°

Wing P 2099.

T.565

2768

A PLAIN account of the persecution, now laid to the charge of the Church of England. [London, 1688.] 4°

Wing P 2339.

T.517

2769

A PLAIN and familiar discourse concerning government. Wherein it is debated, whether monarchy or a common-wealth be best for the people. [London, 1688.] 4°

Wing P 2343.

T.277

2770

POPISH treaties not to be rely'd on: in a letter from a gentleman at York, to his friend in the Prince of Orange's camp. Addressed to all members of the next Parliament. [London, 1688?]. 4°

Wing P 2960.
2 copies.

T.565

2771

POPPLE (*Sir* William)

A letter to Mr. Penn, with his answer. [Anon.] London, T. Sowle, [1688]. 8°

Wing P 2963.

T.444

2772

POPPLE (*Sir* William)

A letter to Mr. Penn, with his answer. [Anon.] [London, 1688.] 4°

Wing P 2964.

T.79

2773

The PRIMITIVE rule of reformation according to the first liturgy of K. Edward VI. 1549. Containing an extract of the same, so far as it is popishly affected ... London, Mary Thompson, 1688. 4°

Wing P 3472.
2 copies.

T.515 T.63

2774

PULTON (Andrew)

Some reflections upon the author [i.e. William Wake] and licenser [i.e. William Needham] of a scandalous pamphlet; called, The missioners arts discover'd. With the reply of A. Pulton to a challenge made him in a letter prefix'd to the said pamphlet... London, Mary Thompson for the author, and are to be sold by Matthew Turner, and John Lane, 1688. 4°

Wing P 4208.

T.515

2775

R. (J.)

Religio laici, or a lay-mans faith, touching the supream head and infallible guide of the Church. In two letters to a friend in the country. By J. R... London, for John Newton, 1688. 4°

Wing R 30.

T.185

2776

The REASONABLENESS of the Church of Englands test, and justness, of her reformation, asserted; in answer to the Bishop of Oxon's fallacious, reasons, and precarious assertions against it... Printed in the year, 1688. 4°

Wing R 463.

T.565

2777

A REPLY to an Answer to the City minister's letter from his country friend. London, for W.M., 1688. 4°

Wing R 1058.
The final leaf is imperfect.

T.264

2778

RIDLEY (Nicholas) *Bishop of London.*

An account of a disputation at Oxford, anno. Dom. 1554. With a treatise of the blessed sacrament: both written by Bishop Ridley, martyr. To which is added a letter written by Mr. John Bradford ... [Edited by Gilbert Ironside.] Oxford, printed at the Theater, anno Dom. 1688. 2 parts. 4°

Wing R 1451.

T.140

2779

RIDLEY (Nicholas) *Bishop of London.*

A brief declaration of the Lords Supper, written by Dr. Nicholas Ridley, Bishop of London, during his imprisonment... London: For Ric. Chiswell, 1688. 4°

Wing R 1452.

T.517

2780

RIDLEY (Nicholas) *Bishop of London.*

The way to peace amongst all protestants: being a letter of reconciliation sent by Bp. Ridley to Bp. Hooper, with some observations upon it. London: for Richard Baldwin, 1688. 4°

Wing R 1453.
2 copies.

T.330 T.185

2781

S.(R.)

A letter to a person of quality, occasion'd by the news of the ensuing Parliament. [London, 1688?] 4°

Wing S 133.
2 copies.

T.565

2782

SABRAN (Lewis)

An answer to Dr. Sherlock's Preservative against popery. Shewing, that protestancy cannot be defended, nor Catholic faith opposed, but by principles which make void all reason, faith, fathers, councils, scripture, moral honesty. [Anon.] London: Henry Hills, 1688. 4°

Wing S 214.

T.515

2783

SABRAN (Lewis)

The challenge of R.F. Lewis Sabran, of the Society of Jesus, made out against the historical discourse [by Edward Gee] concerning invocation of saints. The first part. London, Henry Hills, 1688. 4°

Wing S 215.

T.515

2784

SABRAN (Lewis)

Dr. Sherlock's Preservative considered ... In two letters of F. Lewis Sabran of the Society of Jesus. London, Henry Hills, 1688. 4°

Wing S 217.

T.185

785

SABRAN (Lewis)

A letter to Dr. William Needham, in answer to the
Third letter [by Edward Gee] by him licensed written
to Father Lewis Sabran... Wherein the said letter is
examined and confuted. London, Henry Hills, 1688.
4°

Wing S 219.

T.515

786

SAVILE (George) *Marquess of Halifax.*

The anatomy of an equivalent. [Anon.]
[London, 1688.] 4°

Wing H 291.
3 copies.

T.199 T.565

787

SAVILE (George) *Marquess of Halifax.*

The character of a trimmer. His opinion of I. The
laws and government. II. Protestant religion.
III. The papists. IV. Foreign affairs. By the
Honourable Sir W. C. London, printed in the year,
1688. 4°

Wing H 296.
2 copies.

T.332 T.201

788

SAVILE (George) *Marquess of Halifax.*

A letter from a clergy-man in the city, to his friend
in the country, containing his reasons for not
reading the declaration. [Anon.] [London, 1688.]
4°

Wing H 308.
5 copies.

T.509 T.137

2789

SAYWELL (William)

The reformation of the Church of England justified,
according to the canons of the Council of Nice ...
Being an answer to a paper reprinted at Oxford,
called the Schisme of the Church of England
demonstrated ... [by John Sergeant] ... [Anon.]
Cambridge, John Hayes: for Edward Hall. And are to
be sold by Luke Meredith, 1688. 33pp. 4°

Wing S 803.
3 copies.

T.393 T.185 T.140

2790

SAYWELL (William)

The reformation of the Church of England justified,
according to the canons of the Council of Nice ...
Being an answer to apaper reprinted at Oxford, called
the Schism of the Church of England demonstrated
... [by John Sergeant] ... Cambridge, John Hayes:
for Edward Hall. And are to be sold by Luke
Meredith, 1688. 29pp. 4°

Wing S 804.

T.24

2791

SCOTT (John)

A sermon preach'd at the funeral of Sir John
Buckworth, at the parish-church of St. Peter's le
Poor in Broadstreet, December 29. 1687. London, for
Walter Kettilby; and Thomas Horne, 1688. 4°

Wing S 2072.

T.618

2792

A SECOND collection of papers relating to the
present juncture of affairs in England ... Printed
in the year, 1688. 4°

Wing S 2264.

T.137

2793

SERGEANT (John)

The fourth Catholick letter in answer to Dr.
Stillingfleet's sermon, preach't at Guild-hall ...
entituled, Scripture & tradition compared ...
London, Matthew Turner, 1688. 4°

Wing S 2569.
2 copies.

T.184 T.63

2794

SERGEANT (John)

The schism of the Church of England &c. demonstrated
in four arguments. Formerly propos'd to Dr. Gunning
and Dr. Pearson ... by two Catholick disputants,
in a celebrated conference upon that point. [Anon.]
Oxon, Henry Cruttenden, 1688. 4°

Wing S 2591.

T.140

2795

The SEVERAL declarations, together with the several
depositions made in Council on Monday, the 22d of
October, 1688. Concerning the birth of the Prince
of Wales... London: printed, and sold by the
booksellers of London and Westminster, [1688?]
40pp. 8°

Not in Wing. cf. S2760.

T.413

2796

SHADWELL (Thomas)

The squire of Alsatia. A comedy, as it is acted
by their Majesty's servants... London, for
James Knapton, 1688. 4°

Wing S 2874.

T.502

2797

SHERLOCK (William)

An answer to a discourse intituled, Papists protesting against Protestant-Popery [by John Gother];
being a vindication of Papists not misrepresented by
Protestants... [Anon.] 2nd ed. London: for
John Amery, and William Rogers, 1688. 4°

Wing S 3260.

T.760

2798

SHERLOCK (William)

A discourse concerning the nature, únity, and
communion of the Catholick Church. Wherein most of
the controversies relating to the Church, are briefly
and plainly stated. Part I. London: for William
Rogers, 1688. 4°

Wing S 3291.

T.744

2799

SHERLOCK (William)

A letter to a member of the convention. [Anon.]
[London, 1688?] 4°

Wing S 3298.

T.565

2800

SHERLOCK (William)

A preservative against popery: being some plain
directions to unlearned protestants, how to dispute
with Romish priests, The first part, London: for
William Rogers, 1688. 4°

Wing S 3326.
2 copies.

T.286 T.178

2801

SHERLOCK (William)

A preservative against popery: being some plain
directions to unlearned protestants, how to dispute
with Romish priests. The first part. 5th ed.
London: for William Rogers, 1688. 4°

Wing S 3330.

T.185

2802

SHERLOCK (William)

The second part of the preservative against popery:
shewing how contrary popery is to the true ends of
the Christian religion ... London: for William
Rogers, 1688. 4°

Wing S 3342.

T.178

2803

SHERLOCK (William)

The second part of the preservative against popery:
shewing how contrary popery is to the true ends of
the Christian religion ... 2nd ed. London: for
William Rogers, 1688. 4°

Wing S 3343.
2 copies.

T.265 T.185

2804

SHERLOCK (William)

A vindication of both parts of the Preservative
against popery: in answer to the cavils of
Lewis Sabran, Jesuit. London: for William Rogers,
1688. 4°

Wing S 3370.
3 copies.

T.178 T.185 T.286

2805

SHERLOCK (William)

A vindication of some protestant principles of
Church-unity and Catholick-communion, from the
charge of agreement with the Church of Rome ...
London: for William Rogers, 1688. 4°

Wing S 3372.

T.180

2806

SMITH (Thomas) *of Magdalen College, Oxford.*

A pacifick discourse of the causes and remedies
of the differences about religion, which distract
the peace of Christendom. [Anon.] London, for Sam.
Smith, 1688. 4°

Wing S 4226.

T.604

2807

SOCIETY OF JESUS. *Collegium S.J. Coloniae.*

Sol in occasu, siue serenissimus et reuerendissimus
princeps Maximilianus Henricus Archi-episcopus
Colon ... M.DC.LXXXVIII. die 3.Junij Bonnae
mortuus ... Lessu funebri deploratus, a musis
Collegij Soc. Iesu Colon. Bonn. et Noues. Coloniae,
typis Petri Alstorff, [1688]. Fol.

T.810

2808

SOME reflections upon his Highness the Prince of
Oranges declaration. London, printed in the year,
1688. 4°

Wing S 4589.

T.511

2809

STILLINGFLEET (Edward) *Bishop of Worcester.*

The Council of Trent examin'd and disprov'd by
Catholick tradition. In the main points in
controversie between us and the Church of Rome...
Part I... 2nd ed. corrected. With an appendix
in answer to some late passages of J.W... Concerning
the prohibiting of scripture in vulgar languages.
London, for H. Mortlock, 1688. 4°

Wing S 5570.

T.786

2810

STILLINGFLEET (Edward) *Bishop of Worcester.*

A discourse concerning the nature and grounds of
the certainty of faith, in answer to J. S. his
Catholick letters. London: for Henry Mortlock,
1688. 4°

Wing S 5582.

T.178

2811

STILLINGFLEET (Edward) *Bishop of Worcester.*

Scripture and tradition compared; in a sermon
preached at Guild-hall chappel, Novemb. 27. 1687.
London, for Henry Mortlock, 1688. 4°

Wing S 5632.

T.756

2812

TENISON (Thomas) *Archbishop of Canterbury.*

A defence of Dr. Tenison's Sermon of discretion in
giving alms. Written in a letter to the author
[i.e. John Williams] of the Apology for the pulpits.
[London, 1688.] 4°

Wing T 693.

T.760

2813

TENISON (Thomas) *Archbishop of Canterbury.*

Popery not founded on scripture: or, The texts which
papists cite out of the Bible, for the proof of the
points of their religion, examin'd, and shew'd to be
alledged without ground. [The introduction by Thomas
Tenison.] London; for Richard Chiswell, 1688. 4°

Wing T 707.
Incomplete.

T.606

2814

The TEXTS examined which papists cite out of the Bible for the proof of their doctrine of the sacrifice of the Mass. London, J. D. for Richard Chiswel, 1688. 4°

Wing T 826.
Part II, pp. 397-432 only.

T.140

2815

THIRTY plain, but sound reasons why protestants dissent from popery... London, printed in the year 1688. 4°

Wing T 918.

T.236

2816

The TRUE test of the Jesuits: or, The spirit of that society, disloyal to God, their king, and neighbour. Amsterdam: printed in the year 1688. 4°

Wing T 3122.

T.406

2817

TULLY (George)

An answer to A discourse [by Abraham Woodhead] concerning the celibacy of the clergy, printed at Oxford... [Anon.] Oxford, printed at the Theater, for Richard Chiswell, 1688. 4°

Wing T 3235.

T.743

2818

VOX cleri pro rege: or the rights of the imperial soveraignty of the crown of England vindicated. In reply to a late pamphlet pretending to answer a book, entituled the Judgment and doctrine of the clergy ... In a letter to a friend ... [London], printed in the year 1688. 4°

Wing V 715.
3 copies.

T.509   T.199

2819

WAKE (William) *Archbishop of Canterbury.*

A defence of the Exposition of the doctrine of the Church of England, against the exceptions of Monsieur de Meaux [Bossuet], and his vindicator... 2nd ed., corrected. [Anon.] London: for Richard Chiswell, 1688. 4°

Ch.Ch.W236+
Signature of S. Jebb.

T.276

2820

WAKE (William) *Archbishop of Canterbury.*

A discourse concerning the nature of idolatry: in which a late author's true and onely notion of idolatry is considered and confuted... [Anon.] London: for William Rogers, 1688. 4°

Wing W 239.

T.178

2821

WHITBY (Daniel)

A demonstration that the Church of Rome, and her councils have erred... [Anon.] London, J. Leake, and are to be sold by Randal Taylor, 1688. 4°

Wing W 1721.

T.140

2822

WILLIAM III, *King of England.*

The Prince of Orange his declaration: shewing the reasons why he invades England. With a short preface, and some modest remarks on it. London: Randal Taylor, 1688. 4°

Wing W 2331.
2 copies.

T.511   T.66

2823

WILLIAM III, *King of England.*

The Prince of Orange his third declaration. [London, 1688?] 4°

Wing W 2487.
2 copies.

T.511   T.66

2824

WILLIAMS (Daniel) *D.D.*

The Kingdom of God in power. A sermon preached before the... Lord Mayor of the city of London; at Grocers-hall, November the 20th, 1687. London: for J. Robinson, and Tho. Cockerill, 1688. 4°

Wing W 2652.

T.765

2825

WILLIAMS (John) *Bishop of Chichester.*

An answer to the address presented to the ministers of the Church of England. [Anon.] London: for Ric. Chiswell, 1688. 4°

Wing W 2680.
2 copies.

T.178   T.236

2826

WILLIAMS (John) *Bishop of Chichester.*

An apology for the pulpits: being in answer to a late book, intituled, Good advice to the pulpits. Together with an appendix, containing a defence of Dr. Tenison's sermon about alms ... [Anon.] London: for Dorman Newman, 1688. 2 parts. 4°

Wing W 2681.
2 copies.

T.760   T.184

2827

WILLIAMS (John) *Bishop of Chichester.*

Pulpit-popery, true popery: being an answer to a book intituled, Pulpit-sayings [by John Gother]: and in vindication of the Apology for the pulpits, and the stater of the controversie against the representer. [Anon.] London, Randall Taylor, 1688. 4°

Wing W 2721.

T.760

2828

WITT (Cornelius de)

A letter from Holland, touching liberty of conscience, &c. [Signed C.D.W.] Printed with allowance, for E.R., 1688. 4°

Wing W 3223.

T.509

2829

YOUNG (Edward) *Dean of Salisbury.*

A sermon exhorting to union in religion. Preach'd at Bow-church, May 20th... London, for Walter Kettilby, 1688. 4°

Wing Y 64.

T.756

1689

2830

The ADDRESS of John Dryden, laureat, to his Highness the Prince of Orange. [Attributed to Thomas Shadwell.] London, printed in the year, 1689. 4°

Not in Wing, cf. A 544 A.

T.407

2831

B. (A.)

Gloria Britannica; or, The boast of the British seas. Containing a true and full account of the Royal Navy of England ... Carefully collected and digested by a true lover of the seamen, and of long experience in the practices of the Navy and Admiralty. London: for Thomas Howkins, 1689. 4°

Wing B7.

T.328

2832

B.(A.)

Some remarks upon government, and particularly upon the establishment of the English monarchy relating to this present juncture. In two letters, written by, and to a member of the great convention, holden at Westminster the 22d. of January, 1688/9. [The first letter signed A.B., the answer signed N.T.] [London, 1689.] 4°

Wing B 31.
2 copies.

T.197   T.511

2833

BEHN (Aphra)

A congratulatory poem to her sacred Majesty Queen Mary, upon her arrival in England. London, R.E. for R. Bentley, and W. Canning, 1689. Fol.

Wing B 1723.

T.699

2834

BEHN (Aphra)

A pindaric poem to the Reverend Doctor Burnet, on the honour he did me of enquiring after me and my muse. London, for R. Bentley, and are to be sold by Richard Baldwin, 1689. 4°

Wing B 1754.

T.407

2835

BENNET (Joseph)

A true and impartial account of the most material passages in Ireland since December 1688. With a particular relation of the forces of Londonderry ... [Anon.] London: for John Amery, 1689. 4°

Wing B 1885 A.

T.328

2836

BETTER late than never. [No imprint, 1689?] 4°

Wing B 2083.

T.510

2837

BEVERIDGE (William) *Bishop of St. Asaph.*

Concio ad synodum ab episcopis & clero provinciae Cantuariensis celebratam ... Londini, excudebat S. Roycroft, sumptibus Roberti Clavell, 1689. 4°

Wing B 2091.
2 copies.

T.494   T.273

2838

BIRCH (Peter)

A sermon preached before the honourable House of Commons, November 5, 1689. In the Savoy: E. Jones; and are to be sold by W. Nott, and R. Taylor, 1689. 4°

Wing B 2938.

T.173

2839

A BREVIATE of the state of Scotland in its government, supream courts, officers of state... burroughs royal, and free corporations.. London, for Ric. Chiswell, 1689. Fol.

Wing B 4415.

T.531

2840

BURNET (Gilbert) *Bishop of Salisbury.*

An enquiry into the present state of affairs: and in particular, whether we owe allegiance to the King in these circumstances? And whether we are bound to treat with him, and call him back again, or not? [Anon.] London: for John Starkey; and Ric. Chiswell, 1689. 4°

Wing B 5811.

T.328

2841

BURNET (Gilbert) *Bishop of Salisbury.*

An exhortation to peace and union, in a sermon preached at St. Lawrence-Jury, on Tuesday the 26th of Novemb. 1689. London, for Richard Chiswell, 1689. 4°

Wing B 5788.

T.173

2842

BURNET (Gilbert) *Bishop of Salisbury.*

A letter to Mr. Thevenot, containing a censure of Mr. Le Grand's history of King Henry the Eighths divorce, to which is added a censure of Mr.de Meaux's history of the variations of the protestant churches... London, for John Starkey and Richard Chiswell, 1689. 4°

Wing B 5823.
Wanting all before p.7.

T.743

2843

BURNET (Gilbert) *Bishop of Salisbury*.

A pastoral letter writ by... Gilbert, Lord Bishop
of Sarum, to the clergy of his diocess, concerning
the oaths of allegiance and supremacy to K. William
and Q. Mary. London: for J. Starkey; and Ric.
Chiswell, 1689. 4°

Wing B 5842.

T.754

2844

BURNET (Gilbert) *Bishop of Salisbury*.

The royal martyr lamented, in a sermon preached
at the Savoy, on King Charles the Martyr's day,
1674/5. London, for Luke Meredith, 1689. 4°

Wing B 5870.

T.514

2845

BURNET (Gilbert) *Bishop of Salisbury*.

A sermon preached at the coronation of William III.
and Mary II... in the abby-church of Westminster,
April II. 1689. London: for J. Starkey; and
Ric. Chiswell, 1689. 4°

Wing B 5888.

T.756

2846

BURNET (Gilbert) *Bishop of Salisbury*.

A sermon preached before the House of Commons, on
the 31st of January, 1688. Being the thanksgiving-
day for the deliverance of this Kingdom from popery
and arbitrary power... London: for John Starkey;
and Ric. Chiswell, 1689. 4°

Wing B 5885.
2 copies.

T.742 T.756

2847

BURNET (Gilbert) *Bishop of Salisbury*.

A sermon preached before the House of Peers in the
Abbey of Westminster, on the 5th. of November 1689
... London, for Ric. Chiswel, 1689. 4°

Wing B 5889.

T.173

2848

BURNET (Gilbert) *Bishop of Salisbury*.

A sermon preached in the chappel of St. James's,
before his Highness the Prince of Orange, the
23d of December, 1688. London; for Richard
Chiswell, 1689. 4°

Wing B 5881.
2 copies.

T.494   T.756

2849

BURNET (Gilbert) *Bishop of Salisbury*.

Six papers. To which is added, I. An apology for
the Church of England, &c. and II. An enquiry into
the measures of submission to the supream authority,
&c. London; printed in the year 1689. 3 parts.
4°

Wing B 5913.

T.744

2850

BURNET (Gilbert) *Bishop of Salisbury*.

Subjection for conscience-sake asserted: in a
sermon preached at Covent-Garden-church,
December the sixth, 1674. London, for Luke
Meredith, 1689. 4°

Wing B 5929.

T.514

2851

BURNET (Gilbert) *Bishop of Salisbury*.

A word to the wavering: or an answer to the enquiry
into the present state of affairs: whether we owe
allegiance to the king in these circumstances? &c.
With a postscript of subjection to the higher powers;
by Dr. G. B. London, printed in the year, 1689. 4°

Wing B 5941.

T.199

2852

C.

A friendly conference concerning the new oath of
allegiance to K. William and Q. Mary wherein the
objections against taking the oaths are impartially
examined, and the reasons of obedience confirm'd
from the writings of... Bishop Sanderson, and
proved to agree to the principles of the Church of
England and the laws of the land. By a divine of
that Church. London, for Samuel Smith, 1689. 4°

Wing C 1 A.
Wanting the first gathering.

T.513

2853

CAMP (Abraham)

Aquila grandis magnarum alarum ... Hoc est ... Maria
Anna Iosepha Archidux Austriae ... Ioannis Wilhelmi
Iosephi, lectissima conjux ... Funebri panegyri
repraesentata à R. P. Abrahamo Camp. Cöllen, Arnold
Metternich, 1689. Fol.

T.810

2854

The CHARITY and loyalty of some of our clergy. In
a short view of Dr. M[eggott]'s sermon before their
Majesties at Hampton-Court, July the 14th, 1689...
London,for Richard Janeway, 1689. 4°

Wing C 2068.

T.173

2855

CHILD (*Sir* Josiah)

A discourse concerning trade, and that in
particular of the East-Indies, wherein several
weighty propositions are fully discussed, and the
state of the East-India Company is faithfully
stated. [Anon.] London, Andrew Sowle, 1689. 4°

Wing C 3854.

T.324

2856

CHILD (*Sir* Josiah)

A supplement, 1689. to a former treatise, concerning
the East-India trade, printed 1681. [Anon.]
[London, 1689.] 4°

Wing C 3865.

T.324

2857

CHURCH OF ENGLAND.

Additional prayers to be used together with those
appointed in the service for the fifth of November.
London, Charles Bill and Thomas Newcomb, 1689. 4°

Not in Wing.
4 copies.

T.461

2858

CHURCH OF ENGLAND.

A form of prayer to be used on Wednesday the
twelfth day of March... being the fast-day appointed
... for supplicating almighty God for the pardon
of our sins, and for imploring his blessing and
protection in the preservation of his Majesties sacred
person, and the prosperity of his arms in Ireland...
London, Charles Bill and Thomas Newcomb, 1689. 4°

Wing C 4150.
2 copies.

T.461 T.463

2859

CHURCH OF ENGLAND.

A form of prayer to be used on Wednesday the fifth
day of June... being the fast day appointed... to
implore the blessing of almighty God upon their
Majesties forces by sea and land, and success in
the war now declared against the French King. London,
Charles Bill, and Thomas Newcomb, 1689. 4°

Wing C 4151.
2 copies.

T.461 T.463

2860

CLEVELAND (John)

Majestas intemerata. Or, The immortality of the
king ... [Anon.] Printed in the year 1689. 4°

Wing C 4680.
2 copies.

T.199 T.328

2861

COLLIER (Jeremy)

Animadversions upon the modern explanation of
II Hen. 7. cap. I. or, A king de facto. [Anon.]
[London, 1689.] 4°

Wing C 5241.
2 copies.

T.328   T. 64

2862

COLLIER (Jeremy)

The desertion discuss'd. In a letter to a country
gentleman. [Anon.] [No imprint, 1689.] 4°

Wing C 5249.

T.328

2863

COLLIER (Jeremy)

Vindiciae juris regii: or, Remarques upon a paper,
entituled, An enquiry into the measures, of
submission to the supream authority [by Gilbert
Burnet]. [Anon.] London, printed in the year
1689. 4°

Wing C 5267.
4 copies.

T.511   T.328 T.199   T. 64

2864

COMBER (Thomas)

A letter to a bishop concerning the present
settlement, and the new oaths. [Anon.]
London: for Robert Clavel, 1689. 4°

Wing C 5476.

T.513

2865

A CONGRATULATORY poem to his Royal Highness the
Prince of Orange, on his happy arrival. London,
for Anthony Baskervile, 1689. 4°

Not in Wing.

T.407

2866

COOKE (Shadrach)

An exhortation to firmness and constancy in true
religion. In a sermon preached at St. Mary
Islington, Feb. 2. 1689/90 ... London, J. Redmayne,
1689. 4°

Wing C 6037.

T.173

2867

DILLINGHAM (William)

The mystery of iniquity anatomized ... London, for
Jonathan Robinson, 1689. 4°

Wing D 1483.

T.173

2868

The DILUCIDATION of the late commotions of
Turkey ... Printed in Italian at Venice, and
translated in English by the author of the Monthly
account ... London, printed by J. B. and
publish'd by Randal Taylor, 1689. 4°

Wing D 1491.

T.328

2869

A DISCOURSE concerning the nature, power, and proper
effects of the present conventions in both kingdoms
called by the Prince of Orange. In a letter to a
friend. London: for J. L. and are to be sold by
Richard Baldwin, 1689. 4°

Wing D 1588.

T.197

2870

ENGLAND. *Parliament*.

Die Martis, 12° Februarii, 1688/9. The declaration
of the Lords spiritual and temporal, and Commons
assembled at Westminster. [London, 1689.] Fol.

cf. Wing E 1489.

T.694

2871

ENGLAND. *Parliament.*

The Lords & Commons reasons and justifications for
the deprivation and deposal of James II. from the
imperial throne of England ... London, for
Thomas Tilliar, 1689. 4°

Wing E 1641 (=L 3060 A)

T.328

2872

EYRE (Elizabeth)

A letter from a person of quality in the North to
a friend in London, concerning Bishop Lake's
late declaration of his dying in the belief of
the doctrine of passive obedience, as the
distinguishing character of the Church of England.
[Anon.] London, for Awnsham Churchill, 1689. 4°

Wing E 3940.

T.260

2873

FERGUSON (Robert)

A brief justification of the Prince of Orange's
descent into England, and of the Kingdoms late
recourse to arms ... [Anon.] London: for J. S. and
sold by Richard Baldwin, 1689. 4°

Wing F 732.

T.328

2874

FERGUSON (Robert)

A brief justification of the Prince of Orange's
descent into England, and of the kingdoms late
recourse to arms. With a modest disquisition of
what may become the wisdom and justice of the
ensuing Convention, in their disposal of the crown.
London: for J. S. and are to be sold by R. Baldwin,
1689. 4°

Wing F 733. 2 copies

T.197 T.199

2875

FERGUSON (Robert)

The late proceedings and votes of the Parliament
of Scotland; contained in an address delivered to
the King, signed by the plurality of the members
thereof, stated and vindicated ... [Anon.]
Glasgow, Andrew Hepburn, anno Dom. 1689. 4°

Wing F 728A.
2 copies, one with the misprint 'Parliamemt'.

T.60   T.328

2876

FERGUSON (Robert)

A representation of the threatning dangers, impending
over protestants in Great Britain, before the coming
of his Highness the Prince of Orange... [Anon.]
Printed in the year, 1689. 4°

Wing F 757.

T.744

2877

FLEETWOOD (William) *Bishop of Ely.*

A sermon preached before the University of Cambridge,
in Kings-College Chapel; on the 25th of March, 1689
... Cambridge, John Hayes; for William Graves, 1689.
4°

Wing F 1251.
3 copies.

T.771   T.618   T.173

2878

FOURTEEN papers ... London: Richard Baldwin, 1689.
4°

Wing F 1682.
Reprints of fourteen pamphlets, mostly published
in 1688.

T.332

2879

FOWLER (Edward) *Bishop of Gloucester.*

A vindication of the divines of the Church of
England, who have sworn allegiance to K. William
α Q. Mary, from the imputations of apostasy and
perjury, which are cast upon them upon that account,
in the now published History of passive obedience
[by Abednego Seller]. By one of those divines ...
London, for Brabazon Aylmer, 1689. 4°

Wing F 1728.

T.516

2880

A FREE conference concerning the present revolution
of affairs in England. London, R. Baldwyn, 1689.
4°

Wing F 2111.

T.197

2881

FULLWOOD (Francis)

Obedience due to the present King, notwithstanding
our oaths to the former. Written by a divine of
the Church of England. [Anon.] London, for
Awnsham Churchill, 1689. 4°

Wing F 2511.
2 copies.

T.260 T.328

2882

GEE (Edward) *the Younger.*

The catalogue of all the discourses published
against popery, during the reign of King James II.
by the members of the Church of England, and by
the non-conformists. With the names of the authors
of them. [Anon.] London: R. Baldwin, 1689. 4°

Wing G 454.

T.393

2883

GOODMAN (John)

The leaven of pharisaism and sadducism purged out.
A sermon preached before the court of aldermen and
city of London at their Guild-hall chappel on
Sunday Decemb. 16. 1688. London, S. Roycroft, for
Robert Clavel, 1688/9. 4°

Wing G 1110.

T.494

2884

GRASCOMBE (Samuel)

A letter to Dr. W. Payne. [Anon.] [London, 1689.]
4°

Wing G 1574.
Manuscript attribution to "Mr Spinckes" [i.e.
Nathaniel Spinckes].

T.60

2885

GROVE (Robert) *Bishop of Chichester.*

The protestant and popish way of interpreting
scripture, impartially compared. In answer to
Pax vobis, &c. [by John Gordon, or Evan Griffith].
[Anon.] London, for Walter Kettilby, 1689. 4°

Wing G 2155.

T.393

2886

HAMMOND (Henry)

Dr. Hammond's brief resolution of that grand case
of conscience, (necessary for these times)
concerning the allegiance due to a prince
ejected by force out of his kingdoms...
[London, 1689?] 4°

Wing H 517.
2 copies.

T.64   T.509

2887

HICKES (George)

A letter to the author of a late paper [by Edward
Fowler], entituled, A vindication of the divines
of the Church of England, &c. In defence of the
History of passive obedience [by Abednego Seller].
[Anon.] Printed in the year,1689. 4°

Wing H 1856.

T.516

2888

The HISTORY and transactions of the English nation:
more especially by their representatives assembled
in Parliament in the reign of King Charles ...
By a person of quality, and true lover of his
countrey. London, Richard Janeway, 1689. 4°

Wing H 2110.

T.531

2889

The HISTORY of the most illustrious William, Prince
of Orange: deduc'd from the first founders of the
ancient house of Nassau: together with the most
considerable actions of this present prince. 2nd
ed. Printed in the year 1689. 8°

Wing H 2171.

T.447

2890

The HISTORY of the plot anatomised: or, the late
sham fanatical-plot, briefly and plainly laid open
... In a letter to a friend ... London, for M. R.
in the year 1689. 4°

Wing H 2175.

T.137

2891

HOOPER (George) *Bishop of Bath and Wells.*

The parsons case under the present land tax,
recommended in a letter to a member of the House
of Commons. [Anon.] London, printed in the year
1689. 4°

Wing H 2704.

T.754

2892

HUNTON (Philip)

A treatise of monarchy: containing two parts.
1. Concerning monarchy in general. II. Concerning
this particular monarchy. Wherein all the main
questions occurrent in both, are stated, disputed
and determined. Done by an earnest desirer of
his countries peace. London: for, and sold by
Richard Baldwin, 1689. 4°

Wing H 3783.

T.277

2893

HUNTON (Philip)

A treatise of monarchy: containing two parts.
I. Concerning monarchy in general. II. Concerning
this particular monarchy. Also a vindication of the
said treatise. Done by an earnest desirer of his
countries peace. London, for E. Smith, and are
sold by Randal Taylor, 1689. 4°

Wing H 3783A.
2 copies.

T.199

2894

The INTREIGUES of the French King at Constantinople,
to embroil Christendom: discovered in several
dispatches past betwixt him and the late Grand
Seignior, Grand Vizier, and Count Teckily ...
London: for Dorman Newman, 1689. 4°

Wing I 279.
2 copies.

T.332   T.357

2895

IRELAND, *Parliament.*

An exact list of the lords spiritual & temporal,
who sate in the pretended Parliament at Dublin ...
on the 7th of May, 1689 ... London, T. B. and are
to be sold by Randal Taylor, 1689, 4°

Wing E 3657.

T. 11

2896

JANE (William)

A letter to a friend, containing some quaeries about
the new commission for making alterations in the
liturgy, canons, &c. of the Church of England.
[Anon.] [London, 1689.] 4°

Wing J 453.

T.327

2897

JEFFREYS (George) *Baron Jeffreys.*

The argument of the lord chief justice of the court
of King's Bench concerning the great case of
monopolies, between the East-India Company, plaintiff,
and Thomas Sandys, defendant ... London, Randal
Taylor, 1689. Fol.

Wing J 526.

T.531

2898

JOHNSON (Samuel) *Rector of Corringham.*

The opinion is this: that resistance may be used, in
case our religion and rights should be invaded.
[Anon.] London: for J. Watts, 1689. 4°

Wing J 836.

T.260

2899

JOHNSON (Samuel) *Rector of Corringham.*

Remarks upon Dr. Sherlock's book, intituled, The case of resistance of the supreme powers stated and resolved ... London: printed for the author, and are to be sold by Richard Baldwin, 1689. 8°

Wing J 839.
2 copies.

T.367   T.141

2900

JURIEU (Pierre)

Monsieur Jurieu's judgment upon the question of defending our religion by arms, with Reflections upon the affairs of England, in his ninth pastoral letter of the third year. Faithfully translated out of French. London: for John Lawrence, and are to be sold by Richard Baldwin, 1689. 4°

Wing J 1204.

T.315

2901

JURIEU (Pierre)

Seasonable advice to all protestants in Europe of what persuasion soever. For uniting and defending themselves against popish tyranny ... Done out of French. London, for R. Baldwin, 1689. 4°

Wing J 1213.

T.248

2902

KEN (Thomas) *Bishop of Bath and Wells.*

Lacrymae Ecclesiae Anglicanae: or, A serious and passionate address of the Church of England, to her sons, especially those of the clergy. Printed in the year, 1689. 4°

Wing K 350.

T.604

2903

KING William's toleration: being an explanation of that liberty of religion, which may be expected from his Majesty's declaration. With a bill for comprehension & indulgence, drawn up in order to an act of Parliament. London: for Robert Hayhurst, 1689. 4°

Wing K 580.

T.744

2904

L. (N.)

A letter from a minister in the country, to a member of the Convocation. London: for Richard Baldwin, 1689. 4°

Wing L 46.

T.327

2905

The LATE plot on the fleet, detected: with the Jacobites memorial to the French king: and an account of those gentlemen, who invited the French fleet to invade our English coasts, &c. [London, 1689.] 4°

Wing L 555.

T 510

2906

A LETTER from a clergy-man in the country, to a minister in the city, concerning ministers intermedling with state-affairs in their sermons & discourse. London: printed in the year 1689. 4°

Wing L 1368.

T.328

2907

A LETTER from a loyal member of the Church of England to a relenting abdicator ... London, printed in the year 1689. 4°

Wing L 1410.

T.511

2908

A LETTER to his Highness the Prince of Orange. London, for R.J., 1689. 4°

Wing L 1706.

T.328

2909

LETTRE de Geneve contenant une relation exacte au sujet des petits prophetes de Dauphiné. A Rotterdam, chez Abraham Acher, 1689. 4°

T.12

2910

LLOYD (William) *Bishop of Worcester.*

A sermon preached before their Majesties at Whitehall, on the fifth day of November, 1689 ... By the Bishop of St. Asaph ... London, for Robert Clavell, 1689. 4°

Wing L 2713.
2 copies.

T.771   T.173

2911

LOCKE (John)

A letter concerning toleration: humbly submitted, &c. [Anon.] London, for Awnsham Churchill, 1689. 4°

Wing L 2747.

T.604

2912

LONG (Thomas)

Reflections upon a late book [by Samuel Masters] entituled, The case of allegiance consider'd: Wherein is shewn, that the Church of England's doctrine of non-resistance and passive obedience, is not inconsistent with taking the new oaths to their present Majesties. [Anon.] London: for Richard Baldwin, 1689. 4°

Wing L 2979.

T.513

2913

M. (M.)

A letter from the member of Parliament, in answer to the Letter of the divine, concerning the Bill for uniting protestants. [London, 1689?] 4°

Wing M 56.
2 copies.

T.517   T.744

2914

MACKENZIE (*Sir* George)

A memorial for his Highness the Prince of Orange, in relation to the affairs of Scotland: together with the address of the presbyterian-party in that kingdom to his Highness; and some observations on that address. By two persons of quality ... London, for Randal Taylor, 1689. 4°

Wing M 169.

T.511

2915

MANLEY (Thomas)

The present state of Europe briefly examined and found languishing, occasioned by the greatness of the French monarchy: for cure whereof a remedy ... is humbly proposed to ... William Henry Prince of Orange, and to the great convention ... London: for Richard Baldwin, 1689. 4°

Wing M 445.

T.328

2916

MASTERS (Samuel)

The case of allegiance in our present circumstances consider'd. In a letter from a minister in the city, to a minister in the country... [Anon.] London: for Ric. Chiswell, 1689. 4°

Wing M 1067.

T.513

2917

MAURICE (Henry)

The lawfulness of taking the new oaths asserted. [Anon.] London, for J. Mills, and are to be sold by Randal Taylor, 1689. 4°

Wing M 1364.
2 copies.

T.315   T.328

2918

MAURICE (Henry)

A letter out of the country, to a member of this present parliament: occasioned by a late letter to a member of the House of Commons, concerning the bishops lately in the Tower, and now under suspension. [Anon.] London, for Awnsham Churchill, 1689. 4°

Wing M 1365.
2 copies.

T.260   T.328

2919

MAURICE (Henry)

A letter to a member of the House of Commons, concerning the bishops lately in the Tower, and now under suspension. [Anon.] London: printed in the year, 1689. 4°

Wing M 1366.

T.260

2920

MEGGOTT (Richard)

A sermon preached before the King and Queen at Hampton-Court, July 14th. 1689. London, for Tho. Bennet, 1689. 4°

Wing M 1628.
2 copies.

T.618   T.173

2921

A MODEST examination of the new oath of allegiance. By a divine of the Church of England. London, for Randal Taylor, 1689. 4°

Wing M 2363.

T.328

2922

The MURMURERS. A poem... London, for R. Baldwin 1689. Fol.

Wing M 3103.
Signature of Edward Garrett, 1722.

T.699

2923

N.(N.)

A letter to a member of Parliament, in favour of the Bill for uniting protestants. London: Randal Taylor, 1689. 4°

Wing N 43.

T.517

2924

The NECESSITY of parliaments: with seasonable directions for the more regular election of parliament-men ... By a true protestant, and English man. London, Rich. Janeway, 1689. 4°

cf. Wing N 371.

T.328

2925

PATRICK (Symon) *Bishop of Ely.*

A sermon preached at St. Paul's Covent Garden on the day of thanksgiving Jan. XXXI. 1688... London, for Richard Bentley, 1689. 4°

Wing P 847.
3 copies.

T.173   T.339   T.756

2926

PATRICK (Symon) *Bishop of Ely.*

A sermon preached at St. Paul's Covent-Garden, on the first Sunday in Lent; being a second part of the sermon preached before the Prince of Orange. London, for Richard Chiswell, 1689. 4°

Wing P 851.

T.494

2927

PATRICK (Symon) *Bishop of Ely.*

A sermon preach'd before the Queen at Whitehall, March 1. 1688/9. London, for Richard Chiswell, 1689. 4°

Wing P 848.
2 copies.

T.494   T.756

2928

PATRICK (Symon) *Bishop of Ely.*

A sermon preached in the chappel of St. James's, before his Highness the Prince of Orange, the 20th of January, 1688. London: for Richard Chiswell, 1689. 4°

Wing P 846
2 copies.

T.494   T.756

2929

PATRICK (Symon) *Bishop of Ely.*

Two sermons; one against murmuring, the other against censuring, preached at St. Paul's Covent-Garden.   London, for Richard Chiswell, 1689.   4°

Wing P 863.

T.494

2930

PERSE (William)

A sermon preached in the cathedral of St. Peters in York, on the fifth day of Novemb. 1689.   York, John Bulkley for Francis Hildyard, 1689.   4°

Wing P 1654.

T.742

2931

A POLITICAL conference between Aulicus, a courtier; Demas, a country-man; and Civicus, a citizen: clearing the original of civil government, the powers and duties of soveraigns and subjects ...   London: for J. L. and are to be sold by Richard Baldwin, 1689.   4°

Wing P 2765.
2 copies.

T.277   T.197

2932

The PRESENT conjuncture: in a dialogue between a church-man and a dissenter...   London, Randal Taylor, 1689.   4°

Wing P 3239.

T.744

2933

The PRESENT policies of France, and the maxims of Lewis XIV. plainly laid open; detecting the management of his intrigues against the princes and states of Europe.   London, printed in the year 1689.   4°

Wing P 3249.

T.332

2934

PRO populo adversus tyrannos: or the sovereign right and power of the people over tyrants, clearly stated, and plainly proved...   By a true protestant English-man, and well-wisher to posterity.   London, printed in the year, 1689.   4°

Wing M 2164 (attributed to John Milton).
3 copies.

T.277   T.328   T.509

2935

The PROCEEDINGS of the present parliament justified by the opinion of the most judicious and learned Hugo Grotius; with considerations thereupon ...   By a lover of the peace of his country.   London: Randal Taylor, 1689.   4°

Wing G 2124.

T.328

2936

R.(J.)

Vox laici: or, The layman's opinion touching the making alterations in our establish'd liturgy, in answer to a letter from a member of the Convocation.   With some remarks on the (pretended) answer [by William Payne] of Vox Clerici.   London, printed, and are to be sold by the booksellers of London and Westminster, 1689.   4°

Wing R 36.

T.327

2937

REFLECTIONS upon our late and present proceedings in England.   London: printed in the year 1689.   4°

Wing R 722.

T.509

2938

The RELATION of the rejoycings made in Rome for the birth of the most serene Prince of Wales, only son of James the second...   Faithfully translated into English, from the Italian impression, as it was printed at Rome and Genoa.   London, for Randal Taylor, 1689.   4°

Wing R 863.

T.315

2939

A REMONSTRANCE and protestation of all the good protestants of this Kingdom, against deposing their lawful sovereign King James II.   With reflections thereupon...   London: Randall Taylor, 1689.   4°

Wing R 970.

T.511

2940

RESBURY (Nathanael)

A sermon preach'd before the Right Honourable the Lord Mayor, and court of aldermen, in Guild-hall chappel.   On Sunday the xxi. of October. 1688.   London, for W. Kettilby, 1689.   4°

Wing R 1131.

T.756

2941

ROYSE (George)

A sermon preached before the Right Honourable the Lord Mayor, and the court of aldermen, at Guild-hall-chapel upon Good-Friday the 29th of March, 1689.   London: for Samuel Crouch, 1689.   4°

Wing R 2162.

T.756

2942

SCOTT (John)

A sermon preached at Fulham, on Sunday, Oct. 13. 1689,.at the consecration of ... Edward Lord Bishop of Worcester, Simon Lord Bishop of Chichester, & Gilbert Lord Bishop of Bristol.   London, for Walter Kettilby, and Thomas Horne, 1689 .   4°

Wing S 2074.
4 copies.

T.757   T.618   T.732   T.73

2943

SCOTT (John)

A sermon preached at the funeral of Sir John Chapman, late Lord Mayor of London at St. Lawrence's Church, March 27. 1689.   London, for Walter Kettilby, and Thomas Horne, 1689.   4°

Wing S 2073.
3 copies.

T.618   T.93   T.132

2944

SEASONABLE considerations.   Printed in the year 1689.   4°

Wing S 2224.
2 copies.

T.517   T.60

2945

The SECOND and last collection of the dying speeches, letters and prayers, &c. of those eminent protestants who suffered in the west of England, (and elsewhere), under the cruel sentence of the late ... Lord Chief Justice Jefferys ...   London, for John Dunton; and are to be sold by R. Janeway, 1689.   4°

Wing S 2256.

T.137

2946

SELDEN (John)

Table-talk: being the discourses of John Selden Esq; or his sence of various matters of weight and high consequence relating especially to religion and state ...   London, for E. Smith, 1689.   4°

Wing S 2437.

T.328

2947

SELLER (Abednego)

The history of passive obedience since the Reformation.   [Anon.]   Amsterdam: for Theodore Johnson, 1689.   4°

Wing S 2453.
5 copies.

T.66   T.328   T.509   T.516

2948

SELLER (Abednego)

A plain answer to a popish-priest, questioning the orders of the Church of England.   Drawn up for the satisfaction of his parishioners, by a minister of that Church.   2nd ed.   To which is now annext, An answer to the Oxford animadverter's reflections upon it.   By the same author.   London: for Samuel Smith, 1689.   4°

Wing S 2459.

T.393

2949

SEVEN papers, viz.   I. The grounds and reasons of the laws against popery.   II. The character of popery.   III. A letter to the author of the Dutch design anatomized ...   London, R. Baldwin, 1689.   4°

Wing S 2738.

T.197

2950

SHAKESPEARE (William)

The history of King Lear, acted at the Queen's theatre.   Reviv'd with alterations.   By N. Tate.   London, for R. Bentley, and M. Magnes, 1689.   4°

Wing S 2919.
Wanting the first gathering and the final leaf; all supplied in a near-contemporary hand.

T.564

2951

SHERLOCK (William)

Observations upon Mr. Johnson's Remarks upon Dr. Sherlock's book of non-resistance...   [Anon.]   London, printed in the year, 1689.   4°

Wing S 3305.

T.513

2952

SHERLOCK (William)

A sermon preached before the Right Honourable the Lord Mayor and aldermen of the city of London, at Guild-hall-chappel, on Sunday, Nov. 4. 1688.   London: for William Rogers, 1689.   4°

Wing S 3348.
2 copies.

T.494   T.756

2953

SHOWER (*Sir* Bartholomew)

The magistracy and government of England vindicated: or, A justification of the English method of proceedings against criminals, by way of answer to the defence [by Sir Robert Atkyns] of the late Lord Russel's innocence, &c.   [Anon.]   London, printed in the year 1689.   4°

Wing S 3653.
2 copies.

T.277   T.64

2954

SHOWER (*Sir* Bartholomew)

A second vindication of the magistracy and government of England, by way of answer to the several replies, &c.   [Anon.]   [London, 1689?]   4°

Wing S 3658.

T.64

2955

SHOWER (*Sir* Bartholomew)

The third and last part of the magistracy and governmentof England vindicated: with reasons for a general act of indemnity, &c.   [Anon.]   [London, 1689?]   4°

Wing S 3660.

T.64

2956

A SIXTH collection of papers relating to the present juncture of affairs in England ...   London, Richard Janeway, 1689.   4°

Wing S 3930.

T.137

2957

SMYTH (Edward) *Bishop of Down and Connor.*

A sermon preached before the right worshipful the deputy-governour, and the Company of Merchants trading to the Levant-Seas, at St Bartholemew-Exchange, May 1. 1689. London: For Sam. Crouch, 1689. 4°

Wing S 4023.

T.732

2958

SOME observations concerning the regulating of elections for parliament, found among the Earl of Shaftsbury's papers after his death, and now recommended to the consideration of this present parliament. London: Randall Taylor, 1689. 4°

Wing S 4534.

T.328

2959

SPRAT (Thomas) *Bishop of Rochester.*

The Bishop of Rochester's second letter to the Right Honourable the Earl of Dorset and Middlesex, Lord-Chamberlain of his Majesty's houshold. In the Savoy, Edward Jones, 1689. 4°

Wing S 5049.
3 copies.

T.137 T.139 T.328

2960

The STATE-prodigal his return; containing a true state of the nation. In a letter to a friend. [London, 1689.] 4°

Wing S 5326.
2 copies.

T.328 T.64

2961

STEPHENS (Edward)

A caveat against flattery, and profanation of sacred things to secular ends: upon sight of the order of the Convention for the thanksgiving... [Anon.] London, printed in the year 1689. 4°

Wing S 5424.

T.374

2962

STEPHENS (Edward)

Important questions of state, law, justice and prudence, both civil and religious, upon the late revolutions and present state of these nations ... By Socrates Christianus. London, printed in the year, 1689. 4°

Wing S 5427.

T.197

2963

STEPHENS (Edward)

Reflections upon the occurrences of the last year, From 5. Nov. 1688. to 5. Nov. 1689. Wherein, the happy progress of the late Revolution, and the unhappy progress of affairs since, are considered ... [Anon.] London, printed in the year, 1689. 4°

Wing S 5437.
3 copies.

T.604 T.328 T.60

2964

STEPHENS (Edward)

A specimen of a declaration against debauchery, tendered to the consideration of his Highness the Prince of Orange, and of the present convention of the nation. [Anon.] [London, 1689.] 4°

Wing S 5442.
2 copies.

T.374 T.197

2965

STILLINGFLEET (Edward) *Bishop of Worcester.*

A discourse concerning the unreasonableness of a new separation, on account of the oaths. With an answer to the History of passive obedience [by Abednego Seller], so far as relates to them. [Anon.] London, for Richard Chiswell, 1689. 4°

Wing S 5584.

T.516

2966

STILLINGFLEET (Edward) *Bishop of Worcester.*

Proposals tender'd to the consideration of both Houses of Parliament, for uniting the protestant interest for the present; and preventing divisions for the future... [Anon.] London, for Henry Clark, and sold by the booksellers of London and Westminster, 1689. 4°

Wing S 5621.
2 copies.

T.328 T.393

2967

STILLINGFLEET (Edward) *Bishop of Worcester.*

A sermon preached before the Queen at White-hall February 22d. 1688/9. London, for Henry Mortlocke, 1689. 4°

Wing S 5660.
2 copies.

T.494 T.756

2968

TAYLOR (James)

A letter of enquiry to the reverend fathers of the Society of Jesus. Written in the person of a dissatisfied Roman Catholick. [Anon.] London: for William Rogers; and Samuel Smith, 1689. 4°

Wing T 284.

T.393

2969

TENISON (Thomas) *Archbishop of Canterbury.*

A discourse concerning the Ecclesiastical Commission, open'd in the Jerusalem-chamber, October the 10th, 1689. [Anon.] London: for Ric. Chiswell, 1689. 4°

Wing T 697.

T.327

2970

TENISON (Thomas) *Archbishop of Canterbury.*

A sermon against self-love, &c. Preached before the honourable House of Commons, on the 5th of June, 1689. Being the fast-day, appointed to implore the blessing of Almighty God upon their Majesties forces... London, for Richard Chiswell, 1689. 4°

Wing T 708.

T.756

2971

THREE letters. I. A letter from a Jesuit at Liege, to a Jesuit at Fribourg, giving an account of the happy progress of religion in England. [London, 1689.] 4°

Wing T 1099.

T.565

2972

TILLOTSON (John) *Archbishop of Canterbury.*

A sermon preached at Lincolns-Inn-Chappel, on the 31th of January, 1688. Being the day appointed for a publick thanksgiving ... for having made ... the Prince of Orange the glorious instrument of the great deliverance of this Kingdom from popery and arbitrary power. London, for Brabazon Aylmer; and William Rogers, 1689. 4°

Wing T 1236.
3 copies.

T.756 T.488 T.173

2973

TILLOTSON (John) *Archbishop of Canterbury.*

A sermon preach'd before the King and Queen at Hampton-Court, April the 14th. 1689. London, for B. Aylmer; and W. Rogers, 1689. 4°

Wing T 1238.

T.709

2974

TILLOTSON (John) *Archbishop of Canterbury.*

A sermon preach'd before the Queen at White-hall, March the 8th, 1688/9. London: for Brabazon Aylmer; and Will. Rogers, 1689. 4°

Wing T 1237.
2 copies.

T.709 T.173

2975

TITUS (Silas)

Killing no murder: briefly discoursed in three questions. By William Allen [i.e. Silas Titus] ... Reprinted in the year 1689. 4°

Wing T 1312 (=K 474).

T.60

2976

A TRUE account of the present state of Ireland... By a person that with great difficulty left Dublin, June the 8th 1689. (A letter from Colonel Walker, giving a full account of the treachery of the late governour of Londonderry.) [London], Edw. Jones, for Robert Clavel, 1689. 4°

Wing W 349.

T.328

2977

A TRUE relation of the manner of the deposing of King Edward II. Together with the articles which were exhibited against him in Parliament. As also, an exact account of the proceedings and articles against King Richard II... London, Richard Baldwin, 1689. 4°

Wing T 3002.

T.199

2978

TULLY (George)

Moderation recommended in a sermon preached before the Lord Mayor and court of aldermen at Guild-hall chappel, May 12th. 1689. London, for Ric. Chiswell, 1689. 4°

Wing T 3241.

T.756

2979

VESEY (John) *Archbishop of Tuam.*

A sermon preach'd to the protestants of Ireland, in and about the city of London, at St. Mary le Bow in Cheapside, Octob.23.1689... London, for Robert Clavel, 1689. 4°

Wing V 283.

T.494

2980

WAKE (William) *Archbishop of Canterbury.*

An exhortation to mutual charity and union among protestants. In a sermon preach'd before the King and Queen at Hampton-Court, May 21. 1689. London: for Ric. Chiswell: and W. Rogers, 1689. 4°

Wing W 242.
2 copies.

T.618 T.756

2981

WAKE (William) *Archbishop of Canterbury.*

A sermon preach'd before the honourable House of Commons at St. Margaret's Westminster June 5th. 1689 ... London: for Ric. Chiswell, and William Rogers, 1689. 4°

Wing W 263.

T.756

2982

WALKER (George) *of Londonderry.*

The substance of a discourse being an incouragement for protestants, or a happy prospect of glorious success... Occasionally on the protestants victory over the French and Irish papists before London-Derry, in raising that desperate siege. London, Alex. Milbourn, 1689. 4°

Wing W 347.

T.144

2983

WELLWOOD (James)

A vindication of the present great revolution in England; in five letters pass'd betwixt James Welwood, M.D. and Mr. John March, Vicar of Newcastle upon Tyne. Occasion'd by a sermon preach'd by him on January 30. 1688/9... for passive obedience and non-resistance. London, R. Taylor, 1689. 4°

Wing W 1310.

T.616

1689 (Cont'd)

2984

WHISTON (James)

To the honourable the Commons of England assembled in Parliament. A short account of one of the grand grievances of the nation, humbly presented by James Whiston. [London, 1689?] Fol.

Wing W 1688.

T.531

2985

WHITBY (Daniel)

A letter from a city-minister to a member of the high and honourable court of Parliament, concerning the present affairs. Being a vindication of the Church of England-clergy, for their owning and praying for K. William & Q. Mary. [Anon.] London, for Thomas Newborough, 1689. 4°

Wing W 1730.

T.328

2986

WHITBY (Daniel)

A treatise of traditions. Part II... [Anon.] London, J. Leake, for Awnsham Churchill, 1689. 4°

Wing W 1742.

T.393

1690

2987

An ACCOUNT of what past on Monday the 28th. of October, 1689. in the House of Commons, and since at the King's-Bench-bar at Westminster, in relation to the Earl of Castlemaine. London, for Matthew Granger, 1690. 4°

Wing A 436.

T.328

2988

The ANATOMY of a Jacobite-Tory: in a dialogue between Whig and Tory, occasioned by the Act for recognizing King William and Queen Mary. London: for Richard Baldwin, 1690. 4°

Wing A 3053.

T.604.

2989

ATWOOD (William)

An apology for the East-India Company: with an account of some large prerogatives of the Crown ... in relation to foreign trade and foreign parts. By W. A. ... London, printed for the author, 1690. 4°

Wing A 4169.

T.324

2990

BEAUMONT (Francis) and FLETCHER (John)

The prophetess: or, the history of Dioclesian. With alterations and additions, after the manner of an opera. Represented at the Queen's Theatre by their Majesties servants. London, for Jacob Tonson, 1690. 4°

Wing B 1605.

T.501

2991

BOYSE (Joseph)

Vox populi: or, the sense of the sober lay-men of the Church of England, concerning the heads proposed in his Majesties commission to the Convocation. [Anon.] London, for Randall Taylor, 1690. 4°

Wing B 4084.

T.327

2992

BRETHREN in iniquity: or, The confederacy of papists and sectaries, for the destroying of the true religion, as by law establish'd, plainly detected ... London, Randal Taylor, 1690. 4°

Wing B 4382.

T.178

2993

BROWN (Thomas) of Shifnal.

The late converts exposed: or the reasons of Mr. Bays's [i.e. John Dryden's] changing his religion. Considered in a dialogue. Part the second ... [Anon.] London, for Thomas Bennet, 1690. 4°

Wing B 5061.

T.501

2994

BROWN (Thomas) of Shifnal.

The reasons of Mr. Joseph Hains the player's conversion & re-conversion. Being the third and last part to the dialogue of Mr. Bays ... [Anon.] London, for Richard Baldwin, 1690. 4°

Wing B 5071.

T.501

2995

BROWNE (Thomas) Fellow of St. John's College, Cambridge.

The case of allegiance to a king in possession. [Anon.] Printed in the year, 1690. 4°

Wing B 5183.
4 copies.

T.512 T.513 T.329

2996

BURNET (Gilbert) Bishop of Salisbury.

Injunctions for the arch-deacons of the diocess of Sarum ... Together with a letter from their diocesan Gilbert Lord Bishop of Sarum. London, for Ric. Chiswel, 1690. 4°

Wing B 5806

T. 78

2997

BURNET (Gilbert) Bishop of Salisbury.

A sermon preached at Bow-Church, before the court of aldermen, on March 12. 1689/90 ... London: for Richard Chiswell, 1690. 4°

Wing B 5891.

T.145

2998

C. (T. van)

Min Heer T. Van C's answer to Min Heer H. Van L's letter of the 15th of March, 1689. Representing the true interests of Holland, and what they have already gained by our losses. [London, 1690.] 4°

cf. Wing C 138.
3 copies.

T.511   T. 64

2999

CHURCH OF ENGLAND.

A form of prayer and solemn thanksgiving... for the wonderful preservation of his Majesties person, and his good success towards the reducing of Ireland ... London, Charles Bill and Thomas Newcomb, 1690. 4°

Wing C 4123.
5 copies (three different impressions)

T.78   T.461 T.489

3000

CHURCH OF ENGLAND.

A form of prayer with thanksgiving, to be used yearly upon the fifth day of November; for the happy deliverance of King James I... and also for the happy arrival of his present Majesty on this day for the deliverance of our Church and nation. London, Charles Bill and Thomas Newcomb, 1690. 4°

Wing C 4178.

T.461

3001

COTTON (Sir Robert Bruce)

A discourse of foreign war: with an account of all the taxations upon this kingdom, from the conquest to the end of the reign of Queen Elizabeth ... London, for Henry Mortlock, 1690. 8°

Wing C 6488.

T.443

3002

CUNNINGHAM (Alexander)

Some questions resolved concerning episcopal and presbyterian government in Scotland ... [Anon.] London, printed for the author, and are to be sold by Randal Taylor, 1690. 4°

Wing C 7592.

T.142

3003

D. (C.)

New-England's faction discovered; or, A brief and true account of their persecution of the Church of England ... Being, An answer to a most false and scandalous pamphlet lately published; intituled, News from New-England, &c. London, for J. Hindmarsh, 1690. 4°

Wing D 6.

T. 94

3004

A DISCOURSE of schism for the benefit of humble Christians. London, for W. Crook, 1690. 4°

Wing D 1602.

T. 72

3005

DRYDEN (John)

Amphitryon; or, The two Socia's. A comedy. As it is acted at the Theatre Royal ... To which is added, The musick of the songs. Compos'd by Mr. Henry Purcel. London, for J. Johnson; and M. Tonson, 1690. 2 parts. 4°

Wing D 2234.

T.501

3006

DRYDEN (John)

Don Sebastian, King of Portugal: a tragedy acted at the Theatre Royal ... London: for Jo. Hindmarsh, 1690. 4°

Wing D 2262.

T.501

3007

EYRE (William)

A vindication of the Letter out of the North, concerning Bishop Lake's declaration of his dying in the belief of the doctrine of passive obedience, &c. In answer to a late pamphlet, called, The defence of the profession, &c. of the said bishop. As far as it concerns the person of quality. [Anon.] London; for Awnsham Churchill, 1690. 4°

Wing E 3944.

T.260

3008

A FAITHFUL history of the northern affairs of Ireland: from the K. James accession to the crown, to the siege of Londonderry ... By a person who bore a great share in those transactions. London: Randall Taylor, 1690. 4°

Wing F 271.

T. 60

3009

FOWLER (Edward) Bishop of Gloucester.

An answer to the paper delivered by Mr. Ashton at his execution to Sir Francis Child ... Together with the paper it self. [Anon.] London: for Robert Clavell, 1690. 4°

Wing F 1695.
Manuscript attribution to "Dr. Stanley" [perhaps William Stanley, Dean of St. Asaph].
2 copies.

T.509 T. 60

3010

G. (J.)

A seasonable sermon preach'd January 26. 1689. And publish'd for the common benefit of all true English men. London, S. Roycroft, for R. Clavell, 1690. 4°

Wing G 39.

T.173

3011

H. (T.)

Political aphorisms: or, The true maxims of
government displayed... By way of challenge to
Dr. William Sherlock, and ten other new dissenters,
and recommended as proper to be read by all
protestant Jacobites... London, for Tho. Harrison,
1690. 4°

Wing H 140.

T.512

3012

HOW far the clergy and other members of the Church
of England ought to communicate with the non-
swearing bishops. London, printed in the year
1690. 4°

Wing H 2958.

T. 64

3013

The INTRIGUES of the conclave, set forth in a
relation of what passed therein at the election of
Sixtus V. & Clement VIII ... London, for J. C.,
1690.

Wing I 277.

T.248

3014

ITTIGIUS (Thomas)

Thomae Itigii Lipsiensis... de haeresiarchis aevi
apostolici & apostolico proximi... dissertatio.
Lipsiae, sumpt. haeredum Friderici Lanckisii, typis
Viduae Johannis Wittigau, 1690. 4°

T.818

3015

J. (N,)

A letter from N.J. to E.T. Esq; his representative
in Parliament. [No imprint, 1690.] 4°

Wing J 23.

T.136

3016

JENKIN (Robert)

A defence of the profession which the Right
Reverend ... John, late Lord Bishop of Chichester,
made upon his death-bed; concerning passive
obedience, and the new oaths. Together with an
account of some passages of his lordship's life.
[Anon.] London: printed in the year 1690. 4°

Wing J 567.
2 copies.

T.509 T.64

3017

JENKIN (Robert)

The title of an usurper after a thorough settlement
examined; in answer to Dr. Sherlock's Case of
the allegiance due to sovereign powers, &c ...
[Anon.] London: printed in the year 1690. 4°

Wing J 573.

T.141

3018

JOHNSON (Samuel) *Rector of Corringham.*

Remarks upon Dr. Sherlock's book, intituled, The case
of the allegiance due to sovereign princes, stated
and resolved, &c. [Anon.] London, for J. Humphries,
1690.   4°

Wing J 840.

T.512

3019

JOHNSON (Samuel) *Rector of Corringham.*

Remarks upon Dr. Sherlock's book, intituled, The case
of the allegiance due to sovereign princes, stated
and resolved, &c. [Anon.] 2nd ed. London, for
J. Humphries, 1690.   4°

Wing J 841.

T.141

3020

A JUST censure of the answer [by William Payne] to
Vox cleri [by Thomas Long.] In a letter to a
friend. London, printed in the year 1690. 4°

Wing J 1230.
2 copies.

T.199 T.327

3021

LAMBE (John)

A sermon preached before the King and Queen at
Whitehall, Jan. 19. 1689. London, for Walter Kettilby,
1690.   4°

Wing L 222.

T.494

3022

L'ESTRANGE (*Sir* Roger)

Some queries concerning the election of members
for the ensuing Parliament. [Anon.] London,
printed in the year 1690. 4°

Wing H 833 (attributed to James Harrington).

T.60

3023

A LETTER sent to Dr. Tillotson several months ago.
And now made publick, by reason the author has not
heard of any discourse publish'd since in answer.
[London, 1690.] 4°

Wing L 1616.

T.194

3024

A LETTER to a dissenting clergy-man of the Church of
England, concerning the oath of allegiance and
obedience to the present government. London: for
Richard Baldwin, 1690.   4°

Wing L 1634.

T.604

3025

LITTLETON (Edward)

The management of the present war against France
consider'd. In a letter to a noble lord. By a
person of quality. [Anon.] London, for R. Clavel,
C. Wilkinson and J. Hindmarsh, and are to be sold
by Randal Taylor, 1690. 4°

Wing L 2579.

T.64

3026

LLOYD (William) *Bishop of Worcester.*

A sermon preached before the King & Queen at White-
hall, March the twelfth, 1689/90. being the fast-
day. London, for Robert Clavell, 1690.   4°

Wing L 2714.

T.494

3027

LOCKE (John)

A second letter concerning toleration. [Anon.]
London: for Awnsham and John Churchill, 1690.   4°

Wing L 2755.

T.604

3028

LONG (Thomas)

Vox cleri: or, The sense of the clergy, concerning the
making of alterations in the established liturgy ...
To which is added, An historical account of the whole
proceedings of the present Convocation ... [Anon.]
London: R. Taylor, 1690.   4°

Wing L 2986.
2 copies.

T.327 T.328

3029

MASTERS (Samuel)

The Christian temper of moderation, described and
recommended, in a sermon before the Right Honourable
the Lord Mayor, &c. in Guild-hall-chappel, on...
Jan.26.1689/90.   London, for Awnsham Churchill,
1690.   4°

Wing M 1068.

T.618

3030

MAURICE (Henry)

Remarks from the country; upon the two letters
relating to the Convocation and alterations in the
liturgy. [Anon.] London, printed, and are to
be sold by most booksellers, 1689/90. 4°

Wing M 1369.
2 copies.

T.327 T.509

3031

MEGGOTT (Richard)

A sermon preached before the King & Queen, at
Windsor-castle, Sept. 21. 1690.   London, for
Tho. Bennet, 1690.   4°

Wing M 1629.

T.618

3032

MISHNAH. *Zeraim.*

Misnae pars: ordinis primi Zeraim tituli septem.
Latine vertit & commentario illustravit Gulielmus
Guisius. Accedit Mosis Maimonidis Praefatio in
Misnam Edv. Pocockio interprete. Oxoniae, e
Theatro Sheldoniano, 1690. 2 parts. 4°

Wing M 2250.

T.787

3033

A MODEST attempt for healing the present animosities
in England.   Occasion'd by a late book, entituled, A
modest enquiry, &c...   London, for R. Janeway, 1690.
4°

Wing M 2359.

T.604

3034

A MODEST enquiry into the causes of the present
disasters in England. And who they are that
brought the French fleet into the English Channel,
described. London: for Richard Baldwin, 1690. 4°

Wing M 2367.
2 copies.

T.328 T.60

3035

MONTAGU (Charles) *Earl of Halifax.*

An epistle to the Right Honourable Charles Earl of
Dorset and Middlesex, Lord Chamberlain of his
Majesties houshold. [Anon.] London, for Francis
Saunders, 1690. Fol.

Wing H 287.

T.699

3036

MOORE (John) *Bishop of Ely.*

Of the wisdom and goodness of providence. Two
sermons preached before the Queen, at White-hall,
on August 17/24 1690. London: for W. Rogers,
1690.   4°

Wing M 2551.

T.618

3037

MORER (Thomas)

An account of the present persecution of the Church
in Scotland, in several letters. [Anon.] London:
for S. Cook, 1690. 4°

Wing M 2722.
3 copies (one copy wanting pp.1-6).

T.31   T.142 T.604

3038

N.(N.)

Several letters written by some French protestants
now refug'd in Germany, from the tyrannical
persecution of France, concerning the unity of
the Church... Translated from the French, by
P.B. gent. London, Langley Curtiss,1690.   4°

Wing N 56.

T.328

3039

A NEW history of the succession of the crown of
England. And more particularly, from the time of
King Egbert, till King Henry the eighth ... London,
for Ric. Chiswell, 1690. 4°

Wing N 646.

T.60

3040

An OLD cavalier turned a new courtier. Being a
suppressed letter to a member of Parliament
retrived. [No imprint, 1690]. 4°

Wing O 200.

T.60

3041

PARKER (Samuel) *Bishop of Oxford.*

A discourse sent to the late King James, to persuade him to embrace the Protestant religion. To which are prefixed two letters; the first, from Sir Leolyn Jenkins, on the same subject; the second, from the said bishop ... London: Randal Taylor, 1690. 4°

Wing P 461.
2 copies.

T.60 T.140

3042

PAYNE (William) *D.D.*

An answer to a printed letter to Dr. W. P. concerning non-resistance, and other reasons for not taking the oathes ... London, J. R. for Brabazon Aylmer, 1690. 4°

Wing P 895.

T.260

3043

PAYNE (William) *D.D.*

An answer to Vox cleri, &c. [by Thomas Long] examining the reasons against making any alterations and abatements, in order to a comprehension, and shewing the expediency thereof. [Anon.] London, for Brabazon Aylmer, 1690. 4°

Wing P 896.
3 copies.

T.327 T.328 T.604

3044

PELLING (Edward)

A sermon preached before the King & Queen at Whitehall, Decemb. 8th. 1689. London, for Walter Kettilby, 1690. 4°

Wing P 1100.

T.618

3045

The PLAIN case as it now stands in reference to subjection to the present government ... London, R. Baldwin, 1690. 4°

Wing P 2345.

T.277

3046

A PRESERVATIVE against apostacy from the communion of the Church of England ... London, printed in the year 1690. 4°

Wing P 3292.

T.64

3047

PRIDEAUX (Humphrey)

A letter to a friend relating to the present convocation at Westminster. [Anon.] London, for Brabazon Aylmer, 1690. 4°

Wing P 3413.
2 copies.

T.327 T.133

3048

PROAST (Jonas)

The argument of the Letter concerning toleration, [by John Locke] briefly consider'd and answer'd. [Anon.] Oxford, printed at the Theatre, for George West, and Henry Clements, booksellers in Oxford, A.D. 1690. 4°

Wing P 3538.

T.327

3049

REFLECTION, in vindication of one arch-deacon [i.e. Francis Fullwood], (and consequently of all) from the scurrilous and groundless invectives against him... in a late scandalous pamphlet, intituled, A pretended visitor visited. In a letter, &c... London, for Awnsham Churchill, 1690. 4°

Wing R 693.

T.328

3050

REFLECTIONS on the petition & apology for the six deprived bishops. With a vindication of those that refused to subscribe the said petition. London, for J. Johnson, 1690. 4°

Wing R 709.

T.260

3051

REFLECTIONS upon a form of prayer, lately set forth [by Abednego Seller] for the Jacobites of the Church of England. And of an abhorrance tendred by the late King, to some of our dissenting bishops, upon his present Majesty's landing. London: for Richard Baldwin, 1690. 4°

Wing R 714.

T.461

3052

SAGE (John) *Bishop.*

The case of the present afflicted clergy in Scotland truly represented... By a lover of the Church and his country... London, for J. Hindmarsh, 1690. 4°

Wing S 285.
3 copies.

T.604 T.31 T.142

3053

SANCROFT (William) *Archbishop of Canterbury.*

Modern policies, taken from Machiavel, Borgia, and other choice authors, by an eye-witness. [The dedication signed W. Blois.] London, for J. Hindmarsh, 1690. 4°

Wing S 560.
2 copies.

T.328 T.60

3054

A SECOND modest enquiry into the causes of the present disasters in England... Being a farther discovery of the Jacobite plot. Together with a list of those noble-men, gentlemen, and others now in custody. London, for John Dunton, and John Harris, 1690. 4°

Wing S 2292.

T.328

3055

The SECOND part of Dr. Sherlock's two kings of Brainford, at the importunity of his vindicator. London, for W. Rayner, 1690. 4°

Wing S 2294 A.
Attributed in the MS catalogue of the tract collection to "Mr. Atwood", presumably William Atwood.
2 copies.

T.512 T.141

3056

SELLER (Abednego)

A continuation of the history of passive obedience since the Reformation. (An appendix.) Amsterdam: for Theodore Johnson, 1690. 2 parts. 4°

Wing S 2449.
3 copies (copy T.339 wanting the appendix).

T.64 T.339 T.516

3057

SELLER (Abednego)

A form of prayer and humiliation for God's blessing upon his Majesty [James II], and his dominions, and for the removing and averting of God's judgments from this Church and State. [Anon.] London, printed in the year, 1690. 4°

Wing S 2452.
2 copies.

T.461 T.463

3058

SELLER (Abednego)

The history of self-defence, in requital to the History of passive obedience. [Anon.] London, for D. Newman, 1680 [1690?]. 4°

Wing S 2456.

T.260

3059

SHARP (John) *Archbishop of York.*

A sermon preached before the Queen at Whitehall, on the 11th of April, 1690. London, for Walter Kettilby, 1690. 4°

Wing S 2989.

T.625

3060

SHOWER (*Sir* Bartholomew)

The magistracy and government of England vindicated. In three parts. Containing I. A justification of the English method of proceedings against criminals, &c. II. An answer to several replies, &c. III. Several reasons for a general act of indempnity. [Anon.] [London, 1690?] 4°

Not in Wing, but cf. S 3653-5.
26p. Wanting the first gathering; title taken from the head of p.1.

T.199

3061

STILLINGFLEET (Edward) *Bishop of Worcester.*

A sermon preached before the King & Queen at White-hall, March 23. 1689/90. London, for Henry Mortclocke, 1690. 4°

Wing S 5661.
2 copies.

T.494 T.173

3062

STRUTTON (Richard)

A true relation of the cruelties and barbarities of the French, upon the English prisoners of war. Being a journal of their travels from Dinan in Britany, to Thoulon in Provence... London: for Richard Baldwin, 1690. 4°

Wing S 6018.

T.357

3063

T.(N.)

A modest and just apology for; or, Defence of the present East-India-Company. Against the accusations of their adversaries... London, printed anno Domini, 1690. 4°

Wing T 34A.

T.324

3064

TENISON (Thomas) *Archbishop of Canterbury.*

A sermon concerning doing good to posterity. Preach'd before their Majesties at White-hall, on February 16. 1689/90. London: for Richard Chiswell, 1690. 4°

Wing T 711.

T.494

3065

TILLOTSON (John) *Archbishop of Canterbury.*

A sermon preach'd before the Queen at White-hall, March the 7th, 1689/90. London, for Brabazon Aylmer: Will. Rogers: and John Tillotson bookseller, 1690. 4°

Wing T 1240.

T.173

3066

TO the reverend and merry answerer [i.e. William Payne] of Vox cleri. To be left at Mr. Brabazon Aylmer's at the Three pigeons in Cornhill. With a bundle. [London, 1690.] 4°

Wing T 1601.

T.327

3067

The TRIMMING court-divine, or reflexions on Dr. Sherlock's book of the lawfulness of swearing allegiance to the present government. London, printed in the year 1690. 4°

Wing T 2279.

T.512

3068

The TRUE friends to corporations vindicated; in answer to a letter concerning the disabling clauses lately offered to the House of Commons for regulating corporations. London: printed in the year 1690. 4°

Wing T 2702.

T.328

3069

A TRUE vindication of the reverend Dr. Sherlock: being a reply to the pretended answers of his late book, intituled, The case of allegiance due to sovereign powers, stated and resolved, &c. London, Randal Taylor, 1690. 4°

Wing T 3126.

T.141

3070

TURNER (John) *Hospitaller.*

A memorial humbly presented to the Right Honorable the Lord Chief Justice of the King's-Bench in behalf of the hospitaller and his friends. London, printed in the year, 1690. 4°

Wing T 3311.

T.280

3071

VOX regis & regni: or a protest against Vox cleri [by Thomas Long]; and a perswasive (thereby occasion'd) to make such alterations as may give ease to our dissenting brethen ... London, for G.C. and are to be sold by Richard Baldwin, 1690. 4°

Wing L 2987 A (entered under Long, Thomas). 2 copies.

T.327   T.604

3072

WAGSTAFFE (Thomas)

An answer to a late pamphlet [by Zachary Taylor], entituled Obedience and submission to the present government, demonstrated from Bp. Overall's convocation-book. With a poscript [sic] in answer to Dr. Sherlock's Case of allegiance. [Anon.] London, for Jos. Hindmarsh, 1690. 2 parts. 4°

Wing W 202.

T.513

3073

WAGSTAFFE (Thomas)

An answer to a late pamphlet [by Zachary Taylor], entituled,Obedience and submission to the present government, demonstrated from Bishop Overall's convocation-book. Together with a particular answer to Dr. Sherlock's late Case of allegiance, &c. [Anon.] London, printed in the year 1690. 2 parts. 4°

Wing W 203
3 copies.

T.64   T.512

3074

WAGSTAFFE (Thomas)

A letter to the author [i.e. Henry Maurice] of the late Letter out of the countrey, occasioned by a former Letter to a member of the House of Commons, concerning the bishops lately in the Tower, and now under suspension. [Anon.] [London, 1690.] 4°

Wing W 211.

T.260

3075

WAGSTAFFE (Thomas)

Sherlock against Sherlock. The Master of the Temple's reasons for his late taking the oath to their Majesties, answered, by the rector of St. George Botolph-Lane. With modest remarks on the Doctors celebrated notions of allegiance to sovereign powers... [Anon.] London, for Edward Gosling, 1690. 4°

Wing W 216.
2 copies.

T.512   T.513

3076

WAKE (William) *Archbishop of Canterbury.*

A sermon preach'd at the reviving of the general meetings of the gentlemen and others of the county of Dorset: in the church of St. Mary-le-Bow, Decemb. the 2d. 1690. London, for Richard Sare, 1690. 4°

Wing W 267.

T.618

3077

WAKE (William) *Archbishop of Canterbury.*

A sermon preach'd before the King and Queen at White-hall, May the 4th. M.DC.XC... London: for Ric. Chiswell: and W. Rogers, 1690. 4°

Wing W 266.

T.618

3078

WAKE (William) *Archbishop of Canterbury.*

A sermon preach'd before the Lord Mayor, and court of aldermen, at S. Sepulchres-church, on Wednesday in Easter-week, A.D. M.DC.XC. London: for Ric. Chiswell: and W. Rogers, 1690. 4°

Wing W 265.

T.618

3079

WAKE (William) *Archbishop of Canterbury.*

A sermon preached before the Queen at White-hall April 2. 1690... London: for Ric. Chiswell: and W. Rogers, 1690. 4°

Wing W 264.

T.618

3080

WHITBY (Daniel)

An historical account of some things relating to the nature of English government, and the conceptions which our fore-fathers had of it ... [Anon.] London, for Awnsham Churchill, 1690. 4°

Wing W 1729.

T.260

3081

WILLES (John)

Brevissimum metaphysicae compendium, secundum mentem nominalium... [Anon.] Oxonii, typis L. Lichfield, sumptibus Hen. Clements bibliop. Oxoniensis, an. Dom. 1690. 8°

Wing W 2301.

T.391

3082

WILLIS (John)

The judgment of the foreign reformed churches concerning the rites and offices of the church of England: shewing there is no necessity of alterations. In a letter to a member of the House of Commons... [Anon.] London; for Robert Jenkinson, A.D. 1690. 4°

Wing W 2807.

T.461

3083

A WORD to a wandering levite: or an answer to Dr. Sherlock's reasons concerning the taking of the oaths, with reflections thereupon. By a London apprentice of the Church of England. London, printed in the year 1690. 4°

Wing W 3564.
2 copies.

T.512   T.513

1691

3084

ABRAHAM, ben Mordecai Farisol.

[Hebrew] id est, Itinera mundi, sic dicta nempe cosmographia, autore Abrahamo Peritsol. Latina versione donavit & notas passim adjecit Thomas Hyde. Calce exponitur [Tractatus Alberti Bobovii de] Turcarum liturgia, peregrinatio Meccana, aegrotorum visitatio, circumcisio... Oxonii, e Theatro Sheldoniano, 1691. Impensis Henrici Bonwick bibliopolae Londinensis. 2 parts. 4°

Wing F 438.

T.787

3085

AMES (Richard)

A farther search after claret; or, A second visitation of the vintners. A poem ... [Anon.] London, for E. Hawkins, 1691. 4°

Wing A 2977.

T.501

3086

AMES (Richard)

The search after claret; or, A visitation of the vintners. A poem in two canto's. 2nd ed ... [Anon.] London, for E. Hawkins, 1691. 4°

Wing A 2990.

T.501

3087

An ANSWER to a treatise out of ecclesiastical history, translated from an ancient Greek manuscript... by Humfrey Hody, and published under the title of The unreasonableness of a separation from the new bishops... [Attributed to Nathaniel Bisbie and to Thomas Browne.] London: J. Wells, 1691. 4°

Wing B 2980.
2 copies. A manuscript attribution on copy T.374 to "Mr Jenkins".

T.131   T.374

3088

The ANTI-weesils. A poem. Giving an account of some historical and argumental passages happening in the Lyon's Court... London, Randal Taylor, 1691. 4°

Wing A 3516.

T.513

3089

ASHBY (Sir John)

The account given by Sir John Ashby Vice-Admiral, and Reere-Admiral Rooke to the Lords Commissioners, of the engagement at sea, between the English, Dutch, and French fleets, June the 30th, 1690 ... London, for Randal Taylor, 1691. 4°

Wing A 3937.

T.145

3090

ASHTON (John)

A copy of Mr. Ashton's paper, delivered to the sheriff at the place of execution, January 28. 1690/1. [No imprint, 1691.] brs.

Wing A 3991.

T. 60

3091

ASHTON (John)

A true copy of part ofthat paper, which Mr. Ashton left in a friend's hands: together with the letter in which he sent it enclosed. [London, 1691.] brs.

Wing A 3992.

T.60

3092

BANCROFT (John)

King Edward the third, with the fall of Mortimer Earl of March. An historicall play, as it is acted at the Theatre-Royall, by their Majesties servants. [Anon.] London, for J. Hindmarsh, R. Bently, and Randall Taylor, 1691. 4°

Wing B 635.

T.501

3093

BROWN (Thomas) *of Shifnal.*

Novus reformator vapulans: or, The Welch levite tossed in a blanket. In a dialogue between Hick--of Colchester, David J--nes and the ghost of Wil. Pryn ... [Anon.] London: printed for the assigns of Will. Pryn, next door to the Devil, 1691. 4°

Wing B 5067.

T.501

3094

BROWNE (Thomas) *Fellow of St. John's College, Cambridge.*

An answer to Dr. Sherlock's Case of allegiance to sovereign powers, in defence of the Case of allegiance to a king in possession. In a letter to a friend ... [Anon.] London: printed in the year 1691. 4°

Wing B 5182.
4 copies.

T.512   T.513   T.329

3095

BURY (Arthur)

The naked Gospel. Discovering, I. What was the Gospel which our Lord and his Apostles preached ... Part I. Of faith... London, for Nathanael Ranew, 1691. 4°

Wing B 6202.

T.564

3096

CHURCH OF ENGLAND.

A form of prayer to be used next after the prayer
in the time of war and tumults... as often as
there is divine service, during the time of their
Majesties fleets being at sea. London, Charles
Bill and the executrix of Thomas Newcomb, 1691. 4°

Wing C 4138.

T.461

3097

CHURCH OF ENGLAND.

A form of prayer to be used on Wednesday the twenty
ninth day of this present April, throughout the
whole Kingdom, being the fast-day... for supplicating
almighty God for the pardon of our sins, and for
imploring his blessing and protection in the
preservation of their Majesties sacred persons, and
the property of their arms both at land and sea.
London, Charles Bill, and the executrix of Thomas
Newcomb, 1691.   4°

Wing C 4153.

T.461

3098

CHURCH OF ENGLAND.

A form of thanksgiving to be used in all churches
within the city of London, at Morning and evening
prayer till farther order. London, Charles Bill
and Thomas Newcomb, 1691. 4°

Wing C 4180.

T.461

3099

COCKBURN (John)

An historical relation of the late general assembly,
held at Edinburgh ... In a letter from a person in
Edinburgh, to his friend in London. [Anon.] London,
for J, Hindmarsh, 1691. 4°

Wing C 4809.

T.135

3100

COCKBURN (John)

An historical relation of the late Presbyterian
general assembly, held at Edinburgh... In a
letter from a person in Edinburgh, to his friend
in London... [Anon.] London, for J. Hindmarsh,
1691. 4°

cf. Wing C 4809.

T.60

3101

COLLIER (Jeremy)

Dr. Sherlock's Case of allegiance considered.
With some remarks upon his Vindication.
[Anon.] London, printed in the year 1691.   4°

Wing C 5252.

T.513

3102

COOKE (Shadrach)

Christian supports under the terrours of death ...
[Anon.] London; B. Griffin, for Sam. Keble,
1691.   4°

Wing C 6035.

T.514

3103

D'ANVERS (Alicia)

Academia: or, The humours of the University of
Oxford. In burlesque verse. London, Randal
Taylor, 1691. 4°

Wing D 220.

T.269

3104

A DISCOURSE of toleration: with some
observations upon the late Act of Parliament.
Printed in the year 1691. 4°

Wing D 1610.

T.308

3105

DR, Sherlock's two kings of Brainford brought upon
the stage. In a congratulatory letter to Mr.
Johnson. Occasioned by the Doctor's vindication
of himself, in taking the oath of allegiance...
London: for the author, and are to be sold by
Rich. Humpheries, 1691. 4°

Wing D 1767.
Attributed in the MS catalogue of the tract colln.
to "Mr. Atwood" presumably William Atwood.
2 copies.

T.512   T.141

3106

DOVE (Henry)

A sermon preached before the Queen at White-Hall,
February the fifteenth, 1690/1. London, T, M,
for Robert Clavel, 1691. 4°

Wing D 2052.

T. 93

3107

DOWNES (Theophilus)

An examination of the arguments drawn from scripture
and reason, in Dr. Sherlock's Case of allegiance,
and his Vindication of it. [Anon.] London, printed
in the year 1691.   4°

Wing D 2083.

2 copies.

T.512   T.513

3108

D'URFEY (Thomas)

Love for money: or, The boarding school. A comedy.
As it is acted at the Theatre Royal. London:
for Abel Roper, and are to be sold by Randal Taylor,
1691.   4°

Wing D 2741.

T.501

3109

D'URFEY (Thomas)

The weesil trap'd: a poem: being a reflection on
the late satyrical fable... [Anon.] London, for
Abel Roper, and Joseph Fox, 1691.   4°

Wing B 5076, attributed to Thomas Brown. Attributed
to D'Urfey by *Poems on affairs of state*, vol,5,
p.246.

T.513

3110

D'URFEY (Thomas)

The weesils. A satyrical fable: giving an account
of some argumental passages happening in the Lion's
Court about Weesilion's taking the oaths...
[Satirical verses on Dr Sherlock. Anon.] London,
printed in the year 1691. 4°

Wing B 5077, attributed to Thomas Brown. Attributed
in *Poems on affairs of state*, vol.5, p.245, to
D'urfey.

T.512

3111

E. (N.)

The great question: or, How religion, property and
liberty are to be best secured. Humbly offered to
the consideration of all who are true lovers of
the peace of church and state ... London, for
John Southby, and sold by Randal Taylor, 1691. 4°

Wing E 21.

T.277

3112

An EASIE method for satisfaction concerning the late
revolution & settlement: with a particular respect
to two treatises of Dr. Sherlock's; viz. The case
of resistance, and The case of allegiance. In a
letter to a friend. London, Richard Baldwin,
1691. 4°

Wing E 108.

T.141

3113

ENGLAND must pay the piper. Being a seasonable
discourse about raising of money this session. In
a letter to a member of the honourable House of
Commons. [London, 1691.] 4°

Wing E 2935.
2 copies.

T.511   T.328

3114

The ENGLISH-MAN'S allegiance: or, Our indispensable
duty by nature, by oaths, and by law, to our
lawful king. [No imprint, 1691?] 4°

Wing E 3099.
3 copies. Attributed by Bowdler to the Earl of
Castlemaine.

T.64 T.328 T.511

3115

An ENTIRE vindication of Dr. Sherlock, against his
numerous and uncharitable adversaries, to his late
book, called, The case of allegiance, &c.
London: Randal Taylor, 1691.   4°

Wing E 3138.
Wanting the title-page and preface.

T.141

3116

FLEETWOOD (William) *Bishop of Ely.*

A sermon preached at Christ-Church, before the
governors of that hospital, on St. Stephen's day.
London: for Edw. Brewster, and Ric. Chiswell,
1691.   4°

Wing F 1250.

T.618

3117

FLEETWOOD (William) *Bishop of Ely.*

A sermon preached before the honourable House of
Commons, at St, Margaret Westminster, on Thursday,
the 5th of November, 1691, London, for Tho, Bassett,
and Tho. Dring, 1691, 4°

Wing F 1252,
2 copies.

T.618   T,145

3118

GRASCOMBE (Samuel)

An admonition for the fifth of November. [Anon.]
[London, 1691?] 8°

Wing G 1565.

T.426

3119

GRASCOMBE (Samuel)

Epistola ad Humfredum Hody ..., De tractatu è
scriniis Baroccianis Bibliothecae Bodleianae eruto,
& ab illo nuper edito, conscripta, [Anon,]
Londini, anno 1691. 4°

Wing G 1570.

T,131

3120

GRASCOMBE (Samuel)

A reply to A vindication of A discourse concerning
the unreasonableness of a new separation, &c. [by
John Williams, Bishop of Chichester]. [Anon.]
London, printed in the year 1691.   4°

Wing G 1576.

T.509

3121

GRASCOMBE (Samuel)

The resolution of a case of conscience, wherein
some persons of piety and sincerity seem to be at
a loss. Viz. The case whether, as matters now
stand, it be lawful to frequent our parish-churches
for communion in divine worship? [Anon.]
[No imprint, 1691.] 4°

Wing G 1577.
Wing supplies the imprint and date [Oxford, 1688.].
2 copies.

T.131 T,197

3122

GRASCOMBE (Samuel)

The separation of the Church of Rome from the Church
of England, founded upon a selfish and unchristian
interest. By a presbyter in the diocese of
Canterbury ... London, for Richard Northcott, 1691.
4°

Wing G 59.
2 copies.

T.131

3123

HEADS of agreement assented to by the united ministers in and about London: formerly called presbyterian and congregational. London: R.R. for Tho. Cockerill, and John Dunton, 1691. 4°

Wing H 1282 A.

T.509

3124

HICKES (George)

An apology for the new separation: in a letter to Dr. John Sharpe, Archbishop of York; occasioned by his farewell-sermon ... [Anon.] London, printed in the year 1691. 4°

Wing H 1841.

T.135

3125

HODY (Humfrey)

Anglicani novi schismatis redargutio seu tractatus ex historiis ecclesiasticis quo ostenditur episcopos, injuste licet depositos, orthodoxi successoris communionem nunquam refugisse. Graece & Latine ex cod. mso. editore Humfredo Hody. Oxonii, e Theatro Sheldoniano, 1691. 4°

Wing H 2337.

T.260

3126

HODY (Humfrey)

The unreasonableness of a separation from the new bishops: or, A treatise out of ecclesiastical history... Translated out of an ancient Greek manuscript in the publick library at Oxford, by Humfrey Hody. London, J. Heptinstall, for Henry Mortlock, 1691. 4°

Wing N 1076 (attributed to Nicephorus).

T.308

3127

HOFMANN (Johann) *of Nurnberg.*

Denckwürdige Begebenheiten von dem neuesten Glücks - und Unglücks-Stand, unterschiedlicher berühmten Städte und Vestungen... [Nürnberg?], im Jahr Christi 1691. 4°

T.820

3128

HOPKINS (William)

Animadversions on Mr Johnson's answer to Jovian [by George Hickes], in three letters to a country-friend ... [Anon.] London, for Walter Kettilby, 1691. 8°

Wing H 2753.
2 copies.

T.367 T.157

3129

JENKIN (Robert)

The title of a thorough settlement examined; in answer to Dr. Sherlock's Case of the allegiance due to sovereign powers, &c. With an appendix in answer to Dr. Sherlock's Vindication. [Anon.] London: John Wells, 1691. 2 parts. 4°

Wing J 572.

T.329

3130

KETTLEWELL (John)

Christianity, a doctrine of the cross: or, Passive obedience, under any pretended invasion of legal rights and liberties. [Anon.] London: for Jos. Hindmarsh, and Rob. Kettlewell, 1691. 4°

Wing K 358.

T.64

3131

KETTLEWELL (John)

The duty of allegiance settled upon it s true grounds, according to scripture, reason, and the opinion of the Church: in answer to a late book of Dr. William Sherlock, entituled, The case of the allegiance due to sovereign powers ... [Anon.] London, printed in the year 1691. 4°

Wing K 366.

T.141

3132

A LATE letter concerning the sufferings of the episcopal clergy in Scotland. London: for Robert Clavel, 1691. 4°

Wing L 554.

T.142

3133

A LETTER to a friend [against excises]. [No imprint], 1691. 4°

Not in Wing.
3 copies.

T.510 T.511 T.136

3134

LLOYD (William) *Bishop of Worcester.*

A letter to Dr. Sherlock, in vindication of that part of Josephus's history, which gives an account of Iaddus the high priest's submitting to Alexander the Great while Darius was living. Against the Answer [by Thomas Wagstaffe] to the piece intituled, Obedience and submission to the present government. [Anon.] London, for Thomas Jones, 1691. 4°

Wing L 2686.   2 copies.

T.513 T.604

3135

LOUIS XIV, *King of France.*

The late treaty made between Lewis XIV. of France, and the States General, about the exchange and ransom of the prisoners of war ... London, for Randal Taylor, 1691. 4°

Wing L 3139 A.

T.4

3136

The LOYAL martyr [John Ashton] vindicated [against Edward Fowler's Answer to the paper delivered by Mr Ashton]. [London, 1691.] 4°

Wing F 1710.
"Written by John Sargeant, & others." Attributed by Wing to Edward Fowler; Halkett & Laing and the B. M. suggst Roger North.

T. 60

3137

LUCAS (Richard)

A sermon preached at the assizes held at Horsham in the county of Sussex, August 23d. 1691 ... London: for Samuel Smith, 1691. 4°

Wing L 3418.

T.489

3138

MACHIAVELLI (Niccolò)

Machiavel's vindication of himself and his writings, against the imputation of impiety, atheism, and other high crimes; extracted from his letter to his friend Zenobius. [London, 1691,] 4°

Wing M 142.

T.80

3139

MACKENZIE (*Sir* George)

A vindication of the government in Scotland, During the reign of King Charles II. Against mis-representations made in several scandalous pamphlets ... London, for J. Hindmarsh, 1691. 4°

Wing M 213.

T.60

3140

MEGGOTT (Richard)

A sermon preached before the Queen, at White-hall, on the fast, July 19. 1691. London, for Tho. Bennet, 1691. 4°

Wing M 1631.

T.618

3141

MONRO (Alexander)

Presbyterian inquisition; as it was lately practised against the professors of the Colledge of Edinburgh ... [Anon.] London, for J. Hindmarsh, 1691. 4°

Wing M 2443.

T.31

3142

MOUNTFORT (William)

Greenwich-Park: a comedy. Acted at the Theatre-Royal, by their Majesties servants. London: for Jo. Hindmarsh, R. Bently, and A. Roper, and are to be sold by Randal Taylor, 1691. 4°

Wing M 2973.

T.501

3143

The OXFORD-antiquity examined: wherein is briefly shewn the notorious falshoods in the Greek manuscript, said to be translated by Humphry Hody ... which the better to recommend to the world, he entitles, The unreasonableness of a separation from the new bishops, &c. London, printed in the year 1691. 4°

Wing O 849.

T.131

3144

The PARABLE of the bear-baiting. London, for J. Johnson, 1691. 4°

Wing P 320.

T.325

3145

PARKINSON (James) *Fellow of Lincoln College.*

An examination of Dr. Sherlock's book, entituled, The case of the allegiance due to sovereign powers, stated and resolved, &c. London: for David Hay, 1691. 4°

Wing P 493.

T.141

3146

PASSIVE obedience in actual resistance. Or, Remarks upon a paper fix'd up in the cathedral church of Worcester, by Dr. Hicks. With reflections on the present behaviour of the rest of the family ... London: for E. Hawkins, 1691. 4°

Wing P 663.

T.260

3147

PRIDEAUX (Humphrey)

The case of clandestine marriages stated ... In a letter to a person of honour. [Anon.] London, printed in the year, 1691. 4°

Wing P 3412.

T.145

3148

PROTEUS ecclesiasticus: or, Observations on Dr. Sh---'s. late Case of allegiance, &c. In a letter to Mr. P. W. merchant in London, London: for Jos. Hindmarsh, 1691. 4°

Wing P 3875.
2 copies.

T.512 T.141

3149

A REVIEW of Dr. Sherlock's Case of allegiance due to sovereign powers, &c. With an answer to his vind-ication of that case ... London: printed in the year, 1691. 4°

Wing R 1197.
2 copies.

T.512 T.141

3150

ROYSE (George)

A sermon preached before the King at Belfast in Ireland on the 14th day of June, 1690. London: for Samuel Crouch, 1691. 4°

Wing R 2163.

T.625

3151

SHARP (John) *Archbishop of York.*

A sermon preached before the lords spiritual and temporal in Parliament assembled, in the Abbey-Church at Westminster, on the fifth of November, 1691. London, for Walter Kettilby, 1691. 4°

Wing S 2995.

T.172

3152

SHARP (John) *Archbishop of York.*

A sermon preached on the 28th. of June, at St. Giles in the Fields, by John Sharp... at his leaving yt parish... London: for Walter Kettilby, 1691. 4°

Wing S 2992.

T.742

1691 (Cont'd)

3153

SHARP (Lewes)

The Church of England's doctrine of non-resistance, justified and vindicated, as truly rational and Christian ... London, Randal Taylor, 1691. 4°

Wing S 3006.
Incomplete.

T.260

3154

SHEFFIELD (John) *Duke of Buckingham.*

An essay on poetry: by the Right Honourable, the Earl of Mulgrave. 2nd ed. London, for Jo. Hindmarsh, 1691. Fol.

Wing B 5337.
Another copy is included in the collection of poems published by Nahum Tate in 1697. T.529

T.699

3155

SHERLOCK (William)

The case of the allegiance due to soveraign powers, stated and resolved, according to scripture and reason, and the principles of the Church of England ... London: for W. Rogers, 1691. 4°

Wing S 3269,
2 copies.

T.512   T.141

3156

SHERLOCK (William)

The case of the allegiance due to soveraign powers, stated and resolved, according to scripture and reason and the principles of the Church of England... 2nd ed. London: for W. Rogers, 1691. 4°

Wing S 3271.

T.328

3157

SHERLOCK (William)

The case of the allegiance due to soveraign powers, stated and resolved, according to scripture and reason, and the principles of the Church of England ... 3rd ed. London: for W. Rogers, 1691. 4°

Wing S 3273.

T.339

3158

SHERLOCK (William)

The case of the allegiance due to soveraign powers, stated and resolved, according to scripture and reason, and the principles of the Church of England... 6th ed. London: for W. Rogers, 1691. 4°

Wing S 3276.

T.512

3159

SHERLOCK (William)

The case of the allegiance due to soveraign powers, further consider'd, and defended ... London, for W. Rogers, 1691. 4°

Wing S 3277.

T.141

3160

SHERLOCK (William)

The case of the allegiance due to soveraign powers, further consider'd and defended... London, for W. Rogers, and are to be sold by the booksellers in London and Westminster, 1691. 4°

cf. Wing S 3277.

T.512

3161

SHERLOCK (William)

A vindication of the Case of allegiance due to soveraign powers, in reply to an answer to a late pamphlet, intituled, Obedience and submission to the present government ... London: for W. Rogers, 1691. 4°

Wing S 3375.
3 copies.

T.339   T.141

3162

SOME considerations about the most proper way of raising money in the present conjuncture. [London, 1691.] 4°

Wing S 4479.

T.145

3163

SOME modest remarks on Dr. Sherlocks new book about the case of allegiance due to sovereign powers. &c. In a letter to a friend.   London: printed and sold by the booksellers of London, and Westminster, 1691. 4°

Wing S 4526.

T.512

3164

SOME modest remarks on Dr. Sherlocks new book about the case of allegiance due to sovereign powers, &c. In a letter to a friend.   2nd ed. corrected and enlarged.   London: printed and sold by the booksellers of London, and Westminster, 1691. 4°

Wing S 4525.

T.141

3165

STEPHENS (Edward)

An appeal to heaven and earth, against the Christian epicureans, who have betrayed their king and country and exposed them to the judgments of God ... By Socrates Christianus. London, printed in the year 1691. 4°

Wing S 5419.

T.187

3166

STEPNEY (George)

An epistle to Charles Montague Esq; on his Majesty's voyage to Holland.   London, for Francis Saunders, 1691. Fol.

Wing S 5467.
Another copy is included in the collection of poems published by Nahum Tate in 1697. T.529

T.699

3167

STILLINGFLEET (Edward) *Bishop of Worcester.*

The Bishop of Worcester's charge to the clergy of his diocese, in his primary visitation, begun at Worcester, Sept. II. 1690. London, for Henry Mortlock, 1691. 4°

Ch. Ch. S 5565+.

T.190

3168

TAYLOR (Zachary)

The vindication of a late pamphlet, (entituled, Obedience and submission to the present government, demonstrated from Bp. Overal's convocation-book) from the false glosses, and illusive interpretations of a pretended answer [by Thomas Wagstaffe]. By the author of the first pamphlet. London: for Ric. Baldwin, 1691. 4°

Wing T 602

T.513

3169

TENISON (Richard) *Bishop of Meath.*

A sermon preach'd to the protestants of Ireland in the city of London, at St. Helen's, Octob. 23. 1690 ... By Richard, Lord Bishop of Killala... London: for Robert Clavel, 1691. 4°

Wing T 684.

T.489

3170

THOMPKINS (Edward)

The parable of the black-birds. And the magpies vindicated. [Anon.] London, for Edward Thompkins, a lover of the magpies, 1691. 4°

Wing T 997.

T.325

3171

TILLOTSON (John) *Archbishop of Canterbury.*

A sermon preached at White-Hall before the Queen on the monthly fast-day, September 16th 1691, London: for Brabazon Aylmer; and Will. Rogers, 1691, 4°

Wing T 1244,

T.93

3172

TILLOTSON (John) *Archbishop of Canterbury.*

A sermon preached before the Queen, at White-hall, February the 27th 1690/1. London: for Brabazon Aylmer; and William Rogers, 1691. 4°

Wing T 1243.

T.488

3173

The VINDICATION of the dead: or, Six hours reflections upon the six weeks labour in answer to Mr. Ashton's speech published by authority. [London, 1691.] 4°

Wing V 502.
2 copies.

T.509   T.60

3174

WAKE (William) *Archbishop of Canterbury.*

A sermon preach'd before the Lord-Mayor and court of aldermen, in the church of St. Mary le Bow; on Thursday the 26th of November... London, for R. Sare, 1691. 4°

Wing W 269.

T.618

3175

WAKE (William) *Archbishop of Canterbury.*

A sermon preach'd before the Queen at Whitehall: May Xth. M.DC.XC.I.   London, for Richard Sare, 1691. 4°

Wing W 268.

T.618

3176

WILLIAMS (John) *Bishop of Chichester.*

A vindication of a discourse [by Humfrey Hody] concerning the unreasonableness of a new separation, on account of the oaths, from the exceptions made against it [by Samuel Grascombe] in a tract called, A brief answer to a late discourse, &c... [Anon.] London: for Ric. Chiswell, 1691. 4°

Wing W 2738.

T.260

3177

WORTHINGTON (John)

Charitas evangelica. A discourse of Christian love ... London, J. M. for Walter Kettilby, 1691. 8°

Wing W 3620.

T.39

1692

3178

ATTERBURY (Francis) *Bishop of Rochester.*

A sermon before the Queen at White-hall, May 29. 1692.   London, for Tho. Bennet, 1692. 4°

Wing A 4153.

T.771

3179

B.(A.)

A letter out of the country, to the clergy in and about the city of London.   [London, 1692?] 4°

Wing B 16.
A manuscript date 25 July 1696 at end of this tract. Another copy.

T.11   T.509

3180

BARTON (Samuel)

A sermon preached before the Right Honourable the Lord Mayor and aldermen of the city of London, at St. Mary-le-Bow, Octob.27th.1692.... London, J. Richardson, for Brabazon Aylmer, 1692. 4°

Wing B 992.

T.625

3181

BISBIE (Nathaniel)

Unity of priesthood necessary to the unity of
communion in a church. With some reflection on the
Oxford manuscript, and the preface annexed ...
[Anon.] London, printed in the year 1692. 4°

Wing B 2985.

T.131

3182

BRYAN (Matthew)

St. Paul's triumph in his sufferings for Christ.
With some directions how a Christian ought to behave
himself under, and may reap advantage by his
sufferings. London: printed, for the author, 1692.
4°

Wing B 5248.
2 copies.

T.198   T.181

3183

BURNET (Gilbert) *Bishop of Salisbury.*

A sermon preached at the funeral of the Honourable
Robert Boyle; at St, Martins in the Fields, January
7. 1691/2. London: for Ric. Chiswell, and John
Taylor, 1692. 4°

Wing B 5899.
Another copy, of a different type-setting.

T.356   T.145

3184

The CAMPAIGN 1692. [A poem.]
[London, 1692?] 4°

Wing C 399 A.

T.69

3185

CHURCH OF ENGLAND.

A form of prayer and thanksgiving, to be used
immediately before the general thanksgiving...
as often as there is divine service, and to be
continued till further order. London, Charles
Bill, and the executrix of Thomas Newcomb, 1692.
4°

cf. Wing C 4128.

T.461

3186

CHURCH OF ENGLAND.

A form of prayer to be used next after the prayer
in the time of war and tumults... as often as
there is divine service, during the time of their
Majesties fleets being at sea. London, Charles
Bill, and the executrix of Thomas Newcomb, 1692. 4°

Wing C 4139.

T.461

3187

CHURCH OF ENGLAND.

A form of prayer to be used on Friday the eighth
day of April next... being the fast-day... for
supplicating almighty God for the pardon of our
sins, and for imploring his blessing and protection
in the preservation of their Majesties sacred persons
and the prosperity of their arms both at land and
sea. London, Charles Bill, and the executrix of
Thomas Newcomb, 1692. 4°

Wing C 4154.

T.461

3188

CONSIDERATIONS upon the proclamation for the
thanksgiving. In a letter to a friend.
[London, 1692?] 4°

Wing C 5926.

T.509

3189

A DIARY of the siege & surrender of Lymerick: with
the articles at large, both civil & military.
London, for R. Taylor, 1692. 4°

Wing D 1376.

T.145

3190

DODWELL (Henry)

A vindication of the deprived bishops, asserting
their spiritual rights against a lay-deprivation,
against the charge of schism, as managed by the late
editors of an anonymous Baroccian MS ... [Anon.]
London, printed in the year, 1692. 4°

Wing D 1827.
4 copies.

T.260   T.131   T.135

3191

DRYDEN (John)

Eleonora: a panegyrical poem: dedicated to the
memory of the late Countess of Abingdon ...
London: for Jacob Tonson, 1692.

Wing D 2270.

T.501

3192

FLEETWOOD (William) *Bishop of Ely.*

A sermon preach'd before the Right Honourable the
Lord Mayor and court of Aldermen, at St. Mary
le Bow, on Friday the 11th of April, 1692 ...
London: for Thomas Newborough, 1692. 4°

Wing F 1253.
2 copies.

T.618   T.273

3193

FOWLER (Edward) *Bishop of Gloucester.*

A sermon preach'd at the meeting of the sons of
the clergy in S. Mary-le-Bow church, on Tuesday
the sixth of December, 1692. London, T.M. for
B. Aylmer, and A. and J. Churchil, 1692.   4°

Wing F 1722.

T.742

3194

The GENERAL-excise consider'd. [London, 1692.]
4°

Wing G 498.

T.194

3195

GOSTWYKE (William)

Pray for the peace of Jerusalem. A sermon, preach'd
at St. Mary's in Reading, at the visitation of the
reverend Mr. William Richards, Arch-deacon of Berks,
April the 12th, 1692. London, for Randal Taylor,
1692.   4°

Wing G 1322.

T.752

3196

GRASCOMBE (Samuel)

A farther account of the Baroccian manuscript,
lately published at Oxford, together with the
canons omitted in that edition. In a letter to
his friend in London. [Anon.] [No imprint, 1692.]
4°

Wing G 1571.
2 copies.

T.260   T.131

3197

GRASCOMBE (Samuel)

An appendix to the foregoing letter, being an
answer to Mr. Humphrey Hody's letter, concerning
the canons at the end of the Baroccian manuscript
... [Anon.] [No imprint, 1692.] 4°

Part of Wing G 1571?
2 copies.

T.260   T.131

3198

GRASCOMBE (Samuel)

Two letters written to the author of a pamphlet
[i.e. Samuel Hill], entituled, Solomon and Abiathar:
or, The case of the deprived bishops and clergy
discussed ... [Anon.] London, printed in the year
1692. 4°

Wing G 1579.

T.374

3199

HICKES (George)

A vindication of some among our selves against the
false principles of Dr. Sherlock. In a letter to
the Doctor, occasioned by the sermon which he
preached at the Temple-Church, on the 29th of May,
1692 ... [Anon.] London, printed in the year
1692.   4°

Wing H 1878.

T.512

3200

HILL (Samuel)

Solomon and Abiathar: or, The case of the deprived
bishops and clergy discussed, between Eucheres a
conformist, and Dyscheres a recusant ... [Anon.]
London, for Ric. Chiswell, 1692. 4°

Wing H 2012.
3 copies.

T.374   T.260   T.135

3201

HODY (Humfrey)

A letter from Mr. Humphry Hody, to a friend,
concerning a collection of canons said to be
deceitfully omitted in his edition of the Oxford
treatise against schism ... Oxford, L. Lichfield,
for Ant. Pisly, 1692. 4°

Wing H 2342.
2 copies.

T.652   T.131

3202

The HUMBLE petition of the common people of England,
to the Lords and Commons assembled in Parliament,
particularly to their representatives the House
of Commons. [London, 1692.] 4°

Wing H 3494 (?)

T.136

3203

JAMES II, *King of England.*

The late King James's letter to his privy-counsellors.
With just reflections upon it, and upon the
pretended Prince of Wales ... London: for Ric.
Chiswell, 1692. 4°

Wing J 203.

T.200

3204

JEFFERY (John)

A sermon preached in the cathedral church of Norwich:
at the primary visitation of ... John, Lord Bishop
of Norwich. May 18. 1692. London: Samuel Roycroft,
for Robert Clavell, 1692. 4°

Wing J 519.

T.198

3205

JOHNSON (Samuel) *Rector of Corringham.*

An argument proving, that the abrogation of King
James by the people of England from the regal throne,
and the promotion of the Prince of Orange ... was
according to the constitution of the English
government, and prescribed by it ... London,
printed for the author, 1692. 4°

Wing J 821.
2 copies.

T.329   T.136

3206

JONES (David) *Vicar of Marcham.*

A farewel-sermon preached to the united parishes of
St. Mary Woolnoth, & St. Mary Woolchurch Haw in
Lombard-street ... London, for Thomas Parkhurst; and
Brab. Aylmer, 1692. 4°

Wing J 931.

T.145

3207

LESLIE (Charles)

An answer to a book [by William King], intituled, The
state of the protestants in Ireland under the late
King James's government ... [Anon.] London, printed
in the year 1692. 2 parts.   4°

Wing L 1120.

T.511

3208

A LETTER to Mr. Samuel Johnson, occasion'd by his
argument, proving that the abrogation of King
James, &c. [London, 1692.]   4°

Wing L 1719.

T.509

3209
LLOYD (William) *Bishop of Worcester.*

The pretences of the French invasion examined. For the information of the people of England. [Anon.] London, for R. Clavel, 1692. 4°

Wing L 2690.
2 copies.

T.510 T.200

3210
MEGGOTT (Richard)

A sermon preached before the Queen, at White-Hall, March 11th. 1691/2. London: for Tho. Bennet, 1692. 4°

Wing M 1632.

T.618

3211
MONRO (Alexander)

A letter to a friend, giving an account of all the treatises that have been publish'd, with relation to the present persecution against the Church of Scotland ... [Anon.] London: for Joseph Hindmarsh, 1692. 4°

Wing M 2440.
2 copies.

T.135 T.142

3212
PELLING (Edward)

A sermon preached before the King & Queen at White-hall December 13th. 1691. London, for John Everingham, 1692. 4°

Wing P 1102.

T.620

3213
RUSSELL (Edward) *Earl of Orford.*

Admiral Russel's letter to the Earl of Nottingham: containing an exact & particular relation of the late happy victory and success against the French fleet. In the Savoy: Edward Jones, 1692. Fol.

Wing O 419.

T.543

3214
SCOTT (John)

A sermon preached before the Queen the 22d of May, 1692. Upon occasion of the late victory obtained by their Majesties fleet over the French. London; for Walter Kettilby, 1642 [i.e. 1692]. 4°

Wing S 2076.

T.732

3215
SETTLE (Elkanah)

The second part of the notorious impostor, compleating the history of the life, cheats, &c. of William Morrell, alias Bowyer, sometime of Banbury, chirurgeon ... [Anon.] London, for Abel Roper, 1692. 4°

Wing S 2703 (part).

T.145

3216
SHERLOCK (William)

The charity of lending without usury. And the true notion of usury briefly stated. In a sermon preach'd before the... Lord Mayor, at St. Bridget's Church, on Tuesday in Easter-week, 1692. 2nd ed. London: for William Rogers, 1692. 4°

Wing S 3279.

T.742

3217
SHERLOCK (William)

A letter to a friend, concerning a French invasion, to restore the late King James to his throne. And what may be expected from him, should he be successful in it. [Anon.] London, Randall Taylor, 1692. 4°

Wing S 3295.

T.604

3218
SHERLOCK (William)

A second letter to a friend, concerning the French invasion. In which the declaration lately dispersed under the title of His Majesty's most gracious declaration... is entirely and exactly published... [Anon.] London: Randal Taylor, 1692. 4°

Wing S 3339.
2 copies.

T.510 T.137

3219
SHERLOCK (William)

A second letter to a friend, concerning the French invasion. In which the declaration lately dispersed under the title of His Majesty's most gracious declaration ... is entirely and exactly published ... [Anon.] 2nd ed. London: Randal Taylor, 1692. 4°

Wing S 3340.

T.200

3220
SHERLOCK (William)

A sermon preach'd before the honourable House of Commons, at St. Margaret's Westminster, January the XXXth, 1691/2. London: for William Rogers, 1692. 4°

Wing S 3350.

T.145

3221
A SPECIMEN of the state of the nation, humbly represented to both Houses of Parliament. [London, 1692.] 4°

Wing S 4846.

T.80

3222
SPRAT (Thomas) *Bishop of Rochester.*

A relation of the late wicked contrivance of Stephen Blackhead and Robert Young, against the lives of several persons, by forging an association under their hands ... In the Savoy: Edward Jones, 1692. 4°

Wing S 5046.
2 copies.

T.328 T.139

3223
STEPHENS (Edward)

A letter to the author [i.e. Henry Dodwell] of the Vindication of the deprived bishops, in reply to his reasons for the validity of the lay-deprivation of the bishops ... [London, 1692?] 4°

Not in Wing.
3 copies.

T.260 T.72

3224
TILLOTSON (John) *Archbishop of Canterbury.*

A sermon preached before the King and Queen at White-Hall, the 27th of October, being the day appointed for a publick thanksgiving to Almighty God, for the signal victory at sea ... 2nd ed. London: for Brabazon Aylmer: and William Rogers, 1692. 4°

Wing T 1246.

T.93

3225
The TUNNAGE bank compared with Doctor Chamberlen's land-fund of credit. London, T. Sowle, 1692. 4°

Not in Wing.

T.70

3226
VICTOR AMADEUS II, *King of Sardinia.*

The Duke of Savoye his declaration or the act of re-establishment, granted to the Vaudois. Done out of French. London, H. Hills, 1692. 4°

Wing V 664.

T.11

3227
WAGSTAFFE (Thomas)

An answer to A letter to Dr. Sherlock, written [by William Lloyd] in vindication of that part of Josephus's History which gives the account of Jaddus's submission to Alexander, against the Answer to the piece [by Zachary Taylor], entituled, Obedience and submission to the present government. By the same author. London, printed in the year, 1692. 4°

Wing W 204

T.512

3228
WAGSTAFFE (Thomas)

An answer to Dr. Sherlock's Vindication of the case of allegiance due to sovereign powers, which he made in reply to An answer to a late pamphlet, intituled, Obedience and submission to the present government... By the same author. London, for Joseph Hindmarsh, 1692. 4°

Wing W 205.
2 copies.

T.329 T.512

3229
WALKER (Anthony)

A true account of the author of a book entituled Εἰκων Βασιλικη [sic], or, The pourtraiture of his sacred Majesty in his solitudes and sufferings. With an answer to all objections made by Dr. Hollingsworth and others, in defence of the said book... [Anon.] London, for Nathanael Ranew, 1692. 4°

Wing W 310.

T.200

1693

3230
An ACCOUNT of Mr. Blunts late book, entituled, King William and Queen Mary conquerors, now under the censure of the Parliament. London, printed in the year, 1693. 4°

Wing A 213.

T.135

3231
ANTIQUITY reviv'd: or the government of a certain island antiently call'd Astreada... London, printed in the year 1693.   8°

Wing A 3510.

T.455

3232
BEDA, *the Venerable.*

Bedae Venerabilis opera quaedam theologica, nunc primum edita, necnon historica, antea semel edita. Accesserunt Egberti Dialogus de ecclesiastica institutione, et Aldhelmi Liber de virginitate... Londini, typis S. Roycroft, impensis Roberti Clavell, 1693. 4°

Wing B 1658.
Signature of T. Scott.

T.477

3233
BENTLEY (Richard)

The folly and unreasonableness of atheism demonstrated ... in eight sermons preached at the lecture founded by the Honourable Robert Boyle... London, J.H. for H. Mortlock, 1693. 8 parts. 4°

Wing B 1930.
the general t.p. is bound at the end of the eighth part.

T.489

3234
BLOUNT (Charles)

The oracles of reason ... In several letters to Mr. Hobbs and other persons of eminent quality, and learning. By Char. Blount; Mr. Gildon and others. London, printed 1693. 8°

Wing B 3312.

T.211

3235
BLOUNT (Charles)

Reasons humbly offered for the liberty of unlicens'd printing. To which is subjoin'd, the just and true character of Edmund Bohun, the licenser of the press. In a letter from a gentleman in the country, to a member of Parliament. [Anon.] London, printed in the year 1693. 4°

Wing B 3313.
2 copies.

T.262 T.137

3236
BOOTH (Henry) *1st Earl of Warrington.*

The charge of the Right Honourable Henry Earl of
Warrington, to the grand jury at the quarter
sessions held for the county of Chester, on the 11th
of October, 1692. London: for Richard Baldwin, 1693.
4°

Wing D 874.

T.200

3237
BURNET (Gilbert) *Bishop of Salisbury.*

A letter writ by the Lord Bishop of Salisbury, to the
Lord Bishop of Cov. and Litchfield, concerning a
book lately published, called, A specimen of some
errors and defects in the history of the reformation
of the Church of England, by Anthony Harmer [i.e.
Henry Wharton]. London: for Ric. Chiswell, 1693.
4°

Wing B 5824.

T.604

3238
BYNNS (Richard)

A sermon preached before the honourable House of
Commons January 30. 1692. In the Savoy, Edw.
Jones, for William Crooke, 1693. 4°

Wing B 6403.

T.489

3239
CHAMBERLEN (Hugh)

Papers relating to a bank of credit upon land
security proposed to the Parliament of Scotland
... [Edinburgh, 1693], 4°

Wing C 1877 A.

T.70

3240
A CHRISTIANS sure anchor and comfort in times of
troubles and dangers. Being a sermon preached on
the 16. day of June. By a divine of the Church
of England... Lonnon [sic], for S. Keble, 1693.
4°

Wing C 3961.

T.514

3241
CHURCH OF ENGLAND.

A form of prayer and thanksgiving to almighty God,
to be used... on Sunday the 12th day of this
instant November... for the preservation of his
Majesty from the great and manifold dangers to
which his royal person was exposed during his late
expedition... London, Charles Bill, and the
executrix of Thomas Newcomb, 1693. 4°

Wing C 4129.

T.461

3242
CHURCH OF ENGLAND.

A form of prayer to be used on Wednesday the tenth day
of May... being the fast-day... for supplicating
almighty God for the pardon of our sins, and for imploring his blessing and protection in the preservation
of their Majesties sacred persons, and the prosperity
of their arms both at land and sea. London, Charles
Bill, and the executrix of Thomas Newcomb, 1693. 4°

Wing C 4156.
2 copies.

T.463 T.489

3243
COMBER (Thomas)

The protestant mask taken off from the Jesuited
English-man; being an answer to a book [by Sir
James Montgomery], entituled, Great-Britain's
just complaint. [Anon.] London, William Wilde,
for Robert Clavel, 1692/3. 4°

Wing C 5484.
Wanting the title-page.

T.510

3244
A COPY of a letter sent to the commissioners of
accounts: and now published for information of
the Lords and Commons of England. [London,
1693.] 4°

Wing C 6157.

T.510

3245
CROSFEILD (Robert)

England's glory reviv'd, demonstrated in several
propositions. Shewing an easie and speedy
method for fully manning the Royal Navy with
saylers; without charge, or obstruction to
trade ... London: printed in the year 1693. 4°

Wing C 7243.

T.325

3246
DEFOE (Daniel)

An answer to the late K. James's last declaration,
dated at St. Germains, April 17. S.N. 1693. [Anon]
London, for Richard Baldwin, 1693. 4°

Wing W 1302 (attrib. to James Welwood). Moore 12.
2 copies.

T.200 T.510

3247
DEFOE (Daniel)

A dialogue betwixt Whig and Tory, alias Williamite
and Jacobite. Wherein the principles and practices
of each party are fairly and impartially stated...
[Anon.] Printed in the year 1693. 4°

Wing D 1361. Moore 10b.

T.509

3248
DUCROS (Simon)

A letter from Monsieur de Cros ... which may serve
for an answer to the impostures of Sir Wm Temple
... Together with some remarks upon his memoirs
... London, printed in the year 1693. 8°

Wing D 2436 (Ch. Ch. C 7238+).

T. 52

3249
DUCROS (Simon)

A letter from Monsieur de Cros ... which may serve
for an answer to the impostures of Sir Wm Temple
... Together with some remarks upon his memoirs
... London, for Abel Roper, 1693. 8°

Wing D 2437.

T.351

3250
EDWARDS (John) *D.D.*

Crispianism unmask'd; or, A discovery of the several
erroneous assertions, and pernicious doctrins
maintain'd in Dr. Crisp's sermons. Occasion'd by
the reprinting of those discourses. [Anon.]
London: for Richard Baldwin, 1693. 4°

Wing C 6960.

T.200

3251
EDWARDS (Jonathan) *Principal of Jesus College, Oxford.*

A preservative against Socinianism: shewing the
direct and plain opposition between it, and the
religion revealed by God in the holy scriptures, The
first part. 2nd ed. Oxon, printed at the Theater for
Henry Clements, 1693. 4°

Wing E 217.

T. 76

3252
ENGLAND. *Parliament. House of Lords.*

Some passages of the House of Lords in the Winter
sessions of Parliament in the year 92, [London,
1693.] 4°

Wing E 2847.
4 copies.

T.267 T.136

3253
An ENQUIRY into the nature and obligation of legal
rights: with respect to the popular pleas of the
late K. James's remaining right to the Crown.
London, Thomas Hodgkin, 1693. 4°

Wing I 218.

T.509

3254
An ENQUIRY; or, a discourse between a yeoman of
Kent, and a knight of a shire, upon the prorogation
of the Parliament to the second of May, 1693.
[London, 1693.] 4°

Wing I 220.
2 copies.

T.200 T.136

3255
FELL (John) *Bishop of Oxford.*

A specimen of the several sorts of letter given
to the University by Dr. John Fell late Lord
Bishop of Oxford. To which is added the letter
given by Mr. F. Junius. Oxford, printed at the
Theater, 1693. 8°

Wing F 622.

T. 12

3256
FLEETWOOD (William) *Bishop of Ely.*

A sermon preach'd before the Queen, at White-hall,
February the 12th. 1692/3. London, for Thomas
Newborough, 1693. 4°

Wing F 1255.

T.742

3257
FREKE (William)

A dialogue by way of question and answer, concerning
the deity. [Anon.] [London, 1693.] 4°

Wing F 2163.

T.149

3258
GRASCOMBE (Samuel)

An appeal of murther from certain unjust judges,
lately sitting at the Old Baily, to the righteous
judge of heaven and earth; and to all sensible
English-men, containing a relation of the tryal,
behaviour, and death of Mr. William Anderton,
executed June 16. 1693. at Tyburn, for pretended
high-treason. [Anon.] [London, 1693.] 4°

Wing G 1566.
4 copies.

T.509 T.652 T.660   T.197

3259
GRASCOMBE (Samuel)

Considerations upon the second canon in the book
entituled Constitutions and canons ecclesiastical,
&c. [Anon,] London, printed in the year 1693.
4°

Wing G 1569.
2 copies.

T.200   T.131

3260
HODY (Humfrey)

The case of sees vacant by an unjust or
uncanonical deprivation, stated. In reply to a
treatise [by Henry Dodwell] entituled A vindication
of the deprived bishops, &c... London, J.H. for
Henry Mortlock, 1693. 4°

Wing H 2339.

T.652

3261
IRELAND. *Parliament.*

An account of the sessions of Parliament in
Ireland, 1692. London, for J. T., 1693. 4°

Wing I 297.
2 copies.

T.200 T.22

3262
JAMES II. *King of England.*

His Majesties most gracious declaration to all his
loving subjects... Given at St. Germanies en Laye,
April 17th S.N. 1693... [No imprint, 1693.] brs.

cf. Wing J 217. Perhaps part of Wing R 1066.
5 copies.

T.200 T.510

3263
KETTLEWELL (John)

Of Christian communion, to be kept on in the unity
of Christs church, and among the professors of
truth and holiness ... [Anon.] Printed anno Dom.
1693. 3 parts. 4°

Wing K 377.

T.260

3264

KIDDER (Richard) *Bishop of Bath and Wells.*

A sermon preached before the King & Queen, at White-hall, the fifth of November, 1692. London: for Tho. Parkhurst, 1693. # 4°

Wing K 415
2 copies.

T.742

3265

LAWTON (Charlwood)

A French conquest neither desirable nor practicable. Dedicated to the King of England. [Anon.] London: printed by his Majesty's servants, 1693. 4°

Wing L 739.

T.511

3266

LAWTON (Charlwood)

The Jacobite principles vindicated, in answer to a letter sent to the author. [Anon.] Re-printed at London in the year 1693. 4°

Wing H 1834; attributed to [Hickes?].

T.200

3267

LONG (Thomas)

Dr. Walker's true, modest, and faithful account of the author of Εἰκων Βασιλικη, strictly examined, and demonstrated to be false, impudent, and deceitful. In two parts, the first disproving it to be Dr. Gauden's. The second proving it to be King Charles the first's ... London: R. Talor, 1693. 4°

Wing L 2965.

T.200

3268

MONRO (Alexander)

An apology for the clergy of Scotland, chiefly oppos'd to the censures, calumnies, and accusations of a late Presbyterian vindicator, in a letter to a friend ... [Anon.] London: for Jos. Hindmarsh, 1693. 4°

Wing M 2437.

T.135

3269

N.(N.)

A letter from Oxford, concerning Mr. Samuel Johnson's late book... Oxford, printed in the year 1693. 4°

Wing N 40.

T.329

3270

N. (N.)

Some reasons for annual parliaments, in a letter to a friend. [London, 1693?] 4°

Wing N 58.
2 copies. One copy has list of errata.

T.136

3271

NYE (Stephen)

Considerations on the explication of the doctrine of the Trinity, by Dr. Wallis, Dr. Sherlock, Dr. S——th, Dr. Cudworth, and Mr. Hooker ... Written to a person of quality. [Anon.] Printed in the year 1693. 4°

Not in Wing, cf. Ch. Ch. N 1505+.
2 copies.

T.149   T.9

3272

The PARIS relation of the Battel of Landen, July 29th. 1693, between the French, commanded by the D. of Luxemburg, and the Confederates, by the K. of Great Britain. Publish'd by the French King's authority ... London, for H. Rhodes: and of J. Harris, 1693. 4°

Wing P 360.

T.263

3273

The POOR man's petition to the Lords and gentlemen of the kingdom: or, Englands cry for peace. [London, 1693.] 4°

Wing P 2868.

T.137

3274

The PRICE of the abdication. [No imprint, 1693.] 4°

Wing P 3403.
3 copies.

T.328   T.511

3275

ROSENTHAL (Christian Friedrich)

Q.D.B.V. Paratitla philologico-historica, ad S. Regiae Majestatis Sueciae Caroli Gustavi glor. m. instructionis visitatorum Eccles. Pomeran. & Rugiae... Gryphiswaldiae, literis Danielis Benjaminis Starckii, [1693]. 4°

T.793

3276

ST. LO (George)

England's safety: or, A bridle to the French King. Proposing a sure method for encouraging navigation, and raising qualified seamen for the well manning their Majesties fleet... London: for W. Miller, 1693. 4°

Wing S 341.

T.325

3277

SCOTT (John)

An abstract (with remarks) of Dr. Scot's sermon, preached at Chelmsford assizes, Aug.31.1685. Wherein the Doctor prophetically gives his opinion of the consequences of the late Revolution... London, printed in the year 1693. 4°

Wing S 2037.
2 copies.

T.33   T.374

3278

SENTENTIE van den Hove van Hollandt, Zeelandt ende Vrieslandt, jegens Robbert de Pille du Plessis, gepronunchieert den 31. Julii 1693. In 's Graven-Hage, Jacobus ende Paulus Scheltus, 1693. 4°

T.280

3279

SHARP (John) *Archbishop of York.*

A sermon preach'd before the King & Queen, at White-hall, the 12th. of November, 1693. Being the day appointed for a publick thanksgiving... for the gracious preservation of his Majesty, and his safe return. London, T.W. for Walter Kettilby, 1693. 4°

Wing S 2998.

T.489

3280

A SHORT state of our condition, with relation to the present Parliament. [London, 1693.] 4°

Wing S 3630.
2 copies.

T.194   T.136

3281

SLATER (Samuel)

A sermon preached on the thanksgiving day. The 27th day of October, 1692. at Crosby-square, London: for John Lawrence, 1693. 4°

Wing S 3974.

T.625

3282

SPRAT (Thomas) *Bishop of Rochester.*

The second part of the relation of the late wicked contrivance against the lives of several persons, by forging an association under their hands ... In the Savoy: Edward Jones, 1693. 4°

Wing S 5051.

T.139

STILLINGFLEET (Edward) *Bishop of Worcester.*

The case of an oath of abjuration considered. 1693.

See no. 3789.

3283

TILLOTSON (John) *Archbishop of Canterbury.*

A sermon preached before the Queen at White-hall, April the 9th, 1693. Concerning the sacrifice and satisfaction of Christ. London: for B. Aylmer: and W. Rogers, 1693. 4°

Wing T 1248.

T.709

3284

TILLOTSON (John) *Archbishop of Canterbury.*

Sermons concerning the divinity and incarnation of our blessed Saviour: preached in the church of St. Lawrence Jewry, London, for Br. Aylmer, and W. Rogers, 1693. 8°

Wing T 1255.
"Charles Alchorn/ he bought them for R. S."

T.56

3285

The TRUE and genuine explanation of one King James's declaration. [A poem, attributed to Charles Montagu.] London: printed in the year 1693. brs.

Wing T 2484.
Attributed by Bowdler to "Mr. Mountague", and by *Poems on affairs of state* to Charles Montagu?

T.510

3286

A TRUE copy of a speech made by an English colonel to his regiment, immediately before their late transportation for Flanders at Harwich. [No imprint, 1693?] 4°

Not in Wing.

T.200

3287

VILLIERS (Jacob de)

Nobilis pharmacopola. Historia si non vera, jucunda tamen, nunc demum Latinitate donata: cum nonnullis epistolis... [Anon.] Londini: ex officina M.C. prostant apud bibliopolas, 1693. 12°

Wing V 391.

T.456

3288

WAGENSEIL (Johann Christoph)

Ad Johannem Fechtium... Joh. Christophori Wagenseilii de infundibuli sui occasione, consilio, & instituto, dissertatio epistolica... Altdorfi Noricorum typis Johannis Henrici Schönnerstaedt, 1693. 4°

T.818

3289

WAGSTAFFE (Thomas)

A supplement to his Majesties most gracious speech. Directed to the honourable House of Commons, by the Commons of England. [Anon.] [London, 1693.] 4°

Wing W 217.

T.267

3290

WALKER (Thomas)

A sermon preached at Great St. Marie's Church in Cambridge, before ... the Lord Chief-Justice Holt, at the Assizes held there ... Cambridge, John Hayes, for William Graves, 1693. 4°

Wing W 416.

T.8

3291

WALLIS (John)

A defense of the Christian Sabbath. Part the first. In answer to a treatise of Mr. Thomas Bampfield pleading for Saturday-Sabbath. 2nd ed. Oxford, Leonard Lichfield, 1693. 4°

Ch. Ch. W 570+.

T.827

3292

WELCHMAN (Edward)

A defence of the Church of England, from the charge of schism and heresie, as laid against it by the vindicator of the deprived bishops [i.e. Henry Dodwell]... [Anon.] London: Randal Taylor, 1693. 4°

Wing W 1320.

T.374

3293

WORM (Christen)

Christiani Wormii Wilh: fil: de corruptis antiquitatum Hebraearum apud Tacitum et Martialem vestigiis liber primus. Hafniae, typis Joh. Phil. Bockenhoffer. Prostat apud J.M. Liebe, 1693. 4°

T.818

3294

YOUNG (Edward) *Dean of Salisbury.*

A sermon concerning the wisdom of fearing God; preach'd at Salisbury, on Sunday, July xxx. 1693 ... London, T. W. for Walter Kettilby, 1693. 4°

Wing Y 63.
2 copies.

T.709   T.181

3295

YOUNG (Edward) *Dean of Salisbury.*

A sermon preached before the Queen, at White-hall, on Easter-day, 1693. London: for Walter Kettilby, 1693. 4°

Wing Y 69.

T.181

1694

3296

An ACCOUNT of a most horrid and barbarous murther and robbery, committed on the body of Captain Brown, a gentleman of eight hundred pound a year, near Shrewsbury ... Printed for J. Smith, 1694. 4°

cf. Wing A 187.

T.262

3297

ARWAKER (Edmund) *the Younger.*

An elegy on his Excellency Lieutenant-General Tolmach. London, for Francis Saunders, and sold by Randal Taylor, 1694. Fol.

Wing A 3906.

T.699

3298

ARWAKER (Edmund) *the Younger.*

An epistle to Monsieur Boileau, inviting his muse to forsake the French interest, and celebrate the King of England. London, Tho.Warren for Francis Saunders, 1694. Fol.

Wing A 3907.
Another copy is included in the collection of poems published by Nahum Tate in 1697. T.529.

T.699

3299

ATTERBURY (Francis) *Bishop of Rochester.*

The scorner incapable of true wisdom. A sermon before the Queen at White-hall, October 28. 1694. London: for Thomas Bennet, 1694. 4°

Wing A 4152.

T.771

3300

BAUDAN DE VESTRIC (Pierre)

Les devoirs des ambassadeurs de Christ. Seconde edition augmentée ... A Delf, chez Henry de Krooneveld, 1694. 8°

2 copies.

T.500

3301

BIRCH (Peter)

A sermon preached before the honourable House of Commons, at St Margarets Westminster, January 30. 1694. London, for Tho. Nott, and are to be sold by Randal Taylor, 1694. 4°

Wing B 2939.
4 copies.

T.771   T.637   T.489   T.273

3302

A BRIEF answer to several popular objections against the present established clergy of the Church of England. London, for Randal Taylor, 1694. 4°

Wing B 4544.

T.308

3303

BRISCOE (John)

A discourse on the late funds of the Million-Act, Lottery-Act, and Bank of England ... By J. B. ... 2nd ed., with large additions. London, J. D. and sold by R. Baldwin, 1694. 4°

Wing B 4747.

T. 16

3304

CAMPION (Abraham)

A sermon concerning national providence, preach'd at the assizes held at Ailesbury... March 13. 1693/4. Printed for Anthony Piesley bookseller in Oxford, 1694. 4°

Wing C 406.

T.771

3305

CHURCH OF ENGLAND.

A form of prayer to be used on Wednesday the three and twentieth day of this instant May... being the fast-day appointed... for supplicating almighty God for the pardon of our sins, and for imploring his blessing and protection in the preservation of their Majesties sacred persons, and the prosperity of their arms both at land and sea. London, Charles Bill, and the executrix of Thomas Newcomb, 1694. 4°

Wing C 4157.

T.489

3306

CHURCH OF ENGLAND.

A form of thanksgiving to almighty God, for the preservation of his Majesty from the manifold dangers to which his royal person was exposed during his late expedition... London, Charles Bill and the executrix of Thomas Newcomb, 1694. 4°

Not in Wing.

T.489

3307

CHURCH OF ENGLAND.

Prayers to be used during the Queens sickness, in the cities of London and Westminster. London, Charles Bill and the executrix of Thomas Newcomb, 1694. 4°

Not in Wing.

T.489

3308

EVERETT (George)

The path-way to peace and profit: or, Truth in its plain dress. Wherein is methodically set forth a sure and certain way for the more speedy and effectual building and repairing théir Majesties Royal Navy ... London, printed for the author; and are to be sold by Randal Taylor, 1694. 4°

Wing E 3548.

T.325

3309

HALE (*Sir* Matthew)

A treatise, shewing how usefull, safe, reasonable and beneficial, the inrolling & registring of all conveyances of lands, may be to the inhabitants of this kingdom. By a person of great learning and judgment. London, for Mat. Wotton, 1694. 4°

Wing H 263.

T. 16

3310

JOHNSON (Samuel) *Rector of Corringham.*

An essay concerning parliaments at a certainty; or, The Kalends of May,.. 2nd ed. London, printed for the author; to be sold by Richard Baldwin, 1694. 4°

Wing J 827.

T.136

3311

JOHNSON (Samuel) *Rector of Corringham.*

An essay concerning parliaments at a certainty; or, The Kalends of May ... 2nd ed. London; printed for the author, 1694. 4°

cf. Wing J 827.

T.329

3312

JOHNSON (Samuel) *Rector of Corringham.*

Notes upon the phoenix edition of the pastoral letter. Part I. London, printed for the author, 1694. 4°

Wing J 835.
2 copies.

T.329   T.136

3313

KING (William) *Archbishop of Dublin.*

An admonition to the dissenting inhabitants of the diocess of Derry: concerning a book lately published by Mr. J. Boyse, entituled, Remarks on a late discourse of William Lord Bishop of Derry ... London, for William Keblewhite, 1694. 8°

Wing K 521.

T.454

3314

KNIGHT (*Sir* John)

The following speech being spoke off hand upon the debates in the House of Commons; you cannot expect in it the exactness of Roman eloquence ... [Anon.] [London, 1694.] 4°

Wing K 686 (?)

T.136

3315

LESLIE (Charles)

Tempora mutantur. Or, The great change from 73 to 93 In the travels of a professor of theology at Glasgow, from the primitive and episcopal loyalty, through Italy, Geneva, &c. to the deposing doctrine, under papistico-phanatico-prelatico colours at Salisbury ... [Anon.] Printed in this year, 1694. 4°

Wing L 1160.

T.510

3316

A LETTER to the members of parliament for the county of --- concerning the Triennial Bill ... By some electors of members of parliament. [No imprint, 1694?] 4°

Not in Wing.

T.136

3317

MARONITE CHURCH.

Ordo benedictionis, ac processionis palmarum juxta ritum ecclesiae nationis Maronitarum, a Syriaco textu Latinitati donatus ab Elia Simonio Hesronita. Romae, ex typographia Dominici Antonü Herculis, 1694.

2 copies.

T.461   T.520

3318

N. (H.)

A letter concerning Sir William Whitlock's bill for trials in case of treason, written Oct. 1693. upon the request of a friend who is an honest member of the House of Commons; and now committed to the press ... [London, 1694?] 4°

Wing N 19.

T.136

3319

OSBORNE (Peregrine) *2nd Duke of Leeds.*

A journal of the Brest-expedition, by the Lord Marquiss of Caermarthen. London, for Randal Taylor, 1694. 4°

Wing L 917.

T.4

3320

The PRESENT state of England. [London, 1694.] 4°

Wing P 3260.

T.510

3321

PROPOSALS for raising a million of money out of the forfeited estates in Ireland: together, with the answer to the same, and a reply thereto. London: for T. Goodwin, 1694. 4°

Wing P 3739.

T.22

3322

A REPLY to the answer Doctor Welwood has made to King James's declaration ... dated at St. Germaines, April 17th. S. N. 1693 ... [London, 1694.] 4°

Wing R 1066.
3 copies.

T.510   T.200

3323

ST. LO (George)

England's interest; or, a discipline for seamen: wherein is proposed, a sure method for raising qualified sea-men, for the well manning their Majesties fleet on all occasions... London: for Richard Baldwin, 1694.   4°

Wing S 340.

T.325

3324

SANCROFT (William) *Archbishop of Canterbury.*

Occasional sermons preached by the most reverend father in God William Sancroft... With some remarks of his life and conversation; in a letter to a friend. London, T.B. for Thomas Bassett, 1694.   8°

Wing S 561.

T.386

3325

SAVILE (George) *Marquess of Halifax.*

A rough draught of a new model at sea. [Anon.] London, for A. Banks, 1694. 4°

Wing H 319.
2 copies. On the t.p. of copy T.200 is Bowdler's note: "Sir Hen. Shere. little in it, but words."

T.325   T.200

3326

SERGEANT (John)

An historical romance of the wars, between the mighty giant Gallieno, and the great knight Nasonius, and his associates ... [Anon.] Dublin: printed in the year 1694.   4°

Wing S 2570.
2 copies.

T.510   T.80

3327

SHARP (John) *Archbishop of York.*

A sermon about the government of the thoughts, preach'd before the King & Queen, at White-hall, the 4th of March... 1693/4. London, Tho. Warren, for Walter Kettilby, 1694.   4°

Wing S 2980.

T.625

3328

SHARP (John) *Archbishop of York.*

A sermon about the government of the thoughts, preach'd before the King & Queen, at White-hall, the 4th of March... 1693/4. 2nd ed. London, Tho. Warren, for Walter Kettilby, 1694. 4°

Wing S 2981.

T.709

3329

SHARP (John) *Archbishop of York.*

A sermon about the government of the thoughts, preach'd before the King & Queen, at White-hall, the 4th of March... 1693/4. 3rd ed. London, Tho. Warren, for Walter Kettilby, 1694.   4°

Wing S 2982.

T.771

3330

A SHORT and true relation of intrigues transacted, both at home and abroad, to restore the late King James ... London, printed in the year, 1694.   4°

Wing S 3557.

T.200

3331

SOME useful reflections upon a pamphlet [by William Paterson] called a Brief account of the intended Bank of England. [London, 1694.] 4°

Wing S 4631.

T.70

3332

STEPHENS (William)

A sermon preached before the right honourable the Lord Mayor, and aldermen of the city of London, at St. Mary-le-Bow, Jan 30th. 1693/4. London: for John Lawrence; and Brab. Aylmer, 1694.   4°

Wing S 5462.

T.489

3333

STILLINGFLEET (Edward) *Bishop of Worcester.*

A sermon concerning sins of omission, preached before the King and Queen at White-hall, on March 18th. 1693/4... London, for J.H. for Henry Mortlock, 1694. 4°

Wing S 5636.

T.771

TATE (Nahum)

A poem on the late promotion of several eminent persons... 1694.

See no. 3479.

3334

TILLOTSON (John) *Archbishop of Canterbury.*

A sermon preached before the King and Queen at White-hall February the 25th 1693/4... 2nd ed. London, for Brabazon Aylmer: and William Rogers, 1694.   4°

Wing T 1250.

T.709

3335

TUTCHIN (John)

An epistle to Mr. Benjamin Bridgwater, occasion'd by the death of the late Queen Mary.   London: for Richard Baldwin, 1694.   Fol.

Wing T 3374.

T.699

3336

WAGSTAFFE (Thomas)

A letter out of Lancashire to a friend in London, giving some account of the late tryals there... [Anon.] Printed in the year, 1694.   4°

Wing W 208
2 copies.

T.510   T.511

3337

WAGSTAFFE (Thomas)

A letter out of Suffolk to a friend in London. Giving some account of the last sickness and death of Dr. William Sancroft, late Lord Archbishop of Canterbury. [Anon.] London; printed in the year, 1694. 4°

Wing W. 209.
2 copies.

T.509   T.190

3338

WALLIS (John)

A defense of the Christian Sabbath. Part the second. Being a rejoinder to Mr. Bampfield's Reply to Doctor Wallis's discourse concerning the Christian-Sabbath. Oxford, Leon. Lichfield, 1694.   4°

Wing W 571.

T.827

3339

WILLIAM III, *King of England.*

Injunctions given by the Kings Majesty to the archbishops of this realm, to be communicated by them to the Bishops and the rest of the clergy. London, Charles Bill and the executrix of Thomas Newcomb, 1694.   4°

Wing W 2340

T.461

3340

YOUNG (Edward) *Dean of Salisbury.*

The great advertisement, that a religious life is the best way to present happiness: in two sermons preach'd at White-hall ... London, Tho. Warren, for Walter Kettilby, 1694.   4°

Wing Y 60.
2 copies.

T.709   T.181

3341

ADAMS (John) *Provost of King's College, Cambridge.*

A sermon preach'd at White-hall on Sunday, September 8. 1695. being the day of thanksgiving for the taking of Namur, and the safety of his Majesty's person. London: for Thomas Bennet, 1695.   4°

Wing A 485.

T.771

3342

ADVICE to electors; by a well-wisher to Parliaments, and one who will live and dye a friend to his country. [No imprint], 1695. 4°

Not in Wing.

T.136

BELLERS (John)

Proposals for raising a colledge of industry. 1695.

See no. 8301.

3343

BRIDGWATER (Benjamin)

A poem upon the death of her late Majesty, Queen Mary, of blessed memory. Occasioned by An epistle to the author, from Mr. J. Tutchin. London: for Richard Baldwin, 1695.   Fol.

Wing B 4485.

T.699

3344

The CASE of all the non-commionssi'd [sic] officers... and private horsemen of Colonel Theodore Russel's late regiment... [No imprint, 1695.] 4°

Wing C 878.

T.22

3345

CHURCH OF ENGLAND.

A form of prayer to be used on Wednesday the eleventh of this instant December... being the fast-day appointed... for imploring a blessing upon the consultations of this present Parliament. London, Charles Bill and the executrix of Thomas Newcomb, 1695.   4°

Wing C 4159.

T.463

3346

COLLIER (Jeremy)

A perswasive to consideration, tender'd to the royalists; particularly those of the Church of England; with a vindication of the same. [Anon.] London, printed in the year, 1695.   8°

Not in Wing (cf. C 5260).
2 copies

T.412   T.449

3347

D. (P.)

A letter from an English merchant at Amsterdam, to his friend at London, concerning the trade and coin of England. London: for S. Crouch, 1695. 4°

Wing D 77.

T. 16

3348

D. (P.)

A letter from an English merchant at Amsterdam, to his friend at London, concerning the trade and coin of England. London: printed in the year 1695. 4°

Not in Wing.

T.267

3349

A DISCOURSE concerning the fishery within the British seas ... and more especially, as it relates to the trade of the Company of the Royal Fishery of England ... London, for the Company of the Royal Fishery of England, 1695. 4°

Wing D 1585.
Incomplete.

T. 18

3350

DODWELL (Henry)

A defence of the Vindication of the deprived
bishops ... In a reply to Dr. Hody and another
author. To which is annexed, The doctrine of the
Church of England, concerning the independency of the
clergy on the lay-power ... By the author of
the Vindication of the deprived bishops. London,
printed 1695,97. 2 parts. 4°

Wing D 1805 (including   D 1813).

T.135

3351

ENGLAND. *Parliament.*

A collection of some memorable and weighty
transactions in Parliament, in the year 1678, and
afterwards; in relation to the impeachment of
Thomas Earl of Danby ... London, printed in the
year, 1695. 4°

Wing E 1280.

T.139

3352

ENGLAND. *Parliament.*

A collection of the debates and proceedings in
Parliament, in 1694, and 1695. Upon the inquiry
into the late briberies and corrupt practices ...
(A supplement ...) London, printed in the year
1695. 2 parts. 4°

Wing E 1281.

T.267

3353

ENGLAND. *Parliament.*

The examinations and informations upon oath, of
Sir Thomas Cooke, and several other persons:
lately taken before a committee of both Houses
of Parliament, touching divers indirect practices,
to procure by corrupt and unlawful means, a new
charter, and act of Parliament for the East-
India Company. [London, 1695.] 4°

Wing E 3730.

T.188

3354

ENGLAND. *Parliament.*

The examinations and informations upon oath, of
Sir Thomas Cooke, and several other persons:
lately taken before a committee of both Houses of
Parliament, touching divers indirect practices, to
procure by corrupt and unlawful means, a new
charter, and act of Parliament for the East-
India Company. As also the articles of
impeachment ... against the Duke of Leeds. With
his Grace's answer thereunto. [London, 1695.] 4°

Not in Wing.
2copies.

T.267 T.324

3355

ENGLAND'S appeal, to her high court of Parliament;
against Irish and Scottish evidence. [No imprint,
c.1695.] 4°

Not in Wing.

T.510

3356

FERGUSON (Robert)

A brief account of some of the late incroachments
and depredations of the Dutch upon the English; and
of a few of those many advantages which by fraud
and violence they have made of the British nations
since the revolution ... [Anon.] [London, 1695.]
4°

Wing F 731.

T.511

3357

FERGUSON (Robert)

Whether the Parliament be not in law dissolved by
the death of the Princess of Orange? And how the
subjects ought, and are to behave themselves in
relation to those papers emitted since by the stile
and title of acts? With a brief account of the
government of England. In a letter to a country
gentleman, as an answer to his second question.
[Anon.] [London, 1695.]   4°

Wing F 765.   2 copies

T.511

3358

FERGUSON (Robert)

Whether the preserving the protestant religion was
the motive unto, or the end, that was designed in
the late revolution? In a letter to a country
gentleman, as an answer to his first query. [Anon.]
[London, 1695.]   4°

Wing F 766.

T.511

3359

A FUNERAL eclogue sacred to the memory of her most
serene Majesty, our late gracious Queen Mary: who
departed this life at Kinsington: on Friday the
28th of December 1694. London, for John Whitlock,
1695. Fol.

Wing F 2531.

T.699

3360

GLEANE (Peter)

An elegy on the death of the Queen. London: for
Sam. Heyrick, 1695. Fol.

Wing G 848.

T.699

3361

HODGES (William)

Great Britain's groans: or, An account of the
oppression, ruin, and destruction of the loyal
seamen of England ... [Anon.] Printed in the
year 1695. 4°

Wing H 2327.

T.325

3362

An HUMBLE address offer'd to the consideration of
the Lords and Commons touching a law concerning
perjury. [London, 1695.]   4°

Wing H 3387.

T.510

3363

KEN (Thomas) *Bishop of Bath and Wells.*

A letter to the author [i.e. Thomas Tenison] of a
sermon, entitled, A sermon preach'd at the funeral
of her late Majesty Queen Mary ... [Anon.] [London,
1695.] 4°

Wing K 265.
2 copies.

T.489 T.200

3364

LA RUE (Charles de)

A funeral oration or sermon upon the most high, most
potent lord, Francis Henry de Montmorancy, Duke of
Luxembourg and Piney ... From the French original.
London, Richard Baldwin, 1695.   4°

Wing L 455.

T.489

3365

LESLIE (Charles)

The charge of Socinianism against Dr. Tillotson
considered ... To which is added Some reflections
upon the second of Dr. Burnet's four discourses,
concerning the divinity and death of Christ ... To
which is likewise annexed, A supplement ... By a true
son of the Church. [Anon.] Edenburgh: printed 1695.
4°

Wing L 1124.

T.509

3366

LESLIE (Charles)

Gallienus redivivus or, Murther will out &c. Being
a true account of the de-witting of Glencoe,
Gaffney, &c ... [Anon.] Edinburgh, printed in the
year, 1695. 4°

Wing L 1134.

T.80

3367

LESLIE (Charles)

Querela temporum: or, The danger of the Church of
England. In a letter from the Dean of   to
Prebend of   . [Anon.] London, printed in the
year 1695. 4°

Wing L 1143.
7 copies.

T.11 T.72 T.510

3368

LESLIE (Charles)

Remarks on some late sermons; and in particular,
on Dr. Sherlock's sermon at the Temple, December
30th, MDCXCIV. In a letter to a friend. [Anon.]
[London, 1695.]   4°

Wing L 1147 (?)
Wanting title-page (?)

T.489

3369

LESLIE (Charles)

Remarks on some late sermons; and in particular on
Dr. Sherlock's sermon at the Temple, Decemb.30.
1694. In a letter to a friend. [By Charles Leslie.]
2nd ed., with additions. Together with a letter to
the author of a pamphlet, entitled, A defence of
the Archbishop's sermon... [by Thomas Wagstaffe].
London, printed in the year 1695. 4°

Wing L1148.
3 copies.

T.24 T.489 T.512

3370

A LETTER from a gentleman in Yorkshire, to his
country-man in London: concerning the Duke of
Leeds. With an answer to the said letter.
London: printed in the year, 1695. 2 parts. 4°

Wing L 1396.
3 copies.

T.139 T.188 T.200

3371

A LETTER to a friend in the country [about a
dissolution of Parliament on the death of Queen
Mary]. London, printed in the year 1695. 4°

Wing L 1651.

T.200

3372

LOCKE (John)

Further considerations concerning raising the value of
money. Wherein Mr. Lowndes's arguments for it in his
late report concerning An essay for the amendment of
the silver coins, are particularly examined. [Anon.]
London, for A. and J. Churchil, 1695.   8°

Wing L 2745.

T.443

3373

LOCKE (John)

Further considerations concerning raising the value
of money. Wherein Mr. Lowndes's arguments for it
in his late report concerning An essay for the
amendment of the silver coins, are particularly
examined. [Anon.] 2nd ed. corrected. London, for
A. and J. Churchil, 1695. 8°

Wing L 2746.

T.219

3374

LOWNDES (William)

A report containing an essay for the amendment of
the silver coins. London, Charles Bill, and the
Executrix of Thomas Newcomb, 1695. 8°

Wing L 3323.

T.16

3375

MAURICE (Henry)

An impartial account of Mr. John Mason of Water-
Stratford, and his sentiments ... London, Tho.
Warren, for Walter Kettilby, 1695. 4°

Wing M 1363.

T.139

3376

MURRAY (Robert)

A proposal for a national bank, consisting of land,
or any other valuable securities or depositums ...
[London, 1695.] 4°

Wing M 3117 (?)

T.70

3377

ON the death of the Queen, a poem.   London:
John Whitlock, 1695. Fol.

Wing O 311.

T.699

1695 (Cont'd)

3378

PARTRIDGE (William)

A consolatory poem: address'd to his most sacred Majesty... London, for R. Baldwin, 1695. Fol.

Wing P 635.

T.699

3379

PEACHAM (Henry)

The worth of a penny: or, A caution to keep money ... London, for Samuel Keble, 1695. 4°

Wing P 956.

T.70

3380

PETTY (*Sir* William)

Sir William Petty's quantulumcunque concerning money, 1682. To the Lord Marquess of Halyfax. London, printed in the year 1695. 4°

Wing P 1935.

T.16

3381

A POEM, occasion'd by the death of her late Majesty of ever happy and sacred memory. By a private hand. London, J. Whitlock, 1695. Fol.

Wing P 2678A.

T.699

3382

A POEM occasioned by the death of her Majesty. By a person of honour. London, J. Whitlock, 1695. Fol.

Wing P 2679.

T.699

3383

A POETICAL essay devoted to the glorious memory of our late Queen, occasion'd by a number of poems, and sermons, upon her death... London, printed in the year 1695. Fol.

Wing P 2736.

T.699

3384

RAWSON (Joseph) *and* SMITH (Robert)

Poems on the lamented death of her most excellent Majesty, Queen Mary... London, for Tho. Bennet, 1695. Fol.

Wing R 378.

T.699

3385

SAVILE (George) *Marquess of Halifax.*

Some cautions offered to the consideration of those who are to chuse members to serve in the ensuing parliament. [Anon.] London: printed in the year 1695. 4°

Wing H 322.
2 copies.

T.200 T.136

3386

SEGAR (Simon)

Threno-Maria. A rapsodicall essay on the death of our late gracious soveraign Queen Mary... London: for Thomas Leving, 1695. Fol.

Wing S 2413.

T.699

3387

SERGEANT (John)

A letter from a trooper in Flanders, to his comrade: shewing, that Luxembourg is a witch, and deals with the devil. [Anon.] London, printed in the year 1695. 4°

Wing S 2574.

T.263

3388

SOME remarks on a report containing an essay for the amendment of the silver coins, made to the Right Honourable the Lords Commissioners of His Majesties Treasury, by Mr. William Lowndes ... London, for W. Whitlock, 1695. 4°

Wing S 4598.

T.16

3389

STEELE (*Sir* Richard)

The procession. A poem on her Majesties funeral. By a gentleman of the army... London, for Thomas Bennet, 1695. Fol.

Wing S 5381.

T.699

3390

STEPHENS (Edward)

Positions concerning the differences between the true English liturgy, and the deformed disordered Cranmerian changeling, by which it was supplanted. [Anon.] [London, 1695?] 4°

Not in Wing.
2 copies.

T.72

3391

STRODE (S.)

A poem on the death of her most sacred Majesty, Queen Mary. London, J. Whitlock, 1695. Fol.

Wing S 5979.

T.699

3392

URANIAE metamorphosis in Sydus: or, The transfiguration of our late gracious sovereign Queen Mary. Discover'd in a miraculous vision since the celebration of her funeral. A poem... Written by a doctor of physick... London, for D. Browne, and R. Baldwin, 1694/5. Fol.

Wing U 125.

T.699

3393

URANIA'S temple: or, A satyr upon the silent-poets ... London, J.M. and B.B. and are to be sold by Rich. Baldwin, 1695. Fol.

Wing U 126.

T.699

3394

W. (*Sir* D.)

Some reflections on the oaths & declaration appointed in an act past in the first year of the reign of King William and Queen Mary, in reference to the Roman Catholicks of England. London, printed in the year 1695. 4°

Wing W 12.

T.197

3395

YOUNG (Edward) *Dean of Salisbury.*

Piety's address to the magistrate. Delivered in a sermon at the assizes held in Winchester, July 11th. 1695. London, for Walter Kettilby, 1695. 4°

Wing Y 62.
2 copies.

T.709 T.181

3396

YOUNG (Edward) *Dean of Salisbury.*

Two assize sermons preached at Winchester ... London: for Walter Kettilby, 1695. 4°

Wing Y 70.
2 copies.

T.709 T.181

1696

3397

ADAMS (John) *Provost of King's College, Cambridge.*

A sermon preached before the honourable House of Commons, at St. Margarets Westminster, November the fifth, 1696. London: Sam. Bridge; for Thomas Bennet, 1696. 4°

Wing A 486.

T.172

3398

An ANSWER to a libel entituled, A dialogue between Dr. H.C. and a country-gentleman. [Attributed to Hugh Chamberlen.] London, T. Sowle, 1696. 4°

Wing A 3321.

T.70

3399

ASGILL (John)

Remarks on the proceedings of the Commissioners for putting in execution the Act past last sessions, for establishing of a land-bank. [Anon.] London, printed, and sold by the booksellers of London and Westminster, 1696. 8°

Wing A 3930.

T.212

3400

BARTON (Samuel)

A sermon preach'd before the honourable House of Commons, at St. Margaret's Westminster, upon the 16th of April, 1696 ... London: for Tho. Cockerill, Senr and Junr, 1696. 4°

Wing B 993.

T.172

3401

BASTON (Samuel)

A dialogue between a modern courtier, and an honest English gentleman. [Anon.] Printed in the year 1696. 4°

Wing C 7242 (attributed to Robert Crosfeild).

T.136

3402

C. (W.)

A discourse (by way of essay) humbly offer'd to the consideration of the Honourable House of Commons, towards the raising moneys by an excise ... London, printed for the author, 1696. 4°

Wing C 150.
Attributed by Bowdler to William Culliford.

T.16

3403

CARY (John)

An essay towards the setlement of a national credit, in the Kingdom of England, humbly presented to the two honourable Houses of Parliament. London: Freeman Collins, and are to be sold by S. Crouch, and E. Whitlock, 1696. 8°

Wing C 731.

T.219

3404

CHAMBERLEN (Hugh)

A collection of some papers writ upon several occasions, concerning clipt and counterfeit money, and trade, so far as it relates to the exportation of bullion. London, for Benj. Tooke, 1696. 4°

Wing C 1870.

T.16

3405

CHURCH OF ENGLAND.

A form of prayer and thanksgiving, to almighty God: to be used on Thursday the sixteenth of April next... for discovering and disappointing a horrid and barbarous conspiracy of papists... and for delivering this Kingdom from an invasion intended by the French. London, Charles Bill, and the executrix of Thomas Newcomb, 1696. 4°

Wing C 4134.

T.461

3406

CHURCH OF ENGLAND.

A form of prayer to be used... on Friday the twenty sixth day of June next; being the fast-day... for supplicating almighty God for the pardon of our sins, and for imploring his blessing and protection in the preservation of his Majesties sacred person, and the prosperity of his arms both at land and sea. London, Charles Bill, and the executrix of Thomas Newcomb, 1696. 4°

Wing C 4160.

T.461

3407

CLEMENT (Simon)

A dialogue between a countrey gentleman and a merchant, concerning the falling of guinea's: wherein the whole argument relating to our money is discuss'd. [Anon.] London, John Astwood for Samuel Crouch, 1696. 4°

Wing C 4637.

T, 16

3408

COCKBURN (John)

An enquiry into the nature, necessity, and evidence of Christian faith, in several essays. Part I. Of faith in general, and of the belief of a deity. By J. C ... London, for William Keblewhite, 1696. 8°

Wing C 4810.

T.150

3409

COLLIER (Jeremy)

An answer to the Animadversions on two pamphlets lately publish'd by Mr. Collier, &c. [London, 1696.] 4°

Wing C 5242.
2 copies.

T.509   T.374

3410

COLLIER (Jeremy)

A defence of the absolution given to Sr. William Perkins, at the place of execution, April the 3d. 1696. [London, 1696.] 4°

Wing C 5247 (?)

T.200

3411

COLLIER (Jeremy)

A defence of the absolution given to Sr. William Perkins, at the place of execution ... With a farther vindication thereof, occasioned by a paper [by John Williams], entitled a Declaration of the sense of the archbishops and bishops, &c. [London, 1696.] 4°

Wing C 5247 (?)
4 copies.

T.509   T.197   T.374

3412

COLLIER (Jeremy)

A reply to The absolution of a penitent, according to the directions of the Church of England, &c. [by P. H. J.]. [London, 1696.] 4°

Wing C 5261.
5 copies.

T.509   T.197   T.374

3413

The COUNTRY gentleman's notion concerning governments. In a letter to his friend at Leeds in Yorkshire. London, printed, 1696. 4°

Wing C 6532.

T.277

3414

DAVANZATI (Bernardo)

A discourse upon coins ... Translated out of Italian by John Toland. London; J. D. for Awnsham and John Churchill, 1696. 4°

Wing D 301.

T, 10

3415

DAVENANT (Charles)

An essay on the East-India-trade. By the author of The essay upon wayes and means. London, printed anno, 1696. 8°

Wing D 307.
2 copies.

T.32   T.324

3416

DAWES (*Sir* William) *Archbishop of York.*

A sermon preach'd before the King at White-hall, Novemb. 5. 1696 ... London: for Thomas Speed, 1696. 4°

Wing D 456.

T.489

3417

ELYS (Edmund)

A letter to the Honourable Sir Robert Howard. Together with some animadversions upon a book entituled, Christianity not mysterious [By John Toland] ... London: for Richard Wilkin, 1696. 8°

Wing E 678 A.

T, 32

3418

ELYS (Edmund)

Refutatio erroris execrabilis, symbolum Nicaenum impugnantis, qui occurrit in fallaci isto libello, cui titulus est Animadversions on Mr. Hill's book [by Gilbert Burnet] ... An Dom, 1696. 8°

Not in Wing.

T, 32

3419

FLEETWOOD (William) *Bishop of Ely.*

A sermon of the education of children, preach'd before the ... Lord Mayor, and court of aldermen, at Guild-hall chapel, on Sunday, Novemb. 1. 1696. London, for Thomas Newborough, 1696. 4°

Wing F 1249.

T.709

3420

FOWLER (Edward) *Bishop of Gloucester.*

A sermon preached before the House of Lords in the Abby-Church at Westminster, upon Thursday the sixteenth of April, 1696 ... London, for B. Aylmer, 1696. 4°

Wing F 1724.

T,172

3421

The FREE state of Noland. London: for J. Whitlock, 1696. 4°

Wing F 2120.
Manuscript attribution to "Mr. Littleton" [perhaps Edward Littleton].

T, 80

3422

FULLER (William)

A brief discovery of the true mother of the pretended Prince of Wales known by the name of Mary Grey ... London, printed for the author, anno Dom. 1696. 8°

Wing F 2479.

T.282

3423

An IMPARTIAL account of the horrid and detestable conspiracy to assassinate his sacred Majesty King William, raise a rebellion ... and to encourage an invasion from France. London, for John Salusbury, 1696. 4°

Wing I 70.

T.510

3424

KUSTER (Ludolph)

Historia critica Homeri, qua de scriptis ejustam deperditis, quam exstantibus, spuriis & genuinis... Francofurti ad Viadrum, impensis Jerem. Schrey & haeredum Henrici Johannis Meyeri, 1696. 8°

T.796

3425

LOWTH (Simon)

Historical collections concerning church affairs ... By a presbyter of the Church of England. London, printed in the year 1696. 4°

Wing L 3326.
2 copies.

T.199   T,76

3426

LUDOLF (Heinrich Wilhelm)

[Grammatika Rossiiskaia... V Oksfordi, 1696.] 8°

Not in Wing (cf. L 3463).
Wanting the title-page.

T.148

3427

MAUNDRELL (Henry)

A sermon preach'd before the honourable Company of Merchants trading to the Levant-Seas. At St. Peter-Poor, Dec. 15. 1695. London: for Daniel Brown, 1696. 4°

Wing M 1356.

T.732

3428

MOORE (John) *Bishop of Ely.*

A sermon preach'd before the King at St. James's, April 16. 1696... By... John Lord Bishop of Norwich. London: for Will. Rogers, 1696. 4°

Wing M 2554.

T.172

3429

MURRAY (Robert)

A proposal for the more easie advancing to the crown, any fixed sum of money, to carry on the war against France ... [London, 1696.] 4°

Wing M 3121.

T,70

3430

OATES (Titus)

Εἰκων Βασιλικη: or, The picture of the late King James drawn to the life... London: for Richard Baldwin, 1696. 4°

Wing O 36.

T.77

3431

PATRICK (Symon) *Bishop of Ely.*

A sermon preached before the lords spiritual and temporal, in the Abby-Church at Westminster, on the 5th of November, 1696 ... London: for Ric. Chiswell, 1696. 4°

Wing P 855.

T.172

3432

PENINGTON (John)

The people called Quakers cleared by Geo. Keith, from the false doctrines charged upon them by G. Keith, and his self-contradictions laid open in the ensuing citations out of his books ... London: T. Sowle, 1696. 8°

Wing P 1229.

T.79

3433

PENINGTON (John)

Reflections upon George Keith's late advertisement of a meeting to be held by him and his friends, at Turner's-Hall on the eleventh of the fourth month, 1696 ... [Anon.] London, T. Sowle, 1696. 4°

Wing P 1231.

T.79

3434

PHILLIPS (Daniel)

Disputatio medica inauguralis de variolis ... Lugduni Batavorum, apud Abrahamum Elzevier, 1696.

T.12

3435

PIGGOTT (John)

A good king and his people, the special care of heaven. A sermon preached the 16th of April, 1696... London; J.D. for Andrew Bell; and Eben. Tracy, 1696. 4°

Wing P 2220 B.

T.625

3436

PITT (Moses)

An account of one Ann Jefferies, now living in the county of Cornwall, who was fed for six months by a small sort of airy people call'd fairies...   In a letter from Moses Pitt to...   Dr. Edward Fowler, Lord Bishop of Glocester...   London, for Richard Cumberland, 1696.   8°

Wing P 2301.

T.454

3437

A POEM occasion'd by the happy discovery of the horrid and barbarous conspiracy to assassinate his most sacred Majesty, and to incourage an invasion from France.   Publish'd by Elizabeth Whitlock, 1696.   Fol.

Wing P 2680.

T.529

3438

REMARKS upon an advertisement, of a meeting at Turners-Hall.   [London, 1696.]   4°

Wing R 942.

T.79

3439

ROYAL COLLEGE OF PHYSICIANS.

An appendix to the statutes of the College of Physicians, London.   Wherein are contained several more new laws promulgated in the College, Sept. 30. 1696.   [London, 1696.]   8°

Not in Wing.

T.455

3440

SHOWER (John)

A thanksgiving sermon upon Thursday the sixteenth of April, 1696.   2nd ed.   London; for B. Aylmer; and J. Lawrence, 1696.   4°

Wing S 3694.

T.765

3441

SOME considerations about the raising of coin.   In a second letter to Mr. Locke ... London, for A. and J. Churchill, 1696.   8°

Wing S 4481.

T.219

3442

SOME reflections on a pamphlet [by John Pollexfen], intituled, England and East-India inconsistent in their manufactures.   [By John Gardner?]   London, printed anno 1696.   8°

Wing G 251.
2 copies.

T.219   T.324

3443

SPRAT (Thomas) *Bishop of Rochester.*

A discourse made by the Ld Bishop of Rochester to the clergy of his diocese, at his visitation in the year 1695 ... In the Savoy: Edw. Jones, 1696. 4°

Wing S 5031.

T.190

3444

STEPHENS (Edward)

The Cranmerian liturgy, or, The subtilty of the serpent, in corrupting the true English liturgy, by Cranmer and a faction of Calvinists.   [Anon.] [London, 1696?] 4°

Not in Wing.
2 copies.

T.72

3445

STEPHENS (William)

An account of the growth of deism in England. [Anon.]   London: printed for the author, 1696.   4°

Wing S 5459.
2 copies.

T.9 T.72

3446

STEPHENS (William)

A thanksgiving sermon preach'd before the... Lord Mayor, court of aldermen, sheriffs and companies of the city of London, at St. Mary-le-Bow, April 16. 1696...   London: for B. Aylmer; and J. Lawrence, 1696.   4°

Wing S 5465.

T.172

3447

STORY (Thomas) *and* BEALING (Benjamin)

Reasons why those of the people called Quakers, challenged by George Keith, to meet him at Turner's Hall the eleventh of this month called June, 1696, refuse their appearance at his peremptory summons.   London, T. Sowle, 1696.   brs.

Wing S 5754.

T.79

3448

A TRUE relation of the horrid conspiracy, against the life of the king.   With an exact list of the prisoners committed to the Tower...   upon the account of the plot.   In a letter to a friend. Sold by E. Whitlock, 1696.   4°

Wing T 2968.

T.510

3449

WHISTON (James)

England's calamities discover'd: with the proper remedy to restore her ancient grandeur and policy ... London: printed for the author, and are to be sold by Joseph Fox, R. Clavel, and T. Minton, 1696. 4°

Wing W 1686.

T.80

3450

WILLES (John)

The unlawfulness of bonds of resignation.   First written in the year 1684.   for the satisfaction of a private gentleman.   And now made publick for the good of others...   [Anon.]   London: E. Whitlock, 1696.   8°
Wing W 2304.

T.441

3451

WILLIAMS (John) *Bishop of Chichester.*

A brief exposition of the Church-catechism.   With proofs from scripture.   6th ed.   London: R. Roberts for the author: and are to be sold by Ri. Chiswell, 1696.   8°

Not in Wing.

T.454

3452

WILLIAMS (John) *Bishop of Chichester.*

A declaration of the sense of the archbishops and bishops; ... concerning the irregular and scandalous proceedings of certain clergy-men at the execution of Sir John Freind and Sir William Parkins.   [London], for John Everingham, 1696.   4°

Wing W 2699.
2 copies.

T.374 T.200

3453

WILLIS (Richard) *Bishop of Winchester.*

Reflexions upon a pamphlet [by William Stephens], intituled, An account of the growth of deism in England...   [Anon.]   London: for John Newton, 1696. 4°

Wing W 2816.

T.72

3454

WOODWARD (John)

Brief instructions for making observations in all parts of the world: as also for collecting, preserving, and sending over natural things...   Drawn up at the request of a person of honour: and presented to the Royal Society.   [Anon.]   London: for Richard Wilkin, 1696.   4°

Wing W 3509.

T.262

3455

ATTERBURY (Francis) *Bishop of Rochester.*

A letter to a Convocation-man concerning the rights, powers, and priviledges of that body. [Anon. Also attributed to Sir Bartholomew Shower.]   London, for E. Whitlock, 1697.   4°

Wing S 3652.

T.133

3456

BRADY (Nicholas)

Church-musick vindicated.   A sermon preach'd at St. Bride's church, on Monday November 22. 1697 ...   London, for Joseph Wilde, 1697.   4°

Wing B 4169.

T.771

3457

CHURCH OF ENGLAND.

A form of prayer to be used...   on Wednesday the the twenty eighth day of April next; being the fast-day appointed...   for the imploring a blessing from almighty God, upon his Majesty, and all his dominions...   London, Charles Bill and the executrix of Thomas Newcomb, 1697.   4°

Wing C 4162.

T.461

3458

DEFOE (Daniel)

Some reflections on a pamphlet [by John Trenchard] lately publish'd, entituled, An argument shewing that a standing army is inconsistent with a free government...   [Anon.]   London: for E. Whitlock, 1697.   4°

Wing D 847. Moore 15.

T.200

3459

DODWELL (Henry)

The doctrine of the Church of England, concerning the independency of the clergy on the lay-power... By the author of The vindication of the depriv'd bishops.   London: printed, 1697.   4°

Wing D 1813.
2 copies.   A copy of another edition, wanting the title-page.

T.76   T.260   T.283

3460

'ΕΙΚΩΝ βροτολοιγου: or, The picture of Titus Oates, D.D. Drawn to the life.   In a letter to himself ... 2nd ed., with additions.   London: printed, and are to be sold by the booksellers of London and Westminster, 1697.   4°

Wing E 313.

T.139

3461

H. (P.)

The Bank of England, and their present method of paying, defended from the aspersions cast on them in a late book, entituled, A review of the universal remedy for all diseases incident to coin ... London, for Thomas Speed, 1697.   8°

Wing H 101.

T.219

3462

HELLIER (Henry)

A treatise concerning schism and schismaticks; wherein the chief grounds & principles of a late separation from the Church of England, are considered and answered.   London, Richard Smith for Jo. Crosley bookseller in Oxford, 1697.   4°

Wing H 1381.
2 copies.

T.374   T.260

3463

K. (W.)

A letter on George Keith's advertisement of an intended meeting at Turners-Hall, the 29th of April, 1697.   London: T. Sowle, 1697.   4°

Wing K 26.
2 copies.

T.79

3464

The LATE King James's manifesto answer'd paragraph by paragraph. Wherein the weakness of his reasons is plainly demonstrated. London: Richard Baldwin, 1697. 4°

Wing L 550.
2 copies.

T.510   T.200

3465

LESLIE (Charles)

A discourse proving the divine institution of water-baptism: wherein the Quaker-arguments against it, are collected and confuted ... By the author of, The snake in the grass ... London: for C. Brome, W. Keblewhite, and H. Hindmarsh, 1697. 4°

Wing L 1128.

T.79

3466

LESLIE (Charles)

Satan dis-rob'd from his disguise of light: or, The Quakers last shift to cover their monstrous heresies, laid fully open. In a reply to Thomas Ellwood's answer... to George Keith's Narrative of the proceedings at Turners Hall... By the author of The snake in the grass... London: for C. Brome; W. Keblewhite; and H. Hindmarsh, 1697. 2 parts. 4°

Wing L 1149A.

T.79

3467

LESLIE (Charles)

Some seasonable reflections upon the Quakers solemn protestation against George Keith's proceedings at Turner's-Hall, 29. Apr. 1697 ... By an impartial hand. London, for Charles Brome, 1697. 4°

Wing L 1159.

T.79

3468

A LETTER to a friend, in vindication of the proceedings against Sir John Fenwick, by bill of attainder ... London, for Samuel Heyrick, 1697. 4°

Wing L 1653.

T.200

3469

A LIST of King James's Irish and popish forces in France, ready, (when called for:) in answer to an argument against a land-force, writ by A,B,C,D,E,F,G, or to whatever has been, or ever shall be writ upon that subject. Printed by Edw. Jones in the Savoy, 1697. Fol.

Wing L 2398.

T.695

3470

POLLEXFEN (John)

England and East-India inconsistent in their manufactures. Being an answer to a treatise [by Charles Davenant], intituled, An essay on the East-India trade... [Anon.] London, printed in the year, 1697. 8°

Wing P 2779.

T.324

3471

PRINCE of O's declaration, p.1.col.2. [No imprint, 1697?] brs.

Not in Wing.
Apparently against the appointment to office in 1697 of the Earl of Sunderland, who had served James II and had become a Catholic.

T.267

3472

PROPOSALS for a national bank ... To which is added, A compleat catalogue of all the books lately published concerning the coin. London, for Richard Cumberland, 1697. 8°

Wing P 3724.

T.219

3473

PUCKLE (James)

A new dialogue between a burgermaster and an English gentleman. London, J. Southby, 1697. 8°

Wing P 4163.

T.443

3474

RIDPATH (George)

A dialogue betwixt Jack and Will, concerning the Lord Mayor's going to meeting-houses with the sword carried before him, &c. [Anon.] London, printed in the year 1697. 4°

Wing R 1461.

T.200

3475

A SHORT account of the proceedings of the College of Physicians, London, in relation to the sick poor of the said City and suburbs thereof ... London, printed in the year 1697. 4°

Wing S 3543.

T.280

3476

A SOLEMN protestation against George Keith's advertisement, arbitrary summons and proceedings against certain persons, and a meeting of the people called Quakers. [London, 1697.] 4°

Not in Wing.
2 copies.

T.79

3477

SOME queries for the better understanding of a list of King James's Irish and Popish forces in France, ready (when called for:) in answer to an argument against a land-force ... Printed by Edw. Jones, 1697. brs.

Wing S 4561.

T.80

3478

SOMERS (John) *Baron Somers.*

A letter, ballancing the necessity of keeping a land-force in times of peace: with the dangers that may follow on it. [Anon.] Printed in the year 1697. 4°

Wing S 4642.

T.200

3479

TATE (Nahum)

An essay on poetry; written by the Marquis of Normanby... With several other poems... [By Charles Montagu, George Stepney, Edmund Arwaker, Nahum Tate and another. Collected and published by Nahum Tate.] London, for F. Saunders, 1697. 6 parts. Fol.

Wing B 5338.

T.529

3480

TO the citizens of London, June the 24th, 1697. [No imprint.] brs.

Not in Wing.

T.136

3481

TRENCHARD (John)

An argument, shewing, that a standing army is inconsistent with a free government, and absolutely destructive to the constitution of the English monarchy ... [Anon.] London; printed in the year 1697. 4°

Wing T 2110.
3 copies.

T.267   T.200   T.80

3482

TRENCHARD (John)

A letter from the author of the Argument against a standing army [i.e. John Trenchard], to the author of the Balancing letter ... [i.e. Lord Somers]. London, printed in the year, 1697. 4°

Wing T 2113.

T.200

3483

The TRYAL and condemnation of Capt. Thomas Vaughan for high-treason in adhering to the French-King, and for endeavouring the destruction of his Majesty's ships in the Nore... London, for John Everingham, 1697. Fol.

Wing T 2136.
Wanting t.p.

T.690

3484

WAGSTAFFE (Thomas)

A vindication of King Charles the Martyr, proving that his Majesty was the author of Εἰκὼν Βασιλικη. Against a memorandum said to be written by the Earl of Anglesey ... 2nd ed., with additions. [Anon.] London: for H. Hindmarsh, 1697. 8°

Wing W 219.

T.15⁷

3485

WILLIAM III, *King of England.*

Articuli pacis ... Articles of peace between ... William the third, King of Great Britain, and ... Lewis the fourteenth, the most Christian King, concluded in the royal palace at Ryswicke the 10/20 day of September, 1697. London, Charles Bill and the executrix of Thomas Newcomb, 1697. Fol.

Wing W 2309.

T.695

3486

WRIGHT (James)

Three poems of St. Paul's Cathedral: viz. The ruins, The rebuilding, The choire... [Anon.] London, Ben Griffin for Sam. Keble, 1697. Fol.

Wing W 3700.

T.699

1698

3487

AESOP at Tunbridge. Or, A few select fables in verse. By no person of quality. London: E. Whitlock, 1698. 8°

Wing A 739.

T.212

3488

AESOP return'd from Tunbridge: or, Aesop out of his wits. In a few select fables in verse. London: printed for J.F. in Bedlam, [1698]. 8°

Wing A 745.

T.212

3489

ALINGHAM (William)

A short account, of the nature and use of maps. As also some short discourses of the properties of the earth, and of the several inhabitants thereof ... [Anon.] London, printed, and are to be sold by Mr. Mount; Mr. Lea; Mr. Worgan; and by William Alingham, 1698. 8°

Wing A 930 (?)

T.391

3490

An ANSWER to a letter from a gentleman in the country, to a member of the House of Commons: on the votes of the 14th. instant relating to the trade of Ireland. London: for George Huddleston, 1698. 8°

Wing A 3314.

T.443

3491

B.(F.)

A letter to a member of the House of Commons on a proposal for regulating and advancing the woollen-manufactory, &c... London, for Geo. Huddleston, 1698. 8°

Not in Wing (cf. Wing B 62A).

T.443

3492

BARON (William)

The Dutch way of toleration, most proper for our English dissenters. [Anon.] London, printed for the author, 1698. 4°

Wing B 895.
Wanting the title-page.

T.517

3493

BREWSTER (*Sir* Francis)

A discourse concerning Ireland and the different interests thereof, in answer to the Exon and Barnstaple petitions ... [Anon.] London, for Tho, Nott, and are to be sold by E. Whitlock, 1697/8. 4°

Wing B 4433.

T.22

3494

CLARK (Joshua)

A sermon, preached in the parish church of Grantham, July 12. 1697. at the primary visitation of... James, Lord-Bishop of Lincoln... London: for John Everingham, 1698. 4°

Wing C 4480.

T.752

3495

COCKBURN (John)

Bourignianism detected: or the delusions and errors of Antonia Bourignon, and her growing sect ... Narrative I. London, for C. Brome; W. Keblewhite; and H. Hindmarsh, 1698. 4°

Wing C 4804.

T, 79

3496

CONCUBINAGE and poligamy disprov'd: or, The divine institution of marriage betwixt one man, and one woman only, asserted. In answer to a book, writ by John Butler ... London: for R. Baldwin, 1698. 8°

Wing C 5714.

T.322

3497

CONSIDERATIONS on the nature of parliaments, and our present elections. [London, 1698.] 4°

Wing C 5905.

T.136

3498

CROSS (Walter)

The taghmical art: or, The art of expounding scripture by the points, usually called accents, but are really tactical ... London, S. Bridge, for the author, and are to be sold by A. and J. Churchill, 1698. 2 parts. 8°

Wing C 7265.

T.391

3499

DODWELL (Henry)

Reflexions on a pamphlet [by Thomas Milles] entitled, Remarks on the occasional paper, numb.VIII. Relating to the controversy betwixt Dr. Hody and Mr. Dodwell. And on another entitl'd A defence of the vindication of the depriv'd bishops [by Henry Dodwell]... With an answer to a third call'd Historical collections concerning church affairs [by Simon Lowth]. [Anon.] London, T. Snowden, for John Everingham, 1698. 4°

Wing D 1816.

T.374

3500

DU CHASTELET DE LUZANCY (Hippolite)

A conference between an orthodox Christian and a Socinian. Wherein the late distinction of a real and nominal trinitarian is considered. London, Tho. Warren, for Thomas Bennet, 1698. 8°

Wing D 2417.

T.454

3501

EMES (Thomas)

A dialogue between alkali and acid: containing divers philosophical and medicinal considerations wherein a late pretended new hypothesis [of John Colbatch], asserting the cause, and acid the cure of all diseases; is proved groundless and dangerous ... By T. E. chirurgo-medicus ... London: for R. Cumberland, 1698. 8°

Wing E 708.

T.212

3502

GARRET (Walter)

De vera ecclesia hodierna spiritus sancti testimonium: sive, quarti, quintique Apocalypseos capitum interpretatio paraphrastica, cum notis Gual. Garreti ... Londini, impensis Rob. Clavell; prostant apud J. Nutt, 1698. 8°

Not in Wing.

T. 39

3503

GARRET (Walter)

Decimum caput Apocalypseos: sive Reformatio Anglicana. Cum notis Gualteri Garretti... Londini, prostat venalis apud insigne clavium decussatarum & bibliorum, 1698. 8°

Wing G 266.

T.39

3504

GASTRELL (Francis) *Bishop of Chester.*

Some considerations concerning the Trinity: and the ways of managing that controversie. 2nd ed. Together with a defence of them against the objections of the Dean of St. Pauls. [Anon.] London: for T. Bennet, 1698. 2 parts. 8°

Wing G 304 (incl. G 302).

T.149

3505

HALLEY (George)

A sermon preach'd in the cathedral and metropolitica church of St. Peter, in York: on Friday, the fifth of November, 1697 ... London: printed for, and sold by Tho. Baxter, bookseller in York, 1698. 4°

Wing H 456.

T.172

3506

HARRIS (John) *D.D., F.R.S.*

The atheist's objection, that we can have no idea of God refuted. A sermon preach'd at the cathedral-church of St. Paul, February the 7th. 1697/8 ... London, J. L. for Richard Wilkin, 1698. 4°

Wing H 846.
Boyle lectures.

T.181

3507

HARRIS (John) *D.D., F.R.S.*

The atheist's objections, against the immaterial nature of God, and incorporeal substances, refuted. In two sermons preach'd at the cathedral-church of St. Paul, April 4th. and May 2d. 1698 ... London, J. L. for Richard Wilkin, 1698. 4°

Wing H 847.
Boyle lectures.

T.181

3508

HARRIS (John) *D.D., F.R.S.*

Immorality and pride, the great causes of atheism. A sermon preach'd at the cathedral-church of St. Paul, January the 3d. 1697/8 ... London, J. L. for Richard Wilkin, 1698. 4°

Wing H 850.
Boyle lectures.

T.181

3509

HARRIS (John) *D.D., F.R.S.*

The notion of a god, neither from fear nor policy. A sermon preach'd at the cathedral-church of St. Paul, March the 7th. 1697/8 ... London, J. L. for Richard Wilkin, 1698. 4°

Wing H 852.
Boyle lectures.

T.181

3510

HARRIS (John) *D.D., F.R.S.*

A refutation of the atheistical notion of fate, or absolute necessity. In a sermon preach'd at the cathedral-church of St. Paul, November the seventh, 1698 ... London, J. L. for Richard Wilkin, 1698. 4°

Wing H 853.
Boyle lectures.

T.181

3511

HARRIS (John) *D.D., F.R.S.*

A refutation of the objections against moral good and evil. In a sermon preach'd at the cathedral-church of St. Paul, October the third, 1698 ... London, J. L. for Richard Wilkin, 1698. 4°

Wing H 854.
Boyle lectures.

T.181

3512

HARRIS (John) *D.D., F.R.S.*

A refutation of the objections against the attributes of God in general. In a sermon preach'd at the cathedral-church of St. Paul, September the fifth, 1698 ... London, J. L. for Richard Wilkin, 1698. 4°

Wing H 855.
Boyle lectures.

T.181

3513

HILL (Samuel)

The rites of the Christian Church further defended, in answer to the appeal of Dr. Wake. With a letter to Mr. Hill Rector of Kilmington, on the account of the Municipium ecclesiasticum. As also an answer ... Sold by the booksellers of London and Westminster, 1698. 8°

Wing H 2011.

T.32

3514

HOWE (John) *of Magdalen College, Oxford.*

A sermon on the much lamented death of that reverend and worthy servant of Christ Mr. Richard Adams ... London: S. Bridge, for Tho. Parkhurst, 1698. 8°

Wing H 3040.

T. 32

3515

JOHNSON (Samuel) *Rector of Corringham.*

A confutation of a late pamphlet intituled, A letter ballancing the necessity of keeping a land-force in times of peace; with the dangers that may follow on it.[Anon.] London, for A. Baldwin, 1698. 4°

Wing J 824.

T.80

3516

JONES (John), *M.D., Chancellor of Llandaff.*

De morbis Hibernorum; speciatim vero de dysenteria Hibernica; exercitatio medica; apud Academiam Dubliniensem ... pro gradu doctoratus in medicina, recitata ... Londini: impensis S. Keble, 1698. 4°

cf. Wing J 975.

T.280

3517

LESLIE (Charles)

Considerations of importance to Ireland, in a letter to a member of Parliament there; upon occasion of Mr. Molyneux's late book: intituled, The case of Ireland's being bound by Acts of Parliament in England, stated. [Anon.] [London, 1698.] 4°

Wing L 1125.

T.72

3518

LESLIE (Charles)

A discourse; shewing, who they are that are now qualify'd to administer baptism and the Lord's - Supper ... By the author of A discourse proving the divine institution of water-baptism ... [Anon.] London, for C. Brome; W. Keblewhite; and H. Hindmarsh, 1698. 4°

Wing L 1130.
3 copies.

T.266 T.72

3519

LESLIE (Charles)

The history of sin and heresie attempted, from the first war that they rais'd in heaven ... to the final victory over them, and their eternal condemnation in hell ... [Anon.] London: for H. Hindmarsh, 1698. 4°

Wing L 1135.
2 copies.

T.404 T.72

3520

LESLIE (Charles)

Primitive heresie revived, in the faith and practice of the people called Quakers... To which is added, A friendly expostulation with William Penn, upon account of his Primitive Christianity... [Anon.] London: printed for C. Brome, W. Keblewhite. And H. Hindmarsh, 1698.   4°

Wing L 1140.
6 copies (2 wanting the first gathering).

T.9 T.72 T.746

3521

LESLIE (Charles)

Satan disrob'd from his disguise of light: or, The Quakers last shift to cover their monstrous heresies ... In a reply to Thomas Ellwood's answer ... to George Keith's Narrative of the proceedings at Turners-Hall ... 2nd ed; with some improvements. By the author of, The snake in the grass ... London, for C. Brome; W. Keblewhite; and H. Hindmarsh, 1698. 4°

Wing L 1150.   2 copies.

T.404   T.9

3522

LESLIE (Charles)

A short and easie method with the deists. Wherein the truth of the Christian religion is demonstrated ... In a letter to a friend. [Anon.] London: W. Onley, for H. Hindmarsh, 1698.   8°

Wing L 1152.
2 copies (one wanting title-page).

T.441 T.801

3523

A LETTER from a gentleman of the city of New-York to another, concerning the troubles which happen'd in that province in the time of the late happy revolution. Printed and sold by William Bradford at the sign of the Bible in New-York, 1698. 4°

Wing L 1397.

T.94

3524

A LETTER from a lawyer of the Inner Temple, to his friend in the country, concerning the East-India stock, and the project of uniting the new and old companies. London: printed in the year 1698.   4°

Wing L 1409.

T.324

3525

A LETTER to a friend, concerning the nature of the divine persons in the Holy Trinity ... London: for S. Manship, 1698. 4°

Wing L 1643.

T.149

3526

A LETTER to Mr. Congreve on his pretended amendments, &c. of Mr. Collier's Short view of the immorality and prophaneness of the English stage. London: for Samuel Keble, 1698.   8°

Wing L 1713A.

T.385

3527

The MISTAKEN murderer: being a just vindication of William Lewis of St. Botolph Bishopsgate from the distruction of Mr. Sheppards child, and a true relation of the matter of fact, and necessary observations thereon. London, Edw. Poole, 1698. 4°

Not in Wing.

T.283

3528

OLIVER (Edward)

A sermon preach'd in St. Paul's Cathedral, before the Lord-Mayor, aldermen, &c. on Sunday, October 23. 1698. London: for Edward Castle, 1698. 4°

Wing O 272.

T.198

3529

P.(R.)

A letter from a merchant in London, to his friend, a merchant in Exeter, about subscribing to the two millions. [No imprint, 1698.] 4°

Not in Wing (cf. L 1414).
2 copies.

T.324

3530

POVEY (Josiah)

A sermon preached in the colledge church of St Katharin's, Februaei [sic] the 13th 1698. London: J. Mayos, 1698.   4°

Wing P 3041.

T.702

3531

S.(F.)

The anatomy of a project for raising two millions. [London, 1698.] 4°

Wing S 21.

T.324

3532

SHEERES (Sir Henry)

An essay on the certainty and causes of the earth's motion on its axis, &c. [Anon.] London: for Jacob Tonson, 1698. 4°
Wing S 3059.
Wanting pp. 3-6.

T.12

3533

SOME remarks upon, and instances of the usages of former parliaments, in relation to taxes. [No imprint, 1698?] 4°

Not in Wing.

T.136

3534

STAFFORD (Richard)

Hear this word, o ye princes, ye priests and people of England; especially, such of ye as assemble at Westminster at this your session begun December 3. 1697. [Anon.] [London, 1698.] 8°

Wing S 5120.
Badly cropped.

T.32

3535

TATE (Nahum)

A consolatory poem to the Right Honourable John Lord Cutts, upon the death of his most accomplished lady... London: R.R. for Henry Playford, 1698.   Fol.

Wing T 179.

T.699

3536

TOLAND (John)

The danger of mercenary parliaments. [Anon.] [London, 1698.] 4°

Wing T 1765.

T.136

3537

TRENCHARD (John)

A short history of standing armies in England ... [Anon.] London, printed in the year 1698. 4°

Wing T 2115.
3 copies.

T.267   T.200 T.80

3538

WELCHMAN (Edward)

A second defence of the Church of England from the charge of schism and heresy, as laid against it by the vindicator of the deprived bishops. In answer to two discourses [by Henry Dodwell], entitul'd, A defence of the Vindication of the deprived bishops, and, The doctrine of the Church of England concerning the independency of the clergy on the lay-power. [Anon.] London: for Will. Rogers, 1698. 4°

Wing W 1322.
2 copies.

T.135 T.374

3539

A WORD to the well-inclin'd of all perswasions. Together with a coppy of a letter from William Penn to George Keith, upon his arbitrary summons and unjust proceedings, at Turners-Hall, against the people called Quakers. London, T. Sowle, 1698. 4°

Not in Wing.

T.79

3540

WYETH (Joseph)

Primitive Christianity continued in the faith and practice of the people called Quakers: being in answer to a pamphlet, entituled, Primitive heresie [by Charles Leslie] ... London, T, Sowle, 1698. 8°

cf. Wing W 3761.

T.32

1699

3541

An APOLOGY for the English Presbyterians, with a defence of the heads of agreement assented to by the United Ministers, in the year 91. London, printed, and are to be sold by the booksellers of London and Westminster, 1699. 8°

Wing A 3548.

T. 32

3542

An APOLOGY for the English presbyterians, with a defence of the heads of agreement assented to by the united ministers, in the year 91. London, for John Nutt, 1699. 8°

Not in Wing, cf. A 3548.

T.322

3543

BLACKALL (Offspring) Bishop of Exeter.

A sermon preached before the honourable House of Commons, at St. Margaret's Westminster, January 30th. 1698/9. London, J. Leake, for Walter Kettilby, 1699.   4°

Wing B 3053.
2 copies.

T.702 T.732

3544

BLACKMORE (Sir Richard)

A short history of the last parliament. [Anon.] London: for Jacob Tonson, 1699. 4°

Wing B 3088.
MS attribution to Charles Montagu is incorrect.

T.136

3545

D. (P.)

The Hertford letter; containing several brief observations on a late printed tryal concerning the murder of Mrs. Sarah Stout. London, printed, and sold by the booksellers of London and Westminster, 1699. 8°

Wing D 75.
Damaged by damp.

T.147

3546

A DECLARATION of the congregational ministers in and about London, against antinomian errours, and ignorant and scandalous persons intruding themselves into the ministry. London, printed, and are to be sold by the booksellers of London and Westminster, 1699. 8°

cf. Wing D 655.

T.230

3547

A DEFENCE of the Scots settlement at Darien. With an answer to the Spanish memorial against it... [The dedication signed Philo-Caledon. Attributed to Andrew Fletcher and to Archibald Foyer.] Edinburgh, printed in the year 1699. 8°

Wing F 1292.

T.358

3548

An ESSAY upon excising several branches that have hitherto escaped the duty of the brewing trade to make good the deficiency of the malt-tax, and other funds ... [London, 1699?]   8°

Wing E 3298.

T.443

3549

GARTH (Sir Samuel)

The dispensary; a poem. [Anon.] London, John Nutt, 1699. 4°

Wing G 273.

T.269

1699 (Cont'd)

3550

GRASCOMBE (Samuel)

An appeal to all true English-men, (if there be any such left,) or, A cry for bread. [Anon.] [London, 1699.] 4°

Wing G 1567.

T.136

3551

GUIDE (Philip)

An essay concerning nutrition in animals. Proving it analogical to that of plants ... London: printed for the author, and are to be sold by H. Rhodes, 1699. 8°

Wing G 2183.

T.442

3552

JEFFERY (John)

A plain and short discourse concerning the nature of the Lord's Supper: and the end of celebrating it... London: for W. Rogers, 1699. 8°

Wing J516.

T.622

3553

JONES (David) *Vicar of Marcham.*

A sermon upon Ember-week, preached before the University of Oxford, at Christ-Church in Oxford, 1698 ... London: for Tho. Parkhurst, 1699. 4°

Wing J 939.

T.754

3554

KING (William) *Student of Christ Church.*

Dialogues of the dead. Relating to the present controversy concerning the epistles of Phalaris. By the author of the Journey to London. London: A. Baldwin, 1699. 8°

Wing K 544.

T.212

3555

KING (William) *Student of Christ Church.*

The furmetary. A very innocent and harmless poem. In three canto's. [Anon.] London: A. Baldwin, 1699. 4°

Wing K 545.

T.269

3556

A LETTER to a person of quality, concerning the Archbishop of Canterbury's sentence of deprivation against the Bishop of St. Davids. London, printed in the year, 1699. 4°

Not in Wing.

T.76

3557

A LETTER to the reverend Dr. Bentley. Upon the controversie betwixt him and Mr. Boyle. London, J. Nutt, 1699. 4°

Wing L 1746.

T.77

3558

LLOYD (William) *Bishop of Worcester.*

A chronological account of the life of Pythagoras, and of other famous men his contemporaries. With an epistle to the Rd Dr. Bentley, about Porphyry's and Jamblichus's lives of Pythagoras. London, J. H. for H. Mortlock; and J. Hartley, 1699. 8°

Wing L 2674.
2 copies.

T.402   T.162

3559

LOCHNER (Jacobus Hieronymus)

Terrae natantis, in ducatus Bremensis tractu Waakhusano, phaenomena, per caussas e naturali scientia deducta... Bremae, typis Brauerianis, [1699]. 4°

T.793

3560

MOORE (John) *Bishop of Ely.*

Of religious melancholy. A sermon preach'd before the Queen at White-hall, March the VIth. 1691/2. By... John, Lord Bishop of Norwich. 4th ed. London: for William Rogers, 1699. 8°

Wing M 2549.

T.622

3561

OATES (Titus)

A sermon preached in an Anabaptist meeting in Wapping, on Sunday the 19th. of February, by the Reverend T.O.D.D. ... Printed, at the request of his congregation, for Zachariah Marshal near the Long-Cellar in Wapping, 1699. 4°

Wing O 55.

T.139

3562

The SEAMAN'S opinion of a standing army in England, in opposition to a fleet at sea, as the best security of this kingdom. In a letter to a merchant, written by a sailor. London, for A. Baldwin, 1699. 4°

Wing S 2189.

T.80

3563

SELECT maxims of state: directing how to establish the government of the court and kingdom of England upon a firm and unalterable basis.   By a late eminent person of quality. London, printed in the year 1699. 8°

Not in Wing.

T.443

3564

SHIELDS (Alexander)

A proper project for Scotland. To startle fools, and frighten knaves, but to make wise-men happy ... By a person neither unreasonably Cameronian, nor excessively Laodicean ... Printed in a land where self's cry'd up, and zeal's cry'd down ... [Edinburgh]. Anno Dom: 1699. 4°

Wing S 3433.

T.142

3565

SMITH (Thomas) *of Magdalen College, Oxford.*

Clarissimi ac doctissimi viri, Joannis Gravii, olim astronomiae in Academia Oxoniensi professoris Saviliani, vita... Londini, 1699. 4°

Wing S 4234.

T.12

3566

SMITH (Thomas) *of Magdalen College, Oxford.*

Two compendious discourses: the one concerning the power of God: the other about the certainty and evidence of a future state ... [Anon.] London: for S. Smith and B. Walford, 1699. 4°

Wing S 4254.

T.181

3567

The STATE of the Navy consider'd in relation to the victualling, particularly in the Straits, and the West Indies ... Humbly offer'd to the honourable House of Commons, by an English sailor. 2nd ed. London, for A. Baldwin, 1699. 4°

Wing S 5323.
3 copies.

T.325 T.194 T.200

3568

STEPHENS (William)

A letter to his most excellent Majesty King William III. shewing, I. The original foundation of the English monarchy . II. The means by which it was remov'd from that foundation ... 2nd ed. enlarg'd. [Anon.] London, J. Darby, and sold by A. Baldwin, 1699. 4°

Ch. Ch. S 5460+.

T.136

3569

UTRUM horum, mavis, accipe. A dialogue between T[itus] O[ates] and C[aptain] G[eorge] P[orter] as they met in the Privy-garden. London: printed in the year 1699. 4°

Wing Gallery O U230A.

T.487

3570

WAGSTAFFE (Thomas)

A defence of the Vindication of K. Charles the Martyr; justifying his Majesty's title to Ἐικὼν Βασιλικη. In answer to a late pamphlet [by John Toland] intituled Amyntor. By the author of the Vindication. London, W. Bowyer: and sold by most booksellers in London and Westminster, 1699. 4°

Wing W 206.

T.285

3571

WHATELEY (Solomon)

An answer to a late book written against the learned and reverend Dr. Bentley, relating to some manuscript notes on Callimachus. Together with an examination of Mr. Bennet's appendix, to the said book. [Anon.] London: printed in the year, 1699. 8°

Wing W 1583.

T.92

1700

3572

An ACCOUNT of the doctrine and discipline of Mr. Richard Davis, of Rothwell..., and those of his separation. With the canons of George Fox, appointed to be read in all the Quakers meetings. London, printed in the year, 1700. 4°

Wing A 280.

T.9

3573

An ANSWER to the case of the old East-India Company; as represented by themselves to the Lords spiritual and temporal in Parliament assembled. London, K. Astwood, for the author, 1700. 4°

Wing A 3395.

T.324

3574

ASTELL (Mary)

Some reflections upon marriage, occasion'd by the Duke & Dutchess of Mazarine's case; which is also consider'd.[Anon.] London: for John Nutt, 1700. 4°

Wing A 4067.

T.323

3575

BEVERIDGE (William) *Bishop of St. Asaph.*

Of the happiness of the saints in heaven: a sermon preach'd before the Queen at White-Hall, October 12, 1690. 4th ed. London, for Thomas Speed, 1700. 4°

Wing B 2099.

T. 93

3576

BIBLIOTHECA annua: or, The annual catalogue for the year, 1699. Being an exact catalogue of all English and Latin books, printed in England from January, 1698/9, to March 25. 1700 ... Published ... by A. Roper and W. Turner. Sold by J. Nutt, 1700. 4°

T.263

3577

BLACKALL (Offspring) *Bishop of Exeter.*

No reason to desire now revelations;   a sermon preach'd... October 7th. 1700. Being the seventh, for the year 1700, of the lecture founded by the Honourable Robert Boyle. (New revelations would probably be unsuccesful... Being the eighth ...) London, J. Leake, for Walter Kettilby, 1700. 4°

Wing B 3047.

T.757

3578

BLACKALL (Offspring) *Bishop of Exeter.*

The sufficiency of the scripture-revelation, as to the matter of it. A sermon preach'd... February the 5th. 1699/700. Being the second, for the year 1700, of the lecture founded by the Honourable Robert Boyle. London, J. Leake, for Walter Kettilby, 1700. 4°

Wing B 3057.

T.757

3579

BLACKALL (Offspring) *Bishop of Exeter*.

The sufficiency of the scripture-revelation, as
to the proof of it. Part I. A sermon preach'd
... March the 4th. 1699/700. Being the third,
for the year 1700, of the lecture founded by the
Honourable Robert Boyle. London, J. Leake, for
Walter Kettilby, 1700. 4°

Wing B 3058.

T.757

3580

BLACKALL (Offspring) *Bishop of Exeter*.

The sufficiency of the Scripture-revelation, as
to the proof of it. Part II. Two sermons preach'd
... April 1st. and May 6th. 1700. Being the
fourth and fifth, for the year 1700, of the lecture
founded by the Honourable Robert Boyle. London,
J. Leake, for Walter Kettilby, 1700. 4°

Wing B 3059.

T.757

3581

BLACKALL (Offspring) *Bishop of Exeter*.

The sufficiency of the scripture-revelation, as to
the proof of it. Part III. A sermon preach'd...
September 2d. 1700. Being the sixth, for the year
1700, of the lecture founded by the Honourable
Robert Boyle. London, J. Leake, for Walter Kettilby,
1700. 4°

Wing B 3060.

T.757

3582

BRADFORD (Samuel) *Bishop of Rochester*.

The imperfect promulgation of the gospel, consider'd.
A sermon preach'd in the church of St. Mary le
Bow, January 7. 1699/700 ... London: for Tho.
Parkhurst, 1700. 4°

Wing B 4115.

T.198

3583

BRAY (Thomas)

Apostolick charity, its nature and excellence consider'd. In a discourse upon Dan. 12.3... To
which is prefixt, A general view of the English
colonies in America, with respect to religion...
London, E. Holt for William Hawes, 1700. 4°

Wing B 4287.
2 copies (one copy incomplete).

T.340 T.754

3584

CALEDONIA; or, The pedlar turn'd merchant. A
tragi-comedy, as it was acted by his Majesty's
subjects of Scotland, in the King of Spain's
province of Darien. London: printed, and sold by
the booksellers of London and Westminster, 1700.
8°

Wing C 282.

T.358

3585

The CITY-wive's petition against coffee. Presented
to publick consideration, the grand inconveniences
that accrue to their sex, from the excessive
drinking of that drying, enfeebling liquor ...
Printed for the booksellers of London and
Westminster, 1700. 4°

cf. Wing C 4362 A.

T.262

3586

CONJECTURES politiques sur le conclave de MDCC.
& sur ce qui s'est passé à Rome pendant la
maladie, & aprés la mort du Pape Innocent XII.
pour l'election d'un successeur. A Parme, chez
Innocent Treize, 1700. 8°

T.444

3587

CROMWELL (Oliver)

Oliver Cromwell's letters to foreign princes and
states, for strengthning and preserving the
Protestant religion and interest. With an
appendix. London, for John Nutt, 1700. 4°

Wing C 7116 A.

T.201

3588

DEFOE (Daniel)

The true-born Englishman. A satyr ... [Anon.]
Printed in the year 1700. 4°

Wing D 849. Moore 28.

T.269

3589

EIGENTLICHE Beschreibung der Welt-berühmten Dom-Kirchen
zu Magdeburg /... samt einem vollständigen Catalogo
aller gewesenen Ertz-Bischöffe... zum vierten mahl
heraus gegeben von einem Liebhaber der Antiquität.
Magdeburg / gedruckt auff Kosten der Dem-Küster / bey
Johann Röbern anno 1700. 4°

T.820

3590

ENGLAND. *Parliament. House of Commons*.

The report made to the Honourable House of Commons,
Decemb. 15. 1699, by the Commissioners appointed
to enquire into the forfeited estates of Ireland.
London; printed in the year 1700. 4°

Not in Wing
(cf. E 2231/2 and Ch. Ch. E 2231+).

T. 22

3591

An ENQUIRY into the causes of the miscarriage of
the Scots colony at Darien. Or an answer to a
libel entituled A defence of the Scots abdicating
Darien ... Glasgow, 1700. 8°

Wing I 213.

T.358

3592

F. (S.)

Mr. Toland's Clito dissected. And Fuller's plain
proof of the true mother of the pretended Prince of
Wales, made out to be no proof. In two letters
from a gentleman in the country to his friend in
London ... London: printed in the year 1700. 4°

Wing F 60.

T.351

3593

A FULL account of the rise, progress, and advantages
of Dr Assheton's proposal ... for the benefit of
widows of clergymen and others; by settling
jointures and annuities at the rate of thirty per
cent ... London: for B. Aylmer, 1700.   8°

Wing F 2271.

T.455

3594

FULLER (William)

A plain proof of the true father and mother of the
pretended Prince of Wales ... London, printed for
the author; and sold by the booksellers of
London and Westminster, 1700. 8°

Wing F 2485.

T.282

3595

GANDY (Henry)

An answer to some queries, concerning schism,
toleration, &c. In a letter to a friend ... [Anon.]
London, printed in the year 1700. 4°

Wing G 197.

T. 76

3596

GARRET (Walter)

Theorems; evincing, that the subject of the fourth
and fifth chapters of the Revelation, is the Church
of England... London, printed and are to be sold
by the booksellers of London and Westminster, [1700?]
4°

Not in Wing.

T.39

3597

GASKARTH (John)

A description of the unregenerate and the truly
Christian temper or state; in a sermon preach'd
before the University of Cambridge, on commencement
Sunday ... Cambridge, at the University Press, for
Edmund Jeffery, 1700. 4°

Wing G 286.

T. 73

3598

GASKARTH (John)

Insanientis sapientiae, sive enthusiasmi refutatio.
Concio habita ad clerum Academiae Cantabrigiensis
in feriis Divi Petri, triduo ante comitiorum
solennem diem, an. 1700. pro gradu doctoratus in
s. theologia ... Cantabrigiae, typis academicis,
impensis Edmundi Jeffery, 1700. 4°

Wing G 287.

T. 73

3599

HARE (Francis) *Bishop of Chichester*.

A sermon preach'd at St. Marys church in Cambridge,
January the 6th... Cambridge, printed at the
University Press, for Edmund Jeffery, bookseller
in Cambridge, 1700. 4°

Wing H 757.

T.771

3600

HODGES (James)

A defence of the Scots abdicating Darien:
including an answer to the Defence of the Scots
settlement there. Authore Britanno sed Dunensi
... Printed in the year, 1700. 8°

Wing H 2298.

T.358

3601

JOHNSON (Samuel) *Rector of Corringham*.

The second part of the confutation of the
ballancing letter. Containing an occasional
discourse in vindication of Magna Charta. [Anon.]
London, for A. Baldwin, 1700, 4°

Wing J 844.

T.80

3602

KEITH (George)

A sermon preach'd at the parish-church of St. Helen's,
London, May the 19th. 1700 ... London, for J. Gwillim,
1700. 4°

Wing K 211.

T.198

3603

KING (William) *Student of Christ Church*.

The transactioneer with some of his philosophical
fancies: in two dialogues ... [Anon.] London;
printed for the booksellers of London and Westminster,
1700. 8°

Wing K 546.

T.148

3604

LESLIE (Charles)

A parallel between the faith and doctrine of the
present Quakers, and that of the chief hereticks
in all ages of the Church ... [Anon.] London, for
G. Strahan, 1700. 4°

cf. Wing L 1139.
2 copies.

T.9 T.79

3605

A LETTER to a member of the late Parliament,
concerning the debts of the nation. Printed in the
year 1700. 4°

Wing L 1687.

T.267

3606

LORD'S PRAYER.

Oratio dominica... Nimirum, plus centum linguis,
versionibus, aut characteribus reddita & expressa.
Editio novissima, speciminibus variis quam priores
comitatior... [Edited by B. Motte.] Londini:
prostant apud Dan. Brown, & W. Keblewhite, 1700.
4°

Wing M 2944.

T.763

3607

LOUIS XIV, *King of France*.

A memorial from his Most Christian Majesty ...
containing his reasons for accepting the late King
of Spain's will, in favour of the Duke of Anjou.
London, printed, and sold by J. Nutt, 1700. 4°

Wing L 3128.

T.4

3608

LOUIS XIV, *King of France*.

The treaty betwixt the Most Christian King, the
King of Great Britain, and the States General of
the United Provinces, for settling the succession
of the Crown of Spain ... London, for A. Baldwin,
1700. 4°

Wing L 3139.

T.4

3609

MODO dell'elettione del serenissimo prencipe di Venezia. Con il nome, & cognome di tutti i prencipi fino al sereniss. Silvestro Valier... In Venezia, per il Valuasense in Frezaria a S. Marco, [1700?] 4°

T.383

3610

PARKER (Samuel) *of Trinity College, Oxford.*

Homer in a nutshell: or, His War between the frogs and the mice paraphrastically translated. In three cantos. By Samuel Parker... London: for Tho. Newborough, 1700. Fol.

Wing P 465.

T.543

3611

PRIOR (Matthew)

Carmen saeculare, for the year 1700. To the King... [Anon.] London, for Jacob Tonson, 1700. Fol.

Wing P 3507.

T.543

3612

PUBLICK services in, or relating to the Royal Navy; wherein Mr. Richard Gibson, has been employed since the year of our Lord 1652. [No imprint, 1700?] 4°

Not in Wing.

T.280

3613

PUCKLE (James)

England's path to wealth and honour in a dialogue between an English-man and a Dutch-man... the second edition with additions. London: for Sam. Crouch, 1700. 8°

Wing P 4161.

T.443

3614

RALEIGH (*Sir* Walter)

A discourse of sea-ports; principally of the port and haven of Dover: written by Sir Walter Rawleigh ... Never before made publick. London, John Nutt, 1700. 4°

Wing R 157.

T.12

3615

REMARKS on the present condition of the Navy, and particularly of the victualling. In which the notion of fortifying of garisons is exploded... In a letter from a sailor to a member of the House of Commons. [By John Tutchin?] London, printed in year 1670 [i.e. 1700]. 4°

Wing R 935 and R 935A.
Another copy, with the correct date.

T.194 T.325

3616

REMARKS upon the Navy. The second part. Containing a reply to the observations on the first part ... In a letter from a sailor to a member of the honourable House of Commons ... [By John Tutchin?] London, printed in the year 1700. 4°

Wing R 949 A.
2 copies.

T.194 T.325

3617

SCOTS COMPANY TRADING TO AFRICA AND THE INDIES.

The original papers and letters, relating to the Scots Company, trading to Africa and the Indies: from the memorial given in against their taking subscriptions at Hamburgh, by Sir Paul Ricaut ... to their last address sent up to his Majesty in December, 1699 ... Printed anno 1700. 8°

Wing O 434.

T.103

                                              T.103

3618

SCOTS COMPANY TRADING TO AFRICA AND THE INDIES.

A supplement of original papers and letters, relating to the Scots Company trading to Africa and the Indies. Anno Dom. 1700. 8°

Wing S 6183.

T.103

3619

SHARP (John) *Archbishop of York.*

The reasonableness of believing without seeing. A sermon preach'd before the King in St. James's Chappel, on Palm-Sunday, March 24. 1699/700. London: for Walter Kettilby: and William Rogers, 1700. 4°

Wing S 2979.
2 copies.

T.757   T.93

3620

SHARP (John) *Archbishop of York.*

A sermon preached before the lords spiritual and temporal in Parliament assembled, in the abbey-church at Westminster, on the thirtieth of January, 1699/700. London, J. Leake, for Walter Kettilby, 1700. 4°

Wing S 2999.
2 copies.

T.771 T.93

3621

SHARP (John) *Archbishop of York.*

A sermon preached before the lords spiritual and temporal in Parliament assembled, in the abbey-church at Westminster, on the thirtieth of January, 1699/700. 2nd ed. London, J.Leake, for Walter Kettilby, 1700. 4°

Wing S 3000.

T.732

3622

A SHORT account how the kingdom of Denmark became hereditary and absolute, by a difference betwixt the lords and commons ... London, for A, Baldwin, 1700. 4°

Not in Wing.

T.80

3623

SMITH (Matthew)

Remarks upon the D[uke] of S[hrewsbury]'s letter to the House of Lords concerning Capt. Smyth. Being a vindication of his services from the imputations there-in laid upon them... London; printed, and sold by the booksellers of London and Westminster, 1700. 4°

Wing S 4132.

T.351

3624

STEPHENS (Edward)

An abstract of common principles of a just vindication of the rights of the Kingdom of God upon earth, against the politick machinations of Erastian hereticks; out of the Vindication of the deprived bishops, &c. By a very learned man of the Church of England. [Anon.] London, printed anno Domini, 1700. 4°

Wing S 5414.
2 copies.

T.197 T.72

3625

STEPHENS (Edward)

The case of the Church of England by law established, necessary to be considered, in order to a more firm and full settlement of peace at home and abroad. In a letter to a bishop of the present constitution, by an English Catholick. [Anon.] [London, 1700?] 4°

Wing S 5423.
2 copies.

T.190   T.72

3626

STEPHENS (Edward)

A compleat and unexceptionable form of liturgy, or divine service, for the celebration of the holy communion... [Anon.] [No imprint, 1700?] 4°

Not in Wing.
2 copies.

T.461

3627

STEPHENS (Edward)

An expedient to extricate one's self out of the guilt of schism, and enter effectually into a virtual Catholick communion... In a letter to a friend. [Anon.] [No imprint, 1700?] 4°

Not in Wing.

T.72

3628

STEPHENS (Edward)

The great question, of the authority of the arch-bishops, bishops & clergy, of the present constitution of the Church of England... faithfully examined, and clearly resolved. [Anon.] [No imprint, 1700?] 4°

Not in Wing.

T.72

3629

STEPHENS (Edward)

A preparative for the reception of truth, for a prologue to certain discourses, design'd for a true reformation, and restitution of primitive Christianity. [Anon.] [No imprint, 1700?] 4°

Not in Wing.

T.72

3630

TUTCHIN (John)

The foreigners. A poem. Part I. [Anon.] London, for A. Baldwin, 1700. Fol.

Wing T 3375.

T.695

3631

WARD (Edward)

Labour in vain: or, What signifies little or nothing ... [Anon.] London, printed, and sold by most booksellers in London and Westminster, 1700. 4°

Wing W 744.

T.16

1701

3632

ALDRICH (Henry)

A narrative of the proceedings of the lower house of Convocation, relating to prorogations and adjournments; from Monday, Feb. 10. 1700 ... to Wednesday June 25. 1701 ... [Anon.] London: for Tho. Bennet, 1701. 2 parts. 4°

T.76

3633

ALLIX (Peter)

De Messiae duplici adventu dissertationes duae adversus Judaeos. Londini: prostant apud Joh. Taylor, 1701. 12°

T.441

3634

An ANSWER to the black-list: or, The Vine-tavern queries. [A reply to A list of the one unanimous club of members of the late Parliament ...] London, printed in the year, 1701. 4°

T.267

3635

An ARGUMENT against war: in opposition to some late pamplets, particularly; the first and second [parts] of The Duke of Anjou's succession consider'd ... The 2d edition. London: printed in the year, 1701. 4°

T.4

3636

An ARGUMENT proving, that the imposition of the sacrament of the Lord's Supper, as a qualification for a secular office, is I. contrary to the express law of God. II. Contrary to the doctrines of the Church of England ... London, for A. Baldwin, 1701. 4°

T.509

3637

ARTICLES of peace, or A parcel of safe resolutions over a glass of claret. London, printed in the year, 1701.   4°

T.69

3638

ATTERBURY (Francis) *Bishop of Rochester.*

Additions to the first edition of the Rights, powers, and privileges of an English convocation, stated and vindicated. In answer to a late book of Dr. Wake's, entituled, The authority of Christian princes over their ecclesiastical synods asserted... London: for Tho. Bennet, 1701. 2 parts. 8°

T.550

3639

ATTERBURY (Francis) *Bishop of Rochester.*

A letter to a clergyman in the country, concerning the choice of members, and the execution of the Parliament-writ, for the ensuing Convocation. (A second letter ... about the execution of the Parliament-writ, for the ensuing Convocation.) [Anon.] London: for Thomas Bennet, 1701.   4°

T.267

3640

ATTERBURY (Francis) *Bishop of Rochester.*

The power of the lower house of Convocation to adjourn it self, vindicated from the misrepresentations of a late paper [by Edmund Gibson], entitled, A letter to a friend in the country, concerning the proceedings of the present Convocation. [Anon.] London: for Thomas Bennet, 1701.   4°

2 copies.

T.76   T.195

3641

B.(F.)

The way whereby the Quakers may approve themselves Christians, (in answer to a book [by George Whitehead] called, The Christianity of the people commonly called Quakers, asserted, &c.) ... With a preface by the author of The snake in the grass [i.e. Charles Leslie]. London: for J. Hartley, and sold by E. Mallet, 1701.   12°

T.480

3642

The BALLAD, or: Some scurrilous reflections in verse [by Daniel Defoe], on the proceedings of the honourable House of Commons: answered stanza by stanza. With the Memorial, alias legion [by Daniel Defoe], reply'd to paragraph by paragraph. London, D. Edwards, and sold by the booksellers of London and Westminster, 1701.   8°

T.351

3643

BERTHIER (David Nicolas) *Bishop of Blois.*

Two letters, one from the Bishop of Blois to Monsieur de la Vallette, with promises and threatnings to prevent his turning protestant. The other from Monsieur de la Vallette, to his brethren the clergy of Blois... Done into English by Mr. Hale. London: for R. Bassett, 1701.   4°

T.201

3644

BINCKES (William)

An expedient propos'd: or, The occasions of the late controversie in Convocation consider'd, and a method of adjournments pointed out consistent with the claims of both houses ... In a letter to the author [i.e. Edmund Gibson] of a late book entitled, The right of the Archbishop to continue and prorogue the whole Convocation asserted ... By a country-divine. London, T. Warren for Thomas Bennet, 1701.   4°

T.195

3645

BROWN (George)

A compendious, but a compleat system of decimal arithmetick, containing more exact rules for ordering infinites, than any hitherto extant. First course. Edinburgh, printed for the author, in the year, 1701.   4°

T.280

3646

C. (E.)

The Taunton-Dean letter, from E.C. to J.F. at the Grecian coffee-house. (The Exeter queries.) London: printed in the year, 1701.   brs.

T.695

3647

CHETWOOD (Knightly)

A sermon preach'd at St. Paul's cathedral, before the gentlemen educated at Eton, and King's-College, December the 6th. 1700. London: for Samuel Carr, and sold by Benj. Tooke, 1701.   4°

T.771

3648

The CONGRATULATIONS of several kings and princes of Europe to King James the II. on the birth of the Prince of Wales, who was born on the 10th of June 1688 ... London: printed in the year 1701.   8°

T.212

3649

The CORRUPTION and impiety of the common members of the late House of Commons. Printed in the year 1701. 4°

T.267

3650

DAVENANT (Charles)

The true picture of a modern Whig. Set forth in a dialogue between Mr. Whiglove & Mr. Double, two under-spur-leathers to the late ministry. [Anon.] London: printed in the year, 1701.   8°

2 copies.

T.385   T.212

3651

DEFOE (Daniel)

An enquiry into the occasional conformity of dissenters, in cases of preferment. With a preface to Mr. How [signed D.F.] ... London: printed anno Dom. 1701. 4°

Moore 17.

T.201

3652

DEFOE (Daniel)

The history of the Kentish petition. [Anon.] London, printed in the year, 1701.   8°

Moore 37.

T.136

3653

DEFOE (Daniel)

[Legion's memorial.] Mr. S[peake]r. The enclosed memorial you are charg'd with, in the behalf of many thousands of the good people of England ... [Anon.] [No imprint, 1701.]   4°

Moore 35.
2 copies.

T.194   T.267

3654

DEFOE (Daniel)

A letter to Mr. How, by way of reply to his Considerations of the preface to An enquiry into the occasional conformity of dissenters. By the author of the said preface and enquiry. London: printed in the year 1701.   4°

Moore 31.

T.14

3655

DEFOE (Daniel)

The succession to the Crown of England. Further considered ... Abstracted from the 6d. book, intituled the Succession of the crown of England considred. [Anon.] London, printed in the year, 1701.   8°

cf. Moore 29.

T.412

3656

DEFOE (Daniel)

Ye true-born Englishmen proceed ... [Anon.] [No imprint, 1701.]   4°

Moore 36.

T.69

3657

The DISSERTATOR in burlesque. London, for Bernard Lintott, 1701.   8°

T.58

3658

ELYS (Edmund)

Edmundi Elisii ad Arthurum Bury, S.T.D. epistola... Londini: typis J.M. & prostant venales apud R. Wilkin, 1701.   4°

T.747

3659

ELYS (Edmund)

Socinianismus purus putus Antichristianismus: seu Omnimodae Socinianismi iniquitatis demonstratio ... (Edmundi Elisii Paraenesis ad protestantes quos vocant, apud Gallos.) Londini: typis J.M. & prostant venales apud R. Wilkin, 1701. 2 parts.   8°

T.28

3660

ENGLAND. *Parliament. House of Commons.*

The several proceedings and resolutions of the House of Commons. In relation to the Bill for taking, examining and stating the publick accounts of the Kingdom, together with a copy of the Bill. London, printed in the year, 1701. Fol.

T.267

3661

ENGLAND. *Parliament. House of Commons.*

A state of the proceedings in the House of Commons, with relation to the impeached lords: and what happened thereupon between the two houses. London, for Edward Jones, and Timothy Goodwin, 1701.   Fol.

T.695

3662

ENGLAND. *Parliament. House of Lords.*

The several proceedings and resolutions of the House of Peers, in relation to the lords impeached or charged. London, Charles Bill, and the executrix of Thomas Newcomb, deceas'd, 1701.   Fol.

T.695

3663

A FULL account of the proceedings in relation to Capt. Kidd. In two letters. Written by a person of quality to a kinsman of the Earl of Bellomont in Ireland. The second eddition. London, printed and sold by the booksellers of London and Westminster, 1701.   8°

Attributed by Bowdler to Lord Somers.

T.139

3664

FULLER (William)

The life of William Fuller, Gent. Being a full and true account of his birth, education, employs, and intreagues ... and the occasion of his coming into the service of the present government. Written by his own hand ... London: A. Baldwin, 1701.   8°

T.282

3665

GARRET (Walter)

The usefulness of the study of the Revelation. By W.G. Humbly offer'd to the pious consideration of all sincere lovers of peace and unity. Printed February, 1700/1.   4°

T.39

3666

GATTON (Benjamin)

An essay towards a comprehension or, A perswasive to unity amongst protestants ... By a lover of peace and unity ... London: for J. Hartley, 1701.   8°

T.57

3667

GIBSON (Edmund) *Bishop of London.*

The right of the Archbishop to continue or prorogue the whole Convocation: asserted in a second letter; by way of reply to a pamphlet [by Francis Atterbury], entitled, The power of the lower house of Convocation to adjourn it self ... [Anon.] London, for Awnsham and John Churchill, 1701.   4°

T.195

3668

H.(P.)

A true and demonstrative way to union, by the education of youth in the establish principles of the Church of England. Humbly presented to the consideration of this present Parliament. London: R. Janeway, and sold by J. Nutt, 1701.   4°

T.265

3669

HIGDEN (William)

The case of sureties in baptism. In which is shewn, that schismaticks ought not to be admitted as godfathers and godmothers in the ministration of that holy sacrament. [Anon.] London: for Sam. Keble, 1701.   4°

4 copies.

T.76 T.77 T.192 T.197

3670

HOLLAND (Richard) *Chaplain to the Duke of Richmond.*

Haman and Mordecai. A fast-sermon, preach'd in the parish church of St. Magnus the Martyr, by London-bridge, on Friday, April 4. 1701 ... London: R. Janeway, and are to be sold by Walter Kettilby, and John Back, 1701.   4°

T.198

3671

HOOPER (George) *Bishop of Bath and Wells.*

A sermon preach'd before the honourable the House of Commons, at St. Margaret's Westminster, on Friday the 4th of April, 1701. Being the day of publick fast and humiliation. London, J. Leake, for Walter Kettilby, 1701.   4°

T.198

3672

An INSCRIPTION intended to be set up for the E[ar]l of R[ocheste]r, when by happy effects of his ministry, the chappel of St. Stephen's is become a chappel to the Jesuites ... Printed in the year, &c. [1701]. 4º

Incorrectly included by Wing as I 424.

T.139

3673

JAMES II, *King of England.*

The last dying-words of the late King James to his son and daughter, and the French King. Who sickned the 22d of August, and died the 5th of September, 1701. [No imprint, 1701?] brs.

T.695

3674

A JUSTIFICATION of the proceedings of the honourable the House of Commons, in the last sessions of Parliament. [Attributed to Sir Humphrey Mackworth.] London: printed, and are to be sold by the booksellers of London and Westminster, 1701. Fol.

T.695

3675

KENNET (White) *Bishop of Peterborough.*

An occasional letter on the subject of English convocations. By the author of Ecclesiastical synods and parliamentary convocations in the Church of England. London: for A. and J. Churchill, 1701. 8º

T.550

3676

LEOPOLD I, *Holy Roman Emperor.*

The Emperor's manifesto: plainly setting forth, the right of the House of Austria to the Crown of Spain. Done from the original printed at Vienna. London: for A. Roper, 1701. 4º

T.4

3677

LESLIE (Charles)

The present state of Quakerism in England. Wherein is shew'd, that the greatest part of the Quakers in England are so far converted, as to be convinced. Upon occasion of the relapse of Sam. Crisp to Quakerism... [Anon.] London, for Char. Brome. And Geo. Strahan, 1701. 8º

2 copies.

T.101 T.302

3678

A LETTER from a peer to a member of the House of Commons, about the Countess of Anglesey's bill. [No imprint, 1701.] 4º

Attributed by Bowdler to Lord Haversham.

2 copies.

T.280 T.194

3679

A LETTER sent to a gentleman in Gloucestershire, about electing a new Parliament. London, printed in the year, 1701. Fol.

T.695

3680

A LETTER to a peer concerning the power and authority of metropolitans over their comprovincial bishops... London, for A. Baldwin, 1701. 4º

T.195

3681

The LIFE of William Fuller, by original a butcher's son ... by vote of Parliament an impostor, by title of his own making a colonel, and by his own demerits, now a prisoner at the Fleet ... London, printed to prevent his further imposing upon the publick, 1701. 12º

T.282

3682

A LIST of one unanimous club of members of the late Parliament, Nov. 11. 1701. that met at the Vine-Tavern in Long-Acre ... Printed in the year 1701. 4º

T.136

3683

M. (J.) *and* P. (W.)

A whip for the Spaniards, and a scourge for the French, in two satyrs. Written by J.M. and W.P. ... London, printed in the year, 1701. 8º

T.212

3684

MACKWORTH (*Sir* Humphrey)

A vindication of the rights of the Commons of England. By a member of the honourable the House of Commons [i.e. Humphrey Mackworth]... 2nd ed. London: F. Collins; and are to be sold by J. Nutt, 1701. Fol.

T.695

3685

MILLES (Thomas) *Bishop of Waterford.*

The happiness of those that suffer for righteousness sake: in a sermon preached at St. Maries in Oxford, on the XXXth. of January 1700/01. Oxford, printed at the Theater, for H. Clements, 1701. 4º

T.708

3686

A NEW dialogue between Monsieur Shaccoo [i.e. John Grubham Howe], and the Poussin doctor [i.e. Charles Davenant]. London, printed in the year, 1701. 4º

T.695

3687

OATES (Titus)

A new discovery of Titus Oates: being a collection of his letters to the church of the Baptists, with remarks upon them... London, for John Nut, 1701. 4º

T.139

3688

OWEN (R.)

An account of the birth parentage, education, life, and conversation of Captain William Kidd, the late famous English pirate. Who was executed on Friday the 23d of May, 1701 ... London, for Richard Briggs, 1701. 8º

T.139

3689

PASCHALL (John)

Mr. Paschall's letter to a friend in the country, stating the case of Mr. Parkhurst and himself, together with the rest of the principal commissioners for prizes. London, for A. Bell, J. Barnes, and B. Lintot, 1701. Fol.

T.695

3690

PITTIS (William)

Canterbury tales. Rendred into familiar verse... Written by no body... [Anon.] London, printed in the year, 1701. 8º

T.212

3691

PITTIS (William)

Chaucer's whims: being some select fables and tales in verse, very applicable to the present times... [Anon.] London: D. Edwards, and sold by the booksellers of London and Westminster, 1701. 8º

T.212

3692

PITTIS (William)

The true-born Englishman: a satyr [by Daniel Defoe], answer'd, paragraph by paragraph ... [Anon.] London: printed in the year 1701. 8º

T.212

3693

POMFRET (John)

Two love poems. I. Strephon's love to Delia. Justified; in a letter to Celadon. II. Strephon's address to Delia. By the author of the Choice. London: for J. Place; and are to be sold by J. Nutt, 1701. Fol.

T.699

3694

The PRESENT disposition of England considered. The second edition. With the addition of a preface, occasioned by a late pamphlet, intituled, England's enemies exposed, &c. London, printed in the year 1701. 4º

T.80

3695

The PRESENT state of physick & surgery in London. With an estimate of the prizes of all the medicines now in use. In a letter from a merchant in London, to a dispensary physician ... London, for Thomas Speed, 1701. 4º

T.12

3696

RALEIGH (*Sir* Walter)

An essay on ways and means to maintain the honour and safety of England ... With useful remarks and observations on our harbours, ports and havens, principally those of Kent: by Sir Henry Sheers. London: printed in the year, 1701. 4º

T.194

3697

The REGAL supremacy in ecclesiastical affairs asserted in a discourse occasioned by the Case of the regale and pontificat [by Charles Leslie]... London: for Will. Rogers, 1701. 8º

Manuscript attribution to "Mr Wellstead of Merton College."

Another copy.

T.43 T.101

3698

A ROD for Tunbridge beaus, bundl'd up at the request of the Tunbridge ladies, to jirk fools into more wit, and clowns into more manners. A burlesque poem ... London, printed, and are to be sold by the booksellers of London and Westminster, 1701. 4º

T.69

3699

The SECOND part of the life of William Fuller ... By way of appendix ... London: printed to prevent his farther imposing upon the publick, 1701. 8º

T.282

3700

SEVEN queries. London, printed in the year, 1701. brs.

T.695

3701

SOME queries which deserve no consideration, answer'd paragraph by paragraph, only to satisfie the ridiculous enquiries of the trifling p---r that made 'em publick. [No imprint, 1701.] 4º

2 copies.

T.267 T.139

3702

SOME queries, which may deserve consideration. London, printed in the year, 1701. brs.

T.695

3703

SOMERS (John) *Baron Somers.*

Jura populi Anglicani: or The subject's right of petitioning set forth. Occasioned by the case of the Kentish petitioners ... [Anon.] London, printed in the year 1701. 4º

T.80

3704

STANHOPE (George) *Dean of Canterbury.*

The duty of juries. A sermon preached at the Lent-assizes, holden at Maidstone... April the 1st, 1701. London: for R. Knaplock, R. Wilkin, and T. Leigh and D. Midwinter, 1701. 4º

T.757

3705

The TRUE patriot vindicated, or a justification of his Excellency, the Earl of Rochester, Lord lieutenant of Ireland. From several false and scandalous reports. The first part. [London, 1701.] brs.

T.695

3706

TUTCHIN (John)

The apostates: or, The revolters. A poem. Against foreigners. Written by the author of the Foreigners. London, printed in the year, 1701. 4º

T.69

3707

WARD (Edward)

Aesop at Paris, his letters and fables. Translated from the original French. [Anon.] Printed in the year 1701.   8°

T.202

3708

WHARTON (Henry)

A treatise of the celibacy of the clergy, wherein its rise and progress are historically considered. London, Thomas Bennet, 1701.   4°

T.265

1702

3709

ADAMS (John) *Provost of King's College, Cambridge.*

A sermon preach'd at St. Paul's cathedral, the 8th of December, 1702. before the gentlemen educated at Eton College. London, for Thomas Beckett, 1702.   4°

T.771

3710

ALTHAM (Roger)

A sermon preach'd before ... the Lord Mayor, aldermen, and citizens of London. At the cathedral church of St. Paul, on January 30th 1702 ... London, Tho. Warren for Thomas Bennet, 1702.   4°

T.273

3711

An ANSWER to Mr. Toland's Reasons for addressing his Majesty to invite into England ... the Electress Dowager, and the Electoral Prince of Hanover ... London, printed in the year 1702.   4°

T.80

3712

ATTERBURY (Francis) *Bishop of Rochester.*

A faithful account of some transactions, in the three last sessions of the present Convocation. Numb. I. [Anon.] London, for John Nutt, 1702.   4°

T.192

3713

ATTERBURY (Francis) *Bishop of Rochester.*

The parliamentary original and rights of the lower house of Convocation cleared, and the evidences of its separation from the upper house produc'd ... To which is added a preface, giving an account of the dishonest methods of answering books, taken up by the chief asserter [i.e. Edmund Gibson] of the Archbishop's sole power ... [Anon.] London: for T. Bennet, 1702.   4°

T.195

3714

ATTERBURY (Francis) *Bishop of Rochester.*

A third letter to a clergyman in the country, in defence of what was said in the two former, about the entry of the Parliament-writ in the journals of convocation, and the insertion of a certain clause in the archiepiscopal mandate. [Anon.] London: for Thomas Bennet, 1702.   4°

T.74

3715

B. (R.)

An answer to the Mock mourners. By way of reflection on a late satyr, pretended to be written by the author of The true-born English-man [i.e. Daniel Defoe]. London, printed, 1702.   8°

T.220

3716

BINCKES (William)

A prefatory discourse to an examination of a late book, entituled An exposition of the thirty nine articles of the Church of England, by Gilbert, Bishop of Sarum... By a presbyter of the Church of England. London, for Robert Clavell, 1702.   4°

3 copies.

T.2   T.190   T.827

3717

BINCKES (William)

A sermon preach'd on January the 30th. 1701/2. in King Henry the VIIth's chapel, before the reverend clergy of the lower house of Convocation. London, for R. Clavel, 1702.   4°

T.827

3718

BRECK (Thomas)

The reasonableness of the augmentation of poor vicarages; with the proposals thereunto ... [Anon.] Cambridge, John Hayes, for the author. And are to be sold by Robert Knaplock, and by Richard Thurlbourn, 1702.   4°

2 copies.

T.283   T.137

3719

BRUCE (Alexander) *4th Earl of Kincardine.*

A speech in the Parliament of Scotland, in relation to Presbyterian government. By S.A.B. [No imprint, 1702?]   4°

2 copies.

T.267   T.11

3720

The CASE of the abjuration oath endeavoured to be cleared, to the satisfaction of those who are required to take it. London, for J. Nutt, 1702.   4°

T.509

3721

CHAILLOT. *Monastère de la Visitation Sainte Marie.*

The memoirs of King James II. Containing an account of the transactions of the last twelve years of his life: with the circumstances of his death. Translated from the French original. Printed by D. Edwards, and sold by the booksellers of London and Westminster, 1702.   8°

T.57

3722

The CHARACTER of a country-committee-man, or the mixt assembly of the club-divines. London, printed in the year 1702.   4°

Partly based on a pamphlet by John Cleveland (1649).

T.136

3723

COCK (John)

A sermon preach'd at the cathedral church of Durham; November 18th 1688 ... By a presbyter of the Church of England. London, printed in the year 1702.   12°

T.39

3724

DAVENANT (Charles)

The old and modern Whig truly represented. Being a second part of his picture. And a real vindication of ... the Earl of Rochester ... and of several other true patriots of our Establish'd Church ... from the gross forgeries, and foul calumnies, falsly and maliciously cast upon them in their late libels ... [Anon.] 2nd ed. London: printed in the year 1702.   4°

T.139

3725

DAVENANT (Charles)

Saul and Samuel; or, The common interest of our king and country; in an impartial address to a member of Parliament ... [Anon.] London, for J. Nutt, 1702.   4°

T.197

3726

DAVENANT (Charles)

Tom Double return'd out of the country: or, The true picture of a modern Whig. Set forth in a second dialogue between Mr. Whiglove & Mr. Double, at the Rummer Tavern in Queen-street ... [Anon.] London: printed in the year, 1702.   8°

2 copies.

T.385   T.212

3727

DAWES (*Sir* William) *Archbishop of York.*

The pains and terrors of a wounded conscience insupportable. A sermon preach'd before the Queen ... on the 3d of March, 1701/2 ... London: H. Hills, [1702].   8°

T.491

3728

DEFOE (Daniel)

The mock mourners. A satyr, by way of elegy on King William. The fifth edition corrected. By the author of The true-born Englishman. London, printed 1702.   8°

Moore 42.

T.212

3729

DEFOE (Daniel)

A new test of the Church of England's loyalty: or, Whiggish loyalty and Church loyalty compar'd. [Anon.] Printed in the year 1702.   4°

Moore 44.

T.193

3730

DEFOE (Daniel)

Reformation of manners, a satyr ... [Anon.] Printed in the year 1702.   4°

Moore 43.

T.69

3731

DEFOE (Daniel)

The shortest-way with the dissenters: or proposals for the establishment of the Church. [Anon.] London: printed in the year 1702.   4°

Moore 50.

T.193

3732

A DIALOGUE between the author of the Observator [i.e. John Tutchin] and William Fuller, after an entertainment made at the charge of the latter, in his appartment at the pallace of Bridewel. [Attributed to Daniel Defoe.] London, printed and sold in the year 1702.   4°

T.283

3733

DIVISION our destruction: or, A short history of the French faction in England ... London, John Nutt, 1702.   4°

T.80

3734

DRAKE (James)

Some necessary considerations relating to all future elections of members to serve in Parliament, humbly offer'd to all electors, whether they be true sons of the Church of England ... or modest portestant dissenters ... The second edition; with the addition of a preface in answer to a pamphlet [by Daniel Defoe] call'd, A new test of the Church of England's loyalty, &c. By a true English-man. London: printed in the year 1702.   4°

T.11

3735

E. (T.)

Vindiciae mentis. An essay of the being and nature of mind ... By a gentleman. [The dedication is signed T.E.] ... London, for H. Walwyn, 1702.   8°

T.416

3736

EDWARDS (Jonathan) *Principal of Jesus College, Oxford.*

The exposition given by my Lord Bishop of Sarum, of the second article of our religion, examined. [Anon.] London, for Tho. Bennet, 1702.   4°

T.827

3737

ENGLAND. *Parliament.*

The bill, entituled, An act for preventing occasional conformity, with the amendments... and the reports of the several conferences relating thereunto; and the proceedings thereupon... Printed for Edward Jones in the Savoy, and Timothy Goodwin, 1702. Fol.

2 copies.

T.543   T.690

3738

ENGLAND. *Parliament. House of Commons.*

The evidence given at the bar of the House of Commons, upon the complaint of Sir John Pakington, against William Lord Bishop of Worcester and Mr. Lloyd, his son. Together with the proceedings of the House of Commons thereupon. London, for Edward Jones, and Timothy Goodwin, 1702.   Fol.

T.543

3739

ENGLAND. *Parliament. House of Lords.*

An account of the proceedings of the House of Peers, upon the observations of the Commissioners for taking, examining and stating the publick accounts of the kingdom ... London, Charles Bill, and the executrix of Thomas Newcomb, 1702. Fol.

T.543

3740

ENGLAND. *Parliament. House of Lords.*

An account of the proceedings of the Lords spiritual and temporal in Parliament assembled, in relation to the Bill, intituled, An Act for preventing occasional conformity. London, Charles Bill, and the executrix of Thomas Newcomb, 1702. Fol.

T.543

3741

An EXPLANATION of some passages in Dr. Binckes's sermon preached before the lower house of Convocation, January the 30th, 1701/2. With part of a sermon [by Henry Leslie] publish'd, anno 1649 ... intituled, The martyrdom of King Charles: or, his conformity with Christ in his sufferings... London, for R. Clavel, 1702. 4°

T.827

3742

F.(S.)

Remarks upon Fuller's full demonstration, that the pretended Prince of Wales was the son of Mrs. Mary Grey, &c. In a letter to a friend. To which is added Mr. Toland's Clito dissected. And Fuller's plain proof of the true mother of the pretended Prince of Wales, made out to be no proof. London: printed in the year 1702. 8°

T.282

3743

FERGUSSON (B.)

Mr. B. Fergusson's consolatory letter to Thomas Culpeper, Esq, and all the Kentish petitioners, as also to their London abettors. London, printed in the year 1702. 4°

T.139

3744

G.(D.F.)

The royal family described, or; The character of King James I, King Charles I, King Charles II, King James II, with the pedegree of Queen Anne. Written by the author of The rights of the king and subject briefly stated, &c. London, Benj. Bragg, 1702. 4°

Attributed by Bowdler to D.F. G[errald], i.e. Fitzgerald (?)

T.11

3745

GIBSON (Edmund) *Bishop of London.*

The parallel continu'd, between a presbyterian assembly, and the new model of an English provincial synod. Occasioned by a letter from the borders of Scotland, lately made publick. [Anon.] [No imprint, 1702.] 4°

2 copies.

T.74

3746

GIBSON (Edmund) *Bishop of London.*

Reflexions upon a late paper [by William Binckes], entitl'd An expedient propos'd. Shewing the unreasonableness thereof, and particularly the misrepresentations concerning the Archbishop's schedule... In a letter to the author... [Anon.] London: for A. and J. Churchill, 1702. 4°

T.195

3747

GIBSON (Edmund) *Bishop of London.*

The schedule review'd. Or, The right of the Archbishop to continue or prorogue the whole Convocation, clear'd from the exceptions of a late Vindication of the narrative of the lower-house, as to the point of adjournments ... And of a book [by Francis Atterbury] entitl'd, The case of the schedule stated ... [Anon.] London, for A. and J. Churchill, 1702. 4°

T.195

3748

GIBSON (Edmund) *Bishop of London.*

A sermon preach'd in Lambeth-chapel, at the consecration of... William Lord Bishop of Carlisle, on Sunday, June 14th, 1702. London: for Awnsham and John Churchill, 1702. 4°

2 copies.

T.192 T.708

3749

GIBSON (Edmund) *Bishop of London.*

A sermon preach'd in Lambeth-chapel, at the consecration of ... William Lord Bishop of Carlisle, on Sunday, June 14th, 1702. 2nd ed. London: for Awnsham and John Churchill, 1702. 4°

T.273

3750

GRASCOMBE (Samuel)

The character of a true Church-of-England-man. [Anon.] London, D. Edwards for N.C. in the year 1702. 4°

T.193

3751

KEITH (George)

The doctrine of the holy apostles & prophets the foundation of the Church of Christ, as it was delivered in a sermon at her Majesties chappel, at Boston in New-England, the 14th of June 1702. Boston, for Samuel Phillips, 1702. 4°

T.637

3752

KEITH (George)

A refutation of a dangerous & hurtful opinion maintained by Mr. Samuell Willard, an Independent minister at Boston ... [New York, William Bradford, 1702.] 4°

T.264

3753

KENNET (White) *Bishop of Peterborough.*

The history of the Convocation of the prelates and clergy of the province of Canterbury, summon'd to meet ... on February 6. 1700 ... [Anon.] London: for A. and J. Churchill, 1702. 4°

T.195

3754

KENNET (White) *Bishop of Peterborough.*

The present state of Convocation. In a letter, giving the full relation of the proceedings in several of the late sessions ... Correcting the mistakes and slanders of the pretended Faithful accounts, numb. 1, 2 [by Francis Atterbury]. [Anon.] London: for A. and J. Churchill, 1702. 4°

T.195

3755

KIMBERLEY (Jonathan)

A sermon preach'd before the lower house of Convocation, in Henry the seventh's chapel, November the fifth, 1702 ... London: for Thomas Bennet, and sold by T. Hart, bookseller in Coventry, 1702. 4°

2 copies.

T.172 T.192

3756

A LETTER from a clergy-man in the country, to a dignified clergy-man in London, vindicating the Bill brought in the last sessions of Parliament for preventing the translation of bishops. London; printed in the year 1702. 4°

T.509

3757

A LETTER from a country gentleman, to his friend in London, plainly shewing the frailty of all state oaths and tests. London, printed in the year, 1702. 4°

T.197

3758

A LETTER from a souldier to the Commons of England, occasioned by an address now carrying on by the protestants in Ireland, in order to take away the fund appropriated for the payment of the arrears of the army. London, for E. Mallet, 1702. 4°

T.22

3759

A LETTER from the borders of Scotland, concerning somewhat of agreement between a Scotch general assembly, and an English provincial convocation. By an episcopal divine [i.e. White Kennet?]. London: for A. Baldwin, 1702. 4°

2 copies.

T.74

3760

A LETTER to a new member of the ensuing Parliament. London: printed in the year, 1702. 4°

2 copies.

T.267 T.136

3761

A LETTER to Sir Humphrey Mackworth, on his book in vindication of the House of Commons. By a true lover of his countrey, and constitution of laws, liberties and properties of all English men. London, printed for the author, and are to be sold by the booksellers of London and Westminster, 1702. Fol.

T.695

3762

MACKENZIE (George) *Earl of Cromarty.*

Parainesis pacifica; or a perswasive to the union of Britain ... By a person of quality. London; re-printed, and sold by John Nutt, 1702. 4°

T.142

3763

MAXWELL (Henry)

Anguis in herba: or the fatal consequences of a treaty with France ... [Anon.] London, for A. Baldwin, and sold by the booksellers of London and Westminster, 1702. 4°

T.357

3764

MODESTY mistaken: or, A letter to Mr. Toland, upon his declining to appear in the ensuing Parliament ... Sold by J. Nutt, 1702. 4°

T.248

3765

The MOURNFUL congress, a poem, on the death of the illustrious King William III. of glorious memory. By a sincere lover of his prince and country... London, for John Nutt, 1702. Fol.

T.699

3766

The MOUSE grown a rat: or the story of the city and country mouse newly transpos'd. In a discourse betwixt Bays [i.e. Charles Montagu], Johnson, and Smith. London, E. Mallet, 1702. 4°

T.139

3767

NEEDHAM (William)

A sermon preach'd at Westminster, Nov.12.1702. in K. Henry the VII's chapel, before the reverend clergy of the lower house of Convocation. Being the day appointed by her Majesty for thanksgiving to Almighty God for the signal successes vouchsafed to her forces both by sea and land. London, for R. Knaplock, 1702. 4°

T.172

3768

A NEW dialogue between a member of Parliament, a divine, a lawyer, a freeholder, a shopkeeper, and a country farmer, upon the present juncture of affairs. [No imprint, 1702?] 8°

T.416

3769

A NEW project to make England a flourishing kingdom. Proposed as worthy the consideration of the ensuing parliament. London, printed in the year 1702. 4°

T.137

3770

NICOLSON (William) *Bishop of Carlisle.*

A letter to the Reverend Dr. White Kennet, D.D. in defence of The English historical library: against the unmannerly and slanderous objections of Mr. Francis Atterbury ... London: for Timothy Childe, 1702. 4°

T.137

3771

PAULDEN (Thomas)

Pontefract castle. An account how it was taken: and how General Rainsborough was surprised in his quarters at Doncaster, anno 1648. In a letter to a friend ... In the Savoy: Edward Jones, 1702. 4°

T.6

3772

PHILLIPS (Samuel)

The German Caesar. A panegyrick on Prince Eugene of Savoy, relating to the present posture of affairs in Italy, especially before Mantua... London: printed, and are to be sold by John Nutt, 1702. Fol.

T.699

3773

PHILLIPS (Samuel)

The grove, or, Muse's paradise: a dream. Wherein are describ'd the pleasures that attend a colledge-life... London, printed, and are to be sold by John Nutt, 1702. Fol.

"E. Libris Ed. Garrett Trinitatis Collegia 1715/16."

T.699

3774

The POPISH pretenders to the forfeited estates in Ireland unmask'd, and lay'd open. Being an answer to a letter from a member of Parliament ... London, printed and sold by the booksellers of London and Westminster, 1702. 4º

T.22

3775

The PRESENT condition of the English Navy set forth in a dialogue betwixt young Fudg of the Admiralty, and Capt. Steerwell, an Oliverian commander. London, E. Mallet, 1702. 4º

2 copies.

T.325   T.194

3776

REMARKS upon a late scurrilous pamphlet, [attributed to John Trenchard] intituled, An address of some Irish-folks to the House of Commons. London, printed in the year, 1702. 4º

Attributed by Bowdler to Sir Henry Sheeres.

T.22

3777

SACHEVERELL (Henry)

The character of a Low-Church-man: drawn in an answer to the True character of a Church-man [by Richard West]: shewing the false pretences to that name. Humbly offer'd to all the electors of the ensuing Parliament and Convocation ... [Anon.] Printed in the year, 1702. 4º

T.193

3778

SACHEVERELL (Henry)

The new association of those called, moderate-Church-men, with the modern-Whigs and fanaticks, to under-mine and blow-up the present Church and government. Occasion'd, by a late pamphlet [by John Dennis], entituled, The danger of priest-craft, &c. With a supplement, on occasion of the new Scotch Presbyterian covenant. By a true-Church-man... Printed and sold by the booksellers of London and Westminster, 1702. 2 parts. 4º

2 copies.

T.14   T.193

3779

SACHEVERELL (Henry)

The political union. A discourse shewing the depend-ance of government on religion in general: and of the English monarchy on the Church of England in particular. Oxford: Leonard Lichfield, for George West, and Henry Clements, 1702. 4º

T.192

3780

SACHEVERELL (Henry)

A sermon preach'd before the University of Oxford on the tenth day of June 1702. Being the fast appointed for the imploring a blessing on her Majesty and allies engag'd in the present war against France and Spain. Printed for Geo. West, and Henry Clements, at the Theatre in Oxford, anno 1702. 4º

T.192

3781

SHARP (John) Archbishop of York.

A sermon preach'd at the coronation of Queen Anne, in the abby-church of Westminster, April XXIII. MDCCII. London: for Walter Kettilby and William Rogers, 1702. 4º

T.273

3782

SHARP (John) Archbishop of York.

A sermon preach'd at the coronation of Queen Anne, in the abby-church of Westminster, April XXIII. MDCCII. 2nd ed. London: for Walter Kettilby and William Rogers, 1702. 4º

T.765

3783

SHARP (John) Archbishop of York.

A sermon, preached on Saint George's day, in Westminster Abby; on the coronation of her most sacred Majesty Queen Ann. London: James Read, 1702. 8º

Described by Bowdler as "The sham sermon at the Coronation of Q. Ann."

T.212

3784

A SHORT narrative of the proceedings against the Bp. of St. A ... London, printed in the year 1702. 8º

T.57

3785

SOME observations on the tryal of Spencer Cowper, J. Marson, E. Stevens, W. Rogers, that were tried at Hertford, about the murder of Sarah Stout ... London printed, and sold by the booksellers of London and Westminster, 1702. 4º

T.283

3786

SOME remarks on the Bill for taking, examining and stating the publick accounts of the Kingdom: and on the proceedings thereon in both houses, the last session. London: printed in the year, 1702. 4º

Attributed by Bowdler to Lord Somers.
2 copies.

T.267   T.136

3787

A SPEECH without doors, concerning the most effectual way of providing forty thousand landmen, as England's quota in the present Grand Confederacy. Printed for E. Mallet, 1702. 4º

T.136

3788

STEPHENS (Edward)

A petition and demand of right and justice by one of the Commons of England, on behalf of himself and the rest. In a letter to his representative in the present House of Commons. To M.C. Esq. [Signed E.S.] [No imprint, 1701/2.] 4º

T.11

3789

STILLINGFLEET (Edward) Bishop of Worcester.

The case of an oath of abjuration considered. [Anon.] London, A. Baldwin, 1702. 4º

T.509

3790

The TAVERN hunter: or, A drunken ramble from the Crown to the Devil. [No imprint, 1702.] 4º

T.69

3791

TENISON (Thomas) Archbishop of Canterbury.

A true copy of the Arch-bishop of Canterbury's speech in Jerusalem chamber, on Thursday, February 19. 1701/2. London, for Ri. Chiswell, [1702]. 4º

T.78

3792

TOLAND (John)

I. Reasons for addressing his Majesty to invite into England... the Electress Dowager and the Electoral Prince of Hanover. And likewise, II. Reasons for attainting and abjuring the pretended Prince of Wales ... With arguments for making a vigorous war against France... [Anon.] London, John Nutt, 1702. 4º

T.80

3793

TRELAWNEY (Jonathan) Bishop of Winchester.

A sermon preach'd before the Queen, and both Houses of Parliament ... Nov. 12. 1702. Being the day of thanksgiving; for the signal successes vouchsafed to her Majesties forces ... By ... Jonathan Lord Bishop of Exeter. London, for Tho. Bennet, 1702. 4º

T.192

3794

TRELAWNEY (Jonathan) Bishop of Winchester.

A sermon preach'd before the Queen, and both Houses of Parliament ... Nov. 12. 1702. Being the day of thanksgiving; for the signal successes vouchsafed to her Majesties forces ... By ... Jonathan Lord Bishop of Exeter. London, for Tho. Bennet, 1702. And sold by C. Yeo, in Exon. 4º

T.172

3795

The TRYAL, sentence, and condemnation of fidelity, as it was lately acted on the publick stage. With a dialogue between corruption and fidelity ... London, printed, and sold by the booksellers of London and Westminster, 1702. 4º

T.139

3796

A VINDICATION of the Whigs. In a familiar discourse between Restless, Reasonable, and Wretched. In opposition to a late pamphlet [by Charles Davenant] called the true picture of a modern Whig. Printed and sold by the booksellers of London and Westminster, 1702. 8º

T.52

3797

WAGSTAFFE (Thomas)

The present state of Jacobitism in England. A second part. In answer to the first [by Daniel Defoe]. [Anon.] London: printed in the year 1702. 4º

3 copies.

T.80   T.510

3798

WHINCOP (Thomas)

A sermon preach'd before the honourable House of Commons, at St. Margaret's Westminster, on Thursday the 5th of November, 1702... London, J.L. for Walter Kettilby, 1702. 4º

T.172

1703

3799

An ACCOUNT of the manner of execution: together with the lives, actions, and last dying words of Collonel Richard Kirkby, and Capt. Cooper Wade; who were shot ... for cowardize and neglect of duty, in diserting the Honourable Admiral Bembow, during six days ingagement with Monsieur Du Casse... London, for C. Barnet, 1703. 8º

T.416

3800

ASTREA triumphans. The temple of gratitude, and the trophies of Vigo; being a congratulatory poem to his Grace the Duke of Ormond, on his happy accession to the lieutenancy of the kingdom of Ireland. London, sold by A. Baldwin, 1703. Fol.

T.699

3801

B.(B.)

The exorbitant grants of William the III. examin'd and question'd ... London, printed in the year 1703. 4º

Attributed by Bowdler to F. Gerrald (cf. The royal family described).

T.11

3802

BALZAC (Jean Louis Guez) Sieur de.

A survey of princes and their favourites, by the ingenious Monsieur de Balzack, in his Aristippus abridg'd and translated. London: printed in the year 1703. 4º

4 copies.

T.72

3803

BARRINGTON (John Shute) Viscount.

The interest of England consider'd, in respect to protestants dissenting from the Establish'd Church. With some thoughts about occasional conformity. [Anon.] London, printed in the year 1703. 4º

T.517

3804

BRYDALL (John)

Noli me tangere. The young student's letter to the old lawyer in the country. Containing several other authenticks, to corroborate, and confirm the explication... of that royal maxim; the king can do no wrong... [Anon.] London: for J. Nutt, 1703. 4º

T.11

3805

BURD (Richard)

Concio ad clerum being a sermon preach'd at the Lord Bishop of Winton's visitation at Andover... on the 27th of September, 1703. London: for Edward Brewster, 1703. 4º

T.625

3806

COLLIER (Jeremy)

Mr. Collier's Dissuasive from the play-house; in a letter to a person of quality, occasion'd by the late calamity of the Tempest. London: for Richard Sare, 1703.   8°

T.248

3807

CONGREVE (William)

A satyr against love. Revis'd and corrected by Mr. Congreve... London: printed in the year, 1703. Fol.

T.699

3808

The DANGEROUS consequence to the Queen, and kingdom arising, from an Act voted by the Parliament in Scotland, to which the royal assent is not yet given. [No imprint, 1703?]   4°

T.11

3809

DEFOE (Daniel)

More reformation. A satyr upon himself. By the author of The true born English-man. London: printed in the year, 1703.   4°

Moore 56.

T.69

3810

ENGLAND. *Parliament. House of Commons.*

The report of the conferences and free conference, relating to the message from the Lords the 4th of February, 1702. touching the Commissioners of accounts, and the proceedings thereupon ... London: for Edward Jones; and Timothy Goodwin, 1703. Fol.

Incomplete.

T.543

3811

ET tu Brute? Or, The m[itr]'d c[aba]l. [No imprint, 1703?]   4°

T.69

3812

FERGUSON (Robert)

The extraordinary case of the Bp. of St. David's, further clear'd and made plain, from the several views that have been made of it ... [Anon.] Printed in the year 1703.   4°

T.76

3813

FIDDES (Richard)

A sermon preached on the thanksgiving day: December, 3d. 1702 ... York, John White, for Francis Hildyard, 1703.   4°

T.172

3814

FLETCHER (Andrew) *of Saltoun.*

Speeches, by a member of the Parliament, which began at Edinburgh the 6th of May 1703. [Anon.] Edinburgh; printed in the year 1703.   8°

T.57

3815

FULLER (Thomas) *Rector of Bishops-Hatfield.*

A sermon preached at the triennial visitation of... James, Lord Bishop of Lincoln, held at Stevenage, August the 6th. 1703. London, J.H. for Henry Mortlock, 1703.   4°

T.752

3816

FULLER (William)

The whole life of Mr. William Fuller; being an impartial account of his birth, education, relations, and introduction into the service of the late King James ... Impartially writ, by himself, during his confinement in the Queen's-Bench. Printed and sold by the booksellers in London and Westminster, 1703.   8°

T.282

3817

GANDER (Joseph)

The glory of her sacred Majesty Queen Anne, in the Royal Navy, and her absolute sovereignty as empress of the sea, asserted and vindicated. Also a treatise of navigation ... London: printed for the authour, 1703.   4°

T.18

3818

GARRET (Walter)

An exposition of Rev. ix. Containing a prophecy of the Saracen vexations of Italy from the year 830 to 980 ... By W.G. Printed Feb. 1702/3.   8°

T.39

3819

GARRET (Walter)

An exposition of Rev. xi. Containing the famous prophecy of the witnesses; as also a prediction of the passing-away of the Turkish wo; and of the destruction of the Papacy. By W.G. Printed, November, 1703.   8°

T.39

3820

GIBSON (Edmund) *Bishop of London.*

The pretended independence of the lower-house upon the upper, a groundless notion. And the obligation of presbyters in an English provincial synod, to act in subordination to their metropolitan and bishops... [Anon.] London: for A. and J. Churchill, 1703.   4°

T.74

3821

GIBSON (Edmund) *Bishop of London.*

A short state of some present questions in Convocation: particularly, of the right to continue or prorogue. By way of commentary upon the schedule of continuation. [Anon.] London: for A. and J. Churchill, 1703.   4°

T.74

3822

The GOLDEN age from the fourth eclogue of Virgil, &c. [Wrongly attributed to William Walsh.] London: printed in the year 1703.   4°

T.69

3823

The GOLDEN age from the fourth eclogue of Virgil, &c. [Wrongly attributed to William Walsh.] London, printed in the year 1703.   8°

T.220

3824

HARRIS (John) *D.D.,F.R.S.*

A sermon preach'd in the parish church of St. Mary Magdalen, Old Fish-street, on Wednesday the twenty sixth of May, 1703. Being the fast-day appointed by proclamation... London, for Richard Wilkin, 1703. 4°

T.757

3825

HICKERINGILL (Edmund)

The parliament-tacks inquir'd into ... London, printed; and are to be sold by B. Bragge, [1703?] 4°

T.194

3826

An HISTORICAL and political treatise of the Navy: with some thoughts how to retrieve the antient glory of the Navy of England. Humbly offer'd to the consideration of both Houses of Parliament. London, B. Bragg, 1703. 4°

T.325

3827

HODGES (James)

The rights and interests of the two British monarchies, inquir'd into, and clear'd; with a special respect to an united or separate state. Treatise I ... [Anon.] London: printed in the year 1703.   4°

T.11

3828

HORE (Charles)

A true and exact account of many great abuses committed in the victualling her Majesties Navy, from February 3, 1702/3. to July 1703... [Anon.] London, printed in the year, 1703. Fol.

T.543

3829

HUGHES (John) *Poet.*

An ode in praise of musick, set for variety of voices and instruments by Mr. Philip Hart... London; for B. Lintot, and sold by J. Nutt, 1703. 4°

T.639

3830

INFORMATION for Mr. Robert Bennet, Dean of Faculty, and the other advocates complained upon at the instance of her Majesty's Advocate. [No imprint, 1703?]   4°

T.11

3831

JAMES II, *King of England.*

The late King James his advice to his son. Written with his own hand, and found in his cabinet after his death... London: printed in the year 1703.   12°

T.507

3832

JOHNSON (Richard)

A treatise of the genders of Latin nouns: by way of examination of Lilly's grammar rules... London: John Matthews, for George Sawbridge, 1703.   8°

T.416

3833

KENNET (White) *Bishop of Peterborough.*

The glory of children in their fathers. A sermon preach'd in the cathedral church of St. Paul London, before the Sons of the clergy, December the 3d 1702 ... London: for Henry Bonwicke; and Richard Sare, 1703. 4°

T.73

3834

LESLIE (Charles)

A case of present concern. In a letter to a member of the House of Commons. [Anon.] [No imprint, 1703.] 4°

T.193

3835

A LETTER from a gentleman of Swisserland to a counsellor of Friburgh. [No imprint, 1703.]   4°

T.283

3836

A LETTER to my lords the bishops, concerning the Bill for preventing occasional conformity. [No imprint, 1703.]   4°

T.264

3837

A LETTER to Sir J.P. [John Pakington?] Bart., a member for the ensuing Parliament, relating to the union of England and Scotland. [No imprint, 1703?]   4°

3 copies.

T.11 T.193 T.267

3838

MAXWELL (Henry)

An essay towards an union of Ireland with England ... [Anon.] London: for Timothy Goodwin, 1703.   4°

T.11

3839

MY Lord Bishop of Sarum's Exposition of the twenty third article of the Church of England, defended and cleared from the exceptions of a late book [by William Thornton], entituled, The vindication of the twenty third article of the Church of England, from my Lord Bishop of Sarum's exposition. London, for Awnsham and John Churchill, 1703.   4°

T.191

3840

A NEW dialogue between the horse at Charing-Cross, and the horse at Stocks-market. Printed in the year 1703.   4°

T.69

3841

OWEN (James)

Moderation a virtue: or, The occasional conformist justify'd from the imputation of hipocrisy ... [Anon.] London: for A. Baldwin, 1703.   4°

Annotated by George Hickes and another.
2 copies.

T.517 T.14

3842

PAKINGTON (*Sir* John)

A speech for the Bill against occasional conformity. [Anon.] [No imprint, 1703.]   4°

2 copies.

T.264 T.193

3843

ROQUETTE (Henri Emmanuel de)

A funeral oration upon the death of... James the second, King of Great-Britain. Spoken the 19th day of September, 1702. in the Church of St. Mary de Chaillot, where his Majesty's heart is deposited. Done out of the 13th edition of French. Printed in the year 1703.   4°

T.192

3844

SACHEVERELL (Henry)

The new association. Part.II. With farther improvements ... An answer to some objections in the pretended D. Foe's explication, in the reflections upon the shortest way ... (A supplement.) [Anon.] Printed and sold by the booksellers of London and Westminster, 1703. 2 parts.   4°

2 copies.

T.14 T.193

3845

SCOTLAND. *Parliament.*

The Act of the Parliament of Scotland, for the security of the kingdom ... With a short account of it, and some few remarks ... London, printed in the year 1703.   4°

3 copies.

T.11

3846

SCOTLAND. *Parliament.*

Two speeches; the one relating to trade. (Spoken in the present Parliament of Scotland.) The other relating to the limitations of the Crown thereof. Edinburgh, printed in the 1703.   4°

T.11

3847

The SECOND part of The mouse grown a rat: or, The story of the city and country mouse. Newly transpos'd. In a dialogue betwixt Bays [i.e. Charles Montagu], Johnson, and Smith, in the present reign. London, B. Bragg, 1703.   4°

T.283

3848

A SECOND select collection of letters of the anctients ... Whereby is discovered the morality, gallantry, wit, humour, manner of arguing; and in a word the genius both of the Britains, Normans and English ... London: P.B. for X.Y.A.Z. monster, murther, and ghostsellers, [1703].   4°

T.283

3849

SHARP (John) *Archbishop of York.*

A serious exhortation to repentance and a holy life. A sermon preach'd before the Queen at St. James's chappel, on Ashwednesday, February 10. 1702/3. London: for Walter Kettilby: and William Rogers, 1703.   4°

T.757

3850

STEPHENS (Edward)

A good and necessary proposal for the restitution of Catholick communion between the Greek churches and the Church of England. [Anon.] [No imprint, 1703?] brs.

T.137

3851

STEPHENS (Edward)

The more excellent way: or, A proposal of a compleat work of charity. For the accomodation of some devout women ... [Anon.] [No imprint, 1703?]   4°

Includes a list of Stephens' publications.

T.137

3852

STUBS (Philip)

God's dominion over the seas, and the seaman's duty, consider'd. In a sermon preached at Long-reach, on board her Majesty's capital ship the Royal Soveraign... 4th ed. London; for Richard Mount, 1703.   8°

T.448

3853

TATE (Nahum)

The song for new-years-day, 1703. Perform'd before her Majesty. Set by Mr. Eccles, master of her Majesty's musick. The words by Mr. Tate, poet-laureat to her Majesty. Printed for J. Nutt, 1703.   4°

T.69

3854

The TRUE-born-Huguonot: or, Daniel de Foe. A satyr. [Attributed to William Pittis.] [No imprint, 1703.]   4°

T.69

3855

The TRYAL, examination, and condemnation, of occasional conformity, &c. at a sessions of oyer and terminer, held at Troynovant, before Mr. Justice Upright, and Mr. Baron Integrity ... the 26th of J —— y, 1702/3. London: printed in the year, 1703.   4°

T.264

3856

The TRYAL, examination, and condemnation, of occasional conformity, &c. at a sessions of oyer and terminer, held at Troynovant, before Mr Justice Upright, and Mr. Baron Integrity... the 26th of J---y, 1703. London, printed in the year, 1703.   8°

T.416

3857

WARD (Edward)

English Lucian; or, Modern dialogues between a vintner and his wife, and a captain of the guards... [Anon.] Numb.I. May. London: for John Nutt, 1703.   4°

T.283

3858

The WOLF in sheeps cloathing: or, A new way to play an old game. [No imprint, 1703.]   4°

T.69

1704

3859

An ACCOUNT of the Scotch plot. In a letter, from a gentleman in the City, to his friend in the country. London, printed in the year, 1704.   4°

T.11

3860

AESOP at Portugal: being a collection of fables, apply'd to the present posture of affairs ... London: printed in the year, 1704.   8°

T.57

3861

AESOP in Scotland, exposed in ten select fables relating to the times ... London, printed in the year, 1704.   8°

T.220

3862

Les ARTICLES de la societé de plusieurs refugiez, de l'Assemblée de S. Quentin, & de ces dépendances, qui s'assembloient à Haucourt, en Picardie. [No imprint, 1704.]   4°

T.77

3863

ASTELL (Mary)

A fair way with the dissenters and their patrons. Not writ by Mr. L —— y [i.e. Charles Leslie], or any other furious Jacobite, whether clergyman or lay-man; but by a very moderate person and dutiful subject to the Queen. [Anon.] London: E.P. for R. Wilkin, 1704.   4°

2 copies.

T.193 T.264

3864

ASTELL (Mary)

An impartial enquiry into the causes of rebellion and civil war in this kingdom: in an examination of Dr. Kennett's sermon, Jan. 31. 1703/4. and vindication of the Royal Martyr. [Anon.] London: E.P. for R. Wilkin, 1704.   4°

2 copies.

T.11 T.73

3865

ASTELL (Mary)

Moderation truly stated: or, A review of a late pamphlet [by James Owen], entitul'd, Moderation a vertue. With a prefatory discourse to Dr. D'aveanant, concerning his late Essays on peace and war... [Signed Tom. Single.] London: J.L. for Rich. Wilkin, 1704. 2 parts.   4°

3 copies.

T.14 T.193 T.517

3866

ATTERBURY (Francis) *Bishop of Rochester.*

A sermon preached before the honourable House of Commons, at St. Margaret's Westminster, on Wednesday, March 8. 1703/4. Being the day of her Majesty's happy accession to the throne. London, for Tho. Bennet, 1704.   4°

T.192

3867

ATTERBURY (Francis) *Bishop of Rochester.*

D.F.A.'s. vindication of the Bp. of Sarum, from being the author of a late printed speech. In a letter to a friend. London: John Nutt, 1704.   4°

T.193

3868

BEVERIDGE (William) *Bishop of St. Asaph.*

A sermon preach'd before the House of Peers, in the abbey-church of Westminster, on Sunday, November the 5th. 1704 ... London, J. Leake, 1704.   4°

T.78

3869

BIRKENHEAD (*Sir* John)

The assembly-man. Written in the year 1647 [by Sir John Birkenhead]. But proves the true character of (Cerberus) the Observator, MDCCIV ... To which is added, An exact list of the royal martyrs that were slain in the unnatural rebellion ... London: printed in the year 1704.   4°

T.487

3870

BISSET (William)

More plain English. In two sermons preach'd for reformation of manners: in the year 1701 ... With a large preface by the author in his own vindication. London: A. Baldwin, 1704.   8°

T.57

3871

BISSET (William)

Plain English. A sermon preached at St. Mary-le-Bow, on Monday, March 27. 1704. for reformation of manners ... London: printed for the author; and sold by A. Baldwin, 1704.   8°

T.57

3872

B[I]SS[E]T b-sh-t. Or; The foulness of More plain English, in two sermons, for r-f-rm-t--n of m-nn-rs... London: printed in the year 1704.   4°

2 copies.

T.78 T.227

3873

BLACKALL (Offspring) *Bishop of Exeter.*

A sermon preach'd at Brentwood in Essex, October the 7th. 1693. at the visitation of... Henry Lord Bishop of London. 3rd ed. London: for Will. Rogers, 1704.   4°

T.752

3874

BROWN (Thomas) *of Shifnal.*

Faction display'd. A poem [by William Shippen]. Burlesqu'd by the late ingenious Mr. Thomas Brown. London: printed in the year 1675 [i.e. 1704?]. 4°

See *Poems on the affairs of state*, vol. 6, p.649, where this poem is described as having circulated only in manuscript.

T.69

3875

BURNET (Gilbert) *Bishop of Salisbury.*

The Bishop of Salisbury's speech in the House of Lords, upon the Bill against occasional conformity. London: for Ri. Chiswell, 1704. 4°

T.193

3876

BUTLER (Lilly)

A sermon preach'd at the anniversary meeting of the Sons of clergymen, in the cathedral church of St. Paul, on Thursday, Nov. 30. 1704. London: for Brabazon Aylmer, 1704. 4°

T.625

3877

C.(A.B.)

A letter from a country justice of the peace to an alderman of the city of London, &c. concerning the Bishop of Salisbury's speech in the House of Lords, upon the Bill against occasional conformity. London: printed in the year 1704. 4°

T.193

3878

The CALVES-HEAD Club. A sermon preached at Maggot-Hall, in Good-Old-Cause-Lane on the 30th of January, 1704 ... By that revernd and pious divine Dr. Hipocrit ... London, printed in the year, 1704. 8°

T.11

3879

CHURCH OF ENGLAND.

A form of prayer with thanksgiving to almighty God; to be used in all churches and chapels within this realm, every year, upon the eighth day of March: being the day on which her Majesty began her happy reign. London, Charles Bill, and the executrix of Thomas Newcomb, 1704. 8°

T.78

3880

CHURCH OF ENGLAND. *Convocation. Lower House.*

A representation made by the lower house of Convocation to the Archbishop and bishops, anno 1703. London: for Tho. Bennet, 1704. 4°

2 copies.

T.74 T.133

3881

COBB (Samuel)

The Portugal expedition. To which is added, Dr. G[art]h's epigram on the same subject ... London: for R. Basset; and sold by John Nutt, 1704. 4°

T.269

3882

The COBLER of Gloucester [i.e. Ralph Wallis] reviv'd; in a letter to the Observator's countrey-man. London, H. Hills, [1704]. 4°

T.487

3883

COCK (John)

A sermon preach'd at the cathedral church of Durham. London, printed in the year, 1704. 12°

2 copies.

T.519 T.36

3884

The C[OMMO]NER'S, in answer to the P[ee]r's [i.e. Lord Haversham's] sp[ee]ch. [No imprint, 1704.] 4°

T.193

3885

DEFOE (Daniel)

The address. [Anon.] London, printed in the year 1704. 4°

Moore 77.

T.69

3886

DEFOE (Daniel)

The Christianity of the High-Church consider'd. Dedicated to a noble peer [Lord Haversham]. [Anon.] London, printed in the year, 1704. 4°

Moore 75.

T.193

3887

DEFOE (Daniel)

The dissenters answer to the High-Church challenge. [Anon.] London, printed in the year 1704. 4°

Moore 67.

T.193

3888

DEFOE (Daniel)

A hymn to victory. London, for J. Nutt, 1704. 4°

Moore 85.

T.69

3889

DEFOE (Daniel)

A new test of the Church of England's honesty. [Anon.] London: printed in the year 1704. 4°

Moore 80.
2 copies.

T.264 T.193

3890

DEFOE (Daniel)

Royal religion; being some enquiry after the piety of princes. With remarks on a book, entituled, A form of prayers us'd by King William. [Anon.] London: printed in the year 1704. 4°

Moore 72.

T.11

3891

DE LAUNE (Thomas)

A narrative of the tryal and sufferings of Thomas Delaune, for writing, printing and publishing a late book, called, A plea for the non-conformists ... Directed to Doctor Calamy; in obedience to whose call, that work was undertaken ... Printed for the author, 1683. And re-printed 1704. 4°

T.261

3892

DENNIS (John)

The person of quality's answer to Mr. Collier's letter, being a disswasive from the play-house. In which are inserted the apologies of a young lady, and young gentleman, in behalf of the ladies and gentlemen who frequent the play-house. [Anon.] London: printed and are to be sold by the booksellers of London and Westminster. 1704. 4°

T.77

3893

A DIALOGUE between the Observator, the Weekly review, and the Dayly courant. London, printed in the year, 1704. 4°

T.487

3894

A DIARY of the several reports as well true as false, daily spread throughout the nation, from Sept. 24. 1688, to the coronation of K. William Apr. 11th 1689 ... London, printed in the year 1704. 8°

T.416

3895

The DISSENTERS address of thanks to the bishops, for casting out the Bill against occasional conformity. London: printed in the year 1704. 4°

T.193

3896

A DRAM of the bottle for the French King and the Elector of Bavaria. Being a comical new dialogue between a courier sent from Bavaria, and the French King. London, for R. Rogers, 1704. 8°

T.220

3897

DUKE (Richard)

Of Christ's kingdom. A sermon preach'd at the assizes held at Guilford, July 24. 1704 ... London: E.P. for Tho. Bennet, 1704. 4°

T.192

3898

DUKE (Richard)

Of the imitation of Christ. A sermon preach'd before the Queen, at Bath. Aug. 29th 1703. London: T.W. for Thomas Bennet, 1704. 4°

T.771

3899

E.(E.)

A letter to Henry Hingeston. To which are annexed a few lines to the learned author of the Snake in the grass. [No imprint, 1704?] 8°

T.101

3900

E. (H.)

The orator display'd: or, Remarks on the B[isho]p of S[alis]bury's speech. Upon the Bill against occasional conformity... [The dedication signed H.E.] London: printed in the year 1704. 4°

2 copies.

T.639 T.660

3901

ENGLAND lampoon'd, or a hint upon the times. London. Printed in the year, 1704. 4°

T.69

3902

ENRIQUEZ DE CABRERA (Juan Tomas)

The Almirante of Castile's manifesto. Containing, I. The reasons of his withdrawing himself out of Spain ... Faithfully translated from the original printed in Spanish at Lisbon ... London: John Nutt, 1704. 4°

T.11

3903

FINA (Ferdinand)

A sermon on the occasion of the late storm. Preach'd in Spanish, before the Worshipful Society of Merchants Trading to Spain ... on the 7th of January, 1703/4. Rendred into English from the original Spanish ... London: for John Nutt, 1704. 4°

2 copies.

T.765 T.273

3904

FLETCHER (Andrew) *of Saltoun.*

An account of a conversation concerning a right regulation of governments for the common good of mankind. In a letter to the Marquiss of Montrose, the Earls of Rothes, Roxburg, and Hadington, from London the 1st of December, 1703. [Anon.] Edinburgh; printed in the year 1704. 8°

T.57

3905

FOWLER (Edward) *Bishop of Gloucester.*

A sermon preached in the chappel at Guild-hall, upon Thursday the 7th of September, 1704. Being the day of publick thanksgiving to Almighty God, for the late glorious victory, obtained over the French and Bavarians, at Blenheim ... London: for Brab. Aylmer; and John Wyat, 1704. 4°

2 copies.

T.192 T.198

3906

FULLER (William)

The sincere and hearty confession of Mr. William Fuller: being a true account of the persons that assisted him in the design of imposing Mrs. Mary Grey upon the world, as the mother of the pretended Prince of Wales ... London, printed, and to be sold by most booksellers in London and Westminster, 1704. 8°

T.282

3907

GANDY (Henry)

Some remarks, or, short stictures, upon A compassionate enquiry into the causes of the Civil War. In a sermon preach'd ... by White Kennet ... [Anon.] London, for C. Brome, 1704. 4°

2 copies.

T.73

3908

GASTRELL (Francis) *Bishop of Chester.*

A sermon preach'd before the honourable House of Commons, on Wednesday, Jan. 19th 1703/4. Being the fast-day appointed for the imploring of a blessing from Almighty God upon her Majesty and her allies engaged in the present war ... London: T.W. for Thomas Bennet, 1704. 4°

T.192

3909

GRASCOMBE (Samuel)

The mask of moderation pull'd off the foul face of occasional conformity: being an answer to a late poisonous pamphlet [by James Owen], entitul'd Moderation still a vertue... [Anon.] London: for G. Sawbridge, 1704. 4°

4 copies.

T.14   T.193   T.264   T.266

3910

GRASCOMBE (Samuel)

Occasional conformity a most unjustifiable practice. In answer to a late pamphlet [by James Owen], entituled, Moderation a virtue. With... a postscript, in answer to the eleventh section of Dr. Davenant's Essays of peace at home and war abroad... [Anon.] London: for S. and W. Keble, 1704. 2 parts. 4°
Attributed by Bowdler to William Higden.
4 copies.

T.193   T.266   T.517   T.745

3911

HEREDITARY succession in the protestant line, unalterable. In answer to the Scots bill of security. London: for William Rogers, 1704. 4°

T.487

3912

The HIGH-LANDER'S answer to the L[or]d H[aversha]m's Sp[ee]ch. [No imprint, 1704.] 4°

2 copies.

T.487   T.267

3913

An HISTORICAL account of the principles of the high-flyers in all ages. Shewing how destructive they have been, and Daily are, to the peace and union both of Church and State in every government ... By no zealot, nor a luke warm Christian ... London, B. Bragg, 1704. 4°

T.193

3914

IN imitation of Hudibras. The dissenting hyprocrite or occasional conformist; with reflections on two of the ring-leaders, &c ... London, printed in the year 1704. 8°

T.220

3915

JAMES I, *King of England.*

The royal censure of partial conformity, truly representing the case of Church-men and dissenters, in the time of King James the first, in his proclamations, declarations and conferences, relating thereunto. London: G. Croom, for Sam. and Will. Keble, 1704. 4°

2 copies.

T.264   T.193

3916

The JUBILEE necklace: or, a present from C.III. to the D. of M[arlborough]. A satyr. [No imprint, 1704.] 4°

T.69

3917

KEITH (George)

An answer to Mr. Samuell Willard (one of the ministers at Boston in New-England) his reply to my printed sheet, called, A dangerous and hurtful opinion maintained by him ... Printed and sold by William Bradford in New-York, 1704. 4°

T.264

3918

KENNET (White) *Bishop of Peterborough.*

A compassionate enquiry into the causes of the Civil War. In a sermon preached in the church of St. Botolph Aldgate, on January XXXI, 1703/4... London: for A. and J. Churchil, 1704. 4°

2 copies.

T.73

3919

KENNET (White) *Bishop of Peterborough.*

A compassionate enquiry into the causes of the Civil War. In a sermon preached in the church of St. Botolph Algate, on January XXX1, 1703/4... London, H. Hills, [1704?] 8°

T.519

3920

KENNET (White) *Bishop of Peterborough.*

A sermon preached in the church of St. Botolph Aldgate, in London, on September VII. 1704. the day of solemn thanksgiving for the late glorious victory... London: for Awnsham and John Churchill, 1704. 4°

T.765

3921

LEGION'S humble address to the Lords [by Daniel Defoe], answer'd paragraph by paragraph. [No imprint, 1704.] 4°

2 copies.

T.267   T.193

3922

LESLIE (Charles)

The Bishop of Salisbury's proper defence, from a speech cry'd about the streets in his name, and said to have been spoken by him in the House of Lords, upon the Bill against occasional conformity. [Anon.] Sold by the booksellers of London and Westminster, 1704. 4°

3 copies.

T.2   T.5   T.193

3923

LESLIE (Charles)

Cassandra. (But I hope not) telling what will come of it ... In answer to the Occasional letter. Num. I. Wherein the new-associations, &c. are considered. [Anon.] London: printed and sold by the booksellers of London and Westminster, 1704. 2 numbers. 4°

2 sets.

T.143   T.193

3924

LESLIE (Charles)

Cassandra. (But I hope not) telling what will come of it. Numb. II. In answer to the Occasional letter. Numb. I. wherein the new-associations, &c. are considered. [Anon.] London: printed and sold by the booksellers of London and Westminster, 1704. 4°

T.668

3925

LESLIE (Charles)

The wolf stript of his shepherd's cloathing. In answer to a late celebrated book [by James Owen] intituled Moderation a vertue ... By one call'd an High-Church-man ... (The appendix.) Sold by the booksellers of London and Westminster, 1704. 2 parts. 4°

T.143

3926

LESLIE (Charles)

The wolf stript of his shepherd's cloathing. In answer to a late celebrated book [by James Owen] intituled Moderation a vertue... 2nd ed. By one call'd an High-Church-man... (The appendix.) Sold by the booksellers of London and Westminster, 1704. 2 parts. 4°

T.404

3927

LIEBEL (Isaac)

... [Hebrew] sive Fletum super Thammuz Ezech. VIII. comm. 14... Vitembergae, literis Christiani Gerdesii, [1704]. 4°

T.819

3928

The LOCUSTS: or, Chancery painted to the life, and the laws of England try'd in forma pauperis. A poem ... London: printed in the year, 1704. 4°

T.69

3929

The LORD'S people, commonly miscall'd Quakers, their friendly advice to the Observator, February the 5th. 1704. Concerning his remarks on the dissenters address to the creatures, known by the name of bishops. London: printed in the year 1704. 4°

T.283

3930

The LOW-FLYER'S new declaration. [No imprint, 1704.] 4°

T.487

3931

LUCAS (Richard)

Of humility. A sermon preached before the Queen, at St. James's, on Wednesday March 15th, 1703/4. London: for S. Smith, and B. Walford, 1704. 4°

T.192

3932

The LYING-Jacks, a dialogue [between Partridge and his servant, about Gadbury]. [No imprint, 1704?] 4°

T.283

3933

M.(J.C.)

A copy of a letter concerning the siege of Landaw, presented to a minister of state the 22th of September last, with some observations thereupon ... London, printed in the year of our Lord 1704. 4°

T.194

3934

MACKWORTH (*Sir* Humphrey)

Free parliaments: or, A vindication of the fundamental right of the Commons of England in Parliament assembled to be sole judges of all those privileged of the electors and of the elected; which are absolutely necessary to preserve free parliaments, and a free people ... London: J. Nutt, 1704. 8°

2 copies.

T.267   T.147

3935

MACKWORTH (*Sir* Humphrey)

A treatise concerning the happiness of a religious life: by way of dialogue. 2nd ed. London: Freeman Collins, for George Strahan, 1704. 8°

T.57

3936

MANDEVILLE (Bernard de)

Typhon: or the wars between the gods and giants: a burlesque poem in imitation of the comical Mons. Scarron. [The dedication signed B.M.] London: for J. Pero, and S. Illidge, and sold by J. Nutt, 1704. 4°

T.562

3937

A MANIFESTO, asserting and clearing the legal right of the Princess Sophia, and her issue, the serene house of Hanover, to the succession of Scotland. London: for William Rogers, 1704. 4°

T.487

3938

MARESCHAL Tallard's aid-de-camp: his account of the battle of Bleinheim. In a letter written by him from Strasburg, to Monsieur de Chamillard... and intercepted, and sent over to a foreign minister, residing in England... [Attributed to Antoine de Pas.] London, John Nutt, 1704. 4°

T.487

3939

MEMOIRS relating to the famous Mr. Tho. Brown. With a catalogue of his library. London, B. Brag, 1704. 4°

T.69

3940

MILBOURNE (Luke)

Christian good-fellowship. A sermon preach'd at the meeting of the nobility, gentry, and others of the county of Warwick, at their yearly feast, December the 7th, 1704 ... London: for A. Roper, 1704. 4°

T.78

3941

MODERATION pursued, by a paper written for the vindicating of our liturgy and Church from any malevolence to meetings ... Upon occasion of the book [by James Owen], call'd, Moderation a virtue ... By one that holds communion with the Church ... London: for J. Robinson; and sold by B. Bragg, 1704. 4°

T.14

3942

A NARRATIVE of Sir George Rooke's late voyage to the Mediterranean, where he commanded as admiral of the confederate fleet... In a letter to a person of quality. London: for Benj. Tooke, 1704. 4°

T.487

3943

NORRIS (Richard)

A sermon preach'd on September 7. 1704. being a day of publick thanksgiving for the glorious victory... London: for John Lawrence, 1704. 4°

T.765

3944

NORTH (Francis) *1st Baron Guilford.*

An argument of a learned judge in the Exchequer-chamber upon a writ of error out of the King's-Bench, in a cause, wherein Sir Samuel Barnadiston [sic] was plaintiff against Sir William Soame... wherein the privilege of the House of Commons, in determining matters relating to the right of elections of their own members, is justified... [Anon.] London: for Geo. Sawbridge, and sold by J. Nutt, 1704. 4°

T.283

3945

OBSERVATIONS upon the case of William Rose an apothecary, as represented by him to the ... House of Lords, upon his bringing the case before the said House by a writ of error, in order to have the judgment obtain'd against him by the College of Physicians ... reversed ... London, printed in the year 1704. 4°

T.248

3946

The OCCASIONAL letter. Number I. Concerning several particulars in The new association: the occasional bill; a MS. history, &c ... With a postscript, relating to Sir Humphrey Mackworth's book, intituled, Peace at home: or his defence of the occasional bill. London: printed in the year 1704. 4°

T.14

3947

The OCCASIONALISTS. (Occasional conformity.) London; printed in the year, 1704. 4°

Another copy printed on a single leaf.

T.261 T.264

3948

OWEN (James)

Moderation still a virtue: in answer to several bitter pamphlets: especially two, entituled, Occasional conformity a most unjustifiable practice [by Samuel Grascombe]. And The wolf stripp'd of his shepherd's cloathing [by Charles Leslie]... By the author of Moderation a virtue... London: for J. Taylor, 1704. 4°

T.14

3949

The PICTURE of a high-flyer. London: printed in the year 1704. 4°

T.193

3950

The PICTURE of a low-flyer. [No imprint, 1704.] 4°

T.193

3951

The PICTURE of the Observator drawn to the life. London: printed in the year 1704. 4°

T.69

3952

The POOR furbelow'd ladies lamentation. Or, a pleasant new dialogue between a play-house beau, and a mask'd furbelow'd lady, upon the especial order of their being banished from the play-houses. London, for R. Rogers, 1704. 4°

T.69

3953

The PORTUGUESE arms justified: in vindication of the Spanish liberties oppress'd by a French power. As also, The title of ... Charles III. to the crown of Spain, asserted. Translated from the original copy printed at Lisbon ... London, J. Nutt, 1704. 4°

T.11

3954

The PRINCIPLE of the protestant reformation explain'd, in a letter of resolution concerning Church-communion. London, printed in the year 1704. 4°

T.192

3955

REFLECTIONS on a late speech by the Lord Haversham, in so far as it relates to the affairs of Scotland... In a letter to a friend. London: B. Bragg, 1704. 4°

T.487

3956

RELATION de la bataille de Bleinheim, ou lettre écrite par un aide de camp du Maréchal de Tallard, à Monsieur de Chamillard... et interceptée, & envoyée à un ministre etranger, en Angleterre... [Attributed to Antoine de Pas.] A Londres, chez Jean Nutt, [1704]. 4°

T.261

3957

A REPRESENTATION of the impiety & immortality of the English stage, with reasons for putting a stop thereto: and some questions addrest to those who frequent the play-houses. London, J. Nutt, 1704. 8°

T.204

3958

ROBERT against Ferguson: or a new dialogue between Robert an old independant Whig, and Ferguson a new Tory Jacobite ... London, printed in the year, 1704. 8°

T.416

3959

SACHEVERELL (Henry)

The nature and mischief of prejudice and partiality stated in a sermon preach'd at St. Mary's in Oxford, at the assizes held there, March 9th, 1703/4. Oxford: Leon. Lichfield, for John Stephens: and are to be sold by James Knapton, London, 1704. 4°

T.198

3960

SAVAGE (John) *D.D.*

Christ's body the Church. A sermon preach'd at the yearly visitation held at Welwyn in Hertfordshire, May the 3d. 1704, by the Reverend White Kennet. Cambridge: printed at the University-Press, for Edmund Jeffery, 1704. 4°

T.752

3961

SCOTLAND. *Parliament.*

The proceedings of the Parliament of Scotland: begun at Edinburgh, 6th May, 1703. With an account of all the material debates which occur'd during that session ... Printed in the year 1704. 4°

T.11

3962

SHARPE (John) *Curate of Stepney.*

Plain-dealing: in answer to Plain-English, a sermon preached ... by W. Bisset. In which his vile aspersions are censur'd, his sly innuendo's rebuk'd, his inveterate malice exposed, and his loose arguments confuted. In a second Hampstead-conference betwixt a stanch Church-man and a moderate one ... By the author of the Animadversions on Mr. Calamy's Abridgment of Mr. Baxter's Life, &c. London: E.P. for R. Wilkin, 1704. 4°

T.192

3963

SHERLOCK (William)

A sermon preach'd before the Queen, at the cathedral church of St. Paul, London, on the seventh of September, 1704. Being the thanksgiving-day for the late glorious victory obtain'd over the French and Bavarians at Bleinheim ... London: for W. Rogers, 1704. 4°

2 copies.

T.192 T.198

3964

SHERWILL (Thomas)

Church-conformity asserted and vindicated. A sermon preach'd before the University of Cambridge, upon the feast of St. Simon and St. Jude. MDCCIII. Cambridge, printed at the University-Press, for Edmund Jeffery, 1704. 4°

T.192

3965

SHERWILL (Thomas)

The degeneracy of the present age as to principles. A sermon preach'd before the University of Cambridge ... June 25. 1704. Cambridge: printed at the University-Press, for Edmund Jeffery and Thomas Webster, 1704. 4°

2 copies.

T.192 T.198

3966

SHIPPEN (William)

Faction display'd. A poem... [Anon.] London: printed in the year 1704. 4°

2 copies.
Another copy, wanting title-page.

T.69 T.269 T.354

3967

SHIPPEN (William)

Moderation display'd: a poem... By the author of Faction display'd. London: printed in the year 1704. 4°

3 copies.

T.69 T.269 T.354

3968

SMITH (John) *Vicar of Westham.*

The judgment of God upon atheism and infidelity, in a brief and true account of the irreligious life, and miserable death of Mr. George Edwards... who murder'd himself January the 4th, 1703/4... London: G. Croom, for D. Brown, and J. Taylor, 1704. 8°

T.416

3969

A SOBER enquiry. Whether it can be for the interest of any sort of people in England, to have, the pretended, King James the third advanced to the throne of this kingdom ... London: printed in the year, 1704. 4°

T.197

3970

SOME reflections on the eleventh section of Dr. D'Avenant's late book of essays, intituled, Peace at home, and war abroad, in a letter to a member of the honourable House of Commons. Printed in the year, 1704. 4°

T.193

3971

SPARROW (Anthony) *Bishop of Norwich.*

Confession of sins, and the power of absolution. In a sermon preach'd before the University of Cambridge in the year, 1637. London: for J.C., and are to be sold by Sam. Keble, 1704. 4°

T.192

3972

A SPEECH against the Bill, brought into the House of Commons, for recruiting her Majesty's land forces. London: printed in the year, 1704. 4°

T.283

3973

A SPEECH without doors. London: printed in the year 1704. 4°

T.193

3974

STEPHENS (Edward)

Achan and Elymas: or, The troublers of Israel, the enemies of righteousness, and perverters of the right ways of the Lord detected ... By a faithful monitor and friend to his country, and well-wisher to all. Printed in the year 1704. 2 parts 4°

T.190

3975

STEPHENS (Edward)

Questions concerning the proper and peculiar Christian worship. [Anon.] [No imprint, 1704?] 4°

T.461

3976

STEPHENS (Edward)

A second letter to William Pen, George Whitehead, T. Eccleston, and the rest of the ministers of the Quakers at their general yearly meeting. [No imprint, 1704.]   4°

T.283

3977

STEPHENS (Edward)

The suppression of popery recommended to her Majesty. (The application of a paper remedy for an effectual cure of popery... A charge of treason against the Roman Catholick missioners in England ...) [London, 1704?]   4°

T.7

3978

STEPHENS (Edward)

A vindication of Christianity from and against the scandals of popery. In a letter to a Roman Catholick gentleman ... And an answer to eight questions concerning the Church, wherein The spirit of a Roman Catholick missioner is try'd and discover'd ... Printed in the year 1704. 2 parts.   4°

T.7

3979

STUBS (Philip)

The Church of England, under God, an impregnable bulwark against popery. A sermon preach'd at St. Paul's cathedral before ... the lord-mayor, and court of aldermen, November the 5th. 1703 ... London, J. Leake, for Henry Mortlock, 1704.   4°

T.71

3980

TALBOR (John)

England's safety and Europe's liberty, by the happy accession of our gracious Q. Ann to the throne of her ancestors. Declared in a sermon ... March 8th, 1703/4 ... London: H. Clark, for Timothy Childe, 1704.   4°

T.192

3981

THOMPSON (Francis) B.D.

A true state of the case concerning the election of a provost of Queens-College in Oxford. [Anon.] Oxford: Leon. Lichfield, and are to be sold by Henry Clements, 1704.   4°

T.12

3982

THOMPSON (John) Baron Haversham.

The Lord Haversham's speech in the House of Peers, on Thursday, November 23. 1704. London: for B. Bragg, 1704.   4°

2 copies.

T.487   T.267

3983

THOMPSON (John) Baron Haversham.

The speech of a noble peer upon the reading of the Bill for preventing occasional conformity. [Anon.] London, printed in the year, 1704.   4°

T.193

3984

TINDAL (Matthew)

Reasons against restraining the press. [Anon.] London; printed in the year 1704.   4°

T.283

3985

TOM Double against Dr. D[a]v[e]n[an]t; or; That learned author of the Essays on peace at home and war abroad, consider'd... Also the several heads of Sir Humphry Mackworth's vindication of the proceedings of the House of Commons upon the bill for preventing the danger from occasional conformity.. Printed in the year 1704, and sold by the booksellers of London and Westminster.   8°

2 copies.

T.385   T.416

3986

TRIMNELL (Charles) Bishop of Winchester.

An account of the proceedings between the two houses of Convocation which met November 1702. Particularly of the several proposals made for putting an end to the present differences ... By a member of the lower house. London: for Richard Sare, 1704.   4°

November has been altered to Oct. 20.

T.133

3987

A TRIP to the d——l's summer-house: or, A journey to the wells: with the old preaching Quaker's sermon to the London-mobb. [No imprint, 1704?]   4°

Incorrectly included by Wing as T 2285A.

2 copies.

T.69 T.269

3988

A TRUE state of the controversy betwixt the present Bishop [i.e. William Nicolson] and Dean [i.e. Francis Atterbury] of Carlile, touching the regal supremacy. In a letter from a northern divine, to a member of the University of Oxford. London: printed in the year 1704.   4°

T.137

3989

The TRUE Tom Double: or, An account of Dr. Davenant's late conduct and writings, particularly with relation to the XIth section of his Essays on peace at home, and war abroad ... Part I ... London: G. Croom, and sold by J. Nutt, [1704].   4°

A copy of another edition, wanting title-page.

T.280 T.193

3990

VOELSCHOW (Joachim)

Historia ecclesiae collegiatae S. Nicolai Gryphiswaldensis... Gryphiswaldiae, litteris Danielis Benjaminis Starckii, [1704].   4°

T.793

3991

WAKE (Robert)

Courage and sincerity the main proof of a faithful shepherd: a sermon preached at the triennial visitation of the Dean of Sarum, holden at Hungerford in the county of Berks, May 12. 1704. London, W.S. for R. Clavel, 1704.   4°

2 copies.

T.192 T.198

3992

WARD (Edward)

All men mad: or, England a great bedlam. A poem. [Anon.] London, printed in the year, 1704.   4°

T.69

3993

WESLEY (Samuel) the Elder.

A defence of a letter concerning the education of dissenters in their private academies ... Being an answer to the Defence of the dissenters education [by Samuel Palmer] ... London, for Robert Clavel and James Knaplock, 1704.   4°

T.283

3994

The WHIGS scandalous Address [by Daniel Defoe] answered stanza by stanza. By one who thinks it an honour to be called a high-flyer ... Printed in the year 1704.   8°

T.57

3995

WHITE against Kennet: or, Dr. Kennet's panegyrick upon the late King James: being an extract... from his preface to an address of thanks to a good prince: presented in the Panegyrick of Pliny upon Trajan... By a gentleman. London, J. Nutt, 1704.   4°

2 copies.

T.11 T.73

3996

WILLIAM III, King of England.

A form of prayers, used by his late Majesty K. William III. when he receiv'd the holy sacrament, and on other occasions. With a preface by... John Lord Bishop of Norwich... London, for J. Barnes; and sold by J. Nutt, 1704.   12°

T.448

1705

3997

An ACCOUNT of the transaction between Admiral Benbow and Monsieur Du Cass. With the proceedings thereupon in the case of Colonel Kirkby, who was shot to death in Plimouth Sound, on board the Bristol man of war, April 16. 1703. London, printed in the year 1705.   4°

T.487

3998

An ADDRESS to the clergy of the Church of England, answer'd paragraph by paragraph. [No imprint, 1705?]   4°

T.487

3999

ALLIBOND (John)

Rustica Academiae Oxoniensis nuper reformatae descriptio, in visitatione fanatica Octobris sexto, &c. ann. Dom. 1648 ... London printed, and are to be sold at the Green-Dragon, 1705. brs.

T.225

4000

ALTHAM (Roger)

Norma veritatis orthodoxae. Concio habita coram reverendis dno Episcopo & clero Londinensi, in Collegio Sionensi, Maij Iº A.D. 1705. Londini, impensis Thomae Bennet, 1705.   4°

T.273

4001

An ANSWER paragraph by paragraph, to the Memorial of the Church of England [by James Drake]. London: printed the year, 1705.   8°

T.348

4002

ATTERBURY (Francis) Bishop of Rochester.

A continuation of the faithful account of what past in Convocation. Numb. 4. In a fourth letter to a friend. [Signed N.N.] London, for John Nut, 1705.   4°

T.133

4003

ATTERBURY (Francis) Bishop of Rochester.

A sermon preached before her Majesty, at St. James's chapel, on Sunday, October 28. 1705 ... London: for Tho. Bennet, 1705.   4°

T.8

4004

B.(F.)

Stockings out at heels: or, A full answer to twenty seven queries propos'd by a dislocated hosier, upon the Bill against occasional conformity. London, printed: and sold by Benj. Bragg, 1705.   4°

T.283

4005

B.(J.) Esquire.

Αυτοφονια, or; Self-murther arraign'd and condemn'd as utterly unlawful; by the judgment of learned heathens, Jews, and Christians ... London: for Geo. Sawbridge, 1705.   4°

T.191

4006

BARON (William)

An historical account of comprehension, and toleration ... Part I. By the author of the Dutch way of toleration ... London: for J. Chantry, 1705.   4°

T.191

4007

The BATTLES. A poem. On the late successes of her Majesty's arms by sea and land... London: for John Nutt, 1705. Fol.

T.699

4008

BERLIN. Königliche Akademie der Wissenschaften.

The ordinances, statutes, and privileges, of the Royal Academy, erected by his Majesty the King of Prussia, in his capital city of Berlin. Translated from the original [by John Toland]. London; John Darby, 1705.   8°

2 copies.

T.416 T.522

4009

BEVERIDGE (William) *Bishop of St. Asaph.*

A sermon preach'd before the lords spiritual and temporal ... on the 30th day of January, 1705/6 ... London, for F. Thorn, 1705.   8°

T.519

4010

BINCKES (William)

A sermon preach'd before the honourable House of Commons at St. Margaret's Church in Westminster, Novemb. 5. 1704. London, for R. Clavel, 1705.   4°

T.78

4011

BLACKALL (Offspring) *Bishop of Exeter.*

The lawfulness and the right manner of keeping Christmas, and other Christian festivals: a sermon preached at the parish-church of St. Dunstan in the West, upon Christmas-day, 1704. London: for Walter Kettilby, 1705.   4°

T.757

4012

BLACKALL (Offspring) *Bishop of Exeter.*

St. Paul and St. James reconcil'd. 'A sermon preach'd before the University of Cambridge ... on Commencement Sunday in the afternoon, June 30. 1700 ... 4th ed. London, H. Hills, [1705?]   8°

T.519

4013

BLACKALL (Offspring) *Bishop of Exeter.*

The subjects duty. A sermon preach'd at the parish-church of St. Dunstan in the West, on Thursday, March the 8th 1704/5... London, J. Leake, for Walter Kettilby, 1705.   4°

2 copies.

T.8 T.757

4014

The BOND of resignation-man: in the true picture of a splitter of freeholds. [No imprint, 1705?] 4°

T.194

4015

BROUGHTON (John)

A letter to a member of the present honourable House of Commons, relating to the credit of our government, and of the nation in general. [Anon.] London: A.R.; and are to be sold by J. Nutt, 1705.   4°

T.194

4016

BROUGHTON (John)

Remarks upon the Bank of England, with regard more especially to our trade and government. Occasion'd by the present discourse concerning the intended prolongation of the Bank. Humbly address'd to the honourable House of Commons. By a merchant of London... London, for A. Baldwin, 1705.   8°

T.70

4017

BROWNE (Joseph)

The moon-calf: or, Accurate reflections on the Consolidator [a pamphlet by Daniel Defoe]: giving an account of some remarkable transactions in the lunar world, transmitted hither in a letter to a friend. By the man in the moon. London, printed in the year 1705. 8°

T.416

4018

BUGG (Francis)

A Quaker catechism. [Anon.] London, Henry Hills, [1705?] 8°

T.79

4019

C.(P.)

The three establishments concerning the pay of the sea-officers. To which is prefix'd an introduction for the better understanding by what occasions they came to be produc'd ... London, printed in the year 1705.   8°

T.522

4020

The CASE of Capt. Tho. Green, commander of the ship Worcester, and his crew, tried and condemned for pyracy & murther, in the High Court of Admiralty of Scotland. London: printed in the year 1705.   4°

2 copies.

T.77 T.487

4021

The CASE of Mr. Vaughan, vicar of Dunchtew, truly stated; and his innocence vindicated, from the aspersions of Tho. Overton; and the misrepresentations of Sir Thomas Wheate ... London: printed in the year 1705.   4°

T.72

4022

The CHARACTER of a sneaker. London printed in the year 1705.   4°

2 copies.

T.487 T.267

4023

CHURCH OF ENGLAND.

A form of prayer, and thanksgiving to Almighty God: to be used on Thursday the twenty third of August... for the late glorious success in forcing the enemies lines in the Spanish Netherlands... London, Charles Bill, and the executrix of Thomas Newcomb, 1705.   4°

T.461

4024

CHURCH OF ENGLAND.

A form of prayer, to be used in all churches and chapels ... on Wednesday the fourth day of April, being the fast-day appointed ... for imploring the continuance of a blessing from Almighty God upon her Majesty, and her allies, engaged in the present war ... London, Charles Bill, and the executrix of Thomas Newcomb, 1705.   4°

T.461

4025

CHURCH OF ENGLAND. *Convocation.*

A collection of papers, concerning what hath been transacted in the Convocation, summon'd A.D. 1702. And dissolv'd 1705. London, J. Nut, 1705.   4°

T.133

4026

CHURCH OF ENGLAND. *Convocation. Lower House.*

The humble representation and complaint of the lower house of Convocation, against the Right Reverend the Bishop of Sarum. London, for George Sawbridge, and sold by J. Nutt, 1705.   4°

2 copies.

T.78

4027

CHURCH OF ENGLAND. *Convocation. Lower House.*

A representation made by the lower house of Convocation, to the arch-bishops and bishops, December. 1704. London, for George Sawbridge, and sold by J. Nutt, 1705.   4°

2 copies.

T.78 T.133

4028

The CITY candidates, or, Peace and union in nubibus, in a sermon, preach'd to the congregation of electors, lately held at the Crown-tavern in the favour of the worthy four gentlemen and patriots, propos'd and agreed to there as candidates for the City of London. By a clyster-pipe turn'd broker ... London: printed in the year 1705.   4°

T.487

4029

COLLINS (Richard)

The danger of ungovern'd zeal. A sermon preached at the visitation holden at Rochester in Kent, April the 24th. 1705... London, S.H. for R. Vincent, 1705.   4°

T.771

4030

DEFOE (Daniel)

The dyet of Poland, a satyr. [Anon.] Printed at Dantzick, in the year 1705.   4°

Moore 100.

T.269

4031

DEFOE (Daniel)

Good advice to the ladies: shewing, that, as the world goes and is like to go, the best way for them is to keep unmarried. With the character of a beau. By the author of the True born English-man. The second edition corrected. London: for R. Smith: and are sold by J. Nutte, 1705.   4°

Moore 46.

T.261

4032

DEFOE (Daniel)

A journey to the world in the moon, &c. By the author of the true born English-man. [Anon.] London, printed in the year, 1705.   4°

Moore 96.

T.487

4033

DEFOE (Daniel)

A letter from the man in the moon. To the author of the True born English-man. [Anon.] London, printed in the year, 1705.   4°

Moore 97.

T.487

4034

DEFOE (Daniel)

Persecution anatomiz'd: or, An answer to the following questions ... [Anon.] London, printed in the year, 1705.   4°

Moore 92.

T.264

4035

The DISSENTERS conscientious objections against the Episcopal Church. Together with their reasonable proposals for a compliance with her discipline ... London, 1705.   4°

Title-page incomplete.

T.517

4036

The DISTINCTION of High-Church and Low-Church, distinctly consider'd and fairly stated. With some reflections upon the popular plea of moderation ... London: for Samuel Manship, 1705.   8°

T.34

4037

DR. Blackhall's offspring ... London: printed for the use of the vestry of St. Dunstans in the West, 1705. 4°

T.190

4038

DRAKE (James)

The memorial of the Church of England, humbly offer'd to the consideration of all true lovers of our Church and constitution. [Anon.] London: printed in the year 1705.   4°

4 copies.

T.191 T.266 T.564 T.708

4039

DRAKE (James)

The memorial of the Church of England, humbly offer'd to the consideration of all true lovers of our Church and constitution, with remarks upon the whole paragraph by paragraph. [Anon.] 2nd ed. London: printed in the year, 1705.   8°

2 copies.

T.34 T.348

4040

The DUTCHMAN'S answer to the L[or]d H[aversha]ms sp[ee]ch. London, printed and sold by the booksellers of London and Westminster, 1705.   4°

T.194

4040A

An ELEGY on the burning of the Church memorial [i.e. the pamphlet by James Drake]. [No imprint], 1705. brs.

T.266

4041

EMLYN (Thomas)

A review of the case of Judah and Ephraim, and its application to the Church of England and the dissenters ... In a letter to the Reverend Dr. Willis ... occasion'd by his thanksgiving-sermon on the 23d of August, 1705 ... [Anon.] London, for A. Baldwin, 1705.   4°

T.8

4042

ENGLISH advice to English freeholders. [No imprint, 1705?]   4°

T.487

4043

An ESSAY upon government. Wherein the republican schemes reviv'd by Mr. Lock, Dr. Blackal, &c. are fairly consider'd and refuted ... London, for G. Sawbridge, 1705.   8°

2 copies.

T.101   T.34

4044

The EXAMINER, examined; or, A modest examination of the D[ea]n of St. P[au]l's thanksgiving sermon. September 7th. 1704. In a letter to a friend. London, printed in the year 1705.   4°

T.78

4045

The EXERCEESE of the muckle goon and saundaleero's. Gin owte by Alaster the Cabden, the yaar by-past. [No imprint, 1705?] brs.

T.269

4046

FERGUSON (Robert)

The Bishop of St. David's vindicated, the author [i.e. Sir John Cooke] of The summary view expos'd, his post-script answer'd, and the Letter to a peer defended. By way of free conference between two bold Britons ... [Anon.] London: printed in the year 1705. 2 parts.   4°

T.77

4047

FIDDES (Richard)

A thanks-giving sermon on the 23 of August, 1705. Or A discourse showing that God in the government of the world acts by particular wills. York, John White, for Francis Hildyard, and are to be sold by Thomas Bennet in London, 1705.   4°

T.172

4048

FIRE and faggot, or the City bon-fire. [No imprint], 1705.   4°

T.269

4049

FREE thoughts concerning occasional conformity for an office. [Attributed to Benjamin Loveling the Elder.] London, printed, and sold by the book-sellers of London and Westminster, 1705.   4°

T.283

4050

GIBSON (Edmund) *Bishop of London.*

The complainer further reprov'd: in the observations made by the president and his suffragan bishops, upon a paper presented to them by the prolocutor of the lower-house, Dec. 1. 1704. [Anon.] And his Grace's speech, deliver'd to those of the lower-clergy who were present at the time of his proroguing the Convocation, March 15. 1704 ... London: for A. and J. Churchill, 1705.   4°

2 copies.

T.78   T.133

4051

GIBSON (Edmund) *Bishop of London.*

The complainer reprov'd: in answer to a partial and unseasonable preface of the publisher of A representation made by the lower-house of Convocation to the Archbishop and bishops, anno 1703. [Anon.] With his Grace's speech upon that subject ... London, for A. and J. Churchil, 1705.   4°

T.133

4052

GRASCOMBE (Samuel)

Concordia discors: or, Some animadversions upon a late treatise [by Joshua Basset]; entituled, An essay for Catholick communion. In a letter to a friend at Westminster, by a presbyter of the Church of England. London: for George Sawbridge, 1705.   8°

2 copies.

T.416   T.479

4053

GREAT Britain's union, and the security of the Hanover succession, consider'd. In a letter from Windsor... to a member of Parliament in London. By a person of quality... London: B. Bragg, 1705.   4°

T.248

4054

HARRIS (John) *D.D.,F.R.S.*

The modest Christian's duty, as to indifferent things in the worship of God. A sermon preached before the Lord Mayor, at Guild-hall chapel, on Sunday, October 28. 1705. London: for R. Wilkin, 1705.   4°

T.757

4055

HIGDEN (William)

The case of the admission of occasional conformists to the holy communion, before they renounce their schism, consider'd ... [Anon.] London: for Samuel Keble, and Francis Coggan, 1705.   4°

2 copies.

T.266   T.283

4056

HOADLY (Benjamin) *Bishop of Winchester.*

A sermon preach'd before ... the lord mayor, and aldermen, livery-men, of the several companies of London. At the parish church of St. Laurence Jewry, before the election of the lord mayor, September 29th, 1705 ... London, H. Hills, [1705].   8°

T.8

4057

HOADLY (Benjamin) *Bishop of Winchester.*

A sermon preach'd before ... the lord mayor, aldermen, and livery-men of the several companies of London ... September 29th. 1705. The second edition. London: H. Clark, for Tim. Childe, 1705.   4°

T.14

4058

HOADLY (Benjamin) *Bishop of Winchester.*

A sermon preach'd on the eighth of March, 1704-5. being the anniversary day of... the Queen's accession to the crown. London: H. Clark, for Timothy Childe, 1705.   4°

T.771

4059

HOUGH (John) *Bishop of Worcester.*

A sermon preach'd at the church of St. Mary-le-Bow, before the societies for reformation of manners, on Monday, Jan. 1. 1704. By ... John, Lord Bishop of Litchfield and Coventry. London, for Jacob Tonson, 1705.   4°

T.71

4060

HUMFREY (John)

A draught for a national Church accomodation; whereby the subjects of England and Scotland, however different in their judgments concerning episcopacy and presbytery, may yet be united ... in one church and kingdom of Great Britain. [Anon.] London; for A. Baldwin, 1705.   4°

T.142

4061

ISHAM (Zachary)

A discourse of confirmation: preach'd at Coleshill, Apr. 21. 1705. at the triennial visitation of... John, Lord Bishop of Coventry and Litchfield. London, for Robert Clavell, and Walter Kettilby, 1705.   4°

T.752

4062

JONES (Charles) *Rector of Nettlecomb.*

Against hypocrisie. A sermon preach'd at St Mary Magdalen's in Taunton ... at the Assizes held there, March 20. 1704/5 ... London: John Matthews, for William Hawes; and Henry Chaulklin, bookseller in Taunton, 1705.   4°

T.8

4063

JONES (Charles) *Rector of Nettlecombe.*

Against indifference in religion. A sermon preach'd in the cathedral church of Wells ... at the Assizes held there, August 15. 1705 ... London: John Matthews, for William Hawes; and Henry Chaulklin, bookseller in Taunton, 1705.   4°

T.8

4064

A KIT-KAT c[lu]b describ'd... London, printed in the year 1705.   4°

T.487

4065

KNAGGS (Thomas)

A sermon against the French King. Preach'd at Trinity-chappel... London, on Wednesday, Febr. the 14th. 1704/5... London: for John Barnes, and sold by A. Baldwin, 1705.   4°

T.8

4066

L.(W.)

A letter from a commoner of England, to a member of the honourable H[ouse] of C[ommons]. London: printed in the year 1705.   4°

T.267

4067

LAWTON (Charlwood)

Civil comprehension, &c. in a letter to a friend, from one who wishes the general good of England, and particularly well to the Establish'd Church. [Anon.] Sold by the booksellers of London and Westminster, 1705.   4°

2 copies.

T.194

4068

LESLIE (Charles)

Cassandra. (But I hope not) telling what will come of it. Num. I. In answer to the Occasional letter. Num. I. Wherein the new-associations, &c. are considered. [Anon.] 3rd ed. London: printed and sold by the booksellers of London and Westminster, 1705.   4°

T.404

4069

LESLIE (Charles)

Cassandra. (But I hope not.) Telling what will come of it. Numb. II. In answer to the Occasional letter. Numb. I. wherein the new-associations, &c. are considered. [Anon.] The second edition corrected. London, printed; and sold by the booksellers of London and Westminster, [1705].   4°

2 copies.

T.404   T.356

4070

LESLIE (Charles)

The principles of the dissenters, concerning toleration and occasional conformity ... With seasonable advice to the dissenters. In a preface. [Signed N.N.] London: printed in the year 1705.   4°

The text is taken mainly out of William Assheton's *Toleration disapprov'd* (1670).
3 copies.

T.264   T.283

4071

A LETTER from a citizen of Bath, to his Excellency Dr. R[adcliffe] at Tunbridg ... Printed in the year 1705.   8°

T.220

4072

A LETTER from a dissenter in the City, to his country-friend. Wherein moderation and occasional conformity are vindicated ... and all the treasonable designs of the tackers are expos'd to common view. London: printed, and are to be sold by the booksellers of London, 1705.   4°

T.283

4073

A LETTER from the South, by way of answer to the late
letter from a northern divine; giving an account of
a very strange attempt made by Dr. A[tterbury] towards
antedating the resignation of his predecessor in
the deanery of Carlisle. [No imprint, 1705?] 4°

See also *A true state of the controversy...* 2nd ed.
1705.
3 copies.

T.137

4074

A LETTER to Sir J.P. [John Pakington?] Baronet, a
member of Parliament, relating to the union of
England and Scotland. The second edition, with short
additions. [No imprint, 1705.] 4°

2 copies.

T.490 T.142

4075

MACKWORTH (*Sir* Humphrey)

A letter from a member of Parliament to his friend
in the country. Giving a short account of the
proceedings of the tackers, upon the occasional
and self-denying bills... [Anon.] 2nd ed. London:
printed and are to be sold by the booksellers of
London and Westminster, 1705. 4°

T.487

4076

MANDEVILE (John)

A sermon preached before the Queen, at St. James's
chappel, on Whitsunday, May 27, 1705. London:
for A. and J. Churchill, 1705. 4°

T.771

4077

MANDEVILLE (Bernard de)

The grumbling hive: or, Knaves turn'd honest. [Anon.]
Printed in the year, 1705. 4°

T.69

4078

MANLEY (Mary De la Riviere)

The secret history of Queen Zarah, and the Zarazians;
being a looking-glass for —— —— in the
kingdom of Albigion... [Anon.] Albigion, printed
in the year 1705. 2 parts. 12°

2 copies of the first part only.

T.220 T.456

4079

MIEGE (Guy)

Utrum Horum? Tyranny, or liberty; oppression, or
moderation. In answer to Dr. Chamberlayn's High-
Church principles, and the late fallacious preface
of Mr. Chamberlayn, his son, to the Present state
of England. By G.M ... London, B. Bragg, 1705.
8°

T.34

4080

MODERATION display'd: A poem. By the author of
Faction display'd [i.e. William Shippen]. Answered
paragraph by paragraph ... London: B. Bragg, 1705.
4°

T.69

4081

MODERATION unmask'd: in answer to a bundle of
republican queries, lately faggotted together for the
use of the no-Church party, and the common hangman.
London: for John Morphew, [1705?] 4°

T.264

4082

A MODEST proof of the order and government settled by
Christ and his Apostles in the Church ... London:
for John Wyat, 1705. 4°

T.137

4083

MOSS (Robert) *Dean of Ely.*

The Christian's overthrow prevented, and conquest
gain'd. A sermon preach'd before the Queen, at
St. James's chappel, on Sunday, April 22, 1705...
London, for Richard Sare; and Jacob Tonson, 1705.
4°

T.8

4084

MOSS (Robert) *Dean of Ely.*

The Christian's overthrow prevented, and conquest
gain'd. A sermon preach'd before the Queen, at St.
James's chappel, on Sunday, April 22, 1705...
London: Hen. Hills, [1705]. 8°

T.519

4085

N. (N.)

Advice from Switzerland: giving a full and true
account how far the Switzers are engaged in the
French interest against the confederates. In a
letter sent of late from Switzerland to London,
by a gentleman of honour, to a person of quality.
[Signed N.N.] London: printed in the year 1705.
4°

T.487

4086

NAKED truth: or, Phanaticism detected. Recommended
to the serious considerations of all true protestants,
particularly to the electors of members to serve in
the ensuing Parliament... By a gentleman of the
Church of England... London, printed: and sold by
B. Bragg, 1705. 4°

T.487

4087

The NECESSITY of Church-communion vindicated, from
the scandalous aspersions of a late pamphlet,
entituled, The principle of the protestant reformation
explained ... Humbly offered to the consideration of
the ... clergy, assembled in Convocation.
[Attributed to Robert Nelson.] London, for A. and J.
Churchil, 1705. 4°

2 copies.

T.517 T.192

4088

The OBSERVATOR toss'd in a blanket: dialogue between
Parson Lesley; Haraclitus, the Observator and his
hog, &c. London, printed and sold by the booksellers
of London, and Westminster, 1705. 4°

T.69

4089

PAKINGTON (*Sir* John)

A speech for the Bill against occasional conformity,
by Sir J.P. Baronet. With a preface and short notes,
by W.S. M.A. of Magdalen College, Oxon. [No imprint,
1705.] 4°

T.283

4090

PITTIS (William)

The case of the Church of England's Memorial [by
James Drake] fairly stated: or, A modest enquiry
into the grounds of those prejudices that have
been entertain'd against it... [Anon.] London:
printed in the year, 1705. 4°

T.191

4091

PITTIS (William)

The Dyet of Poland, a satyr [by Daniel Defoe].
Consider'd paragraph by paragraph. To which is
added a key to the whole... [Anon.] London,
printed: and sold by Ben. Bragg, 1705. 8°

T.220

4092

PITTIS (William)

A hymn to confinement. Written by the author of
the Case of the Church of England's memorial
fairly stated, &c. while in durance... London,
printed in the year 1705. And sold by the
booksellers. 4°

T.191

4093

The POWER and prerogative of the inexpressible I
know not what: or, A brief essay upon the unknown
and unintelligible something, exemplified in
variety of modern instances, in private transactions,
and publick affairs. London: B. Bragg, 1705. 8°

T.416

4094

PREGON sonoro, en que manda la magestad de naestro
catolico monarca Carlos tercero al Duque de Anjou, le
restitvya la corona, pues sabe que no es suya.
Barcelona: por Francisco Guasch, 1705. 4°

T.269

4095

SACHEVERELL (Henry)

The new association of those called, moderate-Church-
men, with the modern-Whigs and fanaticks, to under-
mine and blow-up the present Church and government ...
By a true-Church-man ... The fourth edition corrected.
Printed and sold by the booksellers of London and
Westminster, 1705. 4°

2 copies.

T.14 T.404

4096

SACHEVERELL (Henry)

The new association. Part.II. With farther
improvements ... The second edition with additions.
Printed and sold by the booksellers of London and
Westminster, 1705. 4°

2 copies.

T.14 T.404

4097

SACHEVERELL (Henry) *and* PERKS (John)

The rights of the Church of England asserted and prov'd:
in an answer to a late pamphlet [by John Shute
Barrington], intitl'd The rights of the protestant
dissenters, in a review of their case ... [Anon.]
Printed in the year, 1705. 2 parts. 4°

2 copies.

T.266 T.283

4098

The SECRET intrigues of the Duke of Savoy. With a
faithful relation of of [sic] the ill treatments
which Monsieur de Phelippeaux, ambassador of France,
receiv'd from his Royal Highness, against the law
and right of nations. Done into English, from the
original in French... London: sold by J. Nutt,
1705. 4°

2 copies.

T.194

4099

SEDLEY (*Sir* Charles)

The happy pair: or, A poem on matrimony. The second
edition, corrected. London, for John Chantry; and
sold by Benj. Brag, 1705. Fol.

T.699

4100

SHARP (John) *Archbishop of York.*

Christ's resurrection sufficiently proved by chosen
witnesses. A sermon preached before the Queen, at
St. James's chappel, on Easter-day, 1705. London:
for W. Kettilby, and W. Rogers, 1705. 4°

T.757

4101

SHARP (John) *Archbishop of York.*

The design of Christianity. A sermon preach'd before
the Queen at St. James's chappel on Christmas-day,
1704. London: for Walter Kettilby, and William
Rogers, 1705. 4°

T.757

4102

SHUTE (Henry)

A sermon preach'd at the funeral of Mrs. Catherine
Lorrain... in the parish-church of St. Andrew in
Holborn, on Wednesday the 27th. of June, 1705...
London, for Robert Whitledge, T. Davis, and
J. Downing, 1705. 4°

2 copies.

T.8 T.273

4103

SMALRIDGE (George) *Bishop of Bristol.*

A sermon preached before the Queen, at St. James's
chapel, on November the 5th. 1705. The second
impression. London: for Tho. Bennet, 1705. 4°

T.172

4104

SMALWOOD (James)

A sermon preach'd before his Grace the D. of
Marlborough, in the camp at Ulierberg-Abby, near
Louvain, in Brabant, July 15. 1705. Just after the
passing the French lines ... London: T. Mead, for
Andrew Bell, 1705. 4°

T.8

4105

SMEATON (Samuel)

Christian zeal recommended: in a sermon preached at Andover, on May the 15th 1704. being the visitation of the Reverend Mr. Ralph Brideoake, Arch-deacon of Winton. London: for Philip Monckton, 1705. 4°

T.752

4106

SOME plain observations recommended to the consideration of every honest English-man; especially, to the electors of Parliament-members. Printed in the year 1705. 4°

T.487

4107

SOME reasons by a divine of the Kirk of Scotland, proving that their clergy there cannot with a safe conscience swear the English oath of abjuration. [No imprint, 1705?] 4°

T.142

4108

STANHOPE (George) *Dean of Canterbury.*

A sermon preach'd before the honourable House of Commons, at St. Margarets-Westminster, on Tuesday the 30th of January, 1704/5 ... London, W.B. for R. Sare, and M. Wotton, 1705. 4°

T.78

4109

STEPHENS (Edward)

The case of the poor Grecian seamen. [Anon.] [No imprint, 1705?] brs.

T.137

4110

STEPHENS (Edward)

A compleat and unexceptionable form of liturgy, or divine service, for the celebration of the holy communion... For the use of a society of English Catholick, daily communicants. [Anon.] The second edition corrected and enlarged. London: printed for the author, 1704/5. 8°

T.461

4111

STEPHENS (Edward)

The confusion of popery in England, or a great and divine conviction of the deceit and imposture of the papal agents here ... [Anon.] [London, 1705?] 4°

T.7

4112

STEPHENS (William)

A letter to the author [i.e. John Toland] of the Memorial of the state of England. [Anon.] London, printed in the year 1705. 4°

T.191

4113

THOMPSON (John) *Baron Haversham.*

The Lord Haversham's speech in the House of Peers, on Thursday, November 15. 1705. London: B. Bragg, [1705]. 4°

3 copies.

T.267 T.194

4114

THOMPSON (John) *Baron Haversham.*

The Lord Haversham's vindication of his speech in Parliament, November 15. 1705. London, Dr. Leach, for W.H. and sold by B. Bragg, 1705. 4°

2 copies.

T.267 T.194

4115

TILLY (William)

The Church's security, from the providence of God defending her, and the goodness of her own cause and constitution. A sermon preach'd before the mayor, and corporation of Oxford ... November the fifth, 1705. Oxford: Leonard Lichfield, for John Stephens: and are to be sold by James Knapton, London, 1705. 4°

T.8

4116

TILLY (William)

The nature and necessity of religious resolution, in the defence and support of a good cause, in times of danger and trial. A sermon preach'd at the assizes... July 19th. 1705. Oxford: Leonard Lichfield, for John Stephens: and are to be sold by James Knapton, London, 1705. 4°

2 copies, one copy inscribed "Mr. Nelson, Aug. 10. 1705. A.C."

T.8 T.71

4117

TILLY (William)

The nature and necessity of religious resolution, in the defence and support of a good cause, in times of danger and trial. A sermon preach'd at the assizes... July 19th. 1705. 3rd ed. Oxford: Leonard Lichfield, for John Stephens: and are to be sold by James Knapton, London, 1705. 4°

T.708

4118

TOLAND (John)

The memorial of the state of England. In vindication of the Queen, the Church, and the administration: design'd to rectify the mutual mistakes of protestants, and to unite their affections in defence of our religion and liberty. [Anon.] London: printed and sold by the booksellers of London and Westminster, 1705. 4°

T.266

4119

TOM-TELL-TRUTH'S letter to a dissenter, in vindication of the l[aw]s against the tackers. [No imprint, 1705?] 4°

T.487

4120

TRENCHARD (John)

Free thoughts concerning officers in the House of Commons. [Anon.] [No imprint, 1705?] 4°

Incorrectly included by Wing as T 2112 A.

T.194

4121

A TRUE state of the controversy betwixt the present Bishop [i.e. William Nicolson] and Dean [i.e. Francis Atterbury] of Carlisle, touching the regal supremacy, in a letter from a northern divine, to a member of the University of Oxford. The second edition: to which is added, A letter from the South... giving an account of a very strange attempt made by Dr. A. towards antedating the resignation of his predecessor in the deanery of Carlisle. London: printed in the year 1705. 2 parts. 4°

T.487

4122

TUFTON (Sackville)

The Devil's cloven-foot peeping out from the Parson of Colchester's garment. By way of answer to his first and second part of Priest-craft, its character and consequences ... By the author of the History of faction, alias hypocrisy, alias moderation. [Signed H.G.] London, for B. Bragge, 1705. 4°

T.191

4123

TUFTON (Sackville)

The history of faction, alias hypocrisy, alias moderation, from its first rise down to its present toleration in these kingdoms ... [Anon.] London: Ben. Bragg, 1705. 8°

T.115

4124

A VINDICATION of the London clergy, from the aspersions cast upon them by Mr. Hoadly. In a sermon preach'd on March the 8th 1704 ... London, printed 1705. 4°

T.72

4125

WAGSTAFFE (Thomas)

The case of moderation and occasional communion to the true sons of the Church of England. [Anon.] London, for R. Wilkin, 1705. 4°

Attributed by Bowdler to Mary Astell.

T.283

4126

WALL (William)

A vindication of the Apostles, from a very false imputation, laid on them in several English pamphlets. Viz. That they refused constant, and held only occasional communion with one another ... By a presbyter of the Church of England. London: E.P. for H. Bonwicke, 1705. 4°

2 copies.

T.191 T.264

4127

WARD (Edward)

A fair shell, but a rotten kernel: or, A bitter nut for a factious monkey... [Anon.] London, printed: and sold by B. Bragge, 1705. 4°

T.660

4128

WARD (Edward)

Hudibras redivivus: or, A burlesque poem on the times. Part the second. [Anon.] London, printed: and sold by B. Bragge, 1705. 4°

T.261

4129

WARD (Edward)

The secret history of the Calves-Head club, complt. or, The republican unmask'd... [Anon.] The fifth edition, with large additions, corrected. To which is annext, A vindication of the royal martyr King Charles I... Written in the time of the usurpation, by the celebrated Mr. Buttler, author of Hudibras... London, printed: and sold by the booksellers of London and Westminster, 1705. 8°

T.482

4130

WAUGH (John) *Bishop of Carlisle.*

A sermon preach'd at the consecration of ... George Lord Bishop of St. David's, in Lambeth-chappel, on Sunday, April 29. 1705. London: for A. and J. Churchill, 1705. 4°

T.71

4131

WELBE (John)

An answer to Captain Dampier's vindication of his voyage to the South-Seas, in the ship St. George. With particular observations on his ungenerous, false, and barbarous usage to his ship's crew. London, B. Bragge, [1705]. 4°

T.77

4132

WELLS (Zachary)

The advantages of a learned and religious education. In a sermon preach'd at St. Austin's church, December the 6th 1705. before the gentlemen educated at Eton-Coll ... London, T. Warren, for Walter Kettilby, 1705. 4°

T.71

4133

A WHIP for the Whiggs. Buckinghamshire, printed at the Catherine-wheel, for... the mayor of Chipping Wiccomb, 1705. 4°

T.69

4134

WILLIAM III, *King of England.*

A memorial drawn by King William's special direction, intended to be given in at the treaty of Reswyck: justifying the Revolution, and the course of his government, In answer to two memorials that were offer'd there in King James's name. [Attributed to Gilbert Burnet.] London: H. Hills, [1705?] 8°

T.507

4135

WILLIAMSON (Joseph)

A vindication of the thanksgiving-sermon of the Reverend Dr. Willis... from the reflections of a late pamphlet [by Thomas Emlyn]; entitled a Review of the case of Ephraim and Judah... London, John Nutt, 1705. 4°

T.8

4136

WILLIS (Richard) *Bishop of Winchester.*

A sermon preach'd before the honourable House of Commons, at St. Margaret's Westminster, on Monday, the 5th of November, 1705... London: J.L. for Mat. Wotton, 1705. 4°

4 copies.

T.8 T.172 T.273 T.708

1705 (Cont'd)

4137

WILLIS (Richard) *Bishop of Winchester*.

A sermon preach'd before the Queen, at the cathedral church of St. Paul, London, on the 23d of August 1705. Being the thanksgiving-day for the late glorious success in forcing the enemies lines in the Spanish Netherlands ... London, for Mat. Wotton, 1705.   4°

T.198

4138

WILLIS (Richard) *Bishop of Winchester*.

A sermon preached before the Queen, at the cathedral church of St. Paul, London, on the 23 day of August 1705 ... London, E.B. and sold by the booksellers of London and Westminster, for the benefit of the poor, [1705].   8°

"A Madam Bowdler."

T.8

4139

A WORD of advice to the citizens of London and Westminster, and to all the free-holders in England: concerning the choice of members of Parliament at the ensuing election. London: printed in the year, 1705.   4°

2 copies.

T.267 T.487

4140

WOTTON (William)

A defense of the Reflections upon ancient and modern learning, in answer to the objections of Sir W. Temple, and others. With observations upon The tale of a tub [by Jonathan Swift]. London: for Tim. Goodwin, 1705.   8°

T.402

1706

4141

An ACCOUNT of charity-schools lately erected in England, Wales, and Ireland: with the benefactions thereto... London, Joseph Downing, 1706.   4°

2 copies.

T.71 T.78

4142

An ACCOUNT of the Society for Propagating the Gospel in Foreign Parts ... London, Joseph Downing, 1706.
4°

T.12

4143

AESOP in Europe. Or a general survey, of the present posture of affairs ... By way of fable and moral; adapted suitably, to the circumstances of each kingdom ... London, B. Bragg, 1706.   8°

T.89

4144

ANSTIS (John)

Letters to a peer, concerning the honour of earl-marshal. Letter I. Shewing, that no earl-marshal can be made during the minority, or other incapacity, of an hereditary earl-marshal ... London: printed, and sold by the booksellers of London and Westminster, 1706.   8°

T.323

4145

ATTERBURY (Francis) *Bishop of Rochester*.

A sermon preach'd at the Guild-hall chapel, London, Septemb. 28. 1706. being the day of the election of ... the lord mayor. London: E.P. for Jonah Bowyer, 1706.   8°

T.519

4146

ATTERBURY (Francis) *Bishop of Rochester*.

A sermon preach'd in the cathedral church of St. Paul; at the funeral of Mr. Tho. Bennet, Aug. 30. MDCCVI. London: E.P. for Jonah Bowyer, 1706.   4°

Another copy, in 8°

4147

ATTERBURY (Francis) *Bishop of Rochester*.

A sermon preach'd in the Guild-hall chapel, London, Septemb. 28. 1706. being the day of the election of ... the Lord Mayor. London: E.P. for Jonah Bowyer, 1706.   4°

T.71

4148

The AXE laid to the root of Christianity: or, A specimen of the prophaneness and blasphemy that abounds in some late writings. [Attributed to Francis Atterbury or to Charles Leslie.] London: for John Morphew, 1706.   4°

2 copies.

T.72 T.190

4149

BAKER (Daniel)

The history of Job: a sacred poem. In five books ... London: for Robert Clavel, 1706.   8°

T.58

4150

BRAMHALL (John) *Archbishop of Armagh*.

A warning for the Church of England ... [Anon.] London printed, and sold by the booksellers of London and Westminster, 1706.   4°

2 copies.

T.404 T.266

4151

BROME (Richard)

The northern lass, or, The nest of fools. A comedy... The sixth impression. London: for H. N. and are to be sold by James Round, 1706.   4°

Wanting the title-page and other leaves.

T.559

4152

BROUGHTON (John)

An essay upon the national credit of England; introductory to a proposal prepar'd for establishing the public credit ... Humbly submitted to the honourable House of Commons. [Anon.] London: A.R.; and are to be sold by B. Bragg, [1706].   8°

T.70

4153

BROWNE (Joseph)

A dialogue between Church and no-Church: or, A rehearsal of the Review. Containing many necessary reflections on the state of affairs, both at home and abroad. Vol. I, numb. 3. London, printed for the author, and sold by B. Bragge, 1706.   4°

T.194

4154

BROWNE (Joseph)

A letter to the Right Honourable Mr. Secretary Harley, by Dr. Browne: occasion'd from his late commitment to New-gate. Together with his interpretation of that paper call'd, The country parson's advice to my Lord Keeper, laid to his charge. London; printed in the year, 1706.   4°

T.267

4155

BURNET (Gilbert) *Bishop of Salisbury*.

A sermon preach'd at the cathedral church of Salisbury, on the xxviith day of June, MDCCVI. Being the day of thanksgiving ... 2nd ed. London: J.R. for Rich. Chiswell, 1706.   8°

2 copies.

T.519

4156

CHURCH OF ENGLAND.

A form of prayer and thanksgiving to Almighty God: to be used on Thursday the twenty seventh of June ... for having given to the arms of her Majesty ... a signal and glorious victory in Brabant, over the French army ... London, Charles Bill, and the executrix of Thomas Newcomb, 1706.   4°

T.461

4157

CHURCH OF ENGLAND.

A form of prayer and thanksgiving, to be used on Tuesday the one and thirtieth day of December next ... for rendring most hearty thanks to Almighty God, for the great and wonderful successes vouchsafed this year to the arms of her Majesty and her allies ... London, Charles Bill, and the executrix of Thomas Newcomb, 1706.   4°

T.461

4158

CLARKE (Samuel) *Rector of St. James's, Westminster*.

The great duty of universal love and charity. A sermon preached before the Queen, at St James's chapel. On Sunday December the 30th, 1705. London, Will. Botham, for James Knapton, 1706.   4°

T.708

4159

CLARKE (Samuel) *Rector of St. James's, Westminster*.

A letter to Mr Dodwell; wherein all the arguments in his Epistolary discourse against the immortality of the soul are particularly answered ... London, W. Botham; for James Knapton, 1706.   8°

2 copies.

T.673 T.507

4160

A CLEAR and full vindication of some particulars contained in my worthy friend Mr. Dowley's letter to Dr. Wells. [Subscribed D —— Somebody.] London, B. Bragg, 1706.   12°

T.507

4161

COLLIER (Jeremy)

A letter to a lady concerning the new play house. [Anon.]   London, Joseph Downing, 1706.   8°

T.220

4162

COLTON (T.)

A sermon, preach'd at York on the day of publick thanksgiving, June 27th, 1706. appointed by her Majesty for the glorious victory in Brabant, and the great successes in Spain. London: for J. Robinson, 1706.   4°

T.172

4163

The COUNTRY parson's advice to those little scribblers, who pretend to write better sense than great secretaries: or, Mr. Stephens's triumph over the pillory. [No imprint, 1706?] brs.

T.699

4164

CRADOCK (Zachary)

The great end and design of Christianity: in a sermon... London: for Sam. Crouch, 1706.   4°

T.771

4165

CROSFEILD (Robert)

The umpire: or, England the ballance of Europe. Containing a brief account of the evils which have been brought upon this nation, by members of Parliament taking publick employments upon them... [Anon.] London, printed, and sold by the booksellers of London and Westminster, 1706.   8°

2 copies.

T.34 T.385

4166

DEFOE (Daniel)

A collection from Dyers letters, concerning the elections of the present Parliament: with an appendix, relating to some other publick matters. [Anon.] London: B. Bragg, 1706.   4°

Moore 104.

T.194

4167

DEFOE (Daniel)

Jure divino: a satyr. In twelve books. By the author of the True-born-Englishman. London: printed in the year. 1706. 12 parts.   8°

Moore 115.

T.220

4168

DEFOE (Daniel)

A reply to a pamphlet entituled, The L[or]d H[aversham]'s vindication of his speech, &c. By the author of the Review. London: printed in the year 1706.   4°

Moore 110.

T.194

4169

DEFOE (Daniel)

A sermon preach'd by Mr. Daniel Defoe: on the fitting up of Dr. Burges's late meeting-house. Taken from his Review of Thursday the 20th of June, 1706. [No imprint, 1706.] 4°

Moore 117.

T.194

4170

A DISCOURSE on a land-bank: or, Ways and means to increase the coin of this Kingdom ... London, for Charles Smith: and sold by J. Nutt, 1706.   4°

T.194

4171

DODWELL (Henry)

A short discourse concerning sacerdotal absolution: whereby the independent rights of the Church, and the necessity of avoiding schism, are briefly cleared. London: J. Nutt, 1706.   4°

T.754

4172

DORRINGTON (Theophilus)

The regulations of play propos'd and recommended: in a sermon preached at the chapel of Tunbridge-Wells, August the 19th, 1706. London: M. Jenour, for John Wyat, 1706.   8°

T.519

4173

DOWLEY (Peter)

A true copy of a letter lately written by Mr. Dowley to Dr. Wells, and now published by Dr. Wells, together with the Doctor's answer. 3rd ed. Oxford, for John Stephens, and are to be sold by James Knapton, 1706. 8°

T.322

4174

DRAKE (James)

The memorial of the Church of England, humbly offer'd to the consideration of all true lovers of our Church and constitution, with remarks upon the whole paragraph by paragraph. [Anon.] The second edition corrected. London: printed in the year, 1706.   8°

T.169

4175

ENGLAND. *Commissioners nominated to treat of a Union between England and Scotland.*

Articles of the treaty of union agreed on by the commissioners of both kingdons, on the 22nd of July 1706. Printed at Edinburgh by the heirs and successors of Andrew Anderson, and reprinted at London for Andrew Bell: and sold by B. Bragg, [1706?]. 8°

T.34

4176

ENGLAND. *Commissioners nominated to treat of a Union between England and Scotland.*

A true copy of the articles of union agreed on the twenty second day of July ... by the Commissioners nominated on behalf of the kingdom of Scotland ... and the Commissioners nominated on behalf of the kingdom of England ... Printed at Edinburgh by the heirs and successors of Andrew Anderson, and reprinted for John Morphew, 1706.   8°

T.248

4177

An ENQUIRY into the nature of the liberty of the subject, and of subjection to the supreme powers. In a letter to the Reverend Mr. Hoadly, upon occasion of his sermon... Sept. 29. 1705. [Attributed to Francis Atterbury.] London: for John Nutt, 1706.   4°

2 copies.

T.8   T.264

4178

An EPISTLE to Sir Richard Blackmore, Kt. on occasion of the late great victory in Brabant. [A poem.] London, for John Chantry, 1706.   Fol.

T.699

4179

An ESSAY upon government. Wherein the republican schemes reviv'd by Mr. Lock, Dr. Blackal, &c. are fairly consider'd and refuted ... The second edition corrected. London, for G. Sawbridge, 1706.   8°

T.403

4180

FERGUSON (Robert)

The history of the Revolution. [Anon.] London, printed in the year, 1706.   4°

T.77

4181

FLEMING (Robert) *the Younger.*

Seculum Davidicum redivivum; or, The divine right of the Revolution evinc'd and apply'd: in a discourse, occasion'd by the late glorious victory at Ramilly... The sum whereof was delivered in a sermon on the general thanksgiving-day, June 27, 1706... London, for Andrew Bell, 1706.   8°

T.413

4182

GIBSON (Edmund) *Bishop of London.*

A sermon against speaking evil of princes, and those in authority under them: preach'd at the assizes held at Croydon in Surrey, March 7th. 1705/6... London: for A. and J. Churchill, 1706.   4°

2 copies.

T.71   T.273

4183

GIBSON (Edmund) *Bishop of London.*

A sermon of the growth and mischiefs of popery: preach'd at the assizes held at Kingston in Surrey, Sept. 5th 1706 ... London: for A. and J. Churchill, 1706.   4°

Another copy, in 8°

T.519   T.71

4184

HAMILTON (John) *2nd Baron Belhaven.*

The Lord Beilhaven's speech in the Scotch Parliament, Saturday the second of November, on the subject-matter of an union betwixt the two kingdoms... Printed in the year 1706.   8°

T.34

4185

HARRIS (John) *D.D., F.R.S.*

The lawfulness and use of publick feasting. A sermon preached... December 4. 1705. being the anniversary meeting of the natives of the county of Southampton. London: for R. Wilkin, 1706.   4°

T.757

4186

HASLEWOOD (John)

St. Paul, no mover of sedition: or, A brief vindication of that Apostle, from the false and disingenous exposition of Mr. Hoadly, in a sermon preach'd before the lord mayor ... [Anon.] London: printed 1706.   4°

T.8

4187

HOADLY (Benjamin) *Bishop of Winchester.*

A letter to the Reverend Dr. Francis Atterbury: occasion'd by the doctrine lately deliver'd by him in a funeral sermon ... August 30. 1706 ... [Anon.] London: for A. Baldwin, 1706.   8°

T.39

4188

HOADLY (Benjamin) *Bishop of Winchester.*

A letter to the Reverend Dr. Francis Atterbury: occasion'd by the doctrine lately deliver'd by him in a funeral sermon... August 30. 1706... [Anon.] London: H. Hills, [1706].   8°

T.519

4189

HUMFREY (John)

De justificatione: being a letter to a friend, upon a passage in one of the printed sermons of his Grace, the present Archbishop of York ... London, J. Darby for Walter Kettilby, 1706.   4°

T.137

4190

INTERPRETATION ancienne & nouvelle du songe de Louis X1V... Imprimé dans le Mercure Galand, & dans la Gazette de Paris, du onziéme de Novembre 1689. Première interprétation faite par feu Mr. Brousson... A Cologne, chez les héritiers de Pierre Marteau, 1706.   12°

T.444

4191

KEITH (George)

A journal of travels from New-Hampshire to Caratuck, on the continent of North-America. London, Joseph Downing, for Brab. Aylmer, 1706.   4°

2 copies.

T.194   T.12

4192

KENNET (White) *Bishop of Peterborough.*

Dr. Kennet's character of the late King James, in his preface to an address of thanks: with a postscript concerning his late sermons. Printed in the year 1706. 4°

2 copies.

T.155   T.194

4193

KENNET (White) *Bishop of Peterborough.*

The charity of schools for poor children recommended in a sermon preach'd in the parish-church of St. Sepulchers, May 16. 1706 ... London, Joseph Downing: and are to be sold by John Churchill, 1706.   4°

2 copies.

T.71   T.78

4194

KENNET (White) *Bishop of Peterborough.*

The duties of rejoycing in a day of prosperity. Recommended in a sermon preach'd before the Queen at her royal chapel in Windsor. On Sunday, June 23. 1706. London: for A. and J. Churchil, 1706.   4°

T.198

4195

KENNET (White) *Bishop of Peterborough.*

The office and good work of a bishop. A sermon preach'd in Lambeth-chappel, at the consecration of ... William, Lord Bishop of Lincoln, on Sunday, Octob. 21. 1705 ... London: for A. and J. Churchill, and R. Sare, 1706. 4°

On the verso of the title-page is the draft of a letter from Geo. Hickes to Kennet.

T.71

4196

KENNET (White) *Bishop of Peterborough.*

A sermon preach'd before the honourable House of Commons, at St. Margaret's Westminster, on Wednesday, January XXX, 1705/6 ... London, J.H. for John Churchill, 1706.   4°

Annotated by George Hickes.

T.71

4197

KENNET (White) *Bishop of Peterborough.*

A sermon preach'd before the honourable House of Commons, at St. Margaret's Westminster, on Wednesday, January XXX, 1705/6... London, F. Thorn, 1706.   8°

3 copies.

T.82   T.519   T.622

4198

KING (William) *Archbishop of Dublin.*

The advantages of education, religious and political. In a sermon preach'd at St. Margaret's Westminster, January the 13th. 1705. Being the day for the annual collection for the poor children of the Grey-Coat Hospital ... London: H. Meere, for Charles King, 1706.   4°

T.8

4199

LAWTON (Charlwood)

A second letter concerning civil comprehension: by the author of the first. Sold by J. Nutt, and the booksellers of London and Westminster, 1706.   4°

3 copies.

T.194

4200

LE CLERC (Jean)

The life and character of Mr. John Locke, author of the Essay concerning humane understanding. Written in French, by Mr. Le Clerc. And done into English, by T.F.P. London: for John Clark. And are to be had at J. Nutts, 1706. 4°

2 copies.

T.137 T.194

4201

LESLIE (Charles)

The history of the Church, in respect both to its ancient and present condition. To which is added, A continuation of the same ... By one called an High-Churchman ... London, printed, and sold by the booksellers, 1706. 2 parts. 4°

T.137

4202

A LETTER from an Hollander, to one of his friends in Paris. Touching the underhand-proposals of peace made by France. Both in French and English. London: for B. Bragg, 1706. 4°

T.194

4203

A LETTER [by William Stephens] to the author [i.e. John Toland] of the Memorial of the state of England, answer'd paragraph by paragraph. London: printed in the year 1706. 8°

T.34

4204

MACKENZIE (George) Earl of Cromarty.

Two letters concerning the present Union, from a peer in Scotland to a peer in England. [E.C. to E.W.] Printed in the year 1706. 4°

T.490

4205

A METHOD propos'd, for easing her Majesties subjects, of the charge of fines and recoveries. [No imprint, 1706.] 4°

T.194

4206

The MODERATION, justice, and manners of the Review, exemplify'd from his own works... London: for B. Brag, 1706. 4°

2 copies.

T.267 T.652

4207

MOORE (John) Bishop of Ely.

The objections against the duty of prayer, answer'd. In a sermon preach'd before the Queen, at St. James's chappel, on Sunday, February 17. 1705/6. By... John Lord Bishop of Norwich. London: for W. Rogers, 1706. 4°

T.625

4208

MORER (Thomas)

A short account of Scotland. Being a description of the nature of that kingdom, and what the constitution of it is in Church and state ... [Anon.] London, B. Bragg, 1706. 8°

T.34

4209

NO-Church establish'd: or, The schismatick unmask'd. Being an impartial answer to The rights of the Christian Church asserted [by Matthew Tindal]... London: Benj. Bragg, 1706. 8°

T.417

4210

OLDMIXON (John)

Iberia liberata: a poem. Occasion'd by the success of her Majesties arms in Catalonia, Valentia, &c. under the command of ... Charles, Earl of Peterborough and Monmouth ... London: for Anthony Barker; and sold by John Nutt, 1706. 8°

T.220

4211

OSBORNE (Peregrine) 2nd Duke of Leeds.

A copy of the Marquiss of Carmarthen's method for the speedy manning her Majesty's Royal Navy; and for encouraging seamen, Feb. 12. 1705. London, John Humfreys, and sold by B. Bragg, 1706. 8°

T.522

4212

PATIENCE. A present to the press-yard. A poem ... London: printed in the year 1706. 4°

T.261

4213

PEAD (Deuel)

Annus victoriis mirabilis: a thanksgiving sermon preach'd on Tuesday, Dec. 31. 1706. at St. James's Clerkenwell. Occasion'd by the signal victories obtain'd over the French... London: W.D. for T. Brown: and are to be sold by B. Bragge, 1706. 8°

T.519

4214

PEAD (Deuel)

Annus victoriis mirabilis: a thanksgiving sermon preach'd on Tuesday, Dec. 31. 1706. at St. James's Clerkenwell. Occasion'd by the signal victories obtain'd over the French ... London: H. Hills, [1706.] 8°

T.82

4215

PITCAIRNE (Archibald)

Gualteri Dannistoni ad Georgium Buchananum epistola, conscripta anno aerae Christianae MDCCVI. [The imprint is cut away.] [1706.] 8°

The letters VI in the date have been blocked out. cf. Wing O D 1047 A.

T.148

4216

The PLEA of publick good not sufficient to justifie the taking up arms against our rightful and lawful sovereigns. In a letter to the Reverend Mr. Hoadly ... Sold by the booksellers of London and Westminster, 1706. 4°

2 copies.

T.72 T.261

4217

PROCEEDINGS in the present Convocation: relating to the dangers of the Church, and the protestation against the irregularities of some of the lower-clergy. London: printed in the year 1706. 4°

T.133

4218

PROPOSALS for establishing a charitable fund in the city of London ... to relieve necessitous persons from the oppressions and evil practices of ill men ... London, printed at the charge of several charitable persons, 1706. 8°

2 copies.

T.29 T.163

4219

The QUEEN an empress, and her three kingdoms one empire: or, Brief remarks upon the present; and a prospect of the future state of England, Scotland, and Ireland, in a happy union. In a letter to a noble peer. London; for A. Baldwin, 1706. 4°

T.194

4220

REVERENTIAL love: or, God honour'd by the pious decency of the Minister's humbly bowing the head when he approaches to, or comes from, the altar... London: W.B. for William Carter, 1706. 8°

T.441

4221

The REVIEW and Observator review'd. With some observations thereon. By a layman of the Church of England. London, for John Nutt, 1706. 4°

T.194

4222

SACHEVERELL (Henry)

The character of a Low-Church-man: drawn in an answer to the True character of a Church-man [by Richard West]: shewing the false pretences to that name. Humbly offer'd to all electors of Parliament and Convocation. [Anon.] 2nd ed ... Printed in the year 1706. 4°

T.191

4223

SHARPE (John) Curate of Stepney.

The case of non-residency, with the usual pleas for it, considered and censur'd ... In a letter to the Honourable Sir H. Mackworth ... By a hearty lover of the Church Establish'd. Sold by the booksellers of London and Westminster, 1706. 4°

T.191

4224

A SHORT way with the papists. Shewing, what is the most proper, and most effectual method to extirpate popery ... In a dialogue between Mr. Zealous ... and Mr. Moderate ... London, printed for the author, 1706. 4°

T.191

4225

SOPHIA, Electress of Hanover.

A letter from her Royal Highness, the Princess Sophia, Electress of Brunswic and Luneburg, to ... the Archbishop of Canterbury. With another from Hannover, written by Sir Rowland Gwynne to ... the Earl of Stamford. London, B. Bragge, 1706. 4°

2 copies.

T.194 T.267

4226

The SOURSE of our present fears discover'd: or, Plain proof of some late designs against our present constitution and government ... The third edition, much enlarg'd. To which is added, by another hand, A word to the wise ... London: for S.B. and sold by B. Bragg, 1706. 8°

T.34

4227

SPADEMAN (John)

Deborah's triumph over the mighty. A sermon preach'd on the day of publick thanksgiving, June 27. 1706... for the glorious victory in Brabant, and great successes in Spain. With the gratulatory address of the dissenting ministers in and about London. London: R. Tookey, for Tho. Parkhurst, 1706. 4°

T.765

4228

STANHOPE (George) Dean of Canterbury.

Concio coram rrmo archiepiscopo, reverendis admodum episcopis, et clero provinc. Cantuar. synodice congregatis, habita ... mensis Octobris die XXV. A.D. MDCCV ... Londini, typis W.B. impensis vero R. Sare, & R. Knaplock, 1706. 4°

T.8

4229

STANHOPE (George) Dean of Canterbury.

A sermon preach'd before the... archbishop, and the... bishops, and the clergy of the province of Canterbury, assembled in synod. In the cathedral church of St. Paul, London, October the 25th, 1705. Done from the Latin. London: for Rich. Sare; and Rob. Knaplock, 1706. 4°

T.8

4230

STANHOPE (George) Dean of Canterbury.

A sermon preach'd before the Queen at the cathedral church of St. Paul, London, the xxvii th day of June MDCCVI. Being the day appointed for a general thanksgiving for the success of her Majesty's arms in Flanders and Spain... London: W.B. for R. Sare, M. Wotton, T. Speed, and R. Knaplock, 1706. 4°

Another copy, in 8°

T.8 T.36

4231

The SWAN tripe-club in Dublin. A satyr. Dedicated to all those who are true friends to her present Majesty and her government, to the Church of England, and the succession as by law establish'd ... Printed at Dublin, and sold by the booksellers in London and Westminster, 1706. 4°

Teerink 836. Sometimes attributed to Swift.

T.261

4232

TALLENTS (Francis)

Some few considerations upon Mr. S[amuel] G[rascombe]'s large answer to the Short history of schism... London: for W. Boulter, 1706. 8°

T.507

4233

TERRICK (Samuel)

A sermon preached in the cathedral... in York. June 27th, 1706. Being the day of thanksgiving for the late signal and glorious victory, obtain'd by the forces of her Majesty... York, John White, for Francis Hildyard, and are to be sold by Tho. Bennet, London, [1706]. 4°

T.172

4234

TILLY (William)

A sermon preach'd before the University of Oxford, at St. Mary's on Monday, January XXXI. 1703/4 ... 2nd ed. Oxford, L. Lichfield for J. Stephens, and are to be sold by James Knapton, 1706. 4°

T.8

4235

TURNER (John) *Vicar of Greenwich.*

Justice done to human souls, in a short view of Mr. Dodwell's late book, entitul'd, An epistolary discourse; proving from the Scriptures and the first fathers, that the soul is a principle naturally mortal, &c. In a letter to a friend. London: for John Wyat, 1706. 8°

2 copies.

4236

WAKE (William) *Archbishop of Canterbury.*

A sermon preached before the House of Lords, at the abbey-church in Westminster, on Monday, Nov. the 5th, 1705. By... William, Lord Bishop of Lincoln. London: for R. Sare, 1706. 4°

3 copies.

T.8 T.172 T.273

4237

WARD (Edward)

Hudibras redivivus: or, A burlesque poem on the times. Part the sixth. [Anon.] London, printed: and sold by Benj. Bragge, 1706. 4°

2 copies.

T.668 T.261

4238

WELLS (Edward)

Dr. Wells's examination of the remarks on his letter to Mr. Peter Dowley. Part I. In a letter to a dissenting parishioner. Oxford, Leon. Lichfield, for John Stephens: and are to be sold by James Knapton, 1706. 8°

T.322

4239

WELLS (Edward)

Dr. Wells's examination of the Remarks on his letter to Mr. Peter Dowley. Part II. Sect. I. In a letter to the Remarker. Oxford, Leon. Lichfield, for John Stephens: and are to be sold by James Knapton, 1706. 8°

T.322

4240

WELLS (Edward)

A letter from a minister of the Church of England, to a dissenting parishioner of the presbyterian perswasion. 4th ed. Oxford, for John Stephens, and are to be sold by James Knapton, 1706. 8°

T.322

4241

WELLS (Edward)

A letter from a minister of the Church of England, to Mr Peter Dowley, a dissenting teacher of the presbiterian or else independent perswasion. 3rd ed. Oxford, for John Stephens, and are to be sold by James Knapton, 1706. 8°

T.322

4242

WELLS (Edward)

Dr. Wells's letter to a dissenting parishioner, in reference to the Remarks on his first letter to the same. Oxford, Leon. Lichfield, for John Stephens: and are to be sold by James Knapton, London, 1706. 8°

T.322

4243

WELLS (Edward)

Dr. Wells's letter to the Remarker, in reference to his remarks on the Doctor's letter to a dissenting parishioner. Oxford, Leon. Lichfield, for John Stephens: and are to be sold by James Knapton, London, 1706. 8°

T.322

4244

WELLS (Edward)

Some testimonies of the most eminent English dissenters, as also of foreign reformed churches and divines, concerning the lawfulness of the rites and ceremonies of the Church of England, and the unlawfulness of separating from it. 2nd ed. Oxford, printed at the Theater for Jo. Stephens, and are to be sold by James Knapton, London, 1706. 8°

T.322

4245

WHAT are you mad? Or strange doings at Westminster. [No imprint, 1706?] brs.

T.89

4246

A WONDERFUL account from Orthez, in Bearne, and the Cevennes, of voices heard in the air, singing the praises of God, in the words and tunes of the psalms; used by those of the Reformed Religion: at the time of their cruel and inhumane persecution ... by the French king: credibly [sic] attested, by the certificates of Monsieur Jerieu, and many other ministers... London: for H. Preston, 1706. 8°

T.383

4247

WOTTON (William)

The rights of the clergy in the Christian Church asserted. In a sermon preached at Newport Pagnel ... September 2. 1706. at the primary visitation of... William Lord Bishop of Lincoln... London: for Tim. Goodwin, 1706. 4°

T.753

4248

WOTTON (William)

The rights of the clergy in the Christian Church asserted. In a sermon prrach'd [sic] at Newport Pagnel... September 2. 1706... London: H. Hills, [1706]. 8°

T.491

4249

WRIGHT (William) *of Kilmarnock.*

The comical history of the marriage-union betwixt Fergusia and Heptarchus ... [Anon.] Printed in Scotland upon that occasion; and reprinted in England, 1706. 4°

2 copies.

T.490 T.142

1707

4250

The ABSTRACT or state of the case before the general court of St. Bartholomew's hospital, by the advocate of the defendant. [No imprint, 1707?] 4°

T.194

4251

ADAMS (John) *Provost of King's College, Cambridge.*

A sermon preach'd before the Queen at St. James's chappel, on Wednesday the 19th of March, 1706/7. London: for Jonah Bowyer, 1707. 4°

T.771

4252

ADAMSON (John)

A sermon preached at the funeral of Sir Edmund Turnor, Kt. at Stoke in Lincolnshire, on Monday the 14th of April 1707 ... London, for Sam. Keble, 1707. 8°

2 copies.

T.622 T.519

4253

ANCIENNE prediction du celebre prophete Merlin. Copiée sur une traduction en Vieux Gaulois, qui en fut faite sous le regne d'Henry VIII... (Nouvelle prophetie d'Elie Marion... Fidellement transcrite, & maintenant publiée par l'autheur du premier dialogue touchant les prophetes Cevennois.) [No imprint, 1707.] 4°

T.269

4254

An ANSWER to a late pamphlet [by Daniel Defoe], entitled, The experiment; or, The shortest way with dissenters exemplified ... Wherein all the misrepresentations ... contain'd in that pamphlet, are clearly detected and proved, by authentick and undeniable evidence. London: for J. Morphew, 1707. 4°

T.191

4255

ARBUTHNOT (John)

A sermon preach'd to the people, at the Mercat-Cross of Edinburgh; on the subject of the Union ... [Anon.] London, re-printed for Andrew Bell, 1707. 8°

T.519

4256

ATTERBURY (Francis) *Bishop of Rochester.*

An account and defence of the protestation made by the lower-house of Convocation, April 30th. 1707. in behalf of the Queen's supremacy ... [Anon.] London, printed in the year, 1707. 4°

3 copies.

T.74 T.191 T.266

4257

AYMON (Jean)

A letter to Monsieur N ———, professor of divinity in the Protestant University of N ———, from Monsieur Aymon, chaplain to the famous Cardinal Camus, Bishop of Grenoble. London: for R. Burrough and J. Baker, 1707. 4°

T.140

4258

BALDWIN (Robert)

A sermon preach'd at the arch-deacon's visitation at Burnham-Westgate, in the county of Norfolk, October 9, 1706. Printed in the year 1707. 4°

T.753

4259

BARKER (Richard)

The danger of pleasing men: a sermon preached in the cathedral-church of Winchester at the annual visitation of... Jonathan Lord Bishop of that diocese, upon Monday, Sept. 22. 1707. London, W. Sayes, and sold by John Morphew, 1707. 4°

T.752

4260

BLACKALL (Offspring) *Bishop of Exeter.*

The way of trying prophets. A sermon preach'd before the Queen at St. James's, November 9. 1707. London: for W. Rogers, 1707. 8°

2 copies.

T.519

4261

BROWNE (Joseph)

London belles: or, A description of the most celebrated beauties in the city of London... [Anon.] London: printed in the year, 1707. 8°

T.89

4262

BRYDALL (John)

The oracles of the dissenters: containing forty five relations of pretended jugdments [sic], prodigies, and apparitions, in behalf of the non-conformists: in opposition to the Establish'd Church. Publish'd in order to make the Church of Endgland [sic] as odious in the eyes of the vulgar, as popery ... By an impartial hand. Part I. London, B. Bragg, 1707. 4°

T.191

4263

BURNET (Gilbert) *Bishop of Salisbury.*

A sermon preach'd before the Queen, and the two houses of Parliament, at St. Paul's on the 31st of December, 1706. The day of thanksgiving for the wonderful successes of this year. London: W.B. for A. and J. Churchill, 1707.   8°

3 copies.

T.82   T.519

4264

CANNON (Robert)

A sermon preach'd before the Queen at New-market, Octob. 5th 1707. Cambridge: printed, at the University-Press; for Richard Thurlbourn, 1707.   4°

T.771

4265

CARROLL (William)

A letter to the Reverend Dr. Benjamin Prat ... wherein, the dangerous errors in a late book [by Anthony Collins], intituled, An essay concerning the use of reason ... are detected, confuted, and gradually deduc'd from the very basis of all atheism ... London; for Richard Sare; and sold by the booksellers of London and Westminster, 1707.   8°

T.153

4266

CHURCH OF ENGLAND.

A form of prayer and thanksgiving, to be used on Thursday the first day of May ... for rendring most hearty thanks to Almighty God, for the ... conclusion of the treaty for the union of her Majesties two kingdoms of England and Scotland ... London, Charles Bill, and the executrix of Thomas Newcomb, 1707.   4°

T.461

4267

CHURCH OF ENGLAND.

A form of prayer, to be used in all churches and chapels ... on Wednesday the fourteenth day of January, being the day appointed ... for a general fast ... for ... imploring Gods blessing and assistance on the arms of her Majesty, and her allies ... London, Charles Bill, and the executrix of Thomas Newcomb, 1707.   4°

T.461

4268

CHURCH OF ENGLAND.

A form of prayer, to be used in all churches and chapels ... on Wednesday the ninth day of April, being the fast-day appointed ... for imploring the continuance of Gods blessing and assistance on the arms of her Majesty, and her allies ... London, Charles Bill, and the executrix of Thomas Newcomb, 1707.   4°

T.461

4269

The CHURCH of England not in danger: or, A serious answer to several false and seditious suggestions, deliver'd by Mr. Higgins, in a sermon preach'd at White-hall ... By a divine of the Church of England. London, printed: and are to be sold by J. Morphew, 1707.   8°

T.519

4270

COCK (John)

A description of true religion; in a sermon preach'd at the cathedral church of Durham, August 24, 1669, before Bishop Cosins. London: for George Sawbridge, 1707.   8°

2 copies.

T.36   T.519

4271

COCK (John)

A serious exhortation to avoid such as cause divisions in Christ's Church; in a sermon preach'd at the cathedral church of Durham ... in the year 1672 ... London: for George Sawbridge, 1707.   8°

T.36

4272

COLLINS (Anthony)

A letter to the learned Mr. Henry Dodwell; containing some remarks on a (pretended) demonstration of the immateriality and natural immortality of the soul, in Mr. Clark's answer to his late Epistolary discourse, &c. [Anon.] London: for A. Baldwin, 1707.   8°

T.301

4273

COLLINS (Anthony)

Reflections on Mr. Clark's Second defence of his letter to Mr. Dodwell ... [Anon.] London, J. Darby, 1707.   8°

T.151

4274

COLLINS (Anthony)

A reply to Mr. Clark's Defence of his letter to Mr. Dodwell. With a postscript relating to Mr. Milles's answer to Mr. Dodwell's Epistolary discourse ... [Anon.] London; printed in the year 1707.   8°

T.151

4275

A CONVINCING reply to the Lord Beilhaven's speech, in relation to the pretended independency of the Scottish nation, from that of England ... London, B. Bragg, 1707.   8°

T.34

4276

A COPY of the country-man's letter to the Speaker of the last House of Commons, as it was sent to him as soon as the last Parliament rose. The country-man's complaint. [Signed Patriarchus Hodge.] [No imprint, 1707.]   4°

T.194

4277

DAMPIER (William)

Capt. Dampier's vindication of his voyage to the South-Seas in the ship St. George. With some small observations for the present on Mr. Funnel's chimerical relation of the voyage round the world; and detected in little, until he shall be examin'd more at large. London, J. Bradford, 1707.   8°

T.89

4278

DAWES (*Sir* William) *Archbishop of York.*

The nature and excellency of the duty of alms-giving. A sermon preach'd at the parish church of St. Giles's in the Fields. Sunday, Nov. 17. 1706. on behalf of the charity-schools settled in that parish... London: for Thomas Speed, 1707.   4°

T.8

4279

DAWES (*Sir* William) *Archbishop of York.*

The nature and excellency of the duty of alms-giving. A sermon preach'd at the parish church of St. Giles's in the Fields. Sunday Nov. 17th, 1706. on behalf of the charity-schools settled in that parish... 2nd ed. London: for Thomas Speed, 1707.   8°

T.519

4280

A DEFENCE of the doctrine of the man-Christ Jesus his descent from heaven, as it is laid down and prov'd in the Bishop of Gloucester's discourse upon that subject ... By a presbyter of the Church of England. To which is annex'd by the publisher a second defence of that doctrine ... London: for John Wyat, 1707.   8°

T.149

4281

DEFOE (Daniel)

Caledonia, a poem in honour of Scotland, and the Scots nation. In three parts. London: J. Matthews, and sold by John Morphew, 1707.   8°

Moore 129.

2 copies.

T.417   T.89

4282

DEFOE (Daniel)

A true relation of the apparition of one Mrs. Veal, the next day after her death, to one Mrs. Bargrave, at Canterbury, the 8th of September, 1705. Which apparition recommends the perusal of Drelincourt's book of Consolations against the fears of death. 3rd ed. London, for B. Bragg, 1707.   8°

Moore 107.

T.44

4283

DODWELL (Henry)

A further prospect of the Case in view, in answer to some new objections not there considered. [Anon.] London: printed, and sold at the publishing-office in Bearbinder-lane; and by most booksellers in London and Westminster, 1707.   8°

T.361

4284

DODWELL (Henry)

A preliminary defence of the Epistolary discourse, concerning the distinction between soul and spirit ... London, for George Strahan, 1707. 2 parts. 8°

T.156

4285

DUBOURDIEU (Jean Armand)

L'orgueuil de Nebucadnetzar abbatu de la main de Dieu: avec quelques applications particulieres aux affaires du temps. Ou sermon sur Daniel, ch. iv. vers. 29, 30, 31, 32 ... A Londres, chez Henry Ribotteau, 1707.   8°

2 copies.

T.322   T.82

4286

DUBOURDIEU (Jean Armand)

The triumphs of providence in the downfal of Pharoah, renew'd in the late battle of Ramellies: being a sermon ... preach'd at the Savoy-Church. London, for Bernard Lintott, 1707.   4°

T.198

4287

ECKHART (Johann Georg von)

Joannis Georgii Eccardi de usu et praestantia studii etymologici in historia dissertatio inauguralis habita... Helmestadii, typis Georg. Wolffgangi Hammii, 1707.   4°

T.793

4288

EDWARDS (John) *D.D.*

The heinousness of England's sins represented in that of Jerusalem's ... A sermon design'd to be preached (but prevented by sickness) on April the 9th, 1707 ... London, for Jonathan Robinson, John Lawrence, and John Wyat, 1707.   8°

T.36

4289

ENGELBRECHT (Johann)

The German Lazarus; being a plain and faithful account of the extraordinary events that happened to John Engelbrecht of Brunswick: relating to his apparent death, and return to life... All written by himself. And done from the original High-Dutch... London: for Ben. Bragg, 1707.   8°

T.383

4290

FOULKS (Isabella)

[Begins] Isabella Foulks a very aged poor woman swears, That Mr. Higgins utter'd in his sermon at White-hall on Ash-Wednesday last, these following words ... [No imprint, 1707.] brs.

T.519

4291

FOURTEEN quaeries. With a word to the wise. Left by Mr. Higgins, for the better instruction of the people of London. London, J. Jones, 1707.   8°

T.147

4292

FOX (Bohun)

Agrippa almost perswaded to be a Christian: or, the self-condemn'd Quaker. Being a true copy of two papers lately printed by Thomas Beaven, in relation to the Quakers. With a preface and some reflections on the last of them, entituled, His second thoughts ... London: for John Wyat, 1707.   8°

T.79

4293

FRANCKE (Augustus Hermannus)

Pietas Hallensis: or, An abstract of the marvellous footsteps of divine providence, in the building of a very large hospital ... for charitable and excellent uses ... With a preface written by Josiah Woodward ... To which is added, A short history of pietism [by A.W. Boehme]. The second edition enlarged. London, J. Downing, 1707. 2 parts.   12°

T.444

4294

FRESH warning to England. Being an account of the wonderful appearance of a blazing-star ... With the judgments and opinions of Dr. Flamsted, Dr. Partridge, and several other eminent astrologers, relating to a general peace. London: for Sam. Smith, [1707?] 8°

T.44

4295

G. (M.)

Mercurius Oxoniensis; or, the Oxford intelligencer, for the year of our Lord 1707. By M.G. London, for Egbert Sanger, 1707. 8°

T.442

4296

GANDY (Henry)

Jure divino: or an answer to all that hath or shall be written by republicans, against the old English constitution. Part the first ... [Anon.] London: printed in the year 1707. 4°

T.197

4297

GASTRELL (Francis) *Bishop of Chester.*

The religious education of poor children recommended, in a sermon preach'd... June 5. 1707... at the anniversary meeting of the gentlemen concerned in promoting the charity-schools lately erected in the cities of London and Westminster... London, Joseph Downing, for J. Bowyer, and H. Clement, 1707. 8°

T.804

4298

GASTRELL (Francis) *Bishop of Chester.*

Some considerations concerning the Trinity: and the ways of managing that controversie. 3rd ed. Together with an answer to some reflections made upon them, in a late pamphlet [by Anthony Collins] entituled, &c. in a letter to the author. [Anon.] London: for Henry Clements, 1707. 2 parts. 8°

T.149

4299

GIBSON (Edmund) *Bishop of London.*

An account of the proceeding in Convocation, in a cause of contumacy, commenc'd April 10. 1707. occasion'd by the publishing a protestation made against it, in one of the common news-papers. [Anon.] London: J. Morphew, 1707. 4°

2 copies.

T.74 T.191

4300

GRASCOMBE (Samuel)

Schism triumphant: or, A rejoinder to a reply of Mr. Tallents, entituled, Some considerations on Mr. S.G's large answer to his Short history of schism, &c. By the same S.G ... London, H. Meere for G. Sawbridge, 1707. Sold also by B. Bragge. 8°

2 copies.

T.507 T.230

4301

The GREAT sin and folly of drunkenness. With a particular address to the female sex... London: W.B. for R.S. and to be sold by John Morphew, 1707. 12°

T.459

4302

GRIFFITH (John) *Curate of Edensor.*

A sermon occasioned by the death of the late Duke of Devonshire, who departed this life, August the 18th, 1707... London: Dryden Leach, and sold by J. Morphew, 1707. 8°

T.519

4303

HACKET (Laurence)

A sermon preach'd at St. Bennet-Finct church, on Thursday, October the 24th. 1707. before the Honourable Company of Merchants trading to the Levant-seas. London, Tho. Warren, for Jonah Bowyer, 1707. 4°

T.765

4304

HARDT (Richard von der)

Holmia literata auctior & emendatior cum appendice de variis rerum Suecicarum scriptoribus. [Anon.] [No imprint], 1707. 4°

T.793

4305

HASLEWOOD (John)

A sermon preach'd at the assizes held at Kingston upon Thames, on Thursday March the 13th, 1706/7. London: H. Hills, [1707]. 8°

2 copies

T.491 T.519

4306

HIGGINS (Francis)

The prayer of the Reverend Mr. Higgins, before his text, and his case. Printed in the year 1707. 8°

T.147

4307

HIGGINS (Francis)

A sermon preach'd at the royal chappel at White-hall; on Ash-Wednesday, Feb. 26, 1706/7... London, E.P. for B. Barker, and C. King, 1707. 8°

3 copies.

T.36 T.82 T.519

4308

HIGGINS (Francis)

A sermon preach'd before their excellencies the lords justices, at Christ-Church, Dublin; on Tuesday the 28th of August, 1705. Being the day appointed for a solemn thanksgiving... London: for Jonah Bowyer, 1707. 8°

2 copies.

T.519 T.622

4309

HOADLY (John) *Archbishop of Armagh.*

The nature and excellency of moderation. A sermon preach'd in the cathedral church of Sarum, at the assizes held for the county of Wilts, March 9. 1706/7 ... 2nd ed. London, for Timothy Childe, 1707. 8°

2 copies.

T.519 T.36

4310

HUMAN souls naturally immortal. Translated from a Latin manuscript, by S.E. With a recommendatory preface, by Jeremy Collier. London: for Robert Gosling, 1707. 8°

2 copies.

T.507 T.377

4311

JEGON (William)

The following sermon was preach'd some time since at an episcopal visitation in Norfolk, and is now publish'd upon occasion of the vile things very freely vented against the clergy... Norwich: H. Cross-grove, 1707. 4°

T.752

4312

JOHNSON (Richard)

A defence of the grammatical commentaries, against the animadversions of Mr. Edward Leeds, master of Bury school, under the name of (An old man, and who that old man is, if it be worth while to look the following pages will discover)... London: for S. Keeble, 1707. 8°

T.416

4313

KEITH (George)

The necessity of faith, and of the revealed Word of God; to be the foundation of all divine and saving-faith: in a sermon, preach'd at the lecture in Lewis in Sussex, the fourth of 6eptember, 1707 ... London, for W. Haws, 1707. 8°

2 copies.

T.519 T.101

4314

KENNET (White) *Bishop of Peterborough.*

A sermon preach'd at the funeral of the Right Noble William Duke of Devonshire, in the church of All-Hallows in Derby, on Fryday Septemb. 5th. MDCCVII... London: H. Hills, 1707. 8°

T.519

4315

LACY (John)

The prophetical warnings of John Lacy, Esq; pronounced under the operation of the spirit; and faithfully taken in writing, when they were spoken. London: for B. Bragge, 1707. 8°

T.382

4316

LACY (John)

Warnings of the eternal spirit, by the mouth of his servant John, sirnam'd Lacy. The second part. London; for B. Bragg, 1707. 8°

T.382

4317

LESLIE (Charles)

A postscript to Mr. Higgins's sermon, very necessary for the better understanding it. In a dialogue. [Anon.] London, printed, and are to be sold by the booksellers of London and Westminster, 1707. 8°

3 copies.

T.36 T.82 T.519

4318

LESLIE (Charles)

The second part of the wolf stript of his shepherds cloathing: in answer to a late celebrated book [by Matthew Tindal] intituled The rights of the Christian Church asserted... By one call'd an High-Church-man. The second edition, with an addition of several letters from the pastors of the Church of Geneva... Sold by the booksellers of London and Westminster, 1707. 2 parts. 4°

T.2

4319

A LETTER to Mr. Baldwin, occasioned by his sermon preach'd at the arch-deacons visitation at Burnham Westgate in the county of Norfolk, Octob. 9. 1706. Norwich: printed in the year, 1707. 4°

T.753

4320

The LIFE and glorious actions of that right honourable Sir George Rook, Kt. sometime admiral of the English fleet... London: for R. Johnson, 1707. 8°

T.89

4321

LORRAIN (Paul)

A sermon preach'd in the morning at St. Dunstan's in the West; and in the afternoon ... at Newgate, on the second day of September, 1707. being the fast-day for the fire of London. Sold by B. Bragg, 1707. 8°

2 copies.

T.519 T.82

4322

MARION (Elie)

Prophetical warnings of Elias Marion, heretofore one of the commanders of the protestants, that had taken arms in the Cevennes: or, Discourses uttered by him in London, under the operation of the spirit ... London, for Ben. Bragge, 1707. 8°

T.382

4323

MILBOURNE (Luke)

The people not the original of civil-power, proved from God's word, the doctrine and liturgy of the Establish'd-Church, and from the laws of England. In a sermon preach'd ... on Thursday, Jan. 30, 1706/7 ... London, for R. Burrough, and J. Baker, 1707. 8°

2 copies.

T.519 T.36

4324

MILLES (Thomas) *Bishop of Waterford.*

The natural immortality of the soul asserted, and proved from the Scriptures, and first fathers: in answer to Mr Dodwell's Epistolary discourse ... Oxford, printed at the Theater for Ant. Peisley, 1707. 8°

T.301

4325

The MISFORTUNES of royal favourites. London: printed in the year 1707. 8°

T.89

4326

MISSON (François Maximilien)

A cry from the desart: or, Testimonials of the miraculous things lately come to pass in the Cevennes, verified upon oath, and by other proofs. [Anon.] Translated from the originals. 2nd ed. With a preface by John Lacy. London, for B. Bragg, 1707.   8°

T.382

4327

MORLEY (George) *Bishop of Winchester.*

Two letters to the most learned Janus Ulitius: wherein ... it is abundantly proved, that neither St. Augustine, nor any one of those fathers, who flourished in the ages before him, did ... countenance the invocation of saints ... Now made English, by a divine of the Church of England. With a letter to the translator, by Geo. Hickes. London: John Morphew, 1707.   4°

T.191

4328

MOSS (Robert) *Dean of Ely.*

A sermon preach'd before the House of Commons at St. Margaret's Westminster. On Thursday, Jan. 30, 1706/7... London: for Richard Sare; and J. Tonson, 1707.   8°

3 copies.

T.82   T.345   T.519

4329

A NEW way to raise soldiers. In a dialogue between a politick captain, and his inquisitive friend Faggot. London printed, and sold at the publishing-office, in Dove Court, 1707.   4°

T.194

4330

NICOLSON (William) *Bishop of Carlisle.*

A sermon preach'd at Bow-church, London. On Monday, Dec. 30. 1706. before the societies for reformation of manners ... London, for A. and J. Churchill, 1706./7.   4°

T.71

4331

NICOLSON (William) *Bishop of Carlisle.*

A sermon preach'd at Bow-church London, on Monday, Decemb. 30. 1706. before the societies for the reformation of manners... London: H. Hills, [1707?] 8°

T.491

4332

The OLD and true way of manning the Fleet: or how to retrieve the glory of the English arms by sea, as it is done by land ... In a letter from an old Parliament sea-commander, to a member of the present House of Commons ... London, printed in the year 1707.   4°

T.194

4333

PARRIET (Thomas)

The doctrine of the martyrs of the Church of England, vindicated from the misrepresentations of Dr. Edwards, in his book, entituled, Evangelical truths restored ... London, printed: and are to be sold by J. Morphew, 1707.   4°

T.137

4334

PEAD (Deuel)

The honour, happiness, and safety of union. Or, a sermon upon the uniting of England & Scotland, preach'd at the parish church of St. James Clerkenwell, May 1. 1707. London: W. Downing, and are to be sold by B. Bragge, 1707.   4°

T.771

4335

PEARSON (William) *Archdeacon of Nottingham.*

The case of the Curate of Penrith's taking upon him the office of church-warden, considered. 1706. In a letter from the Archdeacon of Nottingham to the Bishop of Carlile. London, for A. and J. Churchill, 1707.   4°

T.137

4336

PERKINS (Joseph)

Primitive purity: or, Singleness of heart, recommended in a sermon, preach'd in Poplar-chappel in the county of Middlesex ... London: G.C., 1707.   4°

T.82

4337

PITT (Robert)

The calamities of all the English in sickness; and the sufferings of the apothecaries from their unbounded increase, with the sovereign legal remedies, presented to the governours of St. Bartholomew's-Hospital ... [Anon.] Lonfon , for John Morphew, 1707.   4°

T.194

4338

PRIDEAUX (Humphrey)

An award of King Charles the first, under his broad-seal, settling two shillings of the pound out of the rents of the houses in Norwich, for the maintenance of the parochial clergy ... London: for Robert Clavel, 1707.   4°

T.280

4339

PSALMANAZAR (George)

A dialogue between a Japonese and a Formosan, about some points of the religion of the time. By G. P ——— m ——— r ... London: for Bernard Lintott, 1707. 8°

T.153

4340

REASONS offer'd against the continuance of the Bank. In a letter to a member of Parliament. London, printed in the year 1707.   8°

T.70

4341

RODERICK (Richard)

Concio ad clerum Londinensem, habita in ecclesia parochiali S. Alphagi, mensis Maii vi. A.D. MDCCVII ... Londini, impensis S. Smith, & B. Walford, 1707. 4°

T.754

4342

The SCOTCH echo to the English legion: or, The union in danger, from the principles of some old and modern Whigs in both nations, about the power of parliaments. Being every word collected from their own writings... Edinburgh: printed 1707.   4°

Includes *Legion's humble address to the Lords*, by Defoe.

T.490

4343

SCOTLAND. *Parliament.*

The articles of the union as they pass'd with amendments in the Parliament of Scotland, and ratify'd by the touch of the royal scepter at Edinburgh, January 16. 1707. by James Duke of Queensberry ... (The Act for securing the protestant religion and presbyterian church-government ...) London: for Andrew Bell, 1707. 2 parts.   4°

2 copies of the first part only.

T.490   T.142

4344

SHARP (John) *Archbishop of York.*

A sermon preach'd June 28, 1691. at St. Giles's in the Fields... 2nd ed. London: H. Hills, 1707.   8°

T.519

4345

A SHORT view of the apparent dangers and mischiefs from the Bank of England. More particularly address'd to the country gentlemen. London, for Benjamin Bragg, 1707.   4°

T.194

4346

SNAPE (Andrew)

Of the relative engagement between ancestry and posterity. A sermon preach'd before the University of Cambridge... on the 25th of March 1707. being the anniversary for commemorating King Henry VI... Cambridge: printed at the University-Press, for Corn. Crownfield; and are to be sold by Jeffery Wale, London, 1707.   4°

T.771

4347

SNAPE (Andrew)

A sermon preach'd before... the Lord Mayor of London, the court of aldermen, and the governours of the several hospitals of the City... on Wednesday in Easter week, 1707. Being one of the anniversary spittal sermons. London: for Richard Sare, 1707.   4°

Another copy, in 8°

T.519   T.771

4348

SOME impartial reflections on Mr. Baldwin's sermon, and the letters concerning it. Norwich: H. Cross-grove, 1707.   4°

T.753

4349

STANHOPE (George) *Dean of Canterbury.*

Christianity the only true comfort for troubled minds. A sermon preach'd before the Queen in her chapel royal at St. James's. Sunday November the 3d 1706. London: W.B. for Rich. Sare, and Tho. Speed, 1707.   8°

2 copies.

T.622   T.519

4350

STANHOPE (George) *Dean of Canterbury.*

A sermon preach'd before the Queen in the chapel royal at St. James's, November the 5th 1706... London: W.B. for R. Sare, 1707.   8°

T.519

4351

STEPHENS (William)

A sermon preach'd at Sutton in Surrey, on December 31. 1706. London: B. Bragg, 1707.   4°

Another copy, in 8°

T.519   T.625

4352

STRICTURAE breves in epistolas d. d. Genevensium & Oxoniensium nuper editas, iterumque juxta exemplar Oxoniense typis mandatas ... Londini, apud Jonath. Robinson, 1707.   4°

T.12

4353

TALBOT (William) *Bishop of Durham.*

The duty and advantage of setting God always before us. A sermon preach'd before the Queen at St. James's chappel, on Sunday the second of March, 1706/7. By... William Lord Bishop of Oxford. London: for Jonah Bowyer, 1707.   8°

T.519

4354

TALBOT (William) *Bishop of Durham.*

A sermon preach'd before the Queen at the cathedral-church of St. Paul, on May the first, 1707. Being the day appointed... for a general thanksgiving for the happy union of the two kingdoms of England and Scotland. By... William Lord Bishop of Oxford. London: J.B. for Jonah Bowyer, 1707.   8°

3 copies.

T.82   T.172

4355

TENISON (Thomas) *Archbishop of Canterbury.*

His Grace the Lord Arch-bishop of Canterbury's circular letter, to the... bishops of his province: in which is inserted her Majesties gracious letter to him, of the eighth of April, 1707. Relating to matters in Convocation. London, Charles Bill, and the executrix of Thomas Newcomb, 1707.   4°

2 copies.

T.74   T.133

4356

THOMPSON (John) *Baron Haversham.*

The Lord Haversham's speech in the House of Peers, on Saturday, February 15. 1706/7. London: B. Bragg, 1707.   4°

3 copies.

T.142   T.194   T.267

4357

TINDAL (Matthew)

A defence of The rights of the Christian Church, against a late visitation sermon, intitled, The rights of the clergy in the Christian Church asserted; preached at Newport Pagnell ... by W. Wotton ... [Anon.] London, printed in the year 1707.   8°

2 copies.

T.507   T.153

4358

TYLER (John) *Bishop of Llandaff.*

A sermon preach'd before the lords... on the 30th day of January, 1706/7... London: for Dan. Midwinter, 1707.   8°

T.519

4359

VULPONE: or, Remarks on some proceedings in Scotland, relating both to the Union, and protestant succession since the Revolution. In a letter to a member of Parliament. Printed 1707.   4°

2 copies.

T.490 T.142

4360

WAKE (William) *Archbishop of Canterbury.*

The Bishop of Lincoln's charge to the clergy of his diocese, in his primary visitation, begun at Lincoln May the 20th, 1706. London: for Richard Sare, 1707. 4°

T.190

4361

WAKE (William) *Archbishop of Canterbury.*

A sermon preach'd in the parish church of St. James Westminster, on Sunday the 29th of September, 1706. By... William Lord Bishop of Lincoln, at his taking his leave of the said parish. London, W.B. for Richard Sare, 1707.   8°

T.519

4362

WELLS (Edward)

The invalidity of presbyterian ordination proved from the presbyterians own doctrine of the twofold order: or a summary view of what has passed in controversy between Dr Wells and Mr Peirce concerning the invalidity of presbyterian ordination. Oxford, printed at the Theater for Jo. Stephens, and are to be sold by James Knapton, 1707.   8°

T.322

4363

WELLS (Edward)

Some animadversions on Mr. Barker's answer to Dr. Wells's letter to a dissenting parishioner. Oxford: Leon. Lichfield, for John Stephens: and are to be sold by James Knapton, 1707.   8°

T.322

4364

WELLS (Edward)

Dr. Wells's theses against the validity of presbyterian ordination proved to hold good. And Mr. Peirce's theses for the validity of presbyterian ordination proved not to hold good. Oxford, Leon. Lichfield, for John Stephens: and are to be sold by J. Knapton, 1707. 4 vols.   8°

T.322

4365

WHITBY (Daniel)

Reflections on some assertions and opinions of Mr. Dodwell, contain'd in a book, entituled, An epistolary discourse ... To which is added, An answer to a pamphlet, entituled, Some passages on Dr. Whitby's paraphrase, and annotations on the New Testament ... London: H. Clark, for Awnsham and John Churchill, 1707. 2 parts.   8°

T.338

4366

WHO wou'd have thought it? A collection of some remarkable passages out of a late pamphlet [by Daniel Defoe], entituled, The dissenters vindicated, or, A short view of the present state of the protestant religion in Britain... in answer to some reflections in Mr. Webster's two books publish'd in Scotland. London: for John Morphew, 1707. 4°

2 copies.

T.142 T.194

4367

WILLIAMS (Daniel) *D.D.*

A thanksgiving-sermon, occasioned by the union of England and Scotland, preach'd at Hand-Alley, May the 1st, 1707. London, J. Humfreys, [1707]. 8°

T.519

4368

The WISDOM of Solomon explain'd; from several discourses upon some of his selected proverbs: by way of dialogue ... Numb. I. London: for R. Sare, and sold by John Morphew, 1707.   4°

T.137

1708

4369

An ACCOUNT of charity-schools lately erected in those parts of Great Britain called, England and Wales: with the benefactions thereto... The seventh edition, with large additions. London, Joseph Downing, 1708.   4°

2 copies.

T.273 T.702

4370

ADAMS (Rice)

The excellency, wisdom, and usefulness of an upright and sincere conversation, recommended in a sermon preach'd in the cathedral church of Sarum, at the triennial visitation there, on April the 20th, 1708 ... London: H.Hills, 1708.   8°

T.71

4371

AGATE (John)

The plain truth: or, An answer to Mr. Withers's defence, wherein the Jesuitism and Donatism of the dissenters is laid open ... The third and last part ... Exon: Sam. Farley, and sold by the booksellers in Exon, 1708.   8°

T.230

4372

ALDENARDUM carmen Duci Malburiensi, datum, donatum, dedicatumque anno salutis humanae, 1708 ... Londini: impensis H. Clements, [1708].   8°

T.350

4373

APOTHEOSIS basilike: or, A Pindarick ode, upon the pious and blessed transit of... James the II. King of Great Britain. Who departed this life upon the fifth of Sept. S.N. at St. Germains, A.D. 1701. Written at the court of St. Germains in the same year, 1701. And printed in this present year, 1708. 4°

T.660

4374

ARENDS (Wilhelm Erasmus)

Early piety recommended in the life and death of Christlieb Leberecht von-Exter... Written soon after his decease... And recommended by Augustus Hermannus Franck... Render'd from the High-Dutch into English. London, J. Downing, [1708?] 12°

T.444

4375

ATTERBURY (Francis) *Bishop of Rochester.*

An acquaintance with God the best support under afflictions. A sermon preach'd before the Queen at St. James's, October 31. 1708. London: J.B. for Jonah Bowyer, 1708.   4°

T.71

4376

ATTERBURY (Francis) *Bishop of Rochester.*

An acquaintance with God the best support under afflictions. A sermon preach'd before the Queen at St. James's, October 31. 1708 ... London: H. Hills, 1708.   8°

T.491

4377

ATTERBURY (Francis) *Bishop of Rochester.*

Some proceedings in the Convocation, A.D. 1705. faithfully represented. To which is prefix'd, An account of the several ineffectual attempts at divers times made by the lower clergy, towards quieting all disputes, and proceeding upon synodical business. [Anon.] London: for Jonah Bowyer, 1708.   4°

Appended is a list of books on the Convocation question published 1697-1708.
3 copies.

T.74 T.78 T.133

4378

BISSE (Philip) *Bishop of Hereford.*

A sermon preach'd at the anniversary meeting of the Sons of the clergy; in the cathedral church of St. Paul, on Thursday December 2d ... London, for Jonah Bowyer, 1708.   4°

T.198

4379

BISSE (Thomas)

A defence of episcopacy. A sermon preach'd before the University of Oxford, at St. Mary's on Trinity-Sunday 1708. Oxford, printed at the Theater for Jo. Stephens, and are to be sold by James Knapton, 1708.   4°

2 copies.

T.71

4380

BLACKALL (Offspring) *Bishop of Exeter.*

The subjects duty. A sermon preach'd at the parish-church of St. Dunstan in the West, on Thursday, March the 8th 1704/5 ... 2nd ed. London: H. Hills, 1708.   8°

T.491

4381

BOILEAU DESPREAUX (Nicolas)

Boileau's Lutrin: a mock-heroic poem. In six canto's. Render'd into English verse [by John Ozell]. To which is prefix'd some account of Boileau's writings, and this translation. By N. Rowe ... London: for E. Sanger and E. Curll, 1708.   8°

T.58

4382

BRADFORD (Samuel) *Bishop of Rochester.*

A sermon preach'd in Lambeth chapel, at the consecration of the right reverend fathers in God Offspring, Lord Bishop of Exeter, and Charles, Lord Bishop of Norwich, on Saturday Feb. 8. 1707/8. London, for R. Burrough, and J. Baker, 1708.   8°

T.36

4383

BRADY (Nicholas)

The antiquity and usefulness of episcopal confirmation: a sermon preach'd at Richmond, in Surry: on Sunday, the 11th day of April, 1708. at a confirmation administred by ... Jonathan, Lord Bishop of Winchester. London: for John Chantry, 1708.   4°

T.273

4384

BROKESBY (Francis)

Some proposals towards promoting the propagation of the Gospel in our American plantations. Humbly offered in a letter to Mr. Nelson ... To which is added a postscript. [Anon.] London: for G. Sawbridge: and sold by B. Bragg, 1708. 4°

2 copies.

T.137   T.9

4385

BULKELEY (Sir Richard)

An answer to several treatises lately publish'd on the subject of the prophets. The first part ... London; for B. Bragg, and are to be sold by most booksellers in London and Westminster, 1708.   8°

T.382

4386

BURNET (Gilbert) *Bishop of Salisbury.*

The Bishop of Salisbury's speech to the House of Lords. London: for N. Saunders, 1708.   brs.

T.2

4387

C. (J.)

Lettre à un gentilhomme allemand, touchant le genie & la force de la langue angloise. [French and English.] [London, Joseph Downing, 1708.] 4°

Wanting title-page (?)

T.12

4388

The CASE of John Palmer and Thomas Symonds, gentlemen, executed near Worcester on the 7th of May 1708... With the letter of the said two gentlemen to the Lord Bishop of Oxon, asserting their innocence... [London], for B. Bragge, 1708. 4°

2 copies.

T.77 T.194

4389

CHURCH OF ENGLAND.

A form of prayer and thanksgiving, to be used on Thursday the seventeenth day of February ... for rendring most hearty thanks to Almighty God, for protecting her Majesty this year from many great attempts and treacherous designs of her enemies ... London, Charles Bill, and the executrix of Thomas Newcomb, 1708. 4°

T.461

4390

CHURCH OF ENGLAND.

A form of prayer and thanksgiving, to be used on Thursday the nineteenth day of August ... for rendring most hearty thanks to Almighty God, for the happy success of her Majesties councils and forces ... As also for the late great victory obtain'd over the French army near Audenarde ... London, Charles Bill, and the executrix of Thomas Newcomb, 1708. 4°

T.461

4391

CHURCH OF ENGLAND.

A form of thanksgiving, to be used throughout the cities of London and Westminster ... on Sunday the eighteenth day of this instant April; and in all other places ... on Sunday the ninth day of May ... London, Charles Bill, and the executrix of Thomas Newcomb, 1708. 4°

4 copies.

T.461

4392

CLARKE (Samuel) *Rector of St. James's, Westminster.*

A defense of an argument made use of in a letter to Mr Dodwel, to prove the immateriality and natural immortality of the soul. [Anon.] 2nd ed. London, W.B. for James Knapton, 1708. 8°

T.301

4393

CLARKE (Samuel) *Rector of St. James's, Westminster.*

A third defense of an argument made use of in a letter to Mr Dodwel, to prove the immateriality and natural immortality of the soul. In a letter to the author [i.e. Anthony Collins] of the Reflexions on Mr Clarke's Second defense, &c ... [Anon.] London, W.B. for James Knapton, 1708. 8°

T.151

4394

CLARKE (Samuel) *Rector of St. James's, Westminster.*

A fourth defense of an argument made use of in a letter to Mr Dodwel, to prove the immateriality and natural immortality of the soul. In a letter to the author [i.e. Anthony Collins] of the Answer to Mr Clark's Third defense, &c ... [Anon.] London, W.B. for James Knapton, 1708. 8°

T.151

4395

CLARKE (William) *Dissenting Minister.*

The sheep in his own cloathing: or, Mr. William Clark's narrative of the High-Church treatment of himself and the dissenters in Lambeth. London, printed for the author, and sold by most booksellers, 1708. 4°

T.267

4396

COLLINS (Anthony)

An answer to Mr. Clark's Third Defence of his letter to Mr. Dodwell ... [Anon.] London, for A. Baldwin, 1708. 8°

T.151

4397

COOPER (Anthony Ashley) *3rd Earl of Shaftesbury.*

A letter concerning enthusiasm, to my Lord *****. [Anon.] London, for J. Morphew, 1708. 8°

2 copies.

T.102 T.153

4398

DANGEROUS positions: or, Blasphemous, profane, immoral, and Jesuitical assertions, faithfully discovered by way of information to the Christian magistrate; as they are industriously dispers'd throughout the nation in a late book [by Matthew Tindal] falsly entitled, The rights of the Christian Church asserted ... 2nd ed ... London: for W. Hawes, 1708. 8°

T.153

4399

DEFOE (Daniel)

Advice to the electors of Great Britain; occasioned by the intended invasion from France. [Anon.] London: printed in the year 1708. 4°

Moore 156.

T.267

4400

DEFOE (Daniel)

The true-born Englishman. A satyr. [Anon.] London, printed in the year, 1708. 4°

Moore 28.

T.689

4401

DENT (Giles)

A sermon occasion'd by the death of ... Prince George of Denmark, preach'd at Westminster, November the 7th, 1708. London, J. Humfreys, for John Lawrence, 1708. 8°

T.82

4402

A DIALOGUE between Adam and John, two citizens of Bristol, about electing of Parliament-men. London: for J. Morphew, 1708. 4°

T.267

4403

A DIALOGUE between Jest, an East-India stock-jobber, and Earnest, an honest merchant. London: printed in the year, 1708. 12°

T.455

4404

The DISSENTING laity pleading their own cause against the clamours & calumnies of the highflying clergy... Occasioned by some late invective pamphlets writ against them, by Dr. Wells, Mr. Jago of Looe, Mr. Agate... and others of the highflying class... By a country Roger, in his socks and buskins... London, for Joseph Marshall, 1708. 4°

T.14

4405

DODWELL (Henry)

The Scripture account of the eternal rewards or punishments of all that hear of the Gospel, without an immortality necessarily resulting from the nature of the souls themselves... London, for George Straughan, 1708. 8°

T.156

4406

DONNEAU DE VISE (Jean)

The history of the siege of Toulon ... Written in French by Monsieur Devize ... Done into English, from the Paris edition ... By Mr. A. Boyer. London: for Arthur Collins; and J. Morphew, 1708. 2 parts. 4°

T.194

4407

DUBOURDIEU (Jean Armand)

L'épée de Gedeon soutenue par l'épée de l'eternel; ou sermon d'action de graces, a l'occasion de la glorieuse victoire remportée sur les François prés d'Oudenarde ... A Londres, Antoine Meure, 1708. 8°

T.82

4408

DUNTON (John)

The hazard of a death-bed-repentance, fairly argued, from the late remorse of W—— late D—— of D—— with serious reflections on his adulterous life ... Publish'd by way of answer to Dr. K[ennet]'s sermon, preach'd at the funeral of W[illiam] late D[uke] of D[evonshire] ... [Anon.] London: printed in the year 1708. 8°

2 copies.

T.520 T.34

4409

DUNTON (John)

The hazard of a death-bed-repentance, further argued, from the late remorse of W[illiam] late D[uke] of D[evonshire] with serious reflections on his adulterous life. Being a second answer to Dr. K[ennet]'s sermon preach'd at the D[uke]'s funeral ... [Anon.] London: R. Tookey, and are to be sold by John Morphew, 1708. 8°

T.520

4410

EYRE (Robert)

A sermon preach'd before the honourable House of Commons, at St. Margaret Westminster, on Friday, Jan. 30. 1707/8... London, J.B. for Benj. Walford, 1708. 8°

2 copies.

T.519 T.622

4411

A FARTHER instruction for those who have learnt the Church catechism. Wherein, by an explanation of the festivals and fasts of the Church of England, Christians are reminded and fix'd in the profession of the articles of the Apostles creed ... London, Joseph Downing, 1708. 12°

T.444

4412

FLEETWOOD (William) *Bishop of Ely.*

A sermon preach'd before the Queen at St. Paul's, August the 19th. 1708. The day of thanksgiving ... for the victory obtain'd near Audenard. By William Lord Bishop of St. Asaph. London: T.H. for Charles Harper, 1708. 8°

2 copies.

T.491 T.36

4413

The FLIGHT of the Pretender, with advice to the poets. A poem, in the Arthurical,-Jobical,-Elizabethecal style and phrase of the sublime poet Maurus ... [Attributed to Sir Richard Blackmore.] London, for Bernard Lintot, [1708]. 8°

T.344

4414

GILDON (Charles)

Threnodia virginea: or the apotheosis. A poem occasion'd by the much lamented death of Mrs. Hester Buckworth, only daughter of Sir John Buckworth, Kt. and Bar. [The preface signed C.G.] London: H. Hills, 1708. 8°

T.89

4415

The GLORIOUS life and actions of St. Whigg: wherein is contain'd an account of his country, parentage, birth, kindred, education, marriage, children, &c... Faithfully done from original writ, by a fryar at Geneva, and printed by a Jesuit at Edinburgh. London: printed in the year, 1708. 8°

T.89

4416

HILL (Samuel)

A thorough examination of the false principles and fallacious arguments, advanc'd against the Christian Church, priest-hood, and religion: in a late pernicious book [by Matthew Tindal], ironically intituled, The rights of the Christian Church asserted ... London: for W. Taylor, 1708. 8°

T.110

4417

HOADLY (John) *Archbishop of Armagh.*

The abasement of pride: a sermon preach'd in the cathedral of Salisbury, at the assizes held for the county of Wilts, July 18th. 1708. Upon occasion of the late victory... London: for Tim. Childe, 1708. 8°

T.491

4418

JONES (Samuel) *Rector of St. John's, Norwich.*

A sermon preached at the arch-deacons visitation. Held at St. Michaels at Plea, in the city of Norwich, Octob. 11. 1708. Norwich: the administrator of E. Burges, for Fr. Oliver, 1708. 4°

T.753

4419

KENNET (White) *Bishop of Peterborough.*

Memoirs of the family of Cavendish. London: H. Hills, 1708. 8°

T.522

4420

KING (William) *Student of Christ Church.*

The art of cookery: a poem. In imitation of Horace's Art of poetry. By the author of a Tale of a tub. London: printed, and are to be sold by the booksellers of London and Westminster, 1708. 8°

T.89

4421

KNAGGS (Thomas)

A sermon against self-murder. Preach'd at St. Giles's Church in the Fields... September 19, 1708... London: J. Bradford, [1708?] 8°

T.491

4422

KNAGGS (Thomas)

A sermon preach'd at St. Margarets, Westminster, August the 19th. 1708. Being the thanksgiving day for the late great victory obtain'd... near Audenarde... London, for C. King, 1708. 8°

T.491

4423

KNOX (Thomas)

Some thoughts humbly offer'd towards an union between Great-Britain and Ireland. [Anon.] London: for John Morphew, 1708. 4°

T.194

4424

LAMBERT (Ralph) *Bishop of Meath.*

A sermon preach'd to the protestants of Ireland, now residing in London: at their anniversary meeting on October XXIII. 1708 ... London: for Tim. Goodwin, 1708. 4°

T.71

4425

LESLIE (Charles)

Mr. Leslie's answer to the Remarks [by Thomas Emlyn] on his first dialogue against the Socinians. [London, 1708.] 4°

2 copies.

T.1   T.14

4426

LESLIE (Charles)

A letter from a gentleman in Scotland to his friend in England, against the sacramental test; as inconsistent with the union ... [Anon.] London: Benj. Bragg, 1708. 4°

Incomplete.

T.266

4427

LESLIE (Charles)

A letter from a gentleman in the City to his friends in the country, concerning the threaten'd prosecution of the Rehearsal, put into the news-papers. [Anon.] [No imprint, 1708.] 4°

2 copies.

T.194 T.267

4428

LESLIE (Charles)

A reply to the Vindication of the Remarks [by Thomas Emlyn] upon Mr. Leslie's first dialogue on the Socinian controversy. By the author of the dialogues. London, for Geo. Strahan, 1708. 4°

T.14

4429

LESLIE (Charles)

The Socinian controversy discuss'd: wherein the chief of the Socinian tracts (publish'd of late years here) are consider'd. London, for G. Strahan, 1708. 6 parts. 4°

2 copies of each part.

The general title-page and prelims. are bound in T.14

T.1 T.9 T.78

4430

A LETTER to a friend. Occasion'd by the presentment of the grand jury for the county of Middlesex, of the author, printer, and publisher, of a book, entitul'd, The rights of the Christian Church asserted [by Matthew Tindal] ... London, printed in the year 1708: and sold by the booksellers. 4°

T.191

4431

LITTELL (Thomas)

The clergyman's remembrancer. A sermon preach'd at a visitation held at Boston in Lincoln-shire; April 23. 1708 ... London: for Jonah Bowyer, 1708. 4°

T.71

4432

LUCAS (Richard)

The influence of conversation, with the regulation thereof; being a sermon preach'd at Saint Clement Dane. To a religious society... London: H. Hills, 1708. 8°

T.491

4433

LUPTON (William)

The eternity of future punishment proved and vindicated. In a sermon preach'd before the University of Oxford, at St. Mary's, Novemb. 24th. 1706. Oxford, printed at the Theatre for John Wilmot, and are to be sold by James Knapton, London, 1708. 8°

"Dr Hicks."

3 copies.

T.36 T.491 T.804

4434

M.(A.)

An account of a dream at Harwich. In a letter to a member of Parliament about the Camisars ... London, for B. Bragg, 1708. 8°

2 copies.

T.44 T.89

4435

MANNINGHAM (Thomas) *Bishop of Chichester.*

A sermon preach'd before the Queen at Windsor, July the 11th, 1708. Being the first Sunday after the account of the late great victory... near Audenarde... London: for T. Prince, [1708?] 8°

T.491

4436

MANNINGHAM (Thomas) *Bishop of Chichester.*

A sermon preach'd before the Queen at Windsor, September the 12th, 1708. London: J.B. for Benj. Walford, 1708. 8°

T.491

4437

MILNER (William)

A sermon at the consecration of... William Lord Bishop of Chester. Preach'd in K. Henry VII's chappel in Westminster, upon Sunday, February 8. 1707/8... 2nd ed. London: J.R. for Thomas Speed, 1708. 8°

T.622

4438

MILNER (William)

A sermon at the consecration of... William Lord Bishop of Chester. Preach'd in K. Henry VII's chappel in Westminster, upon Sunday, February 8. 1707/8... 3rd ed. London: H.H., 1708. 8°

T.491

4439

MOSS (Robert) *Dean of Ely.*

The providential division of men into rich and poor, and the respective duties thence arising, briefly consider'd in a sermon preach'd... at the anniversary meeting of the chief promoters of the charity-schools ... London: for Richard Sare; and Jacob Tonson, 1708. 4°

2 copies.
Another copy, in 8°

T.273 T.622 T.702

4440

MOSS (Robert) *Dean of Ely.*

A sermon preach'd at the parish-church of St. Laurence-Jewry, London. October 5, 1708. London: for Richard Sare; and Jacob Tonson, 1708. 8°

2 copies.

T.491 T.622

4441

MULLINER (John)

A testimony against perriwigs and perriwig-making, and playing on instruments of musick among Christians, or any other in the days of the Gospel... Printed in the year 1677, and re-printed in the year 1708. 4°

T.9

4442

NARBOUEL (   )

The tryal and conviction of the French committee, appointed for the management of the national charity to the poor French refugees, but fully proved guilty of mal-administration... Written originally in French by Monsieur Narbouel... and now done into English... Lonodn [sic], printed in the year 1708. 8°

T.444

4443

NELSON (Henry)

Charity and unity. In a sermon preach'd at the Hertford school-feast, August 19. 1707. London, for G. Strahan, 1708. 4°

2 copies.

T.273 T.78

4444

The OBSERVATOR'S new trip to Scotland; being an exact description of the country, and a true character of the people and their manners. Written from thence by an English gentleman. [No imprint, 1708.] 4°

T.11

4445

PARTRIDGE (John)

Mr. Partridge's answer to Esquire Bickerstaff's strange and wonderful predictions for the year 1708 ... London: E. Beer, 1708. 8°

Teerinck 1022.

T.44

4446

PHILIPS (John) *Poet.*

Cyder. A poem. In two books ... With the Splendid shilling. Paradise lost, and two songs, &c. [Anon.] London: H. Hills, 1708. 8°

T.89

4447

PITTIS (William)

A funeral poem sacred to the immortal memory of the deceas'd Sir Cloudesly Shovel, Kt. Rear Admiral of Great Britain ... London: Henry Hills, 1708. 8°

T.82

4448

PITTS (John)

A defence of the animadversions on Mr. Chishull's charge of heresie, against Mr. Dodwell's Epistolary discourse. Being a reply to a late tract, intituled, Some testimonies of Justin Martyr set in a true and clear light... London: for G. Sawbridge, and sold by J. Morphew, 1708. 8°

T.151

4449

PITTS (Joseph)

'Η χαρις δοθεισα. II. Tim. I.9. That is, The holy spirit the author of immortality... Proved from the holy Scriptures, and Fathers against Mr. [Samuel] Clark's bold assertion of the soul's natural immortality... Being a vindication of Mr. Dodwell's Epistolary discourse from all the aspersions of the foresaid pretended answerer... By a presbyter of the Church of England...London, for George Sawbridge, and sold by Thomas Bickerton 1708. 2 parts. 8°

Wanting the title-page.

T.338

4450

PITTS (Joseph)

Immortality preternatural to human souls; the gift of Jesus Christ, collated by the Holy Spirit in baptism ... By a presbyter of the Church of England ... London, for George Sawbridge, 1708. 8°

T.338

4451

The PLAIN man's guide to the true Church. Or, An exposition of the ninth article of the Apostles creed. Viz. The holy Catholick Church, the communion of saints... London: B. Motte, for R. Clavel, 1708. 8°

T.444

4452

PRAISE out of the mouth of babes: or, a particular account of some extraordinary pious motions and devout exercises, observ'd of late in many children in Silesia ... London, J. Downing, 1708. 12°

T.383

4453
PRICE (Robert) *Justice of the Common Pleas.*

The speech of an ancient Britain in Parliament, against an exorbitant grant. Together with four more speeches, spoke in the Treasury ... London: Mary Edwards, 1708. 8°

T.147

4454
REMARKS upon the Letter to a lord, concerning enthusiasm [by the Earl of Shaftesbury]. In a letter to a gentleman... London, W.D. for John Wyat, 1708. 8°

2 copies.

T.102   T.153

4455
The RIVAL dutchess: or, Court incendiary. In a dialogue between Madam Maintenon, and Madam M[asham]. London: printed in the year 1708. 8°

T.89

4456
ROGERS (William)

Quakers a divided people distinguished. George Whitehead ... is now discovered to be a hypocrite, and a deceiver ... Also an account of the modern English prophets and prophetesses ... (Quakers (a divided people) distinguished. The second part. 2nd ed.) London: J. Morphew, 1708. 2 parts. 4°

T.9

4457
SACHEVERELL (Henry)

The nature, guilt, and danger of presumptuous sins, set forth, in a sermon, preach'd before the University of Oxford, at St. Mary's, Septemb. 14th. 1707. Oxford: for John Stephens: and are to be sold by James Knapton, London, 1708. 8°

T.519

4458
SALLUSTIUS CRISPUS (Caius)

The speech of Caius Memmius, tribune, to the people of Rome. Translated from Sallust. Amsterdam: printed in the year 1656 [i.e. London, 1708?] 4°

Incorrectly included by Wing as S 410.

T.194

4459
SCANDAL display'd: or, A word in season. Being an answer to a paper [by Daniel Defoe], entituled, Advice to the electors of Great Britain; occasion'd by the intended invasion from France. London, printed for and sold by B. Bragge, [1708]. 4°

T.194

4460
SCOTT (John) *Vicar of Carisbrooke.*

Of spiritual rule. A sermon preach'd at the primary visitation of ... Jonathan Lord Bishop of Winton, August 26. 1708 ... London, for George Strahan, and to be sold by John Morphew, 1708. 4°

2 copies.

T.753   T.273

4461
SCUDERY (Madeleine de)

An essay upon glory. Written originally in French by the celebrated Mademoiselle de Scudery. Done into English by a person of the same sex ... London, for J. Morphew, 1708. 2 parts. 8°

T.148

4462
SMALRIDGE (George) *Bishop of Bristol.*

A sermon preach'd before ... the lord mayor ... and governours of the several hospitals of the city of London, in Christ's-church, on Wednesday in Easter week April 6, 1708. London: J.B. for Jonah Bowyer, 1708. 4°

T.71

4463
SOME testimonies of Justin Martyr, set in a true and clear light: as they relate to Mr. Dodwel's unhappy question, concerning the immortality of the soul. Being a just reproof to a late illiterate animadverter on Mr. Chishull, in his pretended answer to Mr. Clark. London: for Sam. Manship, and James Round, 1708. 8°

T.151

4464
SOUTH (Robert)

A sermon preach'd on the anniversary-fast for the martyrdom of King Charles I. at court in the last century ... [Anon.] London, J. Morphew, [1708]. 8°

2 copies.

T.519   T.82

4465
SQUIRE Bickerstaff detected; or, The astrological imposter convicted, by John Partridge, student in physick and astrology. Part I. [Supposed to have been written by Thomas Yalden, and others.] [No imprint, 1708?] 8°

Teerinck 1025.
2 copies.

T.29 T.44

4466
STANHOPE (Michael)

God the author of victory. A sermon preach'd in the royal-chappel at White-hall, on Thursday the 19th of August, 1708 ... London: for W. Taylor, 1708. 8°

2 copies.

T.491   T.82

4467
STILSMAN (John)

Episcopal authority, with the duty both of clergy and laity, consider'd; in a sermon preached at Leicester October 2. 1707. at the visitation of the ... Arch-deacon of Leicester ... London: for W. Taylor. J. Ward, in Leicester. And C. Ratten, in Harborough, 1708. 4°

2 copies.

T.198

4468
STURMY (Daniel)

A sermon preach'd, &c. October the 31st. 1708. on the death of his Royal Highness the Prince. London, for Dan. Midwinter, 1708. 8°

T.622

4469
SWIFT (Jonathan) *Dean of St. Patrick's.*

Predictions for the year 1708... Written to prevent the people of England from being further impos'd on by vulgar almanack-makers. By Isaac Bickerstaff. Sold by John Morphew, 1708. 8°

Teerinck 483.
2 copies.

T.44   T.89

4470
SWIFT (Jonathan) *Dean of St. Patrick's.*

Squire Bickerstaff's strange and wonderful predictions for the year 1708... Written by Isaac Bickerstaff... London: for J. Morphew, 1708. 8°

T.490

4471
SYMSON (Matthias)

The necessity of a lawful ministry: a sermon preached at Horncastle in Lincolnshire. At the visitation of the reverend the Archdeacon of Lincoln... London, for George Strahan, 1708. 4°

2 copies.

T.72   T.752

4472
TALBOT (James) *Rector of Spofforth.*

The judicial power of the Church asserted. A sermon preached at the visitation at Tadcaster in the archdeaconry of York. May 14. 1707 ... London, for Henry Clements, 1708. 4°

T.198

4473
THWAITES (Edward)

Notae in Anglo-Saxonum nummos. [Anon.] Oxoniae, anno Domini 1708. 8°

T.148

4474
TINDAL (Matthew)

A second defence of The rights of the Christian Church, occasion'd by two late indictments against a bookseller and his servant, for selling one of the said books. In a letter from a gentleman in London to a clergyman in the country ... London, printed in the year 1708. 8°

T.102

4475
TRAPP (Joseph)

The practice of confounding the distinction between good and evil consider'd, and expos'd. In a sermon preached at St. Mary's in Oxford ... at the assizes held there, Mar. 4. 1707/8 ... Oxford: for John Stephens: and are to be sold by J. Knapton, 1708. 8°

T.36

4476
TRIMNELL (Charles) *Bishop of Winchester.*

Partiality detected: or, A reply to a late pamphlet [by Francis Atterbury], entituled, Some proceedings in the Convocation, A.D. 1705. faithfully represented... [Anon.] London: for A. and J. Churchill, 1708. 4°

T.133

4477
TRIMNELL (Charles) *Bishop of Winchester.*

A sermon preach'd at the cathedral church of St. Paul; before the Sons of the clergy, on Tuesday the 2d of December, 1707... London: for T. Chapman, and D. Midwinter, 1708. 8°

T.622

4478
TRIMNELL (Charles) *Bishop of Winchester.*

A sermon preach'd before the honourable House of Commons, at the church of St. Margaret Westminster, on Wednesday, Jan. 14. 1707/8. Being the day appointed by her Majesty for a general fast... London: for Tho. Chapman, and Daniel Midwinter, 1708. 8°

T.519

4479
The TRUE characters of, viz. A deceitful petty-fogger, vulgarly call'd attorney. A know-all astrological quack, or, feigned physician ... London: J. Jones, 1708. 8°

T.350

4480
WAKE (William) *Archbishop of Canterbury.*

The principles of the Christian religion explained: in a brief commentary upon the Church-catechism. By ... William, Lord Bishop of Lincoln. The third edition corrected ... London: for Richard Sare, 1708. 8°

T.349

4481
WAKE (William) *Archbishop of Canterbury.*

A sermon preach'd before the House of Lords, at the abbey-church in Westminster, on Friday, Jan. XXX. MDCCVII. By ... William Lord Bishop of Lincoln. London: W.B. for Richard Sare, 1708. 8°

3 copies.

T.519   T.82

4482
WALLER (John)

Religion and loyalty, or the reverence due both to Church and state, asserted in a sermon, preach'd at the parish-church of Bishop-Stortford... at the anniversary solemnity of the school-feast. Cambridge: printed at the University-Press, for Edmund Jeffery; and are to be sold by James Knapton, London, 1708. 4°

T.625

4483
WARD (Edward)

Honesty in distress; but reliev'd by no party. A tragedy: as it is acted on the stage, &c ... [Anon.] London, J. Morphew, 1708. 8°

T.89

4484
WARD (Edward)

Marriage-dialogues: or, A poetical peep into the state of matrimony... [Anon.] London: printed in the year 1708. 4°

T.689

4485

WELLS (Edward)

Dr. Wells's answer to Mr. Peirce's postscript at the end of his considerations of the sixth chapter of the abridgment of the London cases ... Oxford: Leon. Lichfield, for John Stephens: and are to be sold by James Knapton, 1708.   8°

T.322

4486

WHITFELD (William)

The kingdom of Jesus Christ: in answer to some points treated of, in the Rights of the Christian Church [by Matthew Tindal]. In a sermon preach'd before... Jonathan, Lord Bishop of Winchester, at his primary visitation at Guildford, July 5. 1708... London: for Jonah Bowyer, 1708.   4°

3 copies; a fourth copy in 8°

T.36   T.198   T.273   T.752

4487

WILKINSON (Robert) *Pastor of St. Olave's, Southwark.*

The royal merchant. A sermon preach'd at White-hall, before the King's Majesty, at the nuptials of an honourable lord and his lady... 2nd ed. London: H. Hills, 1708.   8°

T.82

4488

WOOD (Thomas)

Some thoughts concerning the study of the laws of England in the two universities. In a letter to the Reverend ——— Head of ——— College in Oxford. [Anon.] London: printed for and sold by J. Morphew, 1708.   4°

T.77

1709

4489

An ACCOUNT of charity-schools lately erected in Great Britain and Ireland: with the benefactions thereto... The eighth edition, with large additions. London: Joseph Downing, 1709.   4°

T.701

4490

An ACCOUNT of the late Scotch invasion; as it was open'd by my Lord Haversham in the House of Lords, on Fryday the 25th of February, 1708/9 ... In a letter from a gentleman in South-Brittain to his friend in North-Brittain ... Printed in the year 1709.   4°

T.142

4491

An ACCOUNT of the late Scotch invasion; as it was open'd by my Lord Haversham in the House of Lords, on Fryday the 25th of February, 1708/9 ... In a letter from a gentleman in South-Brittain to his friend in North-Brittain ... Sold by the booksellers of London and Westminster, 1709.   8°

T.522

4492

ADAMS (John) *Provost of King's College, Cambridge.*

A sermon preach'd at the cathedral-church of St. Paul, before the ... Lord Mayor ... on Tuesday, Novemb. 22. 1709. Being the day appointed ... for a publick thanksgiving. London: for Henry Clements, 1709.   8°

T.491

4493

ADDISON (Rt. Hon. Joseph)

A letter from Italy, to the Right Honourable Charles, Lord Halifax. 1701. Together with the Mourning muse of Alexis. A pastoral. lamenting the death of our late gracious Queen Mary. By Mr. Congreve. 1695 ... London: H. Hills, 1709.   8°

T.89

4494

AESOP at Oxford: or, a few select fables in verse, under the following heads, viz. Aesop matriculated. Aesop's thanks... London: printed in the year, 1709. and sold by the booksellers.   4°

T.689

4495

ASSHETON (William)

A seasonable vindication of the clergy. (Being an answer to some reflections, in a late book [by Matthew Tindal], entituled, The rights of the Christian Church asserted, &c.) ... By a divine of the Church of England ... London: for H. Clements, 1709.   8°

T.153

4496

ATTERBURY (Francis) *Bishop of Rochester.*

Concio ad clerum Londinensem, habita, in Ecclesia S. Elphegi, Maii XVII. A.D. MDCCIX. Londini: typis J.B. impensis J. Bowyer, 1709.   4°

2 copies.

T.3   T.273

4497

ATTERBURY (Francis) *Bishop of Rochester.*

Concio ad clerum Londinensem, habita, in Ecclesia S. Elphegi, Maij XVII. A.D. MDCCIX ... Londini: typis & impensis H. Hills, 1709.   8°

T.491

4498

ATTERBURY (Francis) *Bishop of Rochester.*

A sermon preach'd before ... the lord mayor, aldermen, and governors of the several City hospitals. At St. Brigit's, on Tuesday in Easter-week, April 26, 1709. London: for Henry Clements, 1709.   4°

"For the Reverend Dr. Hicks."

T.3

4499

ATTERBURY (Francis) *Bishop of Rochester.*

A sermon preach'd before the Sons of the clergy, at their anniversary-meeting in the church of St. Paul, Dec. 6. 1709 ... London: for Jonah Bowyer, 1709.   4°

T.3

4500

ATTERBURY (Francis) *Bishop of Rochester.*

A sermon preach'd before the Sons of the clergy, at their anniversary-meeting in the cathedral-church of St. Paul, Dec. 6. 1709. London: for Jonah Bowyer, 1709.   8°

T.491

4501

AVIS a ceux qui auroient dessein de retourner en France apres la paix. [No imprint, 1709?]   4°

T.269

4502

The BALLANCE of power: or, A comparison of the strength of the Emperor and the French King. In a letter to a friend ... London; for A. Baldwin, 1709.   8°

Teerink 1032.

T.233

4503

BALZAC (Jean Louis Guez) *Sieur de.*

The French favorites: or, The seventh discourse of Balzac's Politicks. Publish'd by the Reverend Dr. Kennet ... London, for C. King, 1709.   8°

2 copies.

T.72   T.89

4504

The BEASTS in power, or Robin's song: with an old cat's prophecy. Taken out of an old copy of verses, suppos'd to be writ by John Lidgate, a monk of Bury. London, printed in the year 1709.   8°

T.58

4505

BERKELEY (George) *Bishop of Cloyne.*

An essay towards a new theory of vision. 2nd ed. Dublin: Aaron Rhames, for Jeremy Pepyat, 1709.   8°

2 copies.

T.284   T.54

4506

BESS o' Bedlam's love to her brother Tom: with a word in behalf of poor brother Ben Hoadly. [A reply to Tom of Bedlam's answer, by Luke Milbourne.] London; for J. Baker, 1709.   8°

T.297

4507

BESS o' Bedlam's love to her brother Tom: with a word in behalf of poor brother Ben Hoadly. [A reply to Tom o' Bedlam's answer, by Luke Milbourne.] London: printed and sold by the booksellers of London and Westminster, 1709.   8°

T.102

4508

BICKERSTAFF redivivus; or, Predictions for the year 1709. With the author's defence of his last year's calculation, particularly against Mr. Partridge's assertion in an almanack for this present year; wherein 'tis averr'd, he is still alive: which is plainly prov'd to be an error. By Isaac Bickerstaff. London, printed: and sold by B. Bragge, 1709.   8°

T.44

4509

BION (Jean)

L'origine, le progres, et la fin tragique des quietistes de Bourgogne, en France. Londres, imprimé pour l'autheur, 1709.   8°

T.383

4510

BISSET (William)

Remarks on Dr. Sach[everell]'s sermon at the cathedral of St. Paul, November the 5th, being design'd as a seasonable antidote against the spreading malignity of that pestilent discourse. London, B. Bragge, 1709.   4°

T.152

4511

BLACKALL (Offspring) *Bishop of Exeter.*

The Lord Bishop of Exeter's answer to Mr. Hoadly's letter ... London: J. Leake for W. Rogers, 1709.   8°

2 copies.

T.297   T.157

4512

BLACKALL (Offspring) *Bishop of Exeter.*

The Lord Bishop of Exeter's answer to Mr. Hoadly's letter ... London: printed and sold by the booksellers of London and Westminster, 1709.   8°

T.102

4513

BLACKALL (Offspring) *Bishop of Exeter.*

The divine institution of magistracy, and the gracious design of its institution. A sermon preach'd before the Queen, at St. James's, on Tuesday, March 8. 1708 ... London: J.R. for W. Rogers, 1709.   8°

4 copies.

T.82   T.101

4514

BLACKALL (Offspring) *Bishop of Exeter.*

Of children's bearing the iniquities of their fathers. A sermon preach'd before the honourable House of Peers, in the Abbey-Church at Westminster, on Monday, January the 31st. 1708... London: J.R. for W. Rogers, 1709.   8°

T.491

4515

BLACKBURNE (Lancelot) *Archbishop of York.*

The blessedness of suffering persecution for righteousness sake. A sermon preach'd before her Majesty at St. James's chappel: on Sunday December 26. 1708. London, J. Dutten, 1709.   8°

2 copies.

T.491   T.82

4516

BOEHM (William) *and others.*

Propagation of the Gospel in the East: being an account of the success of two Danish missionaries, lately sent to the East-Indies, for the conversion of the heathens in Malabar ... [Anon.] Rendred into English from the High-Dutch ... London, J. Downing, 1709.   8°

T.29

4517

BOEHME (Anton Wilhelm)

The life of a Christian: a sermon on the occasion of the death of his Royal Higness Prince George of Denmark ... who departed this life at Kensington, October the 28th, 1708 ... Now done into English. London: Joseph Downing, 1709.   8°

T.491

1709 (Cont'd)

4518
BRADFORD (Samuel) *Bishop of Rochester.*

Unanimity and charity, the characters of Christians. A sermon preached in the parish-church of St. Sepulchre, June 16th, 1709... at the anniversary meeting of the children educated in the charity-schools, in and about the cities of London and Westminster. London: Joseph Downing, for John Wyat, 1709. 4°

T.701

4519
BRADFORD (Samuel) *Bishop of Rochester.*

Unanimity and charity, the characters of Christians. A sermon preach'd in the parish-church of St. Sepulchre, June 16th, 1709... at the anniversary meeting of the children educated in the charity-schools, in... London and Westminster. London, Joseph Downing for John Wyat, 1709. 8°

T.622

4520
BRAY (Thomas)

Fight the good fight of faith, in the cause of God against the kingdom of Satan, exemplified, in a sermon preach'd at the parish-church of St. Clements Danes, Westminster ... at the funeral of Mr. John Dent ... London, Joseph Downing, 1709. 8°

T.152

4521
BRAY (Thomas)

For God, or for Satan: being a sermon preached at St. Mary le Bow, before the Society for reformation of manners, December 27. 1708 ... London, J. Downing, 1709. 4°

2 copies.

T.702 T.198

4522
BROWN (Joseph) *Historian.*

The tryal of Thomas Duke of Norfolk by his peers, for high treason against the Queen; on Wednesday the 16th day of January... 1571... London: for J. Morphew, 1709. 8°

T.522

4523
BROWNE (Joseph)

The circus: or, British olympicks. A satyr on the ring in Hide-Park... [Anon.] London, printed: and sold by the booksellers of London and Westminster, 1709. 8°

T.89

4524
BRYDGES (Henry)

A sermon preach'd before the Queen, at St. James's Chappel, on Monday, January 31. 1708/9... London: G.J. for Jonah Bowyer, 1709. 4°

Two other copies, in 8°

T.3 T.491 T.622

4525
BURGESS (Daniel)

A sermon preach'd at the wedding of John Smith, Esq: in New Court, Little Lincolns-Inn-Fields, on Wednesday, September 28, 1709 ... London: for J. Andrews, 1709. 8°

T.36

4526
CANARY-birds naturaliz'd in utopia. A canto ... London printed: and sold by the booksellers, [1709]. 30pp. 8°

"Ex libris Ed. Gayer 1710."

T.204

4527
CANARY-birds naturaliz'd in utopia. A canto... London: printed and sold by the booksellers of London and Westminster, 1709. 16pp. 8°

T.89

4528
CARROLL (William)

Spinoza reviv'd: or, A treatise, proving the book [by Matthew Tindal], entitled, The rights of the Christian Church, &c ... to be the same with Spinoza's Rights of the Christian clergy ... [Anon.] London, J. Morphew, 1709. 8°

Pages 1-64 only.

T.226

4529
CAVENDISH (William) *1st Duke of Devonshire.*

The charms of liberty: a poem. By the late Duke of D[evonshire]. To which is added, epigrams, poems and satyrs. Written by several hands. London: printed in the year, 1709. 8°

T.204

4530
CHANDLER (Henry)

An effort against bigotry, and for Christian Catholicism. The second edition, corrected ... London: for John Lawrence, 1709. 4°

T.190

4531
CHARITY and peace: or, A reconciliatory letter to a friend; who had been, for some considerable time, at variance with his parochial minister ... Exon: Sam. Farley, for Philip Bishop, 1709. 12°

T.459

4532
The CHERUBIM with a flaming sword, that appear'd on the fifth of November last ... Being a letter to my Lord M[ayor], with remarks upon Dr. Sa[cheverel]l's sermon ... London, printed in the year 1709. 8°

T.147

4533
CHURCH OF ENGLAND.

September 5. 1709. A form of prayer and thanksgiving to Almighty God; ... for the late great success vouchsafed to the forces of her Majesty and her allies, at Blaregnies in Hainault ... London, Charles Bill, and the executrix of Thomas Newcomb, 1709. 4°

T.461

4534
CHURCH OF ENGLAND.

October 3. 1709. A form of prayer and thanksgiving, to be used on Tuesday the twenty second day of November... for rendring most hearty thanks to Almighty God, for continuing to her Majesty his protection and assistance in the just and necessary war in which she is engaged... London, Charles Bill, and the executrix of Thomas Newcomb, 1709. 4°

T.461

4535
CHURCH OF ENGLAND.

Prayers to be used next after the prayer in time of war and tumults... on all Sundays, Wednesdays, and Fridays, during the present war: for imploring the continuance of God's blessing on the arms of her Majesty and her allies... London, Charles Bill, and the executrix of Thomas Newcomb, 1709. 4°

2 copies.

T.461

4536
CLARKE (Samuel) *Rector of St. James's, Westminster.*

A sermon preach'd at the parish-church of St. Mary White-chapel, on Tuesday, October 11. 1709. at the funeral of Dame Mary Cooke ... London: J.B. for James Knapton, 1709. 8°

T.152

4537
CLARKE (Samuel) *Rector of St. James's, Westminster.*

A sermon preach'd before the honourable House of Commons, at the church of St. Margaret Westminster. On Tuesday, Nov. 22. 1709. being the day of thanksgiving for the ... victory obtained near Mons ... London, W.B. for James Knapton, 1709. 8°

T.152

4538
COOPER (Anthony Ashley) *3rd Earl of Shaftesbury.*

Sensus communis: an essay on the freedom of wit and humour. In a letter to a friend ... [Anon.] London, for Egbert Sanger, 1709. 8°

T.402

4539
The COURT in mourning. Being the life and worthy actions of Ralph Duke of Montague, master of the great wardrobe to Queen Anne ... London: for J. Smith, 1709. 8°

T.29

4540
DAWES (Sir William) *Archbishop of York.*

A sermon preach'd before ... the lord-mayor, the aldermen, sheriffs, and governors of the several hospitals of the city of London, in St. Bridget's church ... April 25. 1709. By ... William Lord Bishop of Chester ... London: for Anne Speed, 1709. 8°

T.152

4541
DAWES (Sir William) *Archbishop of York.*

A sermon preach'd before the Society for the Propagation of the Gospel in Foreign Parts, at St. Mary-le-Bow, on Friday, February 18. 1708/9. By... William Lord Bishop of Chester. London: for Anne Speed, 1709. 8°

3 copies.

T.82 T.491 T.622

4542
The DREAM of the Solan goose, with advice to Robin red-breast, sent in a packet from Leith. London, printed in the year 1709. 8°

T.58

4543
The DUKE of M[arlborough's] catechism. London: printed in the year, 1709. 8°

2 copies.

T.417 T.89

4544
The EAGLE and the robin. An apologue. Translated from the original of Aesop, written two thousand years since, and now rendred into familiar verse. By H.G. L.Mag. [The preface is signed Horat. Gram.] London: J. Bradford, [1709]. 8°

T.89

4545
ENGLAND. *Parliament.*

The proceedings of the Lords and Commons in the year 1628. against Roger Manwaring ... (the Sacheverell of those days) for two seditious high-flying sermons, intitled, Region and allegiance. London, for Ben. Bragge, 1709. 8°

T.102

4546
An EXACT narrative of many surprizing matters of fact uncontestably wrought by an evil spirit or spirits, in the house of Master Jan Smagge, farmer, in Canvy-Island, near Leigh in Essex, upon the 10th, 13th, 14th, 15th and 16th of September last ... In a letter from Malden in Essex, to a gentleman in London. London, John Morphew, 1709. 8°

T.383

4547
An EXERCISE for the charity schools; explaining the nature of confirmation, by way of question and answer, with prayers suited to that solemn occasion ... London: W.B. for A. and J. Churchill, 1709. 12°

T.459

4548
An EXERCISE for the charity schools; explaining the nature of confirmation, by way of question and answer, with prayers suited to that solemn occasion. 2nd ed... London: W.B. for A. and J. Churchill, 1709. 12°

T.383

4549
EXTRACT of the process of treason, at the instance of Sir James Steuart, her Majesties advocate; and as having special warrant for that effect, against James Stirling of Keir, and others. London: printed in the year, 1709. 4°

T.77

4550
FINCH (Anne) *Countess of Winchilsea.*

The spleen, a Pindarique ode. By a lady. Together with A prospect of death: a Pindarique essay. [By John Pomfret.] ... London: H. Hills, 1709. 8°

T.89

4551

FLEETWOOD (William) *Bishop of Ely.*

A sermon preach'd before the Queen at St. James's, on Sunday, April the 17th. 1709. By William Lord Bishop of St. Asaph. London, T.H. for Charles Harper, 1709.   8°

T.152

4552

FOWLER (Edward) *Bishop of Gloucester.*

Reflections upon a Letter concerning enthusiasm, to my Lord **** [by the Earl of Shaftesbury]. In another letter to a lord ... [Anon.] London: for H. Clements, 1709.   8°

T.153

4553

The GREAT mercy of God in saving people from perishing. A sermon, preached at the camp at Camberwell, to the poor distressed Palatines, on Sunday, July 31. 1709. Translated from the High German tongue into English ... London, printed for, and sold by Benj. Bragge; and by the book-sellers of London and Westminster, 1709. 8°

T.152

4554

GREENSHIELDS (James)

A true copy of a letter from the Reverend Mr. Greenshields. From the goal of Edinburgh, where he now lies, only for reading the English liturgy there in a meeting-house. Directed to a clergy-man in the city of London. [No imprint, 1709.]   4°

T.77

4555

HANCOCK (John)

Patres vindicati: or, Some observations from the fathers, making it probable they did not think the bread and wine, in the sacrament, a true and proper sacrifice ... London: for James Round, 1709. 8°

T.395

4556

HARE (Francis) *Bishop of Chichester.*

A sermon preach'd before the honourable House of Commons, at the church of St. Margaret Westminster, on Thursday, Feb. 17. 1708/9. being the day of thanksgiving ... London: for Benj. Tooke, 1709.   4°

2 copies.

T.273 T.771

4557

HARE (Francis) *Bishop of Chichester.*

A sermon preach'd before the honourable House of Commons, at the church of St. Margaret Westminster, on Thursday, Feb. 17. 1708/9. being the day of thanksgiving... 3rd ed. enlarged. London: for Benj. Tooke, 1709.   8°

3 copies.

T.82 T.491 T.622

4558

HICKES (George)

Three short treatises, viz. I. A modest plea for the clergy, &c. [by Lancelot Addison]. II. A sermon of the sacerdotal benediction, &c. [by Samuel Gibson]. III. A discourse published to undeceive the people in point of tithes, &c. [by Peter Heylyn]. Formerly printed, and now again published by Dr. George Hickes ... against the slanderous and reproachful treatment of the clergy, in a late book ... [by Matthew Tindal], falsely intituled, The rights of the Christian Church ... London, for W. Taylor, 1709. 4 parts.   8°

Annotated by Hickes.

T.157

4559

HIGDEN (William)

A view of the English constitution, with respect to the sovereign authority of the prince, and the allegiance of the subject ... London, for Samuel Keble, 1709.   8°

2 copies.

T.398

4560

HILL (Thomas) *Fellow of Trinity College, Cambridge.*

Nundinae Sturbrigienses. Latin poem. London, 1709. 8°

Gatherings B and C only.

T.58

4561

HILLIARD (Samuel)

A narrative of the prosecution of Mr. Sare and his servant, for selling the Rights of the Christian Church [by Matthew Tindal]. In answer to what relates to that prosecution in the second part of the Defence of the said book. London: for Henry Clements, 1709.   8°

2 copies.

T.414   T.102

4562

HILLIARD (Samuel)

A sermon preach'd at the cathedral-church of St. Paul, before ... the lord-mayor and aldermen. On Sunday October the 9th, 1709.   8°   London, for Henry Clements, 1709.

2 copies.

T.491 T.152

4563

HOADLY (Benjamin) *Bishop of Winchester.*

An humble reply to the Right Reverend the Lord Bishop of Exeter's Answer. In which the considerations lately offered to his Lordship are vindicated ... London: for E. Sanger, and J. Pemberton, 1709. 8°

2 copies.

T.102 T.297

4564

HOADLY (Benjamin) *Bishop of Winchester.*

Some considerations humbly offered to the Right Reverend the lord Bishop of Exeter. Occasioned by his Lordship's sermon preached before her Majesty, March 8. 1708. London: printed and sold by the booksellers of London, and Westminster, 1709.   8°

2 copies.

T.82 T.102

4565

HOADLY (Benjamin) *Bishop of Winchester.*

Some considerations humbly offered to the Right Reverend the Lord Bishop of Exeter. Occasioned by his Lordship's sermon preached before her Majesty, March 8. 1708. London, for J. Morphew, 1709.   8°

T.101

4566

HOADLY (Benjamin) *Bishop of Winchester.*

Some considerations humbly offered to the Right Reverend the Lord Bishop of Exeter. Occasioned by his Lordship's sermon preached before her Majesty, March 8. 1708. 3rd ed. London, for J. Morphew, 1709.   8°

T.297

4567

HODGES (Abraham)

A sermon held forth at the funeral of George Wansey, head Quaker of the West, in a meeting at Warminster ... February the 6th, 1708/9. London: printed in the year, 1709.   8°

2 copies.

T.82 T.101

4568

HOLDSWORTH (Edward)

Muscipula, sive Kambromyomaxia ... Londini: impensis E. Curll; & Sanger, 1709.   8°

2 copies.

T.58   T.347

4569

HOLDSWORTH (Edward)

Muscipula: sive Cambro-muo-maxia. [Anon.] Apud Londini: anno Domini. 1709.   8°

T.204

4570

HOLDSWORTH (Edward)

The mouse-trap: or, The Welshmen's scuffle with the mice. [Translated from the Latin.] London: printed in the year, 1709.   8°

2 copies.

T.89 T.204

4571

HOUGH (John) *Bishop of Worcester.*

A sermon preach'd before the Lords... in the abbey church at Westminster, on the 22d of November, 1709. Being the thanksgiving-day. By... John Ld. Bp. of Litchfield and Coventry. London: for Egbert Sanger, 1709.   4°

T.3

4572

HOUGH (John) *Bishop of Worcester.*

A sermon preach'd before the Lords ... in the abby church at Westminster, on the 22d of November, 1709. Being the thanksgiving-day. By ... John Ld. Bp. of Litchfield and Coventry. London: for Egbert Sanger, 1709.   8°

T.152

4573

An out of the road visit to the Lord Bishop of Exeter: or, A better answer than The best answer ever was made [by Charles Leslie]. Wherein not only Mr. Hoadly is reprimanded for his rudeness to his Lordship; but also, his Lordship's seconds are unmask'd... London: for John Baker, 1709.   8°

T.297

4574

KEITH (George)

Geography and navigation compleated; being a new theory and method whereby the true longitude of any place in the world may be found ... London: for B. Aylmer, 1709.   4°

"Dr H at Mr Taylors a Laceman at the Golden Ball in ye Strand near Arundell Street"

T.12

4575

KENNET (White) *Bishop of Peterborough.*

Glory to God, and gratitude to benefactors. A sermon preach'd before the Queen ... the 22d. of Nov. 1709. The day of publick thanksgiving. For the signal and glorious victory at Blaregnies ... London: for John Churchill, 1709.   8°

2 copies.

T.491 T.152

4576

KENNET (White) *Bishop of Peterborough.*

A true answer to Dr. Sacheverell's sermon before the Lord Mayor, Nov. 5. 1709. In a letter to one of the aldermen ... [Anon.] 2nd ed. London; A. Baldwin, 1709.   8°

T.229

4577

KENNET (White) *Bishop of Peterborough.*

A vindication of the Church and clergy of England, from some late reproaches rudely and unjustly cast upon them. [Anon.] London: J. Baker, 1709.   8°

T.230

4578

KING (William) *Archbishop of Dublin.*

Divine predestination and fore-knowledg, consistent with the freedom of man's will. A sermon preach'd at Christ-Church, Dublin; May 15. 1709. before his Excellency Thomas Earl of Wharton... Printed at Dublin, and reprinted at London, for J. Baker, 1709. 8°

T.491

4579

KNAGGS (Thomas)

A thanksgiving sermon for our many deliverances, particularly the victory obtain'd near Mons ... Preach'd in the chapel at Knightsbridge, Nov. 22. 1709. London: B. Bragg, 1709.   8°

T.152

4580

KNIGHT (*Sir* John)

A speech spoke by Sir J. K--t, in the House of Commons, against the Bill for naturalizing foreigners. [No imprint, 1709?]   8°

T.522

1709 (Cont'd)

4581

LAUD (William) *Archbishop of Canterbury*.

Archbishop Laud's funeral sermon, preached by himself, from the scaffold on Tower-hill, on Friday Jan. 10. 1644... Published at this time to vindicate the memory of that... prelate, from the malicious and scandalous aspersions of those vile, paltry scribblers, who write the Review and Observator. London: for W. Hawes; and sold by J. Morphew, 1709. 8°

T.82

4582

LE CLERC (Jean)

De eligenda inter dissentientes sententia. [Extracted from GROTIUS: De veritate religionis Christianae. Amsterdam, 1709.] 8°

T.388

4583

LESLIE (Charles)

The best answer ever was made. And to which no answer ever will be made. (Not to be behind Mr. Hoadly in assurance) in answer to his bill of complaint exhibited against the Lord Bishop of Exeter, for his lordship's sermon preach'd before her Majesty, March 8. 1708... By a student of the Temple... London printed, and sold by the booksellers of London and Westminster, [1709]. 8°

3 copies.

T.102 T.169 T.297

4584

LESLIE (Charles)

The best answer ever was made. And to which no answer ever will be made. (Not to be behind Mr. Hoadly in assurance) in answer to his bill of complaint exhibited against the Lord Bishop of Exeter, for his lordship's sermon preach'd before her Majesty, March 8. 1708 ... By a student of the Temple ... London: J. Morphew, 1709. 8°

T.101

4585

LESLIE (Charles)

Best of all. Being the student's thanks to Mr. Hoadly. Wherein Mr. Hoadly's second part of his Measures of submission... is fully answer'd... In a letter to himself... [Anon.] London printed, and sold by the booksellers of London and Westminster, 1709. 8°

5 copies. (Copy T.297 has a variant title-page.)

T.101 T.102 T.297 T.663

4586

LESLIE (Charles)

The constitution, laws and government, of England, vindicated. In a letter to the Reverend Mr. William Higden... By a natural born subject... London printed, and sold by the booksellers of London and Westminster, 1709. 8°

3 copies.

T.41 T.46 T.398

4587

LESLIE (Charles)

A letter to the Reverend Mr. William Higden. On account of his View of the English constitution, with respect to the soveraign authority of the prince, &c ... By a natural born subject ... London, printed and sold by the booksellers of London and Westminster, 1709. 8°

T.398

4588

LESLIE (Charles)

A letter to the Reverend Mr. William Higden. On account of his View of the English constitution, with respect to the soveraign authority of the prince, &c... By a natural born subject... London, J. Morphew, 1709. 8°

T.46

4589

A LETTER of advice, presented to Mr. Hoadly, with abundance of that modern sort of humility, for which his own writings are remarkable. [Signed Ignotus.] London: for J. Bowyer, 1709. 8°

T.229

4590

A LETTER to a noble lord, about his dispersing abroad Mr. Hoadly's remarks upon the Bishop of Exeter's sermon before the Queen, humbly recommending to his Lordship's persual an answer to it [by Charles Leslie]; entitul'd; The best answer ever was made, &c. London, John Baker, 1709. 8°

2 copies.

T.297 T.157

4591

A LETTER to Mr. Bisset, eldest brother of the Collegiate Church of St. Catherines; in answer to his remarks on Dr. Sacheverell's sermon. [Signed Amicus.] London: for J. Baker, 1709. 8°

T.229

4592

A LETTER to the Reverend Dr. George Hickes, occasion'd by a late book [by Joseph Pitts], entitled, The character of a primitive bishop, &c. Printed in the year 1709. 8°

T.417

4593

A LETTER to the Reverend Dr. Moss, in behalf of The rights of the Christian Church [by Matthew Tindal]. Together with a poetick rhapsody. By a young Oxford-scholar. London, for B. Bragg, 1709. 8°

2 copies.

T.102 T.153

4594

The LIFE and adventures of Capt. John Avery, the famous English pirate, (rais'd from a cabbin-boy, to a king) now in possession of Madagascar ... Written by a person who made his escape from thence, and faithfully extracted from his journal. London printed, and sold by the booksellers, 1709. 16 pp. 8°

T.275

4595

The LIFE and bold adventures of Capt. John Avery, the famous English pirate (rais'd from a cabbin-boy to a king) now in possession of Madagascar... Written by a person who made his escape from thence, and faithfully extracted from his journal. London: for J. Bagnall, 1709. 8pp. 8°

T.29

4596

The LIFE and death of Charles the first, King of Great Britain, France and Ireland: containing an account of his sufferings; his tryal, sentence, and dying words... London: J. Bradford, [c. 1709?] 8°

T.522

4597

The MALL: or, The reigning beauties. Containing the various intrigues of Miss Cloudy, and her governante Madam Agility ... London: printed in the year, 1709. 8°

T.89

4598

MANNINGHAM (Thomas) *Bishop of Chichester*.

A sermon preach'd before the Queen at St. James's on Thursday the 17th of February, being appointed for a day of thanksgiving to almighty God, for our many and great successes throughout this last year. London, H. Meere, for Edward Place; and sold by B. Bragge, 1709. 8°

2 copies.

T.491 T.82

4599

MANNINGHAM (Thomas) *Bishop of Chichester*.

A sermon preach'd before the Queen at Windsor, September the 12th, 1708... London: H. Hills, 1709. 8°

T.622

4600

MIDSUMMER moon or, Tom o'Bedlam's thanks to his sister Bess: with a letter of recommendation to poor brother Ben, in order to repair his sister's looking-glass ... London, printed: and sold by most booksellers of London and Westminster, 1709. 8°

2 copies.

T.297 T.102

4601

MILBOURNE (Luke)

Melius inquirendum. Or, A fresh enquiry into St. Paul's behaviour toward the civil magistrate. A sermon... January the 31st, 1708/9. London, printed: and sold by J. Morphew, [1709]. 8°

T.491

4602

MILBOURNE (Luke)

Tom of Bedlam's answer to his brother Ben Hoadly, St. Peter's-Poor parson, near the exchange of principles ... [Anon.] London, printed: and sold by B. Bragge, 1709. 8°

T.297

4603

MORSELLI (Adriano)

Pyrrhus and Demetrius. An opera. [With an English translation from the Italian by Owen Mac Swinny.] London: for Jacob Tonson, 1709. 4°

The musical score, by Scarlatti, is not included.

T.24

4604

NARBOUEL (   )

The tryal and conviction of the French committee, appointed for the management of the national charity to the poor French refugees, but fully proved guilty of mal-administration... Written originally in French by Monsieur Narbouel... and now done into English... 2nd ed... London, printed in the year 1709. And sold by the booksellers of London and Westminster. 8°

2 copies.

T.383 T.442

4605

OLDISWORTH (William)

A vindication of ... the Lord Bishop of Exeter, occasioned by Mr. Benjamin Hoadly's reflections on his Lorship's two sermons of government, preached ... March 8, 1704, and ... March 8, 1708 ... [Anon.] London: printed and sold by the booksellers of London, and Westminster, 1709. 8°

2 copies.

T.297 T.102

4606

PEAD (Deuel)

Parturiunt montes, &c. or, Lewis and Clement taken in their own snare. A sermon preach'd in the parish church of St. James Clerkenwell, on Thursday February the 17th, 1708/9 ... London: for E. Curll, 1709. 8°

2 copies.

T.491 T.82

4607

PEAD (Deuel)

A sermon preach'd at St. James's, Clerkenwell, on Sunday, Septem 25. 1709. on the sad occasion of Mr. Preston's being torn in pieces by his own bear... London: for T. Smith, 1709. 8°

T.491

4608

PELLING (John)

A sermon preach'd before the honourable House of Commons, at St. Margaret's Westminster, on Monday, Jan. 31. 1708/9... London: J.B. for Jonah Bowyer, 1709. 8°

2 copies.

T.491 T.622

4609

REFLEXIONS sur l'etat present de l'Eglise. [No imprint, 1709.] 4°

2 copies.

T.266 T.77

4610

RICHARDS (Thomas) *Rector of Llanfyllin*.

Χοιροχωρογραφια: sive, Hoglandiae descriptio ... [Anon.] Londini: anno Domini 1709. 8°

The dedication is signed M.C., i.e. Maredydius Caduganus. The pamphlet is a reply to Holdsworth's Muscipula.

T.58

4611
RIDPATH (George)

The peril of being zealously affected, but not well: or, Reflections on Dr. Sacheverel's sermon preach'd ... on the fifth of November, 1709 ... [Anon.] London, for J. Baker, 1709.   8°

T.229

4612
ROWE (Nicholas)

Epilogue spoken by Mrs. Barry, April the 7th, 1709. At a representation of Love for love: for the benefit of Mr. Betterton at his leaving the stage. [Anon.] London, for E. Sanger, and E. Curll, 1709. 8°

T.58

4613
The RULE for finding Easter explain'd and vindicated. Wherein is shew'd the rubrick's agreement with the Council of Nice; and that Dr. Wallis's exceptions are mistaken and groundless. London: for H. Clements, 1709.   8°

T.522

4614
S.(M.)

A letter to a friend: occasion'd by the contest between the Bishop of Exeter, and Mr. Hoadly. London: for A. Baldwin, 1709.   8°

T.297

4615
SACHEVERELL (Henry)

The communication of sin: a sermon preach'd at the assizes held at Derby, August 15th, 1709. London: for Henry Clements, 1709.   8°

2 copies.

T.491 T.152

4616
SACHEVERELL (Henry)

The perils of false brethren, both in Church, and State: set forth in a sermon preach'd before... the lord mayor, aldermen, and citizens of London, at the cathedral-church of St. Paul, on the 5th of November, 1709... London: for Henry Clements, 1709. 24pp. 8°

T.102

4617
SACHEVERELL (Henry)

The perils of false brethren, both in Church and State: set forth in a sermon preach'd before ... the lord-mayor, aldermen, and citizens of London, at the cathedral-church of St. Paul. On the 5th of November, 1709 ... London: printed in the year, 1709. 16 pp. 8°

T.152

4618
SHARPE (John) *Curate of Stepney.*

The Church of England's complaint against the irregularities of some of its clergy. By a presbyter of the Church of England ... Sold by the booksellers of London and Westminster, 1709.   8°

T.41

4619
SHARPE (John) *Curate of Stepney.*

The wou'd be bishop: or, The lying dean. Being a defence of the Curate of Stepney, against the infamous slanders of Dr. K[enne]t, the (pretended) vindicator of the Church of England. In a letter to a friend ... [Anon.] London printed: and sold by the booksellers of London and Westminster, 1709.   8°

Incomplete.

T.155

4620
SHOWER (John)

Winter meditations: or, A sermon concerning frost, and snow, and winds, &c. and the wonders of God therein. 2nd ed. London, for J. Laurence, 1709. 8°

T.152

4621
SIBBALD (*Sir* Robert)

A letter from Sir R[obert] S[ibbald], to Dr. Archibald Pitcairn. Edinburgh, printed in the year, 1709. 8°

T.294

4622
SMALRIDGE (George) *Bishop of Bristol.*

A sermon preach'd before... the court of aldermen, at the cathedral church of St. Paul, London, on Monday, January 31. 1708/9... London: G.J. for Jonah Bowyer, 1709.   4°

Three other copies, in 8°

T.3 T.82 T.491 T.622

4623
SMITH (John) *Prebendary of Durham.*

An apology to Christians for the Gospel, and its ministers. In a sermon preach'd at the cathedral church of Durham, upon the XIth. Sunday after Trinity. London; for Henry Clements, and Will. Freeman, 1709. 4°

"To ye. Revd. Dr. Hicks."

T.3

4624
STOUGHTON (William) *Prebendary of St. Patrick's.*

A sermon preach'd before the State in Christ-Church in Dublin, on Monday January 31. 1708/9 ... Printed at Dublin, and reprinted at London, for John Baker, 1709.   8°

2 copies.

T.491 T.101

4625
STUBS (Philip)

The sea-assize; or, Sea-faring persons to be judged according to their works. A sermon preach'd ... on the occasion of the most lamented decease of his Royal Highness Prince George ... London: J.L. for R. Smith, 1709.   8°

2 copies.

T.491 T.82

4626
A SUBMISSIVE answer to Mr. Hoadly's humble reply, to my Lord Bishop of Exeter. By a student at Oxford [i.e. John Gaynam?] ... London, printed; and sold by the booksellers of London and Westminster, 1709. 8°

T.297

4627
SWIFT (Jonathan) *Dean of St. Patrick's.*

A letter from a member of the House of Commons in Ireland to a member of the House of Commons in England, concerning the sacramental test. [Anon.] London: for John Morphew, 1709.   4°

Teerink 511.

T.266

4628
SWIFT (Jonathan) *Dean of St. Patrick's.*

A vindication of Isaac Bickerstaff Esq; against what is objected to him by Mr. Partridge, in his almanack for the present year 1709. By the said Isaac Bickerstaff. London: printed in the year 1709.   8°

Teerink 498.
2 copies.

T.44 T.323

4629
TEMPLE (*Sir* William)

Memoirs. Part III. From the peace concluded 1679. to the time of the author's retirement from publick business... Publish'd by Jonathan Swift. London: printed and sold by the booksellers of London and Westminster, 1709.   8°

Teerink 475.

T.522

4630
TENISON (Thomas) *Archbishop of Canterbury.*

To the reverend the minister of   [Royal brief on behalf of the protestant immigrants from the Palatinate.] London, Charles Bill, and the executrix of Thomas Newcomb, 1709.   4°

T.137

4631
THOMPSON (John) *Baron Haversham.*

The Lord Haversham's speech in the House of Peers, Wednesday the 12th of January, 1708/9. On the late intended invasion of Scotland. London, Benj. Bragge, 1709.   4°

3 copies.

T.267 T.194

4632
TILLOTSON (John) *Archbishop of Canterbury.*

A sermon preach'd at the morning-exercise at Cripple-gate ... London, for A. Baldwin, 1709.   8°

T.152

4633
TILLOTSON (John) *Archbishop of Canterbury.*

A sermon preach'd at the morning exercise, at Cripple-gate, about the year, 1660... London: H. Hills, 1709.   8°

T.491

4634
TINDAL (Matthew)

New High-Church turn'd old Presbyterian ... [Anon.] London: B. Bragg, 1709.   8°

2 copies.

T.231 T.102

4635
TRIMNELL (Charles) *Bishop of Winchester.*

A sermon preach'd at the parish-church of St. James's Westminster, on Sunday the 30th of January, 1708. By... Charles, Lord Bishop of Norwich... London: for Tho. Chapman, 1709.   8°

T.82

4636
TRIMNELL (Charles) *Bishop of Winchester.*

A sermon preach'd before the House of Lords, at the abbey-church in Westminster, on Thursday, Feb. 17. 1708. Being the day appointed for a publick thanksgiving, &c. By ... Charles Lord Bishop of Norwich. London: for D. Midwinter, 1709.   8°

2 copies.

T.491 T.82

4637
TURRETINUS (Johannes Alphonsus)

Joh. Alphonsi Turrettini... de variis Christianae doctrinae fatis, oratio academica, dicta statis Academiae Genevensis solennibus, XI. Mai. an. M.DCCVIII... [Latin & English.] London: for William Taylor, 1709.   4°

3 copies.

T.12 T.78 T.564

4638
The VILLANOUS principles of [Matthew Tindal's pamphlet, entitled] The rights of the Christian Church asserted, &c. confuted by Scripture. London, J. Humfreys, for James Round, 1709.   8°

2 copies.

T.102 T.153

4639
WARD (Edward)

Mars strip't of his armour: or, the army display'd in all its true colours ... By a lover of the mathematicks. London, J. Read, 1709.   8°

T.89

4640
WARD (Edward)

The wars of the elements. Or, A description of a sea-storm. To which are added, I. The contemplative angler [and other poems]. By the author of the London-spy. London: printed in the year, 1709. 4°

T.689

4641
WARREN (Erasmus)

An essay towards shewing the reasonableness of the doctrine of the ... Trinity: or, at least, the great reasonableness of believing it ... London, J.H. for Henry Mortlock, 1709.   8°

T.149

4642
WELLS (Edward)

A specimen of an help for the more easy and clear understanding of the holy Scriptures: being St Paul's two Epistles to the Thessalonians, and his Epistle to the Galatians ... Oxford, printed at the Theater, for J. Stephens, and are to be sold by James Knapton, London, 1709.   4°

T.190

4643

An ACCOUNT of charity schools lately erected in
Great Britain and Ireland: with the benefactions
thereto... The ninth edition, with large additions.
London: Joseph Downing, 1710.   4°

2 copies.

T.3 T.700

4644

An ACCOUNT of the late proceedings in the council of
the Royal Society, in order to remove from Gresham-
College into Crane-Court, in Fleet-Street. In a
letter to a friend. London: for J. Morphew, 1710.
8°

T.522

4645

ADAMS (John) *Provost of King's College, Cambridge.*

A sermon preached in Lambeth-chapel, November the 19th,
1710. at the consecration of ... John Lord Bishop of
Bristol, and Philip Ld Bp of St. David's. London:
for Jonah Bowyer, 1710.   8°

T.104

4646

An ADDRESS to the Church of England clergy,
concerning resistance. London: S. Popping, 1710.
8°

T.418

4647

An ADDRESS to the Oxfordshire addressors, and all
others of the same strain ... London, for A. Baldwin,
1710.   8°

T.299

4648

ADVICE to the gentlemen freeholders, citizens and
burgesses, and all others that have a just right to
send representatives to Parliament in South-Britain.
Printed in the year 1710.   8°

T.91

4649

AMICABLE SOCIETY FOR A PERPETUAL ASSURANCE-OFFICE.

The charter of the Corporation of the Amicable Society
for a Perpetual Assurance-office; together with the
by-laws thereunto belonging ... London: for Geo.
Sawbridge, 1710.   8°

T.163

4650

AMINADAB: or, The Quaker's vision. [Printed] in
the year 1710.   8°

2 copies.

T.102 T.204

4651

AMINADAB: or the Quaker's vision, explained and
answer'd paragraph by paragraph. The second edition,
with amendments. London: Edw. Midwinter, 1710. 8°

T.418

4652

An ANSWER to the address of the Oxford-University, as
it was printed at London, intituled, The humble
address of the University of Oxford, &c. London:
B. Bragge, 1710.   8°

T.299

4653

An APPEAL from the city to the country, for the
preservation of her Majesty's person, liberty,
property, and the protestant religion ... Occasionally
written upon the late impudent affronts offer'd to
her Majesty's royal crown and dignity by the people
of Banbury, and Warwick ... London printed, and sold
by A. Baldwin, 1710.   8°

T.91

4654

ASGILL (John)

The assertion is, that the title of the House of
Hanover to the succession of the British monarchy (on
failure of issue of her present Majesty) is a title
hereditary, and of divine institution ... London,
printed in the year 1710.   8°

Half-title: Mr. Asgill de jure divino.
2 copies.

T.417 T.227

4655

ASGILL (John)

The assertion is, that the title of the House of
Hanover to the succession of the British monarchy (on
failure of issue of her present Majesty) is a title
hereditary, and of divine institution. The second
edition corrected ... London, J. Darby, 1710. 8°

Half-title: Mr. Asgill de jure divino.

T.414

4656

ATTERBURY (Francis) *Bishop of Rochester.*

A sermon preach'd before the London-clergy at
Saint Alphage, May the 17th. 1709... Translated
from the Latin. London: printed for, and sold by
H. Hills, 1710.   8°

T.662

4657

ATTERBURY (Francis) *Bishop of Rochester.*

The voice of the people, no voice of God: or, The
mistaken arguments of a fiery zealot, in a late
pamphlet entitl'd Vox populi, vox Dei, since publish'd
under the title of the Judgment of whole kingdoms and
nations, &c. fully confuted ... By F.A. Sold by the
booksellers, 1710.   8°

T.231

4658

B.(A.)

An answer to the arguments in the Lord Bishop of
Oxford's speech, on the impeachment of Dr. Henry
Sacheverell, in favour of resisting the supreme
power. Humbly offer'd to his Lordship's
consideration in a letter from A.B. London: printed
in the year, 1710.   8°

T.49

4659

B.(A.)

A letter to the good people of Great Britain ...
London, for A. Baldwin, 1710.   8°

T.299

4660

BEDFORD (Hilkiah)

A seasonable and modest apology in behalf of the
Reverend Dr. George Hickes, and other Non-jurors:
in a letter to Thomas Wise, D.D. On occasion of
his late visitation-sermon... [Anon.] London:
for Sam. Keble, 1710.   8°

4 copies.

T.36 T.104 T.408

4661

BEDFORD (Hilkiah)

A vindication of the Church of England from the
aspersions of a late libel [by Anthony Collins]
intituled, Priestcraft in perfection ... With a
preface containing some remarks upon the Reflections
on that pamphlet. By a priest of the Church of
England ... London: W.B. for R. Wilkin, 1710.   8°

2 copies.

T.153 T.159

4662

BENTLEY (Richard)

The present state of Trinity College in Cambridg, in
a letter from Dr. Bentley, master of the said College,
to the Right Reverend John Lord Bishop of Ely ...
London; for A. Baldwin, 1710.   8°

T.415

4663

BICKERSTAFF (Isaac) *pseud.*

The famous prophesie of the white king and the dead
man explain'd to the present times ... By Isaac
Bickerstaffe. London, for J. Morphew, [1710?]   8°

T.44

4664

BISSE (Philip) *Bishop of Hereford.*

A sermon preach'd before the honourable House of
Commons, at St. Margaret's Westminster, on Wednesday,
March, 15, 1709/10. Being the day appointed by her
Majesty for a general fast ... London: J.B. for
Jonah Bowyer, 1710.   4°

T.273

4665

BISSET (William)

The modern fanatick. With a large and true account
of the life, actions, endowments, &c. of the
famous Dr. Sa[cheverel]l... London: printed: and
sold by A. Baldwin: and T. Harrison, 1710.   8°

3 copies.

T.244 T.336 T.361

4666

BISSET (William)

The modern fanatick. Part II. Containing what is
necessary to clear all the matters of fact in the first
part; and to confute what has been printed in the
pretended vindication of Dr. Sacheverell, relating to
myself ... London: printed; and sold by A. Baldwin;
and T. Harrison, 1710.   8°

T.361

4667

BLACKMORE (*Sir* Richard)

The Kit-Cat club, a poem. Written by Sir R.B. [No
imprint, 1710?]   8°

T.204

4668

BLOMER (Thomas)

A full view of Dr. Bentley's letter to the Lord Bishop
of Ely. In a discourse to a friend ... London: for
R. Knaplock, and R. Wilkin, 1710.   8°

T.415

4669

BODKINS and thimbles: or, 1645 against 1710.
Containing the opinions of the old and new
presbyterians, touching toleration, separation, schism;
and the necessity of uniformity in a national church
... London: Geo. James, and sold by John Morphew,
1710.   8°

T.231

4670

BOTH sides pleas'd: Or, A dialogue between a
Sacheverelite parson, and an Hoadlean gentleman ...
London: S. Popping, 1710.   8°

2 copies.

T.229 T.41

4671

BOWTELL (John)

A defence of the LVth canon, in answer to some
passages in a book intituled, Reflections upon Mr.
Bennet's History of joint prayer; by a presbyter of the
Church of England ... London, for R. Knaplock, 1710.
8°

T.439

4672

BRADFORD (Samuel) *Bishop of Rochester.*

An exhortation to purity and peace. A sermon preach'd
in the parish-church of St. Mary le Bow, on Sunday
March 26. 1710. London: for J. Wyat, 1710.   8°

T.152

4673

A BRIEF account of the Apostle's creed; together with
an explanation of the several articles, according to
the doctrine of the Church of England. London, for
Chr. Coningsby; and sold by J. Morphew, 1710.   8°

T.520

4674

BRITANNIA'S summons to the old genius of the nation.
Or, glorious candidates for the new elections. London
printed: and sold by John Morphew, 1710.   8°

T.350

4675

BROUGHTON (John)

The vindication and advancement of our national
constitution and credit: attempted in several tracts
... [Anon.] London: for Jonah Bowyer, 1710.   8°

2 copies.

T.279 T.147

4676

BROWN (Robert) *Vicar of Sligo.*

The subjects sorrow; or, Lamentations upon the death
of Britain's Josiah, King Charles I ... [Anon.] To
which is added, A form of prayer used in King Charles
IIds chapel at the Hague, upon Tuesdays throughout the
year ... London, J. Morphew, [1710].   12°

T.390

4677

BROWN (Thomas) *of Shifnal.*

Azarias. A sermon held forth in a Quakers meeting, immediately after Aminadab's vision. With a prayer for rooting out the Church and university, and blessing tripe and custard. [Anon.] London printed in the year 1710.   8º

T.418

4678

BUCHANAN (Charles)

Unity and unanimity. A sermon preach'd at Loddon April 26. 1710. at the visitation held there by the Reverend Dr Cannon, archdeacon of Norfolk. Norwich: Fr. Collins, for Fr. Oliver, 1710.   4º

T.754

4679

BURGESS (Cornelius)

The presbyterians not guilty of the unjust charge of being concern'd in the murther of King Charles I ... [Anon.] London, A. Baldwin, 1710.   8º

T.231

4680

BURNET (Gilbert) *Bishop of Salisbury.*

The royal martyr and the dutiful subject, in two sermons. The royal martyr lamented ... 1674/5. (Subjection for conscience-sake asserted ... 1674.) London, reprinted by W. Redmayne for J. Meredith, are to be sold by S. Keble, and J. Morphew, 1710.   4º

T.273

4681

BURNET (Gilbert) *Bishop of Salisbury.*

A sermon preach'd in the cathedral-church of Salisbury, on the 29th day of May, in the year 1710. London: J.M. for J. Churchill, 1710.   8º

3 copies.

T.36   T.101   T.206

4682

BURNET (Gilbert) *Bishop of Salisbury.*

The Bishop of Salisbury his speech in the House of Lords, on the first article of the impeachment of Dr. Henry Sacheverell. London: printed in the year, 1710.   8º

3 copies.

T.49   T.102   T.169

4683

BURNET (Gilbert) *Bishop of Salisbury.*

Two sermons, preached in the cathedral church of Salisbury: the first, on the fifth of November ... The second, on the seventh of November, being the thanksgiving day: in the year 1710. London: for John Churchill, 1710.   8º

2 copies.

T.206   T.101

4684

BURNET (Gilbert) *Bishop of Salisbury.*

A vindication of the Bishop of Salisbury and passive obedience, with some remarks upon a speech which goes under his Lordship's name. And a postscript, in answer to a book just publish'd, entitul'd, Some considerations humbly offer'd to ... the Lord Bishop of Salisbury, &c. [Anon.] Printed in the year 1710.   8º

2 copies.

T.49   T.169

4685

BYNNS (Richard)

Conscience void of offence. A sermon preach'd at the assizes held at Stafford, August the 9th. 1710 ... London: for John Morphew, 1710.   8º

T.206

4686

The CALAMITY of the Church of England, under a presbyterian government; made visable. Or, The measures they took for securing their Common-wealth ... London: printed in the year, 1710. 8º

T.52

4687

CALAMY (Benjamin)

Passive obedience the doctrine of the Church of England; and doing evil that good may come, a damnable sin. A sermon preach'd ... September 30th. 1683 ... London: for John Morphew, 1710.   8º

T.491

4688

CAMBRIDGE. *University. Trinity College.*

A true copy of the articles against Dr. Bentley, exhibited to... John, Lord Bishop of Ely, by many fellows of Trinity College in Cambridge... London, John Morphew, 1710.   8º

T.415

4689

The CHALLENGER answered: or, A reply to the Answer to a letter from a citizen of New Sarum; which answer is suppos'd to be written by Mr. H[oad]ly, concerning the affront offer'd to the B[isho]p there. In answer to a second letter from a gentleman in London, to the said citizen. London: J. Morphew, 1710.   8º

T.166

4690

CHAMBRE (Richard)

A sermon preach'd at the cathedral-church of St. Paul, before the ... Lord Mayor, and the aldermen and citizens of London. On Tuesday, Novemb. 7. 1710. Being the day appointed ... for a publick thanks-giving. London: for John Wyat, 1710.   8º

T.206

4691

CHANDLER (Edward) *Bishop of Durham.*

A sermon preach'd at the cathedral church of Worcester, on the twenty-second day of November being the day appointed for a general thanksgiving for... the signal victory at Blaregnies... Worcester: S. Bryan for J. Mountfort, 1710.   8º

T.622

4692

A CHARACTER of Don Sacheverellio, knight of the fire-brand; in a letter to Isaac Bickerstaff Esq; censor of Great Britain. [Signed John Distaff.] Dublin: Francis Higgins; and to be had of A. Baldwin, in London, [1710].   8º

T.229

4693

CHURCH OF ENGLAND.

A form of prayer and thanksgiving, to be used on Tuesday the seventh day of November ... for the great goodness and mercy of Almighty God, in continuing to us his protection and assistance in the just and necessary war in which we are engaged ... London, the assigns of Thomas Newcomb, and Henry Hills, 1710.   4º

T.461

4694

CHURCH OF ENGLAND.

A form of prayer, to be used in all churches and chapels ... on Wednesday the fifteenth day of March, being the day appointed by her Majesty for a general fast ... for ... imploring Gods blessing and assistance on the arms of her Majesty, and her allies ... London, the assigns of Thomas Newcomb, and Henry Hills, 1709/10.   4º

T.461

4695

CHURCH OF ENGLAND. *Convocation.*

A true copy of the humble address of the two houses of Convocation, as proposed by the Lord Archbishop and suffragan bishops to the inferior clergy ... London: for J. Churchill, 1710.   4º

T.133

4696

The CHURCH of England's address, to all the worthy m---rs against the hereditary rights of kings and queens ... Humbly preseuted [sic] by the true sons of the Church of England, clergy and laity ... London: Edm. Powell; and sold by J. Morphew, 1710.   8º

T.302

4697

CLARKE (Samuel) *Rector of St. James's, Westminster.*

A second defense of an argument made use of in a letter to Mr Dodwel, to prove the immateriality and natural immortality of the soul. In a letter to the author [i.e. Anthony Collins] of A reply to Mr Clarke's Defense, &c. [Anon.] 2nd ed. London, W.B. for James Knapton, 1710.   8º

T.151

4698

CLARKE (Samuel) *Rector of St. James's, Westminster.*

A sermon preach'd at the parish-church of St. James's Westminster. On Tuesday November 7. 1710. Being the day of thanksgiving for the successes of the fore-going campaign ... London: Will. Botham, for James Knapton, 1710.   8º

T.206

4699

CLARKE (Samuel) *Rector of St. James's, Westminster.*

A sermon preach'd before the Queen at St James's chapel, on Wednesday the 8th of March. 1709/10. Being the anniversary of her Majesties happy accession to the throne. London, W.B. for James Knapton, 1710. 8º

T.152

4700

CLEMENT (Simon)

Faults on both sides: or, An essay upon the original cause, progress, and mischievous consequences of the factions in this nation... By way of answer to The thoughts of an honest Tory [by Benjamin Hoadly]... [Anon. Also attributed to Richard Harley, probably an error for Robert Harley.] 2nd ed. London: printed and sold by the booksellers of London and Westminster, 1710.   8º

3 copies.

T.41   T.348   T.363

4701

CLEMENT (Simon)

Faults on both sides: part the second. Or, An essay upon the original cause, progress, and mischievous consequences of the factions in the Church... By the way of letter to a new member of Parliament... [Anon.] London: printed and sold by the booksellers of London and Westminster, 1710.   8º

T.547

4702

A COLLECTION of poems, for and against Dr. Sacheverell. London, printed in the year 1710. 40 pp.   8º

2 copies.

T.336   T.350

4703

A COLLECTION of poems, for and against Dr. Sacheverell. London, printed in the year 1710. 39 pp.   8º

T.336

4704

A COLLECTION of poems, &c. for and against Dr. Sacheverell. The second part. London, printed in the year 1710.   8º

T.350

4705

A COLLECTION of poems, &c. for and against Dr. Sacheverell. The third part. London, printed in the year 1710.   8º

T.350

4706

A COLLECTION of poems, &c. for and against Dr. Sacheverell, and on other affairs of state; most of them never before printed. The fourth part. London, printed in the year 1710.   8º

T.350

4707

A COLLECTION of some letters, written from the 14th of June, 1709. to the 24th of May, 1710. concerning his Eminency the Cardinal de Bouillon ... Together with Considerations upon the letter written to the French king by the said Cardinal, upon his departure from France ... London: for John Morphew, 1710.   4º

T.77

4708

COLLINS (Anthony)

Priestcraft in perfection: or, A detection of the fraud of inserting and continuing this clause (The Church hath power to decree rites and ceremonys, and authority in controversys of faith) in the twentieth article ... of the Church of England ... [Anon.] London; for B. Bragg, 1710.   8º

T.41

4709
COLLINS (Anthony)

Priestcraft in perfection: or, A detection of the fraud of inserting and continuing this clause (The Church hath power to decree rites and ceremonys, and authority in controversys of faith) in the twentieth article ... of the Church of England. [Anon.] The second edition corrected ... London; for B. Bragg, 1710.   8°

T.159

4710
COLLINS (Anthony)

Priestcraft in perfection: or, A detection of the fraud of inserting and continuing this clause (The Church hath power to decree rites and ceremonys, and authority in controversys of faith) in the twentieth article ... of the Church of England. [Anon.] The third edition corrected ... London; for B. Bragg, 1710.   8°

T.153

4711
COMPTON (Henry) *Bishop of London.*

A letter concerning allegiance, written by the Lord Bishop of L[ondo]n, to a clergy-man in Essex, presently after the Revolution... To which are added some queries, occasion'd by the late address of his lordship and the clergy of London and Westminster. London, S. Popping, 1710.   8°

3 copies.

T.41   T.159   T.299

4712
COMPTON (Henry) *Bishop of London.*

Seasonable advice to the ministers of the Church of Great Britain ... not to meddle, as some have done, with matters of state, or controversial preaching. Taken verbatim out of the present Bishop of London's seventh letter of the conference with his clergy, held in the year 1686 ... London: R. Halsey, 1710.   8°

T.302

4713
CONEY (Thomas)

Honesty and plain-dealing an usual bar to honour and preferment. A sermon preach'd at St. Mary's before the University of Oxford, upon Act-Sunday July IX. 1710. Oxford, printed at the Theater, for Anth. Peisley; and are to be sold by Jam. Knapton, Hen. Clements, and J. Morphew, London, 1710.   8°

3 copies.

T.36   T.101   T.662

4714
CONEY (Thomas)

Honesty and plain-dealing an usual bar to honour and preferment. A sermon preach'd at St. Mary's before the University of Oxford, upon Act-Sunday July IX. 1710. 3rd ed. Oxford, printed at the Theater, for Anth. Peisley; and are to be sold by Jam. Knapton, Hen. Clements, and J. Morphew, London, 1710.   8°

"Rev. Mr. Harriott."

T.751

4715
The CRITERION: or, Touchstone, by which to judge of the principles of High and Low Church. In a letter to a friend ... London: B. Bragge, 1710.   8°

T.231

4716
CURLL (Edmund)

The case of Dr. Sacheverell. Represented in a letter to a noble lord ... [Anon.] London: printed in the year 1710.   8°

T.229

4717
CURLL (Edmund)

An impartial examination of ... the Lord Bishop of Lincoln's and Norwich's speeches at the opening of the second article of Dr. Sacheverell's impeachment ... In two letters to their lordships ... [Anon.] London, for E. Curll, 1710.   8°

T.49

4718
CURLL (Edmund)

Some considerations humbly offer'd to ... the Ld. Bp. of Salisbury. Occasion'd by his Lordship's speech, upon the first article of Dr. Sacheverell's impeachment ... By a lay hand ... London: for J. Morphew, 1710.   8°

T.49

4719
CURLL (Edmund)

The white crow: or, An enquiry into some more new doctrines broach'd by the Bp. of Salisbury, in a pair of sermons utter'd in that cathedral, on the V. and VII. of November, 1710 ... [Anon.] Printed in the year, 1710.   8°

2 copies.

T.244   T.166

4720
CURLL (Edmund)

The white crow: or, An enquiry into some more new doctrines broach'd by the Bp. of Salisbury, in a pair of sermons utter'd in that cathedral, on the V. and . VII. days of November, 1710 ... [Anon.] The second edition corrected. Printed in the year of Grace, 1710. 8°

T.523

4721
DAVENANT (Charles)

New dialogues upon the present posture of affairs, the species of mony, national debts, publick revenues, Bank and East India Company, and the trade now carried on between France and Holland. Vol. II. By the author of The essay on ways and means ... London: for John Morphew, 1710.   8°

3 copies.

T.418   T.445   T.549

4722
DAVENANT (Charles)

Sir Thomas Double at court, and in high preferments. In two dialogues, between Sir Thomas Double and Sir Richard Comover, alias Mr. Whiglove: on the 27th of September, 1710. Part I... [Anon.] Printed, and sold by John Morphew, 1710.   8°

3 copies.

T.418   T.445   T.549

4723
The DECLARATION of an honest churchman, upon occasion of the present times. London: J. Morphew, 1710. 8°

2 copies.

T.418   T.159

4724
DEFOE (Daniel)

A condoling letter to the Tattler: on account of the misfortunes of Isaac Bickerstaff, Esq; a prisoner in the ———— on suspicion of debt. [Anon.] London, S. Popping, [1710].   8°

Moore 190.
2 copies.

T.418   T.204

4725
DEFOE (Daniel)

A dialogue betwixt Whig and Tory. Wherein the principles and practices of each party are fairly and impartially stated ... [Anon.] London, printed in the year, 1710.   8°

Moore 10b.

T.363

4726
DEFOE (Daniel)

An essay upon publick credit: being an enquiry how the publick credit comes to depend upon the change of the ministry, or the dissolutions of parliaments... [Anon.] London: printed, and sold by the booksellers, 1710.   8°

Moore 187.
2 copies.

T.147   T.279

4727
DEFOE (Daniel)

Four letters to a friend in North Britain, upon the publishing the tryal of Dr. Sacheverell... [Anon.] London: printed in the year 1710. 35pp. 8°

Moore 184.
2 copies.

T.147   T.336

4728
DEFOE (Daniel)

Four letters to a friend in North Britain, upon the publishing the tryal of Dr. Sacheverell ... [Anon.] London, printed in the year 1710. 27 pp.   4°

Moore 184.

T.490

4729
DEFOE (Daniel)

A letter from a dissenter in the City to a dissenter in the country: advising him to a quiet and peaceable behaviour in this present conjuncture. [Signed Irenaeus Americus.] [Anon.] London: for A. Baldwin, 1710.   8°

Moore 186.

T.302

4730
DEFOE (Daniel)

A letter from a gentleman at the Court of St. Germains, to one of his friends in England; containing a memorial about methods for setting the Pretender on the throne of Great Britain ... Translated from the French copy ... [Anon.] London, printed in the year 1710.   8°

Moore 189.
2 copies.

T.418   T.344

4731
DEFOE (Daniel)

The modern addresses vindicated, and the rights of the addressers asserted, by D. De Foe. Extracted out of his book, intitled, The original right of the people of England examined and asserted. London: for J. Morphew, 1710.   8°

Moore 177.

T.299

4732
DEFOE (Daniel)

A new test of the sence of the nation: being a modest comparison between the addresses to the late King James, and those to her present Majesty ... [Anon.] London, printed in the year 1710.   8°

Moore 188.

T.299

4733
DEFOE (Daniel)

Queries to the new hereditary right-men. [Anon.] Printed and sold by the booksellers of London and Westminster, 1710.   8°

Moore 191.
4 copies.

T.41   T.169   T.413   T.418

4734
DEFOE (Daniel)

Seldom comes a better: or, A tale of a lady and her servants ... [Anon.] London, printed in the year 1710.   8°

Moore 185.
2 copies.

T.445   T.204

4735
DEFOE (Daniel)

A speech without doors ... [Anon.] London, for A. Baldwin, 1710.   8°

Moore 168.

T.229

4736
DEFOE (Daniel)

A supplement to the Faults on both sides [by Simon Clement]: containing the compleat history of the proceedings of a party ever since the Revolution... [Anon.] London: for J. Baker, 1710.   8°

Moore 194.
3 copies.

T.348   T.363   T.547

4737
The DESCRIPTION of a presbyterian; humbly address'd to those gentlemen, that by the imputation of the High Church are lately added to that famous party ... Printed, in the year 1710.   8°

T.227

4738

A DETECTION of the true meaning and wicked design of a book, intitul'd, A plain and easie method with the deists. Wherein is prov'd, that the author's (Lesley) four marks are the marks of the beast ... In a letter to a friend. London, B. Bragge, 1710. 8°

2 copies.

T.101 T.226

4739

A DIALOGUE between Jack High and Will Low; proper for the perusal of those who have a right to choose members for the ensuing Parliament. London: printed in the year 1710. 8°

T.297

4740

DICK and Tom: a dialogue about addresses. London; for B. Bragg, 1710. 8°

T.299

4741

The DISSENTERS loyalty display'd, and their principles both in Church and State examined, from their own writings... Being an answer to a book [by Cornelius Burgess] lately publish'd, entitl'd The presbyterians not guilty of the unjust charge of being concern'd in the murther of King Charles I... London: J. Morphew, [1710]. 8°

2 copies.

T.231 T.622

4742

The DIVINE rights of the British nation and constitution vindicated. In remarks on the several papers publish'd against the Reverend Mr. Hoadly's considerations upon the Bishop of Exeter's sermons ... London, for J. Baker, 1710. 8°

T.231

4743

The DOCTRINE of passive obedience and nonresistance, as established in the Church of England ... London, printed in the year, 1710. 8°

T.229

4744

The DOCTRINE of passive-obedience, by Dr. Tillotson, [and others] ... London: printed in the year 1710. 8°

T.229

4745

DREWE (Patrick)

The Church of England's late conflict with, and triumph over the spirit of fanaticism ... By a lover of the Church of England. London, J. Morphew, 1710. 8°

T.302

4746

EDWARDS (John) D.D.

Great things done by God for our ancestors, and us of this island. A sermon preach'd before the University of Cambridge, (tho refus'd to be licens'd there) at St. Mary's, November 5, 1709 ... 2nd ed. London, J.H. for Jonathan Robinson, John Lawrence, and John Wyat, 1710. 8°

T.36

4747

An ENTIRE confutation of Mr. Hoadley's book, of The original of government; taken from the London Gazette, published by authority. London: reprinted in the year, 1710.

2 copies.

T.297 T.102

4748

ERSKINE (George)

Speculum pastorale; or, The duty of pastors and people in times of prevailing defections. In a sermon preached at St. Mary's church in the Savoy, on Sunday the twelfth day of March 1709/10 ... London, John Morphew, 1710. 4°

T.273

4749

An ESSAY towards the history of the last ministry and Parliament: containing seasonable reflections on I. Favourites, II. Ministers of state... London: for J. Baker, 1710. 8°

2 copies.

T.91 T.547

4750

EVANS (Abel)

The apparition. A poem... [Anon.] Printed in the year 1710. And are to be sold by the booksellers of London and Westminster. 8°

4 copies.

T.58 T.89 T.204

4751

EVANS (Abel)

The apparition. A poem. Or, A dialogue betwixt the devil and a doctor, concerning the rights of the Christian Church. [Anon.] 2nd ed. Printed in the year 1710. And are to be sold by the booksellers of London and Westminster. 8°

T.665

4752

EYRE (Elizabeth)

The opinion of the pious and learned Mrs. Eyre ... concerning the doctrine of passive-obedience, as the distinguishing character of the Church of England ... London: printed in the year 1689. Now re-printed, as seasonable for these times, 1710. Sold by A. Baldwin. 8°

2 copies.

T.229 T.102

4753

The FAIR question, or Who deserves an impeachment now? A poem ... London, printed in the year 1710. 8°

T.350

4754

The FANATICK feast. A pleasant comedy. As it was acted at a wedding-dinner in Gr ——— ... London, printed; and sold by J. Morphew, 1710. 8°

T.350

4755

FARMERIE (William)

God the only judge, and our only hope in war. As deliver'd in a sermon preached at the new chappel in St. Margarets Westminster, on Wednesday the 15th day of March ... London, for D. Browne, and sold by J. Morphew, 1710. 8°

T.152

4756

FAULTS in the fault-finder: or, A specimen of errors in the pamphlet [by Simon Clement], entitul'd Faults on both sides. London: A. Baldwin, 1710. 8°

T.363

4757

FAULTS in the fault-finder: or, A specimen of errors in the pamphlet [by Simon Clement], entitul'd Faults on both sides. 2nd ed. London: A. Baldwin, 1710. 8°

T.547

4758

FISHER (Edward)

An appeal to thy conscience ... Which cannot be answer'd but by rebellion and murder, and is an unanswerable answer to a late pamphlet intituled ... The judgment of whole kingdoms and nations ... [Anon.] London, printed in the year, 1710. 8°

T.418

4759

FLEETWOOD (William) *Bishop of Ely.*

A sermon preach'd before the right honourable the Lords Spiritual and Temporal, January the 30th, 1709/10. at Westminster-Abby. By William, Lord Bishop of St. Asaph. London: T.H. for Charles Harper, 1710. 8°

3 copies.

T.152 T.345 T.491

4760

FLEETWOOD (William) *Bishop of Ely.*

The thirteenth chapter to the Romans, vindicated from the abusive senses put upon it. Written by a curate of Salop; and directed to the clergy of that county, and the neighbouring ones of North-Wales... London: for A. Baldwin, 1710. 8°

2 copies.

T.367 T.302

4761

FREIND (Robert)

A sermon preach'd before the Honourable House of Commons, at St. Margaret's Westminster, on Tuesday, January 30. 1710/11... By Robert Friend [sic]. London: G.J. for Jonah Bowyer, 1710. 4°

T.700

4762

FREIND (Robert)

A sermon preach'd before the Honble House of Commons, at S. Margaret's Westminster, on Tuesday, January 30. 1710/11 ... London: G.J. for Jonah Bowyer, 1710. 8°

2 copies.

T.293 T.104

4763

G.(R.)

Doctor Sacheverell's defence, in a letter to a member of Parliament. Or, Remarks upon two famous pamphlets, the one [by White Kennet] entituled, A true answer to Doctor Sacheverell's sermon ... The other (a sham-pamphlet), Doctor Sacheverell's recantation. London: for John Reade, 1710. 8°

2 copies.

T.102 T.229

4764

GANDY (Henry)

Remarks on Mr. Higden's utopian constitution; or, An answer to his unanswerable book. By an Englishman. With an appendix... London; printed, and sold by the booksellers of Westminster and London, [1710?] 8°

4 copies.

T.46 T.398 T.640 T.650

4765

A GENERAL view of our present discontents. London: A. Baldwin, 1710. 8°

T.405

4766

GODDARD (Thomas)

The guilt, mischief, and aggravations of censure: set forth in a sermon preach'd in St. George's chapel ... 25th of June, 1710. London: for Bernard Lintott, 1710. 8°

T.206

4767

GODDARD (Thomas)

The mercy of God to this Church and Kingdom ... A sermon, preach'd in St. George's chapel in Windsor, on Tuesday the 7th of November, 1710. being appointed as a day of thanksgiving to Almighty God for ... a signal and glorious victory in Spain ... London: for Bernard Lintott; and sold by A. Baldwin, 1710. 8°

T.206

4768

A GOOD husband for five shillings, or, Esquire Bickerstaff's lottery for the London-ladies. Wherein those that want bed-fellows, in an honest way, will have a fair chance to be well-fitted. London: James Woodward; and John Baker, 1710. 8°

Teerink 1595.

T.204

4769

GORDON (William) *Rector of St. James's, Barbados.*

A sermon preach'd at the funeral of the Honourable Colonel Christopher Codrington, late Captain General and Governor in Chief of her Majesty's Carribbee Islands ... London: for G. Strahan, 1710. 4°

T.273

4770

GRAHAM (James) *Marquess of Montrose.*

The Scotch souldier's speech, concerning the king's coronation oath. Made in the year 1647. By the Marquis of Montross. With a preface, shewing the necessity of an act of Parliament to prevent the further growth of schism... London: John Morphew, [c. 1710]. 8°

T.385

4771

A GRANADEER Quaker set in a true light. Being, some remarks on a late scandalous libel, entitul'd, High-Church antipathy to protestant liberty: or, An abstract of [Claridge] the Tottenham school-master's case ... London: printed in the year, 1710. 8°

T.302

1710 (Cont'd)

4772

GREAT BRITAIN. *Parliament. House of Lords.*

The reasons of those lords that enter'd their protest, in Dr. Sacheverell's case, &c. London: printed in the year 1710. 8°

T.102

4773

H.(L.)

A true answer to the Bishop of Salisbury's speech in the House of Lords on the first article of impeachment of Dr. Hen. Sacheverell. Paragraph by paragraph ... London, for W. Dolphin, and sold by John Morphew, 1710. 8°

T.49

4774

HARBIN (George)

The English constitution fully stated: with some animadversions on Mr. Higden's mistakes about it, in a letter to a friend... [Anon.] London, printed, and sold by the booksellers of London and Westminster, 1710. 8°

Attributed by Bowdler to Francis Cholmondeley.

3 copies.

T.274 T.398 T.640

4775

HIGDEN (William)

A defence of the view of the English constitution with respect to the sovereign authority of the prince, and the allegiance of the subject ... London, for S. Keble, and R. Gosling, 1710. 8°

3 copies.

T.398 T.274

4776

The HIGH Church mask pull'd off: or, Modern addresses anatomized. Designed chiefly for the information of the common people ... London: for A. Baldwin, 1710. 8°

T.299

4777

HIGH-Church politicks: or the abuse of the 30th of January consider'd. With remarks on Mr. Luke Milbourne's railing sermons, and on the observation of that day... London: B. Bragge, 1710. 8°

T.520

4778

HOADLY (Benjamin) *Bishop of Winchester.*

The election-dialogue, between a gentleman, and his neighbour in the country, concerning the choice of good members for the next Parliament. [Anon.] London, A. Baldwin, 1710. 8°

2 copies.

T.231 T.547

4779

HOADLY (Benjamin) *Bishop of Winchester.*

The fears and sentiments of all true Britains; with respect to national credit, interest and religion. [Anon.] London: A. Baldwin, 1710. 8°

2 copies.

T.417 T.549

4780

HOADLY (Benjamin) *Bishop of Winchester.*

The Jacobite's hopes reviv'd by our late tumults and addresses: or, Some necessary remarks upon a new modest pamphlet of Mr. Lesly's against the government, entituled, The good old cause: or, Lying in truth, &c. [Anon.] London printed, and sold by A. Baldwin, 1710. 8°

2 copies.

T.417 T.418

4781

HOADLY (Benjamin) *Bishop of Winchester.*

The thoughts of an honest Tory, upon the present proceedings of that party. In a letter to a friend in town. [Anon.] London, sold by A. Baldwin, 1710. 8°

2 copies.

T.363 T.547

4782

The IMPARTIAL secret history of Arlus, Fortunatus, and Odolphus, ministers of state to the Empress of Grand-Insula ... Printed in the year, 1710. 8°

T.147

4783

The INSTRUCTIVE library: or, An entertainment for the curious ... By a friend of the author of the Tale of a tub. Dedicated to Isaac Bickerstaffe Esq; Printed for the man in the moon, 1710. 8°

Teerink 1002B.

T.350

4784

J.(J.)

A letter to the Bishop of Oxford, occasion'd by his Lordship's speech on the first article of impeachment against Dr. Henry Sacheverell. Printed and sold by the booksellers, 1710. 8°

T.49

4785

JAMES I, *King of England.*

The judgment of K. James the first, and King Charles the first, against non-resistance, discover'd by their own letters, and now offer'd to the consideration of Dr. Sacheverell, and his party. London; for J. Baker, 1710. 8°

T.231

4786

JEACOCKE (Abraham)

Submission to governours considered, in a letter to a friend and admirer of Dr. Sacheverell; occasion'd by the late reviv'd doctrine of unlimited passive obedience. London, for A. Baldwin, 1710. 8°

2 copies.

T.229

4787

JEKYLL (*Sir* Joseph) *and others.*

The speeches of four managers upon the first article of Dr. Sacheverell's impeachment. London, for John Baker, 1710. 8°

T.49

4788

JOHN, the Churchman's vision. Oxford, printed in the year, 1710. 8°

T.297

4789

The JUDGMENT of whole kingdoms and nations, concerning the rights, power, and prerogative of kings, and the rights, priviledges, and properties of the people ... Written by a true lover of the Queen and country ... The third edition corrected, with additions. London: printed for, and sold by T. Harrison, 1710. 8°

Variously attributed to Daniel Defoe, Lord Somers and John Dunton.

T.227

4790

... The JUDGMENTS of whole kingdoms & nations, concerning the rights, power, and prerogative of kings, and the rights priviledges, & properties of the people ... Written by a true lover of the Queen & country ... The third edition corrected with additions. London, T. Harrison, 1710. 8°

Title-page and contents only (an advertisement).

T.413

4791

KELSALL (Edward)

Mistakes about moderation detected, and the true nature of it explain'd. In a sermon preach'd the 27th day of August. 1710. in the parish church of Boston ... London: for Jonah Bowyer, and sold by George Barton, bookseller in Boston, 1710. 8°

T.206

4792

KENNET (White) *Bishop of Peterborough.*

Concio ad Synodum ab Archiepiscopo episcopis & clero provinciae Cantuariensis celebrandam habita... xxv. Novembris, MDCCX. Londini, impensis J. Churchill, 1710. 4°

T.133

4793

KING (John) *Rector of Chelsea.*

The case of John Atherton, Bishop of Waterford in Ireland: fairly represented. Against a late partial edition of Dr. Bernard's relation, and sermon at his funeral ... [Anon.] London: for Luke Stokoe, and sold by J. Morphew, 1710. 8°

T.101

4794

KING (William) *Archbishop of Dublin.*

Divine predestination and fore-knowledg, consistent with the freedom of man's will. A sermon preach'd at Christ-Church, Dublin, May 15. 1709. before his Excellency Thomas Earl of Wharton... Printed at Dublin, and reprinted at London, for A. Bell, and J. Baker, 1710. 8°

T.804

4795

KING (William) *Student of Christ Church.*

A friendly letter from honest Tom Boggy, to the Reverend Mr. G[oddar]d, Canon of Windsor; occasion'd by a sermon against censure... London: printed in the year 1710. 8°

3 copies.

T.29 T.402 T.520

4796

KING (William) *Student of Christ Church.*

A second letter from Tom Boggy, to the Canon of Windsor; occasion'd by the late panegyrick given him by the Review of Thursday, July 13. 1710... London: printed in the year, 1710. 8°

3 copies.

T.29 T.402 T.520

4797

KNAGGS (Thomas)

A sermon preach'd in Chelsea church, June the first, 1710. at the funeral of the Honourable Mrs. Elizabeth Roberts ... London: J.B. and sold by J. Morphew, 1710. 8°

T.206

4798

L.(W.)

A letter to a new member of the honourable House of Commons; touching the rise of all the imbezzlements and mismanagements of the kingdom's treasure, from the beginning of the Revolution ... Amsterdam: printed in the year 1710. 4°

2 copies.

T.267 T.13

4799

LAURENCE (Roger)

Lay baptism invalid: or, An essay to prove that such baptism is null and void ... The second edition corrected and enlarged, with an appendix. By a lay hand. To which is prefix'd a letter to the author by the Reverend Geo. Hickes ... London: W. Taylor, 1710. 8°

T.409

4800

LAY-CRAFT exemplified in a discovery of that weakness of the late attempts of the author [i.e. Anthony Collins] of Priest-craft in perfection and Mr. Benjamin Robinson minister of the Gospel, to prove the English clergy guilty of forgery. In a letter to Mr. Robinson. London: for Richard Wilkin, 1710. 8°

T.153

4801

A LAY-MAN'S lamentation on the thirtieth of January; for the horrid, barbarous, and never to be forgotten murder of King Charles the first ... Address'd to Mr. Hoadley, as a confutation of his principles ... London: for M. Corbett, and sold by John Baker, 1710. 8°

T.297

4802

LE CLERC (Jean)

Mr. Le Clerc's account of the Earl of Clarendon's History of the Civil Wars. Done from the French printed at Amsterdam. By J.O. Part I. London, for Bernard Lintott, 1710. 8°

T.522

4803

LESLIE (Charles)

Mr. Leslie his answer, to the examination of his last dialogue, relating to the satisfaction of Jesus Christ. In a letter to the author [Thomas Emlyn]. With A supplement in answer to Mr. Clendon's treatise of the word person. London, printed and sold by the booksellers of London and Westminster, 1710. 2 parts. 4º

3 copies.

T.1 T.14 T.639

4804

LESLIE (Charles)

Beaucoup de bruit pour une aumelette, or, Much a do about nothing, being a tryal of skill betwixt the Jacobite's hopes revived [by Benjamin Hoadly], and the Good old cause. By a true Trojan. London printed: and sold by the booksellers of London and Westminster, 1710. 8º

3 copies.

T.159 T.191 T.370

4805

LESLIE (Charles)

The good old cause, further discuss'd. In a letter to the author [i.e. Benjamin Hoadly] of the Jacobite's hopes reviv'd ... [Anon.] London printed: and sold by the booksellers of London and Westminster, 1710. 8º

3 copies.

T.418 T.191 T.370

4806

LESLIE (Charles)

The good old cause, or, lying in truth, being a second defence of the Lord Bishop of Sarum, from a second speech... By one Miso-dolos... London, printed and sold by the booksellers of London and Westminster, 1710. 2 parts. 4º

3 copies.

T.2 T.5 T.191

4807

LESLIE (Charles)

Now or never: or, A project under God, to secure the Church [and monarchy] of England. In a congratulatory letter to... Lord D[artmouth], upon his late promotion: answer'd paragraph by paragraph. By a well-meaning Tory, who is willing to clear the Church of England from Jacobitism. London: for J. Baker, 1710. 8º

3 copies.

T.41 T.159 T.299

4808

A LETTER from a gentleman in London to a citizen of New-Sarum. With his answer to the same. [Relating to Bishop Burnet.] London, printed: and sold by the booksellers of London and Westminster, 1710. 8º

2 copies.

T.523 T.49

4809

A LETTER to Mr. B—— a North-Wiltshire clergyman, relating to an address from that archdeaconry to the Queen. Wherein a character is given of the Bishop of Sarum, and an account of the clergy's behaviour towards him. London, for S. Popping, 1710. 8º

2 copies.

T.166 T.52

4810

A LETTER to the French refugees concerning their behavior to the government... London, John Morphew, 1710. 8º

T.442

4811

LEWIS (Henry) *D.D.*

The methods, unreasonableness, and danger of sinners enticing others to sin. A sermon preach'd before the University of Oxford, at St. Mary's... July IX. 1710. Being Act-Sunday. Oxford, printed at the Theater, for Edw. Whistler; and are to be sold by Rich. Wilkin, and Rob. Gosling, [1710]. 8º

"Rd Dr Hicks: 25 July 1710."

T.36

4812

LEWIS (John) *Vicar of Minster.*

The clergy of the Church of England vindicated, in a sermon preach'd in the metropolitical church of Christ, Canterbury, on Tuesday, May 16. 1710. London: for R. Wilkin, 1710. 8º

T.206

4813

LEWIS (John) *Vicar of Minster.*

Presbyters not always an authoritative part of provincial synods. Being an examination of a part of Dr. Brett's chapter of provincial synods, in his late Account of church-government ... [Anon.] London: printed in the year 1710. 4º

T.133

4814

The LIFE and character of that eminent and learned prelate, the late Dr. Edw. Stillingfleet, Lord Bishop of Worcester. Together with some account of the works he has publish'd. [Variously attributed to Richard Bentley, Timothy Goodwin and Nathaniel Spinckes.] London, J. Heptinstall, for Henry and George Mortlock, 1710. 8º

2 copies.

T.162 T.822

4815

The LIFE and history, of Sarah, Dutches of Marlborough, containing her birth, family, and education: her rise and progress at court ... and other secret maters [sic] ... never before publish'd. London, J. Read, [1710]. 8º

T.281

4816

The LIFE, birth and education of the Reverend Mr. Benjamin Hoadly, Rector of St. Peters-Poor ... who wrote against Dr. Sacheverell's sermon and High-church; together with his writing, preaching, and character. Written by a student of the University of Cambridge. London: for J.R., [1710]. 8º

T.297

4817

LONDON.

The poll of the livery-men of the city of London, at the election for members of Parliament: begun Monday, October 9th, 1710. and ended the Saturday following ... London: for John Morphew, 1710. 8º

2 copies.

T.163 T.29

4818

The LD Bishop of Oxford vindicated from the abuse of a speech lately published under his Lordship's name. London: printed in the year 1710. 8º

4 copies.

T.49 T.102 T.147

4819

LOVELL (*Sir* Salathiel)

Mr. Baron Lovell's charge to the grand jury for the county of Devon, the 5th of April, 1710. At the castle of Exon. London, for A. Baldwin, 1710. 8º

T.229

4820

LOVELL (*Sir* Salathiel)

Mr. Baron L[ovell]'s charge to the grand jury for the county of Devon, the 5th of April, 1710... The famous speech-maker of England: or, Baron (alias Barren) L[ovell]'s charge, at the assizes at Exon, April 5th, 1710... London: printed and sold by the booksellers of London and Westminster, 1710. 16pp. 8º

T.29

4821

The LOYAL catechism: wherein, every English subject may be truly instructed in their duty to their prince, according to the apostolick doctrine of passive obedience and non-resistance. In a dialogue between Dr. Sacheverell and a young pupil ... London, John Morphew, 1710. 8º

T.229

4822

The LUNACY. A poem, address'd to the burroughs of Southwark and Bramber, against their next choice of members to serve in Parliament. London: J. Baker, [1710]. 8º

2 copies.
Wrongly attributed to Defoe.

T.204 T.350

4823

LYNFORD (Thomas)

Seasonable advice in quarrelsome times. A sermon preach'd in the parish church of St. Edmund the King, on Wednesday March 15. 1709. being the fast-day. London, Joseph Downing, 1710. 8º

T.152

4824

MAITTAIRE (Michael)

The doctrine of passive obedience, and non-resistance stated; and its consistence with theology, reason, justice, the Revolution, our laws and policy, impartially consider'd ... [Anon.] London: for John Morphew, 1710. 8º

2 copies.

T.367 T.297

4825

MARVELL (Andrew) *Junior, pseud.*

The Limehouse dream; or, The Churches prop. London, for J. Woodward, 1710. 8º

T.363

4826

MILBOURNE (Luke)

The measures of resistance to the higher powers, so far as becomes a Christian: in a sermon, preach'd on January the 30th, 1709/10 ... London: for George Sawbridge, 1710. 8º

3 copies.

T.491 T.101 T.152

4827

MILLER (Edmund)

Some remarks upon a letter entituled, The present state of Trinity College in Cambridge: written by Richard Bentley ... With some remarks also upon the preface pretended to be written, and publish'd together with the letter, by a gentleman of the Temple ... London, for John Morphew, 1710. 8º

T.415

4828

The MODERATION and loyalty of the dissenters exemplify'd from the historians, and other writers of their own party, as well as from their late proceedings ... London: printed in the year, 1710. 8º

2 copies.

T.301 T.211

4829

A MODEST answer to the four immodest letters to a friend in North-Britain. London: printed in the year, 1710. 8º

3 copies.

T.231 T.413 T.417

4830

MODEST reflection on the Right Reverend the Bishop of Norwich his late charge to the reverend clergy of his diocess. By a Catholick... [Attributed to William Nokes.] Printed for the author, anno 1710. 4º

T.190

4831

The MODESTY and moderation of the dissenters set in a true light; or, A specimen of their proposals for a comprehension ... Humbly offer'd to the consideration of the moderate sons of the Church of England. London: for J. Morphew, 1710. 8º

2 copies.

T.301 T.101

4832

MOSS (Robert) *Dean of Ely.*

A sermon preach'd before the Queen at St. James's chapel, on Wednesday, March 15, 1709/10. being the day appointed... for a general fast and humiliation... London: for Richard Sare; and Jacob Tonson, 1710. 4º

2 copies.

T.3 T.771

4833

A MOST humble and seasonable proposal to the Queen, to raise money without any tax, sufficient to rebuild her royal palace of White-hall, in greater magnificence than ever... To be sold by the booksellers; and by L. Beardwell, [c.1710]. 8º

T.147

4834

N.(J.)

The rights of the scholars of Trinity-College asserted, and several abuses detected. In a second letter to the Reverend John, Ld. Bp. of Ely. By a master of arts and fellow of the said College ... Sold by the booksellers of London and Westminster, [1710]. 8º

T.415

4835

N. (J.)

Some considerations humbly offer'd in a letter
to John, Lord Bishop of Ely; on a book,
entituled, The present state of Trinity-College
in Cambridge. By Dr. Bentley. By a master of
arts, and fellow of the said College... London:
for J. Morphew, [1710].   8°

T.415

4836

NEEDHAM (John) *Rector of Bedhampton.*

Considerations concerning the origine and cure of
our Church-divisions. In two sermons ... London:
J.L. for R. and J. Bonwicke, 1710.   8°

T.206

4837

A NEW catechism, with Dr. Hickes's thirty nine
articles ... London, for Ben. Bragg, 1710.   8°

T.408

4838

A NEW catechism, with Dr. Hickes's thirty nine
articles ... The second edition corrected. London,
for Ben. Bragg, 1710.   8°

2 copies.

T.102 T.157

4839

A NEW extempore-prayer, fitted for the use of all
conventicles; where rebellion has its rise, and
loyalty its downfall. London: J. Baker, 1710.   8°

T.58

4840

The NEW ill designs of sowing sedition, detected;
and the pretended friends, but private enemies of the
Church and State, discover'd and expos'd. Or, A
vindication of the Lord Bishop of Salisbury's speech
in the House of Lords, at the tryal of Dr.
Sacheverell... In a modest reply to a scurrilous
pamphlet [by Charles Leslie], entitul'd, The good
old cause, or, Lying in truth; London: for J.
Baker, 1710.   4°

3 copies.

T.2   T.5   T.190

4841

The NEW scheme consider'd, to which is added The
Cheshire address with reflections. London: for J.
Baker, 1710.   8°

T.299

4842

NEWCOME (Peter)

A sermon preach'd to the societies for reformation of
manners, at St. Mary-le-Bow. On Monday, December the
26th. 1709. London: J.L. for John Wyat, 1710.   8°

T.152

4843

NO conquest, but the hereditary right of her Majesty,
and her declar'd protestant successors, from their
Saxon predecessors, and acts of settlement, asserted.
In a postscript to a treatise entitl'd, A prelude to
the tryal of skill between Sacheverelism, and the
constitution of the monarchy of Great Britain ...
London, printed: and sold by John Baker, 1710.   8°

T.231

4844

OLDISWORTH (William)

Annotations on the Tatler. Written in French by
Monsieur Bournelle; and translated into English
by Walter Wagstaff... London: for Bernard Lintott,
1710. 2 parts.   12°

2 copies.

T.448 T.456

4845

OLDMIXON (John)

A complete history of addresses, from the first
original under Oliver Cromwell, to this present year
1710 ... By one very near a-kin to the author of the
Tale of a tub. 2nd ed. London, printed in the year
1710, and sold by the booksellers of London and
Westminster.   8°

T.299

4846

OLLYFFE (George)

A Christian alarm, to the enemies of charity and
moderation. In a sermon, occasion'd by the late
disturbances, and preach'd at St. Andrews Holborn,
March 19. 1710. London: J. Downing, and J. Baker,
1710.   8°

T.293

4847

OSWALD (John)

Mr. John Oswald's vindication of himself against
the lyes and slanders of his enemies, in a letter
to the Lord Bishop of Sarum. [No imprint, 1710?]
8°

T.522

4848

OXFORD. *University.*

University loyalty: or, The genuine explanation of
the principles and practices of the English clergy,
as established and directed by the decree of the
University of Oxford, past in their Convocation
21 July 1683... London, for A. Baldwin, 1710.   8°

2 copies.

T.231 T.549

4849

P.(J.)

A refutation of the doctrine of passive obedience
and non-resistance. Written by J.P. one of the laity
of Marlborough. London: S. Popping, 1710.   8°

T.157

4850

P. (W.)

A brief epistle to Henry Sacheverel, the high-flying
doctor. In behalf of the peaceable people called
Quakers, whom he damns by wholesale. In a sermon
(as he calls it) preach'd at Paul's, November. 5.
1709... London: for T. King, [1710].   8°

T.229

4851

PALMER (Charles)

A defence of passive obedience and non-resistance,
to supreme and soveraign powers ... London, W.S.
for J. Ward, and sold by J. Morphew, 1710.   8°

T.231

4852

A PARAPHRASE on the fourteenth chapter of Isaiah,
only appropriating what is there meant of the King of
Babylon to Oliver the Protector. A pindarique. Humbly
dedicated to D[avi]d P[olhi]ll ... [Signed Philo
Dear-heart.] London: printed in the year, 1710.   8°

T.350

4853

PARIS (John) *and* WHITE (Samuel)

The true state of Trinity College, in a letter to a
residing fellow of that society: wherein the trifling
impertinencies, malicious aspersions, and bold
falsehoods of Dr. Bentley, are answer'd in such a
manner as they deserve ... [Anon.] London: for
John Morphew, 1710.   8°

T.415

4854

PARKER (Henry)

A political catechism: or, Certain questions
concerning the government of this land; answered in
his Majesties own words... [Anon.] London:
printed in the year 1643. And re-printed and sold
by J. Baker, 1710.   8°

T.403

4855

The PARLIAMENT arraigned, convicted; wants nothing but
execution ... Written in the year of wonders ... by
Tom Tyranno-Mastix; alias, Mercurius Melancholicus ...
Printed for the publick view of all his Majesty's
faithful subjects; and are to be sold at the old sign
of You may go look, anno Dom. 1648. [Reprinted 1710.]
24 pp.   8°

T.231

4856

A PENNY cord for the pretended Prince of Wales, or;
A Scotch cordial to cure the French King of the
griping of the guts. Reprinted from the original
copy of Edinburgh, [*c.* 1710].   4°

T.269

4857

The PERILS of false brethren: set forth in the fable
of the boy and wolf ... London, printed in the year,
1710.   8°

T.350

4858

PETERS (Hugh)

The perfect pattern of true worldly happiness; or the
only path-way to become rich, great, splendid and
glorious. As it was deliver'd in a funeral sermon,
preach'd at the death of Oliver Cromwell ... London:
printed in the year 1658. And now reprinted by Tho.
Simmons, 1710.   8°

T.82

4859

The PICTTRE [sic] of malice, or a true account of
Dr. Sacheverell's enemies, and their behaviour with
regard to him since the fifth of November last.
London, printed and are to be sold by J. King, 1710.
8°

T.229

4860

The PICTURE of malice, or a true account of Dr.
Sacheverell's enemies, and their behaviour with
regard to him since the fifth of November last.
London, J. King, 1710.   8°

Incomplete.

T.147

4861

The PICTURE of malice, or a true account of Dr.
Sacheverell's enemies, and their behaviour with regard
to him since the fifth of November last. London,
printed for, and are to sold [sic] by J. Read, 1710.
8°

T.102

4862

PITTIS (William)

The seven extinguishers. A poem.[Anon.] London,
printed in the year 1710.   4°

2 copies.

T.261 T.269

4863

PLACE (Conyers)

The true English revolutionist, or; The happy turn,
rightly taken ... London: for W. Taylor, 1710. 8°

T.403

4864

The PLAY-HOUSE scuffle, or, Passive obedience kickt
off the stage. Being a true relation of a new tragi-
comedy, as it was acted last week at the play-house in
Drury-lane ... London: for J. Bethel, and sold by
John Morphew, 1710.   8°

T.350

4865

A PRELUDE to the tryal of skill between Sacheverelism,
and the constitution of the monarchy of Great Britain.
Occasion'd by the printing Dr. Sacheverell's answer to
his impeachment ... London, printed in the year 1710,
and sold by the booksellers.   8°

T.229

4866

A PROPOSAL humbly offered for the laying a tax upon
liberty of conscience written by a dissenter for the
preventing all hypocrisie and occasional conformity.
Printed in the year 1710.   8°

T.390

4867

PROPOSALS for supplying the loss of soldiers,
by a new million-lottery, wherein all are certain
of getting. Invented for the benefit of ladies
that want husbands, and younger brothers that stand
in need of rich wives... London, printed: and
sold by J. Morphew, 1710.   8°

T.490

4868

PRYNNE (William)

The title of kings proved to be jure divino... In
a short essay, written by W. Prynne Esquire. And
published in the year 1660. and now reprinted...
London, A. Baldwin, [*c.*1710].   8°

T.344

4869

QUEVEDO Y VILLEGAS (Francisco Gomez de)

The controversy about resistance and non-resistance, discuss'd in moral and political reflections on Marcus Brutus... Written in Spanish by Don Francisco de Quevedo Villegas... Translated into English. And publish'd in defence of Dr. Henry Sacheverell... London, for J. Baker, 1710. 8°

T.231

4870

REASONS against receiving the Pretender, and restoring the popish line. Together with some queries of the utmost importance to Great Britain. [This pamphlet has been attributed to Hoadly and to Defoe.] London: A. Baldwin, 1710. 8°

2 copies.

T.413   T.91

4871

REASONS for a total change of a certain m[ember] and the dissolution of the P[arliament] ... With a word to the Bank of England, on account of some undutiful proceedings amongst the right worshipfuls and worshipfuls that govern it. London: for J. Baker, [1710]. 4°

T.267

4872

REASONS to prove the complying clergy, and those that adhere to them, guilty of schism. Printed in the year 1710. brs.

Folded inside *The difference between the Nonjurors.*

T.439

4873

REASONS why a certain great g[enera]l has not yet receiv'd the thanks of either of the two houses of Parliament ... In a letter to the mayor of St. Albans. Printed in the year, 1710. 8°

T.281

4874

REBELLION sainted: or, King-killing openly avow'd and justify'd. Being the dying words and sentiments of the regicides that were executed for the impious murder of their sovereign K. Charles ... London: B. Bragg, 1710. 8°

T.302

4875

REFLECTIONS on Dr. Sacheverell's answer to the articles of impeachment, exhibited against him by the honourable House of Commons paragraph by paragraph ... London: sold by B. Bragge, 1710. 4°

T.2

4876

RESISTANCE and non-resistance stated and decided: in a dialogue betwixt a Hotspur-high-flyer, a canting-Low-Church man, and B[ickerstaf]f censor of Great Britain. London: J. Baker, 1710. 8°

3 copies.

T.41   T.157   T.231

4877

RICHMOND (Henry)

Two sermons preached at the assizes held at Lancaster, on Sunday Aug. 27. 1710 ... London: for Jonah Bowyer, and sold by Joseph Eaton bookseller in Leverpoole, 1710. 2 parts. 8°

T.205

4878

The ROASTING of a parson [i.e. Henry Sacheverell]. A ditty, that may be sung by the High-Church, and said by the Low. In imitation (and to the tune) of Chevy Chace. London: printed and sold by the booksellers of London and Westminster, 1710. 8°

T.204

4879

ROBERTS (William) *Rector of Jacobstow.*

The divine institution of the Gospel ministry, and the necessity of episcopal ordination, asserted. In a sermon, preach'd at the primary visitation of ... Ofspring Lord Bishop of Exon, held at Okehampton, August 19th, 1709. 2nd ed ... Exon: Sam. Farley, for Philip Bishop, 1710. 8°

T.36

4880

RULES of government: or, a true balance between sovereignty and liberty. Written by a person of honour, immediately after the late Civil War. And now published, to prevent another. [Attributed to —— Lund, or to Sir Philip Warwick.] London: for Bernard Lintott, 1710. 8°

T.231

4881

S.(H.)

Reasons why the Duke of Marlborough cannot lay down his commands, deduced from the principles of loyalty, gratitude, honour, interest, &c. In a letter from the country to a friend in London. London: J. Baker, 1710. 4°

T.267

4882

SACHEVERELL (Henry)

The answer of Henry Sacheverell, D.D. to the articles of impeachment, exhibited against him by the honourable House of Commons... Printed in the year 1710. 8°

5 copies (three different impressions)

T.49   T.102   T.147

4883

SACHEVERELL (Henry)

Collections of passages referr'd to by Dr. Henry Sacheverell in his answer to the articles of his impeachment ... 2nd ed. London: for H. Clements, 1710. 8°

T.169

4884

SACHEVERELL (Henry)

A defence of her Majesty's title to the Crown, and a justification of her entring into a war with France and Spain: as it was deliver'd in a sermon preach'd before the University of Oxford on the 10th day of June, 1702 ... 2nd ed. London: for Henry Clements, 1710. 8°

2 copies.

T.491   T.82

4885

SACHEVERELL (Henry)

The nature, obligation, and measures of conscience, deliver'd in a sermon preach'd at Leicester, at the assizes held there, July 25th, 1706... London: J. Bradford, 1710. 8°

T.491

4886

SACHEVERELL (Henry)

Dr. Sacheverel's prayers and meditations on the day of his tryal, being February 27th. 1709/10. London, for George Sawbridge, [1710]. 8°

2 copies.

T.229   T.336

4887

SACHEVERELL (Henry)

Dr. Sacheverel's prayers of thanksgiving, for his great deliverance out of his troubles. London, for George Sawbridge, 1710. 8°

T.229

4888

SACHEVERELL (Henry)

The speech of Henry Sacheverell, D.D. upon his impeachment at the bar of the House of Lords, in Westminster-Hall, March 7. 1709/10. London: printed in the year 1710. Fol.

T.543

4889

SACHEVERELL (Henry)

The speech of Henry Sacheverell, D.D. made in Westminster-Hall, on Tuesday, March 7, 1709/10. London: for J. Baker, 1710. 8°

2 copies.

T.169   T.345

4890

SACHEVERELL (Henry)

The speech of Henry Sacheverell, D.D. upon his impeachment at the bar of the House of Lords, in Westminster-Hall, March 7. 1709/10. London, printed in the year 1710. 8°

T.49

4891

SACHEVERELL (Henry)

Dr. Sacheverel's speech upon his impeachment at the bar of the House of Lords, in Westminster-Hall, March 7. 1709/10. With reflections thereupon, paragraph by paragraph. Wherein the charge of the Commons against him is fully justify'd ... London, for B. Bragg, 1710. 8°

T.49

4892

ST. JOHN (Henry) *Viscount Bolingbroke.*

A letter to the Examiner. [Anon.] Printed in the year, 1710. 8°

3 copies.

T. 51   T.159   T.348

4893

ST. JOHN (Pawlet)

The promise and advantages of Christ's presence within his Church. A sermon preach'd before the reverend archdeacon and clergy of the county of Bedford, at the visitation ... 2nd ed. London: for J. Bowyer, 1710. 8°

T.206

4894

ST. LEGER (Sir John)

The manager's pro and con: or, An account of what is said at Child's and Tom's coffee-houses for and against Dr. Sacheverell... (Reflections on a late pamphlet [by Anthony Collins], intitled, Priestcraft in perfection.) [Anon.] London: A. Baldwin, 1710. 2 parts. 8°

T.49

4895

ST. LEGER (Sir John)

The managers pro and con: or, An account of what is said at Child's and Tom's coffee-houses for and against Dr. Sacheverell ... The third edition corrected. (Reflections on a late pamphlet [by Anthony Collins], intitled, Priestcraft in perfection.) [Anon.] London: A. Baldwin, 1710. 8°

T.169

4896

ST. LEGER (Sir John)

The manager's pro and con: or, An account of what is said at Child's and Tom's coffee-houses for and against Dr. Sacheverell ... 5th ed. (Reflections on a late pamphlet [by Anthony Collins], intitled, Priestcraft in perfection.) [Anon.] London: A. Baldwin, 1710. 8°

T.147

4897

ST. Paul and her Majesty vindicated. In proving from the Apostle's own words, Rom. XIII. that the doctrine of non-resistance, as commonly taught, is none of his ... 2nd ed. London: first printed Feb. 25. Sold by A. Baldwin, and most booksellers in London and Westminster, 1710. 8°

T.231

4898

The SALISBURY quarrel ended: or, The last letter of the citizen of New Sarum to Mr. Hoadly. In which the true notions of passive obedience and hereditary right are more fully explain'd. London: for W. Taylor, 1710. 8°

T.166

4899

A SECOND test offer'd to the electors of Great Britain. Impartially collected out of the addresses of both parties ... London: printed in the year 1710. 8°

T.299

4900

The SECRET history of Arlus and Odolphus, ministers of state to the Empress of Grandinsula... Printed in the year, 1710. 8°

2 copies.

T.281   T.418

4901

SELLER (Abednego)

A defence of Dr. Sacheverell. Or, Passive-obedience prov'd to be the doctrine of the Church of England, from the Reformation, to these times ... [Anon.] 2nd ed. London printed: and sold by J. Baker, 1710. 8°

T.229

4902

A SERMON [on Titus III.1] preach'd on the anniversary-fast for the martyrdom of King Charles I. in the last century. London, printed, and sold by the booksellers, 1710. 8°

Not the sermon by Robert South, nor that by John Sharp.

T.152

4903

SHARP (John) *Archbishop of York*.

A sermon preach'd before the Lords ... in the abbey-church at Westminster, on the thirtieth of January, 1699/700 ... London: H. Hills, 1710. 8°

T.82

4904

SHERLOCK (Thomas) *Bishop of London*.

A sermon preach'd before the Sons of the clergy, at their anniversary-meeting in the church of St. Paul, December 5. 1710. 2nd ed. London: for John Pemberton, 1710. 8°

2 copies.

T.206 T.104

4905

A SHORT essay towards the promoting of love and unity amongst Christians of different persuasions in the lesser matters of religion ... London: for Jonathan Robinson; and sold by A. Baldwin, 1710. 8°

T.302

4906

A SHORT historical account of the contrivances and conspiracies of the men of Dr. Sacheverell's principles, in the late reigns. London, A. Baldwin, 1710. 8°

T.229

4907

SMALBROKE (Richard) *Bishop of Lichfield and Coventry*.

The doctrine of an universal judgment asserted. In a sermon preach'd before the University at St. Mary's in Oxford, June the 9th, 1706. In which the principles of Mr. Dodwell's late Epistolary discourse ... are consider'd ... London: H. Hills, 1710. 8°

T.345

4908

SMALRIDGE (George) *Bishop of Bristol*.

Not as pleasing men, but God. A sermon preach'd at the cathedral church of St. Paul, before ... the lord mayor, the judges and aldermen, Jan. 29. 1709/10. London: for Jonah Bowyer, 1710. 4°

2 copies.
Another copy, in 8°

T.3 T.78 T.152

4909

SMALRIDGE (George) *Bishop of Bristol*.

The royal benefactress: or, the great charity of educating poor children. In a sermon preached in the parish-church of St. Sepulchre, June 1. 1710... at the anniversary meeting of the children educated in the charity-schools, in and about the cities of London and Westminster... London, J. Downing, for Jonah Bowyer, 1710. 4°

2 copies.

T.3 T.700

4910

SMALRIDGE (George) *Bishop of Bristol*.

The thoughts of a country gentleman upon reading Dr. Sacheverell's tryal. In a letter to a friend ... [Anon.] London: printed and sold by the booksellers of London and Westminster, 1710. 8°

3 copies.

T.417 T.336 T.147

4911

SNAPE (Andrew)

A sermon preach'd before ... the lord-mayor, the aldermen and citizens of London, at the cathedral-church of St. Paul, on Monday the 30th of Jan. 17[0]9/10 ... London: for Jonah Bowyer, 1710. 8°

2 copies.

T.491 T.152

4912

SOLOMON against Welton: or, That prince's authority brought against the insolence of the White-chappel priest ... By way of remarks on the Dr's sermon preached before the lieutenancy ... November 19. 1710. [London], sold by John Baker, [1710]. 8°

T.104

4913

SOME queries propos'd to the publisher of a certain pamphlet called the Bishop of S[aru]m's speech, in the House of Lords, on the first article of the impeachment, of Dr. Henry Sacheverell ... London: printed and sold by the booksellers, [1710]. 8°

T.49

4914

SOME reflections on a letter occasion'd by Bishop Lake's dying declaration, and entituled, The opinion of the pious and learned Mrs. Eyre, &c. concerning the doctrine of passive obedience, as the distinguishing character of the Church of England. London, for Richard Wilkin, 1710. 8°

2 copies.

T.417 T.157

4915

A SPECIMEN of the wholesom severities, practis'd in Queen Elizabeth's reign, against her protestant dissenters; in the examination of Henry Barrow ... Recommended by Dr. Henry Sacheverell, as proper for the present times ... London, for J. Baker, 1710. 8°

T.336

4916

The SPEECH of the Lord Haversham's ghost. London: printed in the year 1710. 8°

T.162

4917

SPEED (Robert)

The counter-scuffle. A poem. [Anon.] London, printed, and sold by the booksellers of London and Westminster, 1710. 8°

T.29

4918

SPINCKES (Nathaniel)

The new pretenders to prophecy re-examined: and their pretences shewn to be groundless and false. And Sir R. Bulkeley and A. Whitro convicted of very foul practices, in order to the carrying on their imposture. London: for Richard Sare, 1710. 8°

T.382

4919

STACY (Edmund)

The black-bird's tale. A poem... [Anon.] London: printed in the year, 1710. 8°

2 copies.

T.89 T.350

4920

STACY (Edmund)

The black-bird's second tale. A poem. By the author of the first... London, printed for and sold by Ed. Lewis, 1710. 8°

T.350

4921

STACY (Edmund)

The black-bird's third tale. A poem. By the author of the first... London, John Morphew, 1710. 8°

T.350

4922

STACY (Edmund)

The tale of the Robin-red-breast. A poem. By the author of The black bird's tale... London: printed and sold by most booksellers of London, and Westminster, 1710. 8°

T.35

4923

STANHOPE (George) *Dean of Canterbury*.

The common obstructions to faith, and a good life considered. A sermon preached in the chapel-royal at St. James's, Novemb. the 6th, 1709. London: for Richard Sare, 1710. 8°

2 copies.

T.491 T.152

4924

STANHOPE (George) *Dean of Canterbury*.

A sermon preached before the Queen in the chapel-royal at St. James's; November the 7th 1710. Being the day of thanksgiving to Almighty God, for the successes of this campaign... London: W. Bowyer, for Richard Sare, 1710. 8°

3 copies.

T.101 T.104 T.206

4925

The STATE bell-mans collection of verses for the year 1711 ... London, John Morphew, 1710. 8°

T.350

4926

The STATE of the Palatines for fifty years past to this present time... London: for J. Baker, 1710. 8°

T.44

4927

SWIFT (Jonathan) *Dean of St. Patrick's*.

A meditation upon a broom-stick, and somewhat beside; of the same author's ... [Anon.] London: for E. Curll; and sold by J. Harding, 1710. 8°

Teerinck 1A.

T.347

4928

SWIFT (Thomas)

Noah's dove. An earnest exhoration to peace: set forth in a sermon preach'd on the 7th of November, 1710. A thanksgiving day ... London: for Bernard Lintott; and sold by A. Baldwin, [1710]. 8°

2 copies.

T.104 T.206

4929

SWINFEN (John)

The objections of the non-subscribing London clergy, against the address from the Bishop of London, and the clergy of London and Westminster... Humbly offerr'd in a letter from a clergy-man in London, to a member of Parliament in the country. By the author of the Reasons of the absenting clergy. London: A. Baldwin, 1710. 8°

5 copies.

T.159 T.230 T.299 T.417

4930

SWINFEN (John)

The reasons of the absenting clergy, for not appearing at St. Paul's, on Monday, August 21. 1710. When the address from the bishop and clergy of London was propos'd and sign'd. Humbly offer'd in a letter from a clergy-man in the City to a member of Parliament in the country. London: for A. Baldwin, 1710. 8°

3 copies.

T.299 T.230 T.41

4931

SYNGE (Edward) *Archbishop of Tuam*.

The divine authority of church-government, and episcopacy, stated and asserted, upon principles common to all Christians. In a sermon at the consecration of... Peter Brown, late Provost of Trinity College, Dublin, and now Lord Bishop of Corke and Rosse... London, for Richard Sare, 1710. 8°

2 copies.

T.36 T.622

4932

TALBOT (William) *Bishop of Durham*.

The Bishop of Oxford his speech in the House of Lords on the first article of the impeachment of Dr. Henry Sacheverell. London: for Jonah Bowyer, 1710. 8°

4 copies.

T.49 T.102 T.147 T.169

4933

TEAGUE'S everlasting glory, set forth in St. Patrick's giving a true character of Ireland ... London, for W. Dolphin, and sold by J. Morphew, 1710. 8°

T.58

4934

THOMAS (John) *Minister of Yately*.

Fear God and the King. A sermon preach'd at the assizes held at Winchester, the 19th day of July ... London, for T. Bever, and J. Morphew, 1710. 8°

T.206

4935
THOMPSON (John) *Baron Haversham.*

The Lord H[aversham]'s speech in the House of Lords, on the first article of the impeachment of Dr. Henry Sacheverell. London: for A.R. and sold by John Morphew, 1710. 8°

2 copies.

T.147 T.336

4936
The THOUGHTS of an honest Whig, upon the present proceedings of that party. In a letter to a friend in town. London: printed in the year, 1710. 8°

T.363

4937
TILLY (William)

A return to our former good old principles and practice, the only way to restore and preserve our peace. A sermon preach'd before the University of Oxford, at St. Mary's, on Sunday, May the 14th 1710. With a letter to Dr. Sacheverell. Oxford: L. Lichfield, for Anth. Peisley: and are to be sold by J. Knapton, H. Clements and J. Morphew, 1710. 8°

T.36

4938
TILLY (William)

A return to our former good old principles and practice, the only way to restore and preserve our peace. A sermon preach'd before the University of Oxford, at St. Mary's, on Sunday, May the 14th 1710. With a letter to Dr. Sacheverell. 4th ed. Oxford: L. Lichfield, for Anth. Peisley: and are to be sold by J. Knapton, H. Clements and J. Morphew, 1710. 8°

T.622

4939
TILLY (William)

The sins and vices of mens lives, the chief cause of their ignorance and corrupt opinions in religion. A sermon preach'd before the University of Oxford, at St. Mary's, on December the 11th, 1709. London, for Anthony Peisley, and are to be sold by J. Knapton and Hen. Clements, 1710. 8°

T.622

4940
TINDAL (Matthew)

The merciful judgments of High Church triumphant on offending clergymen, and others, in the reign of Charles I ... [Anon.] London, for Ben. Bragg, 1710. 8°

T.231

4941
TINT for taunt. The manager managed: or, The exemplary moderation and modesty, of a Whig Low-Church-preacher discovered, from his own mouth. In remarks ... upon a sermon, preach'd on Sunday, the fifth of November last past ... by the self-call'd, Honourable Robert Lumley Lloyd ... London: printed in the year 1710. 8°

2 copies.

T.336 T.230

4942
TO the Wh[ig]s nineteen queries, a fair and full answer, by an honest Torie; purely for the publick good of his country. [Attributed to Francis Atterbury.] London: for J. Baker, 1710. 8°

3 copies.

T.281 T.348 T.418

4943
TO the Wh[ig]s nineteen queries, a fair and full answer, by an honest Torie; purely for the publick good of his country. [Attributed to Francis Atterbury]. Printed in the year 1710. 8°

T.417

4944
TOLAND (John)

The Jacobitism, perjury, and popery of High Church priests ... [Anon.] London; for J. Baker, 1710. 8°

T.302

4945
TOLAND (John)

Mr. Toland's reflections on Dr. Sacheverells sermon preach'd at St. Paul's, Nov. 5. 1709. In a letter from an English-man to an Hollander. Lately publish'd in French in Holland, and translated into English, to let the world know how Dr. Sacheverell's case is represented abroad. London, J. Baker, 1710. 8°

T.229

4946
TRAPP (Joseph)

A letter out of the country, to the author [Sir John St. Leger] of The managers pro and con, in answer to his account of what is said at Child's and Tom's in the case of Dr. Sacheverell, article by article ... [Anon.] London, for J. Morphew, 1710. 8°

2 copies.

T.231 T.147

4947
TRAPP (Joseph)

Most faults on one side: or, The shallow politicks, foolish arguing, and villanous designs of the author [i.e. Simon Clement] of a late pamphlet, entitul'd Faults on both sides consider'd and expos'd... [Anon.] London: for John Morphew, 1710. 8°

2 copies.

T.363 T.547

4948
TRAPP (Joseph)

An ordinary journy no progress: or, A man doing his own business no mover of sedition. Being a vindication of Dr. Sacheverell, from the slanders rais'd against him, upon the account of the late honours which have been paid him in the country. [Anon.] London: printed in the year 1710. 8°

T.336

4949
TRIMNELL (Charles) *Bishop of Winchester.*

A charge deliver'd to the clergy of the diocess of Norwich. At the visitation of that diocess, in the year, 1709. By ... Charles, Lord Bishop of Norwich. London: F. Collins, and are to be sold by Maurice Atkins, 1710. 4°

Annotated [by George Hickes?].

T.190

4950
TROUTBECK (John)

The good old principles the safest way to salvation: deliver'd in a sermon at the assizes held at Northampton, on Wednesday July 19. 1710 ... London: for Henry Clements, 1710. 8°

T.206

4951
A TRUE and faithful account of the last distemper and death of Tom. Whigg, Esq; who departed this life on the 22d day of September last, anno Domini 1710 ... Part I. London: printed in the year 1710. 8°

T.363

4952
A TRUE and faithful account of the last distemper and death of Tom. Whigg, Esq; who departed this life on the 22d day of September last, anno Domini 1710... The second edition, corrected... Part I. London: printed in the year 1710. 8°

T.641

4953
A TRUE defence of Henry Sacheverell, D.D. in a letter to Mr. D——n ... By L.M.N.O. London, W. Dolphin, 1710. 8°

T.229 T.102

4954
A TRUE description of the Mint. Giving an account of its first becoming a place of refuge for debtors ... The manners, ways, and customs of the inhabitants: with their character, nature and temper ... London, A. Baldwin, and T. Harrison, 1710. 8°

T.163

4955
TRUE passive obedience restor'd in 1710. In a dialogue between a country-man and a true patriot. London: S. Popping, 1710. 8°

T.418

4956
A TRUE state of the case of the Rev. Mr. Greenshields ... now prisoner in the Tolbooth of Edinburgh, for reading common prayer in an episcopal congregation there ... With copies of several original papers. London, J. Bowyer, 1710. Fol.

Wanting title-page.

T.77

4957
A TRUE state of the case of the Reverend Mr. Greenshields, now prisoner in the Tolbooth in Edinburgh, for reading common-prayer, in an episcopal congregation there ... With copies of several original papers ... London: for Jonah Bowyer, 1710. 8°

T.349

4958
The TRUE use of a stanch Church-jury, practically explain'd by an eminent attorney at law [i.e. Robert South]: for which he is now under confinement by order of the High Court of Chancery. In answer to a letter a friend. London; for A. Baldwin, 1710. 8°

T.405

4959
The TRYALS of Peter Messenger [and others] for high treason, in tumultuously assembling themselves in Moor-Fields, and other places, under colour of pulling down of bawdy-houses. At the sessions-house in the Old-Baily on Saturday, April 4. 1688 ... London, for S. Popping, 1710. 8°

T.207

4960
UNDONE again; or, The plot discover'd. Being a detection of the practices of papists with sectaries, for overthrowing the government, and the national church ... Humbly inscrib'd to all the true lovers of Old England; and may serve for an answer to all the scandalous pamphlets and reflexions thrown upon Dr. Sacheverell. London: printed in the year 1710. 8°

T.91

4961
The VOICE of the addressers: or, A short comment upon the chief things maintain'd, or condemn'd, in our late modest addresses. London: A. Baldwin, 1710. 8°

T.299

4962
VOX dilectionis: or, The young nonconformist charitably call'd back. In a short and kind letter to such a one, who was ordain'd by his brethren, to be a preacher, August 23. 1710. At Southmolton, in Devon. By a true friend of his. Exon: Joseph Bliss, for Philip Bishop, 1710. 8°

T.377

4963
WAKE (William) *Archbishop of Canterbury.*

The Bishop of Lincoln's charge, to the clergy of his diocese, in his triennial visitation begun at Leicester, June the 1st. 1709. London: for Richard Sare, 1710. 4°

T.190

4964
WAKE (William) *Archbishop of Canterbury.*

The danger and mischief of a mis-guided zeal: a sermon preach'd at the parish church of St. James Westminster, April the 2d, 1710. By ... William Lord Bishop of Lincoln. London: for R. Sare, 1710. 8°

2 copies.

T.36 T.152

4965
WAKE (William) *Archbishop of Canterbury.*

The Bishop of Lincoln's and Bishop of Norwich's speeches in the House of Lords, March the 17th. at the opening of the second article of the impeachment against Dr. Sacheverell. London: for John Morphew, 1710.

3 copies.

T.49 T.102 T.169

4966
WALKER (John) *Vicar of Ledbury.*

Not Baal, but the Lord: or the prophet's plea for truth. A sermon preach'd in the parish-church of Ledbury in Herefordshire, April the 23d. 1710 ... London, for R. Knaplock, 1710. 8°

T.152

4967
WALPOLE (Robert) *Earl of Orford.*

A letter from a foreign minister in England, to Monsieur Pettecum. Containing the true reasons of the late changes in the ministry... Translated from the French original. [Anon.] London: for J. Baker, 1710. 8°

2 copies.

T.418 T.547

4968

WARD (Edward)

The galloper: or, Needs must when the Devil drives.
A poem. [Anon.] London: for John Morphew, 1710. 4°

T.269

4969

WARD (Edward)

Pulpit-war: or, Dr. S[achevere]ll, the High-Church
trumpet, and Mr. H[oad]ly, the Low-Church drum,
engaged. By way of dialogue between the fiery
dragon, and aspiring grashopper. [Anon.] London,
J. Baker, 1710. 8°

2 copies.

T.350 T.89

4970

WARD (Edward)

Vulgus Britannicus: or, The British Hudibrass ...
[Anon.] London: for James Woodward; and John Morphew,
1710. 5 parts. 8°

T.347

4971

WATTS (Robert)

The lawfulness and right manner of keeping Christmas:
shewn in a familiar conference between a Church-man
and a dissenter... [Anon.] London: Joseph Downing,
1710. 8°

T.455

4972

The WELCHMAN'S tales concerning the times ... London:
printed in the year, 1710. 8°

T.89

4973

WELLS (Edward)

The duty of being grieved for the sins of others.
Briefly set forth in a sermon preached in St. Martin's
church in Leicester, April the 26th, 1710 ... London,
W.B. for James Knapton; and sold by John Ward,
bookseller in Leicester, 1710. 8°

T.206

4974

WELTON (Richard)

The wise man's counsel upon the test. In a sermon
preach'd before the honourable the lieutenancy of the
city of London ... November the 19th, 1710. London:
for Samuel Manship, 1710. 8°

3 copies.

T.206 T.101 T.104

4975

WENTWORTH (Thomas) *Earl of Strafford.*

A scheme for an absolute and tyrannical government.
Written by Thomas Earl of Strafford, and sent by him
to King Charles I ... London: printed in the year,
1710. 8°

T.403

4976

WEST (Richard) *Prebendary of Winchester.*

A sermon preached before the honourable House of
Commons, at St. Margarets Westminster, on Munday,
Jan. 30. 1709/10... London, for J. Churchill,
1710. 8°

2 copies.

T.152

4977

WHALEY (Nathaniel)

The gradation of sin both in principles and practice.
A sermon preach'd before the University of Oxford,
at St Mary's on the XXXth of January 1709/10...
Oxford, printed at the Theater, for Anth. Peisley:
and are to be sold by Jam. Knapton, Hen. Clements,
and J. Morphew, 1710. 8°

3 copies.

T.36 T.152 T.491

4978

WHAT has been, may be again: or an instance of
London's loyalty, in 1640, &c. Being the substance of
a traiterous play, acted in the guild-hall of that
City, by some of the aldermen and chief leaders of
the party, in the year 1642... Address'd to the
modern Whigs... London: Edm. Powell, and sold by
J. Morphew, 1710. 2 parts.

Another copy of Part 1 only.

T.231 T.344

4979

WHITEAR (William)

An apology for the Church of England against the
defamations of deists, with an address to the
dissenters. A sermon preached at the primary
visitation of... Thomas Lord Bishop of Chichester
... June the 27th. 1710. London, for S. Keble,
1710. 4°

T.752

4980

The WHOLE life and actions. Of John Dolben Esquire
one of the chief managers against Dr. Henry
Sacheverel... who departed this life... the 29th
of May 1710. With a true elegy written by one
of his friends. London, for J. Smith, 1710. 8°

T.35

4981

WILLIAMSON (Joseph)

A modest essay upon the character of her late Grace,
the Dutchess-Dowager of Devonshire. London: for A.
Roper, 1710. 4°

T.490

4982

WISE (Thomas)

The faithful stewards: or the pastoral duty open'd:
in a visitation-sermon preach'd at St. Margaret's
church in Canterbury, June the first, 1710.
London: for E. Curll, and R. Gosling, 1710. 8°

2 copies.

T.36 T.104

4983

WITHERS (John)

The history of resistance, as practis'd by the Church
of England ... Written upon occasion of Mr. Agate's
sermon at Exeter ... London: for J. Robinson: and
sold by A. Baldwin, 1710. 8°

T.231

4984

The WOLF stript of his shepherd's clothing, address'd
to Dr. Sacheverell. By a Salopian gentleman. London:
for J. Baker, 1710. 8°

T.350

4985

The WORCESTERSHIRE address: with an account of some
remarks upon it in Dyer's news letter of April 27.
1710. London, for A. Baldwin, 1710. 8°

T.299

4986

YATES (Henry)

Letters upon the untimely death of Mrs. Elizabeth
Yates. Published by Henry Yates esquire. London:
printed for the use of the booksellers of London
and Westminster, 1710. 8°

T.29

1711

4987

An ACCOUNT of charity-schools in Great Britain
and Ireland: with the benefactions thereto...
The tenth edition, with large additions. London,
Joseph Downing, 1711. 4°

T.700

4988

An ACCOUNT of the Earl of Galway's conduct in Spain
and Portugal ... London, J. Baker, 1711. 8°

2 copies.

T.162

4989

ALLIX (Peter)

Remarks upon some places of Mr. Whiston's books,
either printed or in manuscript. London: for John
Wyat, 1711. 8°

T.305

4990

ALLIX (Peter)

The answer to Mr. Whiston's Reply. [London, for
John Wyat, 1711.] 8°

The pagination and register continue on from the
end of Allix' pamphlet *Remarks upon some places of
Mr. Whiston's books.* There is no title-page.

T.305

4991

ANIMADVERSIONS upon, or an impartial answer to the
Secret history of Arlus and Odolphus ... [The
dedication is signed Philalethes.] London: printed in
the year 1711. 8°

T.418

4992

ANNE, *Queen of Great Britain.*

Her Majesty's letter to the Arch-bishop of Canterbury;
and his Grace's letter to the bishops of his province.
[No imprint, 1711.] brs.

T.133

4993

ANNE, *Queen of Great Britain.*

Her Majesties most gracious letter to the Arch-bishop
of Canterbury; to be communicated by his Grace to
the bishops of his province. London: for Abel Roper;
and sold by John Morphew, [1711]. Fol.

T.133

4994

ANNE, *Queen of Great Britain.*

The preambles to the patents for advancing...
William Lord Dartmouth to the dignity of Viscount
Lewisham... Thomas Lord Raby, Viscount Wentworth
... and Robert Lord Ferrers, Viscount Tamworth...
London: for J. Morphew, 1711. 4°

T.2

4995

ANNE, *Queen of Great Britain.*

The reasons which induc'd her Majesty to create...
Charles Earl of Orrery, and James Duke of Hamilton,
peers of Great Britain... London: for J. Morphew,
1711. 4°

T.2

4996

ANNE, *Queen of Great Britain.*

The reasons which induc'd her Majesty to create the
Right Honourable Sir Simon Harcourt a peer of
Great-Britain. London; for J. Morphew, 1711. 4°

T.2

4997

An ANSWER to a letter to Mr. Hoadly, entituled, Faith
and obedience. Wherein the two arguments from the
XIII th. to the Romans, and the providence of God,
against the reasonableness of resisting supreme
magistrates in any case whatever, are consider'd.
London: printed: and sold by A. Baldwin, 1711. 8°

T.297

4998

An APOLOGETICAL vindication of the present bishops,
from the calumnies and invectives us'd against them in
some late pamphlets. By a presbyter of the Church of
England ... London: John Morphew, 1711. 4°

T.266

4999

ARCHER (Edmond)

A sermon preach'd in King Henry VII's chapel at
Westminster, January XXXth 1710. before the reverend
clergy of the lower house of Convocation ... London:
J. Leake, for Richard Wilkin, 1711. 8°

2 copies.

T.293 T.104

5000

ASPLIN (Samuel)

The divine rights and duties of the Christian
priesthood, as they are contain'd in the holy
Scriptures, deliver'd in a farewel sermon, at
Morden-College upon Black-heath, the 29th of
April, 1711. London, for George Sawbridge, 1711.
8°

T.293

5001

ATTERBURY (Francis) *Bishop of Rochester.*

The mitre and the crown; or, A real distinction between them. In a letter to a reverend member of the Convocation. [Anon.] London: for Henry Clements, 1711.   8°

Attributed by Bowdler to Mr. Wm. Robertson.
3 copies.

T.159 T.405 T.506

5002

The BALLAD of The King shall enjoy his own again. With a learned comment thereupon, at the request of Capt. Silk, dedicated to Jenny Man. By the author of Tom Thumb ... London: printed in the year, 1711.   8°

2 copies.

T.225 T.35

5003

BARRET (John)

The evil and remedy of scandal. A practical discourse on Psalm CXIX. clxv. London: for Nath. Cliff, and Daniel Jackson, 1711.   8°

T.293

5004

BASSET (Joshua)

Ecclesiae theoria nova Dodwelliana exposita in epistola ad authorem clariss. super paraenesi sua ad exteros, tam reformatos quam etiam pontificios, de nupero schismate Anglicano. [Anon.] [No imprint, 1711.]   8°

T.361

5005

BAYLY (Benjamin)

The true notion of moderation; In a sermon preach'd in the church of St. James in Bristol, October the 1st. 1710. London: for John Wyat, 1711.   8°

2 copies.

T.622 T.206

5006

BEDFORD (Hilkiah)

A defence of the Church of England from priestcraft, in vindication of the contested clause of the XXth article. Extracted out of the Vindication of the Church of England from the aspersions of a late libel [by Anthony Collins], entituled, Priestcraft in perfection, &c. By the author of the Vindication ... London: for R. Wilkin, 1711.   8°

2 copies.

T.226   T.41

5007

BENSON (William)

A letter to Sir J[acob] B[anks], by birth a Swede, but naturaliz'd, and a m[embe]r of the present P[arliamen]t: concerning the late Minehead doctrine ... [Anon.] London; for A. Baldwin, 1711.   8°

2 copies.

T.50 T.367

5008

BENSON (William)

A second letter to Sir J[acob] B[anks], by birth a Swede, but naturaliz'd, and a m[embe]r of the present P[arliamen]t. Wherein the late Minehead doctrine is further consider'd ... [Anon.] London: printed in the year 1711.   8°

Different from A second letter ... concerning the Minehead doctrine.

T.50

5009

BEVERLAND (Adriaan)

Seign. Perin del Vago's discovery of a most horrid and most cruel plot, contrived this twenty years, continually, against Hadr. Beverland, doctor in the Civil Law. [No imprint, 1711?]   8°

T.161

5010

BISSE (Philip) *Bishop of Hereford.*

A sermon preach'd before the right honourable House of Peers, on Tuesday the 29th of May, 1711... By Philip, Lord Bishop of St. David's. London: J. Leake, for Jonah Bowyer, 1711.   8°

3 copies.

T.104 T.293 T.622

5011

BISSE (Thomas)

Jehoshaphat's charge. A sermon preach'd at the assizes held at Oxford, July 12. 1711 ... Oxford, printed at the Theatre for Hen. Clements, 1711.   8°

T.293

5012

B[ISSE]T b-sh-t, part II. or the character of that inoffensive creature, who calls himself a moderate plain-dealing protestant ... Being an answer to what Mr. B[isse]t and his seconds have said, can, or dare say. Together with a letter to Dr. Josiah Woodward, upon his late wonderful performance against Dr. H. Sach[evere]ll ... London: printed and sold by the booksellers, 1711.   8°

2 copies.

T.336   T.227

5013

BLOMER (Ralph)

A sermon preach'd in King Henry VII's chapel at Westminster, on Thursday the 8th of March, 1710. before the lower house of Convocation ... London: J. Leake, for Rob. Knaplock, 1711.   8°

T.293

5014

BOYER (Abel)

An account of the state and progress of the present negotiation of peace. With the reasons for and against a partition of Spain, &c. In a letter to a noble lord in Worcestershire ... [Anon.] London, A. Baldwin, 1711.   8°

T.233

5015

BRADFORD (Samuel) *Bishop of Rochester.*

A sermon preach'd before ... the Lord Mayor, and court of aldermen, and the citizens of London, in the cathedral church of St. Paul, January the 30th, 1710. London: for John Wyat, 1711.   8°

T.293

5016

BRETT (Thomas)

A letter to the author of Lay-baptism invalid [i.e. Roger Laurence]: wherein the popish doctrine of lay-baptism, taught in a sermon, said to have been preach'd by the B[ishop] of S[alisbury], the 7th of November, 1710. is censur'd and condemn'd ... London; for Henry Clements, 1711.   8°

2 copies.

T.409 T.395

5017

BRETT (Thomas)

A sermon on remission of sins, according to the Scriptures and doctrine of the Church of England ... London; J. Matthews, for John Wyat, 1711.   8°

2 copies.

T.395   T.104

5018

BRIEF remarks on the late representation of the lower house of Convocation; as the same respects the Quakers only ... London: printed in the year 1711. 8°

T.506

5019

BROWNE (Simon)

The guilt and provocation of taking encouragement to sin, from the mercies of God. Represented in a sermon preach'd Nov. 7. 1710. Being a day of publick thanksgiving for the successes in Spain and Flanders. London: for Nath. Cliff, and Daniel Jackson, 1711. 8°

T.206

5020

BURNET (Gilbert) *Bishop of Salisbury.*

A sermon preach'd at St. Brides before the Lord-Mayor and court of aldermen: on Monday in Easter-week, 1711. London: for John Churchill, 1711.   8°

T.293

5021

BURSCOUGH (William) *Bishop of Limerick.*

A sermon freach'd [sic] at the funeral of Catherine Duchess of Rutland ... the 10th. day of November, 1711. London: for Sam. Crouch, and Tim. Childe, 1711.   8°

T.364

5022

CARROLL (William)

Spinoza reviv'd. Part the second. Or, A letter to Monsieur Le Clerc, occasioned by his Bibliotheque choisie, tom. 21 ... London: printed; and to be sold by John Morphew, 1711.   8°

2 copies.

T.110 T.150

5023

The CASE of insufficiency discuss'd; being the proceedings at large, touching the divorce between the Lady Frances Howard, and Robert Earl of Essex ... As it was heard before a court of delegates ... anno 1613 ... London: for E. Curll, 1711.   8°

2 copies.

T.522 T.103

5024

The CASE of Mr. Greenshields, fully stated and discuss'd, in a letter from a commoner of North Britain, to an English peer. London: printed in the year, 1711.   4°

2 copies.

T.77 T.103

5025

A CAVEAT to the treaters; or, The modern schemes of partition examin'd, with relation to the safety of Europe in general, and of Great-Britain and Ireland in particular ... [By William Wagstaffe?] London: for S. Popping, 1711.   8°

T.113

5026

The CHARACTER and declaration of the October-club. Printed in the year 1711.   8°

T.50

5027

The CHARACTER of a true churchman. In a letter from a gentleman in the city, to his friend in the country. London, for John Baker, 1711.   8°

T.91

5028

CHISHULL (Edmund)

The orthodoxy of an English clergy-man ... Being a sermon preach'd in the chapel of Rumford, at the visitation held, on the 4th of May, 1711 ... London: for Samuel Manship; and James Round, 1711.   8°

T.293

5029

CHURCH OF ENGLAND.

A form of prayer, to be used in all churches and chapels ... on Wednesday the twenty eighth day of this instant March, being the day appointed ... for a general fast ... for ... imploring Gods blessing and assistance on the arms of her Majesty, and her allies ... London, the assigns of Thomas Newcomb, and Henry Hills, 1710/11.   4°

T.461

5030

CHURCH OF ENGLAND. *Convocation.*

A representation, of the present state of religion with regard to the late excessive growth of infidelity, heresy, and profaneness: drawn up by the upper house of Convocation ... London: for Jonah Bowyer, 1711. Fol.

T.133

5031

CHURCH OF ENGLAND. *Convocation.*

A representation, of the present state of religion, with regard to the late excessive growth of infidelity, heresy, and profaneness: unanimously agreed upon by a joint committee of both houses of Convocation ... and afterwards rejected by the upper house, but passed in the lower house ... London: for Jonah Bowyer, 1711. Fol.

T.133

5032

CHURCH OF ENGLAND. *Convocation.*

A representation of the present state of religion, with regard to the late excessive growth of infidelity, heresy and profaneness: as it passed the lower house of Convocation... To which is added, The representation, as drawn up by the upper-house. London: for John Morphew, 1711.   8°

T.133

5033

CHURCH OF ENGLAND. *Convocation.*

A true and exact list of the members of both houses of this present Convocation, summon'd to meet on the twenty fifth day of November, A.D. 1710 ... London, W. Sayes, for Richard Wilkin, 1711. brs.

T.133

5034

CLARKE (Samuel) *Rector of St. James's, Westminster.*

The government of passion. A sermon preach'd before the Queen at St. James's chapel, on Sunday the 7th of January, 1710/11. London, Will. Botham, for James Knapton, 1711. 8º

T.293

5035

CLARKE (Samuel) *Rector of St. James's, Westminster.*

A letter to Mr Dodwell; wherein all the arguments in his Epistolary discourse against the immortality of the soul are particularly answered ... 4th ed. London, Will. Botham; for James Knapton, 1711. 8º

T.301

5036

CLARKE (William) *Dissenting Minister.*

An epistolary debate between Mr. William Clarke, a dissenting minister, and Mr. William Richardson, now of the Church of England; concerning episcopal ordination. London: Rich. Newcomb, 1711. 4º

T.2

5037

COCKBURN (John)

A sermon preach'd at Westminster-Abby, March the 8th, 1710/11, the anniversary of the Queen's inauguration. London: for George Strahan, 1711. 8º

T.293

5038

A COLLECTION of hymns and poems, for the use of the October Club. By Dr. S[acheverel]l, Dr. A[tterbur]y, Dr. S[nap]e, Dr. M[o]ss, and little T[rap]p of Oxford, ch——ns to the said Club. London: printed in the year 1711. 8º

T.347

5039

A COLLECTION of poems, &c. for and against Dr. Sacheverell. The fourth [sic, i.e. fifth] part. London, printed in the year 1711. 8º

T.350

5040

The CONSIDERABLE advantages of a South-Sea trade to our English nation. Humbly offer'd, with other particulars, to the consideration of this present Parliament ... London: for S. Popping, [1711?] 8º

T.272

5041

CONSIDERATIONS relating to our choice, and the qualifications of our members of Parliament. By a Church of England-man. London, for W. Freeman, 1711. 8º

T.390

5042

The COURT and city vagaries, or intrigues, of both sexes. Written by one of the fair sex. London, printed: and sold by J. Baker, [1711?] 8º

T.410

5043

CREFFIELD (Edward)

The duty of the subject to his prince set forth; and passive obedience, and non-resistance maintain'd and recommended. In a sermon preached at the parish-church of Witham in Essex. On Tuesday the 30th January, 1710/11 ... London: for Ch. Brome; and sold by J. Morphew, and Francis Blith, bookseller in Colchester, [1711]. 4º

T.196

5044

CUNINGHAME (James)

Hymns by James Cuninghame, under the influence of the Holy Spirit. London: printed in the year, 1711. 8º

T.383

5045

The CURATE of Dorset's answer to the curate of Salop's [i.e. William Fleetwood] exposition of the 13th chapter to the Romans. By way of dialogue ... London: for J. Baker, 1711. 8º

T.302

5046

DAVYS (John)

A sort of an answer to a piece of a book [by Charles Leslie] entitled A battle royal. In a dialogue ... By a man of business. Oxford, for Stephen Fletcher, and are to be sold by James Knapton, Sam. Keble, Will. Taylor, and John Morphew, 1711. 8º

2 copies.

T.398   T.115

5047

DAWES (*Sir* William) *Archbishop of York.*

A sermon preach'd before ... the lords spiritual & temporal at Westminster-abbey, on January the XXXth, 1710 ... By ... William, Lord Bishop of Chester. London: for Anne Speed, 1711. 8º

2 copies.

T.364   T.104

5048

DEAN (Jasper)

A narrative of the sufferings, preservation and deliverance, of Capt. John Dean and company; in the Nottingham-Gally of London, cast away on Boon-Island, near New England, December 11, 1710. London: R. Tookey, and sold by S. Popping, [1711.] 8º

T.161

5049

DEFOE (Daniel)

Armageddon: or, The necessity of carrying on the war, if such a peace cannot be obtained as may render Europe safe, and trade secure ... [Anon.] London: for J. Baker, [1711]. 8º

Moore 218.

T.233

5050

DEFOE (Daniel)

Atalantis Major. [Anon.] Printed in Olreeky, the chief city of the north part of Atalantis Major. Anno mundi 1711. 8º

Moore 196.

T.363

5051

DEFOE (Daniel)

The ballance of Europe: or, An enquiry into the respective dangers of giving the Spanish monarchy to the Emperour as well as to King Philip ... [Anon.] Printed for John Baker, 1711. 8º

Moore 219.

T.233

5052

DEFOE (Daniel)

The British visions: or, Isaac Bickerstaff senr; being twelve prophecies for the year 1711. [Anon.] Printed first in the North, and now reprinted at London; and sold by John Baker, 1711. 8º

Moore 195.

T.91

5053

DEFOE (Daniel)

The British visions: or, Isaac Bickerstaff, sen. Being twelve prophesies for the year 1711. [Anon.] Printed in the North, and reprinted at London, and sold by J. Baker, 1711. 8º

Moore 195.

T.385

5054

DEFOE (Daniel)

An essay at a plain exposition of that difficult phrase a good peace. By the author of the Review. Printed for J. Baker, 1711. 8º

Moore 221.
2 copies.

T.233 T.551

5055

DEFOE (Daniel)

The felonious treaty: or an enquiry into the reasons which moved his late Majesty King William ... to enter into a treaty ... with the King of France for the partition of the Spanish monarchy ... By the author of the Review. London, J. Baker, 1711. 8º

Moore 222.

T.113

5056

DEFOE (Daniel)

Reasons for a peace: or, The war at an end. [Anon.] London: printed in the year, 1711. 8º

Moore 209.

T.233

5057

DEFOE (Daniel)

Reasons why a party among us, and also among the confederates, are obstinately bent against a treaty of peace with the French at this time. By the author of the Reasons for putting an end to this expensive war ... Printed for John Baker, 1711. 8º

Moore 217.

T.233

5058

DEFOE (Daniel)

Reasons why this nation ought to put a speedy end to this expensive war ... [Anon.] Printed for J. Baker, 1711. 8º

Moore 216.

T.551

5059

DEFOE (Daniel)

Reasons why this nation ought to put a speedy end to this expensive war ... [Anon.] 2nd ed. Printed for J. Baker, 1711. 8º

Moore 216.

T.233

5060

DEFOE (Daniel)

The representation examined: being remarks on the state of religion in England. [Anon.] London: for A. Baldwin, 1711. Fol.

Moore 208.

T.133

5061

DEFOE (Daniel)

R[ogue]'s on both sides. In which are the characters of some r[ogue]'s not yet describ'd; with a true description of an old Whig, and a modern Whig; an old Tory, and a modern Tory... as also of a minister of state. By the same author. London, for John Baker, 1711. 8º

Moore 198.

T.547

5062

DEFOE (Daniel)

R[ogue]'s on both sides. In which are the characters of some r[ogue]'s not yet describ'd; With a true description of an old Whig, and a modern Whig; an old Tory, and a modern Tory ... as also of a minister of state. By the same author. [Anon.] 2nd ed. London, for John Baker, 1711. 8º

Moore 198.

T.363

5063

DEFOE (Daniel)

The Scotch medal decipher'd, and the new hereditary-right men display'd: or, Remarks on the late proceedings of the Faculty of Advocates at Edinburgh, upon receiving the Pretender's medal ... [Anon.] London: for S. Popping, 1711. 8º

Moore 211.

T.169

5064

DEFOE (Daniel)

The secret history of the October club: from its original to this time. By a member. London: printed in the year, 1711. 8º

Moore 204.
3 copies.

T.50 T.414 T.445

5065

DEFOE (Daniel)

The secret history of the October-club, from its original to this time. By a member. Part II. London: for J. Bbker [sic], 1711. 8°

Moore 207.

T.50

5066

DEFOE (Daniel)

A spectators address to the Whigs, on the occasion of the stabbing Mr. Harley. [Anon.] Printed in the year 1711. 8°

Moore 203.

T.348

5067

DEFOE (Daniel)

A speech for Mr. D[unda]sse Younger of Arnistown, if he should be impeach'd of h ―― t ―― n for what he said and did about the Pretender's medal, lately sent to the Faculty of Advocates at Edinburgh. [Anon.] London; for J. Baker, 1711. 8°

Moore 212.
2 copies.

T.29 T.169

5068

DEFOE (Daniel)

The succession of Spain consider'd: or, A view of the several interests of the princes and powers of Europe, as they respect the succession of Spain and the Empire. [Anon.] London, J. Baker, 1711. 8°

Moore 205.

T.363

5069

DEFOE (Daniel)

A true account of the design, and advantages of the South-Sea trade: with answers to all the objections rais'd against it. A list of the commodities proper for that trade: and the progress of the subscription towards the South-Sea Company. [Anon.] London: J. Morphew, 1711. 8°

Moore 213.

T.272

5070

DEFOE (Daniel)

The true state of the case between the government and the creditors of the Navy, &c. as it relates to the South-Sea-trade ... [Anon.] London: J. Baker, 1711. 8°

Moore 215.

T.272

5071

DEFOE (Daniel)

Worcestershire-queries about peace. By Tom Flockmaker, clothier of Worcester. London: for S. Popping, 1711. 8°

Moore 220

T.233

5072

DENT (Giles)

A thanksgiving sermon, preached November 5. 1711. London: for S. Popping, 1711. 8°

T.364

5073

A DIALOGUE between the eldest brother of St. Katharines [i.e. William Bisset], and a London-curate. Wherein several things, relating to the present state of the Church of England and the universities, are consider'd. London: for John Morphew, 1711. 8°

T.361

5074

The DISSENTING teachers address to the J[un]to against the Bill for building fifty new churches, in and about the cities of London and Westminster: and the L[or]d W[harton's] answer ... London, printed in the year, 1711. 8°

T.115

5075

DODWELL (Henry)

The case in view, now in fact, proving, that the continuance of a separate communion, without substitutes in any of the late invalidly-deprived sees, since the death of William late Lord Bishop of Norwich, is schismatical. With an appendix ... By the author of the Case in view. London, for S. Keble, and M. Atkins, 1711. 2 parts. 8°

T.110

5076

DODWELL (Henry)

A discourse concerning the use of incense in divine offices ... In a letter to a friend. London, J. Heptinstall, for James Holland, 1711. 8°

T.361

5077

D'OYLY (Robert)

Providence vindicated, as permitting wickedness and mischief. In a sermon preach'd at Bath, on September the 17th, 1710 ... 2nd ed. London: for H. Clements, 1711. 8°

T.206

5078   T.405

EDWARDS (Jonathan) *Principal of Jesus College, Oxford.*

The doctrine of original sin, as it was always held in the Catholick Church, and particularly in the Church of England, asserted and vindicated from the exceptions and cavils of ... Daniel Whitby ... Oxford, printed at the Theatre, for Hen. Clements; and are to be sold by Hen. Clements, 1711. 8°

T.405

5079

An ESSAY towards advancing the interest of the Establish'd Church and state, humbly offered, in several considerations, to the Queen, and both houses of Parliament. 2nd ed. London: for John Baker, 1711. 8°

T.390

5080

An ESSAY towards the life of Lawrence, Earl of Rochester; late Lord President of her Majesty's most honourable Privy Council ... London: for John Morphew, 1711. 8°

T.275

5081

An EXAMINATION of the Management of the War [a pamphlet by Francis Hare]. In a letter to my Lord ***... London: J. Morphew, 1711. 8°

2 copies.

T.551

5082

An EXAMINATION of the third and fourth letters [by Francis Hare] to a Tory member. Relating to the negociations for a treaty of peace in 1709. In a second letter to my Lord *** ... London: for J. Morphew, 1711. 8°

2 copies.

T.551

5083

An EXPLANATION of the design of the Oxford almanack for the year 1711. Taken from the most occult hieroglyphicks of Kircher, Pignorius, Pierius ... and from several other antient as well as modern writers ... London: A. Baldwin, 1711. 8°

T.363

5084

FAITH and obedience: or, A letter to Mr. Hoadley, occasioned by his doctrin of resistance, and dispute with the Bishop of Exeter ... Norwich: Hen. Crossgrove for Mrs. Oliver, 1711. 8°

2 copies. Attributed by Bowdler to Sir Algernon Potts of Norwich.

T.367 T.377

5085

FANATICAL moderation: or, Unparalell'd villainy display'd. Being a faithful narrative of the barbarous murther committed upon... Dr. James Sharpe, Lord Archbishop of St. Andrews, by the Scotch Presbyterians, May the 3d 1679... London: for E. Curll, and R. Gosling, 1711. 8°

T.348

5086

FELTON (Henry)

The hope of Christians an argument of comfort for their death. A sermon preach'd at the funeral of his grace John late Duke of Rutland. Who was interr'd at Bottesford in Leicestershire, February 23. 1710/11. London: for Jonah Bowyer: and sold by John Ward bookseller in Leicester; and William Ward bookseller in Nottingham, 1711.

T.293

5087

FENTON (Elijah)

An epistle to Mr. Southerne, from Mr. El. Fenton. From Kent, Jan. 28. 1710/11. London: for Benj. Tooke; and Bernard Lintott, 1711. 8°

T.347

5088

FERGUSON (Robert)

An account of the obligations the states of Holland have to Great-Britain, and the return they have made both in Europe and the Indies ... [Anon.] London: printed in the year, 1711. 8°

2 copies.

T.337   T.113

5089

FERGUSON (Robert)

Of the qualifications requisite in a minister of state ... [The dedications to Robert Harley signed R.F.] London, printed; and sold by John Morphew, 1711. 3 parts. 8°

2 sets.

T.50 T.162 T.418

5090

The FIFTEEN comforts of a good Parliament, and the fifteen plagues of a bad one... London, printed in the year, 1711. 8°

T.547

5091

FINCH (Anne) *Countess of Winchilsea.*

Free-thinkers. A poem in dialogue ... [Anon.] London, printed and sold by the booksellers of London and Westminster, 1711. 8°

T.58

5092

FLEETWOOD (William) *Bishop of Ely.*

A sermon preached before the Society for the Propagation of the Gospel in Foreign Parts, at the parish church of St. Mary-le-Bow, on Friday the 16th of February, 1710/11... By... William Lord Bishop of St. Asaph. London, Joseph Downing, 1711. 4°

T.3

5093

FLEMING (Robert) *the Younger.*

The history of hereditary-right. Wherein its indefeasibleness, and all other such late doctrines, concerning the absolute power of princes, and the unlimited obedience of subjects, are fully and finally determin'd, by the Scripture standard of divine right ... [Signed F.T.] London, for J. Baker, [1711]. 8°

T.227

5094

FORTY one in miniature: an elegiack poem. Inscrib'd to the honourable Matthew Prior, Esq; ... London; printed in the year 1711. 4°

2 copies.

T.261 T.269

5095

A FULL answer to the depositions, and to all other the pretences and arguments whatsoever, concerning the birth of the pretended Prince of Wales ... Printed in the year 1711. 8°

T.362

5096

GANDY (Henry)

A conference between Gerontius and Junius. In which Mr. Dodwell's Case in view now in fact is consider'd ... [Anon.] London: printed in the year 1711. 8°

T.169

1711 (Cont'd)

5097

GARNET (John)

A sermon preach'd in the parish-church of St. Mary in Lambeth, on Sunday, Aug. 12. 1711. London: J.L. for John Wyat, 1711. 8°

T.293

5098

GARRET (Walter)

Of the usefulness of the prophecy of the Revelation, in disputes about religious matters ... In a letter to Mr. William Whiston. [Signed W.G.] London: printed in the year 1711. 8°

T.25

5099

The GATES of hell opend: in a dialogue between the Observator and Review. Dedicated to Aminadab. Written in the time of the late dissolv'd Parliament. By a friend of the light. London, printed; and sold by J. Morphew, 1711. 8°

T.347

5100

GATTON (Benjamin)

The doctrine of non-resistance stated and vindicated: in a sermon preach'd November 5. 1710 ... in the parish church of Ailesbury ... London, for Richard Wilkin, 1711. 4°

T.196

5101

GAY (John)

The present state of wit, in a letter to a friend in the country. [Signed J.G.] London printed in the year, 1711. 8°

T.347

5102

GERMANY.

The form of proceeding in the choice and coronation of an emperor of Germany, extracted from the Golden Bull of Pope Gregory. To which is added the Elector of Mentz's proclamation ... And other particulars relating to the present election. London: J. Morphew, 1711. 8°

T.363

5103

GRABE (Johann Ernst)

An essay upon two Arabick manuscripts of the Bodleian Library, and that ancient book call'd, The doctrine of the apostles, which is said to be extant in them; wherein Mr. Whiston's mistakes about both are plainly prov'd. Oxford, for Henry Clements, 1711. 8°

3 copies.

T.25 T.149 T.211

5104

The GRAND-point lately carried by the Common-Council [of London], has lost the main-point ... In a dialogue betwixt a Whig-alderman, and a Church-common-council-man ... London: S. Popping, 1711. 8°

T.163

5105

GREAT BRITAIN. *Commissioners of Accounts.*

The report of the Commissioners for taking, examining, and stating, the publick accounts of the Kingdom, with the depositions at large of Sir Solomon Medina [and others] mentioned in the report. Printed in the year 1711. 36 pp. 8°

Another copy, with 16 pp.

T.279

5106

GREAT BRITAIN. *Parliament.*

A compleat list of the lords spiritual and temporal, with a list of the Commons of Great Britain, both of the late Parliament, dissolved September the 23d 1710. and that summoned to meet November the 25th 1710. [With those that voted for or against Henry Sacheverell noted.] London: for J. Baker, 1711. 8°

2 copies.

T.29 T.417

5107

GREENSHIELDS (James)

A brief history of the revival of the Arian heresie in England since the Reformation... To which is added, Mr. Dodwell's sentiment of Mr. Whiston's heresie, in a letter to a friend... London: for J. Morphew, 1711. 8°

2 copies.

T.25 T.150

5108

HARE (Francis) *Bishop of Chichester.*

The allies and the late ministry defended against France, and the present friends of France. In answer to a pamphlet [by Jonathan Swift], intituled, The conduct of the allies... [Anon.] London, for A. Baldwin, 1711. 8°

Teerink 1041.

T.113

5109

HARE (Francis) *Bishop of Chichester.*

The allies and the late ministry defended against France, and the present friends of France. Part II... [Anon.] London: for A. Baldwin, 1711. 8°

T.113

5110

HARE (Francis) *Bishop of Chichester.*

The allies and the late ministry defended against France, and the present friends of France. Part III... [Anon.] London: for A. Baldwin, 1711. 8°

T.113

5111

HARE (Francis) *Bishop of Chichester.*

The charge of God to Joshua: in a sermon preach'd before his Grace the Duke of Marlborough, at Avenes le Sec, September 9. 1711, being the day of thanksgiving for passing the lines, and taking Bouchain. London, for John Baker, 1711. 8°

T.364

5112

HARE (Francis) *Bishop of Chichester.*

The management of the War. In a letter to a Tory-member... [Anon.] 2nd ed. London: for A. Baldwin, 1711. 8°

T.547

5113

HARE (Francis) *Bishop of Chichester.*

The Management of the War. In a second letter to a Tory-member... [Anon.] 2nd ed. London: for A. Baldwin, 1711. 8°

T.547

5114

HARE (Francis) *Bishop of Chichester.*

The negotiations for a treaty of peace, in 1709, consider'd, in a third letter to a Tory-member. Part the first... [Anon.] 2nd ed. London: for A. Baldwin, 1711. 8°

T.547

5115

HARE (Francis) *Bishop of Chichester.*

The negotiations for a treaty of peace, from the breaking off of the conferences at the Hague, to the end of those at Gertruydenberg, consider'd, in a fourth letter to a Tory-member. PartII... [Anon.] London, for A. Baldwin, 1711. 8°

T.551

5116

HIGDEN (William)

A sermon preached at the Queen's chappel at St. James's on the 30th of January 1710/11... London, for Sam. Keble, 1711. 4°

Two other copies, in 8°

T.104 T.196 T.622

5117

HIGH-Church aphorisms, written by those twin-brothers in scandal, the author of the Examiner, and modest Abel ... [Extracts from the Examiner and the Post-boy.] Printed in the year 1711. 8°

T.363

5118

HILL (William) *of Lincoln's Inn.*

A full account of the life and visions of Nicholas Hart: who has every year of his life past, on the 5th of August, fall'n into a deep sleep, and cannot be awakened till five days and nights are expired, and then gives a surprising relation of what he hath seen in the other world... London: for John Baker, 1711. 8°

T.522

5119

HOADLY (Benjamin) *Bishop of Winchester.*

A serious enquiry into the present state of the Church of England: or, The danger of the Church from the rashness of the clergy. In a letter to Dr. Atterbury... [Anon.] London, J. Baker, 1711. 8°

T.506

5120

HOFFMAN (Francis)

Secret transactions during the hundred days Mr. William Gregg lay in Newgate under sentence of death for high-treason, from the day of his sentence, to the day of his execution. London: printed in the year 1711. 8°

2 copies.

T.414 T.348

5121

HOFFMANN (Christian Gottfried)

Dissertatio historico-philosophica de senio eruditorum... Lipsiae, literis Brandenburgerianis, [1711]. 4°

T.793

5122

HONESTY the best policy: or the mischiefs of faction shewed in the character of an High, and a Low-Church clergy-man. London, for John Morphew, 1711. 8°

2 copies.

T.230 T.159

5123

HORNBY (Charles)

A caveat against the Whiggs, in a short historical view of their transactions ... [Anon.] The second edition corrected. London, J. Morphew, 1711. 8°

T.337

5124

HOTMAN (François)

Franco-Gallia: or, An account of the ancient free state of France, and most other parts of Europe, before the loss of their liberties. Written originally in Latin by... Francis Hotman, in the year 1574. And translated into English by the author of the Account of Denmark [i.e. Lord Molesworth]. London: for Tim. Goodwin, 1711. 8°

T.111

5125

HOWELL (William) *of Wadham College, Oxford.*

The doctrine of the Trinity prov'd from Scripture. A sermon preach'd before the University of Oxford, at St. Mary's on Sunday, May 13. 1711. By the author of the collection intituled, The Common-prayer-book the best companion, &c. Oxford, printed at the Theatre for Anth. Peisley, and are to be sold by James Knapton, Hen. Clements and J. Morphew, 1711. 8°

T.39

5126

HUMFREY (John)

A seasonable suggestion arising from the grateful reflexion upon her Majesties resolution, the Lords agreement, and the Commons determination on it, to let the dissenters quietly enjoy that indulgence which the law hath allowed them to improve our union ... London: for W. Wyat, and sold by J. Morphew, 1711. 8°

T.302

5127

IBBOT (Benjamin)

The dissolution of this world by fire. A sermon preach'd before ... Sir Gilbert Heathcote, knight, Lord-Mayor ... at the cathedral-church of St. Paul, on Monday, September 3. 1711. the day of humiliation for the dreadful fire, in the year, 1666. London: J.L. for John Wyat, 1711. 8°

T.293

5128

INNOCENTIA patefacta, & malitia detecta: being the case of Mr Charles Dean, practicer at law. Who was lately (but innocently) executed at Tyburn, for breaking open the house of Mr. John Stone, at Shepperton ... Printed in the year, 1711.   8°

T.161

5129

JENINGS (John)

The case of King Charles before the regicides at Westminster, parallel to St. Paul's before Felix at Caesarea. In a sermon preach'd at Gamlingay in Cambridgeshire, on Tuesday, January 30th 1710 ... London: for John Wyat, 1711.   8°

T.293

5130

JENINGS (John)

The promises of God to royal David and his line, adapted to Queen Anne and the protestant succession. In a sermon preach'd at Great Gransden in Huntingdonshire. On Thursday, March the 8th 1710... London: for John Wyat, 1711.   8°

T.622

5131

KEN (Thomas) *Bishop of Bath and Wells.*

Expostulatoria: or, The complaints of the Church of England ... London, J. Baker, 1711.   8°

T.274

5132

KENNET (White) *Bishop of Peterborough.*

An argument in defence of passive obedience, in opposition to all manner of tenets advanc'd by several pretended fathers of the Church ... 2nd ed. London: for John Morphew, 1711.   8°

T.408

5133

KENNET (White) *Bishop of Peterborough.*

The Christian neighbour. A sermon preach'd in the church of St. Lawrence-Jewry ... upon the election of a mayor for the year ensuing, on the feast of St. Michael, MDCCXI. London: for J. Churchill, 1711.   8°

T.364

5134

KENNET (White) *Bishop of Peterborough.*

A sermon preach'd before the Arch-bishop, bishops and clergy of the province of Canterbury, in convocation assembled, in the cathedral church of St. Paul in London. Translated from the Latin ... London: for J. Churchill, 1711.   8°

3 copies.

T.36   T.104   T.206

5135

KENNET (White) *Bishop of Peterborough.*

A sermon preach'd before the Convocation held by the Archbishop, bishops, and the clergy of the province of Canterbury, in St. Paul's cathedral, on Saturday the 25th of November, 1711 ... Made English for the benefit of the dissenting teachers, with some cursory remarks. London, J. Morphew, 1711.   8°

T.206

5136

KING (William) *Student of Christ Church.*

An answer to a second scandalous book, that Mr. B[isse]t is now writing, to be publish'd as soon as possible ... Part I. [Anon.] London: for J. Morphew, 1711.   8°

T.361

5137

KING (William) *Student of Christ Church.*

Mr. B[isse]t's recantation: in a letter to the Reverend Dr. Henry Sacheverell. Occasion'd by his reading the Doctor's Vindication, lately publish'd ... [Anon.] London: printed, and may be sold by A. Baldwin, and J. Harrison, 1711.   8°

T.361

5138

KING (William) *Student of Christ Church and* LAMBE (Charles)

A vindication of the Reverend Dr. Henry Sacheverell, from the false, scandalous and malicious aspersions cast upon him in a late infamous pamphlet [by William Bisset], entitled, The modern fanatick... [Anon.] London: for H. Clements, [1711].   8°

2 copies.

T.336   T.361

5139

KNIGHT (James)

Considerations on Mr. Whiston's historical preface. Being an answer to his plain questions, and other most material passages therein contain'd. In a letter to the author of The history of Montanism [i.e. Francis Lee] ... [Anon.] London, J.L. for R. and J. Bonwicke, 1711.   8°

3 copies.

T.305   T.211   T.150

5140

LACY (John)

A letter from John Lacy, to Thomas Dutton, being reasons why the former left his wife, and took E. Gray a prophetess to his bed. [No imprint, 1711?] 12°

T.383

5141

The LAITY'S remonstrance to the late representation of the lower h[ouse] of C[onvocatio]n: with a turn of the tables... London printed in the year 1711. 8°

2 copies.

T.506   T.523

5142

LANGMAN (Christopher) *and others.*

A true account of the voyage of the Nottingham-Galley of London, John Dean commander, from the River Thames to New-England ... With an account of the falsehoods in the Captain's Narrative ... The whole attested upon oath, by Christopher Langman, mate; Nicholas Mellen, boatswain; and George White, sailor in the said ship. London: for S. Popping, 1711. 8°

T.161

5143

LAURENCE (Roger)

Sacerdotal powers: or the necessity of confession, penance, and absolution. Together with the nullity of unauthoriz'd lay baptism asserted. In an essay. Occasion'd by the publication of two sermons preached [by Gilbert Burnet] at Salisbury the 5th and 7th of November. 1710. By the author of Lay baptism invalid ... London, for Henry Clements, 1711.   8°

T.409

5144

LE CLERC (Jean)

The rights of the Christian Church adjusted: being the extract and judgment of Mr. Le Clerc upon those authors who have written against the book intitul'd The rights of the Christian Church asserted, &c. [by Matthew Tindal] ... Translated from the French. To which is added a letter to the Reverend Dr. George Hickes. London: for E. Curll; and E. Sanger, 1711. 8°

2 copies.

T.110   T.159

5145

LESLIE (Charles)

The finishing stroke. Being a vindication of the patriarchal scheme of government, in defence of the Rehearsals, Best answer, and Best of all ... [Anon.] London: printed and sold by the booksellers of London, and Westminster, 1711.   8°

2 copies.

T.403   T.274

5146

LESLIE (Charles)

The truth of Christianity demonstrated. With a dissertation concerning private judgment and authority. To which is prefixed a vindication of the short method with the deists. In answer to a book lately publish'd with this title. [A detection of the true meaning and wicked design of a book...] London, printed: and sold by E. Pool, and G. Strahan, 1711.   8°

3 copies.

T.101   T.159   T.226

5147

A LETTER concerning the affair of Mr. Greenshields ... London printed: and sold by J. Baker, 1711.   8°

2 copies.

T.402   T.103

5148

A LETTER from a country-gentleman, to his friend in London: concerning what a king or queen may lawfully and justly do, to preserve and maintain the Church, against those that would establish an unlimited toleration. London: for John Pemberton, 1711.   8°

T.302

5149

A LETTER to a clergy-man: concerning Mr. Hoadly's doctrine, about the homilies, and resistance... London: printed in the year 1711   8°

3 copies.
"4 October 1711 Given me by Mr Stamp" (Bowdler's hand).

T.157   T.297   T.367

5150

A LETTER to a gentleman, concerning the South Sea trade. Printed for J. Morphew, 1711. Fol.

T.272

5151

A LETTER to a High-Churchman, in answer to a pamphlet [by Daniel Defoe], intitled, Reasons why this nation should put a speedy end to this expensive war ... London; for A. Baldwin, 1711.   8°

T.233

5152

A LETTER to a member of Parliament, on the settling a trade to the South-Sea of America. [Attributed to Daniel Defoe.] Printed for J. Phillips, and are to be sold by A. Baldwin, [1711].   8°

T.272

5153

A LETTER to a member of the October-club: shewing, That to yield Spain to the Duke of Anjou by a peace, wou'd be the ruin of Great Britain ... London; for A. Baldwin, 1711.   8°

T.50

5154

The LETTER to Sir J. B[anks] examined ... In a letter to Mr. Benson. By Irenaeus Philalethes, an Oxford scholar [i.e. Johann Georg Burchard?] ... London: for J. Baker, 1711.   8°

T.50

5155

A LETTER to the author of the Vindication of the Reverend Dr. Sacheverell, from the malicious aspersions cast on him, by Mr. William Bisset ... London: for J. Baker, 1711.   8°

T.361

5156

A LETTER to the Bishop of Lincoln, occasion'd by his Lordship's speech in the House of Lords on the second article of the impeachment. (A letter to the Bishop of Norwich ...) Printed and sold by the booksellers, 1711.   8°

T.49

5157

A LETTER to the Bishop of Salisbury, occasion'd by his Lordship's speech on the first article of impeachment against Dr. Henry Sacheverell. Printed and sold by the booksellers, 1711.   8°

T.49

5158

A LETTER to the eldest brother of the Collegiate Church of St. Katherine [i.e. William Bisset], in answer to his scurrilous pamphlet entitul'd the Modern fanatick, &c ... London, for J. Baker, 1711.   8°

2 copies.

T.345   T.361

5159

A LETTER to the Reverend Dr. Sacheverel. With a post-script, concerning the late Vindication of him; in answer to Mr. B[isse]t's Modern phanatick ... By an inferior clergyman. London: for A. Baldwin, 1711.   8°

T.361

1711 (Cont'd)

5160

LLOYD (Robert Lumley)

A sermon preach'd at St. Paul's Covent Garden, on the 5th of November, 1711 ... London: for A. Baldwin, 1711.   8°

2 copies.

T.364   T.104

5161

LONDON.

A true and impartial account of the poll of the inhabitants of the ward of Broad Street, upon the nomination of an alderman in the room of Sir Joseph Woolfe, deceas'd... London: sold by James Woodward, 1711.   8°

2 copies.

T.29   T.163

5162

LOVELL (*Sir* Salathiel)

Mr. Ba[ron] L[ovel]l's ch[ar]ge to the grand-jury for the county of Devon, the fifth of April, 1710 ... The famous speech-maker of England, Ba[ro]n, (alias Barren) L[ovel]l's ch[a]rge at the assizes at Exon, April 5. 1710. Printed in the year 1711.   15 pp. 8°

T.229

5163

LUPTON (William)

The resurrection of the same body. A sermon preach'd before the University of Oxford, at St. Mary's, on Easter-Monday, Apr. 2. 1711. Oxford, printed at the Theatre for John Wilmot, and are to be sold by James Knapton and J. Morphew, booksellers in London, [1711]. 8°

2 copies.

T.39   T.804

5164

MAINWARING (Arthur)

Remarks on the preliminary articles offer'd by the French King, in order to procure a general peace. As publish'd in the Daily Courant, and postscript to the Post-boy ... [Anon.] London: printed in the year, 1711.   8°

T.233

5165

MAITTAIRE (Michael)

An essay against Arianism and some other heresies: or, A reply to Mr. William Whiston's Historical preface and appendix to his Primitive Christianity revived. London, for H. Clements, 1711.   8°

T.305

5166

MAITTAIRE (Michael)

The present case of Mr. William Whiston, humbly represented: in a letter to the reverend clergy now assembled in convocation. London: for H. Clements, 1711.   8°

T.25

5167

MAITTAIRE (Michael)

Remarks on Mr. Whiston's Account of the Convocation's proceedings, with relation to himself: in a letter to ... George, Lord Bishop of Bath and Wells. London: printed in the year 1711.   8°

2 copies.

T.228   T.150

5168

MANLEY (Mary De la Riviere)

The D[uke] of M[arlborou]gh's vindication: in answer to a pamphlet [by Francis Hare] lately publish'd, call'd Bouchain, or a dialogue between the Medley and the Examiner. [Anon.] London: for John Morphew, 1711.   8°

T.281

5169

MANLEY (Mary De la Riviere)

A learned comment upon Dr. Hare's excellent sermon preach'd before the D. of Marlborough, on the surrender of Bouchain. By an enemy to peace ... London, for John Morphew, 1711.   8°

Teerink 538. Sometimes attributed to Swift.

T.104

5170

MANLEY (Mary De la Riviere)

A true narrative of what pass'd at the examination of the Marquis de Guiscard, at the Cock-pit, the 8th of March, 1710/11. His stabbing Mr. Harley, and other precedent and subsequent facts, relating to the life of the said Guiscard. [Anon.] London: for John Morphew, 1711.   8°

T.414

5171

MANLEY (Mary De la Riviere)

A true relation of the several facts and circumstances of the intended riot and tumult on Queen Elizabeth's birth-day ... [Anon.] London, for John Morphew, 1711.   8°

T.50

5172

MARTYN (Richard)

A modest representation of the past and present state of Great Britain, occasion'd by the late change in the administration. By Eubulos. London: for A. Baldwin, 1711.   8°

T.363

5173

MAXWELL (Henry)

Anguis in herba: or the fatal consequences of a treaty with France ... [Anon.] London, printed in the year 1711.   8°

Also attributed to Lord Somers.

T.233

5174

MEMORIALS on both sides, from the year 1687, to the death of K. James II. With divers original papers never before publish'd, useful for such as desire to be fully inform'd in the true state of the Revolution and the birth of the Pretender ... London printed, and are to be sold by the booksellers of London and Westminster, 1711.   8°

T.362

5175

MILBOURNE (Luke)

The impiety and folly of resisting lawful governours by force or arms, demonstrated in a sermon preach'd on the thirtieth of January, 1710/11 ... London: for George Sawbridge, 1711.   8°

2 copies. One copy inscribed: "Alex. Scott ex dono Authoris."

T.293   T.345

5176

MR. Hoadly's Measures of submission to the civil magistrate enquired into, and disprov'd. By a presbyter of the Church of England ... London, for R. Smith; and W. Taylor, 1711.   8°

Attributed by Bowdler to Samuel Grascombe.

T.297

5177

The MODERATION and justice of modern Whigs, &c. exemplify'd. In a letter from a friend in the City to a friend in the country. Sold by J. Morphew, 1711. 4°

T.267

5178

MODERATION turn'd into madness, prov'd by the proceedings of a moderate corporation, in a plain, and familiar letter, to a burgess of Derby. Sold by John Morphew, [1711].   4°

T.267

5179

A MODEST vindication of the Right Honourable Sir Gilbert Heathcote, Knight, late lord-mayor of the city of London ... London, for John Baker, 1711.   8°

T.163

5180

NON-RESIDENCY of the clergy proved to be against right reason, Scripture and antiquity. Humbly offer'd to the consideration of the... members of the lower house of Convocation... By a true Churchman. Printed, and sold by the booksellers of London and Westminster, [1711?]   4°

T.461

5181

OBEDIENCE to civil government clearly stated: wherein the Christian religion is rescu'd from the false notions pretended to be drawn from it; and Mr. Hoadly's new scheme, in his last book Of the origin and form of government; is fully consider'd. London: for George Strahan, 1711.   8°

2 copies.

T.297   T.157

5182

OCKLEY (Simon)

The dignity and authority of the Christian priesthood, asserted; in a sermon preached at Ormond chapel, December 10, 1710. London: for James Round, 1711.   8°

3 copies.

T.36   T.206   T.622

5183

The OLD French way of managing treaties ... London, for A. Baldwin, 1711.   8°

T.233

5184

OLD stories which were the fore-runners of the Revolution in 88, reviv'd ... London, John Morphew, 1711.   8°

T.362

5185

OLDISWORTH (William)

Reasons for restoring the Whigs. [Anon.] London, printed in the year 1711.   8°

T.363

5186

OLDMIXON (John)

The history of addresses. With remarks serious and comical. In which particular regard is had to all such as have been presented since the impeachment of Dr. Sacheverell. Part II. By the author of the first. London, for J. Baker, 1711.   8°

T.299

5187

OLDMIXON (John)

A letter to the seven lords of the committee, appointed to examine Gregg. [Anon.] London, for J. Baker, 1711.   8°

T.414

5188

OLIVER'S pocket looking-glass, new fram'd and clean'd, to give a clear view of the great modern Colossus, begun by K. C[harles]; carry'd on by K. J[ames]; augmented by K. W[illiam]; and now finish'd, in order to be thrown down in the glorious r[eign] of Q. A[nne]... Printed in the year 1711.   8°

T.281

5189

OPINION and matter of fact: or, A seasonable caution to the present Conv[ocatio]n. London: for A. Baldwin, 1711.   8°

T.506

5190

The OXFORD almanack of 1712, explain'd: or, The emblems of it unriddl'd. Together with some prefatory account of the emblems of the two preceding years. In a letter to a friend. London: for S. Popping, 1711. 8°

T.363

5191

A PAIR of spectacles for Oliver's looking-glass maker. London printed; and sold by J. Baker, 1711. 8°

T.281

5192

PARIS (John)

A true and impartial account of the present differences between the Master and fellows of Trinity College in Cambridge, consider'd. In a letter to a gentleman sometime member of that society ... [Anon.] London: for John Morphew, 1711.   8°

T.415

5193

The PEACE-HATERS: or, A new song, for the illumination of those that won't see ... London: printed in the year 1711.   8°

T.58

5194

PITTIS (William)

Aesop at the Bell-tavern in Westminster, or, A present from the October-club, in a few select fables from Sir Roger L'Estrange, done into English verse... [Anon.] London: printed in the year 1711.

2 copies.

T.347 T.35

5195

PITTIS (William)

The history of the present Parliament and Convocation ... [The dedication signed W.P.] London: for John Baker, 1711.   8°

T.91

5196

PLACE (Conyers)

The arbitration: or, The Tory and Whig reconcil'd ... London: for J. Baker, [1711].   8°

T.363

5197

A PLOT discover'd; or, The protestant succession in danger: to which is added, A new character of a popish successor. London printed, and sold by the booksellers of London and Westminster, 1711.   8°

T.362

5198

POSTSCRIPT for postscript, by way of answer to Dr. Kennet's gentleman-like treatment of the person that translated and explain'd his sermon for him ... In a letter to that Reverend Doctor; not forgetting his last Ash-Wednesday sermon ... London, John Morphew, 1711.   8°

2 copies.

T.206   T.155

5199

The PRESENT state of Mr. Greenshields case, now before ... the House of Lords. In a letter from a commoner of North-Britain, to his friend in Edenburgh. London, for John Baker, 1711.   8°

T.77

5200

The PRETENDER an impostor: being that part of the memorial from the English protestants to ... the Prince and Princess of Orange, concerning their grievances, and the birth of the pretended Prince of Wales ... London, printed and sold by the booksellers, 1711. 8°

T.362

5201

A PROPOSAL for carrying on the war. In a letter to a nobleman. London: for A. Baldwin, 1711.   8°

T.233

5202

PSEUDARCHOMASTIX: or, A censure on some mistakes about civil government... London: for Richard Wilkin, 1711.   8°

T.403

5203

The QUAKERS abhorrence and detestation of Aminadab's vision and declaration. Given at a general meeting this Pentecost. London: printed; and sold by J. Baker, 1711.   8°

T.115

5204

R.(A.)

Jura regiae majestatis in Anglia: or, The rights of the English monarchy. With reflections on Mr. Hoadly's book, entituled, A defence of his sermon. In a letter to a person of quality. London: printed in the year 1711.   8°

T.297

5205

REASON and Gospel against matter of fact: or, Reflections upon two letters to Sir J. B[anks]. London: for J. Morphew, 1711.   8°

2 copies.

T.50 T.147

5206

The RECEPTION of the Palatines vindicated: in a fifth letter to a Tory member ... [Attributed to Francis Hare.] London: printed and sold by the booksellers of London and Westminster, 1711.   8°

T.363

5207

REFLECTIONS upon some passages in Mr. Le Clerc's life of Mr. John Locke: in a letter to a friend ... London: for J. Morphew, 1711.   4°

T.137

5208

REFLECTIONS upon the Examiner's scandalous peace. London: for A. Baldwin, 1711.   8°

Teerink 1036 B.

T.233

5209

REMARKS on a false, scandalous, and seditious libel [by Jonathan Swift], intituled, The conduct of the allies, and of the late ministry, &c ... London, for A. Baldwin, 1711.   8°

Teerink 1040.
2 copies.

T.551 T.113

5210

REMARKS on two late sermons, preach'd [by Gilbert Burnet] in the cathedral-church of Salisbury: in a letter to a friend ... London: for J. Morphew, 1711.   4°

T.196

5211

REMARKS upon remarks: or the Barrier-Treaty and the protestant succession vindicated. In answer to the false and treasonable reflections of the author [i.e. Jonathan Swift] of The conduct of the allies ... London: for A. Baldwin, 1711.   8°

Teerink 1045.

T.113

5212

RICHARDSON (William) *formerly a Dissenting Minister.*

God's call of his ministers, in a sermon preach'd in the parish-church of St. Mary White-chappel, on Sunday the 16th of September, 1711... London: J. Applebee, for George Strahan, and J. Philips; and sold by J. Morphew, 1711.   4°

T.3

5213

RICHARDSON (William) *formerly a Dissenting Minister.*

God's call of his ministers, in a sermon preach'd in the parish-church of St. Mary White-chappel, on Sunday the 16th of Septemb. 1711 ... London: J. Applebee, for Geo. Strahan, and J. Philips: and sold by John Morphew, [1711].   8°

2 copies.

T.364   T.104

5214

ROBINSON (John) *Bishop of London.*

An account of Sueden: together with an extract of the history of that kingdom. [Anon.] 2nd ed. London: for Tim. Goodwin, 1711.   8°

T.50

5215

ROBINSON (John) *Bishop of London.*

A sermon preach'd at St. James's, on Thursday, March 8. 1710. Being the anniversary of her Majesty's happy accession to the throne. By ... John Lord Bishop of Bristol. London: for Sam. Crouch, 1711.   8°

2 copies.

T.293   T.36

5216

ROGERS (Francis)

Orationes ex poetis Latinis excerptae. Argumenta singulis praefixa sunt, quae causam cujusque & summam ex rei gestae occasione explicant. Vol. I. Oxoniae, e Theatro Sheldoniano, 1711.   8°

"Georgio Hicks ... [Latin verse]."

T.204

5217

ROPER (Abel)

Cursory but curious observations of Mr. Ab-1 R--er, upon a late famous pamphlet [by Arthur Mainwaring], entituled, Remarks on the preliminary articles offer'd by the F.K. in hopes to procure a general peace. London: for John Morphew, 1711.   8°

T.233

5218

ROSEWELL (H.)

The religious revel. A sermon. Being a defence and vindication of keeping the annual feast of the dedication, finishing, and consecration of our churches ... London, J. Morphew, 1711.   8°

T.39

5219

The ROYAL family of the Stuart's vindicated, from the false imputation of illegitimacy formerly laid upon it by Buchanan, and maliciously reviv'd in a late pamphlet, intitul'd, The judgment of whole kingdoms and nations ... London: for E. Curl, and E. Sanger, 1711.   8°

2 copies.

T.413   T.344

5220

SACHEVERELL (Benjamin)

Sacheverell against Sacheverell; or, The detector of false brethren prov'd unnatural and base to his own grandfather, and other relations. In a letter to Dr. Henry Sacheverell, from his uncle ... London: printed and sold by A. Baldwin: and T. Harrison, 1711.   8°

T.361

5221

ST. JOHN (Pawlet)

The wisdom of integrity. A sermon preach'd at St. Saviour's Southwark, for the Reverend Dr. Henry Sacheverell, on Sunday, May 6. 1711 ... London: for J. Bowyer, 1711.   8°

2 copies.

T.196   T.104

5222

A SEASONABLE address to the citizens of London: which may serve indifferently for every inhabitant of Great-Britain ... London: T. Harrison, and A. Baldwin, 1711. 8°

T.299

5223

A SECOND letter to Sir J[acob] B[anks], by birth a Swede, but naturaliz'd, and a m[embe]r of the present P[arliamen]t: concerning the Minehead doctrine ... [Signed Philo. Tory.] London, for S. Popping, [1711].   8°

Different from A second letter ... Wherein the late Minehead doctrine is further consider'd. [By William Benson.]

T. 50

5224

SERIOUS considerations on the state of religion, as perform'd in the Church of England, and by the dissenters of all kinds ... London, R. Wilkin; and J. Baker, 1711.   4°

T.266

5225

SHARP (John) *Archbishop of York.*

A sermon preach'd before the Queen at St. James's chapel, on Ashwednesday, Feb. 14. 1710/11. London: for W. Kettilby; and for W. Rogers: and sold... by R. Wilkin, 1711.   8°

2 copies.

T.104   T.293

5226

SMALBROKE (Richard) *Bishop of Lichfield and Coventry.*

Reflections on the conduct of Mr. Whiston, in his revival of the Arian heresy. [Anon.] London: for Timothy Childe, 1711.   8°

2 copies.

T.25 T.150

1711 (Cont'd)

5227

SMALRIDGE (George) *Bishop of Bristol.*

A sermon, preached at the parish-church of St. Dunstan in the West, on Sunday Dec. the 23d. 1711 ... London, printed for, and sold by Chr. Coningsby; and Jonah Bowyer, 1711.   4°

Another copy, in 8°

T.3   T.364

5228

SMITH (John) *Prebendary of Durham.*

A sermon preached to the Sons of the clergy, upon their first solemn meeting at St. Nicolas church, in Newcastle upon Tine, Sept. 10th, 1711 ... Newcastle upon Tine, John White, [1711].   4°

T.198

5229

SNAPE (Andrew)

A sermon preach'd before the honourable House of Commons, on Wednesday the 28th of March, 1711 being the day appointed ... for a general fast. London: for Jonah Bowyer, 1711.   8°

T.293

5230

SNAPE (Andrew)

A sermon preach'd in the parish-church of St. Sepulchre, May the 24th, 1711... at the anniversary-meeting of the children educated in the charity schools in and about the cities of London and Westminster... London: J. Downing; and are to be sold by Jonah Bowyer, 1711.   8°

3 copies.
Another copy, in 4°

T.104   T.293 T.622   T.700

5231

The SOLICITOUS citizen: or, The Devil to do about Dr. Sach[evere]ll. A comedy as it was publickly acted last year, in London, and several other places. By John-a-Noaks, and Tom-a-Stiles. London: printed, to be sold at the Blew-Ball ... and J. Baker, [1711].   8°

T.231

5232

SOME observations upon a late pamphlet [by Richard Martyn], intitled, A modest representation of the past and present state of Great Britain... London, for A. Baldwin, 1711.   8°

T.363

5233

SOME remarks by way of answer to a late pamphlet, entituled, A letter to Sir J. B[anks] ... London: for Jonah Bowyer, 1711.   8°

T.50

5234

SOME short remarks upon the late address of the Bishop of London and his clergy, to the Queen. In a letter to Dr. Sm[a]l[rid]ge. [Attributed to Benjamin Hoadly.] London: for A. Baldwin, 1711.   8°

2 copies.

T.159   T.299

5235

SOME thoughts on the representation of the lower house of Convocation. In a letter to the Reverend Dr. Atterbury, prolocutor. London, for J. Baker, 1711.   8°

T.506

5236

SOUTH SEA COMPANY.

A list of the commissioners names appointed by her Majesty to take subscriptions to the Corporation for carrying on a trade to the South-Seas. London, for S. Popping, 1711.   brs.

T.272

5237

SOUTH SEA COMPANY.

List of the Governors and directors appointed by her Majesty for the South-Sea Company. London, for S. Popping, 1711.   brs.

T.272

5238

The SPECTATOR inspected: or, A letter to the Spectator. From an officer of the Army in Flanders, touching the use of French terms, in relations from the Army ... London: printed in the year 1711.   8°

T.410

5239

SPRAT (Thomas) *Bishop of Rochester.*

Two letters written in the year 1689... to... the late Earl of Dorset, concerning his sitting in the Ecclesiastical Commission in the reign of K. James II. London, printed in the year 1711.   8°

T.822

5240

A SPY upon the Spectator. Part I. London, for John Morphew, 1711.   8°

T.410

5241

STACY (Edmund)

Assassination display'd in the fable of the robin red-breast and vulture. By the author of The black-bird's tale... London printed, and sold by J. Morphew, 1711.   8°

T.347

5242

STACY (Edmund)

The picture of a Church militant. An original, after the modern manner. For the use of St. Stephen's chapel, and humbly inscrib'd to a member of the lower house of Convocation. By the author of The blackbird's tale. London, for S.B. and sold by J. Morphew, 1711.   8°

2 copies.

T.58   T.414

5243

STAR-BOARD and lar-board: or, Sea-politicks. An allegory. Written by a gentleman that has made himself merry on board the Fleet ... London, printed in the year 1711.   8°

T.50

5244

STRYPE (John)

The thankful Samaritan. A sermon preached at the cathedral church of S. Paul, before ... the Lord Mayor, and the aldermen of the city of London, September the 16th. 1711. London: for J. Wyat, 1711.   8°

T.364

5245

STUBS (Philip)

The divine mission of Gospel-ministers; with the obligations upon all pious and rich Christians to promote it, set forth; in a sermon preach'd ... on Trinity-Sunday, May 27. 1711. The day appointed by her Majesty for a collection ... towards the more effectual propagation of the Gospel in foreign parts ... London, for R. and J. Bonwicke, 1711.   8°

2 copies.

T.293   T.39

5246

SWIFT (Jonathan) *Dean of St. Patrick's.*

A new journey to Paris, together with some secret transactions between the Fr[enc]h K[in]g, and an Eng[lish] gentleman. By the Sieur du Baudrier [i.e. Jonathan Swift]. Translated from the French. London, for John Morphew, 1711.   8°

Teerink 536.

T.233

5247

SWIFT (Jonathan) *Dean of St. Patrick's.*

A new journey to Paris: together with some secret transactions between the Fr[enc]h K[in]g, and an Eng[ligh] gentleman. By the Sieur du Baudrier [i.e. Jonathan Swift]. Translated from the French. The second edition, corrected. London, for John Morphew, 1711.   8°

Teerink 536.

T.29

5248

SWIFT (Jonathan) *Dean of St. Patrick's.*

A short character of his Ex. t[he] E[arl] of W[harton], L[ord] L[ieutenant] of I[reland]. With an account of some smaller facts, during his government, which will not be put into the articles of impeachment. [Anon.] London: for William Coryton, 1711.   8°

Teerink 527.

2 copies.

T.29   T.385

5249

The TAXES not grievous, and therefore not a reason for an unsafe peace. London: A. Baldwin, 1711.   8°

T.233

5250

A TEST of the truest Church man. Humbly offer'd at this time of our unhappy distinctions, to the consideration of all those who call themselves sons of the Church. By a sincere and hearty lover of his Queen and country ... London: for John Morphew, 1711.   4°

T.266

5251

THOMPSON (John) *Baron Haversham.*

Memoirs of the late Right Honourable John Lord Haversham, from the year 1640 to 1710 ... To which are added all his speeches in Parliament ... The whole publish'd from his Lordship's original papers. London, for J. Baker, 1711.   8°

T.162

5252

The THOUGHTS of a Church of England divine, upon those words in an act made in King Charles IId's. reign, That it was not lawful upon any pretence whatsoever to take up arms against the King. In a letter to a student at Oxford, who had some doubts thereupon. London, for S. Popping, 1711.   8°

T.297

5253

The THOUGHTS of a learned divine concerning the present state of religion, and interest of the nation; humbly offered to the consideration of the ensuing Parliament and Convocation. London: for John Baker, 1711.   4°

T.266

5254

The THOUGHTS of a member of the October Club, about a partition of Spain... Printed for John Baker, [1711?]   8°

T.401

5255

THREE articles of the Grand Alliance. With the late preliminaries of peace, in the year 1709. And an account of the several successes gain'd by his Grace the Duke of Marlborough since that time. London; printed in the year 1711.   8°

T.233

5256

TINDAL (Matthew)

The nation vindicated, from the aspersions cast on it in a late pamphlet, intitled, A representation of the present state of religion, with regard to the late excessive growth of infidelity, heresy and profaneness, as it pass'd the lower house of Convocation. [Anon.] Part I. ... London; for A. Baldwin, 1711.   8°

T.506

5257

TODD (Hugh)

A sermon preach'd before the honourable House of Commons, on Tuesday, the 29th of May, 1711 ... London: for Jonah Bowyer, 1711.   8°

2 copies.

T.293

5258

TOLAND (John)

The description of Epsom, with the humors and politicks of the place: in a letter to Eudoxa [signed Britto-Batavus]... There is added a translation of four letters out of Pliny. London: for A. Baldwin, 1711.   8°

T.410

5259

TRAPP (Joseph)

The character and principles of the present set of Whigs... [Anon.] London: for John Morphew, 1711. 8°

2 copies.

T.348 T.547

5260

TRAPP (Joseph)

A sermon preach'd at Christ-Church in Dublin, before their excellencies the lords justices: on Tuesday the 29th of May 1711... London: for H. Clements, 1711. 4°

Another copy, in 8°

T.3 T.293

5261

TRAPP (Joseph)

A sermon preach'd at Christ-Church in Dublin, before their excellencies the lords justices: on Tuesday the 29th of May, 1711... 2nd ed. London, for Henry Clements, 1711. 8°

T.622

5262

TRIMNELL (Charles) *Bishop of Winchester.*

A sermon preach'd in the chappel at Tunbridge-Wells upon Sunday the 19th of August, 1711 ... By ... Charles Lord Bishop of Norwich. London: for D. Midwinter, 1711. 8°

T.293

5263

A TRUE account of what past at the Old-Bailey, May the 18th, 1711. Relating to the tryal of Richard Thornhill, Esq; indicted for the murther of Sir Cholmley Deering, Bar. London: for John Morphew, 1711. 8°

2 copies.

T.29 T.161

5264

A TRUE and particular account of a storm of thunder & lightning, which fell at Richmond in Surrey, on Whit-Sunday last in the afternoon, being May 20th, 1711 ... London: for John Morphew, 1711. 8°

T.111

5265

The TRUE patriots vindicated: or, A justification of the late Earl of Rochester, Lord President of her Majesty's Council, &c. from several false and scandalous reports. London: printed in the year, 1711. 8°

T.50 T.103

5266

A VIEW of the Queen and Kingdom's enemies, in the case of the poor Palatines: to which is added a list of the persons appointed commissioners and trustees of that charity... as also of those members of the late Parliament that voted for the Naturalization-Bill. In a letter from a gentleman in London to his friend in the country. Sold by the booksellers, [1711]. 8°

2 copies.

T.29 T.91

5267

A VINDICATION of his Grace the Duke of Leeds, from the aspersions of some late fanatical libellers. London, for John Morphew, 1711. 8°

The pamphlet consists of reprints of B.(J.) *Some reflections upon the Earl of Danby.* (1679), and CHRISTIAN (E.) *Reflections upon a paper* (1679). 2 copies.

T.275 T.162

5268

A VINDICATION of the last Parliament. In four dialogues between Sir Simon [Harcourt] and Sir Peter [King]. London, printed in the year 1711. 8°

T.91

5269

A VINDICATION of the present m[inistr]y, from the clamours rais'd against them upon occasion of the new preliminaries ... London, printed in the year 1711. 8°

Teerinck 1039.
2 copies.

T.547 T.113

5270

W.

A letter from a foreign minister at Vienna, to another of the same quality at the Hague, concerning the death of the late Emperour of the Romans ... London: J. Morphew, 1711. 8°

T.363

5271

WAGSTAFFE (Thomas)

A vindication of K. Charles the Martyr: proving that his Majesty was the author of Εἰκων Βασιλικη. Against a memorandum, said to be written by the Earl of Anglesey... [Anon.] 3rd ed., with large additions... London: for R. Wilkin, 1711. 4°

2 copies.

T.196 T.660

5272

WAGSTAFFE (William)

A comment upon the history of Tom Thumb ... [Anon.] London, for J. Morphew, 1711. 8°

T.347

5273

WAGSTAFFE (William)

Crispin the cobler's confutation of Ben Hoadly, in an epistle to him. [Anon.] London: printed in the year, 1711. 8°

T.361

5274

WATTS (Robert)

The rule for finding Easter, in the Book of common prayer, explain'd ... [Anon.] London, for J. Downing, and J. Holland, 1711. 8°

2 copies.

T.442 T.323

5275

WATTS (Robert)

The true time of keeping St. Matthias's day in leap-years, further shewn in a second familiar conference between a Church man and a dissenter. Wherein is inserted Arch-bishop Sancroft's order concerning the time of keeping the same, A.D. 1684. with a vindication thereof ... [Anon.] London: printed and sold by J. Downing, J. Knapton, J. Wyat, R. Knaplock, J. Bonwick, W. Carter, H. Clements, and J. Holland, and J. Bowyer and T. Baker, [1711]. 8°

T.323

5276

WATTS (Robert)

The true time of keeping St. Matthias's-day in leap-years: shewn in a familiar conference between a Church-man and a dissenter. Wherein is inserted Dr. Wallis's letter to Bp. Fell, written on that subject A.D. 1684... [Anon.] Oxford: L.L. 1711. And are to be sold by Joseph Downing, J. Knapton, J. Wyat, J. Bonwick, H. Clements, W. Carter, and W. Meadows. 8°

2 copies.

T.323 T.442

5277

The WAY to bring the world to rights: or, Honesty the best policy at all times, and in all places ... London: for John Morphew, 1711. 8°

2 copies.

T.417 T.348

5278

WELLS (Edward)

Harmonia grammaticalis, or, a view of the agreement between the Latin and Greek tongues as to the declining of words... [The preface signed E.W.] London: for James Knapton, 1711. 8°

T.788

5279

WEST (Richard) *Prebendary of Winchester.*

A sermon preach'd before ... the Lord Mayor ... and governors of the several hospitals of the city of London, at St. Bridget's church in Easter-week, 1711. Being one of the anniversary spittal sermons. London: for John Churchill, 1711. 8°

T.293

5280

The WHIGS appeal to the Tories. In a letter to Sir T[homas] H[anmer]. With a postscript concerning the proceedings in P——t. London: for S. Popping, 1711. 8°

T.113

5281

WHISTON (William)

An account of the Convocation's proceedings with relation to Mr. Whiston. With a postscript, containing a reply to the Considerations on the historical preface [by James Knight], and the Premonition to the reader ... London: printed for the author; and sold by A. Baldwin, 1711. 8°

T.150

5282

WHISTON (William)

An historical preface to Primitive Christianity reviv'd. With an appendix containing an account of the author's prosecution at, and banishment from the University of Cambridge ... London: printed for the author, and are to be sold by the booksellers of London and Westminster, 1711. 2 parts. 8°

T.305

5283

WHISTON (William)

Remarks on Dr. Grabe's Essay upon two Arabick manuscripts of the Bodleian Library, &c. London, printed for the author, and sold by A. Baldwin, 1711. 8°

T.25

5284

WHISTON (William)

Remarks on Dr. Grabe's Essay upon two Arabick manuscripts of the Bodleian Library, &c. 2nd ed. London, printed for the author, and sold by A. Baldwin, 1711. 8°

T.149

5285

WHISTON (William)

A reply to Dr. Allix's Remarks on some places of Mr. Whiston's books, either printed or manuscript ... London: printed for the author, and sold by A. Baldwin, 1711. 8°

T.305

5286

WHISTON (William)

A second reply to Doctor Allix. With two postscripts: the first to Mr. Chishull; the second to the author of the Reflections on Mr. Whiston's conduct, &c. [i.e. Richard Smalbroke]. London: printed for the author; and sold by A. Baldwin, 1711. 8°

T.305

5287

WILSON (Thomas) *Bishop of Sodor and Man.*

A sermon preach'd before the Queen at St. James's, on Holy-Thursday, May 10. 1711. London: for Jonah Bowyer, 1711. 8°

T.293

5288

WINCHESTER COLLEGE.

The plea of the fellows of Winchester-College, against the Bishop of Winchester's local, and final visitatorial power over the said college. London: Geo. James, for Jonah Bowyer, 1711. 4°

T.2

5289

WITHERS (W.)

A general apology for the lies made use of against Dr. Sacheverell. Occasion'd by the pretended answer to Mr. Bisset ... London: printed in the year, 1711. 8°

T.361

5290

WITHERS (W.)

Some thoughts concerning suicide, or self-killing: with general directions for the more easie dispatch of that affair. Written for the benefit of all malecontents in Great-Britain. London: printed in the year, 1711. 8°

T.520

5291

A WORD to the wise: in a letter to a City-clergyman: recommended to the consideration of his brethren of the clergy, especially those of the younger sort ... [Attributed to Joseph Rawson.] London; for John Morphew, 1711. 8°

T.405

1711 (Cont'd)

5292

WOTTON (William)

The case of the present Convocation consider'd; in answer to the Examiner's unfair representation of it, and unjust reflections upon it... [Anon.] London: for John Churchill, 1711. 8°

3 copies.

T.506 T.523 T.603

5293

WRIGHT (Samuel)

A funeral sermon, upon the sudden and much lamented death of Dr. Francis Upton; who died September 4th, 1711... London: W. Hurt, for John Clark, 1711. 8°

T.364

5294

Z.(X.)

A letter from an old Whig in town, to a modern Whig in the country, upon the late expedition to Canada. London, printed: and sold by J. Morphew, [1711]. 4°

T.161

1712

5295

An ACCOUNT of charity-schools in Great Britain and Ireland: with the benefactions thereto... The eleventh edition, with large additions. London, Joseph Downing, 1712. 4°

T.701

5296

An ACCOUNT of the damnable prizes in Old Nicks lottery, for men of honour only... In a gradation of familiar thoughts, arising, upon the not passing of the Duelling Bill, brought in last session of Parliament... London: for John Morphew, 1712. 8°

T.161

5297

An ACCOUNT of the life and writings of Mr. John Le Clerc ... to this present year MDCCXI. To which is added, a collection of letters, from J.G. Graevius, and Baron Spanheim, to Mr. Le Clerc ... London: for E. Curll: and E. Sanger, 1712. 8°

2 copies.

T.522 T.159

5298

An ALARUM to the Christian Church: a discourse concerning the great and wonderful events now approaching ... London: J. Baker, and S. Noble, 1712. 4°

T.266

5299

ALLEN (Joseph)

The danger of evil communication. In two sermons, preach'd at Sir George Wheler's chappel, in Spittle-fields: on the 25th of May and the 22d of June, 1712 ... London: for J. Morphew; and J. Hodgson, bookseller in Chester, 1712. 2 parts. 4°

T.196

5300

ALLEN (Robert)

An essay on the nature and methods of carrying on a trade to the South-Sea. London: John Baker, 1712. 8°

T.272

5301

ALTHAM (Roger)

A sermon preach'd before the Honourable House of Commons ... on Wednesday, Jan. 16. 1711/12. being the fast-day for a general peace. London: for Geo. Strahan, 1712. 8°

2 copies.

T.364 T.104

5302

The ANCIENT amity restor'd: or, France the best friend. Containing an historical account of the fair and friendly dealings of the French towards the English, for these 600 years past ... London: for A. Baldwin, 1712. 8°

T.337

5303

ANNE, *Queen of Great Britain.*

A collection of all her Majesty's speeches, messages, &c. from her happy accession to the throne, to the twenty first of June 1712. London, printed in the year 1712. 8°

T.205

5304

ANNE, *Queen of Great Britain.*

Her Majesty's reasons for creating the Electoral Prince of Hanover a peer of this realm ... with remarks upon the same. London: for A. Baldwin, 1712. 4°

T.2

5305

ANNE, *Queen of Great Britain.*

The reasons which induced her Majesty to create Samuel Massam Esq; a peer of Great-Britain: also the reasons which induc'd ... King William III. to create Charles Mountague Esq; a peer of England, anno M.DCC. London: for E. Curll, 1712. 4°

T.2

5306

An ANSWER to that part of Dr. Brett's sermon which relates to the incapacity of persons not episcopally ordain'd to administer Christian baptism. In a letter to the Doctor. London: W.D. for John Morphew, 1712. 8°

T.360

5307

An APOLOGY for the clergy of the city of Bristol. In their petitioning an act of Parliament, for their better and more certain maintenance. In a letter to a gentleman of Bristol ... London: for John Wyat, 1712. 8°

T.164

5308

ARBUTHNOT (John)

John Bull in his senses: being the second part of Law is a bottomless-pit. Printed from a manuscript found in the cabinet of the famous Sir Humphrey Polesworth. [Anon.] London: for John Morphew, 1712. 8°

T.29

5309

ARBUTHNOT (John)

John Bull in his senses: being the second part of Law is a bottomless-pit. Printed from a manuscript found in the cabinet of the famous Sir Humphry Polesworth. [Anon.] 2nd ed. London: for John Morphew, 1712. 8°

T.147

5310

ARBUTHNOT (John)

Law is a bottomless-pit. Exemplify'd in the case of the Lord Strutt, John Bull, Nicholas Frog, and Lewis Baboon. Who spent all they had in a law-suit. Printed from a manuscript found in the cabinet of the famous Sir Humphry Polesworth. [Anon.] London: for John Morphew, 1712. 8°

A satire on the Spanish succession; the characters are identified in Bowdler's hand.

T.29

5311

ARBUTHNOT (John)

Law is a bottomless-pit. Exemplify'd in the case of the Lord Strutt, John Bull, Nicholas Frog, and Lewis Baboon. Who spent all they had in a law-suit. Printed from a manuscript found in the cabinet of the famous Sir Humphry Polesworth. [Anon.] 2nd ed. London: for John Morphew, 1712. 8°

T.147

5312

ARBUTHNOT (John)

Proposals for printing a very curious discourse, in two volumes in quarto, intitled, Ψευδολογια πολιτικη; or, A treatise of the art of political lying, with an abstract of the first volume of the said treatise. [Anon.] London: for John Morphew, 1712. 8°

2 copies.

T.337 T.51

5313

ARGUMENTS relating to a restraint upon the press, fully and fairly handled in a letter to a bencher from a young gentleman of the Temple. With proposals humbly offer'd to the consideration of both houses of Parliament. London: for R. and J. Bonwicke, 1712. 8°

T.205

5314

ASGILL (John)

Mr. Asgill's defence upon his expulsion from the House of Commons of Great Britain in 1707. With an introduction, and a postscript... London, A. Baldwin, 1712. 8°

3 copies.

T.414 T.548 T.798

5315

ASGILL (John)

An essay for the press. [Anon.] London, for A. Baldwin, 1712. 8°

T.205

5316

ATTERBURY (Francis) *Bishop of Rochester.*

A continuation of the mitre and the crown; or, A real distinction between them. In a second letter to a reverend member of the Convocation. By the author of the first letter. London: for Henry Clements, 1712. 8°

3 copies.

T.506 T.405 T.159

5317

AYERST (William)

The duty and motives of praying for peace. A sermon preach'd before their Excellencies ... her Majesty's plenipotentiaries at the Congress of Utrecht. In St. John's church, Utrecht. January 27. 1711/12 ... London: for Jonah Bowyer, 1712. 8°

2 copies.

T.364 T.104

5318

BARNES (Joshua)

Aristarchus ampullans in curis Horatianis; sive querimonia epistolaris de intempestive ista corrigendi libidine, tum de ea opportune cohibenda, ne indies pessime inquinati prodeant optimi auctores ... [Signed Philargyrius Cantab.] Londini, 1712. 8°

T.402

5319

The BARRIER-treaty vindicated. London: for A. Baldwin, 1712. 8°

Teerink 1047.
Variously attributed to Lord Bolingbroke, Lord Townshend and Francis Hare.

T.171

5320

BECKETT (William)

New discoveries relating to the cure of cancers ... in a letter to a friend ... 2nd ed., with additions. London: for George Strahan, 1712. 8°

T.44

5321

BENTLEY (Richard)

Dr. Bentley's dedication of Horace, translated. To which is added, a poem ... inscribed to the Right Honourable the Lord Hallifax ... 2nd ed. London: for John Morphew, [1712]. 8°

T.92

5322

BERKELEY (George) *Bishop of Cloyne.*

Passive obedience, or, The Christian doctrine of not resisting the supreme power, proved and vindicated upon the principles of the law of nature ... 2nd ed. London: for H. Clements, 1712. 8°

2 copies.

T.229 T.39

5323

BETTESWORTH (Charles)

A sermon preach'd at Petworth in Sussex, on Wednesday, September the 3d, 1712. at a confirmation held there by Thomas Lord Bishop of Chichester. London: H. Meere for A. Bettesworth; and sold by W. Webb in Chichester, Joseph Jaques in Midhurst, and W. Browne in Horsham, 1712. 4°

T.752

5324

BEVERIDGE (William) *Bishop of St. Asaph.*

The opinion of the Right Reverend Father in God William Beveridge, D.D. late Lord Bishop of St. Asaph, concerning the apostolical constitutions. London, for John Morphew, 1712.   8°

T.228

5325

BICKERSTAFF (Isaac) *pseud.*

Predictions for the year, 1712. By Isaac Bickerstaff, Esq; in a letter to the author of the Oxford almanack. Printed in the year, 1712.   8°

Teerink 1029.

T.417

5326

BINGHAM (Joseph)

A scholastical history of the practice of the Church in reference to the administration of baptism by laymen ... With an appendix containing some remarks on the historical part of Mr. Lawrence's writings touching the invalidity of lay-baptism ... London: W. Downing, for R. Knaplock, 1712.   8°

T.365

5327

BLE (Nicolas de) *Marquis d'Uxelles and* POLIGNAC (Melchior de) *Cardinal.*

The French plenipotentiaries letter to the Grand Pensionary of Holland, upon the rupture of the treaty at Gertruydenberg. With observations ... London: John Morphew, 1712.   8°

T.147

5328

BRADBURY (Thomas)

The ass: or, The serpent. A comparison between the tribes of Issachar and Dan, in their regard for civil liberty. Nov. 5. 1712 ... London: for N. Cliff and D. Jackson: and sold by J. Baker; and T. Harrison, [1712].   8°

T.160

5329

BRADBURY (Thomas)

Theocracy: the government of the judges, consider'd and applied to the Revolution, 1688. In a sermon November 5. 1711 ... London: for Nat. Cliff and Dan. Jackson, 1712.   8°

T.364

5330

BRAGGE (Francis)

A defense of the proceedings against Jane Wenham, wherein the possibility and reality of witchcraft are demonstrated from Scripture ... In answer to two pamphlets, entituled, I. The impossibility of witchcraft, &c. II. A full confutation of witchcraft ... London: for E. Curll, 1712.   8°

T.48

5331

BRAGGE (Francis)

A full and impartial account of the discovery of sorcery and witchcraft, practis'd by Jane Wenham of Walkerne in Hertfordshire ... Also her tryal at the assizes at Hertford before Mr. Justice Powell ... [Anon.] London: for E. Curll, 1712.   8°

T.48

5332

BRAGGE (Francis)

A full and impartial account of the discovery of sorcery and witchcraft, practis'd by Jane Wenham of Walkerne in Hertfordshire ... Also her tryal at the assizes at Hertford before Mr. Justice Powell ... [Anon.] 2nd ed. London: for E. Curll, 1712.   8°

T.103

5333

BRAGGE (Francis)

Witchcraft farther display'd. Containing I. An account of the witchcraft practis'd by Jane Wenham of Walkerne, in Hertfordshire... II. An answer to the most general objections against the being and power of witches... [The introduction signed F.B.] London, for E. Curll, 1712.   8°

2 copies.

T.48 T.622

5334

BRETT (Thomas)

The doctrine of remission of sins, and the power of absolution, as set forth in a late sermon, explain'd and vindicated: in remarks on Dr. Cannon's Account of his two motions in the lower house of Convocation. London: for John Wyat, 1712.   8°

T.395

5335

BRETT (Thomas)

The extent of Christ's commission to baptize. A sermon shewing the capacity of infants to receive, and the utter incapacity of our dissenting teachers to administer Christian baptism ... London: J. Matthews, for John Wyat, 1712.   8°

T.39

5336

BRETT (Thomas)

A sermon of the honour of the Christian priesthood, and the necessity of a divine call to that office ... London; J. Matthews, for John Wyat, 1712.   8°

2 copies.

T.395 T.104

5337

BRETT (Thomas)

A sermon on remission of sins, according to the Scriptures and the doctrine of the Church of England... 2nd ed. London: J. Matthews, for John Wyat, 1712.   8°

Signature of Tho: Fairfax.

T.641

5338

A BRIEF answer to a late pamphlet [by John Turner], entituled, A defence of the doctrine and practice of the Church of England, against some modern innovations ... London: W. Bowyer, for J. Morphew, 1712.   8°

T.395

5339

BROOKE and Hellier. A satyr. London: J. Baker, 1712. 8°

T.410

5340

BURNET (*Sir* Thomas)

A letter to the people, to be left for them at the booksellers; with a word or two of the Bandbox plot. [Anon.] London: for J. Baker, 1712.   8°

T.51

5341

BURNET (*Sir* Thomas)

Truth, if you can find it: or, A character or the present m[inistr]y and P[arliamen]t. In a letter to a member of the March club... [Anon.] London: printed, and sold by the booksellers, 1712.   8°

T.205

5342

BURRIDGE (Richard)

Religio libertini: or, The faith of a converted atheist. Occasionally set forth by Mr. Richard Burridge, who was lately convicted of blasphemy, before ... Sir Thomas Parker ... London: for Sam. Briscoe, and sold by John Graves, and J. Morphew, 1712.   8°

T.161

5343

BUTLER (William) *Rector of St Ann's within Aldersgate.*

A sermon preach'd before the Right Honourable Sir Robert Beachcroft, Kt. Lord-mayor ... on Wednesday, January 16th. 1711/12. Being the day appointed by her Majesty for a publick fast. London, J.H. for Sam. Crouch, 1712.   8°

T.364

5344

C.(A.B.)

A short history of the Revolution in Scotland. In a letter from a Scotch gentleman in Amsterdam to his friend in London. London printed: and sold by the booksellers of London and Westminster, 1712.   8°

2 copies.

T.413 T.103

5345

CANNON (Robert)

An account of two motions made in the lower house of Convocation. London: for E. Sanger, 1712.   8°

T.395

5346

CANNON (Robert)

An account of two motions made in the lower house of Convocation, concerning the power of remitting sins. London: for E. Sanger, 1712.   8°

2 copies.

T.603 T.506

5347

The CASE of ordination consider'd ... By a Catholick ... London: for John Baker, 1712.   8°

Attributed by Bowdler to Dr. Clark.

T.230

5348

The CASE of the dissenters, and others in office, with respect to the laws now in force ... London, for John Lawrence, 1712.   8°

T.363

5349

A CATECHISM, that is to say, an instruction to be learned of every person, before he be brought to be confirmed by the bishop. To which are prefixed brief and plain rules for reading the Irish language. London, E. Everingham, [1712?]   8°

T.441

5350

CHAUCER (Geoffrey)

The carpenter of Oxford. Or, The miller's tale, from Chaucer. Attempted in modern English, by Samuel Cobb ... To which are added, Two imitations of Chaucer, I. Susannah and the two elders. II. Earl Robert's mice. By Matthew Prior. London: for E. Curll, R. Gosling, and J. Pemberton, 1712. 2 parts. 8°

T.35

5351

CHISHULL (Edmund)

Against duelling. A sermon preach'd before the Queen in the royal chapel at Windsor-castle, on November the 23rd, 1712. London: for J.Round, 1712. 8°

T.160

5352

CHURCH OF ENGLAND.

A form of prayer, to be used in all churches and chapels ... on Wednesday the sixteenth day of January next, being the day appointed ... for a general fast ... for ... imploring Gods blessing ... and his assistance on the arms and forces of her Majesty, and her allies ... London, the assigns of Thomas Newcomb, and Henry Hills, 1711/12.   4°

T.461

5353

CHURCH OF IRELAND. *Convocation.*

A representation of the present state of religion, with regard to infidelity, heresy, impiety, and popery: drawn up and agreed to by both houses of Convocation in Ireland ... 2nd ed. London, for John Hyde, bookseller in Dublin; and are to be sold by Henry Clements, 1712. 8°

2 copies.

T.506 T.523

5354

CHURCHILL (John) *Duke of Marlborough.*

The case of his Grace the D[uke] of M[arl]borough]. As design'd to be represented by him to the honourable House of Commons, in vindication of himself from the charge of the Commissioners of Accounts; in relation to the two and half per cent. bread and bread waggons. The third edition corrected. Printed in the year 1712.   8°

T.281

5355

The CITY Shushan perplexed. Or, The perplexity of the present protestant dissenters considered. In a sermon preach'd Jan. 16th. 1711/12. upon occasion of the late publick fast for a peace ... By a protestant dissenting divine ... London, A. Baldwin, 1712.   8°

T.364

5356

CLARKE (Samuel) *Rector of St. James's, Westminster.*

The dedication of Dr Clarke's edition of Caesar's Commentaries, to his Grace the Duke of Marlborough. In Latin and English. Translated by R.T. London, printed: and sold by John Morphew, 1712.   8°

T.281

5357

A COLLECTION of poems on state-affairs, several never before printed. Part I. London printed: and sold by the booksellers, 1712.   8°

T.347

5358

The COMPARISON or Whiggish fulsom flattery exemplifyed in his G[race] the D[uke] of M[arlborough]. By way of dialogue betwixt a Whig and a Tory. Touching the late examination of a late g[enera]l. London, printed, and sold by the booksellers of London and Westminster, 1712.   4°

T.267

5359

COOKE (Thomas) *Curate of Kingston.*

The way to peace consider'd and recommended. In a sermon preach'd in the parish church of Kingston in Surry January 16. 1711/12... (Lamentation for the fall of the righteous. A sermon... preach'd... January 30. 1711/12.) London, for Samuel Keble, and Henry Clements, 1711/12.   8°

T.364

5360

COOPER (Anthony Ashley) *1st Earl of Shaftesbury.*

Delenda est Carthago, or the Lord Chancellor Shaftsbury's speeches in Parliament about the second war with the Dutch in 1672, and 1673. London: for J. Baker, 1712.   8°

T.275

5361

COSIN (John) *Bishop of Durham.*

An additional letter 'from Dr. John Cosin, afterwards Bishop of Durham, to Mr. Cordel, who scrupled to communicate with the French-protestants, upon some of the modern pretences.'

pp. 51-57 of the second edition of Fleetwood (W.) The judgment of the Church of England. 1712.

T.302

5362

CRISPE (H.)

To the honourable Mathew Prior, Esq; on his promotion to the commission of her Majesty's customs, and first coming to the board. January 28. 1711. London: for E. Curll, 1712.   4°

T.269

5363

CROMWELL (Oliver)

A most learned, conscientious, and devout exercise, or sermon, held forth the last Lords-day of April, in the year 1649. at Sir P[eter] T[emple]'s house in Lincolns-Inn-Fields. As it was faithfully taken in characters by Aaron Guerdon. Reprinted in the year, 1712. and sold by John Morphew.   8°

T.520

5364

CUNINGHAME (James)

A warning of the eternal spirit, pronounc'd by the mouth of James Cuninghame, June 25th, 1712. upon reading Math. XXII. from verse 15. to verse 23. [No imprint, 1712.]   8°

T.383

5365

DAVENANT (Charles)

A report to the honourable the Commissioners for putting in execution the act, intitled, An Act, for the taking, examining, and stating the publick accounts of the Kingdom. London: printed in the year, 1712. 2 parts.   8°

T.279

5366

DEFOE (Daniel)

The conduct of parties in England, more especially of those Whigs who now appear against the new ministry, and a treaty of peace. [Anon.] Printed in the year 1712.   8°

Moore 228.

T.401

5367

DEFOE (Daniel)

A defence of the allies and the late ministry: or, Remarks on the Tories new idol. Being a detection of the manifest frauds and falsities, in a late pamphlet [by Jonathan Swift], entituled, The conduct of the allies ... [Anon.] London: J. Baker, 1712.   8°

Moore 225.

T.113

5368

DEFOE (Daniel)

An essay on the South-Sea trade. With an enquiry into the grounds and reasons of the present dislike and complaint against the settlement of a South-Sea Company. By the author of the Review. London: for J. Baker, 1712.   8°

Moore 214.

T.272

5369

DEFOE (Daniel)

A farther search into the conduct of the allies, and the late ministry, as to peace and war ... [Anon.] London: printed in the year 1712.   8°

Moore 242.

T.401

5370

DEFOE (Daniel)

Hannibal at the gates: or, The progress of Jacobitism. With the present danger of the Pretender ... [Anon.] London: for J. Baker, 1712.   8°

Moore 246.

T.362

5371

DEFOE (Daniel)

Imperial gratitude, drawn from a modest view of the conduct of the Emperor Ch[arl]es VI. and the King of Spain Ch[arl]es III ... [The preface is signed Philopax.] London: printed in the year 1712.   8°

Moore 233.

T.401

5372

DEFOE (Daniel)

A justification of the Dutch from several late scandalous reflections ... [Anon.] London, for J. Baker, 1712.   8°

Moore 226.

T.233

5373

DEFOE (Daniel)

No queen: or, No general. An argument, proving the necessity her Majesty was in ... to displace the D[uke] of M[arl]borough. [Anon.] London: printed, and sold by the booksellers of London and Westminster, 1712.   8°

Moore 227.

T.281

5374

DEFOE (Daniel)

Peace, or poverty. Being a serious vindication of her Majesty and her ministers consenting to a treaty for a general peace ... [Anon.] London: John Morphew, 1712.   8°

Moore 229.

T.401

5375

DEFOE (Daniel)

Reasons against fighting. Being an enquiry into the great debate, Whether it is safe for her Majesty, or her ministry, to venture an engagement with the French ... [Anon.] Printed in the year 1712.   4°

Moore 238.

T.551

5376

DENNIS (John)

An essay on the genius and writings of Shakespear: with some letters of criticism to the Spectator ... London: for Bernard Lintott, 1712.   8°

T.410

5377

DIAPER (William)

Nereides: or, Sea-eclogues... [Anon.] London, J.H. for E. Sanger, 1712.   8°

T.410

5378

DIBBEN (Thomas)

A sermon preach'd at Shaftsbury, May 24. 1711. at the primary visitation of ... John, Lord Bishop of Bristol ... London: W.B. for Richard Sare, 1712.   8°

2 copies.

T.293   T.104

5379

The DISMAL consequences of delighting in war. In a sermon preach'd on Wednesday January 16. 1711/12. Being the fast day for a general peace. By a presbyter of the Church of England ... London, printed for, and sold by J. Morphew, 1712.   8°

T.364

5380

DODWELL (Henry)

A letter from the learned Mr. Henry Dodwell to the Right Reverend the Bishop of Sarum, in which he owns his spiritual character, but not his temporal. Together with the Bishop's answer. London: for John Baker, 1712.   8°

T.367

5381

DUCKETT (George)

A new project, dedicated neither to the Q——n nor the Lord T——r, nor any of the Houses of P——nt, but to the unbelieving club at the Grecian ... [Anon.] London: printed for the booksellers, 1712.   8°

2 copies.

T.205   T.147

5382

The D[UKE] of M[arlborough]'s confession to a Jacobite priest: as it was taken in short-hand the 6th of February last, 1711 ... London, for J. Smith, 1712.   8°

Wanting title-page.

T.281

5383

DUMMER (Jeremiah)

A letter to a friend in the country, on the late expedition to Canada: with an account of former enterprizes, a defence of that design, and the share the late m——rs had in it. [Anon.] London, for A. Baldwin, 1712.   8°

T.161

5384

DUNTON (John)

The preaching-weathercock: a paradox, proving Mr. W[illiam] R[ichar]dson (lately a dissenting minister, and now a presbiter of the Church of England) will cant, recant, and re-recant ... London, R. Tookey, for the author, and sold by the booksellers of London and Westminster, [1712].   8°

T.548

5385

The DUTCH riddle: or, A character of a h——ry monster. Often found in Holland, &c. London: J. Read, [1712?]   4°

T.261

5386

EDWARDS (John) *D.D.*

Some brief observations and reflections on Mr. Whiston's late writings, falsly entitul'd Primitive Christianity reviv'd ... London: for J. Lawrence; and J. Wyat, and R. Robinson, 1712.   8°

T.25

5387
EMLYN (Thomas)

The previous question to the several questions about valid and invalid baptism, lay-baptism, &c. consider'd, viz Whether there be any necessity ... for the continual use of baptism among the posterity of baptiz'd Christians ... [Anon.] London, for S. Popping, 1712. 8°

T.395

5388

An ESSAY towards an impartial account of the Holy Trinity, and the deity of our Saviour... In which are some remarks on the Scripture account lately publish'd by Dr. Clark... [Attributed to Edward Wells.] London: for H. Clements, 1712. 8°

T.546

5389

An EXHORTATION to the love of our country: with some reflections on a late protest ... London, for John Morphew, 1712. 8°

T.51

5390
FAIRMAN (Arthur)

A full confutation of witchcraft: more particularly of the depositions against Jane Wenham, lately condemned for a witch; at Hertford. In which the modern notions of witches are overthrown ... proving that, witchcraft is priestcraft ... In a letter from a physician in Hertfordshire, to his friend in London. London: for J. Baker, 1712. 8°

T.48

5391

The FATE of M. Manlius Capitolinus; translated from approved historians. Printed in the year 1712. 4°

T.267

5392

A FEW orthodox remarks upon a late H[igh] Ch[urch] preface, publish'd before some occasional sermons [by William Fleetwood]. London, for J. Baker, 1712. 8°

T.520

5393
FLEETWOOD (William) Bishop of Ely.

The Bishop of St. Asaph's charge to the clergy of that diocese, in 1710. and now made publick, by his Lordship's permission. London, for Sam. Buckley: and sold by D. Midwinter, 1712. 12°

2 copies.

T.520 T.523

5394
FLEETWOOD (William) Bishop of Ely.

Four sermons: I. On the death of Queen Mary, 1694. II. On the death of the Duke of Gloucester, 1700. III. On the death of King William, 1701. IV. On the Queen's accession ... 1703. By William Lord Bishop of St. Asaph. 2nd ed. London: for Charles Harper, 1712. 8°

T.520

5395
FLEETWOOD (William) Bishop of Ely.

The judgment of the Church of England in the case of Lay-baptism and of dissenters baptism. [Anon.] London: A. Baldwin, 1712. 8°

T.409

5396
FLEETWOOD (William) Bishop of Ely.

The second part of The judgment of the Church of England, in the case of lay-baptism, and dissenters baptism. [Anon.] London, sold by A. Baldwin, 1712. 8°

T.365

5397
FLEETWOOD (William) Bishop of Ely.

A sermon on the fast-day, January the sixteenth, 1711/12. against such as delight in war. By a divine of the Church of England. London: for Sam. Buckley, 1712. 8°

T.364

5398
FOWLER (Edward) Bishop of Gloucester.

Memoirs on the life and death of our late most gracious Queen Mary. 2nd ed. With some small corrections and additions. London: for B. Aylmer; and J. Wyat, 1712. 8°

T.275

5399

A FULL answer to the Conduct of the allies [by Jonathan Swift]: to which is added, Some observations on the remarks on the Barrier Treaty. By the same author. London: printed in the year 1712. 8°

Teerink 1044.

T.71

5400

A FULL vindication of the ... Lord Bishop of Edinburgh, and other administrators of the charities there, from the calumnies ... of Mr. George Barclay, in his defamatory libel, publish'd in the Flying post ... London: G. Strahan, 1712. 4°

2 copies.

T.142 T.2

5401
GAY (John)

The Mohocks. A tragi-comical farce. As it was acted near the Watch-house in Covent-Garden. By his Majesty's servants ... [The dedication is signed W.B.] London: for Bernard Lintott, 1712. 8°

T.410

5402

The GENERAL history of all revolutions, rebellions, and murders of sovereign princes, that have been in all countries, from the creation to this present time. London: for J. Baker, 1712. 8°

T.115

5403
GOOCH (Sir Thomas) Bishop of Ely.

A sermon preach'd before the honourable House of Commons, at St. Margaret's Westminster, on Wednesday the 30th of January 1711 ... London: J.R. for Jonah Bowyer, 1712. 4°

2 copies.
Another copy, in 8°.

T.364 T.3

5404
GRABE (Johann Ernst)

Some instances of the defects and omissions in Mr. Whiston's collection of testimonies from the scriptures and the fathers, against the true deity of the Son and the Holy Ghost... To which is premised a discourse... By George Hickes. London, W. Bowyer, for Henry Clements, 1712. 8°

2 copies.

T.25 T.768

5405

GRANDSIRE Hambden's ghost. And peace, or, no peace. Two poems. Together with a prefatory answer, to some late Whiggish scurrility, especially, a certain dedication. London: for J. Woodward, 1712. 8°

T.225

5406
GREAT BRITAIN. Commissioners of Accounts.

The second report of the Commissioners for the taking, examining and stating the publick accounts, &c. London: printed in the year 1712. 8°

T.279

5407
GUYBON (Francis)

An essay concerning the growth of empiricism; or the encouragement of quacks. Wherein the present state of physick in this kingdom is fairly represented ... London: for R. Parker; and sold by J. Morphew, 1712. 8°

T.294

5408
H.(A.)

A funeral poem upon the much lamented death of Lieutenant-General Wood, who departed this life at his house at Kensington the 17th of May, 1712 ... Written by a female. A.H. London, John Morphew, 1712. 4°

T.269

5409
HARE (Francis) Bishop of Chichester.

The allies and the late ministry defended against France, and the present friends of France. Part IV... [Anon.] London. for E. Sanger, 1712. 8°

T.113

5410
HARE (Francis) Bishop of Chichester.

Frauds and abuses at St. Paul's. In a letter to a member of Parliament ... [Anon.] London: printed in the year 1712. 8°

2 copies.

T.402 T.163

5411
HAYLEY (Thomas)

A sermon preach'd at the parish-church of St. James Westminster, on Wednesday January 16. 1711/12. Being the day appointed ... for a general fast ... London, for Matt. Wotton, 1712. 8°

T.364

5412

The HISTORY of the proceedings of the Mandarins and Proatins of the Britomartian empire at their last general diet, with the characters of the chief members ... London: printed for the booksellers of London and Westminster, 1712. 8°

T.205

5413
HOLDSWORTH (Edward)

The mouse-trap: a poem. Written in Latin by E. Holdsworth. Made English by Samuel Cobb ... London: for E. Curll, and E. Sanger, 1712. 8°

T.347

5414
HORATIUS FLACCUS (Quintus)

Horatius reformatus: sive, emendationes omnes quibus editio Bentleiana a vulgaribus distinguitur summa fide in unum collectae ... Editio altera emendatior. Londini: impensis J. Bowyer; et vaeneunt per J. Morphew, 1712. 8°

T.92

5415
HORNBY (Charles)

A second part of the Caveat against the Whiggs, &c. With a preface to both parts ... [Anon.] London: J. Morphew, 1712. 8°

T.337

5416
HORNBY (Charles)

A third part of the Caveat against the Whiggs, in a short historical account of their transactions since the Revolution ... [Anon.] London: J. Morphew, 1712. 8°

T.348

5417
HORNBY (Charles)

A third part of the Caveat against the Whiggs, in a short historical account of their transactions since the Revolution ... [Anon.] 2nd ed. London: J. Morphew, 1712. 8°

T.337

5418
HORNBY (Charles)

The fourth and last part of a Caveat against the Whiggs, &c. In a short historical account of their behaviour in the reign of her Majesty Queen Anne ... [Anon.] London: J. Morphew, 1712. 8°

2 copies.

T.337 T.348

5419
HOUGH (John) Bishop of Worcester.

A sermon preach'd at St. Bride's, before the lord-mayor, and court of aldermen, on Monday in Easter-week, 1712. By ... John, Lord Bishop of Litchfield and Coventry. London: for Egbert Sanger, 1712. 4°

T.3

1712 (Cont'd)

5420

HOWELL (William) of *Wadham College, Oxford.*

Peace and unity recommended. A sermon preach'd before the University of Oxford, at St. Mary's, on Sunday, Aug. 17th. 1712. By the author of a collection intitled, The Common-prayer-book the best companion &c. Oxford, printed at the Theatre, for Anthony Peisley: and are to be sold by J. Knapton, H. Clements, and J. Morphew, booksellers in London, 1712. 8°

T.39

5421

HUMPHREYS (Thomas)

The divine authority of the New Testament prov'd and vindicated, in a sermon preach'd before the University of Oxford, at St. Mary's, Septemb. 30th. 1711. Oxford, printed at the Theatre, for Anthony Peisley: and are to be sold by J. Knapton, H. Clements, and J. Morphew, 1712. 8°

T.39

5422

IBBETSON (Richard)

The divinity of our Blessed Saviour prov'd from Scripture and antiquity. A sermon preach'd before the University of Oxford... Jan. 6th. 1711/12. In which Mr. Whiston's attempt to revive the Arian heresy is consider'd. 2nd ed. Oxford, printed at the Theater, for Anthony Peisley: and are to be sold by J. Knapton, H. Clements, and J. Morphew, 1712. 8°

3 copies.

T.39 T.364 T.804

5423

The IMPOSSIBILITY of witchcraft further demonstrated. Both from Scripture and reason .... By the author of the Impossibility of witchcraft ... London: for J. Baker, 1712. 8°

T.48

5424

The IMPOSSIBILITY of witchcraft, plainly proving, from Scripture and reason, that there never was a witch ... In which the depositions against Jane Wenham ... are confuted and expos'd ... 2nd ed. London, J. Baker, 1712. 8°

T.48

5425

The IMPOSTOR painted in his own colours; or, The base birth and parentage of the Chevalier de St. George, alias the Pretender, now truly brought to light ... London: J. Read, [1712?] 8°

T.205

5426

The INFANTS advocate or, The ministers address to parents to bring their children to church baptism ... London: for Geo. Strahan, 1712. 8°

T.395

5427

The INFORMATION against the Duke of Marlborough. And his answer. London, J. Bradford, 1712. 8°

T.281

5428

The JUDGMENT of the Reformed in France, extracted out of the acts of their publick synods ... concerning the invalidity of lay-baptisms. In a letter to the author of Lay-baptism invalid [i.e. Roger Laurence]. By a priest of the Church of England... London: for Henry Clements, 1712. 8°

2 copies.

T.365 T.395

5429

JUS sacrum, or, A discourse wherein it is fully prov'd and demonstrated, that no prince ought to be depriv'd of his natural right on account of religion, &c. London printed, and sold by John Baker, 1712. 8°

T.344

5430

JUS sacrum, or, A discourse wherein it is fully prov'd and demonstrated, that no prince ought to to [sic] depriv'd of his natural right on account of religion, &c. 2nd ed. London printed, and sold by John Baker, 1712. 8°

T.205

5431

KENNET (White) *Bishop of Peterborough.*

The lets and impediments in planting and propagating the Gospel of Christ. A sermon preach'd before the Society for the Propagation of the Gospel ... on Friday the 15th of February, 1711/12 ... London: Joseph Downing, 1712. 8°

T.39

5432

KING (William) *Student of Christ Church.*

Rufinus: or an historical essay on the favourite-ministry under Theodosius the Great and his son Arcadius. [Anon.] To which is added, a version of part of Claudian's Rufinus ... London, John Morphew, 1712. 8°

2 copies.

T.281 T.205

5433

KNAGGS (Thomas)

God governs the world. A sermon preach'd at St Giles's church in the Fields, on the 16th of January, 1711/12 ... London: for Daniel Midwinter, 1712. 8°

T.364

5434

KNIGHT (James)

Primitive Christianity vindicated, in a second letter to the author of the history of Montanism [i.e. Francis Lee], against the Arian misrepresentations of it, and Mr. Whiston's bold assertions in his late books... By the author of the Considerations on Mr. Whiston's Historical preface. London: for R. and J. Bonwicke, 1712. 8°

3 copies.

T.305 T.546 T.768

5435

The LAND-leviathan; or, Modern hydra: in burlesque verse, by way of letter to a friend ... London: for John Morphew, 1712. 8°

T.410

5436

LAURENCE (Roger)

The Bishop of Oxford's charge, consider'd ... By the author of Lay-baptism invalid. London: for H. Clements, 1712. 8°

2 copies.

T.365 T.1

5437

LAURENCE (Roger)

Dissenters, and other unauthoriz'd baptisms null and void, by the articles, canons and rubricks of the Church of England. In answer to a pamphlet [by William Fleetwood], call'd, The judgment of the Church of England, in the case of lay-baptism, and of dissenters baptism. By the author of lay baptism invalid ... London: for Henry Clements, 1712. 8°

T.365

5438

LESLIE (Charles)

Natural reflections upon the present debates about peace and war. In two letters to a member of Parliament from his steward in the country. [Anon.] London: John Morphew, 1712. 8°

3 copies.

T.401 T.417 T.551

5439

LESLIE (Charles)

Salt for the leach. In reflections upon reflections ... [Anon.] London: printed in the year 1712. 4°

T.523

5440

A LETTER from a merchant in Amsterdam to a friend in London, about the South Sea trade. London: John Baker, 1712. 8°

T.87

5441

A LETTER from a Whig gentleman in the country, to his friend in town; concerning a printed memorial, under the name of his Excellency the Baron de Bothmar, envoy from the court of Hannover. London, for John Baker, 1712. 8°

2 copies.

T.401 T.344

5442

A LETTER to a friend, occasion'd by the Bishop of St. Asaph's preface to his Four sermons. By a true born Englishman... [Signed Tom Trueman.] London: John Morphew, 1712. 8°

3 copies.

T.39 T.520 T.523

5443

The LIFE and conversation of Richard Bentley, delivered in his own words, for the most part from his own writings ... London: for John Morphew, 1712. 8°

T.402

5444

The LIFE and reign of Henry the sixth ... London: for A Baldwin, 1712. 8°

T.362

5445

LLOYD (Robert Lumley)

A sermon preach'd at St. Paul's Covent-Garden, on the 30th of January, 1711 ... London, for A Baldwin, 1712. 8°

T.364

5446

LLOYD (Robert Lumley)

A sermon preach'd at St. Paul's Covent-garden, on the 5th of November 1712 ... London, for A. Baldwin, 1712. 8°

T.160

5447

LONDON.

Tory partiality detected: or, A true state of the poll and scrutiny of Broad-Street ward, on the election of an alderman in the room of Sir Joseph Wolfe ... London, for J. Baker, 1712. 8°

T.163

5448

LORRAIN (Paul)

Popery near a-kin to paganism and atheism: or, Which is the purer religion, the Romish, or the Reformed; set forth in a sermon, preach'd in the chapel of Newgate ... London, for Sam. Briscoe, and sold by J. Morphew, and J. Graves, 1712. 8°

T.334

5449

MACARTNEY (George)

A true and impartial account of the murder of his Grace the Duke of Hamilton and Brandon, by Mr. Mackartney. London, John Morphew, 1712. 4°

T.490

5450

MACKWORTH (*Sir* Humphrey)

The Mine-Adventurers case; in order to explain a proposal for raising a stock of 200001. for carrying on the undertaking. [Anon.] [No imprint, 1712.] 8°

T.442

5451

MAINWARING (Arthur) *and others.*

The British Academy: being a new-erected society for the advancement of wit and learning: with some few observations upon it ... [Anon.] London: printed in the year 1712. 8°

T.161

5452

MARSHALL (Nathaniel)

A sermon preach'd before the Sons of the clergy, at their annual assembly in the cathedral-church of St. Paul, London. Upon Thursday Dec. 6, 1711 ... London: Geo. James, for Richard Sare, and Tho. Baker, 1712. 4°

T.3

5453

MAYO (Richard)

Several hundred texts of holy Scripture, plainly proving, that our Lord Jesus Christ is the most high God; collected, composed and disposed in a proper method, by a presbyter of the Church of England ... London, for J. Lawrence, and J. Downing, 1712. 8°

T.228

5454

The MEDAL: or, A full and impartial account of the late proceedings of the dean and Faculty of Advocates in Scotland, relating to that affair. London: for E. Curll; and J. Morphew, 1712.   8°

T.169

5455

MEMOIRS of the Chevalier de St. George: with some private passages of the life of the late King James II. Never before publish'd. London: printed in the year 1712.   8°

T.413

5456

A MERRY new year's gift; or, The captain's letter to the colonel about the late election in Southwark. London, for S. Popping, 1712.   8°

T.205

5457

MESECH and Kedar. Or, Reflections on a scurrilous pamphlet, entitl'd, Mr. Trapp's sermon, preach'd at ... St. Martin in the Fields, on the general fast ... London: for Bernard Lintott; and sold by A. Baldwin, and the booksellers in Oxford, 1712.   8°

T.364

5458

MILBOURNE (Luke)

The curse of regicides: or Simeon and Levi's doom, in a sermon preached on the thirtieth of January, 1711/12 ... London: for George Sawbridge, 1712.   8°

2 copies.

T.364   T.334

5459

The MISERABLE case of poor old England fairly stated, in a letter to a member of the honourable House of Commons ... Amsterdam, printed in the year 1712. 4°

T.13

5460

MR. Hoadly's measures of submission to the civil magistrate enquired into, and disproved. Part. II ... By a presbyter of the Church of England ... London: for W. Freeman, and R. Wilkin, 1712.   8°

T.297

5461

A MODEST survey of that celebrated tragedy the Distrest mother [by Ambrose Philips], so often and so highly applauded by the ingenious Spectator ... London, William Redmayne, and John Morphew, 1712.   8°

T.410

5462

A MORNING'S discourse of a bottomless tubb, introducing the historical fable of the oak and her three provinces ... Written by a lover of the loyal, honest, and moderate party. London: for John Morphew, 1712.   8°

T.51

5463

MOSS (Robert) *Dean of Ely.*

A sermon preach'd at the assizes holden at Kingston upon Thames, on Wednesday 30th of July, 1712 ... London: for Richard Sare, 1712.   4°

T.3

5464

NAYLOR (William)

A strange and true account of one Mr. William Naylor, a Minister, lately come from the University of Oxford. Who fell in a trance... in which he lay three days and three nights... London: J. Read, 1712.   4°

T.490

5465

NEUCHATEL.

The liturgy used in the churches of the principality of Neufchatel: with a letter from the learned Dr. Jablonski, concerning the nature of liturgies ... London, Joseph Downing, 1712.   4°

T.2

5466

The NEW way of selling places at Court. In a letter from a small courtier to a great stock-jobber ... London, for John Morphew, 1712.   8°

Sometimes attributed to Swift.

T.205

5467

NEWTON (Richard)

A sermon preach'd before the honourable House of Commons, at St. Margaret's, Westminster, on Saturday, March 8. 1711/12. Being the anniversary of her Majesty's happy accession to the Crown. London: G. James, for Jonah Bowyer, 1712.   8°

T.334

5468

NO punishment no government: and no danger even in the worst designs ... [Attributed to Daniel Defoe.] London: printed, and sold by the booksellers of London and Westminster, 1712.   8°

T.205

5469

OCCASIONAL poems on the late Dutch war, and the sale of Dunkirk. To which is added, A satyr against the Dutch. London: printed, and sold by the booksellers of London and Westminster, 1712.   8°

T.225

5470

OCKLEY (Simon)

An account of the authority of the Arabick manuscripts in the Bodleian Library, controverted between Dr. Grabe and Mr. Whiston. In a letter to Mr. Thirlby ... London: for H. Clements, 1712.   8°

2 copies.

T.211   T.25

5471

OCKLEY (Simon)

An imitation of the new way of writing, introduc'd by the learned Mr. Asgill. Humbly offer'd to his admirers... [Anon.] London: for John Morphew, 1712. 8°

T.548

5472

OCKLEY (Simon)

Oratio inauguralis habita Cantabrigiae in scholis publicis, Kalend. Februariis anno MDCCXI. Cantabrigiae: typis academicis, impensis Edmundi Jeffery. Prostant venales Londini apud Jac. Knapton, 1712.   4°

T.12

5473

An OLD story that every one knows: or, The religion of the Whigs enquired into. Occasion'd by their charging the Church of England with popery. In a letter from a gentleman in the country, to his friend in town... London: for John Morphew, 1712.   8°

T.227

5474

The OLD wives tales: a poem. Part I. London: J. Morphew, 1712.   8°

2 copies.

T.35   T.410

5475

OLDMIXON (John)

The Dutch barrier our's: or, The interest of England and Holland inseparable. With reflections on the insolent treatment the Emperor and States-General have met with from the author of Conduct [i.e. Jonathan Swift], and his brethren ... [Anon.] London: for A. Baldwin, 1712.   8°

Teerink 1048.

T.171

5476

OLDMIXON (John)

Reflections on Dr. Swift's letter to the Earl of Oxford, about the English tongue. [Anon.] London: sold by A. Baldwin, [1712].   8°

Teerink 1051.
2 copies.

T.103   T.161

5477

ON the death of Mr. Edmund Smith, late student of Christ-Church, Oxon. A poem in Miltonic verse ... 2nd ed. London, for J. Morphew, 1712.   8°

T.347

5478

OVERTON (Benjamin)

Good advice to the Whigs, by an old dying Whig: or, Mr. Overton's last letter to his friends. With an account of his sickness and death. London: for J. Baker, 1712.   8°

T.622

5479

PEIRCE (James)

An enquiry into the present duty of a Low-Church-man; occasion'd by the late Act of Parliament. In a letter from a dissenter in the country, to a Low-Church-man in the city ... [Anon.] London: for John Clark, 1712.   8°

T.363

5480

PHILLIPS (Robert)

Religion and loyalty. A sermon preach'd at St. Margaret's Westminster, before the honourable House of Commons, upon Thursday the 29th of May, 1712 ... London, for Math. Wotton, and Maurice Atkins, 1712. 4°

T.196

5481

PITTIS (William)

The history of the proceedings of the second session of this present Parliament ... London. Printed: and sold by John Baker, [1712].   8°

T.205

5482

PLAIN English, with remarks and advice to some men who need not be nam'd. [Probably by Daniel Defoe.] London, J. Woodward, 1712.   8°

Moore 235.

T.205

5483

PLAXTON (William)

Advice to new-married husbands, in Hudibrastick verse. By the author of the York-shire horse-racers. Printed for John Morphew, 1712.   8°

T.410

5484

The PLEA for toleration, on pretence of tenderness of conscience, proved to be a cheat ... In a letter from a gentleman in the country, to his friend a citizen of London. London, for Henry Clements, 1712.   8°

2 copies.

T.377   T.115

5485

PLUNDER and bribery further discover'd, in a memorial humbly offer'd to the British Parliament. London: printed in the year, 1712.   8°

Sometimes attributed to Defoe.

T.205

5486

The PRESENT state of religion in Ireland. Containing, I. An humble address and apology of the Presbyterian ministers and gentlemen... II. Another from the same persons... III. An address of the protestant dissenting ministers in Dublin... Wherein the dissenters are vindicated from the calumny of being enemies to the present establishment... London, for Andrew Bell, [1712]. 8°

T.506

5487

The PRESENT state of the prison of Ludgate ... To which are added, useful remarks and pertinent observations on the former state thereof ... [The preface signed Philopolites.] London: printed for and sold by A. Baldwin, [1712].   8°

T.163

5488

The PRESS restrain'd: a poem, occasion'd by a resolution of the House of Commons, to consider that part of her Majesty's message to the House, which relates to the great licence taken in publishing false and scandalous libels. London: for John Morphew, 1712.   8°

T.347

5489

PRINCE Eugene not the man you took him for: or, A merry tale of a modern heroe ... London, J. Baker, 1712.   8°

T.51

5490

A PROJECT for establishing the general peace of
Europe, by a more equal partition than has hitherto
been proposed. London: printed in the year, 1712.
8°

T.401

5491

A PROPOSAL to the Governor and Company of the
Mine-Adventurers of England, for raising a stock
of twenty thousand pounds to carry on their
undertaking. [No imprint, 1712?] 8°

T.442

5492

PUNCH turn'd critick, in a letter to the honourable
and (some time ago) worshipful rector of Covent-
Garden [Robert Lumley Lloyd]. With some wooden
remarks on his sermon, preach'd the 30th of January,
1711 ... [Signed Seignioro Punchanello.] Printed in
the year 1712. 8°

T.302

5493

R.(G.)

The belief of witchcraft vindicated: proving, from
Scripture, there have been witches; and from reason,
that there may be such still. In answer to a late
pamphlet, intituled, The impossibility of witchcraft
... London: for J. Baker, 1712. 8°

T.48

5494

RAWSON (Joseph)

A brief admonition to the members of the Church of
England, who attend the publick service of it, that
they repeat not aloud the prayers after the minister,
unless where it is otherwise requir'd in the rubrick.
3rd ed. London: for Tho. Baker, 1712. 8°

T.39

5495

REASONS pro and con: being a debate at the council-
table, between the Treasurer [Lord Burghley] and the
General [the Earl of Essex], for making a peace, or
carrying on the war, in the reign of Queen Elizabeth
... London: for S. Popping, 1712. 8°

T.401

5496

REEVES (William)

The nature of truth and falshood; with some motives to
the practice of mutual sincerity. A sermon preached
before the Queen, in St. George's Chapel at Windsor;
on the 10th day of August 1712 ... London, W. Bowyer,
for Richard Sare, 1712. 4°

T.3

5497

REMARKS on some extracts, published in a paper, called
The supplement of Friday, March 28. 1712. London: for
A. Baldwin, 1712. 8°

T.401

5498

RESPECTFUL observations on a late print, call'd A
memorial; said to be publish'd by the Baron de Bothmar,
in the name of his Electoral Highness of Hanover.
London: for John Morphew, 1712. 8°

2 copies.

T.401 T.344

5499

RICHARDSON (William) *formerly a Dissenting Minister.*

Episcopacy vindicated, in a letter to Mr. W. Clark a
dissenting teacher. To which is prefix'd Mr. Clark's
first letter to Mr. Richardson, upon his conversion;
and Mr. Richardson's answer. London, for George
Strahan, 1712. 8°

T.115

5500

ROBERTS (William) *Rector of Jacobstow.*

The divine institution of the Gospel ministry, and the
necessity of episcopal ordination, asserted. In a
sermon, preach'd at the primary visitation of ...
Ofspring, Lord Bishop of Exon, held at Okehampton,
Aug. 19th, 1709. 3rd ed ... Exon: Jos. Bliss, for
Philip Bishop, 1712. 8°

T.36

5501

RUSSEL (David)

The impeachment [of Dr. Sacheverell]: or, The Church
triumphant. A poem ... [Anon.] London: printed in
the year 1712. 8°

T.350

5502

S. (E.)

All at stake Hannover or Perkin, in a letter to a
country clergy-man. London, for J. Baker, 1712. 8°

T.362

5503

ST. JOHN (Pawlet)

A sermon preach'd before the Queen, at St. James's
chappel, on Wednesday, January 30. 1711/12 ... London:
G.J. for Jonah Bowyer, 1712. 8°

2 copies.

T.364 T.334

5504

A SECRET history of the amours and marriage of
an English nobleman with a famous Italian lady.
2nd ed. London printed, and sold by the booksellers
of London and Westminster, 1712. 12°

T.442

5505

The SECRET history of the Geertrudenbergh negociation.
With several original papers ... Done out of French
... London: printed in the year 1712. 8°

T.401

5506

The SENSE of the court and parliaments of England,
as to the dissenters, ever since the Restoration ...
In a letter to the Right Honourable the E[arl] of
N[ottingham]. By the author of the letter to Sr.
T[homas] H[anmer]. London: for S. Popping, 1712. 8°

T.302

5507

SEWELL (George)

The life and character of Mr. John Philips. Author of
the Splendid shilling, Bleinheim, Cyder, &c. [Anon.]
(Ode, ad Henricum St. John, armig.) London: for E.
Curll, 1712, 13. 2 parts. 8°

T.275

5508

SHARPE (John) *Curate of Stepney.*

The regular clergy's sole right to administer Christian
baptism, asserted: in a familiar dialogue betwixt a
Church-man and a dissenter ... By the author of the
Hamsted-conferences. London, for Richard Wilkin, 1712.
8°

2 copies.

T.395 T.360

5509

A SHORT account, of the many extraordinary mercies,
God in his infinite goodness has conferred upon
Franciscus Bellisomus, as well in his almost ten
years imprisonment in the Inquisition at Rome, as
in his unexpected deliverance. Printed, anno 1712.
8°

T.522

5510

SMALRIDGE (George) *Bishop of Bristol.*

A sermon preach'd at the assizes held at Kingston
upon Thames; on Thursday, March 20. 1711/12 ...
London: G. James, for Jonah Bowyer, 1712. 4°

Another copy, in 8°

T.334 T.198

5511

SMALRIDGE (George) *Bishop of Bristol.*

A sermon, preached at the royal chapel at St. James's,
on Wednesday, January the 16th, 1711/12...
London, J.H. for Jonah Bowyer, 1712. 4°

Another copy, in 8°

T.3 T.364

5512

SMITH (John) *Prebendary of Durham.*

A sermon preach'd at the consecration of the chapel of
Stockton ... August 21. 1712 ... London: for H.
Clements, 1712. 4°

T.3

5513

SOME observations upon Bishop Fleetwood's Four
sermons: wherein his preface is fully consider'd.
London: printed in the year 1712. 8°

2 copies.

T.520 T.523

5514

SOPHIA CHARLOTTE, *Queen of Prussia.*

A letter against popery... Being an answer to a
letter written to her Majesty by Father Vota, an
Italian Jesuit... There is prefixt by the publisher,
a letter [signed J. Londat.] containing the
occasion of the Queen's writing, and an apology for
the Church of England. London: for A. Baldwin,
1712. 8°

T.405

5515

STACY (Edmund)

The parliament of birds... [Anon.] London: for
John Morphew, 1712. 8°

T.410

5516

STRANGE news from Scotland, or, Scotch Presbyterian
piety evidently prov'd by the regard they shew to
consecrated churches, the bodies of the dead, &c.
A late instance whereof, may be seen, at this day,
at Dunglass, belonging to Sir James Hall... Sold
by J. Morphew, 1712. 8°

T.413

5517

STUBS (Philip)

De missione evangelica. Concio habita coram clero
Londinensi, in ecclesia parochiali Sancti Ealfegi.
3to Id. Maij, anno a Christo incarnato M.DCC.XII.
Hagae Comitis, prostat venalis apud Thom. Jonsonium,
1712. 4°

T.198

5518

The SUBSTANCE of all the depositions taken at the
coroners inquest the 17th, 19th, and 21st of
November, on the body of Duke Hamilton. And the
15th, 18th, 20th, and 22d, on the body of my Lord
Mohun... London: for A. Baldwin, 1712. 8°

T.161

5519

A SUCCINCT and methodical history of the proceedings
in the first sessions of this present Parliament,
which begun at Westminster the 25th of November 1710,
and ended the 12th of June 1711 ... London, J. Baker,
1712. 8°

T.91

5520

SUETONIUS TRANQUILLUS (Caius)

The life of Horace, with Dr. Bentley's preface, Latin
and English ,.. London: for John Morphew, [1712].
8°

T.92

5521

SWIFT (Jonathan) *Dean of St. Patrick's.*

The conduct of the allies, and of the late ministry,
in beginning and carrying on the present War ...
[Anon.] London, for John Morphew, 1712. 8°

Teerink 539.
2 copies.

T.551 T.233

5522

SWIFT (Jonathan) *Dean of St. Patrick's.*

The conduct of the allies, and of the late ministry,
in beginning and carrying on the present War ...
[Anon.] The sixth edition, corrected. London, for
John Morphew, 1712. 8°

Teerink 539.

T.147

5523

SWIFT (Jonathan) *Dean of St. Patrick's.*

A letter of thanks from my Lord W*****n to the
Lord Bp of S. Asaph, in the name of the Kit-Cat-Club.
Printed in the year 1712. 8°

Teerink 585A.

T.520

5524

SWIFT (Jonathan) *Dean of St. Patrick's.*

A proposal for correcting, improving and ascertaining the English tongue; in a letter to ... Robert Earl of Oxford and Mortimer, Lord High Treasurer of Great Britain. London: for Benj. Tooke, 1712.   8°

Teerink 577.

T.161

5525

SWIFT (Jonathan) *Dean of St. Patrick's.*

Some advice humbly offer'd to the members of the October club, in a letter from a person of honour. [Anon.] London, for John Morphew, 1712.   8°

Teerink 557.

T.50

5526

SWIFT (Jonathan) *Dean of St. Patrick's.*

Some reasons to prove, that no person is obliged by his principles, as a Whig, to oppose her Majesty or her present ministry. In a letter to a Whig-lord. [Anon.] London, for John Morphew, 1712.   8°

Teerink 578.

T.115

5527

SWIFT (Jonathan) *Dean of St. Patrick's.*

Some remarks on the Barrier Treaty, between her Majesty and the States-General. By the author of The conduct of the allies ... London, for John Morphew, 1712.   8°

Teerink 559.
3 copies.

T.551 T.147 T.171

5528

SYDDALL (Arnold)

The mask pull'd off: or, The dissection of a Whiggish corporation. Being the late Curate of Gravesend's vindication from a villanous and libelling letter inserted some time ago in the Observator ... London printed, and sold by J. Baker, 1712.   8°

T.363

5529

SYNGE (Edward) *Archbishop of Tuam.*

Thankfulness to almighty God for his more ancient and later mercies and deliverances vouchsafed to the British and protestants, within the kingdom of Ireland. Recommended and press'd in a sermon before the honourable House of Commons, October the 23d, 1711 ... London: John Morphew, 1712.   8°

T.364

5530

TALBOT (William) *Bishop of Durham.*

The Bishop of Oxford's charge to the clergy of his diocese, at his visitation in the year 1712. London: for Jonah Bowyer, 1712.   4°

T.1

5531

THIRLBY (Styan)

An answer to Mr. Whiston's seventeen suspicions concerning Athanasius, in his Historical preface... Cambridge: printed at the University-Press, for Edm. Jeffery: and are to be sold by James Knapton, London, 1712.   8°

2 copies.

T.768 T.546

5532

TINDAL (Matthew)

The nation vindicated, from the aspersions cast on it in a late pamphlet, intitled, A representation of the present state of religion, with regard to the late excessive growth of infidelity, heresy and profaneness... [Anon.] Part II. With some remarks on the representation of the Irish convocation... London, for A. Baldwin, 1712.   8°

2 copies.

T.506 T.523

5533

TRAPP (Joseph)

Her Majesty's prerogative in Ireland; the authority of the government and privy-council there; and the rights, laws, and liberties of the city of Dublin, asserted and maintain'd. In answer to a paper falsly intituled, The case of the city of Dublin in relation to the election of a lord-mayor ... [Anon.] London, for H. Clements, 1712.   8°

2 copies.

T.205 T.523

5534

TRAPP (Joseph)

A sermon preach'd at the parish-church of St. Martin in the Fields; January the 16th 1711. Being the day appointed ... for the general fast: for imploring the blessing of almighty God upon the treaty of peace now in negotiation ... London: for Henry Clements, 1712.   8°

T.364

5535

The TREATY between her Majesty and the States-General, for securing the succession to the Crown of Great-Britain, and for settling the barrier for the States-General against France, consider'd. London, printed in the year 1712.   8°

T.401

5536

TRIMNELL (Charles) *Bishop of Winchester.*

A sermon preach'd before the Lords Spiritual and Temporal ... in the abbey church at Westminster, on the 30th of January, 1711/12 ... By Charles Lord Bishop of Norwich. London: for D. Midwinter, 1712.   8°

2 copies.

T.364 T.334

5537

A TRUE and impartial account of the animosity, quarrel and duel, between the late Duke of Hamilton, and the Lord Mohun ... And, some previous reflections on sham-plots, &c. London: A. Baldwin, 1712.   8°

T.161

5538

The TRUE difference betwixt the principles & practices of the Kirk and Church of Scotland: exemplified in several instances. London: for John Morphew, 1712. 8°

2 copies.

T.211 T.405

5539

The TRYAL and condemnation of Don Prefatio d'Asaven' [i.e. William Fleetwood], for endeavouring to resist, subvert, and totally destroy the doctrines of passive-obedience, indefeasible hereditary-right, and a[rbitrar]y power... London printed: sold by the booksellers of London and Westminster, 1712.   8°

2 copies.

T.520 T.523

5540

The TRYAL, examination and condemnation of occasional conformity, &c. at a sessions of oyer and terminer, held at Westminster, before Mr Just. Upright, and Mr. Bar. Integrity, December the 22d, MDCCXI. London: printed for, and sold by the booksellers of London and Westminster, 1712.   8°

T.115

5541

The TUNBRIDGE-miscellany: consisting of poems, &c. Written at Tunbridge-Wells this summer. By several hands ... London, for E. Curll, 1712.   8°

Half title: The Tunbridge-miscellany, for the year 1712.

T.410

5542

TURNER (John) *Vicar of Greenwich.*

A defence of the doctrine and practice of the Church of England, against some modern innovations ... In a letter to a friend. [Anon.] London: for John Morphew, 1712.   8°

2 copies.

T.395 T.365

5543

TURNER (John) *Vicar of Greenwich.*

New dangers to the Christian priesthood: or, A serious enquiry into the proper administrator of Christian baptism. In a letter to the author of Lay-baptism invalid [i.e. Roger Laurence] ... By the author of the Defence of the principles, and practice of the Church of England, &c. London: for John Morphew, 1712 8°

T.365

5544

VERNEY (George) *Baron Willoughby de Broke.*

The blessedness of doing good. A sermon preached in the parish church of St. Sepulchre, June the 12th, 1712... at the anniversary meeting of the children educated in the charity-schools in and about the cities of London and Westminster. London, Joseph Downing, 1712.   4°

T.701

5545

A VINDICATION of Mesech and Kedar; or, A short answer to some reflections cast thereupon, by the extraordinary author of an extraordinary long sentence. Written by a gentleman, a scholar, and a Christian ... London: for Bernard Lintott, [1712].   8°

T.302

5546

A VINDICATION of Oliver Cromwell, and the Whiggs of forty one, to our modern Low Churchmen. With some reflections upon the Bar[ie]r Treaty ... Printed, and sold by the booksellers of London and Westminster, 1712.   8°

T.171

5547

A VINDICATION of the Reverend Dr. George Hickes, and the author [i.e. Hilkiah Bedford] of the Seasonable and modest apology, &c. from the undeserved reflections of the Reverend Dr. Thomas Wise, in his book, entitled, The Christian Eucharist rightly stated ... By a presbyter of the Church of England. London: J. Morphew, 1712.   8°

T.395

5548

VOX populi: being the sense of the nation, concerning the French king, the Pretender, the faction, and their principles; express'd in the addresses, to his late Majesty King William ... and to our present gracious sovereign Queen Anne. London: for S. Popping, 1712. 8°

T.401

5549

W. (T.)

The K[e]ntish spy: or, A memorial of the C[al]ves H[ea]d Club: particularly of three members of the said Society that absented themselves from the parish church of W-st--ham in Kent, the 30th day of January last ... By T.W. an enemy to faction. London: printed in the year 1712.   8°

T.410

5550

WAGSTAFFE (William)

Crispin the cobler's confutation of Ben H[oa]dly, in an epistle to him ... [Anon.] 2nd ed. London, printed in the year 1712.   8°

T.297

5551

WAGSTAFFE (William)

The story of the St. Alb[a]ns ghost, or the apparition of Mother Haggy... [Anon.] London: printed in the year 1712.   8°

T.281

5552

WARD (Edward)

The poetical entertainer: or, Tales, satyrs, dialogues, and intrigues, &c. serious and comical ... [Anon.] Numb. I. London printed: and sold by J. Morphew, 1712.   8°

T.410

5553

WARD (Edward)

The poetical entertainer: or, Tales, satyrs, intrigues, &c... [Anon.] Numb. II. London printed: and sold by J. Morphew, 1712.   8°

T.410

5554

WARD (Edward)

The poetical entertainer: or, Tales, satyrs, dialogues, &c... [Anon.] Numb. III. London printed: and sold by J. Woodward; and J. Morphew, 1712.   8°

T.410

5555

WATTS (Robert)

The rule for finding Easter in the Book of common-prayer, explain'd and vindicated, against the exceptions of the late learned Dr. Wallis ... (A table of golden numbers and dominical letters.) [Anon.] London: for J. Downing, J. Knapton, J. Wyat, H. Clements, and J. Holland; J. Bowyer; D. Brown; J. Fox; and G. Strahan, 1712.   2 parts.   8°

T.392

1712 (Cont'd)

5556

WATTS (Robert)

The true time of keeping St. Matthias's-day in leap-years ... [Anon.] London, for J. Downing, and J. Holland, 1712.   8°

Bound with this leaflet is a manuscript bearing the signatures of Robert Watts and George Hickes.

T.323

5557

WATTS (Robert)

The true time of keeping St. Matthias's-day in leap-years.   Shewing, that it is to be kept on the 24th, and not on the 25th of February, as some almanacks place it ... [Anon.] London, for J. Downing, J. Knapton, J. Wyat, H. Clements, & J. Holland, J. Bowyer, D. Brown, J. Fox, and G. Strahan, 1712.   8°

The preface only.

T.392

5558

The WHIGS feast: or, The protestant entertainment design'd by the City for the popish general.   London: printed, and sold by the booksellers, 1712.   8°

T.390

5559

WHISTON (William)

Athanasius convicted of forgery.   In a letter to Mr. Thirlby of Jesus-College in Cambridge.   London: printed for the author; and sold by A. Baldwin, 1712.   8°

2 copies.

T.228   T.546

5560

WHISTON (William)

Primitive infant-baptism reviv'd.   Or, An account of the doctrine and practice of the two first centuries, concerning the baptism of infants ... London, printed for the author, and sold by the booksellers of London and Westminster, 1712.   8°

2 copies.

T.395   T.360

5561

WHITE (John) *Counsellor-at-Law*

A new-years gift for the High-Church clergy: being an account of the sufferings of a great number of the clergy of the Church of England... [Anon.] First printed by order of the Parliament in the year 1643; and now reprinted in the year 1712. 8°

T.115

5562

The WHOLE tryal and examination of Mr. Richardson, before... the Lord Bishop of London at Fulham, on Wednesday the 3d of September... London: A. Hinde, 1712.   4°

T.490

5563

WILLIAM III, *King of England.*

A collection of all the speeches, messages, &c. of his late Majesty King William III. of ever glorious memory; to which is added the English declaration of rights. London: for J. Baker, 1712.   8°

T.205

5564

WILSON (Edward) *Vicar of Rye.*

A sermon preach'd in the parish-church of Rye in Sussex, on Wednesday, Jan. 30th, 1711/12 ... London, W.S. for Richard Wilkin, 1712.   8°

T.364

5565

WOLF (Johann Christoph)

Jo. Christophori Wolfii Historia Bogomilorum qua potissimum ex Panoplia dogmatica Euthymii Zigabeni ejusque codice Graeco non edito eorum fata, doctrinae et mores ita exponuntur... Vitembergae, apud Christ. Theophil. Ludovicum, 1712.   4°

T.802

5566

A WORD to the wise: or, Some seasonable cautions about regulating the press.   London: printed in the year 1712.   8°

T.205

5567

WRIGHT (Samuel)

To be every where spoken against, at first the case of the Christians themselves, and now of the protestant dissenters.   Considered in two sermons preach'd at Black Fryers, March the 9th and 16th, 1711/2... 2nd ed.   London, for J. Clark; and E. Matthews, 1712.   8°

T.622

1713

5568

ADDISON (*Rt. Hon.* Joseph)

Cato. A tragedy.   As it is acted at the Theatre-Royal in Drury-Lane, by his Majesty's servants... 2nd ed.   London: for J. Tonson, 1713.   4°

T.564

5569

ADVICE to a young gentleman ... London, for John Morphew, [1713].   8°

T.390

5570

ANNE, *Queen of Great Britain.*

Tractatus navigationis et commerciorum...   Treaty of navigation and commerce between the most serene and potent Princess Anne... and the most serene and most potent Prince Lewis the XIVth, the most Christian King, concluded at Utrecht the 31/11 day of March/April 1713. London, John Baskett, and by the assigns of Thomas Newcomb, and Henry Hills, 1713.   4°

2 copies.

T.564   T.783

5571

ANNE, *Queen of Great Britain.*

Tractatus pacis & amicitiae...   Treaty of peace and friendship between the most serene and most potent Princess Anne... and the most serene and potent Prince Lewis the XIVth, the most Christian King, concluded at Utrecht the 31/11 day of March/April 1713.   London, John Baskett, and by the assigns of Thomas Newcomb, and Henry Hills, 1713.   4°

T.783

5572

The ANSWER of a barrister at law to the Curate of En[g--field], concerning the birth of a suppositious child.   Being a reply to some arguments and printed queries dispers'd in and about Oxford ... London, printed in the year 1713.   8°

T.362

5573

An ANSWER to Mr. Whiston's challenge which he made to Dr. Sacheverell.   Wherein the doctrine of the blessed Trinity is defended against Mr. Whiston.   Written by a communicant belonging to the parish church of St. Andrew's Holborn ... London, J. Morphew, [1713].   8°

T.222

5574

An ANSWER to the Discourse on free-thinking [by Anthony Collins]: wherein the absurdity and infidelity of the sect of free-thinkers is undeniably demonstrated.   By a gentleman of Cambridge...   London, John Morphew; and A. Dodd, 1713.   8°

3 copies.

T.47   T.103   T.226

5575

An ANSWER to the Examiner's cavils against the Barrier Treaty of 1709.   To which are added the articles of the New Barrier Treaty that relate to the Hanover succession ... London: S. Popping, 1713.   8°

Teerink 1576.

T.171

5576

An ANSWER to the exceptions made against the Ld Bp of Oxford's charge, by Mr. L[aurence] and Dr. Brett. In which the justice and reasonableness of the Bishop's advice to his clergy is vindicated ... London: for John Wyat, 1713.   8°

T.360

5577

ANTIDOTUM Sarisburiense: or, A free expostulation with the Bishop of Sarum, (suited to the present time) on some passages in his Lordship's preface, prefixed to the last edition of his Pastoral care. By an High-Church-man... [Signed Philanax Episcopius.] London: for John Morphew, 1713.   8°

Attributed by Bowdler to Mr. Stamp.
2 copies.

T.166   T.523

5578

The ART of lying and rebelling, taught by the Whigs, in an infamous libel, entitled, The judgment of whole kingdoms and nations, &c ... London, printed: and sold by J. Morphew, 1713.   8°

T.227

5579

ASGILL (John)

Mr. Asgill's apology for an omission in his late publication. London, for A. Baldwin. 1713.   8°

2 copies.

T.548   T.414

5580

ASGILL (John)

Mr. Asg..l's congratulatory letter to the L..d B....p of S...m, upon the excellent modern preface just publish'd by his L......p.   2nd ed.   London: for John Morphew, 1713.   8°

2 copies.

T.370   T.48

5581

ASGILL (John)

The Pretender's declaration abstracted from two anonymous pamphlets: the one intitled, Jus sacrum; and the other, Memoirs of the Chevalier St. George ... London, for A. Baldwin, 1713.   8°

2 copies.

T.414   T.205

5582

AYLMER (William)

A recantation-sermon against the errors of popery, particularly transubstantiation.   Preach'd at St. Martin's in Oxford, Sept. 20th, 1713 ... Oxford: L. Lichfield, for Anth. Peisley, and are to be sold by J. Knapton, H. Clements, W. Taylor and J. Morphew, 1713.   8°

T.37

5583

B. (A.)

Her Majesty and her royal father vindicatd.   In answer to a preface to the volume of sermons, &c. now publish'd by the Bishop of Sarum.   In a letter to his Lordship. London, for J. Baker, 1713.   8°

T.166

5584

B. (A.)

A short narrative of modern justice.   Or, a letter from a non-free-man to Mr. Sword-b[ea re]r, Mr. Common-c[rie]r, &c. occasion'd by the grievous complaints of a most useful, necessary, and ancient corporation of freemen in London ... [Signed A.B.] London: for John Morphew, 1713.   8°

Half title: The baker's vindication.

T.442

5585

B. (J.) *of Lynn Regis.*

Cameronian Whigs no patriots: or, Some remarkable exploits of Bob Hush [i.e. Robert Walpole], and his fairylanders, set in a true light.   In a letter to an elector of Lynn Regis... London: for John Morphew, 1713.   8°

T.363

5586

B. (J.) *of Lynn Regis.*

A letter to an elector.   Containing powerful persuasives to vote for our most worthy patriots the Whigs next election. London, for John Morphew, 1713.   8°

T.390

5587

BATEMAN (Thomas)

An abstract of An answer lately publish'd to a pamphlet [by Francis Hare] intitled Frauds and abuses at St. Paul's. [Anon.] London: for John Morphew, 1713. 8°

T.164

5588

BATEMAN (Thomas)

An answer to a pamphlet [by Francis Hare] entitul'd Frauds and abuses at St. Paul's. With an appendix relating to the revenues and repairs of that cathedral. [Anon.] London: for John Morphew, 1713. 8°

T.164

5589

BATEMAN (Thomas) *and* JENNINGS (Richard)

The second part of Fact against scandal; in answer to a pamphlet [by Francis Hare] intitled A continuation of Frauds and abuses at St. Paul's ... [Anon.] London: for John Morphew, 1713. 8°

T.164

5590

BENTLEY (Richard)

Remarks upon a late Discourse of free-thinking [by Anthony Collins]: in a letter to F.H. By Phileleutherus Lipsiensis... London: for John Morphew, 1713. 2 parts. 8°

3 copies.
A third part was published in 1743.

T.47 T.103 T.226

5591

BERKELEY (George) *Bishop of Cloyne.*

Three dialogues between Hylas and Philonous. The design of which is plainly to demonstrate the reality and perfection of humane knowledge, the incorporeal nature of the soul, and the immediate providence of a deity ... London: G. James, for Henry Clements, 1713. 8°

T.228

5592

The BISHOP of Salisbury's new preface consider'd. With respect to King James's male-adminstration ... London: for A. Baldwin, 1713. 8°

T.166

5593

The BISHOP of Salisbury's new preface to his Pastoral care, consider'd. With respect to the following heads, viz. I. The qualifications of the clergy ... 2nd ed. London: for A. Baldwin, 1713. 8°

T.166

5594

The BISHOP of Salisbury's new preface to his Pastoral care, consider'd, with respect to the following head, viz. I. The qualifications of the clergy ... 2nd ed. London: J. Bradford, [1713]. 8°

T.370

5595

BISSE (Thomas)

A sermon preach'd before the University of Oxford on Act-Sunday July 12. 1713 ... Oxford, printed at the Theatre for Henry Clements, 1713. 8°

T.160

5596

BOOKEY (Sacheverell)

In congratulation to Sir John Lake, on the conclusion of the war. A poem ... London: for Henry Clements, 1713. 4°

T.269

5597

BRADFORD (Samuel) *Bishop of Rochester.*

The reasonableness of standing fast in English and in Christian liberty. A sermon preach'd before ... the Lord Mayor, the aldermen, and citizens of London. In the cathedral church of St. Paul, on Thursday November 5th, 1713. 4th ed. London: for John Wyat, 1713. 8°

T.334

5598

BRADY (Nicholas)

Proposals for publishing a translation of Virgil's Aeneids in blank verse. Together with a specimen of the performance. London: printed for the author, 1713. 8°

T.225

5599

BRADY (Nicholas)

A sermon preach'd at Richmond in Surrey, upon July the 7th, 1713. Being the day of thanksgiving ... for a general peace. London: for John Wyat, 1713. 8°

T.160

5600

BRAMSTON (William)

The great sin of lukewarmness in religion; together with reflections upon some late notions of moderation; proving, that those notions do directly lead to that great sin. Set forth in two sermons ... London, for James Woodward, 1713. 8°

2 copies.

T.334 T.335

5601

BRETT (Thomas)

The dangers of a relapse. A sermon preach'd at the royal chapel at St. James's, on May 29. 1713... London: for John Wyat, 1713. 8°

3 copies.

T.160 T.334 T.622

5602

BRETT (Thomas)

An enquiry into the judgment and practice of the primitive Church, in relation to persons being baptized by lay-men. Wherein Mr. Bingham's Scholastical history is considered ... London: for John Wyat, 1713. 8°

2 copies.

T.395 T.365

5603

BRIDGEN (William)

The duty and power of the magistrate in matters of religion vindicated. In a sermon preach'd at East-Grinsted ... at the assizes held there March 9. 1712/3. London, for W. Mears, and are to be sold by J. Morphew, [1713]. 8°

T.160

5604

A BRIEF apology for those divines of the Church of England who have opposed the notion of the bread and wine in the Eucharist being a proper propitiatory sacrifice. In a letter to the Reverend Dr. George Hicks, and the author of the Seasonable apology [i.e. Hilkiah Bedford] ... London: J. Baker, 1713. 8°

2 copies.

T.377 T.390

5605

BROUGHTON (John)

A funeral sermon upon Mr. Noble. By a neighbouring minister. London: for Sam. Buckley, 1713. 8°

T.160

5606

BROWNE (Francis)

A sermon preach'd before... the Lord Mayor, the aldermen, and citizens of London; at the cathedral-church of St. Paul's; on Friday, January 30. 1712/13 ... London: G.J. for Jonah Bowyer, 1713. 4°

2 copies.

T.3 T.160

5607

BURNET (Gilbert) *Bishop of Salisbury.*

The new preface and additional chapter, to the third edition of the Pastoral care... London: for D. Midwinter, and B. Cowse. And sold by A. Baldwin, 1713. 8°

T.523

5608

BURNET (*Sir* Thomas)

Some new proofs by which it appears that the Pretender is truly James the third. [Anon.] 3rd ed. London: for J. Baker, 1713. 8°

T.413

5609

CALUMNY no conviction: or an answer to Mr. Whiston's letter to Mr. Thirlby, entitled, Athanasius convicted of forgery ... [Signed Philalethes.] London, for Henry Clements, 1713. 8°

2 copies.

T.546 T.228

5610

CAMPBELL (Archibald) *Bishop.*

The case restated; or an account of a conversation with a papist, concerning a book [by Charles Leslie?] intitled, The case stated between the Church of Rome, and the Church of England, &c. In a letter from a gentleman in the country to his friend in London. [Signed A.C.]... Printed in the year 1713. 8°

T.405

5611

The CASE of ordination consider'd; being a seasonable essay to rectify some prevailing opinions ... By a lay man of the Church of England. 2nd ed ... London: John Matthews, and are to be sold by John Lawrence, and John Kent, 1713. 8°

T.360

5612

The CASE of St. Winefred open'd; or, An unanswerable confutation of St. Winefred's life, the Bishop's [i.e. William Fleetwood] historical observations, the Examiner, and the Guardian on the same subject... By Dr. Bernardine Bambouzelberg ... London: for John Morphew, 1713. 8°

T.383

5613

The CASE of the Pretender, occasion'd by the late addresses in Parliament for his removal from the territories of the Duke of Lorrain, and other princes in amity with her Majesty ... London, printed for, and sold by John Baker, 1713. 8°

T.362

5614

CHURCH OF ENGLAND. *Convocation. Lower House.*

The proceedings of the lower house of Convocation, upon her Majesty's gracious messages and letters, sent to the Convocation. Being the substance of a report drawn up by a committee of the lower house ... London: J. Morphew, 1713. 8°

2 copies.

T.506 T.603

5615

CLARKE (William) *Dissenting Minister.*

A word to the wise: or, A hint on the times. Deliver'd in three sermons... London: printed for the author, and are to be sold by John Baker, and by most booksellers in London and Westminster, 1713. 8°

T.362

5616

CLEARBROOK (William) *pseud?*

A project for the more effectual compleating the new reformation, or extirpation of the faction, mention'd in the Examiner, no. 36. In a letter to the author of the Examiner. London: for J. Moor, 1713. 8°

T.302

5617

COCKBURN (John)

The blessedness of Christians after death, with the character of ... Henry Compton, D.D. late Lord Bishop of London. Deliver'd in a sermon at St. Martin's in the Fields, July the 19th, 1713 ... London, for George Strahan, 1713. 4°

T.196

5618

COCKMAN (Thomas)

Free-thinking rightly stated; wherein a discourse [by Anthony Collins] (falsly so call'd) is fully consider'd ... [Anon.] London: for George Strahan, 1713. 8°

T.226

5619

COLLIER (Jeremy)

An essay upon gaming, in a dialogue between Callimachus and Dolomedes. London: for J. Morphew, 1713. 8°

T.442

5620

COLLINS (Anthony)

A discourse of free-thinking, occasion'd by the rise and growth of a sect call'd free-thinkers... [Anon.] London, printed in the year 1713. 8°

3 copies.

T.47 T.226 T.798

1713 (Cont'd)

5621
COOPER (Anthony Ashley) *3rd Earl of Shaftesbury.*

A notion of the historical draught or tablature of
the judgment of Hercules, according to Prodicus ...
[Anon.] London, for A. Baldwin, 1713.   8°

T.164

5622
COOPER (Anthony Ashley) *3rd Earl of Shaftesbury.*

A notion of the historical draught or tablature of the
judgment of Hercules, according to Prodicus ... [Anon.]
Printed in the year 1713.   8°

T.148

5623
CUMMINGS (George)

The good of government. A sermon preached in St.
Margaret-Patton's church in Rude-Lane, London, on
Tuesday, July 7, 1713. Being the day appointed ...
for a general thanksgiving for the peace. By G.C ...
London, printed for, and sold by J. Morphew, 1713.
8°

T.160

5624
CURLL (Edmund)

A catalogue of books, sold by Edmund Curll, at his
shop on the Walk at Tunbridge-Wells; and at the Dial
and Bible, against St. Dunstan's Church in Fleet-
street, London. [No imprint, 1713?]   8°

T.410

5625
DAVENANT (Charles)

Dr. D[ave]nant's prophecys ... London; for A. Baldwin,
1713.   8°

T.403

5626
DAWES (*Sir* William) *Archbishop of York.*

The excellency of the charity of charity-schools. In
a sermon preach'd in the parish church of St.
Sepulchre, May 28. MDCCXIII ... at the anniversary
meeting of the children educated in the charity-
schools, in and about the cities of London and
Westminster ... By ... William, Lord Bishop of
Chester. London, J. Downing for Anne Speed, 1713.
4°

T.3

5627
DAWES (*Sir* William) *Archbishop of York.*

A sermon preach'd before ... the lord-mayor, the
aldermen, sheriffs, and governors of the several
hospitals of the city of London, in St. Bridget's
church ... April 6th, 1713. By ... William, Lord
Bishop of Chester. London: for Anne Speed, 1713.   8°

T.160

5628
DECLARATIO et sponsio... Declaration and engagement
concerning the rights and privileges of the British
merchants in the kingdom of Sicily, made at Utrecht
the 25/8 day of February/March 1712/13. London,
John Baskett, and by the assigns of Thomas Newcomb,
and Henry Hills, 1713. 4°

T.783

5629
A DEFENCE of the doctrines of the holy Trinity, of the
divinity, and incarnation of our blessed Saviour;
against the Arian doctrines reviv'd by Mr. Whiston.
London: for R. Wilkin, 1713.   8°

T.228

5630
DEFOE (Daniel)

An account of the abolishing of duels in France:
being extracts out of the edicts of the kings, the
regulations of the marshals, and the records of the
parliaments of France ... [Anon.] London: for John
Morphew, 1713.   8°

Moore 254.

T.161

5631
DEFOE (Daniel)

And what if the Pretender should come? or, Some
considerations of the advantages and real consequences
of the Pretender's possessing the Crown of Great
Britain. [Anon.] **2nd** ed. London: J. Baker, 1713.
8°

Moore 251.

T.51

5632
DEFOE (Daniel)

An answer to a question that no body thinks of, viz.
But what if the Queen should die? [Anon.] London, for
J. Baker, 1713.   8°

Moore 252.

T.51

5633
DEFOE (Daniel)

A general history of trade, and especially consider'd
as it respects the British commerce, as well at home,
as to all parts of the world... [Anon.] [Part I.]
London: for J. Baker, 1713.   8°

Moore 260.

T.279

5634
DEFOE (Daniel)

A letter from a member of the House of Commons to his
friend in the country, relating to the Bill of
commerce. With a true copy of the Bill, and an exact
list of all those who voted for and against engrossing
it. [Anon.] London: J. Baker, 1713.   8°

Moore 265.

T.279

5635
DEFOE (Daniel)

A letter to the dissenters. [Anon.] London: for John
Morphew, 1713.   8°

Moore 269.

T.302

5636
DEFOE (Daniel)

Memoirs of Count Tariff, &c... [Anon.] London: for
John Morphew, 1713.   8°

Moore 262.
2 copies.

T.87 T.147

5637
DEFOE (Daniel)

Not[tingh]am politicks examin'd. Being an answer to
a pamphlet lately publish'd, intituled, Observations
upon the state of the nation. [Anon.] London: for
J. Baker, 1713.   8°

Moore 249.

T.51

5638
DEFOE (Daniel)

Proposals for imploying the poor in and about the city
of London, without any charge to the publick. [Anon.]
London, for J. Baker, 1713.   8°

Moore 270.

T.163

5639
DEFOE (Daniel)

Reasons against the succession of the House of Hanover,
with an enquiry how far the abdication of King James,
supposing it to be legal, ought to affect the person
of the Pretender ... [Anon.] London: for J. Baker,
1713.   8°

Moore 248.
2 copies.

T.344 T.362

5640
DELAUNE (William)

Of original sin: a sermon preach'd before ... the
lord mayor and aldermen, at the cathedral-church of
St. Paul, London, Feb. 22. 1712/13. London: G.
James, for Henry Clements, 1713.   8°

2 copies.

T.198   T.160

5641
DELAUNE (William)

Of original sin: a sermon preach'd before... the
Lord Mayor and aldermen, at the cathedral-church
of St. Paul, London, Feb. 22. 1712/13. 2nd ed.
London: G. James, for Henry Clements, 1713.   8°

T.804

5642
A DIALOGUE between the author of Whigs no Christians
and a country gentleman ... London printed, and are
to be sold by J. Morphew, [1713].   8°

T.227

5643
DINGLEY (William)

Cathedral service decent and useful. A sermon preach'd
before the University of Oxford at St Mary's on
Cecilia's day, 1713. Oxford, for Anthony Peisley: and
are to be sold by J. Knapton, H. Clements, and J.
Morphew, booksellers in London, 1713.   8°

T.334

5644
DODWELL (Henry)

Four letters which pass'd between the Right Reverend
the Lord Bishop of Sarum and Mr. Henry Dodwell.
Printed from the originals. [Edited by Robert Nelson.]
London, for Richard Smith, 1713.   8°

T.367

5645
DUNTON (John)

Neck or nothing: in a letter to the Right Honourable
the Lord —— being a supplement to the short
history of Parliament ... Written by his Grace John
Duke of —— ... London, T. Warner, 1713.   8°

T.29

5646
ECHLIN (John)

The royal martyr. A sermon preach'd before ... the
lords justices of Ireland, in Christ-Church, Dublin,
on the XXXth of January, 1712/13. 2nd ed ... London,
for H. Clements, 1713.   8°

T.160

5647
ELSTOB (Elizabeth)

Some testimonies of learned men, in favour of the
intended edition of the Saxon homilies, concerning
the learning of the author of those homilies; and
the advantages to be hoped for from an edition of
them. In a letter from the publisher to a doctor
of divinity... London, W. Bowyer; and sold by
J. Morphew, 1713.   8°

2 copies (one possibly a proof).

T.148

5648
ENGLISH gratitude: or, The Whig miscellany, consisting
of the following poems. I. On the Duke of Marlborough's
going into Germany ... London: for A. Baldwin, 1713.
8°

T.410

5649
An ENQUIRY into the manner of assenting to the articles
and liturgy of the Church of England; practised and
recommended by Dr. Clarke ... in his introduction to
his Scripture doctrine of the Trinity ... London, for
George Strahan, 1713.   8°

T.546

5650
EVANS (Abel)

Magdalen-grove: or, A dialogue between the Doctor
[Sacheverell] and the Devil. Written in February in
the year 1713. and found among the papers of a
gentleman deceas'd. Humbly dedicated to the author
[i.e. Abel Evans] and admirers of the Apparition, a
poem ... [Anon.] London: J. Carrett, [1713].   8°

2 copies.

T.336 T.350

5651
EYRE (Richard)

The blessing of peace. A sermon preach'd at the
cathedral church of Sarum, July 7. 1713. the day of
thanksgiving for the peace ... Oxford, printed at
the Theater, for Stephen Fletcher; and are to be
sold by John Morphew, 1713.   8°

T.160

5652

FREE thoughts upon the Discourse of free-thinking [by Anthony Collins] ... London: for John Pemberton, 1713.   8°

T.226

5653

A FULL and exact relation of the duel fought in Hyde-Park on Saturday, November 15. 1712. Between his Grace James, Duke of Hamilton, and ... Charles, Lord Mohun. In a letter to a member of Parliament. London: for E. Curll, 1713.   8°

2 copies.

T.622 T.161

5654

GARDINER (James) *Sub-Dean of Lincoln.*

The duty of peace amongst the members of the same State ... or, How a man should behave himself, as becomes a Christian, with respect to High and Low-Church, Whig and Tory. A sermon preached at the cathedral church of Lincoln; July the 7th, 1713. London: for Bernard Lintott, 1713.   8°

T.160

5655

GASKARTH (John)

A sermon preached to the societies for reformation of manners, at St. Mary le Bow, on Monday, December the twenty ninth, MDCCXII ... London: for Richard Wilkin, 1713.   4°

T.198

5656

GOOCH (*Sir* Thomas) *Bishop of Ely.*

A sermon preach'd before ... the Lord Mayor and aldermen at the cathedral-church of St. Paul, London, July 26. 1713. On occasion of the much-lamented death of ... Henry, late Lord Bishop of London ... London: G.J. for Jonah Bowyer, 1713.   8°

T.334 T.335

5657

GREAT BRITAIN. *Commissioners of Accounts.*

A report from the Commissioners appointed to take, examine and state the publick accompts of the Kingdom. Printed in the year 1703 [i.e. 1713].   8°

T.279

5658

GREAT BRITAIN. *Parliament.*

A compleat list of both houses of the last and this present Parliament. London: John Morphew, [1713]. 8°

T.51

5659

GREAT BRITAIN. *Parliament.*

An exact list of the lords spiritual and temporal. As also, A compleat list of the knights ... and burgesses, both of the last and ensuing Parliaments ... London: A. Baldwin, 1713.   8°

T.51

5660

GRONOVIUS (Jacobus)

Recensio brevis mutilationum quas partitur Suidas in editione nupera Cantabrigiae anni MDCCV. ubi varia ejus auctoris loca perperam intellecta illustrantur, emendantur & supplentur. [Anon.] Lugdunum Batavorum, apud Samuelem Luchtmans, 1713.   8°

T.148

5661

HAMILTON (William)

Episcopal the only apostolical ordination: or the case of ordination truly consider'd, in relation to these questions ... [Anon.] To which is prefixed a letter from the Reverend George Hickes ... London, for G. Strahan, 1713.   8°

2 copies.

T.360 T.274

5662

HANCOCK (John)

Arianism not the primitive Christianity: or, The antenicene fathers vindicated ... Design'd as an answer (in part) to Mr. Whiston's Primitive Christianity, reviv'd. London, for R. Halsey; and sold by J. Morphew, 1713.   8°

T.25

5663

HANCOCK (John)

The Christian schoolmaster. Or, A sermon preach'd at St. Augustin's church London, Sept. 30. 1713. at the funeral of ... Mr. John Postlethwait, chief master of St. Paul's school. London: for Charles Humphryes, 1713.   8°

T.335

5664

HARE (Francis) *Bishop of Chichester.*

The clergyman's thanks to Phileleutherus, for his Remarks on the late Discourse of free-thinking. In a letter to Dr. Bentley [signed Philocriticus] ... London, for A. Baldwin, 1713.   8°

2 copies.

T.103   T.47

5665

HARE (Francis) *Bishop of Chichester.*

A continuation of Frauds and abuses at St. Paul's, wherein is consider'd at large, the Attorney General's report, in relation to a prosecution of Mr. Jenings the carpenter: in answer to Fact against scandal [by Richard Jennings] ... [Anon.] London: for A. Baldwin, 1713.   8°

T.163

5666

HARRISON (Joseph)

A sermon preach'd in the parish-church of Cirencester, on Tuesday July the 7th 1713, being the thanksgiving day for the peace. London, for James Knapton; and John Barksdale, in Cirencester, 1713.   8°

T.160

5667

HEINSIUS (Antonius)

An epistle from Mr. H[einsiu]s, P[ensionar]y of H[ollan]d, to Mr. W[alpole], concerning his conduct in the ensuing P[arlia]m[en]t, especially with relation to the Bill of commerce. Translated from the original Dutch. Printed in the year, 1713.   8°

T.147

5668

HILL (Samuel)

Compendious speculations concerning sacerdotal remission of sins. London: for W. Taylor, 1713.   8°

T.360

5669

HILL (Samuel)

Compendious speculations upon valid and invalid baptism. London: for W. Taylor, 1713.   8°

T.360

5670

HILLIARD (Samuel)

A sermon preach'd at the parish-church of St. Margaret Lothbury, London, upon the occasion of the thanksgiving for the peace ... London: for J. Round, 1713.   8°

T.160

5671

HOADLY (Benjamin) *Bishop of Winchester.*

Queries recommended to the authors [i.e. Anthony Collins] of the late Discourse of free thinking. By a Christian. London, for James Knapton, 1713.   8°

T.47

5672

HOLE (Matthew)

Two sermons: I. The danger of arraigning God's ministers ... II. An olive-branch of peace ... London, for J. Morphew, 1713.   8°

T.160

5673

HOOPER (George) *Bishop of Bath and Wells.*

A sermon preach'd before both Houses of Parliament, in the cathedral church of St. Paul, on Tuesday, July 7. 1713. Being the day appointed ... for a general thanksgiving for the peace. London: for Robert Knaplock, 1713.   8°

2 copies.

T.334 T.160

5674

HORNE (Thomas) *Chaplain of St. Saviour's, Southwark.*

A sermon preach'd at the assises held at Kingston upon Thames, on Thursday, March 12. 1712/13 ... London, H. Clark, for Henry Clements, 1713.   4°

T.196

5675

HOUGH (Nathaniel)

A sermon upon the anniversary day of her Majesty's happy accession to the throne. Preach'd at Kensington-church, March 8. 1712/13. London: for B. Barker, and C. King, 1713.   8°

T.160

5676

JENNINGS (Richard)

Fact against scandal: or, A collection of testimonials, affidavits, and other authentick proofs, in vindication of Mr. Richard Jenings carpenter, Langley Bradley clock-maker and Richard Phelps bell-founder: to be referr'd to in an answer which will speedily be publish'd to a late false and malicious libel, entituled; Frauds and abuses at St. Paul's ... London: for John Morphew, 1713.   8°

2 copies.

T.164 T.35

5677

A JUST vindication of the Bp. of W[orceste]r. Or, The new proofs of the Pretender's being truly James the third, proved to be old no proofs. And the author ... prov'd to be an impostor, and truly Fuller the third. London: printed in the year 1713.   8°

T.344

5678

KENNET (White) *Bishop of Peterborough.*

A letter to the Lord Bishop of Carlisle, concerning one of his predecessors Bishop Merks; on occasion of a new volume for the Pretender, intituled, The hereditary right of the Crown of England asserted [by George Harbin]. [The letter is signed W.K.] 2nd ed. London: for Sam. Buckley, 1713.   8°

T.403

5679

KENNET (White) *Bishop of Peterborough.*

A memorial to protestants on the fifth of November, containing a more full discovery of some particulars relating to the happy deliverance of King James I... In a letter to a peer of Great Britain. [Anon.] London: for John Churchill, 1713.   8°

T.548

5680

KER (John) *M.D.*

Quaternae epistolae. Prima & secunda ad Richardum Bentleium: tertia ad ... Ezekielem Spanhemium: quarta ad Ludovicum Fridericum Bonetum. Londini, impensis J. Churchill, 1713.   8°

2 copies.

T.402

5681

KING (Henry) *Bishop of Chichester.*

A sermon preached at White-hall on the 29th of May, 1661. Being the happy day of his Majesties inauguration and birth ... Reprinted in the year 1713, and sold by John Morphew.   8°

T.104

5682

KING (William) *Archbishop of Dublin.*

An answer to all that has ever been said, or insinuated in favour of a popish Pretender. Exhibited in an abstract of The state of the protestants of Ireland, under King James the 2d's government ... London, A. Baldwin, 1713.   12°

T.390

5683

LAURENCE (Roger)

The second part of Lay-baptism invalid ... By the author of Lay-baptism invalid ... London: for H. Clements, 1713.   8°

T.409

1713 (Cont'd)

5684

LAW (William)

A sermon preach'd at Hazelingfield, in the county of Cambridge, on Tuesday, July 7. 1713. Being the day appointed ... for a publick thanksgiving for her Majesty's general peace ... London: for Richard Thurlbourne, bookseller in Cambridge; and sold by R. Knaplock, 1713.   8°

T.160

5685

A LETTER from a member of Parliament to a friend in the country. With a list of those who voted for and against the Bill of trade and commerce: also a copy of the Bill. London: Edw. Midwinter, [1713]. 8°

T.203

5686

A LETTER from an English gentleman at Madrid, to his friend in London. London, H. Meere, and J. Baker, 1713.   8°

T.442

5687

A LETTER from an English Tory to his friend in Town. Chiefly occasioned by the several reflections on Mr. Steele's Guardian of August the seventh. To which is added the said Guardian, by way of appendix. London: E. Smith, [1713].   8°

T.169

5688

A LETTER to a member of the P[arliamen]t of G[rea]t = B[ritai]n, occasion'd by the priviledge granted by the French king to Mr. Crozat. London: for J. Baker, 1713.   8°

T.111

5689

A LETTER to the Examiner, concerning the Barrier-treaty vindicated. London, for John Morphew, 1713. 8°

Teerink 1047A.

T.171

5690

The LIFE and miracles of St. Wenefrede, together with her litanies. With some historical observations made thereon [by William Fleetwood]. London, for Sam. Buckley, 1713.   8°

T.275

5691

LORD'S PRAYER.

Oratio dominica... Nimirum, plus centum linguis, versionibus, aut characteribus reddita & expressa. [Edited by Benjamin Motte.] Editio novissima... Londini: prostant apud Dan. Brown, Chr. Bateman, & W. Innys, 1713.   4°

T.639

5692

LOVELING (Benjamin) *the Elder.*

Peace the gift of God: rest, safety, and opportunities of piety, the fruits of peace. A sermon preach'd at Banbury ... on Tuesday the seventh of July, 1713. It being the day of thanksgiving ... for a general peace ... Oxford: Leon. Lichfield, 1713. 8°

T.160

5693

LOWTH (Simon)

Historical collections, concerning district-successions, and deprivations, during the three first centuries of the Church ... By a presbyter of the Church of England. London: for Hammond Banks, 1713. 8°

T.154

5694

LUPTON (William)

The necessity and measures, the excellency and efficacy of works of charity represented. In a sermon preach'd before ... the lord mayor, the aldermen, sheriffs, and governours of the several hospitals of the city of London ... April 8. 1713. London: D.L. for Isaac Cleave, 1713.   8°

T.160

5695

M.(C.D.L.)

A protestant monument, erected to the immortal glory of the Whiggs and the Dutch. It being a full and satisfactory relation of the late mysterious plot and firing of London ... London, John Morphew, 1713. 4°

T.267

5696

MACARTNEY (George)

A letter from Mr. Maccartney, to a friend of his in London. Dated at Ostend, Dec. 4-15. 1712. Giving a particular account of what pass'd before and at the unfortunate duel between... the D. of Hamilton and L. Mohun. London, for A. Baldwin, 1713.   4°

T.490

5697

MANNINGHAM (Thomas) *Bishop of Chichester.*

The spiritual strength to which a good Christian may arrive. A sermon preach'd in the parish-church of St. Andrew Holborn ... London, H. Meere, for E. Place, 1713.   8°

T.160

5698

MILBOURNE (Luke)

A guilty conscience makes a rebel; or, Rulers no terrour to the good prov'd, in a sermon preached on the thirtieth of January, 1712/13 ... With a preface, reflecting on a late pamphlet [by Thomas Bradbury], call'd, The ass and the serpent. London: L. Beardwell, for George Sawbridge, 1713.   8°

2 copies.

T.334   T.160

5699

MILBOURNE (Luke)

Peace the gift of God, but the terrour of the wicked; in a sermon preach'd on the thanksgiving for the peace, July the 7th, 1713 ... London: L. Beardwell, for George Sawbridge, 1713.   8°

T.160

5700

A MODEST censure on some mistakes concerning civil government, with relation to the late disputes about resistance and nonresistance. London, for Richard Wilkin, 1713.   8°

First published in 1711 as *Pseudarchomastix.*

T.227

5701

NE'ER a barrel the better herring, between Low-Church and no-Church. Occasioned by the modern prefacers ... London: J. Morphew, 1713.   8°

T.166

5702

A NEW voyage to the island of fools, representing the policy, government, and present state of the Stultitians. By a noble Venetian ... Translated from the Italian ... London, for John Morphew, 1713. 8°

T.363

5703

NOTITIA St. Johanniana: or, Genealogical and historical memoirs of the most antient, illustrious and noble family of St. John ... Printed by Rich. Newcomb, and sold by John Baker, 1713.   8°

T.275

5704

OBSERVATIONS upon the state of the nation, in January 1712/3. [Attributed to Daniel Finch, Earl of Nottingham.] London: for John Morphew, 1713. 8°

T.51

5705

OBSERVATIONS upon the state of the nation, in January 1712/3. [Attributed to Daniel Finch, Earl of Nottingham.] 2nd ed. London: for John Morphew, 1713.   8°

T.549

5706

OCKLEY (Simon)

An account of South-West Barbary: containing what is most remarkable in the territories of the King of Fez and Morocco ... London: for J. Bowyer; and H. Clements, 1713.   8°

T.164

5707

OCKLEY (Simon)

The necessity of instructing children in the Scriptures. An anniversary sermon, preached ... May 26. 1713. at St. Ives, Huntingdonshire ... London: for James Round, 1713.   8°

T.37

5708

OF the original and ends of government: the indispensable duty of magistrates, and power of princes, distinguishing them from tyrants ... London: for A. Baldwin, T. Harrison, and A. Dodd, 1713.   8°

T.403

5709

The OXFORD-scholar's answer to the Bishop of Sarum's new preface, in the third edition of his Pastoral care. London: for John Morphew, 1713.   8°

2 copies.

T.370   T.166

5710

P. (J.)

An antidote against the growth of popery, for the year of our blessed Saviour's incarnation, 1713 ... London printed: sold by T. Harrison, 1713.   8°

T.390

5711

PARKER (Ephraim)

Proposals for a very easie tax to raise between two and three millions of money, per annum ... in the room of the land-tax ... London, for John Morphew, 1713. 4°

T.13

5712

PASSIVE obedience establish'd; and resistance confuted ... By a gentleman of the city of Norwich. London: printed, and are to be sold by H. Clements; J. Morphew; and F. Oliver in Norwich, 1713.   8°

T.403

5713

PAUL (George)

An account of a discourse at the Graecian coffee-house, on February the 11th 1712/13. Occasion'd by Dr. B[entle]y's answer to the Discourse of free-thinking. In a letter from George Paul ... to Francis Dickins ... London: for H. Clements, 1713.   8°

2 copies.

T.226   T.47

5714

PHILIP V, *King of Spain.*

The assiento; or contract for allowing to the subjects of Great Britain the liberty of importing negroes into the Spanish America. Sign'd by the Catholick King at Madrid, the twenty sixth of March, 1713. London, John Baskett, and by the assigns of Thomas Newcomb, and Henry Hills, 1713.   4°

T.783

5715

PITTIS (William)

The history of the third session of the last Parliament ... London, John Baker, [1713].   8°

T.51

5716

POINTER (John)

An account of a pavement, lately found at Stunsfield in Oxford-shire, prov'd to be 1400 years old. Oxford: Leonard Lichfield, for Anth. Peisley: and are to be sold by J. Morphew, 1713.   8°

T.164

5717

POPE (Alexander)

The narrative of Dr. Robert Norris, concerning the strange and deplorable frenzy of Mr. John Denn[is], an officer of the custom-house... London: for J. Morphew, 1713.   8°

2 copies.

T.35 T.442

5718

PRAYERS for the distressed estate of Charles, King of Sweden, now a captive in Turkey. London: for John Morphew, 1713.   8°

T.461

5719

The PRINCIPLES and practices of the present sett of Whigs defended. By the censor of Great Britain. London: for John Morphew, 1713.   8°

2 copies.

T.385 T.227

5720

PROSSER (Jacob)

The danger of turning again to folly: a sermon preach'd at the royal chappel in Portsmouth, on Tuesday, July 7. 1713. Being thanksgiving-day for the peace ... London: for James Knapton; Eb. Tracy; and James Wilkison, bookseller at Portsmouth, 1713.   8°

T.160

5721

The PROTESTANT Chevalier a papist in masquerade: or, An antidote against the Pretender. In a dialogue between two friends, a citizen and a country-man. London: for E. Smith; and sold by the booksellers of London and Westminster, [1713].   8°

T.51

5722

R.(T.)

Remarks on the Barrier-treaty vindicated. In a letter to the author. London: for John Morphew, 1713. 8°

T.171

5723

RAPIN (René)

Christus patiens. Carmen heroicum. [Edited by Michael Maittaire.] Londini: ex officina J. Tonson, & J. Watts, 1713.   12°

T.204

5724

REASONS for the clergy's being employ'd in the government, drawn from the great services done by them to this nation in their administration of civil offices; being a vindication of her Majesty's late wisdom... in making the Bishop of Bristol, lord privy seal... [Attributed to John Groome.] London, for J. Baker, [1713].   8°

2 copies.

T.147 T.403

5725

REEVES (William)

The sin and folly of misplacing our affections. A sermon preached before the Queen, in St. George's chapel at Windsor; on the 23d. day of August, 1713... London: W.B. for Richard Sare, 1713.   4°

T.3

5726

REFLECTIONS on a paper [by Sir Richard Steele] lately printed, entit'led, A letter to Sir Miles Wharton, concerning occasional peers. Address'd to the Guardian and Examiner. London: for John Morphew, 1713.   8°

T.51

5727

REFLECTIONS upon the humour of the British nation in religion and politics ... London: John Baker, 1713. 8°

T.403

5728

REFLEXIONS upon Sach[everel]l's thanksgiving-day, and the solemnities of that great festival. In a letter to a friend in the country [signed Philopatrius] ... London, John Baker, 1713.   8°

T.229

5729

REGLEMENT provisionel du commerce dans les Pays-Bas Espagnols, fait à Utrecht le 15/26 jour de Juillet, 1713. A provisional regulation of trade in the Spanish Low-Countries, made at Utrecht the 15/26 day of July, 1713. London, John Baskett, and by the assigns of Thomas Newcomb, and Henry Hills, 1713. 4°

T.783

5730

RICHARDSON (William) *formerly a Dissenting Minister.*

The serpents head bruised. Or a full defence of Mr. Richardson from the aspersions that have been lately cast upon him... London, for J. Baker, [1713]. 8°

T.548

5731

The RIGHT of monarchy asserted; wherein the abstract of Dr. King's book, with the motives for the reviving it at this juncture are fully considered... London: John Morphew, 1713. 8°

4 copies.

T.222 T.344 T.403 T.413

5732

ROBERTSON (William) *formerly a Dissenting Minister.*

The liberty, property, and religion of the Whigs. In a letter to a Whig. Occasion'd by some discourse upon the Reverend Dr. Sacheverell's sermons on Palm-Sunday, and 29th of May, 1713. [Anon.] London, for John Morphew, 1713.   8°

T.363

5733

SACHEVERELL (Henry)

The Christian triumph: or, The duty of praying for our enemies ... In a sermon preach'd at St. Saviour's in Southwark, on Palm-Sunday, 1713. London: W. Bowyer, for Henry Clements, 1713.   4°

T.3

5734

SACHEVERELL (Henry)

The Christian triumph: or, The duty of praying for our enemies ... In a sermon preach'd at S. Saviour's in Southwark. On Palm-Sunday, 1713. London, G. James, for Henry Clements, 1713.   8°

T.334

5735

SACHEVERELL (Henry)

False notions of liberty in religion and government destructive of both. A sermon preach'd before the honourable House of Commons, at St. Margaret's Westminster, on Friday, May 29. 1713. London: for Henry Clements, 1713.   8°

T.334

5736

SACRED miscellanies: or, Divine poems. Upon several subjects. Viz. I. An ode on divine vengeance. Inscrib'd to Mr. Steele. II. On the last judgment ... By N. Rowe ... London: for E. Curll, 1713.   8°

T.410

5737

SEELEN (Johann Heinrich von)

Ioan Henrici von Seelen... Oratio solemnis de praecocibus eruditis... Flensburgi sumtibus et operis Vogelianis, [1713]. 4°

T.793

5738

SERENISSIMAE Magnae Britanniae, Hiberniaeque, Reginae; post gravissimum ab ea confectum bellum, ac labanti tandem restitutam Europae pacem, epinicium. Londini: impensis Gulielmi Redmayne, pro authore, 1713. 4°

T.269

5739

SEWELL (George)

The clergy and the present ministry defended. Being a letter to the Bishop of Salisbury, occasion'd by his Lordship's new preface to his Pastoral care. [Anon.] London, for J. Morphew, 1713.   8°

T.166

5740

SEWELL (George)

Remarks upon a pamphlet intitul'd, [Observations upon the state of the nation, in January, 1712/13.] [Anon.] London, for J. Morphew, 1713.   8°

The half-title: Remarks upon my Lord N——ham's State of the nation.
2 copies.

T.549 T.51

5741

SEWELL (George)

A second letter to the Bishop of Salisbury, upon the publication of his new volume of sermons. Wherein his Lordship's preface concerning the Revolution, and the case of the Lord Russel, are examin'd... London: for E. Curll, and sold by J. Morphew, 1713.   8°

2 copies.

T.166 T.370

5742

SHARPE (John) *Curate of Stepney.*

English protestant dissenters not under persecution, as is suggested by dissenting teachers. With notes on some of their sermons, since the passing the late Act against occasional conformity ... By the author of The regular clergy's sole right to administer baptism. London: for Richard Wilkin, 1713.   8°

2 copies.

T.548 T.39

5743

A SHORT account of the Spanish juros. In a letter to a citizen of London ... London: for S. Popping, 1713. 4°

T.267

5744

SMALRIDGE (George) *Bishop of Bristol.*

A sermon preach'd before ... the Lord Mayor, the aldermen, sheriffs, and governours of the several hospitals of the city of London; in St. Bridget's church... April 7th 1713. London: J.L. for Jonah Bowyer, 1713.   8°

2 copies.
Another copy, in 4°

T.3 T.160 T.334

5745

SOME short reflections upon Mr. Bradbury's late libel intituled, The ass and the serpent ... London, for John Morphew, 1713.   4°

2 copies.

T.264 T.2

5746

SOME Whig-principles demonstrated to be good sense and sound divinity, from their natural consequences ... London: for Samuel Keble, and sold by John Morphew, 1713.   8°

2 copies.

T.348 T.227

5747

STUBS (Philip)

Thankfulness for peace, the subjects duty to God's Vicegerent. A sermon preach'd at St. James Garlick-Hythe, London, and in the oratory of the Royal Hospital, Greenwich, July 1713. on occasion of the general thanksgiving ... for peace. London, for R. and J. Bonwick, 1713.   8°

T.160

5748

SUIDAS.

A very ancient, authentick, and remarkable testimony concerning the priesthood of... Jesus Christ. By Theodosius, a Jew, who liv'd in the time of the Emperor Justinian. Translated from the Greek of Suidas. 2nd ed ... London, for E. Curll, 1713.   8°

T.520

5749

SWINDEN (Tobias)

The usefulness of a general standing liturgy, before either extempore prayer, or forms of each private ministers composing: set forth in a sermon preach'd at the cathedral-church of Rochester. On Sunday the 22d of March, 1712/13. London, H. Clark, for Henry Clements, 1713.   8°

2 copies.

T.334   T.160

5750

SWIFT (Jonathan) *Dean of St. Patrick's.*

Mr. C[olli]ns's Discourse of free-thinking, put into plain English, by way of abstract, for the use of the poor. By a friend of the author. London, for John Morphew, 1713.   8°

Teerink 587.

T.47

5751

SWIFT (Jonathan) *Dean of St. Patrick's.*

Part of the seventh epistle of the first book of Horace imitated: and address'd to a noble peer. [Anon.] 2nd ed. London: for A. Dodd, 1713.   4°

Teerink 589.

T.261

1713 (Cont'd)

5752
SWIFT (Jonathan) *Dean of St. Patrick's*

A preface to the B[isho]p of S[a]r[u]m's introduction to the third volume of The history of the reformation of the Church of England. By Gregory Misosarum... London: for John Morphew, 1713.   8°

Teerink 592.
3 copies.

T.166 T.367 T.370

5753
SYDALL (Elias) *Bishop of Gloucester*.

Of the true uses and ends of religious fasting: with a brief account of the original of Lent... London: for John Wyat, 1713.   12°

T.390

5754
SYNGE (Edward) *Archbishop of Tuam*.

Religion tryed by the test of sober and impartial reason. London, for Richard Sare, 1713.   12°

2 copies

T.377 T.619

5755
TATE (Nahum)

The muse's bower, an epithalamium on the auspicious nuptials of ... the Marquis of Caermarthen, with the Lady Elizabeth Harley ... London: printed for the author, and sold by J. Morphew, 1713.   4°

T.269

5756
The TESTIMONIES of several citizens of Fickleborough, in the kingdom of Fairy-land, concerning the life and character of Robert Hush, commonly called, Bob [i.e. Robert Walpole] ... [Attributed to William Wagstaffe.] London: for John Morphew, 1713.   8°

T.363

5757
THIRLBY (Styan)

A defense of the answer to Mr. Whiston's suspicions, and an answer to his charge of forgery against St. Athanasius. In a letter to Mr. Whiston. Cambridge, printed at the University-Press, for Cornelius Crownfield. And are to be sold by John Morphew, London, 1713.   8°

T.546

5758
THOMSON (Robert)

St. Paul's doctrine of passive obedience. A sermon preach'd at the parish-church of St. Paul's Covent-Garden, on Sunday, November the 16th, 1712. By R. T.   London, John Morphew, 1713.   4°

T.3

5759
THREE essays upon preaching and hearing: containing some few reflexions upon the two late celebrated prefaces [by Gilbert Burnet]; but chiefly intended for the use of those that frequent the evening-lectures and charity-sermons. By a gentleman formerly of St. John's-College, Cambridge ... London printed: and sold by J. Morphew, 1713.   8°

T.166

5760
TILLY (William)

The favour and blessing of God in the appointment, and the people's happiness under the government, of a wise and vertuous prince. A sermon preach'd before the mayor and corporation of Oxford, at St. Martin's church, on Sunday, March the 8th, 1713 ... 2nd ed. Oxford: L. Lichfield, for Anth. Peisley: and are to be sold by J. Knapton, H. Clements, and J. Morphew, booksellers in London, 1713.   8°

T.334

5761
A TRUE relation of the late case in Convocation, concerning an address proposed to be presented to her Majesty upon the conclusion of the peace. Printed for Sam. Buckley, 1713.   8°

T.506

5762
The TRUE Scripture doctrine of the Holy Trinity, the Eucharist, and the satisfaction made for us by our Lord Jesus Christ. In three books. Wherein all the texts in the Old and New Testaments relating thereunto... are collected, compared, explained and vindicated from the errors of Dr. Clarke. London: for George Strahan, 1713.   8°

T.546

5763
The TUNBRIDGE-miscellany: consisting of poems, &c. Written at Tunbridge-Wells, in the year 1713. London: for E. Curll, 1713.   8°

Half-title: The Tunbridge-miscellany, for the year 1713.

T.410

5764
TURNER (John) *Vicar of Greenwich*.

The state and importance of the present controversy, about the validity of lay-baptism, fairly represented: in a letter to the author of Lay-baptism invalid [i.e. Roger Laurence] ... By a country clergy-man. London, for John Morphew, 1713.   8°

2 copies.

T.395 T.360

5765
TWO letters concerning the author of the Examiner [i.e. Jonathan Swift]. London: A. Baldwin, 1713. 8°

T.51

5766
TWO letters with some remarks upon the fourth tome of the English edition of Lewis du Pin's compendious History of the Church. London: for John Morphew, 1713.   8°

T.161

5767
VICKERS (William)

An easie and safe method for curing the king's evil... To which is added, A specimen of success... In a letter to a friend. 9th ed... London, printed, and sold by S. Manship; A. Collins, and at the author's house, 1713.   12°

T.455

5768
WAGSTAFFE (William)

The character of Richard St[ee]le, Esq; with some remarks. By Toby, Abel's kinsman... London, for J. Morphew, 1713.   8°

T.35

5769
WALPOLE (Robert) *Earl of Orford*.

A short history of the Parliament... [Anon.] London: for T. Warner, 1713.   8°

T.547

5770
WAUGH (John) *Bishop of Carlisle*.

The duty of apprentices and other servants. A sermon preach'd ... August 24th, 1713 ... at a meeting of about 1400 persons of both sexes.   Being part of those who had been educated, and afterwards put out to trades and other services, by the trustees of the charity schools, in and about the cities of London and Westminster. London: for G. Strahan; and J. Downing, 1713.   4°

T.3

5771
WAUGH (John) *Bishop of Carlisle*.

Publick worship set forth and recommended in a sermon preached at St. Peter's Cornhill, on Sunday the 18th of Octob. 1713. At the opening of the said parish church after repairing. London, for George Strahan, 1713.   4°

T.3

5772
WAUGH (John) *Bishop of Carlisle*.

Publick worship set forth and recommended in a sermon preached at St. Peter's Cornhill, on Sunday the 18th of Octob. 1713. at the opening of the said parish church after repairing. 2nd ed. London, for George Strahan, 1713.   8°

T.335

5773
WELLS (Edward)

A letter to the Reverend Dr Clarke... in answer to his Letter to Dr Wells... Oxford, for Anthony Peisley; and are to be sold by James Knapton, Henry Clements, William Taylor, and John Morphew, booksellers in London, 1713.   8°

4 copies.

T.546 T.649 T.768 T.821

5774
WELLS (Edward)

Remarks on Dr Clarke's introduction to his Scripture-doctrin of the Trinity. Oxford, printed at the Theatre, for Anthony Peisley, and are to be sold by James Knapton, Henry Clements, William Taylor, and John Morphew booksellers in London, 1713.   8°

3 copies.

T.28 T.655 T.768

5775
WHIGS no Christians. A sermon preach'd at Putney, in Surry, Jan. 30. 1712/3 ... London, John Morphew, [1713].   8°

T.160

5776
WHIGS truly Christians. Occasion'd by a sermon intitled Whigs no Christians, preach'd at Putney in Surry on Jan. 30th, 1712. In which their opinions as to matters of government are fully justify'd by Scripture and reason. London printed: and sold by J. Baker, 1713.   8°

T.227

5777
WHISTON (William)

Mr. Whiston's letter to the Revd. Dr. Henry Sacheverell, rector of St. Andrew's, Holborn. London: printed for the author; and are to be sold by A. Baldwin, [1713]. brs.

T.521

5778
WHISTON (William)

Reflexions on an anonymous pamphlet [by Anthony Collins], entituled, a Discourse of free thinking ... 2nd ed. London: printed for the author; and sold by A. Baldwin, 1713.   8°

T.47

5779
WILLES (*Sir* John)

The speech that was intended to have been spoken by the Terrae-filius, in the Theatre at O[xfor]d, July 13. 1713. Had not his mouth been stopp'd by the V. Ch[ancello]r... [Anon.] London printed: and sold by E. Smith, 1713.   8°

With a letter relating to the pamphlet addressed to Dr Hickes (copy T.35).
2 copies.

T.35 T.410

5780
WITHERS (John)

The Dutch better friends than the French, to the monarchy, church, and trade of England. In a letter from a citizen to a country gentleman. [Anon.] 3rd ed. London, for John Clark, 1713.   8°

T.337

5781
WOODWARD (John)

An account of some Roman urns, and other antiquities, lately digg'd up near Bishops-gate. With brief reflections upon the antient and present state of London. In a letter to Sir Christopher Wren ... London: for E. Curll, 1713.   8°

T.164

5782
A WORD to the present ministry; with two or three in vindication of our High Church House of Commons: and six or seven to the electors of members for the next ensuing Parliament. London: for John Morphew, 1713.   4°

T.267

5783
YOUNG (Edward) *Poet*.

A poem on the last day ... Oxford, printed at the Theatre for Edward Whisler, 1713.   8°

T.410

5784

An ACCOUNT of charity-schools in Great Britain and
Ireland: with the benefactions thereto... The
thirteenth edition, with additions. London, Joseph
Downing, 1714. 4°

T.700

5785

ACRES (Joseph)

The true method of propagating religion and loyalty.
A sermon preach'd in the parish church of St. Mary in
White Chapel, on Sunday the 24th of October, 1714 ...
London: for John Phillips, and sold by J. Roberts,
[1714]. 8°

T.335

5786

ADVOCATES for murther and rebellion, the pest of
government: being an answer to two treasonable libels,
lately publish'd; one, in defence of the murther of
King Charles I. and the other, reasons for abrogating
the fast of that day ... London, John Morphew, 1714.
8°

T.154

5787

ANNE, *Queen of Great Britain.*

Tractatus navigationis et commerciorum... Treaty of
navigation and commerce between the most serene and
most potent Princess Anne... and the most serene and
potent Prince Philip the Vth, the Catholick King of
Spain, concluded at Utrecht the 28/9 day of November/
December 1713. London, John Baskett, and by the
assigns of Thomas Newcomb, and Henry Hills, 1714. 4°

T.783

5788

ANNE, *Queen of Great Britain.*

Tractatus pacis & amicitiae... Treaty of peace and
friendship between the most serene and most potent
Princess Anne... and the most potent Prince Philip
the Vth, the Catholick King of Spain, concluded at
Utrecht the 2/13 day of July, 1713. London, John
Baskett, and by the assigns of Thomas Newcomb, and
Henry Hills, 1714. 4°

T.783

5789

B.(R.)

Longitude to be found out with a new invented
instrument, both by sea and land ... Written by
R.B. secretary to the Honourable Sir Francis Wheeler,
when admiral and general in an expedition to
Martineco. London: for F. Burleigh, 1714. 8°

T.111

5790

BATES (John)

A fast sermon preach'd at Hackney, Novemb. the 3d.
1714. upon account of the present mortality of the
cattle. London: for M. Lawrence, and S. Cliffe, 1714.
8°

T.335

5791

BISSE (Thomas)

A sermon preach'd before the honourable House of
Commons, at St. Margaret's Westminster, on Saturday,
May 29. 1714. London, W. Wilkins, for Henry Clements,
1714. 8°

T.335

5792

BOUGHEN (Edward)

Unanimity in judgment and affection, necessary to unity
of doctrine and uniformity in discipline. A sermon
preached at Canterbury, at the visitation of the Lord
Archbishop's peculiars ... London, R.B. for Robert
Allot, 1635. And reprinted and sold by Samuel Keble,
1714. 8°

2 copies.

T.334   T.335

5793

BRADBURY (Thomas)

The lawfulness of resisting tyrants, argued from the
history of David, and in defence of the Revolution.
Nov. 5. 1713 ... 2nd ed. London: S. Keimer, for
N. Cliff and D. Jackson: and sold by S. Popping; and
T. Harrison, 1714. 8°

T.39

5794

BRADBURY (Thomas)

The lawfulness of resisting tyrants, argued from the
history of David, and in defence of the Revolution.
Nov. 5. 1713 ... 4th ed. London: S. Keimer, for N.
Cliff and D. Jackson: and sold by S. Popping; and T.
Harrison, 1714. 8°

T.335

5795

BRADSHAW (William) *Bishop of Bristol.*

A sermon preach'd before ... Sir William Humfreys,
knight and baronet, lord-mayor, the aldermen, and
citizens of London, at the cathedral-church of St.
Paul, on the fifth of November, 1714. London, for
Bernard Lintott, 1714. 8°

T.335

5796

BRETT (Thomas)

A further enquiry into the judgment and practice of
the primitive Church, in relation to persons being
baptized by lay-men ... London: for John Wyat, 1714.
8°

2 copies.

T.395   T.365

5797

BRETT (Thomas)

A review of the Lutheran principles; shewing, How they
differ from the Church of England ... In a letter to
a friend ... London: for Henry Clements, 1714. 8°

T.395

5798

BRETT (Thomas)

A review of the Lutheran principles... 2nd ed.
To which is added, A postscript, containing some
transient remarks on a late virulent pamphlet [by
Robert Watts], entituled, Two letters, to the Right
Honourable the Lord Viscount Townsend... London:
for Henry Clements, 1714. 8°

T.395

5799

BROUGHTON (John)

Of the house of prayer. A sermon preach'd at the
consecration of the chapel at Kew ... on Wednesday,
May 12. 1714 ... London: W.B. for R. Sare, and E.
Place, 1714. 4°

2 copies.

T.335   T.3

5800

BULL (George) *Bishop of St. David's.*

The corruptions of the Church of Rome. In relation to
ecclesiastical government, the rule of faith, and form
of divine worship. In answer to the Bishop of Meaux's
queries. 4th ed. London: W.B. for Richard Sare,
1714. 8°

T.405

5801

BURCHETT (Josiah)

The ark. A poem. In imitation of du Bartas. By Mr.
Burchett. London: for Edward Castle, 1714. 4°

T.261

5802

BURNET (Gilbert) *Bishop of Salisbury.*

An introduction to the third volume of The history
of the reformation of the Church of England...
London: for John Churchill, 1714. 8°

3 copies.

T.166   T.367   T.370

5803

BURNET (Gilbert) *Bishop of Salisbury.*

A sermon preach'd, and a charge given at the
triennial visitation of the diocese of Salisbury.
London: for J. Churchill, 1714. 4°

T.765

5804

BURNET (Gilbert) *Bishop of Salisbury.*

A sermon preach'd at St. Bridget's-church... March
29. 1714. before... the Lord Mayor, the aldermen
and governours of the several hospitals of the City.
London: for J. Churchill, 1714. 8°

2 copies.

T.334   T.335

5805

CALAMY (Edmund) *D.D.*

The seasonableness of religious societies. A sermon
preach'd to the supporters of the lecture on Lord's-
day mornings, at Little St. Hellen's, upon April the
23d, 1714. London: for John and Joseph Marshall, 1714.
8°

T.335

5806

CARTE (Thomas)

The Irish massacre set in a clear light. Wherein
Mr. Baxter's account of it in the history of his
own life, and the abridgment thereof by Dr. Calamy,
are fully consider'd. Together with two letters
from Mr. Chaundler... to the Reverend Mr. Thomas
Cart at Bath, with his two replies... London: for
George Strahan, [1714]. 4°

T.2

5807

The CASE of Richard Steele, Esq; being an impartial
account of the proceedings against him. In a letter
to a friend. London: for J. Roberts, 1714. 8°

T.169

5808

A CAT may look upon a king [by Sir Anthony Weldon].
Answer'd paragraph by paragragh [sic]. London:
R. Mathard, [1714?] 12°

T.413

5809

A CEREMONIAL for the reception of his most sacred
Majesty George, by the grace of God, King of Great
Britain, &c. upon his arrival from Holland to his
kingdom of Great Britain. Printed by John Nutt, 1714.
Fol.

T.529

5810

CHALMERS (John)

The divine institution and model of the Christian
priesthood. In a sermon preach'd at St. Peter's
church in Colchester, at the visitation of the
reverend the arch-deacon there, April the 13th, 1713.
London: for George Strahan, 1714. 4°

T.752

5811

CHISHULL (Edmund)

The excellency of a proper, charitable relief. A
sermon preach'd before the Sons of the clergy, at
their anniversary-meeting in the cathedral church of
St. Paul, December the 2d, 1714 ... London: for
James Round, 1714. 8°

T.37

5812

CHURCH OF ENGLAND.

A form of prayer and thanksgiving to Almighty God;
to be used... on Thursday the twentieth day of
January next, for bringing his Majesty to a peaceable
and quiet possession of the throne... London, John
Baskett, and by the assigns of Thomas Newcomb, and
Henry Hills, 1714. 4°

T.461

5813

CLARKE (Samuel) *Rector of St. James's, Westminster.*

A letter to the Reverend Dr Wells... In answer to
his Remarks, &c. London, for James Knapton, 1714. 8°

3 copies.

T.28   T.768   T.821

5814

CLARKE (Samuel) *Rector of St. James's, Westminster.*

A reply to the objections of Robert Nelson, Esq;
and of an anonymous author, against Dr Clarke's
Scripture-doctrine of the Trinity... To which is
added, An answer to the remarks of the author [i.e.
Francis Gastrell] of, Some considerations concerning
the Trinity... London, for James Knapton, 1714. 8°

T.821

5815

CLELAND (William)

Some observations, shewing the danger of losing the
trade of the sugar colonies. Humbly offer'd to the
consideration of the Parliament. By a planter.
London: printed in the year, 1714. 8°

T.148

1714 (Cont'd)

5816
COBB (Samuel)

Clavis Virgiliana: or new observations upon the works of Virgil. London: for E. Curll, 1714. 8º

T.410

5817
CONSIDERATIONS upon The secret history of the white staff [by Daniel Defoe]. Humbly address'd to the E[arl] of O[xford]. [Attributed to Lord Bolingbroke.] London: for A. Moore, and sold by the booksellers of London and Westminster, [1714]. 8º

T.385

5818
CONSIDERATIONS upon The secret history of the white staff [by Daniel Defoe]. Humbly address'd to the E[arl] of O[xford]. [Attributed to Lord Bolingbroke.] 4th ed. London: for A. Moore, and sold by the booksellers of London and Westminster, [1714?] 8º

T.392

5819
CRAUFURD (David)

A key to the Memoirs of the affairs of Scotland [by George Lockhart]. [Anon.] London: for J. Moor; and sold by the booksellers of London and Westminster, 1714. 8º

T.412

5820
The CRISIS upon crisis. A poem. Being an advertisement stuck in the lion's mouth at Button's: and addressed to Doctor S[wif]t ... London, for J. Morphew, 1714. 8º

Teerink 1080.

T.267

5821
CROXALL (Samuel)

An original canto of Spencer: design'd as part of his Fairy queen, but never printed. Now made publick by Nestor Ironside ... 2nd ed. London; for James Roberts, 1714. 4º

T.261

5822
DEFOE (Daniel)

Advice to the people of Great Britain, with respect to two important points of their future conduct. I. What they ought to expect from the King. II. How they ought to behave to him. [Anon.] London: for J. Baker, 1714. 8º

Moore 281.

T.207

5823
DEFOE (Daniel)

Impeachment, or no impeachment: or, An enquiry how far the impeachment of certain persons, at the present juncture, would be consistent with honour and justice. [Anon.] London: for J. Baker, 1714. 8º

Moore 285.

T.207

5824
DEFOE (Daniel)

The remedy worse than the disease: or, Reasons against passing the Bill for preventing the growth of schism ... In a letter to a noble earl ... [Anon.] London: for J. Baker, 1714. 8º

Moore 277.

T.302

5825
DEFOE (Daniel)

The Scots nation and union vindicated; from the reflections cast on them, in an infamous libel [by Jonathan Swift], entitl'd, The publick spirit of the Whigs ... [Anon.] London: for A. Bell; and sold by J. Baker, 1714. 4º

Moore 273.

T.490

5826
DITTON (Humphry)

The new law of fluids: or, A discourse concerning the ascent of liquors, in exact geometrical figures, between two nearly contiguous surfaces. To which is added The true state of the case about matter's thinking ... London: J. Roberts, for Benj. Cowse, 1714. 2 parts. 8º

T.111

5827
EGLETON (John)

A vindication of the late House of Commons, in rejecting the Bill for confirming the eigth and ninth articles of the treaty of navigation & commerce between England and France. Humbly recommended to... the Lord Mayor, aldermen, and Common Council of the city of London. By a citizen ... London, for John Clark, 1714. 8º

T.279

5828
An ENQUIRY into the ill designs, errors, &c. of Dr. Clarke's (pretended) Scripture doctrine of the Trinity ... London: printed for, and sold by George Strahan, 1714. 8º

2 copies.

T.228   T.28

5829
An ESSAY to prove women have no souls. Compos'd of several arguments publish'd by S. Clarke. Sold by A. Dodd, [1714]. 8º

T.35

5830
An EXPEDIENT to remove the groundless jealousies and fears of honest meaning people concerning his Majesty, so industriously spread about by Jesuits, Jacobites and other papists ... With a preface to Mr. Steele. By a lover of his country ... London. Printed for D. Jackson, and sold by J. Roberts, [1714]. 8º

T.207

5831
The FALSE alarm: or, Remarks upon Mr. Steele's Crisis. Being a defence of the true constitution, and succession to the crown of England: and the case of the Revolution fully considered. London: printed in the year 1614 [i.e. 1714]. [Col: J. Roberts, 1714.] 4º

T.267

5832
The FALSE steps of the ministry after the Revolution: shewing that the lenity and moderation of that government was the occasion of all the factions which have since endanger'd the constitution ... In a letter to my Lord ----. London: for J. Roberts, 1714. 8º

T.207

5833
The FORM of the proceeding to the royal coronation of his most excellent Majesty King George, from Westminster-Hall to the collegiate church of St. Peter ... the 20th day of this instant October, 1714. Printed by John Nutt, 1714. Fol.

T.529

5834
A FULL account of the proceedings in the last session of Parliament, against Richard Steele, Esq; with a defence of his writings. In a letter to his Excellency the Earl of N[o]tt[ingha]m ... London: for J. Roberts, 1714. 8º

Also published as *The case of Richard Steele, Esq.*

T.402

5835
GASTRELL (Francis) *Bishop of Chester.*

Remarks upon Dr. Clark's Scripture-doctrine of the Trinity. By the author of, Some considerations concerning the Trinity, and the ways of managing that controversy. [Anon.] London: W.B. for Henry Clements, 1714. 8º

T.28

5836
GAY (John)

The fan. A poem. In three books... 2nd ed. London: for J. Tonson, 1714. Fol.

T.529

5837
GEORGE I, *King of Great Britain.*

Directions to our archbishops, and bishops, for the preserving of unity in the Church, and the purity of the Christian faith, concerning the Holy Trinity... London, John Baskett, and by the assigns of Thomas Newcomb, and Henry Hills, 1714. 4º

T.461

5838
GILLANE (John)

The life of the reverend and learned Mr. John Sage. Wherein also some account is given of his writings, both printed and in manuscript ... [Anon.] London, for Henry Clements, 1714. 8º

T.377

5839
GREAT BRITAIN. *Civil Service.*

A new and compleat list of officers, civil and military in Great Britain ... London: for Abel Roper, and Robert Gosling, 1714. 8º

T.51

5840
GREAT BRITAIN. *Commissioners of Accounts.*

A report from the Commissioners appointed to take, examine and state, the publick accompts of the Kingdom. And to determine the debts due to the army ... London: printed in the year 1714. 8º

T.87

5841
HANNIBAL not at our gates: or, An enquiry into the grounds of our present fears of popery and the Pre[ten]der: in a dialogue between my Lord Panick, and George Steady, Esq ... London: for E. Thornhill, 1714. 8º

2 copies.

T.337   T.51

5842
HICKES (George)

The celebrated story of the Thebaean legion no fable. In answer to the objections of Doctor Gilbert Burnet's preface to his translation of Lactantius de mortibus persecutorum ... Written in the year 1687, by a dignify'd clergy-man of the Church of England, and now first publish'd from the author's own MS ... London: printed 1714. 8º

2 copies.

T.370   T.157

5843
An HISTORICAL account of the constitution of the vestry of the parish of St. Dunstan's in the West, London. Wherein are discovered, the secret managements of certain select parish officers, and the abuses of their respective trusts ... London: printed for, and sold by John Morphew, 1714. 8º

T.402

5844
HOFFMAN (Francis)

Two very odd characters tho' the number be even: of the Whigg flesh-fly, and the industrious Tory bee. With a hymn, written by the bee, and set to the musick of his wings. (The demolishing edict.) [Anon.] London: printed for the author, 1714. 4º

T.2

5845
HUYGENS (Christiaan)

Christiani Hugenii libellus de ratiociniis in ludo aleae. Or, The value of all chances in games of fortune; cards, dice, wagers, lotteries, &c. mathematically demonstrated. [Translated by W. Browne.] London: S. Keimer, for T. Woodward, 1714. 8º

T.148

5846
IBBOT (Benjamin)

A sermon preach'd before ... Sir Samuel Stanier Knt. Lord Mayor, the aldermen, and citizens of London, in the cathedral church of St. Paul, on Monday March 8. 1713 ... London: for John Wyat, 1714. 8º

T.335

5847
JOHN Dennis, the sheltring poet's invitation to Richard Steele, the secluded party-writer, and member; to come and live with him in the Mint... London, for John Morphew, 1714. 4º

T.269

5848
KING (Peter) *1st Baron King.*

The speech of Sir Peter King Kt. recorder of London, at St. Margaret's Hill, to the King's most excellent Majesty, upon his royal entry, Sept. 20. 1714. London: for George Grafton, 1714. brs.

T.529

5849

KNIGHT (James)

A letter to the Reverend Dr. Clark ... from the author
of The true scripture doctrine of the Holy Trinity,
the Eucharist, &c. Occasion'd by some passages in a
letter from Dr. Clark to Dr. Wells. London: for
George Strahan, 1714.　　8°

T.28

5850

LACY (John)

The ecclesiastical and political history of Whig-
land, of late years... Londin, for J. Morphew,
1714.　8°

T.548

5851

LESLIE (Charles)

A letter from Mr. Lesly to a member of Parliament in
London. [No imprint, 1714.]　4°

T.190

5852

LESLIE (Charles)

The old English constitution, in relation to the
hereditary succession of the Crown, antecedent to
the Revolution in 1688. [Anon.] London, printed
in the year, 1714.　8°

T.413

5853

A LETTER to the Examiner, suggesting proper heads,
for vindicating his masters. London: for J. Moore,
1714.　8°

T.51

5854

LEWIS (John) *Vicar of Minster.*

A vindication of the Right Reverend the Ld. Bishop of
Norwich, from the undeserved reflections of the
Reverend Mr. John Johnson, in his book entituled The
unbloody sacrifice and altar unvailed and supported
... In a letter to the Reverend Mr. Johnson. By a
Christian ... London: for John Morphew, [1714]. 8°

T.169

5855

LINDSAY (Colin) *Earl of Balcarres.*

An account of the affairs of Scotland, relating to the
Revolution in 1688. As sent to the late King James
II. when in France. By the Right Honourable the Earl
of B —— ... London: for J. Baker, 1714.　8°

T.413

5856

LLOYD (Robert Lumley)

A sermon preach'd at St. Paul's Covent-Garden, on the
30th of January, 1713/14 ... London, for J. Roberts,
1714.　8°

T.335

5857

LOCKHART (George)

Memoirs concerning the affairs of Scotland, from
Queen Anne's accession to the throne, to the
commencement of the union of the two kingdoms of
Scotland and England, in May, 1707... (The appendix.)
[Anon.] London printed: and sold by the booksellers
of London and Westminster, 1714.　8°

T.412

5858

LONG (Roger)

The music speech, spoken at the public commencement
in Cambridge, July the 6th, 1714... 3rd ed.
London: for T. Payne; and W. Thurlbourn, [1714?] 8°

T.651

5859

MACKENZIE (George) *Earl of Cromarty.*

A vindication of the historical account of the
conspiracies by the Earls of Gowry, against K.
James the sixth... from the mistakes of Mr.
John Anderson... Edinburgh: James Watson; and
George Stewart, 1714.　8°

T.403

5860

MANLEY (Mary De la Riviere)

A modest enquiry into the reasons of the joy expressed
by a certain sett of people, upon the spreading of a
report of her Majesty's death. [Anon.] London: for
John Morphew, 1714.　8°

T.51

5861

MANLEY (Mary De la Riviere)

A modest enquiry into the reasons of the joy expressed
by a certain sett of people, upon the spreading of
a rerort [sic] of her Majesty's death. [Anon.]
London: for John Morphew, 1714.　8°

T.154

5862

MARSHALL (Nathaniel)

The royal pattern: or, A sermon upon the death of her
late most excellent Majesty Queen Anne; preach'd
in the parish-church of Finchley ... London: for
W. Taylor; and H. Clements, 1714.　8°

T.37

5863

MERKS (Thomas) *Bishop of Carlisle.*

The late Bishop of Carlisle's speech against the
deposition of kings; and in vindication of hereditary
right, and the lineal succession to the crown of these
realms. London: for John Morphew, 1714.　8°

T.403

5864

MILBOURNE (Luke)

The traytors reward: or, A king's death revenged. In
a sermon preach'd on the thirtieth of January, 1713
... London: L. Beardwell, for George Sawbridge, 1714.
8°

2 copies.

T.334　T.335

5865

MILN (William)

A practical essay, proving the Christian religion to
be from God ... Together with an apology for the
Episcopal Church in Scotland. A sermon preach'd in
one of the meeting-houses of the city of Edinburgh
... By W.M. 2nd ed ... Edinburgh, printed in the
year 1714. And sold at Mr. Stuart's shop: at Mr.
Freebairn's; and at Mr. M'Ewen's.　8°

T.170

5866

N.(N.)

Will-with-a-wisp; or, The grand ignis fatuus of
London. Being a lay-man's letter to a country-
gentleman, concerning the articles lately exhibited
against Mr. Whiston ... By a gentleman formerly of
Queen's College, Oxon ... London: for J. Woodward;
A. Bettesworth; E. Curll, and R. Gosling, 1714. 8°

T.150

5867

NEW discoveries of the dangers of popery. [Attributed
to Defoe.] London: for James Roberts, and A. Dodd,
1714.　8°

T.405

5868

An ODE. Humbly inscribed to the Right Reverend John,
Lord Bishop of London ... London: for R. Gosling,
1714.　8°

T.225

5869

PARKER (Samuel) *Bishop of Oxford.*

A letter sent by Sir Leolyn Jenkins, to the late
King James, to bring him over to the communion of
the Church of England... London, S.K. and sold by
J. Morphew, 1714.　8°

T.405

5870

POPE (Alexander)

The rape of the lock. An heroi-comical poem... In
five canto's ... London: for Bernard Lintott, 1714.
8°

T.35

5871

POTTER (Edward)

A vindication of our Blessed Saviour's divinity;
chiefly against Dr. Clarke... Cambridge, printed
at the University-Press, for R. Thurlbourne; and
are to be sold by R. Knaplock, London, 1714.　8°

T.821

5872

POVEY (Charles)

An inquiry into the miscarriages of the four last years
reign ... Presented to the freeholders of Great
Britain, against the next election of a new Parliament.
[Anon.] 2nd ed. London: printed for the author, and
are to be sold at Mr. Robinson's, 1714.　8°

T.207

5873

The PRESENT ministry justify'd: or, An account of
the state of the several treaties of peace, between
her Majesty and her allies, and France and Spain ...
London, for J. Morphew, 1714.　8°

T.51

5874

The PUBLICK spirit of the Tories, manifested in the
case of the Irish dean [i.e. Jonathan Swift], and his
man Timothy ... London: J. Roberts, 1714.　4°

Teerink 1079.

T.267

5875

R.(B.)

Remarks on Mr. Steele's Crisis, &c. By one of the
clergy. In a letter to the author ... London printed:
and sold by B. Berrington; and E. Smith, 1714.　4°

T.267

5876

REED (Benjamin)

A reply to a pamphlet [by John Withers], entitled,
A caveat against the new sect of anabaptists, lately
sprung up at Exon. In a letter to a friend ... Exon:
S. Farley, for John March; and are to be sold by John
Morphew, 1714.　8°

T.360

5877

REEVES (William)

The great importance of redeeming time. A sermon
preached before the Queen, in St. James's chapel; on
the 3d day of March, 1714. London: W.B. for Richard
Sare, 1714.　8°

T.335

5878

The RESPECTFUL behaviour of the dissenters towards
her late Majesty, the Church and the ministry,
exemplified from their own writings ... Contriv'd to
be bound up with Dr. Calamy's abridgment of Mr.
Baxter's life. London, for John Moor, and sold by
the booksellers of London and Westminster, [1714?]
8°

T.302

5879

ROBINSON (John) *Bishop of London.*

The benefits and duty of the members of Christ's
kingdom. A sermon preach'd in the parish-church
of St. Sepulchre, May 20. MDCCXIV... at the
anniversary meeting of the children educated in
the charity-schools, in and about the cities of
London and Westminster. London, Joseph Downing,
1714.　4°

T.700

5880

RYE (George)

The supremacy of the Crown, and the power of the
Church, asserted and adjusted. A sermon preach'd before
the University of Oxford, at St Mary's, on Sunday Jan.
17. 1713/14. Oxford, printed at the Theatre, for
Anth. Peisley: and are to be sold by J. Churchill,
J. Knapton, W. Taylor, H. Clements, W. Meadows and J.
Morphew booksellers in London, 1714.　8°

T.335

5881

RYMER (Thomas)

Of the antiquity, power & decay of parliaments.
Being a general view of government, and civil policy,
in Europe ... London: sold by J. Roberts. 1714.　8°

T.51

5882

SACHEVERELL (Henry)

The character of a Low-Church-man: drawn in an answer
to the True character of a Church-man [by Richard
West]: shewing the false pretences to that name.
Humbly offer'd to all electors of Parliament and
Convocation. [Anon.] 3rd ed. Printed, and sold by
the booksellers of Great-Brittain, [1714].　8°

T.345

5883

SACHEVERELL (Henry)

A sermon preach'd before the Sons of the clergy, at their anniversary meeting in the cathedral-church of St. Paul, December 10, 1713. London: for Henry Clements, 1714. 8°

2 copies.

T.334 T.335

5884

The SERAPHICK world: or, Celestial hierarchy: being an account of the nature and ministry, the different employments, ranks, and stations of angels and arch-angels ... London, for J. Baker, 1714. 8°

T.377

5885

SEWELL (George)

An introduction to the life and writings of G——t Lord Bishop of S——m. Being a third letter to his Lordship, occasioned by his introduction to the third volume of the History of the Reformation ... By the author of the two former letters ... London: for E. Curll, 1714. 8°

T.48

5886

SEWELL (George)

More news from Salisbury ... By the author of three letters to the Bishop of Salisbury. London: for E. Curll, 1714. 8°

T.370

5887

SEWELL (George)

The reasons for writing against the Bishop of Salisbury. With remarks upon his Lordship's Spittal-sermon preached on Easter-Monday last. London: for E. Curll, 1714. 8°

2 copies.

T.370 T.166

5888

SHERLOCK (Thomas) *Bishop of London.*

A sermon preach'd before the honourable House of Commons, at St. Margaret's Westminster, on Monday, March 8. 1713/4. Being the day of her Majesty's happy accession to the throne. London: for J. Pemberton, 1714. 8°

2 copies.

T.334 T.335

5889

SHORE (John) *M.D.*

A charge, deliver'd at the general quarter sessions of the peace, for the county of Sussex, held at Chichester, on Monday the fifth day of April, 1714. London: for R. Gosling, 1714. 8°

T.402

5890

SLADE (Joseph)

The character of a righteous magistrate. In a sermon preach'd at the assizes held at Reading, in the county of Berks, March the 2d, 1713 ... London: for Benj. Shirley, bookseller in Reading; and are to be sold by Benj. Cowse, 1714. 8°

T.335

5891

SMITH (Elisha)

Preservation from impending judgments, a forcible argument for humiliation, and amendment of life; which is the best thanksgiving unto God. A sermon preached at Wisbeech in the Isle of Ely, February 21. 1713 ... London, John Morphew, 1714. 8°

T.335

5892

SOME few obvious and just reflections on the Bishop of Sarum's charity or spittle sermon: preached at St. Bridget's church, on Monday ... March 29, 1714. By a Tory... London: John Morphew, 1714. 8°

2 copies.

T.334 T.370

5893

SPECULUM Sarisburianum, in remarks on some passages in a pamphlet, entituled, An introduction to the third volume of the History of the Reformation of the Church of England. By... Gilbert, Lord Bishop of Sarum. In a letter to a friend. By Philoclerus ... London: for J. Morphew, 1714. 8°

3 copies. Attributed by Bowdler to Thomas Stamp.

T.367 T.370 T.654

5894

A SPEECH to the people against the Pretender, at the publication of her Majesty's proclamation, and upon the vote of the honourable House of Commons... 2nd ed. London: Ferd. Burleigh, 1714. 8°

T.51

5895

SPINCKES (Nathaniel)

The case truly stated; wherein the Case restated [by Archibald Campbell] is fully consider'd. By a member of the Church of England... London: for George Strahan, 1714. 8°

T.405

5896

STANHOPE (James) *1st Earl Stanhope.*

Mr. Stanhope's answer to the report of the Commissioners sent into Spain, &c. Together with an extract of so much of the said report, as concerns him. Sold by Richard Charret, 1714. 8°

T.279

5897

STEELE (*Sir* Richard)

The crisis: or, A discourse representing, from the most authentick records, the just causes of the late happy Revolution... London: Sam. Buckley; and sold by Ferd. Burleigh, 1714. 4°

3 copies.

T.267 T.553 T.763

5898

STEELE (*Sir* Richard)

The Englishman: being the close of the paper so called. With an epistle concerning the Whiggs, Tories, and new converts ... London: for Ferd: Burleigh, 1714. 4°

T.267

5899

STEELE (*Sir* Richard)

A speech suppos'd to be spoke by R[ichard] St[ee]l, Esq; at the opening this present Parliament. With some remarks in a letter to the bailiff of St[ockbri]dge, very proper to be bound up with the Crisis... London, John Morphew, 1714. 4°

T.267

5900

STRANGE news from Westminster, or, Robin Red-breast fell from his perch ... London: for T. Smith, 1714. 4°

T.261

5901

SWIFT (Jonathan) *Dean of St. Patrick's.*

The first ode of the second book of Horace paraphras'd: and address'd to Richard St[ee]le, Esq ... [Anon.] London: for A. Dodd, 1714. 4°

Teerink 594.

T.269

5902

SWIFT (Jonathan) *Dean of St. Patrick's.*

The publick spirit of the Whigs: set forth in their generous encouragement of the author of the Crisis [i.e. Sir Richard Steele]: with some observations on the seasonableness, candor, erudition, and style of that treatise. [Anon.] London: for John Morphew, 1714. 4°

Teerink 596.

T.267

5903

SWIFT (Jonathan) *Dean of St. Patrick's.*

The publick spirit of the Whigs: set forth in their generous encouragement of the author of the Crisis [i.e. Sir Richard Steele]: with some observations on the seasonableness, candor, erudition, and style of that treatise. [Anon.] 2nd ed. London: for John Morphew, 1714. 4°

Teerink 596.

T.267

5904

SWORDER (William)

For God, or for Baal. The unreasonableness and absurdity of practical atheism, and occasional conformity, demonstrated in three sermons ... London: for Anne Speed, 1714. 8°

T.335

5905

T. (F.)

A short discourse of the canary bird... (Some few rules for angling.) London: printed, and sold (by the author's appointment) by Mr. Bradshaw, 1714. 12°

T.455

5906

TALBOT (William) *Bishop of Durham.*

A sermon preach'd at the coronation of King George, in the abbey-church of Westminster, October the 20th, 1714. London: W. Wilkins for John Churchill, 1714. 8°

Another copy, in 4°

T.771 T.335

5907

A TENDER and hearty address to all the freeholders, and other electors of members for the ensuing Parliament ... In which the conspiracies of the faction, for four years last past, are plac'd in a true light. London: for J. Baker, 1714. 8°

T.207

5908

THACKER (Jeremy)

The longitudes examin'd. Beginning with a short epistle to the longitudinarians, and ending with the description of a smart, pretty machine of my own, which I am (almost) sure will do for the longitude, and procure me the twenty thousand pounds... London: for J. Roberts, 1714. 8°

T.111

5909

TOLAND (John)

The art of restoring. Or, The piety and probity of General Monk in bringing about the last Restoration ... In a letter to a minister of state, at the court of Vienna ... [Anon.] London: J. Roberts, 1714. 8°

T.51

5910

TOLAND (John)

The art of restoring. Or, The piety and probity of General Monk in bringing about the last Restoration ... In a letter to a minister of state, at the Court of Vienna ... [Anon.] 3rd ed. London: J. Roberts, 1714. 8°

T.344

5911

TRIMNELL (Charles) *Bishop of Winchester.*

An answer to a pamphlet entituled, The proceedings of the lower house of Convocation. Wherein the great unfairness of that account is laid open ... [Anon.] London: Sam. Buckley, and sold by Ferd. Burleigh, 1714. 4°

2 copies.

T.74

5912

The TRYALS of the rioters at Bristol, on Friday, Saturday, and Monday, the 26th, 27th, and 29th of November, and Wedneday [sic], the 1st of December, 1714 ... To which is prefix'd, An account of the riot. London: John Smith, [1714]. 8°

T.207

5913

VILLARS (Nicolas Montfaucon de)

The Count de Gabalis: being a diverting history of the Rosicrucian doctrine of spirits, viz. sylphs, salamanders, gnomes, and daemons: shewing their various influence upon human bodies. Done from the Paris edition... London: for B. Lintott and E. Curll, 1714. 8°

T.798

5914

A VINDICATION of the Earl of Nottingham from the vile imputations, and malicious slanders, which have been cast upon him in some late pamphlets. London: for J. Roberts, 1714. 8°

T.462

5915

WAGSTAFFE (William)

A letter from the facetious Doctor Andrew Tripe, at Bath, to the venerable Nestor Ironside. With an account of the reception Mr. Ironside's late present of a Guardian met with from the worshipful Mr. Mayor, and other substantial inhabitants of that ancient city... London, for J. Morphew, 1714.   8°

T.169

5916

WARD (Edward)

The republican procession; or, The tumultuous cavalcade. A merry poem. [Anon.] Printed in the year 1714.   8°

2 copies.

T.35   T.204

5917

WAUGH (John) *Bishop of Carlisle.*

A sermon preached before ... the Lord Mayor, the aldermen, and governours of the several hospitals of the city of London; at St. Bridget's church, on Wednesday in Easter week, 1714. London: for George Strahan, 1714.   8°

T.335

5918

WAUGH (John) *Bishop of Carlisle.*

A sermon preached to the societies for reformation of manners, at St. Mary-le-Bow, on Monday, December the 28th, MDCCXIII ... London: J. Downing, 1714. 4°

T.3

5919

WELCHMAN (Edward)

Dr. Clarke's Scripture doctrine of the Trinity examined. To which are added Some remarks on his sentiments, and a brief explanation of his doctrine by way of question and answer. Oxford: L.Lichfield, for A.Peisley: and are to be sold by J.Knapton, W.Taylor, H.Clements, W.Meadows and J.Morphew booksellers in London, 1714.   8°

Copy T.28 lacks the first two gatherings.

T.28   T.821

5920

WELDON (*Sir* Anthony)

A cat may look upon a king. [Anon.] Amsterdam: printed in the glorious year 1714.   8°

First published in 1652; reprinted with additions.

T.413

5921

WELTON (Richard)

Church-ornament without idolatry vindicated: in a sermon preach'd on occasion of an altar-piece lately erected in the chancel of St. Mary White-chappel... London: for G. Strahan, 1714.   4°

2 copies.

T.3   T.196

5922

WHISTON (William)

An argument to prove that, either all persons solemnly, tho' irregularly set apart for the ministry, are real clergy-men... or else there are now no real clergy-men, or Christians in the world ... 2nd ed. London: printed for the author; and are to be sold by the booksellers of London and Westminster; and by J. Roberts, 1714.   8°

T.360

5923

WHITELOCK (Bulstrode)

Mr. Bulstrode Whitlock's account of his embassy to Sweden, deliver'd to the Parliament in the year 1654. Together with the defensive alliance concluded between Great-Britain and Sweden, in the year 1700... London: John Morphew, 1714.   8°

T.147

5924

WHITGIFT (John) *Archbishop of Canterbury.*

A godlie sermon preached before the Queenes Maiestie at Greenwiche... Imprinted at London by Henry Bynneman, for Humfrey Toy, 1574. And now reprinted with a large preface, shewing the reasons of it, for John Wyat, 1714.   8°

T.36

5925

WILLES (*Sir* John)

The present constitution, and the protestant succession vindicated: in answer to a late book [by George Harbin] entituled, The hereditary right of the Crown of England asserted, &c ... [Anon.] London: for J. Baker, 1714.   8°

2 copies.

T.344   T.403

5926

YOUNG (Edward) *Poet.*

On the late Queen's death, and his Majesty's accession to the throne. [A poem.] Inscribed to Joseph Addison... London: for J. Tonson, 1714. Fol.

T.529

1715

5927

An ADDRESS to the peers of England. [No imprint, 1715?]   4°

T.267

5928

An ANTIDOTE against presbytery: or, A vindication of the rites and ceremonies, the principles and practices of the Church of England ... London: for Richard Smith, 1715.   4°

T.264

5929

An ARGUMENT from the Civil Law, shewing that mere possession cannot give right. [No imprint, c. 1715.]   8°

2 copies.

T.92   T.413

5930

ASPLIN (Samuel)

A sermon preached in the parish-church of St. Mary, Woolwich, in Kent; on Sunday, May 29. 1715 ... London: G. James, for G. Sawbridge, 1715.   8°

T.37

5931

ATTERBURY (Francis) *Bishop of Rochester.*

English advice, to the freeholders of England... [Anon.] Printed in the year 1714. [Col: London, for J. Roberts, 1715.]   8°

T.207

5932

AWBREY (Timothy)

A sermon preach'd before the honble House of Commons on the 29th of May, 1715... London: for William Taylor, 1715.   8°

T.37

5933

B. (A.)

Histrio theologicus: or, An historical-political-theological poetical account of the most remarkable passages and transactions in the life of the late B[isho]p of S[aru]m found among his L[ordshi]p's papers, and inscrib'd to his old friend and admonitor, Mr. L[esle]y ... London: John More, 1715.   8°

T.370

5934

BRAMSTON (William)

A sermon, preach'd at the Temple-Church, upon the 13th of February, 1714 ... London: for Henry Clements, 1715.   8°

T.335

5935

BRETT (Thomas)

Dr Brett's vindication of himself, from the calumnies thrown upon him in some late news-papers, wherein he is falsly charged with turning papist. In a letter to ... Archibald Campbell. London: for John Morphew, 1715.   8°

T.395

5936

BRITONS strike home. The absolute necessity of impeaching somebody. In a letter to Tom. Burnet, Esquire ... London: for E. Smith, 1715.   8°

2 copies.

T.370   T.207

5937

BURNET (*Sir* Thomas)

The British bulwark: being a collection of all the clauses in the several statutes now in force against the Pretender, the Non-jurors and the Papists ... London: W. Wilkins; and sold by J. Roberts, 1715.   12°

T.412

5938

BURNET (*Sir* Thomas)

The necessity of impeaching the late ministry, in a letter to the Earl of Hallifax ... London: for D. Brown, 1715.   8°

T.370

5939

BURNET (*Sir* Thomas)

The necessity of impeaching the late ministry. In a letter to the Earl of Hallifax. 3rd ed ... London: W. Wilkins, and sold by J. Roberts, 1715.   8°

T.207

5940

BURNET (*Sir* Thomas) *and* DUCKETT (George)

Homerides: or, A letter to Mr. Pope, occasion'd by his intended translation of Homer. By Sir Iliad Doggrel ... London: W. Wilkins, and sold by J. Roberts, 1715.   8°

T.35

5941

A CERTAIN dutiful son's lamentation for the death of a certain right reverend. With the certain particulars of certain sums, and goods that are bequeath'd him ... Written in Hudibrastick verse ... London: for J. Morphew; and S. Jeeves, 1715.   8°

T.446

5942

A COLLECTION of white and black lists or, A view of those gentlemen who have given their votes in Parliament for and against the protestant religion, and succession, and the trade and liberties of their country ... [Attributed to Stephen Whateley.] 2nd ed ... London: for S. Popping; and sold by the booksellers of London and Westminster, 1715.   8°

T.462

5943

The CONDUCT of his Grace the Duke of Ormonde, in the campagne of 1712. London: for John Morphew, 1715.   4°

2 copies.

T.564   T.2

5944

DEFOE (Daniel)

An account of the riots, tumults, and other treasonable practices; since his Majesty's accession to the throne ... [Anon.] London: for J. Baker, 1715.   8°

Moore 316a.

T.462

5945

DEFOE (Daniel)

Burnet and Bradbury, or the confederacy of the press and the pulpit for the blood of the last ministry. [Anon.] 2nd ed. London: S. Keimer, 1715.   8°

Moore 302.

T.207

5946

DEFOE (Daniel)

A friendly epistle by way of reproof from one of the people called Quakers, to Thomas Bradbury, a dealer in many words. [Anon.] 2nd ed. London: S. Keimer, 1715.   8°

Moore 305.

T.302

5947

DEFOE (Daniel)

A friendly epistle by way of reproof from one of the people called Quakers, to Thomas Bradbury, a dealer in many words. [Anon.] 4th ed. London: S. Keimer, 1715.   8°

Moore 305.

T.264

5948
DEFOE (Daniel)

His Majesty's obligations to the Whigs plainly proved.
Shewing that he can neither with safety, reason, or
gratitude, depart from them ... [Anon.] London:
for J. Baker, 1715.   8°

Moore 318.

T.207

5949
DEFOE (Daniel)

A letter to a merry young gentleman, intituled,
Tho. Burnet, Esq; in answer to one writ by him to
... the Earl of Halifax; by which it plainly appears,
the said squire was not awake when he writ the
said letter. [Anon.] London, sold by J. Morphew,
1715. . 8°

Moore 301.

T.370

5950
DEFOE (Daniel)

A remonstrance from some country Whigs to a member of
a secret committee. [Anon.] London: for J. Morphew,
1715.   8°

Moore 314.
2 copies.

T.462 T.207

5951
DEFOE (Daniel)

Some reasons offered by the late ministry in defence
of their administration. [Anon.] London: for J.
Morphew, 1715.   8°

Moore 308.

T.207

5952
DENNIS (John)

Priestcraft distinguish'd from Christianity ... [Anon.]
London: for J. Roberts, 1715.   8°

T.302

5953

DR. S[wift]'s real diary; being a true and faithful
account of himself, for that week, wherein he is
traduc'd by the author of a scandalous and
malicious Hue and cry after him ... London, R.
Burleigh, 1715.   8°

Teerinck 886.

T.35

5954
ELLIOT (Robert)

A specimen of the Bishop of Sarum's posthumous History
of the affairs of the Church and State of Great-
Britain, during his life ... Printed in the year,
1715. 70pp.   8°

T.48

5955
ELLIOT (Robert)

A specimen of the Bishop of Sarum's posthumous History
of the affairs of the Church and State of Great
Britain, during his life ... London, J. Morphew,
[1715]. 42pp.   8°

T.48

5956
FLEETWOOD (William) *Bishop of Ely.*

The counsellor's plea for the divorce of Sir
G[eorge] D[owning] and Mrs. F[orrester].
[Anon.] London: sold by R. Burleigh, 1715.
8°

T.402

5957

FOUR Hudibrastick canto's, being poems on four the
greatest heroes that liv'd in any age since Nero's,
Don Juan Howlet, Hudibras, Dicko-ba-nes and Bonniface.
London, for J. Roberts, 1715.   8°

T.242

5958
GIBSON (Edmund) *Bishop of London.*

De excommunicatione: concio ad Synodum, ab
Archiepiscopi commissarijs, episcopis, & clero,
provinciae Cantuariensis, celebratam, habita in
ecclesia cathedrali S. Pauli, London, XXI. die
Martij, A.D. 1714/15. Londini: prostant venales
apud Joannem Churchil, 1715.   4°

T.196

5959
GREAT BRITAIN. *Parliament.*

A list of the lords spiritual and temporal: as
also a very exact and correct double list of the...
knights... and burgesses, returned to serve in the
Parliament of Great Britain, summon'd to meet at
Westminster, March 17, 1714 [1715]... London: for
Abel Roper, and Samuel Butler, and sold by John
Morphew, 1715.   8°

T.462

5960
GREAT BRITAIN. *Parliament.*

A true and exact list of the lords spiritual and
temporal, as also the last House of Commons of
Queen Anne, and the first House of Commons of
King George... London: J. Roberts, 1715.   8°

T.462

5961
GREAT BRITAIN. *Parliament. House of Commons.*

A report from the committee of secrecy, appointed...
to examine several books and papers laid before
the House, relating to the late negotiations of
peace and commerce, &c. Reported on the ninth of
June, 1715. by... Robert Walpole, Esq; chairman...
London; for Jacob Tonson, Timothy Goodwin, Bernard
Lintott, and William Taylor, 1715. 2 parts.   Fol.

T.529

5962
HARE (Francis) *Bishop of Chichester.*

The difficulties and discouragements which attend the
study of the Scriptures in the way of private
judgment ... In a letter to a young clergyman. By
a presbyter of the Church of England. 6th ed. London,
for John Baker, 1715.   8°

T.408

5963
HARLEY (Robert) *Earl of Oxford.*

The answer of Robert Earl of Oxford and Earl
Mortimer, to the articles exhibited by the
knights, citizens and burgesses in Parliament
assembled... in maintenance of their impeachment
against him for high treason... London: for
John Morphew, 1715.   Fol.

T.529

5964
HORATIUS FLACCUS (Quintus)

The odes and satires of Horace, that have been done
into English by the most eminent hands ... With his
Art of poetry, by my Lord Roscommon. London: for
A. Bell, T. Varnam and J. Osborn, J. Brown, and J.
Baker, 1715.   8°

T.204

5965
HOUGH (John) *Bishop of Worcester.*

A sermon on Malachi, chap. iv. ver.2. upon occasion of
the Lady Marow's death. London: for G. Davies, 1715.
4°

T.3

5966
HOWELL (Laurence)

The case of schism in the Church of England truly
stated. [Anon.] [No imprint, 1715.]   8°

2 copies.

T.408 T.439

5967
JAMES EDWARD, *Prince of Wales, the Old Pretender.*

[A declaration by the Pretender dated 3 Jan. 1714/5,
beginning The King having impartially consider'd ...]
8°

2 copies.

T.412 T.368

5968
KENNET (White) *Bishop of Peterborough.*

The witchcraft of the present rebellion. A sermon
preached in the parish church of St. Mary Aldermary,
in the city of London. On Sunday the 25th of
September, 1715. the time of a publick ordination...
London, for John Churchwell, 1715.   8°

3 copies.

T.662 T.37

5969
LAMBE (Charles)

The pretences for the present rebellion, considered.
In a sermon preach'd at St. Katherine Cree-church
and All-Hallows Barkin, on Octob. 16. 1715. London:
for Sam. Crouch, 1715.   4°

T.702

5970
LESLIE (Charles)

Mr. Lesley to the Lord Bishop of Sarum. [No imprint,
1715.]   4°

T.190

5971

A LETTER from a country Whig, to his friend in London
wherein appears, who are the truest friends to their
King and country. London, for J. Morphew, 1715.   8°

T.207

5972

A LETTER from a country Whig, to his friend in London;
wherein appears, who are the truest friends to their
King and country. 2nd ed. London, for J. Morphew,
1715.   8°

T.348

5973

A LIST of the late Queen's Cabinet-council, at
the time when she made the peace... A list of the
secret committee, who thirst after the blood of
the said cabinet, to make room for foreigners.
[No imprint, 1715?] brs.

T.490

5974
LYNFORD (Thomas)

God, a tower of salvation to the King. A sermon
preach'd before the honourable House of Commons
... on Monday the first day of August, 1715.
Being the day of his Majesty's happy accession to
the throne. London: for John Wyat, 1715.   4°

T.765

5975
LYNFORD (Thomas)

God, a tower of salvation to the King. A sermon,
preach'd before the honourable House of Commons ...
on Monday the first of August, 1715. Being the day
of his Majesty's happy accession to the throne.
London: for John Wyat, 1715.   8°

2 copies.

T.170   T.37

5976

A MEMORIAL from a faithful member of the Church of
England; shewing the danger we may be in from a new
set of separatists if not timely prevented. London:
for George Sawbridge, [1715].   8°

T.408

5977

The METHODS used for erecting charity-schools, with
the rules and orders by which they are governed. A
particular account of the London charity-schools:
with a list of those erected elsewhere... The
fourteenth edition, with additions. London, Joseph
Downing, 1715.   4°

T.700

5978
MILBOURNE (Luke)

The danger of changes in Church and state; or, The
fatal doom of such as love them and their associates:
in a sermon preach'd, January 31, 1714/15 ...
London: H. Meere, for George Sawbridge, 1714/15.   8°

T.37

5979
NOSTREDAME (Michel de)

The prophecies of Michael Nostradamus concerning the
fate of all the kings and queens of Great Britain
since the Reformation ... Written originally in
French ... But lately collected and explained by D.D.
And now made English for the speculation of the publick
... London: printed and sold for the author, by
J. Roberts; and at Peter Dunoyer's, a French
bookseller, 1715.   8°

T.275

5980
PARKER (Samuel) *of Lincoln College, Oxford.*

An essay upon the duty of physicians and patients,
the dignity of medicine, and the prudentials of
practice. In two dialogues. [Anon.] London:
G.J. for Henry Clements, 1715.   8°

T.92

5981
PHILIPS (John) *Dramatist.*

The Earl of Mar marr'd. With the humours of Jockey,
the Highlander: a tragi-comical farce. By Mr. Philips.
2nd ed. London: for E. Curll, 1715.   8°

T.399

5982
PHILIPS (John) *Poet*.

Poems by Mr. John Philips, late of Christ-Church,
Oxon. To which is prefix'd his life [by George
Sewell]. London: printed in the year 1715. 2 parts.
8°

T.204

5983
PITTIS (William)

Some memoirs of the life of John Radcliffe, M.D.
Interspersed with several original letters: also a
true copy of his last will and testament. (A
supplement.) [Anon.] London: for E. Curll, 1715.
3 parts. 8°

T.402

5984
A POEM in memory of Robert Nelson Esquire ... London:
Geo. James for Richard Smith, 1715. 8°

T.204

5985
POVEY (Charles)

A memorial of the proceedings of the late
ministery and the lower house of Parliament...
Writ by the author of An inquiry into the
miscarriages of the four last years reign...
London: printed for the author, and sold by
J. Roberts, A. Bell, R. Robinson, Mr. Robinson;
J. Pemberton, J. Smith, and Mrs. Boulter, 1715.
8°

T.462

5986
The PRIVATE sentiments of a member of P[arliamen]t.
In a letter to his friend in London... London:
for J. Morphew, 1715. 8°

T.462

5987
A REPRESENTATION of matters of fact concerning the late
war. Shewing the just reasons for engaging in it, and
the ill consequences that attends Great-Britain by the
late inglorious peace ... London, for John Baker,
1715. 8°

T.207

5988
A REVIEW of the report of the secret committee;
digested into alphabetical order, which
distinguishes the transactions of the late
ministers one from another... London: for Eman.
Matthews, and sold by S. Pipping; A. Dodd, and
J. Harrison. 1715. 8°

T.462

5989
SACHEVERELL (Henry)

A sermon preach'd January 31st. 1714/15. London:
D. Brown, [1715]. 8°

T.335

5990
SAMUEL, *Patriarch of Alexandria*.

Lachrymae & suspiria Ecclesiae Graecae: or, The
distressed state of the Greek Church. Humbly
represented in a letter to her late Majesty Queen
Anne, from the Patriarch of Alexandria; by the hands
of Arsenius Archbishop of Thebais, now residing in
London ... London: printed in the year 1715. 4°

T.137

5991
A SEASONABLE expostulation with the disaffected
clergy, at this juncture. By a presbyter of the
Church of England... London: for J. Roberts,
1715. 8°

T.548

5992
A SECOND letter from a country Whig, to his friend in
London; relating to the matter of impeachments, &c.
London, for J. Morphew, 1715. 8°

T.348

5993
A SERMON preached towards the latter end of the last
century, on the anniversary thanksgiving day for
putting an end to the Great Rebellion ... Printed at
Cambridge, 1715. 8°

2 copies.

T.334

5994
SHOREY (William)

A sermon preach'd before ... the lord-mayor, aldermen,
and citizens of London, in the cathedral church of St.
Paul, on Monday, January xxxi. 1715 ... London: for
W. Innys, 1715. 8°

2 copies.

T.170   T.37

5995
A SHORT state of the war and the peace. 2nd ed.
London: for John Morphew, 1715. 8°

T.207

5996
SOME account of the life and writings of ... Thomas
Sprat, D.D. late Lord Bishop of Rochester, and Dean
of Westminster. With a true copy of his last will and
testament. London: for E. Curll, 1715. 2 parts.
8°

T.402

5997
STACY (Edmund)

The blackbird's song... Robin red-breast's answer.
[Anon.] London; D. Brown, 1715. 8°

T.35

5998
STACY (Edmund)

The former, present, and future state of the Church
of England, a poem. Address'd to a member of the
lower house of Convocation. By the author of The
blackbird's song. The second edition, with
additions. London: J. Morphew, 1715. 8°

T.225

5999
STACY (Edmund)

The tale of the raven and the blackbird. By the
author of the Blackbird's song... London: for R.
Barnham, and sold by J. Morphew, 1715. 8°

T.225

6000
STEELE (*Sir* Richard)

A letter from the Earl of Mar to the King, before
his Majesty's arrival in England. With some
remarks on my Lord's subsequent conduct. London:
for Jacob Tonson, 1715. 8°

T.412

6001
SYNGE (Edward) *Archbishop of Tuam*.

A plain and easy method, whereby a man of a
moderate capacity may arrive at full satisfaction
in all things that concern his everlasting
salvation... London: for Richard Sare, 1715. 12°

T.619

6002
SYNGE (Edward) *Archbishop of Tuam*.

The rule of self-examination; or, The only way of
banishing doubts and scruples, and directing the
conscience in the satisfactory practice of all
Christian duties. London: for Richard Sare, 1715.
12°

T.619

6003
TENISON (Thomas) *Archbishop of Canterbury*.

A declaration of the Arch-bishop of Canterbury, and
the bishops in and near London, testifying their
abhorrence of the present rebellion ... London,
John Baskett, and by the assigns of Thomas Newcomb,
and Henry Hills, deceas'd, 1715. 4°

2 copies.

T.2

6004
A VINDICATION of her late Majesty Queen Anne, of
glorious memory; of his Grace the Duke of Ormonde; and
of the late ministry; from the horrid reflections
cast upon them in a late pamphlet, intitled, The
conduct of his Grace the Duke of Ormonde in the
campaign of 1712. London, for R. Burleigh, 1715. 8°

T.207

6005
WAKE (William) *Archbishop of Canterbury*.

The excellency, and benefits, of a religious
education. A sermon preach'd in the parish-church
of St. Sepulchre, June the ixth, 1715... at the
anniversary meeting of the children educated in
the charity-schools in and about the cities of
London and Westminster. By... William, Lord Bishop
of Lincoln. London, J. Downing for R. Sare, 1715.
4°

T.700

6006
WAKE (William) *Archbishop of Canterbury*.

A sermon preached before the King in St. James's
chapel, upon the thirtieth of January, 1715 ...
London, for Richard Sare, 1715. 8°

T.37

6007
WAKE (William) *Archbishop of Canterbury*.

A sermon preached before the King in St. James's
chapel, upon the first of August 1715: being the
first anniversary return of his Majesty's inauguration.
London: for Richard Sare, 1715. 8°

2 copies.

T.37   T.170

6008
WELLS (Edward)

A second letter to the Reverend Dr. Clarke ... being
an answer to the close of his Reply to Mr. Nelson:
together with part of two letters from Mr. Nelson,
wherein notice is taken of Dr. Clarke's most foul
quotations ... London, for Richard Smith, 1715. 8°

T.28

6009
WELTON (Richard)

The clergy's tears: or, A cry against persecution.
Humbly offer'd in a letter to the Lord Bishop of
London, in our present great distress and danger...
Printed in the year 1715. 8°

2 copies.

T.37   T.412

6010
WHATELY (Robert)

Mr. Burnet's defence: or, More reasons for an impeachment. In remarks on an infamous and trayterous libel,
lately published [by Daniel Defoe], entitled, A letter
to a merry young gentleman. In a second letter to ...
the Earl of Halifax [signed W.R.] ... London: J.
Roberts, 1715. 8°

T.207

6011
The WHOLE art of short and swift writing necessary
for all ministers of state, members of Parliament,
lawyers ... to write down speedily whatever they
hear or see done ... 3rd ed. London, printed in the
year 1715. 8°

T.402

6012
WILLIAMS (John) *Archbishop of York*.

The substance of the Archbishop of York's speech in
the House of Lords on the impeachment of the Earl
of Strafford. London, for R. Burleigh, 1715. Fol.

T.529

6013
WILLIS (Richard) *Bishop of Winchester*.

The way to stable and quiet times: a sermon preach'd
before the King... on the 20th of January, 1714.
Being the day of thanksgiving to almighty God for
bringing his Majesty to a peaceable and quiet
possession of the throne... By Richard Lord Bishop
of Glocester. London, for Matthew Wotton, 1715.
8°

T.37

6014
WITHERS (John)

The Whigs vindicated, the objections that are commonly
brought against them answer'd, and the present
ministry prov'd to be the best friends to the Church,
the monarchy, the lasting peace, and real welfare of
England ... The seventh edition corrected. London:
for John Clark, 1715. 8°

T.348

6015

The ALTERATION in the Triennial Act considered. [Attributed to Daniel Defoe.] London: for R. Burleigh, 1716.   8°

T.224

6016

ASGILL (John)

An abstract of the publick funds granted and continued to the Crown since 1 Wm. & M. and still existing ... 2nd ed. London, for J. Roberts, 1716.   4°

T.13

6017

BARRINGTON (John Shute) *Viscount*.

The layman's letter to the Bishop of Bangor: or, An examination of his Lordship's Preservative against the nonjurors ... [Anon.] London, printed: and sold by J. Roberts; J. Graves; and A. Dodd, 1716.   8°

T.400

6018

BENNET (Thomas) *D.D.*

The case of the reform'd episcopal churches in Great Poland and Polish Prussia consider'd, in a sermon preach'd on Sunday Nov. 18. 1716... London: for W. Innys, 1716.   8°

T.804

6019

BENNET (Thomas) *D.D.*

Dr. Bennet upon schism... London: for J. Smith, 1716.   8°

4 copies.

T.439   T.449   T.673

6020

BENNET (Thomas) *D.D.*

The Nonjurors separation from the public assemblys of the Church of England examin'd, and prov'd to be schismatical, upon their own principles. 2nd ed. London: for W. Innys, 1716.   8°

2 copies.

T.439   T.408

6021

BISSE (Thomas)

The beauty of holiness in the Common-prayer: as set forth in four sermons preach'd at the Rolls chapel. London: W.B. for Henry Clements, 1716.   8°

T.303

6022

BRERETON (Jane)

The fifth ode of the fourth book of Horace, imitated: and apply'd to the King. By a lady. London: for William Hinchliffe; and sold by J. Roberts, 1716. Fol.

T.529

6023

BURCHETT (Josiah)

Strife and envy, since the fall of man. A poem. London: for Edward Castle, 1716.   Fol.

T.529

6024

BURSCOUGH (William) *Bishop of Limerick*.

A sermon preach'd before the honourable House of Commons at St. Margaret's Westminster on the 29th of May 1716 ... London, for Tim. Childe, 1716. 8°

T.37

6025

CALLIERES (François de)

The art of negotiating with sovereign princes. Of the usefulness of negotiations, of the choice of ambassadors and envoys; and of the qualifications necessary for succeeding in those imployments. Translated from the French. London: for Geo. Strahan: Bern. Lintott, and J. Graves, 1716.   12°

T.392

6026

A CATALOGUE of medals from Julius Caesar to the Emperor Heraclius ... (Proposals for printing eleven dialogues explaining the use of medals, inscriptions and other antiquities. Written by Don Antonio Augustino.) London, 1716. 2 parts.   8°

Wanting title-page.

T.148

6027

A COLLECTION of the several papers deliver'd by Mr. J. Gordon, the Earl of Derwentwater [and others] ... As likewise an exact list of the names of all those who suffer'd death on account of the late rebellion ... London: for J. Jones, and sold by most booksellers in London and Westminster, [1716].   8°

2 copies.

T.368   T.224

6028

COLLIER (Jeremy)

A panegyrick upon the Maccabees, by St. Gregory Nazianzen: Of unseasonable diversions, by Salvian: A description of the manners of the pagan world ... by St. Cyprian. Done into English by Jeremy Collier. Together with two essays, viz. Of discontent and of gaming, by the same hand. London: for G. Strahan, 1716. 2 parts.   8°

T.92

6029

COLLIER (Jeremy)

A perswasive to consideration, tender'd to the Royalists; particularly those of the Church of England. [Anon.] The third edition, corrected. London, reprinted in the year, 1716.   8°

T.412

6030

CYPRIAN, *Saint*.

St. Cyprian's discourse to Donatus. Done into English metre, by W[illiam] T[unstall] in the Marshalsea. The second edition corrected... London: printed for the author, by E. Berington, 1716.   8°

T.35   T.225

6031

DAWSON (Thomas) *D.D.*

A vindication of the Church of England against the Nonjurors charge of schism ... London: for Henry Clements, 1716.   8°

T.408

6032

A DEFENSE of the Right Reverend Bishops of Rochester and Bristol: being a full answer to a late virulent pamphlet, entitul'd, Bishop Atterbury's and Bishop Smalridge's reasons for not signing the declaration, lately put forth by the Arch-bishop of Canterbury ... London, for A. Dodd: and sold by the booksellers of London and Westminster, 1716.   8°

T.299

6033

DEFOE (Daniel)

The layman's vindication of the Church of England, as well against Mr. Howell's charge of schism, as against Dr. Bennett's pretended answer to it. [Anon.] London, for A. and W. Bell: and sold by J. Baker, 1716. 8°

Moore 352.

T.439

6034

A DISSUASIVE against joining with the conventicles of Nonjurors; in a serious and earnest address to the subjects of Great Britain ... London, for R. Burleigh, 1716.   8°

2 copies.

T.408   T.439

6035

EARBERY (Matthias)

Elements of policy civil and ecclesiastical, in a mathematical method. By M.E... London: for John Morphew, 1716.   8°

2 copies.

T.155   T.483

6036

An ESSAY concerning the late apparition in the heavens, on the sixth of March. Proving ... that it cou'd not have been produced meerly by the ordinary course of nature, but must of necessity be a prodigy. Humbly offer'd to the consideration of the Royal Society ... London: for J. Morphew, 1716.   8°

T.92

6037

The ESTABLISH'D Church of England vindicated from the imputation of schism; in a serious address to all the members of her communion... London: for John Wyat, 1716.   8°

Attributed by Bowdler to Dr Hare; entered in N.U.C. under name of Benjamin Hoadly.

2 copies.

T.408   T.439

6038

EYRE (Richard)

A sermon preach'd at the funeral of the Honourable Sir Stephen Fox, knight, November 7. 1716. at Farly in Wilts. London: H. Clark, for Jonah Bowyer, 1716. 8°

T.37

6039

FLEETWOOD (William) *Bishop of Ely*.

A charge delivered to the clergy of the diocese of Ely at Cambridge, Aug. the VIIth. MDCCXVI. at his primary visitation. 2nd ed. Cambridge: printed at the University-Press, for Corn. Crownfield: and are to be sold by James Knapton; and J. Morphew, 1716. 4°

T.190

6040

FLEETWOOD (William) *Bishop of Ely*.

A sermon preach'd at Ely-house chapel in Holbourn; on Thursday June 7, 1716. Being the day of publick thanksgiving ... 2nd ed. London: for D. Midwinter, 1716.   8°

T.37

6041

FLEETWOOD (William) *Bishop of Ely*.

A sermon preach'd at Ely-house chapel in Holbourn; on Thursday June 7, 1716. Being the day of publick thanksgiving ... 6th ed. London: for D. Midwinter, 1716.   8°

T.170

6042

GAY (John)

Trivia: or, The art of walking the streets of London ... 2nd ed. London: for Bernard Lintot, [1716?] 8°

T.225

6043

GIBSON (Edmund) *Bishop of London*.

The deliverances and murmurings, of the Israelites, and these nations, compar'd. A sermon preach'd before the... House of Peers... on Thursday June 7, 1716. Being the day of publick-thanksgiving... By... Edmund, Lord Bishop of Lincoln. London: for John Churchill, 1716.   8°

2 copies.

T.37   T.170

6044

GIBSON (Edmund) *Bishop of London*.

The peculiar excellency and reward of supporting schools of charity. A sermon preach'd in the parish-church of St. Sepulchre, May the 24th, 1716 ... at the anniversary meeting of the children educated in the charity-schools in and about the cities of London and Westminster. By... Edmund, Lord Bishop of Lincoln. London, Joseph Downing, 1716.   4°

2 copies.

T.700   T.716

6045

GREAT BRITAIN. *Parliament*.

Several speeches against the Bill for repealing the Triennial Act: as they were spoken in the House of Commons, the 24th day of April, 1716. Together with the reasons given by the lords who protested against the said bill. London: for T. Jones, 1716.   Fol.

T.529

6046

GREAT BRITAIN. *Parliament*.

The tryal of George Earl of Wintoun, upon the articles of impeachment of high treason exhibited against him by the knights, citizens, and burgesses in Parliament assembled... London: for Jacob Tonson, 1716.   Fol.

T.529

6047

GREAT BRITAIN. *Parliament.*

The whole proceedings to judgment upon the articles of impeachment of high treason exhibited by the knights, citizens, and burgesses in Parliament assembled... against James Earl of Derwentwater, William Lord Widdrington [and others]... London: for Jacob Tonson, 1716. Fol.

T.529

6048

GREAT BRITAIN. *Parliament. House of Commons.*

An exact and correct list of the members of the House of Commons who voted for and against the Bill for repealing the Triennial-Act, 24. April 1716... Printed for T. Jones, 1716. Fol.

T.529

6049

HARE (Francis) *Bishop of Chichester.*

A sermon preach'd at the cathedral-church of Worcester, on the 1st of August, 1716... London: S. Buckley, 1716. 4º

T.771

6050

HICKES (George)

The last will and testament of the Reverend Dr. George Hickes. London: for E. Curll, 1716. 8º

T.402

6051

The HISTORY of publick and solemn state oaths. Containing all those that have been taken by the kings of England, at their coronation, or administer'd to the subjects upon several occasions ... London: for A. Bettesworth, and Jonas Browne, 1716. 8º

T.224

6052

HOADLY (Benjamin) *Bishop of Winchester.*

A preservative against the principles and practices of the Nonjurors both in Church and state ... By ... Benjamin, Lord Bishop of Bangor. 2nd ed. London: for James Knapton: and Timothy Childe, 1716. 8º

2 copies.

T.400 T.408

6053

HOADLY (Benjamin) *Bishop of Winchester.*

The restoration made a blessing to us, by the protestant succession. A sermon preach'd before the King at the royal chapel at St. James's, on the 29th of May, 1716 ... By ... Benjamin, Lord Bishop of Bangor. London: for James Knapton; and Timothy Childe, 1716. 8º

T.170

6054

HOADLY (Benjamin) *Bishop of Winchester.*

The restoration made a blessing to us, by the protestant succession. A sermon preach'd before the King at the royal chapel at St. James's, on the 29th of May, 1716 ... By ... Benjamin, Lord Bishop of Bangor. 3rd ed. London, for James Knapton; and Timothy Childe, 1716. 8º

T.37

6055

HOUGH (Nathaniel)

A sermon preach'd at the primary visitation of the Reverend Mr. Arch-deacon of Surrey ... Octob. 25. 1716. Wherein the new nonjuring schism is justly reprehended ... London: for B. Barker, and C. King; and sold by R. Burleigh, 1716. 8º

T.408

6056

KENNET (White) *Bishop of Peterborough.*

The faithful steward. A spital sermon, preach'd before... the Lord Mayor... and the governors of hospitals within the city of London, in St. Bridget's church, on... April 3d, 1716. London: for J. Churchill, 1716. 4º

T.702

6057

KENNET (White) *Bishop of Peterborough.*

A second letter to the Lord Bishop of Carlisle ... upon the subject of Bishop Merks; by occasion of seizing some libels, particularly a collection of papers written by the late R. Reverend George Hickes, D.D. London: Sam. Buckley, 1716. 8º

T.154

6058

KENNET (White) *Bishop of Peterborough.*

A second letter to the Lord Bishop of Carlisle... upon the subject of Bishop Merks; by occasion of seizing some libels particularly a collection of papers written by the late R. Reverend George Hickes, D.D. 2nd ed. London: Sam. Buckley, 1716. 8º

T.408

6059

KENNET (White) *Bishop of Peterborough.*

A thanksgiving-sermon for the blessing of God, in suppressing the late unnatural rebellion. Deliver'd in the parish-church of St. Mary Aldermary, in the city of London, on Thursday, the 7th of June, 1716. London: for J. Churchill, 1716. 8º

2 copies.

T.37 T.170

6060

KNAGGS (Thomas)

A sermon preach'd on Sunday the tenth of June ... at the parish-church of St. Giles in the Fields, 1716 ... London: for J. Pemberton, 1716. 8º

T.170

6061

LEE (Francis)

Considerations concerning oaths. [Anon.] [No imprint, 1716.] 8º

T.154

6062

A LETTER to a country gentleman, shewing the inconveniences, which attend the last part of the Act for triennial Parliaments ... [Attributed to Daniel Defoe.] London, J. Roberts, 1716. 8º

T.224

6063

A LETTER to Doctor Bennet, requiring farther satisfaction in relation to the charge of schism against the Non-jurors. By a lay-man of the Doctor's communion... London, for J. Roberts, [1716]. 8º

Attributed by Bowdler to Matthias Earbery.
2 copies.

T.408 T.439

6064

MARTIN (Josiah)

A letter to the author [i.e. Benjamin Coole] of Some brief observations on the paraphrase and notes of the judicious John Locke, relating to the womens exercising their spiritual gifts in the Church. London: printed in the year, 1716. 8º

T.377

6065

MEMOIRS of the life and times of the most reverend ... Dr. Thomas Tennison, late Archbishop of Canterbury... 3rd ed. London: for J. Roberts, [1716?] 8º

T.822

6066

MEMOIRS relating to the restoration of King James I. of Scotland ... London: for W. Jones, 1716. 8º

2 copies.

T.403 T.412

6067

The METHODS used for erecting charity-schools, with the rules and orders by which they are governed. A particular account of the London charity-schools: with a list of those erected elsewhere... The fifteenth edition, with additions. London, Joseph Downing, 1716. 4º

T.700

6068

MILBOURNE (Luke)

Good princes and faithful counsellors, the blessings of a repenting nation. In a sermon preach'd May the 29th, 1716. at St. Ethelburga's. London: for G. Sawbridge, 1716. 8º

T.37

6069

MR. W----k's speech against the Bill for repealing the Triennial Act, whilst it was depending in the H--se of C----ns. London: for J. Smith, [1716]. 8º

Perhaps the speech of William Wykes, M.P. for Northampton.

T.390

6070

MYNORS (Willoughby)

Comfort under affliction. A sermon preach'd at the parish-church of S. Mary White-chappel, on Thursday, March 15. 1715-16. being the evening when the late disturbance happen'd there. London: for John Morphew, 1716. 8º

T.170

6071

MYNORS (Willoughby)

True loyalty; or, Non-resistance the only support of monarchy. A sermon preach'd at S. Pancras, Middlesex, on Sunday, June 10. 1716. London: for John Morphew, 1716. 8º

3 copies.

T.37 T.100 T.170

6072

N.(N.)

A letter to the Reverend the Dean of Chichester, on occasion of some passages in his thanksgiving-sermon before the House of Commons on June the 7th, 1716 ... London: for E. Matthews, and sold by J. Harrison, and A Boulter, 1716. 8º

T.390

6073

ONANIA, or the heinous sin of self-pollution, and all its frightful consequences, in both sexes, considered. With spiritual and physical advice to those who have already injur'd themselves by this abominable practice. The third edition, corrected ... London: E.R. and sold by P. Varenne, [1716?] 8º

T.148

6074

A PRACTICAL scheme. Of the secret disease ... Dedicated to Dr. Chamberlaine. 15th ed. London: H. Parker, 1716. 8º

T.148

6075

RADCLIFFE (James) *Earl of Derwentwater.*

The speech of James Earl of Derwentwater: who was beheaded on Tower-Hill, for high treason... February the 24th, 1715/16. London, S. Crouch and A. Bell, 1716. Fol.

Wanting title-page.

T.529

6076

RUSSELL (John) *Rector of Postwick.*

A sermon concerning peoples knowing the things that belong to their peace, before they be hid from their eyes. Preach'd in the cathedral church of Norwich: upon the xxxth day of January, 1715. Norwich: W. Chase, 1715/16. 8º

T.170

6077

RUSSELL (Richard)

The obligation of acting according to conscience, especially as to oaths. A farewel sermon preached Jan.22. 1715/6... [Anon.] London, for J. Roberts, 1716. 8º

3 copies.

T.37 T.100 T.154

6078

SAMUEL, *Patriarch of Alexandria.*

Lachrymae & suspiria Ecclesiae Graecae: or, The distressed state of the Greek Church. Humbly represented in a letter to her late Majesty Queen Anne, from the Patriarch of Alexandria; by the hands of Arsenius Archbishop of Thebais, now residing in London... London, printed in the year 1716... 4º

T.660

6079

SANDERSON (Robert) *Bishop of Lincoln.*

A discourse concerning the nature and obligation of oaths. Wherein all the cases which have any relation to oaths enjoyned by governments, are briefly considered. London, for J. Roberts, 1716. 8º

T.154

6080

A SEASONABLE speech made by a worthy member of Parliament in the House of Commons, concerning the Other House. Mar. 1659. [Attributed to Silas Titus and to the Earl of Shaftesbury.] London, John Morphew, 1716. 4º

T.267

6081

A SECOND letter to a friend in Suffolk, occasion'd
by repealing the Triennial Act. With a copy of the
Bill now depending in the House of Commons.
[Attributed to Daniel Defoe.] London: printed in
the year 1716. [Col: for W. Wilkins.]   8°

T.224

6082

SEELEN (Johann Heinrich von)

Q.D.B.V. Lutherus de scholis optime meritus sive
de praeclaris rebus, quibus Lutherus scholas
ornavit, oratio... Accedit Consilium B. Lutheri
de bibliothecis... Flensburgi sumtu Balthasaris
Ottonis Bosseckii, typis Christophori Vogelii,
[1716].   4°

T.793

6083

The SEVERAL depositions concerning the late riot
in Oxford. London: for John Morphew, 1716.   8°

2 copies.

T.238 T.462

6084

SHEFFIELD (John) *Duke of Buckingham.*

The Earl of Mulgrave's speech spoken in the House
of Lords, for the Bill touching free and impartial
proceedings in Parliament. London: for S. Popping,
1716. Fol.

T.529

6085

SHERLOCK (Thomas) *Bishop of London.*

A sermon preach'd before the honourable House of
Commons, at St. Margaret's Westminster, on
Thursday, the 7th of June, 1716. Being the day of
publick thanksgiving to Almighty God, for
suppressing the late unnatural rebellion. 3rd ed.
London: for J. Pemberton, 1716.   8°

2 copies.

T.37 T.170

6086

SMITH (Joseph)

The difference between the Nonjurors and the present
publick assemblies, not a real, but accidental
schism. [Anon.] London: printed for and sold by J.
Morphew, 1716.   8°

"Said to be by Bp Atterbury".

T.439   T.408

6087

SOME arguments made use of in the Bishop of Bangor's
Preservative against the principles and practices of
the nonjurors, briefly consider'd. By a lay-man.
London: for J. Morphew: and E. Berrington, 1716.   8°

2 copies.

T.295 T.400

6088

SOME rules for speaking and action; to be observed
at the bar, in the pulpit, and the senate, and by
every one that speaks in publick. In a letter to
a friend... The third edition, with additions...
London: for W. Mears, 1716.   8°

T.788

6089

SOUTH (Robert)

Comprehension and toleration consider'd; in a sermon
preach'd at the close of the last century. [Anon.]
London: for A. Moore, 1716.   8°

T.804

6090

The SPIRITUAL intruder unmask'd: in a letter from
the orthodox in White-chappel, to Dr. Shippen ...
London: for James Uplit, and sold by the booksellers
of London and Westminster, 1716.   8°

"To the Hond. Mr. Bowdler."

T.92

6091

STILEMAN (Timothy)

A short answer to the charge of schism laid upon the
Church of England, shewing that our adversaries have
not made good their charge ... London: for R. and J.
Bonwicke, 1716.   8°

2 copies.

T.439 T.408

6092

The SUSPENSION of the Triennial Act the certain way to
unite the nation. Printed in the year 1716.   4°

T.267

6093

SYKES (Arthur Ashley)

An answer to the Nonjurors charge of schism upon the
Church of England. Written by a clergyman of the
Church of England. London, for James Knapton, 1716.
8°

2 copies.

T.439 T.408

6094

SYNGE (Edward) *Archbishop of Tuam.*

The sin of schism most unjustly and groundlesly
charged by the Nonjurors upon the present
establish'd Church of England, and the charge made
good against themselves. In a letter to a Nonjuring
clergyman [i.e. Laurence Howell]. [Anon.] London:
for Richard Sare, and sold by John Morphew, 1716.   8°

2 copies.

T.408 T.439

6095

TALBOT (William) *Bishop of Durham.*

A sermon preach'd before the King at St. James's-
chapel, on Thursday, June 7. 1716. Being the day
of publick thanksgiving to almighty God, for
supppressing [sic] the late unnatural rebellion. By
... William Lord Bishop of Sarum. London: for John
Churchill; and Jonah Bowyer, 1716.   8°

2 copies.

T.37 T.170

6096

TIPPING (William)

An account of Tipping's pleasant liquor; which
dissolves the stone in the bladder, or kidneys,
bringing it away visibly ... [No imprint, 1716?] 8°

T.148

6097

The TRIENNIAL Act impartially stated ... [Attributed
to Daniel Defoe.] London: for J. Grantham, 1716.
8°

T.224

6098

A TRUE and particular account of the battle of
Sheriff-muir: with an exact list of all the nobility,
general officers, chiefs of clans, and number of
private men, in the King's army in Scotland... By
an officer of the King's army. Printed in the year
1716.   8°

T.438

6099

TUNSTALL (William)

Ballads and some other occasional poems: by W[illiam]
T[unstall] in the Marshalsea ... London: E. Berington,
for the benefit of the author, 1716.   8°

T.242

6100

A VINDICATION of the Non-juring Church, and the
reasonableness of Mr. Paul, and Esq; Hall's embracing
the communion of those orthodox members ... who have
stood stedfast to the doctrine of ... the Church of
England ... London: printed in the year 1716.   4°

2 copies.

T.637 T.197

6101

WAKE (William) *Archbishop of Canterbury.*

A vindication of the realm, and Church of England,
from the charge of perjury, rebellion & schism,
unjustly laid upon them by the Non-jurors: and the
rebellion and schism shewn to lie at their own doors.
[Anon.] London: for J. Morphew, 1716.   8°

2 copies.

T.439 T.408

6102

WATERLAND (Theodore)

A sermon preach'd before the University of Cambridge,
on Wednesday the 1st of August, 1716. Being the
anniversary of his Majesty's happy accession to the
throne. Cambridge: printed at the University-press,
for Corn. Crownfield: and are to be sold by James
Knapton; and J. Morphew, 1716.   8°

T.170

6103

WEST (Richard) *Lord Chancellor of Ireland.*

A discourse concerning treasons, and bills of
attainder ... [Anon.] London: for J. Roberts, 1716.
8°

T.207

6104

The WHOLE life and character of Richard Gascoigne,
Esq; one of the rebels, who was executed at Tiburn
for high treason, on Friday the 25 of May, 1716...
Printed by E. Beardwell in Fleetstreet, 1716.   8°

T.402

1717

6105

ALI IBN ABI TALIB, *Caliph.*

Sentences of Ali son-in-law of Mahomet, and his fourth
successor. Translated from an authentick Arabick
manuscript in the Bodleian Library at Oxford, by Simon
Ockley ... London, for Bernard Lintot, 1717.   8°

T.92

6106

ALLIBOND (John)

A seasonable sketch of an Oxford reformation. Written
originally in Latin by John Allibond, D.D. and now
reprinted, with an English version [by Edward Ward]
... London printed: and sold by John Morphew, 1717.
8°

T.225

6107

An ANSWER, to this important inquiry, Whether it be
lawful for a Christian, to join in prayers for a
prince in possession, whom he believes in conscience
to be an usurper? ... London: for J. Roberts, 1717.
8°

2 copies.

T.439 T.408

6108

An APOLOGY for such of the episcopal clergy in
Scotland as are non-jurors ... 2nd ed. London: for
A. Smith, 1717.   8°

T.155

6109

BARRINGTON (John Shute) *Viscount.*

The layman's second letter to the Bishop of Bangor: or,
An examination of his Lordship's sermon before the
King. And of Dr. Snape's Letter to his Lordship.
[Anon.] London: J. Roberts; J. Graves; and A. Dodd,
1717.   8°

2 copies.

T.394 T.295

6110

BEDFORD (Hilkiah)

A vindication of the late Archbishop Sancroft, and
of his brethren the rest of the depriv'd bishops,
from the reflections of Mr. Marshal in his Defence
of our constitution in Church and State... In a
letter to a friend. [Anon.] London, for John
Morphew, 1717.   8°

3 copies.

T.245 T.300 T.656

6111

BRETT (Thomas)

Dr. Bennet's concessions to the Non-jurors prov'd to
be destructive of the cause, which he endeavours to
defend ... In a letter to a friend ... [Anon.]
London: for John Morphew, 1717.   8°

2 copies.

T.439   T.408

6112

BRETT (Thomas)

The independency of the Church upon the state, as to
its pure spiritual powers ... London: for Henry
Clements, 1717.   8°

2 copies (one incomplete).

T.525

6113

BROOME (   )

Wednesday club-law: or, The injustice, dishonour,
and ill policy of breaking into parliamentary con-
tracts for publick debts ... [Anon.] London: for
E. Smith, and A. Dodd, 1717.   8°

2 copies.

T.224 T.87

6114

BURDETT (J.)

A letter from Mr. J. Burdett, who was executed on Friday, Febr. 1. at Tyburn, for the murder of Captain Falkner, to some attorneys clerks of his acquaintance... London, for J. Baker and T. Warner, 1717.   8°

T.390

6115

BURNET (*Sir* Thomas)

An answer to A letter to the Bishop of Bangor, written by one Andrew Snap... [Anon.] London, for T. Warner, 1717.   8°

T.400

6116

BURNET (*Sir* Thomas)

An answer to A letter to the Bishop of Bangor, written by one Andrew Snap ... [Anon.] 2nd ed. London: for T. Warner, 1717.   8°

T.295

6117

BURNET (*Sir* Thomas) *and* DUCKETT (George)

A summary of all the religious houses in England and Wales, with their titles and valuations at the time of their dissolution ... [Anon.] London, for James Knapton, and Timothy Childe, 1717.   8°

T.435

6118

BUSBY (Richard)

Hebraicae grammatices rudimenta. In usum Scholae Westmonasteriensis. [Anon.] Londini, 1717.   8°

T.789

6119

CANNON (Robert)

A vindication of the proceedings of the lower house of Convocation, with regard to the King's supremacy. On the 3d and 10th of May, 1717... London, for Jos. Fox, B. Barker, and C. King; and sold by J. Morphew, 1717.   8°

T.603

6120

CHURCH OF ENGLAND. *Book of Common Prayer.*

The form and manner of consecrating and administring the holy communion, according to the liturgy of King Edward VI. called The book of common prayer, and administration of the sacraments ... after the use of the Church of England ... London: H. Parker, for J. Morphew, 1717.   8°

2 copies.

T.303   T.343

6121

CHURCH OF ENGLAND. *Convocation. Lower House.*

A report of the committee of the lower house of Convocation, appointed to draw up a representation to be laid before the Arch-bishop and bishops ... concerning several dangerous positions and doctrines, contained in the Bishop of Bangor's Preservative, and his sermon preach'd March 31, 1717 ... 2nd ed. London: for John Morphew, 1717.   Fol.

T.400

6122

CHURCH OF ENGLAND. *Convocation. Lower House.*

A report of the committee of the lower house of Convocation, appointed to draw up a representation to be laid before the Arch-bishop and bishops ... concerning several dangerous positions and doctrines contained in the Bishop of Bangor's Preservative, and his sermon preached March 31. 1717 ... 5th ed. London: for John Morphew, 1717.   8°

T.400

6123

CLAYTON (David)

A short but thorough search into what may be the real cause of the present scarcity of our silver coin ... By a hearty well-wisher of the peace and prosperity of his country. London, printed for the author, and sold by James Roberts, 1717.   8°

T.484

6124

COCKBURN (John)

Answers to queries concerning some important points of religion. Occasion'd by a late sermon of ... the Lord Bishop of Bangor, at S. James's chappel. London: for John Morphew, 1717.   8°

2 copies.

T.394   T.295

6125

COLLIER (Jeremy)

Reasons for restoring some prayers and directions, as they stand in the communion-service of the first English reform'd liturgy ... [Anon.] London: for John Morphew, 1717.   8°

T.303

6126

COLLIER (Jeremy)

Some considerations on Doctor Kennet's Second and Third letters. Wherein his misrepresentations of Mr. Collier's Ecclesiast. history are lay'd open; and his calumnies disprov'd. London: John Morphew, 1717.   8°

2 copies.

T.155   T.408

6127

COLLINS (Charles)

Howell and Hoadly; or, The Church of England crucify'd between two ———— . Being an account of the fatal effects of religious differences in all ages; with some thoughts of what may be the consequences to the Church of England, from the present dispute... London: for S. Baker, 1717.   8°

T.295

6128

COLLINS (Samuel)

Paradise retriev'd: plainly and fully demonstrating the most beautiful, durable, and beneficial method of managing and improving fruit-trees against walls, or in hedges ... Together with a treatise on mellons and cucumbers ... London: for John Collins; and sold by him, and R. Burleigh, 1717.   8°

T.482

6129

The CONVOCATION anatomized. Being a brief examination of the proceedings against the Ld. Bp. of Bangor's writings: by the lower house of Convocation. London: for T. Warner, 1717.   8°

T.167

6130

CONVOCATION-craft: or, A brief history of the intrigues, and insolence, of English convocations under the Papacy, till restrain'd by King Henry VIII ... Occasion'd by the proceedings of the lower house against the Bishop of Bangor ... London: for S. Baker, 1717.   8°

T.298

6131

CRAVEN (Joseph)

Two letters to the Reverend Dr. Bentley, master of Trinity-College in Cambridge, concerning his intended edition of the Greek Testament. Together with the Doctor's answer ... [Anon.] London: for John Morphew, 1717.   8°

T.92

6132

CUMMINGS (George)

Justice done to the sacred text, and the true nature of the kingdom, or Church of Christ asserted. A sermon preach'd at the chapel in Queen's Square ... on Sunday, May 12, 1717. By G.C. London, printed for the author: and sold by J. Morphew, 1717.   8°

T.298

6133

DEFOE (Daniel)

An argument proving that the design of employing and enobling foreigners, is a treasonable conspiracy against the constitution... [Anon.] London, printed for the booksellers of London and Westminster, 1717. 8°

Moore 359.

2 copies.

T.462   T.484

6134

DEFOE (Daniel)

A declaration of truth to Benjamin Hoadly, one of the high priests of the land, and of the degree whom men call bishops. By a ministring friend, who writ to Tho. Bradbury... London: for E. More, and sold by the booksellers of London and Westminster, 1717.   8°

Moore 379.

T.295

6135

DEFOE (Daniel)

Faction in power: or, The mischiefs and dangers of a High-Church magistracy ... [Anon.] London: for R. Burleigh, 1717.   8°

Moore 357.

T.462

6136

DEFOE (Daniel)

Fair payment no spunge: or, Some considerations on the unreasonableness of refusing to receive back money lent on publick securities ... [Anon.] London, J. Brotherton and W. Meddows, and J. Roberts, 1717. 8°

Moore 363.

T.87

6137

DEFOE (Daniel)

Secret memoirs of a treasonable conference at S[omerset] House, for deposing the present ministry, and making a new turn at court. [Anon.] London, for J. More, 1717.   8°

Moore 354.

T.462

6138

DEFOE (Daniel)

A vindication of Dr. Snape, in answer to several libels lately publish'd against him. With some further remarks on the Bishop of Bangor's sermon... [Anon.] London: for A. Dodd, [1717].   8°

Moore 375.

T.295

6139

DOD (Thomas)

The rule of equity. A sermon preach'd at the assizes held at Oxford, March 14. 1716/17 ... Oxford, printed at the Theatre for Hen. Clements, 1717.   8°

T.170

6140

EARBERY (Matthias)

An historical essay upon the power of the prince, in calling, proroguing and dissolving councils, synods and convocations... London; for J. Morphew, 1717.   8°

3 copies.

T.238   T.482   T.550

6141

EARBERY (Matthias)

The history of the clemency of our English monarchs. The usage prisoners, who surrender'd at discretion, have met with from their hands ... By M.E. London; printed for the author, 1717.   8°

2 copies.

T.412   T.155

6142

EARBERY (Matthias)

The old English constitution vindicated, and set in a true light. Offer'd to the consideration of the Bishop of Bangor... By M.E... London: printed in the year, 1717   8°

3 copies.

T.298   T.400   T.483

6143

EARBERY (Matthias)

A serious admonition to Doctor Kennet, in order to perswade him to forbear the character of an impartial historian. Illustrated with numerous instances of false quotations, collected from his Third letter concerning Bp. Merks... London: for E. Smith, [1717].   8°

3 copies.

T.155   T.300   T.408

6144

An EARNEST exhortation for making up the breach between the Establish'd Church and the Non-jurors. In a letter to the Reverend Mr. Marshall ... Occasioned by his Defence of our constitution against the Non-jurors charge of heresy ... London: for John Morphew, 1717.   8°

T.300

6145

ESSAYS on the national constitution, bank, credit, and trade. London: for John Morphew, 1717.   8°

T.13

6146

FARTHER remarks on the Reverend Dr. Snape's Second letter to ... the Lord Bishop of Bangor ... To which is added, an appendix. Being a full answer to Mr. Law's Letter to ... the Lord Bishop of Bangor, so far as it relates to his Lordship's Preservative against the principles and practices of the Nonjurors. By the author of the former Remarks. London: for Timothy Childe, 1717.   8°

T.295

6147

GAY (John)

Three hours after marriage. A comedy, as it is acted at the Theatre Royal ... London: for Bernard Lintot, 1717.   8°

Apparently by Gay, Pope and Arbuthnot.

T.225

6148

GIBSON (Edmund) *Bishop of London.*

The charge of Edmund Lord Bishop of Lincoln, at his primary visitation, begun in the year 1717. [London, 1717.]   4°

T.340

6149

The GREAT Jesuit swallows the less: or, A defence of Tom o'Bedlam's first letter to Mons. Francis de la Pillonniere, a Jesuit now living with the Bp. of Bangor ... London, John Morphew, [1717].   8°

T.167

6150

GYLLENBORG (Carl) *and others.*

Letters which passed between Count Gyllenborg, the Barons Gortz, Sparre, and others; relating to the design of raising a rebellion in his Majesty's dominions, to be supported by a force from Sweden. London: S. Buckley, 1717.   Fol.

T.529

6151

H. (D.)

A letter to the scholars of Eton: occasioned by their master Dr. Snape's Letter to the Bishop of Bangor. London: J. Roberts, 1717.   8°

2 copies.

T.295 T.400

6152

HART (Edward)

The lay-man's vindication of the Convocations charge against the Bishop of Bangor: being some animadversions on the Report reported, &c. By the author of the Bulwork storm'd ... London: H. Parker, and sold by J. Morphew: and E. Smith, 1717.   8°

T.167

6153

HAYLEY (Thomas)

The liberty of the Gospel explained, and recommended. A sermon preached before the Incorporated Society for the Propagation of the Gospel in Foreign Parts; at their anniversary meeting... 15th of February, 1716. London, Joseph Downing, 1717.   4°

T.625

6154

HENDLEY (William)

An appeal to the consciences and common sense of the Christian laity, whether the Bishop of Bangor in his Preservative, &c. hath not given up the rights of the Church ... London: for J. Morphew, 1717.   8°

T.295

6155

HILLIARD (Samuel)

The nature of the Kingdom, or Church of Christ, as set forth in holy Scripture. In a sermon preach'd at St. Margt. Lothbury, London. June 2. 1717. Occasioned by the Bishop of Bangor's notions lately published upon that subject ... London: printed for the author, and sold by J. Morphew, [1717].   8°

T.170

6156

HIND (Thomas)

The divinity of our Saviour prov'd from the Scriptures of the Old and New Testament. In a sermon preached before the University of Oxford... July 7. 1717... Oxford, printed at the Theater, for Anthony Peisley: and are to be sold by J. Knapton, H. Clements, J. Morphew, and W. Meadows, booksellers in London, [1717].   8°

T.804

6157

HOADLY (Benjamin) *Bishop of Winchester.*

An answer to the Reverend Dr. Snape's Letter to the Bishop of Bangor. By ... Benjamin Lord Bishop of Bangor. 5th ed. London, for James Knapton, and Timothy Childe, 1717.   8°

T.400

6158

HOADLY (Benjamin) *Bishop of Winchester.*

An answer to the Reverend Dr. Snape's Letter to the Bishop of Bangor. By ... Benjamin Lord Bishop of Bangor. 7th ed. London, for James Knapton, and Timothy Childe, 1717.   8°

T.295

6159

HOADLY (Benjamin) *Bishop of Winchester.*

The nature of the kingdom, or Church, of Christ. A sermon preach'd before the King, at the royal chapel at St. James's, on Sunday March 31, 1717. By ... Benjamin Lord Bishop of Bangor. London, for James Knapton, and Timothy Childe, 1717.   8°

T.295

6160

HOADLY (Benjamin) *Bishop of Winchester.*

The nature of the kingdom, or Church, of Christ. A sermon preach'd before the King, at the royal chapel at St. James's, on Sunday March 31, 1717. By... Benjamin Lord Bishop of Bangor. 9th ed. London, for James Knapton, and Timothy Childe, 1717.   8°

T.603

6161

HOADLY (Benjamin) *Bishop of Winchester.*

The nature of the kingdom, or Church, of Christ. A sermon preach'd before the King, at the royal chapel at St. James's, on Sunday March 31, 1717. By ... Benjamin Lord Bishop of Bangor. 10th ed. London, for James Knapton, and Timothy Childe, 1717.   8°

T.400

6162

KENNET (White) *Bishop of Peterborough.*

A third letter to the Lord Bishop of Carlisle ... upon the subject of Bishop Merks; wherein the nomination, election, investiture, and deprivation of English prelates, are shew'd to have been originally constituted and govern'd by the sovereign power of kings ... London: Sam. Buckley, 1717.   8°

T.154

6163

LAMBE (Charles)

Stedfastness to the protestant religion and to the King, recommended upon the alarm of an invasion from Sweden. In a sermon preach'd at Richmond, Sunday March 24 ... the day of the general assize for the county of Surry ... London, for W. Hinchliffe, and J. Walthoe; and sold also by J. Roberts, 1717.   8°

T.170

6164

LA PILLONNIERE (François de)

An answer to the Reverend Dr. Snape's accusation. Containing an account of his behaviour, and sufferings, amongst the Jesuits ... With a preface, by the Lord Bishop of Bangor. London: for James Knapton, and Tim. Childe, [1717]. 2 parts.   8°

T.396

6165

LA PILLONNIERE (François de)

An answer to the Reverend Dr. Snape's accusation. Containing an account of his behaviour, and sufferings, amongst the Jesuits ... With a preface, by the Lord Bishop of Bangor. 2nd ed. London: for James Knapton, and Tim Childe, [1717]. 2 parts.   8°

T.167

6166

● LAURENCE (John) *Rector of Yelvertoft.*

The clergy-man's recreation: shewing the pleasure and profit of the art of gardening... 5th ed. London: for Bernard Lintot, 1717.   8°

T.518

6167

LAURENCE (John) *Rector of Yelvertoft.*

The gentleman's recreation: or the second part of the art of gardening improved... 2nd ed. London: for Bernard Lintot, 1717.   8°

T.518

6168

LAW (William)

The Bishop of Bangor's late sermon, and his letter to Dr. Snape in defence of it, answer'd. And the dangerous nature of some doctrines in his Preservative, set forth in a letter to his Lordship. London, for W. Innys, 1717.   8°

T.662

6169

LAW (William)

The Bishop of Bangor's late sermon, and his letter to Dr. Snape in defence of it, answer'd. And the dangerous nature of some doctrines in his Preservative, set forth in a letter to his Lordship. 2nd ed. London, for W. Innys, 1717.   8°

2 copies.

T.394 T.189

6170

LAW (William)

The Bishop of Bangor's late sermon, and his letter to Dr. Snape in defence of it, answer'd. And the dangerous nature of some doctrines in his Preservative, set forth in a letter to his Lordship. 5th ed. London, for W. Innys, 1717.   8°

T.295

6171

LAW (William)

A second letter to the Bishop of Bangor; wherein his Lordship's notions of benediction, absolution, and Church-communion are prov'd to be destructive of every institution of the Christian religion... London: for W. Innys, 1717.   8°

2 copies.

T.396 T.654

6172

The LAYMAN'S humble address to the bishops and clergy in Convocation assembled, concerning an attempt to subvert the Christian faith, lately made by Sam. Clarke... London: for Charles Rivington; and sold by John Morphew, 1717.   8°

T.400

6173

A LETTER from a gentleman to Dr. Snape, in answer to his Letter to the Bishop of Bangor. London: for John Wyat, 1717.   8°

T.295

6174

A LETTER from the Right Reverend G-lb-rt, late Lord Bishop of S[aru]m, to the Right Reverend B-nj-m-n, L[or]d B[isho]p of B[a]ng[o]r ... London, for J. Morphew, 1717.   8°

This pamphlet is divided between volumes 99 and 238.

T.99 T.238

6175

A LETTER from Tom o'Bedlam, to the B[ishop] of B[ango]r's Jesuit [i.e. François de la Pillonnière] ... London: J. Sackfield, and J. Morphew, 1717.   8°

T.169

6176

A LETTER from Tom o' Bedlam, to the B[ishop] of B[ango]r's Jesuit [i.e. François de la Pillonnière]... 2nd ed. London: J. Sackfield, and J. Morphew, 1717.   8°

T.526

6177

A LETTER to a member of Parliament: shewing the justice of a more equal and impartial assessment on land ... and the ease of reducing by degrees the debts of the nation ... 2nd ed. London: J. Roberts, 1717.   8°

T.87

6178

A LETTER to a Non-juring clergyman, concerning the schism charged upon the Church of England ... London: H.P. for John Morphew, 1717.   8°

T.408

6179

A LETTER to Dr. Andrew Snape, occasioned by his letter to the Bishop of Bangor. 2nd ed. London: J. Roberts, 1717.   8°

2 copies.

T.394 T.295

6180

A LETTER to Dr. Snape, occasion'd by his letter to the Bishop of Bangor. Wherein the doctor is answer'd and expos'd, paragraph by paragraph. By a layman of conscience and common sense. 3rd ed. London, printed; and sold by J. Roberts, 1717.   8°

T.394

6181

A LETTER to the Reverend Dr. Snape; occasion'd by
a passage in his sermon before the honble House of
Commons, on Wednesday, the 29th of May, 1717.
London: for John Morphew, 1717.   8°

Attributed by Bowdler to Mrs Astell.
2 copies.

T.37   T.295

6182

M. (L.)

A short narrative of the life and death of John
Rhinholdt Count Patkul, a nobleman of Livonia,
who was broke alive upon the wheel in Great Poland,
anno 1707... Faithfully translated out of a High
Dutch manuscript... By L.M... [Attributed to
Daniel Defoe.] London: for T. Goodwin, 1717.   8°

T.446

6183

MACKWORTH (*Sir* Humphrey)

Down with the mug: or, Reasons for suppressing the
mug-houses; humbly offer'd to the consideration
of the Parliament of Great-Britain. By Sir H.M.
London: for John Morphew, 1717.   8°

T.462

6184

MARSHALL (Nathaniel)

A defence of our constitution in Church and State: or,
An answer to the late charge of the Non-jurors,
accusing us of heresy and schism ... London: H. Parker
for William Taylor: and Henry Clements, 1717.   8°

T.300

6185

MEIRS (John)

A short treatise compos'd and published by John Meirs,
formerly a Jew, now ... converted to the Christian
faith ... London: reprinted for the author, 1717.   4°

T.340

6186

METHODS used for erecting charity-schools, with
the rules and orders by which they are governed.
A particular account of the London charity-schools:
with a list of those erected elsewhere... The
sixteenth edition, with additions. London, Joseph
Downing, 1717.   4°

T.702

6187

A MODERATE censure of doctrines contain'd in a sermon
preach'd before his Majesty; and a book intituled
A preservative against Nonjurors, by the Lord Bishop
of Bangor, which are fairly and exactly consider'd.
By a lover of the present establish'd government in
Church and State, under his Majesty King George ...
London, for J. Morphew, 1717.   8°

T.298

6188

A MODEST enquiry into the Bishop of Bangor's
Preservative against the Nonjurors. Humbly offer'd
to the consideration of his Lordship ... London: for
C. Rivington; and sold by J. Morphew, 1717.   8°

T.295

6189

MOULD (Bernard)

A sermon preach'd before... the deputy governor and
the Company of Merchants trading to the Levant-seas
... January 8, 1716. London, J. Humfreys, for
Thomas Ward, 1717.   4°

T.765

6190

MYNORS (Willoughby)

A sermon preached May 29. Being the anniversary of
the restoration of K. Charles II. London: printed
for the author, and sold by [the rest is cut away]
[1717].   8°

T.39

6191

NICOLSON (William) *Bishop of Carlisle.*

A collection of papers scatter'd lately about the
town in the Daily-Courant, St. James's-Post, &c.
With some remarks upon them. In a letter from the
Bishop of Carlile to the Bishop of Bangor.
London: for B. Barker and C. King, 1717.   8°

3 copies.

T.169   T.295   T.394

6192

NOAILLES (Louis Antoine de) *Cardinal.*

The act of appeal of his Eminence the Cardinal of
Noailles, Archbishop of Paris... to the Pope better
advis'd, and to the future general council; from
the constitution of our Holy Father, Pope Clement
Xl. London: for J. Roberts, 1717.   8°

T.521

6193

The OECONOMY of his Majesty's Navy-office. Containing
the several duties of the commissioners and principal
officers thereof ... By an officer of the Navy.
London, for Jonas Browne, and Richard Mount, 1717.
12°

T.392

6194

PARKER (Edward) *pseud.*

A complete key to the new farce, call'd Three hours
after marriage. With an account of the authors
[i.e. John Gay, Alexander Pope and John Arbuthnot.]
... (A true character of Mr. Pope, &c. [by John
Dennis].) London: E. Berrington, 1717.   2 parts.
8°

T.225

6195

PATERSON (William)

An enquiry into the state of the union of Great
Britain, and the past and present state of the trade
and publick revenues thereof ... By the Wednesday's
Club in Friday-street. 2nd ed. London: for A. and
W. Bell; and J. Watts: and sold by B. Barker and C.
King; W. Mears and J. Brown; W. Taylor, J. Brotherton
and W. Meddows, and J. Roberts, 1717.   8°

T.87

6196

PEIRCE (James)

A letter to Dr. Bennet, occasion'd by his late
treatise concerning the Non-jurors separation, &c.
2nd ed. London: for John Clark, 1717.   8°

T.300

6197

A PHILOSOPHICAL enquiry into the tenets of the Bishop
of Bangor, as deliver'd in his late inimitable sermon
and answer to Dr. Snape ... By a gentleman ... London:
J. Morphew, 1717.   8°

T.298

6198

A PRESERVATIVE against the Bishop of Bangor's sermon:
or, The Church of England defended, in opposition to
the pernicious doctrines and designs lately advanced
against her ... London: for J. Morphew, 1717.   8°

T.295

6199

PRIOR (Matthew)

The dove. A poem... [Anon.] London: for J.
Roberts, 1717.   Fol.

T.529

6200

RAWLINSON (Richard)

The conduct of the Reverend Dr. White Kennet ... from
the year 1681, to the present time. Being a supplement
to his three letters to the Bishop of Carlisle, upon
the subject of Bishop Merks. By an impartial hand ...
London: Charles King, 1717.   8°

2 copies.

T.408   T.155

6201

The REHEARSAL: or, A brief recapitulation of all,
or most of the arguments for and against the Bishop
of Bangor's sermon preach'd before the King, on
Sunday the 31st day of March, 1717... By a true
lover of our happy constitution both in Church
and State. London: for S. Baker, 1717.   8°

T.167

6202

REMARKS on the Reverend Dr. Snape's Second letter to
... the Lord Bishop of Bangor. With some reflections
on Dr. Sherlock's Answer to a letter, &c ... London:
for Timothy Childe, 1717.   8°

T.295

6203

REMARKS on the State anatomy of Great Britain
[a pamphlet by John Toland]. In a letter to a
member of Parliament; which may serve to obviate
the ill designs, and expose the false reasonings
of that pamphlet. [Attributed to Richard Fiddes.]
London: for J. Morphew, 1717.   8°

T.462

6204

A REPLY to Francis de la Pillonniere the Bishop of
Bangor's reputed Jesuit's, answer to Doctor Snape's
accusation ... In a letter to the Lord Bishop of
Bangor ... London, for S. Baker: and sold by the
booksellers, 1717.   8°

T.396

6205

The REPORT reported: or, The weakness and injustice
of the proceedings of the Convocation in their
censure of the Lord Bp. of Bangor, examin'd and
expos'd ... 2nd ed. London: for S. Baker, 1717.
8°

T.167

6206

A ROD for the Eaton schoolmaster's back: or, A letter
from a country school-boy to Dr. Snape, occasion'd
by one from him to the Bishop of Bangor ... London:
for J. Roberts, 1717.   8°

T.295

6207

A ROD for the Eaton school-master's back: or, A letter
from a country school-boy to Dr. Snape, occasion'd
by one from him to the Bishop of Bangor ... 2nd ed.
London: for J. Roberts, 1717.   8°

T.394

6208

RUTTER (John)

Bethlem hospital. A poem in blank verse. [Anon.]
London, for E. Smith, 1717.   4°

T.668

6209

SALT (Aylmer)

A letter to Mr. Timothy Goodwin, to be communicated
to his friend L.M. author of the narrative of
Count Patkul... London: for John Morphew, 1717.   8°

T.446

6210

SEELEN (Johann Heinrich von)

Commentatio de vita, scriptis et meritis in
rempublicam literariam... Ioan. Christoph.
Wolfii... Stadae, operis Holweinianis, 1717.   4°

T.793

6211

SEELEN (Johann Heinrich von)

Q.D.B.V. Disquisitio de Reformatione Lutheri non
humanis coepta ac promota consiliis... Praemissa
actui oratorio Iubilaeo in Gymn. Stadens... hab.
Stadae, operis Holweinianis, anno Iubilaeo 1717.   4°

T.793

6212

SHARP (John) *D.D.*

The charter of the Kingdom of Christ, explain'd in
two hundred conclusions and corollaries, from the
last words of our blessed Lord to his disciples ...
London: for John Morphew, 1717.   8°

T.298

6213

SHERLOCK (Thomas) *Bishop of London.*

An answer to a letter [by Arthur Ashley Sykes] sent
to the Reverend Dr. Sherlock, &c. relating to his
sermon preach'd before the lord-mayor, November the
5th 1712 ... London: for John Pemberton, 1717.   8°

T.394

6214

SHERLOCK (Thomas) *Bishop of London.*

An answer to a letter [by Arthur Ashley Sykes] sent
to the Reverend Dr. Sherlock, &c. relating to his
sermon preach'd before the lord-mayor, November the
5th 1712 ... 2nd ed. London: for John Pemberton,
1717.   8°

T.167

6215

SHERLOCK (Thomas) *Bishop of London.*

Remarks upon the Lord Bishop of Bangor's treatment of
the clergy and Convocation. By a gentleman ... 3rd
ed. London: for E. Smith, 1717.   8°

T.167

6216

SHERLOCK (Thomas) *Bishop of London.*

Some considerations occasioned by a postscript from ... the Lord Bishop of Bangor to the Dean of Chichester, offered to his Lordship. London: for John Pemberton, 1717.   8°

3 copies.

T.603 T.394 T.167

6217

SNAPE (Andrew)

A letter to the Bishop of Bangor, occasion'd by his Lordship's sermon preach'd before the King of S. James's, March 31st, 1717.   2nd ed. London: for Jonah Bowyer, 1717.   8°

T.662

6218

SNAPE (Andrew)

A letter to the Bishop of Bangor, occasion'd by his Lordship's sermon preach'd before the King at S. James's, March 31st, 1717.   4th ed. London: for Jonah Bowyer, 1717.   8°

T.295

6219

SNAPE (Andrew)

A letter to the Bishop of Bangor, occasion'd by his Lordship's sermon preach'd before the King at S.James's, March 31st, 1717.   8th ed. London: for Jonah Bowyer, 1717.   8°

T.603

6220

SNAPE (Andrew)

A letter to the Bishop of Bangor, occasion'd by his Lordship's sermon preach'd before the King at S. James's, March 31st, 1717.   9th ed. London: for Jonah Bowyer, 1717.   8°

T.400

6221

SNAPE (Andrew)

A second letter to the Lord Bishop of Bangor, in vindication of the former. London: for Jonah Bowyer, 1717.   8°

T.394

6222

SNAPE (Andrew)

A second letter to the Lord Bishop of Bangor, in vindication of the former. 2nd ed. London: for Jonah Bowyer, 1717.   8°

T.295

6223

SNAPE (Andrew)

A sermon preach'd before the honourable House of Commons, at S. Margaret's, Westminster, on Wednesday the 29th of May, 1717 ... 2nd ed. London: for Jonah Bowyer, 1717.   8°

T.37

6224

SNAPE (Andrew)

A sermon preach'd before the honourable House of Commons, at S. Margaret's, Westminster, on Wednesday the 29th of May, 1717 ... 8th ed. London: for Jonah Bowyer, 1717.   8°

T.345

6225

SNAPE (Andrew)

A vindication of a passage in Dr. Snape's Second letter to the Lord Bishop of Bangor, relating to Mr. Pillonniere. London: for Jonah Bowyer, 1717. 8°

T.396

6226

SOUTH (Robert)

Maxims, sayings, explications of Scripture phrases, descriptions and characters, extracted from the writings of the late reverend and learned Dr. South ... London: for J. Roberts, 1717.   8°

T.738

6227

SPINCKES (Nathaniel)

No reason for restoring the prayers and directions of Edward VI's first liturgy. By a Nonjuror ... London, for John Morphew, [1717].   8°

2 copies.

T.303 T.343

6228

STANHOPE (Michael)

The clergy of the Church of England not guilty of the schism charg'd upon them by the Non-jurors. In a sermon preach'd in the parish church of St. Martin in the Fields: on Sunday, December the 9th. 1716 ... London: for John Wyat, 1717.   8°

T.37

6229

A STATE and estimate of the publick debts, to Lady-day 1717, with proposals for redeeming and paying off the same. [No imprint, 1717.] Fol.

T.13

6230

STEPHENS (William) *Vicar of St. Andrew's, Plymouth.*

The personality and divinity of the Holy Ghost prov'd from Scripture, and the Ante-Nicene fathers. A sermon preach'd before the University of Oxford... Feb. 24th 1716/7... Oxford, printed at the Theater for John and Sam. Wilmot: and are to be sold by J. Knapton, W. Taylor, W. Churchill, Jonas Brown, and John Morphew booksellers in London, 1717.   8°

T.804

6231

SYKES (Arthur Ashley)

The difference between the kingdom of Christ, and the kingdoms of this world. Set forth in a sermon preached at the arch-deacon's visitation, in St. Michael's church in Cambridge, December 13. 1716. London: for James Knapton, 1717.   8°

T.400

6232

SYKES (Arthur Ashley)

A letter to a friend. In which is shewn, the inviolable nature of publick securities. By a lover of his country. London: for R. Burleigh, 1717.   8°

T.87

6233

SYKES (Arthur Ashley)

A letter to the Reverend Dr. Sherlock, one of the committee of Convocation, appointed to draw up a representation concerning the Bishop of Bangor's Preservative and sermon ... [Signed A.V.] London, R. Burleigh, 1717.   8°

2 copies.

T.394 T.167

6234

SYKES (Arthur Ashley)

A second letter to the Reverend Dr. Sherlock, being a reply to his answer, &c ... To which is added, a postscript to the Reverend Dr. Sherlock Dean of Chichester, by ... Benjamin Lord Bishop of Bangor. London, for James Knapton, and Timothy Childe, [1717]. 8°

2 copies.

T.394 T.167

6235

SYKES (Arthur Ashley)

Some remarks on Mr. Marshall's Defense of our constitution in Church and State ... London, for James Knapton, 1717.   8°

Incomplete.

T.300

6236

TALBOT (William) *Bishop of Durham.*

A sermon preach'd in the parish-church of St. Sepulchre, June the 13th, 1717... at the anniversary meeting of the children educated in the charity-schools in and about the cities of London and Westminster. By... William, Lord Bishop of Salisbury. London, Joseph Downing, 1717.   4°

T.702

6237

TICKELL (Thomas)

An epistle from a lady in England; to a gentleman at Avignon. 3rd ed. London, for J. Tonson, 1717. Fol.

T.529

6238

TINDAL (Matthew)

The defection consider'd, and the designs of those, who divided the friends of the government, set in a true light ... [Anon.] 5th ed. London, J. Roberts, 1717.   8°

T.224

6239

TOLAND (John)

The state-anatomy of Great Britain. Containing a particular account of its several interests and parties, their bent and genius; and what each of them... may hope or fear from the reign and family of King George. [Signed Patricola.] London: for John Philips, and sold by J. Brotherton, and J. Roberts, [1717].   8°

Wanting the final leaf.

T.462

6240

TOLAND (John)

The state-anatomy of Great Britain. Containing a particular account of its several interests and parties, their bent and genius; and what each of them ... may hope or fear from the reign and family of King George ... [Signed Patricola.] 4th ed. London: for John Philips; and sold by J. Brotherton, and P. Meadows, [1717].   8°

T.169

6241

TOLAND (John)

The state-anatomy of Great Britain. Containing a particular account of its several interests and parties, their bent and genius; and what each of them... may hope or fear from the reign and family of King George... [Signed Patricola.] 5th ed. London: for John Philips; and sold by J. Brotherton, and P. Meadows, [1717].   8°

T.462

6242

TOLAND (John)

The second part of the State anatomy, &c... [signed Patricola.] 2nd ed. London: for John Phillips; and sold by J. Brotherton, and P. Meadows, 1717. 8°

T.462

6243

TRAEINER (Adam Fridericus)

Q.D.B.V. dissertatio historico-moralis de misanthropia eruditorum... Lipsiae, literis Andreae Martini Schedii, [1717].   4°

T.793

6244

TRAPP (Joseph)

The real nature of the Church or kingdom of Christ. A sermon preach'd at the church of S. Martin in the Fields, May 19. and at that of St. Olave Old-Jewry, and St. Martin Ironmonger-Lane June 2. 1717. In answer to the Bishop of Bangor's sermon upon the same text ... 2nd ed. London, for Henry Clements, 1717.   8°

2 copies.

T.400 T.295

6245

The UNINTERRUPTED succession of the ecclesiastical mission asserted; and the appeal (in the Preservative against the principles and practices of the Non-jurors, &c. [by Benjamin Hoadly]) to the consciences and common sense of the Christian laity, discuss'd ... London; John Morphew, 1717.   8°

2 copies.

T.396 T.245

6246

VARILLAS (Antoine)

The pretended reformers: or, The history of the heresie of John Wickliffe, John Huss, and Jerom of Prague. Made English from the French original [by Varillas]. To which is prefixed, an introductory preface ... By Matthias Earbery. London: for A. Smith, 1717.   8°

T.155

6247

A VINDICATION of the honour and prerogative of Christ's Church: as is laid down by ... the Ld. Bishop of Bangor, in his sermon preach'd before the King on the 31st of March last. Being an answer to the cavils of Dr. Snape. The second edition, corrected. London: for T. Warner, 1717.   8°

2 copies.

T.400 T.295

6248

A VINDICATION of the Reverend Dr. Snape; in answer to
the Bishop of Bangor's preface to a pamphlet lately
publish'd, by Father Francis Pillonniere ... With
some considerations on his Lordship's postscript to
the said pamphlet; in defence of the Reverend Dr.
Sherlock. By an Englishman, that never was a Jesuit.
London, for J. Morphew, 1717.   8°

T.167

6249

WARD (Edward)

British wonders: or, A poetical description of the
several prodigies and most remarkable accidents that
have happen'd in Britain since the death of Queen
Anne. [Anon.] London: John Morphew, 1717.   8°

T.410

6250

WATKINS (Thomas)

A table of redemption. Shewing at one view in what
time the principal and interest of any debt from
three to six per cent may be discharged...
By T.W. F.R.S.   London: W.Wilkins; and sold by J.
Roberts, 1717.   4°

T.13

6251

WELLS (Edward)

Forty six propositions briefly proving, that his
present Majesty King George is the only rightful
and lawful king of Great-Britain. And also that
the nonjuring bishops (&c.) were rightfully and
lawfully deprived. London, for James Knapton,
1717.   8°

T.439

6252

WHITBY (Daniel)

An answer to the Reverend Dr. Snape's Second letter
to ... Benjamin Lord Bishop of Bangor. London: for
W. Churchill, 1717.   8°

T.295

1718

6253

ADDISON (*Rt. Hon.* Joseph)

A dissertation upon the most celebrated Roman poets.
Written originally in Latin; made English by
Christopher Hayes. London, for E. Curll, 1718.
8°

T.397

6254

ADDISON (*Rt. Hon.* Joseph)

Two poems viz. I. On the deluge, paradise, the
burning of the world, and of the new heavens and
new earth. An ode to Dr. Burnett. II. In praise
of physic and poetry. An ode to Dr. Hannes.
[With translations from the Latin by Thomas
Newcomb.] London: for E. Curll, 1718.   8°

T.397

6255

AMHURST (Nicholas)

A congratulatory epistle from his Holiness the Pope,
to the Reverend Dr. Snape. Faithfully translated
from the Latin original into English Verse. By the
author of Protestant popery... London: for E. Curll,
1718.   8°

T.98

6256

ASGILL (John)

A short essay on the nature of the kingdom of God within
us. London, for W. Graves, 1718.   8°

T.223

6257

AUCHER (John)

The arraignment of rebellion, or the irresisibility
of sovereign powers vindicated and maintain'd in a
reply to a letter... London: for M.F. for William
Abington, 1684. And reprinted in the year 1718.
And sold by John Morphew.   8°

T.484

6258

B.(H.)

A letter to the Reverend Dr. Sherlock. London: for
J. Roberts, 1718.   8°

T.27

6259

B.(W.)

The juror. A farce ... London; for John Norcock,
1718.   8°

T.225

6260

BELL (George)

A sermon preached before ... the lord mayor and
court of aldermen, at the cathedral church of St.
Paul, on the twenty ninth of May, 1718 ... London:
for Richard Sare, 1718.   8°

T.40

6261

BOURSAULT (Edme)

The fair of St. Germain. As it is acted at the
theatre in Little Lincoln's-Inn-Fields, by the French
company of comedians, lately arriv'd from the Theatre-
Royal at Paris... Done into English by Mr. Ozell.
London, for W. Chetwood, and sold by J. Roberts, 1718.
8°

T.667

6262

BRADLEY (Richard)

The gentleman and gardeners kalendar, directing what
is necessary to be done every month, in the kitchen-
garden, fruit-garden, nursery, management of forest-
trees, green-house and flower-garden... London: for
W. Mears, 1718.   8°

T.518

6263

BRADLEY (Richard)

New improvements of planting and gardening, both
philosophical and practical; explaining the motion
of the sapp and generation of plants ... The second
edition corrected. London: for W. Mears, 1718.
3 parts.   8°

T.518

6264

BRETT (Thomas)

The divine right of episcopacy, and the necessity of
an episcopal commission for preaching God's word ...
proved from the holy scriptures, and the doctrine
and practice of the primitive Church ... London,
for Henry Clements, 1718.   8°

T.99

6265

BRETT (Thomas)

Tradition necessary to explain and interpret the holy
Scriptures. With a postscript, in answer to that part
of a book lately published [by Nathaniel Spinckes]
(called, No sufficient reason for restoring the
prayers and directions of King Edward the VIth's first
liturgy) which seems to depreciate tradition ...
London, for James Bettenham, 1718.   8°

2 copies.

T.524 T.342

6266

BREVAL (John Durant)

A compleat key to the Non-juror [by Colley Cibber].
Explaining the characters in that play, with
observations thereon. By Mr. Joseph Gay ... 2nd ed.
London: for E. Curll, 1718.   8°

2 copies.

T.225 T.242

6267

CAMPBELL (Archibald) *Bishop.*

An answer to a printed letter, said to be written by
Mr. Lesley: against alterations or additions to
the liturgy of the Church of England. In a letter to
a friend. [Anon.] London, H.P. for J. Morphew,
1718.   8°

"Mr Campbell or Mr Lau[rence]". Attributed by Thos.
Wagstaffe to "Mr Campbell", otherwise attributed to
Thomas Linfield and to Roger Laurence.
2 copies.

T.62 T.525

6268

CHANDLER (Edward) *Bishop of Durham.*

A sermon preach'd before the lords spiritual and
temporal in Parliament assembled, in the abbey-church
at Westminster, on the 30th of January, 1717-18 ...
By ... Edward Lord Bishop of Coventry, and Lichfield.
London: for James Knapton, 1718.   8°

T.40

6269

The CHICHESTER Dean, and his Colchester Amazon: or,
Mrs. Anne Roberts's letter to the author of the
Flying-post, in defence of the Master of the Temple:
with an answer to it ... London, S. Popping, 1718.
8°

T.27

6270

The CHURCH of England man's memorial; or, The history
of comprehension and toleration ... London, for J.
Morphew, 1718.   8°

T.302

6271

The CHURCH of England's apology for the principles of
the present dissenters, in Church and state:
particularly with reference to the thirtieth of
January. By a presbyter of the Church of England.
London, printed: and sold by J. Roberts, 1718.   8°

T.525

6272

CIBBER (Colley)

The Non-juror. A comedy. As it is acted at the
Theatre-Royal, by his Majesty's servants ... London:
for B. Lintot, 1718.   8°

T.225

6273

CLAUSWITZ (Benedict Gottlob)

Quaestionem an homines omnes et singuli ad studium
logicae artificialis obligentur? Dissertatione
philosophica... Lipsiae, typis Immanuelis Titii,
[1718].   4°

T.793

6274

COLLIER (Jeremy)

A defence of the reasons for restoring some prayers and
directions of King Edward the sixth's first liturgy:
being a reply to a book [by Nathaniel Spinckes],
entitled, No reason for restoring them ... [Anon.]
London: for John Morphew, 1718.   8°

2 copies.

T.655 T.303

5275

COLLIER (Jeremy)

A defence of the reasons for restoring some prayers
and directions of King Edward the sixth's first
liturgy: being a reply to a book [by Nathaniel
Spinckes], entitled, No reason for restoring them ...
[Anon.] 2nd ed. London: for J. Bettenham, 1718.
8°

T.343

6276

COLLIER (Jeremy)

Reasons for restoring some prayers and directions as
they stand in the communion-service of the first
English reform'd liturgy ... [Anon.] 4th ed. London:
for J. Bettenham, 1718.   8°

2 copies.

T.343 T.62

6277

COLLIER (Jeremy)

A vindication of the Reasons and defence, &c.
Part I. Being a reply to the first part of No
sufficient reason for restoring some prayers and
directions of King Edward VI's first liturgy [by
Nathaniel Spinckes]. By the author of the Reasons
and defence... London: for J. Bettenham, 1718.   8°

4 copies.

T.62 T.239 T.343 T.524

6278

The CONVENTICLE distinguish'd from the Church: in
answer to Dr. Welton's pretended narrative ...
London: printed for the author, 1718.   8°

Attributed by Bowdler to Matthias Earbery.

T.525

6279

COOKE (Shadrach)

Legal obedience the duty of a subject: consider'd in
a sermon at the archdeacon of Canterbury's visitation
at Sittingbourn ... London, for Robert Knaplock, 1718.
8°

T.40

6280

CROMWELL (Oliver)

A most learned, conscientious and devout exercise; held
forth at Sir Peter Temple's in Lincoln's-Inn-Fields.
By Lieut. General Cromwell. As it was faithfully
taken in characters, by Aaron Guerden, July 19th,
1649. Re-printed in the year, 1717/18. 8°

T.383

6281

DALRYMPLE (Gilbert)

A letter from Edinburgh to Dr. Sherlock, rectifying
the committee's notions of sincerity. Defending the
whole of the B. of Bangor's doctrine... London: for
J. Roberts, A. Dodd, and J. Fox, 1718. 8°

T.223

6282

DAWSON (Thomas) *D.D.*

Suspiria sacra: or, The Church of England's memorial:
with an admonition to Jesuits and their patrons,
extracted out of the statute law ... London: for
Char. Rivington, 1718. 8°

T.525

6283

DEFOE (Daniel)

Dr. Sherlock's Vindication of the Test Act examin'd,
and the false foundations of it exposed. In
answer to so much of his book against the Bishop of
Bangor, as relates to the protestant dissenters.
[Anon.] London: for S. Popping, J. Harrison, and
A. Dodd, 1718. 8°

Moore 397.
Incomplete.

T.45

6284

A DESCRIPTION of the great burning-glass made by Mr.
Villette and his two sons, born at Lyons. With some
remarks upon the surprising and wonderful effects
thereof. In French and English. London: for W. Lewis,
1718. 8°

T.446

6285

DUBOURDIEU (Jean Armand)

An appeal to the English nation; or, The body of the
French protestants, and the honest proselytes,
vindicated from the calumnies cast on them by one
Malard and his associates, in a libel entitled, The
French plot found out against the English Church ...
London: for J. Roberts, 1718. 8°

T.165

6286

EARBERY (Matthias)

A review of the Bishop of Bangor's sermon, and his
Answer to the representation of the committee of
the lower-house of Convocation... London: for J.
Bettenham, 1718. 2 parts. 8°

T.223

6287

An EXPOSITION of the XXXIV article of religion, Of
the traditions of the Church: refer'd to in a report
... concerning several dangerous positions and
doctrines contained in the Bishop of Bangor's
Preservative, and his sermon preach'd March 31. 1717.
By a clergyman of the Church of England ... London;
for J. Roberts, 1718. 8°

T.27

6288

FLACHS (Sigismund Andreas)

Vestitum e papyro in Gallia nuper introductum e
scriniis Antiquitatis erutum... Lipsiae, litteris
Schedianis, [1718]. 4°

T.793

6289

FLEETWOOD (William) *Bishop of Ely.*

Two sermons, the one before the King, on March the
2d. 1717 ... The other preach'd in the City, on the
justice of paying debts. London: W.D. for J. Wyat,
1718. 8°

T.40

6290

GORDON (William) *of Aberdeen.*

An apology for the use of the English liturgy and
worship; against the cavils and exceptions of the
Presbyterians in North-Britain: in a letter to Mr.
Francis Melvil... By a citizen of Aberdeen...
London: H.P. for J. Bettenham, 1718. 8°

T.165

6291

GRANVILLE (George) *Baron Lansdowne.*

The Lord Lansdown's speech against the Occasional
conformity Bill [19 December 1718]. [No imprint,
1718.] 8°

T.302

6292

GREAT BRITAIN. *Parliament. House of Commons.*

Three speeches against continuing the Army, &c.
as they were spoken in the House of Commons [by
William Shippen, Edward Jeffreys and Sir Thomas
Hanmer] the last session of Parliament...
London: for John Morphew, 1718. 8°

T.484

6293

HART (Edward)

A preservative against comprehension. Wherein the
heretical notions of Judge Hale's New year's gift,
and some other latitudinarian pamphlets are ...
confuted. By the author of the Bulwark storm'd ...
London, 1718. 8°

Wanting title-page.

T.244

6294

HERNE (Thomas)

The false notion of a Christian priesthood, and the
pretences to sacerdotal oblation, intercession,
benediction, and authoritative absolution. Examined
and confuted: being an answer to Mr. Law's Second
letter to the Bishop of Bangor ... By Phileleutherus
Cantabrigiensis. London, for James Knapton, 1718.
8°

T.396

6295

HERNE (Thomas)

A letter to the Reverend Dr. Edward Tenison, concerning
some citations made from ... the Arch-bishop of
Canterbury's preliminary discourse to the apostolical
fathers, in a paper lately published, intituled, A
letter to the Reverend the Prolocutor: being an
answer to a paper, &c. By the author of that letter.
London: for J. Roberts, 1718. 8°

T.27

6296

HOADLY (Benjamin) *Bishop of Winchester.*

An answer to a calumny cast upon the Bishop of Bangor,
by the Reverend Dr. Sherlock ... at the conclusion of
his new book, entitled, A vindication of the
Corporation and Test Acts, &c. London: W. Wilkins, for
James Knapton, and Tim. Childe, 1718. 8°

T.45

6297

HOADLY (Benjamin) *Bishop of Winchester.*

An answer to a late book, written by the Reverend Dr.
Sherlock, Dean of Chichester, intituled, The
condition and example of our blessed Saviour vindicated, &c.
London: W. Wilkins; for J. Knapton, and Tim. Childe,
1718. 8°

T.223

6298

HOADLY (Benjamin) *Bishop of Winchester.*

An answer to the representation drawn up by the
committee of the lower-house of Convocation concerning
several dangerous positions and doctrines contain'd in
the Bishop of Bangor's Preservative and sermon. London:
W. Wilkins, for J. Knapton, and Tim. Childe, 1718. 8°

T.45

6299

HOADLY (John) *Archbishop of Armagh.*

A sermon preach'd before the honourable House of
Commons at St. Margaret's Westminster, on January
30. 1717-8. London; W. Wilkins, for Tim. Childe,
1718. 8°

T.40

6300

An INTRODUCTION to the Bishop of Bangor's intended
collection of authorities. With a letter from
Sion College, A.D. 1645. Recommended... to the
consideration of his Lordship, Mr. Pillonniere,
and Mr. Toland. By a member of the late
committee in the lower house of Convocation...
London: for Jonah Bowyer, 1718. 8°

T.526

6301

JONES (Samuel) *Gent.*

Whitby, a poem. Occasioned by Mr. Andrew Long's
recovery from the jaundice, by drinking of Whitby
spaw-waters. York: Grace White, for Tho. Hammond,
and sold by A. Bettesworth, A. Dodd, London, 1718.
8°

T.397

6302

KEIMER (Samuel)

A brand pluck'd from the burning: exemplify'd in the
unparallel'd case of Samuel Keimer ... London: W.
Boreham, 1718. 8°

T.383

6303

KINNERSLY (Thomas)

A sermon lately preach'd at the chapel in the King's-
Bench prison ... London: for J. Bettenham, 1718.
8°

T.40

6304

LA PILLONNIERE (François de)

A reply to Dr. Snape's Vindication of a passage in his
Second letter to the Bishop of Bangor, relating to
Mr. Pillonniere ... To which is prefix'd, A letter
to Dr. Snape, by the Lord Bishop of Bangor. London:
W. Wilkins; for James Knapton, and Tim, Childe, 1718.
8°

T.396

6305

LA PILLONNIERE (François de)

A third defense; containing I. A reply to Dr.
Snape's and Mr. Mills's new calumnies, in their
late book. II. A faithful account of Mr. Rouire's
whole conduct... III. A postscript, in answer to
Mr. Armand Dubourdieu's calumnies... London: W.
Wilkins, for J. Knapton, and Tim. Childe, 1718.
8°

T.526

6306

LAURENCE (John) *Rector of Yelvertoft.*

The fruit-garden kalendar: or, A summary of the art
of managing the fruit-garden... London: for Bernard
Lintot, 1718. 8°

T.518

6307

LE NOBLE DE TENNELIERE (Eustache)

Les deux arlequins. Comedie en trois actes... The
two harlequins. A farce of three acts. Written by
Mr. Noble. And acted by the King's Italian comedians
at Paris. And now perform'd by the French comedians
at the theatre in Lincoln's-Inn-Fields. London: for
W. Mears, and W. Chetwood; and sold by J. Roberts,
1718. 8°

T.667

6308

LESLIE (Charles)

A letter from Mr. Lesly to his friend; against
alterations or additions to the liturgy of the Church
of England. London: printed in the year, 1718. 8°

T.100

6309

A LETTER from the Jesuits to Father De La Pillonniere.
In answer to the letter sent to them by that Father,
and published by Dr. Snape, in his Vindication, &c.
London: for T. Warner. 1718. 8°

T.526

6310

A LETTER to Dr. Sherlock, concerning the wickedness
and injustice of making any addition to a divine
institution, by human authority ... Occasion'd by
his late Vindication of the Corporation and Test
Acts ... London, for S. Baker, 1718. 8°

T.27

6311

LOVE'S invention: or, The recreation in vogue.
An excellent new ballad upon the masquerades...
(To the ingenious Mr. Moore, author of the
celebrated worm-powder. By Mr. Pope.) London:
for E. Curll, and R. Francklin, 1718. 8°

The half-title reads: Mr. Pope's Worms: and a new
ballad on the masquerades.

T.397

6312

LOWMAN (Moses)

A defence of the protestant dissenters; in answer to
the misrepresentations of Dr. Sherlock, in his
Vindication of the Corporation and Test Acts. London,
for John Clark, 1718. 8°

T.298

6313

LOWMAN (Moses)

The principles of an occasional conformist, stated
and defended. With a preface in answer to Dr.
Sherlock's reflections on occasional conformity, in
his Vindication of the Corporation and Test Acts.
[Anon.] London, for John Clark, 1718. 8°

T.27

6314

LUPTON (William)

The necessity of positive duty, or actual goodness. A sermon preach'd in the parish-church of St. Sepulchre, June the 5th, 1718... at the anniversary meeting of the children educated in the charity-schools in and about the cities of London and Westminster. London, Joseph Downing, 1718. 4°

T.701

6315

MANGEY (Thomas)

Remarks upon Nazarenus. Wherein the falsity of Mr. Toland's Mahometan gospel, and his misrepresentation of Mahometan sentiments, in respect of Christianity, are set forth... Printed for William and John Innys, 1718. 8°

T.521

6316

MILLS (Henry)

A full answer to Mr. Pillonniere's reply to Dr. Snape and to the Bishop of Bangor's preface, so far as it relates to Mr. Mills... In a letter to the Lord Bishop of Bangor... To which is prefix'd, A letter to his Lordship. By Dr. Snape. London: for Jonah Bowyer, 1718. 2 parts. 8°

T.526

6317

MOLLOY (Charles)

The coquet: or, The English chevalier. A comedy. As it is acted by his Majesty's servants... London: for E. Curll, and R. Francklin, 1718. 8°

T.667

6318

MYNORS (Willoughby)

The subtilty of the serpent, in corrupting the true English liturgy... [Anon.] London: for J. Smith, 1718. 8°

T.431

6319

NORRIS (Charles)

A dialogue between Dr. Sherlock, Dean of Chichester: and Dr. Sherlock, Master of the Temple.... Being a justification of Mr. Sykes's charge ... London: for J. Roberts, 1718. 8°

T.27

6320

NORRIS (Charles)

The reconciler or the Bangorian controversy, abridg'd, made familiar, and brought to a final period; by a full discovery of its being only mere battology ... London, for W. Boreham, 1718. 8°

T.27

6321

PEIRCE (James)

Some reflections upon Dean Sherlock's Vindication of the Corporation and Test Acts. London: for John Clark, 1718. 8°

T.27

6322

REMARKS upon the publick advertisements in the news-papers of last week, concerning Mr. Pillonniere, once a Jesuit ... With a letter from the cookmaids in or about Croydon, to the cookmaid at Streatham. By T[om o'] B[edlam]. London, for W. Peters, and sold by the booksellers of London and Westminster, 1718. 8°

Two press cuttings are inserted in this copy.

T.59

6323

A REPRESENTATION of the state of the Church in North-Britain, as to episcopacy and liturgy... But more especially of the episcopal churches within the diocese and shire of Aberdeen... With original papers and attestations. London: for W. and J. Innys; and sold by James Bettenham, 1718. 8°

2 copies.

T.165 T.240

6324

ROBERTS (Anne)

The Flying-post posted: or, An answer to a late pamphlet of that author's call'd The Chichester dean, and his Colchester Amazon ... London: for N. Mist, 1718. 8°

T.38

6325

S. (J.)

A letter to the Reverend Dr. Snape, occasion'd by the dangerous consequences drawn from the wrong application of the word separation, particularly as it is urg'd by Mr. Pillonniere, in his syllogistic performance against Dr. Snape... By a convert from the Church of Rome to the Church of England. London: for J. Bettenham, 1718. 8°

T.526

6326

The SAINTS congratulatory address: or, Th[oma]s B[ra]dbury's speech, in the name of all the prot[esta]nt diss[ente]rs, to the B[isho]p of B[angor]'s Jesuit; with that r[everen]d father's answer. In Hudibrastick verse. Humbly dedicated to... Sir Rich[ar]d St[ee]le. London, for J.Cuxon, and sold by the booksellers of London and Westminster, 1718. 8°

T.410

6327

SCOT (William)

No necessity to alter the Common-prayer; or, The unreasonableness of the new separation. Being a full answer to two late books [by Jeremy Collier]; the one called, Reasons for restoring some prayers and directions, &c. and the other, The defence of the reasons ... [Anon.] London; John Morphew, 1718. 8°

3 copies.

T.303 T.342

6328

SEWELL (George)

The resigners vindicated: or, The defection re-consider'd. In which the designs of all parties are set in a true light. By a gentleman ... 4th ed. London: for R. Burleigh, 1718. 2 parts. 8°

T.224

6329

SHARPE (John) *Curate of Stepney.*

An historical account of the rise and growth of heresie in the Christian Church, to the sixteenth century and farther... Part I. London, for R. Wilkin, 1718. 8°

T.521

6330

SHERLOCK (Thomas) *Bishop of London.*

The condition and example of our Blessed Saviour vindicated: in answer to the Bishop of Bangor's charge of calumny against the Dean of Chichester. London: for J. Pemberton, 1718. 8°

T.45

6331

SHERLOCK (Thomas) *Bishop of London.*

The Lord Bishop of Bangor's defence of his assertion, viz. That the example of our Lord is much more peculiarly fit to be urged to slaves than to subjects, consider'd. London: for J. Pemberton, 1718. 8°

T.223

6332

SHERLOCK (Thomas) *Bishop of London.*

A vindication of the Corporation and Test Acts. In answer to the Bishop of Bangor's reasons for the repeal of them. To which is added: A second part, concerning the religion of oaths. London: for J. Pemberton, 1718. 8°

2 copies.

T.298   T.45

6333

SMITH (George)

A vindication of lawful authority: against some principles lately advanc'd to undermine the same. Or, A confutation of Hobbism in politicks, as it is reviv'd by some modern doctors; wherein Dr. Broughton's grand apostacy is consider'd... [Anon.] Printed in the year 1718. 8°

T.52

6334

SNAPE (Andrew)

A sermon preach'd before ... the lord-mayor, the aldermen, sheriffs, and governours of the several hospitals of the city of London, in St. Bridget's church, on Easter Wednesday, April 16. 1718. London, for Jonah Bowyer, 1718. 8°

T.40

6335

SNATT (William)

Mr. Collier's desertion discuss'd: or, The holy offices of worship in the liturgy of the Church of England defended ... In a letter to a friend ... [Anon.] London: for C. Rivington, and sold by J. Bettenham, [1718]. 8°

T.221

6336

SOCIETY OF JESUS. *Collegium S.J. Bonnae.*

Societas laetissima laetitias inspirat in adventu serenissimorum principum Caroli Alberti Electoralis utriusque Bavariae Principis... et Ferdinandi Mariae utriusque Bavariae ducis &c. ex fratre nepotum... Josephi Clementis Dei gratia Archi-episcopi Coloniensis... [No imprint, 1718.] Fol.

T.810

6337

SPERBACH (Carl Gottlob)

B.C.D. de obligatione erga eruditos consensu inclyti ordinis philosophici, pro loco in eodem obtinendo... disputabit M. Carolus Gottlob Sperbach. Lipsiae, typis Christiani Scholvini, [1718]. 4°

T.793

6338

SPINCKES (Nathaniel)

The case farther stated, between the Church of Rome and the Church of England, wherein the chief point, about the supremacy is fully discuss'd: in a dialogue beteeen a Roman Catholick, and a member of the Church of England. [Anon.] London: for George Strahan, 1718. 8°

T.525

6339

SPINCKES (Nathaniel)

No sufficient reason for restoring the prayers and directions of King Edward the sixth's first liturgy. Part I. By a non-juror... London: for John Morphew, 1718. 8°

3 copies.

T.62 T.343 T.524

6340

SPINCKES (Nathaniel)

No sufficient reason for restoring the prayers and directions of King Edward VI's first liturgy; Part II. By a Non-juror... London: for James Bettenham, 1718. 8°

3 copies.

T.524 T.343 T.658

6341

SQUIRE (Francis)

The lawfulness of taking oaths: together, with an exposition, of their nature and obligation. Set forth in a sermon, preach'd at the assizes begun at Wells... August 19. 1718. Taunton, W. Norris: and are likewise sold, by Mr. Norris; Mr. Penn, Bristol; Mr. March bookseller in Exon; and Mr. Brown in Wells, [1718?] 4°

T.702

6342

STANHOPE (George) *Dean of Canterbury.*

A letter from the Prolocutor to the Reverend Dr. Edward Tenison, Archdeacon of Carmarthen. London, for R. Sare, and sold by John Morphew, 1718. 8°

2 copies.

T.27 T.603

6343

STANHOPE (George) *Dean of Canterbury.*

The Prolocutor's answer to a letter from a member of the lower house of Convocation [i.e. Robert Moss]; entitled, The report vindicated from misreports. London: for Richard Sare; and sold by J. Morphew, 1718. 8°

4 copies.

T.45 T.74 T.238 T.603

6344

STEBBING (Henry) *Archdeacon of Wilts.*

A defence of the first head of the charge of the committee of the lower house of Convocation against... the Lord Bishop of Bangor. Being remarks upon some positions of his Lordship, contained in his sermon, in his Answer to Dr. Snape, and to the Representation... [Anon] London, for Henry Clements, 1718. 8°

T.603

6345

STEBBING (Henry) *Archdeacon of Wilts.*

Remarks upon a position of... the Lord Bishop of Bangor concerning religious sincerity. Wherein the consequences of this position are fully stated, and his Lordship's pretended demonstration is shewn to be inconclusive... London, for Henry Clements, 1718. 8°

T.223

1718 (Cont'd)

6346
SYKES (Arthur Ashley)

The Dean of Chichester's conduct considered, in his remarks upon the Lord Bishop of Bangor's treatment of the clergy and convocation ... London, for James Knapton, and Tim. Childe, 1718.   8°

T.27

6347
SYKES (Arthur Ashley)

A fourth letter to the Reverend Dr. Sherlock, being an answer to his late book, entitled, The Lord Bishop of B[angor]'s defence of his assertion consider'd ... London: for J. Knapton: and T. Childe, 1718.   8°

T.223

6348
SYNGE (Edward) *Archbishop of Tuam.*

The authority of the Church in matters of religion. [Anon.] London: for Richard Sare, 1718.   8°

T.165

6349
TASSO (Torquato)

The third book of Tasso's Jerusalem. Written originally in Italian. Attempted in English. By Mr. Bond... London: W. Lewis, H. Clements, and T. Warner, 1718.   8°

T.397

6350
TASWELL (E.)

Miscellanea sacra, consisting of three divine poems ... With a proposal for publishing a large collection of the said poems ... London: printed for the author, and sold by J. Morphew, 1718.   8°

T.98

6351
TENISON (Edward) *Bishop of Ossory.*

A protestation made on the 14th day of February, 1717/8, in behalf of the King's supremacy and the protestant doctrines asserted and maintain'd in the Lord Bishop of Bangor's sermon... 2nd ed... London: for J. Wyat, 1718.   8°

2 copies.

T.27   T.603

6352
The THEATRE-Royal turn'd into a mountebank's stage. In some remarks upon Mr. Cibber's quack-dramatical performance, called the Non-juror ... By a Non-juror. London: for John Morphew, 1718.   8°

T.225

6353
TOLAND (John)

Nazarenus: or, Jewish, Gentile, and Mahometan Christianity... London, printed: and sold by J. Brown, J. Roberts, and J. Brotherton, 1718.   8°

T.521

6354
WAGSTAFFE (Thomas) *the Younger.*

The necessity of an alteration... Being a reply to a late tract [by William Scot], entitled, No necessity to alter, &c... London: for J. Bettenham, 1718.   8°

3 copies.

T.221   T.342   T.343

6355
WELTON (Richard)

The Church distinguish'd from a conventicle: in a narrative of the persecution of Dr. Welton and his family, for reading the Common-prayer in his own house... London: printed and sold by the booksellers of London and Westminster, [1718].   8°

T.525

6356
WERENFELS (Samuel)

Three discourses: one, A defence of private judgment; the second, Against the authority of the magistrate over conscience; the third, Some considerations concerning the re-uniting of protestants... [Translated by Thomas Herne.] With a prefatory epistle to the Reverend Dr. Tenison... By Phileleutherus Cantabrigiensis... London, for James Knapton, 1718.   8°

T.27

6357
WHEATLY (Charles)

Bidding of prayers before sermon, no mark of disaffection to the present government: or an historical vindication of the LVth canon ... London, for A. Bettesworth, H. Clements and C. Rivington, 1718.   8°

T.165

1719

6358
ALTHAM (Roger)

The harmony of the sacred and civil polity: or, The soveraignty of Jesus Christ no injury to the civil power. A third charge delivered to the clergy of the arch-deaconry of Middlesex. London: for G. Strahan, 1719.   8°

2 copies.

T.520   T.40

6359
ARBUCKLE (James)

An epistle to the Right Honourable Thomas Earl of Hadington, on the death of Joseph Addison, Esq ... London: for T. Cox, 1719.   8°

T.397

6360
BANKS (*Sir* Jacob)

A letter from Sir J. B[an]ks to W. B[enso]n, Esq; S.O. by birth an Englishman; but unnaturaliz'd and turn'd Swede ... Concerning a late contract, that was endeavour'd to be establish'd by a certain bold officer in Sweden, to the utter undoing of the Board of Works in that kingdom ... London: for A. Moore, 1719.   8°

T.224

6361
BAYNARD (Edward)

Health, a poem. Shewing how to procure, preserve, and restore it. To which is annex'd the Doctor's decade. The second edition, corrected. By Dabry Dawne, M.D. London: James Bettenham, 1719.   8°

T.397

6362
BERRIMAN (William)

A seasonable review of Mr. Whiston's account of primitive doxologies. In his late abusive letter of thanks to ... the Lord Bishop of London, &c. Together with some occasional remarks on ... his Primitive Christianity revived. By a presbyter of the diocese of London ... London, for Thomas Ward; and sold by James Bettenham, 1719.   8°

T.521

6363
BRADFORD (Samuel) *Bishop of Rochester.*

A sermon preach'd before the House of Lords, in the abbey church of Westminst. on the 30th of January, 1718/9 ... By Samuel Lord Bishop of Carlile. London: for John Wyat, 1719.   8°

T.40

6364
BUTLER (*Sir* Francis)

A true and just account of what was transacted in the Commons House at Westminster, anno. Dom. 1648. when that House voted David Jenkins Esq; a Welch judge, and Sir Francis Butler, to be guilty of high treason ... All which matters and things D.T. Esq; had from the mouth and notes of the said Sir Francis Butler. London: printed in the year 1719.   8°

2 copies.

T.434   T.203

6365
CALAMY (Edmund) *D.D.*

The Church and the dissenters compar'd, as to persecution. In some remarks on Dr. Walker's attempt to recover the names and sufferings of the clergy ... London: for John Clark, 1719.   8°

T.38

6366
CAMPBELL (Archibald) *Bishop.*

An answer to A letter from the Reverend Mr. Charles Leslie, concerning what he calls the new separation. [Anon.] London: for John Morphew, 1719.   8°

T.100

6367
CASTLE (A.)

A discourse against false preaching: that is to say, speeching and doubling in the pulpit. In a visitation sermon, address'd (in a preface) to the clergy of the Church of England, by a presbyter of that Church ... London: for John Hooke, [1719].   8°

2 copies.
An incomplete copy of another impression.

T.520   T.244   T.40

6368
The CHURCH of England man's memorial; or, The history of comprehension and toleration ... London, for J. Bettenham and T. Bickerton, 1719.   8°

T.38

6369
COLLIER (Jeremy)

A vindication of the Reasons and defence, &c. Part II. Being a reply to the second part of No sufficient reason for restoring some prayers and directions of King Edward VI's first liturgy [by Nathaniel Spinckes]. By the author of the Reasons and defence ... London: for J. Bettenham, 1719.   8°

3 copies.

T.524   T.239   T.62

6370
A COMPLEAT catalogue of all the plays that were ever yet printed in the English language ... [Perhaps compiled by William Mears, the publisher.] London: for W. Mears, 1719.   8°

T.442

6371
The CONDUCT of the dissenters considered. In a letter to the Bishop of Bangor ... London, for T. Warner, 1719.   8°

T.38

6372
CONSIDERATIONS on the Peerage-bill; address'd to the Whigs. By a member of the lower house ... London: J. Roberts, 1719.   8°

T.203

6373
CROCKATT (Gilbert) *and* MONROE (John)

The Scotch Presbyterian eloquence; or, The foolishness of their teachings discovered from their books, sermon and prayers, and some remarks on Mr. Rule's late Vindication of the Kirk ... [The preface is signed Jacob Curate.] The third edition, with additions. London, for M. Smith, and sold by the booksellers of London and Westminster, 1719.   8°

T.437

6374
CUMMING (John)

Advice to Christians, to contend for the faith once delivered to the saints. A discourse to a society of young men in Jewen-street; on Easter-Monday, 1719 ... London: J. Darby, for A. Bell, and sold by J. Roberts, 1719.   8°

T.40

6375
CYPRIAN, *Saint.*

The unity of the Church, and expediency of forms of prayer; illustrated in two treatises compos'd by St. Cyprian the martyr. To which is prefix'd, a large preface... By the late pious and learned Dr. Grabe... London: for R. Francklin, and J. Bettenham, 1719. 2 parts.   8°

T.59

6376
DEACON (Thomas)

The plaintiff's charge disprov'd, and turn'd upon himself, by the defendant in a letter to the author [i.e. Nathaniel Spinckes] of No just grounds for introducing the new communion office, &c ... [Anon.] London: for James Bettenham, 1719.   8°

2 copies.

T.221   T.100

6377
A DEFENSE of the Ld Bishop of London; in answer to Mr. Whiston's letter of thanks to his Lordship. Address'd to his Grace the Lord Archbishop of Canterbury ... 2nd ed. London: for J. Roberts, 1719.   8°

T.521

6378

DEFOE (Daniel)

The anatomy of Exchange-alley. Or, A systhem of stock-jobbing proving that scandalous trade ... to be knavish in its private practice, and treason in its publick ... By a jobber. London: A. Hinde, [1719]. 8°

Moore 414.

T.366

6379

DEFOE (Daniel)

The anatomy of Exchange-alley: or, A system of stock-jobbing. Proving that scandalous trade ... to be knavish in its private practice, and treason in its publick ... By a jobber. London: for E. Smith, 1719. 8°

Moore 414.

T.484

6380

DEFOE (Daniel)

Some account of the life, and most remarkable actions, of George Henry Baron de Goertz, privy-counsellor, and chief minister of state, to the late King of Sweden. [Anon.] London: for T. Bickerton, 1719. 8°

Moore 415.

T.528

6381

A DESCRIPTION of the great burning-glass made by Mr. Villette and his two sons, born at Lyons. With some remarks upon the surprising and wonderful effects thereof. London: for W. Lewis, 1719. 8°

T.442

6382

A DIALOGUE in vindication of our present liturgy and service: between Timothy a churchman, and Thomas an essentialist. London: for J. Bettenham and T. Bickerton, 1719. 8°

2 copies. Sometimes attributed to Matthias Earbery.

T.26 T.100

6383

DRAKE (Samuel)

Vino Eucharistico aqua non necessario admiscenda. Concio habit ad clerum in templo B. Mariae Cantabrigiae, termino Sancti Michaelis, 1718 ... Londini: impensis Gul. & Joh. Innys, 1719. 8°

T.240

6384

DUNTON (John)

Neck for nothing: or, A satyr upon two great little men now in the ministry ... To which is added, Mordecai's dying groans from the Fleet-Prison: or, Mr. John Dunton's humble appeal to his Majesty's royal honour, justice, gratitude, and the rest of his princely virtues ... London: printed for the author and are to be sold by S. Popping, [1719?] 2 parts. 8°

T.203

6385

EVELEIGH (Josiah)

A defence of the account, &c. In answer to Mr. Peirce's Defence of the case, &c. [Anon.] London: for John Clark, 1719. 8°

T.38

6386

FREIND (John)

Dr. Friend's epistle to Dr. Mead, render'd faithfully into English. Divided into proper chapters; with notes learned and unlearned [attributed to John Woodward] ... London, printed: and sold by J. Roberts; J. Brown; W. Meadows; and A. Dodd, 1719. 8°

T.528

6387

FREIND (John)

A letter to the learned Dr. Woodward. By Dr. Byfielde [i.e. John Freind]... 2nd ed. London: for James Bettenham, 1719. 8°

The letter is signed J. Byefield.

T.397

6388

GORDON (Thomas) of Kirkcudbright.

An apology for the danger of the Church. Proving, that the Church is, and ought to be always in danger ... Being a second part of the Apology for Parson Alberoni. By the same author ... London, for J. Roberts, 1719. 8°

T.296

6389

GORDON (Thomas) of Kirkcudbright.

The character of an independent Whig ... [Anon.] London: for J. Roberts, 1719. 8°

T.203

6390

GORDON (Thomas) of Kirkcudbright.

A dedication to a great man, concerning dedications. Discovering, amongst other wonderful secrets, what will be the present posture of affairs a thousand years hence ... [Anon.] The fourth edition corrected. With a preface. London: for James Roberts, 1719. 8°

T.397

6391

GORDON (Thomas) of Kirkcudbright.

A modest apology for Parson Alberoni, governor to King Philip, a minor; and universal curate of the whole Spanish monarchy; the whole being a short, but unanswerable defence of priestcraft, and a new confutation of the Bishop of Bangor... [Anon.] 11th ed. London: for J. Roberts, 1719. 8°

T.296

6392

H.(J.)

A word in season: being a modest enquiry into the lawfulness of making and imposing creeds. With the plain man's reply to a Socinian paper ... London: Joseph Marshall; and Stephen Dagnal, 1719. 8°

T.38

6393

HARE (Francis) Bishop of Chichester.

Church-authority vindicated, in a sermon preach'd at Putney, May 5, 1719 ... London: J. Roberts, 1719. 8°

T.40

6394

HENDLEY (William) and DEFOE (Daniel)

Charity still a Christian virtue: or, an impartial account of the tryal and conviction of the Reverend Mr. Hendley, for preaching a charity-sermon at Chisselhurst ... [Anon.] London: for T. Bickerton, 1719. 8°

Moore 421.

T.203

6395

HERNE (Thomas)

An account of all the considerable pamphlets that have been published on either side in the present controversy, between the Bishop of Bangor, and others ... By Philanagnostes Criticus. London, for James Knapton, 1719. 8°

T.296

6396

HERNE (Thomas)

A letter to the Reverend Dr Mangey. Occasioned by his sermon on Christmas-day, entitled, Plain notions of our Lord's divinity. By Phileleutherus Cantabrigiensis ... London, for James Knapton, 1719. 8°

T.40

6397

HOADLY (Benjamin) Bishop of Winchester.

The common rights of subjects, defended: and the nature of the sacramental test, consider'd. In answer to the Dean of Chichester's Vindication of the Corporation and Test Acts. London: W. Wilkins, for J. Knapton, and Tim. Childe, 1719. 8°

T.223

6398

HOADLY (Benjamin) Bishop of Winchester.

A sermon preach'd at the funeral of Mrs. Elizabeth Howland, in the parish-church of Streatham in Surry, on Friday, May the first, 1719. London: W. Wilkins, for James Knapton, and Tim.Childe, 1719. 8°

T.40

6399

IBBOT (Benjamin)

The parable of the unjust steward, explain'd. A sermon preach'd before the ... lord-mayor of the city of London ... the aldermen, the sheriffs, and the presidents and governors of the several hospitals ... Apr. 1st. 1719. London, for J. Wyat, 1719. 8°

T.40

6400

KENNET (White) Bishop of Peterborough.

Charity and restitution: a spital sermon preached at the church of St. Bridget, on Easter-Monday, March the 30th, 1719 ... London: for J. Wyat, 1719. 8°

T.40

6401

KILLIGREW (Thomas) the Younger.

Chit-chat. A comedy. As it is acted at the Theatre-Royal in Drury-lane, by his Majesty's servants. London: for Bernard Lintot, [1719?] 8°

T.237

6402

LAURENCE (Roger)

Mr. Leslie's defence from some erroneous and dangerous principles, advanc'd in a letter, said to have been written by him concerning the new separation. By a known friend of Mr. Leslie ... London: for John Morphew, 1719. 8°

T.100

6403

LAW (William)

A reply to the Bishop of Bangor's Answer to the representation of the committee of Convocation. Humbly address'd to his Lordship. London, for William and John Innys, 1719. 8°

4 copies.

T.189 T.349 T.526 T.675

6404

LESLIE (Charles)

A letter from the Reverend Mr. Charles Leslie, concerning the new separation. London: J. Morphew, 1719. 8°

3 copies.

T.26 T.100

6405

A LETTER of thanks from a young clergyman, to the Reverend Dr. Hare, Dean of Worcester, for his visitation-sermon at Putney... [sometimes attributed to Joseph Butler.] London: W. Wilkins, and sold by J. Roberts, 1719. 8°

T.40

6406

A LETTER to a doctor of physick concerning diascordium, &c. London, for J. Bettenham, 1719. 8°

T.528

6407

A LETTER to Mr. John Clark, bookseller; upon his printing on both sides in the present debates among the dissenting ministers. London: for T. Cox, 1719. 8°

T.38

6408

A LETTER to the Reverend Mr. James Peirce, in answer to his Animadversions on the true relation of some proceedings at Salters-hall, as far as the London ministers are concerned in them. By one of the subscribing ministers. London; for E. Matthews, and R. Cruttenden, 1719. 8°

T.38

6409

MANGEY (Thomas)

The eternal existence of our Lord Jesus Christ: set forth in a sermon preached at the Lord-Bishop of Winchester's visitation at Chertsey ... the twenty second of May ... London: for William and John Innys, 1719. 8°

T.40

6410

MANGEY (Thomas)

Plain notions of our Lord's divinity. Set forth in a sermon preached upon Christmas-day, at the royal chapel of Whitehall ... London: for W. and J. Innys, 1719. 8°

T.40

6411

MARTIN (David)

A critical dissertation upon the seventh verse of the fifth chapter of St. John's first epistle ... Written originally in French by Mr. Martin, and now translated into English. London: for William and John Innys, 1719. 8°

T.97

6412

MARTIN (David)

An examination of Mr. Emlyn's Answer to the dissertation upon the seventh verse of the fifth chapter of the first epistle of St. John ... Translated from the French. London: for W. and J. Innys, 1719.   8°

T.97

6413

MARTIN (David)

A second dissertation by Mr. Martin in defence of the testimony given to our Saviour by Josephus ... Translated from the French original. London: for W. and J. Innys, 1719.   8°

T.97

6414

MIDDLETON (Conyers)

A full and impartial account of all the late proceedings in the University of Cambridge against Dr. Bentley ... By a member of that University. London, for J. Bettenham, 1719.   8°

T.238

6415

MIDDLETON (Conyers)

A second part of the Full and impartial account of all the late proceedings in the University of Cambridge against Dr. Bentley ... By a member of the University. London, for J. Bettenham, 1719.   8°

T.415

6416

MILBOURNE (Luke)

Ignorance and folly put to silence by well-doing: Or, A preservative against the Bishop of Bangor's politicks. In a sermon preach'd at the parish-church of St. Ethelburga's ... London, for E. Sawbridge; and sold by A. Bettesworth, 1719.   8°

T.40

6417

A MODEST apology for the Reverend Mr. Thomas Bradbury, in a letter to the dissenting layman. By a gentleman of Exon... London: for J. Roberts, 1719. 8°

T.38

6418

The OXFORD criticks. A satire ... London: for J. Roberts, 1719.   8°

T.397

6419

PEIRCE (James)

The charge of misrepresentations maintain'd against Dean Sherlock's preface to his Answer to the Lord Bishop of Bangor's late book, entitled, The common rights of subjects defended, &c. London: for John Clark, 1719.   8°

T.296

6420

PEIRCE (James)

A second letter to Mr. Eveleigh, in answer to his Sober reply, &c. To which is added, A confutation of a slanderous report. Exon: Andrew Brice, for John March, 1719.   8°

T.38

6421

PRAT (Daniel)

A review of the most considerable writers, in the great controversy with the Bishop of Bangor ... London: for Tim. Childe, 1719.   8°

T.296

6422

RALEIGH (Walter) Dean of Wells.

Certain queries, proposed by Roman Catholicks, and answered by Dr. Walter Raleigh ... With a prefatory account of the author by Laurence Howel. London: W. Redmayne, 1719.   8°

T.42

6423

A REPLY to the subscribing ministers reasons, in their vindication, for declaring their faith at this critical juncture ... Publish'd by agreement of a committee of non-subscribing ministers. London: for John Clark; E. Matthews; and R. Ford. 1719.   8°

T.38

6424

REY (Claudius)

The weavers true case; or, the wearing of printed callicoes and linnen destructive to the woollen and silk manufactures ... Address'd to the members of the honourable House of Commons. By a weaver ... London: W. Wilkins, and sold by J. Noon; J. Roberts; and W. Chetwood, 1719.   8°

T.203

6425

ROGERSON (Thomas)

The controversy about restoring some prayers, &c. Summed up in some plain propositions upon the several heads of it. By a private person, at the request of his friend ... London: for Tho. Bickerton, 1719.   8°

2 copies.

T.26 T.59

6426

SCOT (William)

The new separation from the Church of England groundless; being a vindication of the No necessity of altering the Common-prayer: in answer to a late pamphlet [by Thomas Wagstaffe], entitled The necessity of an alteration... [Anon.] London, for W. Mears; and sold by J. Bettenham, 1719.   8°

3 copies.

T.100 T.221

6427

SHERIDAN (Thomas) D.D.

Ars pun-ica, sive flos linguarum: the art of punning; or, The flower of languages ... By the labour and industry of Tom Pun-sibi. (i.e.) Jonathan Swift, D.D. ... 3rd ed. Printed at Dublin in the year 1719. Reprinted at London for J. Roberts.   8°

Teerink 895.

T.397

6428

SHERLOCK (Thomas) Bishop of London.

An answer to the Lord Bishop of Bangor's late book; entitled, The common rights of subjects defended, &c. London: for John Pemberton, 1719.   8°

T.296

6429

SHERLOCK (Thomas) Bishop of London.

A sermon preach'd in the parish-church of St. Sepulchre, May the 21st, 1719... at the anniversary meeting of the children educated in the charity-schools in and about the cities of London and Westminster. London, Joseph Downing, 1719.   4°

"For Edward Gross Esq."

T.701

6430

SOCIETY OF JESUS. Collegium S.J. Monasteriense.

Fata reverendissimi & serenissimi... Clementis Augusti utriusque Bavariae ducis... in episcopum Monasteriensium non sine divorum numine electi... a musis Monasteriensibus Societatis Jesu. Monasterii Westphaliae: typis Viduae Nagel, 1719. Fol.

T.810

6431

SOCIETY OF JESUS. Collegium S.J. Monasteriense.

... Schema parallelum reverendissimo & serenissimo ... Clementi Augusto... episcopo Monasteriensi, Ratisbonensi ac Paderbornensi... Monasterii Westphaliae typis Viduae Nagel, 1719. Fol.

T.810

6432

SOME remarks upon the late differences among the dissenting ministers and preachers. With a brief answer to Mr. Pierce of Excester. And the subtilty of some to cover heretical principles, discover'd and detected. London: for W. Boreham, 1719.   8°

T.38

6433

SPINCKES (Nathaniel)

No just grounds for introducing the new communion office, or denying communion to those who cannot think themselves at liberty to reject the liturgy of the Church of England for its sake... By a Nonjuror... London, for James Bettenham, 1719.   8°

T.431

6434

STEBBING (Henry) Archdeacon of Wilts.

The true meaning & consequences of a position of ... the Lord Bishop of Bangor concerning sincerity, asserted against his Lordship's general charge of misunderstanding, and the particular exceptions of the Reverend Mr. Pyle ... London: for Henry Clements, 1719.   8°

T.296

6435

STEELE (Sir Richard)

A letter to the Earl of O[xfor]d, concerning the Bill of peerage ... By Sir R[ichar]d S[tee]le. 2nd ed. London: for J. Roberts, 1719.   8°

T.203

6436

THEOBALD (John)

Poems on several occasions. London: for John Morphew, 1719.   8°

T.397

6437

TOPPING (Henry)

A sermon concerning the whole duty of prayer. Preach'd at St. Paul's Covent-garden, the third Sunday in July ... London, for James Knapton, 1719. 8°

T.170

6438

TRENCHARD (John)

The thoughts of a member of the lower house, in relation to a project for restraining and limiting the power of the Crown in the future creation of peers... [Anon. Also attributed to Robert Walpole.] 2nd ed. London, for J. Roberts, 1719.   8°

T.603

6439

WAGSTAFFE (Thomas) the Younger.

Vino Eucharistico aqua necessario admiscenda. Responsio ad concionem habitam ad clerum in templo B. Mariae Cantabrigiae, a Samuele Drake ... Londini: prostat apud T. Bickerton, 1719.   8°

T.240

6440

WAUGH (John) Bishop of Carlisle.

A sermon preach'd before the honourable the House of Commons at St. Margaret's Westminster, on Friday, January the 30th, 1718/19 ... London: for John Wyat, 1719.   8°

T.40

6441

The WEAVERS pretences examin'd. Being a full and impartial enquiry into the complaints of their wanting work, and the true causes assign'd ... By a merchant. London: J. Roberts; and J. Harrison, 1719.   8°

T.203

6442

The WELCHMAN'S last will and testament ... London: Tho. Bickerton, 1719.   8°

T.397

6443

T.203

WEST (Richard) Lord Chancellor of Ireland.

An inquiry into the manner of creating peers ... [Anon.] 2nd ed. London: for J. Roberts, 1719.   8°

T.203

6444

WHISTON (William)

Mr. Whiston's account of Dr. Sacheverell's proceedings in order to exclude him from St. Andrew's church in Holborn. London: for J. Senex, and W. Taylor; and sold by J. Roberts, 1719.   8°

T.521

6445

WHISTON (William)

Mr. Whiston's letter to the Right Honourable the Earl of Nottingham, concerning the eternity of the Son of God and of the Holy Spirit... London: for J. Senex, and W. Taylor, 1719.   8°

T.150

6446

ALTHAM (Roger)

Church authority not an universal supremacy. A
fourth charge deliver'd to the clergy of the archdeaconry of Middlesex ... London, for George
Strahan, 1720.   8°

T.520

6447

AN ANSWER to a printed libel, intitled, A letter to
a member of Parliament concerning the Bill for
regulating the nightly-watch in the city of Westminster
and liberties thereof. London: for J. Roberts, and A.
Dodd, 1720.   8°

T.203

6448

BRETT (Thomas)

A discourse concerning the necessity of discerning
the Lord's body in the holy communion ... London:
for Richard King, 1720.   8°

T.99

6449

BRETT (Thomas)

A vindication of the postscript to a book, called,
The necessary use of tradition to understand the
Holy Scriptures: in answer to a book [by Nathaniel
Spinckes], entitled, No just grounds for introducing
the new communion office, &c. London: for Rich.
King, 1720.   8°

T.26

6450

The CHARACTERS of two independent Whigs, viz. T.
G[ordon] of the North, and Squire T[renchard] of
the West ... London: for John Morphew, 1720.   8°

Teerink 900.

T.203

6451

CHETWOOD (William Rufus)

The stock-jobbers: or, The humours of Exchange-alley.
A comedy, of three acts ... [Anon.] London: for
J. Roberts, 1720.   8°

2 copies.

T.667   T.397

6452

The CHRISTIAN monitor; or, The heathen's conversion,
in six parts... London; J. Lightbody, [c.1720].
8°

T.383

6453

COLLIER (Jeremy)

A farther defence, &c. Being an answer to a reply
[by Nathaniel Spinckes] to the Vindication of the
reasons and defence for restoring some prayers and
directions in King Edward VI's first liturgy. By
the author of the Reasons ... London: for T.
Bickerton, 1720.   8°

2 copies.

T.26 T.62

6454

CONSIDERATIONS on the present state of the nation, as
to publick credit, stocks, the landed and trading
interests ... London: for J. Roberts, and A. Dodd,
1720.   8°

T.366

6455

DEFOE (Daniel)

The chimera: or, The French way of paying national
debts, laid open ... [Anon.] London: for T. Warner,
1720.   8°

Moore 426.

T.366

6456

DENNIS (John)

The characters and conduct of Sir John Edgar [i.e.
Richard Steele], call'd by himself sole monarch of
the stage in Drury-lane; and his three deputy-
governors ... [Anon.] 2nd ed. London: for M. Smith,
1720.   8°

T.397

6457

DESAGULIERS (John Theophilus)

A course of mechanical and experimental philosophy ...
[No imprint, c. 1720.]   8°

T.245

6458

DOWNES (Samuel)

An abridgment of the controversy between the Church
of England, and the new pseudo-primitives ... In a
dialogue between Neophytus, an essentialist
clergyman, and Irenaeus, a layman of the Church of
England ... [The preface signed S.D.] London: for
J. Morphew, 1720.   8°

T.59

6459

EARBERY (Matthias)

Reflections upon modern fanaticism. In two letters
to Doctor Brett, and the author [i.e. Roger Laurence]
of a late pamphlet ironically intitled, Mr. Leslie's
defence from some dangerous and erroneous principles
... London: N. Mist, and sold by J. Morphew, 1720.
2 parts.   8°

2 copies.

T.99   T.26

6460

An EXAMINATION and explanation of the South-Sea
Company's scheme, for taking in the publick debts ...
3rd ed. London: printed, and sold by J. Roberts,
1720.   8°

T.366

6461

GOEBEL (Johann David)

Dissertatio solemnis de devotionibus veterum
Romanorum... Stargardiae, typis Ernestinis,
[1720].   4°

T.819

6462

GORDON (Thomas) of Kirkcudbright.

Considerations offered upon the approaching peace,
and upon the importance of Gibraltar to the British
Empire, being the second part of the independent
Whig ... [Anon.] 3rd ed. London: for J. Roberts,
1720.   8°

T.203

6463

GORDON (Thomas) of Kirkcudbright.

A learned dissertation upon old women, male and
female, spiritual and temporal, in all ages; whether
in Church, state, or Exchange-alley ... [Anon.]
London: for J. Roberts, 1720.   8°

T.397

6464

HODGES (Nathaniel)

Loimologia: or, An historical account of the
plague in London in 1665... To which is added,
An essay on the different causes of pestilential
diseases... By John Quincy. London: for E. Bell;
and J. Osborn, 1720.   8°

T.528

6465

LAW (John) of Lauriston.

Money and trade consider'd; with a proposal for
supplying the nation with money. London: for W. Lewis,
1720.   8°

T.366

6466

A LETTER to a member of Parliament, concerning the
naval store-bill, brought in last session ... London,
printed in the year 1720.   8°

T.203

6467

LUPTON (William)

The omniscience of God. A sermon preached in ... the
Lord Bishop of Durham's chapel at Stene in
Northamptonshire, October 2. 1720 ... London: for Tim.
Goodwin, 1720.   8°

T.40

6468

MEAD (Richard)

A short discourse concerning pestilential contagion,
and the methods to be used to prevent it. London:
for Sam. Buckley, and Ralph Smith, 1720.   8°

T.528

6469

MERES (Sir John)

The equity of Parliaments, and publick faith,
vindicated; in answer to the Crisis of property, and
address'd to the annuitants ... The second edition,
corrected. London: for Chr. Coningsby, 1720.   8°

T.366

6470

MILBOURNE (Luke)

Royal and innocent blood expiated: or, God justified
in punishing a wicked people. In a sermon preach'd
at the parish-church of St. Ethelburga's ... London:
for J. Wilford, 1720.   8°

T.40

6471

MILNER (James)

A letter to a friend, concerning the proposals for the
payment of the nation's debts. [Anon.] London: for
J. Roberts, and A. Dodd, 1720.   8°

T.366

6472

OLDHAM (George)

A sermon preach'd at the visitation at St. Alban's,
April 28. 1720. London: for R. Knaplock, and F. Gyles
1720.   8°

"Donum authoris T. Scott."

T.345

6473

RAMSAY (Allan)

Content. A poem ... London: for E. Curll, 1720. 8°

T.397

6474

RAMSAY (Allan)

Patie and Roger: a pastoral, by Mr. Allan Ramsay, in
the Scots dialect. To which is added, An imitation
of the Scotch pastoral: by Josiah Burchett ... London;
for J. Pemberton, and T. Jauncy, 1720.   8°

T.397

6475

RAMSAY (Allan)

Wealth, or the woody: a poem on the South-Sea. To
which is prefix'd, A familiar epistle to Anthony
Hammond Esq; by Mr. Sewell. The second edition
corrected. London; for T. Jauncy, 1720.   8°

T.397

6476

SIR H. Mackworth's proposal in miniature, as it has been
put in practice in New-York, in America. London: for
W. Boreham, 1720.   8°

T.224

6477

SNATT (William)

Mr. Collier's desertion discuss'd: or the offices of
worship in the liturgy of the Church of England
defended... In a letter to a friend. [Anon.] The
second edition, with considerable enlargements...
London: for W. Boreham, 1720.

T.675

6478

SPINCKES (Nathaniel)

A reply to the Vindication of the Reasons and defence,
&c. [by Jeremy Collier]. Being a farther proof that
there is no reason for restoring the prayers and
directions of K. Edward VI's first liturgy; nor for
introducing a new communion-office in it's stead. By
a Nonjuror... London: for T. Bickerton, 1720.   8°

2 copies.

T.239 T.649

6479

STEELE (Sir Richard)

The state of the case between the Lord-Chamberlain of
his Majesty's household, and the governor of the
Royal Company of Comedians ... 2nd ed. London: for
J. Roberts; J. Graves; and Charles Lillie, 1720. 8°

T.399

1720 (Cont'd)

6480

TOLAND (John)

Reasons most humbly offer'd to the honble House of
Commons, why the Bill sent down to them from the ...
House of Lords, entitul'd, An Act for the better
securing the dependency of the kingdom of Ireland
upon the Crown of Great-Britain, shou'd not pass into
a law ... [Anon.] London: for R. Franklin, 1720. 8°

T.203

6481

TOLAND (John)

Tetradymus. Containing I. Hodegus ... II. Clidophorus
... III. Hypatia ... IV. Mangoneutes ... London
printed: and sold by J. Brotherton and W. Meadows,
J. Roberts, W. Meres, W. Chetwood, S. Chapman, and
J. Graves, 1720.   8°

T.241

6482

TRENCHARD (John)

A letter of thanks from the author of the Comparison
between the proposals of the Bank and the South-Sea,
&c. To the author of the Argument, shewing the
disadvantage which will accrue to the publick, from
obliging the South-Sea to fix what capital stock
they will give the annuitants. [Anon.] London:
printed, and sold by J. Roberts, [1720].   8°

T.366

6483

WALKER (Sir Hoveden)

A journal: or full account of the late expedition to
Canada ... London: for D. Browne, W. Mears, and
G. Strahan, 1720.   8°

T.111

6484

WALKER (Samuel)

The doctrine of the Eucharist stated: and the harmony
between the primitive Church and the reformed Church
of England manifested ... By a presbyter of the Church
of England. [Signed S.W.] Printed for T. Bickerton,
1720. 8°

Attributed by Bowdler to Henry Gandy.
2 copies.

T.26 T.59

1721

6485

An ANSWER to Dr. Ibbot's sermon preach'd before
the lord-mayor on Thursday, September 29. 1720.
By Philoclesius... London, printed for the author
and sold by W. Boreham, and A. Dod, 1721.   4°

2 copies.

T.196 T.564

6486

BECKETT (William)

A collection of very valuable and scarce pieces
relating to the last plague in the year 1665 ... With
a preface shewing the usefulness of this collection;
some errors of Dr. Mead, and his misrepresentations
of Dr. Hodges ... [Anon.] 2nd ed. London: for J.
Roberts, 1721.   8°

2 copies.

T.202

6487

BENTLEY (Richard)

Dr. Bentley's proposals for printing a new edition
of the Greek Testament, and St. Hierom's Latin
version. With a full answer to all the remarks of
a late pamphleteer [i.e. Conyers Middleton]. By a
member of Trinity College in Cambridge... London:
for J. Knapton, 1721.   4°

T.816

6488

The BEST preservative against the plague. With a
short account of the state of this nation, from the
conclusion of the Grand Rebellion of Oliver Cromwel
to the Revolution. By an Englilh-man [sic]...
London: for J. Leminge, 1721.   8°

2 copies.

T.202 T.647

6489

BLACKMORE (Sir Richard)

Just prejudices against the Arian hypothesis. To
which is added, a vindication of this proposition,
Articles of faith depend upon inferences, or are
left to consequences. London: W. Wilkins; for J.
Peele, 1721.   8°

T.738

6490

BURMANNUS (Petrus) the Elder.

An oration by Mr. Peter Burman against the studies of
humanity. Shewing, that the learned languages ...
are not only useless, but also dangerous to the studies
of law, physick, philosophy, and above all divinity ...
Translated into English, and the original annext.
London, for J. W. and sold by J. Roberts, 1721. 12°

Wanting the first gathering.

T.383

6491

CAII spectrum: or, Dr. Keyes's charge against Dr.
M[ead] ... London: for A. Moore, 1721.   8°

T.202

6492

The CASE of observing such fasts and festivals as are
appointed by the King's authority, and of using the
prayers provided for such occasions, considered ...
London: for J. Roberts, 1721.   8°

T.222

6493

The CHARACTER of the Parliament, commonly called the
Rump, &c. begun November 23. in the year 1640. With
a short account of some of their proceedings ...
London: printed; and sold by the booksellers of
London and Westminster, 1721.   8°

2 copies.

T.238 T.169

6494

The CHARACTERS of the four candidates for
M[i]d[dlese]x. Being a letter in the Freeholders
journal of Wednesday Feb. 14, 1721. [Signed
Philo-Britannicus.] [No imprint, 1721.] brs.

T.490

6495

CHICOYNEAU (François) and others.

A succinct account of the plague at Marseilles, its
symptoms, and the methods and medicines used for
curing it ... Translated from the French by a
physician. London: for S. Buckley, and D. Midwinter,
1721.   8°

T.202

6496

CHURCH OF ENGLAND.

A form of prayer, to be used in all churches and chapels
... on Friday the eighth day of December, being the
day appointed ... for beseeching God to preserve us
from the plague ... London, John Baskett, and by the
assigns of Thomas Newcomb, and Henry Hills, deceas'd,
1721.   4°

T.294

6497

COOPER (Anthony Ashley) 3rd Earl of Shaftesbury.

Letters from the Right Honourable the late Earl of
Shaftesbury, to Robert Molesworth ... With two
letters written by the late Sir John Cropley. To
which is prefix'd a large introduction by the editor
[i.e. John Toland]. London: W. Wilkins; and sold by
J. Peele, 1721.   8°

T.222

6498

DOCTOR Mead's Short discourse explain'd. Being a
clearer account of pestilential contagion, and
preventing ... London: W. Boreham, 1721.   8°

T.202

6499

ELLIOT (Robert)

A specimen of the Bishop of Sarum's posthumous
History of the affairs of the Church and State of
Great Britain, during his life ... 3rd ed. London:
J. Morphew, [1721?]   8°

T.222

6500

ELLIS (   )

The sense of the people concerning the present state
of affairs. With remarks upon some passages of our
own and the Roman history. In a letter to a member
of Parliament ... [Anon.] London: for J. Peele,
[1721].   8°

T.272

6501

FIDDES (Richard)

A letter, in answer to one from a free-thinker:
occasion'd by the late Duke of Buckinghamshire's
epitaph ... London: for J. Pemberton, 1721.   8°

T.399

6502

FINCH (Daniel) Earl of Nottingham.

The answer of the Earl of Nottingham to Mr. Whiston's
letter to him, concerning the eternity of the Son of
God, and of the Holy Ghost ... 2nd ed. London: for
Edward Valentine, 1721.   8°

2 copies.

T.244 T.222

6503

FINCH (Daniel) Earl of Nottingham.

The answer of the Earl of Nottingham to Mr. Whiston's
letter to him, concerning the eternity of the Son of
God, and of the Holy Ghost ... 3rd ed. London: for
Edward Valentine, 1721.   8°

T.150

6504

GASTRELL (Francis) Bishop of Chester.

The Bishop of Chester's case, with relation to the
wardenship of Manchester. In which it is shewn,
that no other degrees but such as are taken in the
university, can be deemed legal qualifications for
any ecclesiastical preferment... Cambridge, Corn.
Crownfield, 1721. Fol.

T.690

6505

GODOLPHIN (William) Marquess of Blandford.

A letter from an English traveller at Rome to his
father, of the 6th of May 1721. [An account of the
Pretender.] [Anon.] [No imprint, 1721?]   8°

T.438

6506

GORDON (Thomas) of Kirkcudbright.

The conspirators; or, The case of Catiline, as collected
from the best historians, impartially examin'd; with
respect to his declared and covert abettors ... By the
author of the case of Francis, Lord Bacon. [Anon. The
preface signed Britannicus.] ... 2nd ed. London, for
J. Roberts, 1721.   8°

2 copies.

T.238 T.272

6507

GORDON (Thomas) of Kirkcudbright.

Francis, Lord Bacon: or, The case of private and
national corruption, and bribery, impartially
consider'd. Address'd to all South-Sea directors,
members of Parliament, ministers of state, and Church-
dignitaries. By an Englishman ... 2nd ed. London,
for J. Roberts, 1721.   8°

T.272

6508

GORDON (Thomas) of Kirkcudbright.

Three political letters to a noble lord, concerning
liberty and the constitution. [Anon.] London: for
J. Roberts, 1721.   8°

T.403

6509

GRABE (Johann Ernst)

De forma consecrationis Eucharistiae, &c. Or,
A defence of the Greek Church against the Roman...
And now first published [by Thomas Wagstaffe],
together with a translation... London: for Richard
King, 1721.   8°

T.431

6510

HAMMOND (Anthony)

A modest apology, occasion'd by the late unhappy turn
of affairs, with relation to publick credit. By a
gentleman ... London: J. Peele, 1721.   8°

T.366

6511

HARE (Francis) *Bishop of Chichester.*

Scripture vindicated from the misinterpretations of the Lord Bishop of Bangor: in his answer to the Dean of Worcester's visitation sermon concerning Church-authority. London: for Jonah Bowyer, and sold by J. Roberts, 1721.   8°

T.296

6512

HASLEWOOD (Francis)

A sermon preach'd before ... the lord-mayor, the aldermen, and the citizens of London, in the cathedral church of St. Paul; on November the 5th, 1720 ... London: for Eman. Matthews, 1721.   8°

T.40

6513

HELL broke-loose, or, Devils aboveground, Being a dreadful desription [sic], of the hell-fire club, sulphur-society, demi-red dragons, merry-mohocks... By a true lover of the Church of England. [No imprint, 1721?]   8°

T.490

6514

JACOB (Giles)

Human happiness. A poem. Adapted to the present times. With several other miscellaneous poems: consisting of paraphrases, tales epistles, imitations epigrams, &c. never before printed. [The preface signed G.J.] London, for T. Jauncy, and J. Roberts, 1721.   8°

T.397

6515

JOHNSON (John) *Vicar of Cranbrook.*

The case of a rector refusing to preach a visitation sermon at the archdeacon's command ... London: for R. Knaplock, 1721.   12°

T.222

6516

KING (John) *Rector of Chelsea.*

Tolando-pseudologo-mastix: or, A curry-comb for a lying coxcomb. Being an answer to a late piece of Mr. Toland's, called Hypatia ... [Anon.] London: for Luke Stokoe; and sold by T. Bickerton, 1721.   8°

T.241

6517

KNIGHT (James)

A sermon preach'd in the parish-church of St. Sepulchre, June the 9th, 1720... at the anniversary meeting of the children educated in the charity-schools in and about the cities of London and Westminster. 2nd ed. London, Joseph Downing, 1721. 4°

T.701

6518

The LATE dreadful plague at Marseilles compared with that terrible plague in London, in the year 1665 ... By the author of the Practical scheme ... London: H. Parker, 1721. 2 parts.   8°

T.383

6519

LAWTON (Charlwood)

Three letters concerning civil comprehension, &c. the last of which is occasion'd by the present distresses the directors of the South-Sea Company have brought upon these kingdoms. [Anon.] London, A. Dodd, 1721. 8°

2 copies.

T.203 T.224

6520

LE FEVRE (Tannegui)

A compendious way of teaching the learned languages, and some of the liberal sciences at the same time; us'd formerly by Tanaquil Faber, in teaching one of his sons, and the famous Madam Dacier, his daughter. Done out of French... Printed in London, 1721.   8°

T.484

6521

A LETTER to a leading great man [i.e. Robert Walpole], concerning the rights of the people to petition, and the reasonableness of complying with such petitions ... London: for J. Peele, [1721].   8°

T.272

6522

M. (R.)

Now or never: or, A familiar discourse concerning the two schemes for restoring national credit ... By R.M. London printed: and sold by W. Boreham, 1721.   8°

T.366

6523

MARSEILLES.

A brief journal of what passed in the city of Marseilles, while it was afflicted with the plague, in the year 1720. Extracted from the register of the council-chamber ... kept by Monsieur Pichatty de Croissainte ... Translated from the original ... London: for J. Roberts, 1721.   8°

T.202

6524

MARSHALL (Nathaniel)

A sermon preach'd in the parish-church of St. Sepulchre, June the 1st 1721... at the anniversary meeting of the children educated in the charity-schools in and about the cities of London and Westminster. London, Joseph Downing, 1721.   4°

T.701

6525

MIDDLETON (Conyers)

Remarks, paragraph by paragraph, upon the proposals lately publish'd by Richard Bentley, for a new edition of the Greek Testament and Latin version... By a member of the University of Cambridge. London: J. Roberts, 1721.   4°

T.816

6526

MIDDLETON (Conyers)

Some farther remarks, paragraph by paragraph, upon proposals lately publish'd for a new edition of a Greek and Latin Testament, by Richard Bentley... London: for T. Bickerton, 1721.   4°

2 copies.

T.554 T.816

6527

PEARCE (Zachary) *Bishop of Rochester.*

Epistolae duae ad celeberrimum doctissimumque virum F[ranciscum] V[alckenaer] professorem Amstelodamensem scriptae. Quarum in altera agitur de editione Novi Testamenti a clarissimo Bentleio suscepta... [Anon.] Londini: prostant venales apud Ffranciscum Clay, 1721.   4°

T.816

6528

SOME observations concerning the plague. Occasion'd by, and with some reference to, the late ingenious discourse of the learned Dr. Mead, concerning pestilential contagion, and the methods to prevent it. By a well-wisher to the publick. Printed at Dublin: and reprinted for J. Roberts, 1721.   8°

T.528

6529

SOUTH SEA COMPANY.

The proceedings of the directors of the South-Sea Company, from the first proposal of that Company, for taking in the publick debts, February 1, 1719. to the choice of new directors, February 2, 1720 ... London: for J. Roberts, 1721.   8°

T.366

6530

A SUPPLEMENT to the London Journal of March 25, 1721; being the state of the case relating to the surrender of Mr. Knight, farther considered. London: for J. Peele, 1721.   8°

T.272

6531

SWIFT (Jonathan) *Dean of St. Patrick's*

The wonderfull wonder of wonders; being an accurate description of the birth, education, manner of living... whole a--se. By Dr. Sw-ft... 3rd ed. London: printed from the original copy from Dublin and sold by T. Bickerton, 1721.   4°

Teerink 906. The attribution to Swift is not certain.

2 copies.

T.269 T.397

6532

T. (M.)

A letter from a gentleman at Rome, to his friend in London; giving an account of some very surprizing cures in the king's evil by the touch, lately effected in the neighbourhood of that city ... Translated out of the Italian ... London: for A. Moore, 1721.   8°

T.294

6533

TRAPP (Joseph)

The dignity, and benefit, of the priesthood; the lawfulness of marriage in the clergy; the hardships of them, and their families, in this nation; and the excellency of the charity by which they are relieved, &c. Set forth in a sermon preached before the Sons of the clergy... December 8, 1720... London: for Jonah Bowyer, 1721.   8°

2 copies.

T.40 T.170

6534

TRENCHARD (John) *and others.*

A collection of all the political letters in the London Journal, to December 17, inclusive, 1720 ... [Anon.] London: for J. Roberts, 1721.   8°

T.272

6535

TRENCHARD (John) *and others.*

A second collection of introductions, and letters, in the London Journal. Being the author's account of himself: with humorous essays on several subjects. [Anon.] London, J. Roberts, 1721.   8°

T.272

6536

A VINDICATION of Mary, Queen of Scotland, from the vile reflections and foul aspersions of Buchanan ... Together with the character of Buchanan and his writings ... London: A. Dodd, [1721].   8°

T.222

6537

WALKER (Samuel)

Tradition is no rule now to Christians, either of faith or practice. Being an answer to Dr. Brett's treatise of tradition. By S.W. London: for T. Bickerton, 1721.   8°

T.26

6538

WHEN my lord falls in my lady's lap England beware of a great mishap. Being prophetick predictions, for the years 1722. 1723. and 1744 deduc'd from solid and authentick precedents in history ... London; for J. Roberts, 1721.   8°

T.44

6539

WILLIAMS (Daniel) *Presbyter of the Church of England.*

The succession of protestant bishops asserted; or, The regularity of the ordinations of the Church of England justify'd. Wherein the first protestant bishops are clear'd from the aspersions lately cast upon them by Mr. Thomas Ward, a Romanist, in his book, intituled, The controversy of ordination truly stated ... London: for Charles Rivington, 1721.   8°

2 copies.

T.42 T.767

1722

6540

The ART of parliamenteering ... By the author of The history of the late septennial Parliament. London; for J. Peele, 1722.   8°

T.224

6541

The BENEFIT of farting explained: or, The fundament-all cause of the distempers incident to the fair sex inquir'd into... Wrote in Spanish, by Don Fartinhando Puff-indorst... and translated into English... by Obadiah Fizzle... 7th ed. London: for A. Moore, 1722.   4°

Formerly attributed to Swift.

T.269

6542

The BENEFIT of farting explained: or, The fundament-all cause of the distempers incident to the fair sex inquir'd into... Wrote in Spanish, by Don Fartinhando Puff-indorst... and translated into English... by Obadiah Fizzle... 9th ed. London: for A. Moore, 1722.   4°

Formerly attributed to Swift.

T.269

6543

The BENEFITS and advantages gain'd by the late septennial Parliament, set in a clear light, by their acts and deeds ... By a member of the late Parliament. The fourth edition corrected. London: for A. Moore, [1722].   8°

T.224

6544

BOULTER (Hugh) *Archbishop of Armagh.*

A sermon preach'd in the parish-church of St. Sepulchre, May the 17th, 1722... at the anniversary meeting of the children educated in the charity-schools in and about the cities of London and Westminster. By... Hugh, Lord Bishop of Bristol. London, Joseph Downing, 1722. 4°

T.701

6545

A COMPLEAT history of the late septennial Parliament. Wherein all their proceedings are particularly enquir'd into, and faithfully related ... The third edition, corrected. London; for J. Peele, 1722. 8°

T.224

6546

CORNWALL (C.)

Homeros, homoros. The third book of Homer's Ilias burlesqu'd... London: S. Richardson, for C. Stokes; and sold by the booksellers of London and Westminster, 1722. 8°

2 copies.

T.397 T.653

6547

DOCTOR Mead's Short discourse explain'd. Or, His account of pestiential contagion, and preventing, exploded. 2nd ed... London, J. Peele, 1722. 8°

T.202

6548

DOWNES (Samuel)

An abridgment of the controversy between the Church of England, and the new pseudo-primitives ... In a dialogue between Neophytus, an essentialist clergyman, and Irenaeus, a layman of the Church of England. 2nd ed ... (The appendix.) London: for Charles Rivington, 1722. 2 parts. 8°

T.431

6549

The D[UKE] of B[uckingha]m's pro[phec]y for the year 1722, which was found in his closet a week after his death, foretelling several strange wonders and accidents ... London: Jonathan Parry, [1722?] 8°

T.399

6550

EARBERY (Matthias)

An historical account of the advantages that have accru'd to England, by the succession in the illustrious house of Hanover ... [Anon.] London: printed in the year, 1722. 2 parts. 8°

T.438

6551

EARBERY (Matthias)

A monthly packet of advices from Parnassus, establish'd by Apollo's express authority, and sent to England... (The prosecution of the author [i.e. Zachary Pearce] of the clergyman's letter to the Bishop of Rochester...) [Anon.] London: for the authors, and sold by Katherine Nelthorp, [1722?] 4°

T.10

6552

FAIRCHILD (Thomas)

The city gardener. Containing the most experienced method of cultivating and ordering such ever-greens, fruit-trees... &c. as will be ornamental, and thrive best in the London gardens. London: for T. Woodward, and J. Peele, 1722. 8°

T.518

6553

GREAT BRITAIN. *Army.*

Rules and articles for the better government of our horse and foot-guards, and all other our land-forces in our kingdoms of Great Britain and Ireland, and dominions beyond the seas. London, John Baskett, and by the assigns of Thomas Newcomb, and Henry Hills, deceas'd, 1722. 8°

T.390

6554

GREAT BRITAIN. *Parliament. House of Commons.*

A report from the committee appointed by order of the House of Commons to examine Christopher Layer, and others... Reported on the first of March, 1722, by ... William Pulteney... Together with the appendixes... London: for Jacob Tonson, Bernard Lintot, and William Taylor, 1722. 2 parts. Fol.

T.683

6555

GREY (Zachary)

Presbyterian prejudice display'd. Or; An answer to Mr. Benjamin Bennet's Memorial of the Reformation ... By a hearty well-wisher to the Established Church ... London: for T. Warner, 1722. 8°

T.42

6556

GRIFFIN (John)

The common Christian instructed in some necessary points of religion: in a dialogue between a clergyman and a layman of different communions. In answer to Mr. S[amuel] D[ownes]'s Abridgment of the controversy... [Anon.] London: for E. Morphew, 1722. 8°

2 copies.

T.98 T.62

6557

HUTCHESON (Archibald)

A collection of advertisements, letters and papers, and some other facts, relating to the last elections at Westminster and Hastings. [Anon.] 2nd ed. London: for T. Payne, 1722. 8°

T.224

6558

HUTCHESON (Archibald)

Copies of some letters from Mr. Hutcheson, to the late Earl of Sunderland. And an introduction to the same. 2nd ed. London: for T. Payne, 1722. 8°

T.224

6559

HUTCHESON (Archibald)

A speech made in the House of Commons April the 24th 1716; against the Bill for the repeal of the Triennial Act, and for enlarging the time of continuance of parliaments... [Anon.] London: for J. Jones, and sold by the booksellers of London and Westminster, 1722. 8°

T.242

6560

HUTCHESON (Archibald)

A speech made in the House of Commons April the 25th 1716; against the Bill for the repeal of the Triennial Act, and for enlarging the time of continuance of parliaments. By Ar[chibal]d Hu[tcheso]n. 2nd ed. To which is added, A list of the members who voted for and against the Bill... London: T. Sharpe, and sold by T. Payne, 1722. 2 parts. 8°

T.434

6561

LIVIA'S advice to Augustus, persuading clemency in the case of Cinna, who, was taken in actual rebellion against the government. Collected from the Roman historians... London: for T. Payne, 1722. 8°

T.399

6562

MAITLAND (Charles)

Mr. Maitland's account of inoculating the small pox vindicated, from Dr. Wagstaffe's misrepresentations of that practice, with some remarks on Mr. Massey's sermon. London: J. Peele, 1722. 8°

T.294

6563

MARSHALL (Nathaniel)

The case of the erectors of a chapel, or oratory; in the parish of St. Andrew's, Holborn. And a defense of their proceedings therein ... [Anon.] London: for W. Taylor, 1722. 8°

T.222

6564

MARTIN (David)

The genuineness of the text of the first Epistle of Saint John ... Translated from the French. London: for W. and J. Innys, 1722. 8°

T.97

6565

MASSEY (Edmund)

A sermon against the dangerous and sinful practice of inoculation. Preach'd at St. Andrew's Holborn, on Sunday, July the 8th, 1722. London, for William Meadows, 1722. 8°

2 copies.

T.109 T.170

6566

MASSEY (Edmund)

The signs of the times. A sermon preached before ... the lord-mayor, and court of aldermen, at the cathedral of St. Paul, on Friday the 8th of December, 1721. being the day appointed for a general fast for the prevention of the plague. London: Thomas Bickerton, 1722. 8°

T.100

6567

MASSEY (Edmund)

The signs of the times. A sermon preached before ... the lord-mayor, and court of aldermen, at the cathedral of St. Paul, on Friday the 8th of December, 1721. being the day appointed for a general fast for the prevention of the plague. 6th ed. London: for J. Brotherton and W. Meadows, and sold by T. Bickerton, 1722. 8°

T.109

6568

MASSINGER (Philip)

The Roman actor. A tragedy. Written originally by Philip Massenger; and since reviv'd with alterations. London: for W. Mears, and D. Brown, W. Chetwood, and J. Woodman, S. Chapman, 1722. 8°

T.237

6569

The PARSON and his maid. A mery tale ... (Venus enrag'd.) London: for T. Payne, [1722?] 8°

T.58

6570

PEARCE (Zachary) *Bishop of Rochester.*

A letter to the clergy of the Church of England: on occasion of the commitment of the ... Lord Bishop of Rochester to the Tower of London. By a clergyman of the Church of England. London, J. Roberts, 1722. 4°

2 copies.

T.2 T.24

6571

PHILIPS (William)

Hibernia freed. A tragedy, as it is acted at the theatre in Lincoln's-Inn-Fields. London: for Jonah Bowyer, 1722. 8°

Incomplete.

T.667

6572

The PLOTTERS; a satire. Occasion'd by the proceedings of the Earl of Or[rer]y; the Lord B[ishop] of R[ochester] the Lord N. and G. and others. Containing a true description of all the statesmen belonging to the Chevalier's court... [A poem] London; for A. Moore, 1722. 8°

T.647

6573

RIGHTFUL monarchy: or, Revolution tyranny. A satyr: being a dialogue between High-Dutch illustrious, and Low-Dutch glorious. Printed in the year, 1722. 8°

2 copies.

T.397 T.653

6574

SPRAT (Thomas) *Bishop of Rochester.*

A relation of the wicked contrivance of Stephen Blackhead and Robert Young, against the lives of several persons, by forging an association under their hands ... London: for T. Payne, 1722. 8°

T.238

6575

SYKES (Arthur Ashley)

A letter to the Right Honourable the Earl of Nottingham. Occasioned by a late motion made by the Archdeacon of London, at his visitation for the City clergy to return their thanks to his Lordship for his answer to Mr. Whiston. By a curate of London. London, for J. Roberts, 1722. 8°

T.738

6576

SYNGE (Edward) *Archbishop of Tuam.*

An essay towards making the knowledge of religion easy to the meanest capacity... 5th ed... London: for R. Sare, 1722. 12°

T.619

6577

TRAPP (Joseph)

The case of the patron and rector of St. Andrew's, Holbourn. In answer to a pamphlet [by Nathaniel Marshall], entitled, The case of the erectors of a chapel, or oratory, in the said parish, &c ... [Anon.] London: for Jonah Bowyer, 1722. 8°

T.222

6578

WATERLAND (Daniel)

A sermon preach'd before the Sons of the clergy at their anniversary-meeting in the cathedral church of St. Paul, December 14. 1721. London: for W. and J. Innys, 1722. 8°

T.170

6579

The WHOLE life and history of Benjamin Child, lately executed for robbing the Bristol mail ... London; for A. Moore, 1722. 8°

T.399

6580

The WHOLE life and history of Benjamin Child, lately executed for robbing the Bristol mail... 2nd ed. London; for A. Moore, 1722. 8°

T.111

6581

The WHOLE proceeding upon the arraignment, tryal, conviction and attainder of Christopher Layer, Esq; for high treason, in compassing and imagining the death of the King... London: S. Buckley, 1722. Fol.

T.683

1723

6582

ATTERBURY (Francis) *Bishop of Rochester.*

The entire, true, and genuine, speech of Francis late Lord Bishop of Rochester, at the bar of the House of Lords, on Saturday the 11th of May, 1723. 2nd ed., carefully corrected... London, James Dodd, and A. Rocayrol, [1723]. Fol.

T.683

6583

DELAUNE (William)

A sermon preach'd before the Sons of the clergy, at their anniversary meeting in the cathedral-church of St. Paul, on Thursday, December 12. 1723. London: for Jonah Bowyer, 1723. 4°

T.196

6584

The DUTY of consulting a spiritual guide consider'd: and the practice of it recommended to all Christians ... London: for Jonah Bowyer, 1723. 8°

T.673

6585

ENGLAND. *Laws, Statutes.*

The penal laws against papists and popish recusants, nonconformists and nonjurors: with the statutes relating to the succession of the Crown ... In the Savoy; E. and R. Nutt, and R. Gosling, (assigns of Edw. Sayer) for R. Gosling, 1723. 8°

T.399

6586

FREIND (John)

Johannis Freind ad celeberrimum virum Ricardum Mead, M.D. de quibusdam variolarum generibus epistola. Londini: impensis J. Bowyer, 1723. 8°

T.294

6587

GREAT BRITAIN.

A letter, dated London 20 March 1723, directed a Monsieur Gordon, banquier à Bologne, with draughts of two affidavits inclosed... With depositions of Anthony Sanderson and Roger Garth... Laid before the House of Commons by his Majesty's command... London: for Jacob Tonson, Bernard Lintot, and William Taylor, 1723. Fol.

T.683

6588

GREAT BRITAIN.

Several examinations taken before one of his Majesty's principal secretaries of state: together with two letters referred to in some of the said examinations. Laid before the House of Commons by his Majesty's command... London: for Jacob Tonson, Bernard Lintot, and William Taylor, 1723. Fol.

T.683

6589

GREAT BRITAIN. *Parliament. House of Lords.*

A collection of the several protests in the House of Lords... in the years 1722 and 1723. 2nd ed. To which is added, the heads of the late Bp. of Rochester's speech, before the House of Lords... Printed for A. Moore, and sold by the booksellers of London and Westminster, 1723. Fol.

T.683

6590

GREAT BRITAIN. *Parliament. House of Lords.*

A report from the Lords committees to whom the report and original papers delivered by the House of Commons were referred, and who were impowered by the House of Lords to examine Christopher Layer... London: for Edmund Parker, and Jacob Tonson, 1723. 2 parts. Fol.

T.683

6591

GREY (Zachary)

A letter of thanks to Mr. Benja. Bennet, for his moderate rebuke of the author [i.e. Zachary Grey] of an insolent pamphlet, entituled, Presbyterian prejudice display'd... By one who is neither Jacobite, nor Republican, Presbyterian, nor Papist ... London: for Tho. Osborne, 1723. 8°

T.42

6592

HARE (Francis) *Bishop of Chichester.*

Two sermons on Rom. xiii. 1,2... preached in the cathedral at Worcester, on Novemb. 18, and 25. 1722. London: S. Buckley, 1723. 4°

T.765

6593

The HISTORY of the sheriffdom of the city of London and county of Middlesex ... London: sold by A. Dodd, 1723. 8°

T.399

6594

KELLY (George)

The speech of Mr. George Kelly. Spoke at the bar of the House of Lords, on Thursday, the 2d of May, 1723. in his defence against the bill then depending, for inflicting pains and penalties upon him... London: for A. Moore, 1723. Fol.

T.683

6595

MIDDLETON (Conyers)

Bibliothecae Cantabrigiensis ordinandae methodus quaedam; quam domino procancellario senatuique academico considerandam & perficiendam officii et pietatis ergo proponit. Cantabrigiae: typis academicis, 1723. 4°

T.816

6596

PHIPPS (*Sir* Constantine)

The defence of Francis, late Lord Bishop of Rochester, at the bar of the House of Lords, on Thursday the 9th, and Saturday the 11th, of May, 1723. Against the Bill then depending for inflicting pains and penalties on him... London, for Jonah Bowyer, 1723. Fol.

T.683

6597

REEVE (Thomas)

The replies of Thomas Reeve, Esq; and Clement Wearg, Esq; in the House of Lords, the thirteenth of May, 1723. in behalf of the Bill to inflict pains and penalties on the late Bishop of Rochester, against the defence made by the said late Bishop and his counsel. London, S. Buckley, 1723. Fol.

T.683

6598

ROBINSON (Robert) *Recorder of Scarborough.*

An essay upon kings, poets, stoics, sceptics, fortune, reason, dedications; and for defining the meaning of the term barbarous, &c. In a dedication to the king of clubs ... [Anon.] London: for J. Roberts, 1723. 8°

T.275

6599

SHUCKFORD (Samuel)

Peace and unity recommended to the clergy. A sermon preach'd in the cathedral-church of Norwich, at the primary visitation of... Thomas Lord Bishop of Norwich, on Monday July 1st. 1723. Cambridge: for Corn. Crownfield: and are to be sold by James Knapton, and Robert Knaplock, London, 1723. 4°

T.753

6600

SMITH (John) *C.M.*

The curiosities of common water: or The advantages thereof in preventing and curing many distempers ... The third edition, corrected. London, for John and Barham Clark, 1723. 8°

T.294

6601

SYNGE (Edward) *Bishop of Elphin.*

The constitution of our Establish'd Church, as founded on law divine, and humane, consider'd: in a sermon preach'd at the cathedral church of St. Patrick, Dublin ... at the consecration of ... Theophilus, Lord Bishop of Clonfert. London: for R. Sare, 1723. 8°

T.170

6602

WILLIS (Richard) *Bishop of Winchester.*

The Bishop of Salisbury's speech in the House of Lords, upon the third reading of the Bill to inflict pains and penalties on Francis (late) Bishop of Rochester, the 15th of May, 1723. London, S. Buckley, 1723. Fol.

T.683

6603

WYNNE (William) *Serjeant-at-Law.*

The defence of Francis, late Lord Bishop of Rochester, at the bar of the House of Lords, on Thursday the 9th, and Saturday the 11th, of May, 1723. against the Bill then depending for inflicting pains and penalties on him. London, for Jonah Bowyer, 1723. fol.

T.683

1724

6604

The ART of managing popular elections. Being a complete collection of all the advertisements, papers, letters, advices ... used on behalf of the candidates on both sides, in the late election of common-councilmen for the ward of Farringdon-Without ... London: for T. Warner, 1724. 8°

T.399

6605

BRADY (Nicholas)

Sin display'd in its natural deformity. A sermon preach'd at the assizes held for the county of Surry, at Kingston upon Thames, August 3. 1724. London: for W. Mears; J. Walthoe; and J. Walthoe, in Richmond, 1724. 4°

T.637

6606

BURNET (William)

An essay on Scripture-prophecy, wherein it is endeavoured to explain the three periods contain'd in the XII chapter of the prophet Daniel ... [Anon.] Printed in the year 1724. 4°

T.552

6607

COCKBURN (John)

A specimen of some free and impartial remarks on publick affairs and particular persons, especially relating to Scotland; occasion'd by Dr. Burnet's History of his own times. London: for T. Warner, and sold by the booksellers of London and Westminster, [1724.] 8°

T.370

6608

DEFOE (Daniel)

Considerations on publick credit. In a letter to a member of Parliament. [Anon.] London: for J. Roberts, 1724. 8°

Moore 455. Probably, not certainly, by Defoe.

T.272

1724 (Cont'd)

6609

DOUGHTY (Gregory)

A sermon preach'd before the University of Cambridge, in Kings College Chapel, on the 25th of March 1724 .. Cambridge, printed at the University-Press, for Will. Thurlbourn, and sold by R. Knaplock, 1724. 4°

T.340

6610

DRAKE (Samuel)

Ara ignoto Deo sacra. Concio ad clerum habita in templo beatae Mariae Cantabrigiae VII. Id. Julii MDCCXXIV. pro gradu doctoratus in sacra theologia... Cantabrigiae typis academicis impensis Gulielmi Thurlbourne. Prostant vaenales apud Gul. & Ioh. Innys Londini, 1724. 4°

T.339

6611

EARBERY (Matthias)

Impartial reflections upon Dr. Burnet's posthumous History. By Philalethes ... London: Richard Macey, 1724. 8°

T.370

6612

EDGLEY (Samuel)

A sermon preach'd before the Sons of the clergy, at their anniversary meeting in the cathedral-church of St. Paul, on Tuesday, December 10. 1724. London: for Jonah Bowyer, 1724. 4°

T.196

6613

IBBOT (Benjamin)

A sermon preach'd before... Sir Peter Delmé Kt, Lord Mayor, the aldermen and citizens of London, in the cathedral church of St. Paul, on Saturday, August the first, 1724... London: for John Wyat, 1724. 4°

T.625

6614

LAW (William)

Remarks upon a late book [by Bernard de Mandeville], entituled, The fable of the bees, or Private vices, publick benefits. In a letter to the author... London: for Will. and John Innys, 1724. 8°

2 copies.

T.109 T.658

6615

A LETTER to Mr. William Timms, one of the common-council-men of Cripplegate-Within, London. Containing an answer to the report of a committee of aldermen... in affirmance of the right of the mayor and aldermen to put a negative to bills or acts depending in the Common Council... [Signed Londinensis.] London: for James Roberts, 1724. Fol.

T.685

6616

LUPTON (William)

National sins fatal to prince and people. A sermon preached before the honourable House of Commons at St. Margaret's Westminster, on the 30th day of January, 1724 ... London: for S. Keble, J. Crokatt, and Tho. Worrall, 1724. 4°

T.196

6617

NEWCOME (John)

The sure word of prophecy. A sermon preach'd before the University of Cambridge at St. Mary's church June 24th. 1724. 2nd ed. Cambridge: for Will. and John Innys; and Will. Thurlbourn, 1724. 8°

2 copies.

T.109 T.345

6618

SANNAZARO (Jacopo)

The osiers. A pastoral translated from the Latin of Sannazarius [by Beaupré Bell]. With some account of Sannazarius, and his piscatory eclogues... Cambridge, printed for the author, at the University Press, 1724. 4°

T.554

6619

TRUEMAN (John) *pseud?*

An examination and resolution of the two questions following, viz. First, whether unfreemen can vote in our wardmote elections. Secondly, whether freemen paying to one or more scots, and not to all, shall be qualified to vote in those elections... By a citizen [signing himself John Trueman]... London, for James Roberts, 1724. Fol.

T.685

6620

A VINDICATION of the late Bishop Burnet from the calumnies and aspersions of a libel, entitled, A specimen of some free and impartial remarks, &c. occasioned by Dr. Burnet's History of his own times, by John Cockburn. London: for J. Roberts, 1724. 8°

T.370

6621

WALKER (Samuel)

The Scripture doctrine of the sacred and adorable Trinity. By S.W. London, printed for the author, 1724. 8°

T.109

6622

WESLEY (Samuel) *the Younger.*

The battle of the sexes: a poem... [Anon.] 2nd ed. London: for J. Brotherton; and sold by J. Roberts, 1724. 8°

T.651

6623

WILSON (Thomas) *Bishop of Sodor and Man.*

The true Christian method of educating the children both of the poor and rich, recommended more especially to the masters and mistresses of the charity-schools, in a sermon preach'd in the parish-church of St. Sepulchre, May the 28th, 1724... (The present state of the charity-schools...) London, Joseph Downing, 1724. 4°

2 copies.

T.196 T.700

1725

6624

ANSTIS (John)

Observations introductory to an historical essay, upon the knighthood of the Bath. London: for James Woodman, and sold by J. Roberts, 1725. 2 parts. 4°

T.235

6625

BERKELEY (George) *Bishop of Cloyne.*

A proposal for the better supplying of churches in our foreign plantations, and for converting the savage Americans to Christianity, by a college to be erected in the Summer Islands, otherwise called the Isles of Bermuda... [Anon.] London, H. Woodfall, 1725. 8°

T.383

6626

BERRIMAN (William)

The excellency and reward of charity. A sermon preach'd in the parish-church of St. Sepulchre, May the 20th, 1725... at the anniversary meeting of the children educated in the charity-schools in and about the cities of London and Westminster. (An account of the charity-schools...) London, Joseph Downing, 1725. 4°

T.700

6627

BLUETT (Thomas)

An enquiry whether a general practice of virtue tends to the wealth or poverty, benefit or disadvantage of a people? In which the pleas offered by the author of the Fable of the bees ... [i.e. Bernard de Mandeville] are considered. With some thoughts concerning a toleration of publick stews ... [Anon.] London: for R. Wilkin, 1725. 8°

T.109

6628

BRAMSTON (John)

Private judgment in religion justified, in opposition to implicit faith. A sermon preach'd at the assizes holden at Chelmsford in Essex, July 22d, 1724. London: for J. Pemberton [sic], 1725. 8°

T.662

6629

BROMFIELD (William) *Quaker.*

The faith of the true Christian, and the primitive Quakers faith ... [By W.B.] Printed for the author, 1725. 8°

T.109

6630

The CASE of orphans consider'd, from antiquity. With some remarks on our courts of wards, and why put down ... London: for J. Peele, 1725. 8°

T.527

6631

DENNE (John)

The miraculous success of the Gospel in its first preaching and authority. A sermon preached ... at an ordination held [at St. Margaret's, Westminster] by ... Samuel Lord Bishop of Rochester. London: for R. Knaplock, 1725. 4°

T.72

6632

EARLE (Jabez)

The memory of the just is blessed. A sermon preach'd at Hanover-street, Nov. 4th, 1725. being the birth-day of King William. London: for John Clark and Richard Hett; and Samuel Chandler, 1725. 8°

T.706

6633

ENGLAND. *Parliament.*

A collection of the proceedings in the House of Commons against the Lord Verulam ... for corruption and bribery ... Together with the judgment given by the Lords against the said Lord Chancellor, A.D. 1620. 3rd ed. London: for A. More, [1725?] 8°

T.527

6634

FORMAN (Charles)

Mr. Forman's letter to the Right Honourable William Pulteney, Esq; shewing how pernicious, the Imperial Company of Commerce and Navigation, lately established in the Austrian Netherlands, is likely to prove to Great Britain ... London: printed for, and sold by S. Bussey, 1725. 8°

T.527

6635

GRANDVAL (Nicolas Ragot de)

Le vice puni, ou cartouche, poëme. [Anon.] A Anvers, chez Nicolas Grandveau, 1725. 8°

T.642

6636

GREAT BRITAIN. *Commissioners for Forfeited Estates.*

The final report of the Commissioners and Trustees of the Forfeited Estates in Scotland. Presented to the honourable House of Commons; Saturday the 17th day of April, 1725. London: for Robert Knaplock, Jacob Tonson, and Bernard Lintot, 1725. Fol.

T.685

6637

GREAT BRITAIN. *Court of Chancery.*

The accompts of the several masters of the High Court of Chancery; of the securities, effects, and cash, belonging to the suitors of that court, deposited in their respective hands. Published... by order of ... the Lords Commissioners for the custody of the Great Seal of Great Britain. London: S. Buckley, 1725. Fol.

T.685

6638

GREAT BRITAIN. *Court of Chancery.*

An order of the High Court of Chancery, made by... the Lords Commissioners for the custody of the Great Seal of Great Britain, on the 26th of May, 1725. Fol.

T.685

6639

GREAT BRITAIN. *Court of Chancery.*

An order of the High Court of Chancery, made by the Right Honourable Peter Lord King... on the 4th day of November, 1725. London, S. Buckley, 1725. Fol.

T.685

6640

GREAT BRITAIN. *Parliament.*

Articles exhibited by the knights, citizens, and burgesses in Parliament assembled... against Thomas Earl of Macclesfield, in maintenance of their impeachment against him for high crimes and misdemeanors. (The answer of Thomas Earl of Macclesfield to the Articles...) London, John Baskett, and by the assigns of Henry Hills, 1725. Fol.

T.685

6641

GREAT BRITAIN. *Parliament. House of Lords.*

A compleat collection of all the protests of the Lords during their last session of Parliament. To which is prefix'd the petition against the City-bill. London, for A. Moore, 1725. Fol.

T.685

6642

GREAT BRITAIN. *Trustees for Raising Money on the Estates of the late South Sea Directors.*

The report of the Trustees for raising money on the estates of the late South Sea directors and others... London: for Robert Knaplock, Jacob Tonson, and Bernard Lintot, 1725. Fol.

T.685

6643

HARRIS (William) *Minister of Crutched-friars.*

Some memoirs of the life and character of the reverend and learned Thomas Manton, D.D. Prefix'd to the second edition of his sermons on the CXIXth psalms. London, J. Darby, and sold by R. Ford and S. Chandler, and S. Billingsley, 1725. 8°

T.527

6644

The LIFE and character of the late Lord Chancellor Jefferys... [Attributed to A. More.] 2nd ed. London: R. King, 1725. 8°

T.527

6645

LUPTON (William)

A discourse of murther, preach'd in the chapel at Lincoln's-Inn... London: for S. Keble, J. Crokatt, and Tho. Worrall, 1725. 8°

T.109

6646

MORETON (Andrew)

Every-body's business, is no-body's business; or, Private abuses, publick grievances: exemplified in the pride, insolence, and exorbitant wages of our women-servants, footmen, &c... London: sold by T. Warner; A. Dodd; and E. Nutt, 1725. 8°

T.399

6647

PAXTON (Nicholas)

The report of the state of the offices of the deficient masters of the High Court of Chancery, made to... the Lord Viscount Townshend... (The report made to the... Lord High Chancellor of Great Britain, by Robert Holford... The report... by James Lightboun... The report... by Mark Thurston... The report... by Henry Edwards...) London, Sam. Buckley, 1725. Fol.

T.685

6648

ROBINSON (Nicholas)

A general scheme for a course of medical lectures, intended for the improvement of young physicians, and gentlemen, that are desirous of understanding the laws of the animal oeconomy... [No imprint, 1725?] 4°

T.639

6649

ROPER (Joseph)

A sermon preach'd at the anniversary meeting of the Sons of the clergy, in the cathedral-church of St. Paul, on the 9th of December, 1725. London: for Jonah Bowyer; and W. and J. Innys, 1725. 4°

T.196

6650

The TRYAL of the Czarewitz, Alexis Petrowitz, who was condemn'd at Petersbourg, on the 25th of June, 1718, for a design of rebellion and treason against the life of the Czar his father... London: for James Crokatt, 1725. 8°

T.527

6651

A VINDICATION of the Lord Chancellor Bacon, from the aspersion of injustice, cast upon him by Mr. Wraynham... London; for J. Peele, 1725. 8°

T.527

1726

6652

AHLERS (Cyriacus)

Some observations concerning the woman of Godlyman [Mary Toft] in Surrey. Made at Guilford on Sunday, Nov. 20. 1726. tending to prove her extraordinary deliveries to be a cheat and imposture. London: for J. Roberts, 1726. 8°

T.294

6653

AMHURST (Nicholas)

Terrae-filius: or, The secret history of the University of Oxford; in several essays. To which are added, Remarks upon a late book, entitled, University education, by R. Newton... [Anon.] London: for R. Francklin, 1726. 2 vols. 12°

T.440

6654

ARBUTHNOT (John)

It cannot rain but it pours: or, London strow'd with rarities. Being, an account of the arrival of a white bear ... as also of the Faustina, the celebrated Italian singing woman; and of the copper-farthing dean from Ireland ... [Anon.] London: for J. Roberts, 1726. 4°

Incomplete.

T.490

6655

BROMFIELD (William) *Quaker.*

A reply, to a late pamphlet, published by Henton Brown. Called by him, An examination of William Bromfield's principles. With regard to the conception and mission of Jesus Christ ... London: printed for the author, and sold by G. Strahan, 1726. 8°

T.44

6656

BURROUGHS (Samuel)

The history of the Chancery; relating to the judicial power of that court, and the rights of the masters ... [Anon.] London: for J. Walthoe, 1726. 12°

T.440

6657

COLLIER (Jeremy)

God not the origin of evil. Being an additional sermon to a collection of Mr. Collier's discourses, &c. London: W. Bowyer, 1726. 8°

2 copies.

T.43   T.662

6658

The GRAND mystery, or art of meditating over an house of office, restor'd and unveil'd; after the manner of the ingenious Dr. S[wi]ft ... The second edition corrected. London: for J. Roberts, and sold by the booksellers of London and Westminster, 1726. 8°

T.347

6659

GREAT BRITAIN. *Parliament. House of Lords.*

A collection of all the protests of the Lords during this last session of Parliament. London, for A. Moore, 1726. Fol.

T.685

6660

HOMER.

The Iliad in a nutshell: or, Homer's Battle of the frogs and mice. Illustrated with notes. [By Samuel Wesley.] ... London: for B. Barker; and sold by J. Roberts, 1726. 8°

T.225

6661

KING GEORGE'S COLLEGE.

The articles of the foundation of King George's College, that is to be open'd upon the birthday of ... the ... Princess of Wales. London: for J. Roberts, 1726. 8°

T.44

6662

LUPTON (William)

Christian conversation. A farewell sermon, preach'd in the parish church of St. Dunstan in the West, on Sunday, March 20. 1725/6 ... London: for S. Keble; and T. Worrall, 1726. 8°

T.109

6663

MANGEY (Thomas)

The Gospel preach'd to the poor. A sermon preach'd in the parish-church of St. Sepulchre, June the 2d, 1726... at the anniversary meeting of the children educated in the charity-schools in and about the cities of London and Westminster. London, Joseph Downing, 1726. 4°

T.716

6664

MANNINGHAM (*Sir* Richard)

An exact diary of what was observ'd during a close attendance upon Mary Toft, the pretended rabbet-breeder of Godalming... 2nd ed. London, for Fletcher Gyles, and sold by J. Roberts, 1726. 8°

T.294

6665

The MEMORIAL of the Chevalr. de St. George, on occasion of the Princess Sobieski's retiring into a nunnery: and two original letters, written by the Chevalier to the said Princess, to dissuade her from that design. Translated from the original French. London: for W. Wilkins; and sold by N. Blandford, [1726]. 8°

2 copies.

T.527 T.169

6666

MIDDLETON (Conyers)

De medicorum apud veteres Romanos degentium conditione dissertatio... Prostant venales Cantabrigiae apud Edmundum Jeffery, 1726. 4°

T.816

6667

MR. Law's Unlawfulness of the stage entertainment examin'd: and the insufficiency of his arguments fully demonstrated. By S. Philomusus. London, printed: and sold by J. Roberts, 1726. 8°

T.109

6668

ORENDAYN (Juan Bautista de) *Marques de la Paz.*

The letters of the Marquis de la Paz, Secretary of State to his Catholick Majesty, and Coll. Stanhope.. With some remarks upon the conduct of the British ministry in the present posture of the affairs of Europe. [No imprint, 1726.] 4°

T.490

6669

SYNGE (Edward) *Archbishop of Tuam.*

An answer to all the excuses and pretences which men ordinarily make for their not coming to the communion... By a divine of the Church of England. The twelfth edition corrected. London: for the executors of R. Sare, and sold by R. Williamson, 1726. 12°

T.619

6670

SYNGE (Edward) *Archbishop of Tuam.*

The divine authority of church-government, and episcopacy, stated and asserted, upon principles common to all Christians. In a sermon at the consecration of... Peter Brown, late Provost of Trinity College, Dublin, and now Lord Bishop of Corke and Rosse... London: for the executors of R. Sare, and sold by R. Williamson, 1726. 12°

T.619

1726 (Cont'd)

6671

SYNGE (Edward) *Archbishop of Tuam.*

Plain instructions for the young and ignorant. Comprised in a short and easie exposition of the Church catechism... By the author of the Answer to all the excuses and pretences which men usually make, for their not coming to the holy sacrament... 6th ed. London: for Richard Williamson, 1726. 12º

T.619

6672

SYNGE (Edward) *Archbishop of Tuam.*

A true church-man set in a just and clear light: or, An essay towards the real character of a faithful son of the Establish'd Church. [Anon.] London: for the executors of R. Sare, and sold by R. Williamson, 1726. 12º

T.619

6673

SYNGE (Edward) *Bishop of Elphin.*

The case of toleration consider'd with respect both to religion and civil government, in a sermon preach'd in St. Andrew's, Dublin... October 23. 1725... London: for R. Williamson, 1726. 8º

T.109

6674

THOMSON (James)

Winter. A poem ... 2nd ed. London: N. Blandford, for J. Millan, 1726. 8º

T.397

6675

WAGSTAFFE (William)

Some memoirs of the life of Abel, Toby's uncle. Composed, collated, comprized, compiled, digested, methodized, written, and illustrated by Dr. Andrew Tripe... London: for T. Warner, 1726. 8º

T.527

6676

WARD (Edward)

News from Madrid. The Spanish beauty: or, The tragicomical revenge... A poem... London: printed for the author, and sold by A. Bettesworth, 1726. 8º

T.665

6677

WINTRINGHAM (Clifton)

Observations on Dr. Freind's history of physick; shewing, some false representations of ancient and modern physicians. By C.W... London: for G. Strahan, 1726. 8º

T.294

1727

6678

BAKER (William) *Fellow of St. John's College, Cambridge.*

A sermon preached before the honourable House of Commons, at St. Margaret's Westminster, on the 30th day of January, 1726... London: for W. and J. Innys, 1727. 4º

2 copies.

T.356 T.637

6679

BENNET (Thomas) *D.D.*

Thomas Bennet, S.T.P. Grammatica Hebraea cum uberrima praxi, in usum tironum... Accedit Consilium de studio praecipuarum linguarum Orientalium... instituendo & perficiendo. Londini, sumptibus authoris, 1727. 8º

T.788

6680

The CASE of J[ohn] W[ard]. [No imprint, 1727?] 4º

T.77

6681

FROWDE (Philip)

The fall of Saguntum. A tragedy. As it is acted at the Theatre-Royal in Lindoln's-Inn-Fields... London: for J. Crokatt, and T. Wood; and sold by J. Roberts, 1727. 8º

T.664

6682

HUTCHINSON (Michael)

A sermon preach'd before the Sons of the clergy, at their anniversary meeting in the cathedral-church of St. Paul, February 15, 1727. London: for James Crokatt, 1727. 4º

T.754

6683

A LETTER to the chairman of the East-India Company: in which the facts contained in the memorials to the court of directors ... are fully stated and shown. By a proprietor in the Company's stock ... London: for J. Roberts, 1727. 8º

T.224

6684

MIDDLETON (Conyers)

Dissertationis de medicorum Romae degentium conditione ignobili & servili, contra anonymos quosdam... defensio... Pars prima. Prostant venales Cantabrigiae apud Edmundum Jeffery, 1727. 4º

T.816

6685

PALM (Carl Joseph von)

Translation of the memorial presented in Latin to the King of Great-Britain by Monsieur de Palm the Imperial resident upon the speech which his Britannick Majesty made to the two houses of Parliament on the 28/17 of January, 1726-7. (A letter from the Count Sinzendorf... 20th of February, 1727.) [No imprint, 1727.] 4º

T.490

6686

POPE (Alexander)

Several copies of verses on occasion of Mr. Gulliver's travels. Never before printed. [Anon.] London: for Benj. Motte, 1727. 8º

Teerink 1224.

T.653

6687

POTTER (John) *Archbishop of Canterbury.*

A sermon preach'd at the coronation of King George II. and Queen Caroline, in the abbey-church of Westminster, October 11. 1727. By... John, Lord Bishop of Oxford. London: C. Ackers, for R. Knaplock, 1727. 4º

3 copies.

T.72 T.625 T.637

6688

PULTENEY (William) *Earl of Bath.*

A state of the national debt, as it stood December the 24th, 1716. With the payments made towards the discharge of it out of the sinking fund, &c. compared with the debt at Michaelmas, 1725. [Anon.] London: for R. Francklin, 1727. 4º

T.490

6689

SHIPPEN (William)

A speech against Sir R[obert] W[alpole]'s proposal for increasing the civil list revenue: as it was spoken in the House of Commons, July 3. 1727. By W[illiam] S[hippen], Esq; London: J. Watson, and sold by the booksellers of London and Westminster, [1727]. 8º

T.434

6690

SHIPPEN (William)

A speech against Sir R[obert] W[alpole]'s proposal for increasing the civil list revenue: as it was spoken in the House of Commons, July 3. 1727. By W[illiam] S[hip]p[e]n, Esq; 3rd ed. London: J. Watson, and sold by the booksellers of London and Westminster, [1727]. 8º

T.224

6691

SYNGE (Edward) *Archbishop of Tuam.*

A charitable address to all who are of the communion of the Church of Rome. London, W.B. for R. Williamson, 1727. 12º

T.619

6692

THEOBALD (Lewis)

The rape of Proserpine: as it is acted at the Theatre-Royal in Lincoln's-Inn-Fields. Written by Mr. Theobald. And set to musick by Mr. Galliard... London: T. Wood, 1727. 4º

T.668

1728

6693

BOND (William)

The progress of dulness. By an eminent hand. Which will serve for an explanation of the Dunciad... [Signed H. Stanhope.] (Observations on Windsor Forest, The temple of fame, and The rape of the lock, &c. [By John Dennis].) London: printed in the year 1728. 8º

T.673

6694

The CLERGYMAN'S daughter's new annual tract of youth and age ... Printed in the year 1728. 4º

Incomplete.

T.383

6695

EARLE (Jabez)

Subjection to the father of spirits. Consider'd in a funeral sermon for Mrs. Elizabeth Andrews, who died October 27. Preach'd in Hanover-Street, Nov. 5, 1727. London: printed in the year 1728. 8º

T.706

6696

FIELDING (Henry)

The masquerade. A poem. Inscrib'd to C[oun]t H[ei]d[eg]g[e]r ... By Lemuel Gulliver. London, printed; and sold by J. Roberts, 1728. 4º

T.269

6697

FONTENELLE (Bernard le Bovier de)

Eloge de Monsieur le Chevalier Neuton. Paris, 1728. 4º

T.579

6698

FONTENELLE (Bernard le Bovier de)

The life of Sir Isaac Newton. With an account of his writings ... [Anon.] London: J. Roberts, 1728. 8º

T.275

6699

GIBSON (Edmund) *Bishop of London.*

The Bishop of London's pastoral letter to the people of his diocese... Occasion'd by some late writings in favour of infidelity. London: for Sam. Buckley, 1728. 8º

T.43

6700

LONG (Roger)

The blessedness of believing. A sermon preached before the University of Cambridge... June the 30. 1728... Cambridge, for Corn. Crownfield, and sold by J. Crownfield, London, [1728]. 8º

T.738

6701

MEMOIRS concerning the life and manners of Captain Mackheath ... London: for A. Moore, 1728. 8º

T.275

6702

NEWCOME, *Mrs.*

An enquiry into the evidence of the Christian religion. [Anon.] Cambridge: for William and John Innys, 1728. 8º

Attributed by Bowdler to Dr Newcome of St John's.

T.28

6703

REFLECTIONS on the principal characters in a late comedy [by Colley Cibber] call'd The provok'd husband. By a private gentleman... London: for J. Roberts, 1728. 8º

T.647

6704

REYNOLDS (Richard) *Bishop of Lincoln.*

A sermon preached before the Incorporated Society for the Propagation of the Gospel in Foreign Parts ... on Friday the 16th of February, 1727. London, J. Downing, 1728.   4°

T.72

The SAILORS advocate. [1728?]

See no. 7703.

6705

VANBRUGH (*Sir* John)

A journey to London. Being part of a comedy written by the late Sir John Vanbrugh... which (since his decease) has been made an intire play, by Mr. Cibber. And call'd, The provok'd husband, &c. London: for John Watts, 1728.   8°

T.667

6706

VANE (Guy)

An essay on the consummate and invariable perfection of the Catholick-religion ... London: for John Worrall, 1728.   8°

T.169

6707

WHEATLY (Charles)

Bezaleel and Aholiab: or, Men's abilities and skill the gifts of God, and their professions and trades the ways of serving him. A sermon preach'd before the gentlemen educated at the Merchant-Taylors School... December 7. M.DCC.XXVII... London, for J. Walthoe, 1728.   4°

T.625

1729

6708

AKERBY (George)

The life of Mr. James Spiller, the late famous comedian. In which is interspers'd much of the poetical history of his own time. London: for J. Purser, 1729.   8°

T.665

6709

BETTY (Joseph)

The divine institution of the ministry and absolute necessity of church-government. A sermon preach'd before the University of Oxford: on Sunday the 21st of September, 1729 ... 2nd ed. corrected. Oxford: for Sam. Wilmot: and sold by J. and J. Knapton, R. Knaplock, and T. Astley, S. Birt, and B. and C. Motte, 1729.   8°

T.43

6710

BRAMSTON (James)

The art of politicks, in imitation of Horace's Art of poetry. [Anon.] London: for Lawton Gilliver, 1729.   8°

T.665

6711

BRETT (Thomas)

A chronological essay on the sacred history, from the creation of the world to the birth of Christ: being a defence of the computation of the Septuagint ... London: for Fletcher Gyles, 1729.   8°

T.774

6712

GAY (John)

Polly: an opera. Being the second part of the Beggar's opera... [Includes the score.] London: printed for the author, 1729. 2 parts.   4°

T.559

6713

HAYWOOD (Eliza)

Frederick, Duke of Brunswick-Lunenburgh. A tragedy. As it is acted at the Theatre-Royal in Lincoln's-Inn -Fields... London: for W. Mears, J. Brindley; and sold by the booksellers of London and Westminster, 1729.   8°

T.664

6714

HORLER (Joseph)

Works of charity recommended from the common relation we bear to Christ. A sermon preached at All-Saints church, in Bristol, before the Wiltshire Society... April the 21st 1729. Sarum: Charles Hooton, for the author, and sold by Edward Eastton, [1729].   4°

T.625

6715

JOHNSON (Samuel) *Dancing Master.*

Hurlothrumbo: or, The super-natural. As it was acted at the New-Theatre, in the Hay-market... London: for T. Wotton, and J. Shuckburgh, 1729.   4°

T.559

6716

JONES (Jonathan)

Instructions to the Right Rev. Richard Ld. Bishop of St. Davids, in defence of religious liberty. Being remarks upon his Lordship's dedication, lately publish'd ... London, for R. Walker, and sold by the booksellers of London and Westminster, [1729].   8°

T.43

6717

KNIGHT (Samuel)

The present, and future rewards of charity. A sermon preach'd before... the Lord Mayor, the aldermen, and governors of the several hospitals of the city of London... on Wednesday in Easter-week, April 9. 1729. Cambridge: printed at the University-Press, for John Crownfield, London, [1729].   4°

T.488

6718

The LOSS of liberty: or fall of Rome... London: C. Ackers, for J. Brindley, 1729.   Fol.

T.539

6719

LOWTH (Robert) *Bishop of London.*

The genealogy of Christ; as it is represented in the east-window in the college chappel at Winchester. A poem. By a young gentleman of Winchester school. London: for J. Jackson, 1729.   8°

T.649

6720

MABBUT (George)

Tables for renewing and purchasing of the leases of cathedral-churches and colleges, according to several rates of interest; with their construction and use explain'd ... [Attributed to Sir Isaac Newton.] 3rd ed. corrected ... To which is added, The value of church and college leases consider'd ... London: for Thomas Astley, 1729. 2 parts.   8°

T.44

6721

RALPH (James)

Clarinda: or the fair libertine. A poem... [Anon.] London: for John Gray, 1729.   8°

Incomplete.

T.665

6722

SHERLOCK (Thomas) *Bishop of London.*

The tryal of the witnesses of the resurrection of Jesus. [Anon.] 2nd ed. London: for J. Roberts, 1729.   8°

T.436

6723

SOME considerations against joining with the Nonjurors in private communion, in opposition to the publick one... London: printed 1729.   8°

T.649

6724

SOME remarks upon the Reverend Dr. Marshall's sermon on occasion of the death of the Revd Dr Rogers ... By Philalethes ... London: for James Roberts, 1729.   8°

T.43

6725

STATE law: or, The doctrine of libels, discussed and examined... 2nd ed. In the Savoy: E. and R. Nutt, and R. Gosling, for T. Wotton; and J. Shuckburgh, [1729].   8°

T.44

6726

VANERIUS (Jacobus)

Jacobi Vanerii e Societate Jesu Apes. Londini, apud F. Gyles, Woodman & Lyon, & C. Davis, 1729.   8°

T.649

6727

TRAPP (Joseph)

A sermon preach'd before... the Lord Mayor and aldermen of the city of London, at the cathedral church of St. Paul, on Friday, January 30. 1729... London: for L. Gilliver; and sold by A. Dodd, 1729.   4°

T.72

6728

TWO genuine letters selected from Mist's Weekly-journal. The one bearing date May 27, 1721. the other August 24, 1728... [The second letter is by the Duke of Wharton.] London: A. Moore, 1729.   8°

T.438

6729

WESLEY (Samuel) *the Younger.*

The prisons open'd. A poem occasion'd by the late glorious proceedings of the committee appointed to enquire into the state of the goals [sic] of this kingdom... [Anon.] London: for J. Roberts, 1729.   4°

T.562

1730

6730

B. (A.)

The treaty of Seville, and the measures that have been taken for the four last years, impartially considered. In a letter to a friend. London: for J. Roberts, 1730.   8°

T.376

6731

BEDFORD (Arthur)

A sermon preached in the parish-church of St. Butolph's Aldgate ... Occasioned by the erecting of a play-house in the neighbourhood ... London: Charles Ackers; and sold by J. Hooke; W. Meadows; and T. Cox, 1730.   8°

T.43

6732

The CASE of Dunkirk faithfully stated and impartially considered. By a member of the House of Commons. London: for A. Moore, 1730.   8°

T.376

6733

The CENSORIAD: a poem. Written originally by Martin Gulliver. Illustrated with sundry curious annotations of divers learned commentators, scholiasts and criticks... London; re-printed from the Dublin third edition, for Weaver Bickerton, 1730.   8°

T.653

6734

CHUBB (Thomas)

The comparative excellence and obligation of moral and positive duties, fully stated and considered. In answer to a pamphlet [by Daniel Waterland], entitled, The nature, obligation, and efficacy of the Christian sacraments consider'd... [Anon.] London: for J. Roberts, 1730.   8°

T.663

6735

COLBATCH (*Sir* John)

A dissertation concerning misletoe: a most wonderful specifick remedy for the cure of convulsive distempers ... 5th ed ... London, for Dan. Browne, 1730. 2 parts.   8°

T.44

6736

A COLLECTION of original letters and authentick papers, relating to the Rebellion, 1715. Edinburgh: printed for the publisher, and sold by several booksellers in town, 1730.   8°

T.438

1730 (Cont'd)

6737

A COLLECTION of papers relating to the East India trade: wherein are shewn the disadvantages to a nation, by confining any trade to a corporation with a joint-stock. London: for J. Walthoe, 1730.   8°

T.376

6738

CONSIDERATIONS on the present state of affairs in Europe, and particularly with regard to the number of forces in the pay of Great-Britain. London: for J. Roberts, 1730.   8°

T.376

6739

CROXALL (Samuel)

A sermon preach'd before the honourable House of Commons, at St. Margaret's Westminster, on Friday, January XXX. 1729. London: for J. Roberts, 1730. 4°

T.72

6740

DAILY JOURNAL.

A collection of recipe's and letters lately inserted in the Daily journal ... London: for T. Warner, 1730. 8°

T.44

6741

D'ANVERS (Caleb) *pseud.*

The remembrancer: or, Caleb's seasonable exhortation ... London: for A. Moore, 1730.   8°

T.376

6742

A DISCOURSE historical and critical, on the Revelations ascrib'd to St. John. In which, an enquiry is made whether they were written by that apostle... London: printed in the year, 1730.   8°

T.43

6743

EARBERY (Matthias)

The occasional historian... Numb. I. Contains a vindication of King James the Second's Queen, against the Craftsman. London, for J. Wilford, 1730.   8°

T.774

6744

FENELON (François de Salignac de la Mothe) *Archbishop of Cambrai.*

An essay, founded upon arguments natural and moral, proving the immortality of the soul. Translated from the original manuscript of the Archbishop of Cambray ... London: for L. Gilliver, and F. Cogan, 1730.   8°

T.43

6745

GIBSON (Edmund) *Bishop of London.*

The Bishop of London's pastoral letter to the people of his diocese ... Occasion'd by some late writings in favour of infidelity. 6th ed. London: for Sam. Buckley, 1730.   8°

T.43

6746

GIBSON (Edmund) *Bishop of London.*

The Bishop of London's second pastoral letter to the people of his diocese ... Occasion'd by some late writings, in which it is asserted, "That reason is a sufficient guide in matters of religion, without the help of Revelation. London: for Sam. Buckley, 1730. 8°

T.43

6747

GIBSON (Edmund) *Bishop of London.*

The Bishop of London's second pastoral letter. To the people of his diocese... Occasion'd by some late writings, in which is asserted, "That reason is a sufficient guide in matters of religion, without the help of Revelation. 4th ed. London: printed. And, Dublin re-printed, and sold by George Faulkner, 1730.   8°

T.778

6748

HENLEY (John)

Light in a candlestick, to all that are in the House: Or, The impartial churchman, considering the celebrated discourses on the 30th of January, of ... the Bishop of Bristol ... Dr. Croxall ... and of the Reverend Dr. Trap... London: for J. Roberts, 1730. 8°

T.43

6749

HERVEY (John) *Baron Hervey.*

Observations on the writings of the Craftsman. [Anon.] London: for J. Roberts, 1730.   8°

T.376

6750

MIDDLETON (John)

The duty and excellence of thanksgiving. A sermon preach'd before ... the lord-mayor and aldermen of the city of London, at the cathedral church of St. Paul, on Friday May 29, 1730 ... London: for J. and J. Bonwicke, 1730.   4°

T.72

6751

The OBSERVATIONS on the treaty of Seville examined. London: for R. Francklin, 1730.   8°

T.376

6752

PRIOR (Thomas)

A list of the absentees of Ireland, and the yearly value of their estates and incomes spent abroad. With observations on the present state and condition of that kingdom ... [Anon.] Dublin, printed: and reprinted at London, for Weaver Bickerton, 1730.   8°

T.44

6753

ROBERTS (William) *Rector of Jacobstow.*

The divine institution of the Gospel ministry, and the necessity of episcopal ordination, asserted... In a sermon, preach'd at the primary visitation of ... Offspring Blackall, formerly Lord Bishop of Exon. Held at Okehampton... Aug. 19, 1709. 4th ed. To which is added, A short character of Dr. George Hooper... By the Reverend Thomas Coney. London: for Benjamin Matthews, bookseller, Bath, [and others], [1730?]   8°

T.662

6754

ST. JOHN (Henry) *Viscount Bolingbroke.*

A letter to Caleb D'Anvers, Esq; concerning the state of affairs in Europe as published in the Craftsman, January 4, 1728-9. By John Trott, yeoman. London: for R. Francklin, 1730.   8°

T.376

6755

SHARPE (John) *Curate of Stepney.*

Short remarks on some passages in The life of Dr. Kennet, late Bishop of Peterborough [by William Newton]. In which he is clear'd, and vindicated from the aspersions laid to his charge. In a letter to a clergyman ... By a lover of truth. London, for G. Strahan, and R. Willock, 1730.   8°

T.44

6756

SOUTHALL (John)

A treatise of buggs ... London, for J. Roberts, 1730. 8°

T.44

6757

The SQUIRE and the cardinal [i.e. Horatio Walpole and Cardinal Fleury]. London, 1730.   Fol.

Wanting the title-page.

T.543

6758

STEVENS (Nicholas)

Two letters from a deist to his friend, concerning the truth and propagation of deism, in opposition to Christianity. [Anon.] With remarks [by Samuel Wesley] ... London, for James Roberts, 1730.   4°

T.72

6759

SWIFT (Jonathan) *Dean of St. Patrick's*

A libel on Dr. D[ela]ny, and a certain great lord. By Dr. Sw[if]t, occasion'd by a certain epistle. To which is added I. An epistle to his Excellency John Lord Carteret, by Dr. D[ela]ny II. An epistle on an epistle... III. Dr. Sw[if]t's proposal for preventing the children of poor people being a burthen to their parents or country... Dublin: printed, London: reprinted for Capt. Gulliver, 1730.   8°

Teerink 36.

T.665

6760

SWIFT (Jonathan) *Dean of St. Patrick's*

A vindication of his Excellency the Lord C[artere]t, from the charge of favouring none but Tories, High-Churchmen and Jacobites. By the Reverend Dr. S[wif]t. London: for T. Warner, 1730.   8°

Teerink 697.

T.44

6761

TAYLOR (John) *Archdeacon of Buckingham.*

The music speech at the public commencement in Cambridge, July 6, MDCCXXX. To which is added, an ode designed to have been set to music on that occasion. London, William Bowyer; and sold by W. Thurlbourn in Cambridge, R. Clements in Oxford, and the booksellers of London and Westminster, 1730.   8°

2 copies.

T.672   T.345

6762

TINDAL (Matthew)

An address to the inhabitants of the two great cities of London and Westminster: in relation to a pastoral letter said to be written by the Bishop of London... occasion'd by some late writings in favour of infidelity. [Anon.] The second edition, with alterations and additions... London, J. Peele, 1730.   8°

T.778

6763

TINDAL (Matthew)

A second address to the inhabitants of the two great cities of London and Westminster: occasion'd by a second pastoral letter [by Edmund Gibson]. With remarks on Scripture vindicated [by Daniel Waterland], and some other late writings... [Anon.] 2nd ed. London: for J. Peele, 1730.   8°

T.778

6764

WATERLAND (Daniel)

The nature, obligation, and efficacy, of the Church sacraments, considered; in reply to a pamphlet; intituled, An answer to the Remarks upon Dr. Clarke's Exposition of the Church-catechism [by Arthur Ashley Sykes]... By the author of the Remarks. London: Sam. Aris for John Crownfield; and sold by Cornelius Crownfield, 1730.   8°

3 copies.

T.62   T.656   T.663

6765

WETSTEIN (Johann Jacob)

Prolegomena ad Novi Testamenti Graeci editionem accuratissimam e vetustissimis codd. MSS. denuo procurandam... [Anon.] Amstelaedami, apud R. & J. Wetstenios & G. Smith, 1730.   4°

T.816

1731

6766

An ANSWER to a late pamphlet [by Lord Hervey], intitled, Observations on the writings of the Craftsman. [By Caleb D'Anvers?] London: for R. Francklin, 1731.   8°

T.376

6767

ARNALL (William)

Observations on a pamphlet [by William Pulteney], intitled, An answer to one part of a late infamous libel, &c. In a letter to Mr. P[ulteney]... [Anon.] London: for J. Roberts, 1731.   8°

T.376

6768

BOWMAN (William)

The traditions of the clergy destructive of religion: with an enquiry into the grounds and reasons of such traditions. A sermon preach'd at the visitation held at Wakefield in Yorkshire, June 25. 1731. London: for Stephen Austen, 1731. 8º

T.43

6769

BURROUGHS (Samuel)

An enquiry into the customary-estates and tenant-rights of those who hold lands of Church and other foundations, by the tenure of three lives and twenty-one years ... By Everard Fleetwood ... London: for J. Roberts, 1731. 8º

2 copies.

T.437   T.44

6770

CHANDLER (Samuel)

Plain reasons for being a Christian ... [Anon.] The second edition, corrected. London: for J. Roberts, 1731. 12º

T.480

6771

CONEY (Thomas)

The happiness or misery of a nation dependent upon the principles and conduct of its governors. A sermon preach'd at Taunton, March 14, 1730/1. At the assizes... London, for W. Innys, 1731. 8º

T.751

6772

CRAMBO (Christopher)

Mr. Bowman's sermon, preach'd at Wakefield, in Yorkshire, versify'd ... London: for H. Cook, 1731. 8º

T.43

6773

CUNNINGHAM (John William)

The political duties of the minister of religion in times of great national excitement. London: printed by Ellerton and Henderson: published by J. Hatchard and Son; and sold by S. Collins, Glasgow, 1731. 8º

T.704

6774

DAVIES (Joseph)

An humble proposal for the increase of our home trade, and a defence to Gibraltar... London: printed for the author, 1731. 8º

T.774

6775

A DEFENCE of the measures of the present administration. Being an impartial answer to what has been objected against it: in a letter to ——— ... London: for J. Peele, 1731. 8º

T.376

6776

EARBERY (Matthias)

The occasional historian. Numb. II... Containing instructions to an English baronet in Northamptonshire. Concerning the Craftsman's pretended memoirs of Sir John Oldcastle... London: for J. Wilford, 1731. 8º

T.774

6777

EARBERY (Matthias)

The occasional historian. Numb. III... Containing a vindication of King Charles I. from the Craftsman's charge of cruelty, in relation to the Star-Chamber... London: printed and sold by A. Dodd, 1731. 8º

T.774

6778

ELLIOT (Adam)

The depositions of the ever-memorable Dr. Titus Oates, against the Reverend Mr. Adam Elliot ... With an account of the Doctor's trial and conviction for defamation, at the suit of the said Mr. Elliot: proving the Doctor wilfully forsworn in several instances ... London: for G. Strahan, 1731. Fol.

T.543

6779

GIBSON (Edmund) *Bishop of London.*

The Lord Bishop of London's caveat against aspersing princes and their administration. Applied to William Pulteney Esq; and the Lord Viscount Bolingbroke, occasioned by their present political debates ... London: printed in the year 1731. 8º

T.376

6780

GIBSON (Edmund) *Bishop of London.*

The Bishop of London's third pastoral letter to the people of his diocese... Occasion'd by the suggestions of infidels against the writings of the New Testament, consider'd as a divine rule of faith and manners. The fifth edition, revised. London: Sam. Buckley, 1731. 8º

T.778

6781

HALL (Fayrer)

Remarks upon a book, entituled, The present state of the sugar colonies consider'd. Wherein some of the consequences and effects of restraining our trade are examined. [Anon.] London: for J. Peele, 1731. 8º

T.376

6782

The IMPORTANCE of the Lord's coming to us, and the necessity of our coming to the Lord; set forth from Scripture prophecy and doctrine: in a sermon preached at Bristol on Advent Sunday, 1731. By a presbyter of the Church of England... Sam. Farley, for the booksellers in Bath and Bristol, 1731. 4º

Attributed by Bowdler to "Mr Castel[man?]".

T.668

6783

The IMPORTANCE of the sugar colonies to Great-Britain stated, and some objections against the Sugar colony Bill answer'd. In a letter to a member of the House of Commons. London: for J. Roberts, 1731. 8º

T.376

6784

A KEY to the Craftsman ... London: for J. Roberts, 1731. 8º

T.376

6785

LAW (William)

The case of reason, or natural religion, fairly and fully stated. In answer to a book [by Matthew Tindal], entitul'd, Christianity as old as the creation. Part I. London: for W. Innys, 1731. 8º

T.673

6786

A LETTER to Caleb D'Anvers, Esq; on his Proper reply to a late scurrilous libel [by Sir William Yonge], entitled, Sedition and defamation display'd, &c ... [Perhaps by Lord Hervey.] London, printed: and sold by J. Roberts, 1731. 8º

T.376

6787

A LETTER to Mr. P** [Pulteney] on occasion of his late letter in answer to the Remarks, &c. The second edition corrected. London: for J. Roberts, 1731. 8º

T.376

6788

A LETTER to Richard Arnold, alias Francis Walsingham, Esq; [i.e. William Arnall] in answer to his unparallell'd scurrility and falshood in the Free-Briton, of Sept. 30. 1731 ... London: for G. Smith, and sold by the booksellers of London and Westminster, 1731. 8º

T.376

6789

A LETTER to the person last mentioned in the Craftsman of the 22d of May ... London: for J. Roberts, 1731. 8º

T.376

6790

LORD Pole translated; or The d——l turn'd chimney-sweeper: a ballad. To which is added Bob's soliloquy ... With an elegy upon a meeting-house, and a grave and serious exhortation to the smoaking of tobacco... London: for T. Warner, and sold at the pamphlet shops in London and Westminster, 1731. 8º

T.677

6791

MILLER (James)

Harlequin-Horace: or, The art of modern poetry... [Anon.] London: for Lawton Gilliver, 1731. 8º

T.651

6792

PULTENEY (William) *Earl of Bath.*

An answer to one part of a late infamous libel [by Lord Hervey], intitled, Remarks on the Craftsman's Vindication of his two honourable patrons; in which the character and conduct of Mr. P. is fully vindicated. In a letter to the most noble author... [Anon.] London: for R. Francklin, 1731. 8º

2 copies.

T.376   T.631

6793

SOME few arguments in defence of the Bill now depending in Parliament, for disabling pensioners from sitting in the House of Commons ... London: for A. Moore, and sold by the booksellers in town and country, 1731. 8º

T.376

6794

SOME useful and occasional remarks on a late seditious libel, entitl'd, Considerations on the present state of affairs in Europe; and particularly with regard to the number of forces in the pay of Great-Britain. London: printed for the author, and sold by the booksellers in town and country, 1731. 8º

T.376

6795

SYMONDS (Edward)

Priestly avarice: or, The clergy's kingdom of this world. A visitation sermon, preach'd at Halstead in Essex. London, printed: and sold by J. Roberts, 1731. 8º

Incomplete.

T.773

6796

WALPOLE (Horatio) *1st Baron Walpole.*

The case of the Hessian forces, in the pay of Great-Britain, impartially and freely examin'd; with some reflections on the present conjuncture of affairs. In answer to a late pamphlet, intitled, Considerations on the present state of affairs, &c. [Anon.] London: for R. Francklin, 1731. 8º

2 copies.

T.638   T.376

6797

WETSTEIN (Johann Jacob)

Specimen animadversionum in prolegomena in Novi Testamenti Graeci editionem accuratissimam nuper Amstelaedami edita. [Anon.] Londini: prostant venales apud R. Hett, 1731. 8º

Signature of Swithin Adee.

T.767

6798

WHARTON (Philip) *Duke of Wharton.*

Select and authentick pieces written by the late Duke of Wharton... Boulogne: J. Wolfe, 1731. 8º

T.438

1732

6799

AVERILL (John) *Bishop of Limerick.*

The question about eating of blood stated and examin'd; in answer to two dissertations in a book [by Patrick Delany] entitled, Revelation examin'd with candour. [Anon.] Dublin, printed; London, re-printed for J. Roberts, 1732. 8º

T.773

6800

BASTON (Thomas)

Observations on trade and a publick spirit ... London: for Olive Payne, 1732. 8º

T.242

6801

BELLONI (Giovanni Angelo)

Signior John Angelo Belloni's letter to my Lord ****. [No imprint, 1732.] 8º

T.438

1732 (Cont'd)

6802

EARBERY (Matthias)

The occasional historian. Numb. IV. Being an historical essay upon, and in defence of English hereditary right... London: printed, and sold by W. Wells, bookseller in Oxford, J. Parker, W. Pepper, E. Nutt, and by the booksellers of London and Westminster, 1732. 8°

T.774

6803

An ENQUIRY whether the Christian religion is of any benefit, or only a useless commodity to a trading nation. [Attributed to Swift.] London: for Weaver Bickerton, 1732. 8°

T.437

6804

An EXAMINATION of the facts and reasonings in the Lord Bishop of Chichester's sermon preached before the House of Lords on the 31st of January last... The fourth edition, corrected. London: for J. Peele, 1732.

T.790

6805

The EXAMINER examined: or, An answer to the Examination of the facts and reasonings in the Bishop of Chichester's sermon. With some remarks upon the letter, in answer to the defence. By a friend to monarchy and episcopacy. London: for J. Roberts, 1732. 8°

T.790

6806

FIELDING (Henry)

The lottery. A farce. As it is acted at the Theatre-Royal in Drury-Lane, by his Majesty's servants. [Anon.] With the musick prefix'd to each song. London: for J. Watts, 1732. 8°

T.664

6807

FORMAN (Charles)

A letter to the Right Honourable Sir Robert Walpole, for re-establishing the woollen manufactures of Great Britain upon their ancient footing, by encouraging the linen manufactures of Ireland... London: for T. Warner, 1732. 8°

T.790

6808

FORMS of prayer, proper to be used before, at, and after the receiving of the holy sacrament... 6th ed. London: for Benj. Barker: and sold by A. Bettesworth and C. Hitch, J. Osborn and T. Longman, R. Ware, S. Birt, J. Hazard, and B. Creake; T. Astley; J. Clarke; S. Harding; J. Jackson, and C. King, 1732. 12°

T.795

GIBSON (Edmund) *Bishop of London.*

The dispute adjusted, about the proper time of applying for a repeal of the Corporation and Test Acts... 1732.

See no. 7889.

6809

GRAY (Jeffery)

A proposal fully to prevent the smugling of wool... The third edition. With alterations and addition. London: printed for the author, and sold by W. Meadows, and several pamphlet shops in London and Westminster, 1732. 8°

T.790

6810

HAWLES (Sir John)

The Englishman's right: a dialogue between a barrister at law, and a juryman... London: for Tho. Wotton; and J. Shuckburgh, 1732. 8°

2 copies.

T.790

6811

HICKES (George)

Three short treatises, never before printed. The first, against the dissenters and occasional communion: the second, an answer to a popish letter: both written by ... Dr. George Hickes. The third, a letter against a protestant's marrying a papist: by the late Revd Mr. John Kettlewell. London: for J. Roberts, 1732. 8°

2 copies.

T.656   T.43

6812

The INTERESTS of the protestant dissenters considered. 2nd ed. London: for J. Wilford; and sold by A. Dodd; and H. Whitridge, 1732. 8°

T.790

6813

KELLY (George)

The speech of Mr. George Kelly. Spoke at the bar of the House of Lords, on Thursday, the 2d of May, 1723. in his defence against the bill then depending, for inflicting pains and penalties upon him... 5th ed. London: for T. Payne, 1732. 8°

T.434

6814

LAURENCE (Roger)

The indispensible obligation of ministring expressly and manifestly the great necessaries of publick worship in the Christian Church. Together with a detection of the false reasonings in Dr. B[ret]t's printed letter, to the author of Two discourses... Addressed to the Doctor by one of his friends... London, printed in the year 1732. 8°

Copy T.433 interleaved, and is annotated by Thomas Wagstaffe.

T.62   T.433

6815

A LETTER to a freeholder, on the late reduction of the land tax to one shilling in the pound. By a member of the House of Commons [i.e. William Arnall?] London: for J. Peele, 1732. 8°

T.790

6816

A LETTER to Samuel Holden, Esq; occasioned by his speech delivered from the chair, at a general assembly of dissenters, on the 29th of November, 1732... London: for J. Roberts, 1732. 8°

T.790

6817

LYTTELTON (George) *Baron Lyttelton.*

The progress of love. In four eclogues. I. Uncertainty. To Mr. Pope. II. Hope. To the Honourable George Doddington, Esq... [Anon.] London: for L. Gilliver, 1732. Fol.

T.543

6818

The NATURAL probability of a lasting peace in Europe; shewn from the circumstances of the great powers, as they are now situated... London: for J. Peele, 1732. 8°

T.790

6819

POPE (Alexander)

Of the use of riches, an epistle to the Right Honourable Allen Lord Bathurst. London: J. Wright, for Lawton Gilliver, 1732. Fol.

T.540

6820

PULTENEY (William) *Earl of Bath.*

The case of the revival of the salt duty, fully stated and considered; with some remarks on the present state of affairs. In answer to a late pamphlet, intitled A letter to a freeholder on the late reduction of the land-tax... In a letter from a member of the House of Commons to a gentleman in the country. [Anon.] London: H.Haines at Mr. Francklin's, 1732. 8°

T.790

6821

REMARKS on the occurrences of the years 1720 and 1721; relating to the execution of the South-Sea scheme. London: for J. Roberts, 1732. 8°

T.376

6822

The RIGHTS and liberties of subjects vindicated: in answer to the adjuster of the dispute [i.e. Edmund Gibson] about the proper time of applying for a repeal of the Corporation and Test Acts... London: for J. Roberts, 1732. 8°

T.790

6823

ROBERTSON (Robert)

A detection of the state and situation of the present planters, of Barbadoes and the Leward Islands... [Anon.] London: J. Wilford, 1732. 8°

T.790

6824

SHIPPEN (William)

Four speeches against continuing the Army, &c. as they were spoken on several occasions in the House of Commons. As also, a speech for relieving the unhappy sufferers in the Charitable Corporation; as it was spoken in the House of Commons, May 8. 1732. By W[illiam] S[hippen]. London: for J. Wilford, 1732. 8°

Half title: Five speeches.

T.434

6825

SMITH (George)

Two discourses wherein it is prov'd that the Church of England blesseth and offereth the Eucharistick elements ... [Anon.] Printed in the year 1732. 8°

T.62

1733

6826

BERRIMAN (William)

Some brief remarks on Mr. Chandler's introduction to the History of the Inquisition... London: for T. Ward and A. Wicksteed; and sold by J. Roberts, 1733. 8°

T.436

6827

BRETT (Thomas)

The great necessaries of publick worship in the Christian Church, expressly and manifestly allowed and provided for in the use of the present liturgy; in answer to a late pamphlet [by Roger Laurence], intituled, The indispensible obligation ... [Anon.] London: printed in the year 1733. 8°

T.62

6828

CHAMBRES (Charles)

A sermon preached at the cathedral-church of St. Paul, before... the Lord-Mayor, the aldermen, and citizens of London, on Tuesday the 29th of May, 1733... London: for Tho. Astley, 1733. 8°

T.774

6829

CORPORATION OF THE SONS OF THE CLERGY.

A compleat list, of the stewards, presidents, vice-presidents, and treasurers belonging to the Royal Corporation, for the relief of the poor widows, and children of clergymen, from the time their charter was granted, by King Charles II... [Compiled by William Freeman.] (Books lately printed and sold by W. Mears.) London: for W. Mears, 1733. 2 parts.

T.774

6830

EIGHT speeches made in Parliament, on several important occasions. Recommended to the electors of Great-Britain, as a seasonable preparative for the ensuing elections. London: J.W. and sold by A. Dodd, and the booksellers of London and Westminster, 1733. 2 parts. 8°

Speeches by Sir John Knight, Robert Price, William Shippen and others.

T.434

A FULL and fair discussion of the pretensions of the dissenters to the repeal of the sacramental test... 1733.

See no. 7888.

6831

GREAT BRITAIN. *Parliament.*

Most important transactions of the sixth session of the first Parliament of... George II. anno Domini, MDCXXXIII... The fourth edition, revised and corrected... London: for W. James, and sold by the booksellers and pamphlet-sellers in town and country, [1733]. 4°

T.689

6832

GREAT BRITAIN. *Parliament.*

The most important transactions of the sixth session of the first Parliament of... George II. anno Domini, MDCCXXXlll... 5th ed... London: printed, and Dublin, reprinted and sold by George Faulkner, 1733. 4°

T.562

6833

HUMPHREYS (Samuel)

Ulysses. An opera. As it is perform'd at the Theatre-Royal in Lincoln's-Inn-Fields. The musick compos'd by Mr. John Christopher Smith, junior. The words by Mr. Humphreys. London: for John Watts, 1733. 4°

T.276

6834

LANGTON (Lewis) *and* BABER (Thomas)

Bellus homo et academicus. Recitarunt in Theatro Sheldoniano apud comitia Oxoniensia MDCCXXXIII, Ludovicus Langton, et Thomas Baber... Londini, prostant venales, apud J. Wilford, 1733. Fol.

T.540

6835

LYTTELTON (George) *Baron Lyttelton.*

Advice to a lady. [Anon.] London: for Lawton Gilliver, 1733. Fol.

T.540

6836

A REVIEW of the excise-scheme; in answer to a pamphlet [by Horatio Walpole and Matthew Concanen], intitled The rise and fall of the late projected excise impartially considered. With some proper hints to the electors of Great Britain. [Attributed to William Pulteney.] 2nd ed. London: H. Haines, at Mr. Francklin's, 1733. 8°

T.803

6837

SMITH (George)

An appendix to Two discourses, in answer to a scurrilous libel [by Roger Laurence], entitl'd, The indispensable obligation of ministring expresly and manifestly the great necessaries of publick worship ... [Anon.] Printed in the year 1733. 8°

T.62

1734

6838

BERKELEY (George) *Bishop of Cloyne.*

The analyst; or, A discourse addressed to an infidel mathematician ... By the author of The minute philosopher ... London: for J. Tonson, 1734. 8°

T.464

6839

BRETT (Thomas)

To the Reverend Mr. Roger Laurence. [Signed T.B. and dated Sep. 21. 1734.] [No imprint, 1734?] 8°

T.62

6840

CAREY (Henry)

The tragedy of Chrononhotonthologos: being the most tragical tragedy, that ever was tragediz'd by any company of tragedians. Written by Benjamin Bounce... London: for J. Shuckburgh, and L. Gilliver, J. Jackson; and sold by A. Dodd, and E. Nutt, [1734.] 8°

T.664

6841

CLARKSON (Christopher)

The insufficiency of reason, and necessity of revelation, to assure men of the pardon of sin. A sermon preached at the triennial visitation of... Richard Lord Bishop of Lincoln held at Melton-Mowbray in Leicestershire August 2. 1733. Cambridge, for Cornelius Crownfield, and John Crownfield, 1734. 4°

T.710

6842

DARIUS'S feast: or, The force of truth. A poem, addressed, to... Earls of Salisbury and Exeter. London: for Lawton Gilliver, 1734. Fol.

T.539

6843

DAWSON (Thomas) *D.D.*

Disceptatio epistolaris de coelestibus testimoniis I Joh. V. 7... Londini: prostant apud J. Wilcox, & R. Ware, 1734. 8°

T.738

6844

INCORPORATED SOCIETY FOR PROMOTING ENGLISH PROTESTANT SCHOOLS IN IRELAND.

An account of the proceedings of the Incorporated-Society in Dublin, for promoting English protestant schools in Ireland... In two letters published by order of the Society. (Morning-prayers for a charter-school.) Dublin: George Grierson, 1734. 2 parts. 4°

T.562

6845

JURIN (James)

Geometry no friend to infidelity: or, A defence of Sir Isaac Newton and the British mathematicians, in a letter to the author of the Analyst [i.e. George Berkeley]... By Philalethes Cantabrigiensis. London: for T. Cooper, 1734. 8°

T.464

6846

The LIFE of Sir Robt. Cochran, prime-minister to King James III. of Scotland... London: printed and sold by A. Dodd, and the booksellers of London and Westminster, 1734. 8°

T.631

6847

PANELIUS (Alexander Xaverius)

Alexandri Xaverii Panelii ... de cistophoris. Lugduni, sumptibus fratrum Deville, & Ludov. Chalmette, 1734. 4°

T.276

6848

POPE (Alexander)

An epistle from Mr. Pope, to Dr. Arbuthnot... London: J. Wright for Lawton Gilliver, 1734. Fol.

T.540

6849

POPE (Alexander)

Sober advice from Horace, to the young gentlemen about town. As deliver'd in his second sermon. Imitated in the manner of Mr. Pope. Together with the original text, as restored by the Revd. R. Bentley... [Anon.] London: for T. Boreman; and sold by the booksellers of London and Westminster, [1734]. Fol.

T.539

6850

SHERLOCK (Thomas) *Bishop of London.*

A sermon preached before the House of Lords, in the abbey-church at Westminster, upon Wednesday, Januar 30. 1733... By... Thomas Lord Bishop of Bangor. London: for J. Pemberton, 1734. 4°

T.710

6851

VIRGILIUS MARO (Publius)

The tryal of skill between 'Squire Walsingham and Mother Osborne. An eclogue, in imitation of Virgil's Palaemon. To which are added, Horace to Fannius, and an apology for printing a certain Nobleman's epistle to Dr. S[her]w[i]n... London printed: sold by J. Huggonson, 1734. Fol.

T.539

1735

6852

ANDREWS (John)

An answer to a late pamphlet [by Sir Michael Foster], entitled An examination of the scheme of Church power laid down in the Codex juris ecclesiastici Anglicani, &c. [by Edmund Gibson]... By the author of The parallel ... The second edition corrected. London: for J. Roberts, 1735. 8°

T.485

6853

The ARTICLES against the late Lord B[olingbro]ke, sent from London, March 16. 1716. by the agents of the P[retende]r: in relation to the affairs of Scotland, during the rebellion of the late Earl of Mar ... London; printed: and sold by the booksellers of London and Westminster, 1735. 8°

T.422

6854

BERKELEY (George) *Bishop of Cloyne.*

A defence of free-thinking in mathematics. In answer to a pamphlet of Philalethes Cantabrigiensis [i.e. James Jurin], intituled, Geometry no friend to infidelity ... By the author of The minute philosopher ... London: for J. Tonson, 1735. 8°

T.464

6855

BROOKE (Henry) *Dramatist.*

Universal beauty a poem ... [Anon.] London printed: and sold by J. Wilcox, 1735. 6 parts. Fol.

T.539

6856

COMBER (Thomas)

The plausible arguments of a Romish priest from antiquity, answered; by the author of the Answer to the plausible arguments from Scripture. London: M. Downing, 1735. 8°

T.623

6857

COMBER (Thomas)

The plausible arguments of a Romish priest from Scripture answered, by an English protestant... Published in the year 1686. [Anon.] London: reprinted by M. Downing, 1735. 8°

T.623

6858

DODSLEY (Robert)

Beauty: or the art of charming. A poem... [Anon.] London: for Lawton Gilliver, 1735. Fol.

T.540

6859

DUNKIN (William)

The vice-roy: a poem. To his Grace the Duke of Dorset ... Dublin: George Faulkner, 1735. 4°

T.562

6860

ENGLAND. *Laws, Statutes.*

Carta libertatum Angliae; sive Magna Carta regis Johannis: ex autographo Cottoniano. (The charter of liberties, or the Great Charter granted by King John ...) [No imprint, 1735.] 2 parts. 8°

T.437

6861

HARE (Francis) *Bishop of Chichester.*

A sermon preached before the Incorporated Society for the Propagation of the Gospel in Foreign Parts; at their anniversary meeting in the parish-church of St. Mary-le-Bow; on Friday the 21st of February, 1734. London: S. Buckley, 1735. 4°

T.488

6862

HARTE (Walter)

An essay on reason... [Anon.] 2nd ed. London: J. Wright for Lawton Gilliver, 1735. Fol.

T.539

6863

HORATIUS FLACCUS (Quintus)

The miser, a poem: from the first satire of the first book of Horace. Inscrib'd to Horatio Walpole... London: printed; and sold by A. Dodd; Mr. Penn; E. Nutt; and by the book-sellers of London and Westminster, 1735. Fol.

T.539

6864

MIDDLETON (Conyers)

A dissertation concerning the origin of printing in England... Cambridge: for W. Thurlbourn: and sold by Mess. Knapton, Innys and Manby, C. Rivington, J. Clark, booksellers in London; and S. Harding, Westminster, 1735. 4°

T.816

1735 (Cont'd)

6865

PHELIPS (Paulin)

Of man's chief happiness: a poetical essay...
Northampton: William Dicey, 1735.   4°

T.557

6866

A PROTESTANT'S reasons why he cannot turn papist;
being a full answer to a paper [by Richard
Challoner] industriously dispersed; called, A
Roman Catholick's reasons why he cannot conform
to the protestant religion. London: for M.
Downing, 1735.   8°

T.796

6867

SHERLOCK (Thomas) *Bishop of London.*

The nature and extent of charity. A sermon
preach'd before the... President... Vice-President;
and the other trustees of the Infirmary in James-
Street, Westminster... April 26. 1735. By... Thomas,
Lord Bishop of Salisbury. London: for J. and J.
Pemberton, 1735. 2 parts.   4°

T.488

WRIGHT (Samuel)

A sermon preached in the New Meeting House
in Carter Lane... 1735.

See no. 8385.

1736

6868

An ANSWER to The country parson's plea against the
Quakers tythe-bill. In a letter to the r.r. author
[i.e. Thomas Sherlock]. By a member of the House of
Commons. [Attributed to Lord Hervey and to Thomas
Gordon.] 3rd ed. London: for J. Roberts, 1736.   8°

T.464

6869

ARNALL (William)

The complaint of the children of Israel, representing
their grievances under the penal laws ... In a
letter to a reverend high priest of the Church by law
established. 5th ed. By Solomon Abrabanel, of the
house of David. London: for W. Webb, 1736.   8°

T.430

6870

DALTON (John)

An epistle to a young nobleman from his preceptor ...
[Anon.] London: for Lawton Gilliver, and Robert
Dodsley, 1736. Fol.

T.539

6871

DORMAN (Joseph)

The rake of taste. A poem, dedicated to
Alexander Pope... [Anon.] Dublin printed:
London reprinted; and sold by Mrs. Dodd; Mrs.
Nutt; and by the booksellers in town and country,
[1736?] Fol.

T.539

6872

FLEURY (   )

Les genies, ballet représenté pour la premiere fois,
par l'Academie Royale de Musique; le Jeudy dix-huit
Octobre 1736. [Anon.] De l'imprimerie de Jean-
Baptiste-Christophe Ballard, 1736.   4°

T.559

6873

FOSTER (*Sir* Michael)

An examination of the scheme of Church-power, laid
down in the Codex juris ecclesiastici Anglicani, &c.
[by Edmund Gibson]. [Anon.] Third edition, corrected.
London: for J. Roberts, 1736.   8°

T.485

6874

GREY (Zachary)

English Presbyterian eloquence, &c. in a collection
of remarkable flowers of rhetorick. Humbly
inscribed to those two celebrated historiasters,
Mr. Oldmixon... and Mr. Samuel Chandler... By an
admirer of monarchy, and episcopacy... London:
for J. Roberts, 1736.   8°

T.437

6875

HAMMOND (William)

Advice to a son. A poem... Dublin: R. Reilly.
For A. Bradley, 1736.   4°

T.562

6876

LYNCH (John)

A sermon preached before the Incorporated Society
for the Propagation of the Gospel in Foreign
Parts; at their anniversary meeting in the parish-
church of St. Mary-le-Bow, on Friday, February 20,
1735. London: for J. and J. Pemberton, 1736.   4°

T.488

6877

MOORE (Edward)

Yarico to Inkle. An epistle... [Anon.] London:
for Lawton Gilliver, 1736.   Fol.

T.539

6878

PAPERS relating to the Quakers tythe bill...
4th ed. London: for J. Roberts, 1736.   8°

T.464

6879

POLITICAL dialogues between the celebrated statues
of Pasquin and Marforio at Rome. In which the
origin and views of the late war, the secret
mediation of the present peace, and the genuine
conditions of it, are brought to light. Translated
from the original Italian... London: for T.
Boreman, 1736.   8°

2 copies.

T.434 T.482

6880

SKELTON (Philip)

A vindication of the Right Reverend the Lord Bishop
of Winchester, against the malicious aspersions of
those who uncharitably ascribe the book, intituled,
A plain account of the nature and end of the
sacrament of the Lord's-supper, to his Lordship. By
the author of the proposal for the revival of
Christianity... Dublin printed, London, re-printed
for T. Cooper, 1736.   8°

T.656

6881

SKELTON (Philip)

A vindication of the Right Reverend the Lord Bishop
of Winchester, against the malicious aspersions of
those who uncharitably ascribe the book, intituled,
A plain account of the nature and end of the
sacrament of the Lord's-supper, to his Lordship.
By the author of the Proposal for the revival of
Christianity... 2nd ed. Dublin printed, London,
re-printed for T. Cooper, 1736.   8°

T.464

6882

THOULIER D'OLIVET (Pierre Joseph)

Traité de la prosodie françoise. A Paris, chez
Gandouin, 1736. 12°

T.449

6883

WARD (Henry)

The happy lovers: or, The beau metamorphos'd. An opera.
As it is acted at the Theatre Royal in Lincoln's-Inn-
Fields ... London: for S. Slow, 1736.   8°

T.237

6884

WETSTEIN (Johann Jacob)

Oratio funebris in obitum viri celeberrimi Joannis
Clerici, philosophiae & historiae ecclesiasticae
inter remonstrantes professoris, habita a.d. VIII.
Calend. Martii MDCCXXXVI. Amstelaedami, apud J.
Wetstenium & G. Smith, [1736].   4°

T.714

1737

6885

BRIDGES (   )

Divine wisdom and providence; an essay.
Occasion'd by the Essay on man [by Alexander Pope]...
The second edition, corrected. By Mr. Bridges.
London: J. Huggonson, and sold by J. Roberts, 1737.
Fol.

T.540

6886

CLARKE (Alured)

A sermon preached in... Winchester, before the
governors of the county hospital, at the opening
of the said hospital, Oct. 18, 1736... (A collection
of papers relating to the county-hospital...)
London: for J. and J. Pemberton, 1737. 2 parts.   4°

Wanting the title-page.

T.582

6887

The CONTRAST to the man of honour ... London: for
J. Morgan, 1737. Fol.

T.540

6888

DENNE (John)

A sermon preach'd in Lambeth-chapel, on Sunday,
January 15, 1737. at the consecration of...
Thomas Lord Bishop of Bangor. London: for J. and
J. Pemberton, 1737.   4°

T.710

6889

The EUCHARIST. A poem ... Edinburgh: T. and W.
Ruddimans, 1737.   8°

T.98

6890

An INTRODUCTION of the ancient Greek and Latin measures
into British poetry. Attempted in the following
pieces, viz. A translation of Virgil's first eclogue.
A translation of Virgil's fourth eclogue. Jacob and
Rachel: a pastoral ... London: for T. Cooper, 1737.
8°

T.245

6891

A LETTER to the Right Reverend the Lord Bishop of
London: occasioned by disputing with a Quaker.
London: for J. Roberts, 1737.   8°

T.778

6892

The MAN of honour... London: printed in the year
1737.   4°

2 copies.

T.652 T.668

6893

MANWARING (Edward)

Stichology: or, A recovery of the Latin, Greek and
Hebrew numbers... London: printed for the author,
1737.   4°

T.714

6894

MESTON (William)

Old Mother Grim's tales, found in an old manuscript,
dated 1527. Never before published. Decade I...
[Anon.] London, printed, and sold by the booksellers
in London and Westminster, 1737.   8°

T.449

6895

POPE (Alexander)

The second epistle of the second book of Horace,
imitated by Mr. Pope... London: for R. Dodsley,
1737. Fol.

T.540

6896

SECOND political dialogues between the celebrated
statues of Pasquin and Marforio at Rome. Translated
from the original Italian... London: for T.Boreman,
and to be had at the booksellers and pamphlet shops
of London and Westminster, 1737.   8°

T.434

6897

SYKES (Arthur Ashley)

An enquiry into the meaning of demoniacks in the
New Testament... By T.P.A.P.O.A.B.I.T.C.O.S.
The second edition, corrected and amended. London:
for J. Roberts, 1737.   8°

T.767

6898

SYKES (Arthur Ashley)

A further enquiry into the meaning of demoniacks
in the New Testament. Wherein the enquiry is
vindicated against the objections of the Revd. Mr.
Twells, and of the author of the Essays in answer
to it... [Anon.] London: for J. Roberts, 1737.   8°

T.767

1738

6899

AKENSIDE (Mark)

The voice of liberty; or, A British Philippic: a poem, in Miltonick verse. Occasion'd by the insults of the Spaniards, and the preparations for war... By a free-born Briton. London: printed; and, Dublin reprinted and sold by Edward Waters, 1738. 4°

T.562

6900

An ANSWER to the Pope's bull; with the character of a free mason. In an epistle to... Lord Mountjoy, Grand Master of Ireland. [Signed Philo-Lapidarius.] Dublin: Edward Waters, 1738. 4°

T.562

6901

BATE (James)

The practice of religion and virtue the only sure foundation of friendship. A sermon preach'd at St. Paul's, Deptford, Kent, on the twenty-fourth of June, 1738. before a select number of gentlemen, who stile themselves the Order of Ubiquarians. London: for R. Willock, 1738. 4°

T.710

6902

BRETT (Thomas)

A supplement to the remarks on the Reverend Dr. Waterland's Review of the doctrine of the Eucharist... London: J. Bettenham: and sold by A. Bettesworth and C. Hitch, 1738. 8°

T.662

6903

Les CARACTERES de l'amour; ballet heroique, représenté par l'Academie Royale de Musique, le quinziéme jour d'Avril 1738. De l'imprimerie de Jean-Baptiste-Christophe Ballard, 1738. 4°

T.559

6904

CONYBEARE (John) *Bishop of Bristol.*

A sermon preach'd in the parish-church of Christ-Church, London; on Thursday May the 4th, 1738. Being the time of the yearly meeting of the children educated in the charity-schools... London: M. Downing, 1738. 4°

T.716

6905

A DIALOGUE on one thousand seven hundred and thirty-eight: together with a prophetic postscript as to one thousand seven hundred and thirty-nine. London: for T. Cooper, 1738. Fol.

T.540

6906

HAMILTON (Newburgh)

Saul, an oratorio; or sacred drama. [Anon.] As it is perform'd at the King's Theatre in the Hay-market. Set to musick by George-Frederic Handel... London: for Tho. Wood, and sold by Tho. Astley, J. Shuckburgh, and at the King's Theatre, 1738. 4°

T.559

6907

HAYES (Charles)

A critical examination of the holy Gospels according to St. Matthew and St. Luke, with regard to the history of the birth and infancy of our Lord Jesus Christ. By the author of the Vindication of the history of the Septuagint... London: for T. Woodward, 1738. 8°

T.751

6908

HERRING (Thomas) *Archbishop of Canterbury.*

A sermon preached before the Incorporated Society for the Propagation of the Gospel in Foreign Parts; at their anniversary meeting in the parish-church of St. Mary-le-Bow, on Friday, February 17, 1737/8. By Thomas Lord Bishop of Bangor. London: for J. and J. Pemberton, 1738. 4°

2 copies.

T.716 T.581

6909

HUTCHINSON (Thomas) *Prebendary of Chichester.*

The usual interpretation of δαιμονες and δαιμονια, in the New Testament, asserted. In a sermon preach'd before the University of Oxford, at St. Mary's, on Sunday, March 5. 1737-8. Oxford, printed at the Theatre, for Mr. Clements; and sold by Mess. Innys and Manby, Knapton, Rivington and Roberts, in London; and by Mr. Thurlbourn, in Cambridge, 1738. 8°

"S. Adee MD: e dono authoris."

T.767

6910

PAGE (*Sir* Francis)

The charge of J[udge] P[age] to the grand jury of M[iddlese]x, on Saturday May 22. 1736. London: printed in the year 1738. 8°

T.437

6911

POPE (Alexander)

A sermon against adultery: being Sober advice from Horace, to the young gentlemen about town. As deliver'd in his second sermon. Imitated in the manner of Mr. Pope. Together with the original text, as restored by the Revd. R. Bentley... [Anon.] London: for T. Cooper; and sold by the booksellers of London and Westminster, [1738]. Fol.

T.540

6912

REMARKS on the trial of John-Peter Zenger, printer of the New-York weekly journal, who was lately try'd and acquitted for printing and publishing two libels against the government of that province. London: for J. Roberts, 1738. 4°

T.24

6913

VIEVAR (Alexander)

What is man? An ode, in Pindaric verse. In fifteen stanzas... [Anon.] London: for J. Buckland; and sold by W. Meadows; and R. Dodsley, 1738. Fol.

T.540

6914

VOLTAIRE (François Marie Arouet de)

Epistles translated from the French of Mr. Voltaire. On happiness, liberty, and envy. Inscrib'd to John Comins. By William Gordon. London: for J. Roberts, 1738. 8°

T.665

1739

6915

AUDLEY (Matthew)

The duties, and offices of friendship. A sermon preached at St. Paul's, Deptford, Kent, on the twenty-third of June, 1739. before a select number of gentlemen who stile themselves the Order of Ubiquarians. London: for John Carter, 1739. 4°

T.710

6916

BUTLER (Joseph) *Bishop of Durham.*

A sermon preached before the Incorporated Society for the Propagation of the Gospel in Foreign Parts; at their anniversary meeting in the parish-church of St. Mary-le-Bow, on Friday, February 16, 1738-9. By Joseph Lord Bishop of Bristol. London: for J. and P. Knapton, 1739. 4°

3 copies.

T.716 T.488 T.581

6917

CHARACTERS: an epistle to Alexander Pope Esq; and Mr. Whitehead... London: for T. Cooper; and sold by the booksellers of London and Westminster, 1739. Fol.

T.540

6918

DELANY (Patrick)

Longford's-glyn, or the willow and the brook; a true history. Faithfully translated from the Irish original. [Anon.] 2nd ed. London, for Charles Bathurst, 1739. Fol.

T.540

6919

EPIDEMICAL madness: a poem in imitation of Horace ... London: for J. Brindley; and sold by Mrs. Dodd, and the booksellers of London and Westminster, 1739. Fol.

T.540

6920

An ESSAY towards the character of the late chimpanzee, who died Feb. 23, 1738-9 ... London: for L. Gilliver and J. Clarke, 1739. 8°

T.483

6921

HAMMOND (Henry)

Nineteen letters of the truly reverend and learned Henry Hammond, D.D... written to Mr. Peter Staninough and Dr. Nathanael Ingelo... Now first published... and illustrated with notes by Francis Peck... London: for T. Cooper, 1739. 8°

T.486

6922

HERVEY (John) *Baron Hervey.*

A satire in the manner of Persius: in a dialogue between Atticus and Eugenio. By a person of quality. London: for J. Clarke, and J. Robinson, 1739. Fol.

T.540

6923

The HISTORY of the life and actions of Gustavus Vasa, deliverer of his country. Recommended to the spectators of a tragedy on that subject [by Henry Brooke], now in rehearsal at the Theatre-Royal in Drury-Lane. London: for J. Roberts, 1739. 8°

T.658

6924

HORATIUS FLACCUS (Quintus)

An epistle in verse to a friend, in imitation of the second epistle of the first book of Horace. London: for J. Robinson; and sold by the booksellers of London and Westminster, 1739. Fol.

T.540

6925

A HUE and cry after part of a pack of hounds, which broke out of their kennel in Westminster. To which is added, Modern characters, by another hand. London: for F. Style, and sold by the booksellers of London and Westminster, 1739. 8°

T.631

6926

HUTCHINSON (Thomas) *Prebendary of Chichester.*

Remarks upon a pamphlet [by Gregory Sharpe], intit'l'd, A review of the controversy about the meaning of demoniacs, &c... London, for W. Innys and R. Manby, 1739. 8°

T.767

6927

JOHNSON (Samuel)

Marmor Norfolciense: or an essay on an ancient prophetical inscription, in monkish rhyme, lately discover'd near Lynn in Norfolk. By Probus Britanicus. London: for J. Brett, 1739. 8°

T.434

6928

The LIFE and particular proceedings of the Rev. Mr. George Whitefield... By an impartial hand. [Attributed to Josiah Tucker.] London: for J. Roberts, 1739. 8°

T.483

6929

NUGENT (Robert) *Earl Nugent.*

An ode, to his Royal Highness on his birth-day. [Anon.] London: for R. Dodsley, 1739. Fol.

T.543

6930

OGLE (George)

Gualtherus and Griselda: or, The clerk of Oxford's tale. From Boccace, Petrarch, and Chaucer... London: for R. Dodsley, 1739. 4°

T.557

6931

PEACE and no peace; or, An enquiry whether the late convention with Spain will be more advantageous to Great-Britain than the treaty of Seville... London: for R. Chissen, [1739]. 8°

T.628

1739 (Cont'd)

6932
ROBINSON (Christopher) *Rector of Welby.*

Christianity, the sole, true, and infallible rule of
life ... London: for J. and J. Pemberton, 1739.   8°

T.98

6933
SCHULTENS (Albert)

Oraison funèbre en mémoire du grand Herman
Boerhaave. Prononcée... le IV. Novembre
MDCCXXXVIII. A Leide, chez Jean Luzac, 1739.   4°

T.579

6934
SHARPE (Gregory)

A review of the controversy about the meaning of
demoniacks in the New-Testament... By a lover of
truth... London: for J. Roberts, 1739.   8°

T.767

6935
SIR *'s speech upon the peace with Sp[ai]n.
To the tune of the Abbot of Canterbury. London:
for Jacob Lock, 1739.   Fol.

T.543

6936
The STATUES: or, the trial of constancy. A tale
for the ladies. [Attributed to Laetitia Pilkington.]
London: for T. Cooper, 1739.   Fol.

T.540

6937
VIRGILIUS MARO (Publius)

The Dean and the country parson. An imitation of
the first eclogue of Virgil. By Edward Lonergan.
Dublin: E. Waters, 1739.   4°

Teerink 1322.

T.562

6938
VIRGILIUS MARO (Publius)

The fourth book of Virgil's Aeneid. In four cantos,
with notes. [Translated by John Theobald.] Printed
by T. Aris, for the author, [1739].   4°

T.557

1740

6939
An APOLOGY for the life of Mr. T[heophilus] C[ibber],
comedian. Being a proper sequel to the apology for
the life of Mr. Colley Cibber, comedian. With an
historical view of the stage to the present year.
Supposed to be written by himself ... London: for
J. Mechell, 1740.   8°

T.237

6940
BENSON (Martin) *Bishop of Gloucester.*

A sermon preached before the Incorporated Society for
the Propagation of the Gospel in Foreign Parts; at
their anniversary meeting in the parish-church of
St. Mary-le-Bow, on Friday, February 15, 1739-40.
London: for J. and H. Pemberton, 1740.   4°

T.716

6941
BOISSY (Louis de)

Les dehors trompeurs, ou l'homme du jour, comédie
de Monsieur de Boissy. Représentée pour la
premiere fois, sur le théâtre de la Comédie
Françoise, le 18. Février 1740. A Paris, chez
Prault pere, 1740.   8°

T.237

6942
BUTLER (Joseph) *Bishop of Durham.*

A sermon preached before... the Lord Mayor... and
the governors of the several hospitals of the city
of London... on Monday in Easter-week, 1740. By
Joseph Lord Bishop of Bristol. London: for John
and Paul Knapton, 1740.   4°

T.582

6943
DODSLEY (Robert)

The art of preaching: in imitation of Horace's Art
of poetry. [Anon.] London: for R. Dodsley, [1740?]
Fol.

T.540

6944
ENGLAND. *Laws, Statutes.*

Anno regni Caroli II ... tricesimo ... An act for
burying in woollen. (Anno tricesimo secundo ...
An additional act for burying in woollen.) London,
reprinted by John Baskett, 1740. Fol.

T.530

6945
The GRAND removal. Inscribed to his Grace John Duke
of Argyle, in commemoration of the late glorious
struggle for liberty... London: for T. Cooper,
[1740?] Fol.

T.540

6946
HERRING (Thomas) *Archbishop of Canterbury.*

A sermon preached before the House of Lords, in
the abbey-church of Westminster, on Wednesday,
Jan. 30, 1739-40... By Thomas, Lord Bishop of
Bangor. London: for John Pemberton, 1740.
4°

T.488

6947
HORATIUS FLACCUS (Quintus)

Horace's instructions to the Roman senate: and
character of Caius Asinius Pollio. In two odes.
London: for R. Amey. 1740.   8°

2 copies.

T.651   T.665

6948
An IMPARTIAL relation of the proceedings of the
common-hall and court of aldermen, on Monday the
29th of September, 1740. at the election of a
lord mayor for the year ensuing... By a citizen.
London: for T. Robins, 1740.   8°

T.430

6949
MILLER (James)

Are these things so? The previous question, from
an Englishman in his grotto, to a great man at
court... [Anon.] London: for T. Cooper, 1740.   Fol

T.543

6950
MILTON (John)

The celebrated l'Allegro, il Penseroso, ed il
Moderato; of Milton. [Adapted by Charles Jennens.]
Set to music by Mr. Handel. Bath: Stephen Martin,
[1740?] 4°

T.559

6951
MORRIS (Robert)

Have at you all: being a proper and distinct reply
to three pamphlets just published, intituled,
What of that? The weather-menders; and, They are
not. By the author of Yes, they are... London:
for T. Cooper. 1740.   Fol.

T.543

6952
MORRIS (Robert)

Yes, they are: being an answer to Are these things
so? The previous question from an Englishman in
his grotto to a great man at court [by James Miller]
... London: for T. Cooper, 1740.   Fol.

T.543

6953
A POEM occasioned by the present war with Spain...
London: for M. Steen, 1740.   Fol.

T.540

6954
POULETT (John) *Earl Poulett.*

Earl Poulett's motion in the House of Lords on
Thursday, April 24th, for an humble address to
be presented to his Majesty, that he would be
graciously pleased to lay aside his intentions
of visiting his electoral dominions... 2nd ed.
London: for W. Webb, and sold by the booksellers
of London and Westminster, [1740?] Fol.

T.543

6955
The PRESENT state of the national debt. With remarks
on the nature of our public funds, and the uses which
a large national debt may be of to a sole m——r.
London: for T. Berwick, 1740.   8°

T.242

6956
SMITH (George)

A brief historical account of the primitive invocation
or prayer for a blessing upon the Eucharistic
elements, in confirmation of some things mentioned in
the learned Dr. Waterland's Review, &c. and by way of
supplement to it... [Anon.] London: for T. Cooper,
1740.   8°

T.656

6957
TURNBULL (George)

An impartial enquiry into the moral character of Jesus
Christ: wherein he is considered as a philosopher.
In a letter to a friend ... [Signed Philalethes.]
London: for J. Roberts. Sold by A. Dodd, and E. Nutt,
1740.   8°

T.240

6958
WATTS (Isaac)

Serious considerations concerning the doctrines of
election and reprobation. Extracted from a late
author [by John Wesley]. London: printed in the
year 1740.   12°

T.545

6959
WHAT of that! Occasion'd by a pamphlet [by James
Miller], intitled, Are these things so? And its
answer [by Robert Morris], Yes, they are...
2nd ed. London: for T. Cooper: and sold at the
pamphlet shops of London and Westminster, 1740.
Fol.

T.543

1741

6960
The ART of poetry ... London: for R. Dodsley, 1741.
Fol.

T.540

6961
The BATH miscellany. For the year 1740. Wrote by
the gentlemen and ladies at that place. Containing
all the lampoons, satyrs, panegyrics, &c. for that
year. Bath: for W. Jones, and sold by W. Lobb there;
and by Jacob Robinson; and the pamphlet shops of
London and Westminster, 1741.   8°

T.658

6962
BEDLAM: a poem on his Majesty's happy escape from his
German dominions, and the great wisdom of his conduct
there ... London: for J. Huggonson, 1741. Fol.

T.540

6963
CHANDLER (Samuel)

A vindication of the history of the Old Testament, in
answer to the misrepresentations and calumnies of
Thomas Morgan, M.D. and moral philosopher ... London:
for J. Noon, R. Hett, and J. Davidson, 1741.   8°

T.486

6964
CHARACTERISTICKS: a dialogue ... London: for Charles
Corbett, 1741. Fol.

T.540

6965
CLARKE (Alured)

A sermon preached before the trustees of the charity
schools at the cathedral church of Exeter Oct. 13.
1741. Exon, Andrew Brice, for Edward Score,
bookseller, in Exeter, J. and P. Knapton, and Sam.
Birt, London, 1741.   4°

"Dr Bonithon of Bristol from ye author."

T.581

6966
The CRISIS: a sermon, on Revel. XIV. 9,10,11.
Necessary to be preached in all the churches...
at or before the next general election. Humbly
inscribed to... the bench of bishops. By a lover
of his country. [Attributed to Henry Fielding.]...
London: for A. Dodd; E. Nutt, and H. Chappelle,
1741.   8°

T.662

6967

EUROPE'S catechism. To which are added, The new elect catechis'd; and the catechist catechis'd. With the marriage of the Empire as it is to be celebrated at Francfort ... London: printed and sold at the pamphlet-shops of London and Westminster, 1741. 8°

T.242

6968

FIELDING (Henry)

Της 'Ομηρου Vερνον-ιαδος, ραψωδια η γραμμα α'. The Vernon-iad. Done into English, from the original Greek of Homer. Lately found at Constantinople. With notes in usum, &c. Book the first. [Anon.] London: for Charles Corbett, 1741. 4°

T.652

6969

FINLEY (Samuel)

Christ triumphing, and Satan raging. A sermon on Matth. XII. 28... First preached at Nottingham in Pensilvania, Jan. 20. 1740-1... Philadelphia printed, London reprinted for Samuel Mason, 1741. 8°

T.662

6970

The GROANS of Germany: or, The enquiry of a protestant German into the original cause of the present distractions of the Empire... Translated from the original lately publish'd at the Hague. 2nd ed. London: for J. Huggonson, 1741.

T.484

6971

H. (B.)

Some remarks on a pamphlet, intitled, The morality of religion, in a letter to the B[ishop] of W[inchester]. London: for T. Cooper, 1741. 8°

T.641

6972

HORATIUS FLACCUS (Quintus)

The first ode of the first book of Horace imitated, and inscribed to the Earl of Chesterfield. By John, Earl of Orrery. London: for C. Bathurst, and G. Hawkins, 1741. Fol.

T.540

6973

The LATE gallant exploits of a famous balancing captain: a new song. To the tune of The king and the miller... London: for J. Huggonson, 1741. Fol.

T.540

6974

MADDOX (Isaac) *Bishop of Worcester.*

A sermon preach'd in the parish-church of Christ-Church, London; on Thursday April the 30th, 1741. Being the time of the yearly meeting of the children educated in the charity-schools... By... Isaac Lord Bishop of St. Asaph... London: M. Downing, 1741. 8°

T.716

6975

The MEDALIST. A new ballad... London: for J. Huggonson, 1741. Fol.

T.540

6976

The NEW-YEAR'S-gift; a poem. Address'd to a young lady... London, for T. Cooper, 1741. Fol.

T.540

6977

A PLAIN answer to Dr. Middleton's Letter from Rome: in which the gross misrepresentations contained therein are exposed and set in a just light. By a friend to truth. London: for J. Huggonson, 1741. 8°

T.656

6978

PRATTENBERG (Franz)

Traur- und Lob-Rede uber den Tod des weyland... Römischen Kaysers Caroli des VI. dieses Nahmens ... Hildesheim, Wilhelm Diederichs Schlegels Erben, [1741]. Fol.

T.810

6979

The SCRIPTURE doctrine concerning predestination, election and reprobation. Extracted from a late author. By John Wesley... London: W. Strahan, and sold by Thomas Harris; and at the Foundery, 1741. 12°

T.545

6980

SECKER (Thomas) *Archbishop of Canterbury.*

A sermon preached at King's-Street chapel, in the parish of St. James, Westminster, on Wednesday, Feb. 4. 1740/1. Being the day appointed... for a general fast, on occasion of the present war against Spain. By Thomas Lord Bishop of Oxford. London: for J. and H. Pemberton, 1741. 4°

T.582

6981

SECKER (Thomas) *Archbishop of Canterbury.*

A sermon preached before the Incorporated Society for the Propagation of the Gospel in Foreign Parts; at their anniversary meeting in the parish-church of St. Mary-le-Bow, on Friday, February 20. 1740-1. By Thomas Lord Bishop of Oxford. London: for J. and H. Pemberton, 1741. 4°

T.716

6982

SHENSTONE (William)

The judgment of Hercules, a poem. Inscrib'd to George Lyttelton... [Anon.] London: for R. Dodsley, and sold by T. Cooper, 1741. 8°

T.677

6983

TRAPP (Joseph)

A reply to Mr. Law's Earnest and serious answer (as it is called) to Dr. Trapp's Discourse of the folly, sin, and danger of being righteous over-much. London: for L. Gilliver, 1741. 8°

2 copies.

T.655   T.189

6984

WHITEHEAD (William)

The danger of writing verse: an epistle... London: for R. Dodsley; and sold by T. Cooper, 1741. Fol.

T.540

1742

6985

BRITANNIA in mourning: or, A review of the politicks and conduct of the court of Great Britain with regard to France, the ballance of power, and the true interest of these nations, from the Restoration to the present times... London: for J. Huggonson, 1742. 8°

T.648

6986

CARTE (Thomas)

The blatant-beast. A poem... [Anon.] London: for J. Robinson, 1742. Fol.

T.540

6987

The CHRISTIAN test: or, The coalition of faith and reason. A sacred poem... Book I... London: for R. Amey, 1742. Fol.

"Writ by Morgan".

T.540

6988

CIBBER (Colley)

A letter from Mr. Cibber, to Mr. Pope, inquiring into the motives that might induce him in his satyrical works, to be so frequently fond of Mr. Cibber's name... 2nd ed. London, printed: and sold by W. Lewis, 1742. 8°

T.651

6989

The CONDUCT of a noble duke [i.e. the Duke of Argyle], in regard to his resignation of his posts of honour. In a letter to a certain eminent patriot. London: for S. Lyne, and J. Towers, 1742. 8°

T.635

6990

The CONDUCT of the late administration, with regard to foreign affairs, from 1722 to 1742, wherein that of... the Earl of Orford (late Sir Robert Walpole) is particularly vindicated: in a letter to a certain right honourable gentleman, member of the present Parliament... London: for T. Cooper, 1742. 8°

T.633

6991

A CONFERENCE of a most stupendous nature on the present state of affairs. In a letter from the Hague, to a member of Parliament. London: for J. Brett, 1742. 8°

T.635

6992

CRADOCK (Zachary)

Two sermons: the first preach'd before King Charles II. February 10. 1678. upon the providence of God in the government of the world. The second upon charity... London: for W. and T. Payne, and sold by T. Cooper, 1742. 12°

T.623

6993

A CRITICAL history of the last important sessions of Parliament, which probably put a period to B[riti]sh liberty... By a member of the House of Commons. London: for J. Huggonson, 1742. 8°

T.635

6994

The DANGEROUS consequences of parliamentary divisions. Occasion'd by the refusal of the Place Bill, the Act of Indemnity, &c. London: for J. Huggonson, 1742. 8°

T.631

6995

The DAWN of honour; or, Fountain of liberty... London: for J. Huggonson, 1742. Fol.

T.540

6996

DODSLEY (Robert)

Pain and patience. A poem. London: for R. Dodsley; and sold by M. Cooper, 1742. 4°

T.668

6997

GARRICK (David)

The lying valet; in two acts. As it is performed gratis, at the theatre in Goodman's-Fields. London: printed for and sold by Paul Vaillant; and J. Roberts, 1742. 8°

T.237

6998

GREAT BRITAIN. *Parliament.*

A list of the members of Parliament who voted for and against taking the Hanover troops into British pay, December 10, 1742. To which is added, the Lords protest on that occasion, &c. London: for W. Webb, 1742. 8°

T.635

6999

GREAT BRITAIN. *Parliament. House of Commons.*

A further report from the committee of secrecy, appointed to enquire into the conduct of Robert, Earl of Orford; during the last ten years of his being first commissioner of the Treasury... London: for T. Leech, 1742. 8°

T.633

7000

The HAPPY coalition. A poem. Humbly address'd to his Royal Highness the Prince of Wales on the present conjuncture and joyful reconciliation. By a gentleman of the Inner Temple... London: for J. Huggonson, 1742. Fol.

T.540

7001

HAREN (Willem van)

W. Harenii Leonidas. Herodot. lib. VII. Hagae-Comitum, apud Isaacum Beauregard, 1742. 4°

T.692

7002

HER Grace of Marlborough's party-gibberish explained, and the true sons of the Church vindicated. By an honourable hand. London: for T. Cooper, 1742. 8°

T.658

7003

HERVEY (John) *Baron Hervey*.

Miscellaneous thoughts on the present posture both of our foreign and domestic affairs. Humbly offer'd to the consideration of the Parliament and the people ... [Anon.] London: for J. Roberts, 1742. 8°

T.632

7004

HIRELING artifice detected: or, The profit and loss of Great-Britain, in the present war with Spain, set in its true light; by laying before the publick... a list... of the British ships taken since the beginning of the war... London: for T. Cooper, 1742. 8°

T.632

7005

HOLDSWORTH (Edward)

Pharsalia and Philippi: or the two Philippi in Virgil's Georgics attempted to be explain'd and reconcil'd to history... In several letters to a friend... London: for Paul Vaillant, 1742. 4°

2 copies.

T.692   T.535

7006

HOLMES (William)

The country parson's advice to his parishioners of the younger sort. Explaining what they are to believe, and do, in order to be saved. [Anon.] Oxford: printed at the Theatre, 1742. 12°

T.795

7007

An IMPARTIAL review of the opposition; and the conduct of the late minister [i.e. Robert Walpole] since his secession. With an enquiry whether Britain is likely to be better for the change of the ministry ... In a letter from a West-Country clothier to his representative, one of the Twenty-one. London: for T. Cooper, 1742. 8°

T.632

7008

The INDEPENDANT Briton: or, Free thoughts on the expediency of gratifying the people's expectations; as to securing the liberty of the press; restoring the freedom of the stage... London: for T. Cooper, 1742. 8°

2 copies.

T.635   T.648

7009

An INQUIRY into the revenue, credit, and commerce of France. In a letter to a member of this present Parliament. [Attributed to G. Turner.] London: for J. Roberts, 1742. 8°

2 copies.

T.631   T.648

7010

A KEY to some late important transactions: in several letters from a certain great man, no body knows where, wrote no body knows when, and directed to no body knows who. London: for S. Dial: and sold at all the pamphlet shops in London and Westminster, 1742. 8°

2 copies.

T.631   T.635

7011

A KEY to the business of the present s[essio]n: viz. I. His H[ighness]'s speech to his life-guard... II. Certain important hints deliver'd to an assembly of independents, at the Fountain-Tavern, in the Strand... London: for T. Cooper, 1742. 8°

2 copies.

T.635   T.446

7012

KING (William) *Principal of St. Mary Hall*.

Templum libertatis. Liber primus. [Anon.] Londini: apud C. Bathurst, & G. Hawkins, 1742. Fol.

T.543

7013

The LATE minister unmask'd: or, An answer to a late pamphlet, entitled, The conduct of the late administration, with regard to foreign affairs, from 1722 to 1742. Wherein that of... the Earl of Orford ... is particularly vindicated. In a letter to the reverend author... London: for T. Cooper, 1742. 8°

T.633

7014

LEECHMAN (William)

The temper, character, and duty of a minister of the gospel. A sermon preached before the Synod of Glasgow and Air, at Glasgow, April 7th, 1741. 3rd ed. Glasgow, Robert Foulis, and sold by him, and at London by And. Miller, and the book-sellers in Edinburgh and Glasgow, 1742. 8°

T.623

7015

A LETTER from a member of the last Parliament, to a new member of the present, concerning the conduct of the war with Spain... London: for T. Cooper, 1742. 8°

2 copies.

T.648   T.449

7016

A LETTER to a right honourable member of Parliament, demonstrating the absolute necessity of Great Britain's assisting the House of Austria... By an impartial hand. [Signed Britannicus.] London: for T. Cooper, 1742. 8°

T.648

7017

A LETTER to my Lord Mayor, vindicating the late instructions from the city of London for postponing the subsidies to the redress of grievances... By a citizen of London. London: for T. Cooper, 1742. 8°

T.658

7018

A LETTER to the secret committee. Containing certain extraordinary practices of the late m[iniste]r [Robert Walpole], intended to have been laid before them in a private manner, and now submitted to their publick consideration... London: for S. Dial, 1742. 8°

T.632

7019

LYTTELTON (George) *Baron Lyttelton*.

The affecting case of the Queen of Hungary; in relation both to friends and foes: being a fair specimen of modern history. By the author of the Court-secret... London: for T. Cooper, 1742. 8°

T.632

7020

MADDOX (Isaac) *Bishop of Worcester*.

A sermon preach'd before the House of Lords in the abbey-church of Westminster, on Saturday, May 29. 1742... By Isaac Lord Bishop of St. Asaph. London: for John Stagg, 1742. 4°

Stamp of Edward Mills.

T.715

7021

NATIONAL unanimity recommended: or, The necessity of a constitutional resistance to the sinister designs of false brethren... In answer to a late ministerial pamphlet, intitled, An enquiry into the present state of our domestick affairs... London: for J. Huggonson, 1742. 8°

T.651

7022

OGLE (Margaret)

Mordecai triumphant: or, The fall of Haman prime minister of state to King Ahasuerus: an heroic poem ... London: printed for and sold by the author, and J. Leake, and most of the pamphlet-shops in London and Westminster, 1742. 8°

T. 677

7023

OPPOSITION more necessary than ever: or, A review of the principles, designs, and conduct of the two parties, joined in the opposition to the late minister [Robert Walpole], before and since his resignation... London: for J. Huggonson, 1742. 8°

T.633

7024

OVER shoes, over boots: or, The politicians at their wits-end. With an enquiry, whether any former age has equall'd the present in blunders... London: for J. Huggonson, 1742. 8°

T.632

7025

POPE (Alexander)

A blast upon Bays; or, A new lick at the laureat. Containing, remarks upon a late tattling performance, entitled, A letter from Mr. Cibber to Mr. Pope, &c. ... [Anon.] 2nd ed. London: for T. Robbins, and sold at all the booksellers and pamphlet-shops in town and country, 1742. 8°

T.653

7026

POPE (Alexander)

The new Dunciad: as it was found in the year 1741. With the illustrations of Scriblerus, and notes variorum. [Anon.] London: for T. Cooper, 1742. 8°

3 copies.

T.557   T.558   T.579

7027

The PRESENT state of British influence in Holland, exemplified by the States-General's answer of the 23/11 May, 1742, to the Earl of Stair's memorial for a new alliance... In a letter to... the Lord V[iscount] C[obham]. By a nobleman of Holland. London: for W. Webb, 1742. 8°

3 copies.

T.631   T.632   T.635

7028

PULTENEY (William) *Earl of Bath*.

The conduct of the late and present m[inist]ry compared. With an impartial review of public transactions since the resignation of... the Earl of Orford... In a letter to a friend... [Anon.] London: for T. Cooper, 1742. 8°

T.632

7029

PYM (John)

The remarkable speech of John Pym, Esq; in the House of Lords, upon the impeachment of Thomas Earl of Strafford for high treason... London: for A. Dodd, 1742. 8°

T.635

7030

A REVIEW of a late treatise [by Nathaniel Hooke], entituled An account of the conduct of the Dowager D[uchess] of M[arlborough], &c. In which many misrepresentations are detected... In a letter to a person of distinction... [Signed Britannicus.] London: for J. Roberts, 1742. 8°

T.651

7031

REYNOLDS (George)

A letter to the Reverend Dr. Lisle, prolocutor of the lower house of Convocation. Upon a refusal to receive or read a paper concerning ecclesiastical courts, clandestine marriages... By the Archdeacon of Lincoln. London: for T. Osborne, and sold by T. Cooper, 1742. 8°

T.426

7032

SCHULTENS (Joannes Jacobus)

Q.F.F.Q. Dissertationis academicae de utilitate dialectorum orientalium ad tuendam integritatem codicis Hebraei partem alteram. Praeside patre Alberto Schultens defendet filius Ioannes Iacobus Schultens auctor... Lugduni Batavorum, apud Ioannem Luzac, 1742. 4°

T.714

7033

The SCRIBLERIAD. Being an epistle to the dunces. On renewing their attack upon Mr. Pope, under their leader the Laureat. By Scriblerus... London: for W. Webb, 1742. 8°

T.665

7034

A SHORT account of the late application to Parliament made by the merchants of London upon the neglect of their trade: with the substance of the evidence thereupon; as sum'd up by Mr. Glover. London: for T. Cooper, 1742. 8°

T.632

7035

SIMPSON (Thomas)

The doctrine of annuities and reversions, deduced from general and evident principles ... London: for J. Nourse, 1742. 8°

T.284

7036

STEBBING (Henry) *Archdeacon of Wilts.*

A sermon preached before the Incorporated Society for the Propagation of the Gospel in Foreign Parts; at their anniversary meeting in the parish-church of St. Mary-le-Bow, on Friday, February 19, 1741-2. London: E. Owen, and sold by J. Roberts, 1742. 4°

2 copies.

T.716   T.488

7037

A VINDICATION of the conduct of a certain eminent patriot [i.e. William Pulteney]... In a letter from a member to his friend in the country. London: for S. Lyne, and J. Towers, 1742. 8°

T.631

7038

WEBSTER (William)

A sermon preach'd before the honourable the House of Commons, at St. Margaret's church, Westminster, on Saturday May 29. 1742... London: for James Crokatt, [1742]. 8°

T.662

7039

WESLEY (John)

The character of a Methodist... Bristol: Felix Farley, and sold at his printing-office, and by J. Wilson: in London, by Thomas Trye, and Thomas Harris; and at the Foundery, 1742. 12°

T.545

7040

WESLEY (John)

The principles of a Methodist. Occasion'd by a late pamphlet [by Josiah Tucker], intitled, A brief history of the principles of Methodism. Bristol: Felix Farley. And sold at his shop, and by John Wilson: in London, by Thomas Trye, and Thomas Harris; and at the Foundery, 1742. 12°

T.545

1743

7041

BARKER (John)

A defence of a late treatise intitled, An inquiry into the nature, cause and cure, of the present epidemick fever. In answer to the objections of Dr. Henry Hele... Sarum: for Benjamin Collins, and Edward Easton, 1743. 2 parts. 8°

T.645

7042

BENTLEY (Richard)

Remarks upon a late Discourse of free-thinking [by Anthony Collins]: by Phileleutherus Lipsiensis. Part the third. Cambridge, J. Bentham, for W. Thurlbourn; and sold by Messieurs Knaptons, Manby, and Beecroft, in London, 1743. 8°

The first two parts were published in 1713.

T.767

7043

BRETT (Thomas)

Four letters which passed between a gentleman and a clergyman, concerning the necessity of an episcopal commission, for the valid administration of Gospel ordinances. [Anon.] London: for M. Cooper, 1743. 8°

T.429

7044

BROWN (John) *D.D., Vicar of Newcastle-upon-Tyne.*

Honour. A poem. Inscribed to the Right Honble the Lord Viscount Lonsdale... [Anon.] London: for R. Dodsley, and sold by M. Cooper, 1743. 4°

T.579

7045

BURRINGTON (George)

Seasonable considerations on the expediency of a war with France; arising from a faithful review of the state of both kingdoms... London: for F. Cogan, 1743. 8°

T.633

7046

CARTE (Thomas)

A full and clear vindication of the Full answer to a Letter from a by-stander [by Corbyn Morris]. In which all the Cambridge gentleman's cavils and misrepresentations of that book, in his Letter to Mr. Thomas Carte, are exposed and refuted. By the author of the Full answer. London: for J. Robinson, 1743. 8°

T.654

7047

CIBBER (Colley)

The egotist: or, Colley upon Cibber. Being his own picture retouch'd, to so plain a likeness, that no one, now, would have the face to own it, but himself ... London, printed: and sold by W. Lewis, 1743. 8°

T.653

7048

CHUBB (Thomas)

An enquiry concerning redemption... London: for T. Cox, 1743. 8°

T.778

7049

A CONGRATULATORY letter to a certain right honourable person [i.e. William Pulteney], upon his late disappointment... [Attributed to Lord Bolingbroke.] 4th ed. London: J. Mechell, [1743]. 8°

T.630

7050

DECKER (*Sir* Matthew)

Serious considerations on the several high duties which the nation in general, (as well as it's trade in particular) labours under... By a well-wisher to the good people of Great-Britain. London: sold by John Palairet; S. Birt; H. Chapelle; J. Joliffe: Mrs. Dodd, and other pamphlet shops, 1743. 8°

T.807

7051

A DUEL and no duel; or, The skirmish of the West-India heroes. A burlesque account of the cause, rise and progress of the quarrel between Sir C[halone]r O[g]le, and Governor T[relawn]ey... By an honest sailor... London: for G. Foster, 1743. 8°

T.653

7052

HAMILTON (James) *Viscount Limerick.*

Two speeches on the late famous motion, by the Right Honourable the Lord L[imeric]k. London: for J. Millan, 1743. Fol.

T.543

7053

HICKES (George)

A declaration made by the Right Reverend Dr. George Hickes, concerning the faith and religion in which he lived and intended to die: and referred to in his will... London: printed in the year 1743. 8°

T.673

7054

An IMPARTIAL review of the present troubles of Germany, the conduct of the generals now in the field, and particularly of the late battle of Dettingen... In a letter from a member of the Diet at Ratisbon, to a publick minister at the Hague... Translated from the original French. London: for M. Cooper, 1743. 8°

T.630

7055

A KEY to the present politicks of the principal powers of Europe... Translated from the original lately published at Amsterdam. London: for T. Cooper, 1743. 8°

T.630

7056

KING (William) *Principal of St. Mary Hall.*

Tres oratiunculae habitae in Domo Convocationis Oxon. [Anon.] [No imprint, 1743.] 3 parts. 4°

T.815

7057

LETTER to a great man in France; in which are briefly considered, the following popular points: viz. The conduct of Mr. P[ultene]y. The right of instructing members... London: for J. Roberts, 1743. 8°

T.630

7058

MAWSON (Matthias) *Bishop of Ely.*

A sermon preached before the Incorporated Society for the Propagation of the Gospel in Foreign Parts; at their anniversary meeting in the parish-church of St. Mary-le-Bow, on Friday, February 18, 1742-3. By Matthias Lord Bishop of Chichester. London: for Somerset Draper; and sold by J. Roberts, 1743. 4°

T.716

7059

MORALITY from the devil. Quevedo in England: or, The dreamer. London: for M. Cooper, 1743. 8°

T.658

7060

The MYSTERIOUS congress. A letter from Aix la Chappel, detecting the late secret negociations there; accounting for the extraordinary slowness of the operations of the campaign... and, particularly, for the resignation of the E[ar]l of S[tai]r... By a nobleman. London: for M. Cooper, 1743. 8°

T.630

7061

POPE (Alexander)

Verses on the grotto at Twickenham. By Mr. Pope. Attempted in Latin and Greek. To which is added Horti Popiani: Ode Sapphica. Also The cave of Pope. A prophecy. [By Robert Dodsley]. London: for R. Dodsley; and sold by M. Cooper, 1743. 4°

T.579

7062

PRIOR (Matthew)

Solomon de mundi vanitate, liber secundus, cui titulus inscribitur Voluptas, poema Matthaei Prior Latine traductum; cui adjicitur Alexandri convivium, Drydeni in S. Caeciliam ode, lingua eadem donata a Georgio Bally. Cantabrigiae, typis academicis excudebat J. Bentham. Veneunt apud J. et R. Tonson, P. Vaillant, et R. Dodsley, Londini; Corn. et J. Crownfield, et Gul. Thurlbourn, Cantabrigiae; J. Fletcher Oxonii, et J. Pote Etonae, 1743. 4°

T.692

7063

A PROPER reply to a late infamous and scurrilous libel, intitled, A congratulatory letter to a certain right honourable person upon his late disappointment... London: for J. Robinson, 1743. 8°

T.630

7064

A REVIEW of the whole political conduct of a late eminent patriot [i.e. William Pulteney], and his friends; for twenty years last past: in which is contained, a complete history of the late Opposition: and a full answer to a pamphlet [by John Perceval], entitled, Faction detected by the evidence of facts, &c... London: for M. Cooper, 1743. 8°

T.807

7065

SECKER (Thomas) *Archbishop of Canterbury.*

A sermon preached in the parish-church of Christ-Church, London; on Thursday May the 5th, 1743. Being the time of the yearly meeting of the children educated in the charity-schools, in and about the cities of London and Westminster. By... Thomas Lord Bishop of Oxford... London: M. Downing, 1743. 4°

T.716

7066

STANHOPE (Philip Dormer) *4th Earl of Chesterfield* and WALLER (Edmund) *M.P.*

The case of the Hanover forces in the pay of Great Britain, impartially and freely examined... [Anon.] London: for T. Cooper, 1743. 8°

T.633

7067

STANHOPE (Philip Dormer) *4th Earl of Chesterfield* and WALLER (Edmund) *M.P.*

A vindication of a late pamphlet, intitled, The case of the Hanover troops considered: with some further observations upon those troops; being a sequel to the said pamphlet. [Anon.] London: for T. Cooper, 1743. 8°

T.630

1743 (Cont'd)

7068
TAYLOR (John) *Archdeacon of Buckingham.*

Marmor Sandvicense cum commentario et notis Ioannis Taylori. Cantabrigiae typis academicis excudebat Ios. Bentham, 1743. 4°

T.535

7069
THREE fables. Preferment despised. The usurper punished, and Liberty esteemed. Dedicated to the Right Hon. Earl of Chesterfield, Lord Gower, and George Fox, Esq; London: for M. Cooper, 1743. 8°

T.648

7070
W. (L.)

An Englishman's answer to a German nobleman. Containing some observations upon the political system of the present administration, as it is exposed in the German's letter. London, T. Cooper, 1743. 8°

Wanting the title-page.

T.650

7071
WALLER (Edmund) *M.P.*

A free and impartial enquiry into the extraordinary and advantagious bargain... for remitting money for the pay of the forces abroad, for the year 1743. Being a faithful specimen of the oeconomy and management of the present administration... [Anon.] London: for M. Cooper, 1743. 8°

T.630

7072
WESLEY (John)

The nature, design, and general rules, of the united societies, in London, Bristol, King's-wood, and Newcastle upon Tyne. Newcastle upon Tyne, John Gooding, 1743. 12°

T.545

1744

7073
BEARCROFT (Philip)

A sermon preached before the Incorporated Society for the Propagation of the Gospel in Foreign Parts; at their anniversary meeting in the parish church of St. Mary-le Bow, on Friday February 15, 1744. London: Edward Owen. And sold by J. Roberts; and A. Millar, 1744. 4°

T.716

7074
BENTHAM (Edward)

The connection between irreligion and immorality. A sermon preach'd at St. Mary's in Oxford, at the assizes... on March 1, 1743-4. Oxford, printed at the Theatre for James Fletcher, and sold by John Rivington, 1744. 8°

T.751

7075
BERKELEY (George) *Bishop of Cloyne.*

Siris: a chain of philosophical reflexions and inquiries concerning the virtues of tar-water, and divers other subjects connected together and arising one from another... 2nd ed., improved and corrected by the author. Dublin printed, London re-printed, for W. Innys, and C. Hitch; and C. Davis, 1744. 8°

3 copies.

T.54 T.284 T.645

7076
BULL (George) *Bishop of St. David's.*

A companion for the candidates of holy orders. Or, The great importance and principal duties of the priestly office. London: for J. Rivington, 1744. 8°

T.623

7077
CARY (Mordecai) *Bishop of Killala.*

A sermon preached at Christ-Church, Dublin, on the 18th day of March, 1743. before the Incorporated Society, for promoting English protestant schools in Ireland... Dublin: George Grierson, 1744. 4°

T.581

7078
CASTELMAN (John)

A sermon preached before the subscribers to the Bristol infirmary, at their anniversary meeting in the parish church of St. James, on Tuesday, March the 13th, 1743. London, Thomas Trye, 1744. 4°

T.582

7079
CATCOTT (Alexander Stopford)

The antiquity and honourableness of the practice of merchandize. A sermon preached before the Worshipful Society of Merchants of the city of Bristol... Bristol: printed in the year 1744. 4°

T.582

7080
CHANDLER (Mary)

The description of Bath. A poem. Humbly inscribed to... the Princess Amelia. With several other poems. 6th ed. To which is added, A true tale, by the same author. London: for James Leake, bookseller in Bath, 1744. 8°

T.739

7081
CHURCHILL (Sarah) *Duchess of Marlborough.*

A true copy of the last will and testament of her Grace Sarah, late Duchess Dowager of Marlborough... London, M. Cooper, 1744. 8°

Wanting the title-page.

T.739

7082
COBDEN (Edward)

The duty of a people going out to war. A sermon preached... at the cathedral church of St. Paul, on Wednesday the eleventh of April, 1744. being the day appointed... for a solemn fast. London: for M. Cooper, 1744. 4°

T.717

7083
A COMPLETE view of the birth of the Pretender, as collected from our histories, state tracts, and other authorities... London: T. Gardner; and M. Cooper, 1744. 8°

T.438

7084
A DEFENCE of the people: or, Full confutation of the pretended facts, advanc'd in a late huge, angry pamphlet [by John Perceval]; call'd Faction detected. In a letter to the author of that weighty performance... London: for J. Robinson, 1744. 8°

T.807

7085
DELANY (Patrick)

A sermon preach'd before the Society corresponding with the Incorporated Society in Dublin, for promoting English protestant working-schools in Ireland... in the parish-church of St. Mary le Bow, on Tuesday, March 13th, 1743/44. London: M. Downing, 1744. 4°

T.581

7086
GIBSON (Edmund) *Bishop of London.*

Observations upon the conduct and behaviour of a certain sect, usually distinguished by the name of methodists. [Anon.] [No imprint, 1744.] 4°

T.581

7087
GILBERT (John) *Archbishop of York.*

A sermon preached before the Incorporated Society for the Propagation of the Gospel in Foreign Parts; at their anniversary meeting in the parish-church of St. Mary-le-Bow, on Friday, February 17, 1743-4. By John Lord Bishop of Landaff. London: for J. and J. Pemberton; and sold by J. Roberts, 1744. 4°

T.716

7088
GREY (Richard)

The encouragement to works of charity and mercy, from Christ's acceptance of them as done to himself. A sermon preached in the parish church of All-Saints in Northampton before the president and governors of the county infirmary for sick and lame poor, on Thursday, March 29, 1744. To which are added the statutes of the said infirmary. Northampton: William Dicey; also sold by J. and P. Knapton, C. Hitch, and other booksellers in London, 1744. 2 parts. 8°

T.751

7089
JERUSALEM.

The ancient liturgy of the Church of Jerusalem, being the liturgy of St. James... restored to it's original purity... With an English translation and notes... [Edited by Thomas Rattray.] London: James Bettenham, 1744. 4°

T.556

7090
KING (William) *Principal of St. Mary Hall.*

Epistola objurgatoria ad Guilielmum King, LL.D. (Epistola canonici reverendi admodum ad archidiaconum reverendum admodum...) Londini: apud M. Cooper, 1744. 2 parts. 4°

T.815

7091
A LETTER to the Right Reverend the Bishop of Cloyne. Occasion'd by his Lordship's treatise on the virtues of tar-water. Impartially examining how far that medicine deserves the character his Lordship has given of it. London: for Jacob Robinson, 1744. 8°

Incomplete.

T.54

7092
MERRICK (James)

A dissertation on proverbs, chap. IX.V.1,2,3,4,5,6... Containing occasional remarks on other passages in sacred and profane writers. Oxford, printed at the Theatre, and sold by John Rivington, S. Birt, London; W. Thurlbourn at Cambridge; R. Clements and J. Fletcher at Oxford; J. Newbery at Reading, 1744. 4°

T.824

7093
MILLER (James)

Joseph and his brethren. A sacred drama. [Anon.] As it is perform'd at the Theatre-Royal in Covent-Garden. The musick by Mr. Handel. London: for John Watts: and sold by B. Dod, 1744. 4°

T.559

7094
The NOTIONS of the Methodists fully disprov'd, by setting the doctrine of the Church of England, concerning justification and regeneration, in a true light... In two letters to the Reverend Mr. John Wesley... London: for Jacob Robinson, 1744.

Attributed by Bowdler to "Mr. Smith of Burnhall" [i.e. George Smith].

T.431

7095
The OPERATIONS of the British, and the allied arms, during the campaigns of 1743 and 1744, historically deducted... By an eye-witness. London: for M. Cooper, 1744. 8°

T.807

7096
RIDLEY (Alexander.)

The information, upon oath, of Capt. Alexander Ridley, master of one of his Majesty's pacquet boats at Dover. [No imprint, 1744.] Fol.

T.438

7097
SMITH (George)

A defence of the communion-office of the Church of England, proving there is neither reason nor authority for laying it aside; in a letter to a friend. [Signed G.S.] Edinburgh: printed in the year 1744. 8°

T.673

7098
The TRIAL at large, between James Annesley, Esq; and... the Earl of Anglesea, before the Barons of the Court of Exchequer in Ireland: begun on Friday, November 11. 1743... (The trial of Ja. Annesley and Jos. Redding... for the murder of Thomas Egglestone.) Newcastle upon Tyne: John Gooding, 1744. Fol.

T.696

7099
The TRIAL of the Right Honourable Richard Earl of Anglesey, Francis Annesley Esq; and John Ians Gent. for an assault on the Honourable James Annesley... on Friday, Aug. 3. 1744, at Athy in the county of Kildare... London: for J. and P. Knapton, T. Longman and T. Shewell, C. Hitch, C. Davis, and A. Millar, 1744. Fol.

T.696

7100
WARNING to the Whigs, and to the well-affected
Tories. London: for J. Roberts, 1744.   8°

T.807

7101
WESLEY (John)

Scriptural Christianity: a sermon preached, August,
24, 1744: at St. Mary's church in Oxford, before
the University... 4th ed. London: W. Strahan, and
sold by T. Trye; Henry Butler; and at the Foundery,
1744.   12°

T.623

1745

7102
The ARREST of Marshal Belleisle, in the territories
of Hanover, considered as a violation of the laws
and customs of Germany... Translated from the
original, lately publish'd in Holland... London:
for M. Cooper, 1745.   8°

T.626

7103
ASHBURNHAM (Sir William) Bishop of Chichester.

A sermon preached before the honourable House of
Commons, at St. Margaret's Westminster, on Tuesday,
November 5, 1745. London: for John Jolliffe, 1745.
4°

T.710

7104
BROUGHTON (Thomas) Prebendary of Salisbury.

Hercules. A musical drama. [Anon.] As it is
perform'd at the King's Theatre in the Hay-market.
The musick by Mr. Handel. London: for J. and R.
Tonson and S. Draper, 1745.   8°

T.739

7105
BUTLER (Joseph) Bishop of Durham.

A sermon preached in the parish-church of Christ-
Church, London; on Thursday May the 9th, 1745.
being the time of the yearly meeting of the children
educated in the charity schools, in and about the
cities of London and Westminster. By... Joseph
Lord Bishop of Bristol... London: J. Oliver; and
sold by B. Dod, 1745.   4°

2 copies.

T.716   T.581

7106
The CASE fairly stated: in a letter from a member
of Parliament in the country interest, to one of
his constituents... London: for M. Cooper, 1745.
8°

T.650

7107
The CASE of the Marshal Bellisle truly stated:
in which, the manner of his being seized in
Hanover, the usage he met with there, and his
removal hither, are examined by the law of nations...
London: for M. Cooper, 1745.   8°

T.626

7108
CHRISTMAS chat: or, Observations on the late change
at court, on the different characters of the ins and
outs; and on the present state of publick affairs.
A dialogue spoke at the country seat of one of the
new ministry... London: for M. Cooper, 1745.   8°

T.647

7109
DALTON (John)

Two sermons preached before the University of Oxford,
at St. Mary's on Sept. 15th, and Oct. 20th, 1745...
Oxford, printed at the Theatre for Richard Clements:
and sold by Mr Rivington, Mr Dodsley, London; Mr
Thurlbourn in Cambridge; Mr Leak in Bath, 1745.   4°

T.710

7110
DODSLEY (Robert)

Rex et pontifex: being an attempt to introduce
upon the stage a new species of pantomime. [Anon.]
London: for M. Cooper, 1745.   4°

T.660

7111
DUTCH faith: being an enquiry, founded on facts,
into the probability of the success of the British
arms, on the continent, next campaign. With
considerations on the present state of parties in
England... London: for M. Cooper, 1745.   8°

T.630

7112
GILBERT (John) Archbishop of York.

A sermon preached before his Grace Charles Duke
of Richmond... and the governors of the London
infirmary... at the parish church of St.Lawrence-
Jewry, on Tuesday, March 26, 1745. By... John,
Lord Bishop of Landaff.   2nd ed. London: H.
Woodfall: and sold by J. Brotherton; and J. Stagg,
1745.   4°

T.582

7113
GREAT BRITAIN. Commissioners for Forfeited Estates.

The names of the Roman Catholics, Nonjurors, and
others, who refus'd to take the oaths to his late
Majesty King George... Transmitted to the late
Commissioners for the Forfeited Estates of England
and Wales, after the unnatural rebellion in the
North, in the year 1715... [Compiled by John Cosin.]
London: for J. Robinson, 1745.   8°

T.436

7114
HARPER (William)

The advice of a friend, to the army and people of
Scotland. [Anon.] [No imprint, c. 1745.]   8°

T.368

7115
HUTTON (Matthew) Archbishop of Canterbury.

A sermon preached before the Incorporated Society
for the Propagation of the Gospel in Foreign Parts;
at their anniversary meeting in the parish church
of St. Mary-le-Bow, on Friday February 21, 1745.
By... Matthew Lord Bishop of Bangor. London: Edward
Owen. And sold by J. Roberts; and A. Millar, 1745.
4°

T.716

7116
JENNENS (Charles)

Belshazzar. An oratorio.[Anon.] As it is
perform'd at the King's Theatre in the Hay-
market. The musick by Mr. Handel... London:
J. Watts, and sold by him: and by B. Dod, 1745.

T.559

7117
KILNER (James)

A sermon preach'd at the parish-church of Lexden, in
Essex, on the fifth of November, 1745... London: for
E. Comyns, 1745.   4°

T.710

7118
A LETTER to the Archbishop of York: humbly offering
to his Grace's solution some doubts and scruples
suggested by his late speech to the grand meeting
of the county of York, called to subscribe an
association for supporting the German government in
England... [Signed Philalethes.] [No imprint, 1745.]
8°

T.368

7119
MARTIN (Samuel)

A plan for establishing and disciplining a national
militia in Great Britain, Ireland, and in all the
British dominions of America. [Anon.] London: for
A. Millar, 1745.   8°

T.650

7120
The PLAIN reasoner. Wherein the present state of
affairs are set in a new, but very obvious light;
the separate and connected interests of Great-
Britain and Hanover consider'd... 2nd ed. London:
for M. Cooper, 1745.   8°

T.635

7121
REPLIQUE d'un membre du Parlement de la Grande
Bretagne, a la réponse d'un gentilhomme milanois,
&c. Datée de Milan le 15 Juillet 1744. Et
imprimée à Londres, sur l'article dixiéme du
Traité qui a été conclu à Worms le 13/2 Septembre
1743. Traduite de l'Anglois. A Londres, [1745].
8°

T.807

7122
A REVIEW of the case of the Marshal Belleisle,
in answer to a late pamphlet, intitled The case
of the Marshal Belleisle truly stated... London:
for M. Cooper, 1745.   8°

T.626

7123
THOMPSON (William) of Queen's College, Oxford.

Sickness. A poem. In three books... London:
for R. Dodsley; and sold by M. Cooper, 1745.
3 parts.   4°

T.557

7124
TREVOR (Richard) Bishop of Durham.

A sermon preach'd before the Lords spiritual and
temporal, in the abbey-church at Westminster, on
the 5th of November, 1745... By Richard Lord Bishop
of St. David's. London: for H. Pemberton, 1745.   4°

T.710

7125
The VISIBLE pursuit of a foreign interest, in
opposition to the interests of England, proved from
facts stated in a circular rescript lately publish'd
by the young Elector of Bavaria, setting forth the
negociations of peace at Hanau... In a letter to my
Lord B[olingbrok]e. London: for M. Cooper, 1745.   8°

T.650

7126
WILSON (Thomas) Bishop of Sodor and Man.

The true Christian method of educating the children
both of the rich and poor. London: for J. Osborn,
1745.   12°

T.795

1746

7127
An ACCOUNT of the signal escape of John Fraser. [No
imprint, 1746?] brs.

2 copies.

T.432

7128
An APPEAL to Caesar, on the nature and situation
of our public affairs. London: for W. Webb, 1746.
8°

T.628

7129
BALLARD (Edward)

A sermon preached at the consecration of... Lord
James Beauclerck, Lord Bishop of Hereford. At
Lambeth chapel, on Sunday, May 11. 1746. Eton: for
Joseph Pote, 1746.   4°

T.710

7130
BARNARD (Sir John)

A defence of several proposals for raising of three
millions for the service of the government, for the
year 1746... London: for J. Osborn, 1746.   8°

T.628

7131
BAUMGARTEN (Siegmund Jacob)

Commentatio ad difficiliora verba Rom. VIIII, V. qua
natalem Christi an. MDCCXXXXVI, nomine Senatus
Academici indixit Sigism. Iac. Baumgarten. Halae
litteris Gebauerianis, [1746].   4°

T.714

7132
BENTHAM (Edward)

An introduction to moral philosophy... 2nd ed.
Oxford, printed at the Theater, 1746. For James
Fletcher; and sold by Sam. Birt and M. Senex in
London; and in Cambridge.   8°

Signature of E. Harriott.

T.751

7133
BROOKE (Thomas)

The pleasure and advantage of unity. A sermon
preached in the cathedral-church of Chester, at
the assizes, September 2, 1746... London: printed,
for the author, by Henry Woodfall, jun.; and sold
by Mess. John and Paul Knapton; Mr. R. Dodsley;
and by the booksellers of Chester, 1746.   4°

T.710

7134

BURGH (James)

Britain's remembrancer: or, The danger not over.
Being some thoughts on the proper improvement of
the present juncture... [Anon.] London: for M.
Cooper; and sold at the pamphlet-shops of London
and Westminster, 1746.   8°

T.629

7135

BURTON (John) D.D.

The expostulation and advice of Samuel to the men
of Israel applied. A sermon preach'd before the
University of Oxford, at St. Mary's, Oct. 9. 1746.
Being the day appointed to be kept as a general
thanksgiving... for the suppression of the late
rebellion. Oxford, printed at the Theatre for
James Fletcher, and sold by J. and J. Rivington,
London, 1746.   8°

T.791

7136

BURTON (John) D.D.

Principles of religion the only sufficient restraint
from wickedness. A sermon preach'd at the assizes...
at St. Mary's [Oxford], Aug. 7. 1746. Oxford, printed
at the Theatre for James Fletcher, and sold by J. and
J. Rivington, London, 1746.   8°

T.791

7137

COLDEN (Cadwallader)

An explication of the first causes of action in matter;
and of the cause of gravitation. New-York: printed in
the year, 1745. And London reprinted: for J. Brindley,
1746.   8°

T.284

7138

A COLLECTION of letters, concerning the separation
of the Church of England into two communions, &c.
Printed in the year 1746.   4°

T.671

7139

DENNE (John)

God's regard to man in his works of creation: and
providence. A sermon preached in the parish church
of Saint Leonard Shoreditch... June 4. 1745...
London: J. Oliver, and sold by H. Pemberton, 1746.
4°

T.710

7140

A DISSERTATION on nothing: or, Remarks on a letter
to William Pitt, Esq; wherein is contain'd nothing
... London: for M. Cooper, 1746.   8°

T.627

7141

The DUTY of paying custom, and the sinfulness of
importing goods clandestinely; and of buying the
goods that are so imported. The second edition,
altered and amended. London: for B. Dod, 1746.
12°

T.795

7142

ELPHINSTONE (Arthur) Baron Balmerino.

True copies of the papers wrote by Arthur Lord
Balmerino, Thomas Syddell [and others]; and delivered
by them to the sheriffs at the places of their
execution. [No imprint, 1746.]   8°

T.368

7143

An EXAMINE of the expediency of bringing over
immediately the body of Hanoverian troops taken
into our pay in exchange for the like number of
English to be sent to Flanders, in order to a total
suppression of the Rebellion... London: for M.
Cooper, 1746.   8°

T.628

7144

FLEMING (Caleb)

Another defence of the unity, wherein St. John's
introduction to his Gospel, and his account of the
Word's being made flesh, are considered. With a few
remarks on some very late notable publications,
particularly those of Dr. Benjamin Dawson, and Dr.
Kennicot... [Anon.] London: for T. Longman, 1746.
8°

T.791

7145

FLETCHER (Thomas) Bishop of Kildare.

A sermon preached at Christ-Church, Dublin, on the
23d day of March, 1745. before the Incorporated Society,
for promoting English protestant schools in Ireland ...
Dublin: George Grierson, 1746.   4°

T.581

7146

A FREE examination of a modern romance, intitled,
Memoirs of the life of Lord Lovat. Wherein the
character of that nobleman is set in its true light, and
vindicated ... London: for W. Webb, 1746.   8°

T.368

7147

GREAT BRITAIN. Parliament. House of Lords.

The Lords protest on a motion to address his Majesty
for the keeping our forces at home, till the Dutch
has declared war against France. London: printed in
the year 1746.   8°

T.628

7148

GREAT BRITAIN. Parliament. House of Lords.

The whole proceedings in the House of Peers, upon the
indictments against William Earl of Kilmarnock,
George Earl of Cromertie, and Arthur Lord Balmerino;
for high treason, in levying war against his Majesty
... London: for Samuel Billingsley, 1746. Fol.

2 copies.

T.696

7149

HAMILTON (John) 2nd Baron Belhaven.

My Lord Belhaven's memorable and prophetick speech
against the union in the year 1706... To which
is prefix'd, a prefatory discourse, shewing
the expediency of altering the treaty... London:
for M. Cooper, 1746.   8°

T.434

7150

HAYTER (Thomas) Bishop of London.

A sermon preached before the honourable House of
Commons, at St. Margaret's Westminster, on Wednesday,
June 11, 1746... London: for John and Paul Knapton,
1746.   4°

T.710

7151

HUGHES (Michael)

A plain narrative or journal of the late Rebellion,
begun in 1745 ... London: for Henry Whitridge,
1746.   8°

T.368

7152

HUTTON (Matthew) Archbishop of Canterbury.

A sermon, preached before his Grace Charles Duke
of Richmond... and the governors of the London
infirmary... at the parish church of St. Lawrence-
Jewry, on Thursday, March 20, 1745/6. By...
Matthew, Lord Bishop of Bangor. London: H. Woodfall:
and sold by J. Brotherton; G. Woodfall; and J.
Stagg, 1745/6.   4°

T.582

7153

HUTTON (Matthew) Archbishop of Canterbury.

A sermon preached before the House of Lords, in the
abbey church of Westminster, on Wednesday, June 11,
1746... By Matthew, Lord Bishop of Bangor. London:
for J. and P. Knapton, 1746.   4°

T.710

7154

LAVINGTON (George) Bishop of Exeter.

A sermon preached in the parish-church of Christ-
Church, London; on Thursday May the 1st, 1746.
Being the time of the yearly meeting of the children
educated in the charity-schools, in and about the
cities of London and Westminster... London: J.
Oliver; and sold by B. Dod, 1746.   4°

T.716

7155

A LETTER to Sir John Barnard, upon his proposals
for raising three millions of money for the service
of the year 1746. From a member of the House of
Commons. 3rd ed. London: for John Hinton, [1746].
8°

T.651

7156

A LETTER to the most noble Thomas, Duke of Newcastle,
on certain points of the last importance to these
nations: being an enquiry, I. Into the genuine sources
of disaffection in both parts of Great Britain...
And II. Into the most rational measures for
effectually extinguishing the remains of the present
detestable rebellion... London: for H. Whitridge,
1746.   8°

T.628

7157

MEAD (Norman)

The qualifications and duty of a magistrate set forth,
in a sermon preached before... the Lord Mayor... on
Monday the 29th of September, 1746. Being the day of
the election of a lord mayor for the year ensuing.
London: J. Oliver, 1746.   4°

T.710

7158

MEMOIRS of the life of Lord Lovat. London: for M.
Cooper, 1746.   4°

T.368

7159

The PEACE-offering: an essay, shewing the cession
of Hanover to be the only probable means for
extinguishing the present rebellion, without
farther bloodshed... A late speech spoken before
the most venerable society in the nation, by
Methuselah Whitelock... London: for L. Raymond,
and sold by A. Moore, 1746.   8°

2 copies.

T.629   T.432

7160

PRIOR (Thomas)

An authentic narrative of the success of tar-water, in
curing a great number and variety of distempers; with
remarks, and occasional papers relative to the subject
... A new edition, complete. Dublin printed, London
re-printed, for W. Innys, C. Hitch, and M. Cooper; and
C. Davis, 1746.   8°

T.54

7161

RAY (Charles)

A sermon preach'd at the parish-church of St. Peter's
in St. Alban's, on Thursday the 9th of October, 1746.
being the day appointed for a general thanksgiving...
for the suppression of the late unnatural rebellion.
London: E. Say, for M. Cooper, 1746.   4°

T.715

7162

REASONS, proving the absolute necessity of our
assistance on the continent, in order to stop the
rapid progress of the French. In answer to several
late pamphlets, visibly calculated to serve the
cause of the Pretender and France. By a well-wisher
to the present happy establishment. London: R. Owen,
and sold by the booksellers of London and Westminster,
1746.   8°

T.629

7163

REMARKS on a Letter to Sir John Barnard: in which
the proposals of that worthy patriot are
vindicated, and a late important transaction set
in a true light. By an enemy to jobbs. London:
for J. Hinton, 1746.   8°

T.628

7164

REMARKS upon a letter (just made publick) on
certain points of the last importance to these
nations. Addressed to... the Duke of Newcastle.
In a letter to the author of that pamphlet.
London: for M. Cooper, 1746.   8°

T.628

7165

A REVIEW of Mr. James Foster's account, of the
behaviour, of the late Earl of Kilmarnock, after his
sentence, and on the day of his execution, &c. By a
Westminster scholar. London: for H. Carpenter, 1746.
8°

T.368

7166

RUTHERFORTH (Thomas)

A sermon preached before the honourable House of
Commons at St. Magrarets [sic] Westminster January
30. 1745-6. London: for W. Innys; and sold by W.
Thurlbourn in Cambridge, 1746.   4°

T.710

7167

The SCHEMERS scrutiny. Containing I. Serious considerations on the several high duties, &c. seriously considered. II. The merchant of London's scheme to prevent the running of Irish wools to France, examined... London: for J. Roberts, 1746. 8°

T.628

7168

The SEQUEL of Arms and the man: a new historical ballad. London: for W. Webb, 1746. Fol.

T.543

7169

THEOPHRASTUS.

Θεοφραστου του ερεσιου περι των λιθων βιβλιον. Theophrastus's history of stones. With an English version, and critical and philosophical notes... By John Hill... London, for C. Davis, 1746. 8°

T.772

7170

TUNSTALL (James)

A sermon preached before the honourable House of Commons, at St. Margaret's Westminster, on Thursday May 29, 1746... London, for J. Rivington; and William Thurlbourn in Cambridge, 1746. 4°

T.710

7171

VERNON (Edward) *Admiral.*

A specimen of naked truth, from a British sailor, a sincere wellwisher, to the honour, and prosperity of the present royal family, and his country. [Anon.] London: printed in the year 1746. 8°

T.629

7172

W. (T.)

The natural interest of Great-Britain, demonstrated. In a discourse in two parts. Dedicated to... the Lord Mayor, the court of aldermen... and merchants of the city of London. Part I. London: for J. Robinson, 1746. 8°

T.628

7173

WARBURTON (William) *Bishop of Gloucester.*

The nature of national offences truly stated: and the peculiar case of the Jewish people rightly explained... A sermon preached on the general fast day, appointed to be observed December 18, 1745. London, for J. and P. Knapton, 1746. 8°

T.662

7174

WESLEY (John)

Advice to the people called Methodists... [Anon.] 2nd ed. London: printed in the year 1746. 12°

T.545

7175

WESLEY (John)

The principles of a Methodist farther explain'd: occasioned by the Reverend Mr. Church's second letter to Mr. Wesley... London: W. Strahan; and sold by T. Trye; H. Butler; and at the Foundery, 1746. 12°

T.545

1747

7176

An ANSWER to a dangerous pamphlet, entitled, A candid and impartial account of the behaviour of Simon, Lord Lovat. Fully detecting the clandestine views of that writer; and interspersed with reflections on the principles and practices of the Jacobites ... London: for C. Corbett, [1747]. 8°

T.368

7177

An APOLOGY for the conduct of a late celebrated second-rate minister [i.e. Thomas Winnington], from the year 1729, at which time he commenc'd courtier, till within a few weeks of his death, in 1746... Written by himself and found among his papers... London: for W. Webb, [1747]. 8°

Attributed by Bowdler to "Mr Lynch" [Francis Lynch?]

2 copies.

T.430 T.628

7178

BUTLER (Joseph) *Bishop of Durham.*

A sermon preached before the House of Lords, in the abbey church of Westminster, on Thursday, June 11, 1747. being the anniversary of his Majesty's happy accession to the throne. By Joseph, Lord Bishop of Bristol. London: for John and Paul Knapton, 1747. 4°

T.582

7179

A CANDID and impartial account of the behaviour of Simon Lord Lovat, from the time his death-warrant was deliver'd, to the day of his execution... By a gentleman who attended his Lordship in his last moments... London: for J. Newbery, and W. Faden, 1747. 8°

T.368

7180

The CASE of the Genoese impartially stated; wherein the conduct of that people, the Austrians and Piedmontese, during the late convulsions, is candidly examined... In a letter to a member of Parliament ... London: for L. Gilliver, [1747]. 8°

T.653

7181

CAWTHORN (James)

Abelard to Eloisa. [Anon.] London: for M. Cooper, 1747. 4°

T.811

7182

A CONGRATULATORY letter to John Murray, Esq; late secretary to the young Pretender ... [Signed Atticus.] London: for W. Webb, 1747. 8°

T.432

7183

CRY aloud and spare not; or, Plain useful facts and remarks, as a preparative to the present sudden and general election. Address'd to the worthy independent electors of Westminster... By an independent free agent, and citizen of the world. London: printed in the year 1747. 8°

T.629

7184

DEACON (Thomas)

A full, true, and comprehensive view of Christianity ... The whole succinctly and fully laid down in two catechisms... [Anon.] London: for S. Newton, bookseller in Manchester; and sold by Mess.Rivington [and others], 1747. 8°

T.644

7185

DOUGLAS (William)

The resurrection: a poem. In three parts ... London: printed for, and sold by G. Strahan, R. Hett, R. Dodsley, G. Lewis; and J. Brindley, 1747. Fol.

T.540

7186

An ENQUIRY into the state of affairs on the continent; and what encouragement we have from that to expect happy events from continuing the present dangerous expensive war... London: for H. Carpenter, 1747. 8°

"For Tho. Bowdler Esq."

T.629

7187

FERGUSON (James)

A dissertation upon the phaenomena of the harvest moon. Also, the description and use of a new four-wheel'd Orrery, and an essay upon the moon's turning round her own axis. London: printed for the author, and sold by J. Nourse, and by S. Paterson, 1747. 8°

T.423

7188

The FREE-born Englishman's unmask'd battery; or, a short narrative of our miserable condition... By the author of Cry aloud and spare not. London: printed for and sold by E. Lamb; and to be had at the pamphlet shops in London and Westminster, 1747. 8°

T.629

7189

A GENERAL view of the present politics and interests of the principal powers of Europe; particularly of those at war... In a letter from the Hague, to a foreign minister at London. London: for W. Webb, [1747]. 8°

T.629

7190

GRANT (James)

A letter to the Reverend Mr. Murray at Duffus. [Dated] Edinburgh, September 29. 1747. [No imprint, 1747?] brs.

T.432

7191

GREAT BRITAIN. *Parliament.*

The whole proceedings in the House of Peers, upon the impeachment exhibited by the knights, citizens, and burgesses, in Parliament assembled... against Simon Lord Lovat, for high treason... London: for Samuel Billingsley, 1747. Fol.

2 copies.

T.696 T.697

7192

HERRING (Thomas) *Archbishop of Canterbury.*

A sermon, preached before his Grace Charles Duke of Richmond... and governors of the London infirmary... at the parish church of St. Lawrence-Jewry, on Tuesday, March 31, 1747. By... Thomas Lord Archbishop of York. London: H. Woodfall, [1747]. 4°

T.582

7193

A LETTER to Sir John Phillips, Bart. occasion'd by a bill brought into Parliament to naturalize foreign protestants. [Signed Anglo-nativus.] London: for M. Cooper, 1747. 8°

T.629

7194

A LETTER to the Right Honourable the E[ar]l of T[ra]q[uai]r... London, for R. Freeman, jun., [1747?] 8°

T.432

7195

LYTTELTON (George) *Baron Lyttelton.*

Observations on the conversion and apostleship of St. Paul. In a letter to Gilbert West, Esq; [Anon.] London: for R. Dodsley, and sold by M. Cooper, 1747. 8°

2 copies.

T.656 T.426

7196

MASON (William)

Musaeus: a monody to the memory of Mr. Pope, in imitation of Milton's Lycidas. [Anon.] London: for R. Dodsley, and sold by M. Cooper, 1747. 4°

2 copies.

T.811 T.579

7197

MIDDLETON (Conyers)

An introductory discourse to a larger work, designed hereafter to be published, concerning the miraculous powers which are supposed to have subsisted in the Christian Church, from the earliest ages... [Anon.] London: for R. Manby and H. Cox, 1747. 4°

T.639

7198

MURRAY (William) *Earl of Mansfield.*

The thistle; a dispassionate examine of the prejudice of Englishmen in general to the Scotch nation; and particularly of a late arrogant insult offered to all Scotchmen, by a modern English journalist. In a letter to the author of Old England of Dec. 27, 1746. [Signed Aretine.] 2nd ed. London: for H. Carpenter, [1747]. 8°

2 copies.

T.650 T.432

7199

OBSERVATIONS upon a bill, entituled, An Act for taking away, and abolishing the heritable jurisdictions in... Scotland, and for restoring such jurisdictions to the Crown... Edinburgh, printed: London, re-printed for T. Brown, 1747. 8°

T.432

7200

REMARKS on the people and government of Scotland. Particularly the Highlanders; their original customs, manners, &c. With a genuine account of the Highland regiment that was decoyed to London... Edinburgh: printed for the author, 1747. 8°

T.432

1747 (Cont'd)

7201
RUTHERFORTH (Thomas)

Two sermons preached before the University of Cambridge, one May XXIX: the other June XI: MDCCXLVII. London: for W. Innys; and W. Thurlbourne in Cambridge, 1747. 4°

T.710

7202
STEBBING (Henry) *Archdeacon of Wilts.*

Observations on a book [by Conyers Middleton], intituled, An introductory discourse to a larger work, &c. Containing an answer to the author's prejudices, that miraculous powers were not continued to the Church after the days of the Apostles. [Anon.] London, for C. Davis, 1747. 8°

T.665

7203
THOMAS (John) *Bishop of Salisbury.*

A sermon preached before the Incorporated Society for the Propagation of the Gospel in Foreign Parts; at their anniversary meeting in the parish church of St. Mary-le-Bow, on Friday February 20, 1746. By... John Lord Bishop of Lincoln. London: Edward Owen; and sold by J. Roberts; and A. Millar, 1747. 4°

T.716

7204
VERAX to Adamia. An epistle in Ovid's manner... London: for H. Chapelle; and sold by M. Cooper, 1747. Fol.

T.543

7205
The VISIONS of Aaron, the son of Adriel, which he saw concerning the rise and fall of the sister-nations... London: for Isaac Ben Gideon, [1747?] 8°

T.647

7206
WALPOLE (Horace) *Earl of Orford.*

A letter to the Whigs. Occasion'd by The letter to the Tories... [Anon.] London: for M. Cooper, 1747. 8°

T.629

7207
WARBURTON (William) *Bishop of Gloucester.*

A letter from an author, to a member of Parliament, concerning literary property. [Anon.] London, for John and Paul Knapton, 1747. 8°

T.210

7208
WHITEHEAD (Paul)

Honour. A satire... London: for M. Cooper, 1747. 4°

T.811

1748

7209
The ACCOMPLISH'D hero: or, The Caledonian songsters. From the French of Francis Salignac de la Motte Fenelon ... London: for C. Corbett, 1748. Fol.

T.540

7210
BENTHAM (Edward)

A letter to a young gentleman of Oxford... Oxford: for J. Fletcher, and M. Cooper, London, 1748. 8°

T.751

7211
BROUGHTON (Thomas) *Fellow of Exeter College.*

The Christian soldier: or, The duties of a religious life, recommended to the army, from the example of Cornelius: in a sermon preached before his Majesty's second regiment of Foot-guards. By an assistant chaplain of a garrison. 2nd ed. London: for John and James Rivington, 1748. 12°

T.795

7212
CHURCH (Thomas)

A sermon preached in the parish-church of Wandsworth, in the county of Surrey, on May 16, 1748. at the funeral of the Reverend Thomas Cawley... London: for J. and R. Tonson and S. Draper, 1768 [i.e. 1748]. 4°

T.710

7213
COBDEN (Edward)

The parable of the talents. A sermon preach'd at the parish-church of St. Ann, Westminster, on Thursday, March the 24th, 1748. before the governors of the Middlesex-Hospital... (An account of the Middlesex-Hospital...) London: M. Mechell; J. Newberry, and J. Jolliffe, [1748]. 2 parts. 4°

T.717

7214
The CONGRESS of the beasts... a farce of two acts, now in rehearsal at a new, grand theatre in Germany... Written originally in High-Dutch by the Baron Huffumbourghausen; and translated by J.J. H-d-g-r... London: for W. Webb, 1748. 8°

Signature of Ann French.
Attributed by Bowdler to "Mr. Lynch" [Francis Lynch?]

T.430

7215
DALTON (John)

A sermon preached before the University of Oxford, at St. Mary's, on the fifth of November, 1747. 2nd ed. London: for J. and J. Rivington; and sold by Mr. Dodsley; Mr. Millar, Mr. Clements, at Oxford; Mr. Thurlbourn, in Cambridge; and Mr. Leake, in Bath, 1748. 4°

T.710

7216
DOUGHTY (John)

A plain, friendly farewel to the parishioners of Oddington in the county of Glocester: a sermon preached... July the 6th, 1740... 2nd ed. London: John Oliver, 1748. 4°

T.710

7217
DUVERNEY (Guichard Joseph)

A treatise of the ear: containing an exact description of the several parts thereof, and their respective uses ... By M. Du Verney. Englished and improved by John Marshall ... 2nd ed. London: for John Whiston; and Samuel Baker, 1748. 12°

T.450

7218
ENGLISH liberty in some cases worse than French slavery... Containing a particular relation of the barbarous and oppressive methods made use of in raising the land-tax of this Kingdom... In a letter [signed Philalethes] address'd to the serious consideration of the lesser freeholders and electors of Great Britain... London: for M. Cooper, 1748. 8°

Wanting the title-page (supplied in photocopy).

T.631

7219
FORBES (Robert) *Gent.*

Ajax his speech to the Grecian knabbs. From Ovid's Metam. lib. XIII... Attempted in broad Buchans. By R.F. Gent. Printed in the year 1748. 8°

T.665

7220
FRANCKLIN (Thomas)

A sermon preach'd at the parish church of St. Peter's Cornhill; on the Sunday after the late dreadful fire in that neighbourhood. London: for R. Francklin, 1748. 4°

T.710

7221
HUNT (Thomas) *Regius Professor of Hebrew.*

De usu dialectorum orientalium, ac praecipue Arabice, in Hebraico codice interpretando, oratio habita Oxonii... VII Kalend. Martii, MDCCXLVIII... Oxonii, e Theatro Sheldoniano, impensis Ricardi Clements, 1748. 4°

T.714

7222
A LETTER from a gentleman in London to his friend in the country, concerning the treaty of Aix-la-Chapelle, concluded on the 8th of October, 1748. London: for W. Webb, 1748. 8°

T.634

7223
A LETTER to ***** in favour of short parliaments... London: for R. Naws, and T. Fox, 1748. 8°

T.634

7224
The LIFE of the Reverend Humphrey Prideaux, D.D. Dean of Norwich. With several tracts and letters of his, upon various subjects. Never before published. London: for J. and P. Knapton, 1748. 8°

T.352

7225
LISLE (Samuel) *Bishop of Norwich.*

A sermon preached before the Incorporated Society for the Propagation of the Gospel in Foreign Parts; at their anniversary meeting in the parish-church of St. Mary-le-Bow, on Friday February 19, 1747, by... Samuel Lord Bishop of St. Asaph. London: Edward Owen; and sold by J. Roberts; and A. Millar, 1748. 4°

T.716

7226
MASON (John) *Nonconformist Minister.*

An essay on elocution, or pronunciation. Intended chiefly for the assistance of those who instruct others in the art of reading... 2nd ed. London: for R. Hett; J. Buckland; J. Waugh; and M. Cooper, 1748. 8°

2 copies.

T.788 T.803

7227
MIDDLETON (Conyers)

Remarks on two pamphlets lately published against Dr. Middleton's Introductory discourse. The one [by Henry Stebbing], intituled, Observations on that discourse... The other [by John Chapman], The Jesuit-cabal farther opened... [Anon.] London: for R. Manby and H.S. Cox, 1748. 8°

T.678

7228
The MONOSYLLABLE if! A satire... London: for H. Carpenter; and sold at all the pamphlet-shops in London and Westminster, 1748. Fol.

T.543

7229
MORRIS (Robert)

Rupert to Maria. An heroic epistle. With Maria's genuine answer... [Anon.] London: for W. Webb, 1748. Fol.

T.543

7230
The NATIONAL JOURNAL.

A collection of political and humorous letters, poems, and articles of news, published in an evening paper, intitled, The national journal, or, Country gazette. Which began to be publish'd on Saturday, March 22d, 1746, and was suppress'd on Thursday, June the 12th... London: for J. Clark, and to be sold at the pamphlet-shops in town and country, 1748. 8°

T.432

7231
OBSERVATIONS on Mr. Whiston's Historical memoirs of the life and writings of Dr. Samuel Clarke... London: for W. Owen, 1748. 8°

T.658

7232
PASQUIN and Marforio on the peace: being a discussion, by these celebrated statues at Rome, of the general conduct of England, but particularly pending the late war, and in negociating the present peace... 3rd ed. London: for W. Webb, [1748?] 8°

T.434

7233
The PATRIOT analized; or, A compendious view of the publick criticism on a late pamphlet, called, An apology for the conduct of a late second-rate minister [i.e. Thomas Winnington]... In a letter to a friend at Worcester... London: for M. Cooper, 1748. 8°

2 copies.

T.634

7234
SKINNER (John) *of Longside.*

A preservative against presbytery... [Anon.] Printed in the year 1748. 8°

T.671

7235

SQUIRE (Samuel) *Bishop of St. David's.*

A letter to John Trot-Plaid, Esq; author of the Jacobite journal, concerning Mr. Carte's General history of England; by Duncan Mac Carte a Highlander London: for M. Cooper, 1748. 8°

T.658

7236

The STATE of the nation, with a general balance of the publick accounts... 2nd ed. London: for M. Cooper, 1748. 8°

T.634

7237

TO the memory of that dear, that most holy m[other] the C[hurch] of S[cotland]. [No imprint, 1748.] brs.

2 copies.

T.368 T.655

7238

WALPOLE (Horace) *Earl of Orford.*

A second and third letter to the Whigs. By the author of the first... London, for M. Cooper, 1748. 8°

T.629

7239

WARDLAW (Elizabeth)

Hardyknute, a fragment of an antient Scots poem. [Anon.] Glasgow, Robert Foulis, 1748. 8°

T.288

1749

7240

An ACCOUNT of a medical controversy in the city of Cork, in which five physicians are engaged... To which are subjoined two letters from Dr. Mead and one from Dr. Frewin, to the different persons concern'd. London: R. Dosley, 1749. 8°

Wanting the title-page and pp. 41-60.

T.288

7241

The ACTIVE testimony of the true Presbyterians of Scotland, being a brief abstract of acknowledgment of sins, and engagement to duties ... Printed in the year 1749. 8°

T.432

7242

An AUTHENTIC account of the whole conduct of the Young Chevalier. From his first arrival in Paris, after his defeat at Culloden, to the conclusion of the peace at Aix-la-Chapelle... In a letter from a gentleman residing at Paris, to his friend in London. 3rd ed... London printed: and sold by Dodd, Barnes, and at all the pamphlet-shops in London and Westminster, 1749. 8°

T.640

7243

BENTHAM (Edward)

A letter to a fellow of a college. Being the sequel of a letter to a young gentleman of Oxford... London: for S. Birt and Mary Senex; and J. Fletcher in Oxford, 1749. 8°

Signature of E. Harriott.

T.751

7244

BOYSE (Samuel)

Deity: a poem... [Anon.] London: for C. Corbett, 1749. 8°

T.665

7245

BRISTED (John) *M.A.*

The two late shocks of an earth-quake admonitions to repentance, a sermon preached at the parish-church of St. Michael, in Lewes, Sussex, on Sunday, March 18, 1749... London, for M. Cooper, and sold by J. Rivington, E. Verral and W. Lee at Lewes, and J. Lee at Chichester, [1749]. 4°

T.710

7246

BURTON (John) *of York.*

British liberty endanger'd; demonstrated by the following narrative: wherein is prov'd from facts, that J.B. has hitherto been a better friend to the English constitution... than his persecutors... London: A.B., 1749. 8°

T.432

7247

BYROM (John) *Fellow of Trinity College, Cambridge.*

An epistle to a gentleman of the Temple. Occasioned by two treatises just published, wherein the fall of man is differently represented; viz. I. Mr. Law's Spirit of prayer, II. the Bishop of London's appendix ... [Anon.] London: for R. Spavan, 1749. Fol.

T.543

7248

CHANDLER (Samuel)

St. Paul's rules of charity, and his manner of recommending it, considered: in a sermon preached to the Society for relieving the widows and orphans of protestant dissenting ministers, at the Old Jury, March 1. 1748... London: for J. Noon, 1749. 4°

T.710

7249

CHARLES EDWARD, *the Young Pretender.*

A collection of declarations, proclamations, and other valuable papers. Published by authority at Edinburgh, in the years 1745 and 1746 ... Edinburgh: re-printed in the year 1749. 8°

T.368

7250

COBDEN (Edward)

A persuasive to chastity: a sermon preached before the King, at St. James's, on the 11th of December, 1748. London: for J. Lodge, 1749. 4°

T.717

7251

COHAUSEN (Johann Heinrich)

Hermippus redivivus: or, The sage's triumph over old age and the grave. Wherein, a method is laid down for prolonging the life and vigour of man... [Anon.] [Translated by John Campbell.] The second edition carefully corrected and much enlarged. London: for J. Nourse, 1749. 8°

T.425

7252

COPY of a letter from a French lady at Paris. Giving a particular account of the manner in which Prince Edward was arrested. London: for W. Webb, 1749. 8°

2 copies.

T.438 T.640

7253

DRUMMOND (Robert Hay) *Archbishop of York.*

A sermon preached before the House of Lords, in the abbey church of Westminster, on Tuesday, April 25, 1749. Being the day appointed... for a general thanksgiving for the peace. By Robert, Lord Bishop of St. Asaph. London: for John and Paul Knapton, 1749. 4°

T.710

7254

G. (W.)

A poetick epistle address'd to Sir George Vandeput, Bart. Recommended to the dependent as well as independent electors of Westminster... London: for W. Needham, [1749]. Fol.

T.557

7255

HUGHES (Obadiah)

Distress for the loss of pious friends, considered and improved. In a sermon on occasion of the much-lamented death of Anthony Walburge, Esq; preached at the merchants-lecture at Salters-hall, July 11, 1749 ... London: James Waugh, for Richard Hett; James Buckland; and Mrs. Winbush, 1749. 4°

T.710

7256

HUGHES (Obadiah)

The nativity of Christ considered and improved. In two sermons preached at the merchants lecture at Salters-hall; and at the protestant dissenters chapel in Long-ditch, Westminster. London: James Waugh, for Richard Hett; James Buckland; and Mrs. Winbush, 1749. 4°

T.710

7257

JAMES (Robert)

A dissertation on fevers and inflammatory distempers... 2nd ed. London: for J. Newbery, 1749. 8°

T.450

7258

KING (William) *Principal of St. Mary Hall.*

Oratio in Theatro Sheldoniano habita idibus Aprilibus, MDCCXLIX. die dedicationis Bibliothecae Radclivianae.. Londoni, apud J. Clarke, & W. Owen. Oxonii, apud J. Fletcher, & S. Parker, [1749]. 4°

2 copies.

T.692 T.579

7259

MASON (John) *Nonconformist Minister.*

An essay on the power and harmony of prosaic numbers ... [Anon.] London: James Waugh, for M. Cooper, 1749. 8°

T.682

7260

MASON (John) *Nonconformist Minster.*

An essay on the power of numbers, and the principles of harmony in poetical compositions. [Anon.] London: James Waugh, for M. Cooper, 1749. 8°

T.682

7261

MASON (William)

Isis. An elegy. Written in the year 1748... London: for R. Dodsley and sold by M. Cooper, 1749. 4°

T.811

7262

MASON (William)

Ode performed in the senate-house at Cambridge July 1, 1749. at the installation of his Grace Thomas Holles Duke of Newcastle Chancellor of the University... Set to music by Mr. Boyce. Cambridge, J. Bentham; sold by W. Thurlbourn; and R. Dodsley, London, 1749. 4°

T.811

7263

The NORTHERN election; or, Nest of beasts. A drama of six acts, now in rehearsal near Mittaw, in Courland... Done into English, from the original, by T.N. and B.W... London: for W. Webb, 1749. 8°

Attributed by Bowdler to "Mr. Lynch" [Francis Lynch?]

T.430

7264

The NORTHERN election; or, Nest of beasts. A drama of six acts, now in rehearsal near Mittaw, in Courland... Done into English, from the original, by T.N. and B.W... 2nd ed. London: for W. Webb, 1749. 8°

Attributed by Bowdler to "Mr. Lynch" [Francis Lynch?]

T.636

7265

NUGENT (Robert) *Earl Nugent.*

Considerations upon a reduction of the land-tax. [Anon.] London: for R. Griffith, 1749. 8°

T.634

7266

PEARCE (Zachary) *Bishop of Rochester.*

Concio ad synodum ab Archiepiscopo, episcopis, reliquoque clero provinciae Cantuariensis celebratam, habita in ecclesia cathedrali S. Pauli Londini die 2. Decemb. A.D. 1741. Editio tertia. Londini: J. Watts: et apud B. Dod, 1749. 4°

T.710

7267

PERCEVAL (John) *Earl of Egmont.*

An examination of the principles, and an enquiry into the conduct, of the two b[rothe]rs; in regard to the establishment of their power, and their prosecution of the war... [Anon.] London: for A. Price, 1749. 8°

T.634

1749 (Cont'd)

7268

PERCEVAL (John) *Earl of Egmont.*

An occasional letter from a gentleman in the country, to his friend in Town. Concerning the treaty negotiated at Hanau, in the year 1743... [Anon.] London: for A. Briton, 1749. 8°

T.634

7269

POEMS on several occasions, from genuine manuscripts of Dean Swift, Mr. H----m, Mr. C[ibbe]r... London: for J. Bromage, and sold by the booksellers at Bath and Tunbridge Wells, 1749. 8°

Teerink 913.

T.651

7270

ST. JOHN (Henry) *Viscount Bolingbroke.*

Letters, on the spirit of patriotism: on the idea of a patriot king: and on the state of parties at the accession of King George the first. [Anon.] London: for A. Millar, 1749. 8°

2 copies.

T.186 T.772

7271

A SEASONABLE recapitulation of enormous national crimes and grievances to help the memory, for the use and consideration of all honest men and true Britons... London: for M. Cooper, 1749. 8°

"This is a curiosity as having some passages in it which are not in the copies that were publickly sold" (Bowdler III).

T.430

7272

SQUIRE (Samuel) *Bishop of St. David's*

A sermon preached before... the Duke of Newcastle, Chancellor, and the University of Cambridge, in St. Mary's church, upon commencement Sunday, July 2, 1749. London: for Charles Bathurst, 1749. 4°

T.710

7273

THOMSON (James)

Coriolanus. A tragedy. As it is acted at the Theatre-Royal in Covent-Garden. London, for A. Millar, 1749. 8°

T.667

7274

THORNTON (Bonnell)

An ode upon Saint Caecilia's day, adapted to the ancient British musick. As it was performed on the twenty-second of November... [The preface is signed Fustian Sackbut.] London, for J. and J. Rivington, and C. Corbet, 1749. 4°

T.811

7275

WESLEY (John)

A plain account of the people called Methodists. In a letter to the Revd. Mr. Perronet. 2nd ed. London: W. Strahan; and sold by T. Trye; and at the Foundery, 1749. 12°

T.545

7276

WINGFIELD (Thomas)

The mischiefs of unreasonable opposition to government. A sermon preach'd before... the Lord Mayor... on Monday, January the 30th, 1748-9. London: for John Clarke, 1749. 4°

T.710

1750

7277

ALLEN (Thomas) *Rector of Kettering.*

The way to grow rich, as well as to be high in praise, and in name, and in honour, by a voluntary and religious paying of the first-fruits of all our increase... London: for W. Owen, [1750?] 8°

T.777

7278

BOLTON (Robert) *Dean of Carlisle.*

On the employment of time. Three essays. [Anon.] London: for J. Whiston; R. Dodsley; and W. Russel, 1750. 8°

T.641

7279

BUCKLER (Benjamin)

Οἶνος κριθινος. A dissertation concerning the origin and antiquity of barley wine... [Anon.] Oxford, printed at the Theatre for James Fletcher: and sold by J. and J. Rivington, Lond., 1750. 4°

T.579

7280

COOKE (William) *Dean of Ely.*

The sense of St. Peter, as to the more sure word of prophecy, considered and explained. A sermon preached at the visitation held at Beaconsfield, May 25, 1750. London: for C. Bathurst; and R. Dodsley, 1750. 8°

T.661

7281

A COPY of a letter from a gentleman in London to his friend at Bath. Bath: printed in the year 1750. 8°

3 copies.

T.432 T.438 T.640

7282

COX (James) *D.D.*

God's mercies slighted and neglected, a challenge to his justice. A sermon preached at Hampstead chapel, March the 25th, and at Kensington, April the 1st, 1750. London: for Charles Bathurst, 1750. 4°

T.710

7283

A CURIOUS collection of genuine and authentick letters. Edinburgh: printed for the author, 1750. 8°

T.438

7284

An EXAMINATION of the consequences of Dr. Middleton's Free enquiry, &c. To which are added, some observations, in order to confute what he has objected to the Lord Bishop of London's Discourses on the use and intent of prophecy. London: for W. Owen, 1750. 8°

T.678

7285

FORBES (Duncan)

Reflexions on the sources of incredulity with regard to religion. [Anon.] 2nd ed. Edinburgh: Sands, Murray, and Cochran, for G. Hamilton and J. Balfour, 1750. 8°

T.682

7286

FORBES (Robert) *Bishop.*

A plain, authentick and faithful narrative of the several passages of the Young Chevalier, from the battle of Culloden to his embarkation for France... [Signed Philalethes.] London: for W. Webb, 1750. 8°

T.653

7287

GAY (John)

Acis and Galatea, a serenata. [Anon.] The music composed by Mr. Handel. Bath: M. Martin, [c.1750]. 8°

T.664

7288

GORING (Henry)

A letter from H[enry] G[orin]g, Esq; one of the gentlemen of the bed-chamber to the Young Chevalier... containing many remarkable and affecting occurrences, which happened to the P[rince], during the course of his mysterious progress... London: printed, and sold at the Royal Exchange... and all the pamphlet-shops of London and Westminster, 1750. 8°

T.653

7289

HUBBARD (Henry)

A sermon preached before the governors of the charity for the relief of the poor widows and orphans of clergymen in the county of Suffolk... on Thursday, July 19. 1750. Cambridge, J. Bentham; for W. Thurlbourn: and sold by W. Craighton in Ipswich, J. Gleed in Norwich, M. Watson in Bury, and J. Beecroft in London, 1750. 4°

T.710

7290

JACKSON (Lawrence)

Remarks on Dr. Middleton's examination of the Lord Bishop of London's Discourses, concerning the use and intent of prophecy. In a letter from a country clergyman, to his friend in London... [Anon.] London: for G. Hawkins: and sold by M. Cooper, 1750. 8°

T.663

7291

JENKIN (Thomas)

An impartial examination of the Free inquiry: the primitive fathers vindicated, and the necessity of miracles maintain'd, to the conclusion of the third century. In a letter to Dr. Middleton. Cambridge: J. Bentham; sold by W. Thurlbourn in Cambridge, Mess. Payne and Bouquet, London, J. Fletcher at Oxford, J. Hilyard at York, J. Gleed at Norwich, W. Craighton at Ipswich; Mr. Flacton in Canterbury, Mr. Leake at Bath, and Mr. Hollingworth at Lynn, 1750. 8°

T.678

7292

KING (William) *Principal of St. Mary Hall.*

Oratio in Theatro Sheldoniano habita idibus Aprilibus, MDCCXLIX. die dedicationis Bibliothecae Radclivianae... Londini, apud J. Clarke, & W. Owen. Oxonii, apud J. Fletcher, & S. Parker, 1750. 4°

T.815

7293

A LETTER from a gentleman in Town to his friend in the country, recommending the necessity of frugality. London: for W. Webb, 1750. 8°

Attributed by Bowdler to Mr. Pierce.

T.437

7294

MADDOX (Isaac) *Bishop of Worcester.*

The expediency of preventive wisdom. A sermon preached before... the Lord-Mayor, the aldermen, and governors of the several hospitals of the city of London... on Easter-Monday, 1750... The second edition, with additions. London: H. Woodfall; and sold by H. Whitridge; and G. Woodfall, [1750?] 4°

T.710

7295

A REPLY to Dr. Middleton's Examination of... the Bishop of London's Discourses on the use and intent of prophecy, and of his appendix on the subject of the Fall. In a letter to... the Lord Bishop of ---. London: for John Clarke, 1750. 8°

T.678

7296

SEWARD (Thomas)

The folly, danger, and wickedness of disaffection to the government: an assize sermon preach'd at Stafford on Sunday, August 19, 1750... on occasion of the late seditious riots in that county. London for J. and R. Tonson and S. Draper, 1750. 4°

T.710

7297

SHERLOCK (Thomas) *Bishop of London.*

A letter from the Lord Bishop of London, to the clergy and people of London and Westminster; on occasion of the late earthquakes. London: for John Whiston, 1750. 8°

T.682

7298

TUCKER (Josiah)

A brief essay on the advantages and disadvantages which respectively attend France and Great Britain, with regard to trade... [Anon.] The second edition corrected, with large additions. London: for T. Trye, 1750. 8°

T.636

7299

WATSON (George)

Christ the light of the world. A sermon preached before the University of Oxford, at St. Peter's, on Saturday, October 28. 1749. Oxford, printed at the Theatre for Sackville Parker, and sold by M. Cooper, London, 1750. 4°

T.824

7300

WHITEFIELD (George)

Christ the physician of the soul. A sermon by the Rev. Mr. G. Wh[ite]f[iel]d. Taken by a master of short-hand, word for word as he preached it... [No imprint, 1750?] 8°

T.661

1751

7301

ARMSTRONG (John)

Of benevolence: an epistle to Eumenes. [Anon.]
London: for A. Millar, 1751. Fol.

T.540

7302

BAYLY (Anselm)

The antiquity, evidence, and certainty of Christianity,
canvassed, on Dr. Middleton's examination of the Lord
Bishop of London's Discourses on the use and intent of
prophecy ... London: printed, and sold by J. and J.
Rivington; Mr. Clements in Oxford; Mr. Matthews in
Cambridge; and Mrs. Palmer in Gloucester, 1751. 8°

T.426

7303

BERKELEY (George) *Bishop of Cloyne.*

The querist, containing several queries, proposed
to the consideration of the public... To which
is added, by the same author, A word to the wise:
or an exhortation to the Roman Catholic clergy of
Ireland. 2nd ed. London, for W. Innys, C. Davis,
C. Hitch, W. Bowyer; and sold by M. Cooper, 1751.
8°

T.54

7304

BUCKLER (Benjamin)

A complete vindication of the mallard of All-Souls
College, against the injurious suggestions of the
Rev. Mr. Pointer... [Anon.] 2nd ed. London, for
J. and J. Rivington; and J. Fletcher in Oxford,
1751. 8°

"E libris J. Jeans Coll. Reg. Oxon."

T.573

7305

A COPY of a letter published in Adam's Weekly courant,
printed at Chester, July 16, 1751. [Relating to
a cure of the king's evil.] [No imprint, 1751?]
8°

T.432

7306

GRAY (Thomas)

An elegy written in a country church yard. [Anon.]
The third edition, corrected. London: for R. Dodsley;
and sold by M. Cooper, 1751. 4°

T.811

7307

A GUIDE to the stage: or, Select instructions and
precedents from the best authorities towards
forming a polite audience; with some account of the
players... London: for D. Job; and R. Baldwin, 1751.
8°

T.682

7308

A LETTER from a gentleman in Town to his friend
in the country, recommending the necessity of
frugality. 3rd ed. London: for W. Webb, 1751.
8°

T.658

7309

MONOUX (Lewis)

A sermon preached at Bishop-Stortford, in
Hertfordshire, at the anniversary meeting of the
gentlemen educated at that school, on Tuesday,
August 20th, 1750. London, for W. Thurlbourn,
Cambridge; J. Beechcroft, London; and sold by M.
Bayford, in Bishop-Stortford, 1751. 4°

T.715

7310

SEWARD (Thomas)

The folly, danger, and weakness of certain modern
zealous preachers affecting to be politicians.
Display'd, in an assize-sermon, preach'd at Stafford,
on Sunday, August 19, 1750... London: for W. Webb,
1751. 8°

T.661

7311

A THRENODY. To the memory of a nobleman [i.e.
Lord Blantyre] who dyed at Paris, on the 10/21 of
May 1751... By Philalethes. [No imprint, 1751?]
8°

Attributed by Bowdler to James Elphinston.

T.660

7312

TOWNE (John)

The argument of the Divine legation [by William
Warburton] fairly stated, and returned to the
deists, to whom it was originally addressed...
By an impartial hand. To which is added, an
appendix, containing letters which passed between
the late Dr. Middleton and Mr. Warburton, on the
characters of Moses and Cicero... London: for C.
Davis, 1751. 8°

T.352

7313

WARTON (Thomas)

Ode for music, as performed at the Theatre in
Oxford, on the second of July, 1751... Set to
music by Dr. Hayes. Oxford, for R. Clements and
J. Barrett; W. Thurlbourne in Cambridge; and
R. Dodsley, London, [1751]. 4°

T.811

1752

7314

DALTON (John)

Remarks on XII historical designs of Raphael, and
the Musaeum Graecum et Aegyptiacum, or antiquities
of Greece and Egypt, illustrated by prints, intended
to be published from Mr. Dalton's drawings. In
answer to a letter of inquiry concerning those works.
[Anon.] London: for M. Cooper, 1752. 8°

T.788

7315

DOUGLAS (Gavin) *Bishop of Dunkeld.*

A description of May. From Gawin Douglas, Bishop of
Dunkeld. [With a modern version] by Francis Fawkes
... The third edition corrected. London: for
Lockyer Davis, 1752. 8°

T.288

7316

A FARMER'S letter to the True Briton. [Dated] March
10, 1752. [Signed John Plowshare.] [No imprint,
1752?] 8°

T.432

7317

GIBSON (Edmund) *Bishop of London.*

Serious advice to persons who have been sick, to
be put into their hands as soon as they are
recover'd... 25th ed. London: E. Owen; and
sold by W. Johnston, 1752. 12°

T.544

7318

HARMAN (Ephraim)

A letter to Thomas Randolph, a doctor of Oxford;
occasioned by his discourse intitled Party-zeal
censured... London: for W. Owen, 1752. 8°

T.429

7319

HAWKINS (William) *Professor of Poetry.*

A sermon preach'd before the University of Oxford,
at St. Mary's, on Thursday, January 30. 1752...
Oxford, printed at the Theatre for Sackville Parker;
J. and J. Rivington, and W. Owen, Lond., 1752. 8°

T.661

7320

LAW (William)

The spirit of love, being an appendix to the Spirit
of prayer. In a letter to a friend. London: for
W. Innys, and J. Richardson, 1752. 8°

T.644

7321

MASON (William)

Elfrida, a dramatic poem. Written on the model of
the antient Greek tragedy. London, for J. and P.
Knapton, 1752. 4°

T.811

7322

The ONLY true and authentic trial of John Swan and
Miss Elizabeth Jeffreys, for the murder of her
uncle, Mr. Joseph Jeffreys, of Walthamstow in Essex
... London, printed: and sold by J. Robinson; R.
Baldwin; G. Woodfall; Mrs. Dodd; and Mess. Kingman,
Cooke, and James; and by all booksellers; and of the
hawkers in Town and country, 1752. 4°

T.696

7323

A SERMON on the King's happy return, May 29th, 1660.
Written some time ago, but never preach'd...
London: for A. Morse, 1752. 8°

T.661

7324

SPENCE (Joseph)

Crito: or, A dialogue on beauty. By Sir Harry
Beaumont. London, for R. Dodsley, and sold by
M. Cooper, 1752. 8°

Wanting the title-page.

T.803

7325

STEWART (James) *of Aucharn.*

An authentic copy of thhe [sic] dying speech of
James Stewart, who was executed for the alledged
murder of Colin Campbell of Glenure. 1752.
[No imprint, 1752?] 8°

T.640

1753

7326

DELAFAYE (Theodore)

Inoculation an indefensible practice. A sermon
preached at the united parish-churches of St.
Mildred's and All-Saints, in the city of Canterbury,
on the third and twenty-fourth of June, 1753.
London: for M. Cooper, 1753. 8°

T.661

7327

EDWARDS (Thomas) *Barrister.*

The canons of criticism, and glossary, being a
supplement to Mr. Warburton's edition of Shakespear ...
By the other gentleman of Lincoln's Inn ... 5th ed.
London, for C. Bathurst, 1753. 8°

T.425

7328

FREE (John)

The speech of Dr. John Free, containing a concise
and clear account of the English constitution,
both old and new... Delivered July 30, 1753. to
... the mayor, aldermen, and citizens, at the
town-hall in Oxford, upon taking up his freedom of the
city... 2nd ed. London: E. Owen, for the author; and
sold by Mr. Hodges; Mr. Owen; Mr. Whitworth; and Mr.
Parker, bookseller in Oxford, 1753. 8°

T.665

7329

A GENUINE and authentick account of the behaviour
of Dr. Archibald Cameron, at the place of execution,
on Thursday, June 7, 1753. By an eye and ear-witness.
London: printed in the year 1753. 8°

2 copies.

T.640   T.432

7330

A JOURNAL from Grand Cairo to Mount Sinai and
back again. Translated from a manuscript,
written by the Prefetto of Egypt... To which are
added some remarks on the origin of hieroglyphics...
By... Robert Lord Bishop of Clogher... London,
William Bowyer, 1753. 4°

T.535

7331

KEDINGTON (Roger)

On the folly of heathenism and insufficiency of
reason in religious enquiries: and the consequent
necessity, truth, and excellency of the Christian
religion. A sermon preached at the primary
visitation of... Thomas Lord Bishop of Norwich...
Cambridge; J. Bentham; and sold by W. Thurlbourn in
Cambridge; W. Craighton at Ipswich; J. Gleed at
Norwich; J. Lee at Lynn; M. Steel at Bury; and J.
Beecroft, London, 1753. 4°

T.715

7332

MEADOWCOURT (Richard)

A sermon preached at the cathedral-church of
Worcester, on the 23d of August, 1753. being the
anniversary meeting of the contributors to the
infirmary. London: for W. Sandby, 1753. 8°

T.661

1753 (Cont'd)

7333
NORTH (Roger)

A discourse of the poor. Shewing the pernicious tendency of the laws now in force for their maintenance and settlement... London: for M. Cooper; and sold by W. Craighton in Ipswich, 1753. 8°

T.43°

7334
The REJECTION and restoration of the Jews, according to Scripture, declar'd... By Archaicus. London: for R. Baldwin, jun.; and S. Parker, in Oxford, 1753. 8°

T.656

7335
SOME remarks on the late Lord Bolingbroke's famous letter to Sir William Windham, in a course of letters [signed Philalethes] from a gentleman in town to his friend in the country. London: for M. Cooper, 1753. 8°

T.422

1754

7336
BROWNE (Isaac Hawkins)

De animi immortalitate. Poema... [Anon.] Londini: impensis J. & R. Tonson & S. Draper, 1754. 4°

T.579

7337
COBDEN (Edward)

The religious education of children. A sermon preached in the parish-church of Christ-Church, London, on Thursday May the 16th, 1754: being the time of the yearly meeting of the children educated in the charity-schools, in and about the cities of London and Westminster... London: J. Oliver; and sold by B. Dod, 1754. 4°

T.717

7338
FERGUSON (James)

An idea of the material universe, deduced from a survey of the solar system ... London: printed for the author, 1754. 8°

T.288

7339
MILTON (John)

L'Allegro, ed il Penseroso. By Milton. And a Song for St. Cecilia's day. By Dryden. Set to musick by George Frederick Handel. London: for J. and R. Tonson, [1754?] 4°

T.559

7340
OLIVER (William)

Myra: a pastoral dialogue, sacred to the memory of a lady, who died December 29, 1753, in the twenty-fifth year of her age... [Anon.] Bath: T. Boddely, [1754?] Fol.

T.543

7341
TWO dissertations: the first on the supposed suicide of Samson... The second on Jephtha's vow... London: for W. Innys and J. Richardson, 1754. 2 parts. 8°

T.429

7342
WESLEY (John)

An answer to all which the Revd. Dr. Gill has printed on the final perseverance of the saints. London printed; and sold at the Foundery; by T. Try; by J. Robinson, and by T. James, 1754. 12°

T.545

1755

7343
AYSCOUGH (Francis)

A discourse against self-murder. Preached at South-Audley-chapel, January the 12th, 1755. London: for H. Shute Cox, 1755. 4°

T.717

7344
BAKER (*Sir* George)

De affectibus animi·et morbis inde oriundis dissertatio habita Cantabrigiae... Cantabrigiae, typis academicis excudebat J. Bentham. Veneunt apud Gul. Thurlbourn, et T. Merrill, Cantabrigiae; J. Whiston & B. White, et R. Dodsley, Londini; R. Fletcher, Oxonii; J. Pote, Etonae; et A. Rogers, Stamfordiae, 1755. 4°

T.579

7345
DODD (William)

The sinful Christian condemn'd by his own prayers. A sermon on Luke xix.22... 2nd ed. London: for T. Waller, and E. Dilly, 1755. 8°

T.659

7346
GILPIN (William)

The life of Hugh Latimer, Bishop of Worcester. London: Charles Rivington, for James and John Rivington, 1755. 8°

T.640

7347
HAY (William)

Select epigrams of Martial. Translated and imitated by William Hay, Esq; with an appendix of some by Cowley, and other hands. London: for R. and J. Dodsley, 1755. 8°

T.741

7348
HERNANDEZ (Jaime)

A philosophical and practical essay on the gold and silver mines of Mexico and Peru... Translated from a letter wrote in Spanish, by Father James Hernandez ... London: for J. Scott, 1755. 8°

T.730

7349
HURD (Richard) *Bishop of Worcester.*

On the delicacy of friendship. A seventh dissertation. Address'd to the author of the sixth [i.e. John Jortin] ... [Anon.] London: for M. Cooper, 1755. 8°

T.288

7350
KING (William) *Principal of St. Mary Hall.*

Doctor King's apology: or, vindication of himself from the several matters charged on him by the society of informers... Oxford, printed at the Theatre for S. Parker: and sold by W. Owen, London, 1755. 4°

2 copies.

T.815 T.692

7351
LEWIS (John) *Pamphleteer.*

Advice to posterity, concerning a point of the last importance. Written by a friend to liberty and property. London: for J. Freeman, 1755. 8°

Attributed by Bowdler to "Mr. Heathcote."

T.636

7352
OGLETHORPE ( )

The naked truth. [Anon.] London: for A. Price, 1755. 8°

T.636

7353
OSTERVALD (Jean Frédéric)

An abridgment of the history of the Bible. Written originally in French... Translated into English, with some improvements... London: for B. Dod, 1755. 12°

T.795

7354
SHERLOCK (Thomas) *Bishop of London.*

The tryal of the witnesses of the resurrection of Jesus. [Anon.] 13th ed... London: for John Whiston and Benjamin White, 1755. 8°

T.828

7355
SMITH (George)

Remarks upon the life of the Most Reverend Dr. John Tillotson, compiled by Thomas Birch, D.D. [Anon.] The third edition with additions. London, for W. Owen, 1755. 8°

T.429

7356
STEVENSON (John Hall)

Hymn to Miss Laurence, in the pump-room at Bath. [Anon.] London: for R. and J. Dodsley; and sold by T. Cooper, 1755. 4°

T.579

7357
TALBOT (George)

A sermon preached at the cathedral of Glocester at the opening of the infirmary, on Thursday, August 14, 1755. Glocester, printed for the benefit of the charity; and sold by R. and J. Dodsley, and W. Clarke, London, [1755]. 4°

T.670

7358
WHITE (John) *B.D.*

A new preservative against popery, chiefly extracted from a larger treatise lately published, intituled, The protestant Englishman guarded against the arts and arguments of Romish priests and emissaries... London, for C. Davis, 1755. 12°

T.795

1756

7359
An APPEAL to the people: containing, the genuine and entire letter of Admiral Byng to the Secr. of the Ad[miralt]y: observations on those parts of it which were omitted by the writers of the Gazette... Part the first. London: for J. Morgan, 1756. 8°

T.636

7360
BAYLY (Edward)

A sermon preached at St. James's church in Bath, on Friday, February 6. 1756: being the day appointed... for a general fast... 2nd ed. London: for J. Leake and W. Frederick, booksellers in Bath; and sold by Messrs. Hitch and Hawes, and M. Cooper, 1756. 4°

T.717

7361
BEARCROFT (Philip)

A sermon preached before... the Lord-Mayor, the aldermen and citizens, at the cathedral-church of St. Paul, on Friday, February 6, 1756. being the day appointed... for a general fast. London: Edward Owen, 1756. 4°

T.717

7362
BLACKLOCK (Thomas)

An essay on universal etymology: or, The analysis of a sentence. Containing an account of the parts of speech, as common to all languages... Edinburgh: Sands, Donaldson, Murray, and Cochran. For E. Wilson, bookseller in Dumfries, 1756. 8°

T.789

7363
BOWER (Archibald)

Six letters from A[rchibal]d B[owe]r to Father Sheldon, Provincial of the Jesuits in England; illustrated with several remarkable facts, tending to ascertain the authenticity of the said letters, and the true character of the writer ... [Edited by John Douglas.] London: for J. Morgan, 1756. 8°

T.433

7364
CRADOCK (John) *Archbishop of Dublin.*

A sermon preached in the parish church of St. Paul, Covent Garden, on Friday, February 6, 1756. Being the day appointed... for a general fast. London, for S. Baker; and sold by W. Thurlbourn, T. Merril, and R. Matthews, in Cambridge, 1756. 4°

T.717

7365
DANCE OF DEATH.

La danse des morts, comme elle est depeinte dans la... ville de Basle... Dessinée et gravée sur l'original de feu Mr. Matthieu Merian. On y a ajouté, une description de la ville de Basle... A Basle, chés Jean Rodolphe Imhof, 1756. 4°

T.660

7366
GERMAN cruelty: a fair warning to the people of Great Britain... London: for J. Scott, 1756. 8°

T.430

7367

GRIFFITH (Thomas)

The use and extent of reason in matters of religion. A sermon preached before the University of Oxford, at St. Mary's, on Tuesday in Whitsun-week, June 8. 1756. Oxford, printed at the Theatre for S. Parker; and sold by J. Rivington, London, 1756.   8°

T.751

7368

HALL (Charles)

The Gospel credibility defended against the objection of its decrease by length of time. In a sermon preached before the University of Oxford, at St. Marys church, on Sunday, July 4, 1756. Oxford, printed at the Theatre for James Fletcher; and sold by J. Rivington, and J. Fletcher, London, 1756.   8°

T.751

7369

HALLIFAX (James)

A sermon preach'd in St. John's chapel in the parish of St. Andrew, Holborn, on Sunday February 8, 1756. Being the Sunday after the day appointed... for a general fast and humiliation, on account of the dreadful earthquake at Lisbon. London: J. Hughs, and sold by M. Cooper, and E. Batson, 1756.   4°

T.717

7370

KILNER (James)

The perpetual inter-agency of Providence in all things. A sermon preached at the parish-church of Lexden in Essex, on the sixth of February, 1756; (being the day appointed for a general fast.)... London: for H. Whitridge, 1756.   4°

T.717

7371

A LETTER to a member of Parliament in the country, from his friend in London, relative to the case of Admiral Byng: with some original papers and letters... London: for J. Cooke, 1756.   8°

T.624

7372

LEWIS (John) *Pamphleteer.*

The sequel of Advice to posterity, concerning a point of the last importance. Wherein the subject is farther considered... Written by a friend to liberty and property... London: for J. Freeman, 1756.   8°

T.636

7373

LINDSAY (John)

The grand and important question, about the Church, and parochial communion, fairly and friendly debated, in a dialogue between a worthy country gentleman, and his neighbour, newly returned from London. [Anon.] London: printed in the year 1756.   8°

T.649

7374

MADDOX (Isaac) *Bishop of Worcester.*

The duty and wisdom of remembering past dangers and deliverances: a thanksgiving sermon for the suppression of the late unnatural rebellion; preached at the cathedral church of Worcester, on Thursday the 9th of October, 1746. 4th ed. With a preface, containing some reflections suited to the present situation of public affairs. London: H. Woodfall, 1756.   4°

T.717

7375

MAISTER (Georg)

Panegyricus Francisco et Mariae Theresiae Augustis ob scientias optimasque artes suis in terris instauratas, ornatas, dum senatus populusque academicus Vindobonensis Augusta munificentia splendidissimarum aedium e fundamentis recens conditarum possessione donaretur... Vindobonae, e prelo Joannis Thomae Trattner, 1756.   Fol.

T.810

7376

MOSS (Charles) *Bishop of Bath and Wells.*

A sermon preached at the parish church of St. James, Westminster, on February 6, 1756. being the day appointed... for a general fast, on occasion of the late earthquakes... London: for J. Whiston and B. White; and R. Davis, 1756.   4°

T.717

7377

OLIVEYRA (Francisco Xavier de)

A pathetic discourse on the present calamities of Portugal. Addressed to his countrymen, and, in particular, to... Joseph, King of Portugal, by the Chevalier De Oliveyra. Translated from the French. 2nd ed. London: for R. Baldwin, 1756.   4°

T.717

7378

PETIT (Peter)

Natural occasions of terror considered as intentional warnings of Providence... A sermon preached February the 6th, MDCCLVI, (being the day appointed for a general fast...) in the parish-church of St. John the Baptist, in Royston, Hertfordshire. London: for J. Payne, 1756.   4°

T.717

7379

A PLAIN account of the cause of earthquakes. Being a supplement to a treatise, lately published, on fire. By the same author. London: for W. Innys and J. Richardson, 1756.   8°

T.665

7380

SHEBBEARE (John)

A letter to the people of England, on the present situation and conduct of national affairs. Letter I... [Anon.] 3rd ed. London: printed in the year, 1756.   8°

T.626

7381

SHEBBEARE (John)

A fourth letter to the people of England. On the conduct of the m[iniste]rs in alliances, fleets and armies, since the first differences on the Ohio, to the taking of Minorca by the French... [Anon.] 2nd ed. London: for M. Collyer, 1756.   8°

T.626

7382

SQUIRE (Samuel) *Bishop of St. David's.*

A speedy repentance the most effectual means to avert Gods judgments. A sermon preached at the parish church of St. Anne Westminster, February 6, 1756; being the day appointed for a general fast and humiliation, on account of the late... earthquakes... London: for Charles Bathurst, 1756.   4°

T.717

7383

STEBBING (Henry) *Preacher of Gray's Inn.*

A sermon preached at Gray's Inn chapel, on Friday, February 6, 1756. Being the day appointed... for a public fast. London: for Lockyer Davis and Charles Reymers, 1756.   4°

T.717

7384

TERRICK (Richard) *Bishop of London.*

A sermon preached before the honourable House of Commons, at St. Margaret's, Westminster, on Friday, February 6, 1756; being the day appointed... for a general fast. London: for John Shuckburgh, 1756.   4°

T.717

7385

THOMAS (John) *Bishop of Salisbury.*

A sermon preached before the House of Lords in the abbey-church of Westminster, on Friday, February 6th, 1756. Being the day appointed to be observed as a general fast, on occasion of the late dreadful earthquake. By John Lord Bishop of Lincoln. London: J. Oliver: sold also by Mr. Dod; Mr. Fox; Mr. Dodsley; Mr. Payne; Mr. Chapelle; Mrs. Kingman; and at the pamphlet shops, 1756.   4°

T.717

7386

VERSCHUIR (Johannes Henricus)

Disputatio Philologica exhibens observationes selectas ad origines Hebraeas, quam... praeside Nicol. Guil. Schroeder, publico examini subjicit Johannes Henricus Verschuir, Drentinus. Ad diem V. Maji, MDCCLVI... Groningae, apud Henr. Vechnerum, & Henr. Crebas, [1756].   4°

T.714

7387

VOLTAIRE (François Marie Arouet de)

The history of the war of Seventeen hundred and forty one ... 2nd ed. London, for J. Nourse, 1756.   8°

T.186

7388

WILLATS (Charles)

The religion of nature, which is now set up in opposition to the word of God, proved to be a mere idol from the very text that has been so often produced in its favour. In a sermon preach'd in York-minster, July 8. 1744. at the assizes... The second edition, with a new postscript. London: for W. Innys and J. Richardson, 1756.   8°

2 copies.

T.661 T.751

7389

WINSTANLEY (Thomas)

A sermon preached at Conduit-Street chapel, in the parish of St. George, Hanover-Square. On Sunday, February the 1st, 1756. Being the Sunday before the day appointed for a general fast and humiliation. On occasion of the late dreadful earthquakes at Lisbon, and elsewhere. London: for A. and C. Corbett, 1756.   4°

T.717

7390

WRIGHT (   )

The loss of the handkerchief. An heroic-comic poem, in four cantos... London: for the author, and sold by J. Marshall, 1756.   8°

T.803

1757

7391

An APPEAL to the people: part the second. On the different deserts and fate of Admiral Byng and his enemies... London: for J. Morgan, 1757.   8°

T.636

7392

BROMFIELD (William) *Surgeon.*

An account of the English nightshades, and their effects, also practical observations on the use of corrosive sublimate ... London, R. Baldwin; G. Woodfall, 1757.   12°

Wanting the title-page.

T.450

7393

BROWN (John) *D.D., Vicar of Newcastle-upon-Tyne.*

An estimate of the manners and principles of the times. By the author of Essays on the characteristics, &c... 4th ed. London, for L. Davis, and C. Reymers, 1757.   8°

T.18b

7394

ELLIS (John) *Vicar of St. Catherine's, Dublin.*

An enquiry whence cometh wisdom and understanding to man?... Being the substance of two sermons, preached some years ago before a learned audience. London: for Benjamin Dod, 1757.   8°

T.649

7395

JUSTIN, *Martyr, Saint.*

St. Justin the philosopher and martyr, his exhortations to the gentiles. Translated from the Greek by the Reverend Mr. Thomas Moses... Aberdeen: F. Douglass and W. Murray, sold by C. Hitch and L. Hawes in London, Mr. Charnly in Newcastle, A. Kincaid and A. Donaldson in Edinburgh, and by F. Douglass at Aberdeen, 1757. 8°

T.429

7396

A LETTER from a gentleman, residing in foreign parts, to his godson in England, explaining to him and enforcing the obligations of his baptismal covenant. London: printed in the year 1757.   8°

Possibly by Thomas Wagstaffe, the Younger.

T.641

7397

LUCAS (Charles) *M.P.*

Letters of Doctor Lucas and Doctor Oliver. Occasioned by a physical confederacy discovered in Bath... Bath: printed in the year 1757. And sold by James Leake.   8°

T.645

1757 (Cont'd)

7398

SHEBBEARE (John)

A fifth letter to the people of England, on the subversion of the constitution: and, the necessity of it's being restored... [Anon.] London: for J. Morgan, 1757. 8°

T.626

7399

SHEBBEARE (John)

A sixth letter to the people of England, on the progress of national ruin... [Anon.] London: for J. Morgan, 1757. 8°

T.626

7400

A SHORT explication of the Apocalypse of St. John, and part of Daniel's prophecy, on a new plan. Wherein is shewn, that the present wars may probably terminate in the restoration of the Jews, and in the Millennium... London, for W. Owen, 1757. 8°

T.426

7401

WALPOLE (Horace) Earl of Orford.

A letter from Xo Ho, a Chinese philosopher at London, to his friend Lien Chi at Peking. [Anon.] 4th ed. London: for Josiah Graham, [1757]. Fol.

T.543

1758

7402

ALLEN (John) Vice-President of Magdalen College.

The two-fold evidence of adoption. A sermon preached before the University of Oxford, at St. Mary's church, on Monday in Whitsun-week, May 15. 1758. Oxford, printed at the University Press for Daniel Prince, and sold by Sackville Parker. Also by E. Withers; and J. Rivington and J. Fletcher, London, 1758. 8°

T.661

7403

BACKHOUSE (James)

A sermon preached in Bow-church, London, at the consecration of... Philip [Yonge], Lord Bishop of Bristol. On Thursday, June 29, 1758. Cambridge, J. Bentham; for T. & J. Merrill, and J. Paris. Sold by Benj. Dod, J. Whiston & B. White, in London; and J. Fletcher, and D. Prince, in Oxford, 1758. 4°

T.715

7404

BOWER (Archibald)

One very remarkable fact more, relating to the conduct of the Jesuits, &c. London: printed for and sold by E. Comyns; J. Jackson; J. Gretton; and Z. Stuart, 1758. 8°

T.656

7405

BRETT (John)

Conjugal love and duty: a discourse upon Hebrews xiii.4. preached at St. Ann's, in Dublin, Sept. 11, 1757. With a dedication to... Lady Caroline Russel, asserting the prerogative of beauty, and vindicating the privileges of the fair sex. [Anon.] 5th ed. Dublin, printed: London, reprinted; and sold by J. Wilkie, 1758. 8°

T.661

7406

The CHARACTER of a good ruler: or, An enquiry into the nature and true extent of a laudable ambition, in acquiring the chief dignities and honours in a state. Being a discourse preached at a country parish-church in the diocese of Norwich, in the year M,DCC,LVIII. Ipswich: W. Craighton, 1758. 4°

A manuscript attribution to G. Sheldon, Vicar of Edwardstone.

T.715

7407

LINDSAY (John)

A seasonable antidote against apostasy... [Anon.] London: T. Gardner, for the author, 1758. 8°

T.429

7408

REMARKS on the Right Reverend Lord Bishop of Clogher's Vindication of the histories of the Old and New Testament. In a letter to... the Lord Viscount A[rbuthno]t... London, for W. Owen, 1758. 8°

Attributed by Bowdler to "Mr [David?] Guthrie of [   ] near Forfar."

T.426

7409

A SOLEMN act of confession and intercession, &c. London: printed for the public good, 1758. 8°

T.673

7410

THINGS as they are... [Attributed to John Perceval, Earl of Egmont.] London: for S. Hooper, and A. Morley; G. Woodfall; and J. Staples, 1758. 8°

"Supposed to be by ye Earl of Egmont" (Bowdler).

T.638

1759

7411

BUSHE (Amyas)

Socrates a dramatic poem. As it was corrected from the many errors of the London edition. London: printed, and Kilkenny re-printed, by Edward Crofton and company, [1759?] 4°

T.235

7412

The HONEST grief of a Tory, expressed in a genuine letter from a burgess of ——, in Wiltshire, to the author of the Monitor, Feb. 17, 1759... London: for J. Angel, 1759. 8°

2 copies.

T.638 T.641

7413

A HYMN after sore eyes: composed on Easter-day. London: for W. Owen, 1759. Fol.

T.557

7414

KENRICK (William)

Epistles philosophical and moral. [Anon.] London: for T. Wilcox, 1759. 8°

T.607

7415

A LETTER from the Duchess of M[a]r[lborou]gh, in the shades, to the great man [i.e. William Pitt]... London: for S. Hooper, 1759. 8°

T.651

7416

LINDSAY (John)

The grand and important question, about the Church, and parochial communion, further debated... between a worthy country gentleman, and his neighbour, together with the reverend vicar of the parish also. [Anon.] London: printed in the year 1759. 8°

T.663

7417

MAXWELL (Francis Kelly)

A sermon preached at Christ-Church, Newgate-street, on Friday the 21st of September, 1759, before... the Lord-Mayor, the aldermen and governors, of the royal-hospitals of this city. London, [1759]. 4°

T.637

7418

A SECOND letter from Wiltshire to the Monitor, on the vindication of his constitutional principles... London, sold by S. Hooper, 1759. 8°

2 copies.

T.638 T.641

7419

SPEED (John) M.D.

An impartial by-stander's review of the controversy concerning the wardenship of Winchester College... [Signed Statutophilus] London, for R. Baldwin, 1759. 8°

T.424

7420

SPENCE (Joseph)

A parallel in the manner of Plutarch: between a most celebrated man of Florence [Antonio Magliabechi], and one, scarce ever heard of, in England [Robert Hill]... 2nd ed. London printed: and sold by Messieurs Dodsley; for the benefit of Mr. Hill, 1759. 8°

T.423

7421

TOWNLEY (James) Head Master of Merchant Taylors' School.

A sermon preached before... the Lord-Mayor, the court of aldermen, and the liveries of the several companies of the city of London, in the cathedral church of St. Paul, on Thursday, November 29, 1759; being the day appointed... for a general thanksgiving to God... London: for H. Kent; T. Field; and J. Walter, 1759. 4°

T.637

7422

WELTON (James)

A sermon, preached at the cathedral church at Norwich, on Thursday Nov. 29. 1759. being the day appointed... for a general thanksgiving... for the signal successes of the present year. Norwich: William Chase: sold also by Mrs. Cooper, London; Mr. Merrill, at Cambridge; Mr. Green, at Bury; Mr. Hollingworth, at Lynn; Mr. Carr, at Yarmouth; and Mr. Fortin, at Swaffham, [1759?] 4°

T.715

7423

WILKES (Thomas)

A general view of the stage... London: for J.Coote; and W. Whetstone, Dublin, 1759. 8°

T.607

7424

WITHERSPOON (John)

A letter from a blacksmith, to the ministers and elders of the Church of Scotland. In which the manner of public worship in that church is considered ... [Anon.] London: for J. Coote, 1759. 8°

T.641

1760

7425

An ACCOUNT of the execution of the late Laurence Earl Ferrers, Viscount Tamworth, and of his Lordship's behaviour, from the time of his being delivered into the custody of the sheriffs... until the time of his execution. By the authority of the sheriffs. London: M. Cooper, 1760. Fol.

2 copies.

T.696 T.697

7426

ASHBURNHAM (Sir William) Bishop of Chichester.

A sermon preached before the Incorporated Society for the Propagation of the Gospel in Foreign Parts.. on Friday February 15, 1760. London: E. Owen and T. Harrison; and sold by A. Millar, 1760. 8°

T.659

7427

BATTEUX (Charles)

Principles of translation. Written originally in French... Edinburgh, Sands, Donaldson, Murray, and Cochran. For A. Donaldson, 1760. 8°

T.789

7428

BRETT (Thomas)

A dissertation on the ancient versions of the Bible; shewing why our English translation differs so much from them ... In a letter to a friend. 2nd ed ... London, for W. Owen, 1760. 8°

T.210

7429

COLLINS (William)

The passions, an ode. Written by Mr. Collins. Set to musick by Dr. Hayes. Glocester: R. Raikes, for the benefit of the charity, 1760. 8°

T.672

7430

DODWELL (William)

The doctrine of a particular providence stated, confirmed, defended and applied. In two sermons preached before the University of Oxford, at St. Mary's on Sunday April 20, 1760. Oxford, for J. Fletcher, and sold by Hen. Payne, London, 1760.
8°

T.661

7431

HAY (William)

Religio philosophi: or, the principles of morality and Christianity illustrated from a view of the universe, and of man's situation on it... 3rd ed. London: for R. and J. Dodsley, 1760. 8°

T.671

7432

INSULAE fortunatae ad mare Balthicum priscis ab regibus saepe quaesitae... hodierno a monarcha scientiis, bonis artibus, et pacis olea ornatae. Serenissimo... Friderico V. D.G. Daniae et Norwegiae... regi... [No imprint], 1760. Fol.

"Revermo... Carolo Hilleshem Univers. Colon. Rectori D.D. author poematii F.R.S.J."

T.810

7433

KING (William) *Principal of St. Mary Hall.*

Aviti epistola ad Perillam, virginem Scotam: editoris ecphrasi et annotationibus illustrata. [Anon.] Londini, 1760. 4°

T.815

7434

A LETTER to the great man, occasioned by the Letter [of John Douglas] to two great men... By a citizen of London. A disciple of Sidney and Locke... London: for W. Bristow; and to be had at all the pamphlet shops in London and Westminster, 1760.
8°

Attributed by Bowdler to "Mr. Heathcote".

T.430

7435

MILTON (John)

Samson. An oratorio. As it is perform'd at the Theatre-Royal in Covent-Garden. Alter'd and adapted to the stage from the Samson Agonistes of Milton [by Newburgh Hamilton]. Set to musick by Mr. Handel. London: for J. and R. Tonson, 1760. 4°

T.559

7436

SOCIETY OF JESUS. *Collegium S.J. Mannhemii.*

Basilica Carolina opus grande, non homini, sed Deo praeparata habitatio... duobus a Carolis... Mannhemii Palatina in metropoli aedificata... Ex typographejo Electorali aulico, [1760?] Fol.

T.810

7437

STILLINGFLEET (James)

The Christian ministry and stewardship. A sermon preached before the University of Oxford, at St. Mary's, on Sunday June 8. 1760. Oxford, at the Clarendon Printing House. Sold by J. Fletcher, S. Parker, and D. Prince, in Oxford; by John Rivington in London; by J. Leake and W. Frederick in Bath; and R. Lewis in Worcester, 1760. 8°

T.659

7438

SWANNE (Gilbert)

The advantages of the Jews under their dispensation set forth, and the use they made of them considered. Two sermons preached before the University of Oxford ... Oxford, at the Clarendon Printing House, 1760. Sold by Daniel Prince; and John Rivington, London.
8°

T.751

7439

The TRIAL of Lawrence Earl Ferrers, for the murder of John Johnson, before the right honourable the House of Peers, in Westminster-Hall... London: for Samuel Billingsley, 1760. Fol.

T.696

7440

BENEZET (Anthony)

Thoughts on the nature of war, and its repugnancy to the Christian life. A sermon, on Thursday, Novemb. 29th, 1759; being the day of publick thanksgiving for the successes obtained in the present war. [Anon.] London: for H. Payne, and W. Cropley, 1761. 8°

T.751

7441

BIRCH (Busby)

City Latin, or, Critical and political remarks on the Latin inscription on laying the first stone of the intended new bridge at Black-Fryars... The third edition, with additions and corrections. London, for R. Stevens, 1761. 8°

T.657

7442

EVANS (John) *Dissenting Minister.*

The Christian temper: being a summary of Dr. Evans's Practical discourses, to which are subjoined... some of the leading thoughts, with references to the original: as likewise an appendix, containing the life of this excellent author... [By J.S.] London: for J. Buckland; and E. Dilly, 1761. 2 parts. 8°

T.655

7443

The FORM of the proceeding to the royal coronation of their most excellent Majesties King George III. and Queen Charlotte ... Together with a list of the peers, peeresses, and privy-counsellors. London, William Bowyer. Sold by George Woodfall; and Barnes Tovey, 1761. Fol.

T.543

7444

HORNE (George) *Bishop of Norwich.*

The Christian king. A sermon preached before the University of Oxford, at St. Mary's on Friday, January 30. 1761... Oxford, for S. Parker, and sold by John Rivington, London, and W. Mercer in Maidstone, 1761. 8°

2 copies.

T.659

7445

MEERMAN (Gerard)

Conspectus originum typographicarum, a Meermanno proxime in lucem edendarum. In usum amicorum typis descriptus, 1761. 8°

T.796

7446

A PLAIN account of genuine Christianity. Bristol: William Pine, 1761. 12°

T.545

7447

RIDLEY (Glocester)

De Syriacarum novi foederis versionum indole atque usu dissertatio... Londini, prostant apud J. Clarke; J. Whiston et B. White; R. et J. Dodsley, 1761. 4°

T.714

7448

The RIGHT honourable annuitant vindicated. With a word or two in favour of the other great man, in case of his resignation. In a letter to a friend in the country. London: for J. Morgan, 1761. 8°

T.638

7449

THINGS as they are. Part the second. By the author of the first... [Attributed to John Perceval, Earl of Egmont.] London: for G. Kearsly, 1361 [i.e. 1761]. 8°

T.634

7450

THRENI gregis Coloniensis super rapto archimandrita ... Clemente Augusto, Dei gratia Archi-episcopo Coloniensi... Coloniae Agrippinae, typis Theodori Holtzapfel, [1761]. Fol.

T.810

7451

BERROW (Capel)

A pre-existent lapse of human souls demonstrated from reason... London: for J. Whiston and B. White, 1762. 8°

T.424

7452

The COALITION: or, An historical memorial of the negotiation for peace, between his high mightiness of C[lare]m[on]t [i.e. the Duke of Newcastle] and his sublime excellency of H[a]y[e]s [i.e. William Pitt]... 2nd ed. London: for J. Hinxman, 1762. 4°

T.554

7453

DANICAN (François André) called *Philidor.*

Chess analysed: or instructions by which a perfect knowledge of this noble game may in a short time be acquir'd. By A.D. Philidor. London: for J. Nourse, and P. Vaillant, 1762. 8°

T.666

7454

DOMINICETI (Bartholomew di)

A short and calm apology in regard to the many injuries and repeated affronts he has, uncall'd for, met with during the 6 years he has been in Bristol... Bristol, S. Farley, 1762. 8°

Wanting the title-page.

T.647

7455

GOLDSMITH (Oliver)

The life of Richard Nash, of Bath, Esq; extracted principally from his original papers... [Anon.] London: for J. Newbery; and W. Frederick, at Bath, 1762. 8°

T.646

7456

HEATHCOTE (George)

A letter to the Right Honourable the Lord Mayor, the worshipful aldermen, and common council... of the city of London. From an old servant... London: for W. Owen, R. Baldwin; and C. Pugh, 1762. 8°

Half title: Mr. Heathcote's letter.

T.430

7457

KETTILBY (Joshua)

The excellency and great importance of the Hebrew language, demonstrated by the united testimony of upwards of fifty celebrated authors... London printed: and sold by W. Bristow; T. Hooper; and J. Johnson, 1762. 8°

T.789

7458

MARRIOTT (*Sir* James)

Political considerations; being a few thoughts of a candid man at the present crisis. In a letter to a noble lord retired from power. [Anon.] London, for J. Hinxman, 1762. 8°

T.638

7459

MAUDUIT (Israel)

The parallel: being the substance of two speeches, supposed to have been made in the closet, by two different ministers, some time before a late demise. Humbly submitted to the judgment of those who are to consider of the renewal of our Prussian treaty. [Anon.] London: for William Nicol, 1742 [i.e. 1762].
8°

T.648

7460

MAULDEN (Joseph)

Inoculation for the small-pox, considered, and proved by the word of God to be sinful. In a sermon preached at Burwell, in Cambridge-shire, February 28, 1762... London: printed for the author, and sold by G. Keith, 1762. 8°

T.659

1762 (Cont'd)

7461
MUSGRAVE (Samuel)

Exercitationum in Euripidem libri duo. (Appendix. Emendationes in Euripidem [by Thomas Tyrwhitt].) Lugduni Batavorum, 1762. 8°

pp. 133-176 only, comprising the *Emendationes* of Tyrwhitt.

T.806

7462
ORTHODOX EASTERN CHURCH.

The Orthodox confession of the Catholic and Apostolic Eastern-Church [compiled by Petr Mogila]; faithfully translated from the originals [by Philip Lodvill]... London: printed 1762. 8°

T.420

1763

7463
ANOTHER answer to the letters of the Right Hon. William Pitt, Esq; to Ralph Allen, Esq; in which the reasons are assigned for not venerating the administration of that late secretary of state... By another member of the corporation of Bath... London, 1763. 8°

T.627

7464
CHARNDLER (Samuel)

An answer to the Rev. Mr. John Wesley's letter to William, Lord Bishop of Gloucester; concerning the charges alledged against him and his doctrine, in a book lately published, entitled, The doctrine of grace ... In a letter to the Rev. Mr. John Wesley. London: printed for the author, and sold by W. Nicoll, 1763. 8°

T.288

7465
FERGUSON (James)

A letter to the Rev. Mr. John Kennedy, in answer to his examination of Mr. Ferguson's remarks (inserted in the Critical review for May, 1763) upon Mr. Kennedy's system of astronomical chronology. London: printed in the year 1763. 8°

T.423

7466
A LETTER to a friend. Endeavouring to give a general notion of the Rev. Mr. Kennedy's late System of chronology... Edinburgh: Sands, Murray, and Cochran. Sold by W. Nicol, London, and Drummond, Edinburgh, 1763. 8°

T.424

7467
SHERIDAN (Frances)

The discovery. A comedy. As it is performed at the Theatre-Royal, in Drury-lane. Written by the editor of Miss Sidney Bidulph. London: for T. Davies; R. and J. Dodsley; G. Kearsly; J. Coote; and J. Walter, 1763. 8°

T.288

7468
TOTTIE (John)

The folly and guilt of satyrical slander. A sermon preached before the University of Oxford, at Christ-Church, on Sunday, February 20. 1763... Oxford, printed at the Theatre for James Fletcher; and sold by W. Sandby, and J. Fletcher, London, [1763]. 8°

T.773

7469
TUCKER (Josiah)

The case of going to war, for the sake of procuring, enlarging, or securing of trade, considered in a new light. Being a fragment of a greater work. [Anon.] London: for R. and J. Dodsley; and L. Hawes, W. Clarke, and R. Collins, 1763. 8°

T.638

7470
WALPOLE (Robert) *Earl of Orford.*

A short history of that Parliament which committed Sir Robert Walpole to the Tower, expelled him the House of Commons, and approved of the infamous Peace of Utrecht... London: for J. Almon; and J. Williams, 1763. 8°

Wanting the title-page.

T.628

7471
WATKINSON (Edward)

An essay upon gratitude. Consider'd as a religious duty, and a social virtue... Sheffield: printed for the author, by Wm. Ward, 1763. 8°

T.428

7472
YONGE (Philip) *Bishop of Norwich.*

The charge of... Philip, Lord Bishop of Norwich, delivered to the clergy of his diocese, at his primary visitation, A.D. 1763. Norwich: William Chase, 1763. 4°

T.715

1764

7473
BENTHAM (Edward)

De studiis theologicis. Praelectio habita in Scola Theologica Oxon. Oxonii, e Typographeo Clarendoniano, 1764. 2 parts. 8°

T.767

7474
BRECKNOCK (Timothy)

Droit le roy. Or a digest of the rights and prerogatives of the imperial crown of Great-Britain. By a member of the society of Lincoln's-Inn. London: W. Griffin, 1764. 8°

T.713

7475
FREE (John)

The analysis of man; or the difference between the reasonable and living soul. A sermon preached at St. Mary's in Oxford, before the University, on Sunday, May 20, 1764... London: printed for the author, and sold by W. Sandby, and J. Williams; J. Almon; and S. Parker in Oxford, [1764?] 8°

T.828

7476
FREE (John)

The operations of God and nature, from the beginning of things, to the finishing of the vegetable creation ... A sermon preached before a society of florists, in the parish church of Hackney, July the 25th, 1764 ... 2nd ed. London: printed for the author, and sold by W. Sandby, and J. Williams; and J. Almon, [1764?] 8°

T.828

7477
HOLLAND (J.)

An appeal to Roman Catholicks, and to protestants, as to the charitable Catholick principles of the Church of England... Liverpool: printed in the year 1764. 8°

T.424

7478
KYNASTON (John)

C. Cornelius Tacitus a falso impietatis crimine vindicatus: oratio... habita in sacello Collegii Aenei Nasi Oxon... Londini: prostant venales apud Guilielmum Flexney, 1764. 4°

T.815

7479
PAPPAFAVA (Giovanni Roberto)

Dissertazione [on the family of Carrara]. [Anon.] [No imprint, 1764.] 4°

T.555

7480
A SEASONABLE alarm to the city of London, on the present important crisis; shewing... that the new method of paving the streets with Scotch pebbles... must be... pernicious to the health and morals of the people of England... By Zachary Zeal. London: for W. Nicoll, [1764]. 8°

T.638

7481
SIMPSON (Joseph)

Reflections on the natural and acquired endowments requisite for the study of the law... By a barrister at law... 2nd ed. London, for J. Worrall; T. Waller; and B. Tovey, 1764. 8°

T.624

1765

7482
BELLOY (Pierre Laurent Buirette de)

Le siége de Calais, tragédie... Représentée pour la premiere fois, par les Comédiens Français ordinaires du Roi, le 13 Février 1765. Suivie de notes historiques... A Paris, chez Du Chesne, 1765. 8°

T.677

7483
CARMARTHEN.

Charter for the borough of Carmarthen. Carmarthen, J. Ross, 1765. 8°

T.777

7484
CORBYN (Benjamin)

Reflections upon the fall of a great prince. A sermon, occasioned by the death of his late Royal Highness William Augustus Duke of Cumberland... London: R. Hett; and sold by N. Young; J. Walter; and J. Peyton, [1765]. 8°

T.706

7485
The EASIEST introduction to the Hebrew language, designed for the use of young gentlemen and ladies ... [By Joshua Kettilby?] Part I... London: for W. Faden: and sold by J. Buckland; E. and C. Dilly, and J. Johnson, 1765. 8°

T.777

7486
GREAT BRITAIN. *Parliament. House of Lords.*

The trial of William Lord Byron, Baron Byron of Rochdale, for the murder of William Chaworth, Esq; before... the House of Peers... London: for Samuel Billingsley, 1765. Fol.

2 copies.

T.696   T.539

7487
ISRAEL in Egypt, an oratorio, or sacred drama: as it is performed at the Theatre-Royal in Covent-Garden. The chorus's entire, and the songs from other the works of the late George Frederic Handel, Esq. London: for the administrator of J. Watts: and sold by B. Dodd; G. Woodfall; and S. Hooper, 1765. 4°

T.559

7488
JACKSON (Henry) *Chemist.*

An essay on British isinglass: wherein its nature and properties are compared with the foreign sorts ... London: for J. Newbery, 1765. 8°

T.288

7489
JEACOCKE (Caleb)

A vindication of the moral character of the Apostle Paul, from the charge of insincerity and hypocrisy brought against it by Lord Bolingbroke, Dr. Middleton, and others... (An appendix.) London: for W. Flexney, 1765. 2 parts. 8°

T.641

7490
LESLIE (Charles)

A true and authentic account of the conversion of a Quaker to Christianity, and of her behaviour on her death-bed. Bristol: printed in the year 1765. 8°

T.673

7491
MILTON (John)

L'Allegro, ed il Penseroso. By Milton. Set to musick by George Frederick Handel. (Song of Moses, from Exodus, chap. XV.) London: for the executors of J. Watts, and sold by T. Lowndes, [c.1765?] 2 parts. 4°

T.559

7492
SHARP (Granville)

Remarks on a printed paper [by Benjamin Kennicott] lately handed about, intituled, "A catalogue of the sacred vessels restored by Cyrus..." Addressed to all such gentlemen as have received or read the same. [Anon.] London: W. Richardson and S. Clark, 1765. 8°

T.583

1766

7493

The ANSWER at large to Mr. P[i]tt's speech. London: for W. Nicoll, 1766. 8°

T.638

7494

BETTI (Zaccaria)

Descrizione di un meraviglioso ponte naturale nei monti veronesi. In Verona, nella stamperia di Marco Moroni, 1766. 4°

T.652

7495

BROWN (John) *D.D., Vicar of Newcastle-upon-Tyne.*

A letter to the Rev. Dr. Lowth, occasioned by his late Letter to the right rev. author of The divine legation of Moses. By the author of Essays on the characteristics ... Newcastle upon Tyne: J. White and T. Saint, for L. Davis and C. Reymers, 1766. 8°

T.424

7496

COTES (Humphrey)

An enquiry into the conduct of a late right honourable commoner [i.e. William Pitt]... [Anon.] London: for J. Almon, [1766]. 8°

T.638

7497

DODD (William)

An account of the rise, progress, and present-state of the Magdalen Charity. To which are added the Rev. Dr. Dodd's sermons... 3rd ed. Printed by W. Faden, for the Charity. And sold by J. Whiston and B. White; L. Davis and C. Reymers; J. Newbery; J. Walter; A. Cook; and Mr. Leake at Bath, 1766. 8°

T.428

7498

EDWARDS (Thomas) *D.D.*

Two dissertations: the first, on the absurdity and injustice of religious bigotry... the second, on the principal qualifications and canons, necessary for the right and accurate interpretation of the New Testament... Cambridge: J. Bentham; for W. Thurlbourn & J. Woodyer in Cambridge, and J. Johnson, and sold by J. Beecroft, and T. Cadell, London, 1766. 8°

T.791

7499

HERVEY (Thomas)

A complaint on the part of the Hon. Thomas Hervey, concerning an undue proceeding against him at court: set forth in two letters to... the Princess of Brunswick. London: printed for, and published by the author, and sold by the booksellers of London and Westminster, 1766. 8°

T.647

7500

LOWTH (Robert) *Bishop of London.*

A letter to the right reverend author [i.e. William Warburton] of The divine legation of Moses demonstrated; in answer to the appendix to the fifth volume of that work... By a late professor in the University of Oxford... 2nd ed. London, for A. Millar, and J. Dodsley, 1766. 8°

T.424

7501

MORBUS Anglicanus sanatus: or, A remarkable cure of an inveterate scurvy... In a letter from a country clergyman to his son in London... London: for John and Thomas Curtis, 1766. 8°

T.643

7502

PRICE (Richard)

The nature and dignity of the human soul. A sermon preached at St. Thomas's, January the first, 1766. for the benefit of the charity-school in Gravel-Lane, Southwark. London: for A. Millar; J. Waugh; and M. Young, 1766. 8°

T.828

7503

ROTHERAM (John)

Government a divine institution. A sermon preached before the University of Oxford at St. Mary's on the twenty-ninth of May M.DCC.LXV. London: for W. Sandby, 1766. 8°

T.751

7504

A SECOND letter to a friend. In which some farther objections to the Rev. Mr. Kennedy's System of chronology are pointed out... Edinburgh: Sands, Murray, and Cochran. Sold by W. Nichol, London; and by Drummond, Edinburgh, 1766. 8°

T.424

7505

TAAFFE (Nicholas) *Viscount.*

Observations on affairs in Ireland, from the settlement in 1691, to the present time. London: for W. Griffin. 1766. 8°

T.437

7506

TOTTIE (John)

Two charges delivered to the clergy of the diocese of Worcester, in the years 1763 and 1766; being designed as preservatives against the sophistical arts of the papists, and the delusions of the methodists. Oxford, printed at the Theatre; and sold by J. Fletcher; J. Fletcher and Co., London; and S. Gamidge at Worcester, 1766. 2 parts. 8°

T.773

7507

TRACKEBARNE Gran Mogol, drama... Trackebarn the Great Mogol, an opera to be performed at the King's Theatre, in the Hay-market. Altered by Giovan Gualberto Bottarelli. London: for W. Griffin, [1766?] 8°

T.664

7508

TYRWHITT (Thomas)

Observations and conjectures upon some passages of Shakespeare. [Anon.] Oxford, at the Clarendon Press, 1766. Sold by Dan. Prince, at Oxford; by J. Rivington, and T. Payne. 8°

T.806

1767

7509

DAWSON (Benjamin)

An examination of an Essay on establishments in religion [by John Rotheram]. With remarks upon it, considered as a defence of the Church of England, and as an answer to the Confessional... London, for J. Johnson, 1767. 8°

T.420

7510

FORBES (Robert) *Bishop.*

An essay on the nature of the human body ... in consequence of which, on the growing evil of profaning and defiling kirks, and kirk-yards, and other burying-grounds ... By a ruling elder of the Church of Scotland ... Edinburgh: David Paterson, for John Wilson, 1767. 8°

T.427

7511

FRANKLIN (Benjamin)

The examination of Doctor Benjamin Franklin, relative to the repeal of the American stamp act, in MDCCLXVI. [No imprint], 1767. 8°

T.423

7512

GREEN (John) *Bishop of Lincoln.*

A sermon preached before the Society corresponding with the Incorporated Society in Dublin, for promoting English protestant working-schools in Ireland... March 17, 1767. London: J. and W. Oliver; sold also by J. Rivington, 1767. 4°

T.715

7513

KIMPTON (John)

A faithful narrative of facts, relative to the late presentation of Mr. H[awei]s to the rectory of Al[d]w[inck]le, in Northamptonshire... [Anon.] London: printed for the author, and sold by the booksellers in town and country, 1767. 8°

T.766

7514

LOWTH (Robert) *Bishop of London.*

A sermon preached at the visitation of... Richard Lord Bishop of Durham, held in the parish church of St. Mary le Bow in Durham, on Thursday July 27, 1758. 2nd ed. London: for A. Millar and T. Cadell; and J. Dodsley, 1767. 8°

T.734

7515

MACLAURIN (John) *Lord Dreghorn.*

Considerations on the nature and origin of literary property: wherein that species of property is clearly proved to subsist no longer than for the terms fixed by the statute 8vo Annae. [Anon] Edinburgh: Alexander Donaldson, 1767. 8°

T.573

7516

MADAN (Martin)

An answer to a pamphlet [by John Kimpton], intitled, A faithful narrative of facts relative to the late presentation of Mr H[awei]s, to the rectory of Al[d]w[inck]le, in Northamptonshire... London: for E. and C. Dilly, J. Robson, and J. Mathews, 1767. 8°

T.766

7517

MAYO (Henry)

Aldwinckle. A candid examination of the Rev. Mr. M[adan]'s conduct, as a counsellor and a friend; agreeable to the principles of law and conscience... [Anon.] London, for S. Bladon; and G. Pearch, 1767. 8°

T.766

7518

MERRICK (James)

A second part of annotations, critical and grammatical, on St. John's Gospel, reaching to the end of the third chapter. Reading: J. Carnan and Co. Sold also by Mr. Newbery, London; and by Mr. Fletcher and Mr. Prince, in Oxford, 1767. 8°

T.791

7519

MONK, formerly FLEETWOOD (Martha)

A letter to the Rev. Mr. Madan, occasioned by reading two pamphlets relative to the presentation to the rectory of Aldwinckle. By the widow of the late Mr. Fleetwood. London: for J. Williams; and H. Jackson, [1767]. 8°

T.766

7520

PORTEUS (Beilby) *Bishop of London.*

A sermon preached before the honourable House of Commons, at St. Margaret's, Westminster, on Friday, January XXX, 1767. 2nd ed. London: for Thomas Payne, 1767. 4°

T.715

7521

REMARKS on the answer of the Reverend Mr. M[ada]n, to the Faithful narrative of facts [by John Kimpton], relating to the late presentation of Mr. H[awei]s to the rectory of Al[d]w[inck]le in Northamptonshire... By a by-stander. London: for J. Lee, 1767. 8°

T.766

7522

ROTHERAM (John)

An essay on establishments in religion. With remarks on the Confessional.[Anon.] Newcastle upon Tyne: J. White and T. Saint, for Wm. Sanby, 1767. 8°

T.419

7523

STRICTURES upon modern simony, and the crime of Simon Magus; or, An enquiry into Mr. Madan's account of simony, in his late answer to the Faithful narrative of facts [by John Kimpton] relative to the presentation of Mr. H[awei]s to the rectory of Aldwinckle... London: for T. Vernor and J. Chater, 1767. 8°

T.766

7524

WINGRAVE (John)

A narrative of the many horrid cruelties inflicted by Elizabeth Brownrigg upon the body of Mary Clifford, deceased... London: printed for the author; and J. Williams, 1767. 8°

T.422

1768

7525

ATTERBURY (Francis) *Bishop of Rochester.*

The private correspondence of Dr Francis Atterbury, and his friends, in 1725... Printed in the year 1768. 4°

T.554

1768 (Cont'd)

7526

BICKERSTAFFE (Isaac)

Lionel and Clarissa. A comic opera. As it is performed at the Theatre-Royal in Covent-Garden. [Anon.] London: for W. Griffin, 1748 [i.e. 1768]. 8°

T.624

7527

BURTON (John) *D.D.*

Johannis Burton ad amicum epistola: sive commentariolus Thomae Secker Archiep. Cantuar. memoriae sacer. Oxonii, e typographeo Clarendoniano, 1768. 8°

T.214

7528

The CASE of his Grace the Duke of Portland, respecting two leases, lately granted by the lords of the Treasury, to Sir James Lowther, Bart. With observations on the motion for a remedial bill, for quieting the possession of the subject... 8th ed. London: for J. Almon, 1768. 8°

T.624

7529

CATCOTT (Alexander)

A supplement to a book, entitled, A treatise on the deluge... Bristol: Farley and Cocking, 1768. 8°

T.655

7530

A CAVEAT on the part of public credit, previous to the opening of the budget, for the present year, 1768. London: for J. Almon, 1768. 4°

T.812

7531

DRUMMOND (William Abernethy) *Bishop.*

Remarks upon the second part of Principles political and religious; being intended, as a supplement to the letter from Aberdeen, in answer to Norman Siewwright... [Signed R.S.] Edinburgh, printed for and sold by John Wilson, 1768. 8°

T.673

7532

HALDANE (John)

The second part of the Players scourge exhibited to the world. Wherein is contained the true character of playhouses, play-actors, and play-haunters... By J-n H-ne. Printed in the year 1768. 8°

"For Thomas Bowdler, Esq."

T.427

7533

HOGARTH (William)

Hogarth moralized. The Harlot's progress. (The rake's progress.)

pp. 1-40 of Hogarth moralized, by John Trusler, London, 1768. 8°

T.420

7534

HUNTINGDON, *County of.*

A poll taken before Edward Leeds, Esq; high-sheriff of the county of Huntingdon, March 29th, 30th, 31st, April 1st, 1768... Cambridge, Fletcher and Hodson: and sold by Mr. Jenkinson, in Huntingdon [and by others], [1768]. 8°

T.666

7535

A LETTER to the Right Hon. Thomas Harley, Esq; Lord Mayor of... London. To which is added, A serious expostulation with the Livery, on their late conduct, during the election of the four City members. By an alderman of London... London: for W. Bingley, 1768. 2 parts. 8°

T.624

7536

LUCAS (Charles) *M.P.*

An address to the right Honorable the Lord Mayor, the worshipful the board of aldermen... of Dublin, relating to the intended augmentation of the military force in the kingdom of Ireland. Dublin printed: London reprinted for G. Kearsly, 1768. 8°

T.423

7537

MADAN (Martin)

An exact copy of an epistolary correspondence between the Rev. Mr. M[adan] and S[amuel] B[rewer], concerning the living of A[ldwinckle]. Before the publication of either Mr. K[impton]'s or the Rev. Mr. M[adan]'s narratives... London: for G. Pearch; and W. Davenhill 1768. 8°

T.766

7538

NOWELL (Thomas)

An answer to a pamphlet [by Sir Richard Hill], entitled Pietas Oxoniensis, or A full and impartial account of the expulsion of six students from St. Edmund-Hall, Oxford. In a letter to the author... Oxford, at the Clarendon-Press, 1768. Sold by Daniel Prince. And by John Rivington. 8°

2 copies.

T.791   T.428

7539

PRIESTLEY (Joseph) *LL.D.*

A free address to protestant dissenters, on the subject of the Lord's supper... London: for J. Johnson, 1768. 8°

T.776

7540

ROTHERAM (John)

An essay on faith, and its connection with good works. 2nd ed. London: for W. Sandby, 1768. 8°

T.641

7541

ROTHERAM (John)

An essay on faith, and its connection with good works. 3rd ed. London: for W. Sandby, 1768. 8°

T.435

7542

SCHULTENS (Albert)

Dissertationum philologicarum triga, de verbis et sententiis... Groningae, apud Henricum Crebas, 1768. 4°

T.714

7543

SHARP (Granville)

Remarks on several very important prophecies... London: W. Richardson and S. Clark; and sold by B. White; R. Horsfield; and J. Allix, 1768. 5 parts. 8°

T.584

7544

The TRIAL of Frederick Calvert, Esq; Baron of Baltimore, in the kingdom of Ireland, for a rape on the body of Sarah Woodcock... Taken in short-hand by Joseph Gurney. London: for William Owen; and Joseph Gurney, 1768. Fol.

T.696

7545

UNITED BRETHREN.

A candid declaration of the Church known by the name of the Unitas Fratrum, relative to their labour among the heathen. [Signed by Augustus Gottlieb Spangenberg.] [No imprint, 1768?] Fol.

T.543

7546

WHITEFIELD (George)

A letter to the Reverend Dr Durell, Vicechancellor of the University of Oxford; occasioned by a late expulsion of six students from Edmund Hall... London: for J. Millan; E. and C. Dilly; and M. Folingsby, 1768. 8°

T.750

1769

7547

The BATH contest: being a collection of all the papers, advertisements, &c. published before and since the death of Mr. Derrick, by the candidates for the office of master of the ceremonies, and their friends ... Bath: Archer and Cruttwell, [1769]. 8°

T.422

7548

BETTER late than never. The humble address of Mrs. Hitch-about. [Bath, 1769?] brs.

T.422

7549

BRERETON (William)

[A hand-bill addressed To the ladies and gentlemen, subscribers to the amusements at Bath. Relating to the election of a master of ceremonies.] Bath, Archer and Cruttwell, [1769]. brs.

T.422

7550

The CONCILIADE; being a supplement to the Bath contest: containing the several poetical and other pieces, published since the 14th of April ... Bath: Archer and Cruttwell; also sold, in London, by Mr. F. Newbery; and, in Bristol, by Mr. Cadell, [1769]. 8°

T.422

7551

The CONCILIATING ball for Mr. Plomer, will be at Mr. Simpson's room, on Monday next, the twenty-fourth of April [1769] ... [Bath], S. Hazard, [1769]. brs.

T.422

7552

CROSSMAN (Henry)

Ecclesiastical merchandise shewn to be unlawful, and exceedingly injurious to the church of Christ... in a sermon preached at the archdeacon's visitation in Sudbury... London: J. and W. Oliver; sold also by Mr Merrill at Cambridge, Mr Fletcher at Oxford, Mr Green at Bury, and Mr Keymer at Colchester, 1769. 4°

T.715

7553

FORSTER (Nathaniel) *Rector of All Saints, Colchester.*

An answer to a pamphlet [by Sir William Meredith] entitled, "The question stated, whether the freeholders of Middlesex forfeited their right by voting for Mr. Wilkes at the last election? In a letter from a member of Parliament to one of his constituents... [Anon.] London, for James Fletcher, J. Walter; and J. Robson, 1769. 4°

T.812

7554

GODDARD (Peter Stephen)

A sermon preached at the consecration of Clare-Hall chapel, in Cambridge, July 5, 1769. To which is added, the form of consecration used by the Lord Bishop of London. Cambridge, J. Archdeacon; and sold by J. Woodyer, in Cambridge; J. Beecroft, T. Payne, T. Cadell, M. Hingeston, W. Browne, London; and D. Prince, at Oxford, 1769. 4°

T.715

7555

GOODALL (Walter)

An introduction to the history and antiquities of Scotland. [Translated from the Latin] London: for T. Noteman, 1769. 8°

T.427

7556

GRENVILLE (George)

The speech of a right honourable gentleman, on the motion for expelling Mr. Wilkes, Friday, February 3, 1769. [Anon.] (A list of books and pamphlets, printed for J. Almon.) London: for J. Almon, 1769. 2 parts. 8°

T.624

7557

HARINGTON (Edward)

Nugae antiquae: being a miscellaneous collection of original papers in prose and verse. Written in the reigns of Henry VIII, Edward VI, Mary, Elizabeth, James I, &c. by Sir John Harington... and others who lived in those times... [Edited by Edward Harington.] London: for W. Frederick, at Bath: and sold by J. Robinson and Roberts, 1769. 12°

T.476

7558

HENDERSON (Andrew)

A letter to a noble lord: or, A faithful representation of the Douglas cause. Containing many curious and essential anecdotes... [Anon.] London: for A. Henderson, 1769. 8°

T.657

7559

HORNE (George) *Bishop of Norwich.*

Considerations on the life and death of St. John the Baptist. Oxford, printed at the Clarendon Press, for S. Parker; sold by J. and F. Rivington, and T. Cadell, London, 1769. 8°

T.671

7560

JACOTIUS (Desiderius)

Desiderii Jacotii Vandoperani de philosophorum doctrina libellus ex Cicerone. Oxonii, e Typographeo Clarendoniano, impensis Dan. Prince, 1769. 8°

T.568

7561

A LETTER from Farmer Trusty to his landlord Sir William Worthy, Bart. patron of the living of —, in the county of — . Founded on real matters of fact. To which is annexed, An evening conversation between four very good old ladies over a game at quadrille... London: J. and W. Oliver; sold by G. Keith; E. and C. Dilly; M. Folinsby; and Mr Fletcher, at Oxford, 1769. 8°

T.766

7562

A LETTER to the authors of the Monthly review, which is absolutely necessary to be read by every one who would understand their work... London: for W. Flexney, 1769. 8°

T.428

7563

MEMOIRS of the amours, intrigues, and adventures of Charles Augustus Fitz-Roy, Duke of Grafton, with Miss Parsons. Interspersed with a faithful account of Miss Parson's amours with other persons of distinction. London: for J. Meeres; W. Bingley; T. Peete; and S. Caldicott, 1769. 8°

T.476

7564

MUSGRAVE (Samuel)

Dr. Musgrave's reply to a letter published in the news papers by the Chevalier D'Eon... London, printed for the benefit of the charity-school, at Plymouth, and sold by J. Wilkie, 1769. 8°

T.422

7565

PLOMER (R.H.)

[A hand-bill addressed To the nobility and gentry. Relating to the election of a Master of Ceremonies at Bath.] Archer and Cruttwell, [1769]. brs.

T.422

7566

PRATT (Charles) *Earl Camden.*

A second letter to a noble lord: or the speeches of the Lord Chancellor, and of Lord Mansfield, on February the 27th, 1769, on the Douglas cause... [Compiled by Andrew Henderson.] London, for A. Henderson, [1769]. 8°

T.657

7567

SCIPIO (Quintus Caecilius Metellus Pius)

An epistle to Junius Silanus from Cornelius Scipio... London: for T. Becket and P.A. De Hondt, 1769. 8°

T.422

7568

SECKER (Thomas) *Archbishop of Canterbury.*

A letter to... Horatio Walpole, Esq; written Jan. 9, 1750-1, concerning bishops in America. London: for J. and F. Rivington, 1769. 8°

T.428

7569

STRANGE (Robert)

A descriptive catalogue of a collection of pictures, selected from the Roman, Florentine... French and Spanish schools... Collected and drawn, during a journey of several years in Italy, by Robert Strange. London: printed for the author; sold by E. and C. Dilly; and J. Robson, 1769. 8°

T.476

7570

W. (W.)

The Bath riot described. [No imprint], 1769. brs.

T.422

7571

WARLTIRE (John)

Analysis of a course of lectures in experimental philosophy... 6th ed. London: printed for the author, 1769. 8°

T.777

7572

WARLTIRE (John)

Tables of the various combinations and specific attraction of the substances employed in chemistry... London: printed for the author, 1769. 8°

T.777

1770

7573

ALMON (John)

A new catalogue of books and pamphlets, printed for J. Almon, bookseller and stationer, opposite Burlington-house, Piccadilly. London, 1770. 8°

T.421

7574

ANOTHER letter to Mr. Almon, in matter of libel ... London: for J. Almon, 1770. 8°

T.421

7575

BAINE (James)

The theatre licentious and perverted. Or, A sermon for reformation of manners ... Partly occasioned by the acting of a comedy, entitled, The minor [by Samuel Foote] ... 2nd ed. Edinburgh: J. Reid; and sold at his printing house, and by W. Gray, 1770. 8°

T.433

7576

BURKE (Edmund)

Thoughts on the cause of the present discontents... [Anon.] 2nd ed. London, for J. Dodsley, 1770. 8°

T.773

7577

CAMOES (Luis de)

Proposals for printing by subscription, a translation [by William Julius Mickle] of the Lusiad, from the Portuguese of Camoens, into English verse. Oxford, 1770. 4°

T.536

7578

DRUMMOND (William Abernethy) *Bishop.*

The rebuffer rebuffed; or, A vindication of the Remarks on the second part of principles political and religious, and of several MS. letters sent to the Reverend Mr Sieveright, anno 1767. In answer to that gentleman's exceptions in his pamphlet, intitled, Miscellaneous tracts, no 1. a rebuff ... [Anon.] Edinburgh: Wilson Robertson & Tennent, 1770. 8°

T.427

7579

GOLDSMITH (Oliver)

The deserted village, a poem. 5th ed. London: for W. Griffin, 1770. 4°

Incomplete.

T.536

7580

GOLDSMITH (Oliver)

The traveller, a poem. London: for T. Carnan and F. Newbery junr., 1770. 4°

T.711

7581

JOHNSON (Samuel)

The false alarm. [Anon.] 2nd ed. London: for T. Cadell, 1770. 8°

T.773

7582

LAW (Edmund) *Bishop of Carlisle.*

Observations occasioned by the contest about literary property. [Anon.] Cambridge, J. Archdeacon printer to the University. Sold by T. & J. Merrill, in Cambridge; and by J. Johnson & J. Payne, B. White, T. Cadell, J. Robson, and J. Murray, in London; J. Fletcher, and D. Prince, at Oxford, 1770. 8°

T.573

7583

A LETTER to the Rev. Mr. Augustus Toplady. Written in great part by himself. Relative to part of his late printed letter to the Rev. Mr. John Wesley. London: printed in the year, 1770. 12°

T.545

7584

LORT (Michael)

A sermon preached in Lambeth chapel, at the consecration of... John Hinchliffe, D.D. Lord Bishop of Peterborough, on Sunday, December, 17, 1769. Cambridge, J. Archdeacon; for T. & J. Merrill, in Cambridge; and B. White, in London, 1770. 4°

T.718

7585

MACAULAY (Catharine)

Observations on a pamphlet [by Edmund Burke], entitled, Thoughts on the cause of the present discontents... 5th ed. London: for Edward and Charles Dilly, 1770. 8°

T.421

7586

MILTON (John)

Samson, an oratorio, as it is performed at the Theatre-Royal in Covent-Garden. Altered from the Sampson Agonistes of Milton [by Newburgh Hamilton]. The music composed by George Frederick Handel, Esq. London: J. Hardy, by assignment of Mr. R. Tonson, and sold by T. Lowndes, [c.1770?] 4°

T.559

7587

MORRIS (Robert) *Barrister.*

A letter to Sir Richard Aston, Knt... Containing a reply to his scandalous abuse, and some thoughts on the modern doctrine of libels... 3rd ed. London: for Geo. Pearch, 1770. 8°

T.421

7588

The REAPERS: or the Englishman out of Paris. An opera. [Based on Les Moussonneurs, by Charles Simon Favart.] London: for T. Carnan, 1770. 8°

T.664

7589

A SECOND postscript to a late pamphlet, entitled, A letter to Mr. Almon, in matter of libel. By the author of that letter... London: for J.Miller, 1770. 8°

T.421

7590

TOKE (John)

Five letters on the state of the poor in the county of Kent... [Anon.] [No imprint, 1770?] 8°

T.421

7591

TOPLADY (Augustus Montague)

The doctrine of absolute predestination stated and asserted. By the Reverend Mr. A[ugustus] T[oplady]. London: printed in the year 1770. 12°

T.545

7592

VENN (Henry)

A token of respect to the memory of the Rev. George Whitefield, A.M. Being the substance of a sermon preached on his death, at the... Countess of Huntingdon's chapel at Bath, the 18th of Nov. 1770... London: for E. and C. Dilly, 1770. 8°

T.433

7593

WESLEY (John)

A sermon on the death of the Rev. Mr. George Whitefield. Preached at the chapel in Tottenham-Court-Road, and at the Tabernacle near Moorfields, on Sunday, November 18, 1770... London: J. and W. Oliver. Sold by G. Keith; W. Harris; E. Cabe; P. Jones; M. Englefield; and at the Foundery, 1770. 8°

T.433

7594

WOODWARD (Henry)

Songs, chorusses, &c. As they are performed in the new entertainment of Harlequin's jubilee, at the Theatre Royal in Covent-Garden. London: for W. Griffin. 1770. 8°

T.624

1771

7595
BENTHAM (Edward)

Reflexions upon the study of divinity. To which are subjoined Heads of a course of lectures. Oxford, printed at the Clarendon Press. Sold by Mess. Fletcher, Prince, and Bliss, Oxford; B. White, London, 1771. 2 parts. 8°

T.791

7596
DRUMMOND (William Abernethy) *Bishop*.

Remarks upon Dr. Campbell's sermon, delivered before the synod of Aberdeen, April 9th, 1771. Entitled, The spirit of the Gospel, neither a spirit of superstition, nor of enthusiasm. [Anon.] Edinburgh: for John Wilson, and sold by him, and the booksellers in town, 1771. 8°

2 copies.

T.671 T.433

7597
EELES (Henry)

Philosophical essays... Dublin: for L. Flin, 1771. 8°

Incomplete.

T.680

7598
FOTHERGILL (Samuel)

The grace of our Lord Jesus Christ, the love of God, and a divine communion, recommended and inforced, in a sermon publicly delivered at a meeting of the people called Quakers, held in Leeds, the 26th of ... June, 1769. [Anon.] Carefully taken down ... by James Blakes. London: printed for the editor; and sold by M. Hinde; and W. Nicoll. As also by G. Copperthwaite, in Leeds; and S. Farley, Bristol, 1771. 4°

T.536

7599
JONES (*Sir* William) *the Orientalist*.

Dissertation sur la litérature orientale... [Anon.] A Londres: chez P. Elmsly; & Richardson & Urquhart, 1771. 8°

T.730

7600
LA TROBE (Benjamin)

A succinct view of the missions established among the heathen by the Church of the Brethren, or Unitas Fratrum. In a letter to a friend. London: M. Lewis; and sold by Mess. Dilly; Mr. Beckett; and at all the Brethren's chapels, 1771. 8°

T.671

7601
A LETTER to his Grace the Archbishop of Canterbury, on the subject of the intended petition to Parliament, for relief in the matter of subscription to the thirty-nine articles, and the liturgy of the Church of England. By a clergyman of the Church of England. London: for J. Johnson, 1771. 8°

T.573

7602
MURRAY (Patrick) *Baron Elibank*.

Considerations on the present state of the peerage of Scotland. Addressed to his Grace the Duke of Buccleugh. By a peer of Scotland. London: for T. Cadell, and J. Balfour in Edinburgh, 1771. 8°

T.421

7603
NEWTON (Samuel)

The leading sentiments of the people called Quakers examined... London: S. Burchall, for E. and C. Dilly, 1771. 8°

T.794

7604
RANDOLPH (Thomas)

The reasonableness of requiring subscription to articles of religion from persons to be admitted to holy orders, or a cure of souls, vindicated in a charge delivered to the clergy of the diocese of Oxford, in the year 1771. Oxford, Clarendon Press for J. and J. Fletcher; and sold by Mess. Rivington, London, [1771]. 8°

T.433

7605
SHIRLEY (Walter)

A narrative of the principal circumstances relative to the Rev. Mr. Wesley's late conference, held in Bristol, August the 6th, 1771... In a letter to a friend. Bath: W. Gye, for T. Mills; and to be had of Mrs. Graham, Bristol; Keith, Dilley, and Gurney, London, 1771. 8°

T.433

7606
STUART (James)

Critical observations on the buildings and improvements of London. [Anon.] 2nd ed... London: for J. Dodsley, 1771. 8°

T.421

7607
A SUMMARY view of the laws relating to subscriptions, &c. with remarks, humbly offered to the consideration of the British Parliament. London: printed in the year 1771. 8°

T.573

7608
VELTHUSEN (Johann Caspar)

The authenticity of the first and second chapters of St. Matthew's Gospel, vindicated: in answer to a treatise [by John Williams], intitled, A free enquiry into the authenticity, &c. [Signed I.C.V.] London: for J. Wilkie; and C. Heydinger, 1771. 8°

T.433

1772

7609
BUTLER (John) *Bishop of Hereford*.

A letter to the protestant dissenting ministers, who lately solicited Parliament for further relief. [Anon.] London: for W. Flexney, 1772. 8°

2 copies.

T.214 T.751

7610
COX (James)

A descriptive catalogue of the several superb and magnificent pieces of mechanism and jewellery, exhibited, at Spring Gardens, Charing-Cross... London, 1772. 4°

T.668

7611
FIREBRACE (John)

The plea of the petitioners stated and vindicated from the misrepresentations contained in a late charge delivered by Dr. Balguy to the clergy of the arch-deaconry of Winchester... [Anon.] London: for J. Payne; M. Hingeston, and J. Wilkie, [1772?] 8°

T.773

7612
HALLIFAX (Samuel) *Bishop of St. Asaph*.

Three sermons preached before the University of Cambridge, occasioned by an attempt to abolish subscription to the XXXIX articles of religion... Cambridge, T. & J. Merrill, 1772. 4°

Wanting the title-page.

T.715

7613
JOHN, *Chrysostom, Saint*.

The sin of Sodom, reproved by St. John Chrysostom.. To which is prefixed, a brief account of the life of that saint. By Edward Lewis. London: for E. and C. Dilly, 1772. 8°

T.431

7614
KILLINGWORTH (Grantham)

Paradise regained: or the Scripture account of the glorious Millennium, &c... Unto which is added A consistent explanation of the prophet Daniel's numbers... [Anon.] London: for J. Buckland, and W. Davenhill, 1772. 8°

T.433

7615
KNOWLES (Thomas) *D.D.*

Objections to charity-schools candidly answered: a sermon preached at St. Edmund's-Bury, for the benefit of the charity-schools in that town, on Sunday, October, 11th 1772. Bury: W. Green: and sold by S. Crowder, London; Mess. J. and T. Merrill, at Cambridge; W. Chase, at Norwich; J. Shave, at Ipswich; and the booksellers at Bury, 1772. 4°

T.715

7616
A LETTER to Dr. Hallifax, upon the subject of his three discourses preached before the University of Cambridge, occasioned by an attempt to abolish subscription to the XXXIX articles... [Attributed to Samuel Blackall.] London, for G. Kearsly; and sold by Fletcher & Hodson in Cambridge, and D. Prince in Oxford, 1772. 4°

T.715

7617
LINNAEUS (Carl)

Fundamenta entomologiae: or, An introduction to the knowledge of insects. Being a translation... by W. Curtis. London: printed for the author; and sold by G. Pearch, 1772. 8°

T.646

7618
The MESSIAH, a sacred oratorio, as it is to be perform'd for charity, in the Octogon Chapel, Milsom-street, Bath, on Wednesday the 28th and Thursday the 29th of October... [The words selected from the Bible by Charles Jennens.] Printed for R. Bullman, [1772?] 8°

T.664

7619
NEUCHATEL.

La liturgie, ou la maniere de célébrer le service divin, comme elle est établie dans les eglises de la principauté de Neuchatel et Valengin. Nouvelle édition, augmentée de quelques prieres... A Neuchatel, de l'imprimerie de la Société Typographique, 1772. 8°

T.642

7620
PRICE (Richard)

An appeal to the public, on the subject of the national debt. 2nd ed ... London: for T. Cadell, 1772. 8°

T.214

7621
REMARKS on An introduction to the history of Great Britain and Ireland by James Macpherson... London: for J. Whiston, 1772. 8°

T.435

7622
ROBINSON (Nicholas)

A complete treatise of stones, gravel, and all other sabulous concretions... London: for Messrs. Robinson and Roberts, and W. Frederick at Bath, 1772. 8°

T.643

7623
RUDDER (Samuel)

The history of Fairford Church, in Gloucestershire. [Anon.] 6th ed. Cirencester: S. Rudder, 1772. 8°

T.435

7624
STURGES (John)

A letter to a bishop; occasioned by the late petition to Parliament, for relief in the matter of subscription. [Anon.] London: for J. Wilkie, 1772. 8°

T.573

7625
TALBOT (William) *Vicar of St. Giles, Reading*.

The Rev. Mr. Talbot's narrative of the whole of his proceedings relative to Jonathan Britain. Bristol: S. Farley: sold also, by J. Dodsley [and others], [1772]. 8°

T.214

7626
TOTTIE (John)

A charge relative to the articles of the Church of England, delivered to the clergy of the archdeaconry of Worcester in the year MDCCLXXII... Oxford, printed at the Clarendon Press; for J. and J. Fletcher; and sold by Mess. Rivington in London, and Mess. Merril at Cambridge, [1772?] 8°

T.214

7627

TUCKER (Josiah)

An apology for the present Church of England...
occasioned by a petition said to be preparing by
certain clergymen... for abolishing subscriptions,
in a letter to one of the petitioners. Glocester,
R. Raikes, 1772. 8°

T.433

7628

TUCKER (Josiah)

An apology for the present Church of England...
occasioned by a petition laid before Parliament,
for abolishing subscriptions, in a letter to one
of the petitioners. The second edition, corrected.
Glocester: R. Raikes, 1772. 8°

T.750

1773

7629

CRADOCK (John) *Archbishop of Dublin.*

A charge delivered by John Archbishop of Dublin, to
the clergy of the dioceses of Dublin and Glandelagh,
at his primary visitation... June 17, 1772...
Dublin: William Sleater, 1773. 4°

T.718

7630

DAWSON (Benjamin)

A letter to the clergy of the archdeaconry of
Winchester. Being a vindication of the petition ...
for the removal of subscription to human formularies
of religious faith and doctrine, from the
misrepresentations of Dr. Balguy, in a late charge ...
London: sold by T. Cadell; J. Wilkie; and E. and C.
Dilly, 1773. 8°

T.573

7631

GRIFFITH (Thomas)

The evils arising from misapply'd curiosity. A
sermon preached before the University of Oxford,
at St. Mary's, on Sunday, March 9, 1760... 2nd
ed. Oxford: printed at the Clarendon Press. Sold
by Daniel Prince; and by J. Rivington, London,
1773. 8°

T.567

7632

GRIFFITH (Thomas)

A sermon preached before the University of Oxford,
at St. Mary's, on Act Sunday, July the 11th, 1773...
Oxford: printed at the Clarendon Press. Sold by
Daniel Prince; and by J. Rivington, London, 1773.
8°

T.567

7633

GRIFFITH (Thomas)

The use and extent of reason in matters of religion.
A sermon preached before the University of Oxford,
at St. Mary's, on Tuesday in Whitsun-week, June 8,
1756... 2nd ed. Oxford: printed at the Clarendon
Press. Sold by Daniel Prince; and by J. Rivington,
London, 1773. 8°

T.567

7634

HORNE (George) *Bishop of Norwich.*

The influence of Christianity on civil society. A
sermon preached at St. Mary's, in Oxford, at the
assizes... March 4, 1773. Oxford: at the Clarendon
Press, 1773. Sold by Daniel Prince; and by John and
Francis Rivington, London. 8°

T.659

7635

JONES (*Sir* William) *the Orientalist.*

An oration intended to have been spoken in the
theatre at Oxford, on the 9th of July 1773, by a
member of the University. [Anon.] London:
printed in the year 1773. 8°

T.420

7636

A MOB in the pit: or, Lines addressed to the
D[u]ch[es]s of A[rgy]ll. 2nd ed. London: for
S. Bladon, 1773. 4°

T.558

7637

A NEW and faithful translation [by William Stevens]
of letters from Mr. l'Abbé *** [i.e. Joseph Adolphe
Dumay?], to the Rev. Dr. Benjamin Kennicott. With
an introductory preface, in answer to a late pamphle
published with a view to vindicate Dr. Kennicott
from the arguments and facts alledged against him...
London: for G. Robinson: J. Robson; J. Walter;
E. and C. Dilly; Mr. Prince, at Oxford; and Mr.
Woodyer, at Cambridge, 1773. 8°

T.431

7638

PALMER (John) *Dissenting Minister.*

A letter to Dr. Balguy, on the subject of his
charge, delivered to the archdeaconry of Winchester,
in the year 1772... London, for J. Johnson, 1773.
8°

T.573

7639

PORTEUS (Beilby) *Bishop of London.*

Two sermons preached at the chapel royal, St.
James's. The third edition, corrected. London:
H. Hughs: and sold by T. Payne; and J. and T.
Merrill, 1773. 4°

T.689

7640

PRIESTLEY (Joseph) *LL.D.*

A sermon, preached before the congregation of
protestant dissenters at Mill-Hill-chapel in Leeds,
May 16, 1773. On occasion of his resigning his
pastoral office among them. London: for J. Johnson,
1773. 8°

T.777

7641

RANDOLPH (Thomas)

The excellency of the Jewish law vindicated. In
two sermons preached before the University of
Oxford... Oxford: for J. and J. Fletcher; and
sold by J. and F. Rivington, London; and Messrs
Merril at Cambridge, 1773. 8°

2 copies.

T.435 T.567

7642

ROLT (Richard)

The history of the Island of Man; from the earliest
accounts to the present time. Compiled from the
public archives of the island, and other authentic
materials. London: for W. Nicoll, 1773. 8°

T.647

7643

STEVENS (William)

A treatise on the nature and constitution of the
Christian Church; wherein are set forth the form
of its government, the extent of its powers, and
the limits of our obedience... By a layman.
London: for G. Robinson; and sold by J. Robson; J.
Walter; Mr. Prince, at Oxford; and Mr. Woodyer, at
Cambridge, 1773. 8°

T.435

7644

TUCKER (Josiah)

Letters to the Rev. Dr. Kippis, occasioned by his
treatise, entitled, A vindication of the protestant
dissenting ministers, with regard to their late
application to Parliament. Glocester: R. Raikes;
and sold by S. Bladon, 1773. 8°

T.750

7645

WOLLASTON (Francis)

An address to the clergy of the Church of England
in particular, and to all Christians in general.
Humbly proposing an application to... the bishops...
for such relief in the matter of subscription, as in
their judgements they shall see proper... 2nd ed...
London: for J. Wilkie, 1773. 8°

T.751

1774

7646

BROSSAYS DU PERRAY (Joseph Marie)

Remarques historiques et anecdotes sur le chateau
de la Bastille. [Anon.] [No imprint], 1774. 8°

T.672

7647

BURKE (Edmund)

Mr. Edmund Burke's speeches at his arrival at
Bristol, and at the conclusion of the poll. London:
for J. Wilkie, 1774. 4°

T.812

7648

CRUWYS (Henry Shortrude)

Enquiries into the archetype of the Septuagint
version, its authenticity, and different editions.
London, for B. Law; J. Williams; J. Cooke; and J.
Swan, 1774. 8°

T.214

7649

FRANKLIN (Benjamin)

The way to wealth; as clearly shewn in the preface
of an old Pennsylvania almanack, intitled, Poor
Richard improved. [Signed Richard Saunders.]
[No imprint, 1774.] 8°

T.653

7650

GREAT BRITAIN. *Laws, Statutes.*

An abstract of the Act of Parliament made in the
fourteenth year of... King George III. intitled,
An act for the further and better regulation of
buildings and party walls... Calculated for the
use of builders, and workmen in general. By John
Matthews, surveyor. London: printed for the author,
by W. Strahan, and M. Woodfall; and sold by W. Owen;
and by the author, at Mr. Mylne's, 1774. 8°

T.657

7651

HAWKESWORTH (John)

The fall of Egypt: an oratorio. As it is
performed at the Theatre Royal in Drury-lane.
Written by the late John Hawkesworth. And set
to musick by John Stanley. London, printed:
and sold by Mr. Condell, 1774. 4°

T.559

7652

HORNE (George) *Bishop of Norwich.*

A sermon preached in the chapel of the asylum for
female orphans, at the anniversary meeting of the
guardians of that charity, May 19, 1774. London:
Harriot Bruce; and sold by T. Payne; J. and F.
Rivington; J. Fletcher and D. Prince, at Oxford; and
at the Asylum, Lambeth, [1774]. 4°

T.637

7653

LAW (Edmund) *Bishop of Carlisle.*

Considerations on the propriety of requiring a
subscription to articles of faith. [Anon.]
Cambridge, J. Archdeacon printer to the University;
for T. & J. Merrill, in Cambridge; J. Robson,
B. White, T. Cadell and J. Wilkie, London, 1774.
8°

T.573

7654

MANN (Isaac) *Bishop of Cork and Ross.*

A sermon preached at Christ-church, Dublin, on the
15th of May, 1774, before... the Incorporated
Society in Dublin, for promoting English protestant
schools in Ireland. With an abstract and continuation
of the Society's accounts and proceedings... [Dublin,
1774?] 4°

The title-page is imperfect.

T.715

7655

PRINGLE (*Sir* John)

A discourse on the different kinds of air, delivered
at the anniversary meeting of the Royal Society,
November 30, 1773. London: for the Royal Society,
1774. 4°

T.802

7656

ROBINSON (Matthew) *Baron Rokeby.*

Considerations on the measures carrying on with
respect to the British colonies in North America...
[Anon.] London, sold by R. Baldwin, [1774]. 8°

Incomplete.

T.627

1774 (Cont'd)

7657

SCHULTENS (Hendrik Albert)

Henrici Alberti Schultens, A.M. Oratio de finibus literarum orientalium proferendis, publice dicta... die 15. Novembris MDCCLXXIII... Amstelaedami, apud Petrum Mortier, 1774.   4°

T.714

7658

SOCIETY OF FRIENDS.

The epistle from the yearly-meeting, held in London... from the 23d of the fifth month, 1774, to the 28th of the same, inclusive... [No imprint, 1774.]   4°

T.536

7659

THOMAS (Benjamin) *of Malmesbury.*

A letter to the Right Reverend Father in God, Shute, Lord Bishop of Landaff, from a petitioner... Marlborough: E. Harold, for the author, and sold by J. Johnson, and T. Cadell, 1774.   8°

T.573

1775

7660

AMERICAN CONTINENTAL CONGRESS.

Journal of the proceedings of the Congress, held at Philadelphia, September 5th, 1774... To which is added... an authentic copy of the petition to the King. London: for J. Almon, 1775.   8°

T.773

7661

BIBLE. *Old Testament.   Song of Solomon.*

The song of Solomon paraphrased: with an introduction, containing some remarks on a late new translation of this sacred poem; also, a commentary, and notes... [By Elizabeth Stuart Bowdler.] Edinburgh: for Drummond; and W. Hay, London, 1775.   8°

2 copies.

T.663   T.666

7662

BRYANT (Jacob)

A vindication of the Apamean medal: and of the inscription Νωε... By the author of the Analysis of ancient mythology. London: for T. Payne; P. Elmsly; B. White; and J. Walter, 1775.   4°

T.554

7663

BURKE (Edmund)

The speech of Edmund Burke, Esq; on moving his resolutions for conciliation with the colonies, March 22, 1775. London: for J. Dodsley, 1775.   4°

2 copies.

T.534   T.812

7664

CUTTS, *Mrs.*

Almeria: or, Parental advice: a didactic poem. Addressed to the daughters of Great Britain and Ireland, by a friend to the sex. [Anon.] London: for E. and J. Rodwell: and sold by H. Gardner; Mrs. Denoyer; and by Mr. Smith, in Doncaster, 1775.   4°

T.557

7665

GENIUS Agrippinae consuli, domino, patri optumo cum lacrumis parentans quum... D. Joannes Balthasar Josephus de Mulheim dominus in Schwartzbongart et Boosdorf, liberae imperialis reipublicae Agrippinensis VIII consul regens senior... funus esset... Coloniae Agrippinae, ex typographia Universitatis, [1775].   Fol

T.810

7666

GREAT BRITAIN. *Parliament. House of Commons.*

Motions made in the House of Commons, on Monday, the 27th of March, 1775. Together with a draught of a letter of requisition to the colonies. Printed for J. Almon, [1775].   4°

T.812

7667

HORNE (George) *Bishop of Norwich.*

Christ the object of religious adoration; and therefore, very God. A sermon preached before the University of Oxford, at St. Mary's, on Sunday, May 14, 1775. Oxford: at the Clarendon Press, 1775. Sold by Daniel Prince; and by John and Francis Rivington, London.   8°

2 copies.

T.659   T.567

7668

HORNE (George) *Bishop of Norwich.*

The providence of God manifested in the rise and fall of empires. A sermon preached at St. Mary's, in Oxford, at the assizes... July 27. 1775. Oxford: at the Clarendon Press, 1775. Sold by Daniel Prince; and by John and Francis Rivington, London.   8°

T.659

7669

JEBB (Richard)

Oratio anniversaria in theatro Collegii Regalis Medicorum Londinensium ex Harveii instituto habita die XVIII Octobris, 1774. Londini: apud Gul. Griffin, 1775.   4°

T.554

7670

MILTON (John)

The celebrated l'Allegro, il Penseroso, of Milton. Set to music by Mr. Handel. Bath: M. Martin, 1775.   4°

T.559

7671

The PAMPHLET [by Samuel Johnson], entitled, "Taxation no tyranny," candidly considered, and it's arguments, and pernicious doctrines, exposed and refuted... London: for W. Davis; and T. Evans, [1775].   8°

T.730

7672

PITT (William) *Earl of Chatham.*

Plan offered by the Earl of Chatham, to the House of Lords, entitled, A provisional act, for settling the troubles in America... London: for J. Almon, 1775.   4°

T.812

7673

PITT (William) *Earl of Chatham.*

The speech of the Right Honourable the Earl of Chatham, in the House of Lords, on Friday the 20th of January 1775. London: for G. Kearsly, 1775.   4°

T.812

7674

PRINGLE (*Sir* John)

A discourse on the attraction of mountains, delivered at the anniversary meeting of the Royal Society, November 30, 1775. London: for the Royal Society, 1775.   4°

T.802

7675

PRINGLE (*Sir* John)

A discourse on the torpedo, delivered at the anniversary meeting of the Royal Society, November 30. 1774. London: for the Royal Society, 1775.   4°

T.802

7676

TYRANNY unmasked. An answer to a late pamphlet [by Samuel Johnson], entitled Taxation no tyranny... London: printed for the author; and sold by W. Flexney, 1775.   8°

T.773

1776

7677

ADAMS (Samuel)

An oration delivered at the State-house, in Philadelphia... on Thursday the 1st of August, 1776... Philadelphia printed; London, re-printed for E. Johnson, 1776.   8°

T.773

7678

DALRYMPLE (John) *5th Earl of Stair.*

The state of the national debt, the national income, and the national expenditure... 2nd ed. London: for J. Almon, 1776.   Fol.

T.539

7679

EVELYN (John)

Silva: or, A discourse of forest-trees... [An advertisement, with a specimen gathering, of an edition to be published in York. No imprint, 1776?]

T.536

7680

FORDYCE (James)

The character and conduct of the female sex, and the advantages to be derived by young men from the society of virtuous women ... A discourse in three parts. London, 1776.   8°

Wanting title-page and other leaves.

T.567

7681

GREAT BRITAIN. *Laws, Statutes.*

Anno regni Georgii II... vicesimo sexto... An act for the better preventing of clandestine marriages. London, reprinted by Charles Eyre and William Strahan, 1776.   Fol.

T.530

7682

HEYLIN (John)

A discourse on the Eucharist... Bath: S. Hazard: sold also by T. Mills, Bristol; and S. Chirm, London, 1776.   8°

T.655

7683

JENYNS (Soame)

A view of the internal evidence of the Christian religion... [Anon.] London: for J. Dodsley, 1776. 8°

T.796

7684

PAYNE (Thomas)

A catalogue of the libraries, of the late Bishop of Bangor, the Rev. Dr. Murdock, the Rev. Mr. Barsham, the Rev. Pawlet St. John, and of William Lowndes, Esq; containing near thirty thousand volumes ... which will be sold ... this day 1776, and continue on sale till all are sold, by Tho. Payne and son, booksellers ... [No imprint, 1776.]   8°

T.353

7685

A PLAIN state of the case of her Grace the Duchess of Kingston; with considerations, calling upon the interference of the high powers, to stop a prosecution illegally commenced... London: printed in the year 1776.   4°

T.812

7686

RICHARDSON (F.)

An appeal to the officers of the guards. London: for J. Dodsley, 1776.   4°

2 copies.

T.812   T.536

7687

ROBINSON (Matthew) *Baron Rokeby.*

A further examination of our present American measures and of the reasons and the principles on which they are founded. By the author of Considerations on the measures carrying on with respect to the British colonies in North-America ... Bath: R. Cruttwell, for R. Baldwin; and E. and C. Dilly, London, 1776.   8°

T.773

7688

ROSSI (Giovanni Bernardo de)

De Hebraicae typographiae origine ac primitiis seu antiquis ac rarissimis Hebraicorum librorum editionibus seculi XV. disquisitio historico-critica Johannis Bernardi De Rossi. Parmae, ex Regio Typographeo, 1776.

Wanting the title-page.

T.802

7689

The TRIAL of Joseph Fowke, Francis Fowke, Maha
Rajah Nundocomar, and Roy Rada Churn, for a
conspiracy against Warren Hastings, Esq. And that
of Joseph Fowke, Maha Rajah Nundocomar, and Roy Rada
Churn, for a conspiracy against Richard Barwell,
Esq... London: for T. Cadell, 1776. 4 parts. 4°

T.536

7690
TYRWHITT (Thomas)

Dissertatio de Babrio, fabularum Aesopearum
scriptore... Accedunt Babrii fragmenta.
[Anon.] Londini, apud T. Payne et P. Elmsley,
1776. 8°

T.806

7691
VOLTAIRE (François Marie Arouet de)

Young James or the sage and the atheist. An English
story. From the French of M. de Voltaire. London:
for J. Murray, 1776. 8°

T.681

7692
WATSON (Richard) *Bishop of Llandaff.*

The principles of the Revolution vindicated. In a
sermon preached before the University of Cambridge,
on Wednesday, May 29. 1776. Cambridge, J. Archdeacon;
sold by T. & J. Merrill; B. White, J. Wilkie, T.
Cadell, J. Robson & Co., and Richardson & Urquhart,
1776. 4°

T.726

7693
WHITEHEAD (William)

Variety. A tale, for married people... [Anon.]
3rd ed. London: for J. Dodsley, 1776. 4°

T.536

1777

7694
BIRCH (G.)

Love elegies ... [Anon.] 2nd ed. London: for T.
Becket, 1777. 4°

T.536

7695
COOPER (Samuel) *D.D.*

The necessity and truth of the three principal
revelations demonstrated from the gradations of
science, and the progress of the mental faculties,
in a sermon, preached before the University of
Cambridge... Cambridge, J. Archdeacon; for J.
Woodyer, and T. & J. Merrill, in Cambridge; and
sold by T. Becket, and B. White, T. Cadell; T.
Beecroft, J. Wilkie, and J. Fiske, London, 1777. 4°

T.726

7696
EAST INDIA COMPANY.

Extract of the proceedings of a general court of the
United Company of Merchants of England trading to the
East-Indies, held at their house in Leadenhall Street
... the 23d April, 1777 ... [No imprint, 1777?]
pp. 291-316. 4°

T.554

7697
GREAT BRITAIN. *Laws, Statutes.*

Anno regni Georgii III... decimo septimo...
Cap. LIII. An act to promote the residence of
the parochial clergy... London: Charles Eyre
and William Strahan, 1777. Fol.

T.530

7698
HEY (John)

A sermon preached before the governors of Addenbrooke's
Hospital, on Thursday, June 26, 1777... Cambridge,
J. Archdeacon; and sold by T. & J. Merrill, and J.
Woodyer, in Cambridge; and Lockyer Davis, London, 1777.
2 parts. 4°

T.726

7699
MICKLE (William Julius)

Sir Martyn, a poem, in the manner of Spenser.
London: for Flexney; Evans; and Bew, 1777. 4°

T.558

7700
PAYNE (Thomas)

A catalogue of near thirty thousand volumes of curious
and rare books; in which are included the libraries
of John Danville, Esq; the Rev. Dr. Charlton, and
the Rev. Mr. Beachcroft ... which will be sold ...
this day 1777, and continue on sale till all are sold,
by Thomas Payne and son, booksellers ... [No imprint,
1777.] 8°

T.353

7701
QUINAULT (Philippe)

Armide, drame-héroïque en cinq actes... A
Paris, chés P. de Lormel, 1777. 4°

T.536

7702
ROBINSON (Matthew) *Baron Rokeby.*

Peace the best policy, or reflections upon the
appearance of a foreign war, the present state of
affairs at home and the commission for granting
pardons in America. In a letter to a friend.
London: for J. Almon, 1777. 8°

T.730

7703

The SAILORS advocate. First printed in 1727-8.
To which is now prefixed, some strictures...
relating to the pretended right of taking away
men by force, under the name of pressing seamen.
8th ed., with additions. London: for B. White,
and E. and C. Dilly, 1777. 8°

T.583

7704
STANHOPE (Philip Dormer) *4th Earl of Chesterfield.*

Characters of eminent personages of his own time,
written by the late Earl of Chesterfield; and never
before published. Printed for William Flexney,
1777. 8°

T.796

7705
TAYLOR (Henry)

A full answer to a late View of the internal evidence
of the Christian religion [by Soame Jenyns]. In a
dialogue between a rational Christian and his friend.
By the editor of Ben Mordecai's letters to Elisha
Levi... London: for J. Wilkie, 1777. 8°

T.419

1778

7706
APTHORP (East)

The excellence of the liturgy of the Church of
England; a sermon at the church of St. Mary le
Bow on St. Mark's day, 1778, pursuant to the will
of Mr. John Hutchin... London, for J. Robson, 1778.
4°

T.718

7707
CAMPBELL (George)

The nature, extent, and importance, of the duty of
allegiance: a sermon, preached at Aberdeen, December
12, 1776, being the fast day... on account of the
rebellion in America. The second edition, with notes
and illustrations. Aberdeen: J. Chalmers and Co.,
1778. 12°

T.796

7708
EYRE (Francis)

A few remarks on The history of the decline and
fall of the Roman Empire. Relative chiefly to the
two last chapters. By a gentleman... London:
for J. Robson, 1778. 8°

T.646

7709
HARTLEY (David)

Letters on the American War. Addressed to the
right worshipful the mayor and corporation...
of the town of Kingston upon Hull. 2nd ed.
London: for Almon; Kearseley; Dilly; Crutwell,
Bath; and Mullet, Bristol, 1778. 4°

T.554

7710
JAMES (Robert)

A dissertation on fevers, and inflammatory distempers.
8th ed. To which are now first added... A
vindication of the fever powder, and a short treatise
on the disorders of children. London: for Francis
Newbery, 1778. 8°

T.730

7711
LIVIGNI (Filippo)

La frascatana. La paysanne de Frescati, opéra-
bouffon en trois actes, représenté par l'Academie-
Royale de Musique, le Jeudi 10 Septembre 1778.
[Anon.] La musique, del Signor Paisello. A Paris,
chez P. de Lormel, 1778. 8°

T.672

7712
OBSERVATIONS upon the administration of justice
in Bengal; occasioned by some late proceedings
at Dacca. [No imprint, 1778?] 2 parts. 4°

T.554

7713
PAYNE (Thomas)

A catalogue of near forty thousand volumes of curious
and rare books; containing the libraries of an eminent
prelate, Sir James Porter, W. Negus, Esq; [and others]
... which will be sold ... this day 1778, and
continue on sale till all are sold, by Thomas Payne
and son, booksellers ... [No imprint, 1778.] 8°

T.353

7714
PAYNE (William) *Teacher of Mathematics.*

Maxims for playing the game of whist; with all
necessary calculations, and laws of the game.
[Anon.] A new edition. London: for T. Payne
and Son, 1778. 8°

T.796

7715
PORTEUS (Beilby) *Bishop of London.*

An exhortation to the religious observance of
Good-Friday. By Beilby, Lord Bishop of Chester.
3rd ed. London: for John, Francis, and Charles
Rivington, booksellers to the Society for
Promoting Christian Knowledge, 1778. 12°

T.544

7716
TICKELL (Richard)

The wreath of fashion, or, The art of sentimental
poetry... [Anon.] London: for T. Becket, 1778.

T.558

7717
TRELAWNY (*Sir* Harry)

Ministers, labourers together with God. A sermon
preached at Exeter, before the assembly of the
united dissenting clergy of Devon and Cornwall,
Wednesday, September 9th, 1778. London: for J.
Buckland; and sold by Henry Mugg, at Exon, 1778.
4°

T.703

1779

7718
ANSTEY (Christopher)

A paraphrase or poetical exposition of the thirteenth
chapter of the first book of St. Paul's epistles
to the Corinthians... London: for J. Dodsley,
1779. Fol.

T.543

7719
GUILLARD (Nicolas François)

Iphigénie en Tauride, tragédie en quatre actes,
représenté pour la première fois, par l'Academie-
Royale de Musique, le Mardi 11 Mai 1779... De
l'imprimerie de P. de Lormel, 1779. 4°

T.559

7720
JERNINGHAM (Edward)

The ancient English wake. A poem... London:
William Richardson; for James Robson, 1779. 4°

T.558

7721

KIDDELL (John)

The inspiration of the holy Scriptures asserted and explained: in three dissertations... London: for Edward and Charles Dilly, 1779.   8°

T.705

7722

MÉMOIRE justificatif de la conduite de la Grande Bretagne, en arrêtant les navires étrangers et les munitions de guerre, destinées aux insurgens de l'Amérique. Londres: T. Harrison et S. Brooke, 1779.   4°

T.555

7723

MORLEY (John)

The nineteenth edition, revised, of an essay, on the nature and cure of schrophulous disorders, commonly called the king's evil... London: for James Buckland, 1779.   8°

T.730

7724

PORTEUS (Beilby) *Bishop of London.*

A sermon preached before the Lords spiritual and temporal, in the abbey-church, Westminster; on Wednesday, February 10, 1779: being the day appointed... for a general fast. London: for T. Payne and son. Sold also by J.F. and C. Rivington: J. Dodsley; B. White; T. Cadell; and J. Robson, 1779.   4°

T.637

7725

PROTESTANT ASSOCIATION.

An appeal from the Protestant Association to the people of Great Britain; concerning the probable tendency of the late Act of Parliament in favour of the papists... London: J.W. Pasham; and sold by J. Dodsley; C. Dilly; and J. Mathews, 1779.   8°

T.705

7726

QUINAULT (Philippe)

Alceste, tragedie-opera, en trois actes, représentée, pour la premiere fois, par l'Academie-Royale de Musique, le Mardi 16 Avril 1776... [Anon.] De l'imprimerie de P. de Lormel, 1779.   4°

T.559

7727

ST Paul's opinion of Jesus Christ stated: in a letter to a friend. By a member of the Church of England... London: W. Oliver, 1779.   12°

T.544

7728

SHERLOCK (Martin)

Lettres d'un voyageur Anglois... Geneve, 1779.   8°

T.642

7729

STURGES (John)

Considerations on the present state of the Church-establishment, in letters to... the Lord Bishop of London. London: for T. Cadell, 1779.   8°

Signature of J. Dampier, 1806.

T.569

1780

7730

DRYDEN (John)

Alexander's feast or the power of music: an ode in honour of St. Cecilia's day. [Anon.] Bath: for John Keene, [1780?]   8°

T.664

7731

EAST INDIA COMPANY.

Report of the committee of proprietors of East-India stock, appointed to examine into the Company's affairs, both at home and abroad; and which was made to a general court ... the 20th of December, 1780. [No imprint, 1780.] Fol.

T.539

7732

ERSKINE (David) *Earl of Buchan.*

Speech of the Earl of Buchan, intended to have been delivered at the meeting of the peers of Scotland, for the general election of their representatives, October 17. 1780 ... Edinburgh: for John Bell, 1780.   4°

T.554

7733

FOUR dissertations. I. On eternal punishments ... II. On Christ's cursing the fig-tree ... III. On mistranslations in the New Testament ... IV. On Christ's temptation ... London: for T. Becket and P.A. De Hondt, [1780?]   8°

T.210

7734

PROTESTANT ASSOCIATION.

An appeal from the Protestant Association to the people of Great Britain; concerning the probable tendency of the late Act of Parliament in favour of the papists. A new edition... London: J.W. Pasham; and sold by J. Dodsley; C. Dilly; J. Buckland; and J. Mathews, 1780.   8°

T.615

7735

QUINTO Fabio; a serious opera: as it is performed at the King's Theatre in the Hay-market. With additions by Signor A. Andrei. The translation by Signor Povoleri. The music entirely new by Signor Ferdinando Bertoni. 2nd ed. London: W. Mackintosh, 1780.   8°

T.664

7736

SEWARD (Anna)

Elegy on Captain Cook. To which is added, An ode to the sun. 2nd ed. London: for J. Dodsley, 1780. 4°

T.558

7737

SMITH (Hugh)

A treatise on the use and abuse of mineral waters. With rules for drinking the waters; and a plan of diet for invalids labouring under chronic complaints. The fourth edition, considerably enlarged. London, for G. Kearsley, [1780?].   8°

T.609

7738

WATSON (Richard) *Bishop of Llandaff.*

A sermon preached before the University of Cambridge, on Friday, February 4th, 1780, being the day appointed for a general fast. Cambridge, J. Archdeacon; for J. Deighton, in Cambridge; and sold by Messrs. Rivington, J. Beecroft, T. Cadell, H. Payne, and T. Evans, London, 1780.   4°

2 copies.

T.715   T.726

1781

7739

APTHORP (East)

A sermon in Lambeth chapel, at the consecration of ... Samuel Hallifax, D.D. Lord Bishop of Gloucester, on Sunday, October 28, MDCCLXXXI. London: for T. Cadell, 1781.   4°

T.718

7740

BALDWIN (George)

The memorial of George Baldwin [to the Earl of Hillsborough, secretary of state]. [No imprint, 1781.]   8°

T.596

7741

BALGUY (Thomas)

Divine benevolence asserted; and vindicated from the objections of ancient and modern sceptics ... London: for Lockyer Davis, 1781.   8°

Signature of D. Yonge.

T.568

7742

BRUNS (Paul Jacob)

De eo quod praestandum restat in litteris orientalibus. Oratio... in Academia Iulia Carolina... XXVII. Octobr. MDCCLXXXI. Helmstadii ex officina Michaelis Guntheri Leuckart. [1781]. 4°

2 copies.

T.714   T.802

7743

CATCOTT (Alexander Stopford)

The supreme and inferiour Elahim. A sermon preached before the corporation of Bristol, and the Lord Chief-Justice Hardwicke, at the mayor's chappel, on Sunday the 16th of August, 1735... 2nd ed. Oxford: printed in the year 1781.   8°

T.659

7744

CLARK (John) *F.S.A.*

An answer to Mr Shaw's Inquiry into the authenticity of the poems ascribed to Ossian... Edinburgh: for T. Longman, and T. Cadell, London; and C. Elliot, Edinburgh, 1781.   8°

T.730

7745

The DAILY advertiser, in metre. By Thomas Sternhold, Esq. formerly of the Temple, now of Stonecutter-Street ... London, for G. Kearsly, 1781.   4°

T.558

7746

FIELDING (Charles John)

The brothers, an eclogue ... London: for J. Walters; sold also by Mr. Merrill, at Cambridge, and by Mr. Crutwell, at Bath, 1781.   4°

2 copies.

T.557   T.558

7747

FORSTER (Nathaniel) *Rector of All Saints, Colchester.*

Evil providentially good. A sermon, preached at the parish church of All-Saints, in Colchester, Essex, on Wednesday the 21st. of February, 1781, being a day appointed for a general fast. Colchester: W. Keymer. Sold also by G. Robinson; and J. Robson, London; J. Fletcher, Oxford; and - Deighton, Cambridge, 1781.   4°

T.715

7748

MASON (William)

The English garden: a poem. In four books... York, A. Ward: and sold by J. Dodsley; T. Cadell; and R. Faulder, in London: and J. Todd, in York, 1781. 4 parts.   4°

T.558

7749

ORPHEUS.

Περι λιθων. De lapidibus, poema Orpheo a quibusdam adscriptum, Graece et Latine, ex editione Jo. Matthiae Gesneri. Recensuit notasque adjecit Thomas Tyrwhitt... Londini, typis J. Nichols; apud bibliopolas, Payne, White, et Elmsly, 1781.   8°

"T. Burgess from ye Editor."

T.806

7750

PARKER (William)

A sermon preached in the parish-church of Christ-Church, London: on Thursday, May the 10th, 1781... To which is annexed, An account of the Society for Promoting Christian Knowledge. London: John Rivington, jun; and sold by John, Francis, and Charles Rivington, 1781. 2 parts.   4°

T.637

7751

PRATT (Samuel Jackson)

Sympathy; or, A sketch of the social passion. A poem. Written at the villa of a friend, in his absence. [Anon.] 2nd ed. London: for T. Cadell, 1781.   4°

T.558

7752

TAYLOR (Henry)

Thoughts on the nature of the grand apostacy. With reflections and observations on the XVth chapter of Mr. Gibbon's History of the decline and fall of the Roman Empire... London: for J. Johnson, 1781.   8°

T.419

7753

UNITED BRETHREN.

An address from the Brethren's Society for the furtherance of the Gospel among the heathen, to the members of the congregations and societies of the Brethren, and to all those friends who wish success to the missions... [Signed by Benjamin La Trobe, and others. No imprint, 1781.] 8°

"Mr. Bowdler"

T.657

7754

WILSON (Thomas) *Bishop of Sodor and Man.*

The true way of profiting by the publick worship. A sermon... Bath: R. Cruttwell, 1781. 8°

T.659

1782

7755

EAST INDIA COMPANY.

Second report of the committee appointed by the General Court, on the 8th April, 1782, to examine into the general state of the debts, credits, and effects, both in England and abroad ... [No imprint, 1782.] Fol.

T.539

7756

FREE and apposite observations on one very evident and indecent cause of the present rapid decline of the clerical credit and character; in a letter addressed to... the Lord Bishop of Chester. 2nd ed... London: for J. Johnson, 1782. 8°

T.571

7757

HINTS for the regulation of the convicts in the hulks off Woolwich, and other prisons, with a view to mercy, by rendering them useful as subjects... London: July, 1782. 8°

T.672

7758

JONES (*Sir* William) *the Orientalist.*

The principles of government, in a dialogue between a scholar and a peasant. Written by a member of the Society for Constitutional Information. Printed and distributed gratis by the Society for Constitutional Information, 1782. 8°

T.773

7759

JONES (*Sir* William) *the Orientalist.*

A speech of William Jones, Esq. to the inhabitants of the counties of Middlesex and Surry, the cities of London and Westminster, and the borough of Southwark. XXVIII May, M.DCC.LXXXII. London: for C. Dilly, 1782. 8°

T.773

7760

A LETTER to the Right Honourable the Earl of Shelburne, First Lord of the Treasury... Dublin: for C. Jenkin, T. Walker, J. Exshaw, and P. Byrne, 1782. 8°

T.680

7761

PALEY (William)

Advice addressed to the young clergy of the diocese of Carlisle, in a sermon preached at a general ordination holden at Rose-Castle, on Sunday, July 29, 1781. London: for John, Francis, and Charles Rivington, booksellers to the Society for Promoting Christian Knowledge. 1782. 12°

T.544

7762

POTT (Percivall)

Farther remarks on the useless state of the lower limbs, in consequence of a curvature of the spine... London: for J. Johnson, 1782. 8°

T.643

7763

PRIESTLEY (Joseph) *LL.D.*

Two discourses; I. on habitual devotion, II. on the duty of not living to ourselves... Birmingham: Piercy and Jones, for J. Johnson, 1782. 8°

T.776

7764

ROBERTSON (Abram)

An essay on original composition. [No imprint], 1782. 4°

T.802

7765

SHARP (Granville)

The claims of the people of England... [Anon.] 3rd ed... London: for J. Stockdale, 1782. 8°

T.583

7766

SHARP (Granville)

The claims of the people of England... 4th ed. London: for J. Stockdale, 1782. 8°

T.420

TOOKE (John Horne)

A letter to Lord Ashburton. 1782.

See no. 7968.

7767

TUCKER (Josiah)

Reflections on the present low price of coarse wools, its immediate causes, and its probable remedies... London: for T. Cadell, 1782. 8°

T.713

7768

VELTHUSEN (Johann Caspar)

Populi Iudaici caritas commendatur Christianis. Annectitur epistola consolatoria ad Iudaeos... Helmstadii, excudebat vidua B. Paul. Diet. Schnorr, 1782. 2 parts. 4°

T.802

1783

7769

BARRINGTON (Shute) *Bishop of Durham.*

A charge delivered to the clergy of the diocese of Sarum at the primary visitation of that diocese, in the year MDCCLXXXIII, by Shute Lord Bishop of Sarum. Oxford: 1783. 4°

2 copies.

T.718 T.802

7770

BARRINGTON (Shute) *Bishop of Durham.*

A charge delivered to the clergy of the diocese of Sarum at the primary visitation of that diocese, in the year MDCCLXXXIII, by Shute Lord Bishop of Sarum. Oxford: for J. and J. Fletcher: and sold by T. Cadell, and Mess. Payne and Son, London, 1783. 8°

Signature of D. Yonge.

T.567

7771

BOWEN (Thomas)

An historical account of the origin, progress, and present state of Bethlem Hospital, founded by Henry the eighth, for the cure of lunatics ... London: printed in the year, 1783. 4°

T.554

7772

DALRYMPLE (John) *5th Earl of Stair.*

An argument to prove, that it is the indispensible duty of the creditors of the public to insist, that government do forthwith bring forward the consideration of the state of the nation... London: for J. Stockdale, 1783. 8°

"T. Bowdler Esq."

T.627

7773

EAST INDIA COMPANY.

Observations on a letter to the Court of directors of the East-India Company, from Warren Hastings, Esq. governor-general of Bengal, dated at Fort-William, the 20th March, 1783... Printed, by order of the Court of directors, November 19, 1783. 8°

T.657

7774

GREAT BRITAIN. *Laws, Statutes.*

Anno regni Georgii III... vicesimo tertio... Cap. LXVll. An act for granting to his Majesty a stamp-duty on the registry of burials, marriages, births, and christenings. London: Charles Eyre and William Strahan, 1783. Fol.

T.530

7775

HOOLE (John)

Preface to the Orlando furioso of Ariosto; translated by John Hoole. [No imprint, 1783.] 8°

T.666

7776

JACKSON (William) *Bishop of Oxford.*

A sermon preached in Lambeth-chapel, at the consecration of Edward [Smallwell] Lord Bishop of St. David's, and Christopher [Wilson] Lord Bishop of Bristol, on Sunday July 6, 1783. Oxford, for J. and J. Fletcher; and Mess. Rivington, London, 1783. 4°

T.813

7777

JONES (Thomas) *Lecturer at St. Magnus the Martyr.*

A probation sermon, preached before the united parishes of St. Magnus, the Martyr, and St. Margaret, New Fish-Street, London, January 12, 1783... London: printed for the author, and sold by, Mr. Dodsley; Mess. Buckland; Mess. Richardson and Urquart; Mr. Tilly; London; Mess. Merrill, Cambridge, and Mess. Fletcher, Oxford, [1783]. 4°

T.718

7778

LAW (Edmund) *Bishop of Carlisle.*

A dissertation on the nature and necessity of catechising... London: for John, Francis, and Charles Rivington, booksellers to the Society for Promoting Christian Knowledge, 1783. 12°

T.544

7779

... A LETTER of advice, addressed to all merchants, manufacturers, and traders... concerning the odious and alarming tax on receipts, which is to take place on the first day of September next... With an abstract of the Act. By Oliver Quid, tobacconist... 4th ed. London, for G. Kearsley, 1783. 8°

T.627

7780

MERCIER (Barthélemi)

Lettres de M. l'Abbé de St.- L ***, de Soissons, à M. le Baron de H ***. Sur différentes éditions rares du XVe. siècle. A Paris, chez Hardouin, 1783. 8°

T.809

7781

PAUL (*Sir* George Onesiphorus)

A state of proceedings on the subject of a reform of prisons, within the county of Glocester. Glocester: R. Raikes, 1783. 8°

T.666

7782

PRICE (Richard)

The state of the public debts and finances at signing the preliminary articles of peace in January 1783... London: for T. Cadell, 1783. 8°

T.627

7783

RANDOLPH (John) *Bishop of London.*

De Graecae linguae studio praelectio habita in Schola linguarum, Oxon. III Non. Dec. A.D. MDCCLXXXII... Oxonii: e typographeo Clarendoniano. Prostant apud J. et J. Fletcher, Oxon: et J.F. et C. Rivington, Londini, [1783]. 4°

T.802

7784

SHARP (Granville)

An appendix to the second edition of Mr. Lofft's 'Observations on a late publication, entitled "A dialogue on the actual state of Parliaments"; and on some other tracts equally inimical to the constitution of 'free parliaments'... [No imprint, 1783?] 8°

T.584

1783 (Cont'd)

7785
SIMMONS (Samuel Foart)

An account of the life and writings of the late
William Hunter, M.D.F.R.S. and S.A... London:
printed for the author, by W. Richardson, and sold
by J. Johnson, 1783. 8°

T.646

7786
TYRWHITT (Thomas)

Conjecturae in Strabonem. [London, 1783.] 8°

No title page.

T.806

7787
WATSON (Richard) *Bishop of Llandaff.*

A letter to his Grace the Archbishop of Canterbury.
2nd ed. London: for T. Evans, 1783. 4°

T.711

1784

7788
An APPEAL to the fellows of the Royal Society,
concerning the measures taken by Sir Joseph Banks,
their president, to compel Dr. Hutton to resign the
office of secretary to the Society for their foreign
correspondence. By a friend to Dr. Hutton. London:
for J. Debrett; and sold by R. Baldwin, and J. Bew;
and J. Sewell, 1784. 8°

T.649

7789
ARCHER (John)

Colonel Archer's narrative of the proceedings
relative to the fort at Gill-Kicker, (now called
Fort Monckton) near Portsmouth. January 1784.
[No imprint, 1784?] 4°

T.561

7790
An AUTHENTIC narrative of the dissensions and
debates in the Royal Society. Containing the
speeches at large of Dr. Horsley [and others]...
London: for J. Debrett; and sold by R. Baldwin,
and J. Bew; and J. Sewell, 1784. 8°

T.657

7791
BAGOT (Lewis) *Bishop of St. Asaph.*

A charge delivered to the clergy at the primary
visitation of Lewis, Lord Bishop of Norwich.
MDCCLXXXIV. Norwich: W. Chase and Co., [1784]. 4°

Signature of B. Mills.

T.715

7792
A COLLECTION of letters on the thirtieth of January
and twenty-ninth of May; with the testimonies of
presbyterians, republicans, and churchmen, in favour
of Charles I... London: printed in the year 1784.
8°

T.649

7793
DALRYMPLE (John) *5th Earl of Stair.*

Address to, and expostulation with, the public...
London: for John Stockdale, 1784. 8°

T.627

7794
DARBY (Samuel)

A sermon preached at the primary visitation of...
Lewis, Lord Bishop of Norwich, holden at Bury St.
Edmund's, on Monday, May 17th... London: for Charles
Bathurst, 1784. 4°

3 copies.

T.715 T.718 T.813

7795
HORNE (George) *Bishop of Norwich.*

The antiquity, use, and excellence of church music,
a sermon preached at the opening of a new organ in
the cathedral church of Christ, Canterbury, on
Thursday, July 8, 1784. Oxford: for D. Prince and
J. Cooke: sold also by J.F. and C. Rivington, and
G. Robinson in London; and Mess. Flacton Smith and
Simmons in Canterbury, 1784. 4°

T.813

7796
JONES (William) *of Nayland.*

The religious use of botanical philosophy. A sermon
preached at the church of St. Leonard, Shoreditch...
June 1, 1784... London: for G. Robinson; J.F. and C.
Rivington; and W. Keymer, Colchester, 1784. 4°

T.813

7797
KING (Edward) *F.R.S.*

A speech by Edward King, Esq. president of the
Society of Antiquaries of London, at Somerset Place
on the 23d of April 1784... London: J. Nichols,
1784. 4°

T.554

7798
PAUL (*Sir* George Onesiphorus)

Considerations on the defects of prisons, and their
present system of regulation, submitted to the
attention of the gentlemen of the county of Gloster
... London: for T. Cadell, 1784. 8°

T.647

7799
PLOWDEN (Francis)

An investigation of the native rights of British
subjects... [Anon.] London: printed for the
author; and sold by R. Baldwin; T. Whieldon; and
J. Debrett, 1784. 8°

T.645

7800
RODNEY (George Brydges) *Baron Rodney.*

Letters from Sir George Brydges now Lord Rodney, to
his Majesty's ministers, &c. &c. relative to the
capture of St. Eustatius... and shewing the state
of the war in the West-Indies, at that period.
[London, 1784?] 4°

T.560

7801
SMALLWELL (Edward) *Bishop of Oxford.*

A sermon preached before the Lords spiritual and
temporal, in the abbey church, Westminster, on
Thursday, July 30, 1784, being the day... of
general thanksgiving. By Edward, Lord Bishop of
St. David's. Oxford: for J. and J. Fletcher;
and sold by Mess. Rivington, and Mess. Payne,
London, 1784. 4°

T.813

7802
SOCIETY OF ANTIQUARIES.

Orders and regulations established by the council
of the Society of Antiquaries; concerning forms
and proceedings to be henceforth observed in the
transacting the business of the Society...
London, J. Nichols, 1784. 8°

T.647

7803
TOUCH (P.)

A thanksgiving sermon, preached at St. Lucia, the
Sunday after the hurricane in October, 1780, on
board his Majesty's ship Vengeance... London:
printed for the author, 1784. 8°

T.659

7804
The TRUE state of the question... London: for J.
Debrett, 1784. 8°

T.593

1785

7805
BERKELEY (George) *Vice-Dean of Canterbury.*

The danger of violent innovations in the state
exemplified from the reigns of the two first Stuarts,
in a sermon preached at... Canterbury, on Monday,
Jan. 31, 1785... Canterbury: Simmons and Kirkby;
sold also by J. Johnson in London; Fletcher, at
Oxford; T. and J. Merrill, Cambridge; and Todd, at
York, 1785. 4°

T.813

7806
BLAIR (John)

Lectures on the canon of the Scriptures.
Comprehending a dissertation on the Septuagint
version ... London: for T. Cadell, 1785. 4°

T.556

7807
COOPER (William)

A charge delivered to the clergy at York, June 16th
1784... London: for Lockyer Davis, 1785. 4°

T.813

7808
ELHUYAR (Juan José de) *and* ELHUYAR (Fausto de)

A chemical analysis of wolfram; and examination of a
new metal, which enters into its composition. By
Don John Joseph and Don Fausto de Luyart. Translated
from the Spanish by Charles Cullen... London: for
G. Nicol, 1785. 8°

T.643

7809
FERRIS (Samuel)

A dissertation on milk... Printed by John Abraham;
and sold by T. Cadell; R. Faulder; and C. Elliot,
[1785]. 8°

"For Dr Bowdler with respectful compts."

T.643

7810
KENNEDY (John) *Rector of Langley.*

The first and second advents of our Lord and Saviour
Jesus Christ, considered in their nature, purpose,
and effect, in a sermon preached November 27, 1785...
To which is added, a short appendix, containing some
observations on... Sunday schools... Maidstone:
printed for the author by J. Blake, and sold by G. &
T. Wilkie, and J. Matthews, London, [1785]. 4°

T.813

7811
MOORE (Charles) *Rector of Cuxton.*

A sermon preached in the church of St. Nicholas,
Rochester, on June 24, 1785... on the introduction
of Sunday schools. To which is added a large
appendix... Canterbury: Simmons and Kirkby. Sold
also by J. Johnson, London, 1785. 4°

T.813

7812
NEWTON (John)

A monument to the praise of the Lord's goodness, and
to the memory of dear Eliza Cunningham... London:
H. Trapp; and to be had at Mr. Neal's, [1785]. 8°

T.707

7813
PLOWDEN (Francis)

A supplement to the investigation of the native
rights of British subjects... London, printed for
the author; and sold by R. Baldwin; T. Whieldon;
and J. Debrett, 1785. 8°

T.627

7814
PRIESTLEY (Joseph) *LL.D.*

The importance and extent of free inquiry in matters
of religion: a sermon, preached before the
congregations of the Old and New Meeting of protestant
dissenters at Birmingham. November 5, 1785...
Birmingham: M. Swinney; for J. Johnson, 1785. 8°

T.776

7815
ROSE (George)

The proposed system of trade with Ireland explained.
[Anon.] London: John Nichols; and sold by T. Cadell;
G.G.J. and J. Robinson; and J. Sewell, 1785. 8°

T.713

7816
SKINNER (John) *Bishop.*

The nature and extent of the apostolical commission.
A sermon, preached at the consecration of...
Samuel Seabury, Bishop of the Episcopal Church in
Connecticut. By a bishop of the Episcopal Church
in Scotland. London: for John, Francis, and Charles
Rivington, 1785. 4°

T.813

7817
TOMLINS (*Sir* Thomas Edlyne)

A familiar, plain, and easy explanation of the law
of wills and codicils, and of the law of executors
and administrators... By a barrister, of the Inner
Temple. London: for R. Baldwin; and B.C. Collins,
1785. 8°

T.678

7818
TOULMIN (George Hoggart)

The eternity of the world. London: for T. Cadell,
1785.   8°

T.681

7819
WARREN (John) *Bishop of Bangor*.

The duties of the parochial clergy of the Church of
England considered, in a charge delivered to the
clergy of the diocese of Bangor at the primary
visitation held in the months of August and
September, 1784... London: for Lockyer Davis, 1785.
4°

2 copies.

T.718   T.813

1786

7820
ACLAND (John)

A plan for rendering the poor independent on public
contribution; founded on the basis of the friendly
societies, commonly called clubs... Exeter: R. Thorn.
Sold also by Messrs. Rivington, and T. Cadell, London;
and by all other booksellers, 1786.   8°

Signature of D. Yonge.

T.568

7821
BLAYNEY (Benjamin)

The sign given to Ahaz. A discourse on Isaiah VII.
14, 15, 16. delivered in the parish church of St.
John Devizes, at the triennial visitation of Shute
Lord Bishop of Sarum, on Wednesday July 26. 1786...
Oxford: for D. Prince and J. Cooke, and T. Cadell,
London, 1786.   4°

T.813

7822
CROUCH (Isaac)

The eternity of future punishments. A sermon
preached before the University of Oxford, at St.
Mary's, on Sunday April the ninth, MDCCLXXVI.
Oxford: printed at the Clarendon Press, for J.
Fletcher; and Mess. Rivingtons, London, 1786.   4°

T.813

7823
CROWE (William)

On the late attempt on his Majesty's person, a
sermon preached before the University of Oxford,
at Saint Mary's church, Aug. 6th, MDCCLXXXVI.
Oxford: at the Clarendon Press, for D. Prince and
J. Cooke. Sold by J.F. and C. Rivington, and T.
Cadell, London, 1786.   4°

T.813

7824
DAHLER (Johann Georg)

Animadversiones in versionem Graecam Proverbiorum
Salomonis... Argentorati impensis Bibliopolii
Academici, 1786.   8°

T.785

7825
DARBY (Samuel)

A sermon preached at the visitation of the Reverend
Thomas Knowles... holden at Lavenham, on Thursday,
Sept. 28, 1786. Ipswich: C. Punchard and G. Jermyn.
Sold by T. Payne and son; and J.F. and C. Rivington,
London; and J. and C. Berry, Norwich; J. Merrill,
Cambridge; and P. Gedge, Bury, 1786.   4°

2 copies.

T.715   T.718

7826
GLASSE (Samuel)

The piety, wisdom, and policy, of promoting
Sunday-schools. A sermon preached in the parish
church of Painswick, in the county of Glocester,
on Sunday, the 24th of September, 1786... London:
Mess. Rivington, and Mr. Gardner, 1786.   4°

T.813

7827
HERTZBERG (Ewald Friedrich von)

Two discourses delivered at public meetings of
the Royal Academy of Sciences and Belles Lettres,
at Berlin, in the years 1785 and 1786... Translated
from the French. London: for C. Dilly, 1786.   8°

T.713

7828
HORNE (George) *Bishop of Norwich*.

The duty of contending for the faith. A sermon
preached at the primary visitation of... John
Lord Archbishop of Canterbury... July 1. 1786...
Oxford: sold by D. Prince and J. Cooke, Oxford,
Mess. Flackton and Marrabel in Canterbury, and J.
F. and C. Rivington, G.G.J. and J. Robinson, and
T. Cadell, London, 1786.   4°

T.813

7829
HORNE (George) *Bishop of Norwich*.

Sunday schools recommended in a sermon preached at
the parish church of St. Alphage, Canterbury, on
Sunday, December the eighteenth, MDCCLXXXV...
Oxford: at the Clarendon Press, 1786. Sold by D.
Prince and J. Cooke, Oxford: G. Robinson, J.F. and
C. Rivington, and T. Cadell, London,   4°

T.813

7830
HORSLEY (Samuel) *Bishop of St. Asaph*.

On the incarnation. A sermon, preached in the parish
church of St. Mary Newington, in Surrey, Dec. 25,
1785. London: for James Robson, 1786.   4°

T.813

7831
HURD (Richard) *Bishop of Worcester*.

A sermon preached before... the House of Lords, in
the abbey church of Westminster, on Monday, January
30, 1786... London: for T. Cadell, 1786.   4°

T.813

7832
INCHBALD (Elizabeth)

I'll tell you what. A comedy, in five acts, as it
is performed at the Theatre Royal, Haymarket.
London: for G.G.J. and J. Robinson, 1786.   8°

T.775

7833
JOSEPHUS (Flavius)

Flavii Iosephi de vita sua liber Graece. Recensuit
varietatem lectionis et notas adiecit Henr. Phil.
Conr. Henke. Brunovici in Bibliopolio Orphanotrophei,
1786.   8°

T.785

7834
LUCAS (Robert)

A sermon preached on the 21st of May, 1786, in the
parish-church of Hardingstone, in the county of
Northampton, on the establishment of a Sunday school
at that place... Printed for J. Robson, London,
1786.   4°

T.813

7835
LUCAS (Robert)

A sermon, preached on the 8th of October, 1786, in
the parish-church of Hardingstone, in the county
of Northampton; supplemental to a sermon, preached
there, on the establishment of a Sunday school.
Printed for J. Robson, London, 1786.   4°

T.813

7836
PARR (Samuel)

A discourse on education and on the plans pursued
in charity-schools... Printed for T. Cadell, and
T. Evans, London; and J. and C. Berry, Norwich,
[1786].   4°

T.813

7837
PORTEUS (Beilby) *Bishop of London*.

A letter to the clergy of the diocese of Chester,
concerning Sunday schools. By Beilby, Lord Bishop
of that diocese. London: for T. Payne and Sons,
J. Rivington and Sons, and T. Cadell, 1786.   8°

T.567

7838
PURKIS (William)

The influence of the present pursuits in learning
as they affect religion, considered in a sermon
preached before the University of Cambridge...
July 2, 1786. Cambridge, J. Archdeacon; for J.
& J. Merrill, in Cambridge; T. Cadell; B. White;
T. Payne & Son, and G. & T. Wilkie, London, 1786.
4°

T.813

7839
SAMARITANS.

Epistolam Samaritanam Sichemitarum tertiam ad
Iobum Ludolfum ex autographo quod servatur in
bibliotheca Cl. Buttneri... nunc primum edidit
versionem notasque adiecit... Paulus Iacobus
Bruns. Helmstadii literis viduae B.P.D. Schnorrii,
[1786].   4°

2 copies.

T.802   T.714

7840
STANHOPE (Charles) *Earl Stanhope*.

Observations on Mr. Pitt's plan for the reduction
of the national debt. London: J. Davis, for
P. Elmsly, 1786.   4°

T.561

7841
VANBRUGH (George)

A sermon preached, at the drum-head, in the Queen's
Square, Lancaster, Sunday, October the 1st, 1786,
before Major-General Sir George Osborn, Bart. and
many of the officers and soldiers of the 40th
Regiment... London: for J. Johnson, and T. and
J. Egerton, 1786.   4°

T.813

1787

7842
BRYANT (John Frederick)

Verses by John Frederick Bryant, late tobacco-pipe
maker at Bristol. Together with his life, written
by himself. London: for the author, 1787.   8°

T.677

7843
BUTLER (John) *Bishop of Hereford*.

A sermon preached before the House of Lords, at the
abbey church, Westminster, on Tuesday, January 30,
1787... By John, Lord Bishop of Oxford. London:
for T. Cadell, 1787.   4°

T.813

7844
COWPER (William) *Vicar of Ramsey*.

Peace and holiness; a lecture; delivered in the
parochial chapel of Saint Nicholas, in the borough
of Harwich... Ipswich: Shave and Jackson, and sold
by the booksellers of Suffolk, Norfolk, and Essex,
1787.   4°

T.715

7845
FRANCE. *Assemblée des Notables*.

Collection des mémoires présentés a l'Assemblée
des Notables. Premiere et seconde division. A
Lyon, de l'Imprimerie du Roi, 1787. 2 parts.   8°

T.713

7846
GILPIN (Jeremiah)

A sermon preached in the parochial chapel of
Broughton in Furness, in the county of Lancaster,
on Sunday the 13th. of May 1787. Being the
anniversary of the institution of Sunday-schools in
that place... Kendal: James Ashburner, for J. Bew,
London, 1787.   4°

T.813

7847
GODSCHALL (William Man)

A general plan of parochial and provincial police...
London: for Messrs. T. Payne and Son; J. Robson
and W. Clarke; G.G.J. and J. Robinson; and J.
and S. Russell, 1787.   8°

T.568

7848
GREAT BRITAIN. *Laws, Statutes*.

Anno regni Georgii II... decimo nono... An act
more effectually to prevent profane cursing and
swearing. London: reprinted by Charles Eyre and
Andrew Strahan, 1787.   Fol.

T.530

7849
HAFIZ.

Select odes, from the Persian poet Hafez, translated
into English verse; with notes critical, and
explanatory: by John Nott... London; for T. Cadell;
and sold by J. Payne and sons; J. Fletcher and
Messrs. Prince and Cooke, Oxford, 1787.   4°

T.534

1787 (Cont'd)

7850

HOADLY (Benjamin) *Bishop of Winchester.*

Bishop Hoadly's refutation of Bishop Sherlock's arguments against a repeal of the Test and Corporation Acts: wherein the justice and reasonableness of such a repeal are clearly evinced. London: for Charles Dilly, 1787. 8°

T.741

7851

LEE (Harriet)

New peerage; or, Our eyes may deceive us. A comedy. As it is performed at the Theatre-Royal in Drury-lane. London: for G.G.J. and J. Robinson, 1787. 8°

T.775

7852

LEVI (David)

Letters to Dr. Priestly, in answer to those he addressed to the Jews; inviting them to an amicable discussion of the evidences of Christianity... London, printed for the author; and sold by J. Johnson; J. Walker, and J. Parsons, 1787. 8°

T.740

7853

MARTYNI-LAGUNA (Johann Aloysius)

J.A.M.L. epistola ad virum inclutam C.G. Heyne... Exponitur de libris Lucani editis, qui seculo quintodecimo typographorum formulis descripti sunt. [No imprint, 1787.] 8°

"Viro eximio atque eruditissimo Thomae Burgessio humanitatis & observantiae causa obtulit Jo. Aloys. Martin-Laguna auctor."

T.731

7854

METASTASIO (Pietro Antonio Domenico Bonaventura)

Artaxerxes. An English opera [translated from the Italian of Metastasio]... The musick composed by Tho. Aug. Arne. A new edition. London: for T. Lowndes and J. Condell, [1787?] 8°

T.664

7855

PEARCE (William) *Dean of Ely.*

A sermon preached in Lambeth chapel, at the consecration of the Right Rev. George Pretyman, D.D. Lord Bishop of Lincoln, on Sunday, March 11, 1787. London: H. Goldney, for T. Cadell, 1787. 4°

T.813

7856

PHILLIPS (William Luke)

Clerical misconduct reprobated. A sermon preached at the arch-deacon's visitation, at Danbury, in Essex, June 11th, 1787... Chelmsford: W. Clachar; sold also by Mr. Allen, Witham; Mr. Gibbs, and Mr. Keymer, Colchester; Mr. Brackett, Sudbury; Mr. Smitheman, Braintree; Mr. Goldsmith, London, [1787]. 4°

T.813

7857

PRIESTLEY (Joseph) *LL.D.*

Letters to Dr. Horne, Dean of Canterbury; to the young men, who are in a course of education for the Christian ministry... ; to Dr. Price; and to Mr. Parkhurst; on the subject of the person of Christ... Birmingham, printed for the author by Pearson and Rollason, and sold by J. Johnson, 1787. 8°

T.740

7858

PRIESTLEY (Joseph) *LL.D.*

Letters to the Jews; inviting them to an amicable discussion of the evidences of Christianity. The second edition, with some additions... Birmingham, printed for the author, by Pearson and Rollason; and sold by J. Johnson, London, 1787. 8°

T.740

7859

SHERLOCK (Thomas) *Bishop of London.*

Bishop Sherlock's arguments against a repeal of the Corporation and Test Acts: wherein most of the pleas advanced in a paper now circulating, styled The case of protestant dissenters, &c. are discussed... London: for G.G.J. and J. Robinson; T. Payne; and R. Faulder, 1787. 8°

"Jno. Dampier."
2 copies.

T.741   T.571

7860

STONE (Thomas)

Suggestions for rendering the inclosure of common fields and waste lands a source of population and riches. London: J. Nichols; and sold by G.G.J. and J. Robinson, 1787. 8°

Signature of A.C. Schomberg.

T.713

7861

TOOKE (John Horne)

A letter to a friend, on the reported marriage of his Royal Highness the Prince of Wales. 2nd ed. London: for J. Johnson, 1787. 8°

T.750

1788

7862

COMMERELL, *Abbé de.*

An account of the culture and use of the mangel wurzel, or root of scarcity. Translated from the French of the Abbé de Commerell... [and published by John Coakley Lettsom]. 4th ed. London: for Charles Dilly; and J. Phillips, 1788. 8°

T.730

7863

CONSIDERATIONS on parochial evils: a letter addressed to Thomas Gilbert, Esq. London: for Lockyer Davis, printer to the Royal Society, 1788. 8°

T.567

7864

HARRISON (Richard)

A sermon, preached in the parish-church of St. Lawrence, by Guildhall, before the... Lord Mayor... on the 29th of September, 1788, being the day of the election of the chief magistrate of this City. London: J.W. Galabin, 1788. 4°

T.715

7865

INCHBALD (Elizabeth)

Such things are; a play in five acts. As performed at the Theatre Royal, Covent Garden. London: for G.G.J. and J. Robinson, 1788. 8°

T.775

7866

KEMP (John)

The Gospel adapted to the state and circumstances of man. A sermon preached before the Society in Scotland for Propagating Christian Knowledge... June 5. 1788. To which are added facts serving to illustrate the character of... Thomas late Earl of Kinnoull. Edinburgh: at the Apollo Press, by Martin and M'Dowall, 1788. 8°

T.707

7867

KIPPIS (Andrew)

A sermon preached at the Old Jewry, on the fourth of November, 1788, before the Society for commemorating the glorious Revolution... London: for G.G.J. and J. Robinson, 1788. 8°

T.776

7868

LAYARD (Charles Peter)

A sermon preached in Lambeth chapel, at the consecration of... Samuel Lord Bishop of St. David's, on Whitsunday, May 11, 1788. London: for J. Walter, 1788. 4°

T.718

7869

LOGAN (John)

A review of the principal charges against Warren Hastings Esquire, late governor general of Bengal. [Anon.] London: for John Stockdale; and John Murray, 1788. 8°

T.593

7870

TOWERS (Joseph)

An oration delivered at the London tavern, on the fourth of November, 1788, on occasion of the commemoration of the Revolution... London: for Charles Dilly, 1788. 8°

T.776

1789

7871

BENDTSEN (Benedict)

Specimen exercitationum criticarum in Veteris Testamenti libros apocryphos... quod... in Vniversitate Georgia Augusta auctoritate pro summis in philosophia honoribus obtinendis d.XIV. Septembris anni MDCCLXXXIX. publice defendet Benedictus Bendtsen Hafniensis. Gottingae, typis Jo. Christ. Dieterich, [1789]. 8°

T.785

7872

COMBE (William)

A letter from a country gentleman, to a member of Parliament, on the present state of public affairs: in which the object of the contending parties... are particularly considered... [Anon.] The fifth edition, with additions. London: printed at the Logographic Press, and sold by J. Walter; and W. Richardson, 1789. 8°

Signature of Wm. Avis, 1789.

T.589

7873

GABRIEL (Robert Burd)

Facts relating to the Reverend Dr. White's Bampton lectures. 2nd ed. London: John Bell; and sold by Fletcher, at Oxford; Merrill, at Cambridge; Meyler, at Bath; Woolmer; at Exeter; and Smart and Cowslade, Reading, [1789]. 8°

T.678

7874

GRISDALE (Browne)

A sermon preached in the chapel at Rose Castle, at a public ordination of priests and deacons, on Sunday, August 17, 1788. London: A. Strahan; for T. Cadell, 1789. 4°

T.718

7875

HUNTINGFORD (George Isaac) *Bishop of Hereford.*

A letter addressed to the delegates from the several congregations of protestant dissenters who met at Devizes on September 14, 1789. [Anon.] Salisbury: E. Easton; sold also by Messrs. Wilkie, London, 1789. 8°

T.782

7876

HUNTINGFORD (George Isaac) *Bishop of Hereford.*

A second letter addressed to the delegates from the several congregations of protestant dissenters who met at Devizes on September 14, 1789. By the author of the first letter... Salisbury: E. Easton; sold also by Messrs. Wilkie, London, 1789. 8°

T.782

7877

PRIESTLEY (Joseph) *LL.D.*

The conduct to be observed by dissenters in order to procure the repeal of the Corporation and Test Acts, recommended in a sermon, preached... at Birmingham, November 5, 1789. Birmingham, J. Thompson. Sold by J. Johnson, [1789]. 8°

T.740

7878

SCHWEIGHAEUSER (Johann)

Emendationes et observationes in Suidam. Argentorati, typis Ph. J. Dannbach, [1789]. 8°

T.731

7879

TOMLINE (George Pretyman) *Bishop of Winchester.*

A sermon preached before the lords spiritual and temporal, in the abbey church of Westminster, on Friday, January 30, 1789... By George, Lord Bishop of Lincoln. London: for T. Cadell, 1789. 4°

T.715

7880

WITHERS (Philip)

Alfred's appeal. Containing his address to the Court of King's Bench, on the subject of the marriage of Mary Ann Fitzherbert, and her intrigue with Count Bellois. London: printed in the year 1789. 8°

T.589

1790

7881

B.(W.)

A vindication of the doctrines and liturgy of the Church of England; in answer to a pamphlet [by the Duke of Grafton] entitled, "Hints to the new association," and other late publications of a similar tendency. In a letter from a gentleman in the country to a friend in Town... London: for J. Debrett, 1790. 8°

2 copies.

T.679 T.782

7882

BELL (William)

A practical enquiry into the authority, nature, and design of the Lord's Supper; as they are explained in the New Testament itself. 2nd ed. London: for J.F. and C. Rivington, [c. 1790]. 8°

T.796

7883

A CHURCH of England-man's answer to the arguments and petition of protestant dissenters against the Test. Oxford, for J. Fletcher. Sold, in London, by Rivington; Payne; and B. White, 1790. 8°

T.782

7884

CLERKE (*Sir* William)

Thoughts upon the means of preserving the health of the poor, by prevention and suppression of epidemic fevers. Addressed to the inhabitants of the town of Manchester ... London: for J. Johnson; and J. Edwards, 1790. 8°

T.567

7885

The DANGER of repealing the Test-Act: in a letter to a member of Parliament, from a country freeholder... London, for W. Lowndes, 1790. 8°

T.712

7886

DESTUTT DE TRACY (Antoine Louis Claude) *Comte.*

Translation of a letter from Monsieur de Tracy, member of the French National Assembly, to Mr. Burke, in answer to his remarks on the French Revolution. London, for J. Johnson, 1790. 8°

T.600

7887

FREE English territory in Africa. [No imprint, 1790.] 8°

A manuscript attribution to Granville Sharp. "E. Prowse, 1790."

T.583

7888

A FULL and fair discussion of the pretensions of the dissenters, to the repeal of the sacramental test... First published in 1733, and now reprinted at the Clarendon Press. Oxford: sold by D. Prince and J. Cooke; J.F. and C. Rivington; and P. Elmsly, London, 1790. 8°

T.782

7889

GIBSON (Edmund) *Bishop of London.*

The dispute adjusted, about the proper time of applying for a repeal of the Corporation and Test Acts: by shewing, that no time is proper. [Anon.] First published in the year 1732; again in 1736; now republished at the Clarendon Press. Oxford: sold by D. Prince and J. Cooke; J.F. and C. Rivington; and P. Elmsly, London, 1790. 8°

T.782

7890

HORNE (George) *Bishop of Norwich.*

Observations on The case of the protestant dissenters with reference to the Corporation and Test Acts. [Anon.] Oxford, at the Clarendon Press: printed for D. Prince and J. Cooke. Sold by G.G. and J. Robinson; J.F. and C. Rivington; and T. Cadell, London, 1790. 8°

T.782

7891

HORSLEY (Samuel) *Bishop of St. Asaph.*

An apology for the liturgy and clergy of the Church of England: in answer to a pamphlet, entitled Hints, &c. submitted to the serious attention of the clergy ... by a layman [i.e. the Duke of Grafton]. In a letter to the author, by a clergyman... London: for J.F. and C. Rivington, 1790. 8°

2 copies.

T.782 T.679

7892

HORSLEY (Samuel) *Bishop of St. Asaph.*

A review of The case of the protestant dissenters; with reference to the Corporation and Test Acts... [Anon.] London: for J. Robson, 1790. 8°

T.782

7893

An INQUIRY into the moral and political tendency of the religion called Roman Catholic... London: for G.G.J. and J. Robinson, and R. Faulder, 1790. 8°

Attributed by Halkett and Laing to T. Potts.

T.758

7894

A LOOK to the last century: or, The dissenters weighed in their own scales... London: for B. White and Son; and R. Faulder, 1790. 8°

T.712

7895

OBSERVATIONS on the conduct of the protestant dissenters. 2nd ed. London: for J. Pridden, 1790. 8°

T.712

7896

OBSERVATIONS on the conduct of the protestant dissenters. No. II. By the author of the first number... London: for J. Pridden, 1790. 8°

T.712

7897

PORTEUS (Beilby) *Bishop of London.*

A charge delivered to the clergy of the diocese of London, at the primary visitation of that diocese in the year MDCCXC. London: for J.F. and C. Rivington, 1790. 8°

T.567

7898

PRIESTLEY (Joseph) *LL.D.*

Reflections on death. A sermon, on occasion of the death of the Rev. Robert Robinson, of Cambridge, delivered at the New Meeting in Birmingham, June 13, 1790... Birmingham, J. Belcher, and sold by J. Johnson, London, 1790. 8°

T.776

7899

REES (Abraham)

The doctrine of Christ, the only effectual remedy against the fear of death: and the union of good men in the future world: in two sermons, preached at Cambridge... on the occasion of the death of the late Rev. Robert Robinson... London: H. Goldney, for T. Cadell; T. Longman; J. Johnson; C. Dilly; and J. Bowtell, Cambridge, 1790. 8°

T.776

7900

SHERLOCK (Thomas) *Bishop of London.*

Bishop Sherlock's arguments against a repeal of the Corporation and Test Acts: wherein most of the pleas advanced in a paper now circulating, styled The case of protestant dissenters, &c. are discussed. Oxford: at the Clarendon Press. Sold by D. Prince and J. Cooke. And by J.F. and C. Rivington, and P. Elmsly, London, 1790. 8°

T.608

7901

SHERLOCK (Thomas) *Bishop of London.*

The history of the Test Act: in which the mistakes in some late writings against it are rectified, and the importance of it to the Church explained. [Anon.] London, printed 1732. Oxford, reprinted 1790, and sold by J. Fletcher; and in London by Mess. Rivington. 8°

2 copies.

T.712 T.782

7902

SWIFT (Jonathan) *Dean of St. Patrick's*

Dean Swift's tracts on the repeal of the Test Act, written, and first published, in Ireland, in the years 1731-2... London: re-printed at the Logographic Press; and sold by J. Walter, 1790. 8°

Teerink 124.

T.712

7903

TOULMIN (Joshua)

Christian vigilance. Considered in a sermon, preached at the Baptist chapel, in Taunton, on the Lord's day, after the sudden removal of the learned and reverend Robert Robinson. To which is added, some account of Mr. Robinson, and his writings. London: for J. Johnson, 1790. 8°

T.776

7904

The TRIAL of John Magee, for printing and publishing a slanderous and defamatory libel, against Richard Daly, Esq. Held before the Right Honourable Lord Viscount Clonmel... on Monday, June 28, 1790. Dublin: P. Byrne, 1790. 8°

T.680

7905

TRIST (Jeremiah)

Historical memoirs of religious dissension; addressed to the seventeenth Parliament of Great Britain... [Anon.] London: for J. Murray, 1790. 8°

T.712

7906

VINCENT (William)

Considerations on parochial music. The second edition, with additions. London: for T. Cadell, 1790. 8°

T.568

7907

WATSON (Richard) *Bishop of Llandaff.*

Considerations on the expediency of revising the liturgy and articles of the Church of England... By a consistent protestant... London, for T.Cadell, 1790. 8°

Signature of J. Dampier.
2 copies.

T.679 T.569

7908

WOLLSTONECRAFT (Mary)

A vindication of the rights of men, in a letter to the Right Honourable Edmund Burke; occasioned by his Reflections on the Revolution in France. [Anon. London: for J. Johnson, 1790. 8°

T.600

1791

7909

ASBOTH (Joannes)

Joannis Asboth Commentatio de interpretatione codicis sacri ad communia omnes libros interpretandi principia revocata... Gottingae typis Joann. Christian. Dieterich, [1791]. 4°

T.814

7910

BELCHER (James)

An authentic account of the riots in Birmingham, on the 14th, 15th, 16th, and 17th days of July, 1791; also the judge's charge, the pleadings of the counsel, and the substance of the evidence given on the trials of the rioters... [Anon.] Printed (for the compiler) and sold by J. Belcher, in Deritend; sold also by T. Pearson, and T. Wood; the other booksellers in Birmingham; and by J. Johnson, London, [1791.] 8°

T.593

1791 (Cont'd)

7911
BELSHAM (William)

Historic memoir on the French Revolution: to which are annexed, strictures on the Reflections of the Rt. Hon. Edmund Burke... [Anon.] London: for C. Dilly, 1791.   8°

T.600

7912
FICKER (Wilhelm Anton)

Guilielmi Antonii Ficker Commentatio de temperamentis hominum quatenus ex fabrica corporis et structura pendent... Gottingae typis Joann. Christian. Dieterich, [1791].   4°

T.814

7913
HARDY (Thomas) *D.D.*

The benevolence of the Christian spirit, a sermon, preached in the Tron church of Edinburgh, May 31, 1791. before the Society for the benefit of the sons of the clergy of the Church of Scotland. To which i added an account of the objects and consititution of the Society. Edinburgh: printed for and sold by William Creech, 1791.   8°

T.762

7914
HARTMANN (Johann Melchior)

Joannis Melchioris Hartmann Commentatio de geographia Africae Edrisiana... Gottingae typis Joann. Christian. Dieterich, [1791].   4°

T.814

7915
HEUBACH (Carl Christian)

Caroli Christiani Heubach Commentatio de politia Romanorum seu veteris urbis Romae... Gottingae typis Joann. Christian. Dieterich, [1791].   4°

T.814

7916
HORSLEY (Samuel) *Bishop of St. Asaph.*

The charge of Samuel, Lord Bishop of St. David's, to the clergy of his diocese, delivered at his primary visitation, in the year 1790. 2nd ed. Glocester: R. Raikes, for J. Robson, London, 1791. 4°

Incomplete.

T.711

7917
MARTIN (John) *Solicitor.*

In the press, and in November next will be published, An enquiry into the state of the legal and judicial policy of Scotland... London: for J. Johnson; and W. Creech, Edinburgh, 1791.   8°

The introduction only.

T.595

7918
PRIESTLEY (Joseph) *LL.D.*

Letters to the members of the New Jerusalem Church, formed by Baron Swedenborg. Birmingham, J. Thompson; sold by J. Johnson, 1791.   8°.

T.740

7919
PRIESTLEY (Joseph) *LL.D.*

Letters to the Right Honourable Edmund Burke, occasioned by his Reflections on the Revolution in France, &c. The third edition, corrected... Birmingham, Thomas Pearson; and sold by J. Johnson, London, 1791.   8°

T.600

7920
PRIESTLEY (Joseph) *LL.D.*

A particular attention to the instruction of the young recommended, in a discourse, delivered at the Gravel-Pit meeting, in Hackney... London: for J. Johnson, 1791.   8°

T.567

7921
RABAUT ST. ETIENNE (Jean Paul)

An address to the people of England, by M. Rabaut de St. Estienne, late president of the National Assembly of France. [No imprint, 1791?] 8°

T.594

7922
REMARKS on the manufacturing of maple sugar: with directions for its further improvement. Collected by a society of gentlemen, in Philadelphia... Philadelphia printed, 1790. London: reprinted by James Phillips, 1791.   8°

T.583

7923
SINCLAIR (*Sir* John)

Address to the Society for the Improvement of British Wool; constituted at Edinburgh, on Monday, January 31, 1791... 2nd ed. London: for T. Cadell, 1791.   8°

T.594

7924
WESLEY (John)

Original letters, by the Rev. John Wesley, and his friends, illustrative of his early history, with other curious papers, communicated by the late Rev. S. Badcock. To which is prefixed, An address to the Methodists. By Joseph Priestley. Birmingham, Thomas Pearson; and sold by J. Johnson, 1791.   8°

Incomplete.

T.740

7925
WIESE (Georg)

Georgii Wiese Commentatio de differentia comitiorum S.I.R.G. durante interregno et vivo imperatore... Gottingae typis Joann. Christian. Dieterich, [1791]. 4°

T.814

1792

7926
ALLEY (Jerom)

Observations on the government and constitution of Great Britain, including a vindication of both from the aspersions of some late writers, particularly Dr. Price, Dr. Priestley, and Mr. Paine; in a letter to... Lord Sheffield... Dublin: William Sleater, 1792.   8°

Signature of Geo. Pentland.

T.680

7927
ASHHURST (*Sir* William Henry)

Judge Ashhurst's charge to the grand jury of Middlesex. II. Proclamation of May, 1792. III. Proclamation of Nov. 1792. IV. Lord Grenville's circular letter. V. Thanks of the Common Council of London, to the Lord Mayor. VI. Resolutions of the Corporation of London. Durham: L. Pennington, 1792.   4°

T.384

7928
ASSOCIATION FOR PRESERVING LIBERTY AND PROPERTY AGAINST REPUBLICANS AND LEVELLERS.

I. Inequality of rank and condition the necessary consequence of civil society, and one great source of its happiness... II. Cautions to the sellers and carriers of newspapers and hand bills... Durham: L. Pennington, 1792.   4°

T.384

7929
BAKER (William) *M.P.*

I. Extracts from the speeches of Mr Baker, M.P. [and others] on the King's proclamation, and the expediency of suppressing seditious writings. II. Extract from the Lord Bishop of Durham's charge, on the same subject ... Durham: L. Pennington, 1792.   4°

T.384

7930
BLUSSE (Abraham)

Observationes in Euripidis maxime Hippolytum. Exercitationum academicarum specimen primum... Lugduni Batavorum, apud Henricum Mostert, 1792.   8°

T.731

7931
BOOTHBY (*Sir* Brooke)

A letter to the Right Honourable Edmund Burke. The third edition, with additions. London: for J. Debrett, 1792.   8°

T.600

7932
CALLENDER (James Thomson)

The political progress of Britain; or, An impartial account of the principal abuses in the government of this country, from the Revolution in 1688... Part first. [Anon.] Edinburgh; for Robertson and Berry; and T. Kay, [1792].   8°

T.587

7933
The CONFEDERACY of kings against the freedom of the world; being free thoughts upon the present state of French politics... In three letters to the Right Hon. Edmund Burke... London: for Deighton; and Johnson, 1792.   8°

T.600

7934
The CONTRAST; or, The first part of a word in season, to the traders and manufacturers in Great Britain. Durham: L. Pennington, 1792.   4°

T.384

7935
ECCLESIASTICAL reform. The present state of the clergy of the Established Church considered ... By a beneficed clergyman, of the University of Cambridge. London: for E. Williams; and T. Williams, 1792.   8°

T.420

7936
FULL, true, and particular, account of the conquest & partition of France, by the King of Prussia, Duke of Brunswick... and their glorious overthrow of French anarchy, tyranny and oppression. The second edition, corrected... London: for H.D. Symonds; and J. Ridgway, [1792].   8°

T.586

7937
An INQUIRY into the causes of the insurrection of the negroes in the island of St. Domingo. To which are added, Observations of M. Garran-Coulon on the same subject... London: J. Johnson, 1792. 8°

T.609

7938
MONCRIEFF-WELLWOOD (*Sir* Henry)

The inheritance of a good man's children. A sermon preached in the Tron church of Edinburgh, May 29. 1792. before the Society... for the benefit of the sons of the clergy of the Church of Scotland. To which is added an account of the objects and constitution of the Society. Edinburgh: for William Creech, 1792.   8°

T.762

7939
OLD truths and established facts, being an answer to a Very new pamphlet indeed! [Signed Vindex.] [No imprint, 1792.]   8°

Attributed by Halkett and Laing to Thomas Paine.

T.609

7940
A PARTICULAR account of the insurrection of the negroes of St. Domingo... Translated from the French. The fourth edition: with notes and an appendix... (Speech made to the National Assembly.. by the deputies from... St. Domingo.) London, 1792.   8°

Wanting the title-page.

T.609

7941
A PLAIN and earnest address to Britons, especially farmers, on the interesting state of public affairs, in Great Britain & France. By a farmer ... 2nd ed. Durham: L. Pennington, 1792.   8°

T.384

7942
ROGERS (George)

Five sermons... Ipswich: Shave and Jackson; sold by J. Shave, Ipswich; Evans, Bury; Johnson, London; and the booksellers in Suffolk, Norfolk, and Essex, 1792.   8°

"From the author to J. Lambert Fell. Coll. Trin, Camb."

T.734

7943
SPALDING (Georg Ludwig)

Vindiciae philosophorum megaricorum tentantur subjicitur commentarius in priorem partem libelli de Xenophane Zenone et Gorgia... [No imprint, 1792?]   8°

T.731

7944

A VERY new pamphlet indeed! Being the truth: addressed to the people at large. Containing some strictures on the English Jacobins, and the evidence of Lord M'Cartney, and others, before the House of Lords, respecting the slave trade. London: printed in the year 1792. 8°

T.609

7945

WATSON (Richard) *Bishop of Llandaff.*

A charge delivered to the clergy of the diocese of Landaff, June, 1791. London: for Thomas Evans; J. and J. Merrill, Cambridge; J. Fletcher, and Prince and Cooke, Oxford; P. Hill, Edinburgh; and W. McKenzie, Dublin, 1792. 4°

T.703

1793

7946

AUTHENTIC copies of treaties [between George III and the King of Sardinia, the Empress of Russia and the Landgrave of Hesse Cassel]... London: for J. Debrett, 1793. 8°

T.590

7947

BEADON (Richard) *Bishop of Bath and Wells.*

A sermon, preached before the lords spiritual and temporal, in the abbey church of St. Peter, Westminster, on Friday, April 19, 1793: being the day appointed... for a general fast and humiliation. By Richard Lord Bishop of Gloucester. London: for J. Walter, 1793. 4°

T.726

7948

BOWLES (John)

The real grounds of the present war with France. 5th ed... London: for J. Debrett; and sold by G. Nicol and T.N. Longman, 1793. 8°

T.587

7949

BURNEY, *afterwards* D'ARBLAY (Frances)

Brief reflections relative to the emigrant French clergy: earnestly submitted to the humane consideration of the ladies of Great Britain. By the author of Evelina and Cecilia. London: T. Davison, for Thomas Cadell, 1793. 8°

T.592

7950

CARLYLE (Alexander)

The usefulness and necessity of a liberal education for clergymen, a sermon... preached in the Tron church of Edinburgh, before the Society for the benefit of the sons of the clergy, on the 28. of May, 1793. To which is added, An account of the objects and constitution of the Society. Edinburgh, printed for and sold by William Creech, 1793. 2 parts. 8°

T.762

7951

CARTWRIGHT (John)

A letter from John Cartwright, Esq. to a friend at Boston... and to all other commoners who have associated in support of the constitution... London, printed for James Ridgway, 1793. 8°

T.587

7952

The ERRORS of Mr. Pitt's present administration many, recent, important, and dangerous. By a gentleman, totally unconnected with foreign interests or internal parties... London: for J. Ridgeway, and H.D. Symmonds, 1793. 8°

T.590

7953

FAWCETT (James)

A sermon preached before the University of Cambridge, on January 27, 1793... Cambridge, J. Archdeacon; and sold by J. & J. Merrill, in Cambridge; T. Cadell, B. & J. White, W. Richardson, G. & T. Wilkie, and Thomas Evans and James Evans, London, 1793. 4°

T.726

7954

FOX (Charles James)

A letter from the Right Honourable Charles James Fox, to the worthy and independent electors of the city and liberty of Westminster. 3rd ed. London: for J. Debrett, 1793. 8°

T.598

7955

FRANKLIN (Benjamin)

The way to wealth: or, The admonitions of Poor Richard ... Durham: L. Pennington, 1793. 4°

T.384

7956

GERRALD (Joseph)

A convention the only means of saving us from ruin. In a letter, addressed to the people of England... London: for D.I. Eaton, 1793. 8°

T.599

7957

GREAT BRITAIN. *Parliament. House of Commons.*

Authentic report of the debate in the House of Commons, on the 6th and 7th of May, 1793, on Mr. Grey's motion for a reform in Parliament... To which is added, a correct copy of the petition of the Friends of the People. London: for J. Debrett, 1793. 8°

T.799

7958

HAWLES (*Sir* John)

The Englishman's right: a dialogue, between a barrister at law and a juryman... Re-printed by the London Corresponding Society, 1793, and sold by J. Ridgeway; D.I. Eaton; H.D. Symonds; Thomas Spence; J. Lambeth; C. Rickman: and by all booksellers in town and country. 8°

T.599

7959

JOHNSON (Samuel)

The witticisms, anecdotes, jests, and sayings, of Dr. Samuel Johnson, during the whole course of his life... Collected... by J. Merry... The second edition, greatly improved. London: for D. Brewman; and sold by J. Parsons and H.D. Symonds, 1793. 8°

T.730

7960

MONTGOMERY (James) *Poet.*

The history of a church and a warming-pan. Written for the benefit of the associators and reformers of the age... [Signed J.M.G.] London: for H.D. Symonds, 1793. 8°

T.599

7961

MOORE (William)

Counsel from heaven to God's people, in a time of public danger or calamity. A sermon... London: printed for the author, by W. Smith; sold by J. Mathews, and W. and J. Stratford, 1793. 8°

T.707

7962

MORE (Hannah)

Village politics. Addressed to all mechanics, journeymen, and day-labourers, in Great Britain. [Anon.] Durham: L. Pennington, 1793. 4°

T.384

7963

OBJECTIONS to the war examined and refuted. By a friend to peace. London: for J. Debrett, and T.N. Longman, 1793. 8°

T.592

7964

PARKINSON (James) *F.G.S.*

An address, to the Hon. Edmund Burke. From the swinish multitude... [Signed Old Hubert.] London, for J. Ridgway, 1793. 8°

T.599

7965

RIGHTS of man... or, The second part of a word in season, to the traders and manufacturers in Great-Britain. Durham: L. Pennington, 1793. 4°

T.384

7966

SOCIETY OF THE FRIENDS OF THE PEOPLE.

Proceedings of the Society of Friends of the People; associated for the purpose of obtaining a parliamentary reform, in the year 1792. London, for Mr. Westley, 1793. 8°

T.799

7967

SOCIETY OF THE FRIENDS OF THE PEOPLE.

The state of the representation of England, Scotland, and Wales, delivered to the Society, the Friends of the People, associated for the purpose of obtaining a parliamentary reform, on Saturday the 9th of February, 1793. London: for J. Ridgway, H.D. Symonds, and G. Westley, [1793]. 8°

2 copies.

T.589 T.799

7968

TOOKE (John Horne)

A letter on parliamentary reform; containing the sketch of a plan. 2nd ed. London: for James Ridgway, [c. 1793]. 8°

T.599

7969

TRIALS at large for adultery. The trial of Major Hook, for adultery with his own niece... February 26, 1793. The trial of Sir Matthew White Ridley, Bart. for adultery with Mrs. Bromel... March 4, 1793... Taken in short-hand by a barrister at law. Sold by the booksellers at Newcastle-upon-Tyne, Pater-Noster-Row, and J. Ridgway, London, [1793?]. 8°

T.597

7970

VANSITTART (Nicholas) *Baron Bexley.*

Reflections on the propriety of an immediate conclusion of peace. [Anon.] London: for John Stockdale, 1793. 8°

T.592

7971

WALLACE (Eglantine) *Lady.*

The conduct of the King of Prussia and General Dumourier, investigated by Lady Wallace... London: for J. Debrett, 1793. 8°

T.612

7972

WATSON (Richard) *Bishop of Llandaff.*

A sermon preached before the stewards of the Westminster Dispensary at their anniversary meeting, in Charlotte-street chapel, April 1785. With an appendix. London: for T. Cadell; and T. Evans, 1793. 4°

Signature of Lord Henry Fitzroy, 1793.

T.823

7973

WILKINSON (Joshua Lucock)

Political facts, collected in a tour, in the months of August, September, and October, 1793, along the frontiers of France; with reflexions on the same. London: for James Ridgway, 1793. 8°

T.591

7974

WILSON (Jasper)

A letter, commercial and political, addressed to... William Pitt: in which the real interests of Britain, in the present crisis, are considered... The second edition, corrected and enlarged... London: for G.G. J. and J. Robinson, 1793. 8°

T.587

7975

WYVILL (Christopher)

A letter to the Right Hon. William Pitt, by the Rev. Christopher Wyvill, late chairman of the Committee of association of the County of York. 3rd ed. York: W. Blanchard; for J. Johnson, and J. Stockdale, London; and J. Todd, York, [1793]. 8°

T.586

1794

7976

BOWLES (John)

Reflections submitted to the consideration of the combined powers... London: for J. Debrett; and T.N. Longman, 1794. 8°

T.598

7977

BRISSOT (Jacques Pierre)

J.P. Brissot, deputy of Eure and Loire, to his constituents, on the situation of the National Convention... Translated from the French... A new edition. London: for John Stockdale, 1794. 8°

T.590

1794 (Cont'd)

7978
CONSIDERATIONS on the French War, in which the circumstances leading to it, its object, and the resources of Britain for carrying it on, are examined, in a letter, to... William Pitt, by a British merchant... London, for D.I. Eaton, 1794. 8°

T.590

7979
A DIALOGUE in the shades, between Mercury, a nobleman, and a mechanic... London: for J.S. Jordan, 1794. 8°

T.592

7980
FRANCIS (*Sir* Philip)

Draught of a resolution and plan, intended to be proposed to the Society of the Friends of the People... Printed for the use of the members of the Society, [1794]. 2 parts. 8°

T.799

7981
GISBORNE (Thomas)

A sermon, preached in the parish church of Walsall, in the county of Stafford, at the archdeacon's visitation, May 30, 1794. London: for B. and J. White, 1794. 4°

T.726

7982
HARDY (Thomas) *D.D.*

The importance of religion to national prosperity. A sermon, preached in the High Church of Edinburgh, May 15. 1794, at the opening of the general assembly of the Church of Scotland... Edinburgh: D. Willison, and sold by James Dickson, 1794. 8°

T.762

7983
HILL (George)

The prayer of Jacob for his descendants, a sermon, preached before the Society... for the benefit of the sons of the clergy of the established Church of Scotland... May 28. 1794. To which is added an account of the objects and constitution of the Society Edinburgh: printed for and sold by William Creech, 1794. 2 parts. 8°

T.762

7984
JOYCE (Jeremiah)

A sermon preached on Sunday, February the 23d, 1794. To which is added an appendix, containing an account of the author's arrest... London: printed for the author, and sold by J. Ridgway; H.D. Symonds; and D. Holt, Newark, 1794. 8°

T.588

7985
KNIGHT (Joel Abraham)

The Apostle's prayer for the church at Corinth considered, in a discourse on 2 Cor. xiii. 14. the substance of which was preached at Tottenham-Court-chapel, on Trinity Sunday, June 15, 1794... London: W. Smith; sold by T. Stratton [and others], 1794. 8°

T.707

7986
A LETTER to the K[in]g; containing some observations on his M[ajesty]'s declarations, published in the Gazettes of the 29th of October and 24th of December, 1793... London: for J. Ridgway, and H.D. Symonds. And sold by all the booksellers of London and Westminster, 1794. 8°

T.592

7987
A LETTER to the Right Honourable Charles James Fox, from a Westminster elector. London: for D.I. Eaton, 1794. 8°

T.586

7988
A LETTER to the Right Hon. William Pitt... wherein is demonstrated, by various arithmetic calculations, the injuries that have arisen, and will continue to arise, to the Bank of England... and to the nation in general, from the present erroneous method of calculating interest on money. London: for J. Stockdale, 1794. 8°

T.588

7989
MILES (William Augustus)

A letter to Earl Stanhope from Mr. Miles. With notes... London: for G. Nicol; and J. Sewell, 1794. 8°

T.598

7990
MONTGAILLARD (Jean Gabriel Maurice Rocques) *Comte de.*

State of France, in May, 1794. Translated from the original of le Comte de Montgaillard, by Joshua Lucock Wilkinson. London: for B. Crosby; J. Owen; and T. Boosey, [1794]. 8°

T.589

7991
MORELL (Thomas)

Notes and annotations on Locke on the human understanding... corresponding in section and page with the edition of 1793. London: for G. Sael, 1794. 8°

T.805

7992
O'CONNOR (Arthur)

The measures of ministry to prevent a revolution, are the certain means of bringing it on. [Anon.] London: for D.I. Eaton, 1794. 8°

T.586

7993
SHARP (Granville)

A general plan for laying out towns and townships, on the new-acquired lands in the East Indies, America, or elsewhere... [No imprint], 1794. 8°

T.584

7994
SOCIETY OF THE FRIENDS OF THE PEOPLE.

Friends of the People. Freemasons' Tavern, Wednesday, 9th April, 1794. At an extraordinary general meeting ... the following address and resolutions were unanimously agreed to... [No imprint, 1794.] 8°

T.799

7995
SOCIETY OF THE FRIENDS OF THE PEOPLE.

Friends of the People. Freemason's Tavern, Saturday, May 31, 1794. At a general meeting... the following address to the people of Great Britain was agreed to, and ordered to be published. [No imprint, 1794.] 8°

T.799

7996
SOME account of a very seditious book, lately found upon Wimbledon Common, by one of his Majesty's secretaries of state... London: for J. Owen, 1794. 8°

T.591

7997
STUART (Daniel)

Peace and reform, against war and corruption. In answer to a pamphlet, written by Arthur Young... [Anon.] London: for J. Ridgway, 1794. 8°

T.587

7998
TINDAL (William)

Plain truth, in a plain dress: or, A short admonition to the middle ranks of Great Britain and Ireland... Evesham: J. Agg; T.N. Longman, London; Messrs. Holl and Brandish, Worcester; M. Swinney, Birmingham; and all other booksellers, 1794. 8°

T.591

7999
WAKEFIELD (Gilbert)

An examination of the Age of reason, or an investigation of true and fabulous theology, by Thomas Paine... London: sold by Kearsley, 1794. 8°

T.591

8000
WAKEFIELD (Gilbert)

The spirit of Christianity, compared with the spirit of the times in Great Britain... A new edition. London: for D.I. Eaton, 1794. 8°

T.599

8001
YOUNG (John) *D.D.*

Essays on the following interesting subjects: viz. I. Government. II. Revolutions. III. The British constitution... 4th ed. Glasgow: printed and sold by David Niven; also by W. Creech, and Bell & Bradfute, Edinburgh, and Vernor and Hood, London, 1794. 8°

T.750

1795

8002
An ACCOUNT of the proceedings on a charge of high treason against John Martin, author of the following works; 1. An enquiry into the state of the legal and judicial polity of Scotland... 2. A letter to the Earl of Lauderdale... London: for Smith; and Burks, 1795. 8°

T.588

8003
The AGE of paper; or, An essay on banks and banking... By Colbert, jun... 2nd ed. London: published for the proprietors, by Mr. Parsons; Mr. Mason; and sold by all the booksellers in the kingdom, [1795?]. 8°

T.597

8004
BELCHER (William)

Precious morsels. I. Features of sundry great personages... II. A tit-bit for Billy Pitt, &c. &c. III. America fast a-sleep. IV. The wonders of the hatred of liberty... [No imprint, 1795?] 8°

T.592

8005
BICHENO (James)

A word in season: or, A call to the inhabitants of Great Britain, to stand prepared for the consequences of the present war. Second edition, corrected and improved by the author... London: printed for the author, and sold by Parsons [and others], 1795. 8°

T.583

8006
BLACK (John) *Curate of Butley.*

The famine of Samaria: a sermon, recommending trust in God, and moderation among all parties, at the present crisis. Woodbridge: R. Loder, 1795. 4°

"D. of Grafton 1795."

T.726

8007
CAMBRIDGE. *University.*

Academical contributions of original and translated poetry. Cambridge: for W.H. Lunn, and J. Deighton; J. Cooke, Oxford; T. Egerton, and J. Bell, London, 1795. 8°

T.741

8008
DUNN (Thomas)

A discourse, delivered in the new Dutch church, Nassau Street, on Tuesday, the 21st of October, 1794 before the New York Society, for the information and assistance of persons emigrating from foreign countries ... New York, printed. London, re-printed, and sold by Citizen D.I. Eaton, [1795]. 8°

T.586

8009
DYER (George)

A dissertation on the theory and practice of benevolence... London: for Kearsley, 1795. 8°

T.773

8010
HALHED (Nathaniel Brassey)

A calculation on the commencement of the Millennium, and a short reply to Dr. Horne's pamphlet, entituled, "Sound argument, dictated by common sense." Together with cursory observations on the "Age of credulity"... London: for B. Crosby, 1795. 8°

T.588

8011
HODGSON (William)

The commonwealth of reason... London: printed for and sold by the author, and also by H.D. Symonds; B. Crosby; J. Ridgway; J. Smith; J. Burks, 1795. 8°

T.598

8012

JOYCE (Jeremiah)

An account of Mr. Joyce's arrest for "treasonable practices;" his examination before his Majesty's most honourable Privy Council; his commitment to the Tower, and subsequent treatment... Second edition, corrected and enlarged. London: printed for the author, and sold by J. Ridgway; H.D. Symonds; and D. Holt, Newark, 1795. 8°

"Mr. Lowten from the author."

T.588

8013

NAYLOR (Martin Joseph)

The inanity and mischief of vulgar superstitions. Four sermons, preached at All-Saint's church, Huntingdon... To which is added, some account of the witches of Warboys... Cambridge: B. Flower, for J. Deighton, & W.H. Lunn; sold in London, by Rivingtons; Conder; Clarke; and E. Greenwood, Leeds, 1795. 8°

T.735

8014

PALEY (William)

Dangers incidental to the clerical character, stated, in a sermon, preached before the University of Cambridge... London: for R. Faulder, 1795. 4°

T.726

8015

PEREIRA (Moses Gomez)

The Jew's appeal on the divine mission of Richard Brothers, and N.B. Halhed, Esq. to restore Israel, and rebuid Jerusalem... London: printed for the author, and sold by Mr. Bell, and Mr. Crosby, 1795. 8°

T.588

8016

RAMSEY (David)

An oration, delivered on the anniversary of American independence, July 4, 1794, in Saint Michael's church, to the inhabitants of Charleston, South Carolina... London: printed and sold by Citizen Daniel Isaac Eaton, printer and bookseller to the supreme majesty of the people, 1795. 8°

T.586

8017

RELIGION in danger: addressed to the Archbishop of Canterbury, by the curate of Snowdon; and submitted to the consideration of the clergy of all denominations... [Attributed to Charles Symmons.] London: for E. and T. Williams, 1795. 8°

T.420

8018

A RESOLUTION to act, the only way left us to be free... Par un amie de la liberte. Paris printed, 1795. 8°

T.594

8019

SHORE (John) *Baron Teignmouth.*

The literary history of the late Sir William Jones, in a discourse. London: for Edward Jeffery, 1795. 8°

T.730

8020

SOCIETY OF THE FRIENDS OF THE PEOPLE.

Friends of the People. Freemason's Tavern, Jan.17, 1795. At an extraordinary general meeting... resolved, that the following declaration be published... [No imprint, 1795.] brs.

T.799

8021

SOCIETY OF THE FRIENDS OF THE PEOPLE.

Friends of the People. Freemasons Tavern, 30th May, 1795. At a general meeting... [No imprint, 1795.] 8°

T.799

8022

STANHOPE (Charles) *Earl Stanhope.*

Substance of Earl Stanhope's speech, delivered from the chair, at a meeting of citizens, at the Crown and Anchor... to celebrate the happy event of the late trials, for supposed high treason... London: for J. Burks, J. Smith; T. Spence, [1795]. 8°

T.588

8023

STUART (Daniel)

Peace and reform, against war and corruption. In answer to a pamphlet, written by Arthur Young, entitled "The example of France a warning to Britain." 4th ed... London: for J. Ridgway, 1795. 8°

T.799

8024

STUKELEY (William)

Palaeographia Britannica: or discourses on antiquities in Britain... Cambridge: F. Hodson; sold by Messrs. G. and T. Wilkie, London; J. Deighton, Cambridge; and Mrs. Watson, Royston, 1795. 8°

Signature of David Mackie chirurgeon.

T.750

8025

TOLFREY (Samuel)

An answer to the speech delivered by Mr. Richard Twining, at a court of proprietors, at the East-India-House... New edition with additions. London: for John Stockdale, 1795. 8°

T.586

8026

TRAVELL (Ferdinando Tracy)

A short and simple exposition of the Athanasian creed, tending to remove the usual prejudices against it. London, J. Smeeton; sold by J. Robson [and others], 1795. 8°

T.615

8027

TWINING (Richard)

Observations on the question to be balloted for at the East India House... viz. "That no director be allowed to trade to or from India, in his private capacity..." London: for T. Cadell jun. and W. Davies; J. Sewell; and J. Debrett, 1795. 8°

T.586

8028

WILLIAMS (Thomas) *Calvinist Preacher.*

The age of infidelity: in answer to Thomas Paine's Age of reason. By a layman... London: for W. Button, [1795]. 8°

T.591

1796

8029

BLAIR (Hugh)

The compassion and beneficence of the deity. A sermon, preached before the Society... for the benefit of the sons of the clergy of the established Church of Scotland... May 20, 1796. To which is added, An account of the objects and constitution of the Society. Edinburgh: printed for and sold by William Creech, 1796. 8°

T.762

8030

BOARD OF AGRICULTURE.

Queries relating to live stock. [No imprint, 1796?] 4°

T.561

8031

BOWLES (John)

Two letters, addressed to a British merchant, a short time before the meeting of the new Paraliment [sic] in 1796. The fourth edition, with a preface. London: for T.N. Longman, and J. Owen, 1796. 8°

T.612

8032

BURKE (Edmund)

Thoughts on the prospect of a regicide peace, in a series of letters. [Anon.] London, for J. Owen, 1796. 8°

T.597

8033

BURKE (Edmund)

Two letters addressed to a member of the present Parliament, on the proposals for peace with the regicide Directory of France. London: for F. and C. Rivington, 1796. 8°

T.610

8034

COBBETT (William)

The bloody buoy, thrown out as a warning to the political pilots of America... By Peter Porcupine... Philadelphia printed. London reprinted, and sold by J. Owen, [1796?] 12°

T.797

8035

DESPAZE (Joseph)

Les cinq hommes... A Paris, chez l'auteur; Desenne; Maret; Deroy, 1796. 8°

T.601

8036

GRIEVE (Henry)

The nature and advantages of good education. A sermon, preached before the Society... for the benefit of the sons of the clergy of the established Church of Scotland... June 3d, 1795. To which is added, An account of the objects and constitution of the Society. Edinburgh: printed for and sold by William Creech, 1796. 8°

T.762

8037

MARTIN (John) *Solicitor.*

A letter to the subscribers and non-subscribers to the loan of eighteen millions. London: T. Williams; and J.S. Jordan, 1796. 8°

T.593

8038

O'BRYEN (Denis)

Utrum horum? The government; or the country? 3rd ed. London: for J. Debrett, 1796. 8°

T.595

8039

POLIGNAC (Diane de)

Mémoires sur la vie et le caractere de Mme. la Duchesse de Polignac. Avec des anecdotes intéressantes sur la Révolution Françoise, et sur la personne de Marie-Antoinette, reine de France. A Londres: chez J. Debrett, 1796. 8°

T.775

8040

The REFUGE of an honest Briton, from the apprehensions and dangers of insurrection and anarchy on the one hand, and of military despotism on the other. [No imprint, 1796?] 4°

"Distributed in the Winter of 1796 & 7."

T.561

8041

RENNELL (Thomas) *Dean of Winchester.*

A sermon preached at the anniversary meeting of the Sons of the clergy... on Tuesday, May 10, 1796. To which are added, lists of the nobility, clergy, and gentry, who have been stewards for the feasts... since the year 1721. London: Ann Rivington; and sold by F. and C. Rivington; and T. Cadell, [1796]. 2 parts. 4°

T.726

8042

WADDINGTON (Samuel Ferrand)

Remarks on Mr. Burke's Two letters "on the proposals for peace with the regicide directory of France"... 2nd ed. London: T. Wilkins; and sold by J. Johnson, 1796. 8°

T.610

1797

8043

BARING (*Sir* Francis)

Observations on the establishment of the Bank of England, and on the paper circulation of the country. 2nd ed. London: at the Minerva-Press, for Sewell, Cornhill, and Debrett, 1797. 8°

T.609

8044

BOWDLER (John)

Reform or ruin: take your choice! In which the conduct of the King, the Parliament, the ministry... is considered: and that reform pointed out, which alone can save the country! [Anon.] 2nd ed. London: for J. Hatchard, 1797. 8°

T.609

1797 (Cont'd)

8045

BOWLES (John)

French aggression, proved from Mr. Erskine's "View of the causes of the war"... London: for J. Wright, 1797.   8°

T.612

8046

COBBETT (William)

A letter to the infamous Tom Paine, in answer to his Letter to General Washington. By Peter Porcupine. Philadelphia printed: London reprinted, for David Ogilvy and son, 1797.   8°

T.610

8047

COWE (James)

Religious and philanthropic tracts... London: for J. Robson; F. and C. Rivington; T. and G. Wilkie; and D. Bremner, 1797.   8°

T.769

8048

ERSKINE (Thomas) *Baron Erskine.*

The only genuine edition of the speeches of the Hon. T. Erskine, and S. Kyd, Esq. on the trial of T. Williams, for publishing Thomas Paine's Age of reason; with Ld. Kenyon's charge to the jury. London: for Evans and Bone, [1797].   8°

T.594

8049

ERSKINE (Thomas) *Baron Erskine.*

The speeches of the Hon. Thomas Erskine... on the trial the King versus Thomas Williams, for publishing the Age of reason, written by Thomas Paine; together with Mr. Stewart Kyd's reply, and Lord Kenyon's charge to the jury. London: for J. Debrett, 1797.   8°

T.583

8050

ERSKINE (Thomas) *Baron Erskine.*

A view of the causes and consequences of the present war with France. 7th ed. London: for J. Debrett, 1797.   8°

T.611

8051

ERSKINE (Thomas) *Baron Erskine.*

A view of the causes and consequences of the present war with France. 32nd ed. London: for J. Debrett, 1797.   8°

T.722

8052

GIFFORD (John)

A letter to the Hon. Thomas Erskine; containing some strictures on his View of the causes and consequences of the present war with France. 3rd ed... London: for T.N. Longman, 1797.   8°

T.613

8053

GIFFORD (John)

A letter to the Hon. Thomas Erskine; containing some strictures on his View of the causes and consequences of the present war with France. 7th ed... London: for T.N. Longman, 1797.   8°

T.611

8054

HANNO, *the Carthaginian.*

The voyage of Hanno translated, and accompanied with the Greek text; explained from the accounts of modern travellers... By Thomas Falconer... London: sold by T. Cadell Jun. and Davies, 1797.   8°

"Johannes Wilhelmus Mackie Aedis Christi alumnus 1809."

T.736

8055

JONES (John) *M.B.*

Medical, philosophical, and vulgar errors, of various kinds, considered and refuted... London: for T. Cadell Jun. and W. Davies, 1797.   8°

T.748

8056

MACLAINE (Archibald)

The solemn voice of public events considered in a discourse from Zephaniah iii. 6, 7. Relative to the appointment of the late general fast, on the 8th of March, 1797... Bath, S. Hazard; sold also by Cadell and Davies, London; and by the booksellers in town and country, [1797].   4°

T.703

8057

MANCHESTER AGRICULTURAL SOCIETY.

Rules & conditions of the Manchester Agricultural Society. To which is added a list of premiums offered by the society for the year 1798... Manchester: printed at the office of George Nicholson, 1797.   8°

T.594

8058

PAINE (Thomas)

Agrarian justice, opposed to agrarian law, and to agrarian monopoly being a plan for meliorating the condition of man, by creating in every nation a national fund... [3rd ed.] Paris: W. Adlard. London: reprinted and sold by J. Adlard, and J. Parsons, [1797].   8°

T.749

8059

REASONS against national despondency; in refutation of Mr. Erskine's View of the causes and consequences of the present war. With some remarks upon the supposed scarcity of specie... London: for T. Cadell jun. and W. Davies, 1797.   8°

2 copies.

T.611   T.613

8060

RULHIERE (Claude Carloman de)

The history, or anecdotes, of the revolution in Russia, in the year 1762. Translated from the French of M. de Rulhière. London: for T.N. Longman, 1797.   8°

T.797

8061

SOCIETY FOR BETTERING THE CONDITION AND INCREASING THE COMFORTS OF THE POOR.

The first report of the Society, for bettering the condition and increasing the comforts of the poor. [The preliminary address signed by Sir Thomas Bernard.] London: for T. Becket, 1797.   8°

T.583

8062

The VOICE of truth to the people of England, of all ranks and descriptions, on occasion of Lord Malmesbury's return from Lisle... London: for F. and C. Rivington; sold also by J. Hatchard, 1797.   8°

T.609

1798

8063

COBBETT (William)

Observations on the emigration of Dr. Joseph Priestley, and on the several addresses delivered to him, on his arrival at New York... By Peter Porcupine. 4th ed... Printed at Philadelphia. London: re-printed for J. Wright, 1798.   8°

T.610

8064

COBBETT (William)

The republican judge: or the American liberty of the press, as exhibited, explained, and exposed, in the base and partial prosecution of William Cobbett... before the supreme court of Pennsylvania ... By Peter Porcupine. London: for J. Wright, 1798.   8°

T.610

8065

DUMOURIEZ (Charles François Duperrier)

Tableau speculatif de l'Europe. [No imprint], Fevrier 1798.   8°

T.797

8066

EMIGRATION to America, candidly considered. In a series of letters, from a gentleman, resident there, to his friend, in England. [Edited by Thomas Clio Rickman.] Printed and sold by Thomas Clio Rickman, 1798.   8°

T.593

8067

FITZGIBBON (John) *Earl of Clare.*

The speech of the Right Honourable John, Earl of Clare, Lord High Chancellor of Ireland, in the House of Lords of Ireland, Monday, February 19, 1798, on a motion made by the Earl of Moira... 3rd ed. Dublin: for John Miliken: London: reprinted for J. Wright, 1798.   8°

T.612

8068

GIFFORD (John)

A short address, to the members of the loyal associations, on the present state of public affairs... London: for T.N. Longman, 1798.   8°

T.596

8069

HARPER (Robert Goodloe)

Observations on the dispute between the United States and France, addressed by Robert Goodloe Harper, Esq. one of the representatives in Congress for the state of South Carolina, to his constituents, in May 1797. 3rd ed. Philadelphia printed. London: reprinted for John Stockdale, 1798.   8°

T.610

8070

HINCKLEY (John)

The people's answer to the Lord Bishop of Landaff... London: for J.S. Jordan, 1798.   8°

T.595

8071

JENOUR (Joshua)

Observations on the taxation of property... [Anon.] London: printed for the author, and sold by Carpenter, and Tyndal, 1798.   8°

T.594

8072

LE MESURIER (Havilland)

Thoughts on a French invasion, with reference to the probability of its success, and the proper means of resisting it. 4th ed. London: for J. Wright, 1798.   8°

T.609

8073

MARSTERS (Thomas)

A view of agricultural oppressions: and of their effects upon society. 2nd ed. Lynn Regis, Rd. Marshall, And may be had of the booksellers in Lynn. Sold also by Jordan, and Robinsons, London; March, Norwich; Gregory, Cambridge; and Gedge, Bury, 1798.   8°

T.593

8074

MONROE (James)

A view of the conduct of the executive in the foreign affairs of the United States, as connected with the mission tothe French Republic... 2nd ed. Philadelphia, printed. London: for James Ridgway, 1798.   8°

T.609

8075

O'COIGLY (James)

The life of the Rev. James Coigly, observations upon his trial, an address to the people of Ireland, and several interesting letters, all written by himself during his confinement in Maidstone gaol. [Edited by Valentine Derry.] [No imprint, 1798.]   8°

T.594

8076

PLAIN facts: in five letters to a friend, on the present state of politics... London: for J.S. Jordan, 1798.   8°

T.596

8077

SOUTHOUSE (E.)

... A letter to the Right Hon. Wm. Pitt, as Chancellor of the Exchequer; requiring him as such to do the author justice, in paying... some back salary that he claims, as heretofore attorney general, and judge of common pleas, in Canada... Printed for the author, and sold at Fentum's music shop, and at Wood's news-shop, London, [1798].   8°

T.609

8078

VENN (John) *Rector of Clapham.*

Reflections in this season of danger. A sermon preached in the parish church of Clapham... April 15, 1798. London: sold by F. and C. Rivington; Eglyn and Pepys, and Batten, Clapham, 1798. 8°

T.769

8079

WAKEFIELD (Gilbert)

A letter to Sir John Scott, his Majesty's attorney-general, on the subject of a late trial in Guildhall... Sold by the author, 1798. 8°

T.594

8080

WATSON (Richard) *Bishop of Llandaff.*

An address to the people of Great Britain. London: for R. Faulder, 1798. 8°

T.610

1799

8081

BERTIE (Willoughby) *Earl of Abingdon.*

Constitutional strictures on particular positions advanced in the speeches of... William Pitt, in debates which took place on the union between Great Britain and Ireland... 3rd ed... London: for T. Barnes, [1799]. 8°

T.595

8082

BLANE (Gilbert)

Letters, &c. on the subject of quarantine. London: printed at the Philanthropic Reform, 1799. 4°

With a letter from the author presenting copy [to Lord Pelham?], 1802.

T.561

8083

CONSIDERATIONS on national independence, suggested by Mr. Pitt's speeches on the Irish union... By a member of the Honourable Society of Lincoln's Inn... London: for G.G.J. and J. Robinson, and Thomas Clio Rickman, [1799?] 8°

T.596

8084

COWE (James)

On the advantages which result from Christianity; and on the influence of Christian principles on the mind and conduct. London: for J. Robson; F. and C. Rivington; G. Wilkie; and D. Bremner, 1799. 8°

T.769

8085

DUPPA (Richard)

A journal of the most remarkable occurrences that took place in Rome, upon the subversion of the ecclesiastical government, in 1798. London: for G.G. and J. Robinson, 1799. 8°

T.601

8086

GREAT BRITAIN. *Laws, Statutes.*

An Act (passed 21st March 1799,) for extending the time for returning statements under an Act... intituled, An Act to repeal the duties imposed by an Act... for granting an aid and contribution for the prosecution of the War... by granting certain duties upon income... London: George Eyre and Andrew Strahan, 1799. 8°

T.597

8087

HESLOP (Luke)

Observations on the statute of the thirty-first George II. ch. 29, concerning the assize of bread... London: Bunney & Gold, for Shepperson and Reynolds, 1799. 4°

Signature of Lord Pelham.

T.561

8088

MADDOCK (Henry)

The power of parliaments considered, in a letter to a member of Parliament. 2nd ed... London: for J. Debrett, by Cooper and Wilson, 1799. 8°

T.595

8089

OBSERVATIONS, &c. upon the amended act for taxing income... London: Bunney & Gold, [1799?] 8°

T.597

8090

O'CONNOR (Arthur)

Arthur O'Connor's letter to Lord Castlereagh. [No imprint, 1799.] 8°

T.595

8091

SINCLAIR (*Sir* John)

Proposals for establishing by subscription, a joint stock farming society, for ascertaining the principles of agricultural improvement... London: W. Bulmer, 1799. 4°

T.561

8092

STURGES (John)

Reflections on the principles and institutions of popery, with reference to civil society and government, especially that of this kingdom; occasioned by the Rev. John Milner's History of Winchester. In letters to the Rev. John Monk Newbolt. Printed by Robbins, Winchester; and sold by him, and Cadell, Jun. and Davies, London 1799. 4°

T.534

8093

The SUBSTANCE of the Income Act... By a barrister, of the Middle Temple. London: Thomas Hurst, 1799. 8°

T.596

8094

WYVILL (Christopher)

The secession from Parliament vindicated. York: L. Lund, 1799. 8°

T.594

1800

8095

BARTHELEMY (Jean Jacques)

Catalogue des livres de la bibliothèque de feu l'Abbé Barthélemy... A Paris, chez Bernard [et] Thuret, 1800. 2 parts. 8°

Annotated.

T.809

8096

BURKE (Edmund)

Thoughts and details on scarcity, originally presented to the Right Hon. William Pitt, in the month of November, 1795. London: for F. and C. Rivington; and J. Hatchard, 1800. 8°

T.615

8097

COBBETT (William)

Le maître anglais, ou grammaire régulière, pour faciliter aux Français l'étude de la langue anglaise. Nouvelle édition... A Paris, chez Fayolle, Warée, Laran, an VIII [1799-1800]. 8°

Title-page only.

T.809

8098

GRAHAM (John)

A defence of Scripture doctrines, as understood by the Church of England; in reply to a pamphlet, entitled, "Scripture the only guide to religious truth"... In a series of letters to Mr. D. Eaton. York: William Blanchard: and sold by J. Mathews; W. Tesseyman; Binns, Leeds; Edwards, Halifax; Ware, Whitehaven; and by the booksellers in Hull, Scarborough, &c., 1800. 8°

T.608

8099

HOWARD (Frederick) *Earl of Carlisle.*

The step-mother, a tragedy. London: for R.H. Evans; by G. Woodfall. 1800. 8°

T.775

8100

MADISON (James) *Bishop.*

A discourse on the death of General Washington, late President of the United States: delivered on the 22d of February, 1800, in the church in Williamsburg. The second edition - corrected. New-York, printed. London, re-printed for John Hatchard, by Henry Reynell, 1800. 8°

T.583

8101

POLITICAL essays on popular subjects... London: J. Plymsell; for C. Chapple, 1800. 8°

T.614

8102

POTT (Joseph Holden)

A charge delivered to the clergy of the archdeaconry of St. Alban's, at the visitation, held June 5, A.D.1800. London: for F. and C. Rivington; by Bye and Law, 1800. 4°

T.711

8103

POTT (Joseph Holden)

The pattern of Christian prudence and discretion, urged against hurtful and fantastic schemes of life. London: for F. and C. Rivington; by Bye and Law, 1800. 4°

T.711

8104

REID (William Hamilton)

The rise and dissolution of the infidel societies in this Metropolis... from the publication of Paine's Age of reason till the present period... London: for J. Hatchard, 1800. 8°

T.614

8105

RIGSHAW (Cincinnatus) pseud.

Sans culotides: by Cincinnatus Rigshaw... London: printed for the author, and sold by C. Chapple. By J. Bonsor. 1800. 4°

T.534

8106

ROYAL INSTITUTION OF GREAT BRITAIN.

The prospectus, charter, ordinances and bye-laws, of the Royal Institution of Great Britain... London: W. Bulmer, and sold by Cadell and Davies; Beckett; Payne; Debrett, Stockdale, Wright, and Hatchard; Robson, Faulder, and Hookham; White; Rivingtons; and Vernor, 1800. 4°

T.560

8107

STEVENS (William)

A review of the review of a new preface to the second edition of Mr. Jones's life of Bishop Horne, in the British critic, for February, 1800... By A.I.N. London: T. Crowder; and sold by J. Hatchard, 1800. 8°

"The Rev. Jno. Watson from the author".

T.615

8108

STEVENS (William)

A review of the review of a new preface to the second edition of Mr. Jones's life of Bishop Horne, in the British critic, for February, 1800... By A.I.N. 2nd ed. To which is added a postscript. London: T. Crowder; and sold by J. Hatchard, 1800. 8°

"Rev. J.J. Watson from the author."

T.608

1801

8109

ANSWER to an anonymous letter, (dated September 18, 1777,) on predestination and free-will, with a postscript on eternal punishments. London: R. Balfe, for the author; and sold by White; by Mawman; and at the London Library, by Mr. Taylor, the librarian, 1801. 8°

T.584

8110

ATWOOD (George)

Review of the statutes and ordinances of assize... London; for T. Egerton; G. and J. Robinson; and R. Faulder, 1801. 4°

T.561

1801 (Cont'd)

8111

CLEAVER (William) *Bishop of St. Asaph.*

The origin and utility of creeds considered: with a vindication of the Athanasian Creed: in a sermon preached before the University of Oxford... November 16, 1800. By William Lord Bishop of Bangor. Oxford: printed at the University Press, for Mess. Hanwell and Parker: sold also by J. Cooke [and others], 1801. 8°

T.608

8112

COBBETT (William)

The trial of republicanism: or, A series of political papers, proving the injurious and debasing consequences of republican government, and written constitutions... By Peter Porcupine. London: for Cobbett and Morgan, April, 1801. 8°

T.614

8113

DUBLIN. *King's Inns.*

A catalogue of the library belonging to the Honourable Society of King's Inns, Dublin; to Trinity term 1801. [Compiled by Bartholomew Thomas Duhigg.] Dublin: R.E. Mercier, 1801. 4°

"To Mr. Mason from his friend B.T.D. 1810."
"Sotheby's sale Aug. 1831." (Heber?)

T.693

8114

FRANCKLIN (Thomas)

A letter to a bishop, concerning lectureships. Designed to shew the propriety and necessity of a total abolition of the institution. Written many years ago by the Rev. Dr. Stebbing... London: for T. Becket, 1801. 8°

T.608

8115

HEWLETT (John)

The duty of keeping the Christian Sabbath holy: a sermon, preached in the chapel of the hospital for the maintenance and education of exposed and deserted young children, on Sunday morning, March 8, 1801. London: Luke Hansard, and sold by F. and C. Rivington, and J. Johnson; T. Cadell jun. and W. Davies; and J. Mawman, 1801. 8°

T.608

8116

LE PELETIER DE SAINT-FARGEAU (Louis Michel)

Catalogue du restant des livres, rares et précieux, de feu C. Louis-Michel Le Pelletier de Saint-Fargeau, dont la vente se sera le 7 Floréal an 9... dans la salle du C. Sylvestre... Paris, chez G. Debure, 1801. 8°

Annotated.

T.809

8117

LE PRESTRE (René Charles Hippolyte) *Marquis de Chateaugiron.*

Notice sur la mort de Paul Ier., empereur de Russie. [Anon.] [No imprint, 1801?] 8°

T.601

8118

A LETTER humbly addressed to the most rev. and right rev. the archbishops and bishops of the Church of England. London: Cobbett and Morgan, 1801. 8°

T.615

8119

A LETTER to the Hon. Spencer Perceval... in consequence of the notice given by him, in the last session of Parliament, that he would, in the present, bring forward a bill for the punishment of the crime of adultery. 2nd ed... London: for F. and C. Rivington; W.J. and J. Richardson; Cobbett and Morgan; and J. Wright, and J. Hatchard, [1801]. 8°

T.614

8120

RANDOLPH (Francis)

A sermon preached at Laura Chapel, Bath, on Friday, February 13th, 1801, the day appointed for a general fast. Bath, R. Cruttwell; and sold by F. and C. Rivington, 1801. 8°

T.608

8121

REEVES (John)

Considerations on the coronation oath, to maintain the protestant reformed religion, and the settlement of the Church of England... London: for J. Wright, February 23, 1801. 8°

T.614

8122

TWO addresses to the inhabitants of the several parishes in the deaneries of Louth-Esk, and Ludburgh, Calcewaith, Horncastle, Gartree, Bolingbroke, Candleshoe, and Hill; within the archdeaconry of Lincoln... To which are added forms of morning and evening prayers... By a committee of the clergy of the aforesaid deaneries. London: for F. and C. Rivington; Cobbett and Morgan; Hatchard; and J. Whittle, [1801?] 2 parts. 8°

T.608

1802

8123

BARRINGTON (Shute) *Bishop of Durham.*

A charge, delivered to the clergy of the diocese of Durham, at the ordinary visitation of that diocese, in July, 1801. London: W. Bulmer and Co. Sold by T. Payne, T. Cadell, [and others], London; Hanwell and Parker, Oxford; Deighton, Cambridge; and the booksellers at Durham and Newcastle, 1802. 4°

T.718

8124

BEVAN (Joseph Gurney)

An examination of the first part of a pamphlet [by Thomas Foster], called An appeal to the Society of Friends. By Vindex. London: W. Phillips, 1802. 8°

T.794

8125

BOWLES (John)

Remarks on modern female manners, as distinguished by indifference to character, and indecency of dress; extracted from "Reflections political and moral at the conclusion of the war." London: for F. and C. Rivington. Sold also by W. and J. Richardson; Cobbett and Morgan; and W. Hatchard, 1802. 8°

T.723

8126

COURTENAY (Henry Reginald) *Bishop of Exeter.*

A sermon, preached at the parish church of Saint George, Hanover Square, on Tuesday, the 1st of June, 1802, being the day appointed for a general thanksgiving. London: D.N. Shury; for J. Robson, 1802. 4°

T.718

8127

HOOK (James)

Anguis in herba! A sketch of the true character of the Church of England, and her clergy... 2nd ed. London: D.N. Shury, for J. Ginger. Sold also by Hanwell and Parker, Oxford; and Deighton, Cambridge, 1802. 8°

Signature of J. Dampier.

T.570

8128

HUDDERSFORD (George)

The scum uppermost when the Middlesex porridge-pot boils over!! An heroic election ballad with explanatory notes... Accompanied with an admonitory nod to a blind horse. [Anon.] London: printed for the author, and sold by all booksellers, 1802. 4°

T.561

8129

HUNTER (John)

Governor Hunter's remarks on the causes of the colonial expense of the establishment of New South Wales, &c. Hints for the reduction of such expense, and for reforming the prevailing abuses. London: S. Gosnell, 1802. 4°

T.561

8130

LAW (John) *Archdeacon of Rochester.*

A charge delivered to the clergy of the diocese of Rochester, in the year 1802... London: for T. Payne; F. and C. Rivington; and Nunn; by S. Hamilton, 1802. 4°

T.718

8131

A LETTER, addressed to the Hon. Charles James Fox, in consequence of his speech in the House of Commons, on the character of... Francis Duke of Bedford. [Attributed to John Bowles.] 2nd ed. Printed for F. and C. Rivington; W. and J. Richardson; W. Hatchard; and Cobbett and Morgan; by G. Woodfall, [1802]. 8°

T.615

8132

A LETTER to the Hon. Charles James Fox, on the death of his Grace the late Duke of Bedford... London: R. Bostock; and published by J. Whittle. Sold by Cobbett and Morgan; Chapple; and all other booksellers, 1802. 8°

T.615

8133

PEALE (Rembrandt)

Account of the skeleton of the mammoth, a non-descript carnivorous animal of immense size, found in America. London: E. Lawrence, 1802. 8°

Signature of E. Hawkins.

T.808

8134

POPE (Simeon)

Considerations, political, financial, and commercial, relative to the important subject of the public funds... London, Wilson and Co. Oriental Press, 1802. 8°

T.563

8135

POULTER (Edmund)

Proposals for a new arrangement of the revenue, and residence of the clergy. [Winchester, Jacob, 1802.] 8°

T.570

8136

REMARKS on a pamphlet by Thomas Kipling, D.D. Dean of Peterborough entitled "The articles of the Church of England proved not to be Calvinistic." By Academicus. Cambridge, printed at the University Press; and sold by J. Deighton, Cambridge; J. Mawman; J. Hatchard; J. Matthews; Cooke, Oxford; and Todd, York, 1802. 8°

A manuscript attribution to [Joseph] Jowett LL.D. of Trin. Hall.

T.769

8137

REMARKS on the Rev. Dr. Vincent's defence of public education... By a layman... 2nd ed. London: for J. Hatchard, 1802. 8°

Signature of J. Dampier, 1803.

T.571

8138

SCOTT (William) *Baron Stowell.*

Substance of the speech of the Right Honourable Sir William Scott, delivered in the House of Commons... upon a motion for leave to bring in a bill, relative to the non-residence of the clergy... London: Cobbett and Morgan, and White, May, 1802. 8°

T.615

8139

STURGES (John)

Thoughts on the residence of the clergy and on the provisions of the statute of the twenty-first year of Henry VIII.c.13. The second edition, with additions. Printed by Robbins, Winchester: and sold by him, and Cadell, jun. and Davies, London, 1802. 8°

Signature of J. Dampier. 1803.

T.570

8140

SUMNER (John Bird) *Archbishop of Canterbury.*

An essay tending to show that the prophecies, now accomplishing, are an evidence of the truth of the Christian religion... Cambridge, J. Burges, printer to the University; and sold by J. Deighton [and others], 1802. 8°

T.615

8141

VINCENT (William)

A defence of public education, addressed to... the Lord Bishop of Meath. In answer to a charge annexed to his Lordship's discourse preached at St. Paul's, on the anniversary meeting of the charity children... 3rd ed. London: A. Strahan, for T. Cadell jun. and W. Davies, 1802. 8°

Signature of J. Dampier, 1803.

T.571

8142

WATSON (Richard) *Bishop of Llandaff.*

A charge delivered to the clergy of the diocese of Landaff, in June, 1802. London: for T. Cadell, jun. and W. Davies, 1802. 4°

T.718

1803

8143

The ATROCITIES of the Corsican demon; or a glance at Buonaparte... London: printed at the Minerva-Press, for Lane, Newman, and Co., 1803. 8°

T.563

8144

DAMPIER (Thomas) *Bishop of Ely.*

A charge delivered to the clergy of the diocese of Rochester, at the primary visitation of Thomas, Lord Bishop of Rochester. 1803. London: Luke Hansard; for T. Payne, 1803. 4°

T.718

8145

DIXON (John)

Improvement of the fisheries; letter IV. or, A plan for establishing a nursery for disbanded seamen and soldiers, and increasing the strength and security of the British Empire. London: for G. and W. Nichol; by J. Brettell, 1803. 4°

T.561

8146

GIFFORD (William)

An examination of the strictures of the critical reviewers on the translation of Juvenal... London: for J. Hatchard, 1803. 4°

T.534

8147

GORDON (*Sir* Adam)

The necessity and benefit of preaching the Gospel. A sermon preached at the visitation of... Beilby, Lord Bishop of London, held at Brentwood, on Wednesday, June 1, 1803... London: printed for the author, by Bye and Law: and sold by Messrs. Rivingtons, and Hatchard, 1803. 8°

Stamp of F.I.H. Wollaston.

T.769

8148

HOOK (James)

A sketch of the true character of the Church of England, and her clergy... 3rd ed. London: D.N. Shury, for J. Ginger. Sold also by Hanwell and Parker, Oxford; and Deighton, Cambridge, 1803. 8°

T.570

8149

HOWELL (Thomas Bayly)

Observations on Dr. Sturges's pamphlet respecting non-residence of the clergy; in a letter... to Mr. Baron Maseres... 2nd ed. London: for J. Hatchard; Rivingtons; and Robson, 1803. 8°

Signature of J. Dampier, 1803.

T.570

8150

LETTER to the Rev. Dr. Goodall, head master of Eton School; on the importance of a religious education. London: for John Stockdale, 1803. 8°

Signature of J. Dampier, 1803.

T.571

8151

MACALISTER (Norman)

Historical memoir relative to Prince of Wales Island, in the straits of Malacca: and its importance political and commercial... London: printed, for the author, by J.H. Hart, 1803. 4°

"For Lord Pelham with Sir J. Macpherson's best respects, 1804."

T.561

8152

A REPLY to the Anguis in herba of the Rev. James Hook. Containing a refutation of his defence of pluralities, non-residence, and the employment of substitutes by the beneficed clergy. By a member of the Established Church... London: for J. Mawman, 1803. By T. Gillet. 8°

Signature by J. Dampier, 1803.

T.570

8153

THOUGHTS on non-residence and farming. In a letter to the Bishop of Saint Asaph. By a magistrate... London: J.D. Dewick, for John Cawthorn; and sold by J. Hatchard; C. Chapple, and R. Dutton, 1803. 8°

Signature of J. Dampier, 1803.

T.570

8154

TOMLINE (George Pretyman) *Bishop of Winchester.*

A charge delivered to the clergy of the diocese of Lincoln, at the triennial visitation of that diocese in May and June 1803. London: for Cadell and Davies; Rivingtons; White; Hatchard; Lunn; Deighton, Cambridge; Cooke and Hanwell & Parker, Oxford; Brooke, Lincoln; and Longland, Huntingdon, 1803. 4°

T.718

8155

A VINDICATION of the clergy, in regard to residence; with observations on the bill now before Parliament. By a resident clergyman... London, A. Wilson, for J. Debrett, 1803. 8°

Signature of J. Dampier, 1803. A Manuscript attribution to the Revd. Mr. Greenwood.

T.570

8156

WAKEFIELD (Thomas)

A sermon, on occasion of the threatened invasion, preached at Richmond, Surry, on Sunday, July 31, and... August 7, 1803. Richmond: G.A. Wall. Sold also by T. Hurst; and J. Hatchard, [1803]. 8°

T.723

1804

8157

An ADDRESS to the Society of Friends, commonly called Quakers, on their excommunicating such of their members as marry those of other religious professions ... London, Thomas Clio Rickman; Johnson; Symonds; Griffiths; and all booksellers, 1804. 8°

"To the Editor of the Antijacobin Review, 1804."

T.794

8158

FALCONER (Thomas)

A letter to the Rev. Richard Warner. [Signed T.F.] Bath, R. Cruttwell; and sold by G. and J. Robinson, London, 1804. 8°

T.750

8159

IVERNOIS (*Sir* Francis d')

Immenses préparatifs de guerre qui eurent lieu en France d'abord après le Traité d'Amiens. Fragment d'un exposé historique des événemens qui ont amené la rupture de ce traité. A Londres de l'imprimerie de Cox, Fils, et Baylis. Se trouve chez Deboffe; Dulau et Co.; Prosper; de Conchi, Mars 1804. 8°

T.737

8160

PICTON (*Sir* Thomas)

A letter to the Rt. Hon. Lord Hobart... By Colonel Thomas Picton, late governor and captain general of the island of Trinidad... London: D.N. Shury, for E. Lloyd, 1804. 8°

T.737

8161

SEYER (Samuel)

Observations on the causes of clerical non-residence, and on the Act of Parliament lately passed for its prevention. [Anon.] London: for G. and J. Robinson, 1804. 8°

Signature of J. Dampier, 1804.

T.570

8162

TYRWHITT (Robert)

Baptismal faith explained. A sermon, preached before the University of Cambridge, April 8, 1804. London: for J. Mawman, 1804. By T. Gillet. 4°

Signature of Lord Henry Fitzroy, 1804.

T.823

1805

8163

BENSON (Martin) *Bishop of Gloucester.*

A sermon preached before the House of Lords, in the abbey-church of Westminster, on Monday, January 30th, 1737/8... 4th ed. London: for F.C. and J. Rivington; by Bye and Law, 1805. 8°

T.769

8164

D. (W.)

An authentic narrative of the loss of the Earl of Abergavenny East Indiaman... on the night of the 5th of Feb. 1805... By a gentleman in the East-India-House... London: printed at the Minerva Press; for Lane, Newman, and Co. and sold by Asperne; Symonds; and Chapple, 1805. 8°

T.750

8165

FISHER (John) *Bishop of Salisbury.*

A charge delivered to the clergy of the diocese of Exeter, at the primary visitation of John, Lord Bishop of Exeter, 1804 and 1805. Exeter, Trewman and Son, for T. Beckett, 1805. 4°

T.703

8166

JAMAICA. *House of Assembly.*

House of Assembly. Veneris, 23° die Novembris, 1804. [Report of a committee on the abolition of the slave trade.] [No imprint, 1805?] 4°

T.561

8167

LAW (George)

The limit to our enquiries, with respect to the nature and attributes of the deity. A sermon preached before the University of Cambridge, on commencement Sunday, July 1, 1804. 2nd ed. London: J. Brettell: for R. Faulder; F.C. and J. Rivington; and J. Deighton, Cambridge, 1805. 4°

T.703

8168

LE MESURIER (Thomas)

A serious examination of the Roman Catholic claims, as set forth in the petition, now pending before Parliament. London: Barnard and Sultzer, for F.C. and J. Rivington, and J. Hatchard; J. Cooke, and Hanwell & Parker, Oxford, 1805. 8°

Signature of J.J. Rye.

T.759

8169

M'KENNA (Theobald)

Thoughts on the civil condition and relations of the Roman Catholic clergy, religion and people, in Ireland... London: for J. Budd, Feb. 1805. 8°

T.758

8170

MEDICAL AND CHIRURGICAL SOCIETY OF LONDON.

Statutes of the Medical and Chirurgical Society, of London. London: Phillips and Fardon, 1805. 4°

T.560

1805 (Cont'd)

8171

POPHAM (*Sir* Home)

Concise statement of facts, relative to the treatment experienced by Sir Home Popham, since his return from the Red Sea... London: for John Stockdale, 1805. 8°

T.737

8172

POTT (Joseph Holden)

Considerations on the general conditions of the Christian covenant; with a view to some important controversies. The second edition; with corrections and additions. London: for F.C. and J. Rivington; By Bye and Law, 1805. 8°

T.621

8173

RATHBONE (William)

A memoir of the proceedings of the society called Quakers, belonging to the monthly meeting of Hardshaw, in Lancashire, in the case of the author of a publication, entitled A narrative of events which have lately taken place in Ireland, &c... Liverpool, J. M'Creery, for J. Johnson, London; sold also by Gilbert and Hodges, Dublin, 1805. 8°

T.794

8174

VENN (John) *Rector of Clapham.*

A sermon preached at the parish church of St. Andrew by the Wardrobe... June 4, 1805, before the Society for Missions to Africa and the East... London: C. Whittingham, 1805. 8°

T.769

1806

8175

ASPLAND (Robert)

The fall of eminent men in critical periods a national calamity. A sermon preached at the Gravel-Pit meeting, Hackney... on occasion of the recent death of the Rt. Hon. Charles James Fox... London: C. Stower, for Longman, Hurst, Rees and Orme, 1806. 8°

T.825

8176

CONSTANT DE REBECQUE (Samuel)

Dernieres pensées du grand Frédéric, roi de Prusse, écrites de sa main à Berlin, en 1786. [Anon.] Se vend a Paris, chez Chapelle, Desenne, et chez tous les marchands de nouveautés, an XIV, 1806. 8°

T.601

8177

DAUBENY (Charles)

A sermon, preached at Christ-church, Bath, on Wednesday, February 26, 1806, being the day appointed... for a general fast. London: for F.C. and J. Rivington. Sold also by J. Hatchard, 1806. 4°

T.703

8178

HORSLEY (Samuel) *Bishop of St. Asaph.*

A charge to the clergy at the primary visitation in the month of August 1806, of the late... Samuel ... Lord Bishop of St. Asaph. London: for J. Hatchard, [by S. Gosnell], 1806. 4°

T.718

8179

LAUNAY (Emmanuel Henri Alexandre de) *Comte d'Antraigues.*

Traduction d'un fragment du XVIII livre de Polybe, trouvé dans le monastère de Sainte-Laure au Mont Athos, par le Comte d'Antraigues... Nouvelle edition, avouée par l'auteur. (Requête des bourgeois de la ville d'Anspach a sa Majesté le roi de Prusse...) A Londres: de l'imprimerie de Harper et co., 1806. 2 parts. 8°

T.601

8180

LE MESURIER (Thomas)

A sermon preached before the Archdeacon of Bucks, at his visitation held at Stoney Stratford on Friday, May 2, 1806. Oxford, at the University Press, for the author; sold by J. Cooke, and J. Parker; also by Messrs. Rivington, and J. Hatchard, London; Marlin, Aylesbury; and Inwood, Newport Pagnel, 1806. 8°

Signature of Jos. Jekyll Rye.

T.759

8181

A LETTER to Nathaniel Jefferys... on the subject of his extraordinary pamphlet, entitled, "A review of the conduct of his Royal Highness the Prince of Wales, &c. &c. &c."... London: W. Flint, for J. Mawman; and sold by all the booksellers at the west end of the town, 1806. 8°

T.750

8182

PORTEUS (Beilby) *Bishop of London.*

The beneficial effects of Christianity on the temporal concerns of mankind, proved from history and from facts. London: Luke Hansard, for T. Payne, and T. Cadell and W. Davies, 1806. 8°

Signature of Anne Jesse Cholmley, 1806.

T.723

8183

SKETCH of the character of Mrs Elizabeth Carter, who died in London, on February the 19th, 1806, in the eighty-ninth year of her age. Kelso: A. Ballantyne, 1806. 8°

"Anne Jesse Cholmley - given to her by Mrs. Ord, London, 1806."

T.723

8184

SYMMONS (Charles)

A sermon, preached in the parish church of Richmond, in Surrey, October 12, 1806. London: T. Bensley, 1806. 8°

T.825

1807

8185

BOSANQUET (Charles)

A letter to W. Manning, Esq. M.P. on the causes of the rapid and progressive depreciation of West India property. 2nd ed. London: S. & C. McDowall, and sold by Richardsons; and Stockdale, [1807]. 8°

T.737

8186

DAMPIER (Thomas) *Bishop of Ely.*

A charge delivered to the clergy of the diocese of Rochester, at the ordinary visitation of Thomas, Lord Bishop of Rochester. 1807. London: Luke Hansard and sons, for T. Payne, 1807. 4°

"From the author to R.F. Hallifax."

T.718

8187

FISHER (John) *Rector of Wavendon.*

The utility of the Church establishment, and its safety consistent with religious freedom; a sermon, preached... at the assizes held at Buckingham, on Tuesday 14th July, 1807. Buckingham: J. Seeley; sold also by Inwood, Newport Pagnel; Marlin, Aylesbury; Hunt, Stony Stratford; and Loftus, Banbury, 1807. 8°

T.758

8188

LE MESURIER (Thomas)

A reply to certain observations of the Right Reverend Dr. Milner, upon the sequel to the Serious examination of the Roman Catholic claims... London: T. Curson Hansard. Sold by Messrs. Rivingtons; Hatchard; Richardsons; Cooke and Parker, Oxford; Deighton, Cambridge; and Inwood, Newport Pagnell, 1807. 8°

T.759

8189

LE MESURIER (Thomas)

A sequel to the Serious examination into the Roman Catholic claims... London: T. Curson Hansard. Sold by Messrs. Rivingtons; Hatchard; Richardson's; Cooke and Parker, Oxford; Deighton, Cambridge; and Inwood, Newport Pagnell, 1807. 2 parts. 8°

T.759

8190

PHILLPOTTS (Henry) *Bishop of Exeter.*

A sermon, preached at Durham, July 17, 1806, at the visitation of the Honourable and Right Reverend... Shute, Lord Bishop of Durham. London: W. Bulmer and Co.; and sold by F. and C. Rivington, and J. Hatchard; Hanwell and Parker, Oxford; Deighton, Cambridge; and the booksellers at Durham and Newcastle, 1807. 4°

T.703

8191

SMITH (Sydney)

A sermon preached at the Temple... upon the conduct to be observed by the Established Church towards Catholics and other dissenters. London: for James Carpenter; and Longman, Hurst, Rees, and Orme, 1807. 8°

T.825

8192

SYMMONS (Charles)

An historical memoir of the late Rev. Thomas Wakefield, B.A. minister of Richmond in Surry... London: T. Bensley, 1807. 8°

T.825

8193

SYMONS (Jelinger)

A letter to the Right Honourable Lord Viscount Howick, on the subject of the Catholic Bill; by the author of Unity the bond of peace... London: I. Gold; for Messrs. Rivington; Hatchard; and Richardson, 1807. 8°

Signature of J.J. Rye.

T.758

8194

WILSON (Harry Bristow)

A letter to Lord Grenville upon the repeated publication of his letter to the secretary of the Society for Promoting Christian Knowledge, in consequence of their resolution with respect to his Majesty's late conduct. London: W. Wilson. And sold by Messrs. F.C. and J. Rivington; Messrs. Richardson; and J. Hatchard, 1807. 8°

T.758

1808

8195

CLOWES (John)

Elijah's mantle; or, The double portion of the divine spirit, considered in a sermon. Birmingham, printed for a Society of Gentlemen, by S. and T. Martin, 1808. 8°

T.725

8196

COPENHAGEN. The real state of the case respecting the late expedition. London: for J. Ridgway, 1808. 8°

T.737

8197

HAWKER (Robert)

A letter to a barrister [i.e. James Sedgwick], in answer to Hints to the public and the legislature, on the nature and effect of evangelical preaching... London: J. Dennett; for Williams and Smith, 1808. 8°

T.770

8198

HAWKER (Robert)

A second letter to a barrister [i.e. James Sedgwick], in reply to the second part of his Hints to the public and the legislature, on the nature and effect of evangelical preaching... London: J. Dennett; for Williams and Smith, 1808. 8°

T.770

8199

PEARSON (John Norman)

A critical essay on the ninth book of Bishop Warburton's Divine legation of Moses ... Cambridge: R. Watts, University printer: and sold by Deighton, Cambridge; and Hatchard, London, 1808. 8°

T.352

8200

POTT (Joseph Holden)

Religious education, as it constitutes one branch of the discipline of the Church of England, considered in a charge delivered to the clergy of the archdeaconry of St. Alban's... London: for F.C. and J. Rivington; by Law and Gilbert, 1808. 4°

T.711

8201

STYLES (John)

A vindication of the nature and effect of evangelical preaching; in a letter to a barrister [i.e. James Sedgwick]: occasioned by the first part of his Hints to the public and the legislature... London: for Williams and Smith, [1808]. 8°

T.770

1809

8202

DEALTRY (William)

A sermon preached in the chapel of the East-India College, Herts, on Sunday, November 12, 1809. London: printed for the author, by Ellerton and Byworth, 1809. 8°

T.621

8203

HAWKER (Robert)

A third letter to a barrister [i.e. James Sedgwick], in answer to the third part of his Hints to the public and legislature, on the nature and effect of evangelical preaching... London: W. Nicholson, for Williams & Smith, 1809. 8°

T.770

8204

HULL (William) *and others*.

Discourses delivered at the ordination of the Rev. William Hull, to the pastoral office... in the congregational church at Norwich, June 29, 1809... London: for Williams and Smith: and sold by Annis, Parsons, and Booth, Norwich; Youngman, Witham, and all other booksellers in Norfolk, Suffolk and Essex, [1809]. 8°

T.572

8205

A LETTER addressed to Wm. Smith, Esq. M.P. for Norwich, shewing that his political conduct has rendered him no longer deserving the support of his constituents. By a freeman of the city... Norwich: printed for the author by Booth and Wright, and sold by W. Booth, 1809. 8°

T.563

8206

LUCAS, *pseud*.

Lucas's letters to Earl Moira, as they successively appeared in the British Guardian newspaper; on the present alarming juncture of the country, and particularly as to the necessity of an immediate reform. J. Lettice, and sold at the British Guardian office; and may be had of all the booksellers in town and country, [1809?] 8°

T.737

8207

OPERATIONS of the British army in Spain; involving broad hints to the commissariat, and board of transports... By an officer of the staff. London: J. Dennett; for T. Egerton; and Sherwood, Neely, and Jones, 1809. 8°

T.737

8208

POTT (Joseph Holden)

A charge delivered to the clergy of the archdeaconry of St. Alban's, at the visitation, holden May 24, A.D. 1809. (Connected with a former on religious education.) London: for F.C. and J. Rivington; and R. Floyer; by Law and Gilbert, 1809. 4°

T.711

8209

TWO letters to "a barrister" [i.e. James Sedgwick] containing strictures on his work in three parts, entitled, Hints to the public and the legislature, on the nature and effect of evangelical preaching. By a looker on... Oxford: printed and sold by J. Bartlett; sold also by Black, Parry, and Kingsbury, London, 1809. 8°

T.770

8210

VAUGHAN (Charles Richard)

Narrative of the siege of Zaragoza. The fifth edition, with corrections and additions. London: for James Ridgway, 1809. 8°

T.750

1810

8211

BURDETT (*Sir* Francis)

The address of Sir Francis Burdett to his constituents, in a letter ... denying the power of the House of Commons to imprison the people of England ... London: T. Broom, and sold by all the booksellers, [1810]. 8°

T.563

8212

EXTRACTS from Lord Chatham, Burke, Junius, &c. To which are prefixed remarks on the power of commitment, in cases of libel, recently claimed by the House of Commons... London: for J. Ridgway, 1810. 8°

T.749

8213

HAWKER (Peter)

Journal of a regimental officer during the recent campaign in Portugal and Spain under Lord Viscount Wellington... [Anon.] London: for J. Johnson, 1810. 8°

T.737

8214

HINTS to the public and legislature, on the nature and effect of evangelical preaching. Part the fifth: addressed to the author [i.e. James Sedgwick] of part the fourth... London: published by J. Burditt: printed by Burditt and Morris, 1810. 8°

T.770

8215

HOURGLASS (Humphrey) *pseud*.

The mouse-trap maker and the income tax, a tale, supposed, by anticipation, to be written in the year 2000... By Humphrey Hourglass... London: printed for the author, by W. Newman, [c. 1810?] 8°

"Mr. Smith, with the author's comp."

T.563

8216

LECKIE (Gould Francis)

Historical survey of the foreign affairs of Great Britain, for the year 1810. London: for Edmund Lloyd, 1810. 8°

2 copies.

T.749 T.601

8217

MILLER (Samuel)

Mr. Miller to his constituents [the freemen-householders of the ward of Farringdon Without]. London: W. Burton, [1810]. 8°

T.563

8218

MILNER (John) *Roman Catholic Bishop*.

The substance of a sermon, preached at the blessing of the Catholic chapel of St. Chad, in the town of Birmingham, on Sunday, December 17, 1809. Birmingham; C. Wilks. Also sold by Keating and Co. [and others], [1810?]. 8°

T.566

8219

MONK (James Henry) *Bishop of Gloucester and Bristol*.

A letter to the Rev. Samuel Butler M.A. head master of Shrewsbury school from the Rev. James Henry Monk ... with Mr. Butler's answer. Cambridge: printed at the University Press; and sold by J. Deighton, Cambridge; and T. Payne, and J. Mawman, London, 1810. 8°

Signature of John William Mackie.

T.749

8220

REASONS for reform: or, A brief consideration of our representative system... in a letter, addressed to the freeholders and inhabitants of Cornwall. By a friend to moderate reform. Second edition, with additions... Truro: printed at the Royal Cornwall Gazette office, by T. Flindell, 1810. 8°

T.749

8221

SARRAZIN (Jean)

Réponse du Général Sarrazin au rapport fait au Général Bonaparte par le Général Clarke, ministre de la guerre. A Londres, imprimé pour l'auteur, par R. Juigné, 1810. 8°

T.601

8222

The STATE of the Established Church; in a series of letters to the Right Hon. Spencer Perceval... Second edition, corrected and enlarged... London: for J.J. Stockdale, 1810. 8°

T.569

1811

8223

GOURLAY (William)

Observations on the natural history, climate and diseases of Madeira, during a period of eighteen years. London for J. Callow, by J. Smith, 1811. 8°

T.748

8224

INTERESTING naval trial. Minutes of a court martial ... for the trial of Lieut. W.G. Carlile Kent, late acting commander of H.M.S. Porpoise... on charges exhibited against him by... William Bligh... Portsmouth; Mottley, Harrison, & Miller; and sold in London by W. Kent; J. Miller; and sold by all booksellers at the sea ports, &c., 1811. 8°

T.737

8225

LEMPRIERE (William)

Report on the medicinal effects of an aluminous chalybeate spring, lately discovered at Sandrocks ... in the Isle of Wight... Newport, Musson and Taylor, and sold by John Murray; Nornanville and Fell; and W. and J. Rowdens, Newport, [1811]. 8°

T.748

8226

O'CONNELL (Daniel)

Historical account of the laws against the Roman-Catholics of England... [Anon.] Printed by Luke Hansard & Sons, for Keating, Brown, & Co.; Booker & Faulder; Ridgway; Budd, London; - and Fitzpatrick & Coyne, Dublin, 1811. 8°

T.566

1812

8227

ALLEN (Edward)

An argument addressed to his Majesty's royal commissioners in the island of Jersey... Comprising an epitome of the history of that island, from the remotest periods of antiquity... London: for W. Clarke and Sons, 1812. 8°

T.722

8228

CARSON (William)

A letter to the members of Parliament of the United Kingdom of Great Britain & Ireland, on the address of the merchants and inhabitants of Saint Johns, in the island of Newfoundland, to the Prince Regent. Greenock: William Scott, 1812. 8°

T.722

8229

CATALOGUE of a library of books, to be sold by auction, on Monday the 20th January (and seven following days), at No. 77, Dame-Street... Dublin: Espy & Cross, 1812. 4°

Addressed to Wm. Shaw Mason Esq., Stephen Street.

T.693

8230

A COMMENTARY on the proceedings of the Catholics of Ireland, during the reign of his present Majesty George the third... Dublin, printed: London: reprinted for J.J. Stockdale, 1812. 8°

T.722

1812 (Cont'd)

8231
GANDOLPHY (Peter)

A congratulatory letter to the Rev. Herbert Marsh ... on his judicious inquiry into the consequences of neglecting to give the prayer-book with the Bible ... London: printed and published for the author, by Keating, Brown and Keating: and also sold by Booker; Bartlett, Oxford; Wright, Cambridge; Todd, York; Sharrock, Preston; and Fitzpatrick, Dublin, 1812. 8°

T.566

8232
HACKETT (Maria)

Letters to the Bishop of London, the Dean of Saint Paul's, and other dignitaries of that church, on the present state of the choristers... 2nd ed. London: Nichols, son, and Bentley, 1812. 2 parts. 4°

T.560

8233
HUME (Joseph)

Copy of a letter addressed to... the Chancellor of the Exchequer, and the substance of a speech... on the third reading of the Bill... for preventing frauds and abuses in the frame-work-knitting manufacture... London: for J. Stockdale, 1812. 8°

"To Mr. Smith with Mr. Hume's compts."

T.563

8234
MAUNOIR (Jean Pierre)

Questions de chirurgie, proposées par MM. Ch.-Louis Dumas [and others] pour la chaire de clinique externe, vacante, dans la Faculté de Médecine de Montpellier... présentées à la dispute, le 3 Septembre 1812, par M. Jean-Pierre Maunoir. A Montpellier, de l'imprimerie de J.G. Tournel, 1812. 8°

T.748

8235
NOLAN (Frederick)

Objections of a churchman to uniting with the Bible Society: including a reply to the arguments advanced in favour of that association... London: for F.C. and J. Rivington; by Law and Gilbert, 1812. 8°

T.769

8236
OBSERVATIONS upon commercial terms of peace with France, and our own resources. By a London merchant. London: for Gale and Curtis, 1812. 8°

T.563

8237
TULLY (Edward)

The defence of Lieut. Edward Tully, of the seventy-fifth regiment of Foot. On his trial in Jersey, before a general court-martial. As it was read in court by his counsel Edward Allen... Printed for Goddard, London, and J. Stead, Jersey, 1812. 8°

T.722

8238
WESTON (George)

The defence of George Weston, Esq. paymaster of the 2d Battalion 96th Regiment, on his trial in Jersey, before a general court-martial... as prepared by his counsel, Messrs. Allen, le Couteur, and le Hardy. Jersey, J. De Fries, 1812. 8°

T.722

8239
WYNDHAM (Isabella)

An appeal to the gentlemen of England; or, Facts relating to the transactions between Colonel Greville and Mrs. Wyndham... London: for C. Chapple, 1812. 8°

T.737

1813

8240
BUTLER (Charles)

An address to the protestants of Great Britain and Ireland ... Second edition, with additions. London: sold by Booker; Keating & Co.; Longman & Co.; Ridgway; Cadell & Davies, 1813. Luke Hansard & Sons. 8°

T.566

8241
COOKE (John) *Chaplain to Greenwich Hospital.*

A description of the Royal Hospital for Seamen, at Greenwich; with a short account of the establishment; the chest at Greenwich; and the Royal Naval Asylum... Published by the chaplains, J. Cooke, J. Maule. London, W. Winchester and Son, 1813. 8°

Signature of Wm. Taylor.

T.779

8242
CRAMPTON (Philip)

The description of a newly discovered organ in the eyes of birds... Read before the Royal Society the 23d of January, 1812. Dublin: William Porter, 1813. 4°

T.577

8243
DOUGLAS (Frederic Sylvester North)

An essay on certain points of resemblance between the ancient and modern Greeks... London: for John Murray, 1813. 8°

"John William Mackie A.M. student of Ch. Ch. Oxford."

T.736

8244
EXTRACTS from the speeches and writings of eminent public characters, respecting the Catholic claims: with a few prefatory remarks ... London: sold by Booker, 1813. Luke Hansard & Sons. 8°

T.566

8245
FAVELL (Charles)

A catalogue of the entire collection of antient engravings, and books of prints, portraits, &c. of the Rev. C. Favell... which will be sold by auction, in Liverpool, by Mr. Broster... Bangor, John Broster, 1813. 4°

T.693

8246
FITZGIBBON (John) *Earl of Clare.*

The speech of the late Rt. Hon. John, Earl of Clare, Lord High Chancellor of Ireland: delivered in the Irish House of Peers on the second reading of the bill for the relief of his Majesty's Roman Catholic subjects, in Ireland, March 13, 1793 ... London: for J.J. Stockdale, 1813. 8°

T.576

8247
HOLLAND (Samuel)

The imputation upon the regular clergy of not preaching the Gospel briefly considered, in a visitation sermon, preached in St. Michael's church, Lewes, June 23, MDCCCXIII... Lewes: W. and A. Lee; and sold by them and F.C. and J. Rivington, 1813. 8°

T.705

8248
HORSLEY (Samuel) *Bishop of St. Asaph.*

Protestant authorities against concessions to the Roman Catholics; being speeches of the late Dr. Horsley, Lord Bishop of St. Asaph, and of Lord Ellenborough, delivered in the House of Lords, 13th May 1805... London: for J.J. Stockdale, 1813. 8°

T.576

8249
The RIGHTS of the Church, attested by historical documents. By the author of An analysis of Mr. Canning's speech... London: for J.J. Stockdale, 1813. 8°

T.576

8250
SLATER (Edward)

Letters on Roman Catholic tenets, as they have a reference to the duties of subjects living under Acatholic governments... Sold by Booker, and Hatchard, London; Todd, York; Kirkpatrick, Dublin; Kaye, Robinson, E. Smith, and Wright and Cruickshank, Liverpool, [1813]. 8°

T.566

8251
TOURNAY (William)

A sermon, preached in Lambeth chapel, on Sunday, the 12th of December, 1813, at the consecration of the Right Reverend John Parsons, D.D. Lord Bishop of Peterborough... Oxford: at the University Press, for J. Parker: and sold by Messrs. Rivington, and J. Hatchard, 1813. 4°

T.560

1814

8252
ADAIR (William)

An essay on the construction of penal statutes, with incidental observations on the Act 30 Geo. 2, c.24... Norwich: Stevenson, Matchett, and Stevenson, 1814. 8°

T.727

8253
BEILBY, *and Company.*

Bibliotheca selecta. A catalogue of a choice collection of rare and valuable books, on sale by Beilby and company, High Street, Birmingham. [No imprint, 1814?] 4°

T.693

8254
BROSTER (John)

Broster's catalogue of books, 1814... now selling at the shop of Broster and Son, booksellers and stationers, Exchange, Chester... [No imprint, 1814.] Large Fol.

T.693

8255
HOME (*Sir* Everard)

The Hunterian oration in honour of surgery... London: W. Bulmer, for G. and W. Nicol, 1814. 4°

T.560

8256
HUME (Joseph)

The substance of the speech of Joseph Hume, Esq. at a general court of proprietors at the East-India House... upon the motion for granting a pension of £2000 per annum, for ten years, to the present Lord Melville... London: for John Stockdale, [1814]. 8°

"Mr. Smith with Mr. Hume's Compts."

T.563

8257
HUME (Joseph)

The substance of the speech of Mr. Joseph Hume, at the East-India House... upon the motion for an increase of the salaries to the directors of the East-India Company... London: J. Innes, 1814. 8°

"To Mr. Smith with Mr. Hume's compts."

T.563

8258
NOEL (Gerard Thomas)

A sermon preached at... Christ's Church, Newgate-street, on Thursday, May 5, 1814, before the Prayer Book and Homily Society... London: Taylor and Hessey; and may be had of J. Hatchard, 1814. 8°

T.826

8259
ROYAL IRISH INSTITUTION FOR PROMOTING THE FINE ARTS IN IRELAND.

First exhibition, July 8, 1814. Dublin: John Jones, 1814. 4°

T.693

8260
SHOBERL (Frederic)

Narrative of the most remarkable events which occurred in and near Leipzig, immediately before, during, and subsequent to, the sanguinary series of engagements between the allied armies and the French, from the 14th to the 19th October, 1813... 8th ed. London: for R. Ackermann, by W. Clowes, 1814. 8°

Signature of Jno. Mackie M.D.

T.750

8261
SWIFT (Edmund Lewis Lenthal)

The ecclesiastical supremacy of the Crown proved to be the common law of England... By Basilicus. London: for J.J. Stockdale, 1814. 8°

T.576

8262
WEST (Benjamin)

Christ rejected. Catalogue of the picture, representing the above subject; together with sketches of other scriptural subjects; painted by Benjamin West. Now exhibiting... at... No. 125, Pall-Mall... London: C.H. Reynell, 1814. 8°

T.808

8263

YOUNG (John) *Keeper of the British Institution.*

A descriptive catalogue of the works of Hogarth, placed in the gallery of the British Institution for exhibition... London: William Bulmer, 1814. 4°

T.560

1815

8264

COXE (William)

Letter to John Benett, Esq. of Pyt-House, Wilts, on his essay relative to the commutation of tythes ... Salisbury: Brodie and Dowding; sold also by G. Wilkie, London; and by all other booksellers, [1815]. 8°

T.571

8265

EARDLEY-WILMOT (John)

Historical view of the Commission for enquiring into the losses, services, and claims, of the American loyalists, at the close of the war between Great Britain and her colonies, in 1783... London: J. Nichols, Son, and Bentley; and sold by them; and also by Longman and Co.; Cadell and Davies; and Hatchard, 1815. 8°

T.736

8266

GOURLAY (Robert)

The right to Church property secured, and commutation of tythes vindicated, in a letter to the Rev. William Coxe, Archdeacon of Wilts. London: for Highley and Son, 1815. 8°

T.571

8267

HALL (Robert) *Baptist Minister.*

On terms of communion, with a particular view to the case of the Baptists and pedobaptists... Leicester: Thomas Combe. Sold by Button and son, London; Deighton and sons, Cambridge; James, Bristol; and Combe, Leicester, 1815. 8°

T.575

8268

POLYDORUS (Joannes Gulielmus)

Disputatio medica inauguralis, quaedam de morbo, oneirodynia dicto, complectens... pro gradu doctoris... Edinburgi: excudebat Robertus Allan, 1815. 8°

"C.J. Smyth, from ye author."

T.572

8269

POTT (Joseph Holden)

St. Paul's comparison, between the law and the gospel, considered in a sermon. London, J. Harrison, 1815. 8°

T.621

8270

ROBINS, *Messrs.*

A catalogue of a matchless collection of miscellaneous property consigned from Paris, for absolute sale... Which will be sold by auction, by Messrs. Robins... on Friday, the 19th day of May, 1815... Printed by W. Smith and Co., [1815]. 4°

T.693

8271

VAUGHAN (Edward Thomas)

A sermon preached at the parish church of St. Andrew by the Wardrobe and St. Anne Blackfriars, on Tuesday, May 2, 1815, before the Church Missionary Society for Africa and the East... London: Whittingham and Rowland. Published by L.B. Seeley; and J. Hatchard. Sold, in Dublin, by Martin Keene, J. Parry, and T. Johnson; and, in Edinburgh, by Oliphant [and others], 1815. 8°

T.826

1816

8272

HUME (Joseph)

An account of the Provident Institution for savings, established in the western part of the Metropolis... London: sold by Mrs. Stockdale, 1816. 8°

"Mr. Smith with Mr. Humes compts."

T.563

8273

LLOYD (John) *of Wigfair.*

Collectanea Llwydii. To be sold by auction, by Mr. Broster, at Wygfair, near St. Asaph... January 15th, 1816, and twelve following days... the entire library, philosophical apparatus, &c. of John Lloyd ... Denbigh, Thomas Gee, [1816]. Fol.

Addressed to W.S. Mason, Esq., Dublin, and bearing the St. Asaph postmark.

T.693

8274

POTT (Joseph Holden)

Observations on some controversies respecting baptism. Printed by J. Harrison, 1816. 8°

T.621

8275

PROPOSALS for establishing in the Metropolis, a day school, in which an example may be set of the application of the methods of Dr. Bell, Mr. Lancaster, and others, to the higher branches of education. London: J. M'Creedy, 1816. 8°

Mr. Smith with Mr. Hume's compts."

T.563

8276

REMARKS on a sermon preached by the Rev. T. Le Mesurier... in which the invocation of angels and saints, as now practised in the Church of Rome, is attempted to be shewn to be idolatrous... London: W.E. Andrews; and sold by Sherwood [and others], 1816. 8°

T.572

8277

RYAN (James)

A letter from Mr. James Ryan... on his method of ventilating coal mines... London: for the Society [for the encouragement of arts, manufactures, and commerce], by R. Wilks; and sold by Messrs. Cadell and Davies [and others], 1816. 8°

T.563

1817

8278

CARLISLE (*Sir* Anthony)

An essay on the disorders of old age, and on the means for prolonging human life... London: for Longman, Hurst, Rees, Orme, and Brown, 1817. 8°

"John William Mackie."

T.748

8279

Y DULL yr aeth y byd o chwith: neu'r modd y cynhyddodd trais, ymchwydd, a balchder, nes dwyn y bobl i'r sefyllfa athrist bresenol... [Attributed to Thomas Williams, Gwilym Morganwg.] Merthyr Tydfil: argraphwyd, tros yr awdwr, gan W. Williams, 1817. 8°

T.805

8280

FAWKES (Walter)

The Englishman's manual; or, A dialogue between a Tory and a Reformer. 3rd ed. London: for Longman, Hurst, and Co.; and for the booksellers in York, Leeds, Hull, Halifax, Huddersfield, Bradford, Wakefield, &c. By Edward Baines, Leeds, 1817. 8°

T.781

8281

GASCOIGNE (Henry Barnet)

Suggestions for the employment of the poor of the Metropolis, and the direction of their labours to the benefit of the inhabitants ... London: printed for the author; and published by Baldwin, Cradock, and Joy, 1817. 8°

T.563

8282

GIRDLESTONE (John Lang)

A sketch of the foundation of the Christian Church, according to holy Scripture... Part I. London: for Longman, Hurst, Rees, Orme, and Brown, 1817. 8°

T.572

8283

GREAT BRITAIN. *Parliament. House of Commons.*

Report from the committee of the honourable House of Commons on the employment of boys in sweeping of chimneys... Published under the direction of the Society for superseding the necessity of climbing boys... London: for Baldwin, Cradock, and Joy, 1817. 8°

"Given to me by Mr. W. Tooke."

2 copies.

T.563 T.574

8284

HENSMAN (John)

The faithfulness of Christ to his promise. A sermon preached at Clifton church, May 11th, 1817, on occasion of the death of... Lady Edward O'Bryen... [No imprint, 1817.] 8°

T.826

8285

LEO (Christopher)

An examination of the fourteen verses selected from Scripture, by Mr. J. Bellamy, as a specimen of his emendation of the Bible. Cambridge: J. Smith, printer to the University; and sold by Deighton & sons, and Nicholson & son, and T. Barrett, Cambridge; and F. & C. Rivington, and J. Hatchard, London; and Parker, Oxford, 1817. 8°

T.572

8286

LINGARD (John)

Observations on the laws and ordinances, which exist in foreign states, relative to the religious concerns of their Roman Catholic subjects. London: Keating, Brown and Co. Sold also by Booker; Sherwood and Co; and all other booksellers, 1817. 8°

T.566

8287

MUZARELLI (Alphonsus)

A treatise on the supremacy of St. Peter; the extent of papal jurisdiction; the powers of patriarchs, primates and metropolitans, and the source of episcopal jurisdiction. Translated from the French by the Rev. J. Cunningham. Dublin: printed for the translator, by N. Clarke, 1817. 8°

T.566

8288

PHILLIPS (Charles)

Two speeches on the Catholic question... London: W. Hone, 1817. 8°

T.566

8289

SADLER (Michael Thomas)

A first letter to a reformer, in reply to a pamphlet lately published by Walter Fawkes... entitled The Englishman's manual... London: for Longman, Hurst, Rees, Orme, and Brown; and Robinson, Son, and Holdsworth, Leeds, 1817. 8°

T.781

8290

WILLIAMS (David) *Founder of the Royal Literary Fund.*

Lectures on political principles, the subjects of eighteen books, in Montesquieu's Spirit of laws: read to students under the author's direction. Merthyr Tydfil: W. Williams; and sold in London, by Longman, Hurst, Rees, Orme, and Brown, 1817. 8°

T.805

8291

WILSON (Daniel) *Bishop of Calcutta.*

The doctrine of regeneration practically considered: a sermon, preached before the University of Oxford... London: for J. Hatchard, 1817. 8°

T.826

8292

WILSON (Daniel) *Bishop of Calcutta.*

The duty of contentment under present circumstances: a sermon, preached at St. John's, Bedford Row, London, on Sunday, March 9 and 16, 1817... London: J. Hatchard, 1817. 8°

T.826

1818

8293

BATHURST (Henry) *Archdeacon of Norwich.*

Christianity and present politics how far reconcilable: in a letter to the Right Hon. W. Wilberforce... London: for J. Ridgway, 1818.   8°

Signature of C.J. Smyth.

T.572

8294

BRIGGS (John)

A sermon preached at Brentwood chapel, on Thursday, July 30th, 1818, at the second visitation of... William, Lord Bishop of London... London: printed for the author, and sold by Messrs. Rivingtons; J. Hatchard; and William Walker, 1818.   8°

"The Rev. Archdeacon Wollaston, with the author's kind regards".

T.621

8295

BUXTON (Thomas Fowell)

An inquiry, whether crime and misery are produced or prevented, by our present system of prison discipline... London: for John and Arthur Arch; Butterworth and Sons; and John Hatchard, 1818.   8°

T.727

8296

CLARKE (Liscombe)

A letter to H. Brougham... in reply to the strictures on Winchester College, contained in his letter to Sir Samuel Romilly. London: for J. Hatchard, by W. Jacob, Winchester, 1818.   8°

T.572

8297

DUNDAS (*Sir* David)

The Hunterian oration, delivered before the Royal College of Surgeons ... London: for J. Callow, by W. Bulmer, 1818.   4°

T.560

8298

MACNAB (Henry Grey)

Analysis and analogy recommended as the means of rendering experience and observation useful in education... Paris: M. Nouzou, 1818.   4°

T.560

8299

MASON (Henry Joseph Monck)

An essay on the nature, and symbolical character, of the cherubim of the Jews. Dublin: Graisberry and Campbell, 1818.   4°

"To the Solicitor General from the author."

T.577

8300

MORE remarks on the theatre: addressed to those who will take the trouble to read them. By a churchman... Leeds: printed at the Intelligencer-office, by G. Wright, jun., 1818.   8°

"To Brother Wm. Taylor, P.G. Treas. with the fraternal regards of the author."

T.781

8301

OWEN (Robert)

New view of society. Tracts relative to this subject; viz. Proposals for raising a colledge of industry of all useful trades and husbandry. By John Bellers... Report to the committee of the Association for the relief of the manufacturing and labouring poor. A brief sketch of the religious society of people called Shakers. With an account of the public proceedings connected with the subject, which took place in London in July and August 1817. London: for Longman [and others], 1818. 4 parts.   8°

T.749

8302

POTT (Joseph Holden)

Considerations for the candidates for confirmation, to be used before and after that important period of the Christian life. London: Cood and Adams, 1818.   8°

T.621

8303

POTT (Joseph Holden)

A sermon preached after the notice given of the day fixed for confirmation in the parish of St. Martin in the Fields. London: Cood and Adams, 1818.   8°

T.621

8304

SOTHEBY (William)

Farewell to Italy, and occasional poems. London: W. Bulmer, 1818.   4°

T.560

8305

WAINEWRIGHT (Reader)

Letters to a protestant divine, in defence of Unitarianism; by another barrister... [Anon.] London: Richard and Arthur Taylor: and sold by R. Hunter; and D. Eaton, 1818.   8°

T.572

1819

8306

BARKER (Henry Aston)

Description of a view of the north coast of Spitzbergen, now exhibiting in the large rotunda of Henry Aston Barker's panorama, Leicester-square; painted from drawings taken by Lieut. Beechey... London: Jas. W. and Chas. Adlard, 1819.   8°

T.808

8307

BENNETT (Henry Grey)

Letter to Viscount Sidmouth... on the transportation laws, the state of the hulks, and of the colonies in New South Wales. London: for J. Ridgway, 1819.   8°

T.727

8308

CHRISTIAN (Edward) *Chief Justice of Ely.*

A vindication of the criminal law, and the administration of public justice in England, from the imputation of cruelty... London: Richard Watts, for Clarke and Sons, 1819.   8°

T.727

8309

CROKER (John Wilson)

Substance of the speech of John Wilson Croker, Esq. in the House of Commons ... on the Roman Catholic question. London: John Murray, 1819.   8°

T.576

8310

DEALTRY (William)

The dispositions and conduct required of Christians towards their rulers; and the tendency of infidelity to promote a spirit of disloyalty. A sermon, preached at the parish church of Clapham, in Surrey, on Sunday, November 7, 1819. London: Tilling and Hughes; and sold by H. Batten, 1819.   8°

T.621

8311

HAGUE (Thomas)

The right to punish capitally questioned: with remarks on the uncertainty, inequality, and severity of the criminal laws of England... London: for Darton, Harvey, and Co., 1819.   8°

T.727

8312

HALES (William)

Abridgment of a correspondence between the courts of Rome and Baden, respecting the appointment of Baron Wessenberg, vicar capitular of the diocese of Constance, in the year 1817... Dublin: Grierson and Power. London: F.C. and J. Rivington, 1819.   8°

T.576

8313

MONTAGU (Basil)

Some thoughts upon liberty and the rights of Englishmen. By a lover of order. London: sold by Butterworth and Son; and R. Hunter, 1819.   8°

T.734

8314

The NATURE of the first resurrection, and the character and privileges of those that shall partake of it. A sermon... By a spiritual watchman... London: A. Macintosh. Sold by Seeley; Hatchard; Ogle, Duncan, & Co., and all other booksellers, 1819.   8°

Attributed by Halkett and Laing to C.D. Hawtrey.

T.755

1820

8315

ACKLAND (Thomas Gilbank)

Arraigned doctrine its own advocate. A sermon preached in the parish church of St. James, Colchester, on Sunday, November 7, 1819... London: for F.C. & J. Rivington; R. Jennings; Swinborne and Walter, Colchester; Guy, Chelmsford; and Raw, Ipswich, 1820.   8°

T.621

8316

ACKLAND (Thomas Gilbank)

The Christian king. A sermon... on the death of his Majesty, George the third... London: for F.C. & J. Rivington, and R. Jennings, 1820.   8°

T.621

8317

An ADDRESS to the yeomanry of Westmorland. By a Westmorland yeoman. London: Elizabeth Soulby, 1820.   8°

T.563

8318

BROUGH (Robert)

No valid argument can be drawn from the incredulity of the Jews against the truth of the Christian religion. An essay... Cambridge: J. Smith; sold by Deighton & Sons, Nicholson & Son [and others], 1820.   8°

T.734

8319

DEALTRY (William)

Hezekiah honoured at his death: a sermon preached in the parish church of Clapham, on Wednesday, February 16th, 1820, the day of his late Majesty's funeral. London: for J. Hatchard & Son; and H. Batten, 1820.   8°

T.621

8320

ENGLAND. *Laws, Statutes.*

Magna Charta, the Bill of Rights; with the Petition of Right, presented to Charles I. by the Lords and Commons, together with his Majesty's answer; and the coronation oath... London: J. Bailey, [*c.*1820].   12°

T.779

8321

GASCOIGNE (Henry Barnet)

The old views of society revived; with remarks on the present state and prospects of orphan and pauper children ... London: Ruffy and Evans, [1820].   8°

T.563

8322

LAURENCE (Richard) *Archbishop of Cashel.*

Remarks upon the critical principles, and the practical application of those principles, adopted by writers, who have at various periods recommended a new translation of the Bible as expedient and necessary. [Anon.] Oxford, W. Baxter, for J. Parker; and F.C. and J. Rivington, London, 1820.   8°

T.800

8323

The UNITED Kingdom tributary to France: the real cause of the distresses of the country demonstrated in a letter to... the Earl of Liverpool. London: for F.C. & J. Rivington, 1820.   8°

Signature of John Mackie, M.D.

T.749

8324

BARKER (Henry Aston)

Description of the view of Naples, and surrounding scenery; now exhibited in Henry Aston Barker and J. Burford's panorama, Strand... London, J. and C. Adlard, 1821. 8°

T.808

8325

CRISP (Thomas Steffe)

The insufficiency of human efforts contrasted with the all-sufficiency of divine power, in evangelizing the heathen world. A sermon preached... at the annual meeting of the Baptist Missionary Society, on June 20, 1821. London: sold by John Offor [and others]: sold also in Bristol, by Isaac James, J. & W. Richardson; and by the printer, J.G. Fuller, [1821]. 8°

T.574

8326

The DECLARATION of the people of England to their sovereign lord the King. London: for J. Hatchard and son, 1821. 8°

Signature of G.H. Wollaston.

T.621

8327

DESCRIPTION of the Egyptian tomb, discovered by G. Belzoni. London: John Murray, 1821. 8°

T.808

8328

GRAY (Jonathan)

An inquiry into historical facts, relative to parochial psalmody, in reference to the remarks of... Herbert, Lord Bishop of Peterborough. York: J. Wolstenholme; and sold by L.B. Seeley, London; Deighton & Sons, Cambridge; J. Wolstenholme, J. and G. Todd, York; and Messrs. Gale, Sheffield, 1821. 8°

T.755

8329

IRELAND (John)

Nuptiae sacrae; or, An inquiry into the scriptural doctrine of marriage and divorce. Addressed to the two Houses of Parliament. First published in 1801, and now reprinted by desire. [Anon.] London: John Murray, 1821. 8°

T.621

8330

LAURENCE (Richard) *Archbishop of Cashel.*

A reply to "Some strictures" of Samuel Lee... on a tract entitled, "Remarks upon the critical principles, &c. Oxford, MDCCCXX." By the author of the "Remarks". Oxford, at the University Press, for the author; sold by J. Parker; and F.C. and J. Rivington, London, 1821. 8°

T.800

8331

LEE (Samuel)

A letter to Mr. John Bellamy on his new translation of the Bible, with some strictures on a tract [by Richard Laurence] entitled "Remarks, &c." Oxford, 1820. Cambridge: J. Smith; and sold by Deighton & Sons; by Messrs. Rivington; and Hatchard & Son, London, 1821. 8°

"To the Bishop of St. David's with the author's compliments."

T.800

8332

REMARKS on parliamentary reform... Leeds: Edward Baines, 1821. 8°

"To Wm Taylor Esquire with the fraternal regards of the author."

T.781

8333

SIMEON (Charles)

The conversion of the Jews; or, Our duty and encouragement to promote it. Two discourses preached before the University of Cambridge... London: for T. Cadell, 1821. 8°

T.755

8334

W. (W.)

A letter on the subjects of economical retrenchment, and parliamentary reform, addressed to the middle ranks of the people of England. By a gentleman farmer... London: E. Wilson, 1821. 8°

T.563

8335

WRANGHAM (Francis)

A charge, delivered in July, 1821, at Stokesley, Thirsk, and Malton, to the clergy of the archdeaconry of Cleveland. York: Thomas Wilson and Sons; and sold by Messrs. Baldwin and Co., [and others], 1821. 8°

T.705

8336

BARKER (Henry Aston)

Description of the island and city of Corfu... now exhibiting in H.A. Barker and J. Burford's panorama, Strand. London: J. and C. Adlard, 1822. 8°

T.808

8337

BARKER (Henry Aston)

Description of the procession on the coronation of his Majesty George the fourth... now represented and exhibiting in the great rotunda of Henry Aston Barker's panorama, Leicester-square... London: J. and C. Adlard, 1822. 8°

T.808

8338

BRITISH MUSEUM.

Synopsis of the contents of the British Museum. 20th ed. London: Richard and Arthur Taylor, 1822. 8°

T.808

8339

BUDDICOM (Robert Pedder)

A sermon, preached at St. George's church, Everton, on Sunday, 26th May, 1822, in aid of the fund now raising in Liverpool for the relief of the distressed peasantry of Ireland... Liverpool: G.F. Harris's widow & brothers, and sold by William Grapel and all the booksellers, [1822]. 8°

T.724

8340

FABER (George Stanley)

The conversion of the Jews to the faith of Christ, the true medium of the conversion of the gentile world. A sermon preached before the London Society for promoting Christianity amongst the Jews... London: A. Macintosh. Sold by Seeley; Hatchard; Ogle, Duncan, & Co.; and all other booksellers, 1822. 8°

T.755

8341

The HISTORY of Peter Lacy, and his wife Susan. Dublin: M. Goodwin, 1822. 8°

This tract, together with the others bound in T.719, T.720 and T.721, was published by the Religious Tract and Book Society for Ireland.

T.719

8342

LEE (Samuel)

A vindication of certain strictures on a pamphlet [by Richard Laurence] entitled "Remarks, &c. Oxford, 1820." In answer to "A reply, &c." Oxford, 1821. Cambridge: J. Smith; and sold by J. Deighton & Sons; by Messrs. Rivington; and Hatchard & Son, London, 1822. 8°

"With the author's compliments to the Bishop of St. David's."

T.800

8343

SHERIDAN (Charles Brinsley)

Thoughts on the Greek revolution... London: John Murray, 1822. 8°

"John William Mackie."

T.736

8344

BATHER (Edward)

Saint Paul's views of the Christian ministry considered, in a sermon, preached in the parish church of St. Chad, Shrewsbury... at the visitation of the Venerable Hugh Owen... Shrewsbury: W. Eddowes. Sold also by the different booksellers in the county; and by Longman, Hurst, Rees, Orme, and Brown, London, 1823. 8°

T.735

8345

BLOMFIELD (Charles James) *Bishop of London.*

A remonstrance, addressed to H. Brougham, Esq. M.P. by one of the "working clergy"... [Anon.] London: for J. Mawman, and C. and J. Rivington, 1823. 8°

T.705

8346

The CARE of cattle. Dublin, Bentham & Gardiner, [1823]. 8°

T.721

8347

CHURCH OF ENGLAND. *Articles of Religion.*

The thirty-nine articles of the Church of England, illustrated with notes, and confirmed by texts of the holy Scripture... Written in Latin by the Rev. Mr. Archdeacon Welchman, and now translated into English... by a clergyman of the University of Oxford. 13th ed. London: for C. and J. Rivington, 1823. 8°

T.705

8348

COWPER (William) *Bishop of Galloway.*

Life of William Cowper, Bishop of Galloway, written by himself... Dublin: M. Goodwin, 1823. 12°

T.720

8349

DIVINE titles of our Lord and Saviour Jesus Christ. Dublin: C. Bentham, 1823. 8°

T.719

8350

FARISH (William)

An address to the senate of the University of Cambridge, relative to certain academic proceedings which occasionally take place therein on the Lord's day. [Anon.] Sold by Deighton and Sons, Cambridge; and by Hatchard and Son, London, 1823. 8°

"Rev. Dr. Dany, Caius."

T.734

8351

HINDOO sculpture. Description of a curious piece of ancient sculpture in a cavern in the island Elephanta, near Bombay, in the East Indies. Dublin: M. Goodwin, 1823. 12°

T.720

8352

JONES (John Edmund)

The scriptural doctrine of the last general judgment, as militating against the system of modern millenarianism; the substance of a sermon preached at St. John's church, Gloucester, Oct. 12, 1823... Gloucester: J. Roberts, and sold by I.E. Lea; also by Seeley and Son, London, 1823. 8°

T.755

8353

A LETTER to Henry Brougham, Esq. M.P. upon his Durham speech, and the three articles in the last Edinburgh Review, upon the subject of the clergy. London: for C. & J. Rivington, 1823. 8°

T.705

8354

The LIFE of Cyprian, Bishop of Carthage. Dublin: C. Bentham, 1823. 8°

T.720

8355

The LIFE of Saint Augustine, Bishop of Hippo. Dublin: J. & M. Porteous, 1823. 12°

T.720

1823 (Cont'd)

8356
MARSHALL, *Messrs.*

Description of Messrs. Marshalls' grand historical peristrephic panoramas of the battle of Trafalgar... To which is added, a brief sketch of the life of Lord Nelson... 2nd ed. Norwich: Matchett and Stevenson, 1823.   8°

T.780

8357
NED Delaney. Dublin: M. Goodwin, 1823.   12°

T.719

8358
SOAMES (Henry)

A vindication of the Church and clergy of England from the misrepresentations of the Edinburgh Review. By a beneficed clergyman. London: for C. & J. Rivington, 1823.   8°

T.705

1824

8359
ANDERSON (Christopher)

The Christian spirit which is essential to the triumph of the kingdom of God: a discourse delivered at the annual general meeting of the Baptist Missionary Society, in London, 23d June, 1824... London: B.J. Holdsworth [and others], 1824.   8°

T.574

8360
BAYFORD (John)

A letter, addressed to the Rev. John Edmund Jones, M.A. occasioned by his sermon, preached at St. John's church, Gloucester, October 12, 1823, on the subject of modern millenarianism. London: J. Tilling; and sold by Ogle, Duncan, and Co.; and all other booksellers, 1824.   8°

T.755

8361
CONTEMPLATIONS in a church-yard. Dublin: J. & M. Porteous, 1824.   8°

T.721

8362
DIORAMA... Two views... of Trinity chapel, in Canterbury cathedral, and the valley of Sarnen, in Switzerland, with various effects of light and shade... London: G. Schulze, 1824.   12°

T.808

8363
FLETCHER (Joseph)

A discourse on spirituality of mind, delivered at Chapel Street meeting, Blackburn, February 1st, 1824. London: for Francis Westley; and sold also by Burton [and others], 1824.   8°

T.574

8364
The GOOD minister. Dublin: J. and M. Porteous, 1824.   12°

T.720

8365
JOHN and James, or the winter's fire-side. Dublin: M. Goodwin, 1824.   12°

T.719

8366
LE BAS (Charles Webb)

A sermon, preached in the church... of All Saints... Hertford, on Sunday, May the 16th. 1824, in aid of the funds of the Hertford general dispensary... Hertford: St. Austin, 1824.   8°

T.575

8367
The LIFE of Caroline E. Smelt, who died on the 21st September, 1817, in the city of Augusta, in North America... A narrative of facts. Dublin: M. Goodwin, 1824.   12°

T.719

8368
The REDUCED tradesman. Dublin: J. & M. Porteous, 1824.   12°

T.720

8369
TSCHOOP & Shabasch, Christian Indians, of North America. A narrative of facts... Dublin: M. Goodwin, 1824.   12°

T.719

1825

8370
The ANTIQUITY of the Church of Rome, compared with the novelty of the protestant church... 2nd ed. Dublin: J. & M. Porteus, 1825.   12°

T.720

8371
BURFORD (John) *and* BURFORD (Robert)

Description of a view of the city of Edinburgh, and surrounding country, now exhibiting in the panorama, Leicester-square... London: J. and C. Adlard, 1825.   8°

T.808

8372
A COMPANION for the closet... Dublin: J. and M. Porteous, 1825.   12°

T.720

8373
FLETCHER (Joseph) *and others*.

Discourses delivered at the settlement of the Rev. W. Orme over the congregational church at Camberwell on the 7th October 1824 ... London, for B.J. Holdsworth, 1825.   8°

T.574

8374
The GOOD Catholic, or, The honest farmer. Dublin: J. and M. Porteous, 1825.   12°

T.719

8375
The GRAFTING of fruit trees. Adapted for farmers... Dublin: M. Goodwin, 1825.   8°

T.721

8376
JOHN Pascal: or the temptations of the poor. Dublin: Bentham and Hardy, 1825.   12°

T.719

8377
KINGHORN (Joseph)

Considerations addressed to the Eclectic reviewer, in defence of those who maintain that baptism should precede communion... Norwich: S. Wilkin; and by John Offor: and to be had of all other booksellers, 1825.   8°

T.574

8378
LIGHT in darkness. Intended for the cabin fire side. A narrative of facts. Dublin, Bentham & Hardy, [1825?]   8°

T.721

8379
LOWE (Thomas Hill)

An essay on the absolving power of the Church; with especial reference to the offices of the Church of England for the ordering of priests and the visitation of the sick... Oxford, at the University Press for the author; sold by J. Parker, Oxford; and Messrs. Rivington, London, 1825.   8°

T.755

8380
MOODY (Henry Riddell)

A sermon preached in the church of St. Margaret, Canterbury, on Thursday, May 19th, 1825, at the annual visitation of the archdeacon. Printed [by R. Colegate, Canterbury] for C. and J. Rivington, London: and sold by Parker, Oxford, and Colegate, Cramp, and Cowtan, Canterbury, 1825.   8°

"F.H. Wollaston Esq. with the author's regards."

T.705

8381
ORME (William)

An expostulatory letter to the Rev. Edward Irving, A.M. occasioned by his orations for missionaries after the apostolical school... London: for B.J. Holdsworth, 1825.   8°

T.574

8382
The SAILOR'S return; being an account of Charles Grafton. Dublin: M. Goodwin, 1825.   8°

T.719

8383
The THRIFTINESS of the husbandman, and the diligence of the Christian. Dublin: M. Goodwin, [1825?]   8°

T.721

8384
The TWO friends, or the history of Hugh M'Neil & John Grant. Dublin: Christopher Bentham, [1825?]   12°

T.719

8385
WRIGHT (Samuel)

A sermon, preached at the opening of the place of religious worship, in Carter Lane, Doctors' Commons, on December 5, 1734. To which is prefixed, some account of the author... by John Hoppus... London: Francis Westley; and sold by C.J. Westley and G. Tyrrell, 1825.   8°

T.574

1826

8386
The ADVANTAGES of early instruction. 2nd ed. [Dublin], Napper and White, [1826].   8°

T.721

8387
ANTICHRIST. [Dublin], M. Goodwin, [1826?]   12°

T.720

8388
BERENS (Edward)

Pastoral watchfulness and zeal, particularly in personal instruction and admonition, recommended in two sermons, preached at the bishop's visitation at Abingdon, August 21, 1826, and August 30, 1814. Oxford, W. Baxter. Sold by Messrs. Rivington, London; and Mr. Parker, Oxford, 1826.   8°

Three pencil sketches of Shrivenham are inserted.

T.578

8389
The BEST portion. [Dublin], Napper and White, [1826].   12°

T.720

8390
The BEST purchase. 2nd ed. Dublin, M. Goodwin, [1826?]   8°

T.721

8391
BLIND Mary. [Dublin], J. & M. Porteous, [1826?]   8°

T.721

8392
BROWN (John) *of Edinburgh*.

Sacramental addresses. [Dublin], J. & M. Porteous, [1826?]   8°

T.719

8393
BURNET (Gilbert) *Bishop of Salisbury*.

The life of William Bedell, D.D. Bishop of Kilmore. [Extracted from the work by Gilbert Burnet.] 2nd ed. [Dublin], J. and M. Porteous, 1826.   12°

T.719

8394
The CHRISTIAN'S safety. [Dublin], Napper and White, [1826].   8°

T.721

8395

CLARKE (Liscombe)

A sermon preached in the cathedral church of Salisbury, August 8th, 1826, at the primary visitation of... Thomas, Lord Bishop of Salisbury... 2nd ed. Salisbury: Brodie and Dowding. Sold also by Messrs. Rivington, London, and the country booksellers, [1826]. 8°

T.578

8396

CONCILIATION. Dublin, M. Goodwin, [1826?] 12°

T.719

8397

DALBY (William)

The work of an evangelist in the Church of England, practically considered, in a sermon preached in the parish church of Warminster, Wilts, at the primary visitation of ... Thomas, Lord Bishop of Sarum ... Warminster: J.L. Vardy. Sold also by Baldwin and Co. London; Parker, Oxford; Upham, Bath; and all the booksellers, 1826. 8°

T.578

8398

The DEAF and dumb man cured. 2nd ed. [Dublin], Napper and White, [1826?] 8°

T.721

8399

The DYING Sunday school girl. 2nd ed. Dublin, John Jones, [1826?] 8°

T.721

8400

FISHER (William)

A sermon, preached in the parish church of St. John, Devizes, at the primary visitation, of ... Thomas, Lord Bishop of Salisbury ... Devizes: T.B. Smith, 1826. 8°

T.578

8401

The GLORY of the creation. [Dublin], John Jones, [1826?] 8°

T.721

8402

The GOOD young servant. A narrative of facts. [Dublin], J. & M. Porteous, [1826?] 8°

T.721

8403

The GREAT jubilee of the year 1825. 2nd ed. [Dublin], Napper and White, [1826?] 8°

T.721

8404

The HAPPY poor man... 3rd ed. [Dublin], M. Goodwin, [1826?] 8°

T.721

8405

HARVEST home. Dublin, M. Goodwin, [1826?] 8°

T.719

8406

HELP in need. [Dublin], J. and M. Porteous [1826?] 8°

T.721

8407

HOME. 2nd ed. Dublin, Bentham and Hardy, [1826?] 8°

T.721

8408

ILLICIT distillation. [Dublin], Bentham and Hardy, [1826?] 12°

T.720

8409

The JEW and his daughter, converted to Christianity. From an American publication. 3rd ed. Dublin: J. & M. Porteous, 1826. 8°

T.721

8410

The KING'S visit, as discoursed over by Andrew Walsh, Darby Morris, and John Simpson. 4th ed. Dublin: Bentham and Hardy, 1826. 12°

T.720

8411

The LAUNDRY maid; a narrative of facts. Dublin, M. Goodwin, [1826?] 12°

T.720

8412

LUCY and Ellen. 2nd ed. [Dublin], Bentham and Hardy, [1826?] 12°

T.720

8413

MARTHA and Mary. [Dublin], Napper and White, [1826]. 12°

T.720

8414

MEMOIR of Mr. John B——, late a student in Belfast College. [Dublin], J. and M. Porteous, 1826. 12°

T.720

8415

MEMOIR of William H——, of the county Antrim, who died August 24, 1825, aged 12 years. Dublin: M. Goodwin, 1826. 12°

T.720

8416

The MESSIAH foretold. 2nd ed. [Dublin], Napper and White, [1826]. 12°

T.720

8417

MILMAN (Henry Hart)

The office of the Christian teacher considered: in a sermon preached August 23, 1826... at the primary visitation of the Lord Bishop of Salisbury... Oxford, at the University Press for the author. Sold by J. Parker, Oxford; and John Murray, London, 1826. 8°

T.578

8418

A MORTAL disease, and a remedy. 2nd ed. [Dublin], Napper and White, [1826]. 8°

T.721

8419

MOUNT (Charles Milman)

The Church of England, and the Church of Rome, briefly contrasted; a sermon preached in St. Peter's Church, Marlborough, at the primary visitation of... Thomas, Lord Bishop of Salisbury, August 28th, 1826. Bath, Richard Cruttwell; and sold by C. and J. Rivington, London; Brodie and Dowding, Salisbury; J. Parker, Oxford; and J. Upham, Bath, 1826. 8°

T.578

8420

The MURDER of the Christian Indians in North America, in the year 1782. A narrative of facts. Dublin, Bentham & Hardy, 1826. 8°

T.719

8421

ON the cheerfulness of the husbandman, and the happiness of the true Christian. 2nd ed. Dublin, John Jones, [1826?] 8°

T.721

8422

ON the pope's supremacy. 2nd ed. Dublin, M. Goodwin, [1826?] 12°

T.719

8423

The PRODIGAL son. 2nd ed. [Dublin], J. & M. Porteous, [1826?] 8°

T.721

8424

PROTESTANT doctrine. [Dublin], John Jones, [1826?] 8°

T.721

8425

The REAL fool. 2nd ed. [Dublin], M. Goodwin, [1826?] 8°

T.721

8426

SHORT (William)

A sermon preached in the parish church of Chippenham, August 17, 1826, at the primary visitation of... Thomas, Lord Bishop of Salisbury. Chippenham: J.M. Coombs; sold also by Messrs. Rivington, London, and all country booksellers, [1826]. 8°

T.578

8427

SHORT sermons for family reading. [Dublin], Napper and White; (John Jones), [1826]. 7 parts. 12°

T.720

8428

SLOCOCK (Samuel)

A sermon, preached in the parish church of Newbury, on Friday, August 25, 1826, at the primary visitation of... the Lord Bishop of Salisbury. Newbury: M.P. Price. And sold by Rivingtons, London; and by the booksellers in Newbury and Portsmouth, 1826. 8°

T.578

8429

TREASURE, found in an extraordinary manner, by a young seaman. [Dublin], Napper and White, [1826]. 8°

T.721

8430

A VISIT to a Sabbath school. 2nd ed. [Dublin], Napper and White, [1826]. 8°

T.721

8431

The WIDOW'S son raised from the dead. 2nd ed. [Dublin], Napper and White, [1826?] 8°

T.721

1827

8432

ARARAT. 2nd ed. [Dublin], J. & M. Porteous, [1827?] 8°

T.721

8433

The BIBLE revered. 2nd ed. [Dublin], Napper and White, [1827?] 8°

T.721

8434

BOWRA. 3rd ed. [Dublin], Thomas I. White, [1827?] 8°

T.721

8435

BUDDICOM (Robert Pedder)

The seamen's appeal. A sermon preached at the opening of his Majesty's ship Tees, as a floating episcopal chapel; on the 17th of May, 1827... Liverpool: Thos. Kaye. Sold by all the booksellers, and by Hatchard and Son, and L.B. Seeley and Son, London, [1827]. 8°

"To Rosa Newman from the author."

T.724

8436

The CALLING of St. Peter. 2nd ed. Dublin, Bentham and Hardy, [1827?] 8°

T.721

8437

CARE for posterity. 2nd ed. [Dublin], J. & M. Porteous, [1827?] 8°

T.721

8438

CONVERSATION by the way. 2nd ed. [Dublin], Bentham and Hardy, [1827?] 8°

T.721

8439

The COTTAGE in Connaught. [Dublin], J. & M. Porteous, [1827?] 12°

T.720

8440

CROFT (James William)

Brief sketch of the administration of the maison de force, at Ghent. London; for C. and J.Rivington, by W. Mason, Chichester, 1827. 8°

T.749

8441

DIALOGUES after mass. Dublin: Bentham and Gardiner, [1827?] 12°

T.720

8442

The DYING hour. 2nd ed. Dublin, M. Goodwin, [1827?] 8°

T.721

8443

The FOUNDATION of the Church, against which the gates of hell shall not prevail. 2nd ed. [Dublin], M. Goodwin, [1827?] 8°

T.721

8444

The FRIENDLESS boy. [Dublin], J. & M. Porteous, [1827?] 8°

T.721

8445

GEARY (William)

A letter to Edward Temple Booth, Esq., mayor of Norwich, on the state of education among the poor of that city. Norwich: John Stacy, 1827. 8°

T.741

8446

The GOOD shepherd. 2nd ed. Dublin: Bentham & Gardiner, [1827?] 8°

T.721

8447

The HARD usage of beasts. 2nd ed. Dublin, J. Jones, [1827?] 8°

T.721

8448

JACOB'S well. 2nd ed. [Dublin], J. & M. Porteous, [1827?] 8°

T.721

8449

JANE Bond. A true narrative. 3rd ed. [Dublin], M. Goodwin, [1827?] 8°

T.721

8450

JANE Lindsay, first a scholar and afterwards a teacher in the Tullylish Sunday school, county of Down, Ireland; who died April 16th, 1821, aged 22 years. A narrative of facts. 2nd ed. Dublin: Thomas I. White, 1827. 12°

T.720

8451

LEIGHTON (Robert) *Archbishop of Glasgow.*

A short catechism by Archbishop Leighton. 2nd ed. Dublin: John Jones. [1827?] 8°

T.721

8452

LEIGHTON (Robert) *Archbishop of Glasgow.*

The sower. From the works of Archbishop Leighton. [Dublin], J. & M. Porteous, [1827?] 8°

T.721

8453

MARY Dwyer. [Dublin], J. & M. Porteous, [1827?] 8°

T.721

8454

MEMOIR of the Countess of Huntingdon. [Dublin], M. Goodwin, [1827?] 8°

T.721

8455

MEMOIRS of the Rev. John Berridge. A narrative of facts. Dublin, J. & M. Porteous, [1827?] 12°

T.720

8456

MR. Mollard Lefèvre, the merchant of Lyons. 2nd ed. Dublin: Thomas I. White, 1827. 12°

T.720

8457

A NEW and improved history and description of the Tower of London; including a particular detail of its numerous and interesting curiosities... London: J. King. Sold by H. Steel; L.I. Higham; J. White; and at the armouries, 1827. 8°

T.779

8458

The OLD and the new religions contrasted, in twenty-four particulars... 3rd ed. Dublin: Thomas I. White, 1827. 12°

T.720

8459

The ORPHAN. 3rd ed. [Dublin], Bentham and Hardy, [1827?] 8°

T.721

8460

The PEASANT'S daughter. A true story. 3rd ed. [Dublin], John Jones, [1827?] 8°

T.721

8461

POPES, cardinals and fathers of the Church recommending all classes of persons to read the holy Scriptures. Dublin: M. Goodwin, [1827?] 8°

T.721 .

8462

The RELIGION of the cross. 2nd ed. Dublin: R. Napper, [1827?] 8°

T.721

8463

The RIGHT of private judgment asserted. 4th ed. [No imprint, 1827.] 8°

T.721

8464

ROBERT Shaw. 2nd ed. Dublin, M. Goodwin, [1827?] 8°

T.721

8465

The RULE of faith. 2nd ed. [Dublin], R. Napper, [1827?] 12°

T.719

8466

SARAH Hopkins. 3rd ed. Dublin, J. & M. Porteous, [1827?] 8°

T.721

8467

TRANSUBSTANTIATION condemned by the Fathers of the Church. 2nd ed. Dublin, M. Goodwin, [1827?] 8°

T.721

8468

A TRIP to the country. 2nd ed. [No imprint, 1827?] 8°

T.721

8469

The WINNOWING of corn. 2nd ed. [Dublin], M. Goodwin, [1827?] 8°

T.721

8470

ZACCHEUS. 2nd ed. [Dublin], J. and M. Porteous, [1827?] 8°

T.721

1828

8471

ANSWERS from the holy Scriptures, to questions proposed to Trinitarians. Dublin, Goodwin, [1828?] 12°

T.720

8472

BICKERSTETH (Edward)

A discourse on justification by faith: preached in the course of sermons on the points in controversy between the Romish and the protestant Churches, at Tavistock chapel, Drury Lane, on Tuesday, Dec. 11, 1827. Second edition, corrected. Printed for L.B. Seeley and Sons, London, 1828. 8°

T.792

8473

HINTS respecting divine worship. Dublin: M. Goodwin, [1828?] 8°

T.721

8474

The JOY of harvestmen. 2nd ed. [Dublin], J. & M. Porteous, [1828?] 8°

T.721

8475

KRISHNA, the false god of the Hindoos. 3rd ed. [Dublin], J. and M. Porteous, [1828?] 8°

T.721

8476

The LABOURERS in the vine-yard. Dublin, M. Goodwin, [1828?] 12°

T.720

8477

A LETTER on infant baptism, addressed to Christian parents. By a father. Liverpool: George Smith. Sold by Hatchard & Son, London, 1828. 8°

"Rev. R.P. Buddicom with W.J.'s kind regards."

T.735

8478

MEMOIR of a Sunday School teacher. Dublin, M. Goodwin, [1828?] 8°

T.721

8479

The OLD hawker; a true story. 2nd ed. Dublin, M. Goodwin, [1828?] 8°

T.721

8480

ON dead trees. Good fire-side reading for farmers. [Dublin], M. Goodwin, [1828?] 8°

T.721

8481

PAGES (Pierre Marie François de)

Narrative of a voyage towards the South Pole, in the years 1773 and 1774. 2nd ed. Dublin: J. & M. Porteous, [1828?] 8°

T.721

8482

The PLOUGHING of corn-land. 2nd ed. Dublin, M. Goodwin, [1828?] 8°

T.721

8483

The SCHOOL-BOY. [Dublin], M. Goodwin, [1828?] 8°

T.721

8484

WAINWRIGHT (Jonathan Mayhew) *Bishop.*

A sermon, preached before the Board of directors of
the Domestic and Foreign Missionary Society of the
Protestant Episcopal Church in the United States of
America... on Tuesday, May 13, 1828. New-York:
J. Seymour, 1828.   8°

T.725

1829

8485

CROSTHWAITE (John)

The weeping patriot. A sermon preached in Carysfort
chapel, Black Rock, on Sunday, 8th March, 1829.
With a reprint of a letter from the author, to Henry
Maxwell... Dublin: Richard Moore Tims; and Hatchard
and Son, 1829.   8°

T.735

8486

CULLEN (Charles Sinclair)

A review of the law and judicature of elections,
and of the change introduced by the late Irish
Disfranchisement Bill... London: James Ridgway,
1829.   8°

T.749

8487

SAUMAREZ (Richard)

A letter on the evil effects of absenteeism; being
an answer to Hastings Elwin, Esq. Bath, Benj.
Higman, 1829.   8°

T.749

8488

SUMNER (John Bird) *Archbishop of Canterbury.*

A charge delivered to the clergy of the diocese of
Chester, at the primary visitation in August and
September, MDCCCXXIX. London: J. Hatchard and Son,
1829.   8°

T.735

8489

WILSON (Daniel) *Bishop of Calcutta.* .

The gentleness of the Christian minister an argument
for perseverance in the faith. A sermon occasioned
by the death of the Rev. Samuel Crowther... London:
Saunders and Benning, and G. Wilson, 1829.   8°

T.735

8490

WISNER (Benjamin Blydenburg)

The proper mode of conducting missions to the
heathen. A sermon delivered before the Society
for propagating the Gospel among the Indians and
others in North America, November 5, 1829. Boston:
Putnam & Hunt, 1829.   8°

T.735

1830

8491

An ACCOUNT of Mr. Calderon, formerly a Spanish priest
and a Franciscan. [No imprint, *c.* 1830.]   8°

T.721

8492

BATHER (Edward)

A charge delivered to the clergy of the archdeaconry
of Salop... at the visitation in June 1830... London:
J Hatchard and Son, 1830.   8°

T.735

8493

CROSTHWAITE (John)

A sermon preached in Carysfort chapel, Black Rock,
on Sunday, 4th July, 1830, on occasion of the
accession of... William IV... Dublin: printed
for the author, by Richard Moore Tims, [1830].   8°

2 copies.

T.735

8494

DODSWORTH (William)

Jesus Christ, in his threefold state of sub-angelic
humiliation, heavenly glory, and earthly dominion.
Two sermons... London: James Nisbet, 1830.   8°

T.735

8495

DOUGLAS (James)

Thoughts on prayer at the present time. 3rd ed.
Edinburgh: for Adam Black; and Longman, Rees, Orme,
Brown & Green, London, 1830.   8°

T.735

8496

JESUS Christ is the true God. 2nd ed. [Dublin],
Thomas I. White, [1830?]   12°

T.720

8497

MELVILL (Henry)

A sermon in behalf of the London Association in aid
of the missions of the United Brethren. Preached at
St. Clement's, London, April 26, 1830. London:
L.B. Seeley and Sons, 1830.   8°

T.735

8498

SMITH (Herbert)

A sermon on the holy authority and binding character
of the law of the Sabbath... London: for C.J.G. &
F. Rivington; and sold by J. Hatchard & Son, 1830.
8°

T.792

8499

WARREN (George)

A discourse upon national dietetics... more
particularly upon scrophula, tubercle, and
consumption... London: Longman, Rees, Orme, Brown,
and Green; and T. Butcher, 1830.   8°

T.748

1831

8500

A. (C.)

The farmers and the clergy. Six letters to the
farmers of England, on tithes & Church property.
London: Roake & Varty, [1831?]   8°

T.779

8501

BATHER (Edward)

Considerations upon the growth of infidelity, and
the recent dispersion of infidel publications: a
charge delivered to the clergy of the archdeaconry
of Salop... at the visitation in June, 1831. London:
J. Hatchard and Son, 1831.   8°

T.735

8502

BEVERLEY (Robert Mackenzie)

A letter to his Grace the Archbishop of York, on the
present corrupt state of the Church of England...
5th ed. Beverley: W.B. Johnson; and may be had of
all booksellers, 1831.   8°

T.781

8503

BULTEEL (Henry Bellenden)

A sermon on I. Corinthians II. 12. preached before
the University of Oxford, at St. Mary's, on Sunday,
Feb. 6, 1831... Oxford, W. Baxter, Sold by J.
Hatchard and Son; and J. Nisbet, London; and Messrs.
Deighton, Cambridge, 1831.   8°

"R.P. Buddicom from the Rev. C.L. Livainson."

T.735

8504

BURTON (Edward)

Remarks upon a sermon, preached [by H.B. Bulteel]
at St. Mary's on Sunday, February 6, 1831...
Oxford, W. Baxter. Sold by Messrs. Rivington,
London, 1831.   8°

"R.P. Buddicom from the Rev. C.L. Livainson."

T.735

8505

CAMPBELL (Colin) *M.A.*

A sermon preached in the parish church of Chippenham,
Wilts. on Sunday morning, August 14, 1831. Richmond:
F.H. Wall, 1831.   8°

"To the Rev. R.P. Buddicom with the author's regards."

T.735

8505A

CHALMERS (Thomas)

A sermon, preached in St. George's church, Edinburgh
... on occasion of the death of the Rev. Dr. Andrew
Thomson. Glasgow: for William Collins; Oliver &
Boyd, W. Whyte & Co. and W. Oliphant, Edinburgh;
[and others], 1831.   8°

T.735

8506

A DIALOGUE on parliamentary reform. 2nd ed.
London: Roake and Varty, 1831.   8°

T.779

8507

EVERETT (Edward)

The prospect of reform in Europe. From the North
American review, published at Boston, N.A. July 1,
1831. [Anon.] 2nd ed. London: O. Rich. And sold
by all the booksellers, August, 1831.   8°

Signature of J.W. Mackie, Ch.Ch. Oxford.

T.749

8508

GARBETT (John)

The spirit of the ministerial gift illustrated; a
visitation sermon, preached at Coleshill, June 6,
1831, before the archdeacon of Coventry...
London; Whittaker, Treacher, and Arnot; and Hamilton,
Adams, and Co. Birmingham: Beilby, Knott, and Beilby,
1831.   8°

T.735

8509

GRAY (John Hamilton)

Churchmen and dissenters; or, Plain, popular, and
impartial remarks on the Church of England...
Chesterfield: J. Roberts; Longman, Rees, Orme, Brown,
and Green; Nisbet; Seeley; Rivingtons; and Hatchards,
London: Tait, Edinburgh, 1831.   8°

T.704

8510

GRAY (John Hamilton)

Remarks, addressed to R.M. Beverley, Esq. on his
Letter to his Grace the Archbishop of York. 2nd
ed. Chesterfield: J. Roberts; Longman, Rees, Orme,
Browne, and Green, London; and Tait, Edinburgh,
1831.   8°

T.781

8511

HEATON (George)

A letter to R.M. Beverley, Esq. on the subject of
his late address to his Grace the Archbishop of
York, on the "Present corrupt state of the Church
of England." 3rd ed. Doncaster: Brooke & Co.
Sold also in London by Messrs. Rivington and Co.;
Hatchard and Son; Dennis; J. Chappell; and all other
booksellers, in Town and country, 1831.   8°

T.781

8512

LAW (George Henry) *Bishop of Bath and Wells.*

A pastoral letter, on the present aspect of the
times, addressed to the clergy, the gentry, and
inhabitants, of the diocese of Bath & Wells.
Wells: B. Backhouse; sold also by Rodwell, &
Rivington, London; and Upham, Collings, and Ford,
Bath, [1831].   8°

T.780

8513

M'GHEE (Robert James)

The letter of Doctor Doyle, (Roman Catholic Bishop
of Kildare and Leighlin,) to Lord Farnham, on the
subject of the clergy and revenues of the
Established Church in Ireland, examined and compared
with Dr. Doyle's former professions and writings...
Leeds: Hernaman and Perring, 1831.   8°

T.780

8514

MARSH (Herbert) *Bishop of Peterborough.*

A charge, delivered to the clergy of the diocese of
Peterborough, in July, MDCCCXXXI. London: for
C.J.G. & F. Rivington, 1831.   8°

T.792

8515

The REAL character and tendency of the proposed
reform... 17th ed. London: Roake & Varty,
[1831].   8°

T.779

8516

RHODES (Ebenezer)

The palace of the Peak, or, Chatsworth in 1831.
By the author of "Peak scenery"... Sheffield:
printed for the author, by J.C. Platt, and sold
by him; Mr. Vallance, Matlock Bath; Messrs. Bright
& Sons, and Mr. Moore, Buxton; and Mr. Goodwin,
Bakewell, &c. &c., 1831.   8°

T.779

8517

SCORESBY (William)

Sorrow on the sea: a sermon preached in the mariners'
church, at Liverpool... on occasion of the melancholy
loss of the Rothsay Castle, steamer...   Second edition,
including the personal narrative of John A. Tinne,
Esq...   London; James Nisbet; sold in Liverpool by D.
Marples, W. Grapel, T. Kaye, and other booksellers,
1831.   8°

T.735

8518

SCOTT (John) *Vicar of North Ferriby.*

Reformation, not subversion: an appeal to the people
of England on behalf of their national church. A
sermon, preached before the corporation of Beverley,
on the day of their Majesties' coronation...   London:
L.B. Seeley and Sons; sold also by Kemp, Beverley; and
Wilson, Hull, 1831.   8°

2 copies.

T.704 T.735

8519

SIMEON (Charles)

The offices of the holy Spirit: four sermons preached
before the University of Cambridge, in the month of
November, 1831.   London: for Holdsworth and Ball;
and may be had of the booksellers in Cambridge and
Oxford, 1831.   8°

T.735

8520

SMITH (Sydney)

Mr. Dyson's speech to the freeholders, on reform.
[Anon.] 35th ed. London: James Ridgway, 1831.   8°

T.749

8521

STUART (Moses)

Sermon at the ordination of the Rev. William G.
Schauffler, missionary to the Jews... Andover:
Flagg and Gould, 1831.   8°

T.735

8522

WHEELER (Daniel)

An affectionate address to professing Christians;
more especially the members of the established
Church of England. By one educated in its doctrines.
York: William Alexander and Co; sold also by Harvey
and Darton, and Edmund Fry, London; R. Peart,
Birmingham; D.F. Gardiner, Dublin; and Wethereld
and Co., Belfast, 1831.   8°

2 copies.

T.735 T.781

8523

WILD (William Taylor)

A reply to a letter addressed by R.M. Beverley,
Esquire, to his Grace the Archbishop of York, on
the present state of the Church of England...
2nd ed. Newark: S. and C. Ridge. London: Messrs.
Hatchards [and others], 1831.   8°

T.781

8524

WILSON (Daniel) *Bishop of Calcutta.*

The character of the good man as a Christian
minister. A sermon occasioned by the death of
the Rev. Basil Woodd... London: George Wilson;
and sold by E. Bridgewater, 1831.   8°

T.735

8525

WOODS (Leonard)

Hinderances to the spread of the Gospel. A sermon
delivered at the annual meeting of the American
Board of Commissioners for Foreign Missions, New-
haven, Conn. Oct. 5, 1831. Andover: Flagg and
Gould, 1831.   8°

2 copies.

T.724 T.735

1832

8526

BYRTH (Thomas)

The object of the Christian minister and the means
of its accomplishment. A sermon preached... at the
visitation of the Right Reverend John-Bird, Lord
Bishop of Chester, October X. MDCCCXXXII. Hatchards,
London; Talboys, Oxford; Rowe, Plymouth; Malley,
Warrington, 1832.   8°

"To the Rev. R.P. Buddicom with the author's regards."

T.724

8527

BYRTH (Thomas)

Observations on the neglect of the Hebrew language,
and on the best mode of promoting its cultivation
among the clergy. Hatchards, London; Talboys,
Oxford; Rowe, Plymouth; Malley, Warrington, 1832.   8°

T.735

8528

The DAY-DREAM, or a letter to King Richard, containing
a vision of the trial of Mr. Factory Longhours, at
York Castle. Leeds: T. Inchbold, 1832.   8°

T.779

8529

GASKELL (James Milnes)

Copy of a letter addressed by Milnes Gaskell, Esq.
to the chairman of his committee...   March 28th,
1832. Wakefield: R. Hurst, [1832?]   8°

T.780

8530

HARDING (William)

A word for inquiry previous to decision in the matter
of the present manifestations of, or pretension to,
the gifts of speaking with unknown tongues and
prophesying. By one of the congregation of the
National Scotch Church. With an appendix, containing
extracts from the writings of the Rev. Edward Irving
... London: sold by W. Harding; James Fraser; James
Nisbet; W. Clark; and W. Morrison, 1832.   8°

T.735

8531

PUSEY (Edward Bouverie)

A sermon preached at the consecration of Grove church
on Tuesday, August 14, 1832. Oxford, S. Collingwood,
for the author. Sold by J.H. Parker, Oxford; and by
J.G. and F. Rivington, London, 1832.   8°

T.725

8532

TATTERSHALL (Thomas)

The deity and personality of the holy Spirit: a
sermon preached at St. Andrew's church, Liverpool,
on Wednesday, April 25, 1832. Liverpool: Worrall
and Taylor; sold by Kaye, and Cruickshank; Grapel
and Walmsley; and Davenport, [1832].   8°

"The Rev. R.P. Buddicom with the author's regards."

T.724

1833

8533

COLEMAN (William)

A sermon preached in the parish church of Kingston-
upon-Thames, on Sunday afternoon, August 4th, 1833
... Kingston: James Attfield; sold also by Messrs.
Seeley; & J. Nisbet, [1833].   8°

T.725

8534

COTTON (Henry)

Cui bono? A letter to the Right Hon. E.G. Stanley.
Dublin: Milliken & Son, R.M. Tims, and Curry & Co.
and Roake and Varty, London, 1833.   8°

T.749

8535

SHAW (J.H.)

Local registry of deeds. A speech delivered at
a meeting of solicitors held at Wakefield, on
Friday, May 31, 1833. London, James Ridgway;
and sold by all booksellers, 1833.   8°

T.780

1834

8536

ATCHISON (Thomas)

Statement of Mr. Atchison, late captain in the Royal
Artillery, in defence of his military integrity...
London: J. Hatchard and Son; Seeley and Sons;
Hamilton; Nisbet; Roake and Varty, 1834.   8°

T.780

8537

EDWARDS (Edward)

A letter to Sir R.H. Inglis, Bart. M.P. on the
relative numbers, influence, and benevolence of
churchmen and dissenters. [Signed Presbyter.]
Leeds: printed for the author: may be had at the
Intelligencer office [and others], 1834.   8°

T.779

8538

GOWRING (John William)

The doctrines of free and sovereign grace, being
the substance of two sermons on the seventeenth
article, preached in Witton Church, Northwich,
July 13th & 20th, 1834... Northwich: F. Carnes;
sold also by E. Palmer, [1834].   8°

T.724

8539

INTERCEPTED letter of an archbishop of the Church
by law established; to Mr. Richard Oastler, bailiff
at Fixby-Hall, Huddersfield. Wakefield: Richard
Nichols, 1834.   8°

T.780

8540

LASCELLES (William Sebright)

Speech of the Hon. Wm. Sebright Lascelles, to the
electors of the borough of Wakefield... the sixth
of December, 1834... Wakefield: John Stanfield,
1834.   8°

T.780

8541

OASTLER (Richard)

A papal bull, from Pope Gregory XVI. to King
Joseph, the deluder... the Wood-be-radical...
Huddersfield: Thomas Kemp, 1834.   8°

T.780

8542

PEEL (*Sir* Robert)

An address to the electors of the borough of
Tamworth. London: Roake and Varty, 1834.   8°

T.779

8543

PYM (Robert)

"A caveat against the errors of Calvinism" reviewed
... Wakefield: J. Stanfield; J. Heaton, Leeds; and
J. Ray, Barnsley, 1834.   8°

T.779

8544

TYSON (Edwin Colman)

A few plain remarks addressed to churchmen and
dissenters... London: Whitaker and Co. and
Effingham Wilson; and Rowland Hurst, Wakefield,
1834.   8°

T.780

1835

8545

An APPEAL to patrons on their solemn responsibility
before God and man for the religious exercise of
their sacred trust... London: Geo. Ellerton, 1835.
8°

T.792

8546

BIRD (Charles Smith)

The sword of the spirit. A sermon preached at Burghfield and Shinfield, Berks, October IV, MDCCCXXXV, on occasion of the commemoration of the first translating and printing of the whole Bible in English. Reading: E. Blackwell. London: Hatchard and Co., and Seeley and Co., 1835. 8°

"Rev. R.P. Buddicom."

T.724

8547

BONAR (John James)

Divine judgments considered in their nature and results: two discourses, preached in reference to the late calamitous inundation at Greenock. Greenock: John Thomson. W. Collins and M. Ogle, Glasgow; and W. Whyte & Co., Edinburgh, 1835. 8°

T.725

8548

COLMER (Robert)

Speech of Robert Colmer... at a Conservative dinner at Aldeburgh, on Friday, July 17, 1835; also, a report of the meeting of the Operative Conservative Association, at Manchester, on Monday, August 31, 1835. Wakefield: John Stanfield, 1835. 8°

T.780

8549

CUMMINS (Charles)

A few thoughts on musical festivals; their uses and abuses. By a looker-on, at York... London: Arthur Seguin, 1835. 8°

T.780

8550

FOLLETT (Sir William Webb)

Speech of Sir W.W. Follett, delivered at the grand Conservative dinner, Exeter, on Wednesday Oct. 21st, 1835. Preston, Clarke, [1835?] 8°

T.779

8551

PEEL (Sir Robert)

Speech of the Right Honourable Sir Robert Peel, Baronet, delivered at Merchant Tailors' Hall, London, on Monday, May 10, 1835. Wakefield: John Stanfield, [1835]. 12°

T.779

8552

PEEL (Sir Robert)

The speech of the Right Honourable Sir Robert Peel, Bart. delivered at the Mansion House, December 23, 1834. London: Roake and Varty, 1835. 8°

T.779

8553

TOMKINS (Lydia)

Thoughts on the ladies of the aristocracy... London: Hodgsons, 1835. 8°

T.779

8554

A TRYAL of witches, at the assizes held at Bury St. Edmonds for the county of Suffolk; on the tenth day of March, 1664... Reprinted verbatim from the original edition of 1682. With an appendix... Printed at Charles Clark's private press, Great Totham, Essex. London: Longman and Co.; and P.H. Youngman, Maldon, 1835. 8°

T.780

8555

WATKINS (Henry George)

The established religion a national blessing... 5th ed. London: for Hamilton, Adams & Co., and E. White, 1835. 8°

T.779

1836

8556

COPLEY (John Singleton) *Baron Lyndhurst.*

Summary of the session. Speech of the Right Hon. Lord Lyndhurst, delivered in the House of Lords, on Thursday, August 18, 1836. To which is added, the substance of the speech of his Grace the Duke of Wellington, upon the same occasion. 12th ed. London: James Fraser, [1836]. 8°

T.779

8557

HOSKINS (John)

"Transubstantiation (or the change of the substance of bread and wine) in the supper of the Lord, cannot be proved by holy writ..." A sermon preached at Saint Paul's church, Boughton, near Chester, December XXXI. MDCCCXXXV. Chester: for Longman, Rees, & Co., London; Tims, Dublin; Davenport, Liverpool; and Poole and Boult, Chester, 1836. 8°

T.724

1837

8558

CAMPBELL (Colin) *M.A.*

A pastor's protest against all oppositions to the truth: a sermon preached at Newport, Salop, on Sunday, November 12, 1837. Newport: sold by H.P. Silvester; and by J. Nisbet, London, 1837. 8°

T.725

8559

FELL (Thomas)

The persecuting principles and corrupt doctrines of the Church of Rome. Two sermons, preached in the parish church of Ashby-de-la-Zouch, on Sunday, November 5th, 1837. Ashby-de-la-Zouch: W. Hextall. London: J.G. and F. Rivington, 1837. 8°

"The Rev. R.P. Buddicom with T.F.'s regards."

T.724

8560

HAMILTON (James) *Professor of Midwifery.*

A letter to Dr Edward Rigby, physician in London, from Dr Hamilton, professor of medicine and midwifery in the University of Edinburgh. [No imprint, 1837.] 8°

No title-page.

T.781

8561

HARDING (John) *Bishop of Bombay.*

A sermon, preached in the episcopal chapel, Gray's Inn Lane, St. Pancras, on behalf of the Church Pastoral-Aid Society, on Thursday, September 15, 1837. (Appendix.) London: Seeleys, 1837. 2 parts. 8°

T.725

8562

HOOK (Walter Farquhar)

A farewell sermon, preached in Trinity Church, Coventry, June IV, MDCCCXXXVII... 2nd ed. London: for J.G. & F. Rivington; and sold by Rollason, Price, & Edwards, Coventry; M. Robinson & J. Cross, Leeds; and H.C. Langbridge, Birmingham, 1837. 8°

T.779

8563

HOOK (Walter Farquhar)

On the Church and the establishment. Two sermons. 3rd ed. Leeds: R. Perring. Sold by Rivingtons, London; Talboys, Oxford; and M. Robinson and J. Cross, Leeds, 1837. 8°

T.779

8564

JARVIS (Samuel Farmar)

Christian unity necessary for the conversion of the world: a sermon preached in St. Thomas's church, New York... before... the Board of missions of the Protestant Episcopal Church in the United States of America. New York: Willian Osborn, 1837. 8°

T.725

8565

The POOR-Law Act. Public meeting at Bradford, Yorkshire. Monday, March 6, 1837. Second edition, enlarged. Bradford, T. Inkersley, [1837]. 8°

T.780

8566

RAIKES (Henry)

The mutual dependance of the clergy and laity considered. A sermon preached in the parish church of Warington, on Thursday, July twentieth... London: Hatchard and Son; Nisbet. Sowler & Co., Manchester; Grapell & Davenport, Liverpool; Haddock, Warrington; Seacome, Chester, 1837. 8°

T.725

8567

ROBERSON (Hammond)

A second address to the clergy and influential laity of the West-Riding of the county of York on the subject of "Church accomodation and pastoral superintendence"... Huddersfield: J. Brook, [1837]. 8°

T.780

8568

WATERTON (Charles)

A letter on the Church of England by law established; occasioned by Parson Gregg's unprovoked attack on the Catholic religion... Wakefield: Richard Nichols, 1837. 8°

T.780

8569

WATERTON (Charles)

An ornithological letter to William Swainson, Esq. F.R.S. &c. &c. Wakefield: Richard Nichols, 1837. 8°

T.780

1838

8570

FAUSSETT (Godfrey)

The revival of popery: a sermon preached before the University of Oxford, at St. Mary's, on Sunday, May 20, 1838. 3rd ed. Oxford, at the University Press, for the author. Sold by John Henry Parker: and by J.G. and F. Rivington, London, 1838. 8°

T.724

8571

FLETCHER (William)

Popery not calumniated. A reply to the Rev. T. Sing, by the Rev. W. Fletcher... Derby: Wm. Bemrose, 1838. 8°

"The Rev. R.P. Buddicom."

T.724

8572

"IS there not a cause?" Bristol: published by the Bristol Protestant Association; and sold by Norton; Richardson; Lancaster; Chilcott; and all booksellers, 1838. 8°

T.724

8573

McILVAINE (Charles Pettit) *Bishop.*

The apostolical commission: the sermon at the consecration of... Leonidas Polk, D.D., missionary bishop for Arkansas; in Christ Church, Cincinnati, December 9, 1838. Gambier, G.W. Myers, 1838. 8°

T.725

8574

SING (Thomas)

A most gentle and grave rebuke, administered to the Rev. Wm. Fletcher, on occasion of a recent work entitled "Popery not calumniated"... Debry [sic]: G. Jewitt, 1838. 8°

T.724

8575

WILSON (Roger Carus)

The Christian minister's obligation to preach the Gospel. A sermon, preached at the triennial visitation of... the Lord Bishop of Chester, at Preston, on Tuesday, 12th June, 1838. Preston; Addison: London; Longman & Co., 1838. 8°

T.725

8576

WYLIE (Macleod)

The progress of popery in the British dominions and elsewhere. [Anon.] Reprinted from "Blackwood's magazine" of October. Fourth thousand. London: the Protestant Association: and sold by Nisbet [and others], 1838. 8°

T.724

1839

8577

BUDDICOM (Robert Pedder)

The atonement indispensable to the necessities of guilty man... A lecture, delivered in Christ Church, Hunter Street, Liverpool, on Wednesday evening, March 27, 1839... Liverpool: Henry Perris, and Hamilton, Adams and Co., London, 1839. 8°

T.725

1839 (Cont'd)

8578

CAMPBELL (Colin) *M.A.*

Peace, the gift of God! A farewell sermon, preached in the parish church of Newport, Salop, on Sunday evening, June 23, 1839. Birmingham: H.C. Langbridge; and H.P. Silvester, Newport, 1839. 8°

"To the Rev. R.P. Buddicom with the author's grateful affection."

T.725

8579

MENDHAM (Joseph)

The Church of Rome's traffic in pardons substantiated Extracted from The Church of England quarterly review ... [Anon.] London, Painter, 1839. 8°

T.724

8580

SUMNER (John Bird) *Archbishop of Canterbury.*

Eternal life in Jesus Christ: a sermon preached at the consecration of St. Luke's church, Cheetham Hill. London: J. Hatchard and Son, 1839. 8°

T.725

8581

TATTERSHALL (Thomas)

A sermon, preached at the episcopal Jews' chapel, Cambridge Heath, Bethnal Green... before the London Society for Promoting Christianity amongst the Jews. London: A. Macintosh. Sold at the London Society's office; by Duncan & Malcolm; Hatchard & Son; and B. Wertheim, 1839. 8°

T.725

8582

TWEDDELL (Robert)

Sabbath-profanation and intemperance: or a depraved population, a distracted country, and an offended God... A sermon, preached in the parish church of Halton, on Sunday the 22nd of September, 1839. Liverpool: H. Perris, 1839. 8°

T.725

8583

WOOD (Joseph)

The self-styled reformation society not a religious body, but a detachment of the Orange faction... Wakefield: Rowland Hurst, 1839. 8°

T.780

1840

8584

CAMPBELL (Colin) *M.A.*

The marriage vow. A sermon, preached in St. Paul's chapel, Birmingham, on Sunday morning, February 16, 1840, being the first Sunday after her Majesty's royal nuptials... also by A. Newling, Liverpool: and by Beilby; Knott and Co.; & Langbridge, Birmingham, 1840. 8°

"To the Rev. R.P. Buddicom with the author's grateful affection."

T.725

8585

MENDHAM (Joseph)

Modern evasions of Christianity. A sermon... Birmingham: Knott, Hawker, and Coburn; and Hatchards, London, 1840. 8°

T.725

8586

SANDARS (John)

Justification. A sermon, preached in the parish church of St. Mary, Leicester, on Tuesday, March 31, 1840... Leicester: Combe and Crossley; Hamilton, Adams, and Co., London, 1840. 8°

"The Rev. R.P. Buddicom with the author's affectionate love."

T.725

8587

TATTERSHALL (Thomas)

On the lawfulness of rulers employing their official influence for the promotion of true religion. A sermon preached at St. Augustine's church, Liverpool, 29th January, 1840... Liverpool: J. Perry; Perris; Newling; and J. Crisp, 1840. 8°

T.725

8588

WOODWARK (John)

The love of Christ the true basis of moral reformation. A sermon preached at Paddington chapel April 30th, 1840, on behalf of the British and Foreign Temperance Society. London: printed for the Society, by J. Rider, [1840]. 8°

T.725

1841

8589

GODDARD (Charles)

A charge delivered to the clergy of the archdeaconry of Lincoln, in May and June 1841. London: W. Straker, 1841. 8°

T.792

1842

8590

BAGOT (Richard) *Bishop of Bath and Wells.*

A charge delivered to the clergy of the diocese of Oxford by Richard Bagot, D.D., Bishop of Oxford, at his fourth visitation, May, 1842. 2nd ed. Oxford: John Henry Parker; J.G.F. and J. Rivington, London, 1842. 8°

T.792

8591

INCORPORATED SOCIETY FOR PROMOTING THE ENLARGEMENT, BUILDING, AND REPAIRING OF CHURCHES & CHAPELS.

Annual report, May 23, 1842. London: Rivingtons; Burns, 1842. 8°

T.792

1843

8592

BICKERSTETH (Edward)

The judgment according to works at the coming of Christ. A sermon preached at St. John's chapel, Bedford Row, Bloomsbury... June 15, 1843. For the benefit of the Accident Relief Society. London: Seeley and Co., [1843]. 8°

T.792

8593

BICKERSTETH (Edward)

The real union of all the people of Christ. A sermon, preached at Gray's Inn Lane episcopal chapel, on Thursday, May 11, 1843, in behalf of the Foreign-Aid Society. London: A. Macintosh, 1843. 8°

T.792

8594

INCORPORATED SOCIETY FOR PROMOTING THE ENLARGEMENT, BUILDING, AND REPAIRING OF CHURCHES & CHAPELS.

Twenty-fifth annual report, May 26, 1843. London: Rivingtons; Burns, 1843. 8°

T.792

8595

KAYE (John) *Bishop of Lincoln.*

A charge to the clergy of the diocese of Lincoln... delivered at the triennial visitation, in MDCCCXLIII. 3rd ed. London: J.G.F. and J. Rivington. Lincoln: W. and B. Brooke, 1843. 8°

T.792

8596

MAITLAND (Charles David)

God's testimonies the better portion. A sermon, preached at St. James's chapel, May 21, 1843, on the occasion of the death of its lamented proprietor, Nathaniel Kemp. Brighton: Henry S. King, 1843. 8°

T.792

8597

OAKELEY (*Sir* Herbert)

A charge, delivered to the clergy of the archdeaconry of Colchester, at his first general visitation, in July, 1843. London: for J.G.F. & J. Rivington, 1843. 8°

T.792

UNDATED PAMPHLETS

8598

An ACCOUNT of the rise of silver in this kingdom of England, from the first year of King Edward the first, to this present time. [No imprint, 1689-94?] brs.

Not in Wing.

T.145

8599

A DEFENCE of wearing and reverencing the holy cross. By a young gentleman of the Church of England. [No imprint.] 4°

Wing O D 820.
This pamphlet is dated c.1660 by Wing, but it has the appearance of being rather later, perhaps c.1700.

T.7

8600

The DIMENSIONS and curiosities of St. Paul's cathedral, London... London, M'Gowen, [n.d.]. 8°

Signature of Wm. Taylor, 1814.

T.779

8601

The MASSACRE of Glenco: being a true narrative of the barbarous murder of the Glenco men... on the 13th of February, 1692... [Attributed to George Ridpath.] 2nd ed. London: for J. Johnson, [n.d.] 8°

T.615

8602

MORELL (Thomas)

Jephtha, an oratorio, or sacred drama. [Anon.] Set to music by Mr. Handel. Bath: W. Gye, [n.d.]. 8°

William Gye printed at Bath between about 1770 and 1802.

T.664

8603

OF the much questioned salvability of the English Romanists, and schismatick Non-jurors, if not members of the Church of England established by law. [No imprint, n.d.] 4°

Annotated by George Hickes.

T.265

8604

SAVIGNY (J.)

A treatise on the use and management of a razor; with practical directions relative to its appendages. London: printed for the author, [n.d.]. 8°

T.666

8605

SCHEFFERUS (Johannes)

Iohannis Schefferi Dissertatio de varietate navium. [No imprint.] 4°

Signature of Tho: Bowdler. MS date 1678.

T.168

APPENDIX OF SERIALS

8606

ACTA eruditorum publicata Lipsiae. [No imprint.] 4°

Nos. III and V, 1706.
These numbers carry a lengthy review of George Hickes, *Linguarum Veterum Septentrionalium Thesaurus.*

T.12

8607

The ANTI-ROMAN pacquet: or, Memoirs of popes and popery... [By Henry Care.] [London], A.Godbid for L.C. 4°

no.12   24 Sept.1680.
no.17   29 Oct.   [Another copy in T.150]
no.18   5 Nov.

Continued as *The weekly pacquet of advice from Rome.*

T.105

8608

The ATHENIAN catechism: with the character of a tacker. By John Dunton. London, for S. Malthus. 4°

numb. 17 December 8-13, 1704.

T.487

8609

BIBLIOTHECA curiosa. A catalogue of very curious
and rare books... now on sale by Longman, Hurst,
Rees, Orme, and Brown. [No imprint.] 4°

May 7, 1813.
June 7.
Jan. 1, 1814.
Feb. 1.

T.693

8610

BIBLIOTHECA literaria, being a collection of
inscriptions, medals, dissertations, &c... [Edited
by Samuel Jebb.] London, for W.J. Innys, and T.
Woodward. 4°

nos. I,II. 1722.
nos. III,IV,V. 1723.
no. IX. 1724.
Bound in are five original letters from Samuel Parker
of Oxford to the Rev. Mr Wagstaff, 1721-23.

T.10

8611

A BRIEFE relation of some affaires and transactions,
civill and military, both forraigne and domestique.
[By Walter Frost.] London, for Matthew Simmons. 4°

no.34 9-16 April 1650.
no.44 18-25 June.

T.259

8612

CENSURA temporum. The good or ill tendencies of
books, sermons, pamphlets, &c. impartially consider'd,
in a dialogue between Eubeulus and Sophronius. [By
Samuel Parker.] London, John Morphew. 4°

nos. 1,4 1708.

T.10

8613

A COLLECTION for improvement of husbandry and trade.
By John Houghton. [London], Randal Taylor, and
sold by J. Hindmarsh [and others]. Fol.

Vols. 1-17, nos. 1-240, 290-522, 30 March 1692 -
24 July 1702.

T.541 T.542

8614

A COLLECTION of letters for the improvement of
husbandry & trade. By John Houghton. London, for
John Lawrence. 4°

Vol. I, nos. 1-15 1681-83.
Vol. II, nos. 1- 6 1683.

An incomplete duplicate of Vol. I, no. 1,8 Sept. 1681.

T.53 T.652

8615

The COMMON-WEALHTS [sic] moderate intelligence.
Or, Diurnall occurrences... London, for T. Brewster.
4°

no.1   June 1659.

T.259

8616

A CONTINUATION of the true diurnall of passages in
Parliament. [No imprint]. 4°

no. 6 14-21 Feb. [1641/2].
no. 11 21-28 March [1642].

T.20

8617

The CRITICAL review: or, Annals of literature. By
a society of gentlemen. [Edited by Tobias Smollett.]
London: for A. Hamilton. 8°

Vol. XXV June, 1768.

T.423

8618

ENGLAND. *Parliament. House of Commons.*

Votes of the House of Commons. London, John Leake
for Timothy Goodwin, and Thomas Cockerill. Fol.

numb. 7   28 die Octobris 1696.
      8   30 die Octobris.
     33   30 die Novembris.

T.689

8619

The EVENING post. London, E. Berington; and sold
by J. Morphew. 4°

nos. 1233-1240, June 27-July 13, 1717.

T.394

8620

An EXACT accompt, communicating the chief transactions
of the three kingdomes ... With the daily votes and
resolves in both Houses of Parliament ... London,
John Redmayne. 4°

no. 99 8-15 June [1660].

Formerly *An exact accompt of the daily proceedings
in Parliament.*

T.67

8621

An EXACT accompt of the daily proceedings in
Parliament, with occurrences in foreign parts ...
[London], John Redmayne. 4°

no. 63 3-10 Feb. [1659/60].

Formerly *A particular advice from foreign parts.*
Continued as *An exact accompt, communicating the chief
transactions of the three kingdomes.*

T.67

8622

The FLYING-post: or, The post-master. [Edited by
George Ridpath.] London: T. Tookey: and sold by
S. Popping. Fol.

no. 3977 June 29-July 2, 1717.
no. 3981 July 9-11.

T.394

8623

The GENTLEMAN'S journal for the war: being an
historical account and geographical description of
several strong cities, towns and ports of Europe ...
London, for Abel Swall and Tim. Child; and to be sold
by T. Chapman, R. Parker and R. Taylor. 4°

Part the second, 1693.

T.4

8624

The GENTLEMAN'S magazine. By Sylvanus Urban, Gent.
[i.e. David Henry]. London, for D. Henry, by J.
Lister; and sold by F. Newbery. 8°

February, 1769.
April, 1772 [incomplete].

T.422 T.431

8625

The GRUMBLER. By Squire Gizzard. London: W. Wilkins;
and sold by R. Burleigh. Fol.

numb. XXIX June 24-28, 1715.
      XXX   June 28-July 1.

T.529

8626

HERACLITUS ridens: at a dialogue between jest and
earnest, concerning the times. [By Thomas Flatman.]
London, for B. Tooke. Fol.

no. 22 28 June 1681.

T.532

8627

The HISTORICAL register, containing an impartial
relation of all transactions, foreign and domestick
... London: S. Nevill. Sold also by E. Nutt, R.
Gosling, D. Browne, and J. Stagg. 8°

no. LXXII 1733.

T.803

8628

The HISTORY of the works of the learned. Or, An
impartial account of books lately printed in all
parts of Europe... London: for H. Rhodes;
T.Bennet; A.Bell; D.Midwinter, and T.Leigh. 4°

Vol.II, no.8   August 1700.
Vol.IV, nos.1-12 1702.
Vol.IX, no.2   February 1707.

T.21 T.263 T.505

8629

The INTELLIGENCER, published for satisfaction and
information of the people. [By Sir Roger L'Estrange.]
London, Richard Hodgkinson. 4°

no.3   14 September 1663
no.4   21 September
no.5   28 September
no.6   5 October
no.7   12 October
no.10 2 November
no.17 21 December
no.18 28 December
no.13 15 February 1663[4]
no.25 28 March 1664
no.27 4 April
no.33 25 April
no.39 16 May
no.20 13 March 1664/5
no.45 12 June 1665
no.74 11 September
no.80 2 October
no.82 9 October
no.84 16 October
no.88 30 October
no.90 6 November

Published alternately with *The newes.*

T.258

8630

The KINGDOMES intelligencer of the affairs now in
agitation in England, Scotland and Ireland...
London, R. Hodgkinson. 4°

no.3   14-21 January 1661.
no.5   28 Jan.-4 Feb.
no.6   4-11 February
no.16 22-29 April
no.19 6-13 May
no.29 15-22 July
no.31 29 July-5 August
no.8   16-23 February 1662.
no.9   23 Feb.-2 March [incomplete]
no.11 9-16 March
no.14 30 March-6 April 1663
no.15 6-13 April
no.17 20-27 April
no.32 3-10 August

Formerly *The Parliamentary intelligencer.*

T.258

8631

The KINGDOMES weekly intelligencer, sent abroad to
prevent mis-information. Printed for H.B. 4°

no. 265 13-20 June 1648.

T.20

8632

The LONDON magazine. London. 8°

August, 1753 [incomplete].

T.437

8633

The LONDON review [of English and foreign literature.
By William Kenrick and others]. London. 8°

Vol. I, nos.1,2 January-February, 1775.

T.676

8634

The MAN in the moon, discovering a world of knavery
under the sunne ... [By John Crouch.] [No imprint.]
4°

no.13 4-11 July 1649.
no.17 8-15 Aug.
no.30 14-21 Nov.

T.259

8635

MEMOIRS for the curious: or, An account of what
occurrs that's rare, secret, extraordinary,
prodigious or miraculous, through the world...
London: R. Janeway, for A. Baldwin. 4°

Vol.I. no.1. 1701.

T.10

8636

The MEMOIRS of the present state of Europe: [or,
The monthly account of occurrences... Done into
English from the original printed at the Hague.
London, for Richard Clavell.] 4°

no.8   August 1693 [imperfect]

T.200

8637

MERCURIUS Aulicus, communicating the intelligence
and affaires of the Court, to the rest of the
Kingdome. [By Sir John Birkenhead and Peter Heylyn.]
[No imprint.]   4°

no.4	22-28 Jan [1642/3]	no.32	6-12 Aug.[1643]
no.8	19-25 Feb.	no.34	20-26 Aug.
no.19	7-13 May [1643]	no.37	10-16 Sept.
no.21	21-27 May	no.44	29 Oct. - 4 Nov.
no.22	28 May - 3 June	no.10	3-9 March [1643/4]
no.28	9-14 July	no.23	2-8 June 1644.
no.31	30 July - 5 Aug.		

T.20

8638

MERCURIUS Aulicus: againe, communicating intelligence
from all parts of the Kingdome, touching all affaires
... [By Samuel Sheppard.] [No imprint.] 4°

no.10,11,12 (in 1 part) 30 March - 20 Apr. 1648.

T.20

8639

MERCURIUS bellicus, or, an alarum to all rebels ...
[By Sir John Birkenhead.] [No imprint.] 4°

no.2 22-29 Nov. 1647.

T.20

8640

MERCURIUS Britanicus: communicating the affaires
of great Britaine... [By Thomas Audley.] [London],
G. Bishop, and R. White. 4°

no.6   26 Sept. - 3 Oct. 1643.
no.8   10 - 17 Oct.
no.11 2 - 9 Nov.
no.21 29 Jan. - 5 Feb. 1644.
no.22 5 Feb. - 12 Feb.
no.41 24 - 31 June.
no.51 23 - 30 Sept.

T.20   T.86

8641

MERCURIUS Caledonius. Comprising the affairs now in
agitation in Scotland ... Edinburgh; reprinted at
London.   4°

31 Dec. - 8 Jan. 1661 [i.e. 1660/1].

T.287

8642

MERCURIUS civicus. Londons intelligencer...
London, for Thos. Bates, and I.W.J. 4°

no.113   17 - 24 July 1645.

T.20

8643

MERCURIUS elencticus. Communicating the
unparallell'd proceedings at Westminster, the
head-quarters and other places, discovering their
designes, reproving their crimes, and advising
the Kingdome. [By Sir George Wharton and Samuel
Sheppard.] [No imprint.] 4°

no.4   19-26 Nov. 1647.
no.20 5-12 April 1648.
no.21 12-19 April
no.22 19-26 April

no.46 4-11 October
no.58 26 Dec.-2 Jan. 1648[9].

T.20

8644

MERCURIUS, &c. not - veridicus, nor yet - mutus;
but - Cambro - (or if you please) - honest -
Britannus ... [No imprint.] 4°

no.2 31 Jan. - 6 Feb. 1644.

T.20

8645

MERCURIUS &c. Upon my life new borne, and wants a name,
'troth let the reader impose the same. Veridicus -
I wish thee; if not so, bee - mutus, - for wee lyes
enough doe know. [No imprint.] 4°

17-23 Jan. 1643 [4].

T.86

8646

MERCURIUS melancholicus: or newes from Westminster,
and other parts. [By Martin Parker.] [No imprint.]
4°

no.13 20-29 Nov. 1647.

T.20

8647

MERCURIUS politicus, communicating the chief
transactions of, and advertisements from the three
kingdomes ... [By Oliver Williams, and others.]
London, John Redmayne.   4°

no.20 21-28 June 1660.

T.67

8648

MERCURIUS politicus. Comprising the sum of all
[foreign] intelligence, with the affairs and designs
now on foot in the three nations... [By Marchamont.
Nedham.] London, Tho. Newcomb.   4°

no.221 31 Aug.7 Sept. 1654 [incomplete]
no.233 23-30 Nov.
no.413 22-29 April 1658.
no.415 13-20 May [incomplete]
no.569 26 May-2 June 1659.
no.277[sic] 30 June-7 July

no.580 21-28 July 1659.
no.583 11-18 August
no.593 3-10 November
no.596 24 Nov.-1 December
no.597 1-8 December
no.601 29 Dec.-5 January
no.605 26 Jan.-2 Feb. 1660.
no.606 2-9 February
no.607 9-16 February
no.609 23 Feb.-1 March
no.612 15-22 March

no.613 22-29 March

T.67 T.259

8649

MERCURIUS politicus: or, An antidote to popular
mis-representations; containing reflections on
the present state of affairs. [By James Drake.]
London: for Tho. Hodgson; (James Orme; Samuel
Briscoe). 4°

Vols.I and II, nos. 1-51 12 June-1 December 1705.

T.191

8650

MERCURIUS pragmaticus. Communicating intelligence
from all parts... [By Marchamont Nedham and others.]
[No imprint.] 4°

no.27   26 Sept. - 3 Oct. 1648.

T.20

8651

MERCURIUS publicus: comprising the sum of forraign
intelligence; with the affairs now in agitation in
England, Scotland, and Ireland. [By Giles Dury and
Henry Muddiman.] London, J. Macock, and Tho.
Newcomb. 4°

no.11 8-15 March 1659[60].
no.15 5-12 April 1660.
no.19 3-10 May
no.20 10-17 May

no.23 31 May-7 June
no.24 7-14 June
no.37 6-13 September
no.42 11-18 October
no.53 20-27 December

no.5   31 Jan.-7 Feb. 1661
no.18 2-9 May
no.21 23-30 May

no.16 16-23 April 1663.
no.21 21-28 May

Published alternately with *The Parliamentary
intelligencer.*

T.67 T.258

8652

MERCURIUS Romanus. Londini prostant venales apud
B. Bragge. 4°

num.2 3-10 June 1706. 2 copies.

T.194

8653

MERCURIUS veridicus. Communicating some choice
intelligence domestick and forreign. [London], D.
Maxwell.   4°

no.1   29 May - 5 June 1660.
no.2 5-12 June.

T.67

8654

The MODERATE informer communicating the most
remarkable transactions both civil and military in
the common-wealth of England ... [By Marchamont
Nedham.] London, William Gilberson.   4°

19-25 May [1659].

T.259

8655

The MODERATOR: published for promoting of peace...
and for uniting the hearts of the people to her
Majesty and government. London: S. Malthus.   4°

Vol.I, no.2 May 16-23, 1705.
        no.3 May 23-30.

T.191

8656

The MONETHLY account. [No imprint.] 4°

no.3   December [1687].

no.11 August [1688].

T.263   T.373

8657

The MONTHLY miscellany: or, Memoirs for the
curious. By several hands. London: sold by
J. Morphew.   4°

September, October 1707.
April, May, June 1708.

T.10

8658

The MONTHLY register, or, Memoirs of the affairs of
Europe... London, for Sam. Buckley, and sold by
A. Baldwin.   4°

Vol.III, no.12 December 1705.
Vol.IV, nos.5-8, 10-12 1706.
Vol.V,   nos.1-3 1707.

T.21

8659

The MUSES mercury: or, Monthly miscellany...
[Edited by John Oldmixon.] London, J.H. for
Andrew Bell.   4°

Vol.1,no.6 June 1707.

T.269

8660

The NEWES, published for satisfaction and
information of the people. [By Sir Roger L'Estrange.]
London, Richard Hodgkinson.   4°

no.1   3 Sept. 1663
no.4   24 September
no.28 7 April 1664
no.30 14 April
no.32 21 April
no.90 17 November
no.100 22 December

no.12 9 February 1664/5
no.44 8 June 1665 [incomplete]
no.64 17 August
no.77 21 September
no.93 16 November
no.5   14 December.

Published alternately with *The intelligencer.*

T.258

8661

OCCURRENCES from foreign parts. Also a particular
advice from the Office of Intelligence ... [By Oliver
Williams and other.] London, John Redmayne.   4°

no.32 18-25 Oct. 1659.

The sub-title changes to *With an exact accompt of the
publick transactions of the three nations ...*

no.84 17-24 April 1660.

no.92 15-23 May.
no.96 29 May - 5 June.

Published alternately with *A particular advice from
foreign parts.*

T.67 T.259

8662

The PARLIAMENTARY intelligencer, comprising the sum of
forraign intelligence, with the affairs now in
agitation in England, Scotland, and Ireland ... [By
Henry Muddiman.] London, John Macock and Tho. Newcomb.
4°

no.19	30 April - 7 May 1660.	Published alternately
no.20	7-14 May.	with *Mercurius publicus.*
np.24	4-11 June.	Continued as *The*
no.30	16-23 July.	*Kingdomes intelligencer.*
no.31	23-30 July.	
no.38	10-17 Sept.	

T.67

8663

A PARTICULAR advice from foreign parts, also from the
Office of Intelligence ... London, John Redmayne. 4°

no.47 9-16 Dec. 1659.

Published alternately with *Occurrences from foreign
parts.* Continued as *An exact accompt of the daily
proceedings.*

T.259

8664

A PERFECT diurnall of the passages in Parliament. [London], for William Cook. 4°

[no.8] 28 Feb.-7 March 1641[2].
no.10 14-21 March
no.3 27 June-4 July 1642.
no.9 8-15 August
no.10 15-22 August.

T.20

8665

A PERFECT diurnal of the passages in Parliament... more fully and exactly taken than by any other printed copies... London, for Francis Coules. [Has a woodcut of the Commons in session.] 4°

no.14 12-19 Sept. [1642].
no.35 6-13 Feb. [1642/3].

T.20

8666

A PERFECT diurnall of some passages in Parliament: and from other parts of this Kingdome. [By Samuel Pecke.] [London], for Francis Coles and Laurence Blaiklock. 4°

no.90 14-21 April 1645.
no.91 21-28 April
no.183 25 Jan.-1 Feb. 1646.
no.204 21-28 June 1647.
no.224 8-15 Nov.
no.271 2-9 October 1648.

no.286 1-8 January 1648/9.
no.297 2-9 April 1649.
no.298 9-16 April

T.20 T.259

8667

A PERFECT diurnal of every dayes [or the dayly] proceedings in Parliament. [By Oliver Williams and others.] London, John Redmayne (Tho. Newcomb). 4°

no.1 21 Feb. 1659[60]. no.13 7 March.
no.2 22 Feb. no.18 13 March.
no.4 24 Feb. no.19 14 March.
no.7 29 Feb.
no.8 1 March.
no.11 5 March.

T.67

8668

A PERFECT diurnall of some passages and proceedings of, and in relation to the armies in England and Ireland. [By John Rushworth and Samuel Pecke.] London, Francis Leach, and Edward Griffin. 4°

no.12 25 Feb. - 4 March 1649 [50].
no.98 20-27 Oct. 1651.
no.146 20-27 Sept. 1652.
no.258 13-20 Nov. 1654.
no.268 22-29 Jan. 1655.

T.259

8669

PERFECT occurrences of every daie iournall in Parliament, and other moderate intelligence. Collected by Luke Harruney [i.e. Henry Walker]. London, for I. Coe, and A. Coe.

no.23 4-11 June 1647.

T.20

8670

PERFECT occurrences of the most remarkable passages in the common-wealth of England, Scotland, and Ireland... London, John Redmayne. 4°

no.23 9 - 16 Dec. 1659.

T.259

8671

The POLITICAL register. [Edited by John Almon.] London. 8°

Vol. II, no. 13 April, 1768.
no. 14 May, 1768.

T.423

8672

The POLITICAL state of Great Britain... [By Abel Boyer.] London: for J. Baker. 8°

February, 1710/11. 2nd ed.
April, 1711.
February, 1711/12.

T.414

8673

The POST-angel: or, Universal entertainment... Done by a society of clergy-men, gentlemen, &c. London: printed; and are to be sold by A. Baldwin; and Eliphal Jaye. 4°

Vol. V. no. 2. August 1702.

T.10

8674

The POST boy. [Edited by Abel Roper.] London: L. Beardwell; (for John Morphew). Fol.

no. 2434 December 16-19, 1710.
no. 4335 May 9-11, 1717.
no. 4356 June 27-29.
no. 4357 June 29-July 2.
no. 4388 Sept. 10-12.
no. 4411 November 2-5.

T.133 T.394 T.439

8675

The PRESENT state of Europe: or, The historical and political monthly mercury... Continued monthly from the original published at the Hague... London: for Henry Rhodes, and John Harris; (Eliz.Harris). 4°

Vol.II, nos.8,10 August, October 1691.
Vol.VI, nos.4-11 April - November 1695.
Vol.X, no.2 February 1699.
Vol.XV, nos.8,9,12 1704.
Vol.XVI, nos.1,2,6-12 1705.
Vol.XVII, no.1 January 1706.

T.68 T.145 T.263

8676

The PUBLICK intelligencer, communicating the chief occurrences and proceedings within the dominions of England, Scotland, and Ireland. [By Marchamont Nedham and John Canne.] London, Tho. Newcomb. 4°

no.62 15-22 Dec. 1656.
no.67 19-26 Jan. 1657.
no.74 9-16 March
no.710[sic] 20-27 April
no.113 26 April-3 May 1658.
no.133 5-12 July
no.153 29 Nov.-6 Dec.
no.166 28 Feb.-7 March 1659.
no.178 23-30 May
no.180 6-13 June
no.184 4-11 July
no.187 25 July-1 August
no.191 22-29 August
no.195 19-26 Sept.
no.199 17-24 Oct.
no.200 24-31 Oct.
no.207 12-19 Dec.
no.211 9-16 Jan. 1660
no.216 13-20 Feb.
no.221 5-12 March
no.223 19-26 March

T.67 T.259

8677

The PUBLICK intelligencer: communicating the chief transactions of, and advertisements from the three nations ... [By Oliver Williams and others.] London, John Redmayne.

no.3 23-30 April 1660.

T.67

8678

The PUBLISHER: containing miscellanies in prose and verse. Collected by J. Crokatt. London: for M. Cooper. 8°

nos.1-4 1745.

T.436

8679

The PULPIT. London: Knight & Lacey. 8°

no.114 June 23, 1825.
no.117 July 14.
no.118 July 21.

T.575

8680

The REHEARSAL reviv'd. In a conference between High-Church, Low-Church, no-church, Old-Whig, and crafty. [By Edmund Stacy.] London: printed for the author, and sold by Benj. Bragg. 4°

Vol.I, nos.1-20, 22 September-5 November 1709.
Vol.II, no. 1, 12 November 1709.
Duplicates of all except Vol. I, no. 1. One copy of no. 15 is mis-numbered.

T.191 T.267 T.490

8681

A REVIEW of the state of the British nation. [By Daniel Defoe.] London, John Baker. 4°

Vol.VII, nos.1-155 March 28, 1710 - March 22, 1711.
Vol.VIII, nos.12,18,55,72-76,78-81,83-109,191,193 April 21, 1711 - June 17, 1712.
[A new series entitled] Review.
Vol.I, nos.16,17,22,23,29-34,41-68,70-72,74-82 September 23, 1712 - April 11, 1713.

T.256 T.257 T.268

8682

ROYAL SOCIETY OF LONDON.

Philosophical transactions. [London], for John Martyn, and James Allestry; (for Sam. Smith and Benj. Walford). 4°

no.16 August 1666.
no.273 August 1701.

T.10 T.504

8683

The ST. James's post. London: for J. Baker. Fol.

no.331 March 4-6, 1716-17.
no.33[4] March 11-13.
no.337 March 18-20.
no.341 March 27-29, 1717.
no.342 March 29-April 1.

T.13

8684

SEVERALL proceedings in Parliament ... [London], for Robert Ibbitson. 4°

no. 66 26 Dec. - 2 Jan. 1650[1].
no.146 8-15 July 1652.

Title changes to *Severall proceedings of state affairs.*

no.200 21-28 July 1653.
no.249 29 June - 6 July 1654.

T.259

8685

The STUDENT, or The Oxford monthly miscellany. [Edited by Christopher Smart.] Oxford: for J. Newbery, London; and J. Barrett in Oxford. 8°

nos.1-9 January-September, 1750.

T.676

8686

USEFUL transactions in philosophy [By William King.] London: for Bernard Lintott. 8°

numb.1 January and February, 1708/9.

T.522

8687

The WEEKLY intelligencer of the common-wealth... London, Robert Ibbetson (F. Neile). 4°

no.1 24 Sept.-1 Oct. 1650.
no.91 21-28 Sept. 1652.

T.259

8688

The WEEKLY pacquet of advice from France: or, An account of the present French persecution. London, John Bullord. 4°

no.1. 1689.

T.201

8689

The WEEKLY pacquet of advice from Rome restored: or, The history of popery continued. [London], for Langley Curtis.

no.22 alias 26 3 Dec. 1680.
no.27 10 Dec.
no.40 11 March 1680/1.
no.41 18 March.

Formerly *The anti-Roman pacquet.*

T.105

8690

The WEST Riding magazine; or, Journal of literature, religion, science, and art. Wakefield, Nichols. 8°

no.1 January, 1834.

T.779

2043A

An ACCOUNT of the Bank of Credit in the city of
London. [By John Houghton?] London, John Gain,
and are to be sold by the booksellers every where,
[1682?]   4°

Not in Wing.
T.255

2909A

LITTLETON (Edward)

The groans of the plantations: or a true account
of their grievous and extreme sufferings by the
heavy impositions upon sugar, and other hardships.
Relating more particularly to the island of
Barbados. [Anon.] London, M. Clark, 1689.   4°

Wing L 2577.
T.255

3060A

SOME ways for raising of money, humbly offer'd to
the consideration of the Parliament. By a
person of quality. London: Randall Taylor, 1690.
4°

Wing S 4633.
T.255

3320A

PRICE (Phil.)

Gravamina mercatoris: or, The tradesman's complaint
of the abuses in the execution of the statutes
against bankrupts... [London, 1694?]   4°

Wing P 3398.
T.255

3330A

SOME considerations offered against the continuance
of the Bank of England, in a letter to a member of
the present Parliament. [London, 1694.]   4°

Wing S 4491.
T.255

3345A

CLEMENT (Simon)

A discourse of the general notions of money, trade,
& exchanges, as they stand in relation each to
other... By a merchant. London, printed in the
year, 1695.   4°

Wing C 4638.
T.255

3346A

CROSFEILD (Robert)

Great Britain's tears, humbly offered to the
consideration of the Lords and Commons in
Parliament assembled. London, printed in the year
1695.   4°

Wing C 7244.
T.255

3376A

OBJECTIONS to Mr. Lowndes's proposals about the
amendment of our coin. London, Tho. Hodgkin,
and are to be sold by John Whitlock, 1695.   4°

Wing O 88.
T.255

3383A

POYNTZ (John)

The present prospect of the famous and fertile
island of Tobago... 2nd ed. London, John Astwood
for the author, and sold by William Staresmore,
and at the Marine Coffee-house, 1695.   4°

Wing P 3131.
T.255

3422A

FURTHER proposals for amending and settling the
coyn. By a person of honour. London: M. Whitlock,
1696.   4°

Wing F 2563.
T.255

3437A

The PROPOSAL for the raising of the silver coin of
England, from 60 pence in the ounce to 75 pence,
considered; with the consequences thereof.
London: for Richard Cumberland, 1696.   4°

Wing P 3702.
T.255

3437B

PROPOSALS for national banks; whereby the profits
on usury, tho reduc'd to three per cent. per annum,
will supply his Majesty more plentifully than ever
to carry on the war... The second impression with
corrections and additions. London, printed for
the author, and sold by Peter Parker, and John
Waltho, and John Gouge, 1696.   4°

Wing P 3729.
T.255

3448A

VICKARIS (A.)

An essay, for regulating of the coyn... By A.U.
London, James O. for Richard Cumberland, 1696.
4°

Wing V 337.
T.255

3497A

COX (Sir Richard)

Some thoughts on the Bill depending before... the
House of Lords, for prohibiting the exportation
of the woolen manufactures of Ireland to foreign
parts. Humbly offer'd to their lordships. [Anon.]
London, J. Darby for Andr. Bell, 1698.   4°

Wing C 6724.
T.255

6714A

JAMES II, *King of England.*

Memoirs of the English affairs, chiefly naval, from
the year 1660, to 1673. Written by James, Duke
of York, under his administration of Lord High
Admiral, &c. Published from his original letters,
and other royal authorities. [First collected by
Lord F. Howard.] London, 1729.   8°

Wanting the title-page, prelims. and all pages
following p.272.

T.774

Index

A.(C.) 8500
A.(D.F.) see: Atterbury (Francis)
A.(F.) see: Atterbury (Francis)
A.(M.) 1737
A.(P.) 2335
A.(W.) see: Atwood (William)
Abbot (George) 106
Abbot (Robert) *Bishop of Salisbury* 27
Abbot (Robert) *Minister of St.Austin's* 111
Abelard to Eloisa [J.Cawthorn] 7181
Abingdon (Willoughby Bertie) *Earl of* see: Bertie (Willoughby)
Abrabanel (Solomon) see: Arnall (William)
Abraham ben Mordecai Farisol 3084
Abridgment of the controversy [S.Downes] 6458,6548,6556
Abridgment of the prerogatives of St.Ann 2674
Absalom and Achitophel [Dryden] 1909-10, 2069-70
Absalom senior [E.Settle] 2145
Abstract of An answer lately publish'd [T.Bateman] 5587
Abstract of common principles [E.Stephens] 3624
Abstract of the contents of several letters 1610
Abstract or state of the case 4250
Abtrucke der verwarungs schrifft 3
Academicus see: Remarks on a pamphlet by Thomas Kipling
Accomplish'd hero 7209
Account and defence of the protestation [F.Atterbury] 4256
Account of a conversation concerning right regulation [A.Fletcher] 3904
Account of a dream at Harwich 4434
Account of a medical controversy 7240
Account of a most horrid and barbarous murther 3296
Account of all the considerable pamphlets [T.Herne] 6395
Account of charity-schools 4141,4369,4489,4643, 4987,5295,5784
Account of Mr.Blunts late book 3230
Account of Mr.Calderon 8491
Account of Mr.Ferguson his common-place book [J.Glanvill] 1455
Account of Monsieur de Quesne's late expedition 2164
Account of Sueden [J.Robinson] 5214
Account of the abolishing of duels in France [Defoe] 5630
Account of the arraignment... of the dog 2068
Account of the damnable prizes 5296
Account of the doctrine... of Mr.Richard Davis 3572
Account of the Earl of Galway's conduct 4988
Account of the execution of... Earl Ferrers 7425
Account of the French usurpation [S.Bethel] 1624
Account of the growth of deism [W.Stephens] 3445,3453
Account of the growth of knavery [R.L'Estrange] 1580
Account of the late persecution of the protestants 2675
Account of the late proceedings in the council of the Royal Society 4644
Account of the late Scotch invasion 4490-1
Account of the life and writings of Mr.John Le Clerc 5297
Account of the manner of execution... of Richard Kirkby 3799
Account of the new sheriffs 1738
Account of the obligations [R.Ferguson] 5088
Account of the present persecution of the Church in Scotland [T.Morer] 3037
Account of the proceedings at the Guild-hall 1611
Account of the proceedings between the two houses of Convocation [C.Trimnell] 3986
Account of the proceedings in Convocation [E.Gibson] 4299
Account of the proceedings on a charge of high treason against John Martin 8002
Account of the riots [Defoe] 5944
Account of the rise of silver 8598
Account of the rise... of the Magdalen Charity [W.Dodd] 7497
Account of the Scotch plot 3859
Account of the sessions of Parliament in Ireland 3261
Account of the signal escape of John Fraser 7127
Account of the Society for Propagating the Gospel 4142
Account of the state and progress of the present negotiations of peace [A.Boyer] 5014
Account of the transaction between Admiral Benbow 3997
Account of what past on Monday the 28th of October 1689. 2987
Achan and Elymas [E.Stephens] 3974
Achard (John) see: Eachard (John)
Acis and Galatea [J.Gay] 7287
Ackland (Thomas Gilbank) 8315-6
Acland (John) 7820
Acres (Joseph) 5785
Acta eruditorum publicata Lipsiae 8606
Acte d'appel interjetté par Monsieur le Procureur [A.de Harlay] 2731
Active testimony of the true Presbyterians 7241
Acts of the general assembly of the French clergy 2336
Ad clerum. A sermon [R.Sanderson] 1357
Ad populum: or, A lecture [P.Hausted] 610
Ad Roberti Cardinalis Bellarmini librum 55
Adair (William) 8252
Adams (John) 3341,3397,3709,4251,4492,4645
Adams (Peter) 1499
Adams (Rice) 4370
Adams (Richard) 3514
Adams (Samuel) 7677
Adams (Thomas) 56,69
Adams weekly courant 7305
Adamson (John) 4252
Addison (Joseph) 4493,5568,5926,6253-4,6359
Addison (Lancelot) 1874,4558
Address [Defoe] 3885
Address of John Dryden 2830
Address to the Church of England clergy 4646
Address to the clergy of the Church of England, answer'd 3998
Address to the free-men and free-holders [E.Bohun] 2052
Address to the inhabitants of the two great cities [M.Tindal] 6762
Address to the Oxfordshire addressors 4647
Address to the peers of England 5927
Address to the senate of the University of Cambridge [W.Farish] 8350
Address to the Society of Friends 8157
Address to the yeomanry of Westmorland 8317
Adee (Nicholas) 2337
Adhemar de Monteil de Grignan (Jacques) 1287
Admonition for the fifth of November [S.Grascombe] 3118
Admonition to a deist [W.Assheton] 2341
Admonition to the dissenting inhabitants of the diocess of Derry [W.King] 3313
Advantages of early instruction 8386
Advice from a dissenter 2676
Advice from Switzerland 4085
Advice of a friend, to the army [W.Harper] 7114
Advice to a lady [G.Lyttelton] 6835
Advice to a painter 1612
Advice to a young gentleman 5569
Advice to electors; by a well-wisher 3342
Advice to freeholders and other electors 2552
Advice to new-married husbands [W.Plaxton] 5483
Advice to posterity [J.Lewis] 7351
Advice to the confuter of Bellarmin 2553
Advice to the electors of Great Britain [Defoe] 4399
Advice to the English youth 2677
Advice to the gentlemen freeholders 4648
Advice to the people called Methodists [J.Wesley] 7174
Advice to the people of Great Britain [Defoe] 5822
Advice to the readers of the Common-prayer [T.Seymour] 2146
Advocate 898
Advocates for murther and rebellion 5786
Aedo y Gallart (Diego de) 154
Aesop at Oxford 4494
Aesop at Paris [E.Ward] 3707
Aesop at Portugal 3860
Aesop at the Bell-tavern [W.Pittis] 5194
Aesop at Tunbridge 3487
Aesop in Europe 4143
Aesop in Scotland 3861
Aesop return'd from Tunbridge 3488
Affecting case of the Queen of Hungary [G.Lyttelton] 7019
Agate (John) 4371,4404,4983
Age of infidelity [T.Williams] 8028
Age of paper 8003
Agreement of the associated ministers [R.Gilpin] 962
Agreement of the people 834
Agustin (Antonio) 6026
Ahlers (Cyriacus) 6652
Ainsworth (Henry) 575
Ainsworth (Samuel) 641
Akenside (Mark) 6899
Akerby (George) 6708
Alarum to the Christian Church 5298
Alazonomastix Philalethes see: More (Henry)
Albemarle (George Monck) *Duke of* see: Monck (George)
Alberoni (Giulio) 6391
Alceste, tragedie-opera [P.Quinault] 7726
Aldernardum carmen Duci Malburiensi 4372
Aldrich (Henry) 2554,3632
Aldwinckle. A candid examination [H.Mayo] 7517
Alexander's feast [J.Dryden] 7730
Alexis Petrovich, *Tsarevich* 6650
Ali ibn Abi Talib 6105
Alibone (John) see: Allibond (John)
Alingham (William) 3489
All at stake Hannover or Perkin 5502
All men mad [E.Ward] 3992
Allegations of the Turky Company 1968
Allen (Edward) 8227,8237-8
Allen (John) 7402
Allen (Joseph) 5299
Allen (Ralph) 7463
Allen (Robert) 5300
Allen (Thomas) *Rector of Kettering* 7277
Allen (Sir Thomas) 1272,1360
Allen (William) 1085,2975
Allestree (Charles) 2338
Allestree (Richard) 1301
Alley (Jerom) 7926
Allibond (John) 3999,6106
Allies and the late ministry defended [F.Hare] 5108-10,5409
Allix (Peter) 2678,3633,4989-90,5285-6
Almeria: or, Parental advice [Mrs Cutts] 7664
Almon (John) 7573-4,7589,8671
Alsop (George) 1613
Alsop (Vincent) 1739,1899
Alteration in the Triennial Act 6015
Altham (Michael) 2555-6
Altham (Roger) 3710,4000,5301,6358,6446
Althoven (Joannes Petrus ab) 1286
American Continental Congress 7660
Ames (Richard) 3085-6
Amhurst (Nicholas) 6255,6653
Amicable accomodation of the difference [J.Gother] 2502
Amicable Society for a Perpetual Assurance-office 4649
Amicus see: Letter to Mr.Bisset
Aminadab: or, The Quaker's vision 4650,4677, 5203
Aminadab: or the Quaker's vision, explained 4651
Analyst [G.Berkeley] 6838
Ananias and Saphira discover'd 1614
Anatomy of a Jacobite-Tory 2988
Anatomy of a project 3531
Anatomy of an equivalent [G.Savile] 2786
Anatomy of Dr.Gauden's Idolized non-sence 1102
Anatomy of Exchange-alley [Defoe] 6378-9
Anatomy of warre [R.Ward] 437
Ancienne prediction du celebre prophete Merlin 4253
Ancient amity restor'd 5302
Ancient liturgy of the Church of Jerusalem 7089
Ancilla grammaticae 1253
And what if the Pretender should come? [Defoe] 5631
Anderson (Christopher) 8359
Anderton (William) 3258
Andrei (Antonio) 7735
Andrewes (Lancelot) 70,754,1199
Andrews (Elizabeth) 6695
Andrews (John) 6852
Angell (Philemon) 1870
Anglesey (Arthur Annesley) *Earl of* see: Annesley (Arthur)
Angliae speculum [P.Symon] 1586
Angliara (Juan de) 1
Anglo-nativus see: Letter to Sir John Phillips
Anglorum singultus [E.Peirce] 1159
Anguis in herba [H.Maxwell] 3763,5173
Animadversions by way of answer [J.Reed] 2639
Animadversions on Dr.Burnet's History [T.Comber] 2057,2065
Animadversions on Mr.Johnson's answer [W.Hopkins] 3128
Animadversions on the eight theses [G.Smalridge] 2655
Animadversions upon a late pamphlet [F.Turner] 1519
Animadversions upon, or an impartial answer 4991
Animadversions upon the modern explanation [J.Collier] 2861
Animadversions upon those notes 271
Anne, *Queen* 3781-3,4992-6,5303-5,5570-1, 5787-8,5862,5926,6004
Anne, *Saint* 2674
Annesley (Arthur) *Earl of Anglesey* 995,2060, 2154,2165,2679,3484,5271
Annesley (Catharine) *Countess of Anglesey* 3678
Annesley (James) 7098-9
Annesley (Richard) *Earl of Anglesey* 7098-9
A-Noaks (John) and A-Stiles (Tom) see: Solicitous citizen
Another answer to the letters of... Pitt 7463
Another defence of the unity [C.Fleming] 7144
Another letter to Mr.Almon 7574
Anstey (Christopher) 7718
Anstis (John) 4144,6624
Answer at large to Mr.Pitt's speech 7493
Answer of a barrister at law to the Curate 5572
Answer of a letter from a friend in the country 1875
Answer of the Commissioners of the Navie 691
Answer paragraph by paragraph, to the Memorial 4001
Answer to a book, entituled, Reason and authority [T.Bainbridge] 2561
Answer to a book, intituled, The state of the protestants in Ireland [C.Leslie] 3207
Answer to a dangerous pamphlet 7176
Answer to a discourse concerning the celibacy [G.Tully] 2817
Answer to a discourse intituled, Papists protesting [W.Sherlock] 2530,2797
Answer to a late book written against the learned and reverend Dr.Bentley [S.Whateley] 3571
Answer to a late dialogue between a new Catholick convert [W.Sherlock] 2651
Answer to a late pamphlet, entituled An examination of the scheme [J.Andrews] 6852
Answer to a late pamphlet, entituled, Obedience and submission [T.Wagstaffe] 3072-3,3228
Answer to a late pamphlet, entitled, The experiment 4254
Answer to a late pamphlet, intitled, Observations on the writings of the Craftsman 6766
Answer to a late pamphlet, intituled, The judgment and doctrine 2557
Answer to a letter from a gentleman in the country 3490
Answer to A letter from the Reverend Mr.Charles Leslie [A.Campbell] 6366
Answer to a letter of enquiry into the grounds 1372
Answer to a letter to a dissenter [Anon.] 2558
Answer to a letter to a dissenter [R.L. L'Estrange] 2614
Answer to a letter to Dr.Burnet [G.Burnet] 2359
Answer to A letter to Dr.Sherlock [T.Wagstaffe] 3227
Answer to a letter to Mr.Hoadly 4997
Answer to A letter to the Bishop of Bangor [T.Burnet] 6115-6
Answer to a letter written out of the country 473
Answer to a libel entituled, A dialogue 3398
Answer to a pamphlet entitled, "The question stated [N.Forster] 7553
Answer to a pamphlet entitul'd Frauds and abuses at St.Paul's [T.Bateman] 5588
Answer to a pamphlet entituled, The proceedings of the lower house of Convocation [C.Trimnell] 5911
Answer to a pamphlet intituled the Lord George Digby his apologie 443
Answer to a paper, entituled, A brief account of the designs 1876
Answer to a paper, intituled, Reflections on the Prince of Orange's declaration 2680
Answer to a printed book, intituled, Observations upon some of his Majesties late answers [W.Digges] 317
Answer to a printed letter, said to be written by Mr.Lesley [A.Campbell] 6267
Answer to a printed letter to Dr.W.P. [W.Payne] 3042
Answer to a printed libel 6447
Answer to a proposition in order to the proposing [W.Prynne] 1063
Answer to a question that no body thinks of [Defoe] 5632
Answer to a scandalous pamphlet [H.Payne] 2623
Answer to a second scandalous book [W.King] 5136
Answer to a seditious pamphlet 444
Answer to a speech without doores [Sir J. Birkenhead] 698
Answer to a treatise out of ecclesiastical history 3087
Answer to all the excuses and pretences [E.Synge] 6669
Answer to an anonymous letter 8109
Answer to Doctor Fernes reply [C.Herle] 520
Answer to Dr.Ibbot's sermon 6485
Answer to Dr.Sherlock's Case of allegiance [T.Browne] 3094
Answer to Dr.Sherlock's Preservative [L.Sabran] 2782
Answer to Dr.Sherlock's Vindication [T.Wagstaffe] 3228
Answer to Dr.Stillingfleet's sermon [J.Humfrey] 1790
Answer to Mr.Clark's Third defence [A.Collins] 4396
Answer to Mr.Read's case 2044
Answer to Mr.Toland's Reasons 3711
Answer to Mr.Whiston's challenge 5573
Answer to Monsieur de Meaux's book 2559
Answer to one part of a late infamous libel [W.Pulteney] 6767,6792
Answer to Pereat papa 1877
Answer to some considerations on the spirit of Martin Luther [F.Atterbury] 2560

Answer to some papers lately printed [E.Stillingfleet] 2539
Answer to some queries, concerning schism [H.Gandy] 3595
Answer to that part of Dr.Brett's sermon 5306
Answer to the address of the Oxford-University 4652
Answer to the address presented to the ministers [J.Williams] 2825
Answer to the Amicable accomodation [W.Sherlock] 2507,2531
Answer to the arguments 4658
Answer to the Bishop of Oxford's reasons [W.Lloyd] 2746
Answer to the black-list 3634
Answer to the case of the old East-India Company 3573
Answer to the chief, or materiall heads 801
Answer to the City ministers letter 2777
Answer to the compiler of the Nubes testium [E.Gee] 2724
Answer to The country parson's plea 6868
Answer to the Discourse on free-thinking 5574
Answer to the Examiner's cavile 5575
Answer to the exceptions made against the Ld Bp of Oxford's charge 5576
Answer to the late K.James's last declaration [Defoe] 3246
Answer to the Mock mourners 3715
Answer to the new motions 209
Answer to the Nonjurors charge of schism [A.A.Sykes] 6093
Answer to the paper delivered by Mr.Ashton [E.Fowler] 3009
Answer to the Pope's bull 6900
Answer to the query of a deist 2569
Answer to the representers reflections [W.Clagett] 2701
Answer to the Request to protestants [W.Sherlock] 2652
Answer, to this important inquiry 6107
Answer to this quodlibetical question 1187
Answer to three late pamphlets [W.Sherlock] 2653
Answer to Two letters, concerning the East-India Company 1480
Answer to Vox cleri [W.Payne] 3043
Answers commanded by his Majesty 1894
Answers from the holy Scriptures 8471
Answers of some brethren of the ministerie 186
Anthonie (Francis) 45
Antichrist 8387
Anticoton 53
Antidote against Mr.Baxters palliated cure [E.Bagshaw] 1339
Antidote against presbytery 5928
Antidote against the growth of popery 5710
Antidotum Sarisburiense 5577
Antiquity of the Church of Rome 8370
Antiquity of the protestant religion [E.Pelling] 2624
Antiquity reviv'd 3231
Anti-Roman pacquet 8607
Antithelemite (H.Maurice] 2424
Anti-toleration, or a modest defence 692
Anti-weesils 3088
Antraigues (Emmanuel Henri Alexandre de Launay) *Comte de* see: Launay [E.H.A.de]
Apologetical vindication of the Church [G.Hickes] 2602
Apologetical vindication of the present bishops 4998
Apologie and vindication of the major part 996
Apologie for the Church of England [E.Bohun] 2352
Apology for purchases of lands 1103
Apology for such of the episcopal clergy 6108
Apology for the ancient right and power of the bishops [J.Stephens] 1220
Apology for the builder [N.Barbon] 2344
Apology for the Church of England [G.Burnet] 2685
Apology for the clergy of Scotland [A.Monro] 3268
Apology for the clergy of the city of Bristol 5307
Apology for the conduct of a late celebrated second-rate minister 7177,7233
Apology for the Contemplations [J.Cross] 2577
Apology for the danger of the Church [T.Gordon] 6388
Apology for the East-India Company [W.Atwood] 2989
Apology for the English presbyterians 3541-2
Apology for the life of Mr.T.C. 6939
Apology for the liturgy and clergy [S.Horsley] 7891
Apology for the new separation [G.Hickes] 3124
Apology for the protestants 1878
Apology for the protestants of France 2166
Apology for the pulpits [J.Williams] 2729,2812,2826
Apology for the use of the English liturgy [W.Gordon] 6290
Apostates: or, The revolters [J.Tutchin] 3706
Apotheosis basilike 4373
Apparition. A poem [A.Evans] 4750-1
Appeal from the city to the country 4653
Appeal from the country to the city [C.Blount] 1625
Appeal of murther from certain unjust judges [S.Grascombe] 3258
Appeal to all true English-men [S.Grascombe] 3550
Appeal to Caesar 7128
Appeal to heaven and earth [E.Stephens] 3165
Appeal to patrons 8545
Appeal to the fellows of the Royal Society 7788
Appeal to the people: part the second 7391
Appeal to the people: containing, the genuine and entire letter 7359
Appeal to thy conscience [E.Fisher] 4758
Appeale to thy conscience [E.Fisher] 511
Appendix to the agreement for the people 834
Appendix to the foregoing letter [S.Grascombe] 3197
Appendix to Two discourses [G.Smith] 6837
Appleton (Henry) 908
Apthorp (East) 7706,7739
Aquila Furstenbergica in petra moriens 2045
Ararat 8432
Arbuckle (James) 6359
Arbuthnot (John) 4255,5308-12,6147,6654,6848
Archaicus see: Rejection and restoration of the Jews
Archer (Edmond) 4999
Archer (John) 7789
Arderne (James) 1104,1524
Are these things so? [J.Miller] 6949,6952 6959
Arends (Wilhelm Erasmus) 4374
Aretine see: Murray (William)
Argument against war 3635
Argument for union [T.Tenison] 2242
Argument from the Civil Law 5929
Argument of a learned judge [F.North] 3944
Argument of the Divine legation [J.Towne] 7312
Argument of the Letter concerning toleration [J.Proast] 3048
Argument proving that the design of employing and enobling foreigners [Defoe] 6133
Argument proving, that the imposition 3636
Argument, shewing, that a standing army [J.Trenchard] 3458,3481
Arguments and reasons to prove the inconvenience [J.Aucher] 871
Arguments relating to a restraint 5313
Argyle (Archibald Campbell) *Marquess of* see: Campbell (Archibald)
Ariosto (Lodovico) 7775
Aristarchus ampullans [J.Barnes] 5318
Armageddon: or, The necessity [Defoe] 5049
Armies remembrancer 866
Armstrong (John) 7301
Armstrong (Sir Thomas) 2313
Army's plea for their present practice 997
Arnall (William) 6767,6788,6815,6869
Arne (Thomas Augustine) 7854
Arnold (Richard) see: Arnall (William)
Arraignment and plea of Edw.Fitz-Harris 1879
Arraignment, tryal & condemnation of Algernon Sidney 2260
Arraignment, tryal and condemnation of Stephen Colledge 1880
Arrest of Marshal Belleisle 7102
Arrest rendu en la cour de Parlement 2757
Arsenius 5990, 6078
Art de précher à un abbé [P.de Villiers] 2253
Art of cookery [W.King] 4420
Art of good husbandry 1475
Art of lying and rebelling 5578
Art of managing popular elections 6604
Art of parliamenteering 6540
Art of poetry 6960
Art of politicks [J.Bramston] 6710
Art of preaching [R.Dodsley] 6943
Art of restoring [J.Toland] 5909-10
Artaxerxes. An English opera [P.Metastasio] 7854
Articles against the late Lord Bolingbroke 6853
Articles concerning the surrender of Newark 693
Articles de la societé de plusiers refugiez 3862
Articles for the delivering up of Lichfield-Close 694
Articles of alliance and commerce, between Charles II and Christian V 1380
Articles of impeachment... against Nathaniel Fiennes 445
Articles of peace & alliance between Charles II and Frederick III 1194
Articles of peace, between Charles II and the States General 1421
Articles of peace between his sacred Majesty and the city... of Algiers 1272
Articles of peace, commerce, & alliance 1304
Articles of peace, concluded lately in Italy 576
Articles of peace, or A parcel 3637
Articles of the foundation of King George's College 6661
Articles of the large treaty 217
Articles of the treaty of union 4175
Articles, settlement and officers of the Free Society 2127
Articles stipulated and required from Old Nick 1740
Articuli pacis & confaederationis inter Carolum II et Fridericum III 1195
Arts and pernicious designs of Rome 1825
Arundel (Thomas Howard) *Earl of* see: Howard (Thomas)
Arwaker (Edmund) 2339-40,2484,3297-8,3479
Asboth (Joannes) 7909
Asgill (John) 3399,4654-5,5314-5,5471,5579-81, 6016,6256
Ashburnham (Sir William) 7103,7426
Ashby (Sir John) 3089
Asheton (William) see: Assheton (William)
Ashhurst (William) 802-3
Ashhurst (Sir William Henry) 7927
Ashton (John) 3009,3090-1,3136,3173
Aspland (Robert) 8175
Asplin (Samuel) 5000,5930
Assassination display'd [E.Stacy] 5241
Assembly-man [J.Birkenhead] 1255,3869
Assenters sayings 1881
Assheton (William) 1337-8,1397,2261,2341-2,3593, 4070,4495
Association for Preserving Liberty and Property 7928
Astell (Mary) 3574,3863-5,4125,6181
Aston (Sir Richard) 7587
Aston (Sir Thomas) 1105
Astrea triumphans 3800
Atalantis major [Defoe] 5050
Atchison (Thomas) 8536
Atheist unmasked 2343
Athenian catechism 8608
Atherton (John) 4793
Atkyns (Sir Robert) 2953
Atrocities of the Corsican demon 8143
Atterbury (Francis) 2560,3178,3299,3455, 3638-40,3667,3712-4,3747,3754,3770,3866-7, 3988,4002-3,4073,4121,4145-8,4177,4187-8, 4256,4375-7,4476,4496-4500,4656-7,4942-3, 5001,5038,5119,5235,5316,5931,6032,6086, 6570,6572,6582,6589,6596-7,6602-3,7525
Atterbury (Lewis) 2485
Atticus see: Congratulatory letter to John Murray
Atwood (George) 8110
Atwood (William) 2167-8,2234,2989,3055,3105
Aucher (John) 871,6257
Audley (Matthew) 6915
Audley (Thomas) 8640
Augsburg Confession 3
Aurea dicta 1895
Aurelius (Abraham) 142
Austin (Samuel) 1364
Authentic account of the riots in Birmingham [J.Belcher] 7910
Authentic account of the whole conduct 7242
Authentic copies of treaties 7946
Authentic narrative of the dissensions 7790
Authentic narrative of the loss of the Earl of Abergavenny 8164
Authenticity of the first and second chapters of St.Matthew [J.C.Velthusen] 7608
Authority of the Church in matters of religion [E.Synge] 6348
Autokatakritos: or hypocrisie unvail'd [R.Boreman] 1226
Automachia: or, The selfe-contradiction [L.Du Moulin] 472
Autophonia 4005
Avaux (Jean Antoine de Mesmes) *comte d'* see: Mesmes (Jean Antoine de)
Averill (John) 6799
Avery (John) 4594-5
Avis a ceux qui auroient dessein 4501
Aviti epistola ad Perillam [W.King] 7433
Awbrey (Timothy) 5932
Axe laid to the root of Christianity 4148
Ayerst (William) 5317
Aylmer (William) 5582
Ayloffe (John) 1612
Aymon (Jean) 4257
Ayscough (Francis) 7343
Azaria and Hushai 2046
Azarias. A sermon [T.Brown] 4677
B., *Earl of* see: Lindsay (Colin)
B(A.) 1481,1615,2831-2,3179,4658-9,5583-4,5933, 6730
B.(B.) 3801
B.(E.) see: Bohun (Edmund)
B.(E.) *Esquire* 2277
B.(F.) 3491,3641,4004
B.(F.) see: Bragge (Francis)
B.(G.) see: Burnet (Gilbert)
B.(G.) *Doctor in Physick* 1232
B.(H.) 1741,6258
B.(H.) see: Burton (Henry)
B.(I.) 998
B.(I.) see: Balmford (James)
B.(I.) *Philomathes* 1253
B.(J.) 1616-7,5267
B.(J.) see: Birkenhead (Sir John)
B.(J.) see: Briscoe (John)
B.(Sir J.) see: Banks (Sir Jacob)
B.(J.) *Esquire* 4005
B.(J.) *of Lynn Regis* 5585-6
B.(J.) *of Worcestershire* see: Browne (John) *Quaker*
B.(J.) *Philalelos* 1882
B.(P.) *Gent.* 3038
B.(R.) 1618,3715,5789
B.(R.) see: Boreman (Robert)
B.(Sir R.) see: Blackmore (Sir Richard)
B.(R.) *Seaman* see: Badiley (Richard)
B.(S.) 1742
B.(S.A.) see: Bruce (Alexander)
B.(T.) 1883
B.(T.) see: Brett (Thomas)
B.(W.) 2169,6259,7881
B.(W.) see: Bromfield (William)
B.(W.) see: Gay (John)
Baber (Thomas) 6834
Babrius 7690
Bachiler (John) 735
Backhouse (James) 7403
Backhouse (Robert) 577
Bacon (Francis) *Viscount St Alban's* 28,30 1188,6507,6633,6651
Bacon (Sir Nicholas) 210
Badiley (Richard) 804,908
Bagot (Lewis) 7791
Bagot (Richard) 8590
Bagshaw (Edward) *the Elder* 1106
Bagshaw (Edward) *the Younger* 999,1000,1107, 1156,1225,1238-9,1339
Bagshaw (Henry) 1482
Baillie (Robert) 446
Bainbridge (Thomas) 2561
Baine (James) 7575
Baker (Daniel) 4149
Baker (Sir George) 7344
Baker (Thomas) 1884
Baker (William) *Fellow of St.John's* 6678
Baker (William) *M.P.* 7929
Baker's vindication 5584
Balch, *Justice* 2120
Baldwin (George) 7740
Baldwin (Robert) 4258,4319,4348
Balguy (Thomas) 7611,7630,7638,7741
Ball (Richard) 2047
Ball (William) 695
Ballad of The King shall enjoy his own 5002
Ballad, or: Some scurrilous reflections 3642
Ballance adjusted 2681
Ballance of Europe 5051
Ballance of power 4502
Ballard (Edward) 7129
Bally (George) 7062
Balmerino (Arthur Elphinstone) *Baron* see: Elphinstone (Arthur)
Balmford (James) 107
Baltimore (George Calvert) *Baron* see: Calvert (George)
Balzac (Jean Louis Guez) *Sieur de* 3802,4503
Bambouzelberg (Bernardine) see: Case of St. Winefred open'd
Bampfield (Thomas) 3291,3338
Bancroft (John) 3092
Bank of England 3331,4016,4345
Bank of England, and their present method of paying 3461
Banks (Sir Jacob) 5007-8,5154,5205,5223,5233, 6360
Baptist, *Master of the Queen's Musick* see: Draghi (Giovanni Baptista)
Barbon (Nicholas) 2344
Barclay (George) 5400
Baring (Francis) 8043
Bar-isajah (Eliazar) 909
Barker (Henry Aston) 8306,8324,8336-7
Barker (John) 7041
Barker (Richard) 4259

Barker (Thomas) 4363
Barksdale (Clement) 1280
Barkstead (John) 1040,1246
Barlaamus 23
Barlee (William) 986
Barlow (Thomas) 1619-20,2682
Barlow (William) 37
Barnard (Sir John) 7130,7155,7163
Barnardiston (Sir Samuel) 2330,3944
Barne (Miles) 2048,2170,2262,2345
Barnes (Joshua) 5318
Baron (William) 3492,4006
Barret (John) 5003
Barrier-treaty vindicated 5319
Barrington (John Shute) Viscount 3803,4097,
   6017,6109,7769-70,8123
Barrington (Shute) 7659,7929
Barrow (Henry) 18,1233,4915
Barrow (Isaac) 1365,1525,1621
Barrow (John) 2171
Barry (Catherine) 4612
Barthelemy (Jean Jacques) 8095
Barton (Samuel) 3180,3400
Barton (Thomas) 447
Barzia y Zambrana (Joseph de) 2346
Basilicus see: Swift (Edmund Lewis Lenthal)
Basire (Isaac) 696
Basset (Joshua) 2561,4052,5004
Baston (Samuel) 3401
Baston (Thomas) 6800
Bastwick (John) 176,642
Bate (James) 6901
Bateman (Thomas) 5587-9
Bates (John) 5790
Bath contest 7547
Bath miscellany 6961
Bath riot described 7570
Bather (Edward) 8344,8492,8501
Bathurst (Henry) 8293
Batt upon Batt [J.Speed] 1858
Batteux (Charles) 7427
Battie (William) 1559
Battle of the sexes [S.Wesley] 6622
Battles. A poem 4007
Baudan de Vestric (Pierre) 3300
Baumgarten (Siegmund Jacob) 7131
Baxter (Richard) 946,1083,1108,1189,1209,1226,
   1242,1302,1339,1420,1737,1743,1887,1953,
   1963,2290,2457,5806,5878
Bayford (John) 8360
Baylie (Robert) see: Baillie (Robert)
Bayly (Anselm) 7302
Bayly (Benjamin) 5005
Bayly (Edward) 7360
Bayly (Richard) 202
Bayly (Thomas) 2049
Baynard (Edward) 6361
Bays, Mr. see: Dryden (John)
Beadon (Richard) 7947
Bealing (Benjamin) 3447
Beane (Richard) 1885
Bearcroft (Philip) 7073,7361
Beasts in power 4504
Beauclerk (Lord James) 7129
Beaucoup de bruit pour une aumelette
   [C.Leslie] 4804
Beaulieu (Luke de) 2562
Beaumanoir (Henri Charles de) 2563
Beaumont (Francis) 2990
Beaumont (Sir Harry) see: Spence (Joseph)
Beauty: or the art of charming
   [R.Dodsley] 6858
Beaven (Thomas) 4292
Becanus (Martinus) 57
Beckett (William) 5320,6486
Bede 3232
Bedell (William) 110,8393
Bedford (Arthur) 6731
Bedford (Hilkiah) 4660-1,5006,5547,5604,6110
Bedlam: a poem 6962
Bedloe (William) 1622-3,1769,1827
Beechey (Frederick William) 8306
Behn (Aphra) 2347-8,2833-4
Beilby and Co. 8253
Beilhaven (John Hamilton) Baron see:
   Hamilton (John)
Belcher (James) 7910
Belcher (William) 8004
Belief of witchcraft vindicated 5493
Bell (Andrew) 8275
Bell (Beaupré) 6618
Bell (George) 6260
Bell (James) 12
Bell (John) 1278
Bell (William) 7882
Bellamie (John) 643-4,697
Bellamy (John) 8285,8331

Bellarmino (Roberto) 55,2555,2665,2756
Belle-Isle (Charles Louis Auguste de Fouquet)
   Duc de see:Fouquet (Charles Louis Auguste
   de)
Bellers (Fulk) 958
Bellers (John) 8301
Bellisomus (Franciscus) 5509
Belloni (Giovanni Angelo) 6801
Belloy (Pierre Laurent Buirette de) 7482
Belsham (William) 7911
Belshazzar. An oratorio [C.Jennens] 7116·
Belzoni (Giovanni Battista) 8327
Bendtsen (Benedict) 7871
Benedetto da Mantova 137
Benefit of Christs death [B.da Mantova] 137
Benefit of farting explained 6541-2
Benefits and advantages gain'd 6543
Benett (John) 8264
Benezet (Anthony) 7440
Bennet (Benjamin) 6555,6591
Bennet (Joseph) 2835
Bennet (Robert) 3830
Bennet (Thomas) Bookseller 3571,4146
Bennet (Thomas) D.D. 4671,6018-20,6033,6063,
   6196,6679
Bennett (Henry Grey) 8307
Benson (Martin) 6940,8163
Benson (William) 5007-8,5154,6360
Bentham (Edward) 7074,7132,7210,7243,7473,7595
Bentinck (William Henry Cavendish) Duke of
   Portland 7528
Bentley (Richard) 3233,3557-8,3571,4662,4668,
   4688,4814,4827,4835,4853,5321,5414,5443,
   5520,5590,5664,5680,5713,6131,6414-5,
   6487,6525-7,7042
Berens (Edward) 8388
Berkeley (George) Bishop of Cloyne 4505,5322,
   5591,6625,6838,6845,6854,7075,7091,7303
Berkeley (George) Vice-Dean of Canterbury 7805
Berkenhead (Sir John) see: Birkenhead
   (Sir John)
Berlin. Konigliche Akademie der Wissenschaften
   4008
Bernard, Saint 2349
Bernard (Nicholas) 973,984,1109,1190,4793
Bernard (Sir Thomas) 8061
Berners (Dame Juliana) 73
Berridge (John) 8455
Berriman (William) 6362,6626,6826
Berrow (Capel) 7451
Berthier (David Nicolas) 3643
Bertie (Eleonora) Countess of Abingdon 3191
Bertie (Willoughby) Earl of Abingdon 8081
Beschreibung dess new entsprungnen 75
Bess o'Bedlam's love to her brother 4506-7
Best answer ever was made [C.Leslie] 4573,
   4583-4,4590
Best of all [C.Leslie] 4585
Best portion 8389
Best preservative against the plague 6488
Best purchase 8390
Bethel (Slingsby) 1316,1624
Bethlem Hospital 7771
Bethlem hospital. A poem [J.Rutter] 6208
Better late than never (1689?) 2836
Better late than never (1769?) 7548
Betterton (Thomas) 4612
Bettesworth (Charles) 5323
Betti (Zaccaria) 7494
Betty (Joseph) 6709
Beuttel (Johann Caspar) 1279
Bevan (Joseph Gurney) 8124
Beveridge (William) 2050-1,2263,2837,3575,
   3868,4009,5324
Beverland (Adriaan) 5009
Beverley (Robert Mackenzie) 8502,8510-1,8523
Beverley (Thomas) 2350
Bewick (John) 578
Bèze (Théodore de) 10,11,15,20,38
Bible. Old Testament. Job.11
Bible. Old Testament. Song of Solomon 7661
Bible. New Testament. [Malay] 1526
Bible. New Testament. Epistles. 24
Bible. New Testament. Revelation. 22,3502-3
Bible revered 8433
Bibliotheca annua 3576
Bibliotheca curiosa 8609
Bibliotheca literaria 8610
Bicheno (James) 8005
Bickerstaff (Isaac) 4445,4663,4692,4724,4783,
   see also: Swift (Jonathan).4876,5052-3,5325
Bickerstaff redivivus 4508
Bickerstaffe (Isaac) 7526
Bickersteth (Edward) 8472,8592-3
Billa vera [L.Womock] 2163
Bils (Louis de) 1001
Binckes (William) 3644,3716-7,3741,3746,4010
Bingham (Joseph) 5326,5602
Bion (Jean) 4509

Birch (Busby) 7441
Birch (G.) 7694
Birch (Peter) 2838,3301
Birch (Thomas) 7355
Bird (Charles Smith) 8546
Bird (John) 1254
Birkenhead (Sir John) 448,698-9,732,1255-6,3869
   8637,8639
Bisbie (Nathaniel) 2264,2486,3087,3181
Bishop Atterbury's and Bishop Smalridge's
   reasons 6032
Bishop of Oxford's charge, consider'd
   [R.Laurence] 5436
Bishop of St.David's vindicated [R.Ferguson]
   4046
Bishop of Salisbury's new preface consider'd
   5592
Bishop of Salisbury's new preface to his
   Pastoral care, consider'd 5593-4
Bishop of Salisbury's proper defence
   [C.Leslie] 3922
Bishops courts dissolved [E.Whitaker] 2039
Bisse (Philip) 4378,4645,4664,5010
Bisse (Thomas) 4379,5011,5595,5791,6021
Bisset (William) 3870-2,3962,4510,4591,4665-6,
   5012,5073,5136-8,5155,5158-9,5289
B[isse]t b-sh-t 3872,5012
Black (John) 8006
Blackall (Offspring) 3543,3577-81,3873,4011-3,
   4037,4043,4179,4260,4380,4382,4511-4,
   4563-6,4573,4583-4,4590,4605,4614,4626,
   4742,5084
Blackall (Samuel) 7616
Blackbird's song [E.Stacy] 5997
Black-bird's tale [E.Stacy] 4919-21
Blackburne (Lancelot) 4515
Blackburne (Thomas) 7362
Blackhead (Stephen) 3222,6574
Blacklock (Thomas) 7362
Blackmore (Sir Richard) 3544,4178,4413,4667,
   6489
Blackwell (Elidad) 645
Blackwell (George) 40
Blair (Hugh) 8029
Blair (John) 7806
Blakes (James) 7598
Blane (Gilbert) 8082
Blast upon Bays [A.Pope] 7025
Blatant-beast [T.Carte] 6986
Blaxton (John) 151
Blayney (Benjamin) 7821
Blechynden (Richard) 2351
Blind Mary 8391
Blois (W.) see: Sancroft (William)
Blomer (Ralph) 5013
Blomer (Thomas) 4668
Blomfield (Charles James) 8345
Blount (Charles) 1625,2172,3230,3234-5
Blount (Sir Henry) 162
Bluett (Thomas) 6627
Blussé (Abraham) 7930
Board of Agriculture 8030
Bobovius (Albertus) 3084
Bodkins and thimbles 4669
Boecler (Johann Heinrich) 272
Boehm (William) 4516
Boehme (Anton Wilhelm) 4293,4517
Boerhaave (Hermann) 6933
Bohemia 81
Bohun (Edmund) 2052-3,2173-4,2352,3235
Boileau (Jacques) 2287,2432
Boileau Despréaux (Nicolas) 3298,4381
Boissy (Louis de) 6941
Bolingbroke (Henry St.John) Viscount
   see: St.John (Henry)
Bolton (Robert) 7278
Bolton (Samuel) 700
Bolton (Theophilus) 6601
Bonar (John James) 8547
Bond, Mr.6349
Bond (John) 579
Bond (William) 6693
Bond of resignation-man 4014
Bonhome (Joshua) 1444
Booker (John) 580
Bookey (Sacheverell) 5596
Booth (George) Baron Delamere 1041,2274
Booth (Henry) Earl of Warrington 3236
Booth (William) 273,374
Boothby (Sir Brooke) 7931
Boreel (Willem) 581
Boreman (Robert) 910,1226,1329
Borosky (George) 2155
Borovius (Georgius) 1626
Bosanquet (Charles) 8185
Bossuet (Jacques Benigne) 2265,2353-4,2548-9,
   2559,2819,2842,5800
Both sides pleas'd 4670
Bothmer (Hans Caspar von) 5441,5498

Bottarelli (Giovanni Gualberto) 7507
Boughen (Edward) 646,5792
Bouillon, Cardinal de see: La Tour d'Auvergne
   (Emmanuel Théodose de)
Boulter (Hugh) 6544
Bounce (Benjamin) see: Carey (Henry)
Bourignon (Antonia) 3495
Bournelle, Monsieur see: Oldisworth (William)
Boursault (Edme) 6261
Bowdler (Elizabeth Stuart) 7661
Bowdler (John) 8044
Bowen (Thomas) 7771
Bower (Archibald) 7363,7404
Bowles (Edward) 444,449
Bowles (John) 7948,7976,8031,8045,8125,8131
Bowman (William) 6768,6772
Bowra 8434
Bowtell (John) 4671
Boxhorn (Marcus Zuerius) 805
Boyce (Thomas) 1445
Boyce (William) 7262
Boyd (William) Earl of Kilmarnock 7148,7165
Boyer (Abel) 4406,5014,8672
Boyle (Charles) Earl of Orrery 3557,4995,6572
Boyle (John) Earl of Cork and Orrery 6972
Boyle (Robert) 2192,2266,2564,3183
Boyse (Joseph) 2991,3313
Boyse (Samuel) 7244
Br.(J.) see: Bradshaw (John)
Bradbury (Thomas) 5328-9,5698,5745,5793-4,5946-7,
   6134,6326,6417
Braddon (Laurence) 2331
Bradford (John) 2778
Bradford (Samuel) 3582,4382,4518-9,4672,5015,5597,
   6363
Bradley (Richard) 6262-3
Bradshaw (John) Political Writer 1627
Bradshaw (John) Regicide 1002
Bradshaw (William) 5795
Bradshaw's ghost 1002
Brady (Nicholas) 3456,4383,5598-9,6605
Bragge (Francis) 5330-3
Bramhall (John) 1268,4150
Bramston (James) 6710
Bramston (John) 6628
Bramston (William) 5600,5934
Bray (Thomas) 3583,4520-1
Breck (Thomas) 3718
Brecknock (Timothy) 7474
Brereton (Jane) 6022
Brereton (William) 7549
Brerewood (Edward) 95
Brethren in iniquity 2992
Brett (Arthur) 1330
Brett (John) 7405
Brett (Thomas) 4813,5016-7,5306,5334-7,5576,
   5601-2,5796-8,5935,6111-2,6264-5,6448-9,
   6459,6537,6711,6814,6827,6839,6902,7043,
   7428
Breval (François Durant de) 1340
Breval (John Durant) 6266
Breviate of the state of Scotland 2839
Brevissimum metaphysicae compendium [J.Willes]
   3081
Brewer (Samuel) 7537
Brewster (Sir Francis) 3493
Bridge (Francis) 2355
Bridge (William) 274-5,517
Bridgen (William) 5603
Bridges, Mr. 6885
Bridges (Walter) 701
Bridges (William) 625
Bridgwater (Benjamin) 3335,3343
Bridoul (Toussain) 2565
Brief account of some of the late incroachments
   [R.Ferguson] 3356
Brief account of the Apostle's creed 4673
Brief account of the designs which the papists
   have had 1876,1886
Brief account of the meeting 1003
Brief account of the new sect [S.Patrick] 1243
Brief account of the proceedings of the French
   clergy 2054
Brief and true narration of the late wars 1446
Brief answer to a late pamphlet 5338
Brief answer to several popular objections 3302
Brief apology for those divines 5604
Brief collection out of the records 2105
Brief epistle to Henry Sacheverel 4850
Brief essay on the advantages [J.Tucker] 7298
Brief historical account of the primitive
   invocation [G.Smith] 6956
Brief instructions for making observations
   [J.Woodward] 3454
Brief justification of the Prince of Orange's
   descent [R.Ferguson] 2873-4
Brief method of the law 1744
Brief narrative of the manner how divers members
   [W.Prynne] 1163

Brief reflections relative to the emigrant French clergy [F.Burney] 7949
Brief reflections upon the inconveniencies 2356
Brief relation of the present state of Tangier 1270
Brief remarks on the late representation 5018
Brief vindication of the non-conformists [J.Owen] 1833
Briefe and perfect relation, of the answeres [T.Wentworth] 798
Briefe answer to a late treatise of the Sabbath day [H.Burton] 155
Briefe relation of some affaires 8611
Briggs (John) 8294
Brinsley (John) *the Elder* 171
Brinsley (John) *the Younger* 647
Briscoe (John) 3303
Brissot (Jacques Pierre) 7977
Bristed (John) 7245
Bristol (George Digby) *Earl of* see: Digby (George)
Britain (Jonathan) 7625
Britain's remembrancer [J.Burgh] 7134
Britannia in mourning 6985
Britannia rediviva 1157
Britannia's summons 4674
Britannicus see: Gordon (Thomas)
Britannicus see: Letter to a right honourable member
Britannicus see: Review of a late treatise
British Academy [A.Mainwaring] 5451
British Museum 8338
British visions [Defoe] 5052-3
British wonders [E.Ward] 6249
Britons strike home 5936
Brittish lightning or suddaine tumults 569
Britto-Batavus see: Toland (John)
Brokesby (Francis) 4384
Brome (James) 1628
Brome (Richard) 4151
Bromfield (William) *Quaker* 6629,6655
Bromfield (William) *Surgeon* 7392
Brooke (Henry) *Baron Cobham* 29
Brooke (Henry) *Dramatist* 6855,6923
Brooke (Robert Greville) *Baron* see: Greville (Robert)
Brooke (Thomas) 7133
Brooke and Hellier 5339
Broome 6113
Brossays du Perray (Joseph Marie) 7646
Broster (John) 8245,8254,8273
Brough (Robert) 8318
Brougham (Henry) *Baron* 8296,8345,8353
Broughton (Hugh) 35,42,58
Broughton (John) 4015-6,4152,4675,5605, 5799,6333
Broughton (Thomas) *Fellow of Exeter College* 7211
Broughton (Thomas) *Prebendary of Salisbury* 7104
Brousson (Claude) 4190
Brown, *Captain* 3296
Brown (George) 3645
Brown (Henry) 956
Brown (Henton) 6655
Brown (John) *of Edinburgh* 8392
Brown (John) *of Wamphray* 1560
Brown (John) *Vicar of Newcastle* 7044,7393 7495
Brown (Joseph) *Historian* 4522
Brown (Robert) 4676
Brown (Thomas) *of Shifnal* 2683,2993-4,3093 3109-10,3874,3939,4677
Browne (Francis) 5606
Browne (Isaac Hawkins) 7336
Browne (John) *Quaker* 1887
Browne (Joseph) 4017,4153-4,4261,4523
Browne (Peter) 4931,6670
Browne (Philip) 2055,2267
Browne (Simon) 5019
Browne (Thomas) *Fellow of St.John's* 2684, 2995,3087,3094
Brownrigg (Elizabeth) 7524
Bruce (Alexander) *Earl of Kincardine* 3719
Bruns (Paul Jacob) 7742,7839
Bryan (Matthew) 2357,3182
Bryant (Jacob) 7662
Bryant (John) Frederick) 7842
Brydall (John) 1629,1745,2056,3804,4262
Brydges (Henry) 4524
Buchan (David Erskine) *Earl of* see: Erskine (David)
Buchanan (Charles) 4678
Buchanan (George) 1746,4215,6536
Buckingham, *County of* 262,363,419
Buckingham (George Villiers) *Duke of* see: Villiers (George)
Buckler (Benjamin) 7279,7304
Buckworth (Hester) 4414
Buckworth (Sir John) 2791,4414
Buddicom (Robert Pedder) 8339,8435,8577
Bugg (Francis) 4018
Bulkeley (Richard) 2358
Bulkeley (Sir Richard) 4385,4918
Bull (George) 4130,5800,7076
Bulteel (Henry Bellenden) 8503-4
Burchard (Johann Georg) 5154
Burchett (Josiah) 5801,6023
Burd (Richard) 3805
Burdett (Sir Francis) 8211
Burdett (J.) 6114
Burford (John) 8371
Burgess (Cornelius) 211-2,626,1004,4679,4741
Burgess (Daniel) 4169,4525
Burgh (James) 7134
Burke (Edmund) 7576,7585,7647,7663,7886,7908, 7911,7919,7931,7933,7964,8032-3,8042,8096
Burmannus (Petrus) 6490
Burnet (Gilbert)
Answer to a letter 2359
Answer to the Animadversions 2057
Apology for the Church 2685,2849
Case of compulsion 2686
Citation of Gilbert Burnet 2566
Discourse concerning transubstantiation 2687
Enquiry into the measures 2688,2849,2863
Enquiry into the present state 2840
Enquiry into the reasons 2689
Exhortation to peace 1888,2841
Injunctions for the arch-deacons 2936
Introduction to the third volume 5752,5802, 5885,5893
Letter occasioned by the second letter 2361
Letter to Mr. Simon Lowth 2360,2421
Letter to Mr.Thevenot 2842
Letter writ by the Lord Bishop 3237
Life of William Bedell 8393
Memorial drawn by King William's special direction 4134
Modest survey 1483
New preface 5577,5580,5583,5592-4,5607, 5709,5739.5741
News from France 2058
Pastoral letter 2843
Reflections on the relation 2690
Relation of a conference 2659
Royal martyr and the dutiful subject 4680
Royal martyr lamented 2844,4680
Sermon preach'd, and a charge 5803
Sermon preached at Bow 2997
Sermon preached at St.Brides 5020
Sermon preach'd at St.Bridget's 5804,5887, 5892
Sermon preach'd at the cathedral 4155
Sermon preached at the chappel 2268
Sermon preached at the coronation 2845
Sermon preached at the funeral of James Houblon 2059
Sermon preached at the funeral of R.Boyle 3183
Sermon preached before the aldermen 1889
Sermon preached before the House of Commons 2846
Sermon preached before the House of Peers 2847
Sermon preach'd before the Queen 4263
Sermon preach'd in the cathedral 4681
Sermon preached inthe chappel 2848
Sermon preached on the fast-day 1890
Six papers 2567,2849
Speech in the House of Lords (1704) 3867, 3875,3877,3900,3922
Speech in the House of Lords (1710) 4682, 4718,4773,4840,4913,5157
Speech to the House of Lords (1708) 4386
Subjection for conscience-sake 1447,2850, 4680
Two sermons 4683,4719-20,5016,5143,5210
Vindication of the Bishop 4684
Vindication of the ordinations 2691
Word to the wavering 2851
2065,2318,2375,2616,2834,3315,3418,3716, 3736,3839,4026,4689,4806,4808-9,4847,5380, 5644,5759,5842,5886-7,5933,5954-5,5970, 6174,6499,6607,6620
Burnet (Sir Thomas) 5340-1,5608,5936-40,5949, 6010,6115-7
Burnet (William) 6606
Burnet and Bradbury [Defoe] 5945
Burney (Frances) 7949
Burrell (Andrewes) 691
Burrell (Percival) 128
Burridge (Richard) 5342
Burrington (George) 7045
Burroughes (Jeremiah) 450,517
Burroughs (Samuel) 6656,6769
Burscough (William) 5021,6024
Burthen of Issachar [J.Maxwell] 733
Burton (Edward) 8504
Burton (Henry) 122,155,175,176,182
Burton (John) *D.D.* 7135-6,7527
Burton (John) *of York* 7246
Bury (Arthur) 3095,3658
Bury (Jacob) 2362
Bury (John) 1630
Busby (George) 2028
Busby (Richard) 1000,6118
Bushe (Amyas) 7411
Bushell (Seth) 1398
Butler (Charles) 8240
Butler (Sir Francis) 6364
Butler (James) *1st Duke of Ormonde* 727,1259, 2060,2154
Butler (James) *2nd Duke of Ormonde* 3800,5943 6004
Butler (John) *B.D.* 2175,2269
Butler (John) *Bishop of Hereford* 7609,7843
Butler (John) *Canon of Windsor* 1561
Butler (Joseph) 6405,6916,6942,7105,7178
Butler (Lilly) 3876
Butler (Samuel) *Bishop of Lichfield* 8219
Butler (Samuel) *Poet* 448,883,1005,1891,4129
Butler (Thomas) *Earl of Ossory* 1922
Butler (William) 5343
Buttler see: Butler
Buxton (Thomas Fowell) 8295
Buxtorf (Johann) 1280
By the Kings Maiestie, were accused 213
Byfield (Richard) 155
Byfield (Timothy) 2270,2568
Byfielde(J.) see: Freind (John)
Byng (John) 7359,7371,7391
Bynns (Richard) 3238,4685
Byrom (John) 1892,7247
Byron (William) *Baron* 7486
Byrth (Thomas) 8526-7

C. 1631,2852
C.(A.) 648
C.(A.) see: Campbell (Archibald)
C.(A.B.) 3877,5344
C.(C.) 2176
C.(C.) *of Gray's Inn* 1006
C.(E.) 911,3646
C.(E.) see: Mackenzie (George)
C.(G.) see: Care (George):Cummings (George)
C.(H.) see: Care (Henry)
C.(J.) 2177,2569,4387
C.(J.) see: Cockburn (John) Cross (John)
C.(J.B.) 825
C.(P.) 4019
C.(R.) 974
C.(R.) see: Cudworth (Ralph)
C.(Sir R.) see: Cotton (Sir Robert Bruce)
C.(T.) see: Cooper (Thomas)
C.(T. van) 2998
C.(W.) 3402
C.(W.) see: Crawshaw (William)
Cabala [Sir J.Birkenhead] 1256
Cade (William) 1562
Caduganus (Maredydius) see: Richards (Thomas)
Caii spectrum 6491
Calamities of all the English [R.Pitt] 4337
Calamity of the Church 4686
Calamy (Benjamin) 2178-80,2280,2363,2538,3891, 4687
Calamy (Edmund) *D.D.* 5805,6365
Calamy (Edmund) *the Elder* 276,451,649,975
Caledonia; or, The pedlar 3584
Calfine (Gyles) 1110
Calle (Caleb) 2176
Callender (James Thomson) 7932
Callieres (François de) 6025
Calling of St.Peter 8436
Calumny no conviction 5609
Calvert (Frederick) *Baron Baltimore* 7544
Calvert (George) *Baron Baltimore* 277
Calves-Head club. A sermon 3878
Cambridge University 112,926,1111,1191,1227, 1341,8007
Cambridge University. Trinity College 4662, 4688,4834,4853,5192
Cameron (Archibald) 7329
Cameronian Whigs no patriots 5585
Camfield (Benjamin) 1563,1747,2271,2364
Camoes (Luis de) 7577
Camp (Abraham) 2853
Campaign 1692. 3184
Campanella (Tommaso) 1112
Campbell (Archibald) *Bishop* 5610,5895,5935, 6267,6366
Campbell (Archibald) *Marquess of Argyle* 702, 1192-3,1219
Campbell (Archibald) *Earl of Argyle* 2026,
Campbell (Colin) 8505,8558,8578,8584
Campbell (Elizabeth) *Duchess of Argyll* 7636
Campbell (George) 7596,7707
Campbell (John) *Duke of Argyle* 6945,6989
Campbell (John) *Earl of Loudoun* 703,875
Campbell (John) *LL.D.* 7251
Campion (Abraham) 3304
Canaries (James) 2487
Canary-birds naturaliz'd 4526-7
Candid and impartial account of...Lord Lovat 7179
Canning (William) 2692
Cannon (Robert) 4264,5334,5345-6,6119
Canons of criticism [T.Edwards] 7327
Canterbury tales [W.Pitts] 3690
Capel (Arthur) *Earl of Essex* 1683
Caracteres de l'amour 6903
Cardenas (Alonso de) 452
Care (George) 2365
Care (Henry) 2061,2570-1,2679,2693-5,2745, 8607
Care for posterity 8437
Care of cattle 8346
Carey (Henry) 6840
Carier (Benjamin) 76
Carkesse (James) 1632
Carlingford (Francis Taaffe) *Earl of* see: Taaffe (Francis)
Carlisle (Sir Anthony) 8278
Carlisle (Frederick Howard) *Earl of* see: Howard (Frederick)
Carlton (Mary) 1269
Carlyle (Alexander) 7950
Carmarthen 7483
Carmarthen (Peregrine Osborne) *Marquess of* see: Osborne (Peregrine)
Carmen saeculare [M.Prior] 3611
Carpenter (John) 46
Carrara, *Family of* 7479
Carreus (Johannes) 927
Carroll (William) 4265,4528,5022
Carson (William) 8228
Carte (Thomas) 5806,6986,7046,7235
Carter (Elizabeth) 8183
Carter (John) 203
Carter (Thomas) 453
Carter (William) 278
Carteret (John) *Earl Granville* 6759-60
Cartwright (John) 7951
Cartwright (Thomas) 1484-6,2062,2272,2488-9
Cary (John) 3403
Cary (Lucius) *Viscount Falkland* 214
Cary (Mordecai) 7077
Caryll (John) 1633
Caryll (Joseph) 582,1228
Casaubon (Isaac) 50,135
Casaubon (Meric) 704,1281
Case (Thomas) 215,755
Case concerning the buying of bishops lands [C.Burgess] 1004
Case fairly stated 7106
Case farther stated [N.Spinckes] 6338
Case in view [H.Dodwell] 5075,5096
Case of all the non-commissioned officers 3344
Case of allegiance in our present circumstances [S.Masters] 2912,2916
Case of allegiance to a king [T.Browne] 2995
Case of an oath of abjuration considered [E.Stillingfleet] 3789
Case of Capt. Tho. Green 4020
Case of clandestine marriages stated [H.Prideaux] 3147
Case of compulsion in matters of religion [G.Burnet] 2686
Case of Dr.Sacheverell [E.Curll] 4716
Case of Dunkirk 6732
Case of going to war [J.Tucker] 7469
Case of his Grace the D. of M. [J.Churchill] 5354
Case of his Grace the Duke of Portland 7528
Case of indifferent things [J.Williams] 2257
Case of infant-baptism [G.Hickes] 2199
Case of insufficiency discuss'd 5023
Case of John Atherton [J.King] 4793
Case of John Palmer 4388
Case of J[ohn] W[ard] 6680
Case of kneeling at the holy sacrament [J.Evans] 2190
Case of lay-communion [J.Williams] 2258
Case of Mr.Greenshields 5024
Case of Mr.Vaughan 4021
Case of moderation [T.Wagstaffe] 4125
Case of non-residency [J.Sharpe] 4223
Case of observing such facts 6492
Case of ordination consider'd... By a Catholick 5347
Case of ordination consider'd... By a layman 5611
Case of orphans consider'd 6630
Case of our affaires [Sir J.Spelman] 559
Case of present concern [C.Leslie] 3834
Case of protestants in England [D.Clarkson] 1900
Case of Richard Steele 5807,5834
Case of St.Winefred open'd 5612
Case of schism in the Church [L.Howell] 5966
Case of Sir Robert Viner 1527
Case of succession to the Crown 1658
Case of sureties in baptism [W.Higden] 3669
Case of the abjuration oath 3720
Case of the admission of occasional conformists [W.Higden] 4055
Case of the bankers [T.Turner] 1439
Case of the charter of London stated 2181
Case of the Church of England by law established [E.Stephens] 3625
Case of the Church of England's Memorial [W.Pittis] 4090
Case of the cross in baptism [N.Resbury] 2315
Case of the dissenters 5348
Case of the erectors of a chapel [N.Marshall] 6563,6577
Case of the Genoese impartially stated 7180

Case of the Hanover forces [P.D.Stanhope & E.Waller] 7066
Case of the Hessian forces [H.Walpole] 6796
Case of the Marshal Bellisle 7107,7122
Case of the patron and rector [J.Trapp] 6577
Case of the poor Grecian seamen [E.Stephens] 4109
Case of the present afflicted clergy [J.Sage] 3052
Case of the present Convocation [W.Wotton] 5292
Case of the Pretender 5613
Case of the protestant dissenters 7890,7893, 7900
Case of the purchasers of publick lands 1113
Case of the revival of the salt duty [W.Pulteney] 6820
Case put, concerning the succession [Sir R.L.'Estrange] 1676-7
Case restated [A.Campbell] 5610,5895
Case truly stated [N.Spinckes] 5895
Cassandra. (But I hope not) [C.Leslie] 3923-4,4068-9
Castanaeus (Henricus Ludovicus) *Rupipozaeus* see: Chasteigner de la Roche-Pozai
Castelman (John) 6782,7078
Castile, *Almirante de* see: Enriquez de Cabrera (Juan Tomas)
Castle (A.) 6367
Castlemaine (Roger Palmer) *Earl of* see: Palmer (Roger)
Cat may look upon a king [Sir A.Weldon] 5808,5920
Cat may look upon a king. Answer'd 5808
Catalogue of a library of books 8229
Catalogue of all the cheifest rarities [F.Schuyl] 2649
Catalogue of all the discourses [E.Gee] 2882
Catalogue of medals from Julius Caesar 6026
Catalogue of the damages 1271
Catalogue of the names of the dukes 279
Catcott (Alexander) 7529
Catcott (Alexander Stopford) 7079,7743
Catechism set forth [T.Marshall] 2217
Catechism, that is to say 5349
Catechisme royal [P.Fortin] 720
Catholic balance [S.Hill] 2603
Catholic representer [J.Gother] 2591
Catholick ballad [W.Pope] 1708
Catholick pill to purge popery 1528
Cato 583
Causae veteris epitaphii editio altera 2366
Causae veteris epitaphium 1893
Causton (Peter) 2490
Cave (William) 2273,2367,2494
Caveat against flattery [E.Stephens] 2961
Caveat against the Whiggs [C.Hornby] 5123,5415-8
Caveat on the part of public credit 7530
Caveat to conventiclers 1353
Caveat to the Cavaliers [Sir R. L'Estrange] 1206
Caveat to the treaters 5025
Cavendish, *Family of* 4419
Cavendish (Charles) 1466
Cavendish (Mary) *Duchess of Devonshire* 4981
Cavendish (William) *Duke of Devonshire* 4302, 4314,4408-9,4529
Cawdrey (Daniel) 454,950
Cawdrey (Zachary) 2274
Cawthorn (James) 7181
Cecil (William) *Baron Burghley* 1448,5495
Celebrated story of the Thebaean legion [G.Hickes] 5842
Cellier (Elizabeth) 1748,1837,1864,1979
Censoriad: a poem 6733
Censura temporum 8612
Censure of the Rota [R.Leigh] 1407
Ceremonial for the reception of George I 5809
Certain cases of conscience resolved [J.Scott] 2233
Certain dutiful son's lamentation 5941
Certain queries upon Dr.Pierces sermon 1257
Certain scruples and doubts [J.Gauden] 1132
Certaine considerations touching the better pacification [F.Bacon] 30
Certaine observations touching the two great offices 280
Certificate from Northampton-shire 216
Chaillot. Monastère de la Visitation Sainte Marie 3721
Challenge answered 4689
Challenor (Richard) see: Chaloner (Richard)
Challoner (Richard) *Roman Catholic Bishop* 6866
Chalmers (John) 5810
Chalmers (Thomas) 8505A
Chaloner (Richard) 455
Chaloner (Thomas) 698-9,705,726,732
Chamberlain (Hugh) see: Chamberlen (Hugh)
Chamberlayne (Edward) 2368
Chamberlayne (John) 4079
Chamberlen (Hugh) 3225,3239,3398,3404
Chambers (Humfry) 456
Chambre (Richard) 4690
Chambres (Charles) 6828
Chancery see: Great Britain. Court of Chancery
Chandler (Edward) 4691,6268
Chandler (Henry) 4530,5806
Chandler (Mary) 7080
Chandler (Samuel) 6770,6826,6874,6963,7248
Chap.I. Of magistracy 2696
Chaplin (Sir Francis) 1541
Chapman (George) 138
Chapman (John) 7227
Chapman (Sir John) 2943
Character and declaration of the October-club 5026
Character and principles of the present set [J.Trapp] 5259
Character and qualifications of an honest loyal merchant 2491
Character of a country-committee-man 3722
Character of a good ruler 7406
Character of a London scrivener 1303
Character of a Low-Church-man [H.Sacheverell] 3777,4222,5882
Character of a Quaker [S.Austin] 1364
Character of a sneaker 4022
Character of a trimmer [G.Savile] 2787
Character of a true Church-of-England-man [S.Grascombe] 3750
Character of a true churchman 5027
Character of an independent Whig [T.Gordon] 6389
Character of an informer 2144
Character of Don Sacheverellio 4692
Character of Richard St--le [W.Wagstaffe] 5768
Character of the Parliament 6493
Character or ear-mark of Mr.William Prynne 1007
Characteristicks: a dialogue 6964
Characters: an epistle 6917
Characters and conduct of Sir John Edgar [J.Dennis] 6456
Characters of the four candidates 6494
Characters of two independent Whigs 6450
Charge of a Tory plot maintain'd 2063
Charge of high treason 1193
Charge of Socinianism [C.Leslie] 3365
Charis dotheisa [J.Pitts] 4449
Charis kai Eirene [J.Gauden] 1235
Charity and loyalty of some of our clergy 2854
Charity and peace 4531
Charity still a Christian virtue [W.Hendley & Defoe] 6394
Charles I, *King* 116,123,204,217-221,281-304, 457-462,584,650-1,706,756-7,806-9,849, 850,1236,3229,3267,3484,3570,4596,4679
Charles II, *King* 875,1114,1145,1181,1183, 1194-5,1212,1227,1272,1304,1380,1421, 1529-30,1564,1634-6,1894-6,2182,2335, 2340,2347,7324
Charles III, *Spanish Pretender* see: Charles VI, *Emperor*
Charles V, *Emperor* 6
Charles VI, *Emperor* 3953,4094,5371,6978
Charles VII, *Emperor* 6336
Charles XII, *King of Sweden* 5718
Charles Albert, *Elector of Bavaria* see: Charles VII, *Emperor*
Charles Edward, *the Young Pretender* 7182, 7242,7249,7252,7286,7288
Charleton (Walter) 2172,2183
Charms of liberty [W.Cavendish] 4529
Charndler (Samuel) 7464
Charpentier (François) 1487
Chasteigner de la Roche-Pozai (Henri Louis) 101
Chaucer (Geoffrey) 3691,5350
Chaucer's whims [W.Pittis] 3691
Chaundler (E.) see: Chandler (Edward)
Cherubim with a flaming sword 4532
Chetwood (Knightly) 3647
Chetwood (William Rufus) 6451
Cheynell (Francis) 463-4,585,779
Chichester Dean, and his Colchester Amazon 6269,6324
Chicoyneau (François) 6495
Chifflet (Jules) 154
Child (Benjamin) 6579-80
Child (Sir Josiah) 1317,1897,1948,2855-6
Chillingworth (William) 585,913,1229
Chilmead (Edward) 1112
Chimera [Defoe] 6455
Chishull (Edmund) 4448,4463,5028,5286,5351, 5811
Choice collection of wonderful miracles 1898
Choirochorographia [T.Richards] 4610
Cholmondeley (Francis) 4774
Christian (Edward) *Chief Justice of Ely* 8308
Christian (Edward) *Gentleman to Lord Danby* 5267
Christian monitor 6452
Christian supports under the terrours of death [S.Cooke] 3102
Christian test 6987
Christianissimus Christianandus [M.Nedham] 1585
Christianity, a doctrine of the cross [J.Kettlewell] 3130
Christianity of the High-Church consider'd [Defoe] 3886
Christian's safety 8394
Christians sure anchor and comfort 3240
Christmas chat 7108
Christus Dei [T.Morton] 537
Christus patiens [R.Rapin] 5723
Chubb (Thomas) 6734,7048
Chudleigh (Elizabeth) *Duchess of Kingston* 7685
Church (Thomas) 7175,7212
Church catechism with scripture proofs 2369
Church-government part V [A.Woodhead] 2671
Church-lands not to be sold [J.Warner] 845
Church of England. Articles of religion. 13,2185,2276,8347
Church of England. Book of Common Prayer 6120
Church of England. Constitutions and Canons 31,146,205,3259
Church of England. Convocation 3712,3753-4, 3966,4025,4217,4299,4377,4476,4695, 5030-3,5060,5141,5281,5292,6129-30
Church of England. Convocation. Lower House 3632,3880,4026-7,4256,5018,5235,5256, 5614,5911,6121-2,6298
Church of England. Special prayers 113,124, 1196-7,1565,1637,2184,2275,2370-1,2492, 2572,2697-2700,2857-9,2999,3000,3096-8, 3185-7,3241-2,3305-7,3345,3405-6,3457, 3879,4023-4,4156-7,4266-8,4389-91, 4533-5,4693-4,5029,5352,5812,6496
Church of England-man's answer 7883
Church of England man's memorial 6270,6368
Church of England not in danger 4269
Church of England truly represented 2493
Church of England's address 4696
Church of England's apology 6271
Church of England's complaint [J.Sharpe] 4618
Church of England's late conflict [P.Drewe] 4745
Church of Ireland. Convocation 5353,5532
Church of Rome's traffic [J.Mendham] 8579
Church of Scotland 21,187-8,222,239,305,465, 611,7237
Church-papist (so called) [J.Underwood] 1867
Churchill (John) *Duke of Marlborough* 3916, 4372,4543,4881,5168,5255,5354,5356, 5358,5373,5382,5427,5648
Churchill (Sarah) *Duchess of Marlborough* 4078,4815,7003,7030,7081,7415
Cibber (Colley) 6266,6272,6352,6703,6705, 6939,6988,7025,7047,7269
Cibber (Theophilus) 6939
Circus: or, British olympicks [J.Browne] 4523
Cities propositions 306
Citt and Bumpkin [Sir R.L'Estrange] 1802-3
City candidates 4028
City of London's plea to the quo warranto 2106
City of Londons rejoinder 2107
City Shushan perplexed 5355
City-wive's petition against coffee 3585
Civil comprehension [C.Lawton] 4067
Civil wars of Bantam 2186
Clagett (Nicholas) 2372
Clagett (William) 1899,2187,2573-4, 2605,2701-2
Claims of the people of England [G.Sharp] 7765-6
Clare (John Fitzgibbon) *Earl of* see: Fitzgibbon (John)
Clarendon (Edward Hyde) *Earl of* see: Hyde (Edward)
Claridge (Richard) 4771
Clarinda: or the fair libertine [J.Ralph] 6721
Clark (John) *Bookseller* 6407
Clark (John) *F.S.A.* 7744
Clark (Joshua) 3494
Clark (Margaret) 1749,1869
Clarke (Alured) 6886,6955
Clarke (Liscombe) 8296,8395
Clarke (Samuel) *Minister of Grendon Underwood* 1198
Clarke (Samuel) *Rector of St.James's Westminster* 4158-9,4272-4,4392-4,4396, 4449,4463,4536-7,4697-9,5034-5,5356, 5388,5649,5762,5773-4,5813-4,5828-9, 5835,5849,5871,5919,6008,6172,6764, 7231
Clarke (William) *Dissenting Minister* 4395,5036,5499,5615
Clarke (William) *of North Crawley* 959
Clarkson (Christopher) 6841
Clarkson (David) 1900
Clarret drinkers song [J.Oldham] 1828
Claude (Jean) 2265,2559
Claudianus (Claudius) 5432
Clauswitz (Benedict Gottlob) 6273
Clayton (David) 6123
Clayton (Robert) *Bishop of Clogher* 7330,7408
Clayton (Sir Robert) 1675,2023
Clear and full vindication of some particulars 4160
Clear proof of the certainty and usefulness 2703
Clearbrook (William) 5616
Cleaver (William) 8111
Cleere and full vindication of the late proceedings 758
Cleland (William) 5815
Clemens (Venceslaus) 130
Clemens Augustus, *Archbishop of Cologne* 6430-1, 7450
Clement (Simon) 3407,4700-1,4736,4756-7,4947
Clendon (John) 4803
Clergy and the present ministry defended [G.Sewell] 5739
Clergy vindicated [J.Brydall] 1629
Clergyman's daughter's new annual tract 6694
Clergyman's thanks to Phileleutherus [F.Hare] 5664
Clergy's tears [R.Welton] 6009
Clerke (Sir William) 7884
Cleveland (John 2860,3722
Clifford (Martin) 2575
Clifford (William) 2064
Cloak in its colours 1638
Clowes (John) 8195
Coalition: or, An historical memorial 7452
Cobb (Samuel) 3881,5350,5413,5816
Cobbet (Thomas) 810
Cobbett (William) 8034,8046,8063-4,8097,8112
Cobden (Edward) 7082,7213,7250,7337
Cobler of Gloucester reviv'd 3882
Cochran (Sir Robert) 6846
Cock (John) 3723,3883,4270-1
Cockburn (John) 3099,3100,3408,3495,5037,5617, 6124,6607,6620
Cockman (Thomas) 5618
Codrington (Christopher) 4769
Coffee-house dialogue [A.Yarranton] 1736
Coffin for the good old cause 1115,1158
Coffin opened 1158
Cohausen (Johann Heinrich) 7251
Coigly (James) see: O'Coigly (James)
Colbatch (Sir John) 3501,6735
Colbert, *junior* see: Age of paper
Colden (Cadwallader) 7137
Cole (Robert) 466
Cole (William) 1008
Coleman (Edward) 1604
Coleman (Thomas) 652
Coleman (William) 8533
Colet (John) 1199
Collection for improvement of husbandry and trade 8613
Collection from Dyers letters [Defoe] 4166
Collection of advertisments [A.Hutcheson] 6557
Collection of all the particular papers 467
Collection of all the political letters [J.Trenchard] 6534
Collection of declarations, proclamations [Charles Edward, the Young Pretender] 7249
Collection of hymns and poems 5038
Collection of letters and other writings [Sir G.Treby] 2021
Collection of letters, concerning the separation 7138
Collection of letters for the improvement of husbandry and trade 8614
Collection of letters on the thirtieth of January 7792
Collection of original letters 6736
Collection of papers relating to the East India trade 6737
Collection of papers relating to the present juncture 2704
Collection of poems, for and against Dr. Sacheverell 4702-6,5039
Collection of poems on state-affairs 5357
Collection of political and humorous letters 7230
Collection of recipe's and letters 6740
Collection of several treatises concerning the reasons 1448
Collection of some letters...concerning... Bouillon 4707
Collection of sundry petitions [Sir T.Aston] 1105
Collection of the several papers deliver'd by Mr.J.Gordon 6027
Collection of very valuable and scarce pieces [W.Beckett] 6486
Collection of white and black lists 5942

Collections of notes taken at the Kings tryall 811
College (Stephen) 1880,1901-2,1962,2012
College of Physicians 3475
Collier (Jeremy) 2861-3,3101,3346,3409-12,3526, 3806,3892,4161,5619,6028-9,6125-6,6274-7, 6327,6335,6369,6453,6477,6657
Collinges (John) 1903
Collins (Anthony) 4265,4272-4,4298,4393-4, 4396,4661,4697,4708-10,4800,4894-6,5006, 5574,5590,5618,5620,5652,5671,5778,7042
Collins (Charles) 6127
Collins (Richard) 4029
Collins (Samuel) 6128
Collins (William) 7429
Colmer (Robert) 8548
Colomiès (Paul) 2494
Colton (T.) 4162
Combe (William) 7872
Comber (Thomas) 2057,2065-6,2188,2576,2705-6, 2864,3243,6856-7
Comenius (Johannes Amos) 172
Comical history of the marriage-union [W.Wright] 4249
Commencement of the treaty between the King's Majesty 812
Comment upon the history of Tom Thumb [W.Wagstaffe] 5272
Commentary on the proceedings of the Catholics 8230
Commerell, Abbé de 7862
Commissioners of Accounts see: England. Commissioners of Accounts Great.Britain. Commissioners of Accounts
Common Christian instructed [J.Griffin] 6556
Commoner's, in answer to the peer's speech 3884
Common-wealhts moderate intelligence 8615
Companion for the closet 8372
Company of Royal Adventurers of England Trading into Africa see: Royal African Company
Company of Scotland Trading to Africa and the Indies see: Scots Company Trading to Africa
Company of the Mine-Adventurers of England 5491
Company of the Royal Fishery of England 3349
Comparative excellence and obligation [T.Chubb] 6734
Comparison or Whiggish fulsom flattery 5358
Compendium: or, A short view of the late tryals [R.Palmer] 1700
Complainer further reprov'd [E.Gibson] 4050
Complainer reprov'd [E.Gibson] 4051
Complaint to the House of Commons 307,395
Complaints and queries upon Englands misery 1011
Complaints concerning corruptions 1116
Compleat and true narrative of the manner 1616
Compleat and unexceptionable form of liturgy [E.Stephens] 3626,4110
Compleat catalogue of all the plays 6370
Compleat catalogue of all the stich'd books 1750
Compleat history of the late septennial Parliament 6545
Compleat list of the stewards, presidents 6829
Complete history of addresses [J.Oldmixon] 4845
Complete view of the birth of the Pretender 7083
Complete vindication of the mallard [B.Buckler] 7304
Comprehension and toleration consider'd [R.South] 6089
Compton (Henry) 1459,2088,2695,2718,4711-2, 5617,5656
Conant (Malachi) see: Connant (Malachi)
Conciliade; being a supplement 7550
Conciliating ball for Mr.Plomer 7551
Conciliation 8396
Concordia discors [S.Grascombe] 4052
Concubinage and poligamy disprov'd 3496
Conditions upon which the most Christian King consents 2214
Condoling letter to the Tattler [Defoe] 4724
Conduct of a noble duke 6989
Conduct of his Grace the Duke of Ormonde 5943,6004
Conduct of parties in England [Defoe] 5366 5943
Conduct of the allies [J.Swift] 5108,5209, 5211,5367,5399,5475,5521-2
Conduct of the dissenters considered 6371
Conduct of the late administration 6990,7013
Conduct of the late and present m[inist]ry compared [W.Pulteney] 7028
Conduct of the Reverend Dr.White Kennet [R.Rawlinson] 6200
Coney (Thomas) 4713-4,6753,6771
Confederacy of kings 7933
Conference between Gerontius and Junius [H.Gandy] 5096
Conference between two protestants and a papist [W.Lloyd] 1408
Conference of a most stupendous nature 6991
Confession of faith of the Kirk (1638) 187
Confession of faith, subscrived by the Kingis Maiestie (1590) 21
Confession of the faith, and doctrine (1638)
Confusion of popery [E.Stephens] 4111
Confutation of a late pamphlet [S.Johnson] 3515
Congratulations of several kings 3648
Congratulatory epistle from his Holiness [N.Amhurst] 6255
Congratulatory letter to a certain right honourable person 7049
Congratulatory letter to John Murray 7182
Congratulatory poem on his R.H.'s entertainment 2067
Congratulatory poem to his Royal Highness the Prince of Orange 2865
Congress of the beasts 7214
Congreve (William) 3526,3807,4493
Conjectures politiques sur le conclave de MDCC 3586
Conjugal love and duty [J.Brett] 7405
Connant (Malachi) 1331
Conscience puzzel'd 872
Considerable advantages of a South-Sea trade 5040
Consideration and a resolution [Sir E.Dering] 224
Considerations concerning oaths [F.Lee] 6061
Considerations moving to a toleration 2373
Considerations of importance to Ireland [C.Leslie] 3517
Considerations of present use [H.Hammond] 2087
Considerations offered upon the approaching peace [T.Gordon] 6462
Considerations on Mr.Whiston's historical preface [J.Knight] 5139,5281
Considerations on national independence 8083
Considerations on parochial evils 7863
Considerations on publick credit [Defoe] 6608
Considerations on the expediency of revising the liturgy [R.Watson] 7907
Considerations on the explications of the doctrine [S.Nye] 3271
Considerations on the French War 7978
Considerations on the measures carrying on [M.Robinson] 7656
Considerations on the nature and origin of literary property [J.Maclaurin] 7515
Considerations on the nature of parliaments 3497
Considerations on the Peerage-bill 6372
Considerations on the presentstate of affairs in Europe 6738,6794,6796
Considerations on the present state of the nation 6454
Considerations on the propriety of requiring [E.Law] 7653
Considerations relating to our choice 5041
Considerations upon a printed sheet [Sir R. L'Estrange] 2212
Considerations upon a reduction of the land-tax [R.Nugent] 7265
Considerations upon the proclamation 3188
Considerations upon the second canon [S.Grascombe] 3259
Considerations upon The secret history 5817-8
Consilium quorundam episcoporum Bononiae congregatorum 67
Conspirators; or, The case of Catiline [T.Gordon] 6506
Constable (Robert) 1751
Constant de Rebecque (Samuel) 8176
Constitution, laws and government, of England vindicated [C.Leslie] 4586
Constitutions and canons ecclesiastical 131, 146,205
Contemplations in a church-yard 8361
Continuation of Frauds and abuses [F.Hare] 5589,5665
Continuation of the Coffee-house dialogue [A.Yarranton] 1873
Continuation of the faithful account [F.Atterbury] 4002
Continuation of the German history 147
Continuation of the history of passive obedience [A.Seller] 3056
Continuation of The mitre and the crown [F.Atterbury] 5316
Continuation of the true diurnall 8616
Contrast; or, The first part 7934
Contrast to the man of honour 6887
Controversy about restoring some prayers [T.Rogerson] 6425
Conventicle distinguish'd from the Church 6278
Conversation by the way 8438
Convincing reply to the Lord Beilhaven's speech 4275
Convocation see: Church of England. Convocation
Convocation anatomized 6129
Convocation-craft 6130
Conybeare (John) 6904
Conyers (Tobias) 1117
Cook (Edward) see: Coote (Edmund)
Cook (John) 873
Cooke (Alexander) 96
Cooke (John) 8241
Cooke (Sir John) 4046
Cooke (Shadrach) 2374,2866,3102,6279
Cooke (Thomas) *Curate of Kingston* 5359
Cooke (Sir Thomas) 3353-4
Cooke (William) 7280
Coole (Benjamin) 6064
Cooper (Anthony Ashley) *1st Earl of Shaftesbury* 1077,1449-50,1478,1504,1547-8 1815,1876,1886,1942,1974,1979,1985,1993, 2012,2034,2041,2080,2169,2958,5360,6080
Cooper (Anthony Ashley) *3rd Earl of Shaftesbury* 4397,4454,4538,4552,5621-2, 6497
Cooper (Samuel) 7695
Cooper (Thomas) 17
Cooper (William) 7807
Coote (Edmund) 912
Copenhagen. The real state of the case 8196
Copie of a letter written by a friend 974
Copie of quaeries, or, A comment 1009
Copies of such bills as were presented unto his Majestie 477
Copleston (John) 1200
Copley (John Singleton) *Baron Lyndhurst* 8556
Coppy of a certain large act [L.de Bils] 1001
Coppy of a letter to Generall Monck 1118
Copy of a letter concerning the election of a Lord Protector 928
Copy of a letter concerning the siege of Landaw 3933
Copy of a letter from a French lady 7252
Copy of a letter from a gentleman in London 7281
Copy of a letter published in Adam's Weekly courant 7305
Copy of a letter sent to the Commissioners of Accounts 3244
Copy of some papers past at Oxford [H.Hammond] 779
Copy of the articles for the surrender of... Yorke 586
Copy of the country-man's letter 4276
Corbet (John) 206,1207,1325
Corbett (Edward) 308
Corbyn (Benjamin) 7484
Corker (James) 1752
Corneille (Pierre) 1273
Cornish (Henry) 2464
Cornwall (C.) 6546
Cornwallis (Charles) *Baron* 1665
Cornwallis (Frederick) *Archbishop* 7601
Cornwallis (Sir William) 77
Corporation of the Sons of the Clergy 6829
Corpus disciplinae 653
Correct copy of some notes concerning Gods decrees [T.Pierce] 954
Corrector of the answerer to the speech out of doores [H.Marten] 732
Corruption and impiety of the common members 3649
Cosin (John) *Bishop of Durham* 1173,1230,2501, 5361
Cosin (John) *Secretary to the Commissioners for Forfeited Estates* 7113
Cotes (Humphrey) 7496
Cottage in Connaught 8439
Cottle (Mark) 2083
Cotton (Henry) 8534
Cotton (Sir Robert Bruce) 223,309,3001
Counsellor's plea for the divorce of Sir G.D. [W.Fleetwood] 5956
Count de Gabalis [N.M.de Villars] 5913
Counter-plot against popery 310
Counter-plot, or the close conspiracy 1753
Counter-schuffle [R.Speed] 4917
Country gentleman's notion concerning governments 3413
Country parson's advice to his parishioners [W.Holmes] 7006
Country parson's advice to those little scribblers 4163
Court and city vagaries 5042
Court in mourning 4539
Courten (Sir William) 1418
Courtenay (Henry Reginald) 8126
Courtilz de Sandras (Gatien de) 2707
Covenanters plea against absolvers [T.Gataker] 1203
Coventry (Sir William) 2375,2787
Cowe (James) 8047
Cowley (Abraham) 7347
Cowper (Spencer) 3785
Cowper (William) *Bishop of Galloway* 8348
Cowper (William) *Vicar of Ramsey* 7844
Cox (James) 7610,8084
Cox (James) *D.D.* 7282
Coxe (William) 8264,8266
Crackanthorp (Richard) 102
Cradock (John) 7364,7629
Cradock (Zachary) 1566-7,4164,6992
Cradocke (Francis) 1119
Craftsman 6743,6749,6766,6776-7,6784,6789,6792
Crakanthorp (Richard) see: Crackanthorp
Crambo (Christopher) 6772
Crampton (Philip) 8242
Cranmerian liturgy [E.Stephens] 3444
Crashaw (William) 47,67,79,114
Craufurd (David) 5819
Craven (Joseph) 6131
Creamer (Charles) 1451
Creed of Pope Pius [M.Altham] 2555
Creffield (Edward) 5043
Crisis: a sermon 6966
Crisis upon crisis 5820
Crisp (Samuel) 2495,3677
Crisp (Thomas Steffe) 8325
Crisp (Tobias) 3250
Crispe (H.) 5362
Crispianism unmask'd [J.Edwards] 3250
Crispin the cobler's confutation [W.Wagstaffe] 5273,5550
Criterion: or, Touchstone 4715
Critical examination of the holy Gospels [C.Hayes] 6907
Critical history of the last important sessions 6993
Critical observations on the buildings [J.Stuart] 7606
Critical review 8617
Crockatt (Gilbert) 6373
Croft (Herbert) 1452,1483,1491,1519,1568,1639, 1754
Croft (James William) 8440
Crofton (Zachary) 1120,1132,1201
Crokatt (James) 8678
Croker (John Wilson) 8309
Cromarty (George Mackenzie) *Earl of* see: Mackenzie (George)
Crompton (Richard) 131
Cromwell (Oliver) 929-931,947,952,1009,1045, 1074,1316,1755,1911,2583,3587,4852,4858, 5363,5546,6280
Cromwell (Richard) 1010,1026
Cropley (Sir John) 6497
Cros, *Monsieur de* see: Ducros (Simon)
Crosfeild (Robert) 3245,3401,4165
Cross, alias More (John) 2577
Cross (Walter) 3498
Crossman (Henry) 7552
Crosthwaite (John) 8485,8493
Crouch (Isaac) 7822
Crouch (John) 8634
Crowe (William) 7823
Crowne (John) 2189
Crowne (William) 173
Crowther (Samuel) 8489
Croxall (Samuel) 5821,6739,6748
Crozat (Antoine) 5688
Crusius (Thomas Theodorus) 2277
Cruwys (Henry Shortrude) 7648
Cry aloud and spare not 7183
Cry from the desart [F.M.Misson] 4326
Cudworth (Ralph) 311,3271
Cullen (Charles) 7808
Cullen (Charles Sinclair) 8486
Culliford (William) 3402
Culme (Arthur) 759
Culpeper (Thomas) 3743
Culpeper (Sir Thomas) 1318
Cumberland, *County of* 391
Cumming (John) 6374
Cummings (George) 5623,6132
Cummins (Charles) 8549
Cuninghame (James) 5044,5864
Cunning plot to divide and destroy 468
Cunningham (Alexander) 3002
Cunningham (Eliza) 7812
Cunningham (John William) 6773
Curate (Jacob) see: Crockatt (Gilbert)
Curate of Dorset's answer 5045
Curious collection of genuine and authentick letters 7283
Curll (Edmund) 4684,4716-20,5624
Cursory but curious observations [A.Roper] 5217
Curtis (William) 7617
Cutts, *Mrs.* 7664
Cutts (John) *Baron* 3535
Cyder. A poem [J.Philips] 4446
Cyprian, *Saint* 6028,6030,6375,8354

D***, *Sieur de* see: Villiers (Pierre de)
D.(C.) 3003
D.(D.) 5979
D.(E.) 1011
D.(F.) see: Defoe (Daniel)
D.(J.) 1640,1734

D.(M.) 2068
D.(N.) 654
D.(N.) *Gent* 1144
D.(P.) 3347-8,3545
D.(S.) see: Downes (Samuel)
D.(S.E.) see: Dering (Sir Edward)
D.(T.) see: De Laune (Thomas)
D.(W.) 8164
D.(W.) see: Darrell (William)
D.of B[uckingha]m's pro[phec]y 6549
D.of M[arlborough]'s confession 5382
D.of M[arlboroug]h's vindication 5168
Dahler (Johann Georg) 7824
Daillé (Jean) 913,1756
Daily advertiser, in metre 7745
Daily journal 6740
Dalby (William) 8397
Dalechamp (Caleb) 163
Dalrymple (Gilbert) 6281
Dalrymple (John) *2nd Earl of Stair* 7027, 7060
Dalrymple (John) *5th Earl of Stair* 7678, 7772,7793
Dalton (John) 6870,7109,7215,7314
Dalton (Richard) 7314
Daly (Richard) 7904
Dampier (Thomas) 8144,8186
Dampier (William) 4131,4277
Danby (Thomas Osborne) *Earl of* see: Osborne (Thomas) *Duke of Leeds*
Dance of death 7365
Danger and unreasonableness of a toleration 2376
Danger of mercenary parliaments [J.Toland] 3536
Danger of repealing the Test-Act 7885
Dangerfield (Thomas) 1641,1757,1863,1904, 2377
Dangerous consequences to the Queen 3808
Dangerous consequences of parliamentary divisions 6994
Dangerous plot discovered [A.Wotton] 119
Dangerous positions 4398
Danican (François André) 7453
Danniston (Walter) see: Pitcairne (Archibald)
Danse des morts 7365
Danson (Thomas) 1550,1552,1556
D'Anvers (Alicia) 3103
D'Anvers (Caleb) 6741,6754,6766
Darby (Samuel) 7794,7825
Darcie (Abraham) 135
Darel (William) see: Darrell (William)
Darius's feast 6842
Darley (John) 1231
Darrell (William) 2578,2708
Dartmouth (William Legge) *Earl of* see: Legge (William)
Daubeny (Charles) 8177
Davanzati (Bernardo) 3414
Davenant (Charles) 3415,3470,3650,3686,3724-6, 3796,3910,3970,3985,3989,4721-2,5365,5625
Davenant (Sir William) 2378
Davies (Lady Eleanor) see: Douglas (Lady Eleanor)
Davies (James) 1642
Davies (Sir John) 1422
Davies (Joseph) 6774
Davies (Richard) 3572
Davy du Perron (Jacques) see: Du Perron
Davys (John) 5046
Dawes (Sir William) 3416,3727,4278-9,4437-8, 4540-1,5047,5626-7
Dawn of honour 6995
Dawne (Dabry) see: Baynard (Edward)
Dawson (Benjamin) 7144,7509,7630
Dawson (Thomas) 6031,6282,6843
Day-breaking, if not sun-rising [T.Shepard] 796
Day-dream, or a letter 8528
De animi immortalitate [I.H.Browne] 7336
De Messiae duplici adventu [P.Allix] 3633
Deacon (Thomas) 6376,7184
Deaf and dumb man cured 8398
Dealtry (William) 8202,8310,8319
Dean (Charles) 5128
Dean (Jasper) 5048
Dean (John) 5142
Dear bargain [N.Johnston] 2738
Decker (Sir Matthew) 7050
Declaratio et sponsio 5628
Declaration and vindication of the Lord Mayor 1146
Declaration of an honest churchman 4723
Declaration of the Army in Ireland 1012
Declaration of the congregational ministers 3546
Declaration of the demeanor and cariage of Sir Walter Raleigh 80
Declaration of the general council of the officers of the army 1013
Declaration of the kingdomes of England and Scotland 469
Declaration of the Lord Maior 784
Declaration of the officers of the army 1014
Declaration of the people of England 8326
Declaration of the Pfaltzgraves 174
Declaration of the practises & treasons attempted... by Robert late Earle of Essex [F.Bacon] 28
Declaration of the rebels in Scotland 1643
Declaration of the sense of the archbishops [J.Williams] 3411,3452
Declaration of the state of the colonie and affaires in Virginia 91
Declaration of the true causes which moved his Majestie 116
Declaration of truth to Benjamin Hoadly [Defoe] 6134
Decrees of the Parlement of Paris 1984
Dedication to a great man [T.Gordon] 6390
Defection consider'd [M.Tindal] 6238
Defence of Dr.Sacheverell [A.Seller] 4901
Defence of Dr.Sherlock's Preservative [W.Giles] 2726-7
Defence of free-thinking in mathematics [G.Berkeley] 6854
Defence of the account [J.Eveleigh] 6385
Defence of the allies and the late ministry [Defoe] 5367
Defence of the Church of England from priest-craft [H.Bedford] 5006
Defence of the Church of England from the charge of schism [E.Welchman] 3292
Defence of the communion-office [G.Smith] 7097
Defence of the doctrine and practice of the Church [J.Turner] 5338,5542
Defence of the doctrine of the man-Christ Jesus 4280
Defence of the doctrines of the holy Trinity 5629
Defence of the Duke of Buckingham 2379
Defence of the Duke of Buckingham's book [W.Penn] 2438
Defence of the Exposition of the doctrine of the Church [W.Wake] 2548
Defence of the first head of the charge [H.Stebbing] 6344
Defence of the humble remonstrance [J.Hall] 238
Defence of the measures of the present administration 6775
Defence of the papers written by the late King [J. Dryden] 2498
Defence of the people 7084
Defence of the profession [R.Jenkin] 3007,3016
Defence of the reasons for restoring some prayers [J.Collier] 6274-5,6327
Defence of The resolution of this case [E.Fowler] 2285
Defence of The rights of the Christian Church [M.Tindal] 4357
Defence of the Scots abdicating Darien [J.Hodges] 3600
Defence of the Scots settlement at Darien 3547
Defence of the Vindication of K.Charles the Martyr [T.Wagstaffe] 3570
Defence of the Vindication of the deprived bishops [H.Dodwell] 3350,3538
Defence of wearing and reverencing the holy cross 8599
Defense of an argument made use of [S.Clarke] 4392
Defense of the Ld Bishop of London 6377
Defense of the Right Reverend Bishops of Rochester and Bristol 6032
Defoe (Daniel)
Account of the abolishing 5630
Account of the riots 5944
Address 3885,3994
Advice to the electors 4399,4459
Advice to the people 5822
Alteration in the Triennial Act 6015
Anatomy of Exchange-alley 6378-9
And what if the Pretender 5631
Answer to a question 5632
Answer to the late K.James 3246
Argument proving 6133
Armageddon 5049
Atalantis Major 5050
Ballance of Europe 5051
British visions 5052-3
Burnet and Bradbury 5945
Caledonia 4281
Charity still a Christian virtue 6394
Chimera 6455
Christianity of the High-Church 3886
Collection from Dyers letters 4166
Condoling letter 4724
Conduct of parties 5366
Considerations on publick credit 6608
Declaration of truth 6134
Defence of the allies 5367
Dialogue between the author 3732
Dialogue betwixt Whig 3247,4725
Dissenters answer 3887
Dr.Sherlock's Vindication 6283
Dyet of Poland 4030,4091
Enquiry into the occasional conformity 3651
Essay at a plain exposition 5054
Essay on the South-Sea trade 5368
Essay upon publick credit 4726
Faction in power 6135
Farther search 5369
Felonious treaty 5055
Four letters 4727-8
Friendly epistle 5946-7
General history of trade 5633
Good advice to the ladies 4031
Hannibal at the gates 5370
His Majesty's obligations 5948
History of the Kentish petition 3652
Hymn to victory 3888
Impeachment, or no impeachment 5823
Imperial gratitude 5371
Journey to the world in the moon 4032
Jure divino 4167
Justification of the Dutch 5372
Layman's vindication 6033
Legion's memorial 3642,3653
Letter from a dissenter 4729
Letter from a gentleman 4730
Letter from a member 5634
Letter from the man in the moon 4033
Letter to a country gentleman 6062
Letter to a member 5152
Letter to a merry young gentleman 5949, 6010
Letter to Mr.How 3654
Letter to the dissenters 5635
Memoirs of Count Tariff 5636
Mock mourners 3715,3728
Modern addresses 4731
More reformation 3809
New discoveries of the dangers 5867
New test of the Church of England's honesty 3889
New test of the Church of England's loyalty 3729,3734
New test of the sence 4732
No punishment 5468
No queen 5373
Not [tingh]am politicks 5637
Peace, or poverty 5374
Persecution anatomiz'd 4034
Plain English 5482
Proposals for imploying the poor 5638
Queries to the new hereditary right-men 4733
Reasons against fighting 5375
Reasons against the succession 5639
Reasons for a peace 5056
Reasons why a party 5057
Reasons why this nation 5058-9,5151
Reformation of manners 3730
Remedy worse than the disease 5824
Remonstrance from some country Whigs 5950
Reply to a pamphlet 4168
Representation examined 5060
Review 8681
R[ogue]'s on both sides 5061-2
Royal religion 3890
Scotch medal 5063
Scots nation and union 5825
Second letter to a friend in Suffolk 6081
Secret memoirs of a treasonable conference 6137
Secret history of the October club 5064-5
Seldom comes a better 4734
Sermon preach'd 4169
Short narrative of the life and death of... Patkul 6182
Shortest-way with the dissenters 3731,3844
Some account of the life...of...Goertz 6380
Some reasons offered 5951
Some reflections on a pamphlet 3458
Spectators address 5066
Speech for Mr.D[unda]sse 5067
Speech without doors 4735
Succession of Spain 5068
Succession to the Crown 3655
Supplement to the Faults 4736
Triennial Act impartially stated 6097
True account of the design 5069
True-born Englishman 3588,3692,4400
True relation of the apparition 4282
True state of the case 5070
Vindication of Dr.Snape 6138
Worcestershire-queries 5071
Ye true-born Englishmen proceed 3642,3656
3797,3854,3921,4017,4254,4342,4366,4789, 4822,4870,5485,5817-8
Deity: a poem [S.Boyse] 7244
Delafaye (Theodore) 7326
Delamere (Henry Booth) *Baron* see: Booth (Henry) *Earl of Warrington*
Delany (Patrick) 6759,6799,6918,7085
De Laune (Thomas) 2278-80,3891
Delaune (William) 5640-1,6583
Deliquium: or, The grievances 1905
Dell (William) 655,707
Dellon (Gabriel) 2709
Demonstration how the Latine tongue may be learn't [A.Brett] 1330
Demonstration that the Church of Rome [D.Whitby] 2821
Denham (Sir John) 1015
Denison (Stephen) 139
Denne (John) 6631,6888,7139
Dennis (John) 3778,3892,5376,5717,5847,5952 6194,6456,6693
Denniston (Walter) see: Pitcairne (Archibald)
Dent (Giles) 4401,5072
Dent (John) 4520
Deposition, and farther discovery of the late horrid plot 1631
Depositions made upon the birth of the Prince of Wales 2710
Deputies of the republick of Amsterdam 2281
Derby (Charles Stanley) *Earl of* see: Stanley (Charles)
Dering (Sir Cholmley) 5263
Dering (Sir Edward) 224,313,587
Dernieres pensées du grand Frédéric [S.Constant de Rebecque] 8176
Derrick (Samuel) 7547
Derwentwater (James Radcliffe) *Earl of* see: Radcliffe (James)
Desaguliers (John Theophilus) 6457
Descartes (René) 914
Description of a presbyterian 4737
Description of Epsom [J.Toland] 5258
Description of the Egyptian tomb 8327
Description of the great burning-glass 6284,6381
Desertion discuss'd [J.Collier] 2862
Designs of France against England 2496
Desmarets (Jean) 1453
Despaze (Joseph) 8035
Destutt de Tracy (Antoine Louis Claude) 7886
Detection of the state and situation [R.Robertson] 6823
Detection of the true meaning 4738,5146
Detma basilike 2141
Devereux (Robert) *2nd Earl of Essex* 28
Devereux (Robert) *3rd Earl of Essex* 314,354,470, 548,550,752,5023
Devilish conspiracy [J.Warner] 846
Devil's cloven-foot peeping out [S.Tufton] 4122
Devize (Jean) see: Donneau de Vise (Jean)
Dialogue at Oxford 1906,1995
Dialogue between a countrey gentleman [S.Clement] 3407
Dialogue between a Japonese and a Formosan [G.Psalmanazar] 4339
Dialogue between a modern courtier [S.Baston] 3401
Dialogue between a new Catholic convert 2497,2651, 2653
Dialogue between Adam and John 4402
Dialogue between alkali and acid [T.Emes] 3501
Dialogue between Duke Lauderdale 1644
Dialogue between Jack High and Will Low 4739
Dialogue between Jest...and Earnest 4403
Dialogue between Lod.Muggleton 1531
Dialogue between the author of the Observator 3732
Dialogue between the author of Whigs no Christians 5642
Dialogue between the eldest brother of St. Katharines 5073
Dialogue between the Observator 3893
Dialogue between the Pope and a fanatick 1907
Dialogue between the Pope and a phanatick 1758
Dialogue between two Church of England-men 2579
Dialogue betwixt Jack and Will [G.Ridpath] 3474
Dialogue betwixt Sam. the ferriman 1908
Dialogue betwixt Whig and Tory [Defoe] 3247, 4725
Dialogue by way of question and answer [W.Freke] 3257
Dialogue in the shades 7979
Dialogue in vindication of our present liturgy 6382
Dialogue on one thousand seven hundred and thirty-eight 6905
Dialogue on parliamentary reform 8506
Dialogues after mass 8441
Dialogues of the dead [W.King] 3554
Diaper (William) 5377
Diary of the several reports 3894
Diary of the siege & surrender of Lymerick 3189
Dibben (Thomas) 5378
Dick and Tom: a dialogue 4740
Difference between the church and court of Rome [W.Lloyd] 1430
Difference between the Nonjurors and the present publick assemblies [J.Smith] 6086
Difference betwixt the protestant and Socinian methods [T.Tenison] 2661
Difference of the case [W.Clagett] 2187
Difficulties and discouragements [F.Hare] 5962
Digby (Lady Frances) 2300
Digby (George) *Earl of Bristol* 225,236,258,315,443, 471,708,1423
Digby (John) *Earl of Bristol* 316
Digby (Sir Kenelm) 686
Digges (Dudley) 317,760
Dillingham (William) 960,2867
Dillon (Wentworth) *Earl of Roscommon* 1788,2282, 5964
Dilucidation of the late commotions of Turkey 2868
Dimensions and curiosities of St.Paul's 8600
Dingley (William) 5643
Diorama... Two views 8362
Directory for the publique worship of God 588,660
Discourse about edification [G.Hascard] 2197
Discourse about the charge of novelty [G.Hascard] 2198
Discourse about tradition [S.Patrick] 2227
Discourse against false preaching [A.Castle] 6367
Discourse against transubstantiation [J.Tillotson] 2325-6,2596
Discourse (by way of essay) 3402
Discourse concerning a guide [T.Tenison] 2243, 2662
Discourse concerning a judge [W.Sherlock] 2532-3
Discourse concerning auricular confession [J.Goodman] 2287
Discourse concerning invocation of saints [S.Freeman] 2286
Discourse concerning Ireland [Sir F.Brewster] 3493
Discourse concerning prayer [J.Taylor] 749

Discourse concerning the adoration [W.Payne] 2432
Discourse concerning the celebration [J.Williams] 2479
Discourse concerning the devotions [W.Stanley] 2458
Discourse concerning the Ecclesiastical Commission [T.Tenison] 2969
Discourse concerning the fishery 3349
Discourse concerning the nature of idolatry [W.Wake] 2820
Discourse concerning the nature, power and proper effects 2869
Discourse concerning the necessity of reformation [N.Stratford] 2460
Discourse concerning the object of religious worship [W.Sherlock] 2452,2534
Discourse concerning the second Council of Nice [T.Comber] 2705
Discourse concerning the true notion [R.Cudworth] 311
Discourse concerning the unity of the Catholick Church [W.Cave] 2273
Discourse concerning the unreasonableness [E.Stillingfleet] 2965
Discourse concerning trade [Sir J.Child] 2855
Discourse concerning transubstantiation [G.Burnet] 2687
Discourse concerning treasons [R.West] 6103
Discourse historical and critical, on the Revelations 6742
Discourse of conscience [J.Sharp] 2449
Discourse of free-thinking [A.Collins] 5574, 5590,5620,5652,5671,5750,5778,7042
Discourse of schism 3004
Discourse of the holy Eucharist [W.Wake] 2666
Discourse of the peerage [T.Barlow] 1619
Discourse of the sacrifice of the mass [W.Payne] 2765
Discourse of toleration: in answer to a late book [R.Perrinchief] 1325
Discourse of toleration: with some observations 3104
Discourse on a land-bank 4170
Discourse proving the divine institution of water-baptism [C.Leslie] 3465
Discourse shewing that protestants are on the safer side [L.de Beaulieu] 2562
Discourse; shewing, who they are [C.Leslie] 3518
Discourse touching Tanger [Sir H.Sheeres] 1854
Discourses upon the modern affairs of Europe 1759
Discovery. A comedy [F.Sheridan] 7467
Discovery of the Popish plot 1645
Dismal consequences of delighting in war 5379
Dispensary [Sir S.Garth] 3549
Dispute adjusted [E.Gibson] 7889
Disquisition upon our Saviour's sanction of tithes [T.Beverley] 2350
Dissenters address of thanks 3895
Dissenters, and other unauthoriz'd baptisms [R.Laurence] 5437
Dissenters answer [Defoe] 3887
Dissenters conscientious objections 4035
Dissenters loyalty display'd 4741
Dissenting laity pleading 4404
Dissenting teachers address 5074
Dissertatio de Babrio [T.Tyrwhitt] 7690
Dissertation on nothing 7140
Dissertation sur la litérature orientale [Sir W.Jones] 7599
Dissertator in burlesque 3657
Dissertazione 7479
Dissuasive against joining with the conventicles 6034
Distaff (John) see: Character of Don Sacheverellio
Distinction of High-Church and Low-Church 4036
Ditton (Humphry) 5826
Divers papers from the army 761
Divine rights of the British nation 4742
Divine titles of our Lord and Saviour 8349
Division our destruction 3733
Dixon (John) 8145
Dobson (John) 1258
Dr.Bennet's concessions [T.Brett] 6111
Dr. Bentley's proposals for printing 6487
Dr.Blackhall's offspring 4037
Doctor Mead's Short discourse 6498,6547
Doctor Sacheverell's defence 4763
Dr.Sherlock sifted from his bran [L.Sabran] 2644
Dr.Sherlock's Case of allegiance considered [J.Collier] 3101
Dr.Sherlock's two kings of Brainford brought upon the stage 3105
Dr.Sherlock's Vindication of the Test Act [Defoe] 6283
Dr.S[wift]'s real diary 5953
Doctrine and discipline of divorce [J.Milton] 535
Doctrine of passive obedience and nonresistance as established 4743,4824
Doctrine of passive obedience, and non-resistance stated [M.Maittaire] 4824
Doctrine of passive-obedience, by Dr.Tillotson 4744
Doctrine of the Church of England [H.Dodwell] 3459,3538
Doctrine of the Eucharist stated [S.Walker] 6484
Doctrine of the Trinity and transubstantiation compared [E.Stillingfleet] 2657
Doctrine of the Trinity prov'd [W.Howell] 5125
Doctrines and practices of the Church [E.Stillingfleet] 2540
Dod (Thomas) 6139
Dodd (William) 7345,7497
Dodsley (Robert) 6858,6943,6996,7061,7110
Dodsworth (William) 8494
Dodwell (Henry) 2711-2,3190,3223,3260,3292, 3350,3459,3499,3538,4159,4171,4235,4272-4, 4283-4,4324,4365,4392-4,4396,4405,4448-9, 4463,4697,4907,5004,5035,5075-6,5096,5107, 5380,5644
Dodwell (William) 7430
Doggrel (Sir Iliad) see: Burnet (Sir Thomas)
Dolben (John) Archbishop of York 1282,1297
Dolben (John) the Younger 4980
Dominiceti (Bartholomew di) 7454
Dominis (Marco Antonio de) 78
Dominium maris 899
Donne (John) 148
Donneau de Vise (Jean) 4406
Dorman (Joseph) 6871
Dorrington (Theophilus) 4172
Dorset (Edward Sackville) *Earl of* see: Sackville (Edward)
Dort, Synod of 82
Double (Tom) see: Davenant (Charles)
Doubts concerning the Roman infallibility [H.Maurice] 2749
Doughty (Gregory) 6609
Doughty (John) 7216
Douglas (Lady Eleanor) 589
Douglas (Frederic Sylvester North) 8243
Douglas (Gavin) 7315
Douglas (James) 8495
Douglas (John) 7363,7434
Douglas (William) 7185
Dove (Henry) 1760,2380,2580,3106
Dove. A poem [M.Prior] 6199
Dowley (Peter) 4160,4173,4238-9,4241
Downame (George) 41
Downes (Samuel) 6458,6548,6556
Downes (Theophilus) 3107
Downing (Sir George) *1st Baronet* 1283
Downing (Sir George) *3rd Baronet* 5956
Doyle (James) 8513
D'Oyly (Robert) 5077
Draconia [H.Care] 2570,2693
Draghi (Giovanni Baptista) 2306
Drake (Sir Francis) 125,156
Drake (Sir Francis) *the Younger* 125,156
Drake (James) 3734,4001,4040A,4038-9,4090, 4174,8649
Drake (Samuel) 1342-3,6383,6439,6610
Drake (Sir William) 1147
Dram of the bottle for the French King 3896
Draught for a national Church accommodation [J.Humfrey] 4060
Drayton (Thomas) 976
Dream [a poem] 2713
Dream of the Solan goose 4542
Drelincourt (Charles) 4282
Drewe (Patrick) 4745
Drinkwater 1517
Droit le roy [T.Brecknock] 7474
Drummond (John) *Earl of Melfort* 2581
Drummond (Robert Hay) 7253
Drummond (William Abernethy) 7531,7578,7596
Dryden (John) 1403,1407,1569,1909-11,2069-73, 2414,2498,2575,2582-4,2601,2683,2830,2993, 3005-6,3191,7062,7339,7730
Du Baudrier, *Sieur* see: Swift (Jonathan)
Dublin. King's Inns 8113
Du Bourdieu (Isaac) 2283
Dubourdieu (Jean Armand) 2381,4285-6,4407, 6285,6305
Du Chastelet de Luzancy (Hippolite) 3500
Du Chesne (André) 318
Duckett (George) 5381,5940,6117
Ducros (Simon) 3248-9
Dudley (Alice) *Duchess of Dudley* 1329
Dudley (Robert) *Earl of Leicester* 14
Du Duc (Fronton) 50
Duel and no duel 7051
Du Four de Longuerue (Louis) 2585
Dugdale (Stephen) 1761-2,2009
Duhigg (Bartholomew Thomas) 8113
Duke (Richard) 3897-8
Duke of Anjou's succession considered 3635
D[uke] of B[uckingha]m's pro[phec]y 6549
Duke of M[arlborough's] catechism 4543
D[uke] of M[arlborough]'s confession 5382
D[uke] of M[arlborou]h's vindication [M.Manley] 5168
Dull yr aeth y byd o chwith 8279
Dumay (Joseph Adolphe) 7637
Dummer (Jeremiah) 5383
Du Moulin (Louis) 472,1016,1756,1763-4,1814
Du Moulin (Peter) *d.1676* 1289
Du Moulin (Pierre) *the Elder* 754
Du Moulin (Pierre) *the Younger* 851,1340,1381, 1454
Dumouriez (Charles François Duperrier) 8065
Duncon (Eleazar) 1121
Duncumb (Thomas) 1366
Dundas (Sir David) 8297
Dundas (Robert) *Lord Arniston* 5067
Dunkin (William) 6859
Dunn (Thomas) 8008
Dunton (John) 4408-9,4789,5384,5645,6384, 8608
Du Perron (Jacques Davy) 26
Dupin (Louis Ellies) 5766
Du Plessis-Marly (Philippe de Mornay) *Seigneur* see: Mornay (Phillippe de)
Duport (James) 1488
Duppa (Richard) 8085
Du Quesne (Abraham) 2164
Durel (Jean) 1232
Durell (David) 7546
D'Urfey (Thomas) 3108-10
Durham (William) 900
Dury (Giles) 8651
Dury (John) 226-7,319,590,709,874
Dutch barrier our's [J.Oldmixon] 5475
Dutch better friends [J.Withers] 5780
Dutch design anatomized 2714,2949
Dutch faith 7111
Dutch riddle 5385
Dutch way of toleration [W.Baron] 3492
Dutchman's answer to the L[or]d H[aversha]ms speech 4040
Duty of allegiance settled [J.Kettlewell] 3131
Duty of consulting a spiritual guide 6584
Duty of paying custom 7141
Du Vall (Claude) 1355
Duverney (Guichard Joseph) 7217
Du Vignan, *Sieur* 2715
Dyer (George) 8009
Dyer (John) 4166,4985
Dyet of Poland [Defoe] 4030
Dyet of Poland... consider'd [W.Pittis] 4091
Dying hour 8442
Dying Sunday school girl 8399

E.(E.) 3899
E.(H.) 3900
E.(M.) see: Earbery (Matthias)
E.(N.) 3111
E.(R.) 473,911,1489
E.(S.) 4310
E.(T.) 3735
E.(T.) see: Two seasonable discourses concerning this present Parliament
E.(T.) see: Emes (Thomas)
Eachard (John) 1382
Eagle and the robin 4544
Earbery (Matthias) 6035,6063,6140-3,6246, 6278,6286,6382,6459,6550-1,6611,6743, 6776-7,6802
Eardley-Wilmot (John) 8265
Earle (Jabez) 6632,6695
Earnest exhortation for making up the breach 6144
Earnest request to Mr.John Standish 1490
Easie method for satisfaction 3112
Easiest introduction to the Hebrew language 7485
East India Company 228,1480,1520,1948,1968, 2855,2897,2989,3063,3524,3573,6683,7696, 7731,7755,7773,8025,8027,8256-7
East-India-trade a most profitable trade [R.Ferguson] 1532
Easter not mis-timed [J.Pell] 1276
Eaton (David) 8098
Eaton (Samuel) 879
Eccles (John) 3853
Ecclesiae gemitus [P.Du Moulin] 851
Ecclesiae theoria nova [J.Basset] 5004
Ecclesiastical reform 7935
Ecclesiasticall discipline of the reformed churches 320
Echlin (John) 5646
Eckhart (Johann Georg von) 4287
Eckholt (Jacob) 321
Edgley (Samuel) 6612
Edinburgh review 8353,8358
Edrisi (Muhammad al) 7914
Edward II, *King* 2977
Edwards (Edward) 8537
Edwards (George) 3968
Edwards (John) 3250,4288,4333,4746,5386
Edwards (Jonathan) 3251,3736,5078
Edwards (Thomas) *Barrister* 7327
Edwards (Thomas) *D.D.* 7498
Edwards (Thomas) *Puritan Divine* 762
Eeles (Henry) 7597
Egan (Anthony) 1399,1400
Egerton (Thomas) *Viscount Brackley* 229
Egleton (John) 5827
Egotist: or, Colley upon Cibber
Eick (Franciscus ab) 1241
Eigentliche Beschreibung der Welt-beruhmten Dom-Kirchen zu Magdeburg 3589
Eight and thirty queries propounded 1017
Eight speeches made in Parliament 6830
Eight speeches spoken in Guild-hall 322
Eighteen new court-queries 1018
Eikon brotoloigou: or, The picture of Titus Oates 3460
Eikon tou theriou [T.De Laune] 2278
Election-dialogue [B.Hoadly] 4778
Elegiacall commemoration of the pious life 474
Elegy on the burning of the Church memorial 4040A
Elegy on the usurper O.C. [Dryden] 1911
Elegy written in a country church yard [T.Gray] 7306
Elhuyar (Juan José de) 7808
Elias Levita 2
Elibank (Patrick Murray) *Baron* see: Murray (Patrick)
Elizabeth I, *Queen* 1646
Ellesby (James) 2382
Ellesmere (Thomas Egerton) *Baron* see: Egerton (Thomas)
Elliot (Adam) 2074,6778
Elliot (Robert) 5954-5,6499
Ellis 6500
Ellis (Clement) 2716
Ellis (John) *Rector of Waddesdon* 881
Ellis (John) *Vicar of St.Catherine's, Dublin* 7394
Ellis (Philip) 2499
Ellwood (Thomas) 3466,3521
Elogy, against occasion requires 1912
Elphinston (James) 7311
Elphinstone (Arthur) *Baron Balmerino* 7142,7148
Elstob (Elizabeth) 5647
Elwin (Hastings) 8487
Elys (Edmund) 1765,1913,3417-8,3658-9
Emes (Thomas) 3501
Emigration to America 8066
Emlyn (Thomas) 4041,4135,4425,4428,4803,5387,6412
Emmerton, *Mr.* 2094
Endevour after the reconcilement 813
Engelbrecht (Johann) 4289
England 48
England. Army 470,719,761,771,774-7,788-9,816-8 853,864,997,1013-4,1035,1038-9,1069,1072,1170
England. Commissioners nominated to treat of a Union between England and Scotland 4175-6
England. Commissioners of Accounts 3244,3739,3810
England. Commissioners of the Navy 691
England. Laws, Statutes 475,1122,1401,1570,1647, 6585,6860,6944,8320
England. Parliament 230-2,323-373,476-505,591-601,656-665,710-5,763-7,814-5,875,1019,1123, 1570,1648-9,2717,2870-1,3351-4,3737,4545,6493, 6633
England. Parliament. House of Commons 233-4,374, 506-8,716-8,768,1650,1766-8,3590,3660-1,3738, 3810,8618
England. Parliament. House of Lords 1124,3252, 3662,3739-40
England and East-India inconsistent [J.Pollexfen] 3442,3470
England and Scotlands covenant with their God 666
England lampoon'd 3901
England must pay the piper 3113
England's appeal, to her high court 3355
England's confusion [A.Annesley] 995
England's enemies exposed 3694
England's independency upon the papal power [Sir J.Davies] 1422
Englands interest or the great benefit [R.Verney] 2159
Englands monarchy asserted [Sir E.Peirce] 1160
England's most dreadful calamity 2075
Englands new chains discovered [J.Lilburne] 859
England's path to wealth and honour [J.Puckle] 3613
Englands remembrancers 961
Englands repentance Englands only remedy 1020
Englands safety in the laws supremacy 1021
Englands wants [E.Chamberlayne] 2368
English advice to English freeholders 4042
English advice, to the freeholders [F.Atterbury] 5931
English constitution fully stated [G.Harbin] 4774

English gratitude 5648
English liberty in some cases 7218
English loyalty vindicated 1914
English Lucian [E.Ward] 3857
English Presbyterian eloquence [Z.Grey] 6874
English protestant dissenters [J.Sharpe] 5742
Englishman, or A letter from a universal friend 1344
English-man's allegiance 3114
Englishman's answer to a German nobleman 7070
English-mans right [Sir J.Hawles] 1781,6810
Enquiry into the causes of the miscarriage 3591
Enquiry into the conduct of a late right honourable commoner [H.Cotes] 7496
Enquiry into the evidence of the Christian religion [Mrs.Newcome] 6702
Enquiry into the ill designs 5828
Enquiry into the manner of assenting 5649
Enquiry into the meaning of demoniacks [A.A.Sykes] 6897
Enquiry into the measures of submission [G.Burnet] 2688,2863
Enquiry into the nature and obligation of legal rights 3253
Enquiry into the nature, necessity, and evidence [J.Cockburn] 3408
Enquiry into the nature of the liberty 4177
Enquiry into the occasional conformity of dissenters [Defoe] 3651
Enquiry into the present duty of a Low-Church-man [J.Peirce] 5479
Enquiry into the present state of affairs [G.Burnet] 2840
Enquiry into the present state of our domestick affairs 7021
Enquiry into the reasons for abrogating [G.Burnet] 2689
Enquiry into the state of affairs 7186
Enquiry into the state of the union [W.Paterson] 6195
Enquiry; or, a discourse between a yeoman of Kent 3254
Enquiry whether a general practice of virtue [T.Bluett] 6627
Enquiry whether the Christian religion 6803
Enriquez de Cabrera (Juan Tomas) 3902
Entire confutation of Mr.Hoadley's book 4747
Entire vindication of Dr.Sherlock 3115
Eon de Beaumont (Charles d') 7564
Epicedia, quae clarissimi... Theodoro Bezae charissimi 38
Epidemical madness 6919
Epilogue spoken by Mrs.Barry [N.Rowe] 4612
Episcopal government and the honour 1651
Episcopal the only apostolical ordination [W.Hamilton] 5661
Epistle to a gentleman of the Temple [J.Byrom] 7247
Epistle to a young nobleman [J.Dalton] 6870
Epistle to Sir Richard Blackmore 4178
Epistle to the Right Honourable Charles Earl of Dorset [C.Montagu] 3035
Epistles philosophical and moral [W.Kenrick] 7414
Epistola ad Humfredum Hody [S.Grascombe] 3119
Epistola canonici reverendi admodum [W.King] 7090
Epistola objurgatoria ad Guilielmum King [W.King] 7090
Epistolae duae ad celeberrimum...F.V. [Z.Pearce] 6527
Epithalamia Cantabrigiensia 1227
Erastus (Thomas) 20
Erpenius (Thomas) 164
Errors of Mr.Pitt's present administration 7952
Erskine (David) *Earl of Buchan* 7732
Erskine (George) 4748
Erskine (John) *Earl of Mar* 6000,6853
Erskine (Thomas) *Baron* 8045,8048-53,8059
Essay against Arianism [M.Maittaire] 5165
Essay at a plain exposition [Defoe] 5054
Essay concerning the late apparition 6036
Essay for the press [J.Asgill] 5315
Essay on establishments in religion [J.Rotheram] 7522
Essay on reason [W.Harte] 6862
Essay on Scripture-prophecy [W.Burnet] 6606
Essay on the certainty and causes of the earth's motion [Sir H.Sheeres] 3532
Essay on the East-India-trade [C.Davenant] 3415,3470
Essay on the nature of the human body [R.Forbes] 7510
Essay on the power and harmony of prosaic numbers [J.Mason] 7259
Essay on the power of numbers [J.Mason] 7260
Essay on the South-Sea trade [Defoe] 5368
Essay to ecclesiastical reconciliation 2500
Essay to prove women have no souls 5829
Essay towards a comprehension [B.Gratton] 3666
Essay towards advancing the interest 5079
Essay towards an impartial account 5388
Essay towards an union of Ireland [H.Maxwell] 3838
Essay towards the character of the late chimpanzee 6920
Essay towards the history of the last ministry 4749
Essay towards the life of Lawrence, Earl of Rochester 5080
Essay upon excising several branches 3548
Essay upon government 4043,4179
Essay upon kings, poets [R.Robinson] 6598
Essay upon publick credit [Defoe] 4726
Essay upon the duty of physicians [S.Parker] 5980
Essay upon the national credit [J.Broughton] 4152
Essays on the national constitution 6145
Essex, *County of* 393,826
Essex (Robert Devereux) *Earl of* see: Devereux (Robert)
Essex watchmen's watchword 852
Establish'd Church of England vindicated 6037
Established test 1652
Estimate of the manners [J.Brown] 7393
Estwick (Nicolas) 602
Et tu Brute? 3811
Etherege (Sir George) 1305
Eubulos see: Martyn (Richard)
Eucharist. A poem 6889
Eucharistia. Or, A grateful acknowledgment 2383
Eugene, *Prince* 3772,5489
Euripides 7461,7930
Europe's catechism 6967
Eustace (Sir Maurice) 1202
Euthymius Zigabenus 5565
Evans (Abel) 4750-1,5650
Evans (John) *Dissenting Minister* 7442
Evans (John) *Rector of St.Ethelburga* 2076, 2190
Eveleigh (Josiah) 6385,6420
Evelyn (John) *Diarist* 7679
Evelyn (Sir John) 840
Evening post 8618
Everard (Edmund) 1653
Everett (Edward) 8507
Everett (George) 2077,3308
Exact accompt, communicating the chief transactions 8620
Exact accompt of the daily proceedings 8621
Exact account of Romish doctrine [T.Morton] 1690
Exact account of the trials of the several persons arraigned 1571
Exact account of the whole proceedings against [Henry Compton] 2718
Exact and faithful narrative of the horrid conspiracy [T.Oates] 1827
Exact and most impartial accompt of the indictment [H.Finch] 1127
Exact list of the lords spiritual & temporal who sate in the pretended Parliament 2895
Exact narrative of many surprizing matters 4546
Exact narrative of the tryal and condemnation of John Twyn 1274
Examination and explanation of the South-Sea Company's scheme 6460
Examination and resolution of the two questions [J.Trueman] 6619
Examination of Captain William Bedlow 1769
Examination of Edw. Fitzharris 1915
Examination of the arguments [T.Downes] 3107
Examination of the consequences of Dr. Middleton's Free enquiry 7284
Examination of the facts and reasonings in the Lord Bishop of Chichester's sermon 6804-5
Examination of the first part of a pamphlet [J.G.Bevan] 8124
Examination of the Impartial state of the case of the Earl of Danby 1770,1830
Examination of the Management of the war 5081
Examination of the principles...of the two b[rothe]rs [J.Perceval] 7267
Examination of the scheme of Church-power [Sir M.Foster] 6852,6873
Examination of the third and fourth letters 5082
Examinations and informations upon oath, or Sir Thomas Coke 3353-4
Examinations of Henry Barrow 1233
Examine of the expediency 7143
Examiner 4892,5117,5208,5292,5575,5612,5616, 5689,5726,5765,5853
Examiner, examined; or, A modest examination 4044
Examiner examined: or, An answer to the Examination 6805
Execution of Mr.Rob.Foulks 1654
Exerceese of the muckle goon 4045
Exercise for the charity schools 4547-8
Exercitation answered 876
Exercitation concerning usurped powers [E.Gee] 877
Exhortation to the love of our country 5389
Exorbitant grants of William the III 3801
Expedient propos'd [W.Binckes] 3644,3746
Expedient to extricate one's self [E.Stephens] 3627
Expedient to remove the groundless jealousies 5830
Explanation of some passages 3741
Explanation of the design of the Oxford almanack 5083
Exposition given by my Lord Bishop of Sarum [J.Edwards] 3736
Exposition of Rev.ix [W.Garret] 3818
Exposition of Rev.xi [W.Garret] 3819
Exposition of the doctrine of the Church [W.Wake] 2549
Exposition of the XXXIV article 6287
Extract of the process of treason 4549
Extracts from Lord Chatham 8212
Extracts from the speeches and writings 8244
Extraordinary case of the Bp. of St.David's [R.Ferguson] 3812
Extraordinary deliverance, from a cruell plot [N.Fiennes] 378
Eye-salve for the English army 1142
Eyre (Elizabeth) 2872,4752,4914
Eyre (Francis) 7708
Eyre (Richard) 5651,6038
Eyre (Robert) 4410
Eyre (William) 3007

F.(E.) 1655,1791
F.(G.) see: Fox (George)
F.(R.) see: Ferguson (Robert)
F.(R.) *Gent* see: Forbes (Robert)
F.(S.) 3592,3742
F.(T.) see: Falconer (Thomas)
Faber (George Stanley) 8340
Faber (Tanaquil) see: Le Fevre (Tannegui)
Fact against scandal [R.Jennings] 5665,5676
Faction display'd [W.Shippen] 3874,3966
Faction in power [Defoe] 6135
Fagel (Gaspar) 2719
Fair dealer [J.Trevanian] 1086
Fair of St.Germain [E.Boursault] 6261
Fair payment no spunge [Defoe] 6136
Fair question, or Who deserves an impeachment now? 4753
Fair shell, but a rotten kernel [E.Ward] 4127
Fair way with the dissenters [M.Astell] 3863
Fairchild (Thomas) 6552
Faireclough(John) 1126
Fairfax (Ferdinando) *Baron* 375-6
Fairfax (Henry) 2720
Fairfax (Thomas) *Baron* 667-8,670,681,719,758, 769-777,816-8,853,855
Fairman (Arthur) 5390
Faith and obedience: or, A letter 4997,5084
Faith of the true Christian [W.Bromfield] 6629
Faithful account of some transactions [F.Atterbury] 3712,3754
Faithful history of the northern affairs of Ireland 3008
Faithful narrative of facts [J.Kimpton] 7513, 7516,7521,7523
Faithfull admonition of the Paltsgraves churches 72
Falconer (Thomas) 8054,8158
Falkland (Lucius Cary) *Viscount* see: Cary (Lucius)
False alarm [S.Johnson] 7581
False Alarm: or, Remarks 5831
False notion of a Christian priesthood [T.Herne] 6294
False steps of the ministry 5832
Falsehood of Mr.William Pryn's Truth triumphing [H.Robinson] 684
Familiar, plain, and easy explanation of the law [Sir T.E.Tomlins] 7817
Famous prophesie of the white king [I.Bickerstaff] 4663
Fanatical moderation 5085
Fanatick feast 4754
Fanatique queries 1125
Fannant (Thomas 235
Farewel to popery [W.Harris] 1661
Faria (Francisco de) 1771
Farish (William) 8350
Farisol (Abraham ben Mordecai) see: Abraham
Farmer's letter to the True Briton 7316
Farmerie (William) 4755
Farmers and the clergy 8500
Farther account of the Baroccian manuscript [S.Grascombe] 3196
Farther defence, &c. [J.Collier] 6453
Farther instruction for those who have learnt 4411
Farther remarks on the Reverend Dr.Snape's Second letter 6146
Farther search after claret [R.Ames] 3085
Farther search into the conduct of the allies [Defoe] 5369
Fary (John) 669
Fate of M.Manlius Capitolinus 5391
Faults in the fault-finder 4756-7
Faults on both sides [S.Clement] 4700-1,4756-7, 4947
Faussett (Geoffrey) 8570
Favart (Charles Simon) 7588
Favell (Charles) 8245
Fawcett (James) 7953
Fawkes (Francis) 7315
Fawkes (Walter) 8280,8289
Feake (Christopher) 1022
Fears and sentiments of all true Britains [B.Hoadly] 4779
Featley (Daniel) 1126
Featley (John) 143,165
Fecht (Johann) 3288
Fell (John) 1023,1772,3255
Fell (Phillip) 1491
Fell (Thomas) 8559
Felonious treaty [Defoe] 5055
Felton (Henry) 5086
Fenelon (François de Salignac de la Mothe) 6744,7209
Fenton (Elijah) 5087
Fenwick (Sir John) 3468
Ferdinand, *Infante* 154
Ferguson (James) 7187,7338,7465
Ferguson (Robert) 1455,1532,1916-7,2078-80, 2173,2191,2550,2873-6,3356-8,3812,3958, 4046,4180,5088-9
Fergusson (B.) 3743
Ferne (Henry) 275,377,387,450,509-10,520
Ferris (Samuel) 7809
Few orthodox remarks 5392
Few plain reasons [T.Barlow] 2682
Few remarks on The history of the decline and fall [F.Eyre] 7708
Few thoughts on musical festivals [C.Cummins] 8549
Fiat justitia, & ruat coelum 1656
Ficker (Wilhelm Anton) 7912
Fiddes (Richard) 3813,4047,6203,6501
Fielding (Charles John) 7746
Fielding (Henry) 6696,6806,6966,6968
Fiennes (Nathaniel) 236,378,445,571,977,1010, 1024
Fifteen comforts of a good Parliament 5090
Fifth letter to the people of England [J.Shebbeare] 7398
Fifth ode of the fourth book of Horace, imitated [J.Brereton] 6022
Fina (Ferdinand) 3903
Finch (Anne) *Countess of Winchilsea* 4550,5091
Finch (Daniel) *Earl of Nottingham* 5506,5637, 5704-5,5740,5834,6445,6502-3,6575
Finch (Heneage) *Earl of Nottingham* 1127,1894
Finch (Heneage) *Earl of Winchilsea* 1332
Finishing stroke [C.Leslie] 5145
Finley (Samuel) 6969
Fire and faggot 4048
Firebrace (John) 7611
First anniversary of the government [A.Marvell] 952
First ode of the second book of Horace paraphras'd [J.Swift] 5901
First steps, and following degrees 1918
Fiscus papalis 79
Fisher (Edward) 511,948,4758
Fisher (Jasper) 149
Fisher (John) *Bishop of Salisbury* 8165
Fisher (John) *Rector of Wavedon* 8187
Fisher (William) 8400
Fitz-Geffrey (Charles) 152
Fitzgerald (David) 1773
Fitzgerald (Robert) 2192
Fitzgibbon (John) *Earl of Clare* 8067,8246
Fitz-Harris (Edward) 1879,1915,1919-20,1930,2014, 2023,2027,2035
Fitzroy (Augustus Henry) *Duke of Grafton* 7563, 7881,7891
Fitz-William (John) 2193
Five important queries 1921
Five letters on the state of the poor [J.Toke] 7590
Flachs (Sigismund Andreas) 6288
Flamsteed (John) 4294
Flatman (Thomas) 1922,8626
Fleetwood (Charles) 1025,1051,1084
Fleetwood (Everard) see: Burroughs (Samuel)
Fleetwood (Martha) see: Monk (Martha)
Fleetwood (William) 2877,3116-7,3192,3256,3419, 4412,4551,4759-60,5045,5092,5361,5392-7, 5437,5442,5513,5539,5612,5690,5956,6039-41, 6289
Fleming (Caleb) 7144
Fleming (Robert) 4181,5093
Fletcher (Andrew) 3547,3814,3904
Fletcher (Francis) 156

Fletcher (John) 207,2990

Fletcher (Joseph) 8363,8373

Fletcher (Thomas) 7145

Fletcher (William) 8571,8574

Fleury 6872

Flight of the Pretender 4413

Flockmaker (Tom) see: Defoe (Daniel)

Flying-post 8622

Follett (Sir William Webb) 8550

Following speech being spoken off hand
[Sir J.Knight] 3314

Font guarded with XX arguments [T.Hall] 902

Fontenelle (Bernard le Bovier de) 6697-8

Foote (Samuel) 7575

Forbes (Duncan) 7285

Forbes (Robert) *Bishop* 7286,7510

Forbes (Robert) *Gent.* 7219

Ford (Sir Richard) 1345

Ford (Simon) 1284

Forde (Sir Edward) 1290

Fordyce (James) 7680

Foreigners [J.Tutchin] 3630

Foreman (Charles) see: Forman (Charles)

Fore-warn'd, fore-arm'd 2081

Forfeitures of Londons charter 2082

Form of prayer, &c. Translated from the
Dutch 2721

Form of prayer and humiliation for God's
blessing [A.Seller] 3057

Form of proceeding in the choice and
coronation 5102

Form of the proceeding to the royal
coronation [of George I] 5833

Form of the proceeding to the royal
coronation [of George III] 7443

Forman (Charles) 6634,6807

Forme of common prayer (1625) 113

Forme of government [Sir R.B.Cotton] 309

Forme of prayer, necessary to bee used
(1628) 124

Former, present, and future state of the
Church [E.Stacy] 5998

Forms of prayer, proper to be used 6808

Forster (Nathaniel) 7553,7747

Forster (Richard) 2284

Forth (Patrick Ruthven) *Earl of*
see: Ruthven (Patrick)

Fortin (Pierre) 720

Fortrey (Samuel) 1402

Forty one in miniature 5094

Foster (Henry) 512

Foster (James) 7165

Foster (Sir Michael) 6852,6873

Foster (Thomas) 8124

Fothergill (Samuel) 7598

Foulkes (Robert) 1654,1657

Foulks (Isabella) 4290

Foundation of the Church 8443

Fouquet (Charles Louis Auguste de) *Duc de
Belle-Isle* 7102,7107,7122

Four dissertations 7733

Four Hudibrastick canto's 5957

Four letters to a friend in North Britain
[Defoe] 4727-8

Four letters which passed between a gentleman
[T.Brett] 7043

Fourteen papers 2878

Fourteen quaeries 4291

Fourth defense of an argument [S.Clarke]
4394

Fourth letter to the people of England
[J.Shebbeare] 7381

Fourty four queries to the life of Queen
Dick 1026

Fowke (Joseph) 7689

Fowler (Edward) 2194-5,2221,2285,2384-5,2722,
2879,2887,3009,3136,3193,3420,3436,3905,
4280,4552,5398

Fox (Bohun) 4292

Fox (Charles James) 7954,7987,8131-2,8175

Fox (George) 1128-9,1223,3572

Fox (Sir Stephen) 6038

Foxe (John) 12,1167

Foxes and fire-brands [J.Nalson] 1826

France. Assemblée des Notables 7845

France no friend to England [J.F.P.Retz]
1073

Francis I, *Emperor* 7375

Francis (Sir Philip) 7980

Francis (William) 2501

Francis, Lord Bacon: or, The case [T.Gordon]
6507

Francke (Augustus Hermannus) 4293,4374

Franklin (Benjamin) 7511,7649,7955

Franklin (Thomas) 7220,8114

Franco (Solomon) 1319

François (Claude) 1533

Frascatana [F.Livigni] 7711

Fraser (John) 7127

Fraser (Simon) *Baron Lovat* 7146,7158,7176,7179
7191

Fratres in malo [M.Ogilvy] 1156

Frauds and abuses at St.Paul's [F.Hare] 5410,
5587-8,5676

Frederick, *Elector Palatine* 65,81,87,174

Frederick II, *King of Prussia* 8176

Frederick V, *King of Denmark* 7432

Free (John) 7328,7475-6

Free and apposite observations 7756

Free and impartial enquiry [E.Waller] 7071

Free conference concerning the present
revolution 2880

Free English territory in Africa 7887

Free examination of a modern romance 7146

Free-parliament quaeres [H.More] 1152

Free Society of Traders in Pennsylvania
see: Pennsylvania. Free Society of Traders

Free state of Noland 3421

Free thoughts concerning occasional conformity
4049

Free thoughts concerning officers [J.Trenchard]
4120

Free thoughts of the penal laws 2723

Free thoughts upon the Discourse of free-
thinking 5652

Free-born Englishman's unmask'd battery 7188

Free-born subject [Sir R.L'Estrange] 1678,
2743

Freeman (Elizabeth) 1871

Freeman (John) 513

Freeman (Sir Ralph) 159

Freeman (Samuel) 2083,2286,2586

Freeman (William) 6829

Free-thinkers. A poem [A.Finch] 5091

Free-thinking rightly stated [T.Cockman]
5618

Freher (Marquard) 25

Freind (John) 6386-7,6586,6677

Freind (Robert) 4761-2

Freke (William) 3257

French conquest neither desirable [C.Lawton]
3265

French politician found out 1774

Frese (James) 1027

Fresh warning to England 4294

Frezer (Augustine) 2386

Friend (Robert) see: Freind (Robert)

Friendless boy 8444

Friendly conference concerning the new oath
2852

Friendly epistle by way of reproof [Defoe]
5946-7

Friendly letter from honest Tom Boggy [W.King]
4795

Friendly vindication of Mr.Dryden 1403

Frivolous paper 379

Frost (Walter) 8611

Frowde (Philip) 6681

Fuerstenberg (Franz Egon von) 2045

Fuerstenberg (Wilhelm Egon von) 2241

Fuimus Troes [J.Fisher] 149

Full account of the proceedings in relation
to Capt. Kidd 3663

Full account of the proceedings in the last
session 5834

Full account of the rise, progress, and
advantages 3593

Full and clear vindication of the Full answer
[T.Carte] 7046

Full and exact relation of the duel 5653

Full and fair discussion of the pretensions
7888

Full and impartial account of all the late
proceedings... against Dr.Bentley
[C.Middleton] 6414

Full and impartial account of the discovery
of sorcery [F.Bragge] 5331-2

Full and true account of the penitence of
John Marketman 1775

Full answer to a late View of the internal
evidence of the Christian religion
[H.Taylor] 7705

Full answer to an infamous and trayterous
pamphlet [E.Hyde] 827

Full answer to the Conduct of the allies 5399

Full answer to the depositions 5095

Full answer to the second defence [J.Johnston]
2610

Full confutation of witchcraft [A.Fairman]
5390

Full declaration of the true state [W.Prynne]
1166

Full relation of the contents of the black
box 1776

Full, true, and comprehensive view of
Christianity [T.Deacon] 7184

Full, true, and particular account 7936

Full view of the doctrines and practices of
the ancient Church [S.Patrick] 2764

Full vindication and answer of the XI.
[W.Prynne] 790

Full vindication of the... Lord Bishop of
Edinburgh 5400

Fuller (Thomas) *Prebendary of Salisbury* 380,514

Fuller (Thomas) *Rector of Bishops-Hatfield* 3815

Fuller (William) 3422,3592,3594,3664,3681,3699,
3732,3742,3816,3906

Fuller answer to a treatise written by Doctor
Ferne [C.Herle] 387

Fuller relation of the taking of Bath 670

Fullwood (Francis) 901,1383-4,2881,3049

Funeral eclogue sacred to the memory of
...Queen Mary 3359

Funeral poem upon the much lamented death of
Lieutenant-General Wood 5408

Funeral sermon on the occasion of the death
of Algernon Sidney 2196

Funeral sermon preached on the occasion of
the...Earl of Sh[aftesbur]y's late
interment 2169

Funeral sermon upon Mr.Noble [J.Broughton]
5605

Funnell (William) 4277

Furmetary [W.King] 3555

Further considerations concerning raising
the value of money [J.Locke] 3372-3

Further discoverie of the office [S.Hartlib]
821

Further enquiry into the meaning of demoniacks
[A.A.Sykes] 6898

Further examination of our present American
measures [M.Robinson] 7687

Further prospect of the Case in view
[H.Dodwell] 4283

Fyler (Samuel) 2084

Fysh (Thomas) 2387

G.(A.) see: Golding (Arthur)

G.(C.) see: Gildon (Charles)

G.(D.) see: Grenville (Denis)

G.(D.F.) 3744

G.(E.) see: Griffith (Evan)

G.(H.) 4544

G.(H.) see: Tufton (Sackville)

G.(I.) see: Gregory (John)

G.(J.) 3010

G.(J.) see: Gauden (John)
Gay (John)
Glanvill (Joseph)

G.(J.) *Philomathematikos* see: Gadbury (John)

G.(J.M.) see: Montgomery (James)

G.(M.) 4295

G.(M.) see: Godwyn (Morgan)

G.(R.) 4763

G.(S.) see: Grascombe (Samuel)

G.(W.) 1658,7254

G.(W.) see: Garret (Walter)

G.(W.) *Protestant footman* see: Giles (W.)

Gabriel (Robert Burd) 7873

Gaches (Raymond) 932

Gadbury (John) 1346,2081,2388,2761,3932

Gallienus redivivus [C.Leslie] 3366

Galloper [E.Ward] 4968

Galway (Henri de Massue de Ruvigny) *Earl of*
see: Massue de Ruvigny (Henri de)

Game is up: or, XXXI new quaeries 1028

Gander (Joseph) 3817

Gandolphy (Peter) 8231

Gandy (Henry) 3595,3907,4296,4764,5096,6484

Garbett (John) 8508

Garbrand (John) 2085

Gardiner (James) 5654

Gardner (John) 3442

Garnet (John) 5097

Garran de Coulon (Jean Philippe) 7937

Garret (Walter) 3502-3,3596,3665,3818-9,5098

Garrick (David) 6997

Garth (Sir Samuel) 3549,3881

Garroway (Sir Henry) 515

Garway (Sir Henry) see: Garroway (Sir H.)

Gascoigne (Henry Barnet) 8281,8321

Gascoigne (Richard) 6104

Gascoyne (Sir Thomas) 1865

Gaskarth (John) 2389,3597-8,5655

Gaskell (James Milnes) 8529

Gastrell (Francis) 3504,3908,4297-8,5814,
5835,6504

Gataker (Thomas) 88,103,107,1203

Gates of hell opend 5099

Gatford (Lionel) 819

Gatton (Benjamin) 3666,5100

Gauden (John) 237,820,915,933,1029,1102,
1120,1130-4,1172,1204,1234-6,3267

Gay (John) 5101,5401,5836,6042,6147,6194,
6712,7287

Gay (Joseph) see: Breval (John Durant)

Gaynam (John) 4626

Gayton (Edmund) 2186

Geary (William) 8445

Gee (Edward) *the Elder* 876-9

Gee (Edward) *the Younger* 2587,2595,
2724-5,2783,2785,2882

Gee (John) 108

Genealogy of Christ [R.Lowth] 6719

General-excise consider'd 3194

General history of all revolutions 5402

General history of trade [Defoe] 5633

General, or, no general 1030

General view of our present discontents 4765

General view of the present politics 7189

Generall and particular acts and articles 721

Generall demands concerning the late Covenant
189

Geneva 516

Geneva restituta [F.Spanheim] 160

Geneva University 4352

Genies, ballet [Fleury] 6872

Genius Agrippinae consuli 7665

Gentilis (Robert) 200

Gentleman's journal for the war 8623

Gentleman's magazine 8624

Genuine and authentick account of the behaviour
of Dr.Archibald Cameron 7329

Geometry no friend to infidelity [J.Jurin]
6845

George I, *King* 3711, 3792,5304,5498,5809,5833,
5837,5848,5906

George II, *King* 6687

George III, *King* 7443,7823,7946,7986,8316

George IV, *King* 7861,7880,8181,8326,8337

George, *Prince of Denmark* 4401,4468,4517,4625

Geree (John) 603,854,1135

German cruelty 7366

Germany 5102

Gerrald (Joseph) 7956

Gerrald(F.) 3744,3801

Gerrard (John) 934

Gery (William) 1031

Gesner (Johann Matthias) 7749

Gesta Grayorum [W.Canning] 2692

Gibbon (Edward) 7752

Gibson (Edmund) 3640,3644,3667,3713,3745-9,3820-1,
4050-1,4182-3,4299,5958,6043-4,6148,6699,
6745-7,6762-3,6779-80,6822,6852,6873,6891,7086,
7317,7889

Gibson (Richard) 3612

Gibson (Samuel) 4558

Gideon's fleece [T.Guidott] 2289

Gifford (John) 8052-3,8068

Gifford (William) 8146

Gilbert (John) 7087,7112

Gilbert (Thomas) 7863

Gildon (Charles) 3234,4414

Giles (William) 2726-7

Gill (John) 7342

Gillane (John) 5838

Gilpin (Jeremiah) 7846

Gilpin (John) 949

Gilpin (Richard) 962,981

Gilpin (William) 7346

Girdlestone (John Lang) 8282

Gisborne (Thomas) 7981

Gizzard, *Squire* see: Grumbler

Glanvill (Joseph) 1306-7,1333,1347,1455,1923

Glasse (Samuel) 7826

Gleane (Peter) 3360

Globe notes [R.Holland] 1292

Gloria Britannica 2831

Glorious life and actions of St.Whigg 4415

Glory of the creation 8401

Gloucester, *County of* 261

Glover (Richard) 7034

God and the king [D.Jenkins] 858

God; no impostor [W.Prynne] 136

Goddard (Charles) 8589

Goddard (Peter Stephen) 7554

Goddard (Thomas) 4766-7,4795

Godden (Thomas) 2432,2658

Godfrey (Sir Edmund Berry) 1583,1616-7,1645,1710,
1979,2077,2428

Godolphin (William) *Marquess of Blandford* 6505

Gods love to mankind [S.Hoard] 150

Gods love to man-kinde [S.Hoard] 965

God's wonderful judgment in Lincoln-shire 1659

Godschall (William Man) 7847

Godwin (Francis) 93

Godwyn (Morgan) 1924,2390

Goebel (Johann David) 6461

Goertz (Georg Heinrich) 6150,6380

Goff (Stephen) 708

Golden age from the fourth eclogue 3822-3

Golden rule made plain and easie 1457

Golding (Arthur) 137

Goldsmith (Oliver) 7455,7579-80

Golius (Jacobus) 132

Gondomar, *Count* see: Sarmiento de Acuna (Diego)

Gooch (Sir Thomas) 5403, 5656

Good advice to the Church of England [W,Penn]
2627

Good advice to the ladies [Defoe] 4031

Good advice to the pulpits [J.Gother] 2592, **2826**

Good and necessary proposal for the restitution [E.Stephens] 3850
Good Catholic 8374
Good husband for five shillings 4768
Good minister 8364
Good old cause, further discuss'd [C.Leslie] 4805
Good old cause, or, lying in truth [C.Leslie] 4780,4806
Good old test reviv'd 2588
Good shepherd 8446
Good young servant 8402
Goodall (Joseph) 8150
Goodall (Walter) 7555
Gooden (Peter) 2589
Goodman (John) 1536,1777,2287,2883
Goodrick (John) 2391
Goodwin (George) 89
Goodwin (John) 381,604,671,854,890,917
Goodwin (Thomas) 517
Goodwin (Timothy) 4814,6209
Googe (Barnaby) 1385
Gordon (Sir Adam) 8147
Gordon (James) 2590
Gordon (John) *Bishop of Galloway* 2885
Gordon (John) *Jacobite* 6027
Gordon (Thomas) 6388-91,6450,6462-3,6506-8, 6868
Gordon (William) *A.M.* 6914
Gordon (William) *of Aberdeen* 6290
Gordon (William) *Rector of St.James's Barbados* 4769
Gore (John) 166
Goring (Henry) 7288
Gostwyke (William) 2392,3195
Gother (John) 2393-5,2502-7,2530-1,2535,2540, 2574,2591-6,2620,2624-5,2670,2701,2724-5, 2728-9,2797,2826-7
Gould (Robert) 2414
Gould (William) 1386,1424,1492
Gourlay (Robert) 8266
Gourlay (William) 8223
Government and order of the Church of Scotland [A.Henderson] 239
Gower (Humfrey) 2396
Gowring (John William) 8538
Grabe (Johann Ernst) 5103,5283-4,5404,5470, 6375,6509
Grace of our Lord Jesus Christ [S.Fothergill] 7598
Grafting of fruit trees 8375
Graham (James) *Marquess of Montrose* 4770
Graham (John) 8098
Gram. (Horat.) 4544
Granadeer Quaker set in a true light 4771
Grand and important question [J.Lindsay] 7373, 7416
Grand case of conscience stated [F.Rous] 865
Grand-jurors of the city of Bristoll 1456
Grand-jury-man's oath and office [Sir J.Hawles] 1782
Grand mystery, or art of meditating 6658
Grand-point lately carried 5104
Grand question resolved 1925
Grand removal 6945
Grandsire Hambden's ghost 5405
Grandval (Nicolas Ragot de) 6635
Grant (James) 7190
Granville (George) *Baron Lansdowne* 6291
Grascombe (Samuel) 2730,2884,3118-22,3176, 3196-8,3258-9,3550,3750,3909-10,3948, 4052,4232,4300,5176
Graverol (François) 1425
Gravius (Joannes) see: Greaves (John)
Gray (Jeffery) 6809
Gray (John Hamilton) 8509-10
Gray (Jonathan) 8328
Gray (Thomas) 7306
Great and popular objection [W.Penn] 2766
Great and weighty considerations relating to the D. 1660,1791
Great and weighty considerations, relating to the Duke of York... considered [T.Hunt] 1791
Great Britain 6587-8
Great Britain. Army 6553
Great Britain. Civil Service 5839
Great Britain. Commissioners for Forfeited Estates 6636,7113
Great Britain. Commissioners of Accounts 5105,5354,5365,5406,5657,5840
Great Britain. Court of Chancery 6637-9, 6647,6656
Great Britain. Laws, Statutes 7650,7681, 7697,7774,7848,8086
Great Britain. Parliament 5106,5519,5658, 5715,5959-60,6045-7,6545,6640,6831-2, 6998,7191
Great Britain. Parliament. House of Commons 5961,6048,6292,6554,6999,7666,7957, 8283
Great Britain. Parliament. House of Lords 4772,6589-90,6641,6657,7147-8,7486

Great Britain. Trustees for Raising Money on the Estates of the late South Sea Directors 6642
Great Britain's groans [W.Hodges] 3361
Great Britains misery [G.Smith] 557
Great Britain's union 4053
Great case put home in some modest queries 1926
Great Jesuit swallows the less 6149
Great jubilee of the year 1825 8403
Great mercy of God 4553
Great necessaries of publick worship [T.Brett] 6827
Great question concerning things indifferent [E.Bagshaw] 1107
Great question, of the authority [E.Stephens] 3628
Great question: or, How religion 3111
Great sin and folly of drunkenness 4301
Greatrakes (Valentine) 1298
Greaves (John) 3565
Grebner (Paul) 1778
Green (John) 7512
Green (Thomas) 4020
Greene (Giles) see: Grene (Giles)
Greene (John) 605
Greenshields (James) 4554,4956-7,5024,5107, 5147,5199
Greenwood (John) 18,1233
Gregg (William) 5120,5187
Gregory of Nazianzus 9,6028
Gregory (Francis) 1404
Gregory (Jon) 722
Grene (Giles) 778
Grenville (Sir Bevil) 2307
Grenville (Denis) 2288,2508
Grenville (George) 7556
Grenville (William Wyndham) *Baron* 7927,8194
Greville (Henry Francis) 8239
Greville (Robert) *Baron Brooke* 386,572
Grey (Charles) *Earl* 7957,8193
Grey (Henry) *Earl of Stamford* 366,518,532
Grey (Richard) 7088
Grey (Thomas) 2397
Grey (Zachary) 6555,6591,6874
Grieve (Henry) 8036
Griffin (John) 6556
Griffith (Evan) 2597,2885
Griffith (John) 4302
Griffith (Matthew) 382,1141
Griffith (Thomas) 7367,₩631-3
Grigg (Thomas) 1354
Grisdale (Browne) 7874
Groans of Germany 6970
Gronovius (Jacobus) 5660
Groome (John) 5724
Grotius (Hugo) 97,157,2935,4582
Grounds and motives inducing his Majesty to agree 460
Grove (Robert) 1493,1779,1927,2086,2398-9,2885
Grumbler 8625
Grumbling hive [B.de Mandeville] 4077
Guardian 5612,5687,5726
Guerdon (Aaron) 1755,5363,6280
Guez (Jean Louis) see: Balzac (Jean Louis Guez) *Sieur de*
Guide (Philip) 3551
Guide to the stage 7307
Guidott (Thomas) 2289
Guillard (Nicolas François)7719
Guis (Joseph) 1285
Guiscard (Antoine) *Marquis* 5170
Guise (William) 3032
Gulliver (Lemuel) see: Fielding (Henry)
Gulliver (Martin) see: Censoriad
Gumbleden (John) 117
Gunning (Peter) 1537,1928,2794
Gurnall (William) 963
Gurney (Joseph) 7544
Gustavus Vasa, *King* 6923
Guthrie (David) 7408
Guybon (Francis) 5407
Gwynne (Sir Rowland) 4225
Gyllenborg (Carl) 6150

H., *Lord* see: Thompson (John) *Baron Haversham*
H.(A.) 5408
H.(B.) 6971
H.(C.) 1457
H.(D.) 6151
H.(J.) 6392
H.(J.) see: Howell (James)
H.(J.) *Minister of the Gospel* see: Hoyle (J.)
H.(L.) 4773
H.(P.) 3461,3668
H.(R.) see: Holland (Richard)
H.(S.) see: Hartlib (Samuel)
H.(T.) 3011

H.(W.) 1914,2598
H.(W.) see: Harris (Walter)
Habernfeld (Andreas ab) 1863
Hacket (Laurence) 4303
Hackett (Maria) 8232
Hafiz 7849
Hague (Thomas) 8311
Haine (William) 1240
Hakewill (George) 76
Haldane (John) 7532
Hale (Sir Matthew) 2290,3309,6293
Hales (Sir Edward) 2734
Hales (John) 383,1405
Hales (William) 8312
Halhed (Nathaniel Brassey) 8010,8015
Halifax (Charles Montagu) *Earl of* see: Montagu (Charles)
Halifax (George Savile) *Marquess of* see: Savile (George)
Hall (George) 7368
Hall (Fayrer) 6781
Hall (Joseph) 238,1136
Hall (Robert) 8267
Hall (Thomas) 891,902,935
Halley (George) 3505
Hallifax (James) 7369
Hallifax (Samuel) 7612,7616,7739
Hamilton (James) *1st Duke of Hamilton* 190 868
Hamilton (James) *4th Duke of Hamilton* 4995, 5449,5518,5537,5653,5696
Hamilton (James) *Professor of Midwifery* 8560
Hamilton (James) *Vissount Limerick* 7052
Hamilton (John) *Baron Belhaven* 4184,4275,7149
Hamilton (Newburgh) 6906,7435,7586
Hamilton (William) 5661
Hammond (Anthony) 6510
Hammond (Henry) 606-9,672-4,723,779-80,855, 936,950,950,964,978,1199,2087,2886, 6921
Hammond (William) 6875
Hampden (John) 2329
Hanbury (Dorothy) 641
Hancock (John) 4555,5662-3
Hancocke (Robert) 1780
Handel (George Frederick) 6906,6950,7093,7104, 7116,7287,7339,7435,7487,7491,7586,7618, 7670,8602
Hanmer (Sir Thomas) 5280,5506,6292
Hannibal at the gates [Defoe] 5370
Hannibal not at our gates 5841
Hanno 8054
Happy coalition. A poem 7000
Happy poor man 8404
Harangue au roy 1929
Harbin (George) 4774,5678,5925
Harcourt (Simon) *Viscount* 4996,5268
Hard usage of beasts 8447
Harding (John) 8561
Harding (William) 8530
Hardt (Richard von der) 4304
Hardwick (William) 191
Hardy (Nathaniel) 982,1351
Hardy (Thomas) 7913,7982
Hardyknute, a fragment [E.Wardlaw] 7239
Hare (Francis) 3599,4556-7,5081-2,5108-15, 5168-9,5206,5319,5409-10,5587-9,5664-5, 5676,5962,6037,6049,6393,6405,6511, 6592,6804-5,6861
Haren (William van) 7001
Harington (Edward) 7557
Harlay (Achille de) 2731
Harlequin-Horace [J.Miller] 6791
Harley (Robert) *Earl of Oxford* 4154,4700, 5066,5170,5524,5963,6435
Harley (Thomas) 7535
Harman (Ephraim) 7318
Harmar (John) 856
Harmony of divinity and law [G.Hickes] 2292
Harmony of our oathes 519
Harper (Robert Goodloe) 8069
Harper (William) 7114
Harrington (James) *Barrister* 2732,3022
Harrington (James) *the Elder* 1032-3,1063
Harris (James) *Earl of Malmesbury* 8062
Harris (John) 3506-12,3824,4054,4185
Harris (Robert) 51,118,384,675
Harris (Walter) 1661
Harris (William) 6643
Harrison (John) 81
Harrison (Joseph) 5666
Harrison (Richard) 7864
Harruney (Luke) see: Walker (Henry)
Hart (Edward) 6152,6293
Hart (Nicholas) 5118
Hart (Philip) 3829
Harte (Walter) 6862
Hartley (David) 7709

Hartlib (Samuel) 172,821,916
Hartmann (Johann Melchior) 7914
Harvest home 8405
Harvey (Gideon) 2289
Harvey (William) 2398
Hascard (Gregory) 1662,2197-8,2400
Haslerigg (Sir Arthur) 385
Haslewood (Francis) 6512
Haslewood (John) 4186,4305
Hastings (Francis Rawdon) *Marquess of Hastings* 8067,8206
Hastings (Selina) *Countess of Huntingdon* 8454
Hastings (Warren) 7689,7773,7869
Hausted (Peter) 610
Have at you all 6951
Haversham (John Thompson) *Baron* see: Thompson (John)
Haweis (Thomas) 7513,7516,7521,7523
Hawker (Peter) 8213
Hawker (Robert) 8197-8,8203
Hawkesworth (John) 7651
Hawkins (Francis) 1919,1930,2014,2023
Hawkins (William) 7319
Hawles (Sir John) 1781-2,6810,7958
Hawtrey (C.D.) 8314
Hay (Thomas) *Earl of Kinnoull* 7866
Hay (William) 7347,7431
Hayes (Charles) 6907
Hayes (Christopher) 6253
Hayes (William) 7313,7429
Hayley (Thomas) 5411,6153
Hayley (William) 2599
Hayne (Samuel) 2401
Hayter (Thomas) 7150
Hayward (Roger) 1494
Haywood (Eliza) 6713
Hazard of a death-bed-repentance [J.Dunton] 4408-9
Head of Nile [T.Baker] 1884
Heads of agreement assented to by the united ministers 3123
Healing paper [J.Humfrey] 1574
Hear this word [R.Stafford] 3534
Hearne (Thomas) 880
Heathcote, *Mr.* 7351,7434
Heathcote (George) 7456
Heathcote (Sir Gilbert) 5179
Heaton (George) 8511
Hebraicae grammatices rudimenta [R.Busby] 6118
Heinsius (Antonius) 5667
Hele (Henry) 7041
Hell broke-loose 6513
Hellier (Henry) 2733,3462
Help in need 8406
Henderson (Alexander) 186,239,611
Henderson (Andrew) 7558,7566
Hendley (William) 6154,6394
Henke (Heinrich Philipp Conrad) 7833
Henley (John) 6748
Henry VI, *King* 5444
Henry VIII, *King* 2600,2842
Hensman (John) 8284
Her Grace of Marlborough's party-gibberish explained 7002
Her Majesty and her royal father vindicated 5583
Her Majesty's prerogative in Ireland [J.Trapp] 5533
Heraclitus ridens 1992,8626
Herbert (Sir Edward) 2734
Herbert (Philip) *4th Earl of Pembroke* 386,822, 883
Herbert (Philip) *7th Earl of Pembroke* 1727
Hercules. A musical drama [T.Broughton] 7104
Hereditary succession in the protestant line 3911
Herle (Charles) 387,520-1
Hermippus redivivus [J.H.Cohausen] 7251
Hernandez (Jaime) 7348
Herne (Thomas) 6294-5,6356,6395-6
Herring (Thomas) 6888,6908,6946,7118,7192
Hertford, *County of* 434
Hertford letter 3545
Hertzberg (Ewald Friedrich von) 7827
Hervey (Elizabeth) *Countess of Bristol* see: Chudleigh (Elizabeth) *Duchess of Kingston*
Hervey (John) *Baron* 6749,6766,6786,6792,6868, 6922,7003
Hervey (Thomas) 7499
Hesketh (Henry) 2291,2402
Heslop (Luke) 8087
Hesronita (Elia Simon) 3317
Hess (Joannes Armondus de) 1663
Heu and cry: or, A relation 2118
Heubach (Carl Christian) 7915
Hewlett (John) 8115
Hey (John) 7698
Heydon (John) 983

Heylin (John) 7682
Heylyn (Peter) 175,183-4,522,984,992-3,1137, 1156,2493,4558,8637
Heyne (Christian Gottlob) 7853
Heyrick (Thomas) 2403-4,2601
Hickeringill (Edmund) 1783,1931-3,2088,3093, 3825,4122
Hickes (George)
Apologetical vindication 2602
Apology for the new separation 3124
Case of infant-baptism 2199
Celebrated story 5842
Declaration made 7053
Discourse of the soveraign power 2089
Harmony of divinity 2292
Jovian 2165,2200,3128
Last will and testament 6050
Letter from a person 2405
Letter to the author 2887
Moral schechinah 2090
Peculium Dei 1934
Ravillac Redivivus 1572
Sermon preached at the cathedral 2293
Sermon preached at the church 2294
Sermon preached before the Lord Mayor 2091,2201
Speculum Beatae Virginis 2509
Spirit of enthusiasm 1935,2202
Three short treatises (1732) 6811
Three short treatises (1709) 4558
True notion of persecution 1936
Vindication of some 3199
3146,3266,4327,4592,4660,4799,4837-8,5144, 5404,5547,5604,5661,6057-8,8606
Hickman (Charles) 1937
Hickman (Henry) 1156
Hide (Sir Henry) see: Hyde (Sir Henry)
Hieron (Samuel) 74,104
Higden (William) 3669,3910,4055,4559,4586-8, 4764-5,5116
Higgins (Francis) 4269,4290-1,4306-8,4317
Higgons (Theophilus) 52
High-Church aphorisms 5117
High Church mask pull'd off 4776
High-Church politicks 4777
High-lander's answer 3912
Hildeyard (John) 2203
Hill (George) 7983
Hill (John) 7169
Hill (Joseph) 1406
Hill (Sir Richard) 7538
Hill (Robert) 7420
Hill (Samuel) 2603,3198,3200,3418,3513,4416, 5668-9
Hill (Thomas) *Fellow of Trinity* 4560
Hill (Thomas) *Master of Trinity* 388,523,612-3
Hill (William) 5118
Hilliard (Samuel) 4561-2,5670,6155
Hinchliffe (John) 7584
Hinckley (John) 8070
Hind (Thomas) 6156
Hind and the panther [Dryden] 2882
Hind and the panther transvers'd [M.Prior] 2634
Hinde (John) 615
Hindmarsh (Thomas) 1784
Hindoo sculpture 8351
Hingeston (Henry) 3899
Hinton (John) 2406
Hints for the regulation of convicts 7757
Hints respecting divine worship 8473
Hints to the public and legislature 8214
Hireling artifice detected 7004
His Maiesties declaration to all his loving subjects 123,204,218,291-7,457-8
His Majesty's obligations [Defoe] 5948
Historic memoir on the French Revolution [W.Belsham] 7911
Historical account of comprehension [W.Baron] 4006
Historical account of some things [D.Whitby] 3080
Historical account of the advantages [M.Earbery] 6550
Historical account of the constitution 5843
Historical account of the laws against the Roman-Catholics [D.O'Connell] 8226
Historical account of the principles 3913
Historical and political treatise of the Navy 3826
Historical collections concerning church affairs [S.Lowth] 3425
Historical collections, concerning district-successions [S.Lowth] 5693
Historical examination of the authority [R.Jenkin] 2737
Historical memoirs of religious dissension [J.Trist] 7905
Historical register 8627
Historical relation of the late general assembly [J.Cockburn] 3099
Historical relation of the late Presbyterian general assembly [J.Cockburn] 3100
Historical romance of the wars [J.Sergeant] 3326
History and transactions of the English nation 2888
History of a church and a warming pan [J.Montgomery] 7960
History of addresses [J.Oldmixon] 5186
History of conformity [J.Collinges] 1903
History of faction [S.Tufton] 4123
History of Fairford Church [S.Rudder] 7623
History of hereditary-right [R.Fleming] 5093
History of passive obedience [A.Seller] 2879, 2887,2947,2965
History of Peter Lacy 8341
History of publick and solemn state oaths 6051
History of self-defence [A.Seller] 3058
History of sin and heresie attempted [C.Leslie] 3519
History of the association 2092
History of the Chancery [S.Burroughs] 6656
History of the Church, in respect [C.Leslie] 4201
History of the Convocation [W.Kennet] 3753
History of the Indulgence [J.Brown] 1560
History of the Kentish petition [Defoe] 3652
History of the life and actions of Gustavus Vasa 6923
History of the most illustrious William 2889
History of the plot anatomised 2890
History of the proceedings of the Mandarins 5412
History of the Revolution [R.Ferguson] 4180
History of the sheriffdom 6593
History of the Test Act [T.Sherlock] 7901
History of the works of the learned 8628
Histrio theologicus 5933
Hitch-about (Penelope) see: Better late than never
H-ne (J-n) see: Haldane (John)
Hoadly (Benjamin)
Answer to a calumny 6296
Answer to a late book 6297
Answer to the representation 6298,6403
Answer to the Reverend Dr.Snape's Letter 6157-8
Common rights of subjects 6397,6419,6428
Election-dialogue 4778
Fears and sentiments 4779
Humble reply 4563
Jacobite's hopes 4780,4804-5
Letter to the Reverend Dr.Francis Atterbury 4187-8
Nature of the kingdom 6109,6124,6138,6155, 6159-61,6197-8,6201,6217-22,6244,6247,6351
Preservative against the principles 6017, 6052,6087,6121-2,6154,6188,6245
Queries recommended 5671
Refutation of Bishop Sherlock 7850
Restoration made a blessing 6053-4
Serious enquiry 5119
Sermon preach'd at the funeral 6398
Sermon preach'd before...the Lord Mayor 4056-7,4177,4186
Sermon preach'd on the eighth of March 4058,4124
Some considerations humbly offered 4564-6
Thoughts of an honest Tory 4700,4781
4216,4506,4511-2,4585,4589-90,4602,4605, 4614,4626,4670,4742,4747,4801,4816,4870, 4969,4997,5084,5149,5176,5181,5204,5234, 5273,5550,6037,6115-6,6127,6129-30,6134, 6142,6146,6152,6164-5,6171,6173-4,6179-80 6187,6191,6202,6204-7,6215-6,6225,6233-4, 6248,6252,6281,6283,6286-7,6300,6304, 6316,6320,6330-2,6344-6,6371,6391,6395, 6416,6421,6434,6511,6880-1,6971
Hoadly (John) 4309,4417,4689,4898,6299
Hoard (Samuel) 150,965
Hobbes (Thomas) 1291,1785,3234
Hodges (Abraham) 4567
Hodges (James) 3600,3827
Hodges (Nathaniel) 6464
Hodges (Thomas) 951
Hodges (William) 3361
Hodgson (William) 8011
Hody (Humfrey) 3087,3119,3125-6,3143,3176, 3196-7,3201,3260,3350,3499
Hoffman (Francis) 5120,5844
Hoffman (Christian Gottfried) 5121
Hofmann (Johann) 3127
Hogarth (William) 7533
Hoglandiae descriptio [T.Richards] 4610
Holborne (Robert) 389
Holden (Samuel) *Esq.* 6816
Holden (Samuel) *M.A.* 1495
Holdsworth (Edward) 4568-70,4610,5413,7005
Hole (Matthew) 5672
Holland (Henry Rich) *Earl of* see: Rich (Henry)
Holland (J.) 7477
Holland (Richard) *Chaplain* 3670
Holland (Richard) *Mathematician* 1292
Holland (Samuel) 8247
Holles (Denzil) *Baron* 773,790,1367,1496,1843
Holles (Thomas Pelham) *Duke of Newcastle* 7156,7164,7262,7452
Hollingworth (Richard) 1786,1938,3229
Holloway (James) 2295
Holmes (William) 7006
Holmia literata [R.von der Hardt] 4304
Holy fast of Lent defended 1537
Holy table, name and thing [J.Williams] 183-4
Holy things for holy men [S.Shaw] 994
Holyday (Barten) 133
Home 8407
Home (Sir Everard) 8255
Homer 3424,3610,5940,6546,6660,6968
Homerides [Sir T.Burnet] 5940
Honest grief of a Tory 7412
Honest Hodge & Ralph 1787
Honest informer or Tom-Tell-Troth's observations 390
Honest letter to a doubtfull friend 416
Honesty in distress [E.Ward] 4483
Honesty the best policy 5122
Honesty's best policy [M.Nedham] 1547
Honour. A poem [J.Brown] 7044
Hook (Archibald) 7969
Hook (James) 8127,8148,8152
Hook (Walter Farquhar) 8562-3
Hooke (Nathaniel) 7030
Hooke (Richard) 2296
Hooke (Robert) 1426
Hooker (Richard) 59,3271
Hooker (Thomas) 881
Hoole (John) 7775
Hooper (George) 2093,2891,3671,5167,5673,6753,
Hopkins (William) 3128
Hoppus (John) 8385
Horatius Flaccus (Quintus) 1788,5321,5414, 5520,5751,5901,5964,6022,6710,6849,6851, 6863,6895,6911,6919,6924,6943,6947,6972
Horden (John) 1497
Hore (Charles) 3828
Horler (Joseph) 6714
Hornby (Charles) 5123,5415-8
Horne (George) 7444,7559,7634,7652,7667-8 7795,7828-9,7857,7890,8010,8107-8
Horne (Thomas) *Chaplain of St.Saviour's* 5674
Horne (Thomas) *Fellow of Eton* 2407
Horrid conspiracie of such impenitent traytors 1259
Horsley (Samuel) 7790,7830,7868,7891-2,7916, 8153,8178,8248
Horton (Thomas) 823
Hoskins (John) 8557
Hospinianus (Rodolphus) 1573
Hotman (François) 5124
Houblon (James) 2059
Hough (John) 4059,4571-2,5419,5965
Hough (Nathaniel) 5675,6055
Houghton (John) 8613-4
Hourglass (Humphrey) 8215
Houschone (William) 2204
How far the clergy and other members 3012
How the members of the Church 2604
Howard (Lady Frances) 5023
Howard (Frederick) *Earl of Carlisle* 8099
Howard (Sir Robert) 1831,3417
Howard (Thomas) *Duke of Norfolk* 4522
Howard (Thomas) *Earl of Arundel* 173,240
Howard (William) *Baron Howard of Escrick* 1939,1952
Howard (William) *Viscount Stafford* 1789,2009, 2031
Howe (John) 3514,3651,3654
Howe (John Grubham) 3686
Howe (Obadiah) 1275
Howell (James) 576,824-5,857,1034,1208
Howell (John) 2408
Howell (Laurence) 5966,6033,6094,6127,6422
Howell (Thomas Bayly) 8149
Howell (William) 5125,5420
Howland (Elizabeth) 6398
Hoyle (Joshua) 676
Hubbard (Henry) 7289
Huddersford (George) 8128
Hudibras redivivus [E.Ward] 4128,4237
Hudleston (Richard) 2735
Hudson (Samuel) 677,881
Hue and cry after part of a pack 6925
Huffumbourghausen, *Baron* see: Congress of the beasts
Hugenius (Christianus) see: Huygens (C.)
Hughes (George) 144,781
Hughes (John) *Fellow of Balliol* 2205
Hughes (John) *Poet* 3829
Hughes (Michael) 7151
Hughes (Obadiah) 7255-6
Hull (William) 8204
Human souls naturally immortal 4310
Humble address offer'd to the consideration 3362
Humble advice of the Assembly 799
Humble answer of the general councel 864
Humble petition and address of the Right Honourable the Lord Mayor 1970
Humble petition and address of the officers 1035
Humble petition and representation of the gentry 391
Humble petition of divers well-affected persons 1036
Humble petition of many cordial friends 892
Humble petition of many inhabitants [of London] 1037
Humble petition of many thousands of young men and apprentices 724
Humble petition of the common people of England 3202
Humble petition of the gentry and commons of the county of York 392
Humble petition of the inhabitants of the county of Essex 393
Humble petition of the knights, gentlemen... of Surrey 826
Humble petition of the Lord Mayor 680,831,1048
Humble petition of the Major 399
Humble petition of the ministers 241
Humble petition of the peacefull, obedient, religious, and honest Protestants 394
Humble petition of the protestants of France 1940
Humble petition of the Right Honourable the Lord Mayor 1818
Humble proposal to cause bancrupts 1664
Humble proposals and desires of... Lord Fairfax 817
Humble proposals of sundry learned and pious divines [E.Reynolds] 888
Humble proposals to the Parliament 966
Humble representation and petition of the officers 1038
Humble representation of some officers of the army 1039
Humble tender and declaration of many wel-affected mariners 804
Hume (Joseph) 8233,8256-7,8272
Humfrey (John) 1574,1790,4060,4189,5126
Humphreys (Samuel) 6833
Humphreys (Thomas) 5421
Hungerford (Sir Anthony) 198
Hunt (Thomas) *Lawyer* 1791,2094,2213
Hunt (Thomas) *Regius Professor* 7221
Hunter (John) 8129
Hunter (William) 7785
Hunting of the foxes [J.Lilburne] 860
Huntingdon, *County of* 7534
Huntingford (George Isaac) 7875-6
Hunton (Philip) 524,2892-3
Hurd (Richard) 7349,7831
Hus (Jan) 1167
Hutcheson (Archibald) 6557-60
Hutchinson (C.) 2605
Hutchinson (Michael) 6682
Hutchinson (Thomas) 6909,6926
Hutton (Charles) 7788
Hutton (Matthew) 7115,7152-3
Huxelles see: Blé (Nicolas) *Marquis d'Uxelles*
Huygens (Christiaan) 5845
Hyde (Edward) *Earl of Clarendon* 827,1211,1792, 4802
Hyde (Sir Henry) 882
Hyde (Laurence) *Earl of Rochester* 3672,3705, 3724,5080,5265
Hyde (Thomas) 1526,3084
Hymn after sore eyes 7413
Hymn to confinement [W.Pittis] 4092
Hymn to Miss Laurence [J.H.Stevenson] 7356

I.(P.) 2736
I.(T.) 828
Ibbetson (Richard) 5422
Ibbot (Benjamin) 5127,5846,6399,6485,6613
Iberia liberata [J.Oldmixon] 4210
Ichabod: or, The five groans [T.Ken] 1260
Idrisi see: Edrisi
Iewell for gentrie 73
Ignoramus: an excellent new song 1941
Ignoramus justices [E.Whitaker] 2040
Ignotus see: Letter of advice, presented to Mr.Hoadly
Illicit distillation 8408
Imitation of the new way of writing [S.Ockley] 5471
Immortality preternatural [J.Pitts] 4450
Impartial account of divers remarkable proceedings 1649
Impartial account of the horrid and detestable conspiracy 3423
Impartial account of the nature and tendency of the late addresses 1942,1995
Impartial account of the trial of the Lord Cornwallis 1665
Impartial and exact accompt of the divers Popish books 1575
Impartial by-stander's review of the controversy [J.Speed] 7419
Impartial enquiry into the causes of rebellion [M.Astell] 3864
Impartial enquiry into the moral character of Jesus Christ [C.Turnbull] 6957
Impartial examination of the Right Reverend the Lord Bishop of Lincoln's and Norwich's speeches [E.Curll] 4717
Impartial reflections upon Dr.Burnet's posthumous History [M.Earbery] 6611
Impartial relation of the proceedings of the common-hall 6948
Impartial relation of the whole proceedings against... Magdalen Colledge [H.Fairfax] 2720

Impartial review of the opposition 7007
Impartial review of the present troubles 7054
Impartial secret history of Arlus 4782
Impartial state of the case of the Earl of Danby 1666,1770
Impeachment, or no impeachment [Defoe] 5823
Impeachment: or, The Church triumphant [D.Russel] 5501
Imperial gratitude [Defoe] 5371
Importance of the Lord's coming 6782
Importance of the sugar colonies 6783
Important questions of state [E.Stephens] 2962
Impossibility of witchcraft further demonstrated 5423
Impossibility of witchcraft, plainly proving 5424,5493
Impostor painted in his own colours 5425
In imitation of Hudibras 3914
Inchbald (Elizabeth) 7832,7865
Inchiquin (Murrough O'Brien) *Earl of* see: O'Brien (Murrough)
Inconveniences of toleration [T.Tomkins] 1314
Incorporated Society for Promoting English Protestant Schools in Ireland 6844
Incorporated Society for Promoting the Enlargement, Building, and Repairing of Churches 8591,8594
Independant Briton 7008
Indispensible obligation [R.Laurence] 6814, 6827,6837
Indulgence and toleration considered [J.Owen] 1311
Infants advocate 5426
Information against the Duke of Marlborough 5427
Information for Mr.Robert Bennet 3830
Ingelo (Nathaniel) 1538,6921
Inglis (Sir Robert Harry) 8537
Innocent XII, *Pope* 3586
Innocentia patefacta 5128
Inquest after blood 1348
Inquiry into the causes of the insurrection 7937
Inquiry into the manner of creating peers [R.West] 6443
Inquiry into the miscarriages [C.Povey] 5872
Inquiry into the moral and political tendency 7893
Inquiry into the revenue...of France 7009
Inquisitio Anglicana [A.Sadler] 939
Inscription intended to be set up 3672
Instance of the Church of England's loyalty 2606,2609
Instructive library 4783
Instruments of a king [J.Howell] 824
Insulae fortunatae ad mare Balthicum 7432
Intelligencer, published for satisfaction 8629
Intercepted letter of an archbishop 8539
Interest of England consider'd [J.S. Barrington] 3803
Interest of England stated [J.Fell] 1023
Interest of the three kingdom's 1793-4
Interest of these United Provinces [J.Hill] 1406
Interesting naval trial 8224
Interests of the protestant dissenters considered 6812
Interpretation ancienne & nouvelle du songe 4190
Intimation of the deputies of the States General 1795
Intreigues of the French King 2894
Intrigues of the conclave 3013
Introduction of the ancient Greek and Latin measures 6890
Introduction to the Bishop of Bangor's intended collection 6300
Introduction to the life and writings of G[ilber]t Lord Bishop of S[aru]m [G.Sewell] 5885
Introductory discourse to a larger work [C.Middleton] 7197,7202
Investigation of the native rights of British subjects [F.Plowden] 7799
Invisible John made visible 1040
Ioyfull newes from Ireland 398
Ireland. Parliament 2895, 3261
Ireland (John) 8329
Ireland (William) 1606
Irenaeus Americus see: Defoe (Daniel)
Irenaeus Philalethes see: Burchard (J.G.)
Irenaeus Philalethes see: Du Moulin (L.)
Irish massacre set in a clear light [T.Carte] 5806
Ironside (Gilbert) 2409,2778,2942
Ironside (Nestor) see: Croxall (Samuel)
Irregularitie of a private prayer [R.Sherlock] 1437
Irving (Edward) 8381,8530
Is not the hand of Joab in all this? 1498
"Is there not a cause?" 8572
Isham (Zachary) 4061
Israel in Egypt, an oratorio 7487
It cannot rain but it pours [J.Arbuthnot] 6654
Iter boreale [R.Wild] 1184
Ittigius (Thomas) 3014
Iudicium synodi nationalis 82
Iust complaint, or loud crie 395
Ivernois (Sir Francis d') 8159

J.(A.) 4573
J.(G.) 1626
J.(G.) see: Jacob (Giles)
J.(J.) 4784
J.(N.) 3015
J.(P.H.) 3412
Jablonski (Daniel Ernst) 5465
Jackson (Henry) 7488
Jackson (Lawrence) 7290
Jackson (William) *Bishop of Oxford* 7776
Jackson (William) *D.D.* 1458
Jacob (Giles) 6514
Jacob (Henry) 32
Jacob (John) 1667
Jacobite principles vindicated [C.Lawton] 3266
Jacobite's hopes reviv'd [B.Hoadly] 4780
Jacobitism, perjury, and popery [J.Toland] 4944
Jacob's well 8448
Jacotius (Desiderius) 7560
Jamaica. House of Assembly 8166
James I, *King of England* 16,60,112,115,1943 3915,4785
James II, *King of England* 1539,1610,1656,1660, 1676-7,1736,1792,1798,1812-3,1824,1834, 1836,2067,2085,2113,2123,2131,2327,2339, 2348,2410,2431,2468,2510,2871,2939,3203, 3218,3262,3285,3322,3430,3637,3721,3831, 3843,3995,4192,4373,5174,5455
James I, *King of Scotland* 6066
James VI, *King of Scotland* see: James I, *King of England*
James Francis Edward, *the Old Pretender* 2710, 2795,2938,3203,3422,3594,3648,3742,3906, 3969,4730,4856,5095,5174,5200,5370,5425, 5455,5581,5608,5613,5631,5639,5677-8, 5721,5841,5894,5967,6505,6572,6665,6853, 7083
James (Elinor) 2607-8
James (Francis) 782
James (Henry) 1427
James (John) 1576
James (Robert) 7257,7710
Jämmerliche Zerstörung der uhralten... Residentz-Statt 1540
Jane (William) 1459,1577,1668,2896
Jane Bond. A true narrative 8449
Jane Lindsay, first a scholar 8450
Jang ampat evangelia 1526
Jarvis (Samuel Farmer) 8564
Jeacocke (Abraham) 4786
Jeacocke (Caleb) 7489
Jebb (Richard) 7669
Jebb (Samuel) 8610
Jefferies (Ann) 3436
Jeffery (John) 3204,3552
Jefferys (Nathaniel) 8181
Jeffreys (George) *Baron* 2897,2945,6644
Jeffreys (Sir Robert) 2461
Jegon (William) 4311
Jekyll (Sir Joseph) 4787
Jekyll (Thomas) 1944,2095
Jemson (Nathaniel) 1387
Jenings (John) 5129-30
Jenison (Robert) 1669,1796
Jenkes (Henry) 2206
Jenkin (Robert) 2737,3007,3016-7,3129
Jenkin (Thomas) 7291
Jenkins (David) 842,858,1302,1314,6364
Jenkins (Sir Leoline) 2295,3041,5869
Jenkinson (Robert Banks) *Earl of Liverpool* 8323
Jenkyn (William) 1493,1577,1765,1779,2086
Jennens (Charles) 6950,7116,7618
Jenner (Thomas) 1378
Jennings (Richard) 5589,5665,5676
Jenour (Joshua) 8071
Jenyns (Soame) 7683,7705
Jephtha, an oratorio [T.Morell] 8602
Jerningham (Edward) 7720
Jerusalem 7089
Jesuite countermin'd [J.Bradshaw] 1627
Jesuite in masquerade 1945
Jesuites new discoveries 1670
Jesuites policy to suppress monarchy [C.Stanley] 1597
Jesuits catechism [E.Pasquier] 1986
Jesuits letter of thanks 1671
Jesuits unmasked 1672
Jesus Christ is the true God 8496
Jew and his daughter, converted 8409
Jewel (John) 2411
Jewell for gentrie 73
Joannes Parisiensis 2511
John and James, or the winter's fire-side 8365
John Bull in his senses [J.Arbuthnot] 5308-9
John Chrysostom, *Saint* 7613
John Dennis, the sheltring poet's invitation 5847
John Frederick, *Elector of Saxony* 4
John of Paris see: Joannes Parisiensis
John Pascal: or the temptation 8376
John III Sobieski, *King* 2207
John, the Churchman's vision 4788
Johnson (Francis) 46
Johnson (Sir Henry) 2309
Johnson (John) 5854,6515
Johnson (Ralph) 1253
Johnson (Richard) 3832,4312
Johnson (Samuel) *Dancing Master* 6715
Johnson (Samuel) *LL.D.* 6927,7581,7671,7676,7959
Johnson (Samuel) *Rector of Corringham* 2113,2297, 2609,2898-9,2951,3018-9,3128,3205,3208,3269, 3310-2,3515,3601
Johnson (William) 396
Johnston (Joseph) 2610,2701
Johnston (Nathaniel) 2738
Jolife (Lady Mary) 1731
Jones (Charles) 4062-3
Jones (David) 3093,3206,3553
Jones (Edward) 3784
Jones (Henry) 1673-4
Jones (Inigo) 134
Jones (John) *M.B.* 8055
Jones (John) *M.D.* 3516
Jones (John Edmund) 8352,8360
Jones (Jonathan) 6716
Jones (Michael) 828
Jones (Samuel) *Gent.* 6301
Jones (Samuel) *Rector of St.John's, Norwich* 4418
Jones (Thomas) *Almanack Maker* 1946
Jones (Thomas) *Lecturer at St.Magnus* 7777
Jones (William) *of Nayland* 7796,8107-8
Jones (Sir William) 7599,7635,7758-9,8019
Jonson (Benjamin) 134
Jordan (Thomas) 1460,1541,1675,1797,1947,2096, 2298
Joseph and his brethren [J.Miller] 7093
Josephus (Flavius) 3134,7833
Journal from Grand Cairo 7330
Journal of a regimental officer [P.Hawker] 8213
Journey into the country [C.Creamer] 1451
Journey to the world in the moon [Defoe] 4032
Jovian. Or, an answer [G.Hickes] 2200
Jowett (Joseph) 8136
Joy of harvestmen 8474
Joyce (George) 1074
Joyce (Jeremiah) 7984,8012
Joyful news of opening the Exchequer [T.Turnor] 1555
Joyfull newes from Ireland see: Ioyfull newes from Ireland
Jubilee necklace 3916
Judgement upon the arguments 2208
Judgment and doctrine of the clergy 2557,2818
Judgment of Hercules [W.Shenstone] 6982
Judgment of the Church of England [W.Fleetwood] 5395,5437
Judgment of the foreign reformed churches [J.Willis] 3082
Judgment of the reformed churches 903
Judgment of the Reformed in France 5428
Judgment of whole kingdoms and nations 4657, 4789,5219,5578
Judgments of whole kingdoms & nations 4790
Junius (Franciscus) 22,3255
Jura populi Anglicani [J.Somers] 3703
Jura regiae majestatis in Anglia 5204
Jure divino [Defoe] 4167
Jure divino: or an answer [H.Gandy] 4296
Jurieu (Pierre) 2512,2739,2900-1,4246
Jurin (James) 6845,6854
Juror. A farce 6259
Jus divinum ministerii evangelici 936-7
Jus divinum regiminis ecclesiastici 725
Jus sacrum 5429-30,5581
Just and modest vindication of his Royal Highness 1798
Just and modest vindication of the proceedings of the two last parliaments [R.Ferguson] 2078,2173
Just censure of the answer to Vox cleri 3020
Just complaint, or loud crie 395
Just vindication of the Bp. of W[orceste]r 5677
Just vindication of the principal officers 1428
Justification of a safe and wel grounded answer 726
Justification of the Dutch [Defoe] 5372
Justification of the present war [H.Stubbe] 1391
Justification of the proceedings of [the Commons] 3674
Justin Martyr 4448,4463,7395
Juvenalis (Decimus Junius) 8146
Juxon (Elizabeth) 139

K.(H.) 1948
K.(W.) 3463
K.(W.) see: Kennet (White)
Kaye (John) 8595
Kedarminster-stuff [J.Browne] 1887
Kedington (Roger) 7331
Keimer (Samuel) 6302
Keith (George) 3432-3,3447,3463,3466-7,3476, 3521,3539,3602,3751-2,3917,4191,4313,4574
Kelly (George) 6594,6813
Kelsall (Edward) 4791
Kemp (John) 7866
Kemp (Nathaniel) 8596
Kempster (Bartholomew) 1858
Ken (Thomas) 1260,2097,2412,2483,2639,2740,2902, 3363,5131
Kennedy (John) *Rector of Bradley* 7465-6,7504
Kennedy (John) *Rector of Langley* 7810
Kennet (White)
Argument in defence 5132
Charity and restitution 6400
Charity of schools 4193
Christian neighbour 5133
Compassionate enquiry 3864,3907,3918-9
Concio ad Synodum 4792
Dr.Kennet's character 4192
Duties of rejoycing 4194
Faithful steward 6056
Glory of children 3833
Glory to God 4575
History of the Convocation 3753
Lets and impediments 5431
Letter to the Lord Bishop 5678
Memoirs of the family of Cavendish 4419
Memorial to protestants 5679
Occasional letter 3675
Office and good work 4195
Present state of Convocation 3754
Second letter to the Lord Bishop 6057-8
Sermon preach'd at the funeral 4314,4408-9
Sermon preach'd before the Arch-bishop 5134
Sermon preach'd before the Convocation 5135
Sermon preach'd before the honourable House of Commons 4196-7
Sermon preached in the church 3920
Thanksgiving-sermon 6059
Third letter to the Lord Bishop 6143,6162
True answer to Dr.Sacheverell's sermon 4576, 4763
Vindication of the Church 4577
Witchcraft of the present rebellion 5968
3759,3770,4503,4619,5198,6126,6200,6755
Kennicott (Benjamin) 7144,7492,7637
Kenrick (William) 7414,8633
Kent (William George Carlile) 8224
Kentish conspiracy 678
K[e]ntish spy 5549
Ker (John) 5680
Kettilby (Joshua) 7457,7485
Kettlewell (John) 2299,2300,2513,3130-1,3263,6811
Key to some late important transactions 7010
Key to the business of the present s[essio]n 7011
Key to the Craftsman 6784
Key to the Memoirs of the affairs of Scotland [D.Craufurd] 5819
Key to the present politicks 7055
Kidd (William) 3663,3688
Kiddell (John) 7721
Kidder (Richard) 2611,3264
Killigrew (Henry) 1293
Killigrew (Thomas) 6401
Killing, no murder [S.Titus] 1085,2975
Killingworth (Grantham) 7614
Kilner (James) 7117,7370
Kilvert (Richard) 242
Kimberley (Jonathan) 2209,3755
Kimpton (John) 7513,7516,7521,7523,7537
King (Edward) 7797
King (Henry) 5681
King (John) 4793,6516
King (Peter) *Baron* 5268,5848,6639
King (William) *Archbishop of Dublin* 3207,3313, 4198,4578,4794,5682,5731
King (William) *Principal of St.Mary Hall* 7012, 7056,7090,7258,7292,7350,7433
King (William) *Student of Christ Church* 3554-5, 3603,4420,4795-6,5136-8,5155,5159,5432,8686
King Charles vindicated 1138
King Edward the third [J.Bancroft] 3092
King George's College 6661
King William's toleration 2903
Kingdom of Sweden restored 2098
Kingdomes intelligencer 8630
Kingdomes weekly intelligencer 8631
Kinghorn (Joseph) 8377
Kings cabinet opened 651
Kings march with the Scots 740
King's right of indulgence [A.Annesley] 2679
King's visit, as discoursed 8410
Kingston, *Duchess of* see: Chudleigh (Elizabeth)
Kingston (Richard) 2210
Kinnersly (Thomas) 6303

Kipling (Thomas) 8136
Kippis (Andrew) 7644,7867
Kirkby (Christopher) 1616
Kirkby (Richard) 3799,3997
Kit-Kat c[lu]b describ'd 4064
Knaggs (Thomas) 4065,4421-2,4579,4797,5433, 6060
Knave uncloak'd 1839
Knavery of astrology discover'd 1799
Knell (Paul) 829
Knight (James) 5139,5281,5434,5849,6517
Knight (Joel Abraham) 7985
Knight (Sir John) 3314,4580,6830
Knight (Robert) 6530
Knight (Samuel) 6717
Knott (Edward) 913
Knowles (Thomas) 7615
Knowne lawes. A short examination 525
Knox (Thomas) 1827,4423
Komensky (Jan Amos) see: Comenius (J.A.)
Kreher (Matthias) 2301
Krishna, the false god 8475
Kuster (Ludolph) 3424
Kynaston (John) 7478

L. 397
L.(C.) 1218
L.(J.) see: Gother (John)
L.(J.A.M.) see: Martyni-Laguna (J.A.)
L.(L.) 1949
L.(N.) 2413,2904
L.(R.) see: Laurence (Roger)
Lowth (Robert)
L.(T.) 1950
L.(T.) see: Laxton (Thomas)
L.(W.) 1138,4066,4798
L. N., *Sieur de* 53
Labbe (Philippe) 1470
Labour in vain [E.Ward] 3631
Labourers in the vine-yard 8476
La Brousse (Nicolas de) 1557
Lacrymae Ecclesiae Anglicanae [T.Ken] 2902
Lacy (John) 4315-6,4326,5140,5850
La Guard (Theodore de) see: Ward (Nathaniel)
Laity's remonstrance to the late representation 5141
Lake (Edward) 2302
Lake (John) *Bishop of Chichester* 2872,3007, 3016,4914
Lake (Sir John) 5596
Lambe (Charles) 5138,5969,6163
Lambe (John) 1800,3021
Lambert (John) 1041-2,1058
Lambert (Ralph) 4424
La Motte (François de) 1461
Lamotte (John) 958
Lamplugh (Thomas) 1578-9
Land-leviathan; or, Modern hydra 5435
Laney (Benjamin) 1294
Langbaine (Gerard) *the Elder* 1205
Langbaine (Gerard) *the Younger* 2741
Langlois de Fancan (François) 94
Langman (Christopher) 5142
Langton (Lewis) 6834
Lansdowne (George Granville) *Baron* see: Granville (George)
La Paz (Juan Bautista de Orendayn) *Marques de* see: Orendayn (Juan Bautista de)
La Pillonniére (François de) 6149,6164-5,6175-6, 6204,6225,6248,6300,6304-5,6309,6316,6322, 6325-6
La Placette (Jean de) 2612,2742
La Rue (Charles de) 3364
Lascelles (William Sebright) 8540
Last articles of peace made 727
Last memorial of the Spanish ambassador [P.Ronquillo] 2000
Last speech & behaviour of William late Lord Russel 2211
Last will and testament of the E[ar]l of P[e]mbr[o]ke 883
Late apology in behalf of the papists [W.Lloyd] 1308,1464
Late Bishop of Carlisle's speech [T.Merks] 5863
Late converts exposed [T.Brown] 2993
Late dreadful plague at Marseilles 6518
Late gallant exploits 6973
Late keepers of the English liberties 1801
Late King James's manifesto answer'd 3464
Late letter concerning the sufferings of the episcopal clergy 3132
Late minister unmask'd 7013
Late plot on the fleet 2905
Late proceedings and votes of the Parliament of Scotland [R.Ferguson] 2875
Late proceedings of the Scotish army 614
Lathom (Paul) 1499
Latimer (Hugh) 7346

La Tour d'Auvergne (Anne de) *Vicomtesse de Turenne* 1139
La Tour d'Auvergne (Emmanuel Théodose de) *Cardinal Duc de Bouillon* 4707
La Tour d'Auvergne (Henri de) *Vicomte de Turenne* 1533
La Trobe (Benjamin) 7600,7753
Laud (William) 176,506,615,676,1106,4581
Lauderdale (John Maitland) *Duke of* see: Maitland (John)
Launay (Emmanuel Henri Alexandre de) *Comte d'Antraigues* 8179
Laundry maid 8411
Launoy (Jean de) 1320
Laurel, a poem 2414
Laurence (John) 6166-7,6306
Laurence (Richard) 8322,8330-1,8342
Laurence (Roger) 4799,5016,5143,5326,5428, 5436-7,5543,5576,5683,5764,6267,6402, 6459,6814,6827,6837
La Vallette (François de) 3643
Lavardin (Henri Charles de Beaumanoir) *Marquis de* see: Beaumanoir (Henri Charles de) *Marquis de Lavardin*
Lavington (George) 7154
Law (Edmund) 7582,7653,7778
Law (Edward) *Baron Ellenborough* 8248
Law (George) 8167
Law (George Henry) 8512
Law (John) *Archdeacon of Rochester* 8130
Law (John) *of Lauriston* 6465
Law (William) 5684,6146,6168-71,6294,6403, 6614,6667,6785,6983,7247,7320
Law is a bottomless-pit [J.Arbuthnot] 5310-1
Lawes and statutes of Geneva 516
Lawfulness and right manner of keeping Christmas [R.Watts] 4971
Lawfulness of taking the new oaths asserted [H.Maurice] 2917
Lawrence (John) see: Laurence (John)
Lawton (Charlwood) 3265-6,4067,4199,6519
Lawyer outlaw'd [Sir R.L'Estrange] 2213
Lawyers demurrer 1951
Lawyers demurrer argued [A.Radcliffe] 1998
Laxton (Thomas) 2099
Lay baptism invalid [R.Laurence] 4799
Layard (Charles Peter) 7868
Lay-craft exemplified 4800
Layer (Christopher) 6554,6581,6590
Layman's humble address 6172
Lay-man's lamentation 4801
Layman's letter to the Bishop of Bangor [J.S.Barrington] 6017
Lay-mans opinion [W.Darrell] 2578
Layman's second letter to the Bishop of Bangor [J.S.Barrington] 6109
Layman's vindication of the Church of England [Defoe] 6033
Lay-man's vindication of the Convocation [E.Hart] 6152
Learned comment upon Dr.Hare's excellent sermon [M.Manley] 5169
Learned dissertation upon old women [T.Gordon] 6463
Le Bas (Charles Webb) 8366
Le Camus (Etienne) 2613
Leckie (Gould Francis) 8216
Le Clerc (Jean) 4200,4582,4802,5022,5144, 5207,5297,6884
Ledenbergh (Gillis van) 84
Lee (Sir Charles) 1952
Lee (Francis) 5139,5434,6061
Lee (Harriet) 7851
Lee (Nathaniel) 2415,2584
Lee (Samuel) 8330-1,8342
Leechman (William) 7014
Leeds (Edward) 4312,7534
Leeds (Thomas Osborne) *Duke of* see: Osborne (Thomas)
Le Fevre (Tanneguí) 6520
Legality of the court held by his Majesties [H.Care] 2694
Legge (William) *Earl of Dartmouth* 4807,4994, 5116
Legion's humble address to the Lords answer'd 3921
Legion's memorial [Defoe] 3653
Le Grand (Joachim) 2842
Leicester (Robert Dudley) *Earl of* see: Dudley (Robert)
Leiden University 2649
Leigh (Richard) 1407
Leighton (Robert) 8451-2
Le Mesurier (Havilland) 8072
Le Mesurier (Thomas) 8168,8180,8188-9,8276
Lempriere (William) 8225
Le Noble de Tenneliere (Eustache) 6307
Leo (Christopher) 8285
Leopold I, *Emperor* 1510,3676
Le Peletier de Saint-Fargeau (Louis Michel) 8116
Leporinus (Johannes) 884
Le Prestre (René Charles Hippolyte) *Marquis de Chateaugiron* 8117

Leslie (Alexander) *Earl of Leven* 614,631,728
Leslie (Charles)
Answer to a book 3207
Answer, to the examination 4803
Answer to the Remarks 4425
Axe laid to the root 4148
Beaucoup de bruit 4804
Best answer 4573,4583-4,4590
Best of all 4585
Bishop of Salisbury's proper defence 3922
Case of present concern 3834
Cassandra 3923-4,4068-9
Charge of Socinianism 3365
Considerations of importance 3517
Constitution, laws and government 4586
Discourse proving 3465
Discourse; shewing 3518
Finishing stroke 5145
Gallienus redivivus 3366
Good old cause, further discuss'd 4805
Good old cause, or, lying in truth 4780,4806, 4840
History of sin 3519
History of the Church 4201
Letter from a gentleman in Scotland 4426
Letter from a gentleman in the City 4427
Letter from Mr.Lesly to a member 5851
Letter from Mr.Lesly to his friend 6267,6308
Letter from the Reverend Mr.Charles Leslie 6366,6402,6404
Letter to the Reverend Mr.William Higden 4587-8
Mr.Lesley to the Lord Bishop 5970
Natural reflections 5438
Now or never 4807
Old English constitution 5852
Parallel between the faith 3604
Postscript to Mr.Higgins's sermon 4317
Present state of Quakerism 3677
Primitive heresie 3520,3540
Principles of the dissenters 4070
Querela temporum 3367
Remarks on some late sermons 3368-9
Reply to the Vindication 4428
Salt for the leach 5439
Satan dis-rob'd 3466,3521
Second part of the wolf stript 4318
Short and easie method 3522
Socinian controversy 4429
Some seasonable reflections 3467
Tempora mutantur 3315
True and authentic account 7490
Truth of Christianity 5146
Wolf stript 3925-6,3948
3641,3697,3863,3899,4088,4738,5046,5610,5933
Leslie (Henry) 3741
L'Estrange (Hamon) 243
L'Estrange (Sir Roger)
Accompt clear'd 2100
Account of the growth 1580
Answer to a letter 2614
Apology for the protestants 1878
Case put 1676-7
Casuist uncas'd 1953
Caveat to the Cavaliers 1206
Character of a papist 1954
Citt and Bumpkin 1802-3
Considerations upon a printed sheet 2212
Discovery upon discovery 1804
Dissenter's sayings 1881,1955-8
Free-born subject 1678,2743
Further discovery of the plot 1805
Intelligencer 8629
Interest mistaken 1207
Lawyer outlaw'd 2213
L'Estrange his apology 1140
L'Estrange his appeal 1959
L'Estrange no papist 1960,2416
L'Estrange no papist nor Jesuite 1961
L'Estrange's case 1806
Lestrange's narrative 1807
Modest plea both for the Caveat 1208
Memento: directed to all 1237
Memento. Treating, of the rise 2101
Newes 8660
No blinde guides 1141
Notes upon Stephen College 1962
Observator defended 2417
Physician cure thy self 1142
Plea for limited monarchy 1143
Presbyterian sham 1808
Reformed Catholique 1679
Relaps'd apostate 1209,1963
Remarks on the growth 2102
Reply to the reasons 2615
Reply to the second part 1964
Seasonable memorial 1809
Sermon prepared 2103
Shammer shamm'd 1965
Short answer to a whole litter of libellers 1810
Short answer to a whole litter of libels 1811,1855
Sir Politique uncased 1144
Some queries 3022
State-divinity 1210
State and interest of the nation 1812
To the right honourable, Edward 1211
Tyranny and popery 1581
Whipp a whipp 1238
Whipp for the schismaticall animadverter 1239
Word concerning libels 1966
1741,2215,5194
Let me speak too? 1043
Letter addressed to the delegates [G.I. Huntingford] 7875
Letter, addressed to the Hon.Charles James Fox 8131
Letter addressed to Wm.Smith 8205
Letter ballancing the necessity [J.Somers] 3478,3482,3515
Letter concerning allegiance [H.Compton] 4711
Letter concerning enthusiasm [A.A.Cooper] 4397, 4552
Letter concerning Sir William Whitlock's bill 3318
Letter concerning the affair of Mr.Greenshields 5147
Letter concerning the test 2598
Letter concerning toleration [J.Locke] 2911
Letter, dated London 20 March 1723 6587

Letter desiring information [E.Meredith] 2618
Letter from a blacksmith [J.Witherspoon] 7424
Letter from a citizen of Bath 4071
Letter from a city-minister [D.Whitby] 2985
Letter from a clergy-man in the city [G.Savile] 2788
Letter from a clergy-man in the country, to a dignified clergy-man 3756
Letter from a clergy-man in the country, to a minister 2906
Letter from a commoner of England 4066
Letter from a country gentleman, to a member of Parliament [W.Combe] 7872
Letter from a country-gentleman, to his friend in London: concerning what a king 5148
Letter from a country gentleman, to his friend in London, plainly shewing 3757
Letter from a country justice 3877
Letter from a country Whig 5971-2
Letter from a dissenter in the City to a dissenter in the country [Defoe] 4729
Letter from a dissenter in the City, to his country-friend 4072
Letter from a dissenter to the divines [J.Gother] 2593
Letter from a foreign minister at Vienna 5270
Letter from a foreign minister in England [R.Walpole] 4967
Letter from a gentleman at Rome 6532
Letter from a gentleman at the Court [Defoe] 4730
Letter from a gentleman in Ireland 1542
Letter from a gentleman in London to a citizen of New-Sarum 4808
Letter from a gentleman in London to his friend in the country 7222
Letter from a gentleman in Scotland [C.Leslie] 4426
Letter from a gentleman in the city, to a clergy-man in the country 2744
Letter from a gentleman in the city to his friend in the country [C.Leslie] 4427
Letter from a gentleman in the city, to one in the country 1813
Letter from a gentleman in the country, to his friends [W.Penn] 2628
Letter from a gentleman in Town 7293,7308
Letter from a gentleman in Yorkshire 3370
Letter from a gentleman of quality in the country 1655
Letter from a gentleman of Swisserland 3835
Letter from a gentleman of the city of New-York 3523
Letter from a gentleman of the Romish religion 1429
Letter from a gentleman, residing in foreign parts 7396
Letter from a gentleman to Dr.Snape 6173
Letter from a Jesuit at Paris [J.Nalson] 1691
Letter from a Jesuite [J.A.de Hess] 1663
Letter from a lawyer of the Inner Temple 3524
Letter from a loyal member of the Church 2907
Letter from a member of Parliament to a friend in the country 5685
Letter from a member of Parliament to his friend in the country [Sir H.Mackworth] 4075
Letter from a member of the House of Commons in Ireland [J.Swift] 4627
Letter from a member of the House of Commons to his friend in the country [Defoe] 5634
Letter from a member of the last Parliament 7015
Letter from a merchant in Amsterdam 5440
Letter from a merchant in London 3529
Letter from a minister in the country 2904
Letter from a Parliament man [A.A.Cooper] 1449
Letter from a peer to a member of the House of Commons 3678
Letter from a person of quality in the North [E.Eyre] 2872
Letter from a person of quality to an eminent dissenter [G.Hickes] 2405
Letter from a person of quality to his friend, about abhorrers 2104
Letter from a person of quality, to his friend in the country [A.A.Cooper] 1450,1504
Letter from a souldier to the Commons 3758
Letter from a trooper in Flanders [J.Sergeant] 3387
Letter from a Whig gentleman 5441
Letter from Amsterdam 1582
Letter from an author, to a member of Parliament [W.Warburton] 7207
Letter from an ejected member 840
Letter from an English gentleman at Madrid 5686
Letter from an English merchant 3347-8
Letter from an English Tory 5687
Letter from an English traveller at Rome [W.Godolphin] 6505
Letter from an Hollander 4202
Letter from an old Whig in town 5294
Letter from Farmer Trusty 7561
Letter from H[enry] G[oring] 7288
Letter from Holland [C.de Witt] 2828
Letter from Mercurius Civicus [Sir J.Birkenhead] 448
Letter from N.J. to E.T. 3015

Letter from no body in the city 1680
Letter from Oxford, concerning Mr.Samuel Johnson's late book 3269
Letter from some-body in the country 1681
Letter from the author of the Argument [J.Trenchard] 3482
Letter from the borders of Scotland 3759
Letter from the commanders and officers of the Fleet 1044
Letter from the Duchess of M[a]r[lborou]gh 7415
Letter from the Jesuits 6309
Letter from the man in the moon [Defoe] 4033
Letter from the member of Parliament 2913
Letter from the Prolocutor [G.Stanhope] 6342
Letter from the Right Reverend G[i]lb[e]rt 6174
Letter from the South 4073
Letter from Tom o'Bedlam 6149,6175-6
Letter humbly addressed to the most rev. 8118
Letter intercepted at a court-guard 397
Letter occasioned by the second letter to Dr.Burnet [G.Burnet] 2361
Letter of advice, addressed to all merchants 7779
Letter of advice concerning marriage 1481
Letter of advice, presented to Mr.Hoadly 4589
Letter of comfort to Richard Cromwell 1045
Letter of enquiry to the reverend fathers [J.Taylor] 2968
Letter of November the 16th 1046
Letter of remarkes upon Jovian [A.Annesley] 2165
Letter of resolution concerning Origen [G.Rust] 1218
Letter of thanks from a young clergyman 6405
Letter of thanks from my Lord W*****n [J.Swift] 5523
Letter of thanks from the author of the Comparison [J.Trenchard] 6482
Letter of thanks to Mr.Benja.Bennet [Z.Grey] 6591
Letter on George Keith's advertisement 3463
Letter on infant baptism 8477
Letter on the subjects of economical retrenchment 8334
Letter out of Lancashire [T.Wagstaffe] 3336
Letter out of Suffolk [T.Wagstaffe] 3337
Letter out of the country, to a member of this present Parliament [H.Maurice] 2918
Letter out of the country, to the author [J.Trapp] 4946
Letter out of the country, to the clergy 3179
Letter sent from the Commissioners of Scotland 1176
Letter sent to a gentleman in Gloucestershire 3679
Letter sent to Dr.Tillotson 3023
Letter sent to the Honourable William Lenthall [M.Pindar] 622
Letter sent to the Right Honourable William Lenthall 679,1047
Letter to a bishop concerning the present settlement [T.Comber] 2864
Letter to a bishop; occasioned by the late petition [J.Sturges] 7624
Letter to a clergy-man: concerning Mr.Hoadly's doctrine 5149
Letter to a clergyman in the country, concerning the choice [F.Atterbury] 3639
Letter to a Convocation-man [F.Atterbury] 3455
Letter to a country gentleman 6062
Letter to a dissenter [G.Savile] 2645-7
Letter to a dissenting clergy-man 3024
Letter to a doctor of physick 6406
Letter to a freeholder, on the late reduction of the land tax 6815,6820
Letter to a friend [against excises] 3133
Letter to a friend, concerning a French invasion [W.Sherlock] 3217
Letter to a friend concerning some of Dr.Owens principles [G.Vernon] 1361
Letter to a friend, concerning the proposals for the payment [J.Milner] 6471
Letter to a friend, concerning [the Trinity] 3525
Letter to a friend, containing some quaeries [W.Jane] 2896
Letter to a friend. Endeavouring to give 7466
Letter to a friend, giving an account [A.Monro] 3211
Letter to a friend, in answer to a letter [S.Grascombe] 2730
Letter to a friend in the country [about a dissolution] 3371
Letter to a friend in the country: being a vindication 1983
Letter to a friend in the country, on the late expedition [J.Dummer] 5383
Letter to a friend, in vindication of the proceedings 3468
Letter to a friend, In which is shewn [A.A.Sykes] 6232
Letter to a friend, occasion'd by the Bishop 5442
Letter to a friend: occasion'd by the contest 4614
Letter to a friend. Occasion'd by the presentment 4430
Letter to a friend, reflecting upon the present condition 1834
Letter to a friend relating to the present convocation [H.Prideaux] 3047
Letter to a friend. Shewing, the illegall proceedings 648
Letter to a gentleman, concerning the South Sea trade 5150
Letter to a great man in France 7057
Letter to a High-Churchman 5151
Letter to a lady concerning the new play house [J.Collier] 4161
Letter to a lawyer 2418
Letter to a leading great man 6521
Letter to a member of Parliament concerning the Bill for regulating the nightly-watch 6447
Letter to a member of Parliament, concerning the naval store-bill 6466
Letter to a member of Parliament, in favour of the Bill 2923
Letter to a member of Parliament in the country 7371
Letter to a member of Parliament, on the settling a trade 5152
Letter to a member of Parliament: shewing the justice 6177
Letter to a member of the convention [W.Sherlock] 2799
Letter to a member of the House of Commons, concerning the bishops [H.Maurice] 2919
Letter to a member of the House of Commons on a proposal 3491
Letter to a member of the late Parliament 3605
Letter to a member of the October-club 5153
Letter to a member of the P[arliamen]t 5688
Letter to a member of the present honourable House of Commons [J.Broughton] 4015
Letter to a merry young gentleman 5949,6010.
Letter to a new member of the ensuing Parliament 3760
Letter to a new member of the honourable House of Commons 4798
Letter to a noble lord, about his dispersing abroad 4590
Letter to a noble lord at London 526
Letter to a noble lord: or, A faithful representation [A.Henderson] 7558
Letter to a Non-juring clergyman 6178
Letter to a peer concerning the power 3680
Letter to a person of quality, concerning the Archbishop 3556
Letter to a person of quality, occasion'd by the news 2781
Letter to a right honourable member 7016
Letter to an elector 5586
Letter to an honourable member of the House of Commons 1682
Letter to Anonymus [W.Sherlock] 2167,2234
Letter to Caleb D'Anvers, Esq; concerning the state [H.St.John] 6754
Letter to Caleb D'Anvers, Esq; on his Proper reply 6786
Letter to Dr.Andrew Snape 6179
Letter to Doctor Bennet 6063,6196
Letter to Dr.Burnet [S.Lowth] 2421
Letter to Dr du Moulin 1814
Letter to Dr.Hallifax 7616
Letter to Dr.Sherlock, concerning the wickedness 6310
Letter to Dr.Sherlock, in vindication of that part of Josephus's history [W.Lloyd] 3134,3227
Letter to Dr.Snape 6180
Letter to Dr.W.Payne [S.Grascombe] 2884
Letter to Henry Brougham 8353
Letter to Henry Hingeston 3899
Letter to his Grace the Archbishop of Canterbury 7601
Letter to his Highness the Prince of Orange 2908
Letter to his most excellent Majesty [W.Stephens] 3568
Letter to ****** in favour of short parliaments 7223
Letter to Mr.B--- 4809
Letter to Mr.Baldwin 4319
Letter to Mr.Bisset 4591
Letter to Mr.Congreve 3526
Letter to Mr.How [Defoe] 3654
Letter to Mr.John Clark 6407
Letter to Mr.Penn [Sir W.Popple] 2771-2
Letter to Mr.P[ulteney] 6787
Letter to Mr.S. a Romish priest 1388
Letter to Mr.Samuel Johnson 3208
Letter to Mr.Timothy Goodwin [A.Salt] 6209
Letter to Mr.William Timms 6615
Letter to my Lord Mayor 7017
Letter to my lords the bishops 3836
Letter to Nathaniel Jeffreys 8181
Letter to Richard Arnold 6788
Letter to Samuel Holden 6816
Letter to Sir Humphrey Mackworth 3761
Letter to Sir J[acob] B[anks] [W.Benson] 5007
Letter to Sir J[acob] B[anks] examined 5154
Letter to Sir J.P. Bart 3837,4074
Letter to Sir John Barnard 7155,7163
Letter to Sir John Phillips 7193
Letter to Sir R.H.Inglis [E.Edwards] 8537
Letter to Sir Thomas Osborn [G.Villiers] 1394-5
Letter to the answerer of the Apology 1309
Letter to the Archbishop of York 7118
Letter to the author of a late paper [G.Hickes] 2887
Letter to the author of a sermon [T.Ken] 3363
Letter to the author of Lay-baptism invalid [T.Brett] 5016
Letter to the author of the late Letter out of the countrey [T.Wagstaffe] 3074
Letter to the author of the Memorial [W.Stephens] 4112
Letter to the author of the Memorial... answer'd 4203
Letter to the author of the Vindication of the deprived bishops [E.Stephens] 3223
Letter to the author of the Vindication of the proceedings 2745
Letter to the author of the Vindication of the Reverend Dr.Sacheverell 5155
Letter to the authors of the Monthly review 7562
Letter to the Bishop of Lincoln 5156
Letter to the Bishop of Oxford 4784
Letter to the Bishop of Salisbury 5157
Letter to the chairman of the East-India Company 6683
Letter to the clergy of the Church of England [Z.Pearce] 6570
Letter to the dissenters [Defoe] 5635
Letter to the Earl of O[xfor]d [R.Steele] 6435
Letter to the Earl of Shaftsbury 1815
Letter to the eldest brother 5158
Letter to the Examiner [H.St.John] 4892
Letter to the Examiner, concerning the Barrier-treaty 5689
Letter to the Examiner, suggesting proper heads 5853
Letter to the French refugees 4810
Letter to the good people of Great Britain 4659
Letter to the great man 7434
Letter to the Hon.Charles James Fox 8132
Letter to the Hon.Spencer Perceval 8119
Letter to the Honoble William Lenthal 729
Letter to the K[in]g 7986
Letter to the learned Mr.Henry Dodwell [A.Collins] 4272
Letter to the Lord Bishop of Carlisle [W.Kennet] 5678
Letter to the members of parliament for the county of ---- 3316
Letter to the most noble Thomas, Duke of Newcastle 7156
Letter to the people of England [J.Shebbeare] 7380
Letter to the people to be left for them at the booksellers [Sir T.Burnet] 5340
Letter to the person last mentioned 6789
Letter to the protestant dissenting ministers [J.Butler] 7609
Letter to the Reverend Dr.Bentley 3557
Letter to the Reverend Dr.Clark [J.Knight] 5849
Letter to the Reverend Dr.Edward Tenison [T.Herne] 6295
Letter to the Reverend Dr.Francis Atterbury [B.Hoadly] 4187-8
Letter to the Reverend Dr.George Hickes 4592
Letter to the Rev. Dr.Goodall 8150
Letter to the Reverend Dr. Mangey [T.Herne] 6396
Letter to the Reverend Dr.Moss 4593
Letter to the Reverend Dr.Sacheverel 5159
Letter to the Reverend Dr.Sherlock 6258
Letter to the Reverend Dr.Sherlock, one of the committee [A.A.Sykes] 6233
Letter to the Reverend Dr.Snape; occasion'd by a passage 6181
Letter to the Reverend Dr.Snape, occasion'd by the dangerous consequences 6325
Letter to the Rev.Mr.Augustus Toplady 7583
Letter to the Reverend Mr.James Peirce 6408
Letter to the Reverend Mr.William Higden [C.Leslie] 4587-8
Letter to the Reverend the Dean of Chichester 6072
Letter to the Right Honorable A.Earl of Essex 1683
Letter to the Right Honourable Charles James Fox 7987
Letter to the Right Honourable Edmund Burke [Sir B.Boothby] 7931
Letter to the Right Honourable Lord Viscount Howick [J.Symons] 8193
Letter to the Right Honourable the Earl of Nottingham [A.A.Sykes] 6575
Letter to the Right Honourable the Earl of Shelburne 7760
Letter to the Right Honourable the E[ar]l of T[ra]q[uai]r 7194
Letter to the Right Hon.Thomas Harley 7535
Letter to the Right Hon.William Pitt 7988
Letter to the right reverend author of The divine legation [R.Lowth] 7495,7500
Letter to the Right Reverend Father in God, Shute, Lord Bishop of Landaff [B.Thomas] 7659
Letter to the Right Reverend the Bishop of Cloyne 7091
Letter to the Right Reverend the Lord Bishop of London 6891
Letter to the scholars of Eton 6151
Letter to the secret committee 7018
Letter to the seven lords of the committee [J.Oldmixon] 5187
Letter to the Whigs [H.Walpole] 7206
Letter unto a person of honour [E.Bagshaw] 1225
Letter wherein is shewed, first, what worship is due to images 1742
Letter without any superscription 527
Letter written by a minister 2736
Letter written to Dr.Burnet [Sir W.Coventry] 2375
Letter written to the French King 1967
Letters, on the spirit of patriotism [H.St.John] 7270
Letters to a peer [J.Anstis] 4144
Letters to a protestant divine [R.Wainewright] 8305
Lettre à un gentilhomme allemand 4387
Lettre de Geneve 2909
Lettres de M.l'Abbé de St.-L*** [B.Mercier] 7780
Lettres pastorales addressées aux fideles [P.Jurieu] 2512
Lettsom (John Coakley) 7862
Levant Company 1968
Leven (Alexander Leslie) *Earl of* see: Leslie (Alexander)
Levi (David) 7852
Lewis (Edward) 7613
Lewis (Henry) 4811
Lewis (John) *Pamphleteer* 7351,7372
Lewis (John) *Vicar of Minster* 4812-3,5854
Lewis (Mark) 1462,1543
Lewis (William) *Gent.* 1816
Lewis (William) *of St.Botolph* 3527
Lewys (Henry) 2025
Lex talionis: or, The author of Naked truth [P.Fell] 1491
Lex talionis; sive vindiciae pharmacoporum [H.Stubbs] 1359
Ley (John) 528,741-2
Leyburn (John) 2514
Liberty, property, and religion [W.Robertson] 5732
Liebel (Isaac) 3927
Life and adventures of Capt. John Avery 4594
Life and bold adventures of Capt.John Avery 4595
Life and character of Mr.John Philips [G.Sewell] 5507
Life and character of that eminent and learned prelate 4814
Life and character of the late Lord chancellor Jefferys 6644
Life and conversation of Richard Bentley 5443
Life and death of Charles the first 4596
Life and glorious actions of that right honourable 4320
Life and history, of Sarah, Dutches of Marlborough 4815
Life and miracles of St.Wenefrede 5690
Life and particular proceedings of the Rev.Mr. George Whitefield 6928
Life and reign of Henry the sixth 5444
Life, birth and education of the Reverend Mr. Benjamin Hoadly 4816
Life of Caroline E.Smelt 8367
Life of Cyprian 8354
Life of Richard Nash, of Bath [O.Goldsmith] 7455
Life of Saint Augustine 8355
Life of Sir Isaac Newton [B.le B.de Fontenelle] 6698
Life of Sir Robt. Cochran 6846
Life of the reverend and learned Mr.John Sage [J.Gillane] 5838
Life of the Reverend Humphrey Prideaux 7224
Life of William Fuller 3681
Light in darkness 8378
Light shining out of darknes [H.Stubbe] 1082
Lightfoote (John) 529
Lilburne (John) 730,783,802,859-60
Lilly (William) 616,830,893,2081
Lily (William) 1240,1463,3832
Limehouse dream 4825
Limerick (James Hamilton) *Viscount* see: Hamilton (James)
Lindsay (Colin) *Earl of Balcarres* 5855
Lindsay (John) 7373,7407,7416
Linfield (Thomas) 6267
Linford (Thomas) see: Lynford (Thomas)
Lingard (John) 8286
Lingard (Richard) 1321
Linnaeus (Carl) 7617

Lionel and Clarissa [I.Bickerstaffe] 7526

Lionne (Hughes de) 1322

Lipsius (Justus) 272

Lisle (Samuel) 7031,7225

List of King James's Irish and popish forces in France 3469,3477

List of one unanimous club 3634,3682

List of several ships belonging to English merchants 1544

List of the absentees of Ireland [T.Prior] 6752

List of the late Queen's Cabinet 5973

Littell (Thomas) 4431

Littleton (Adam) 1334,1368

Littleton (Edward) 3025,3421

Liturgie, ou la maniere de célébrer 7619

Livia's advice to Augustus 6561

Livigni (Filippo) 7711

Lloyd (John) of Wigfair 8273

Lloyd (John) Vicar of Writtle 23

Lloyd (Robert Lumley) 4941,5160,5445-6,5492, 5856

Lloyd (William) 1308-9,1323,1369,1408-12, 1430-1,1464,1491,1583,1684-6,1817,2746, 2910,3026,3134,3209,3227,3237,3558,3738, 5677

Lochner (Jacobus Hieronymus) 3559

Locke (John) 2911,3027,3048,3372-3,3441, 4043,4179,4200,5207,6064,7991

Lockhart (George) 5819,5857

Lockyer (Nicholas) 1349

Locmannus see: Lukman

Locusts: or, Chancery 3928

Lodington (Thomas) 1432

Lofft (Capel) 7784

Loftus (Edward) 398

Logan (John) 7869

Logou threskeia [J.Glanvill] 1347

Londinensis see: Letter to Mr.William Timms

London 399,400,408,680,784,831,1048-9, 1145-6,1324,1818-20,1969-72,1989,2105-7, 4817,5161,5447

London Association, for Preserving Liberty against Republicans and Levellers see: Association for Preserving Liberty and Property against Republicans and Levellers

London belles [J.Browne] 4261

London journal 6530,6534-5

London magazine 8632

London review 8633

London's flames 1687

London's glory represented [J.Tatham] 1181

Londons lamentation for her sinnes [W.Crashaw] 114

Lonergan (Edward) 6937

Long (Roger) 5858,6700

Long (Thomas) 2419,2912,3020,3028,3043,3066, 3071,3267

Long Parliament dissolved [D.Holles] 1496

Long Parliament twice defunct 1147

Longford's-glyn [P.Delany] 6918

Longitude to be found out 5789

Longman, publishers 8609

Look to the last century 7894

Looking-glass for all new-converts [St Bernard] 2349

L[or]d Bishop of Oxford vindicated 4818

Lord H[aversham]'s speech 4935

Lord mayor's show [T.Jordan] 2096

Lord Pole translated 6790

Lord's people, commonly miscall'd Quakers 3929

Lord's prayer 3606,5691

Lorenz (Justus) 1389

Lorrain (Paul) 4321,5448

Lort (Michael) 7584

Loss of liberty 6718

Lottery, a farce [H.Fielding] 6806

Loudoun (John Campbell) Earl of see: Campbell (John)

Louis XIV 2108-9,2214,2420,2747,2933,3135, 3607-8,4190

Lovat (Simon Fraser) Baron see: Fraser (Simon)

Love (Christopher) 892,1185

Love (Richard) 1148

Love elegies [G.Birch] 7694

Loveling (Benjamin) 4049,5692

Lovell (Sir Salathiel) 4819-20,5162

Love's invention 6311

Lowe (Thomas Hill) 8379

Low-flyer's new declaration 3930

Lowman (Moses) 6312-3

Lowndes (William) 3372-4,3388

Lowth (Robert) 6719,7495,7500,7514,7729

Lowth (Simon) 2359-60,2421,2616,2730,3425, 3499,5693

Loyal catechism 4821

Loyal martyr vindicated 3136

Loyal Observator 2215

Loyal queries, humbly tendred 1050

Loyal tear dropt [J.Glanvill] 1306

Loyall convert [F.Quarles] 625

Loyalty of the last Long Parliament 1883

Lubin (Eilhard) 785

Lucas (Charles) Baron 1350

Lucas (Charles) M.P. 7397,7536

Lucas (Richard) 2216,3137,3931,4432

Lucas (Robert) 7834-5

Lucas's letters to Earl Moira 8206

Lucida intervalla [J.Carkesse] 1632

Lucilla and Elizabeth 2515,2653

Lucy and Ellen 8412

Ludolf (Heinrich Wilhelm) 3426

Ludolf (Hiob) 7839

Lukman 164

Lunacy. A poem 4822

Lund 4880

Lupton (Willima) 4433,5163,5694,6314,6467, 6616,6645,6662

Lusus Neo-Gamelii 1286

Luther (Martin) 2560,2600,2673,6082,6211

Luyart (John Joseph de) see: Elhuyar (Juan José de)

Luzancy (Hippolite du Chastelet de) see: Du Chastelet de Luzancy (H.)

Lydgate (John) 4504

Lyford (William) 918

Lying-Jacks, a dialogue 3932

Lynch (?Francis) 7177,7214,7263-4

Lynch (John) 6876

Lynford (Thomas) 1688,4823,5974-5

Lyonne, Monsieur de see: Lionne (H.de)

Lysimachus Nicanor see: Corbet (John)

Lyttelton (George) Baron 6817,6835,6982, 7019,7195

M.(A.) 4434

M.(B.) see: Mandeville (Bernard de)

M.(C.D.L.) 5695

M.(G.) see: Miege (Guy)

M.(Sir H.) see: Mackworth (Sir Humphrey)

M.(J.) see: Milner (John)

M.(J.) and P.(W.) 3683

M.(J.C.) 3933

M.(L.) 6182,6209

M.(M.) 2913

M.(P.) 1309

M.(R.) 6522

M.(T.) 29

M.(W.) see: Miln (William)

Mabbut (George) 6720

Macalister (Norman) 8151

Macartney (George) 5449,5696

Macaulay (Catharine) 7585

Mac Carte (Duncan) see: Squire (Samuel)

Macclesfield (Thomas Parker) Earl of see: Parker (Thomas)

M'Ghee (Robert James) 8513

Machiavelli (Niccolo) 3138

McIlvaine (Charles Pettit) 8573

M'Kenna (Theobald) 8169

Mackenzie (George) 1st Earl of Cromarty 3762,4204,5859

Mackenzie (George) 3rd Earl of Cromarty 7148

Mackenzie (Sir George) 2914,3139

Mackheath, Captain 6701

Mackworth (Sir Humphrey) 3674,3684,3761,3934-5, 3946,3985,4075,4223,5450,6183,6476

Maclaine (Archibald) 8056

Maclaurin (John) Lord Dreghorn 7515

Macnab (Henry Grey) 8298

Mac Namara (John) 1852

Macpherson (James) 7621,7744

Macswinny (Owen) see: Swinny (Owen Mac)

Madan (Martin) 7516-7,7519,7521,7523,7537

Maddock (Henry) 8088

Maddox (Isaac) 6974,7020,7294,7374

Madison (James) 8100

Magdalen-grove [A.Evans] 5650

Magdeburg Cathedral 3589

Magee (John) 7904

Magliabechi (Antonio) 7420

Magistracy and government of England vindicated [Sir B.Shower] 2953,3060

Magna Carta 6860,8320

Maimbourg (Louis) 2516

Maimonides see: Moses ben Maimon

Maine (Jasper) see: Mayne (Jasper)

Mainwaring (Arthur) 5164,5217,5451

Maister (Georg) 7375

Maitland (Charles) 6562

Maitland (Charles David) 8596

Maitland (John) Duke of Lauderdale 1644

Maittaire (Michael) 4824,5165-7,5723

Majestas intemerata [J.Cleveland] 2860

Malard (Michel) 6285

Mall: or, The reigning beauties 4597

Mallet (Sir John) 1821

Man in the moon, discovering a world of knavery 8634

Man of honour 6892

Management of the present war against France [E.Littleton] 3025

Management of the war [F.Hare] 5081,5112-3

Manager's pro and con [Sir J.St.Leger] 4894-6, 4945

Manby (Peter) 2617

Manchester (Edward Montagu) Earl of see: Montagu (Edward)

Manchester Agricultural Society 8057

Mandevile (John) 4076

Mandeville (Bernard de) 3936,4077,6614,6627

Mangey (Thomas) 6315,6396,6409-10,6663

Manifesto, asserting and clearing 3937

Manley (Mary De la Riviere) 4078,5168-71,5860-1

Manley (Thomas) 2915

Manlius Capitolinus (Marcus) 5391

Mann (Isaac) 7654

Manner of the impeachment of the XII bishops 401

Manners (Catherine) Duchess of Rutland 5021

Manners (John) Duke of Rutland 5086

Manningham (Sir Richard) 6664

Manningham (Thomas) 1822,2110,2422,2517-8, 4435-6,4598-9,5697

Mansell (Roderick) 1823

Manton (Thomas) 6643

Manwaring (Edward) 6893

Mar (John Erskine) Earl of see: Erskine (John)

March (John) 2983

Mareschal Tallard's aid-de-camp 3938

Maresius (Samuel) 832

Margarita in Anglia reperta [G.Fox] 1128

Margetson (James) 1673

Maria Anna Josepha, Archduchess of Austria 2853

Maria Theresa, Queen of Hungary 7019,7375

Marion (Elie) 4253,4322

Marketman (John) 1775

Marmor Norfolciense [S.Johnson] 6927

Maronite Church 3317

Marprelate (Martin) 17

Marriage-dialogues [E.Ward] 4484

Marriott (Sir James) 7458

Mars stript of his armour [E.Ward] 4639

Marsch der Kayserl. Armée 1545

Marsden (Thomas) 2748

Marseilles 6523

Marsh (Herbert) 8231,8328,8514

Marshall, Messrs 8356

Marshall (John) 7217

Marshall (Nathaniel) 5452,5862,6110,6144, 6184,6235,6524,6563,6577,6724

Marshall (Stephen) 212,244-5,402,530-1,563, 617-9,731

Marshall (Thomas) 2217

Marsters (Thomas) 8073

Marten (Henry) 732,861

Martha and Mary 8413

Martialis (Marcus Valerius) 3293,7347

Martin (David) 6411-3,6564

Martin (Henry) 564

Martin (John) 7917,8002,8037

Martin (Josiah) 6064

Martin (Samuel) 7119

Martini (Matthias) 129

Martyn (Richard) 5172,5232

Martyni-Laguna (Johann Aloysius) 7853

Marvell (Andrew) 952,1392,1500,1584,1973

Marvell (Andrew) Junior 4825

Mary II, Queen 2833,3335,3343,3359-60,3363, 3377-8,3381-4,3386,3389,3391-2,5398

Mary, Queen of Scots 6536

Mary Dwyer 8453

Masham (Abigail) 4455

Masham (Samuel) Baron 5305

Mask of moderation pull'd off [S.Grascombe] 3909

Mask pull'd off [A.Syddall] 5528

Mason (Henry Joseph Monck) 8299

Mason (John) Nonconformist Minister 7226, 7259-60

Mason (John) Rector of Water Stratford 3375

Mason (William) 7196,7261-2,7321,7748

Masquerade [H.Fielding] 6696

Massacre of Glenco 8601

Massey (Edmund) 6562,6565-7

Massinger (Philip) 6568

Massue de Ruvigny (Henri de) Earl of Galway 4988

Master John Goodwin's quere's 917

Masters (Samuel) 2423,2912,2916,3029

Matthews (John) 7650

Mauduit (Israel) 7459

Maulden (Joseph) 7460

Maundrell (Henry) 3427

Maunoir (Jean Pierre) 8234

Maurice, Prince 532

Maurice (Henry) 2111,2424,2749,2917-9,3030,3375

Mawson (Matthias) 7058

Maximilian Henry, Archbishop of Cologne 2807

Maxims for playing the game of whist [W.Payne] 7714

Maxwell (Francis Kelly) 7417

Maxwell (Henry) 3763,3838,5173

Maxwell (John) 620,733,1261

Mayerne (Théodore Turquet de) 951

Maynard (Margaret) Baroness 2097

Mayne (Jasper) 734

Maynwaring (Arthur) see: Mainwaring (A.)

Maynwaring (Everard) 1370

Maynwaring (Roger) 4545

Mayo (Henry) 7517

Mayo (Richard) 5453

Mead (Norman) 7157

Mead (Richard) 6386,6468,6486,6491,6528,6547, 6586,7240

Meadowcroft (Richard) 7332

Mears (William) 6370

Measures of ministry [A.O'Connor] 7992

Medal: or, A full and impartial account 5454

Medalist. A new ballad 6975

Medall. A satyre [Dryden] 2071

Mede (Joseph) 177,192-3,246,403,533

Medical and Chirurgical Society 8170

Meditation upon a broom-stick [J.Swift] 4927

Meerman (Gerard) 7445

Meggott (Richard) 1351,1465,1501,2112,2218,2854, 2920,3031,3140,3210

Meiner genedigsten und genedigen Herrn 4

Meinertzhagen (Geruinus a) 1241

Meirs (John) 6185

Melfort (John Drummond) Earl of see: Drummond (John)

Melvil (Francis) 6290

Melvill (Henry) 8497

Memoir of a Sunday school teacher 8478

Memoir of Mr.John B--- 8414

Memoir of the Countess of Huntingdon 8454

Memoir of William H-- 8415

Memoire justificatif de la conduite 7722

Memoires de Monsieur Du Vall [W.Pope] 1355

Memoirs concerning the affairs of Scotland [G.Lockhart] 5819,5857

Memoirs concerning the life and manners of Captain Mackheath 6701

Memoirs for the curious 8635

Memoirs of Count Tariff [Defoe] 5636

Memoirs of King James II 3721

Memoirs of the amours, intrigues, and adventures 7563

Memoirs of the Chevalier de St.George 5455,5581

Memoirs of the life and times [of Archbishop Tenison] 6065

Memoirs of the life of Lord Lovat'7158

Memoirs of the present state of Europe 8636

Memoirs of the Rev.John Berridge 8455

Memoirs relating to the famous Mr.Tho.Brown 3939

Memoirs relating to the restoration 6066

Memorial drawn by King William's special direction 4134

Memorial for his Highness the Prince of Orange [Sir G.Mackenzie] 2914

Memorial from a faithful member 5976

Memorial from his Most Christian Majesty 3607

Memorial of the Chevalr.de St.George 6665

Memorial of the Church of England [J.Drake] 4001,4038-9,4174

Memorial of the proceedings of the late ministery [C.Povey] 5985

Memorial of the state of England [J.Toland] 4112,4118,4203

Memorial to protestants on the fifth of November [W.Kennet] 5679

Memorials on both sides 5174

Mendham (Joseph) 8579,8585

Mene tekel ou jugement astrologique [J.Partridge] 2761

Mercerus (Johannes) 11

Mercier (Barthélemi) 7780

Merciful judgments of High Church triumphant [M.Tindal] 4940

Mercurius Aulicus 8637-8

Mercurius bellicus 8639

Mercurius Britanicus 8640

Mercurius Caledonius 8641

Mercurius civicus 448,8642

Mercurius Davidicus 534

Mercurius elencticus 8643

Mercurius, &c. not - veridicus 8644

Mercurius &c. Upon my life new borne 8645

Mercurius melancholicus 8646

Mercurius Oxoniensis 4295

Mercurius Philalethes see: Select city quaeries

Mercurius politicus 8647-9

Mercurius pragmaticus 8650
Mercurius publicus 8651
Mercurius Romanus 8652
Mercurius veridicus 8653
Meredith (Edward) 2113,2618,2732,2750
Meredith (Sir William) 7553
Meres (Sir John) 6469
Merian (Matthaeus) 7365
Meriton (John) 1546
Merks (Thomas) 5678,5863,6057-8,6162,6200
Merlin 616, 4253
Merret (Christopher) 1359
Merrick (James) 7092,7518
Merry (J.) 7959
Merry new year's gift 5456
Mesech and Kedar 5457,5545
Mesmes (Jean Antoine de) *comte d'Avaux* 2303
Messenger (Peter) 4959
Messiah, a sacred oratorio 7618
Messiah foretold 8416
Meston (William) 6894
Metastasio (Pietro Antonio Domenico Bonaventura) 7854
Method propos'd, for easing her Majesties subjects 4205
Methods used for erecting charity-schools 5977,6067,6186
Mickle (William Julius) 7577,7699
Middleton (Conyers) 6414-5,6487,6525-6,6595, 6666,6684,6864,6977,7197,7202,7227, 7284,7290-1,7295,7302,7312,7489
Middleton (John) 6750
Midsummer moon 4600
Miege (Guy) 4079
Milbourne (Luke) 2219,2751,3940,4323,4506-7, 4601-2,4777,4826,5175,5458,5698-9,5864, 5978,6068,6416,6470
Miles (William Augustus) 7989
Military orders, and articles, established by his Maiestie 462
Miller (Edmund) 4827
Miller (James) 6791,6949,6952,6959,7093
Miller (Samuel) 8217
Milles (Thomas) 3499,3685,4274,4324
Mills (Henry) 6305,6316
Milman (Henry Hart) 8417
Miln (William) 5865
Milner (James) 6471
Milner (John) 2752
Milner (John) *Roman Catholic Bishop* 8092, 8188,8218
Milner (William) 4437-8
Milton (John) 535,894,1141,1143,2519,2934, 6950,7339,7435,7491,7586,7670
Min Heer T.Van C's answer 2998
Mine-Adventurers case [Sir H.Mackworth] 5450
Miracles no violation of the laws of nature [C.Blount] 2172
Miracles reviv'd 2114
Miraculous recovery of a dumb man 1502
Miscellaneous thoughts on the present posture [J.Hervey] 7003
Mischief of cabals 2425
Mischief of impositions [V.Alsop] 1739
Miser, a poem 6863
Miserable case of poor old England 5459
Misfortunes of royal favourites 4325
Mishnah 3032
Miso-dolos see: Leslie (Charles)
Misosarum (Gregory) see: Swift (Jonathan)
Misson (François Maximilien) 4326
Mistaken murderer 3527
Mr.B[isse]t's recantation [W.King] 5137
Mr.Collier's desertion discuss'd [W.Snatt] 6335,6477
Mr.C[olli]ns's Discourse of free-thinking [J.Swift] 5750
Mr.Dyson's speech to the freeholders [S.Smith] 8520
Mr.Emerton's cause now depending 2115
Mr.Emmertons marriage [T.Hunt] 2094
Mr.Hoadly's Measures of submission 5176,5460
Mr.Law's Unlawfulness of the stage 6667
Mr.Leslie's defence [R.Laurence] 6402,6459
Mr.Mollard Lefevre 8456
Mr.Pryn's good old cause stated [J.Rogers] 1075
Mr.Sidney his self-conviction 2304
Mr.Smirke. Or, the divine in mode [A.Marvell] 1500
Mr.Toland's Clito dissected 3592
Mr.W----k's speech 6069
Mist's weekly journal 6728
Mitchel (Francis) 1369
Mitchel (James) 1572
Mitre and the crown [F.Atterbury] 5001
Mob in the pit 7636
Mock mourners [Defoe] 3715,3728
Moderate answer to Mr.Prins full reply [H.Robinson] 685
Moderate censure of doctrines 6187
Moderate informer communicating the most remarkable transactions 8654
Moderate reply to the Citie-remonstrance [J.Price] 738
Moderation a vertue (1683) 2220
Moderation a virtue (1703) [J.Owen] 3841,3865, 3910,3925-6,3941
Moderation and justice of modern Whigs 5177
Moderation and loyalty of the dissenters 4828
Moderation display'd [W.Shippen] 3967
Moderation display'd... Answered 4080
Moderation, justice, and manners 4206
Moderation pursued 3941
Moderation still a virtue [J.Owen] 3909,3948
Moderation truly stated [M.Astell] 3865
Moderation turn'd into madness 5178
Moderation unmask'd 4081
Moderator expecting sudden peace [T.Povey] 543
Moderator: published for promoting of peace 8655
Modern policies, taken from Machiavel [W.Sancroft] 3053
Modest and just apology for; or, Defence of the present East-India-Company 3063
Modest answer to the four immodest letters 4829
Modest apology for Parson Alberoni [T.Gordon] 6391
Modest apology for the Reverend Mr.Thomas Bradbury 6417
Modest apology, occasion'd by the late unhappy turn [A.Hammond] 6510
Modest attempt for healing 3033
Modest censure on some mistakes 5700
Modest enquiry concerning the election 2116
Modest enquiry into the Bishop of Bangor's Preservative 6188
Modest enquiry into the causes of the present disasters 3034
Modest enquiry into the reasons of the joy expressed [M.Manley] 5860-1
Modest enquiry, whether St.Peter were ever at Rome [H.Care] 2571
Modest examination of the new oath 2921
Modest examination of The resolution 2221,2285
Modest proof of the order 4082
Modest reflection on the Right Reverend the Bishop of Norwich 4830
Modest representation of the past and present state [R.Martyn] 5172,5232
Modest survey of that celebrated tragedy 5461
Modest survey of the most considerable things [G.Burnet] 1483
Modest vindication of the Earl of S[haftesbur]y 1974
Modest vindication of the Right Honourable Sir Gilbert Heathcote 5179
Modesty and moderation of the dissenters 4831
Modesty mistaken 3764
Modo dell'elettione del serenissimo prencipe di Venezia 3609
Mogila (Petr) 7462
Mohocks [J.Gay] 5401
Mohun (Charles) *Baron* 5518,5537,5653,5696
Moira (Francis Hastings) *Earl of* see: Hastings (Francis Rawdon)
Molesworth (Robert) *Viscount* 5124,6497
Molloy (Charles) 6317
Molyneux (William) 3517
Monck (George) *Duke of Albemarle* 1015,1044, 1049,1051-3,1056,1086,1114,1118,1143, 1149-50,1159-60,1170,1176,1184,1341,1362, 5909-10
Moncrieff-Wellwood (Sir Henry) 7938
Monethly account 8656
Monitor 7412,7418
Monk (James Henry) 8219
Monk (Martha) 7519
Monmouth (James Scott) *Duke of* see: Scott (James)
Monosyllable if! 7228
Monoux (Lewis) 7309
Monro (Alexander) 3141,3211,3268
Monro (Andrew) 2753
Monroe (James) 8074
Montagu (Basil) 8313
Montagu (Charles) *Earl of Halifax* 2634,3035, 3166,3285,3479,3544,3766,3847,4493,5305, 5321,5938-9,5949
Montagu (Edward) *Earl of Manchester* 536,564, 786
Montagu (Ralph) *Duke of Montagu* 1689,4539
Montagu (Richard) 119
Montagu (Walter) 642
Montesquieu (Charles de Secondat) *Baron de* 8290
Montgaillard (Jean Gabriel Maurice Rocques) *Comte de* 7990
Montgomery (James) *Poet* 7960
Montgomery (Sir James) 3243
Monthly miscellany 8657
Monthly packet of advices from Parnassus [M.Earbery] 6551
Monthly register 8658
Monthly review 7562
Montmorency (François Henry de) *Duc de Luxembourg* 3364
Montrose (James Graham) *Marquess of* see: Graham (James)
Moody (Henry Riddell) 8380
Moon-calf [J.Browne] 4017
Moon-shine: or the restauration of Jews-trumps [J.Eachard] 1382
Moore (Charles) 7811
Moore (Edward) 6877
Moore (John) *Bishop of Ely* 2117,3036,3428, 3560,3996,4207,4662,4834-5
Moore (John) *of Wechicombe* 1151
Moore (Sir John) 1947,1966
Moore (William) 7961
Moores baffled [L.Addison] 1874
Morality from the devil 7059
Morbus Anglicanus sanatus 7501
More (A.) 6644
More (Hannah) 7962
More (Henry) 1152
More (Sir Thomas) 109
More excellent way [E.Stephens] 3851
More news from Salisbury [G.Sewell] 5886
More reformation [Defoe] 3809
More remarks on the theatre 8300
Morell (Thomas) 7991,8602
Morer (Thomas) 3037,4208
Moreton (Andrew) 6646
Morgan (Thomas) *M.D.* 6963
Morley (George) 1212,1225,1238-9,1242,2316, 4327
Morley (John) 7723
Mornay (Philippe de) *Seigneur du Plessis-Marly* 26,735
Morning-star out of the north 1975
Morning's discourse of a bottomless tub 5462
Morrell (William) 3215
Morris (Corbyn) 7046
Morris (Robert) *Barrister* 7587
Morris (Robert) *Poet* 6951-2,6959,7229
Morselli (Adriano) 4603
Mortal disease 8418
Morton (Thomas) 178,404-5,537,1690
Moses ben Maimon 3032
Moses (Thomas) 7395
Moss (Charles) 7376
Moss (Robert) 4083-4,4328,4439-40,4593,4832 5038,5463,6343
Mosse (Miles) 71
Mossom (Robert) 1153
Most exact and true relation of the proceedings 406
Most faults on one side [J.Trapp] 4947
Most humble and seasonable proposal 4833
Most serious expostulation with several of my fellow citizens 1824
Most true relation of the present state of his Majesties army 407
Motte (Benjamin) 3606,5691
Mould (Bernard) 6189
Mount (Charles Milman) 8419
Mountfort (William) 3142
Mournful congress 3765
Mouse grown a rat 3766
Mouse-trap [E.Holdsworth] 4570,5413
Moyer (Samuel) 1037
Muddiman (Henry) 8651,8662
Muggleton (Lodowick) 1531
Muhammad ibn Muhammad, *al Idrisi* see: Edrisi (Muhammad al)
Mulerius (Carolus) 1310
Mulgrave (John Sheffield) *Earl of* see: Sheffield (John)
Mulheim (Johann Balthasar Joseph von) 7665
Mulliner (John) 4441
Multum in parvo, aut vox veritatis 1976
Munster (Sebastian) 2
Murder of the Christian Indians 8420
Murmurers. A poem 2922
Murray (Sir John) 7182
Murray (Patrick) *Baron Elibank* 7602
Murray (Robert) 1503,3376,3429
Murray (William) *Earl of Mansfield* 7198,7566
Musaeus 120
Musaeus: a monody [W.Mason] 7196
Musarum Cantabrigiensium threnodia 1341
Muscipula [E.Holdsworth] 4568-9
Muses mercury 8659
Musgrave (Samuel) 7461,7564
Mutiny maintained 1154
Muzarelli (Alphonsus) 8287
My Lord Bishop of Sarum's Exposition 3839
Mynors (Willoughby) 6070-1,6190,6318
Myra: a pastoral dialogue [W.Oliver] 7340
Mysterious congress 7060
Mystery of the new fashioned goldsmiths 1498, 1507
N.(A.I.) see: Stevens (William)
N.(D.) *Gent* see: L'Estrange (Sir Roger)
N.(H.) 3318
N.(J.) 4834-5
N.(N.) 1154,1825,2118,2754,2923,3038,3269-70, 4085,5866,6072
Naboth's vinyard [J.Caryll] 1633
Nailour (William) 1466
Naked truth [Oglethorpe] 7352
Naked truth: or, Phanaticism detected 4086
Naked truth. Or, The true state [H.Croft] 1452,1519
Naked truth: the first part [H.Croft] 1754
Naked truth. The second part [E.Hickeringill] 1933
Nalson (John) 1652,1691,1826,1977,2222,2426
Names of the Roman Catholics 7113
Napoleon I 8143,8221
Narbouel 4442,4604
Narrative and declaration of the dangerous design 833
Narrative of Dr.Robert Norris [A.Pope] 5717
Narrative of Sir George Rooke's late voyage 3942
Narrative of the disease and death [of John Pym] 538
Narrative of the proceedings of the lower house of Convocation [H.Aldrich] 3632
Narrative of the siege and surrender of Maestricht 1413
Nash (Richard) 7455
Nation vindicated [M.Tindal] 5256,5532
National journal 7230
National unanimity recommended 7021
Natural interest of Great-Britain 7172
Natural probability of a lasting peace 6818
Natural reflections upon the present debates [C.Leslie] 5438
Nature and extent of the apostolic commission [J.Skinner] 7816
Nature, design, and general rules, of the united societies [J.Wesley] 7072
Nature, obligation, and efficacy, of the Church sacraments [D.Waterland] 6734,6764
Nature of the first resurrection 8314
Naunton (Sir Robert) 247
Naworth see: Wharton (Sir George)
Naylor (Martin Joseph) 8013
Naylor (William) 5464
Necessity of an alteration [T.Wagstaffe] 6354, 6426
Necessity of Church-communion 4087
Necessity of parliaments 2924
Neck or nothing [J.Dunton] 5645
Ned Delaney 8357
Nedham (Marchamont) 1064,1504,1547-8,1585,8648, 8650,8654,8676
Needham (John) 4836
Needham (Robert) 1692
Needham (William) 2774,2785,3767
Ne'er a barrel 5701
Negative voyce: or, A check 1054
Negotiations for a treaty of peace [F.Hare] 5114-5
Nelson (Henry) 4443
Nelson (Horatio) *Viscount* 8356
Nelson (Robert) 2755,4087,4384,5644,5814,5984, 6008
Nereides [W.Diaper] 5377
Neuchatel 5465,7619
Neville (Henry) 885
Neville (Robert) 1693-4
New and compleat list of officers 5839
New and faithful translation of letters 7637
New and improved history and description of the Tower 8457
New association of those called, moderate-Church-men [H.Sacheverell] 3778,3844,4095-6
New Atlantis [T.Heyrick] 2601
New catechism, with Dr.Hickes's thirty nine articles 4837-8
New dangers to the Christian priesthood [J.Turner] 5543
New dialogue between a burgermaster [J.Puckle] 3473
New dialogue between a member of Parliament 3768
New dialogue between Monsieur Shaccoo 3686
New dialogue between the horse 3840
New dialogues upon the present posture of affairs [C.Davenant] 4721
New discoveries of the dangers 5867
New diurnall of passages 539
New Dunciad [A.Pope] 7026
New England's faction discovered 3003
New extempore-prayer 4839
New High-Church turn'd old Presbyterian [M.Tindal] 4634
New history of the succession of the crown 3039
New ignoramus 1978
New ill designs of sowing sedition 4840

New journey to Paris [J.Swift] 5246-7
New letter from Leghorn 2002
New map of England 998
New plot newly discovered 2520
New popish sham-plot discovered 1979
New project, dedicated neither to the Q[uee]n [G.Duckett] 5381
New project to make England 3769
New scheme consider'd 4841
New separation from the Church [W.Scot] 6426
New test of the Church of England's honesty [Defoe] 3889
New test of the Church of Englands loyalty (1687) 2608-9,2619,2641
New test of the Church of England's loyalty (1702) [Defoe] 3729,3734
New test of the sence of the nations [Defoe] 4732
New view of the new directory [H.Hammond] 723
New voyage to the island of fools 5702
New way of selling places at Court 5466
New way to raise soldiers 4329
New-year's-gift; a poem 6976
New-years-gift for the anti-prerogative-men [J.Brydall] 2056
New-years gift for the High-Church clergy [J.White] 5561
Newark (Henry Pierrepont) *Viscount* see: Pierrepont (Henry)
Newcomb (Thomas) 6254
Newcome, *Mrs.* 6702
Newcome (John) 6617
Newcome (Peter) 4842
Newcomen (Matthew) 540,736,787
Newes from the new exchange [H.Neville] 885
Newes, published for satisfaction 8660
News from France [G.Burnet] 2058
Newton (Sir Isaac) 6697-8,6720,6845
Newton (John) 7812
Newton (Richard) 5467,6653
Newton (Samuel) 7603
Newton (Thomas) 171
Newton (William) 6755
Nicephorus 3126
Nichols (Philip) 125
Nicols (Daniel) 1980
Nicolson (William) 2427,3748-9,3770,3988, 4121,4330-1,6057,6162,6191
Nineteen cases of conscience 1055
No blinde guides [Sir R.L'Estrange] 1141
No-Church establish'd 4209
No conquest, but the hereditary right 4843
No just grounds for introducing the new communion [N.Spinckes] 6376,6433,6449
No necessity to alter the Common-prayer [W.Scot] 6327,6354,6426
No new parliament 1155
No protestant-plot [R.Ferguson] 1916
No punishment no government 5468
No queen: or, No general [Defoe] 5373
No reason for restoring the prayers [N.Spinckes] 6227,6274-5
No sufficient reason for restoring the prayers [N.Spinckes] 6265,6277,6339-40, 6369
Noailles (Louis Antoine de) 6192
Nobilis pharmacopola [J.de Villiers] 3287
Noble (Richard) 5605
Noel (Gerard Thomas) 8258
Nokes (William) 4830
Nolan (Frederick) 8235
Noli me tangere [J.Brydall] 3804
Nonconformists plea for the conformists 2177
None but the sheriffs ought to name 1981
Non-residency of the clergy 5180
Norris (Charles) 6319-20
Norris (John) 2223
Norris (Peter) 1766
Norris (Richard) 3943
Norris (Robert) see: Pope (Alexander)
North (Francis) *Baron Guilford* 1769,3944
North (John) 1371
North (Roger) 3136,7333
Northern election; or, Nest of beasts 7263-4
Northern queries from the Lord Gen: Monck 1056
Nostredame (Michael de) 1882,5979
Notae in Anglo-Saxonum nummos [E.Thwaites] 4473
Notes and observations upon some passages of scripture [J.Gregory] 722
Notes of the Church 2756
Notice sur la mort de Paul I [R.C.H.Le Prestre] 8117
Notion of the historical draught [A.A.Cooper] 5621-2
Notions of the Methodists 7094
Notitia St.Johanniana 5703
Notorious impostor [E.Settle] 3215
Nott (John) 7849
Nottingham, *County of* 289,396
Not[tingh]am politicks examin'd [Defoe] 5637
Nouveaux interets des princes de l'Europe [G.de Courtilz de Sandras] 2707
Novus reformator vapulans [T.Brown] 3093
Now or never: or, A familiar discourse 6522
Now or never: or, A project under God [C.Leslie] 4807
Nowell (Thomas) 7538
Nugae antiquae [E.Harington] 7557
Nugent (Robert) *Earl* 6929,7265
Nundinae Sturbrigienses [T.Hill] 4560
Nuptiae Pelei et Thetidos renovatae 1510
Nuptiae sacrae [J.Ireland] 8329
Nye (Philip) 517,2224
Nye (Stephen) 3271

O.(J.) see: Ozell (John)
O.(M.) see: Ogilvy (Michael)
O.(S.) 135
Oakeley (Sir Herbert) 8597
Oastler (Richard) 8528,8539,8541
Oates (Titus) 1645,1695-6,1804-5,1827,2074 2114,2158,3430,3460,3561,3569,3687,6778
Oaths of Irish papists 1982
Oaths of supremacy & allegiance 1182
Obedience due to the present King [F.Fullwood] 2881
Obedience to civil government 5181
O'Beirne (Thomas Lewis) 8141
Objections of the non-subscribing London clergy [J.Swinfen] 4929
Objections to the war examined 7963
Obligation of acting according to conscience [R.Russell] 6077
Obrecht (Ulrich) 1467
O'Brien (Gertrude Grace, Lady Edward) 8284
O'Brien (Murrough) *Earl of Inchiquin* 836
O'Bryen (Denis) 8038
Observations and conjectures upon some passages of Shakespeare [T.Tyrwhitt] 7508
Observations, &c. upon the amended act 8089
Observations occasioned by the contest about literary property [E.Law] 7582
Observations on a book, intituled, An introductory discourse to a larger work [H.Stebbing] 7202
Observations on a pamphlet, intitled, An answer to one part of a late infamous libel [W.Arnall] 6767
Observations on Mr.Whiston's Historical memoirs 7231
Observations on The case of the protestant dissenters [G.Horne] 7890
Observations on the causes of clerical non-residence [S.Seyer] 8161
Observations on the conduct of the protestant dissenters 7895-6
Observations on the conversion and apostleships of St.Paul [G.Lyttelton] 7195
Observations on the last Dutch wars 1697
Observations on the taxation of property [J.Jenour] 8071
Observations on the treaty of Seville examined 6751
Observations on the writings of the Craftsman [J.Hervey] 6749,6766
Observations touching appeals from Chancery 2119
Observations upon a bill 7199
Observations upon commercial terms 8236
Observations upon his Majesties answer 408
Observations upon Mr.Johnson's Remarks [W.Sherlock] 2951
Observations upon some of his Majesties late answers [H.Parker] 317,412-3,428
Observations upon the administration of justice in Bengal 7712
Observations upon the case of William Rose 3945
Observations upon the conduct and behaviour of a certain sect [E.Gibson] 7086
Observations upon the ordinance of the Lords and Commons [E.Boughen] 646
Observations upon the Prince of Orange 409
Observations upon the state of the nation 5637, 5704-5,5740
Observator 410,1992,2063,2133,2215,2254,2319-20,3732,3869,3882,3893,3929,3951,4221,5099
Observator defended [Sir R.L'Estrange] 2417
Observator defended in a modest reply 410
Observator prov'd a trimmer 2428
Observator reproved 2305
Observator toss'd in a blanket 4088
Observator vindicated 2429
Observator's new trip to Scotland 4444
Occasional conformity a most unjustifiable practice [S.Grascombe] 3910
Occasional historian [M.Earbery] 6743,6776-7, 6802
Occasional letter. Number I 3923-4,3946,4068-9,
Occasional letter from a gentleman in the country [J.Perceval] 7268
Occasional letter on the subject of English convocations [W.Kennet] 3675
Occasional poems on the late Dutch war 5469
Occasionalists. (Occasional conformity) 3947
Occurrences from foreign parts 8661
Ockley (Simon) 5182,5470-2,5706-7,6105
O'Coigly (James) 8075
O'Connell (Daniel) 8226
O'Connor (Arthur) 7992,8090
Ode. Humbly inscribed to the...Bishop of London 5868
Ode on Saint Caecilia's day [B.Thornton] 7274
Ode, to his Royal Highness on his birth-day [R.Nugent] 6929
Ode to the King 2306
Oeconomy of his Majesty's Navy-office 6193
Of benevolence: an epistle [J.Armstrong] 7301
Of Christian communion [J.Kettlewell] 3263
Of conscience [H.Hammond] 606
Of resisting the lawfull magistrate [H.Hammond] 607
Of scandall [H.Hammond] 608
Of sinnes of weaknesse [H.Hammond] 673
Of superstition [H.Hammond] 674
Of the authority of councils [C.Hutchison] 2605
Of the incurable scepticism of the Church of Rome [J.La Placette] 2742
Of the much questioned salvability 8603
Of the original and ends of government 5708
Of the power of the keyes [H.Hammond] 780
Of the qualifications requisite in a minister of state [R.Ferguson] 5089
Of the usefulness of the prophecy of the Revelation [W.Garret] 5098
Of will-worship [H.Hammond] 609
Ogilvy (Michael) 1156
Ogle (Sir Chaloner) 7051
Ogle (George) 6930
Ogle (Margaret) 7022
Oglethorpe 7352
Oinos krithinos [B.Buckler] 7279
Old and modern Whig truly represented [C.Davenant] 3724
Old and the new religions contrasted 8458
Old and true way of manning the Fleet 4332
Old cavalier turned a new courtier 3040
Old English constitution [C.Leslie] 5852
Old French way of managing treaties 5183
Old hawker 8479
Old Hubert see: Parkinson (James)
Old Mother Grim's tales [W.Meston] 6894
Old Popery as good as new 2754
Old stories which were the fore-runners 5184
Old story that every one knows 5473
Old truths and established facts 7939
Old wives tales 5474
Oldham (George) 6472
Oldham (John) 1828
Oldisworth (William) 4605,4844,5185
Oldmixon (John) 4210,4845,5186-7,5475-6, 6874,8659
Oliva pacis 926
Oliver (Edward) 3528
Oliver (William) 7340,7397
Oliver's pocket looking-glass 5188
Olivet (Pierre Joseph Thoulier d') see: Thoulier d'Olivet (Pierre Joseph)
Oliveyra (Francisco Xavier de) 7377
Ollyffe (George) 4846
Omnia comesta a bello 1614,1698
On dead trees 8480
On the cheerfulness of the husbandman 8421
On the death of Mr.Edmund Smith 5477
On the death of the Queen 3377
On the delicacy of friendship [R.Hurd] 7349
On the employment of time [R.Bolton] 7278
On the pope's supremacy 8422
Onania, or the heinous sin 6073
One and thirty new orders of Parliament 1057
One and twenty Chester queries 1058
Only true and authentic trial of John Swan 7322
Onslow (Richard) 1829
Operations of the British, and the allied arms 7095
Operations of the British army in Spain 8207
Opinion and matter of fact 5189
Opinion is this [S.Johnson] 2898
Opinions of the barons of the Exchecquer 2120
Opposition more necessary than ever 7023
Oracles of the dissenters [J.Brydall] 4262
Orange (William Henry) *Prince of* see: William III, *King*
Oratio Dominica see: Lord's prayer
Oration intended to have been spoken in the Theatre at Oxford [Sir W.Jones] 7635
Orationes ex poetis Latinis excerptae [F.Rogers] 5216
Orator display'd 3900
Orders for ecclesiastical discipline 411
Ordinary journy no progress [J.Trapp] 4948
Orendayn (Juan Bautista de) *Marques de la Paz* 6668
Original papers and letters, relating to the Scots Company 3617
Originall of popish idolatrie 135
Origine of atheism in the popish and protestant churches [T.T.Crusius] 2277
Orme (William) 8373,8381
Ormonde (James Butler) *Duke of Ormonde* see: Butler (James)
Orphan 8459
Orpheus 7749
Orthodox Eastern Church 7462
Osborne (Peregrine) *Duke of Leeds* 3319,4211
Osborne (Peregrine Hyde) *Duke of Leeds* 5755
Osborne (Thomas) *Duke of Leeds* 1394-5,1616-7, 1644,1648,1666,1689,1706,1770,1830-1,1851, 1912,2056,2121-2,3351,3354,3370,5267
Ostervald (Jean Frédéric) 7353
Oswald (John) 4847
Otes (Titus) see: Oates (Titus)
Otway (Thomas) 1832
Out of the road visit to the Lord Bishop of Exeter 4573
Over shoes, over boots 7024
Overbury (Sir Thomas) 895
Overing (John) 1352
Overton (Benjamin) 5478
Overton (Richard) 683
Ovidius Naso (Publius) 7204,7219
Owen (David) 541
Owen (James) 3841,3865,3909-10,3925-6,3941,3948
Owen (John) 967,1059,1311,1361,1469,1699,1833,2220
Owen (R.) 3688
Owen (Richard) 1295
Owen (Robert) 8301
Owen (Vincent) 2430
Oxford almanack 5083,5190,5325
Oxford-antiquity examined 3143
Oxford criticks 6418
Oxford-scholar's answer 5709
Oxford University 98,241,792,1157,1174-5,1373, 2142,2225,2307,4652,4848
Oxford University. Magdalen College 2695,2720
Oxford University. Queen's College 3981
Oxley (Thomas) 43
Ozell (John) 4381,4802,6261

P. 1834
P.(A.) 834
P.(H.) 264,1158
P.(I.W.) see: Wilson (John)
P.(J.) 1353,1983,4849,5710
P.(J.) see: Page (Sir Francis)
P.(J.) *Somerset Herald* see: Philipot (J.)
P.(R.) 3529
P.(S.) see: Patrick (Symon)
P.(W.) 2431,3683,4850
P.(W.) see: Pittis (William)
Pacifick discourse of the causes [T.Smith] 2806
Pack of old puritans 886
Pack of puritans [Sir P.Wentworth] 265
Pacquet of advices and animadversions [M.Nedham] 1504
Page (Sir Francis) 6910
Pages (Pierre Marie François de) 8481
Pain (George) 2444
Paine (Thomas) 7926,7939,7999,8028,8046,8048-9, 8058,8104
Paine (William) 2077
Pair of spectacles for Oliver's looking-glass 5191
Paire of spectacles for the Citie 835
Pakington (Sir John) 3738,3837,3842,4074,4089
Palace of the Peak [E.Rhodes] 8516
Palatinate 72
Paley (William) 7761,8014
Palm (Carl Joseph von) 6685
Palmer (Charles) 4851
Palmer (John) *Dissenting Minister* 7638
Palmer (John) *Murderer* 4388
Palmer (Roger) *Earl of Castlemaine* 1308-9 1431,1454,1464,1700,2029,2987,3114
Palmer (Samuel) 3993
Pamphlet, entitled, "Taxation no tyranny" 7671
Panegyrick on his Excellency the Lord General George Monck [Sir J.Denham] 1015
Panegyrick on their Royal Highnesses 2123
Panelius (Alexander Xaverius) 6847
Paolo, *Servita* see: Sarpi (Paolo)
Papal bull, from Pope Gregory XVI [R.Oastler] 8541
Papers presented to Parliament, against the Lord Inchiquin 836
Papers relating to the Quakers tythe bill 6878
Papillon (Thomas) 1532
Papist mis-represented and represented [J.Gother] 2393-5,2540

Papist misrepresented and represented [J.Gother] 2503,2594,2620,2670
Papist not misrepresented by protestants [W.Sherlock] 2504-5,2535
Papist represented, and not misrepresented [J.Williams] 2670
Papists no Catholicks [W.Lloyd] 1684
Papists plot of firing discovered 1701
Papists protesting against protestant-popery [J.Gother] 2504,2797
Pappafava (Giovanni Roberto) 7479
Parable of the bear-baiting 3144
Parable of the black-birds [E.Thompkins] 3170
Paradise regained: or the Scripture account [G.Killingworth] 7614
Paradox against liberty 1702
Paraenetick or humble addresse 621
Parainesis pacifica [G.Mackenzie] 3762
Parallel [I.Mauduit] 7459
Parallel between the faith [C.Leslie] 3604
Parallel continu'd [E.Gibson] 3745
Paraphrase on the fourteenth chapter 4852
Pareus (Daniel) 120
Pareus (Joannes Philippus) 248
Paris. Parlement 1984,2757-8
Paris (John) 4853,5192
Paris relation of the Battel of Landen 3272
Parker (Edward) 6194
Parker (Ephraim) 5711
Parker (Henry) 317,412-3,428,542,1677,2759, 4854
Parker (Martin) 8646
Parker (Samuel) *Bishop of Oxford* 1361,1765, 2687,2689,2746,2760,2767,2776,3041, 5869
Parker (Samuel) *of Lincoln College* 5980
Parker (Samuel) *of Trinity College* 3610,8612
Parker (Thomas) *Earl of Macclesfield* 6640
Parker (Thomas) *of Newbury* 737
Parker (Timothy) 1505
Parker (William) 7750
Parkhurst (John) 3689
Parkinson (James) *Fellow of Lincoln College* 3145
Parkinson (James) *F.G.S.* 7964
Parliament see: England. Parliament
Great Britain. Parliament
Parliament arraigned, convicted 4855
Parliament of birds [E.Stacy] 5515
Parliamentary intelligencer 8662
Parliamentary original and rights of the lower house of Convocation [F.Atterbury] 3713
Parliaments plea: or XX. reasons 1060
Parliaments severall late victories 681
Parr (Samuel) 7836
Parriet (Thomas) 4333
Parson and his maid 6569
Parsons (John) 8251
Parsons (Robert) 837,1835,2433
Parsons case under the present land tax [G.Hooper] 2891
Part of the seventh epistle of the first book of Horace imitated [J.Swift] 5751
Partiality detected [C.Trimnell] 4476
Particular account of the insurrection 7940
Particular account of the proceedings at the Old-Bayly 1985
Particular advice from foreign parts 8663
Partington (Thomas) 249
Patridge (John) 2226,2761,3932,4294,4445, 4465,4508
Partridge (Seth) 1213
Partridge (William) 3378
Pas (Antoine de) 3938,3956
Paschall (John) 3689
Pasquier (Etienne) 1986
Pasquin and Marforio on the peace 7232
Passionate satyr upon a devillish great he-whore 1468
Passive obedience establish'd 5712
Passive obedience in actual resistance 3146
Paston (James) 2762
Paston (Robert) *Earl of Yarmouth* 2203
Pastoral letter from the four Catholic bishops 2763
Patern for true Protestants 1703
Paterson (William) 3331,6195
Patience. A present 4212
Patkul (Johann Reinhold) *Count* 6182,6209
Patriarchus Hodge see: Copy of the country-man's letter to the Speaker
Patrick (John) 2620,2764
Patrick (Symon) 1243,1354,1506,1586-8,1987, 2227,2621-2,2925-9,2942,3431
Patricola see: Toland (John)
Patriot analized 7233
Paul I, *Emperor of Russia* 8117
Paul (George) 5713
Paul (Sir George Onesiphorus) 7781,7798
Paulden (Thomas) 3771
Pax vobis: or, Gospel and liberty [E.Griffith] 2597,2885
Paxton (Nicholas) 6647
Payne (Henry) 2623
Payne (Thomas) 7684,7700,7713
Payne (William) *D.D.* 2432,2765,2884,2936,3020, 3042-3,3066
Payne (William) *Teacher of Mathematics* 7714
Peace and no peace 6931
Peace and reform [D.Stuart] 7997
Peace and unity recommended [W.Howell] 5420
Peace-haters: or, A new song 5193
Peace-offering: an essay 7159
Peace, or poverty [Defoe] 5374
Peaceable Christian 1589
Peacham (Henry) 3379
Pead (Deuel) 4213-4,4334,4606-7
Peake (Sir John) 2543
Peale (Rembrandt) 8133
Pearce (William) 7855
Pearce (Zachary) 6527,6551,6570,7266
Pearle found in England [G.Fox] 1129
Pearson (John) 1414
Pearson (John Norman) 8199
Pearson (Richard) 2308
Pearson (William) 4335
Peasant's daughter 8460
Peck (Francis) 6921
Peck (Samuel) 2309
Pecke (Samuel) 8666,8668
Peel (Sir Robert) 8542,8551-2
Peirce (Sir Edmond) 1159-60
Peirce (James) 4362,4364,4485,5479,6196,6321, 6385,6408,6419-20,6432
Pell (John) 1276
Pelling (Edward) 1704-5,2124-5,2228-9,2310, 2433-7,2624-5,3044,3212
Pelling (John) 4608
Pembroke (Philip Herbert) *Earl of* see: Herbert (Philip)
Pendlebury (Henry) 2626
Penington (John) 2432-3
Penn (William) 1378,1433,1982,1988,2126,2157 2373,2438,2521,2552,2627-9,2706,2766,2771 -2,3520,3539,3976
Pennsylvania. Free Society of Traders 2127
Penny cord for the pretended Prince 4856
Penry (John) 1233
Perceval (John) *Earl of Egmont* 7064,7084,7267-7268,7410,7449
Perceval (Spencer) 8119,8222
Pereat Papa 1877
Pereira (Moses Gomez) 8015
Perfect catalogue of all the lords treasurers 1706
Perfect diurnal of every dayes proceedings in Parliament 8667
Perfect diurnal of the passages in Parliament 8665
Perfect diurnall of some passages and proceedings of... the armies 8668
Perfect diurnall of some passages in Parliament 8666
Perfect diurnall of the passages in Parliament 8664
Perfect guide for protestant dissenters [H.Care] 2061
Perfect narrative of the proceedings of the army 828
Perfect occurrences of every daie iournall in Parliament 8669
Perfect occurrences of the most remarkable passages in the common-wealth 8670
Peril of being zealously affected [G.Ridpath] 4611
Perils of false brethren 4857
Peritsol (Abraham) see: Abraham ben Mordecai Farisol
Perkins (Joseph) 4336
Perkins (Sir William) 3410-1,3452
Perrinchief (Richard) 1325
Perronet (Vincent) 7275
Perse (William) 2128,2930
Persecution anatomiz'd [Defoe] 4034
Persius Flaccus (Aulus) 6922
Person of quality's answer to Mr.Collier's letter [J.Dennis] 3892
Persuasive to frequent communion [J.Tillotson] 2246
Perswasion of certaine grave divines 682
Perswasive to an ingenuous tryal [N.Clagett] 2372
Perswasive to consideration [J.Collier] 3346, 6029
Perswasive to moderation to church dissenters [W.Penn] 2521
Pertinent & profitable meditation 887
Pertinent speech made by an honourable member 1161
Peter (John) 2311
Peters (Hugh) 1055,4858
Petit (Peter) 7378
Petition and demand of right and justice [E.Stephens] 3788
Petition and vindication of the officers 788
Petition for peace [R.Baxter] 1189
Petition of divers eminent citizens 1989
Petition of the nobilitie...of Scotland 414
Petition of the officers and souldiers 789
Petre (William) *Baron Petre* 2312
Petter (John) 2439
Pettus (Sir John) 1422
Petty (William) *Marquess of Lansdowne* 7760
Petty (Sir William) 2230,2522,2630-2,3380
Peyto (Edward) 1061
Peyton (Sir Robert) 2042
Phelips (Paulin) 6865
Phelps (Thomas) 2440
Phelypeaux (Raimond Balthasar) *Marquis* 4098
Philalethes see: Animadversions upon, or an impartial answer to the Secret history
Philalethes see: Calumny no conviction
Philalethes see: Earbery (Matthias)
Philalethes see: English liberty in some cases worse than French slavery
Philalethes see: Forbes (Robert)
Philalethes see: Letter to the Archbishop
Philalethes see: Seasonable warneing to the poor persecuted Church
Philalethes see: Some remarks on the late Lord Bolingbroke's famous letter
Philalethes see: Some remarks upon the Reverend Dr.Marshall's sermon
Philalethes see: Threnody
Philalethes see: Turnbull (George)
Philalethes Cantabrigiensis see: Jurin (J.)
Philanagnostes Criticus see: Herne (T.)
Philanax Episcopius see: Antidotum Saris-buriense
Philanax Misopappas see: Tory plot
Philanglus see: Oaths of Irish papists
Philaretus Anthropopolita see: Some seasonable remarks upon the deplorable fall of the Emperour Julian
Philargyrius Cantab see: Barnes (Joshua)
Phileleutherus Cantabrigiensis see: Herne (Thomas)
Phileleutherus Lipsiensis see: Bentley (Richard)
Philidor (A.D.) see: Danican (François A.)
Phililicrines Parrhesiastes see: Some cursory reflexions impartially made upon Mr. Richard Baxter
Philip IV, *King of Spain* 805,979
Philip V, *King of Spain* 3607,3635,4094,5153, 5714
Philip, *Landgrave of Hesse* 4
Philipot (John) 167
Philipps (Fabian) 1244
Philipps (Sir John) 7193
Philips (Ambrose) 5461
Philips (John) *Dramatist* 5981
Philips (John) *Poet* 4446,5507,5982
Philips (William) 6571
Phillips (Charles) 8288
Phillips (Daniel) 3434
Phillips (John) *Milton's nephew* 904,953,1549, 1964,2129,2139,2767
Phillips (Robert) 5480
Phillips (Samuel) 3772-3
Phillips (William Luke) 7856
Phillpotts (Henry) 8190
Philo-Britannicus see: Characters of the four candidates
Philo-Caledon see: Defence of the Scots settlement at Darien
Philoclerus see: Speculum Sarisburianum
Philoclesius see: Answer to Dr.Ibbot's sermon
Philo Dear-heart see: Paraphrase on the fourteenth chapter of Isaiah
Philo-lapidarius see: Answer to the Pope's bull
Philomusus (S.) see: Mr.Law's Unlawfulness of the stage entertainment examin'd
Philonomus Anglicus see: Letter to the author of the vindication of the proceedings
Philopatris see: Child (*Sir* Josiah)
Philopatrius see: Reflexions upon Sach[everel]l's thanksgiving-day
Philopax see: Defoe (Daniel)
Philopolites see: Present state of the prison of Ludgate
Philosophical enquiry into the tenets 6197
Philosophical transactions of the Royal Society 8682
Phipps (Sir Constantine) 6596
Physician cure thy self [Sir R.L'Estrange] 1142
Pichatty de Croissainte 6523
Picton (Sir Thomas) 8160
Picttre of malice 4859
Picture of a high-flyer 3949
Picture of a low-flyer 3950
Picture of malice 4860-1
Picture of the Church militant [E.Stacy] 5242
Picture of the Observator 3951
Pierce (Thomas) 954,985-7,1000,1061,1156,1162, 1214,1258,1262-3,2130
Pierrepont (Henry) *Marquess of Dorchester* 250
Pigna (Giovanni Battista) 7
Piggott (John) 3435
Pilkington (Laetitia) 6936
Pillar and ground of truth [S.Patrick] 2621
Pille du Plessis (Robert de) 3278
Pindar (Martin) 622
Pindar (William) 1707
Pindarique ode, on their Royal Highnesses happy return 2131
Pinkney (Miles) 2732
Piscator (Johannes) 24
Pitcairne (Archibald) 4215,4621
Pitt (Moses) 3436
Pitt (Robert) 4337
Pitt (William) *Earl of Chatham* 7140,7415,7452, 7463,7493,7496,7672-3,8212
Pitt (William) *the Younger* 7840,7952,7974,7975, 7978,7988,8077,8081,8083,8096
Pittis (Thomas) 2132
Pittis (William) 3690-2,3854,4090-2,4447,4862, 5194-5,5481,5715,5983
Pitts (John) 4448
Pitts (Joseph) 4449-50,4592
Pius IV, *Pope* 2555
Place (Conyers) 4863,5196
Plain account of genuine Christianity 7446
Plain account of the cause of earthquakes 7379
Plain account of the persecution 2768
Plain and earnest address to Britons 7941
Plain and familiar discourse by way of dialogue [S.Freeman] 2586
Plain and familiar discourse concerning govern-ment 2769
Plain answer to a popish-priest [A.Seller] 2948
Plain answer to Dr.Middleton's Letter 6977
Plain, authentick and faithful narrative of the several passages of the Young Chevalier [R.Forbes] 7286
Plain case as it now stands 3045
Plain-dealing: in answer to Plain-English [J.Sharpe] 3962
Plain English, with remarks 5482
Plain facts: in five letters 8076
Plain instructions for the young and ignorant [E.Synge] 6671
Plain man's guide to the true Church 4451
Plain reasoner 7120
Plain reasons for being a Christian [S.Chandler] 6770
Plain representation of transubstantiation [H.Pendlebury] 2626
Plain state of the case of her Grace the Duchess of Kingston 7685
Plaine English [E.Bowles] 444,449
Plaintiff's charge disprov'd [T.Deacon] 6376
Plan for establishing and disciplining a national militia [S.Martin] 7119
Plausible arguments of a Romish priest from antiquity, answered [T.Comber] 2576,6856
Plausible arguments of a Romish priest from Scripture answered [T.Comber] 6857
Plaxton (William) 5483
Player (Sir Thomas) 1611
Play-house scuffle 4864
Plea for limited monarchy [Sir R.L'Estrange] 1143
Plea for non-subscribers [E.Gee] 878
Plea for toleration 5484
Plea of publick good 4216
Plea of the petitioners stated and vindicated [J.Firebrace] 7611
Plea to the Duke's answers 1836
Pleasant conference upon the Observator 2133
Pleydell (Josias) 2134
Plinius Caecilius Secundus (Caius) 944,3995, 5258
Plomer (R.H.) 7551,7565
Plot discover'd 5197
Plotters; a satire 6572
Plotting cards reviv'd 1990
Ploughing of corn-land 8482
Plowden (Francis) 7799,7813
Plowshare (John) see: Farmer's letter to the True Briton
Plunder and bribery further discover'd 5485
Plunket (Oliver) 1991,2027,2038
Pocklington (John) 168
Poem in memory of Robert Nelson 5984
Poem, occasion'd by the death of her late Majesty 3381
Poem occasioned by the death of her Majesty 3382
Poem occasion'd by the happy discovery 3437
Poem occasioned by the present war with Spain 6953
Poem upon the death of the late usurper [Dryden] 2583
Poems on several occasions 7269

Poetical entertainer [E.Ward] 5552-4
Poetical essay devoted to the glorious memory of our late Queen 3383
Poetick epistle address'd to Sir George Vandeput 7254
Pointer (John) 5716,7304
Pole (Reginald) 2375
Polhill (David) 4852
Polignac (Diane de) 8039
Political aphorisms 3011
Political catechism [H.Parker] 542,4854
Political conference between Aulicus 2931
Political considerations [Sir J.Marriott] 7458
Political dialogues between the celebrated statues 6879
Political essays on popular subjects 8101
Political progress of Britain [J.T.Callender] 7932
Political register 8671
Political state of Great Britain 8672
Polk (Leonidas) 8573
Poll of the livery-men of the city of London 4817
Pollexfen (John) 3442,3470
Polybius 8179
Polydorus (Joannes Gulielmus) 8268
Pomfret (John) 3693,4550
Pompey the great [P.Corneille] 1273
Pont (Robert) 33
Poole (Matthew) 988
Poor furbelow'd ladies lamentation 3952
Poor-Law Act. Public meeting at Bradford 8565
Poor man's petition to the Lords 3273
Poor Robin's answer to Mr.Thomas Danson 1550
Pope (Alexander) 5717,5870,5940,6147,6194, 6311,6686,6693,6817,6819,6848-9,6871, 6885,6895,6911,6917,6988,7025-6,7033, 7061,7196
Pope (Simeon) 8134
Pope (Walter) 1355,1708
Popery not founded on scripture [T.Tenison] 2813
Popery: or, the principles & positions approved by the Church of Rome [T.Barlow] 1620
Popes brief 568
Popes, cardinals and fathers of the Church 8461
Popes letter, to Maddam Cellier 1837
Pope's supremacy asserted [J.Gother] 2728
Popham (Sir Home) 8171
Popish doctrine of transubstantiation 2633
Popish plot more fully discovered 1709
Popish plot, taken out of several depositions 1838
Popish pretenders to the forfeited estates 3774
Popish treatises not to be rely'd on 2770
Popple (Sir William) 2771-2
Porcupine (Peter) see: Cobbett (William)
Pordage (Samuel) 2046
Porteus (Beilby) 7520,7639,7715,7724,7756, 7837,7897,8182
Portuguese arms justified 3953
Positions concerning the differences between the true English liturgy [E.Stephens] 3390
Post-angel 8673
Post boy 8674
Postlethwait (John) 5663
Postscript for postscript 5198
Postscript to Mr.Higgins's sermon [C.Leslie] 4317
Pott (Joseph Holden) 8102-3,8172,8200,8208, 8269,8274,8302-3
Pott (Percivall) 7762
Potter (Edward) 5871
Potter (John) 6687
Potts (Sir Algernon) 5084
Poulett (John) *Earl* 6954
Poulter (Edmund) 8135
Povey (Charles) 5872,5985
Povey (Josiah) 3530
Povey (Thomas) 543
Power and prerogative of the inexpressible 4093
Power and privilege of juries 1992
Power of the lower house of Convocation to adjourn it self [F.Atterbury] 3640,3667
Practical scheme 6074
Praetorius (Johann) 1356
Praise out of the mouth of babes 4452
Prance (Miles) 1710-1,1960
Prat (Daniel) 6421
Pratt (Benjamin) 4265
Pratt (Charles) *Earl Camden* 7566
Pratt (Samuel Jackson) 7751
Prattenberg (Franz) 6978
Prayers for the distressed estate of Charles, King of Sweden 5718
Prayers to be used in all... churches, and chapels see: Church of England. Special prayers
Precious morsels [W.Belcher] 8004
Predictions for the year 1708 [J.Swift] 4469
Predictions for the year, 1712 [I.Bickerstaff, pseud.] 5325
Preface to the B[isho]p of S[a]r[u]m's introduction [J.Swift] 5752
Prefatory discourse to an examination of a late book [W.Binckes] 3716
Pregon sonoro 4094
Prelude to the tryal of skill 4865
Preparative for the reception of truth [E.Stephens] 3629
Prerogative of man 683
Presbyter see: Edwards (Edward)
Presbyterian inquisition [A.Monro] 3141
Presbyterian prejudice display'd [Z.Grey] 6555,6591
Presbyterian sham [Sir R.L'Estrange] 1808
Presbyterians loyalty 1839
Presbyterians not guilty of the unjust charge [C.Burgess] 4679,4741
Presbyters not always an authoritative part of provincial synods [J.Lewis] 4813
Presbytery display'd [J.Maxwell] 1261
Present alteration in religion 2135
Present condition of the English navy 3775
Present conjuncture 2932
Present constitution, and the protestant succession vindicated [Sir J.Willes] 5925
Present disposition of England 3694
Present interest of England [J.Nalson] 2222
Present ministry justify'd 5873
Present policies of France 2933
Present separation self-condemned [W.Jane] 1577
Present state of British influence 7027
Present state of Christendome 1551
Present state of Convocation [W.Kennet] 3754
Present state of England 3320
Present state of Europe 8675
Present state of Jacobitism in England. A second part [T.Wagstaffe] 3797
Present state of Mr.Greenshields case 5199
Present state of physick 3695
Present state of Quakerism in England [C.Leslie] 3677
Present state of religion in Ireland 5486
Present state of the British sugar colonies consider'd 6781
Present state of the controversie [W.Clagett] 2573
Present state of the national debt 6955
Present state of the prison of Ludgate 5487
Present state of wit [J.Gay] 5101
Preservative against apostacy 3046
Preservative against presbytery [J.Skinner] 7234
Preservative against the Bishop of Bangor's sermon 6198
Press restrain'd: a poem 5488
Preston (John) 140-1
Pretences of the French invasion examined [W.Lloyd] 3209
Pretended independence of the lower-house upon the upper [E.Gibson] 3820
Pretended reformers [A.Varillas] 6246
(Pretended) visitor visited 3049
Pretender see: James Francis Edward
Pretender an impostor 5200
Pretyman (George) see: Tomline (George Pretyman)
Previous question to the several questions about valid and invalid baptism [T. Emlyn] 5387
Price (John) *Citizen of London* 738
Price (John) *D.D.* 1264
Price (Richard) 7502,7620,7782,7857,7926
Price (Robert) 4453,6830
Price of the abdication 3274
Prichard (Sir William) 2096
Pride (Thomas) 1062
Prideaux (Humphrey) 3047,3147,4338,7224
Priestcraft distinguish'd from Christianity [J.Dennis] 5952
Priestcraft in perfection [A.Collins] 4661, 4708-10, 4800,4894-6,5006
Priestley (Joseph) 7539,7640,7763,7814,7852, 7857-8,7877,7898,7918-20,7926,8063
Primitive Christianity vindicated [J.Knight] 5434
Primitive fathers no protestants [J.Gother] 2595
Primitive heresie revived [C.Leslie] 3520, 3540
Primitive rule of reformation 2773
Prince (John) 1434
Prince Eugene not the man 5489
Prince of O's declaration, p.l.col.2 3471
Princely pellican 849
Principle of the protestant reformation explain'd 3954,4087
Principles and practices of the present sett 5719
Principles of an occasional conformist [M.Lowman] 6313
Principles of government [Sir W.Jones] 7758
Principles of the dissenters [C.Leslie] 4070
Pringle (Sir John) 7655,7674-5
Prior (Matthew) 2634,3611,5094,5350,5362,6199, 7062
Prior (Thomas) 6752,7160
Prisons open'd [S.Wesley] 6729
Private prayer to be used in difficult times [S.Patrick] 2622
Private sentiments of a member 5986
Priviledge of our saints [S.Butler] 1891
Priviledges and practice of parliaments 251
Priviledges of the citizens of London 2136
Privileges and practice of parliaments 1840
Privileges of Parliament [W.Prynne] 1066
Pro populo adversus tyrannos 2934
Proast (Jonas) 3048
Probable expedient for present and future publique settlement [W.Prynne] 990
Probus Britanicus see: Johnson (Samuel) *LL.D.*
Proceedings against Mr.J.Reading 1712
Proceedings against Sir Thomas Armstrong 2313
Proceedings at the Guild-hall 1819
Proceedings at the sessions house 1993
Proceedings at the sessions of the peace 2137
Proceedings in the late treaty of peace 544
Proceedings in the present Convocation 4217
Proceedings of the Common-hall of London 1971
Proceedings of the parliament of Paris 2758
Proceedings of the present Parliament 2935
Procession [Sir R.Steele] 3389
Proclamation of his Majesty the King of Spain 979
Prodigal son 8423
Progress of dulness [W.Bond] 6693
Progress of love [G.Lyttelton] 6817
Progress of popery in the British dominions and elsewhere [M.Wylie] 8576
Project for establishing the general peace 5490
Project for the more effectual compleating the new reformation [W.Clearbrook] 5616
Prolegomena ad Novi Testamenti Graeci editionem [J.J.Wetstein] 6765
Prolocutor's answer to a letter from a member [G.Stanhope] 6343
Propagation of the Gospel in the East [W.Boehm] 4516
Proper project for Scotland [A.Shields] 3564
Proper reply to a late infamous and scurrilous libel 7063
Prophecie of a Turk 2635
Prophetia de die novissimo [Lady E.Douglas] 589
Proposal for carrying on the war 5201
Proposal for the advancement of trade [R.Murray] 1503
Proposal for the better supplying of churches [G.Berkeley] 6625
Proposal humbly offered for the laying a tax 4866
Proposal to the Governor and Company 5491
Proposals for a national bank 3472
Proposals for establishing a charitable fund 4218
Proposals for establishing in the Metropolis 8275
Proposals for imploying the poor [Defoe] 5638
Proposals for paying the debts of the nation 6299
Proposals for printing a very curious discourse [J.Arbuthnot] 5312
Proposals for raising a million of money 3321
Proposals for supplying the loss of soldiers 4867
Proposals tender'd to the consideration of both Houses [E.Stillingfleet] 2966
Proposed system of trade with Ireland explained 7815
Propositions agreed upon at a court of common councell 400
Propositions of their excellencies the ambassadours [W.Boreel] 581
Prosopopeia protreptica 1469
Prospect of reform in Europe [E.Everett] 8507
Prosser (Jacob 5720
Protestant admirer 1994
Protestant and popish way of interpreting scripture [R.Grove] 2885
Protestant Association 7725,7734
Protestant Chevalier a papist 5721
Protestant doctrine 8424
Protestant loyalty fairly drawn 1995
Protestant mask taken off [T.Comber] 3243
Protestant monument 5695
Protestant of the Church of England, no Donatist [W.Sherlock] 2536
Protestant petition and addresse 1996
Protestant resolution of faith [W.Sherlock] 2235,2537
Protestants plea for a Socinian [A.Woodhead] 2551,2661
Protestant's reasons why he cannot turn papist 6866
Proteus ecclesiasticus 3148
Prynne (William) 136,155,176,445,545-6,623-4, 654,671,684-5,739,790-1,838,861-4,938, 968-970,989-991,994,1005,1007,1063-71,1075, 1112,1147,1163-8,1215,1997,2231,3093,4868
Psalmanazar (George) 4339
Pseudarchomastix 5202,5700
Publick intelligencer 8676-7
Publick services in, or relating to the Royal Navy 3612
Publick spirit of the Tories 5874
Publick spirit of the Whigs [J.Swift] 5825, 5902-3
Publisher: containing miscellanies 8678
Puckle (James) 3473,3613
Pulpit [periodical] 8679
Pulpit-conceptions, popular deceptions [L.Womock] 1251
Pulpit guarded with XX arguments [T.Hall] 891
Pulpit-popery, true popery [J.Williams] 2827
Pulpit-sayings [J.Gother] 2729,2827
Pulpit-war: or, Dr.S[achevere]ll, the High-Church trumpet [E.Ward] 4969
Pulteney (William) *Earl of Bath* 6554,6634,6688, 6767,6779,6787,6792,6820,6835,7028,7037, 7049,7057,7064
Pulton (Andrew) 2663-4,2750,2774
Punch turn'd critick 5492
Punchanello, *Seignioro* see: Punch turn'd critick
Pun-sibi (Tom) see: Sheridan (Thomas)
Purcell (Henry) 3005
Purkis (William) 7838
Pusey (Edward Bouverie) 8531
Pury Thomas) 252
Pye (John) 1387
Pym (John) 240,253,421,473,515,536,538,564,619, 7029
Pym (Robert) 8543

Quaerees on the proposalls 1072
Quaesumus te, &c. 1169
Quaker catechism [F.Bugg] 4018
Quaker disarmed [T.Smith] 1080
Quakers a dividend people distinguished [W.Rogers] 4456
Quakers abhorrence and detestation 5203
Quakers shaken [J.Gilpin] 949
Quarles (Francis) 625-6
Queen an empress 4219
Querela temporum [C.Leslie] 3367
Queres and coniectures 547
Queries offered by T.W... reprinted and answered [W.Clagett] 2702
Queries recommended to the authors of the late Discourse [B.Hoadly] 5671
Queries relating to live stock 8030
Queries to the new hereditary right-men [Defoe] 4733
Queries upon queries [J.Dobson] 1258
Quesne (Abraham de) see: Du Quesne (A.)
Question about eating blood [J.Averill] 6799
Questions concerning the proper and peculiar Christian worship [E.Stephens] 3975
Questions resolved, and propositions 415
Quevedo y Villegas (Francisco Gomez de) 4869, 7059
Quid (Oliver) see: Letter of advice, addressed to all merchants
Quinault (Philippe) 7701,7726
Quincy (John) 6464
Quinto Fabio; a serious opera 7735

R.(A.) 5204
R.(B.) 5875
R.(G.) 5493
R.(J.) 1498,1507,2775,2936
R.(M.) 1841
R.(S.) 740
R.(T.) 416,5722
R.(W.) see: Whately (Robert)
Rabaut St.Etienne (Jean Paul) 7921
Radcliffe (Alexander) 1998
Radcliffe (James) *Earl of Derwentwater* 6027, 6047,6075
Radcliffe (John) 4071,5983
Raie (C.) 971
Raikes (Henry) 8566
Rainbow (Edward) 158
Rake of taste [J.Dorman] 6871
Raleigh (Walter) *Dean of Wells* 6422
Raleigh (Sir Walter) 80,126,3614,3696
Ralph (James) 6721
Ram (Robert) 2314
Ramsay (Allan) 6473-5
Ramsay (William) 1713,1842
Ramsey (David) 8016
Randolph (Bernard) 2523,2636
Randolph (Francis) 8120

Randolph (John) 7783
Randolph (Thomas) 7318,7604,7641
Rapin (Renè) 1390,5723
Rates of marchandizes 48
Rathbone (William) 8173
Ratio constitutae nuper reipublicae Angliae 955
Rational account given by a young gentleman [J.Corker] 1752
Rattray (Thomas) 7089
Raue (Christian) see: Ravius (Christian)
Ravenscroft (Edward) 2637
Ravillac redivivus [G.Hickes] 1572
Ravius (Christian) 839
Rawlinson (Richard) 6200
Rawson (Joseph) 3384,5291,5494
Ray (Charles) 7161
Raynsford (John) 417
Read (Joseph) 2044
Reading (John) 1712
Real character and tendency of the proposed reform 8515
Real fool 8425
Reapers: or the Englishman 7588
Reason and Gospel against matters of fact 5205
Reasonable defence of The seasonable discourse [W.Lloyd] 1431
Reasonableness of the augmentation of poor vicarages [T.Breck] 3718
Reasonableness of the Church of Englands test 2776
Reasons against fighting [Defoe] 5375
Reasons against national despondency 8059
Reasons against receiving the Pretender 4870
Reasons against restraining the press [M.Tindal] 3984
Reasons against the succession of the House of Hanover [Defoe] 5639
Reasons for a peace [Defoe] 5056
Reasons for a total change 4871
Reasons for abrogating the test [S.Parker] 2760
Reasons for addressing his Majesty [J.Toland] 3711,3792
Reasons for non-conformity examined and refuted 1615
Reasons for reform 8220
Reasons for restoring some prayers [J.Collier] 6125,6276,6327
Reasons for restoring the Whigs [W.Oldisworth] 5185
Reasons for the clergy's being employ'd 5724
Reasons for the repeal of the tests 2638
Reasons humbly offered for the liberty of unlicens'd printing [C.Blount] 3235
Reasons most humbly offer'd to the honble House of Commons [J.Toland] 6480
Reasons of Mr.Bays changing his religion [T.Brown] 2683
Reasons of Mr.Joseph Hains the player's conversion [T.Brown] 2994
Reasons of the absenting clergy [J.Swinfen] 4930
Reasons of the present judgment of the University of Oxford [R.Sanderson] 792, 1174-5
Reasons offer'd against the continuance 4340
Reasons pro and con 5495
Reasons, proving the absolute necessity 7162
Reasons to prove the complying clergy 4872
Reasons which compelled the States of Bohemia 81
Reasons why a certain great g[enera]l 4873
Reasons why a party among us [Defoe] 5057
Reasons why a protestant should not turn papist [R.Boyle] 2564
Reasons why all good Christians should observe the holy fast [P.Gunning] 1928
Reasons why the Duke of Marlborough cannot lay down his commands 4881
Reasons why this Kingdome ought to adhere to the Parliament 418
Reasons why this nation ought to put a speedy end to this expensive war [Defoe] 5058-9,5151
Rebellion sainted 4874
Rebells catechism [P.Heylyn] 522
Rebuffer rebuffed [W.A.Drummond] 7578
Recensio brevis mutilationum [J.Gronovius] 5660
Reception of the Palatines vindicated 5206
Reduced tradesman 8368
Reed (Benjamin) 5876
Reed (John) 2639
Rees (Abraham) 7899
Reeve (Thomas) 6597
Reeves (John) 8121
Reeves (William) 5496,5725,5877
Reflection, in vindication of one archdeacon 3049
Reflections on a late speech by the Lord Haversham 3955
Reflections on a pamphlet, stiled A just and modest vindication [E.Bohun] 2173
Reflections on a paper lately printed 5726
Reflections on Dr.Sacheverell's answer 4875
Reflections on Dr.Swift's Letter to the Earl of Oxford [J.Oldmixon] 5476
Reflections on Mr.Clark's Second defence of his letter to Mr.Dodwell [A.Collins] 4273,4393
Reflections on the conduct of Mr.Whiston [R.Smalbroke] 5226,5286
Reflections on the historical part of Church-government [G.Smalridge] 2656
Reflections on the petition & apology 3050
Reflections on the principal characters 6703
Reflections on the propriety of an immediate conclusion of peace [N.Vansittart] 7970
Reflections on the relation of the English Reformation [G.Burnet] 2690
Reflections upon a form of prayer 3051
Reflections upon a late book entituled, The case of allegiance consider'd [T.Long] 2912
Reflections upon a Letter concerning enthusiasm [E.Fowler] 4552
Reflections upon George Keith's late advertisement [J.Penington] 3433
Reflections upon our late and present proceedings 2937
Reflections upon some passages in Mr.Le Clerc's life 5207
Reflections upon the answer to the Papist misrepresented [J.Gother] 2506
Reflections upon the conduct of the King 2138
Reflections upon the Examiner's scandalous peace 5208
Reflections upon the humour of the British nation 5727
Reflections upon the new test 2640
Reflections upon the use of the eloquence of these times [R.Rapin] 1390
Reflections upon two scurrilous libels 2139
Reflections upon the occurrences of the last year [E.Stephens] 2963
Reflector's defence of his letter [C.Ellis] 2716
Reflexions on a pamphlet [H.Dodwell] 3499
Reflexions on the sources of incredulity with regard to religion [D.Forbes] 7285
Reflexions sur l'etat 4609
Reflexions upon a late paper, entitl'd An expedient propos'd [E.Gibson] 3746
Reflexions upon a pamphlet [R.Willis] 3453
Reflexions upon Sach[evere]l's thanksgiving-day 5728
Reform or ruin [J.Bowdler] 8044
Reformation of church-government in Scotland [A.Henderson] 611
Reformation of manners, a satyr [Defoe] 3730
Reformation of the Church of England justified [W.Saywell] 2789-90
Reformation of the discipline and service of the Church 465
Reformed Catholique [Sir R.L'Estrange] 1679
Refuge of an honest Briton 8040
Refutation of the doctrine of passive obedience 4849
Regal supremacy in ecclesiastical affairs 3697
Regall tyrannie discovered [J.Lilburne] 783
Reglement provisionel du commerce 5729
Regular clergy's sole right to administer Christian baptism asserted [J.Sharpe] 5508
Rehearsal: or, A brief recapitulation 6201
Rehearsal reviv'd 8680
Reid (William Hamilton) 8104
Rejection and restoration of the Jews 7334
Rejoynder to the reply concerning the peerage 1714
Relaçao da vitoria 1216
Relation de la bataille de Bleinheim 3956
Relation of the great success the King of Portugal's army had [M.Sanches] 1265
Relation of the rejoycings made in Rome 2938
Relation succinte de l'estat ou sont maintenant les eglises reformées de France 1296
Relations and observations, historicall and politick [C.Walker] 844
Religio laici 2775
Religion and loyalty supporting each other [T.Comber] 2188
Religion in danger 8017
Religion of the cross 8462
Religious demurrer [N.Ward] 870
Religious Tract and Book Society for Ireland 8341
Remarkes upon a pamphlet [G.Savile] 2648
Remarks from the country [H.Maurice] 3030
Remarks on a false, scandalous, and seditious libel 5209
Remarks on a Letter to Sir John Barnard 7163
Remarks on a pamphlet by Thomas Kipling 8136
Remarks on a printed paper lately handed about [G.Sharp] 7492
Remarks on a sermon preached by T.Le Mesurier 8276
Remarks on An introduction to the history 7621
Remarks on Dr.Middleton's examination of the Lord Bishop of London's Discourses [L.Jackson] 7290
Remarks on Mr.Higden's utopian constitution [H.Gandy] 4764
Remarks on Mr.Steele's Crisis 5875
Remarks on parliamentary reform 8332
Remarks on some extracts 5497
Remarks on some late sermons [C.Leslie] 3368
Remarks on the answer of the Reverend Mr. M[ada]n 7521
Remarks on the Barrier-treaty vindicated 5722
Remarks on the growth and progress of non-conformity [Sir R.L'Estrange] 2102
Remarks on the manufacturing of maple sugar 7922
Remarks on the occurrences of the years 1720 and 1721 6821
Remarks on the people and government 7200
Remarks on the preliminary articles offer'd by the French King [A.Mainwaring] 5164, 5217
Remarks on the present condition of the Navy 3615
Remarks on the proceedings of the Commissioners ...for establishing of a land-bank [J.Asgill] 3399
Remarks on the Reverend Dr.Snape's Second letter 6202
Remarks on the Rev.Dr.Vincent's defence 8137
Remarks on the Right Reverend Lord Bishop of Clogher's Vindication 7408
Remarks on the State anatomy 6203
Remarks on the trial of John-Peter Zenger 6912
Remarks on XII historical designs of Raphael [J.Dalton] 7314
Remarks on two late sermons 5210
Remarks on two pamphlets lately published against Dr.Middleton's Introductory discourse [C.Middleton] 7227
Remarks, paragraph by paragraph, upon the proposals lately publish'd by Richard Bentley [C.Middleton] 6525
Remarks upon a book, entituled, The present state of the sugar colonies consider'd [F.Hall] 6781
Remarks upon a late Discourse [R.Bentley] 5590,5664,7042
Remarks upon a late scurrilous pamphlet 3776
Remarks upon a letter (just made publick) 7164
Remarks upon a pamphlet intitul'd, Observations upon the state of the nation [G.Sewell] 5740
Remarks upon an advertisement 3438
Remarks upon Dr.Campbell's sermon [W.A. Drummond] 7596
Remarks upon Dr.Clark's Scripture-doctrine of the Trinity [F.Gastrell] 5835
Remarks upon Dr.Sherlock's book [S.Johnson] 2899,3018-9
Remarks upon Fuller's full demonstration 3742
Remarks upon my Lord N[otting]ham's State of the nation [G.Sewell] 5740
Remarks upon remarks 5211
Remarks upon the Bank of England [J.Broughton] 4016
Remarks upon the critical principles [R.Laurence] 8322
Remarks upon the Letter to a lord 4454
Remarks upon the life of...Dr.John Tillotson [G.Smith] 7355
Remarks upon the Lord Bishop of Bangor's treatment of the clergy [T.Sherlock] 6215
Remarks upon the Navy 3616
Remarks upon the publick advertisments 6322
Remarks upon the second part of Principles political and religious [W.A.Drummond] 7531
Remarques historiques et anecdotes sur le chateau de la Bastille [J.M.Brossays du Perray] 7646
Remedy worse than the disease [Defoe] 5824
Remembrancer [C.D'Anvers] 6741
Remonstrance, addressed to H.Brougham [C.J.Blomfield] 8345
Remonstrance & address of the armies 1170
Remonstrance and protestation of all the good protestants 2939
Remonstrance and protestation, of the gentry [of Bucks] 419
Remonstrance du clergé 1287
Remonstrance from some country Whigs [Defoe] 5950
Remonstrance of the state of the Kingdom 232
Remonstrance to vindicate his excellence Robert Earle of Essex 548
Rennell (Thomas) 8041
Renuntiation and declaration of the ministers 1217
Replique d'un membre du Parlement 7121
Reply to a most untrue relation [R.Kilvert] 242
Reply to a pamphlet called The mischief of separation [W.Clagett] 1899
Reply to a pamphlet entituled, The L[or]d H[aversham]'s vindication of his speech 4168
Reply to A vindication of A discourse concerning the unreasonableness of a new separation [S.Grascombe] 3120
Reply to an Answer to the City minister's letter 2777
Reply to Dr.Middleton's Examination 7295
Reply to Francis de la Pilloniere 6204
Reply to Mr.Clark's Defence of his letter to Mr.Dodwell [A.Collins] 4274,4697
Reply to "Some strictures" of Samuel Lee [R.Laurence] 8330
Reply to the Anguis in herba 8152
Reply to the answer Doctor Welwood has made 3322
Reply to the answer made upon the three royall papers [J.Leyburn] 2514
Reply to the Answer of the Amicable accommodation [J.Gother] 2507
Reply to the answer of the man of no name [G.Care] 2365
Reply to the new test of the Church of England's loyalty 2641
Reply to the reasons of the Oxford-clergy [Sir R.L'Estrange] 2615
Reply to the subscribing ministers reasons 6423
Reply to the Vindication of the Reasons and defence [N.Spinckes] 6478
Reply to the Vindication of the Remarks upon Mr. Leslie's first dialogue [C.Leslie] 4428
Reply to two discourses [H.Aldrich] 2554
Report reported 6205
Representation examined [Defoe] 5060
Representation of matters of fact 5987
Representation of the impiety & immorality 3957
Representation, of the present state of religion 5030-2,5060,5256,5353,5532
Representation of the state of the Church 6323
Representation of the threatning dangers [R.Ferguson] 2876
Republican procession [E.Ward] 5916
Request to protestants, to produce plain scriptures 2524,2652-3
Request to Roman Catholicks [J.Gordon] 2590
Requete des bourgeois de la ville d'Anspach 8179
Resbury (Nathanael) 1999,2315,2940
Resigners vindicated [G.Sewell] 6328
Resistance and non-resistance stated 4876
Resolution of a case of conscience [S.Grascombe] 3121
Resolution of some cases of conscience [W.Sherlock] 2236
Resolution of the gentry and commonalty in the county of Nottingham [W.Johnson] 396
Resolution of this case of conscience [E.Fowler] 2195,2221
Resolution to act 8018
Respectful behaviour of the dissenters 5878
Respectful observations on a late print 5498
Restauranda: or the necessity of publick repairs [F.Philipps] 1244
Retz (Jean François Paul) 1073
Reverential love: or, God honour'd 4220
Review [Defoe] 4153,4206,4796,5099,8681
Review and Observator review'd 4221
Review of a late treatise, entituled An account of the conduct of the Dowager D. of M[Arlborough] 7030
Review of Dr.Sherlock's Case of allegiance 3149
Review of Mr.James Foster's account 7165
Review of the case of Judah and Ephraim [T.Emlyn] 4041,4135
Review of the case of the Marshal Belleisle 7122
Review of The case of the protestant dissenters [S.Horsley] 7892
Review of the controversy about the meaning of demoniacks [G.Sharpe] 6926,6934
Review of the excise-scheme 6836
Review of the principal charges against Warren Hastings [J.Logan] 7869
Review of the report of the secret committee 5988
Review of the state of the British nation 8681
Review of the whole political conduct of a late eminent patriot 7064
Revision revised 2316
Revolter. A trage-comedy 2642
Rex et pontifex [R.Dodsley] 7110
Rey (Claudius) 6424
Reyner (Samuel) 1843
Reyner (William) 627
Reynolds (Edward) 169,194,420,888,1171
Reynolds (George) 7031
Reynolds (John) 1590
Reynolds (Richard) 6704
Reynor (William) see: Reyner (William)
Rhodes (Ebenezer) 8516
Rich (Henry) *Earl of Holland* 421,549,868
Rich (Robert) *Earl of Warwick* 628
Rich (S.) 2441
Richards (Jacob) 2643
Richards (Thomas) 4610
Richardson (F.) 7686
Richardson (William) 5036,5212-3,5384,5499,5562, 5730
Richmond (Henry) 4877
Rickman (Thomas Clio) 8066
Ridley (Alexander) 7096

Ridley (Glocester) 7447
Ridley (Sir Matthew White) 7969
Ridley (Nicholas) 2778-80
Ridpath (George) 3474,4611,8601,8622
Rigby (Edward) 8560
Right honourable annuitant vindicated 7448
Right of monarchy asserted 5731
Right of private judgment asserted 8463
Right of the Archbishop to continue or prorogue [E.Gibson] 3644,3667
Rightful monarchy 6573
Rights and interests of the two British monarchies [J.Hodges] 3827
Rights and liberties of subjects vindicated 6822
Rights of man 7965
Rights of the Christian Church asserted [M.Tindal] 4209,4318,4398,4416,4430, 4486,4495,4528,4558,4561,4593,4638, 5144
Rights of the Church, attested 8249
Rights of the Church of England asserted [H.Sacheverell] 4097
Rights of the City farther unfolded 2140
Rights of the scholars of Trinity-College asserted 4834
Rigshaw (Cincinnatus) 8105
Rise and fall or degeneracy 1844
Rival duchess 4455
Rivetus (Andreas) see: Marvell (Andrew)
Rix (John) 1074
Ro. (Sma.) see: Turnor (Thomas)
Roasting of a parson 4878
Robartes (Foulke) 66,199
Roberson (Hammond) 8567
Robert against Ferguson 3958
Robert Shaw 8464
Roberts (Anne) 6269,6324
Roberts (Elizabeth) 4797
Roberts (Richard) 2442
Roberts (William) 4879,5500,6753
Robertson (Abram) 7764
Robertson (Robert) 6823
Robertson (William) 5001,5732
Robins, *Messrs.* 8270
Robinson (Benjamin) 4800
Robinson (Christopher) 6932
Robinson (Henry) 684-5,905,919
Robinson (John) *Bishop of London* 4645, 5214-5,5724,5868,5879,6377
Robinson (John) *Congregationalist* 2224
Robinson (Matthew) *Baron Rokeby* 7656,7687, 7702
Robinson (Nicholas) 6648,7622
Robinson (Ralph) 109
Robinson (Robert) *Baptist Minister* 7898-9, 7903
Robinson (Robert) *Recorder of Scarborough* 6598
Rod for the Eaton schoolmaster's back 6206-7
Rod for Tunbridge beaus 3698
Roderick (Richard) 2232,4341
Rodney (George Brydges) *Baron* 7800
Rogers (Francis) 5216
Rogers (George) 7942
Rogers (John) *Canon of Wells* 6724
Rogers (John) *Fifth Monarchy Man* 1064,1075
Rogers (Nehemiah) 145
Rogers (William) 4456
Rogerson (Thomas) 6425
R[ogue]'s on both sides [Defoe] 5061-2
Rolegravius (Johannes) 1435
Rolt (Richard) 7642
Rolte (John) 72,174
Romae ruina finalis 957
Roman Catholic Church 67
Roman wonder 1845
Romes master-peece [W.Prynne] 546
Rome's overthrow 1846
Ronquillo (Pedro) 2000
Rooke (Sir George) 3942,4320
Roper (Abel) 5117,5217,6675,8674
Roper (Joseph) 6649
Roquette (Henri Emmanuel de) 3843
Roscommon (Wentworth Dillon) *Earl of* see: Dillon (Wentworth)
Rose (Alexander) 5400
Rose (George) 7815
Rose (William) 3945
Rosemary & Bayes [H.Stubbe] 1392
Rosenthal (Christian Friedrich) 3275
Rosewell (H.) 5218
Ross (Alexander) 153,686
Ross (John) 2001
Rossi (Giovanni Bernardo de) 7688
Rotheram (John) 7503,7509,7522,7540-1
Rough draught of a new model at sea [G.Savile] 3325
Rouquette (Henri Emmanuel de) see: Roquette (Henri Emmanuel de)
Rous (Francis) 865,870
Rowe (Nicholas) 4381,4612,5736
Royal African Company 1312
Royal apology [W.Assheton] 2261,2342
Royal censure of partial conformity 3915
Royal College of Physicians 3439,3475,3945
Royal family described 3744
Royal family of the Stuart's vindicated 5219
Royal favourite clear'd [J.Garbrand] 2085
Royal guard [R.Hooke] 2296
Royal Institution of Great Britain 8106
Royal Irish Institution for Promoting the Fine Arts in Ireland 8259
Royal religion [Defoe] 3890
Royal Society of London 1358,4644,7788,7790, 8682
Royall legacies of Charles the first 850
Royse (George) 2941,3150,
Rr 866
R----'s on both sides [Defoe] 5061-2
Rudder (Samuel) 7623
Rufinus [W.King] 5432
Rule (Gilbert) 6373
Rule for finding Easter [R.Watts] 5274,5555
Rule for finding Easter explain'd 4613
Rule of faith 8465
Rules and articles for the better government of his Majesties land-forces 2443
Rules and articles for the better government of our horse and foot-guards 6553
Rules of government 4880
Rulhière (Claude Carloman de) 8060
Rupert to Maria [R.Morris] 7229
Rushworth (John) 8668
Russel (David) 5501
Russell (Edward) *Earl of Oxford* 3213
Russell (Francis) *Duke of Bedford* 8131-2
Russell (John) *of Chingford* 1172
Russell (John) *Rector of Postwick* 6076
Russell (Richard) 6077
Russell (William) *Lord* 2211-2,2245,2249, 2254,2953,5741
Rust (George) 1218
Rutherford (Andrew) *Earl of Teviot* 1270,1874
Rutherford (Samuel) 629,687
Rutherforth (Thomas) 7166,7201
Ruthven (Patrick) *Earl of Forth* 550
Rutter (John) 6208
Ryan (James) 8277
Rycaut (Sir Paul) 3617
Rye (George) 5880
Rymer (Thomas) 5881

S.(C.) *Master* see: M.(T.)
S.(E.) 5502
S.(E.) see: Stephens (Edward)
S.(F.) 3531
S.(G.) 840
S.(G.) see: Smith (George)
S.(H.) 4881
S.(J.) 2002,6325,7442
S.(J.) see: Sadler (John)
Sergeant (John)
Streater (John)
S.(M.) 4614
S.(R.) 2781
S.(R.) see: Drummond (William Abernethy)
S.(Sir R.) see: Sibbald (Sir Robert)
S.(R.L.) see: L'Estrange (Sir Roger)
S.(S.) 2444
S.(S.) see: Shaw (Samuel)
S.(T.) 73,1062,1715,2141
S.(T.) see: Smith (Thomas)
S.(T.P.A.P.O.A.B.I.T.C.O.) see: Sykes (Arthur Ashley)
S.(W.) 1372,4089
S.(W.) see: Sancroft (William)
Shippen (William)
Sa (Pantaleao) 920,934
Sabran (Lewis) 2644,2782-5
Sacerdotal powers [R.Laurence] 5143
Sacheverell (Henry)
Answer...to the articles 4865,4875,4882
Character of a Low-Church-man 3777,4222, 5882
Christian triumph 5733-4
Collection of hymns 5038
Collections of passages 4883
Communication of sin 4615
Defence of her Majesty's title 4884
False notions of liberty 5735
Nature and mischief of prejudice 3959
Nature, guilt, and danger 4457
Nature, obligation, and measures 4885
New association 3778,4095
New association.Part II 3844,4096
Perils of false brethren 4510,4532,4576, 4591,4611,4616-7,4850,4944
Political union 3779
Prayers and meditations 4886
Prayers of thanksgiving 4887
Rights of the Church 4097
Sermon preach'd before the Sons of the clergy 5883
Sermon preach'd before the University 3780
Sermon preach'd January 31st 5989
Speech 4888-91
______
4545,4658,4665-6,4670,4682,4692,4702-6, 4716-7,4727-8,4763,4772-3,4784-7,4816, 4821,4840,4843,4859-61,4869,4878,4894-6, 4901,4906,4910,4913,4915,4932,4935,4937-8, 4945-6,4748,4953,4960,4965,,4969,4980, 4984,5012,5039,5106,5137-8,5155-7,5159 5186,5221,5231,5289,5501,5573,5650,5728, 5732,5777,6444
Sacheverell against Sacheverell 5220
Sackbut (Fustian) see: Thornton (Bonnell)
Sackville (Charles) *Earl of Dorset* 2959,3035, 5239
Sackville (Edward) *Earl of Dorset* 422
Sackville (Lionel Cranfield) *Duke of Dorset* 6859
Sacred miscellanies 5736
Sacro-sancta regum majestas [J.Maxwell] 620
Sad, and bloody fight at Westminster 841
Sadler (Anthony) 939
Sadler (John) 208
Sadler (Michael Thomas) 8289
Sage (John) 3052,5838
Sailors advocate 7703
Sailor's return 8382
St.Bartholomew's Hospital 4250,4337
Saint Evremond (Charles Marguetel de Saint-Denis) *Seigneur de* 2445
St.George, *Chevalier de* see: James Francis Edward, *the Old Pretender*
St.James's post 8683
St.John, *Family of* 5703
St.John (Henry) *Viscount Bolingbroke* 4892, 5319,5507,5817-8,6754,6779,6853,7049,7125, 7270,7335,7489
St.John (Pawlet) 4893,5221,5503
St.Leger (Sir John) 4894-6,4946
St.Leger (Sir William) 423
St.Lo (George) 3276,3323
St.Paul and her Majesty vindicated 4897
St.Paul, no mover of sedition [J.Haslewood] 4186
St Paul's opinion of Jesus Christ stated 7727
Saint Quentin, Assemblée de 3862
Saints congratulatory address 6326
Salgado (James) 2003
Salisbury quarrel ended 4898
Sallustius Crispus (Caius) 4458
Salt (Aylmer) 6209
Salt for the leach [C.Leslie] 5439
Saltmarsh (John) 741-2
Salt-water sweetned [R.Fitzgerald] 2192
Salus Britannica 2446
Salus populi, &c. or the case of King and people 2004
Salus populi solus rex 842
Salwey (Humphrey) 441
Sam.Ld.Bp.of Oxon, his celebrated reasons [J.Phillips] 2767
Samaritans 7839
Sambucus (Johannes) 9
Samuel, *Patriarch of Alexandria* 5990,6078
Sanches (Manuel) *Conde de Villa Flor* 1216,1265
Sancroft (William) 1173,1591,3053,3324,3337, 6110
Sanctotisius (Christophorus) 8
Sandars (John) 8586
Sanderson (Robert) 792,921,1174-5,1245,1357, 1373,2142,2852,6079
Sanderson (Sir William) 992-3
Sandys (Sir Edwin) 1415
Sanford (John) 54
Sannazaro (Jacopo) 6618
Sarah Hopkins 8466
Sardi (Alessandro) 1470
Sare (Richard) 4561
Sarmiento de Acuna (Diego) *Count Gondomar* 1096
Sarpi (Paolo) 200
Sarrazin (Jean) 8221
Satan disrob'd [C.Leslie] 3466,3521
Satire in the manner of Persius [J.Hervey] 6922
Satisfaction concerning mixt communions 551
Satyr against hypocrites [J.Phillips] 953, 1549
Saul, an oratorio [H.Newburgh] 6906
Saul and Samuel [C.Davenant] 3725
Saumaise (Claude de) 894
Saumarez (Richard) 8487
Saunders (Sir Edmund) 2447
Saunders (Richard) see: Franklin (Benjamin)
Savage (John) 3960
Savigny (J.) 8604
Savile (George) *Marquess of Halifax* 2005, 2558,2614,2623,2645-8,2786-8,3325,3380, 3385
Savile (Henry) 1612
Savile (Sir Henry) 98
Savoy, *Duke of* see: Victor Amadeus II
Saywell (William) 2006,2789-90
Scandal display'd 4459
Scandalum magnatum [E.Hickeringill] 2088
Scandrett (Stephen) 1374
Scarisbrike (Edward) 2525
Scattergood (Samuel) 1508
Schauffler (William Gottlieb) 8521
Schedule review'd [E.Gibson] 3747
Schefferus (Johannes) 8605
Schemers scrutiny 7167
Schism of the Church of England [J.Sergeant] 2789-90,2794
Schomberg (Armand Frederick) *Duc* 1940
School-boy 8483
Schultens (Albert) 6933,7032,7542
Schultens (Hendrik Albert) 7657
Schultens (Joannes Jacobus) 7032
Schuyl (Frans) 2649
Schweighaeuser (Johann) 7878
Scialitti (Moses) 1266
Scipio (Quintus Caecilius Metellus Pius) 7567
Sclater (Edward) 2007,2526,2587,2624
Sclater (William) 61-3
Scoresby (William) 8517
Scot (William) 6327,6354,6426
Scotch echo to the English legion 4342
Scotch medal decipher'd [Defoe] 5063
Scotch Presbyterian eloquence [G.Crockatt] 6373
Scotch souldiers speech 793,4770
Scotland. Commissioners 710,716,744-5,747-8, 763,794,801,843,1176
Scotland. Parliament 630,743-8,794,1219,1847, 3845-6,3961,4343
Scotland. Privy Council 552,1592
Scotland against popery 1949
Scotland pulling down the gates of Rome [W.Houschone] 2204
Scots army advanced into England 631
Scots Company trading to Africa and the Indies 3617-8
Scots nation and union vindicated [Defoe] 5825
Scott (James) *Duke of Monmouth* 1793-4
Scott (John) *D.D.* 1848,2233,2317,2448,2527-8, 2791,2942-3,3214,3277
Scott (John) *Earl of Eldon* 8079
Scott (John) *Vicar of Carisbrooke* 4460
Scott (John) *Vicar of North Ferriby* 8518
Scott (William) *Baron Stowell* 8138
Scribleriad. Being an epistle 7033
Scriptural catechism 1489
Scripture doctrine concerning predestination 6979
Scripture doctrine of the sacred and adorable Trinity [S.Walker] 6621
Scroggs (Sir William) 1716,1767,2024
Scudery (Madeleine de) 4461
Scum uppermost [G.Huddersford] 8128
Seabury (Samuel) 7816
Seaman's opinion of a standing army 3562
Sea-men undeceived [R.Badiley] 804
Search after claret [R.Ames] 3086
Seasonable address to both houses of Parliament [G.Savile] 2005
Seasonable address to the citizens 5222
Seasonable address to the Right Honourable, the Lord Mayor 1849
Seasonable advice to the citizens [R.Grove] 2399
Seasonable advice to the ministers of the Church of Great Britain [H.Compton] 4712
Seasonable and modest apology in behalf of the Reverend Dr.George Hickes [H.Bedford] 4660,5547
Seasonable alarm to the city 7480
Seasonable antidote against apostasy [J.Lindsay] 7407
Seasonable considerations 2944
Seasonable discourse shewing the necessity [W.Lloyd] 1409-12
Seasonable exhortation of sundry ministers [E.Reynolds] 1171
Seasonable expostulation with the disaffected clergy 5991
Seasonable memento both to king and people 1850,2529
Seasonable memorial in some historical notes [Sir R.L'Estrange] 1809
Seasonable question soberly proposed 1076
Seasonable recapitulation of enormous national crimes 7271
Seasonable review of Mr.Whiston's account [W.Berriman] 6362
Seasonable sermon preach'd 3010
Seasonable speech, made by a worthy member 1077,6080
Seasonable suggestion arising from the grateful reflexion [J.Humfrey] 5126
Seasonable vindication of the clergy [W.Assheton] 4495
Seasonable vindication of the truly Catholick doctrine [W.Atwood] 2167
Seasonable warneing to the poor 2143
Secker (Thomas) 6980-1,7065,7527,7568

Second address to the inhabitants of the two great cities [M.Tindal] 6763
Second and last collection of the dying speeches 2945
Second and third letter to the Whigs [H. Walpole] 7238
Second character of an informer 2144
Second collection of introductions, and letters in the London journal [J.Trenchard] 6535
Second collection of papers 2792
Second defence of the Church of England [E. Welchman] 3538
Second defence of The rights of the Christian Church [M.Tindal] 4474
Second defense of an argument [S.Clarke] 4697
Second dialogue between a new Catholick convert [R.Kidder] 2611
Second dialogue between the Pope and a phanatick [R.Ferguson] 1917
Second letter addressed to the delegates [G.I.Huntingford] 7876
Second letter concerning civil comprehension [C.Lawton] 4199
Second letter concerning toleration [J.Locke] 3027
Second letter from a country Whig 5992
Second letter from Tom Boggy [W.King] 4796
Second letter from Wiltshire to the Monitor 7418
Second letter to a friend, concerning the French invasion [W.Sherlock] 3218-9
Second letter to a friend in Suffolk 6081
Second letter to a friend. In which some farther objections 7504
Second letter to Dr.Burnet 2318
Second letter to Mr.G. [E.Stillingfleet] 2658
Second letter to Mr.Miles Prance [G.Everett] 2077
Second letter to Sir J[acob] B[anks]...concerning the Minehead doctrine 5223
Second letter to Sir J[acob] B[anks]... Wherein the late Minehead doctrine is further considered [W.Benson] 5008
Second modest enquiry into the causes 3054
Second pacquet of advices and animadversions [M.Nedham] 1548
Second part of Dr.Sherlock's two kings of Brainford 3055
Second part of Fact against scandal [T.Bateman] 5589
Second part of Lay-baptism invalid [R.Laurence] 5683
Second part of the Caveat [C.Hornby] 5415
Second part of the confutation of the ballancing letter [S.Johnson] 3601
Second part of the Full and impartial account of all the late proceedings... against Dr. Bentley [C.Middleton] 6415
Second part of the ignoramus justices [E.Whitaker] 2161
Second part of The judgment of the Church of England [W.Fleetwood] 5396
Second part of the life of William Fuller 3699
Second part of The mouse grown a rat 3847
Second part of the notorious impostor [E.Settle] 3215
Second part of the State anatomy [J.Toland] 6242
Second part of the wolf stript [C.Leslie] 4318
Second part of Vox populi 424
Second political dialogues 6896
Second postscript to a late pamphlet 7589
Second select collection of letters 3848
Second test offer'd to the electors 4899
Secret history of Arlus and Odolphus 4900,4991
Secret history of Queen Zarah [M.Manley] 4078
Secret history of the amours 5504
Secret history of the Calves-Head club [E.Ward] 4129
Secret history of the Geertrudenbergh negociation 5505
Secret history of the October club [Defoe] 5064-5
Secret intrigues of the Duke of Savoy 4098
Secret memoirs of a treasonable conference [Defoe] 6137
Secret transactions during the hundred days Mr. William Gregg lay in Newgate [F.Hoffman] 5120
Sedgwick (James) 8197-8,8201,8203,8209,8214
Sedgwick (Joseph) 922
Sedgwick (Obadiah) 425,553,795
Sedgwick (William) 426,554
Sedley (Sir Charles) 4099
Seek and you shall find 1078
Seekers request to Catholick priests 2650
Seelen (Johann Heinrich von) 5737,6082,6210-1
Segar (Simon) 3386
Selden (John) 83,632,1470,2946
Seldom comes a better [Defoe] 4734
Select city quaeries 1177
Select maxims of state 3563
Seller (Abednego) 2879,2887,2947-8,2965,3051, 3056-8,4901
Selneccerus (Nicolaus) 10
Sempill (Sir James) 83
Seneca (Lucius Annaeus) 159
Sennertus (Daniel) 179
Sense of the court and parliaments of England 5506
Sense of the people concerning the present state of affairs [Ellis] 6500
Sensus communis [A.A.Cooper] 4538
Sententie van den Hove van Hollandt 3278
Sentiments. A poem 1851
Separation of the Church of Rome from the Church of England [S.Grascombe] 3122
Sequel of Advice to posterity [J.Lewis] 7372
Sequel of Arms and the man 7168
Seraphick world: or, Celestial hierarchy 5884
Serenissimae Magnae Britanniae... epinicium 5738
Sergeant (John) 1281,2716,2789-90,2793-4, 2810,3136,3326,3387
Serious and faithfull representation of the judgements 867
Serious considerations concerning the doctrines of election and reprobation [I.Watts] 6958
Serious considerations on the several high duties [Sir M.Decker] 7050
Serious considerations on the state of religion 5224
Serious enquiry into the present state of the Church [B.Hoadly] 5119
Serious expostulation with B.E. 1416
Serious review of presbyters re-ordination by bishops [Z.Crofton] 1201
Sermon against adultery [A.Pope] 6911
Sermon lately preached, on 1 Corinth.3.15 [J.Tillotson] 1417
Sermon on the fast-day [W.Fleetwood] 5397
Sermon on the King's happy return 7323
Sermon preach'd at the cathedral church of Durham [J.Cock] 3723
Sermon preached at the funeral of Mr.Francis Mitchel [W.Lloyd] 1369
Sermon preached in the cathedral church of Durham [D.Grenville] 2508
Sermon [on Titus III.1] preach'd on the anniversary-fast 4902
Sermon [on Judges XIX.30] preach'd on the anniversary-fast [R.South] 4464
Sermon preach'd to the people, at the Mercat-Cross [J.Arbuthnot] 4255
Sermon preached towards the latter end 5993
Sermon preached upon the fifth of November [J.Williams] 1609
Sermon prepared to be preach'd at the interment of the renowned Observator [Sir R.L'Estrange] 2103
Seton (George) *Earl of Wintoun* 6046
Settle (Elkanah) 1954,2046,2145,3215
Seven additional quaeres in behalf of the secluded members [W.Prynne] 1168
Seven arguments plainly proving that papists are trayterous subjects 254
Seven extinguishers [W.Pittis] 4862
Seven papers, viz.I. The grounds 2949
Seven queries 3700
Several copies of verses on occasion of Mr. Gulliver's travels [A.Pope] 6686
Several declarations, together with the several depositions 2795
Several depositions concerning the late riot 6083
Several examinations taken before one of his Majesty's principal secretaries 6588
Several hundred texts of holy Scripture [R.Mayo] 5453
Several informations of John Mac-Namarra 1852
Several letters written by some French protestants 3038
Several resolves prepared by the commanding junto 1079
Several speeches of Duke Hamilton 868
Several weighty considerations humbly recommended 1715
Severall proceedings in Parliament 8684
Severall proceedings of state affairs 8684
Severall speeches delivered at a conference [R.Parsons] 837
Seward (Anna) 7736
Seward (Thomas) 7296,7310
Sewell (George) 5507,5739-41,5885-7,5982, 6328,6475
Seyer (Samuel) 8161
Seymour (Thomas) 2146
Shadwell (Thomas) 2796,2830
Shaftesbury (Anthony Ashley Cooper) *Earl of* see: Cooper (Anthony Ashley)
Shakespeare (William) 2637,2950,5376,7327, 7508
Sharp (Granville) 7492,7543,7765-6,7784, 7887,7993
Sharp (James) 1572,1725,5085
Sharp (John) *Archbishop of York* 1436,1509, 1717,1853,2449-50,3059,3124,3151-2,3279, 3327-9,3619-21,3781-3,3849,4100-1,4189, 4344,4903,5225
Sharp (John) *D.D.* 6212
Sharp (Lewes) 3153
Sharpe (Gregory) 6926,6934
Sharpe (John) *Curate of Stepney* 3962,4223, 4618-9,5508,5742,6329,6755
Shaw (J.H.) 8535
Shaw (Samuel) 994
Shaw (William) 7744
Shebbeare (John) 7380-1,7398-9
Sheeres (Sir Henry) 1854,3325,3532,3696,3776
Sheffield (John) *Duke of Buckingham* 2238,3154, 3479,6084,6501,6549
Shelburne (William Petty) *Earl of* see: Petty (William)
Sheldon (George) 7406
Sheldon (Sir Joseph) 1460
Sheldon (Nathaniel) 7363
Sheldon (Richard) 99
Shenstone (William) 6982
Shepard (Thomas) 796
Sheppard (Samuel) 8638,8643
Sherard (Christopher) 2099
Sheridan (Charles Brinsley) 8343
Sheridan (Frances) 7467
Sheridan (Thomas) *D.D.* 6427
Sheridan (Thomas) *Jacobite* 2016
Sheridan (William) 2451
Sheriffs case 2008
Sherlock (Martin) 7728
Sherlock (Richard) 1335,1437
Sherlock (Thomas) 4904,5888,6072,6085,6202, 6213-6,6233-4,6258,6269,6281,6283,6296-8, 6310,6312-3,6319,6321,6324,6330-2,6346-7, 6397,6419,6428-9,6722,6850,6867-8,7247, 7284,7290,7295,7297,7302,7354,7850,7859, 7900-1
Sherlock (William)
Answer to a discourse 2530,2797
Answer to a late dialogue 2661
Answer to a late scandalous pamphlet 1552
Answer to the Amicable accomodation 2507, 2531
Answer to the Request 2652
Answer to three late pamphlets 2653
Case of the allegiance 3017,3069,3072,3094, 3101,3107,3115,3129,3131,3145,3148-9, 3155-8,3163-4
Case of the allegiance... further consider'd 3159-60
Charity of lending without usury 3216
Discourse concerning a judge 2532-3
Discourse concerning the nature 2798
Discourse concerning the object 2452,2534
Letter to a member 2799
Letter to a friend 3217
Letter to Anonymus 2167,2234
Notes of the Church 2756
Observations upon Mr.Johnson's Remarks 2951
Papist not misrepresented 2504-5,2535
Preservative against popery 2726,2782,2784, 2800-1
Protestant of the Church 2536
Protestant resolution 2235,2537
Resolution of some cases 2236
Second letter to a friend 3218-9
Second part of the preservative 2802-3
Sermon preached at the funeral 2538
Sermon preached at St.Margarets 2453
Sermon preach'd before the... House 3220
Sermon preach'd before the Queen 3963,4044
Sermon preached before the... Lord Mayor 2952
Short summary 2654
Some seasonable reflections 2237
Vindication of a passage 2454
Vindication of both parts 2804
Vindication of some protestant principles 2805
Vindication of the brief discourse 2756
Vindication of the Case 3161,3228
1455,1556,2168,2644,2665,2899,3011,3055, 3067,3075,3083,3105,3110,3112,3134,3199, 3227,3271,3368-9,3554
Sherlock against Sherlock [T.Wagstaffe] 3075
Sherman (John) 255
Sherwill (Thomas) 3964-5
Shields (Alexander) 3564
Shippen (Robert) 6090
Shippen (William) 3874,3966-7,4080,6292,6689-90, 6824,6830
Shirley (Laurence) *Earl Ferrers* 7425,7439
Shirley (Walter) 7605
Shoberl (Frederic) 8260
Shore (John) *Baron Teignmouth* 8019
Shore (John) *M.D.* 5889
Shorey (William) 5994
Short (William) 8426
Short account how the kingdom of Denmark 3622
Short account of Scotland [T.Morer] 4208
Short account of the late application 7034
Short account, of the many extraordinary mercies 5509
Short account, of the nature and use of maps [W.Alingham] 3489
Short account of the proceedings of the College of Physicians 3475
Short account of the Spanish juros 5743
Short account, or state of Mr.Sheridan's case 2016
Short addition to the observations concerning trade [Sir J.Child] 1317
Short and easie method with the deists [C.Leslie] 3522
Short and true relation of intrigues 3330
Short answer to his Grace the D.of Buckingham's paper 2455,2471
Short but thorough search into what may be the real cause [D.Clayton] 6123
Short character of his Ex.T.E. of W. [J.Swift] 5248
Short defence of the Church [R.Grove] 1927
Short defence of the orders of the Church of England [L.Milbourne] 2751
Short discourse of the canary bird 5905
Short discourse upon the desires of a friend 1178
Short dull remarks, upon the long dull essay 2238
Short essay towards the promoting of love 4905
Short explication of the Apocalypse 7400
Short historical account of the contrivances 4906
Short history of standing armies in England [J.Trenchard] 3537
Short history of the last parliament [Sir R. Blackmore] 3544
Short history of the Parliament [R.Walpole] 5769,7470
Short history of the Revolution in Scotland 5344
Short narrative of modern justice 5584
Short narrative of the life and death of John Rhinholdt Count Patkul 6182
Short narrative of the proceedings against the Bp. of St.A. 3784
Short plea for the common-wealth 896
Short remarks on some passages in The life of Dr.Kennet [J.Sharpe] 6755
Short reply to M.L'Estrange's short answer 1855
Short sermons for family reading 8427
Short state of our condition 3280
Short state of some present questions in Convocation [E.Gibson] 3821
Short state of the war and the peace 5995
Short summary of the principal controversies [W.Sherlock] 2654
Short treatise of archbishops and bishops 256
Short view of the apparent dangers 4345
Short view of the most gracious providence of God [T.Manningham] 2422
Short way with the papists 4224
Shortest-way with the dissenters [Defoe] 3731
Shovel (Sir Cloudesley) 4447
Shower (Sir Bartholomew) 2953-5,3060,3455
Shower (John) 3440,4620
Shuckford (Samuel) 6599
Shute (Henry) 4102
Shute (Josiah) 474,633,688
Sibbald (Sir Robert) 4621
Sibbs (Richard) 170
Sichemites see: Samaritans
Sictor (Joannes) 195-6,257
Sicurus (Dorotheus) see: Crusius (T.T.)
Sidley (Sir Charles) see: Sedley (Sir C.)
Sidney (Algernon) 2196,2239,2260,2304
Sidney (Henry) *Earl of Romney* 1795
Sidney (Sir Philip) 735
Sievwright (Norman) 7531,7578
Simeon (Charles) 8333,8519
Simmons (Samuel Foart) 7785
Simple cobler of Aggawam [N.Ward] 797
Simpson (Joseph) 7481
Simpson (Sidrach) 517,555
Simpson (Thomas) 7035
Sin of schism most unjustly and groundlesly charged [E.Synge] 6094
Sinclair (Sir John) 7923,8091
Sindercome (Miles) 980
Sing (Thomas) 8571,8574
Single (Tom) see: Astell (Mary)
Sir H.Mackworth's proposal in miniature 6406
Sir Politique uncased [Sir R.L'Estrange] 1144
Sir Thomas Double at court [C.Davenant] 4722
Sir *'s speech upon the peace 6935
Six conferences concerning the Eucharist [J.de La Placette] 2612
Sixth collection of papers relating to the present juncture 2956
Sixth letter to the people of England [J.Shebbeare] 7399
Sixtus V, *Pope* 1593,3013
Skelton (Philip) 6880-1
Sketch of the character of Mrs Elizabeth Carter 8183
Skinner (John) *Bishop* 7816
Skinner (John) *of Longside* 7234
Skippon (Philip) 761
Slade (Joseph) 5890
Slater (Edward) 8250
Slater (Samuel) 3281
Slocock (Samuel) 8428
Smagge (Jan) 4546
Smalbroke (Richard) 4907,5226,5286,6716
Smallwell (Edward) 7776,7801
Smalridge (George) 2655-6,4103,4462,4622,4908-9, 4910,5227,5234,5510-1,5744,6032
Smalwood (James) 4104
Smart (Christopher) 8685

Smart (Peter) 556
Smeaton (Samuel) 4105
Smelt (Caroline Elizabeth) 8367
Smith (Benjamin) 2147
Smith (Edmund) 5477
Smith (Edward) see: Smyth (Edward)
Smith (Elephant) see: Underhill (Cave)
Smith (Elisha) 5891
Smith George) *Gent* 557
Smith (George) *Non-juring Bishop* 6333,6825, 6837,6956,7094,7097,7355
Smith (Herbert) 8498
Smith (Hugh) 7737
Smith (Sir James) 2298
Smith (John) *C.M.* 6600
Smith (John) *of Walworth* 1718,2009
Smith (John) *Prebendary of Durham* 4623,5228, 5512
Smith (John) *Vicar of Westham* 3968
Smith (Joseph) 6086
Smith (Matthew) 3623
Smith (Robert) 3384
Smith (Sydney) 8191,8520
Smith (Thomas) *Librarian* 913,1080,1199
Smith (Thomas) *of Magdalen College* 1471-2, 2148,2456,2806,3565-6
Smith (William) *1756-1835* 8205
Smith (William) *Captain* 558
Smith (William) *Prebendary* 1856,2240
Smith (Sir William) 2010,2137,2149,2161
Smollett (Tobias) 8617
Smyth (Edward) 2957
Smyth (Matthew) see: Smith (Matthew)
Smyth (William) see: Smith (William) *Prebendary*
Smythies (William) 2305,2319-20,2429
Snape (Andrew) 4346-7,4911,5038,5229-30, 6109,6115-6,6138,6146,6151,6157-8, 6164-5,6168-71,6173,6179-81,6197,6202, 6204,6206-7,6217-25,6247-8,6252,6255, 6304-5,6309,6316,6325,6334,6344
Snatt (William) 6335,6477
Snowdon, *Curate of* 8017
Soames (Henry) 8358
Sober advice from Horace [A.Pope] 6849
Sober and seasonable discourse, by way of dialogue 2011
Sober and serious consideration: occasioned by the death of... Charles II 2335
Sober discourse of the honest cavalier [R.Onslow] 1829
Sober enquiry. Whether it can be for the interest 3969
Sobieski (Jan) see: John III Sobieski
Society for Bettering the Condition and increasing the Comforts of the Poor 8061
Society for Propagating the Gospel 4142
Society of Antiquaries 7802
Society of Friends 7658,8157
Society of Jesus 1510,2968
Society of Jesus. Bonn 6336
Society of Jesus. Cologne 2241,2807
Society of Jesus. Dusseldorf 923
Society of Jesus. Mannheim 7436
Society of Jesus. Munster 6430-1
Society of the Friends of the People 7966-7, 7980,7994-5,8020-1
Socrates Christianus see: Stephens (Edward)
Solemn act of confession 7409
Solemn humiliation for the murder of K. Charles [T.Manningham] 2518
Solemn league and covenant discharg'd [J.Russell] 1172
Solemn protestation against George Keith's advertisement 3476
Solicitous citizen: or, The Devil to do about Dr.Sach[evere]ll 5231
Solomon against Welton 4912
Solomon and Abiathar [S.Hill] 3198,3200
Some (Robert) 18
Some account of a very seditious book 7996
Some account of the life, and most remarkable actions, of George Henry Baron de Goertz [Defoe] 6380
Some account of the life and writings of Thomas Sprat 5996
Some advice humbly offer'd to the members of the October club [J.Swift] 5525
Some arguments made use of in the Bishop of Bangor's Preservative 6087
Some cautions offered to the consideration of those who are to chuse members [G.Savile] 3385
Some considerations about the most proper way 3162
Some considerations about the raising of coin 3441
Some considerations against joining with the Nonjurors 6723
Some considerations concerning the Trinity [F.Gastrell] 3504,4298,5814
Some considerations humbly offered in a letter to John, Lord Bishop of Ely 4835
Some considerations humbly offer'd to the Right Reverend the Ld.Bp. of Salisbury [E.Curll] 4684,4718
Some cursory reflexions impartially made 2457
Some few arguments in defence of the Bill 6793
Some few obvious and just reflections 5892
Some few questions concerning the oath of allegiance [P.Walsh] 1224
Some impartial reflections on Mr.Baldwin's sermon 4348
Some memoirs of the life of John Radcliffe [W.Pittis] 5983
Some modest reflections upon the commitment of the Earl of Shaftsbury 2012
Some modest remarks on Dr.Sherlocks new book 3163-4
Some necessary considerations relating to all future elections [J.Drake] 3734
Some new proofs by which it appears that the Pretender is truly James the third [Sir T.Burnet] 5608
Some observations concerning the plague 6528
Some observations concerning the regulating of elections 2958
Some observations on the tryal of Spencer Cowper 3785
Some observations, shewing the danger [W.Cleland] 5815
Some observations upon a late pamphlet 5232
Some observations upon Bishop Fleetwood's Four sermons 5513
Some plain observations recommended 4106
Some proceedings in the Convocation, A.D. 1705 [F.Atterbury] 4377
Some proposals towards promoting the propagation of the Gospel [F.Brokesby] 4384
Some queries concerning the election of members [Sir R.L'Estrange] 3022
Some queries for the better understanding of a list 3477
Some queries propos'd to the publisher 4913
Some queries to the protestants [T.Ward] 2669
Some queries which deserve no consideration 3701
Some queries, which may deserve consideration 3702
Some questions resolved concerning episcopal and presbyterian government [A.Cunningham] 3002
Some reasons by a divine of the Kirk 4107
Some reasons for annual parliaments 3270
Some reasons offered by the late ministry in defence of their administration [Defoe] 5951
Some reasons to prove, that no person is obliged by his principles [J.Swift] 5526
Some reflections on a letter 4914
Some reflections on a pamphlet, intituled, England and East-India 3442
Some reflections on a pamphlet lately published [Defoe] 3458
Some reflections on Mr.Bennet's Discourse of joint prayer 4671
Some reflections on the eleventh section of Dr.D'Avenant's late book 3970
Some reflections on the oaths & declaration 3394
Some reflections upon his Highness the Prince of Oranges declaration 2808
Some reflections upon marriage [M.Astell] 3574
Some reflections upon the author and licenser of a scandalous pamphlet [A.Pulton] 2774
Some reflexions upon a treatise call'd Pietas Romana [J.Harrington] 2732
Some remarks by way of answer to a late pamphlet 5233
Some remarks on a pamphlet, intitled, The morality of religion 6971
Some remarks on a report containing an essay 3388
Some remarks on the Barrier Treaty [J.Swift] 5527
Some remarks on the Bill for taking 3786
Some remarks on the late Lord Bolingbroke's famous letter 7335
Some remarks, or,short strictures [H.Gandy] 3907
Some remarks upon, and instances of the usages 3533
Some remarks upon government 2832
Some remarks upon the late differences 6432
Some remarks upon the Reverend Dr.Marshall's sermon 6724
Some remarques upon a late popular piece of nonsence [E.Meredith] 2113
Some rules for speaking and action 6088
Some seasonable and serious queries upon the late Act [N.Lockyer] 1349
Some seasonable reflections upon the Quakers solemn protestation [C.Leslie] 3467
Some seasonable remarks upon the deplorable fall 2013
Some short but necessary animadversions 2014
Some short reflections upon Mr.Bradbury's late libel 5745
Some short remarks upon the late address of the Bishop of London 5234
Some speciall passages from Hull 427
Some testimonies of Justin Martyr 4448,4463
Some thoughts concerning the study of the laws of England [T.Wood] 4488
Some thoughts humbly offer'd towards an union between Great-Britain and Ireland [T.Knox] 4423
Some thoughts on the representation 5235
Some thoughts upon liberty [B.Montagu] 8313
Some useful and occasional remarks 6794
Some useful reflections upon a pamphlet called a Brief account 3331
Some Whig-principles demonstrated 5746
Somers (John) *Baron* 3478,3482,3515,3663, 3703,3786,4789,5173
Sophia, *Electress of Hanover* 3711,3792,3937, 4225
Sophia (Charlotte) *Queen of Prussia* 5514
Sort of an answer to a piece of a book [J.Davys] 5046
Sotheby (William) 8304
Souldiers catechism [R.Ram] 2314
Sourse of our present fears discover'd 4226
South (Robert) *Attorney* 4958
South (Robert) *D.D.* 1267,1288,1297,1313,4464, 6089,6226
South Sea Company 5069,5236-7,5368,6460, 6519,6529
Southall (John) 6756
Southerne (Thomas) 5087
Southouse (E.) 8077
Sovereign: or a political discourse 1857
Sp., *Mr.* see: Sparrow (Anthony)
Spademan (John) 4227
Spalding (Georg Ludwig) 7943
Spangenberg (Augustus Gottlieb) 7545
Spanheim (Frédéric) 160
Sparrow (Anthony) 180,3971
Specimen animadversionum in prolegomena [J.J.Wetstein] 6797
Specimen of a declaration against debauchery [E.Stephens] 2964
Specimen of naked truth [E.Vernon] 7171
Specimen of the state of the nation 3221
Specimen of the wholesom severities 4915
Spectator 5238,5240
Spectator inspected 5238
Spectators address to the Whigs [Defoe] 5066
Speculum Baxterianum 1737
Speculum Beatae Virginis [G.Hickes] 2509
Speculum crape-gownorum [J.Phillips] 2129, 2139
Speculum Sarisburianum 5893
Speech against the Bill, brought into the House 3972
Speech for Mr.D[unda]sse [Defoe] 5067
Speech for the Bill against occasional conformity [Sir J.Pakington] 3842
Speech in the Parliament of Scotland [A.Bruce] 3719
Speech made in the House of Commons April the 24th 1716 [A.Hutcheson] 6559-60
Speech of a noble peer upon the reading of the Bill [J.Thompson] 3983
Speech of a right honourable gentleman [G.Grenville] 7556
Speech of an ancient Britain [R.Price] 4453
Speech of the Lord Haversham's ghost 4916
Speech of the Right Honourable the Lord Chancellor of Ireland [Sir M.Eustace] 1202
Speech suppos'd to be spoken by R--- St[ee]l [Sir R.Steele] 5899
Speech that was intended to have been spoken by the Terrae-filius [Sir J.Willes] 5779
Speech to the people against the Pretender 5894
Speech without doores defended without reason [Sir J.Birkenhead] 699
Speech without doors (1704) 3973
Speech without doors (1710) [Defoe] 4735
Speech without doors, concerning the most effectual way 3787
Speeches and prayers of some of the late King's judges 1179
Speeches, by a member of the Parliament [A.Fletcher] 3814
Speeches, discourses, and prayers, of Col. John Barkstead 1246
Speed (John) *M.D.* 7419
Speed (John) *1628-1711* 1858
Speed (Robert) 4917
Speght (James) 68
Spelman (Sir John) 428,559
Spence (Joseph) 7324,7420
Spencer (Charles) *Earl of Sunderland* 6558
Spencer (Robert) *Earl of Sunderland* 3471
Spenser (Edmund) 5821
Sperbach (Carl Gottlob) 6337
Spiller (James) 6708
Spinckes (Nathaniel) 4814,4918,5895,6227, 6265,6274-5,6277,6338-40,6369,6376, 6433,6449,6453,6478
Spinoza reviv'd [W.Carroll] 4528,5022
Spirit of a Roman Catholick missioner [E.Stephens] 3978
Spiritual intruder unmask'd 6090
Spittlehouse (John) 924
Spleen, a Pindarique ode [A.Finch] 4550
Sprat (Thomas) 1358,1594-6,2150-1,2321,2959, 3222,3282,3443,5239,5996,6574
Spurtowe (William) 560
Spy upon the Spectator 5240
Squire (Francis) 6341
Squire (Samuel) 7235,7272,7382
Squire and the cardinal 6757
Squire Bickerstaff detected 4465
Squire Bickerstaff's strange and wonderful predictions [J.Swift] 4470
Stacy (Edmund) 4919-22,4241-2,5515,5997-9,8680
Stafford (Richard) 3534
Stafford (William Howard) *Viscount* see: Howard (William)
Stainforth (William) 1511
Stair (John Dalrymple) *Earl of* see: Dalrymple (John)
Stamford (Henry Grey) *Earl of* see: Grey (Henry)
Stamp (Thomas) 5893
Stampe (William) 561
Stanbridge (John) 171
Standard of common liberty 1123
Standfast (Richard) 1512
Standish (John) *Archdeacon of Colchester* 5
Standish (John) *Rector of Conington* 1490, 1513-4
Stanhope (Charles) *Earl* 7840,7989,8022
Stanhope (George) 3704,4108,4228-30,4349-50, 4923-4,6342-3
Stanhope (H.) see: Bond (William)
Stanhope (James) *Earl* 5896
Stanhope (Michael) 4466,6228
Stanhope (Philip Dormer) *Earl of Chesterfield* 7066-7,7069,7704
Stanhope (William) *Earl of Harrington* 6668
Stanley (Charles) *Earl of Derby* 1597
Stanley (John) 7651
Stanley (William) 2458,3009
Stapleton (Sir Miles) 2030
Stapleton (Sir Phillip) 258
Star-board and lar-board 5243
State-anatomy of Great Britain [J.Toland] 6203 6239-42
State and estimate of the publick debts 6229
State and importance of the present controversy [J.Turner] 5764
State and interest of the nation [Sir R. L'Estrange] 1812
State bell-mans collection of verses 4925
State law: or, The doctrine of libels 6725
State of the Established Church 8222
State of the Irish affairs 689
State of the Kingdome represented to the people [W.Ashurst] 803
State of the nation 7236
State of the national debt [W.Pulteney] 6688
State of the Navy consider'd 3567
State of the Palatines 4926
State of the representation of England 7967
State-prodigal his return 2960
Statues: or, the trial of constancy 6936
Statutophilus see: Speed (John) *M.D.*
Staunton (Edmund) 634
Stayley (William) 1605
Stebbing (Henry) *Archdeacon of Wilts* 6344-5, 6434,7036,7202,7227
Stebbing (Henry) *Preacher of Gray's Inn* 7383,8114
Steele (Sir Richard) 3389,5687,5726,5768, 5807,5830-1,5834,5847,5875,5897-9,5901-3, 6000,6326,6435,6456,6479
Stephens (Edward) 2961-4,3165,3223,3390, 3444,3624-9,3788,3850-1,3974-8,4109-11
Stephens (Jeremiah) 1220
Stephens (William) *Rector of Sutton* 3332, 3445-6,3453,3568,4112,4163,4203,4351
Stephens (William) *Vicar of St.Andrew's, Plymouth* 6230
Stepney (George) 3166,3479
Sternhold (Thomas) see: Daily advertiser, in metre
Steuart (Adam) 925
Stevens (Nicholas) 6758
Stevens (William) 7637,7643,8107-8
Stevenson (John Hall) 7356
Stewart (James) *of Aucharn* 7325
Stewart (Robert) *Marquess of Londonderry* 8090
Stileman (Timothy) 6091
Stillingfleet (Edward) 1336,1438,1473,1598-9, 1719-20,1739,1743,1765,1790,1808,1833, 1859,1899,2152,2322,2459,2506,2539-41, 2616,2618,2657-9,2730,2793,2809-11,2942, 2965-7,3061,3167,3333,3789,4814
Stillingfleet (James) 7437
Stilsman (John) 4477
Stirling (James) 4549

Stockings out at heels 4004
Stock-jobbers [W.R.Chetwood] 6451
Stone (Thomas) 7860
Story (Thomas) 3447
Story of the St.Alb[a]ns ghost [W.Wagstaffe] 5551
Stoughton (William) *Prebendary of St.Patrick's* 4624
Stoughton (William) *Professor of Civil Law* 429
Stout (Sarah) 3545,3785
Strabo 7786
Stradling (George) 1474
Strafford (Thomas Wentworth) *Earl of* see: Wentworth (Thomas)
Strange (Robert) 7569
Strange and terrible news from sea 1600
Strange news from Hicks's Hall 2015
Strange news from Scotland 5516
Strange news from Westminster 5900
Stratford (Nicholas) 2460
Streater (John) 1081
Strickland (John) 635
Stricturae breves in epistolas 4352
Strictures upon modern simony 7523
Strode (S.) 3391
Strode (William) 1180
Strutton (Richard) 3062
Strype (John) 5244
Stuart (Charles) *Earl of Traquair* 7194
Stuart (Daniel) 7997,8023
Stuart (James) 7606
Stuart (Moses) 8521
Stuart (Walter) *Lord Blantyre* 7311
Stubbe (Henry) 1082-3,1298,1358-9,1391-2
Stubs (Philip) 3852,3979,4625,5245,5517,5747
Student, or The Oxford monthly miscellany 8685
Study to be quiet 1860
Stukeley (William) 8024
Sturges (John) 7624,7729,8092,8139,8149
Sturmy (Daniel) 4468
Styles (John) 8201
Subjects liberty 562
Subjects sorrow [R.Brown] 4676
Submissive answer to Mr.Hoadly's humble reply 4626
Substance of all the depositions 5518
Substance of the Income Act 8093
Subtilty of the serpent [W.Mynors] 6318
Succession of Spain consider'd [Defoe] 5068
Succession of the Church and sacraments 2542
Succession to the Crown of England [Defoe] 3655
Succinct and methodical history 5519
Suckling (Sir John) 259
Suddaine answer to a suddaine moderatour 430
Suetonius Tranquillus (Caius) 5520
Suidas 5660,5748,7878
Sum of a conference had between two divines [P.Gooden] 2589
Summary of all the religious houses [Sir T. Burnet] 6117
Summary view of the laws relating to subscriptions 7607
Sumner (John Bird) 8140,8488,8580
Sundry considerations touching naturalization 1553
Supplement 5497
Supplement, 1689 [Sir J.Child] 2856
Supplement of original papers and letters, relating to the Scots Company 3618
Supplement to his Majesties most gracious speech [T.Wagstaffe] 3289
Supplement to the Faults on both sides [Defoe] 4736
Supplement to the London Journal 6530
Supplement to the negro's & Indian's advocate [M.Godwyn] 1924
Supplication of certaine masse-priests 34
Surrey, *County of* 826
Suspension of the Triennial Act 6092
Sutton (Robert) *Baron Lexington* 1495
Swan (John) 7322
Swan tripe-club in Dublin 4231
Swanne (Gilbert) 7438
Swedenborg (Emanuel) 7918
Swedish intelligencer 147
Swift (Edmund Lewis Lenthal) 8261
Swift (Jonathan)
Conduct of the allies 5108,5209,5211,5367, 5399,5475,5521-2
Enquiry whether the Christian religion 6803
First ode of the second book 5901
Letter from a member 4627
Letter of thanks 5523
Libel on Dr.D[ela]ny 6759
Meditation upon a broom-stick 4927
Mr.C[olli]ns's Discourse 5750
New journey to Paris 5246-7
Part of the seventh epistle 5751
Predictions for the year 1708, 4469
Preface to the B[isho]p of S[a]r[u]m's Introduction 5752
Proposal for correcting 5476,5524
Publick spirit of the Whigs 5825,5902-3
Short character of his Ex.t[he]E[arl] of W[harton] 5248
Some advice humbly offer'd 5525
Some reasons to prove 5526
Some remarks on the Barrier Treaty 5527
Squire Bickerstaff's strange and wonderful predictions 4470
Dean Swift's tracts 7902
Dr.S[wift]'s real diary 5953
Vindication of his Excellency 6760
Vindication of Isaac Bickerstaff 4628
Wonderfull wonder of wonders 6531
4140,4231,4629,5169,5466,5765,5820,5874, 6427,6541-2,6658,7269
Swift (Thomas) 4928
Swinden (Tobias) 5749
Swinfen (John) 4929-30
Swinny (Owen Mac) 4603
Sworder (William) 5904
Sydall (Elias) 5753
Syddall(Arnold) 5528
Sykes (Arthur Ashley) 6093,6213-4,6231-5, 6319,6346-7,6575,6764,6897-8
Sylla's ghost 2176
Symmons (Charles) 8017,8184,8192
Symmons (Edward) 431,563
Symonds (Edward) 6795
Symonds (Joseph) 260
Symonds (William) 36
Symons (Jelinger) 8193
Sympathy; or, A sketch of the social passion [S.J.Pratt] 7751
Symson (Matthias) 4471
Synge (Edward) *Archbishop of Tuam* 4931,5529, 5754,6001-2,6094,6348,6576,6669-72,6691
Synge (Edward) *Bishop of Elphin* 6601

T.(A.) see: Toplady (Augustus Montague)
T.(F.) 5905
T.(F.) see: Fleming (Robert)
T.(L.) 2016
T.(M.) 6532
T.(N.) 2832,3063
T.(R.) 1475,5356
T.(W.) see: Tunstall (William)
Taaffe (Francis) *Earl of Carlingford* 2323
Taaffe (Nicholas) *Viscount* 7505
Tables for renewing and purchasing of the leases [G.Mabbut] 6720
Tacitus (Publius Cornelius) 272,3293,7478
Talbor (John) 3980
Talbot (Charles) *Duke of Shrewsbury* 3623
Talbot (George) 7357
Talbot (James) 4472
Talbot (William) *Bishop of Durham* 4353-4, 4658,4784,4818,4932,5436,5530,5576, 5906,6095,6236
Talbot (William) *Vicar of St.Giles, Reading* 7625
Tale of the raven and the blackbird [E.Stacy] 5999
Tale of the Robin-red-breast [E.Stacy] 4922
Tallents (Francis) 4232,4300
Tasso (Torquato) 6349
Taswell (E.) 6350
Tate (Nahum) 2950,3479,3535,3853,5755
Tatham (John) 1181
Tatler 4724,4844
Tattershall (Thomas) 8532,8581,8587
Taubman (Matthew) 2461,2543
Taunton-Dean letter 3646
Tavern hunter 3790
Taxes not grievous 5249
Taylor (Henry) 7705,7752
Taylor (James) 2968
Taylor (Jeremy) 432,749,869,972,1221,1247, 1268,2660
Taylor (John) *Archdeacon of Buckingham* 6761, 7068
Taylor (John) *the Water-Poet* 105
Taylor (Zachary) 3072-3,3168,3227
Teague's everlasting glory 4933
Tears wip'd off, or the second essay 2431
Tedder (Richard) 181
Temple (Sir William) 3248-9,4140,4629
Templer (John) 1515
Templum libertatis [W.King] 7012
Tempora mutantur [C.Leslie] 3315
Ten queares, upon the ten new commandements [W.Prynne] 1069
Tender and hearty address to all the free-holders 5907
Tenison (Edward) 6295,6342,6351,6356
Tenison (Richard) 3169
Tenison (Thomas) 2017,2242-3,2661-4,2668, 2750,2812-3,2826,2969-70,3064,3363, 3791,4050-1,4355,4630,6003,6065
Terrae-filius [N.Amhurst] 6653
Terrick (Richard) 7384
Terrick (Samuel) 4233
Tertullianus (Quintus Septimius Florens) 956
Test of the truest Church man 5250
Testimonies of several citizens of Fickle-borough 5756
Teviot (Andrew Rutherford) *Earl of* see: Rutherford (A.)
Texts examined which papists cite 2814
Thacker (Jeremy) 5908
Theatre-Royal turn'd into a mountebank's stage 6352
Theobald (John) 6436,6938
Theobald (Lewis) 6692
Theodosius, *a Jew* 5748
Theophilus Rationalis see: Multum in parvo
Theophilus Timorcus see: Gataker (Thomas)
Theophrastus 7169
Things as they are 7410
Things as they are. Part the second 7449
Third commandment; an essay 2462
Third defense of an argument [S.Clarke] 4393
Third dialogue between the Pope and a phanatick 2324
Third letter from a gentleman in the country [W.Penn] 2629
Third letter to a clergyman in the country [F.Atterbury] 3714
Third letter to a person of quality [E.Pelling] 2625
Thirlby (Styan) 5470,5531,5559,5609,5757
Thirteenth chapter to the Romans, vindicated [W.Fleetwood] 4760,5045
Thirty plain, but sound reasons 2815
Thirty-nine Articles see: Church of England. Articles of religion
Thistle [W.Murray] 7198
Thomas (Benjamin) 7659
Thomas (John) *Bishop of Salisbury* 7203,7385
Thomas (John) *Minister of Yately* 4934
Thomas (Thomas) *Lexicographer* 90
Thomas (William) 1601
Thompkins (Edward) 3170
Thompson (Francis) 3981
Thompson (John) *Baron Haversham* 3678,3884,3886, 3912,3955,3982-3,4040,4113-4,4168,4356, 4490-1,4631,4916,4935,5251
Thompson (Richard) 2463
Thompson (William) 7123
Thomson (James) 6674,7273
Thomson (Robert) 5758
Thomson (William) 2018,2244
Thornhill (Richard) 5263
Thornton (Bonnell) 7274
Thornton (William) 3839
Thorpe (George) 1554
Thoughts of a Church of England divine 5252
Thoughts of a country gentleman upon reading Dr.Sacheverell's tryal [G.Smalridge] 4910
Thoughts of a learned divine concerning the present state of religion 5253
Thoughts of a member of the lower house [J.Trenchard] 6438
Thoughts of a member of the October Club 5254
Thoughts of an honest Tory [B.Hoadly] 4700
Thoughts of an honest Whig 4936
Thoughts on non-residence and farming 8153
Thoughts on the cause of the present discontents [E.Burke] 7576
Thoughts on the nature of war [A.Benezet] 7440
Thoughts on the prospect of a regicide peace [E.Burke] 8032
Thoulier d'Olivet (Pierre Joseph) 6882
Three articles of the Grand Alliance 5255
Three considerations proposed to Mr.William Pen [T.Comber] 2706
Three essays upon preaching and hearing 5759
Three establishments concerning the pay of the sea-officers 4019
Three fables. Preferment despised 7069
Three great questions concerning the succession 1841
Three letters. I. A letter from a Jesuit 2971
Three letters concerning civil comprehension [C.Lawton] 6519
Three letters to Dr.Sherlock [W.Atwood] 2168
Three poems of St.Paul's Cathedral [J.Wright] 3486
Three political letters to a noble lord [T.Gordon] 6508
Three seasonable considerations upon his Majesty's gracious letters patents [T.Turnor] 1608
Three speeches against continuing the Army 6292
Three speeches delivered at a common-hall 564
Three speeches made to the right honorable the Lord Maior 1084
Threni Cantabrigienses in funere 1191
Threni gregis Coloniensis 7450
Threnodia virginea [C.Gildon] 4414
Threnody. To the memory of a nobleman 7311
Thriftiness of the husbandman 8383
Thurlin (Thomas) 2544
Thwaites (Edward) 4473
Thwing (Thomas) 2030
Thynne (Thomas) 2155
Tickell (Richard) 7716
Tickell (Thomas) 6237
Tillotson (John) 1417,1476-7,1516,1602-3,1721-2, 1861,2019,2245-7,2325-6,2545,2596,2972-4, 3023,3065,3171-2,3224,3283-4,3334,3365, 4632-3,4744,7355
Tilly (William) 4115-7,4234,4937-9, 5760
Timms (William) 6615
Tindal (Matthew) 3984,4209,4318,4357,4398,4416, 4430,4474,4486,4495,4528,4558,4561,4593, 4634,4638,4940,5144,5256,5532,6238,6762-3, 6785
Tindal (William) 7998
Tinne (John A.) 8517
Tint for taunt 4941
Tipping (William) 6096
Title of a thorough settlement examined [R.Jenkin] 3129
Title of an usurper [R.Jenkin] 3017
Titus (Silas) 1077,1085,2975,6080
To his Royal Highness the Duke of York 2327
To the citizens of London, June the 24th, 1697 3480
To the Kings most excellent Majestie. The humble petition of the inhabitants [of Glos.] 261
To the Kings most excellent Majesty. The humble petition...of the Lord Mayor 1820
To the Kings most excellent Majestie. The petition of the inhabitants [of Bucks.] 262
To the memory of that dear, that most holy m[other] 7237
To the Prince of Orange,upon the opening of the campagne 2328
To the reverend and merry answerer of Vox cleri 3066
To the Reverend Mr.Roger Laurence [T.Brett] 6839
To the Wh[ig]s nineteen queries 4942-3
Todd (Hugh) 5257
Toft (Mary) 6652,6664
Toke (John) 7590
Toland (John) 3414,3417,3536,3570,3592,3711,3742 3764,3792,4008,4112,4118,4203,4944-5,5258, 5909-10,6203,6239,6300,6315,6353,6480-1, 6497,6516
Tolando-pseudologo-mastix [J.King] 6516
Toleration and liberty of conscience considered [J.Nalson] 2426
Toleration disapprov'd and condemned [W.Assheton] 1337-8
Toleration intolerable 2248
Toleration not to be abused [F.Fullwood] 1384
Tolfrey (Samuel) 8025
Tollemache (Thomas) 3297
Tolleration iustified 750
Tom Double against Dr.D[a]v[e]n[an]t 3985
Tom Double return'd out of the country [C.Davenant] 3726
Tom o' Bedlam see: Letter from Tom o' Bedlam
Tom o' Bedlam's answer to his brother [L.Milbourne] 4506-7,4602
Tom Tell-Troth see: Letter to the Earl of Shaftsbury
Tom-Tell-Truth's letter to a dissenter 4119
Tombes (John) 731
Tomkins (Lydia) 8553
Tomkins (Thomas) 1314
Tomline (George Pretyman) 7855,7879,8154
Tomlins (Sir Thomas Edlyne) 7817
Tompkins (Nathaniel) 565
Tonge (Ezerel) 1690
Tonge (Simson) 1965
Tooke (John Horne) 7861,7968
Toplady (Augustus Montague) 7583,7591
Topping (Henry) 6437
Torriano (Giovanni) 452
Torshell (Samuel) 636-7
Tory partiality detected 5447
Tory plot: or the discovery 2153
Tosier (John) 1723
Tottie (John) 7468,7506,7626
Touch (P.) 7803
Touchet (James) *Earl of Castlehaven* 2060
Toulmin (George Hoggart) 7818
Toulmin (Joshua) 7903
Tournay (William) 8251
Towers (Joseph) 7870
Towne (John) 7312
Townley (James) 7421
Trackebarne Gran Mogol, drama 7507
Tract concerning schisme [J.Hales] 383
Tractatus pacis & amicitiae 5571,5788
Tracy (Antoine Louis Claude Destutt de) see: Destutt de Tracy (A.L.C.)
Trade of England revived 2020
Traeiner (Adam Fridericus) 6243
Tragedy of Christopher Louc [R.Wild] 1185
Tragical history of Jetzer [Sir W.Waller] 1730
Transactioneer with some of his philosophical fancies [W.King] 3603

Transubstantiation condemned 8467
Transubstantiation contrary to scripture [R.Nelson] 2755
Transubstantiation defended [J.Gother] 2596, 2724
Transubstantiation no doctrine of the primitive fathers [J.Patrick] 2620
Trapnel (Anna) 940
Trapp (Joseph) 4475,4946-8,5038,5259-61, 5457,5533-4,6244,6533,6577,6727,6983
Travell (Ferdinando Tracy) 8026
Tray (Richard) 565
Treason, popery, &c. 1862
Treasure, found in an extraordinary manner 8429
Treatie of peace, concluded the 29. of September, 1642 433
Treatise of monarchie [P.Hunton] 524,2892, 2893
Treatise of the perpetuall visibilitie [G.Abbot] 106
Treatise of traditions [D.Whitby] 2986
Treatise on the nature and constitution of the Christian Church [W.Stevens] 7643
Treatise, shewing how usefull, safe, reasonable and beneficial [Sir M.Hale] 3309
Treatise touching the East-Indian trade [F.Charpentier] 1487
Treatise wherein is demonstrated [Sir J.Child] 1897
Treatise written by an author of the communion of the Church of Rome [L.Du Four de Longuerue] 2585
Treaty between her Majesty and the States-General 5535
Treaty betwixt the Most Christian King 3608
Treaty marine between Charles II and Lewis XIV 1530
Treaty of Seville... considered 6730
Treby (Sir George) 2021-3
Trelawney (Jonathan) 3793-4
Trelawny (Sir Harry) 7717
Trenchard (John) 3458,3481-2,3537,3776,4120, 6438,6450,6482,6534-5
Tres oratiunculae habitae in Domo Convocationis Oxon [W.King] 7056
Trevanian (John) 1086
Trevor (Richard) 7124
Trial at large, between James Annesley 7098
Trial of Frederick Calvert 7544
Trial of John Magee 7904
Trial of Joseph Fowke 7689
Trial of Lawrence Earl Ferrers 7439
Trial of the Right Honourable Richard Earl of Anglesey 7099
Trial of William Lord Byron 7486
Trials at large for adultery 7969
Triennial Act impartially stated 6097
Trimming court-divine 3067
Trimnell (Charles) 3986,4382,4476-8,4635-6, 4717,4830,4949,4965,5156,5262,5536, 5854,5911
Trip to the country 8468
Trip to the d[evi]l's summer-house 3987
Tripe (Andrew) see: Wagstaffe (William)
Trist (Jeremiah) 7905
Triumphs of justice over unjust judges 2024
Trott (John) see: St.John (Henry)
Troutbeck (John) 4950
True account from Chichester 2100
True account of the author of a book [A.Walker] 3229
True account of the design, and advantages of the South-Sea trade [Defoe] 5069
True account of the late bloody and inhumane conspiracy 941
True account of the present state of Ireland 2976
True account of the tryal of Mrs.Mary Carlton 1269
True account of the whole proceedings betwixt his Grace 2154
True account of what past at the Old-Bailey 5263
True and demonstrative way to union 3668
True and exact account of many great abuses [C.Hore] 3828
True and exact particulars of the articles of peace 1087
True and faithful account of the last distemper 4951-2
True and genuine explanation of one King James's declaration 3285
True and impartial account of the animosity 5537
True and impartial account of the most material passages in Ireland [J.Bennet] 2835
True and impartial account of the poll of the inhabitants...of Broad Street 5161
True and impartial account of the present difference [J.Paris] 5192
True and impartial narrative of the eminent hand of God 1393
True and impartiall relation of the battaile neare Newbery [G.Digby] 471
True and particular account of a storm 5264
True and particular account of the battle of Sheriff-muir 6098
True and perfect relation of Elizabeth Freeman [R.Wilkinson] 1871
True and wonderful relation of the dreadful fighting 2025
True answer to Dr.Sacheverell's sermon [W.Kennet] 4576
True answer to the Bishop of Salisbury's speech 4773
True-born Englishman [Defoe] 3588
True-born Englishman: a satyr, answer'd [W.Pittis] 3692
True-born-Huguonot: or, Daniel de Foe 3854
True Briton 7316
True character of Mr.Pope [J.Dennis] 6194
True character of, viz.A deceitful petty-fogger 4479
True church-man [E.Synge] 6672
True copy of a letter (intercepted) going for Holland 1741
True copy of a project for the reunion of both religions in France [J.A.Dubourdieu] 2381
True copy of a speech made by an English colonel 3286
True copy of the articles of union 4176
True copy of the indictment which is preferred 2026
True defence of Henry Sacheverell 4953
True description of the Mint 4954
True difference betwixt the principles & practices of the Kirk 5538
True discovery of those treasons of which Geilis van Ledenberch was a practiser 84
True friends to corporations vindicated 3068
True good old cause rightly stated [W.Prynne] 1071
True narrative of the late design [J.Bury] 1630
True narrative of the popish-plot 1863
True narrative of the proceedings at Guild-hall 1972
True narrative of the proceedings at the sessions 1724
True narrative of the proceedings in Parliament 1088
True narrative of the proceedings of his Majesties Privy-Council in Scotland 1592
True narrative of what pass'd at the examination of... Guiscard [M.Manley] 5170
True notion of government 1950
True passive obedience restor'd 4955
True patriot vindicated (1701) 3705
True patriots vindicated (1711) 5265
True picture of a modern Whig [C.Davenant] 3650,3796
True portraiture of the kings of England [H.Parker] 2759
True relation of a wicked-plot [R.Backhouse] 577
True relation of the apparition of one Mrs. Veal [Defoe] 4282
True relation of the confession and execution of Drinkwater 1517
True relation of the horrid conspiracy 3448
True relation of the late case in Convocation 5761
True relation of the late great and bloudy fight 1277
True relation of the late victory [H.Grey] 518
True relation of the manner of deposing of King Edward II 2977
True relation of the several facts and circumstances of the intended riot [M.Manley] 5171
True relation of the terrible earthquake which happaned at Ragusa 1315
True relation of the unexpected proceedings of the King of Denmark 1518
True relation of the unjust accusation [D.Holles] 1367
True relation of the victory and happy success 1360
True relation of what is discovered concerning the murther 1725
True Scripture doctrine of the Holy Trinity 5762
True state of the case between the government and the creditors of the Navy [Defoe] 5070
True state of the case concerning the election of a provost [F.Thompson] 3981
True state of the case of the Commonwealth of England 942,955
True state of the case of the Reverend Mr. Greenshields 4956-7
True state of the controversy betwixt the present Bishop 3988,4121
True state of the question 7804
True state of Trinity College [J.Paris] 4853
True test of the Jesuits 2816
True time of keeping St.Matthias's-day [R.Watts] 5275-6,5556-7
True Tom Double 3989
True use of a stanch Church-jury 4958
True vindication of the reverend Dr.Sherlock 3069
Trueman (John) 6619
Trueman (Tom) see: Letter to a friend, occasion'd by the Bishop
Truth and honesty in plain English 1726
Truth, if you can find it [Sir T.Burnet] 5341
Truth tried: or, Animadversions [J.Wallis] 572
Truth vindicated: or A detection [Sir G. Treby] 2023
Tryal and condemnation of Capt.Thomas Vaughan 3483
Tryal and condemnation of Don Prefatio 5539
Tryal and condemnation of Edw.Fitz-Harris 2027
Tryal and condemnation of George Borosky 2155
Tryal and condemnation of George Busby 2028
Tryal and conviction of John Hambden 2329
Tryal and conviction of Sr.Sam Bernardiston 2330
Tryal and examination of a late libel [S.Johnson] 2609
Tryal and sentence of Elizabeth Cellier 1864
Tryal, examination, and condemnation, of occasional conformity 3855-6,5540
Tryal of Edward Coleman 1604
Tryal of George Earl of Wintoun 6046
Tryal of Laurence Braddon and Hugh Speke 2331
Tryal of Philip Earl of Pembroke 1727
Tryal of Roger Earl of Castlemaine 2029
Tryal of Sir Henry Vane 1248
Tryal of Sr.Miles Stapleton 2030
Tryal of Sr.Tho.Gascoyne 1865
Tryal of skill between 'Squire Walsingham and Mother Osborne 6851
Tryal of the Czarewitz 6650
Tryal of the witnesses of the resurrection [T.Sherlock] 6722,7354
Tryal of William Stayley 1605
Tryal of William Viscount Stafford 2031
Tryal of witches 8554
Tryal, sentence, and condemnation of fidelity 3795
Tryals of Henry Cornish 2464
Tryals of Peter Messenger 4959
Tryals of Sir George Wakeman 1728
Tryals of such persons as under the notion of London-apprentices 1326
Tryals of the rioters at Bristol 5912
Tryals of Thomas Walcot, William Hone 2249
Tryals of William Ireland, Thomas Pickering 1606
Tschoop & Shabasch 8369
Tucker (Josiah) 6928,7040,7298,7469,7627-8, 7644,7767
Tuckney (Anthony) 567
Tufton (Sackville) 4122-3
Tuke (Sir Samuel) 1375
Tully (Edward) 8237
Tully (George) 2756,2817,2978
Tunbridge-miscellany 5541,5763
Tunbrigialia [P.Causton] 2490
Tunnage bank compared with Doctor Chamberlen's land-fund 3225
Tunstall (James) 7170
Tunstall (William) 6030,6099
Turbervill (Edward) 1866,2009
Turenne (Anne de la Tour d'Auvergne) *Vicomtesse de* see: La Tour d'Auvergne (Anne de)
Turenne (Henri de la Tour d'Auvergne) *Vicomte de* see: La Tour d'Auvergne (Henri de)
Turkey Company see: Levant Company
Turkish secretary [Sieur Du Vignan] 2715
Turnbull (George) 6957
Turner (Bryan) 1607,2032
Turner (Francis) 1519,2033,2156,2250,2332-3, 2465-8,2546
Turner (G.) 7009
Turner (John) *Hospitaller* 1729,2251,3070
Turner (John) *Vicar of Greenwich* 4235,5338, 5542-3,5764
Turner (Thomas) *D.D.* 1381,2469
Turner (Thomas) *of Gray's Inn* see: Turnor (Thomas)
Turnor (Sir Edmund) 4252
Turnor (Thomas) 1439,1555,1608
Turretinus (Johannes Alphonsus) 4637
Tutchin (John) 3335,3343,3615-6,3630,3706, 3732
Tweddell (Robert) 8582
Twells (Leonard) 6898
Twelve queries humbly proposed 1089
Twelve seasonable quaeries 1090
Twenty five modest, and sober queries 1091
XXV queries: modestly and humbly...propounded 1092
Twenty four queries touching the Parliament 1093
Twenty quaking queries 1094
Twenty seven queries relating to the general good 1095
XXIII. puntilio's or caprichio's 1096
Twining (Richard) 8025,8027
Two addresses to the inhabitants 8122
Two associations. One subscribed by CLVI members 2034
Two compendious discourses [T.Smith] 3566
Two discourses concerning the adoration of our B.Saviour [A.Woodhead] 2672
Two discourses for the furtherance of Christian piety and devotion [E.Wetenhall] 1377
Two discourses: of purgatory, and prayers [W.Wake] 2667
Two discourses. The first, concerning the spirit of Martin Luther [A.Woodhead] 2673
Two discourses wherein it is prov'd [G.Smith] 6825
Two dissertations: the first on the supposed suicide of Samson 7341
Two friends, or the history of Hugh M'Neil 8384
Two genuine letters selected from Mist's Weekly-journal 6728
Two letters concerning the author of the Examiner 5765
Two letters concerning the East-India Company 1480,1520
Two letters concerning the present Union [G.Mackenzie] 4204
Two letters containing a further justification of the Church [T.Pierce] 2130
Two letters from a deist to his friend [N.Stevens] 6758
Two letters, one from the Bishop of Blois [D.N.Berthier] 3643
Two letters; the one sent by the Lord Mayor 1049
Two letters to "a barrister" 8209
Two letters to a friend, concerning the distempers of the present times 2547
Two letters to the Reverend Dr.Bentley [J.Craven] 6131
Two letters with some remarks 5766
Two letters written to the author of a pamphlet [S.Grascombe] 3198
Two love poems [J.Pomfret] 3693
Two petitions, of the knights, gentlemen [of Herts.] 434
Two seasonable discourses concerning this present Parliament 1478
Two treatises the first, proving both by history & record [L.Womock] 1872
Two useful cases resolved [R.Blechynden] 2351
Two very odd characters tho' the number be even [F.Hoffman] 5844
Twyn (John) 1274
Tyler (John) 4358
Typhon: or the wars [B.de Mandeville] 3936
Tyranno-Mastix (Tom) see: Parliament arraigned, convicted
Tyranny and popery lording it [Sir R. L'Estrange] 1581
Tyranny unmasked 7676
Tyrwhitt (Robert) 8162
Tyrwhitt (Thomas) 7461,7508,7690,7749,7786
Tyson (Edwin Colman) 8544

Udall (Ephraim) 263,688
Ulmorum Acherons 2157
Umpire: or, England the ballance of Europe [R.Crosfeild] 4165
Underhill (Cave) 1977,2158
Underwood (John) 1867
Undone again; or, The plot discover'd 4960
Unhappy game at Scotch and English [J.Lilburne] 730
Unhappy marks-man 1097
Uninterrupted succession of the ecclesiastical mission asserted 6245
Union of Christ and the Church [R.Cudworth] 312
United Brethren 7545,7600,7753,8497
United Kingdom tributary to France 8323
Unitie, truth and reason 264
Unity of priesthood necessary [N.Bisbie] 3181
Universal beauty a poem [H.Brooke] 6855
University loyalty 4848
University queries 1098
Universum totale 1327
Unlawfulness of bonds of resignation [J.Willes] 3450
Unreasonableness of a separation from the new bishops [H.Hody] 3087,3126,3143
Unto the questions sent me last night [J.Owen] 1059
Upton (Francis) 5293
Uraniae metamorphosis in Sydus 3392
Urania's temple: or, A satyr 3393
Urban VIII, *Pope* 568
Use and great moment of The notes 2665
Useful transactions in philosophy 8686
Usefulness of the study of the Revelation [W.Garret] 3665
Ussher (James) 197,906,973,984,1190
Utrecht, *Treaty of* 5570-1,5628,5729,5787-8
Utrum horum, mavis, accipe 3569
Utrum horum? Tyranny, or liberty [G.Miege] 4079

V.(A.) see: Sykes (Arthur Ashley)

V.(G.L.) 569

V.(I.C.) see: Velthusen (Johann Caspar)

V.(J.) see: Vicars (John)

V.(T.) see: Vicars (Thomas)

Vago (Perin del) see: Beverland (Adriaan)

Vanbrugh (George) 7841

Vanbrugh (Sir John) 6705

Vandeput·(Sir George) 7254

Vane (Guy) 6706

Vane (Sir Henry) 1083,1248

Vanerius (Jacobus) 6726

Vaniere (Jacques) see: Vanerius (Jacobus)

Vansittart (Nicholas) *Baron Bexley* 7970

Variety. A tale [W.Whitehead] 7693

Varillas (Antoine) 6246

Vaughan (Charles Richard) 8210

Vaughan (Edward Thomas) 8271

Vaughan (Meredith) 4021

Vaughan (Thomas) 3483

Velthusen (Johann Caspar) 7608,7768

Venice looking-glasse [J.Howell] 825

Venn (Henry) 7592

Venn (John) 8078,8174

Verax to Adamia 7204

Verbum diei: or, A word in season 2470

Veritable relation en forme de lettre 1521

Veritable response a l'Anticoton 53

Veritas pacifica 897

Verney (George) *Baron Willoughby de Broke* 5544

Verney (Robert) 2159

Vernon (Edward) 7171

Vernon (George) 1361

Vernon-iad [H.Fielding] 6968

Verschuir (Johannes Henricus) 7386

Vertues reward wherein the living are incouraged 201

Very new pamphlet indeed! 7939,7944

Vesey (John) 2252,2979

Veteres vindicati [E.Gee] 2587

Vicars (John) 570

Vicars (Thomas) 121

Vice puni, ou cartouche [N.R.de Grandval] 6635

Vickers (William) 5767

Victor Amadeus II, *King of Sardinia* 3226,4098

Vievar (Alexander) 6913

View of a printed book intituled Observations upon his Majesties late answers and expresses [Sir J.Spelman] 428

View of the internal evidence of the Christian religion [S.Jenyns] 7683,7705

View of the Queen and kingdom's enemies 5266

View of the whole controversy between the representer and the answerer [W.Clagett] 2574

Villa Flor (Manuel Sanches) *Conde de* see: Sanches (Manuel)

Village politics [H.More] 7962

Villanous principles of The rights of the Christian Church 4638

Villars (Nicolas Montfaucon de) 5913

Villette (François) 6284,6381

Villiers (George) *Duke of Buckingham* 1394-5, 2352,2365,2373,2379,2424,2438,2455, 2471-2

Villiers (Jacob de) 3287

Villiers (Pierre de) 2253

Vincent (Nathaniel) 2473

Vincent (William) 7906,8137,8141

Vindex see: Bevan (Joseph Gurney)

Vindex see: Old truths and established facts

Vindication and advancement of our national constitution and credit [J.Broughton] 4675

Vindication of a discourse concerning the unreasonableness of a new separation [J.Williams] 3120,3176

Vindication of a late pamphlet (entituled, Obedience and submission) [Z.Taylor] 3168

Vindication of a late pamphlet, intituled, The case of the Hanover troops considered [P.D.Stanhope] 7067

Vindication of a passage in Dr.Sherlock's sermon [W.Sherlock] 2454

Vindication of a printed paper, entituled, An ordinance 751

Vindication of Christianity from and against the scandals of popery [E.Stephens] 3978

Vindication of Dr.Snape [Defoe] 6138

Vindication of her late Majesty 6004

Vindication of his Excellency the Lord C--t [J.Swift] 6760

Vindication of his Grace the Duke of Leeds 5267

Vindication of King Charles the Martyr [T.Wagstaffe] 3484,5271

Vindication of lawful authority [G.Smith] 6333

Vindication of Mary, Queen of Scotland 6536

Vindication of Mesech and Kedar 5545

Vindication of Mr.Sherlock 1556

Vindication of Oliver Cromwell 5546

Vindication of some among our selves [G.Hickes] 3199

Vindication of that prudent and honourable knight, Sir Henry Vane [H.Stubbe] 1083

Vindication of the Apamean medal [J.Bryant] 7662

Vindication of the Apostles [W.Wall] 4126

Vindication of the Bishop of Salisbury [G.Burnet] 4684

Vindication of the Church and clergy of England (1709) [W.Kennet] 4577

Vindication of the Church and clergy of England (1823) [H.Soames] 8358

Vindication of the Church of England from the aspersions of a late libel [H.Bedford] 4661

Vindication of the Church of England from the foul aspersions of schism [M.Altham] 2556

Vindication of the clergy, in regard to residence 8155

Vindication of the conduct of a certain eminent patriot 7037

Vindication of the conforming clergy [R.Grove] 1493

Vindication of the dead 3173

Vindication of the deprived bishops [H.Dodwell] 3190,3223,3260

Vindication of the divines of the Church of England [E.Fowler] 2879,2887

Vindication of the doctrines and liturgy of the Church of England 7881

Vindication of the Earl of Nottingham 5914

Vindication of the honour and prerogative 6247

Vindication of the honourable the sheriffs 2035

Vindication of the imprisoned and secluded Members [W.Prynne] 864

Vindication of the King 435

Vindication of the last Parliament 5268

Vindication of the late Archbishop Sancroft [H.Bedford] 6110

Vindication of the late Bishop Burnet 6620

Vindication of the late House of Commons [J.Egleton] 5827

Vindication of the Letter out of the North [W.Eyre] 3007

Vindication of the London apprentices 1099

Vindication of the London clergy 4124

Vindication of the Lord Chancellor Bacon 6651

Vindication of the Lord Russell's speech 2254

Vindication of the Non-juring Church 6100

Vindication of the ordinations of the Church [G.Burnet] 2691

Vindication of the Parliament 436

Vindication of the presbyteriall-government 889

Vindication of the present m[inistr]y 5269

Vindication of the principles of the author of the Answer [E.Gee] 2725

Vindication of the proceedings of his Majesties Ecclesiastical Commissioners [H.Care] 2695,2745

Vindication of the realm, and Church [W.Wake] 6101

Vindication of the Reasons and defence, &c. [J.Collier] 6277,6369,6453,6478

Vindication of the Reverend Dr.George Hickes 5547

Vindication of the Reverend Dr.Henry Sacheverell [W.King] 5138,5155,5159

Vindication of the Reverend Dr.Snape 6248

Vindication of the Right Reverend the Lord Bishop of Exeter [W.Oldisworth] 4605

Vindication of the Right Reverend the Ld. Bishop of Norwich [J.Lewis] 5854

Vindication of the Right Reverend the Lord Bishop of Winchester [P.Skelton] 6880

Vindication of the rights of men [M.Wollstonecraft] 7908

Vindication of the Whigs 3796

Vindiciae Caroli Regis 654

Vindiciae juris regii [J.Collier] 2863

Vindiciae mentis 3735

Viner (Sir Robert) 1527

Vines (Richard) 752

Vinsemius (Dominicus) 49

Violet (Thomas) 1222

Virgilius Maro (Publius) 153,5598,5816,6851, 6890,6937-8,7005

Virginia 91

Visible pursuit of a foreign interest 7125

Visions of Aaron 7205

Visit to a Sabbath school 8430

Vittorio Amedeo see: Victor Amadeus

Voelschow (Joachim) 3990

Voice of liberty [M.Akenside] 6899

Voice of the addressers 4961

Voice of truth to the people of England 8062

Voltaire (François Marie Arouet de) 6914, 7387,7691

Vorstius (Conradus) 60

Vossius (Gerardus Joannes) 943-4,1299

Vota (Carolus Mauritius) 5514

Votes of the House of Commons 8618

Vowell (Peter) 934

Vox Cleri: or, the sense of the clergy [T.Long] 3020,3028,3043,3066,3071

Voc cleri pro rege 2818

Vox dilectionis: or, The young nonconformist 4962

Vox lachrymae [C.Underhill] 2158

Vox laici 2936

Vox patriae 2036

Vox populi: being the sense of the nation 5548

Vox populi, fax populi [J.Nalson] 1977

Vox populi: or the peoples claim 2037

Vox populi: or, the sense of the sober lay-men of the Church of England [J.Boyse] 2991

Vox regis & regni 3071

Vox regis: or, The difference [James I] 1943

Vox rugientis leonis [G.Borovius] 1626

Vulgus Britannicus [E.Ward] 4970

Vulpone: or, Remarks on some proceedings in Scotland 4359

W. 5270

W.(C.) see: Wintringham (Clifton)

W.(C.D.) see: Witt (Cornelius de)

W.(Sir D.) 3394

W.(E.) 1418

W.(E.) see: Wells (Edward) Whitaker (Edward)

W.(G.) see: Wall (George)

W.(I.) see: Wallis (John)

W.(J.) 957,2283

W.(L.) 7070

W.(R.) 2547

W.(R.) see: Ware (Richard)

W.(S.) see: Walker (Samuel)

W.(T.) 1182,5549,7172

W.(T.) see: Savile (George) Ward (Thomas) Webster (Thomas)

W.(T.) *F.R.S.* see: Watkins (Thomas)

W.(W.) 7570,8334

Waad (John) 1223

Waddington (Samuel Ferrand) 8042

Wadsworth (James) 110

Wagenseil (Johann Christoph) 3288

Wagstaffe (Thomas) *the Elder* 2255,2474-5, 3072-5,3134,3168,3227-8,3289,3336-7,3369, 3484,3570,3797,4125,5271

Wagstaffe (Thomas) *the Younger* 6354,6426, 6439,6509,7396

Wagstaffe (William) 5025,5272-3,5550-1,5756, 5768,5915,6562,6675

Wahrhafftige Erzehlung von Hinrichtung... de La Brosse 1557

Wahrhafftige Erzehlungen...von der Campagnia dises 1676-sten Jahrs 1522

Waighty and demonstrative reasons 1289

Wainewright (Reader 8305)

Wainwright (Jonathan Mayhew) 8484

Wake (Robert) 3991

Wake (William) 2548-9,2666-7,2774,2819-20, 2980-1,3076-9,3174-5,3513,3638,4195,4236, 4360-1,4480-1,4717,4963-5,5156,6005-7,6101

Wakefield (Gilbert) 7999,8000,8079

Wakefield (Thomas) 8156,8192

Wakeman (Sir George) 1728

Walburge (Anthony) 7255

Walcot (Thomas) 2211,2249

Walker (Anthony) 3229,3267

Walker (Clement) 445,571,844

Walker (George) 2976,2982

Walker (H.) 811

Walker (Henry) 8669

Walker (Sir Hoveden) 6483

Walker (John) *D.D.* 6365

Walker (John) *Vicar of Ledbury* 4966

Walker (Samuel) 6484,6537,6621

Walker (Thomas) 3290

Wall (George) 161

Wall (Thomas) 2160

Wall (William) 4126

Wallace (Eglantine) *Lady* 7971

Waller (Edmund) *M.P.* 7066-7,7071

Waller (Sir Edmund) 1183,1300

Waller (Henry) 144

Waller (John) 4482

Waller (Sir William) 489,1575,1630,1730

Wallis (John) 572,3271,3291,3338,4613,5276, 5555

Wallis (Ralph) 3882

Walpole (Horace) *Earl of Orford* 4967,7206, 7401

Walpole (Horatio) *Baron* 6757,6796,6836,6863, 7568

Walpole (Robert) *Earl of Orford* 5585,5667, 5756,5769,5961,6438,6521,6689-90,6807, 6990,6999,7007,7013,7018,7023,7238,7470

Walsh (Peter) 1224,1451

Walsh (William) 3822-3

Walsingham (Sir Francis) 2640

Warburton (William) 7173,7207,7312,7327,7464, 7500,8199

Ward (Edward) 3631,3707,3857,3992,4127-9,4237, 4483-4,4639-40,4968-70,5552-4,5916,6106, 6249,6676

Ward (Hamnet) 1440

Ward (Henry) 6883

Ward (John) 6680

Ward (Nathaniel) 797,870

Ward (Sir Patience) 1797,1868

Ward (Richard) 437

Ward (Seth) 1362,1419,1441

Ward (Thomas) 2668-9,2702,6539

Wardlaw (Elizabeth) 7239

Warltire (John) 7571-2

Warmington (William) 64

Warmstry (Thomas) 438

Warner (John) *Bishop of Rochester* 845-6

Warner (John) *Jesuit* 2316

Warner (Richard) 8158

Warning for servants 1869

Warning for the Church of England [J.Bramhall] 4150

Warning to the Whigs 7100

Warren (Albertus) 945

Warren (Erasmus) 2476,4641

Warren (George) 8499

Warren (John) 7819

Wars of the elements [E.Ward] 4640

Warton (Thomas) 7313

Warwick (Sir Philip) 4880

Warwick (Robert Rich) *Earl of Warwick* see: Rich (Robert)

Washington (George) 8100

Waterhouse (Thomas) 925

Waterhouse (William) 1249

Waterland (Daniel) 6578,6734,6763-4,6902,6956

Waterland (Theodore) 6102

Waterton (Charles) 8568-9

Watkins (Henry George) 8555

Watkins (Thomas) 6250

Watkinson (Edward) 7471

Watson (George) 7299

Watson (Richard) 7692,7738,7787,7907,7945,7972, 8070,8080,8142

Watson (Thomas) 3556,3812,4046

Watson (William) 1448

Watts (Isaac) 6958

Watts (Robert) 4971,5274-6,5555-7,5798

Waugh (John) 4130,5770-2,5917-8,6440

Way of peace: or, A discourse 1870

Way to bring the world to rights 5277

Way to good success 2413

Way whereby the Quakers may approve themselves Christians 3641

Weavers pretences examin'd 6441

Weavers true case [C.Rey] 6424

Webster (James) 4366

Webster (Thomas) 2600

Webster (William) 7038

Wednesday club-law [Broome] 6113

Weekly intelligencer of the common-wealth 8687

Weekly pacquet of advice from France 8688

Weekly pacquet of advice from Rome restored 8689

Weesil trap'd [T.D'Urfey] 3109

Weesils [T.D'Urfey] 3110

Welbe (John) 4131

Welchman (Edward) 3292,3538,5919,8347

Welchman's last will and testament 6442

Welchman's tales concerning the times 4972

Weldon (Sir Anthony) 5920

Weldon (Robert) 847

Wellesley (Arthur) *Duke of Wellington* 8213, 8556

Wells (Edward) 4160,4173,4238-44,4362-4,4404, 4485,4642,4973,5278,5388,5773-4,5813,6008, 6251

Wells (Zachary) 4132

Wellstead (Stephen) 3697

Wellwood (James) 2983,3246,3322

Welton (James) 7422

Welton (Richard) 4912,4974,5921,6009,6278,6355

Wendelin (Marcus Frederik) 848

Wenham (Jane) 5330-3,5390,5424

Wensley (Robert) 2550

Wentworth (Sir Peter) 265

Wentworth (Thomas) *Earl of Strafford* 266-7,798, 4975,6012,7029

Were (John) 638

Werenfels (Samuel) 6356

Werge (Richard) 2477

Wesley (John) 6958,6979,7039-40,7072,7094,7101, 7174-5,7275,7342,7464,7583,7593,7605,7924

Wesley (Samuel) *the Elder* 3993

Wesley (Samuel) *the Younger* 6622,6660,6729,6758

West (Benjamin) 8262

West (Gilbert) 7195

West (Richard) *Lord Chancellor of Ireland* 6103,6443

West (Richard) *Prebendary of Winchester* 3777, 4222,4976,5279,5882

West (Richard) *Rector of Shillingston* 1376

West (Thomas) *Baron de la Warre* 47

West Riding Magazine 8690

Westminster Assembly of Divines 799,814

Weston (George) 8238

Wetenhall (Edward) 1328,1377

Wetstein (Johann Jacob) 6765,6797,6884

Weyer (Florence) 2038

Whaley (Nathaniel) 4977

Whalley (Peniston) 1442

Wharton (Sir George) 580,8643

Wharton (Henry) 3237,3708

Wharton (Sir Miles) 5726

Wharton (Philip) *Baron Wharton* 322,439

Wharton (Philip) *Duke of Wharton* 6728,6798

Wharton (Thomas) *Marquess of Wharton* 5074, 5248,5523

What are you mad? 4245

What has been, may be again 4978

What is man? [A.Vievar] 6913

What of that! 6951,6959

Whateley (Solomon) 3571

Whateley (Stephen) 5942

Whately (Robert) 6010

Whately (William) 85-6

Wheatly (Charles) 6357,6707

Wheeler (Daniel) 8522

When my lord falls in my lady's lap 6538

Whetenhall (Thomas) 39

Whether the Parliament be not in law dissolved [R.Ferguson] 3357

Whether the preserving the protestant religion was the motive [R.Ferguson] 3358

Whichcot (Benjamin) 2247

Whigg (Tom) 4951-2

Whigs appeal to the Tories 5280

Whigs feast 5558

Whigs no Christians 5642,5775

Whigs scandalous Address answered 3994

Whigs truly Christian 5776

Whincop (John) 690

Whincop (Thomas) 3798

Whip for the Spaniards 3683

Whip for the Whiggs 4133

Whipper whipt [F.Quarles] 626

Whiston (James) 2984,3449

Whiston (William) 4989-90,5098,5103,5107,5139, 5165-7,5226,5281-6,5386,5404,5422,5434, 5470,5531,5559-60,5573,5609,5629,5662, 5757,5777-8,5866,5922,6362,6377,6444-5, 6502-3,6575,7231

Whitaker (Edward) 2039-40,2161

Whitbourne (Richard) 92,100

Whitby (Daniel) 2478,2821,2985-6,3080,4365, 5078,6252

White (Francis) 155,182

White (John) *B.D.* 7358

White (John) *Counsellor at Law* 268,5561

White (John) *of Dorchester* 753

White (Joseph) 7873

White (Samuel) 4853

White (Thomas) 1250

White against Kennet 3995

White crow [E.Curll] 4719-20

White rose: or a word for the House of York [J.Brydall] 1745

Whitear (William) 4979

Whitefield (George) 6928,7300,7546,7592-3

Whitehead (George) 1378,3641,3976,4456,6984

Whitehead (Paul) 7208

Whitehead (William) 6917,7693

Whitelock (Bulstrode) 1084,5923

Whitelock (Methuselah) see: Peace-offering

Whitfeld (William) 4486

Whitfield (John) 2162

Whitfield (William) see: Whitfeld (William)

Whitgift (John) 5924

Whitlock (Sir William) 3318

Whitro (Abraham) 4918

Who would have thought it? 4366

Whole art of short and swift writing 6011

Whole business of Sindercome 980

Whole life and actions. Of John Dolben 4980

Whole life and character of Richard Gascoigne 6104

Whole life and history of Benjamin Child 6579-80

Whole proceeding upon the arraignment...of Christopher Layer 6581

Whole tryal and examination of Mr.Richardson 5562

Wib.(Ios.) see: Wybarne (Joseph)

Widow's son raised from the dead 8431

Wiese (Georg) 7925

Wilbee (Amos) 800

Wilberforce (William) 8293

Wilcock (James) 440

Wild (Robert) 1184-5,1382,1396

Wild(William Taylor) 8523

Wilde (John) 441

Wilkens (Johann) 2256

Wilkes (John) 7553,7556

Wilkes (Thomas) 7423

Wilkins (John) 1363,1379

Wilkinson (Henry) *Canon of Christ Church* 269,573,639

Wilkinson (Henry) *Captain* 2041

Wilkinson (Joshua Lucock) 7973,7990

Wilkinson (Richard) 1871

Wilkinson (Robert) 4487

Will-with-a-wisp 5866

Willard (Samuel) 3752,3917

Willats (Charles) 7388

Willes (John) 3081,3450

Willes (Sir John) 5779,5925

Willes (Samuel) 1731

Willet (Andrew) 65

William III, *King* 2328,2680,2808,2822-3, 2830,2845,2865,2873-4,2889,2908,3339, 3485,3728,3765,3801,3996,4134,5563

William II, *Prince of Orange* 409

William Augustus, *Duke of Cumberland* 7484

Williams (Daniel) *D.D.* 2824,4367

Williams (Daniel) *Presbyter of the Church of England* 6539

Williams (David) *Founder of the Royal Literary Fund* 8290

Williams (Griffith) 574

Williams (John) *Archbishop of York* 115,127, 183-4,856,6012

Williams (John) *Bishop of Chichester* 1609, 1732,2257-8,2334,2479-80,2670,2812, 2825-7,2827,3120,3176,3411,3451-2

Williams (John) *LL.D.* 7608

Williams (John) *Roman Catholic Writer* 1765

Williams (Oliver) 8647,8661,8667,8677

Williams (Roger) 621

Williams (Thomas) *Calvinist Preacher* 8028

Williams (Thomas) *Gwilym Morganwg* 8279

Williams (Thomas) *Publisher* 8048-9

Williams (William) *Minister* 2481

Williams (Sir William) 2042

Williamson (Joseph) 4135,4981

Willis (John) 3082

Willis (Richard) 3453,4041,4135-8,6013,6602

Willoughby de Broke (George Verney) *Baron* see: Verney (George)

Wilmot (John) *Earl of Rochester* 1835

Wilson (Christopher) 7776

Wilson (Daniel) 8291-2,8489,8524

Wilson (Edward) 5564

Wilson (Harry Bristow) 8194

Wilson (Jasper) 7974

Wilson (John) 57

Wilson (Roger Carus) 8575

Wilson (Thomas) *Bishop of Sodor and Man* 5287,6623,7126,7754

Wilson (Thomas) *Rector of Arrow* 1733

Wiltshire-petition for tythes explained 911

Winchester College 5288,7419

Winchilsea (Heneage Finch) *Earl of* see: Finch (Heneage)

Windebank (Sir Francis) 230

Wing (Vincent) 1346

Wingfield (Thomas) 7276

Wingrave (John) 7524

Winifred, *Saint* 5612,5690

Winnington (Thomas) 7177,7233

Winnowing of corn 8469

Winstanley (Thomas) 7389

Winter dreame [J.Howell] 857

Wintringham (Clifton) 6677

Wisdom of Solomon explain'd 4368

Wise (Thomas) 4660,4982,5547

Wisner (Benjamin Blydenburg) 8490

Witchcraft farther display'd [F.Bragge] 5333

Wither (George) 1100

Withers (John) 4371,4983,5780,5876,6014

Withers (Philip) 7880

Withers (W.) 5289-90

Witherspoon (John) 7424

Witt (Cornelius de) 2828

Wolf (Johann Christoph) 5565,6210

Wolf in sheeps cloathing 3858

Wolf stript of his shepherd's cloathing [C.Leslie] 3925-6,3948

Wolf stript of his shepherd's clothing, address'd to Dr.Sacheverell 4984

Wolfgang Wilhelm, *Count Palatine of Neuburg* 923

Wollaston (Francis) 7645

Wollstonecraft (Mary) 7908

Women's petition against coffee 1443

Womock (Laurence) 1251,1872,2130,2163

Wonder of this age 1558

Wonderful account from Orthez 4246

Wood (Joseph) 8541,8583

Wood (Thomas) 4488

Woodd (Basil) 8524

Woodhead (Abraham) 2551,2554,2560,2605,2655-6, 2661,2671-3,2817

Woodroffe (Benjamin) 2482

Woods (Leonard) 8525

Woodward (Henry) 7594

Woodward (John) 3454,5781,6386-7

Woodward (Josiah) 4293,5012

Woodwark (John) 8588

Woolley (John) 1479

Worcestershire address 4985

Worcestershire-queries about peace [Defoe] 5071

Word for inquiry previous to decision [W.Harding] 8530

Word in due season to the ranting royallists 1186

Word in season: being a modest enquiry into the lawfulness of making and imposing creeds 6392

Word in season: or, A letter from a reverend divine 1618

Word of advice to the citizens 4139

Word to a wandering levite 3083

Word to Mr.Wil Prynn [H.Marten] 861

Word to purpose 1006

Word to the present ministry 5782

Word to the wavering [G.Burnet] 2851

Word to the well-inclin'd 3539

Word to the wise: in a letter 5291

Word to the wise: or, Some seasonable cautions 5566

Word within-doors 1734

Word without-doors 1640,1734,1798

World encompassed by Sir Francis Drake 156

World's mistake in Oliver Cromwell [S.Bethel] 1316

Worm (Christen) 3293

Worse and worse newes from Ireland [T. Partington] 249

Worthington (John) 3177

Wotton (Anthony) 119

Wotton (William) 4140,4247-8,4357,5292

Wou'd be bishop [J.Sharpe] 4619

Wrangham (Francis) 8335

Wray (Sir John) 270

Wreath of fashion [R.Tickell] 7716

Wren (Sir Christopher) 5781

Wren (Matthew) 1252

Wright, *Mr.* 7390

Wright (James) 3486

Wright (Leonard) 19

Wright (Samuel) 5293,5567,8385

Wright (William) 4249

Wyatt (William) 1735

Wybarne (Joseph) 44

Wyeth (Joseph) 3540

Wykes (William) 6069

Wylie (Macleod) 8576

Wyllys (J.) 1523

Wyndham (Isabella) 8239

Wynell (Thomas) 442

Wynne (Edward) 100

Wynne (William) 6603

Wyvill (Christopher) 7975,8094

Xo Ho see: Walpole (Horace)

Yalden (Thomas) 4465

Yarico to Inkle [E.Moore] 6877

Yarranton (Andrew) 1736,1873,2043

Yates (Henry) 4986

Yates (John) 185

Ye true-born Englishman proceed [Defoe] 3656

Yes, they are [R.Morris] 6952,6959

Yet more worke for a masse-priest [A.Cooke] 96

Yong souldier [J.Raynsford] 417

Yonge (Philip) 7403,7472

Yonge (Sir William) 6786

York, *County of* 392

York (James Stuart) *Duke of* see: James II

Young (Arthur) 7997,8023

Young (Edward) *Dean of Salisbury* 2259,2483, 2829,3294-5,3340,3395-6

Young (Edward) *Poet* 5783,5926

Young (John) *D.D.* 8001

Young (John) *Keeper of the British Institution* 8263

Young (Thomas) 640

Your servant gentlemen 1101

Z.(X.) 5294

Zaccheus 8470

Zeal (Zachary) see: Seasonable alarm to the city of London

Zealous and impartial protestant [J.Glanvill] 1923

Zenger (John Peter) 6912

Ziegler (Caspar) 907